# Oh My Goddess!

## OMNIBUS 2

ああっ女神さまっ

### STORY AND ART BY
## Kosuke Fujishima

#### TRANSLATION BY
### Dana Lewis, Alan Gleason, AND Toren Smith

#### LETTERING AND TOUCHUP BY
### Susie Lee AND Betty Dong WITH Tom2K

**DARK HORSE MANGA**

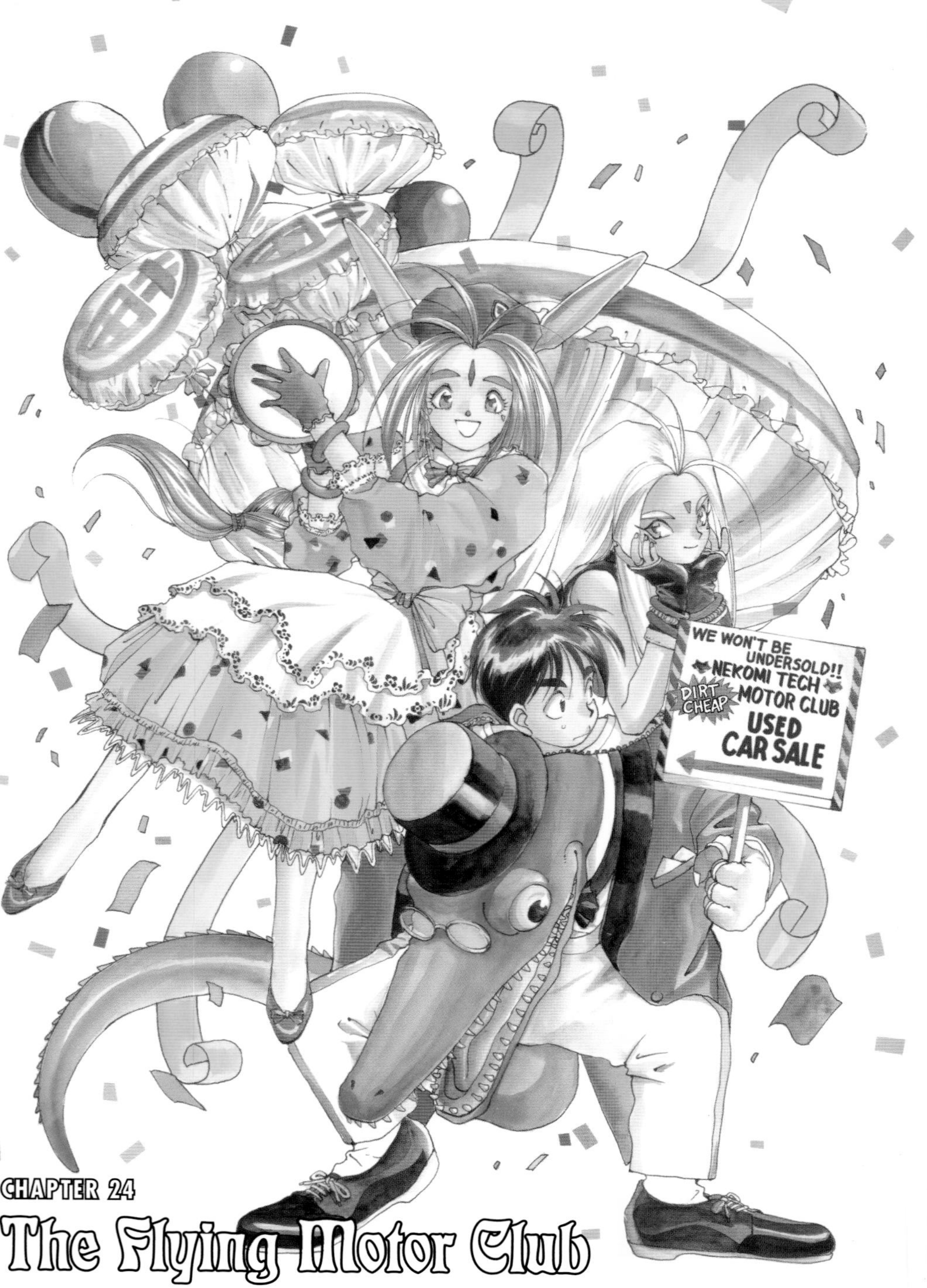
WE WON'T BE UNDERSOLD!!
NEKOMI TECH MOTOR CLUB
DIRT CHEAP
USED CAR SALE

CHAPTER 24

# The Flying Motor Club

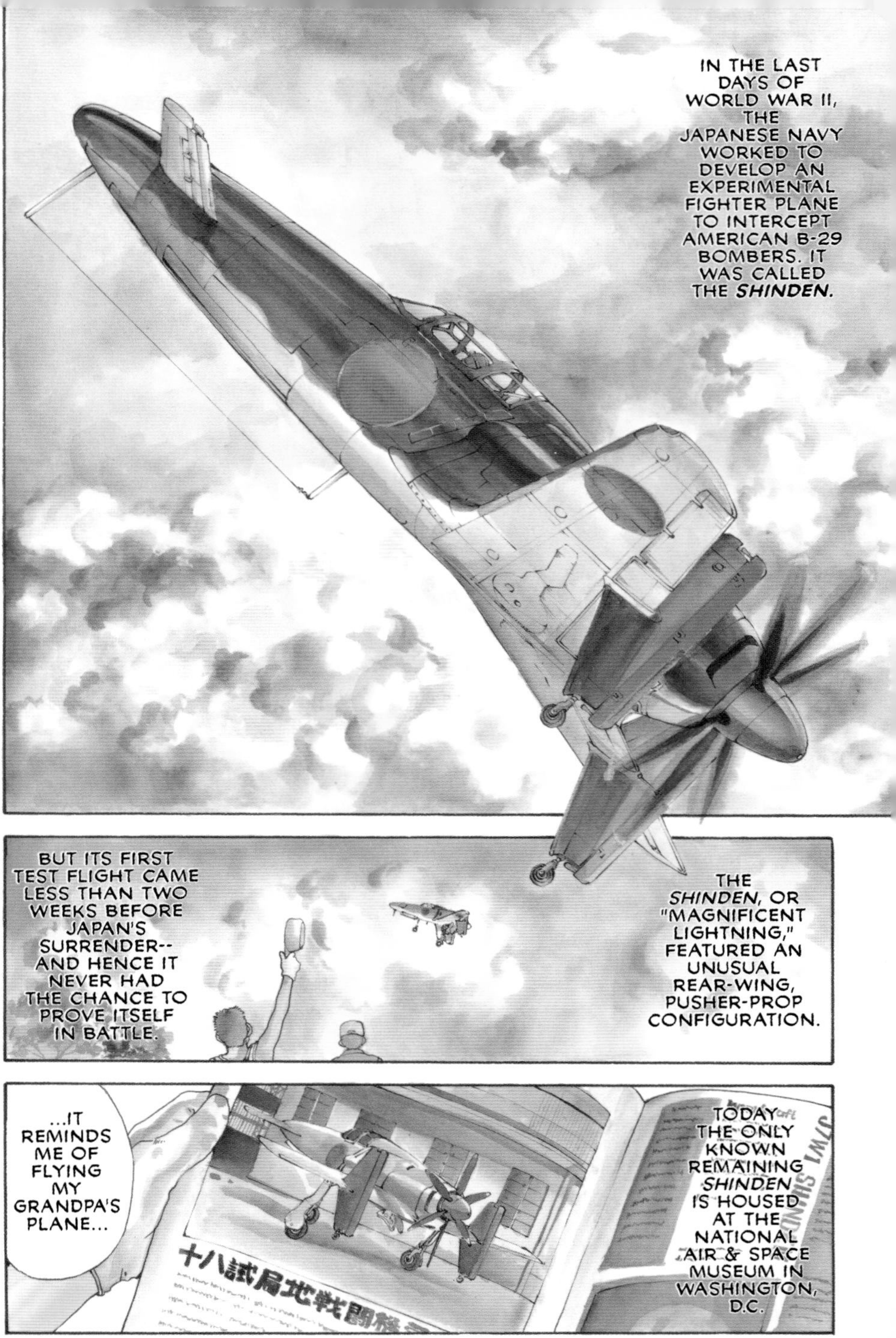
IN THE LAST DAYS OF WORLD WAR II, THE JAPANESE NAVY WORKED TO DEVELOP AN EXPERIMENTAL FIGHTER PLANE TO INTERCEPT AMERICAN B-29 BOMBERS. IT WAS CALLED THE *SHINDEN.*
THE *SHINDEN*, OR "MAGNIFICENT LIGHTNING," FEATURED AN UNUSUAL REAR-WING, PUSHER-PROP CONFIGURATION.
BUT ITS FIRST TEST FLIGHT CAME LESS THAN TWO WEEKS BEFORE JAPAN'S SURRENDER-- AND HENCE IT NEVER HAD THE CHANCE TO PROVE ITSELF IN BATTLE.
TODAY THE ONLY KNOWN REMAINING *SHINDEN* IS HOUSED AT THE NATIONAL AIR & SPACE MUSEUM IN WASHINGTON, D.C.
十八試局地戦闘
...IT REMINDS ME OF FLYING MY GRANDPA'S PLANE...

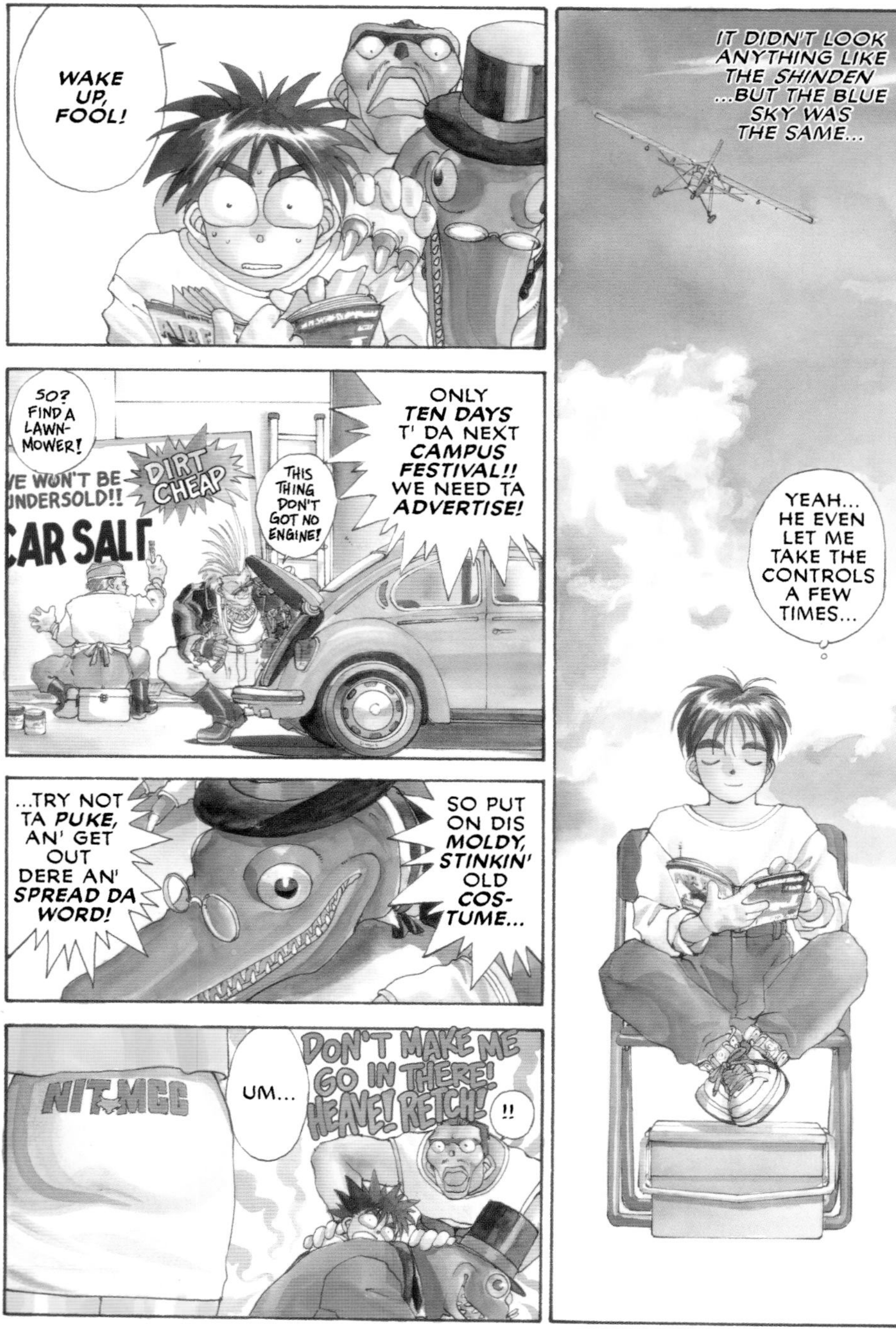
IT DIDN'T LOOK ANYTHING LIKE THE SHINDEN ...BUT THE BLUE SKY WAS THE SAME...
YEAH... HE EVEN LET ME TAKE THE CONTROLS A FEW TIMES...
WAKE UP, FOOL!
ONLY TEN DAYS T' DA NEXT CAMPUS FESTIVAL!! WE NEED TA ADVERTISE!
THIS THING DON'T GOT NO ENGINE!
SO? FIND A LAWN-MOWER!
DIRT CHEAP
E WON'T BE
NDERSOLD!!
CAR SALT
SO PUT ON DIS MOLDY, STINKIN' OLD COS-TUME...
...TRY NOT TA PUKE, AN' GET OUT DERE AN' SPREAD DA WORD!
DON'T MAKE ME GO IN THERE! HEAVE! RETCH!
!!
UM...
NIT-MCC

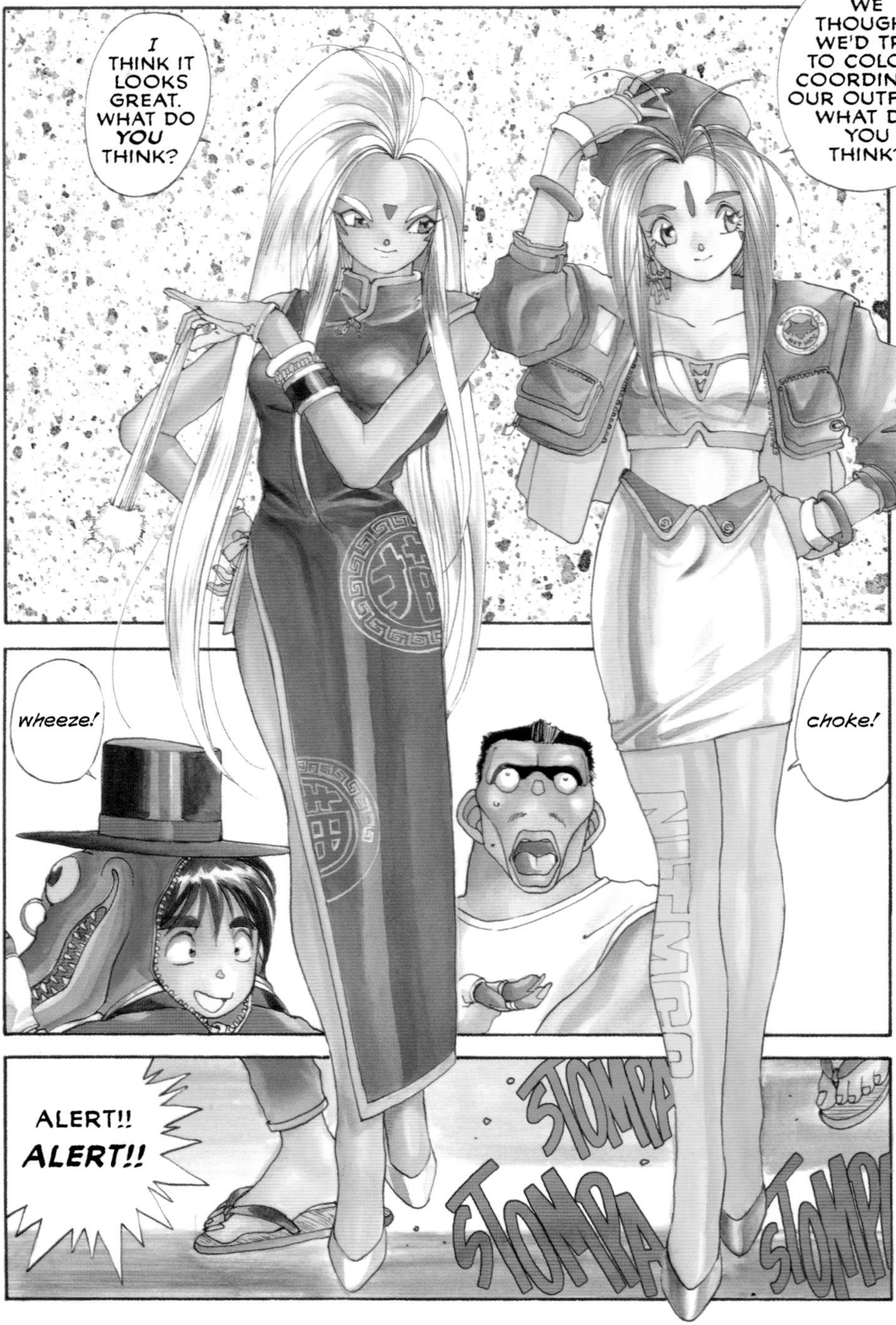
WE THOUGHT WE'D TRY TO COLOR-COORDINATE OUR OUTFITS--WHAT DO YOU THINK?
I THINK IT LOOKS GREAT. WHAT DO *YOU* THINK?
*choke!*
*wheeze!*
STOMP
STOMPA
STOMPA
STOMPA
ALERT!!
***ALERT!!***

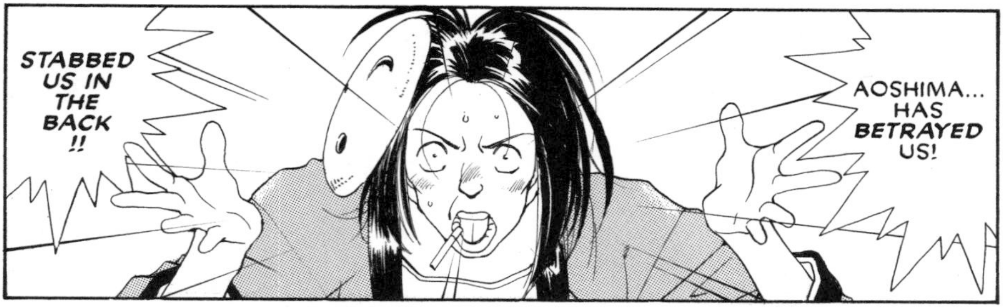
AOSHIMA... HAS BETRAYED US!
STABBED US IN THE BACK !!

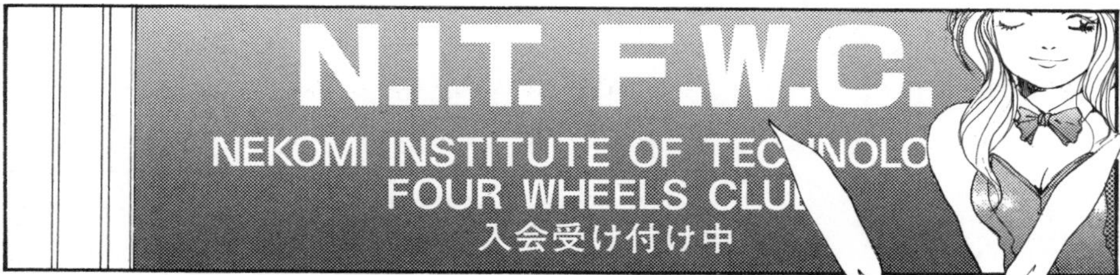
N.I.T. F.W.C.
NEKOMI INSTITUTE OF TECHNOLO
FOUR WHEELS CLUB
入会受け付け中

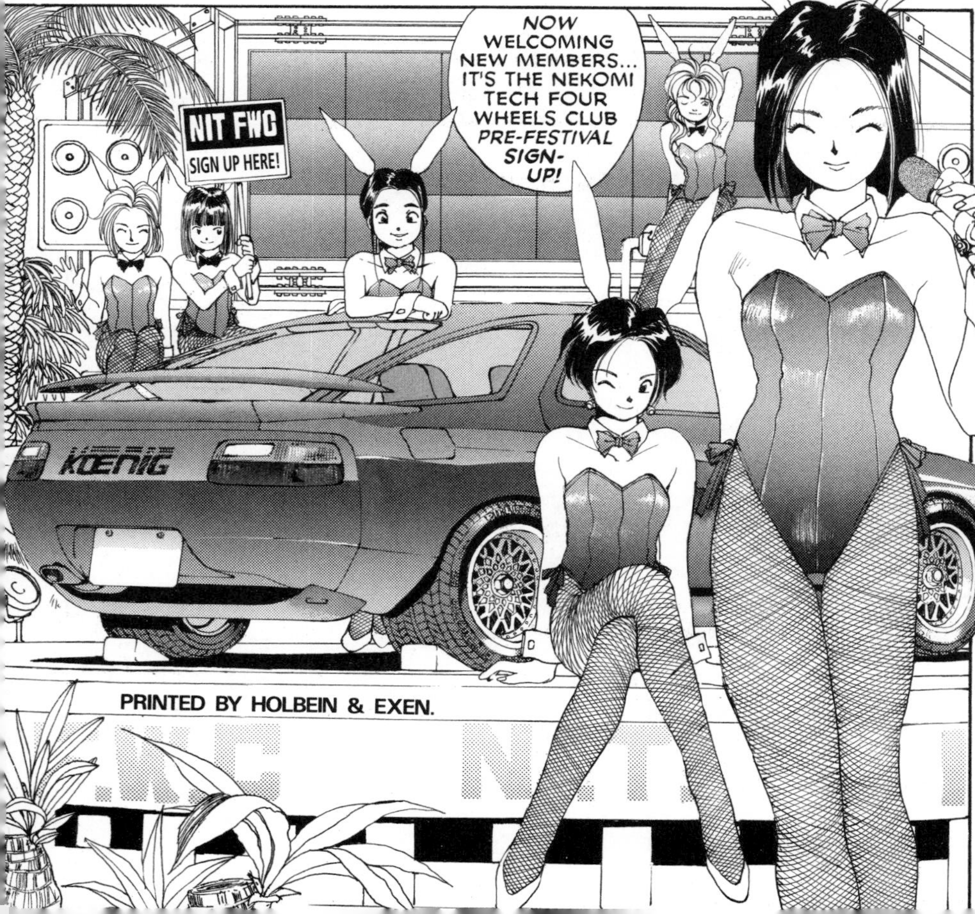
NOW WELCOMING NEW MEMBERS... IT'S THE NEKOMI TECH FOUR WHEELS CLUB PRE-FESTIVAL SIGN-UP!
NIT FWC
SIGN UP HERE!
KOENIG
PRINTED BY HOLBEIN & EXEN.

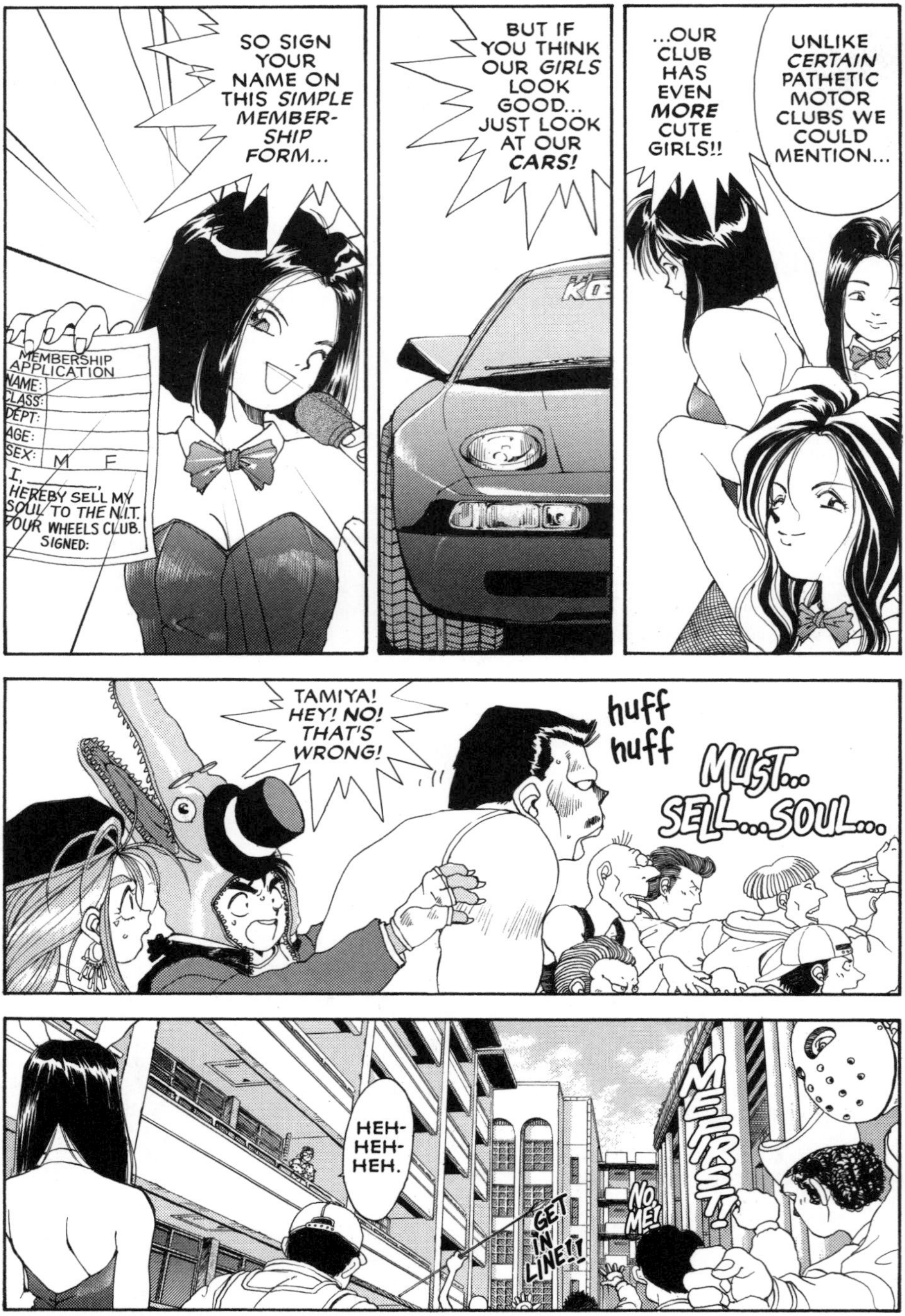
UNLIKE CERTAIN PATHETIC MOTOR CLUBS WE COULD MENTION...
...OUR CLUB HAS EVEN MORE CUTE GIRLS!!
BUT IF YOU THINK OUR GIRLS LOOK GOOD... JUST LOOK AT OUR CARS!
SO SIGN YOUR NAME ON THIS SIMPLE MEMBER-SHIP FORM...
MEMBERSHIP APPLICATION
NAME:
CLASS:
DEPT:
AGE:
SEX: M F
I, ____, HEREBY SELL MY SOUL TO THE N.I.T. FOUR WHEELS CLUB.
SIGNED:
huff huff
MUST... SELL...SOUL...
TAMIYA! HEY! NO! THAT'S WRONG!
ME FIRST!
NO ME!
GET IN LINE!!
HEH-HEH-HEH.

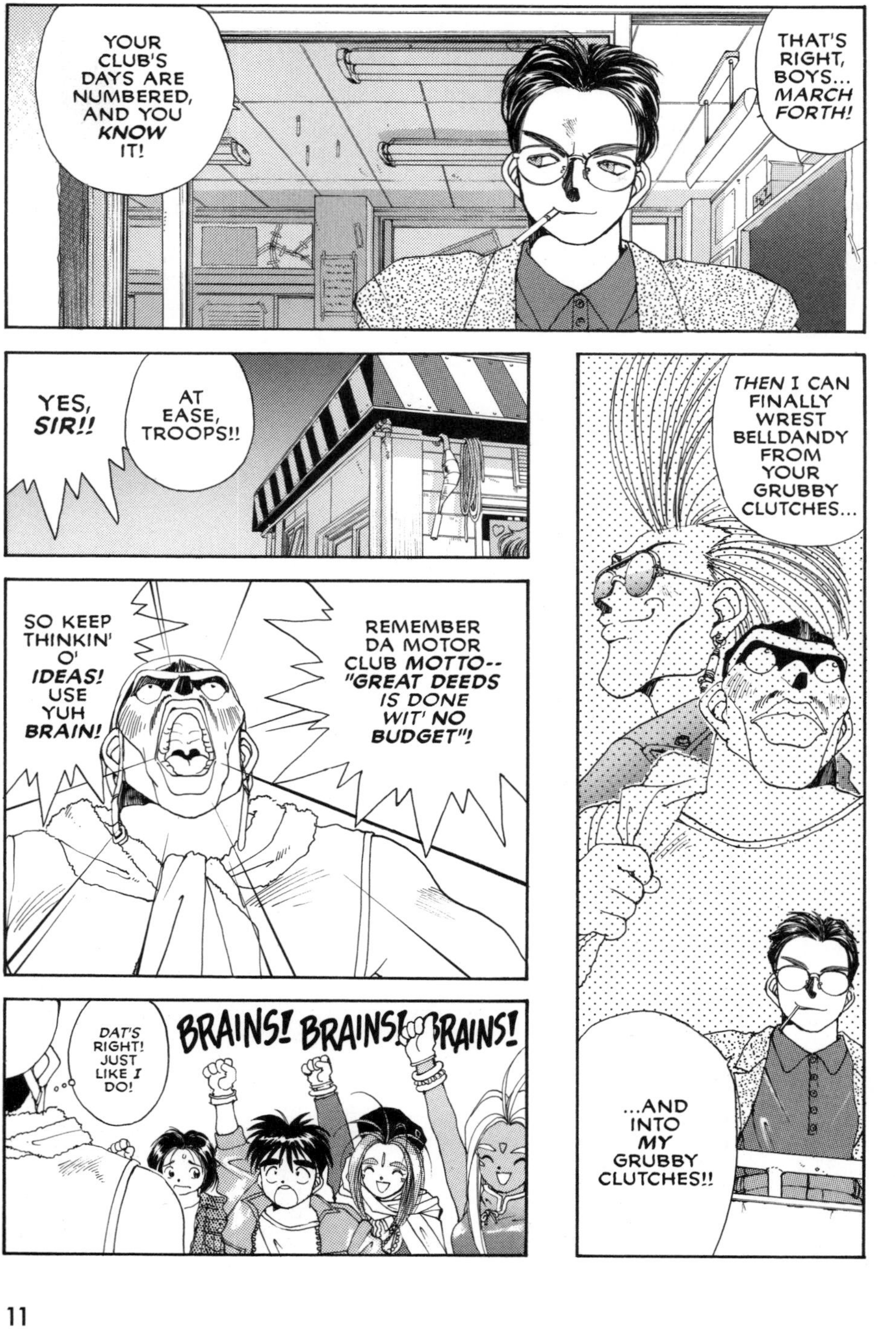
THAT'S RIGHT, BOYS... MARCH FORTH!
YOUR CLUB'S DAYS ARE NUMBERED, AND YOU KNOW IT!
THEN I CAN FINALLY WREST BELLDANDY FROM YOUR GRUBBY CLUTCHES...
...AND INTO MY GRUBBY CLUTCHES!!
AT EASE, TROOPS!!
YES, SIR!!
REMEMBER DA MOTOR CLUB MOTTO-- "GREAT DEEDS IS DONE WIT' NO BUDGET"!
SO KEEP THINKIN' O' IDEAS! USE YUH BRAIN!
BRAINS! BRAINS! BRAINS!
DAT'S RIGHT! JUST LIKE I DO!

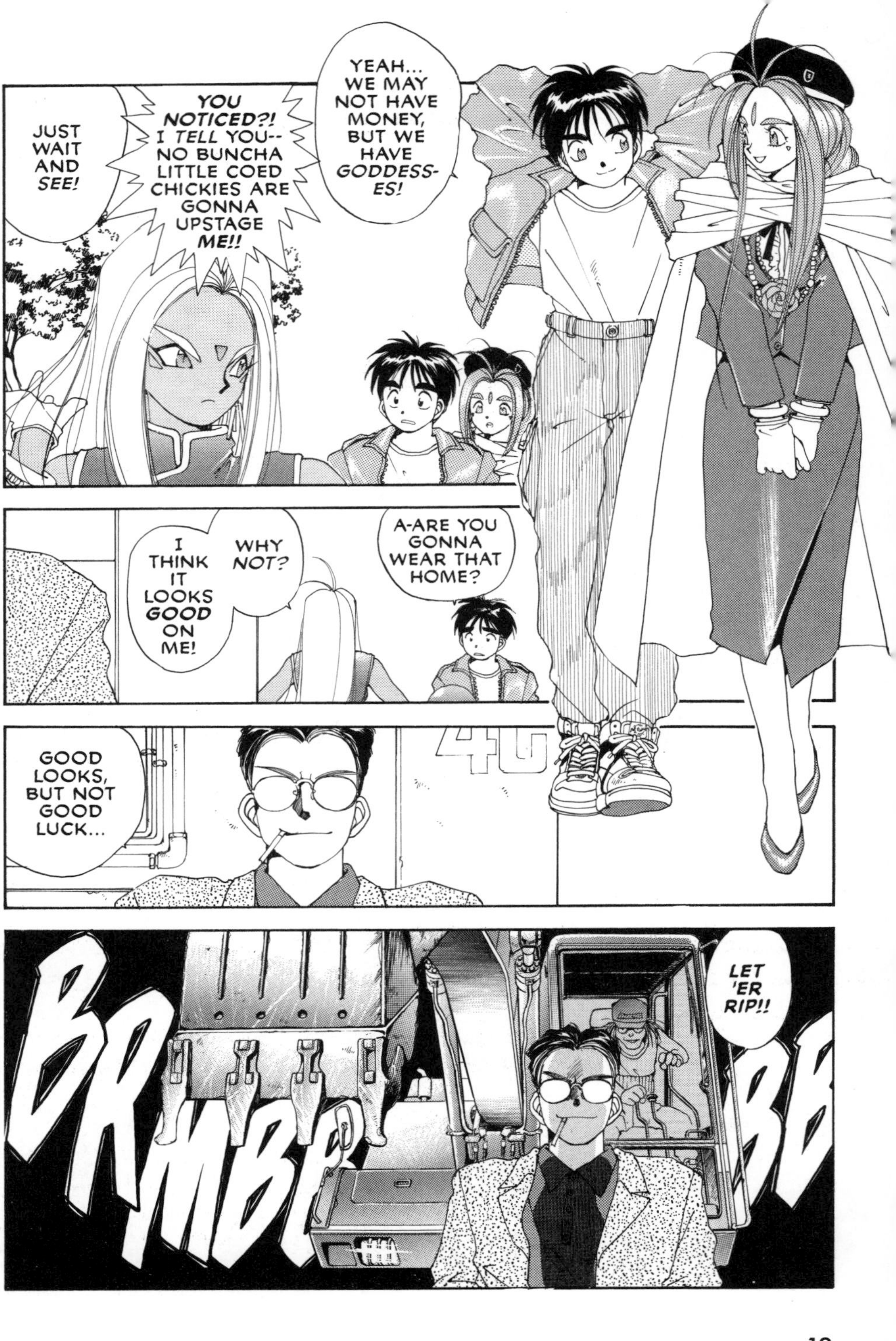
YEAH... WE MAY NOT HAVE MONEY, BUT WE HAVE GODDESSES!
YOU NOTICED?! I TELL YOU-- NO BUNCHA LITTLE COED CHICKIES ARE GONNA UPSTAGE ME!!
JUST WAIT AND SEE!
A-ARE YOU GONNA WEAR THAT HOME?
WHY NOT?
I THINK IT LOOKS GOOD ON ME!
GOOD LOOKS, BUT NOT GOOD LUCK...
LET 'ER RIP!!
BB
BRMBB

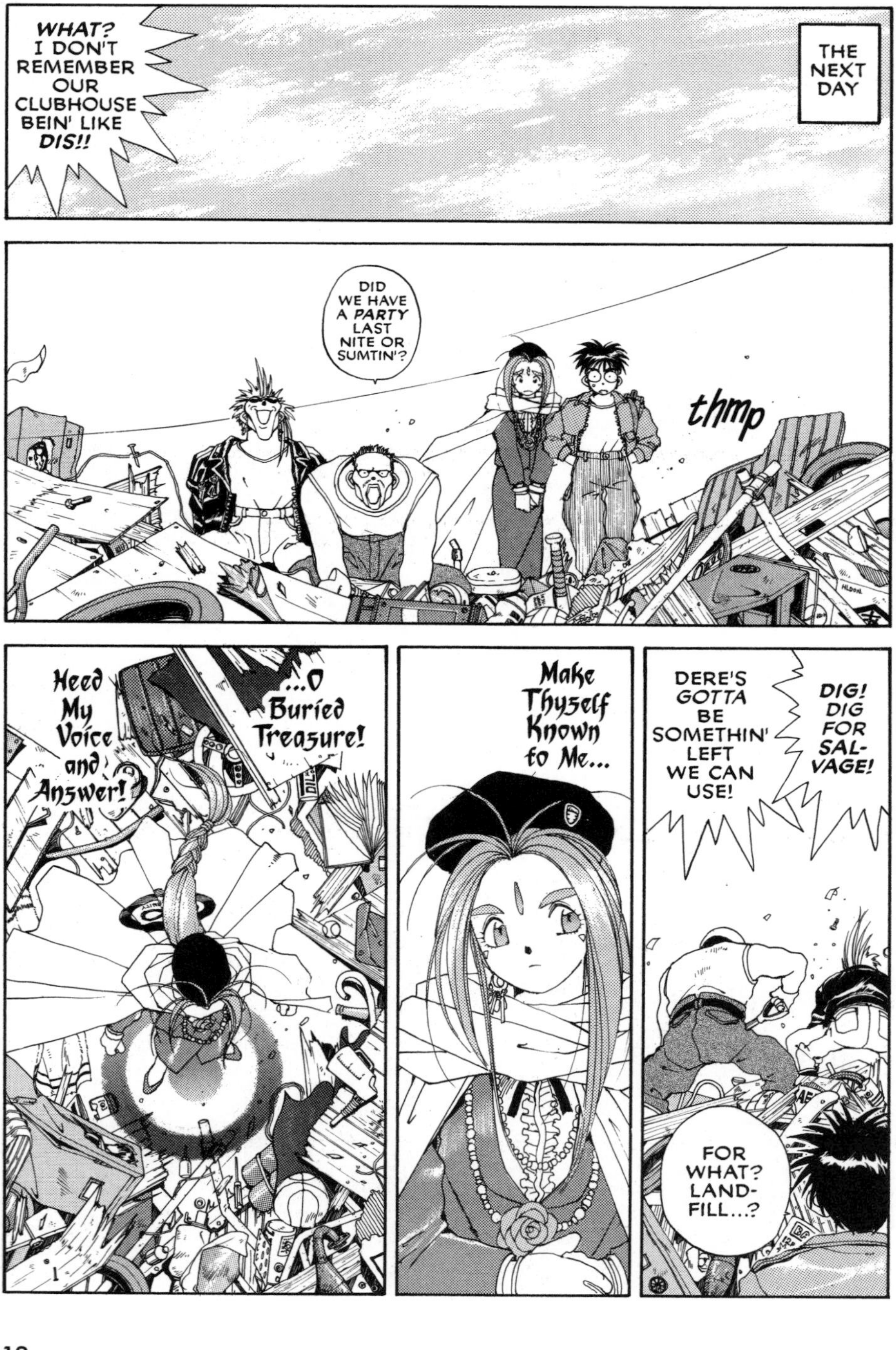
THE NEXT DAY
WHAT? I DON'T REMEMBER OUR CLUBHOUSE BEIN' LIKE DIS!!
DID WE HAVE A PARTY LAST NITE OR SUMTIN'?
thmp
DERE'S GOTTA BE SOMETHIN' LEFT WE CAN USE!
DIG! DIG FOR SAL-VAGE!
FOR WHAT? LAND-FILL...?
Make Thyself Known to Me...
Heed My Voice and Answer!
...O Buried Treasure!

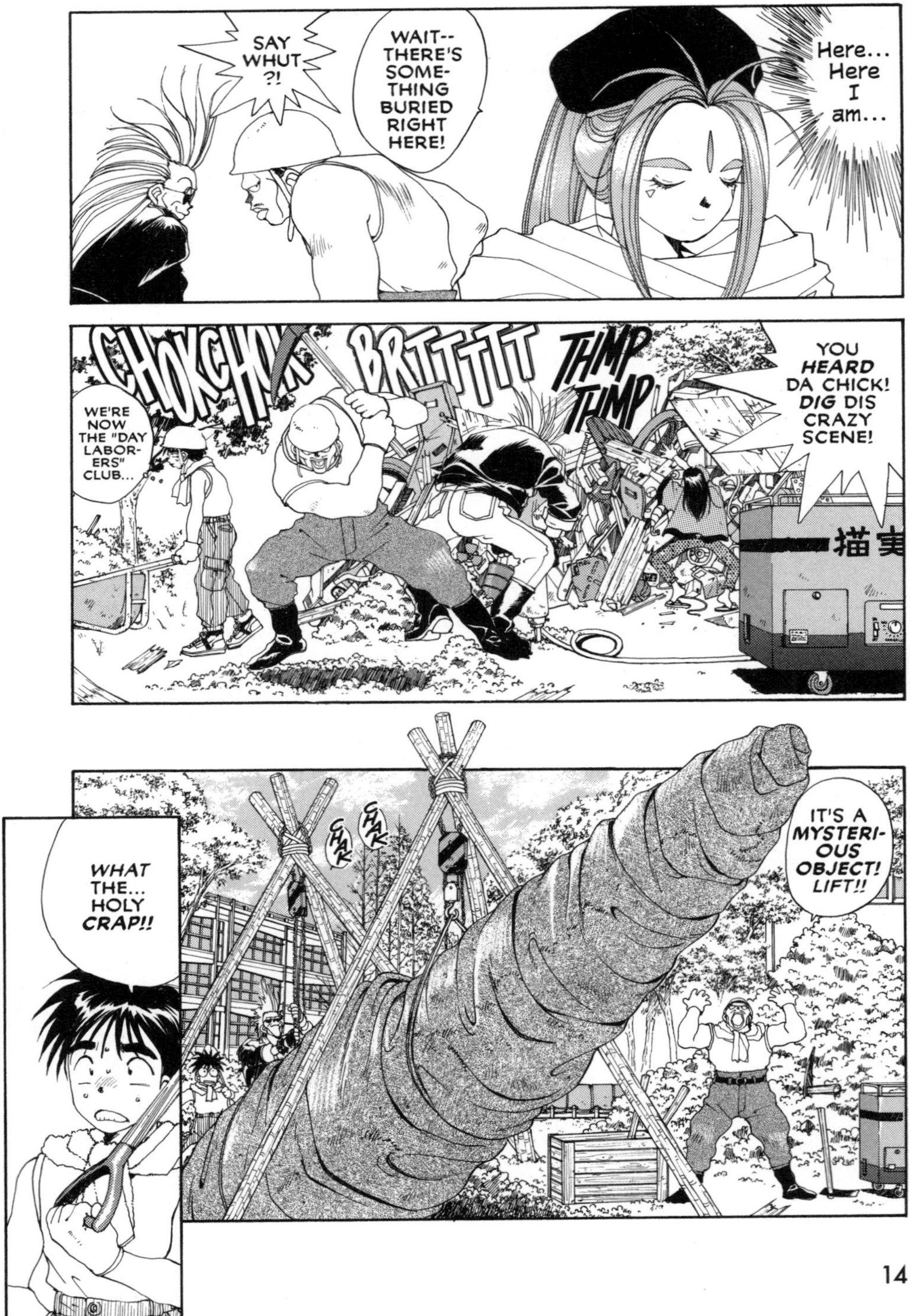
Here... Here I am...
WAIT-- THERE'S SOME-THING BURIED RIGHT HERE!
SAY WHUT ?!
YOU *HEARD* DA CHICK! *DIG* DIS CRAZY SCENE!
猫実
THMP THMP
BRTTTTTT
CHOKCHOK
WE'RE NOW THE "DAY LABOR-ERS" CLUB...
IT'S A *MYSTERI-OUS OBJECT! LIFT!!*
CHAK
CHAK
*WHAT THE... HOLY CRAP!!*

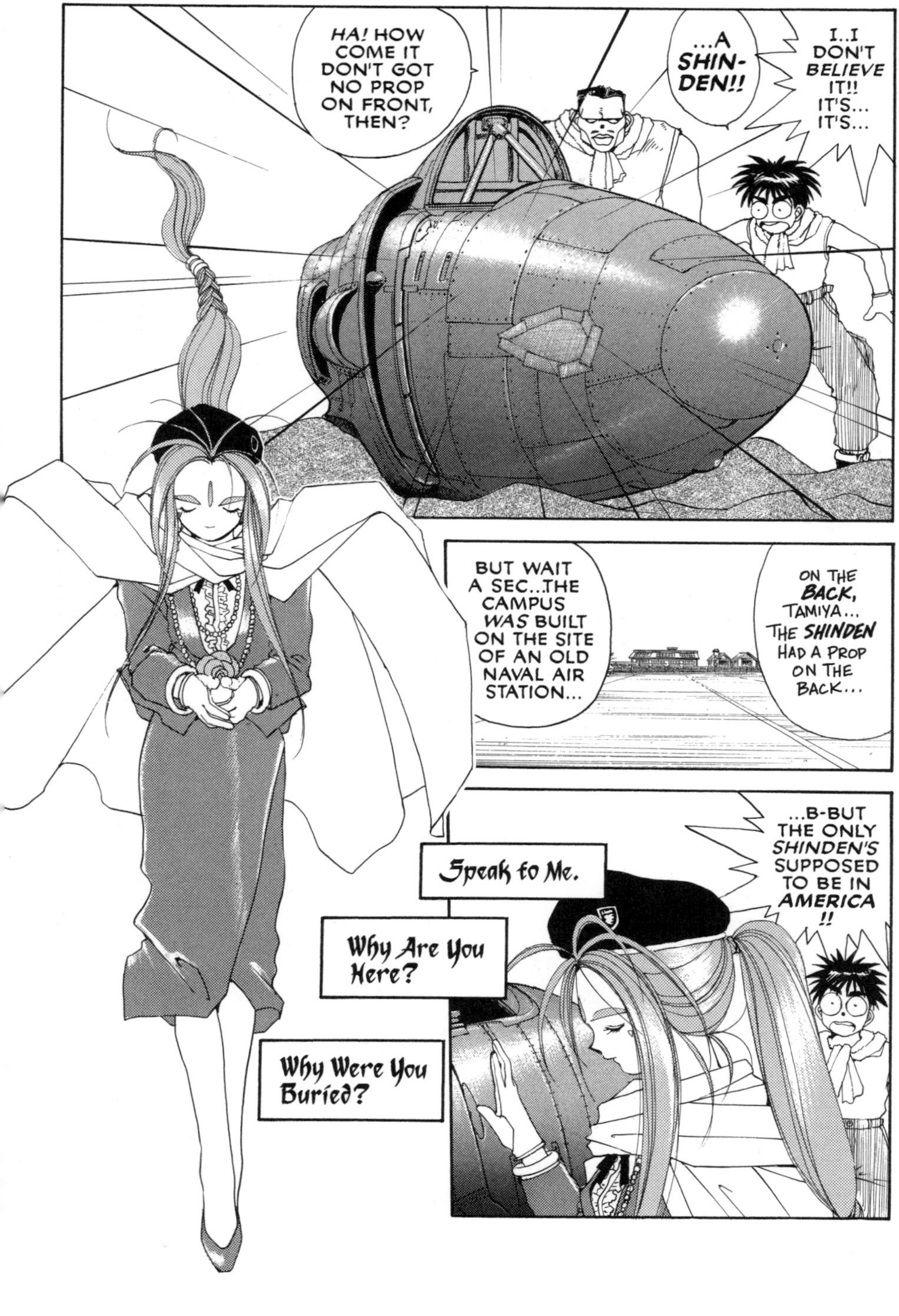
I..I DON'T BELIEVE IT!! IT'S... IT'S...
...A SHINDEN!!
HA! HOW COME IT DON'T GOT NO PROP ON FRONT, THEN?
ON THE BACK, TAMIYA... THE SHINDEN HAD A PROP ON THE BACK...
BUT WAIT A SEC...THE CAMPUS WAS BUILT ON THE SITE OF AN OLD NAVAL AIR STATION...
...B-BUT THE ONLY SHINDEN'S SUPPOSED TO BE IN AMERICA!!
Speak to Me.
Why Are You Here?
Why Were You Buried?

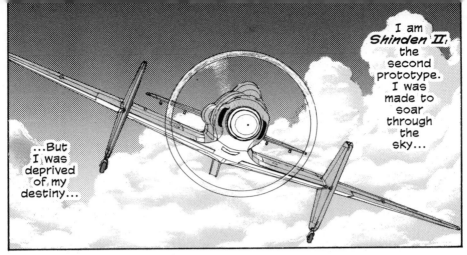

I am *Shinden II*, the second prototype. I was made to soar through the sky...
...But I was deprived of my destiny...
...before I ever had the chance.
My makers hid me deep within the earth...
I beg thee, let me fly.
KEIICHI...
...LET'S GIVE THE *SHINDEN* A CHANCE!
HUH ?!
DAT'S *IT!!*
Kyaa!

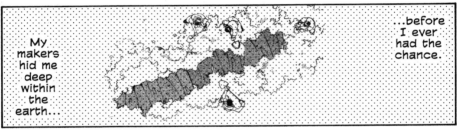

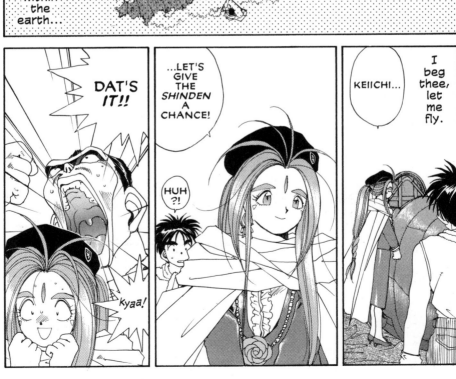

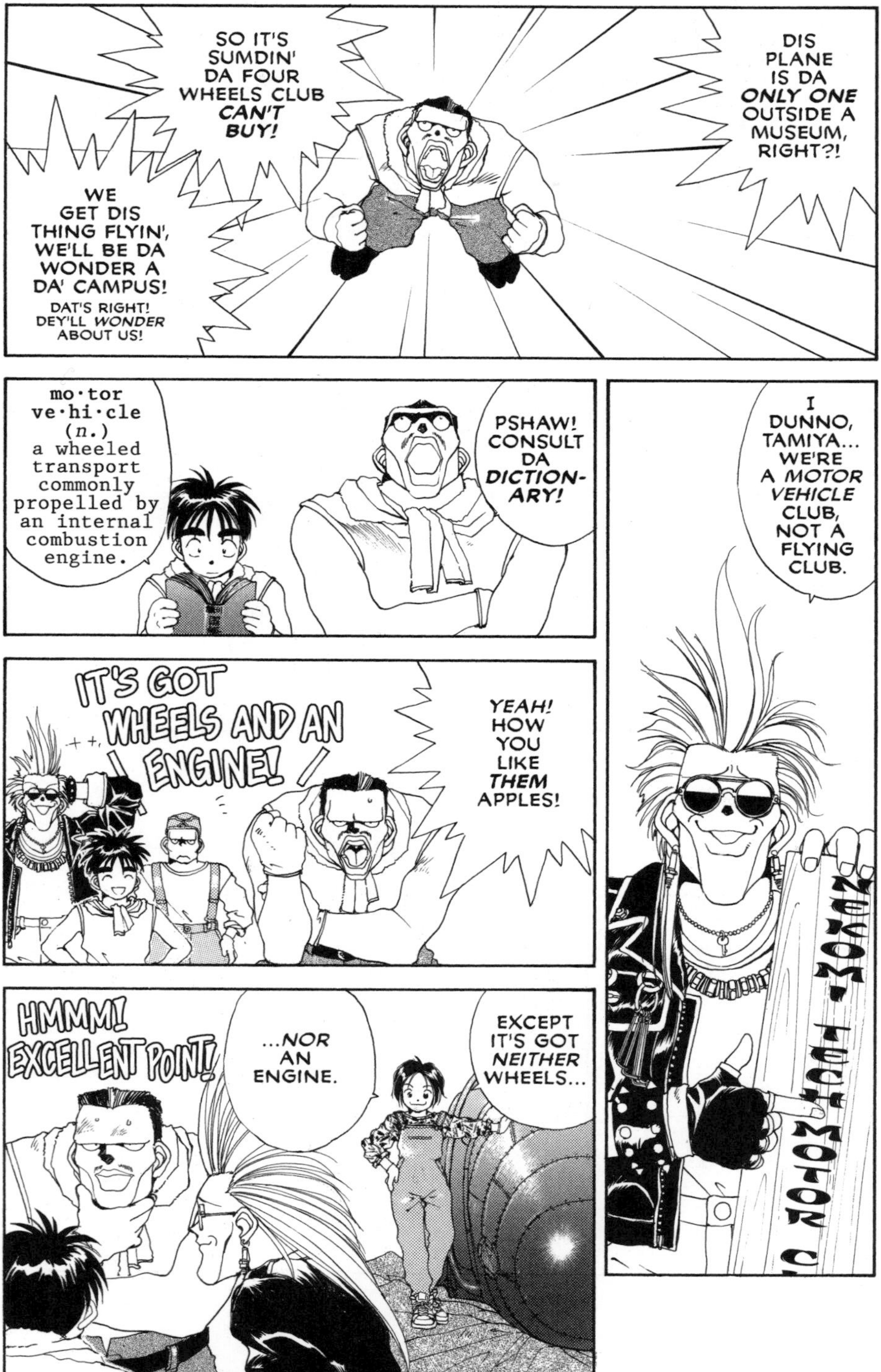
DIS PLANE IS DA *ONLY ONE* OUTSIDE A MUSEUM, RIGHT?!
SO IT'S SUMDIN' DA FOUR WHEELS CLUB *CAN'T BUY!*
WE GET DIS THING FLYIN', WE'LL BE DA WONDER A DA' CAMPUS!
DAT'S RIGHT! DEY'LL *WONDER* ABOUT US!
I DUNNO, TAMIYA... WE'RE A *MOTOR VEHICLE* CLUB, NOT A FLYING CLUB.
NEKOMI TECH MOTOR C
PSHAW! CONSULT DA *DICTIONARY!*
mo·tor ve·hi·cle (*n.*) a wheeled transport commonly propelled by an internal combustion engine.
*YEAH!* HOW YOU LIKE *THEM* APPLES!
IT'S GOT WHEELS AND AN ENGINE!
EXCEPT IT'S GOT *NEITHER* WHEELS...
...*NOR* AN ENGINE.
HMMM! EXCELLENT POINT!

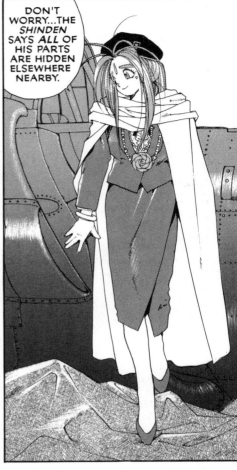

DON'T WORRY...THE *SHINDEN* SAYS **ALL** OF HIS PARTS ARE HIDDEN ELSEWHERE NEARBY.
DIG IT, MAN!
WELL DEN, BACK TA SUMTIN' WE *KNOW* WE'RE GOOD AT-- ***DITCH DIGGIN'!***
WAIT !!
YOU WON'T GET ANYWHERE JUST DIGGING AT RANDOM...
twtch
twtch
Wings, O Wings...
WHOA! *DOWSIN'*, EH?
twtch twtch
twtch
*HERE!*

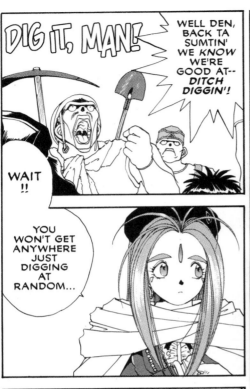

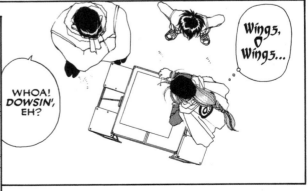

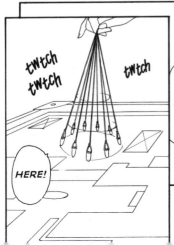

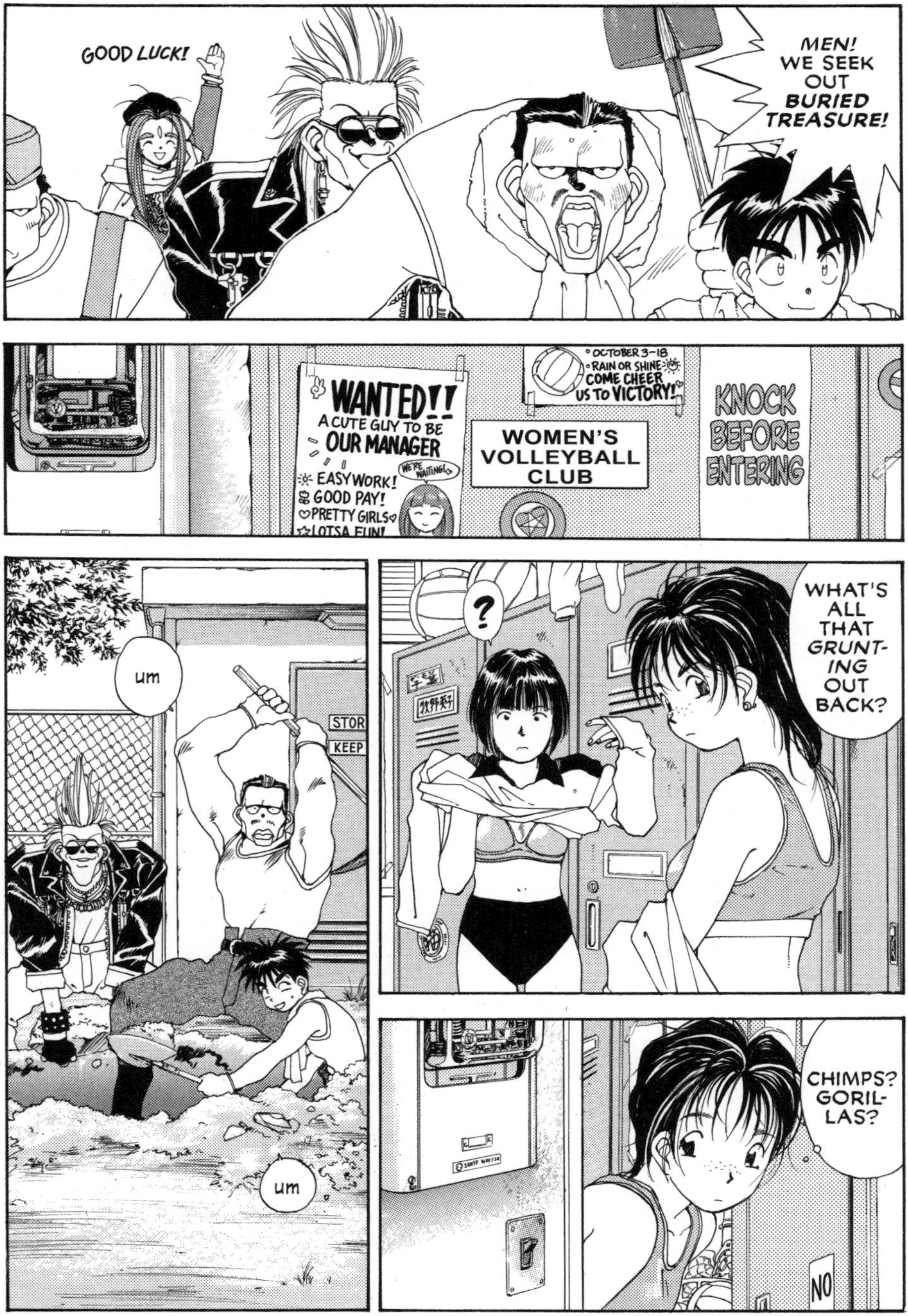

MEN! WE SEEK OUT BURIED TREASURE!
GOOD LUCK!
KNOCK BEFORE ENTERING
WOMEN'S VOLLEYBALL CLUB
OCTOBER 3-18
RAIN OR SHINE
COME CHEER US TO VICTORY!
WANTED!!
A CUTE GUY TO BE OUR MANAGER
WE'RE WAITING!
EASY WORK!
GOOD PAY!
PRETTY GIRLS
LOTSA FUN!
WHAT'S ALL THAT GRUNTING OUT BACK?
?
CHIMPS? GORILLAS?
um
um

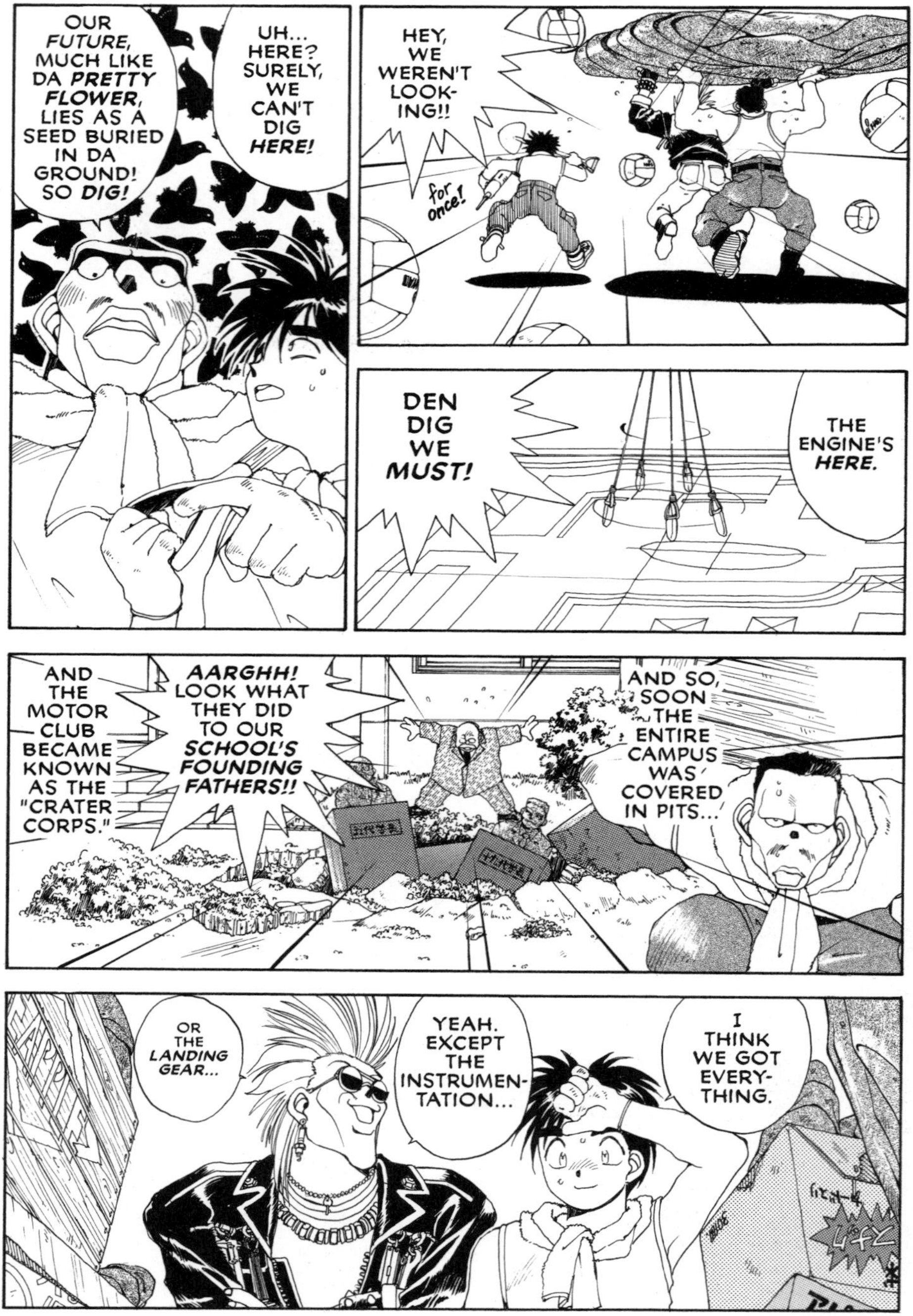
HEY, WE WEREN'T LOOKING!!
for once!
THE ENGINE'S HERE.
DEN DIG WE MUST!
UH... HERE? SURELY, WE CAN'T DIG HERE!
OUR FUTURE, MUCH LIKE DA PRETTY FLOWER, LIES AS A SEED BURIED IN DA GROUND! SO DIG!
AND SO, SOON THE ENTIRE CAMPUS WAS COVERED IN PITS...
AARGHH! LOOK WHAT THEY DID TO OUR SCHOOL'S FOUNDING FATHERS!!
AND THE MOTOR CLUB BECAME KNOWN AS THE "CRATER CORPS."
I THINK WE GOT EVERYTHING.
YEAH. EXCEPT THE INSTRUMENTATION...
OR THE LANDING GEAR...

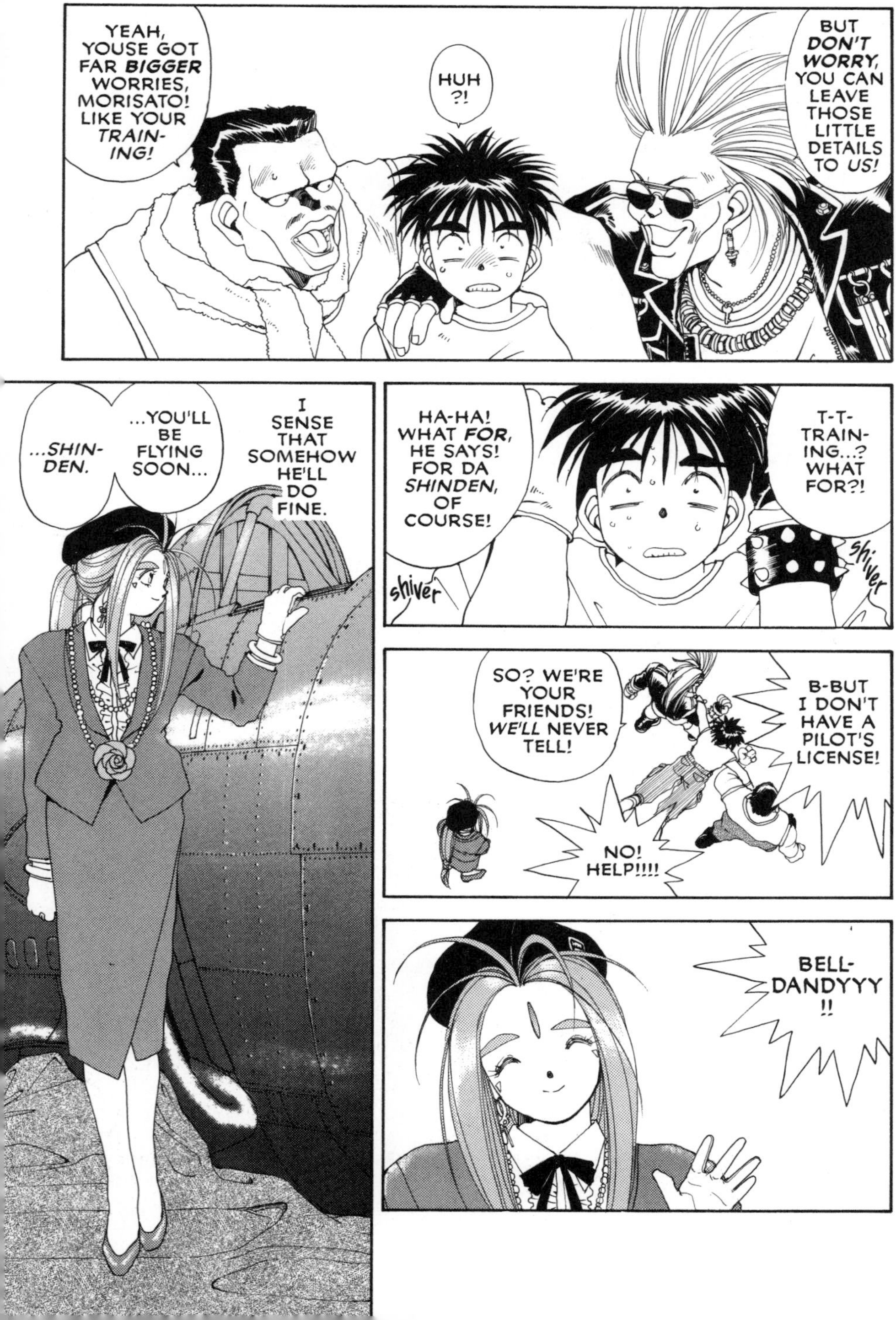
BUT DON'T WORRY, YOU CAN LEAVE THOSE LITTLE DETAILS TO US!
HUH ?!
YEAH, YOUSE GOT FAR BIGGER WORRIES, MORISATO! LIKE YOUR TRAIN-ING!
T-T-TRAIN-ING...? WHAT FOR?!
HA-HA! WHAT FOR, HE SAYS! FOR DA SHINDEN, OF COURSE!
shiver
shiver
B-BUT I DON'T HAVE A PILOT'S LICENSE!
SO? WE'RE YOUR FRIENDS! WE'LL NEVER TELL!
NO! HELP!!!!
BELL-DANDYYY !!
I SENSE THAT SOMEHOW HE'LL DO FINE.
...YOU'LL BE FLYING SOON...
...SHIN-DEN.

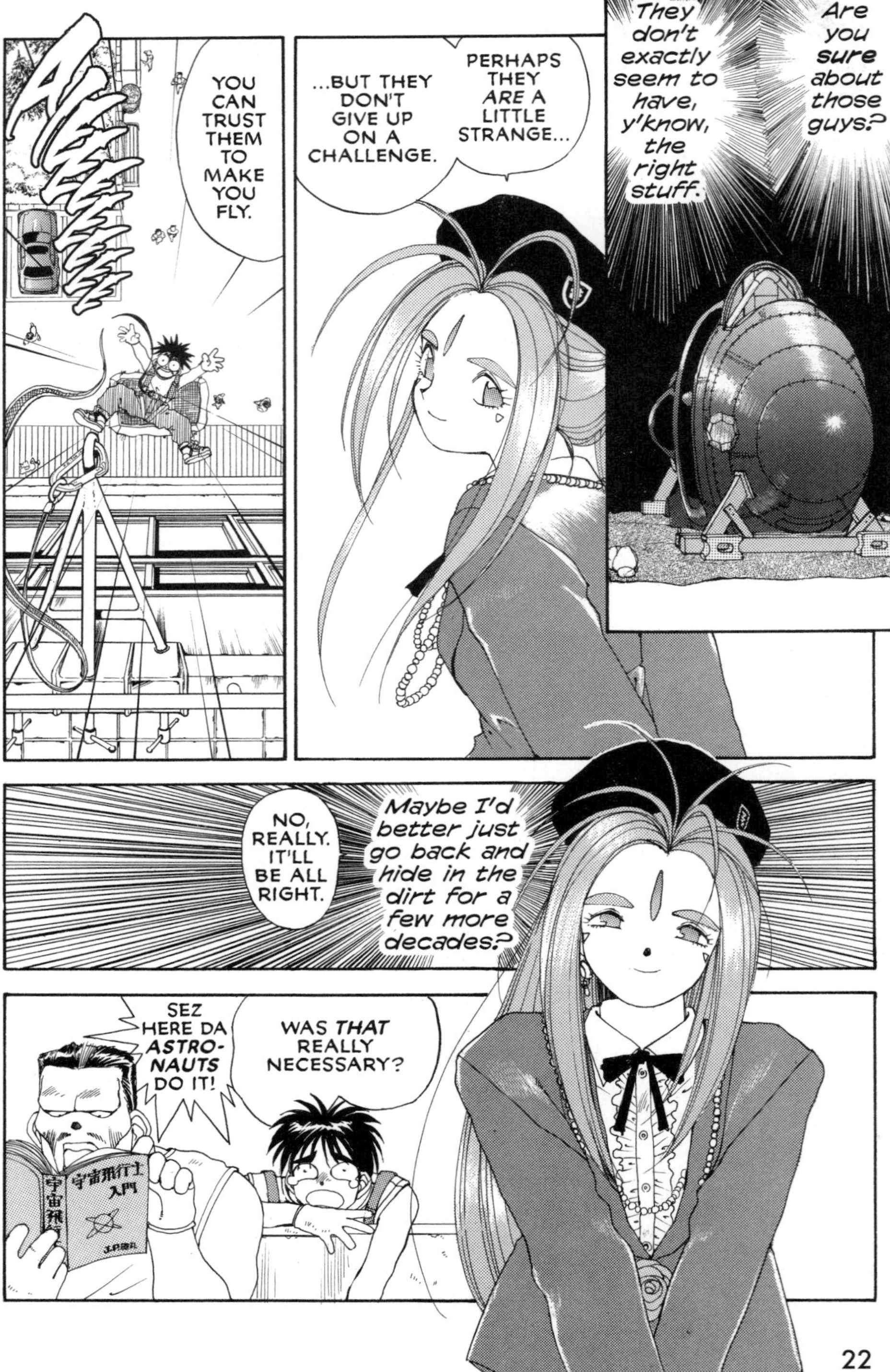
Are you sure about those guys?
They don't exactly seem to have, y'know, the right stuff.
PERHAPS THEY ARE A LITTLE STRANGE...
...BUT THEY DON'T GIVE UP ON A CHALLENGE.
YOU CAN TRUST THEM TO MAKE YOU FLY.
Maybe I'd better just go back and hide in the dirt for a few more decades?
NO, REALLY. IT'LL BE ALL RIGHT.
WAS THAT REALLY NECESSARY?
SEZ HERE DA ASTRONAUTS DO IT!
宇宙飛行士入門

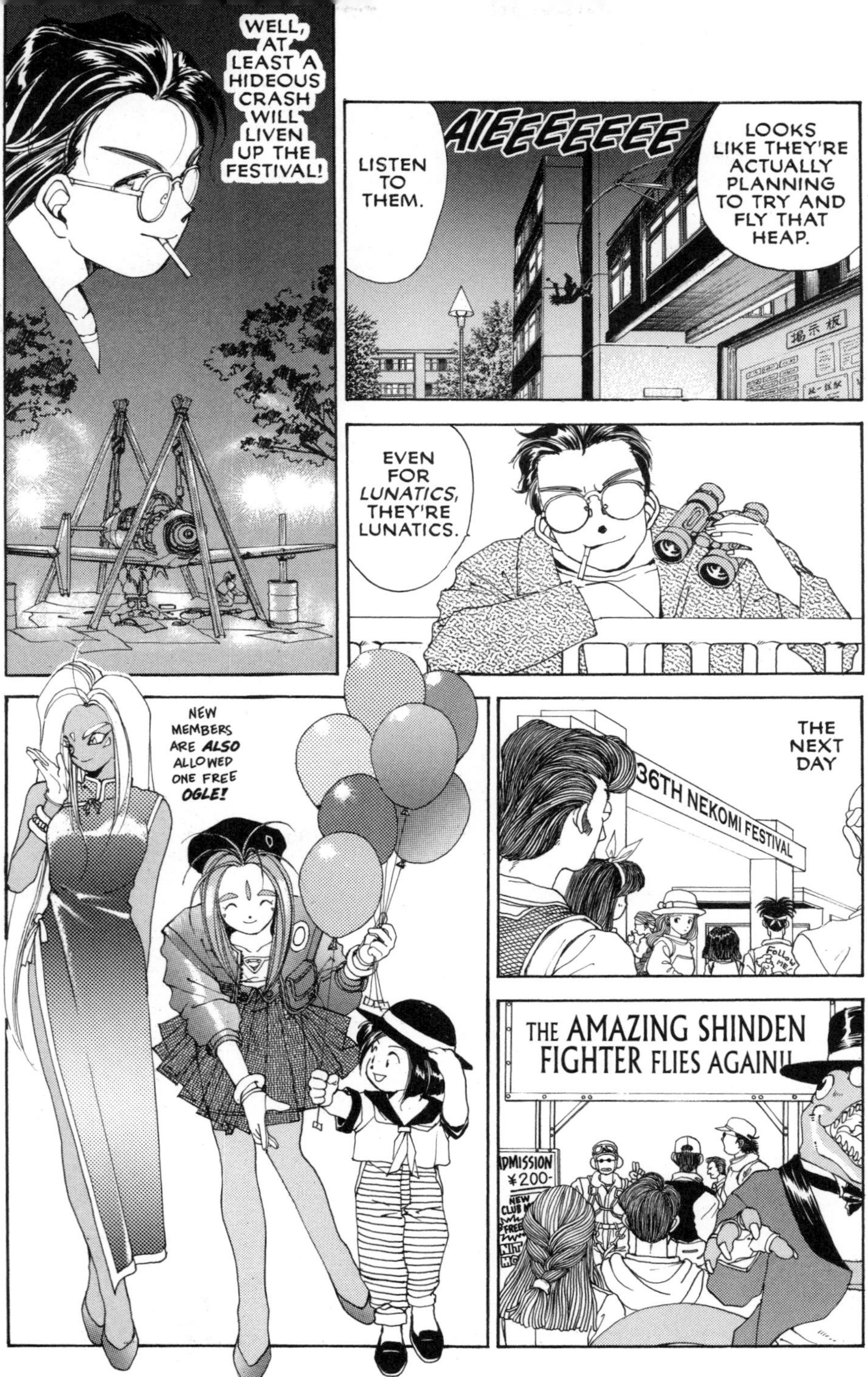
LOOKS LIKE THEY'RE ACTUALLY PLANNING TO TRY AND FLY THAT HEAP.
AIEEEEEEEE
LISTEN TO THEM.
EVEN FOR *LUNATICS*, THEY'RE LUNATICS.
WELL, AT LEAST A HIDEOUS CRASH WILL LIVEN UP THE FESTIVAL!
THE NEXT DAY
36TH NEKOMI FESTIVAL
THE AMAZING SHINDEN FIGHTER FLIES AGAIN!!
ADMISSION ¥200-
NEW MEMBERS ARE **ALSO** ALLOWED ONE FREE **OGLE!**

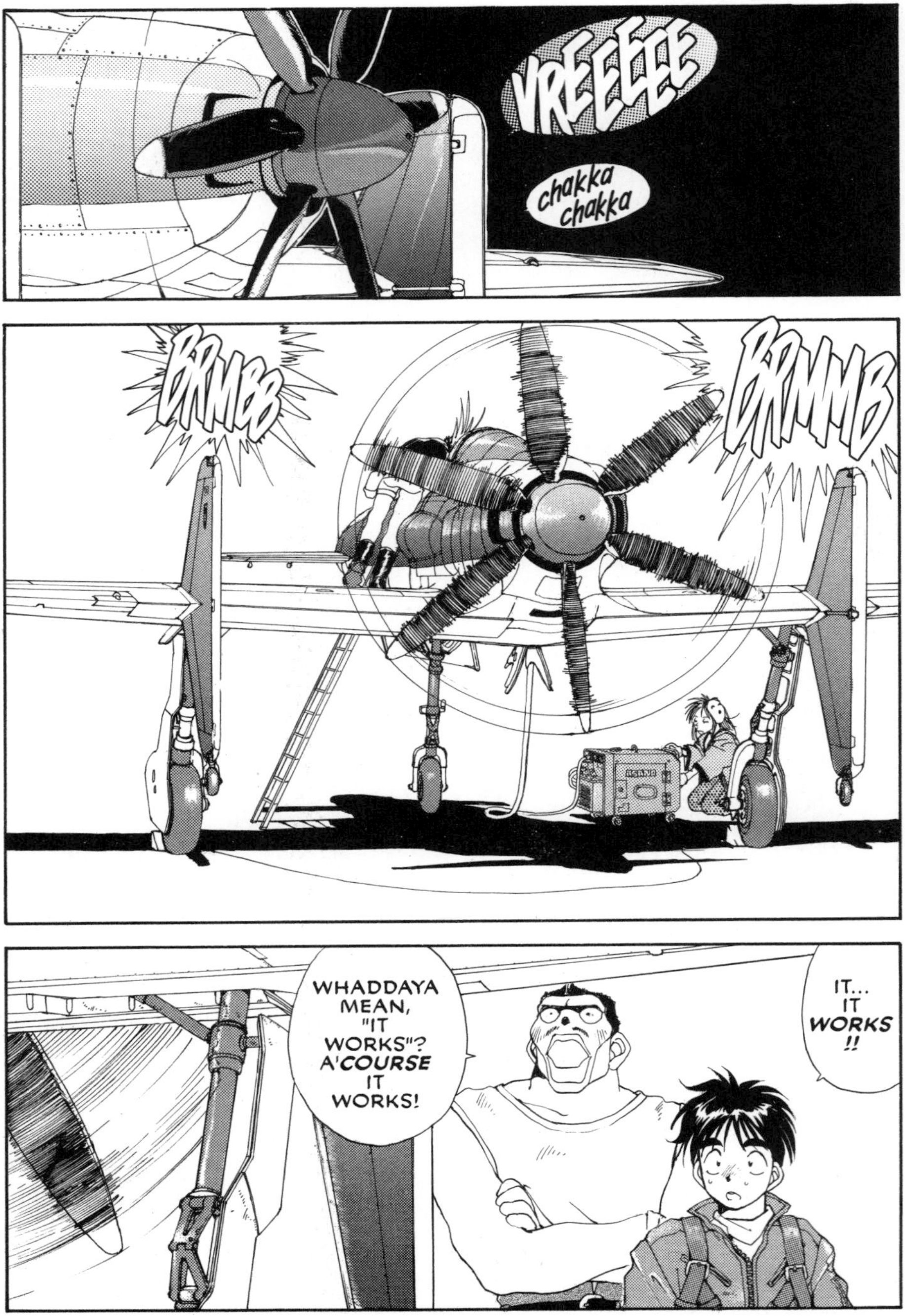
VREEEEE
chakka chakka
BRMMB
BRMBB
IT... IT WORKS!!
WHADDAYA MEAN, "IT WORKS"? A'COURSE IT WORKS!

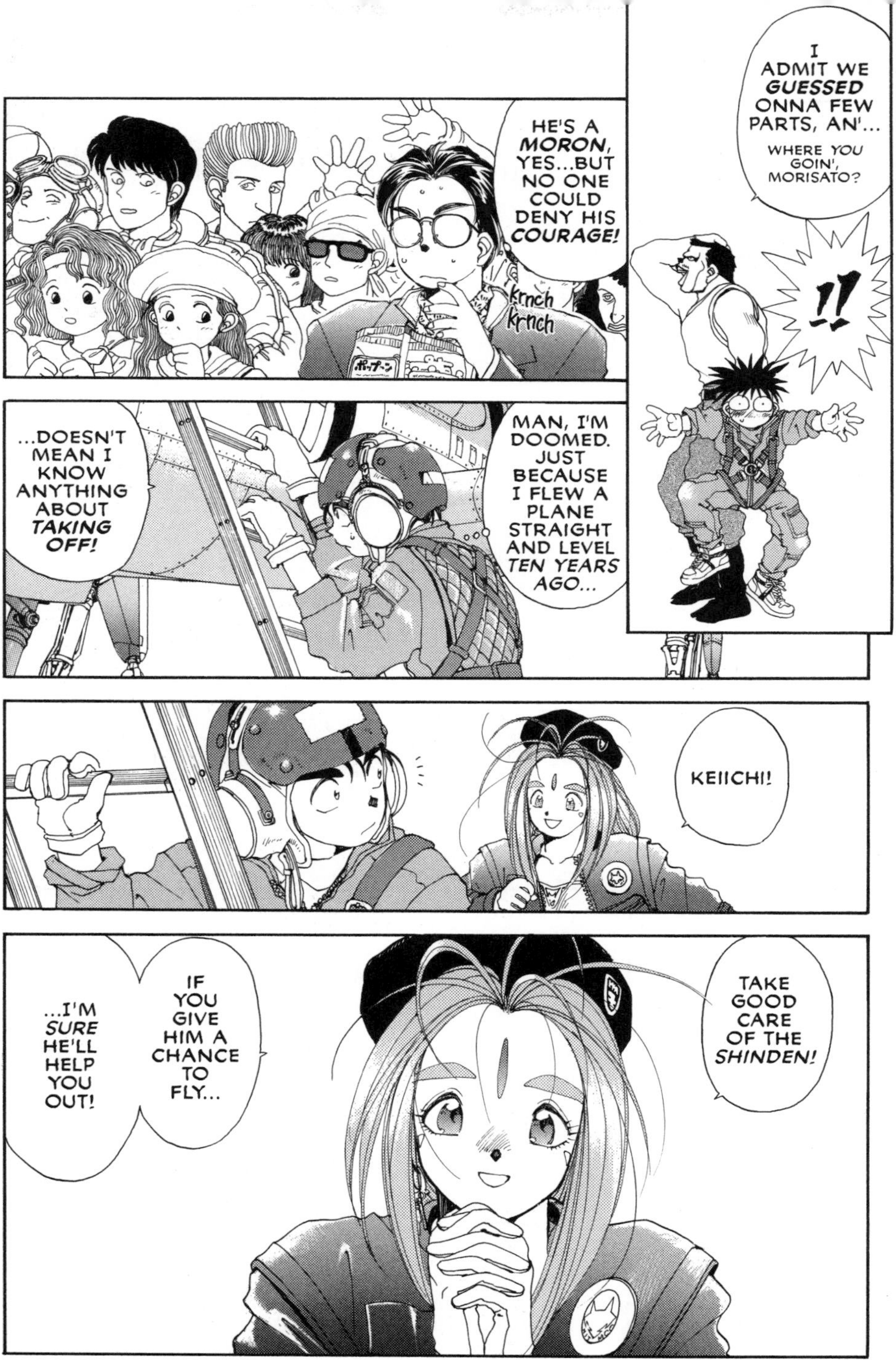
I ADMIT WE GUESSED ONNA FEW PARTS, AN'...
WHERE YOU GOIN', MORISATO?
!!
HE'S A MORON, YES...BUT NO ONE COULD DENY HIS COURAGE!
krnch krnch
MAN, I'M DOOMED. JUST BECAUSE I FLEW A PLANE STRAIGHT AND LEVEL TEN YEARS AGO...
...DOESN'T MEAN I KNOW ANYTHING ABOUT TAKING OFF!
KEIICHI!
TAKE GOOD CARE OF THE SHINDEN!
IF YOU GIVE HIM A CHANCE TO FLY...
...I'M SURE HE'LL HELP YOU OUT!

HOW CAN I REFUSE... A MISSION FROM A GODDESS?!
LEAVE IT TO ME, BELL-DANDY!
pat
....
BRAAAAAAAA
LET'S GO, SHIN-DEN!!
chak
OKAY, THEN...
GREAT... THEY JUST BOLTED ON A BUNCH OF MOTOR-CYCLE AND TRUCK GAUGES...
WELL... AT LEAST I CAN READ THEM...

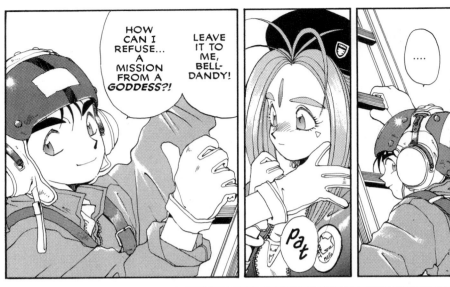

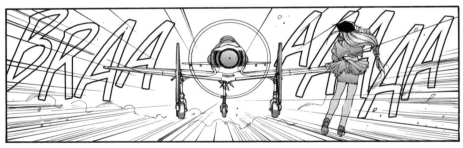

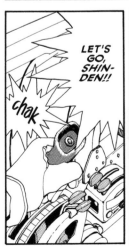

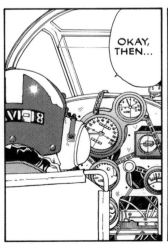

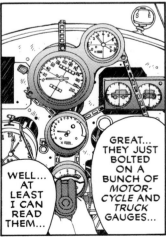

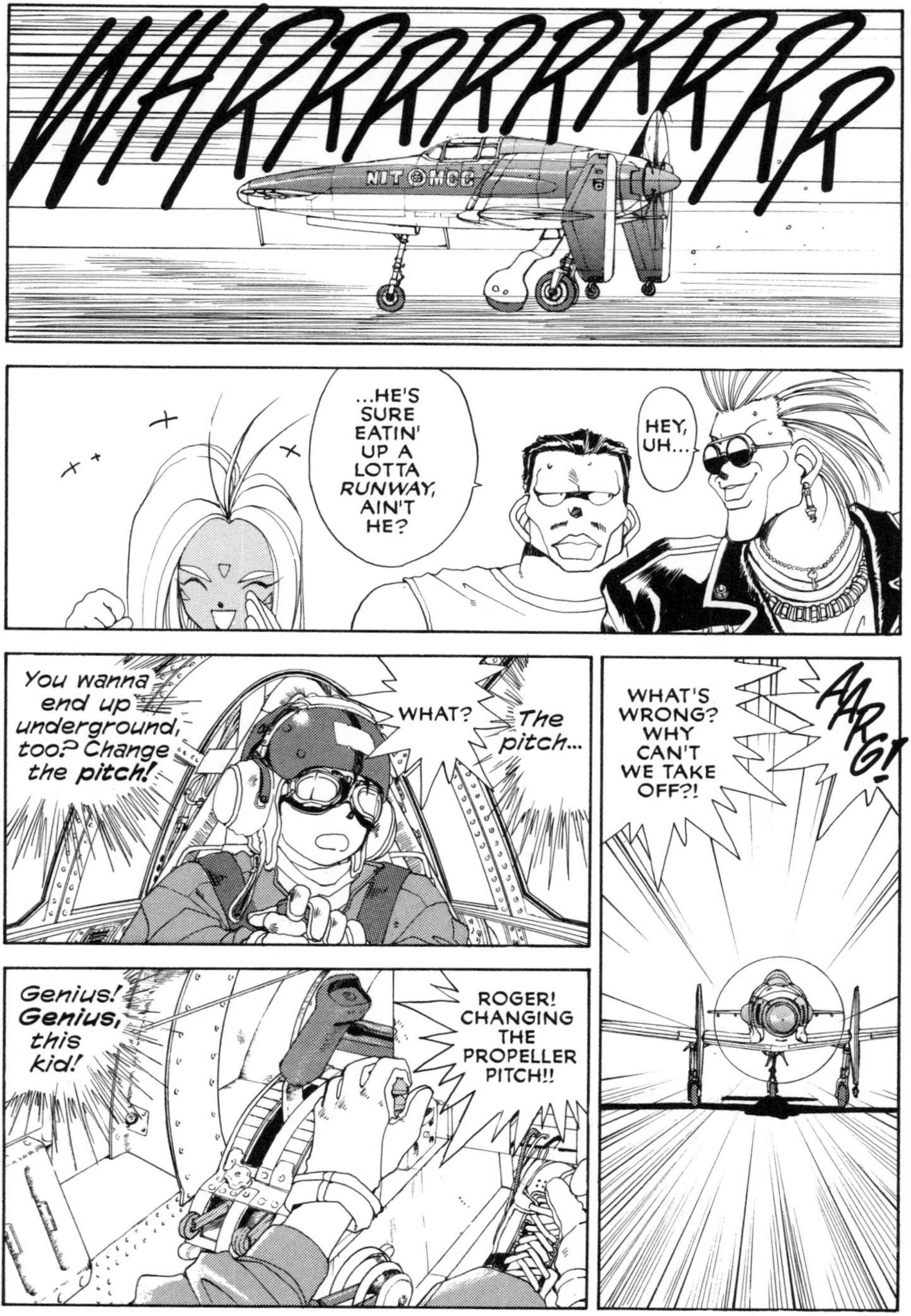
WHRRRRRRRRRRR
HEY, UH...
...HE'S SURE EATIN' UP A LOTTA RUNWAY, AIN'T HE?
WHAT'S WRONG? WHY CAN'T WE TAKE OFF?!
AARG!
The pitch...
WHAT?
You wanna end up underground, too? Change the pitch!
ROGER! CHANGING THE PROPELLER PITCH!!
Genius! Genius, this kid!

FLY, SHINDEN! AND CARRY OUR DREAMS WITH YOU...

SKff

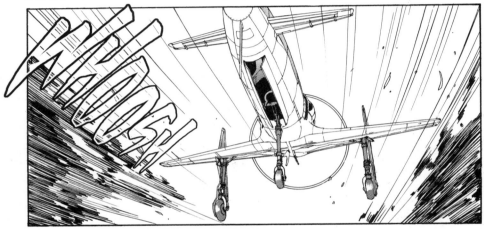

WHOOSH!

HURAAAAAAH!

YOU REALLY *DID* WANT TO FLY... DIDN'T YOU, SHINDEN?

WOW...

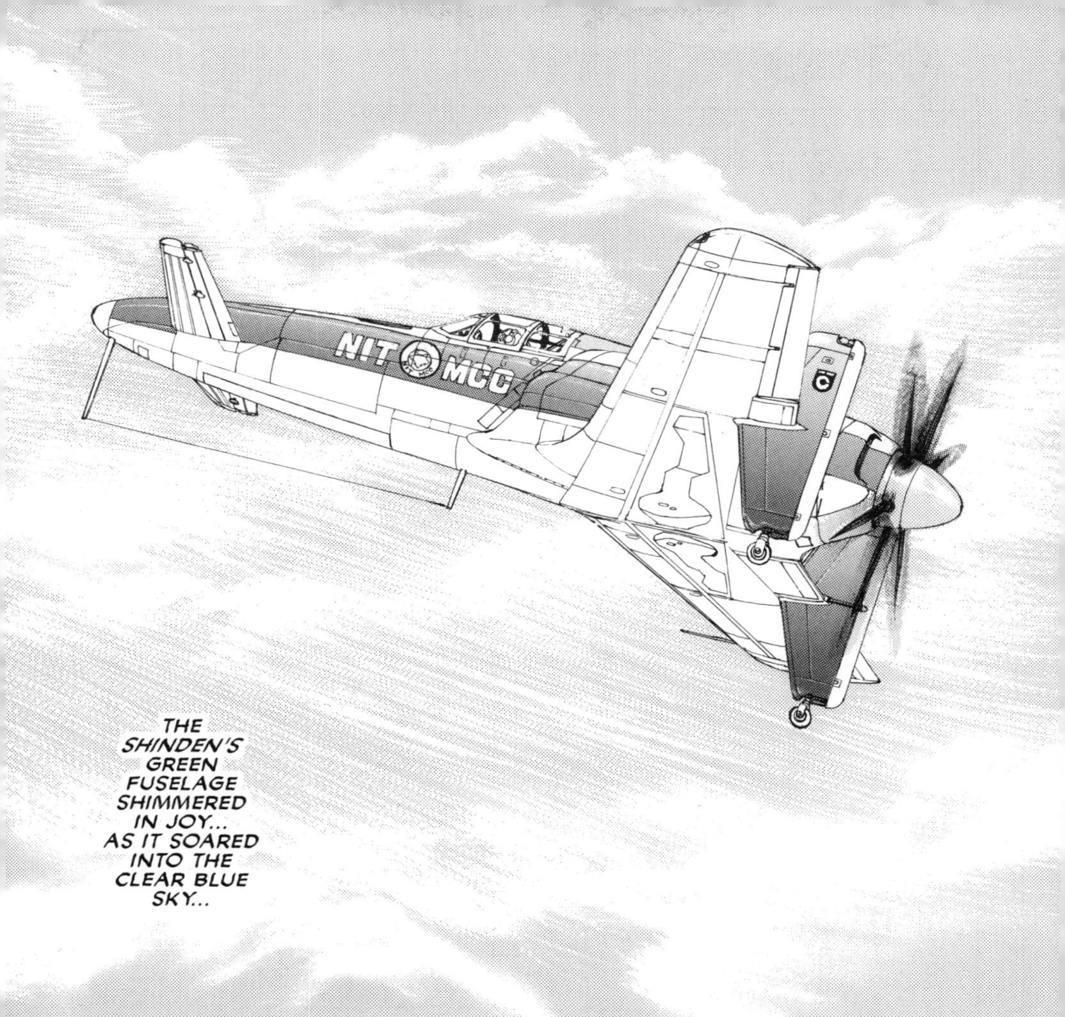
NIT MCC
THE SHINDEN'S GREEN FUSELAGE SHIMMERED IN JOY... AS IT SOARED INTO THE CLEAR BLUE SKY...

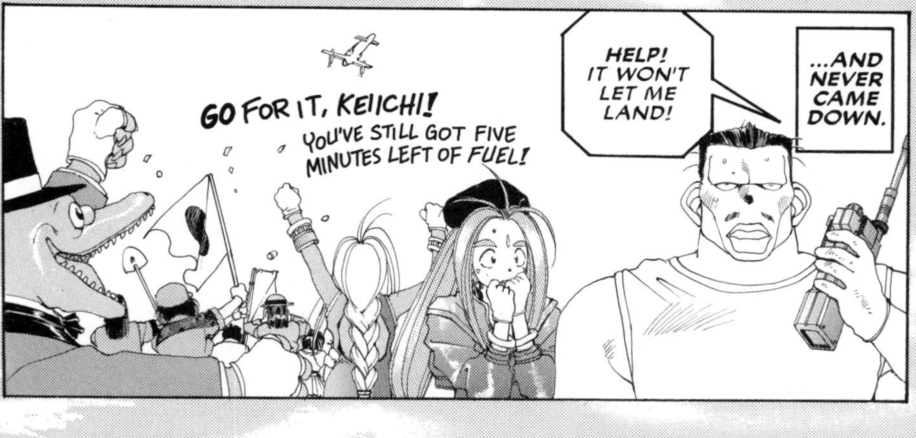
...AND NEVER CAME DOWN.
HELP! IT WON'T LET ME LAND!
GO FOR IT, KEIICHI!
YOU'VE STILL GOT FIVE MINUTES LEFT OF FUEL!

# THE ADVENTURES OF MINI-URD
## PART 2

1/24

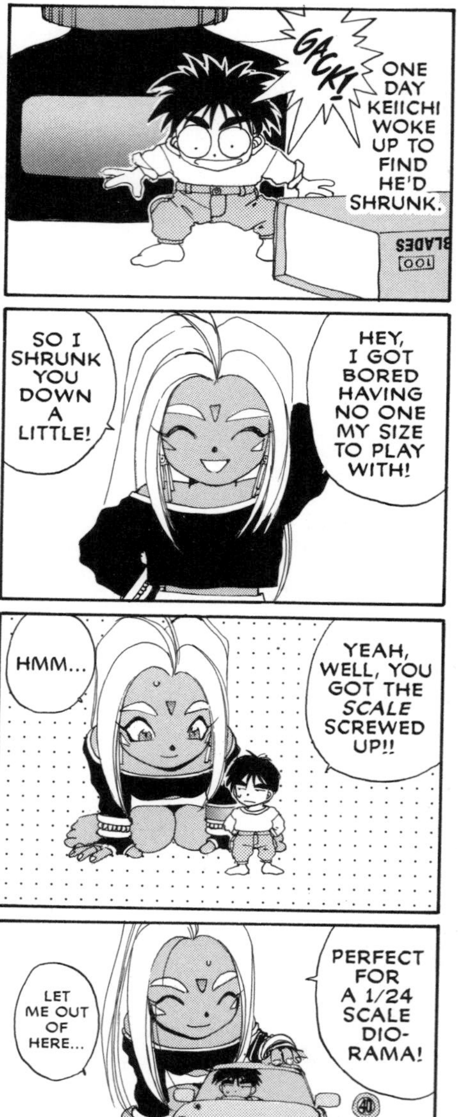
ONE DAY KEIICHI WOKE UP TO FIND HE'D SHRUNK.
GACK!
HEY, I GOT BORED HAVING NO ONE MY SIZE TO PLAY WITH!
SO I SHRUNK YOU DOWN A LITTLE!
YEAH, WELL, YOU GOT THE *SCALE* SCREWED UP!!
HMM...
PERFECT FOR A 1/24 SCALE DIO-RAMA!
LET ME OUT OF HERE...

1/35

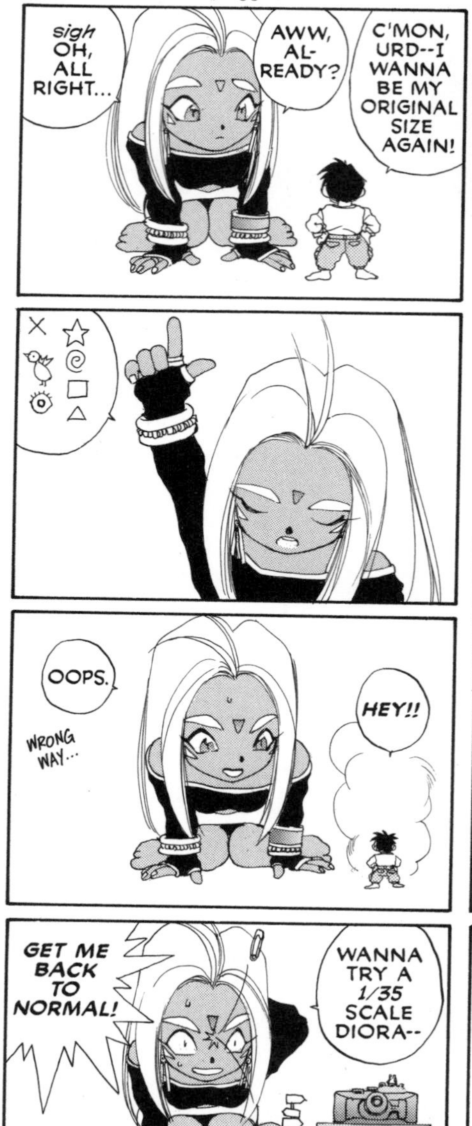
C'MON, URD--I WANNA BE MY ORIGINAL SIZE AGAIN!
AWW, AL-READY?
*sigh* OH, ALL RIGHT...
HEY!!
OOPS.
WRONG WAY...
WANNA TRY A *1/35* SCALE DIORA--
GET ME BACK TO NORMAL!

SEE YOU NEXT TIME!

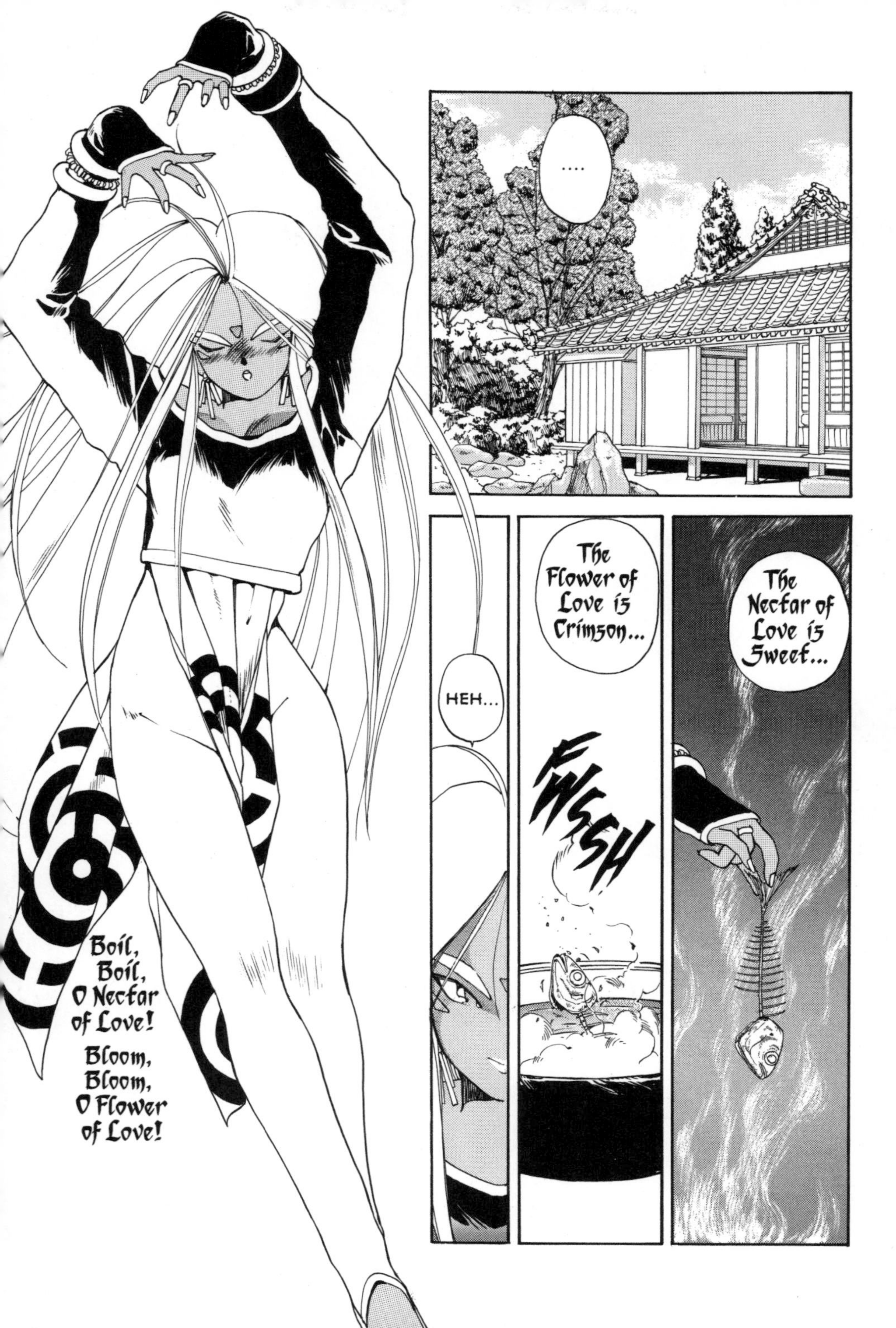
....
The Nectar of Love is Sweet...
The Flower of Love is Crimson...
FWSSH
HEH...
Boil, Boil, O Nectar of Love!
Bloom, Bloom, O Flower of Love!

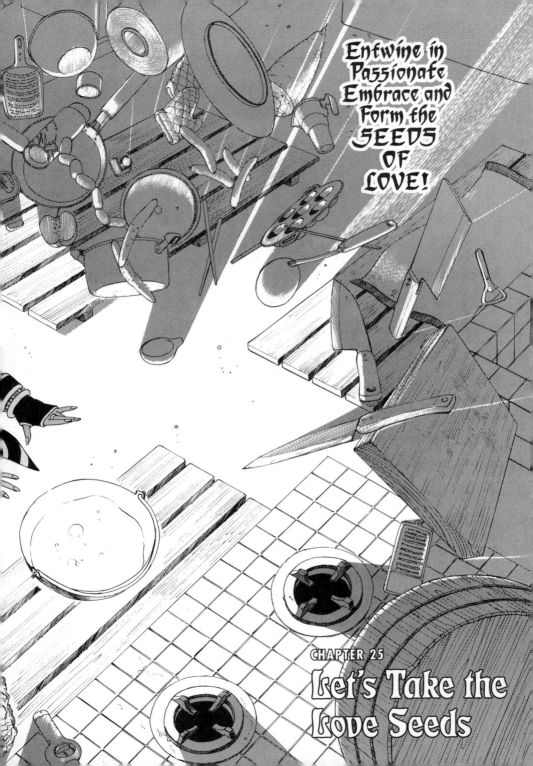

Entwine in Passionate Embrace and Form the SEEDS OF LOVE!

CHAPTER 25
Let's Take the Love Seeds

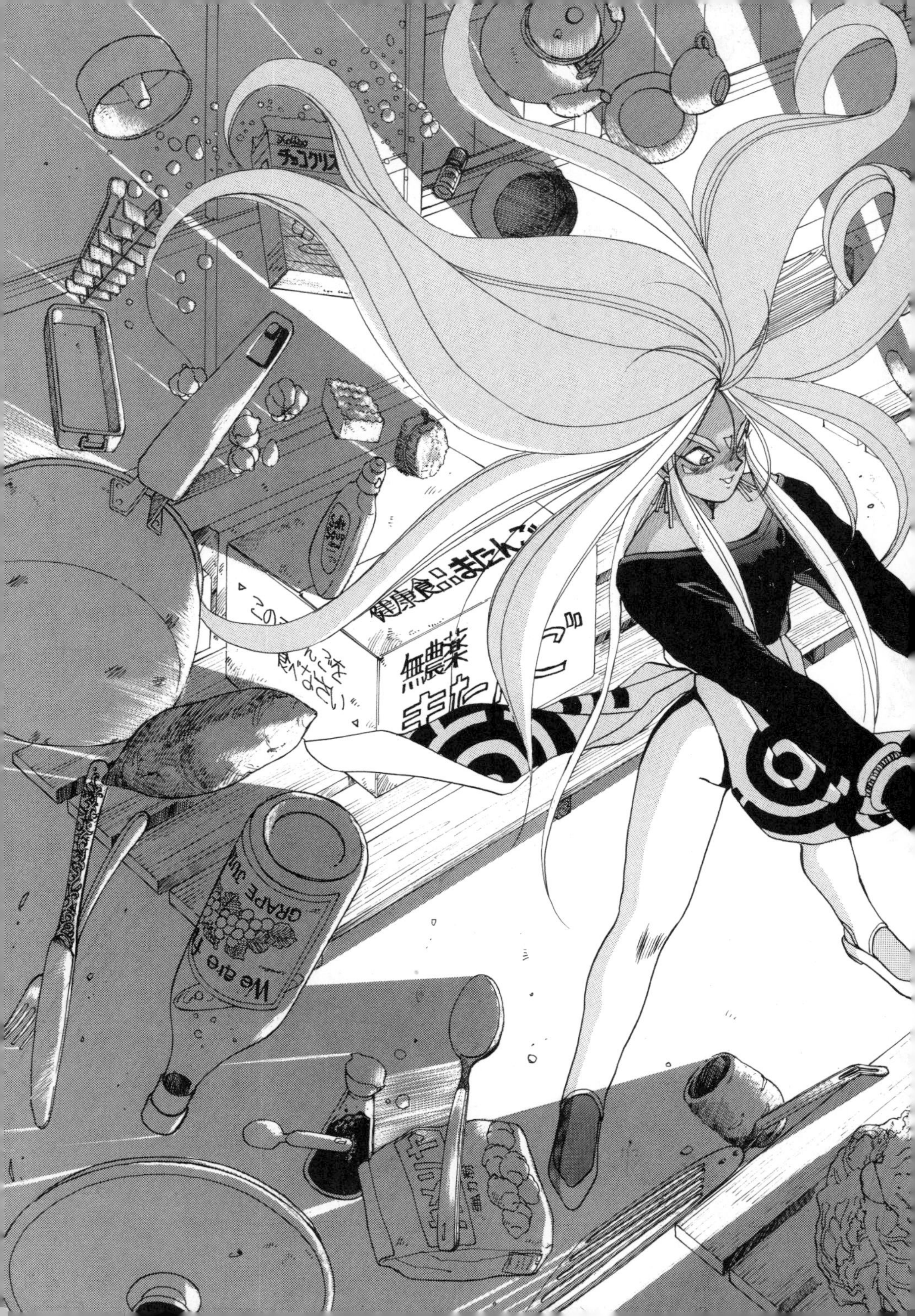
チョコクリス
健康食品
無農薬
GRAPE
We are

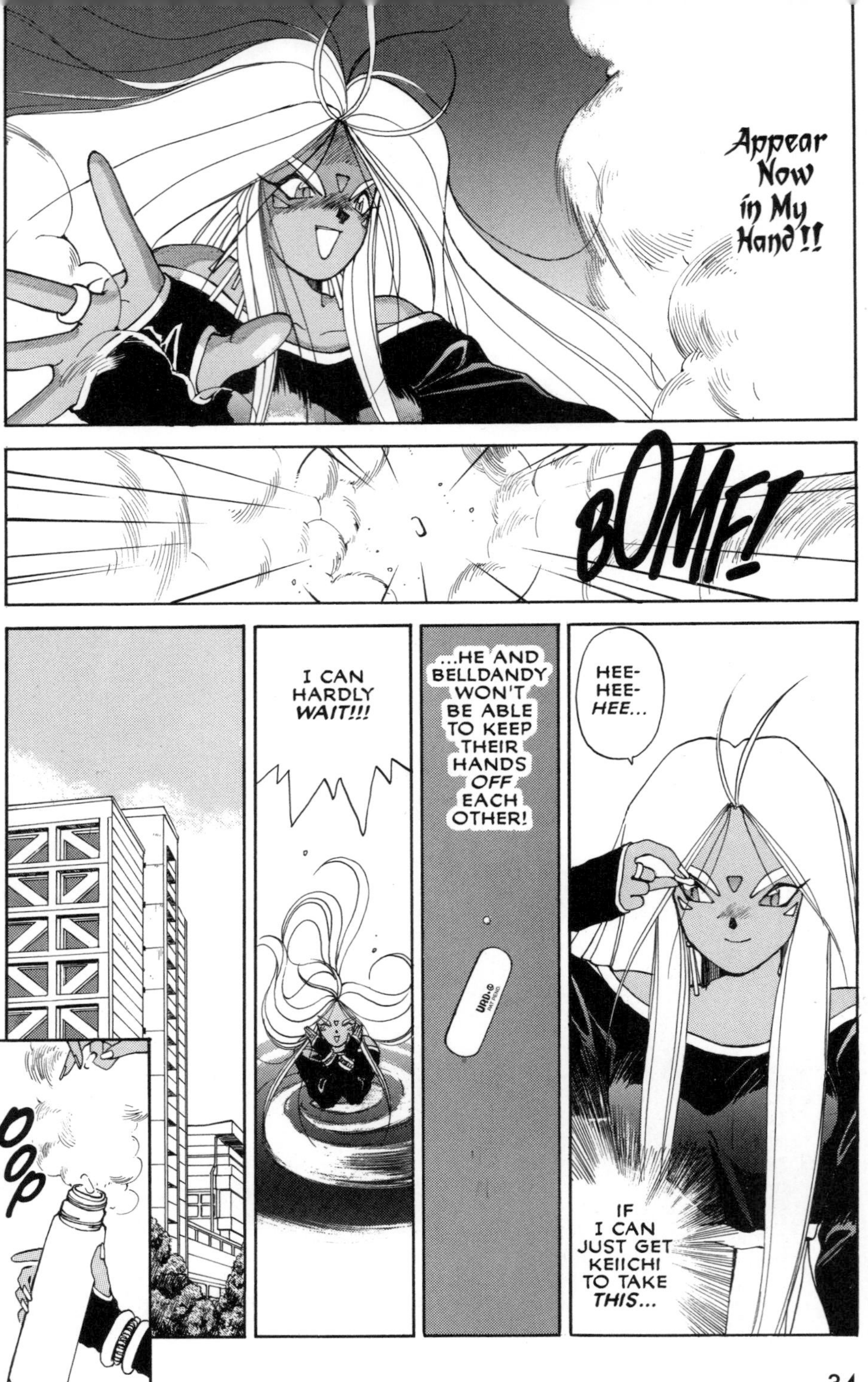
Appear Now in My Hand!!
BOMF!
HEE-HEE-HEE...
IF I CAN JUST GET KEIICHI TO TAKE THIS...
...HE AND BELLDANDY WON'T BE ABLE TO KEEP THEIR HANDS OFF EACH OTHER!
I CAN HARDLY WAIT!!!
POP

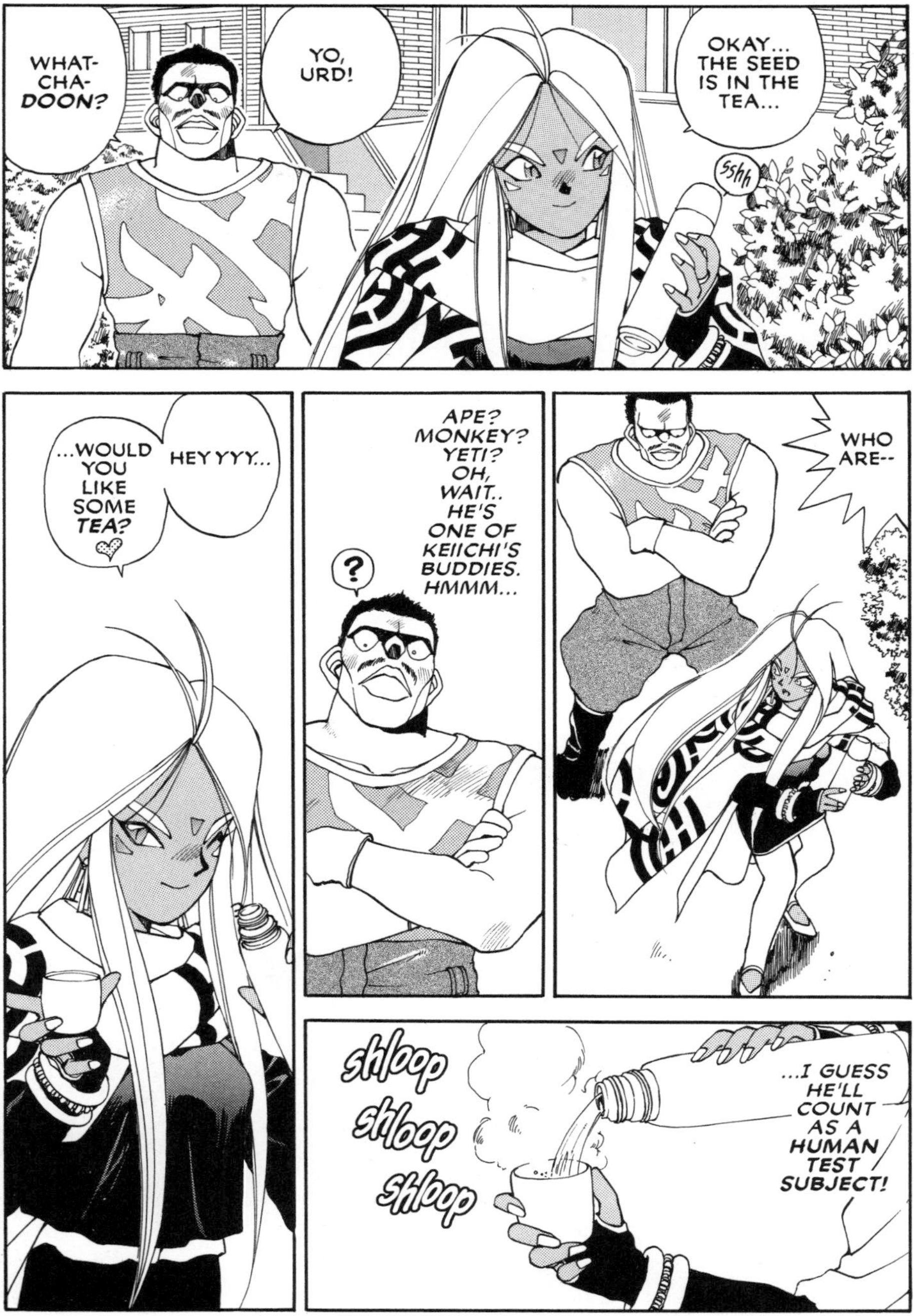
OKAY... THE SEED IS IN THE TEA...
YO, URD!
WHAT-CHA-DOON?
sshh
WHO ARE--
APE? MONKEY? YETI? OH, WAIT.. HE'S ONE OF KEIICHI'S BUDDIES. HMMM...
?
...I GUESS HE'LL COUNT AS A HUMAN TEST SUBJECT!
shloop
shloop
shloop
HEYYYY...
...WOULD YOU LIKE SOME TEA?

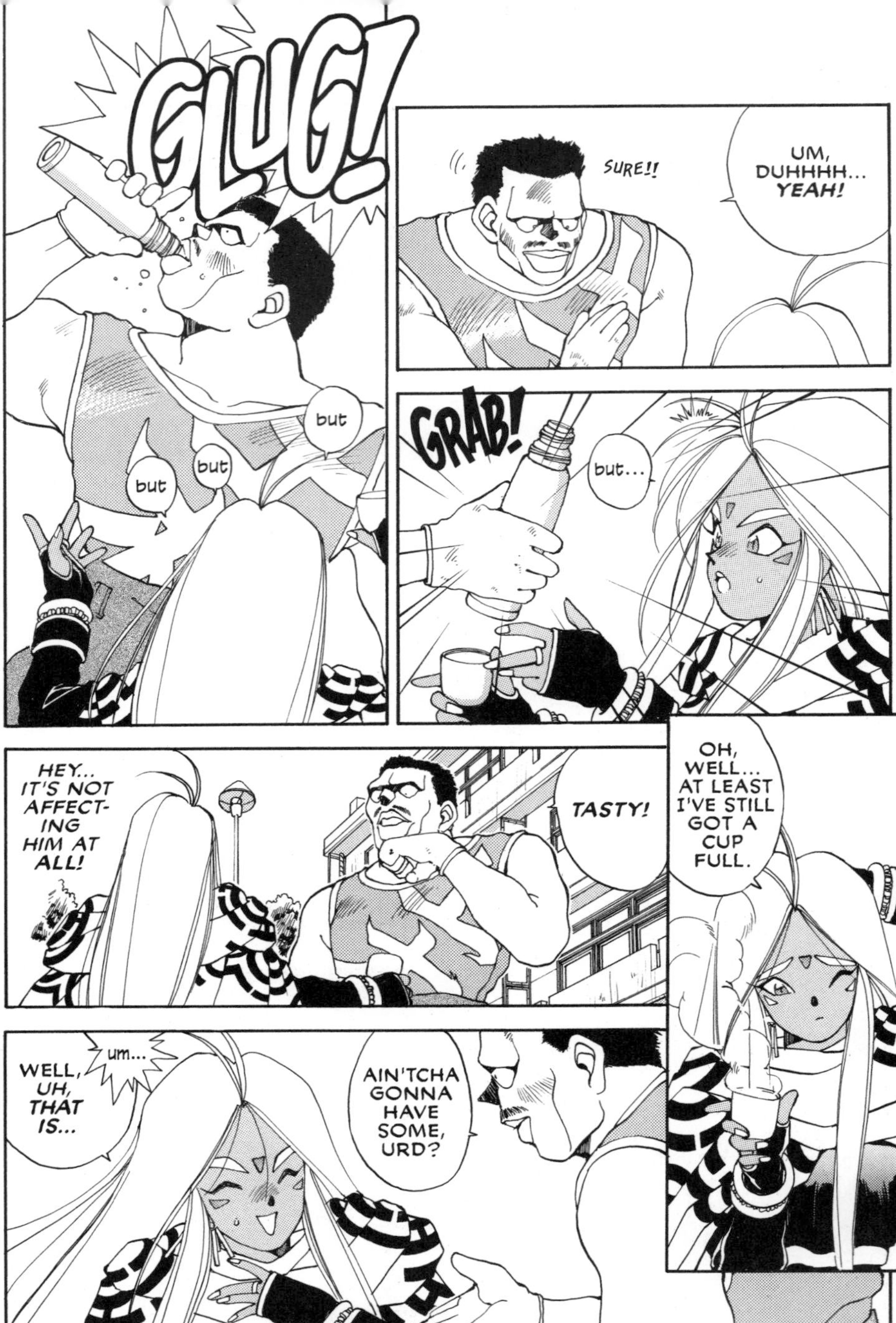
UM, DUHHHH... YEAH!
SURE!!
GRAB!
but...
GLUG!
but
but
but
OH, WELL... AT LEAST I'VE STILL GOT A CUP FULL.
TASTY!
HEY... IT'S NOT AFFECT-ING HIM AT ALL!
AIN'TCHA GONNA HAVE SOME, URD?
um...
WELL, UH, THAT IS...

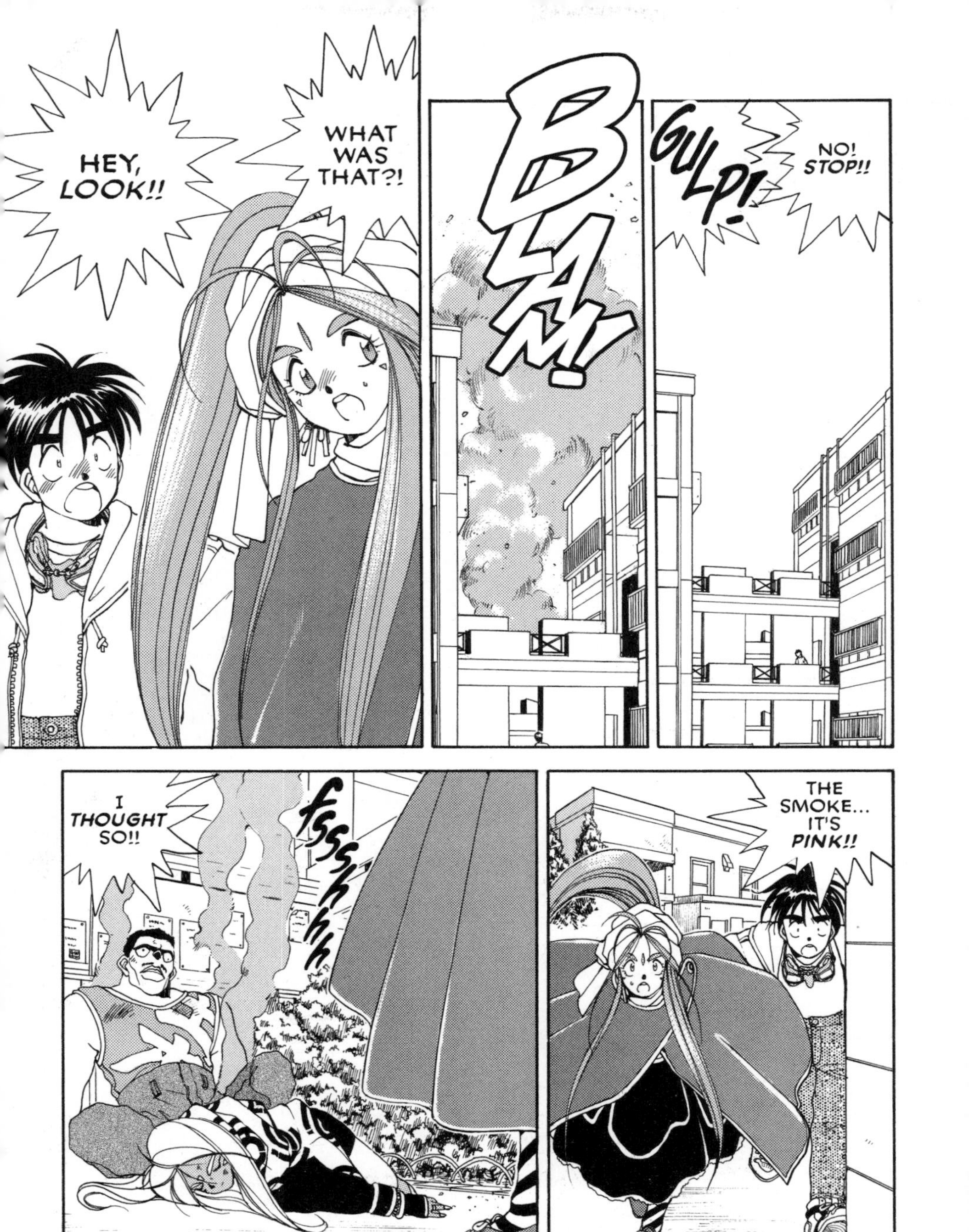
GULP!
NO! STOP!!
BLAM!
WHAT WAS THAT?!
HEY, LOOK!!
THE SMOKE... IT'S PINK!!
I THOUGHT SO!!
fssshhh

UH-OH! OUR FELLOW STUDENTS!

MUTTER MUTTER

muh

WHAT WAS IN THE TEA, SIS? IT WAS *LOVE SEEDS*, WASN'T IT?!

THERE!

WHAT CAUSED IT?

A MYSTERIOUS EXPLOSION!

C'MON... WHILE WE STILL GOT A *SCAPE-GOAT!!*

TAMIYA!

OBVIOUSLY, HE MUST BE TO BLAME!

THAT EXPLAINS IT!

SO, WHAT EXACTLY *ARE* THESE "LOVE SEEDS"?

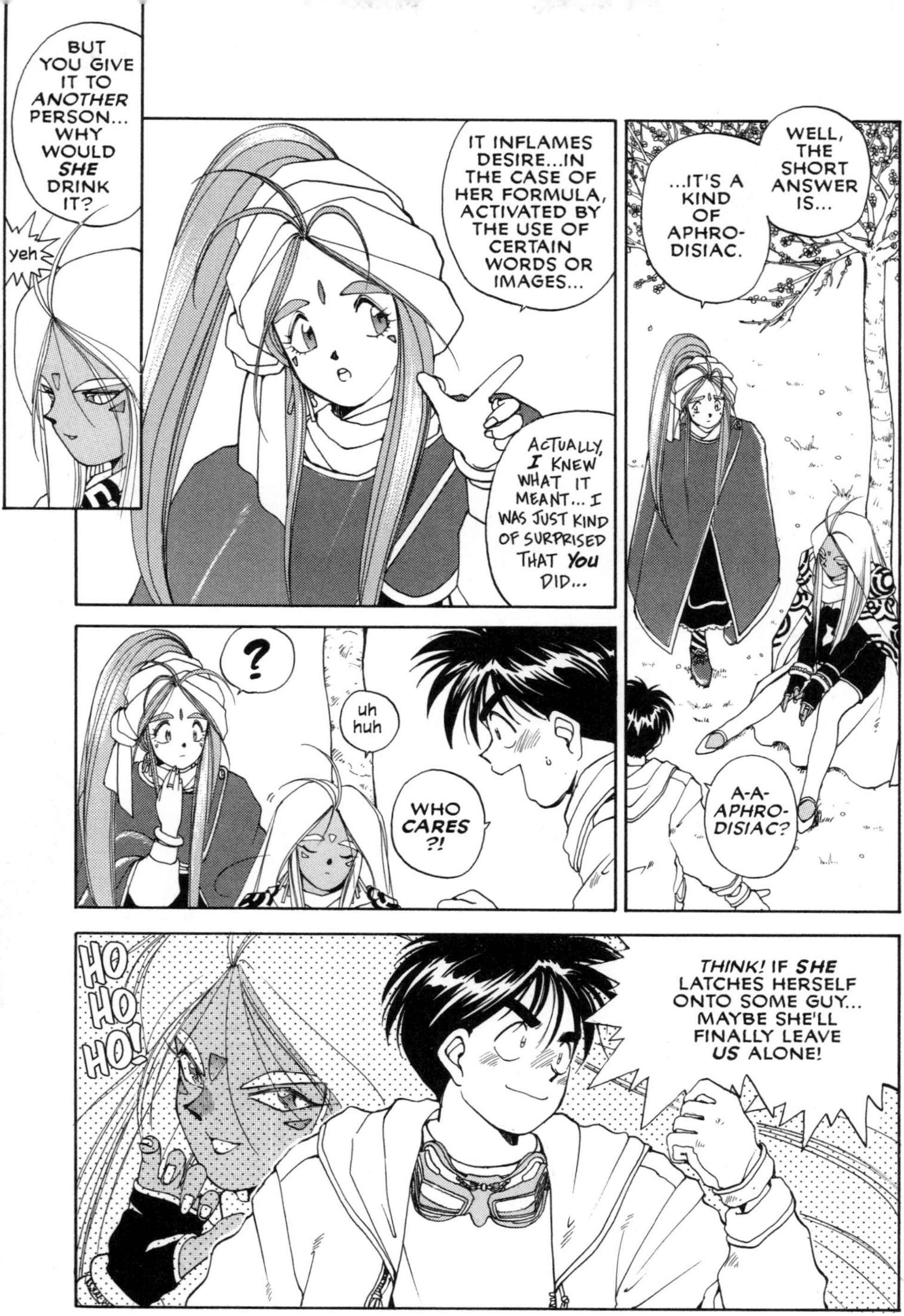
WELL, THE SHORT ANSWER IS...
...IT'S A KIND OF APHRO-DISIAC.
A-A-APHRO-DISIAC?
IT INFLAMES DESIRE...IN THE CASE OF HER FORMULA, ACTIVATED BY THE USE OF CERTAIN WORDS OR IMAGES...
ACTUALLY, I KNEW WHAT IT MEANT... I WAS JUST KIND OF SURPRISED THAT YOU DID...
BUT YOU GIVE IT TO ANOTHER PERSON... WHY WOULD SHE DRINK IT?
yeh
?
uh huh
WHO CARES?!
HO HO HO!
THINK! IF SHE LATCHES HERSELF ONTO SOME GUY... MAYBE SHE'LL FINALLY LEAVE US ALONE!

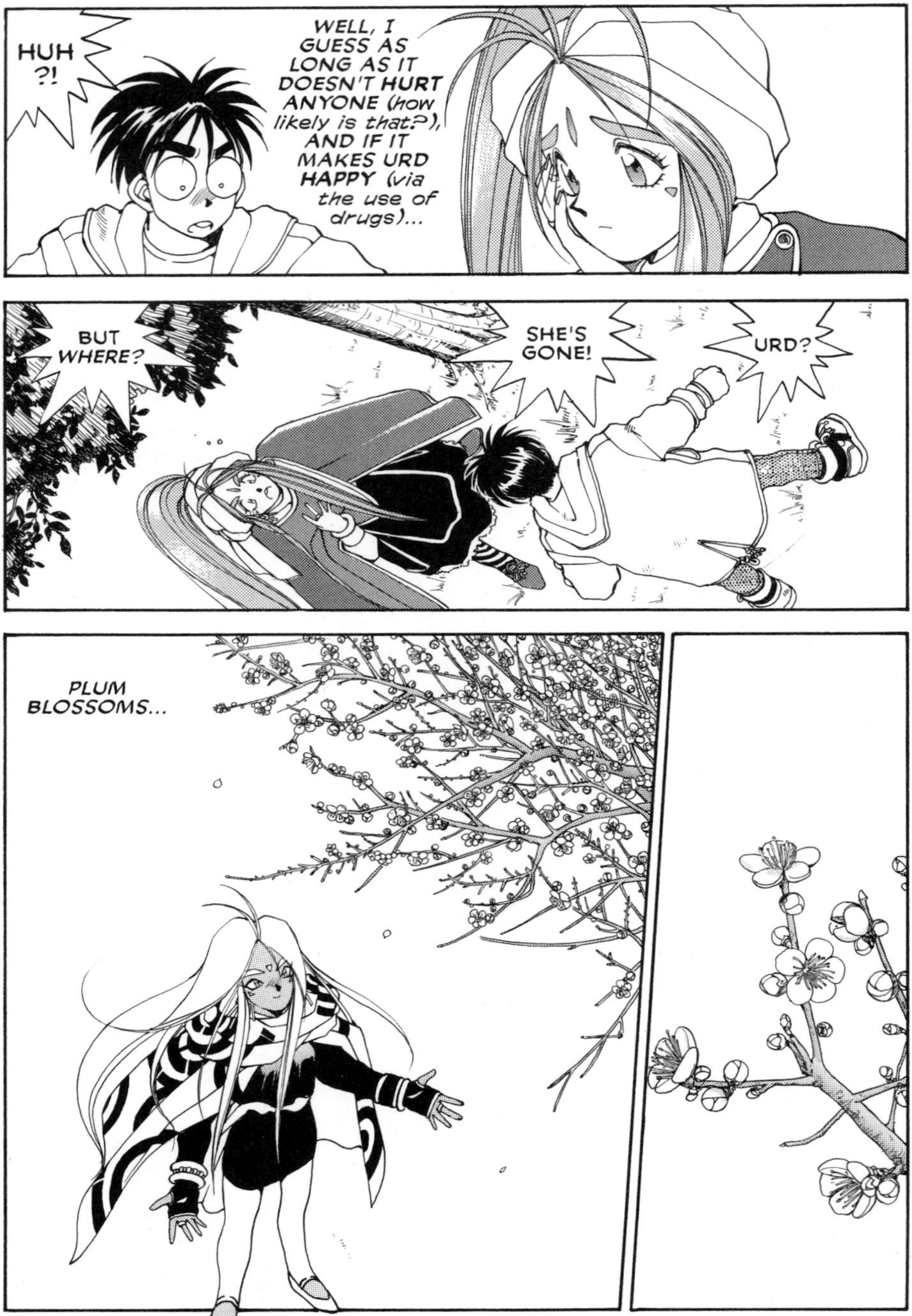
WELL, I GUESS AS LONG AS IT DOESN'T **HURT** ANYONE *(how likely is that?)*, AND IF IT MAKES URD **HAPPY** *(via the use of drugs)*...
HUH ?!
URD?
SHE'S GONE!
BUT WHERE?
PLUM BLOSSOMS...

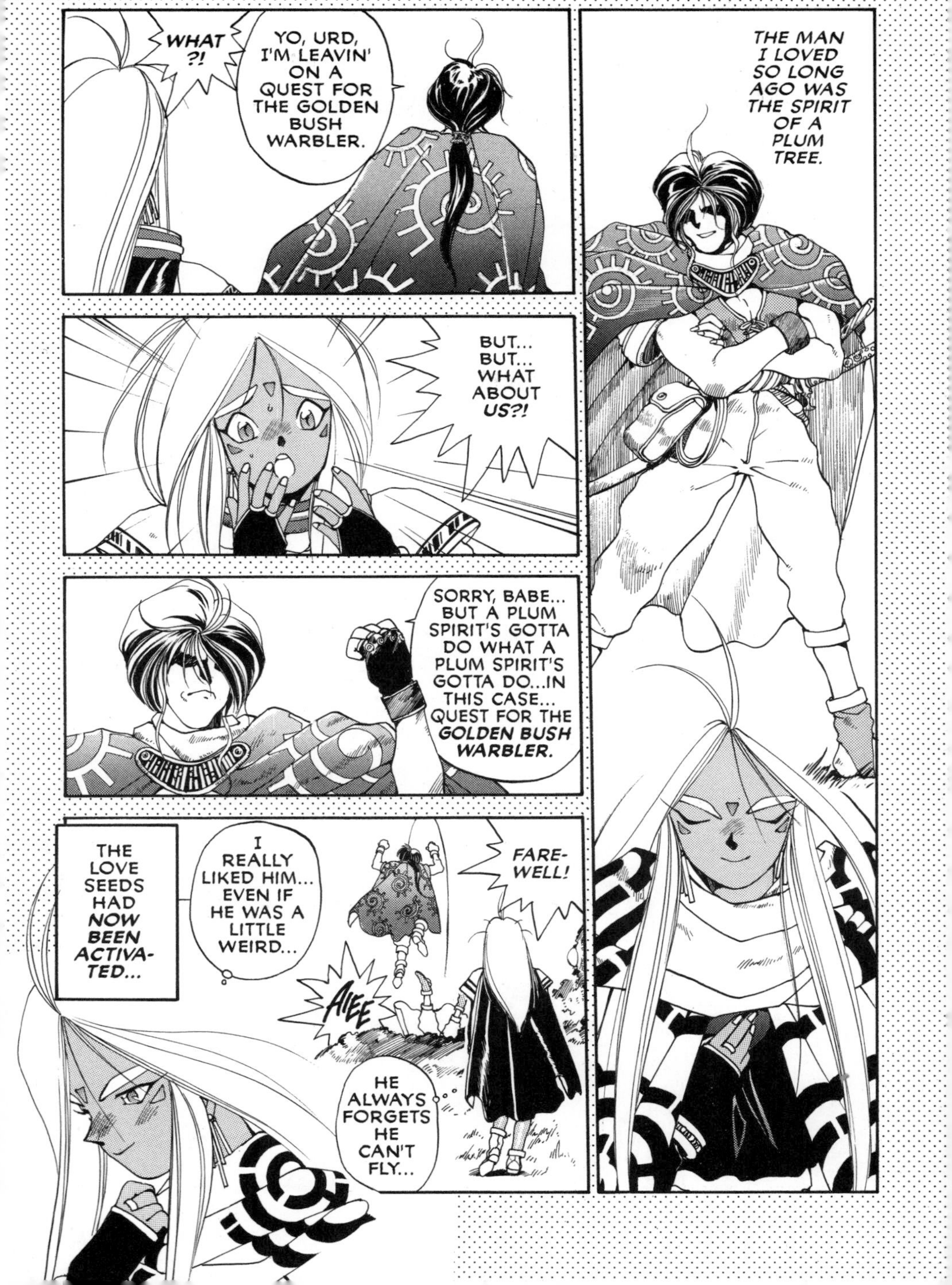
THE MAN I LOVED SO LONG AGO WAS THE SPIRIT OF A PLUM TREE.
YO, URD, I'M LEAVIN' ON A QUEST FOR THE GOLDEN BUSH WARBLER.
WHAT?!
BUT... BUT... WHAT ABOUT US?!
SORRY, BABE... BUT A PLUM SPIRIT'S GOTTA DO WHAT A PLUM SPIRIT'S GOTTA DO...IN THIS CASE... QUEST FOR THE GOLDEN BUSH WARBLER.
FARE-WELL!
I REALLY LIKED HIM... EVEN IF HE WAS A LITTLE WEIRD...
THE LOVE SEEDS HAD NOW BEEN ACTIVATED...
AIEE
HE ALWAYS FORGETS HE CAN'T FLY...

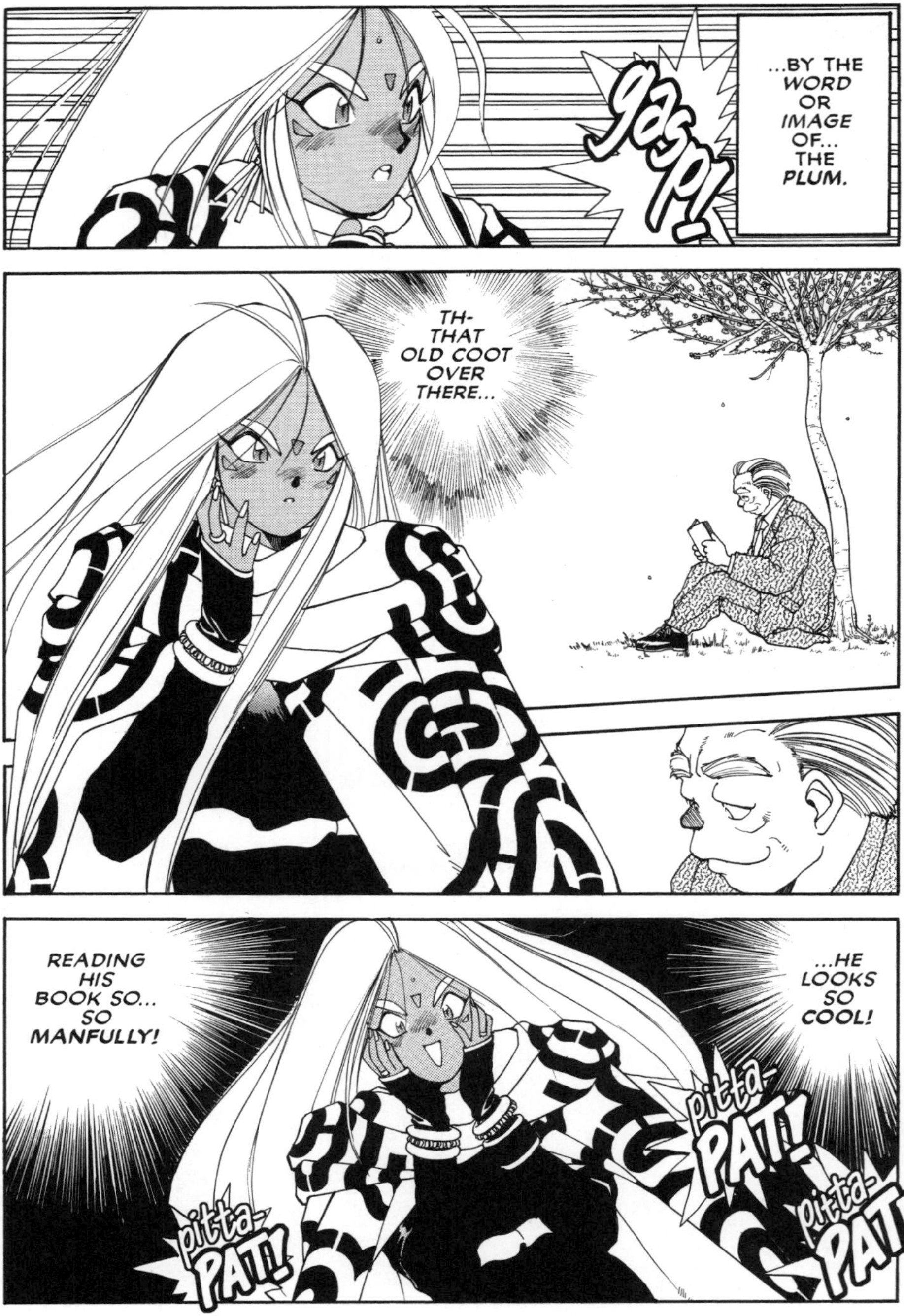
...BY THE WORD OR IMAGE OF... THE PLUM.
gasp!
TH-THAT OLD COOT OVER THERE...
...HE LOOKS SO COOL!
READING HIS BOOK SO... SO MANFULLY!
pitta-PAT!
pitta-PAT!
pitta-PAT!

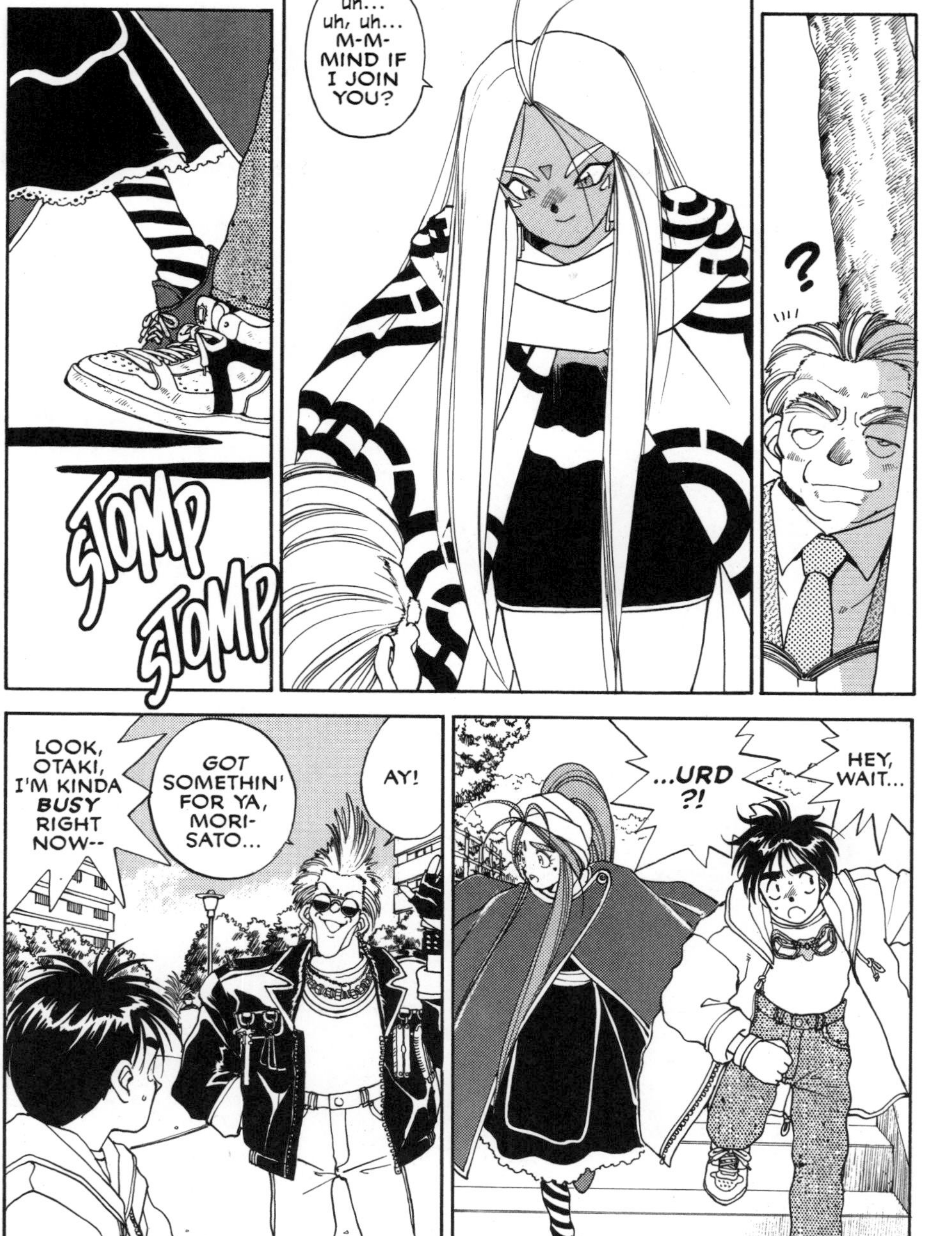
?
uh... uh, uh... M-M-MIND IF I JOIN YOU?
STOMP STOMP
HEY, WAIT...
...URD ?!
AY!
GOT SOMETHIN' FOR YA, MORI-SATO...
LOOK, OTAKI, I'M KINDA BUSY RIGHT NOW--

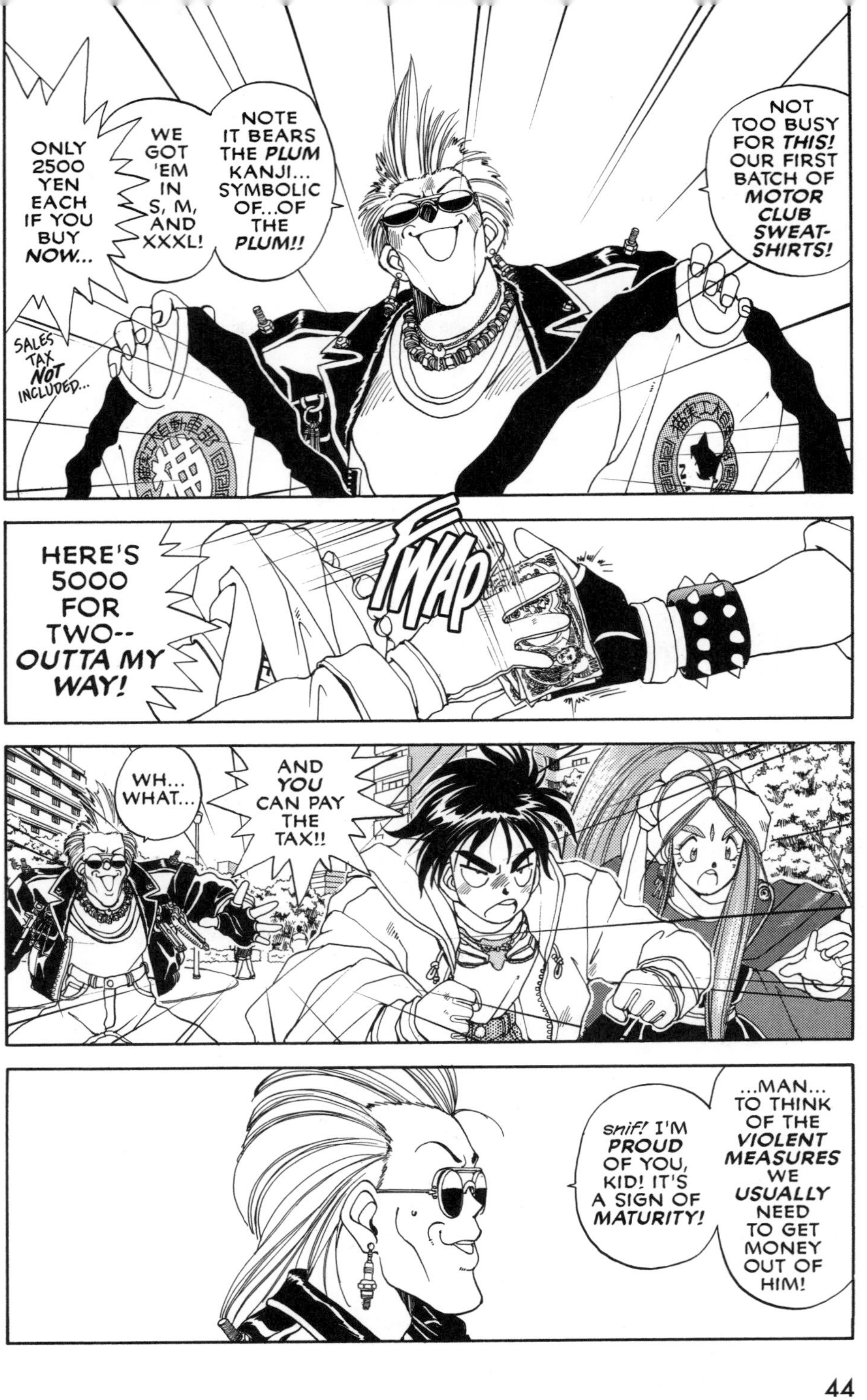
NOT TOO BUSY FOR THIS! OUR FIRST BATCH OF MOTOR CLUB SWEAT-SHIRTS!
NOTE IT BEARS THE PLUM KANJI... SYMBOLIC OF...OF THE PLUM!!
WE GOT 'EM IN S, M, AND XXXL!
ONLY 2500 YEN EACH IF YOU BUY NOW...
SALES TAX NOT INCLUDED...
FWAP
HERE'S 5000 FOR TWO-- OUTTA MY WAY!
AND YOU CAN PAY THE TAX!!
WH... WHAT...
...MAN... TO THINK OF THE VIOLENT MEASURES WE USUALLY NEED TO GET MONEY OUT OF HIM!
snif! I'M PROUD OF YOU, KID! IT'S A SIGN OF MATURITY!

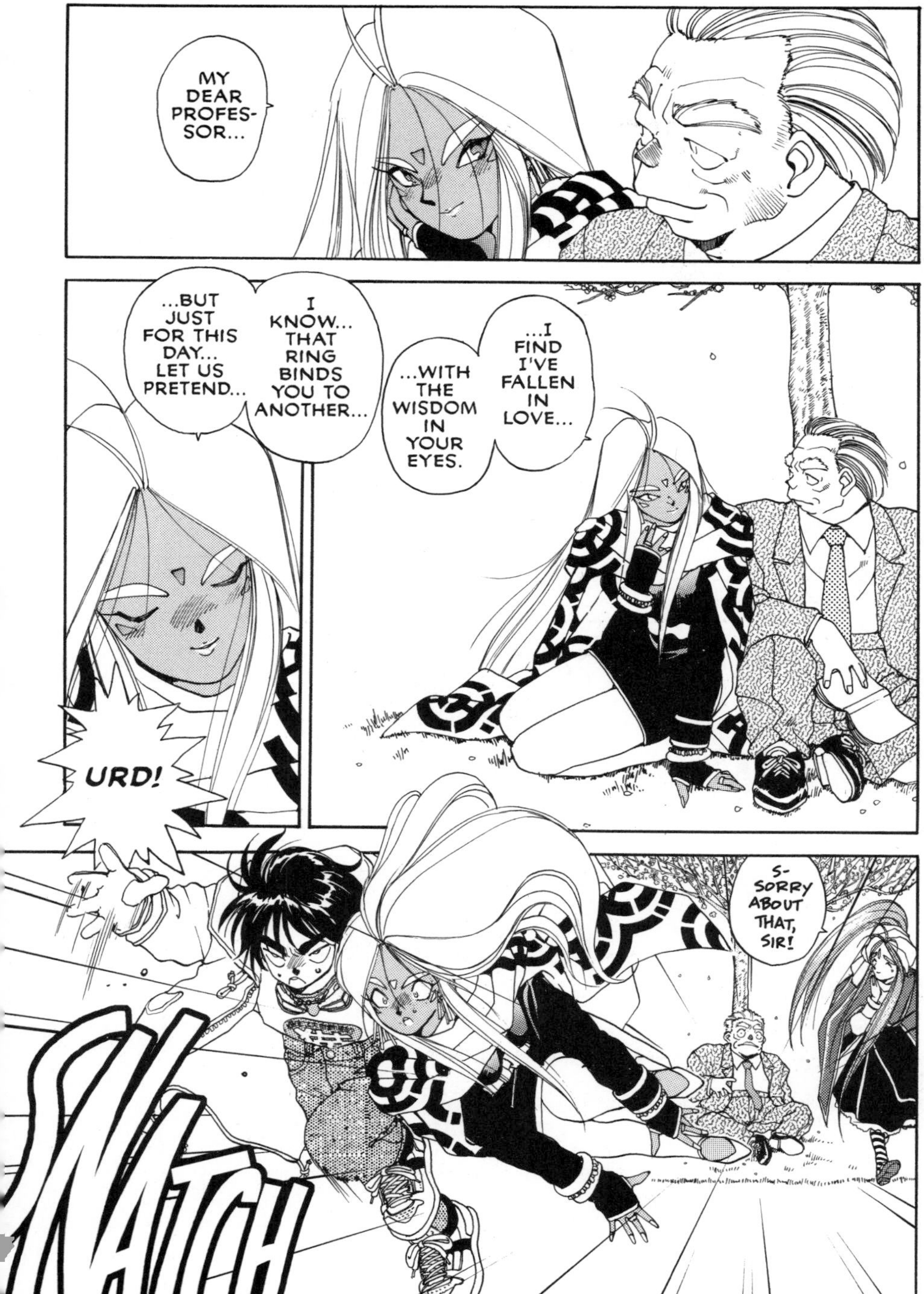
MY DEAR PROFES-SOR...
...I FIND I'VE FALLEN IN LOVE...
...WITH THE WISDOM IN YOUR EYES.
I KNOW... THAT RING BINDS YOU TO ANOTHER...
...BUT JUST FOR THIS DAY... LET US PRETEND...
URD!
S-SORRY ABOUT THAT, SIR!
SNATCH

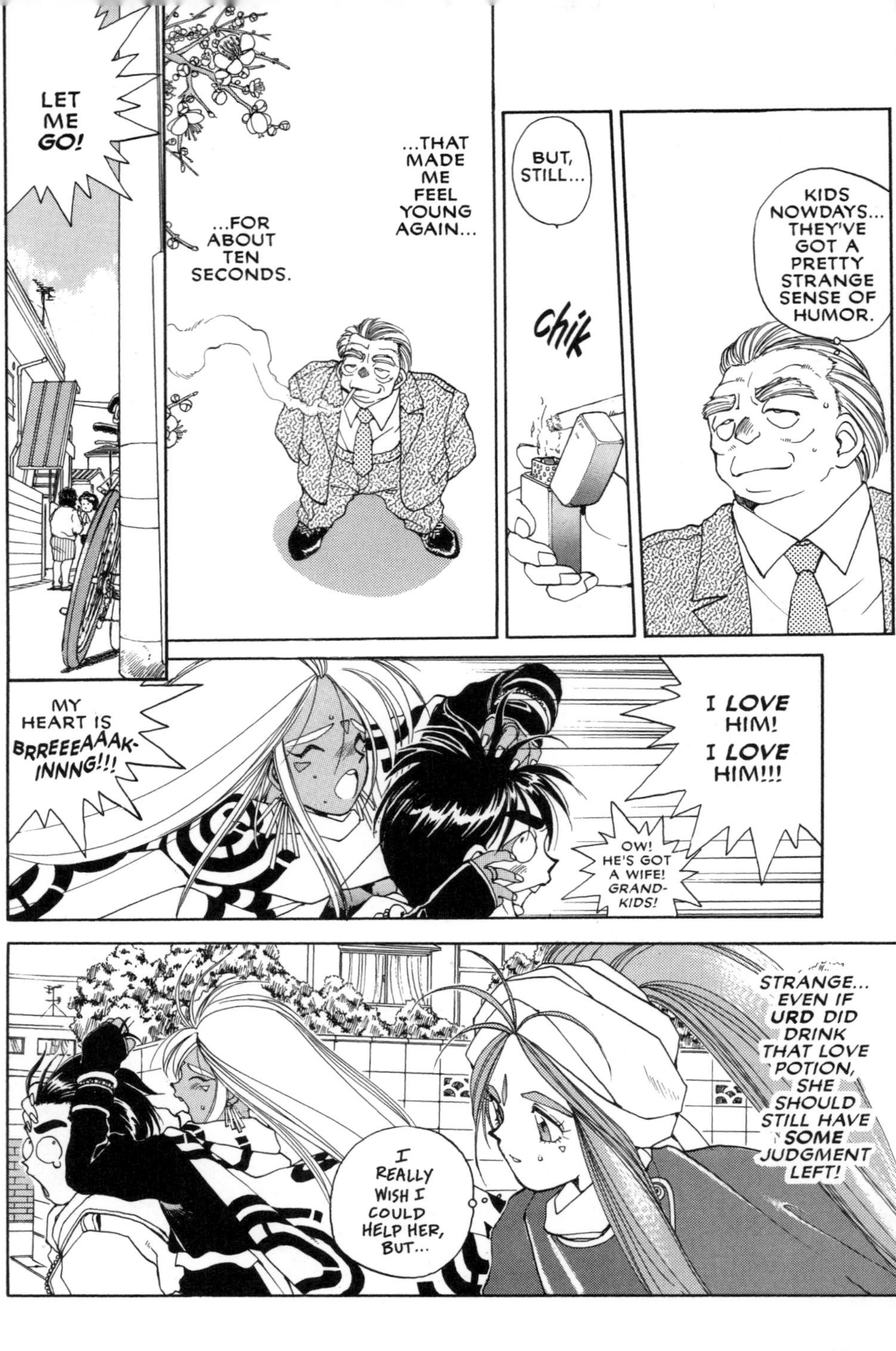
KIDS NOWDAYS... THEY'VE GOT A PRETTY STRANGE SENSE OF HUMOR.
BUT, STILL...
Chik
...THAT MADE ME FEEL YOUNG AGAIN...
...FOR ABOUT TEN SECONDS.
LET ME GO!
I LOVE HIM! I LOVE HIM!!!
OW! HE'S GOT A WIFE! GRAND-KIDS!
MY HEART IS BRREEEAAAK-INNNG!!!
STRANGE... EVEN IF URD DID DRINK THAT LOVE POTION, SHE SHOULD STILL HAVE SOME JUDGMENT LEFT!
I REALLY WISH I COULD HELP HER, BUT...

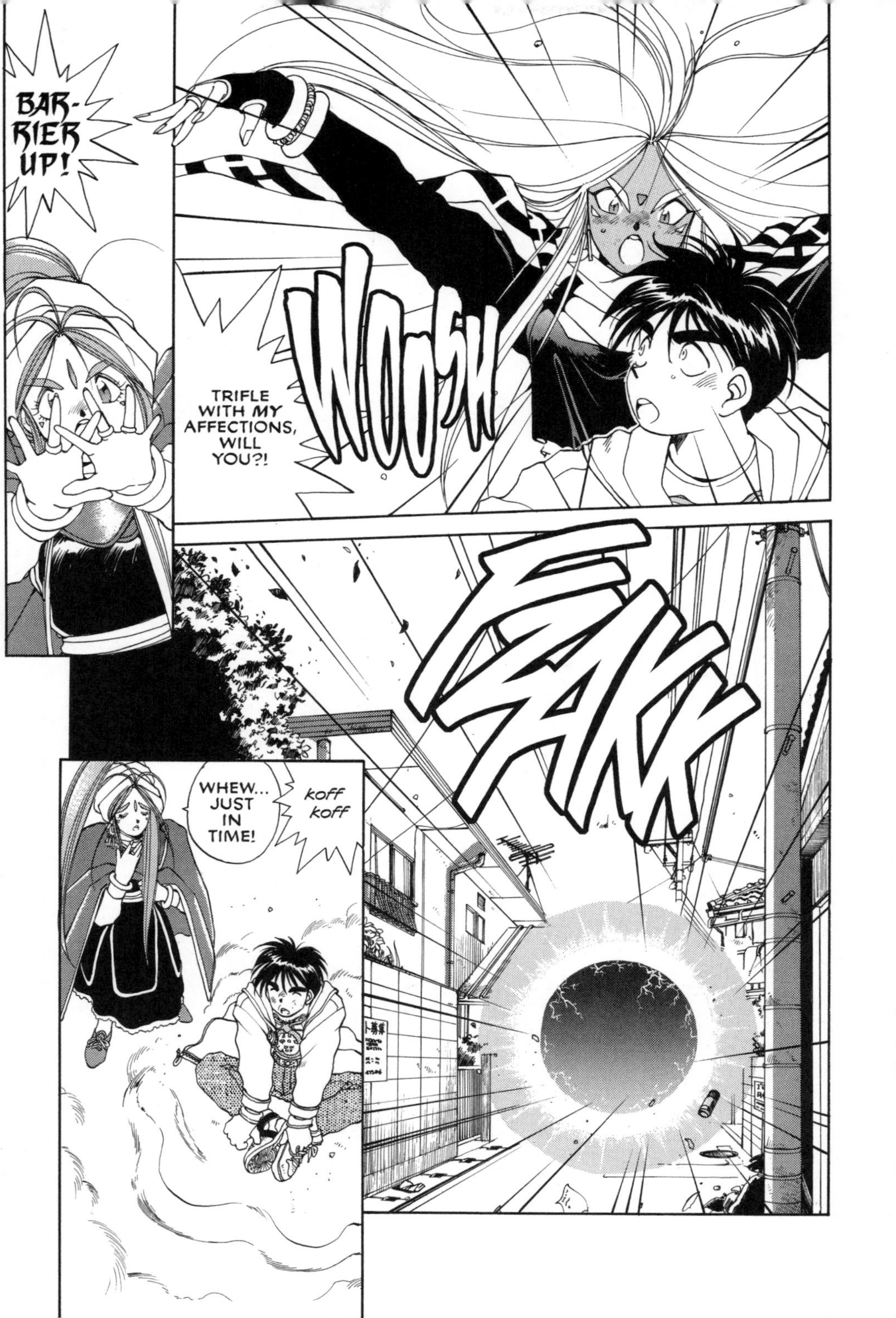
TRIFLE WITH MY AFFECTIONS, WILL YOU?!
WOOSH
BAR-RIER UP!
FZAKK
WHEW... JUST IN TIME!
koff koff

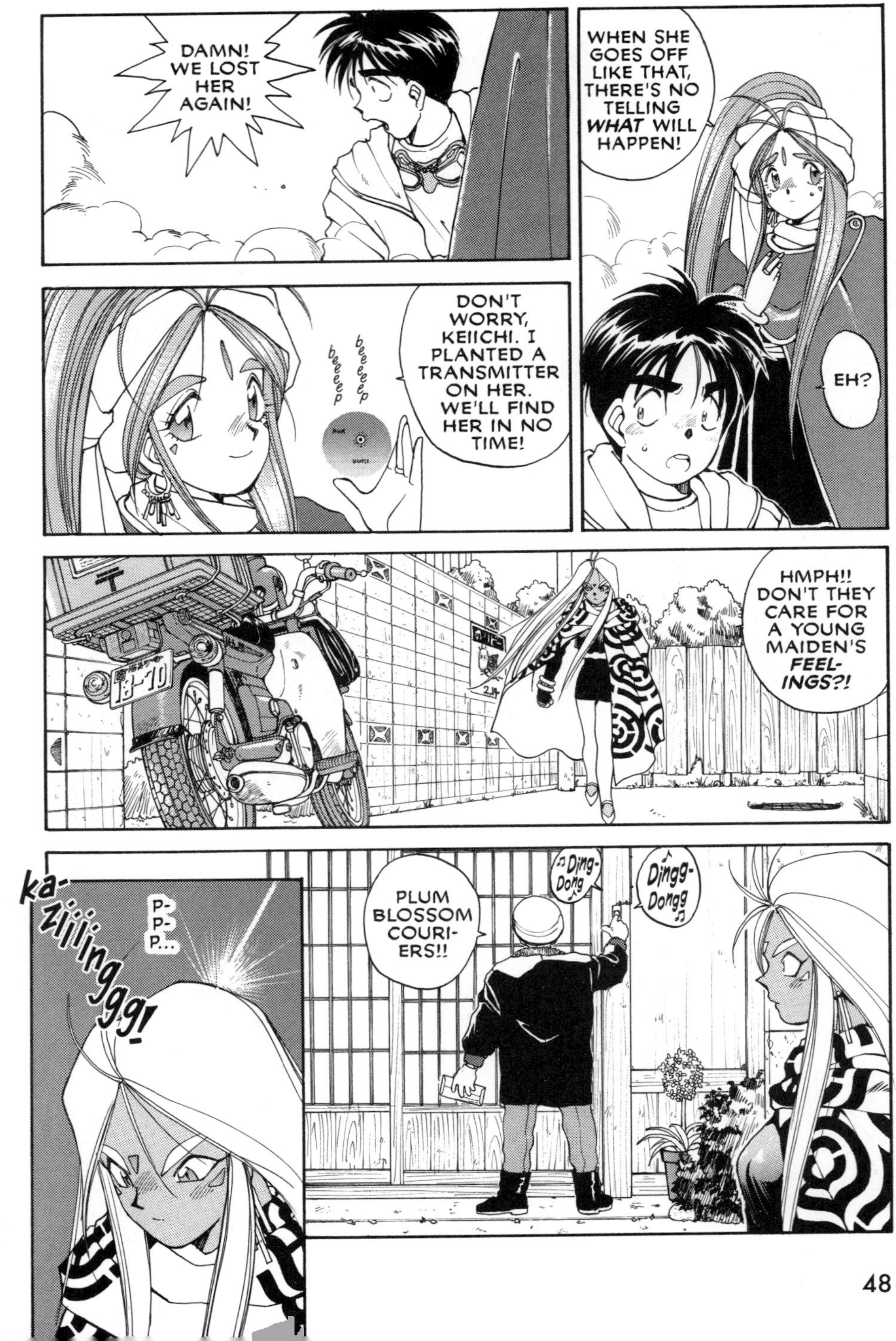
WHEN SHE GOES OFF LIKE THAT, THERE'S NO TELLING *WHAT* WILL HAPPEN!
EH?
DAMN! WE LOST HER AGAIN!
DON'T WORRY, KEIICHI. I PLANTED A TRANSMITTER ON HER. WE'LL FIND HER IN NO TIME!
beeeep
beeeep
HMPH!! DON'T THEY CARE FOR A YOUNG MAIDEN'S *FEEL-INGS?!*
Dingg-Dongg
Ding-Dong
PLUM BLOSSOM COURI-ERS!!
P-P-P...
ka-ziiiinggg!

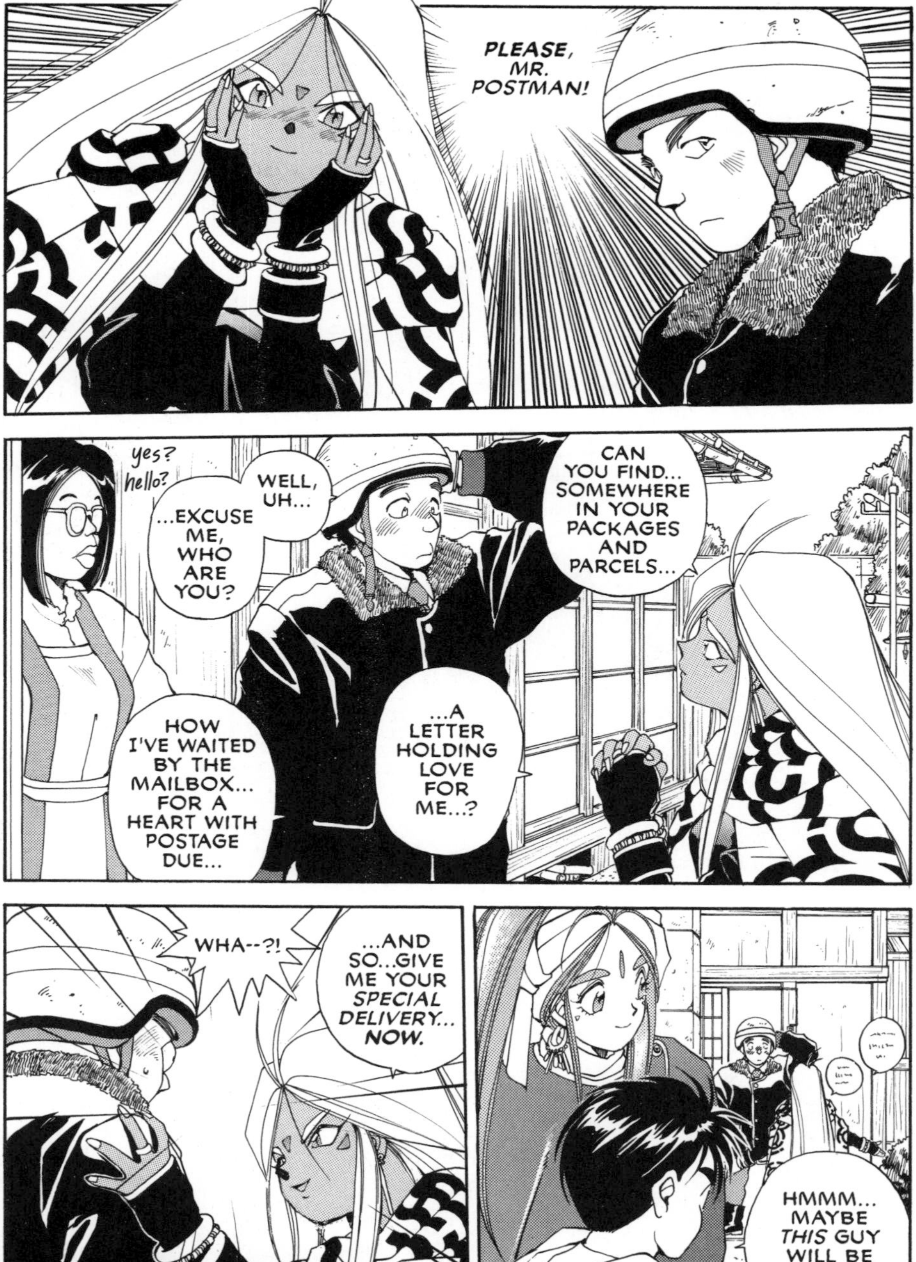

PLEASE, MR. POSTMAN!
CAN YOU FIND... SOMEWHERE IN YOUR PACKAGES AND PARCELS...
WELL, UH...
yes? hello?
...EXCUSE ME, WHO ARE YOU?
...A LETTER HOLDING LOVE FOR ME...?
HOW I'VE WAITED BY THE MAILBOX... FOR A HEART WITH POSTAGE DUE...
HMMM... MAYBE *THIS* GUY WILL BE SAFE FOR HER...
...AND SO...GIVE ME YOUR *SPECIAL DELIVERY*... NOW.
WHA--?!

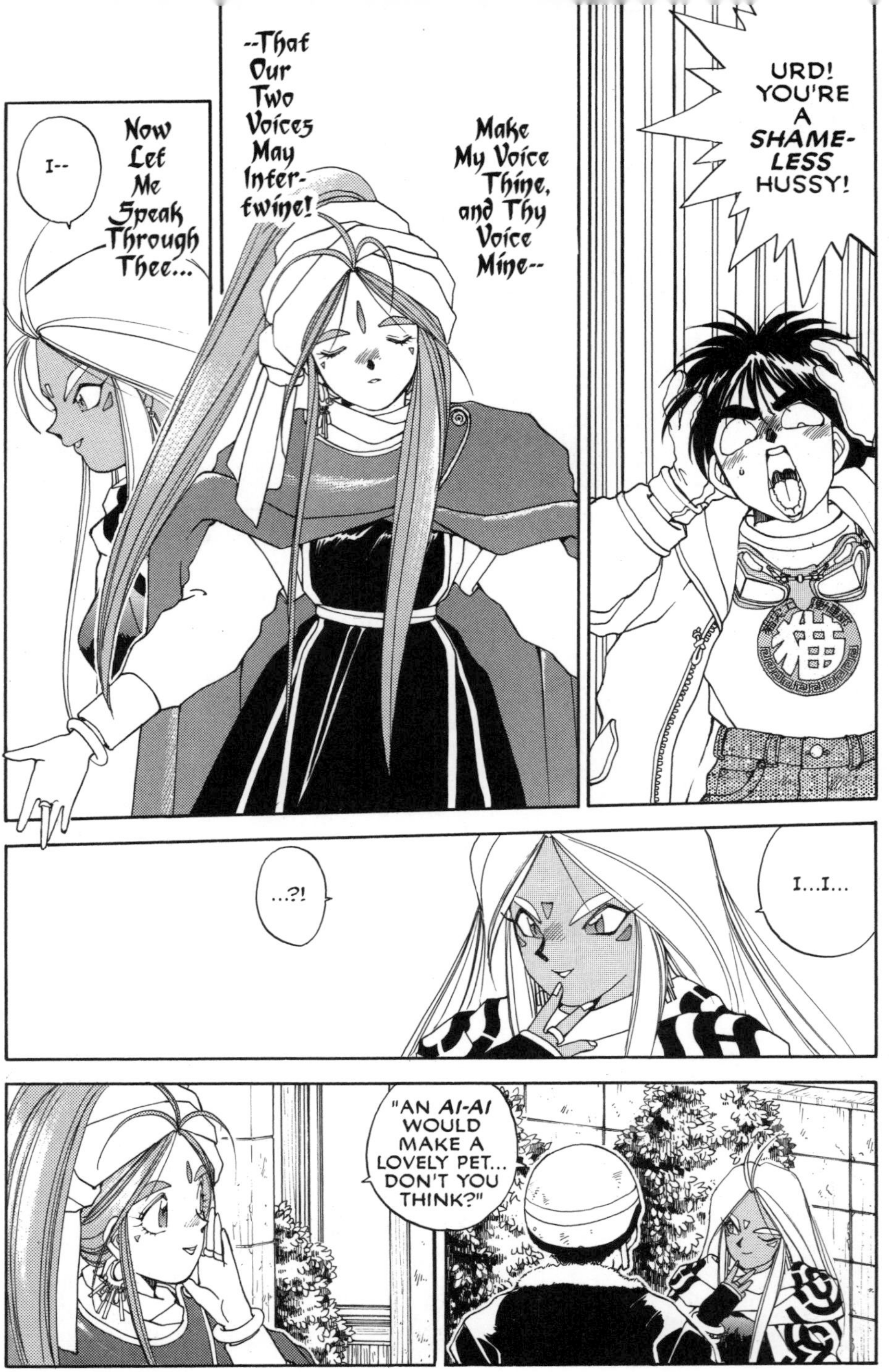
URD! YOU'RE A SHAMELESS HUSSY!
Make My Voice Thine, and Thy Voice Mine--
--That Our Two Voices May Intertwine!
Now Let Me Speak Through Thee...
I--
I...I...
...?!
"AN AI-AI WOULD MAKE A LOVELY PET... DON'T YOU THINK?"

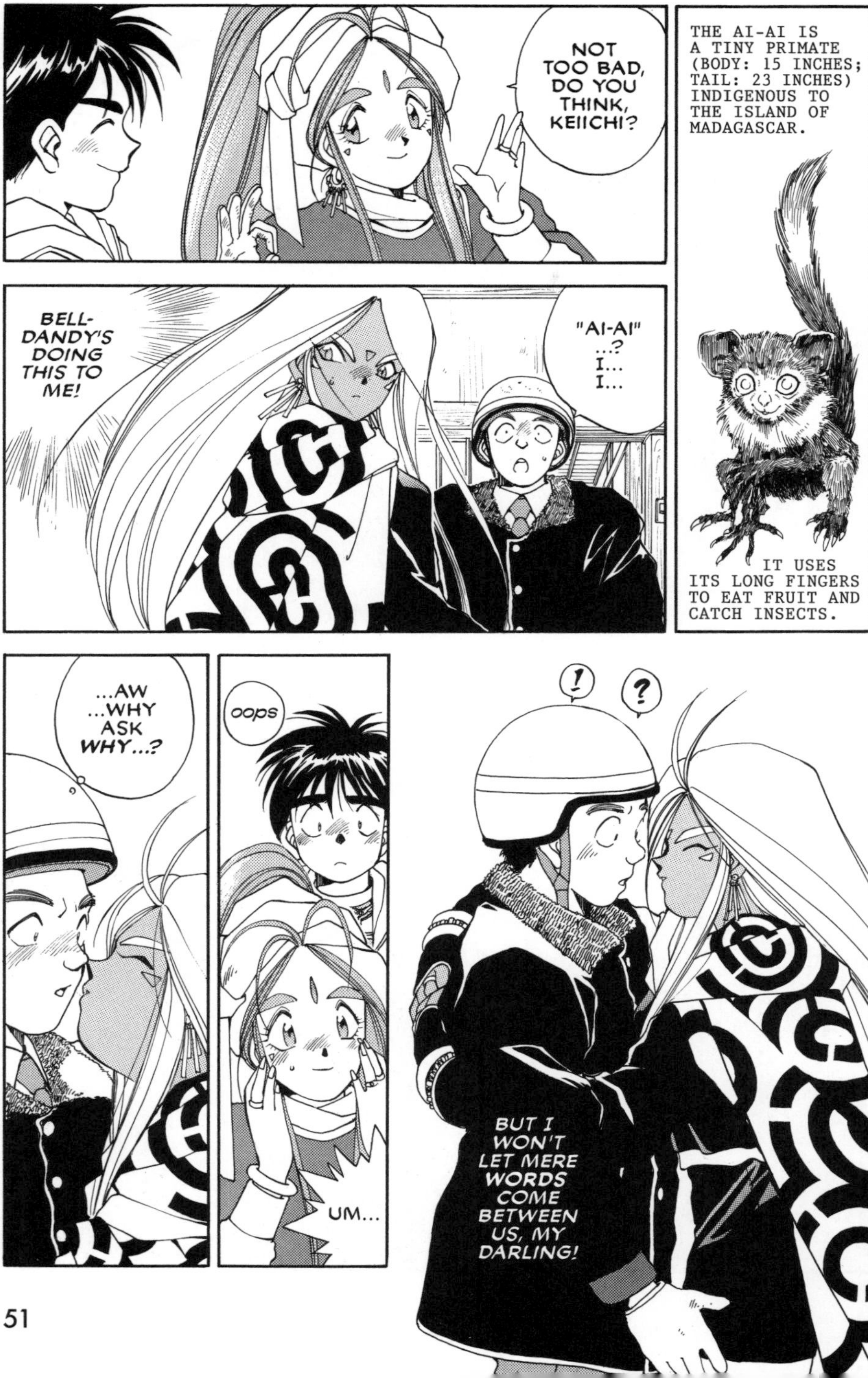
THE AI-AI IS A TINY PRIMATE (BODY: 15 INCHES; TAIL: 23 INCHES) INDIGENOUS TO THE ISLAND OF MADAGASCAR.
IT USES ITS LONG FINGERS TO EAT FRUIT AND CATCH INSECTS.
NOT TOO BAD, DO YOU THINK, KEIICHI?
"AI-AI" ...? I... I...
BELL-DANDY'S DOING THIS TO ME!
!
?
BUT I WON'T LET MERE WORDS COME BETWEEN US, MY DARLING!
oops
UM...
...AW ...WHY ASK WHY...?

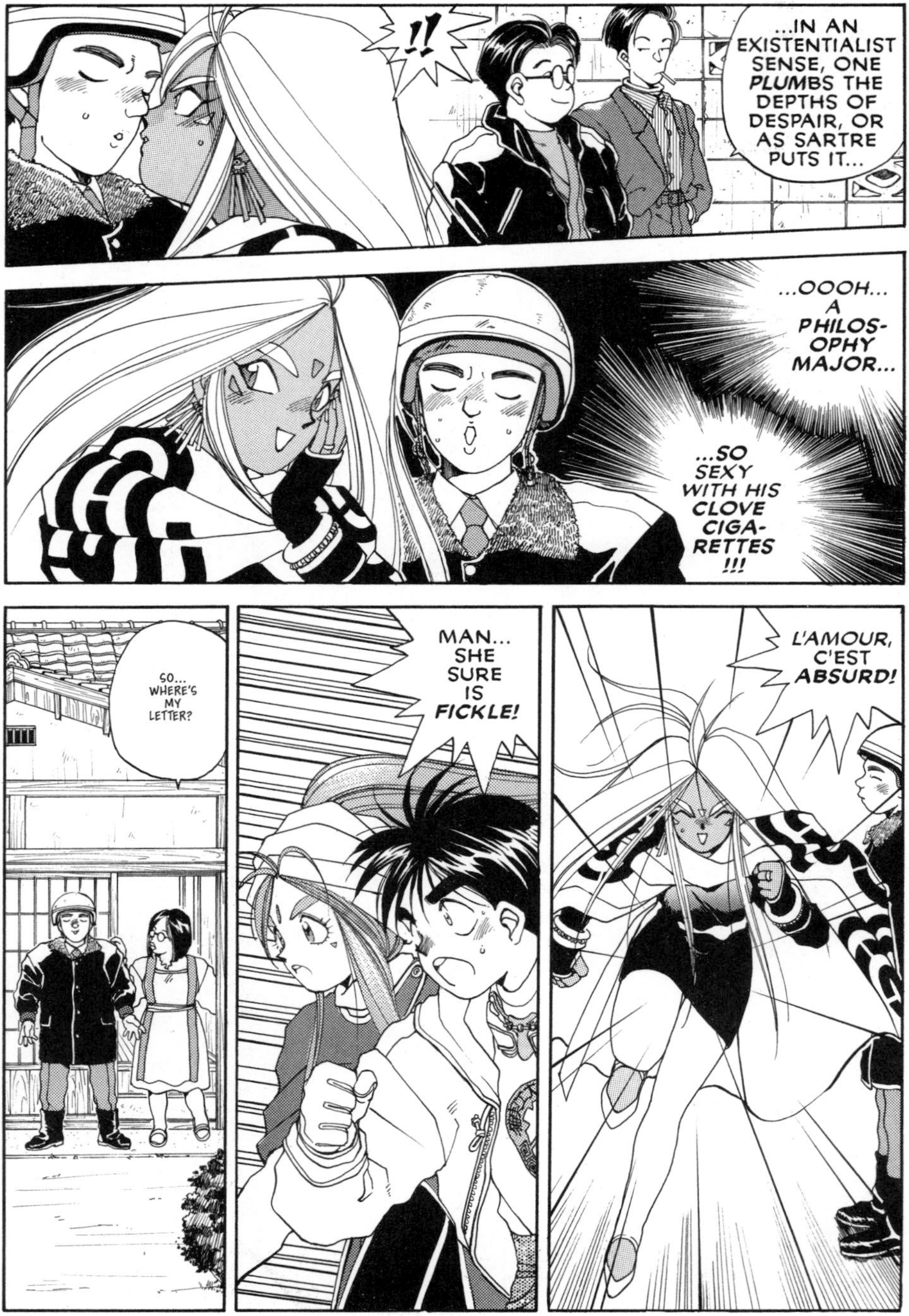
...IN AN EXISTENTIALIST SENSE, ONE PLUMBS THE DEPTHS OF DESPAIR, OR AS SARTRE PUTS IT...
!!
...OOOH... A PHILOSOPHY MAJOR...
...SO SEXY WITH HIS CLOVE CIGARETTES!!!
L'AMOUR, C'EST ABSURD!
MAN... SHE SURE IS FICKLE!
SO... WHERE'S MY LETTER?

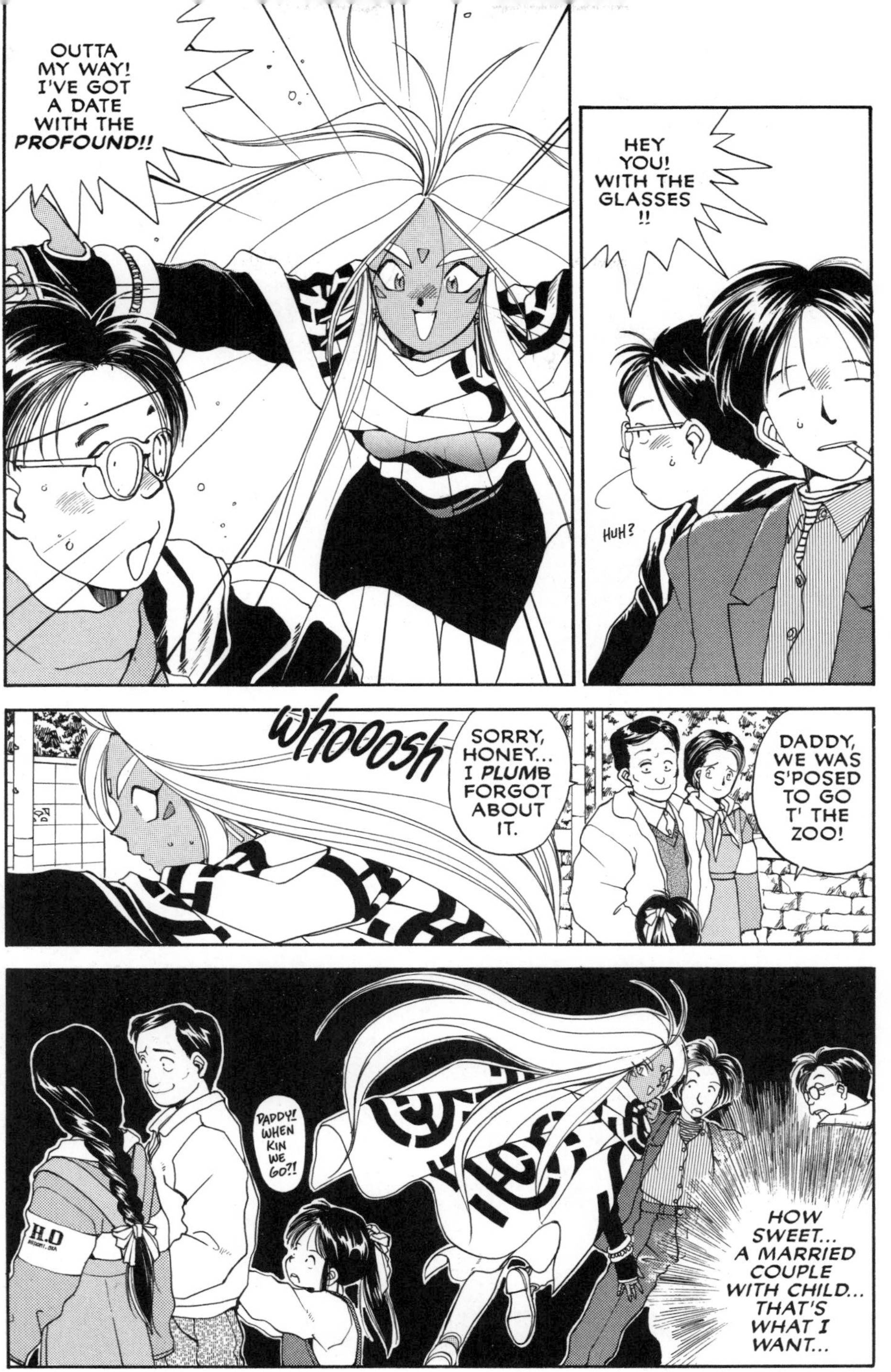
HEY YOU! WITH THE GLASSES !!
HUH?
OUTTA MY WAY! I'VE GOT A DATE WITH THE PROFOUND!!
DADDY, WE WAS S'POSED TO GO T' THE ZOO!
SORRY, HONEY... I PLUMB FORGOT ABOUT IT.
whoooosh
HOW SWEET... A MARRIED COUPLE WITH CHILD... THAT'S WHAT I WANT...
DADDY! WHEN KIN WE GO?!

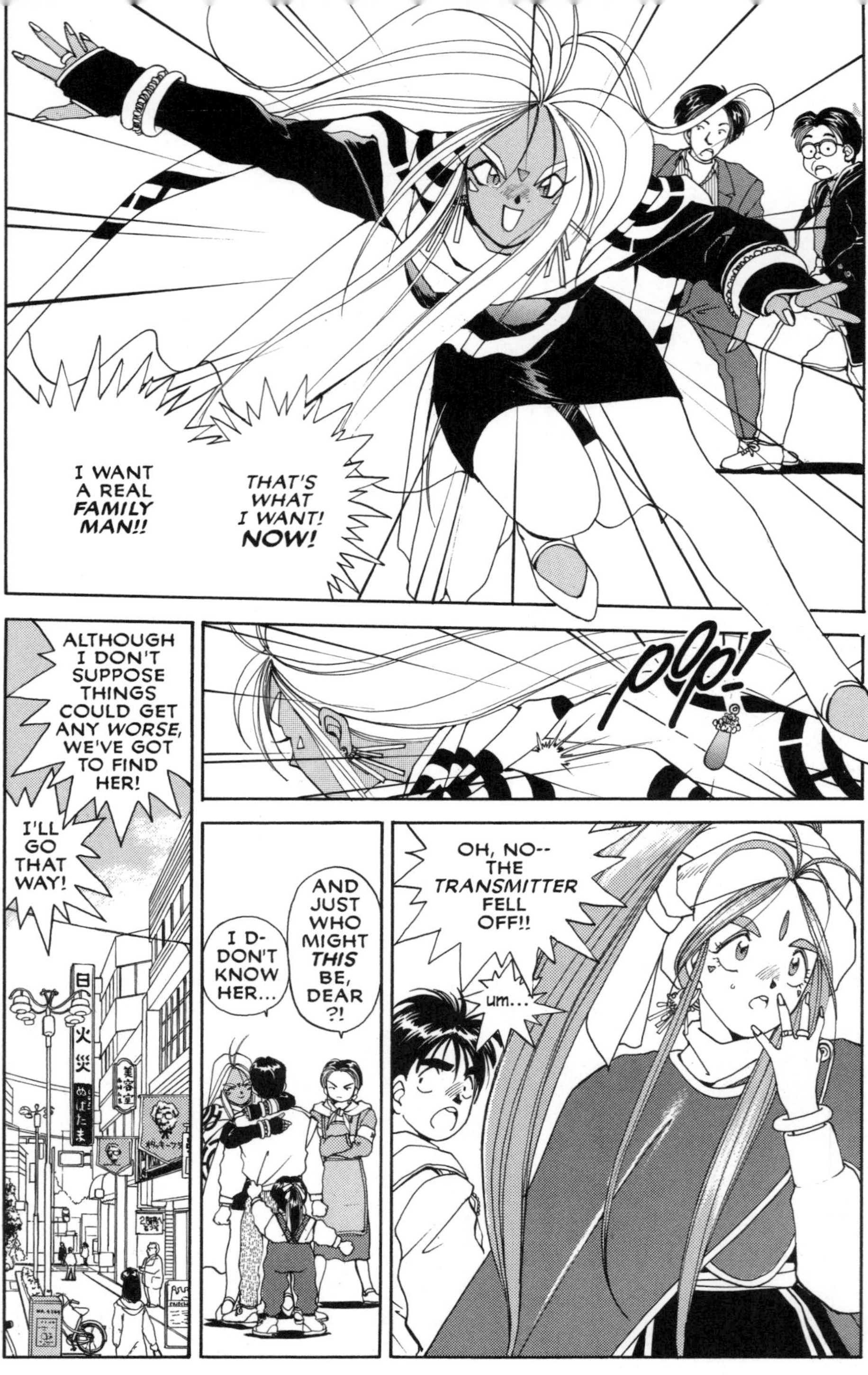
THAT'S WHAT I WANT! NOW!
I WANT A REAL FAMILY MAN!!
POP!
OH, NO-- THE TRANSMITTER FELL OFF!!
um...
AND JUST WHO MIGHT THIS BE, DEAR?!
I D-DON'T KNOW HER...
ALTHOUGH I DON'T SUPPOSE THINGS COULD GET ANY WORSE, WE'VE GOT TO FIND HER!
I'LL GO THAT WAY!

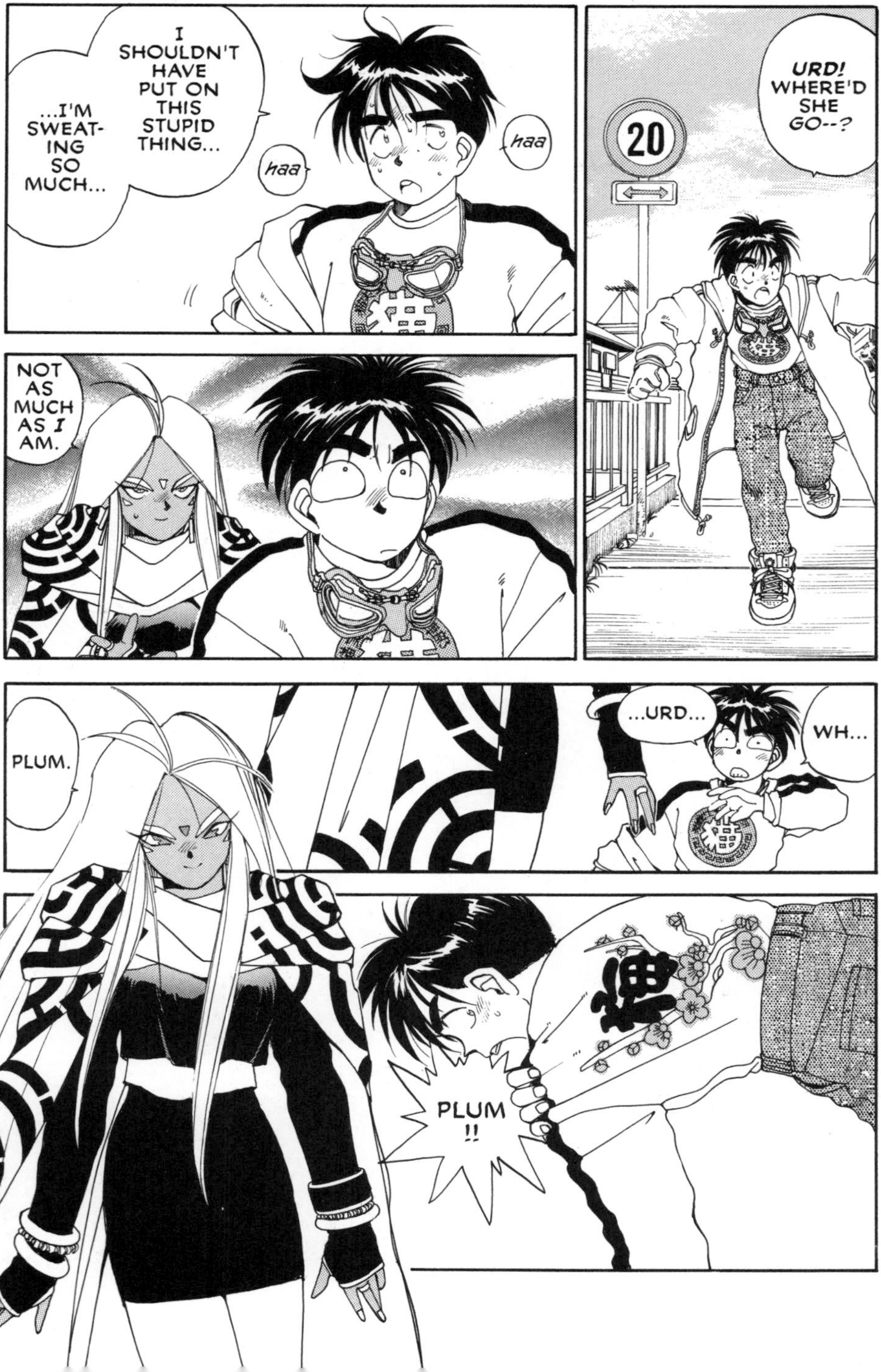
URD! WHERE'D SHE GO--?
haa
I SHOULDN'T HAVE PUT ON THIS STUPID THING...
haa
...I'M SWEAT-ING SO MUCH...
NOT AS MUCH AS I AM.
WH...
...URD...
PLUM.
PLUM !!
20

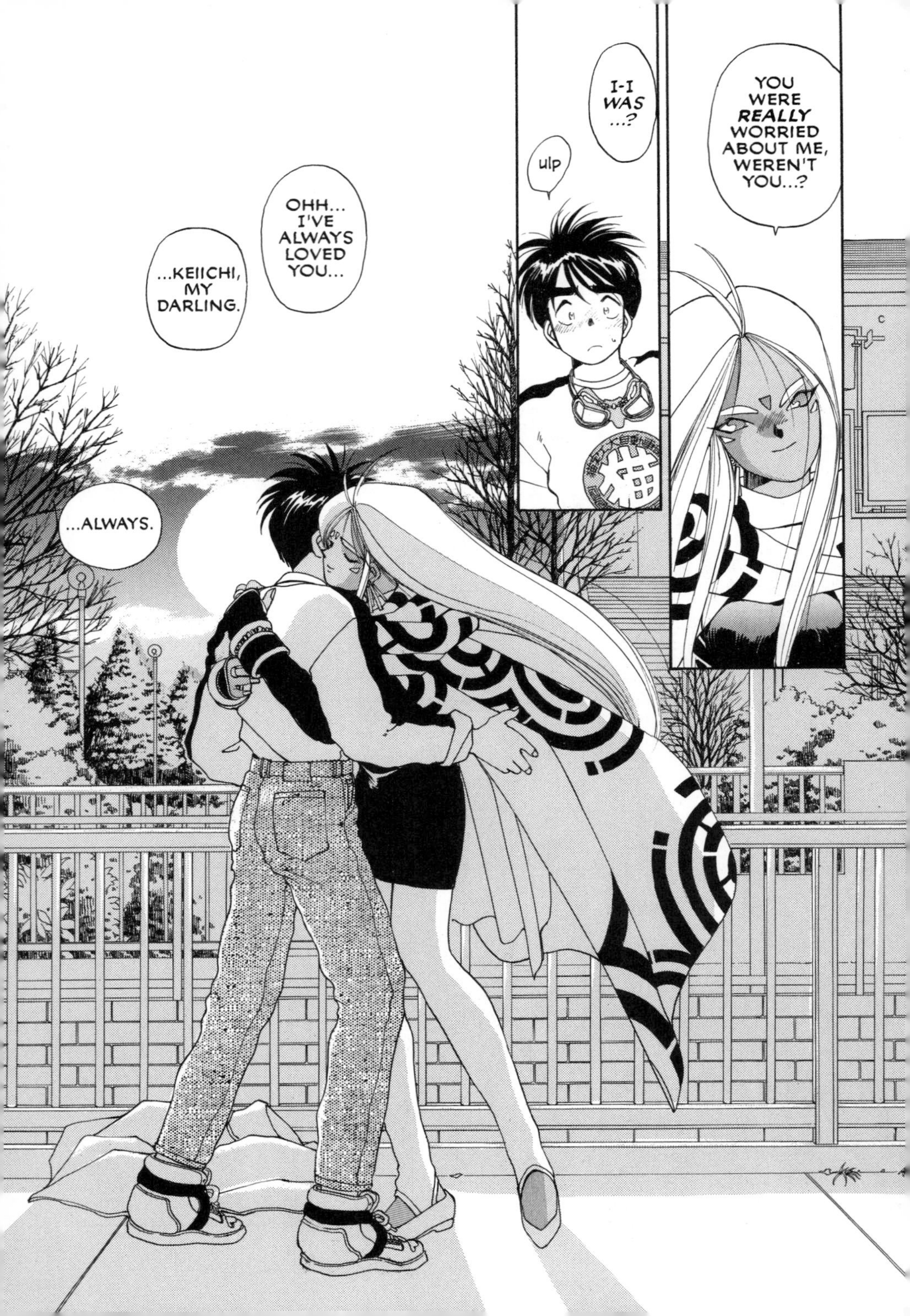
YOU WERE **REALLY** WORRIED ABOUT ME, WEREN'T YOU...?
I-I *WAS* ...?
ulp
OHH... I'VE ALWAYS LOVED YOU...
...KEIICHI, MY DARLING.
...ALWAYS.

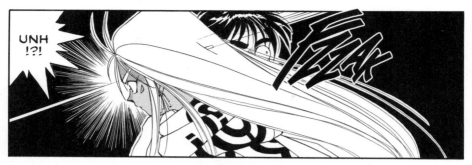

UNH !?!
URD !!
ooog...
E-EVEN IF YOU *ARE* MY BIG SISTER...
...I-I JUST CAN'T LET YOU...
huh?
...T-TAKE MY KEIICHI.
HE'S...
HE'S MY...

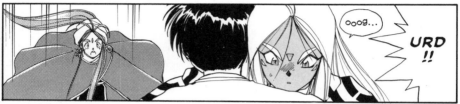

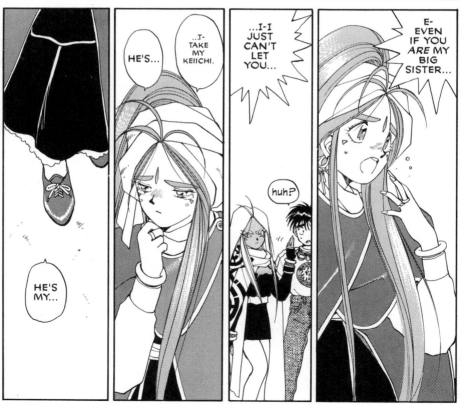

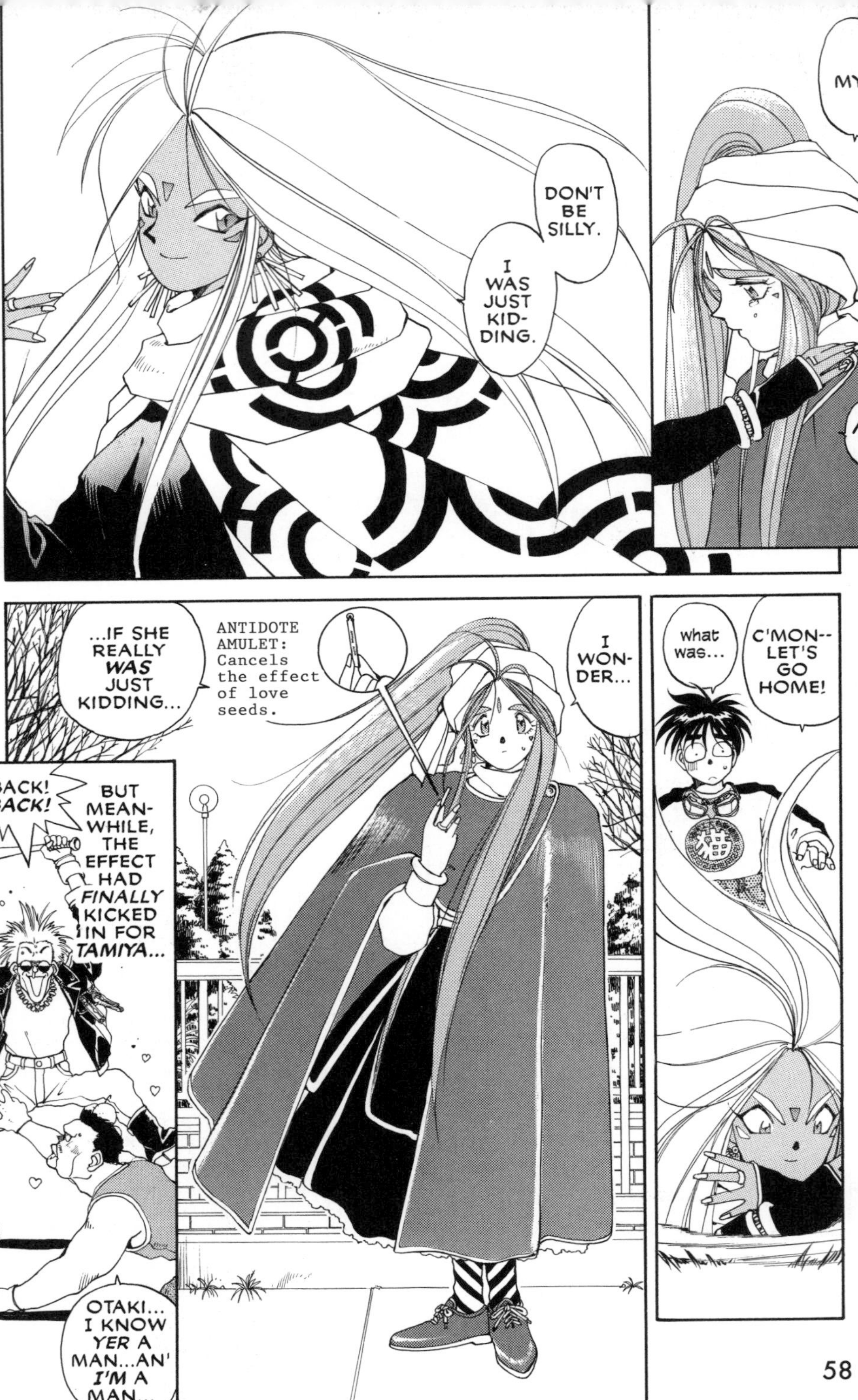
MY...
pat
DON'T BE SILLY.
I WAS JUST KID-DING.
C'MON-- LET'S GO HOME!
what was...
I WON-DER...
ANTIDOTE AMULET: Cancels the effect of love seeds.
...IF SHE REALLY WAS JUST KIDDING...
BUT MEAN-WHILE, THE EFFECT HAD FINALLY KICKED IN FOR TAMIYA...
BACK! BACK!
OTAKI... I KNOW YER A MAN...AN' I'M A MAN...

CHAPTER 26

# The Nemesis

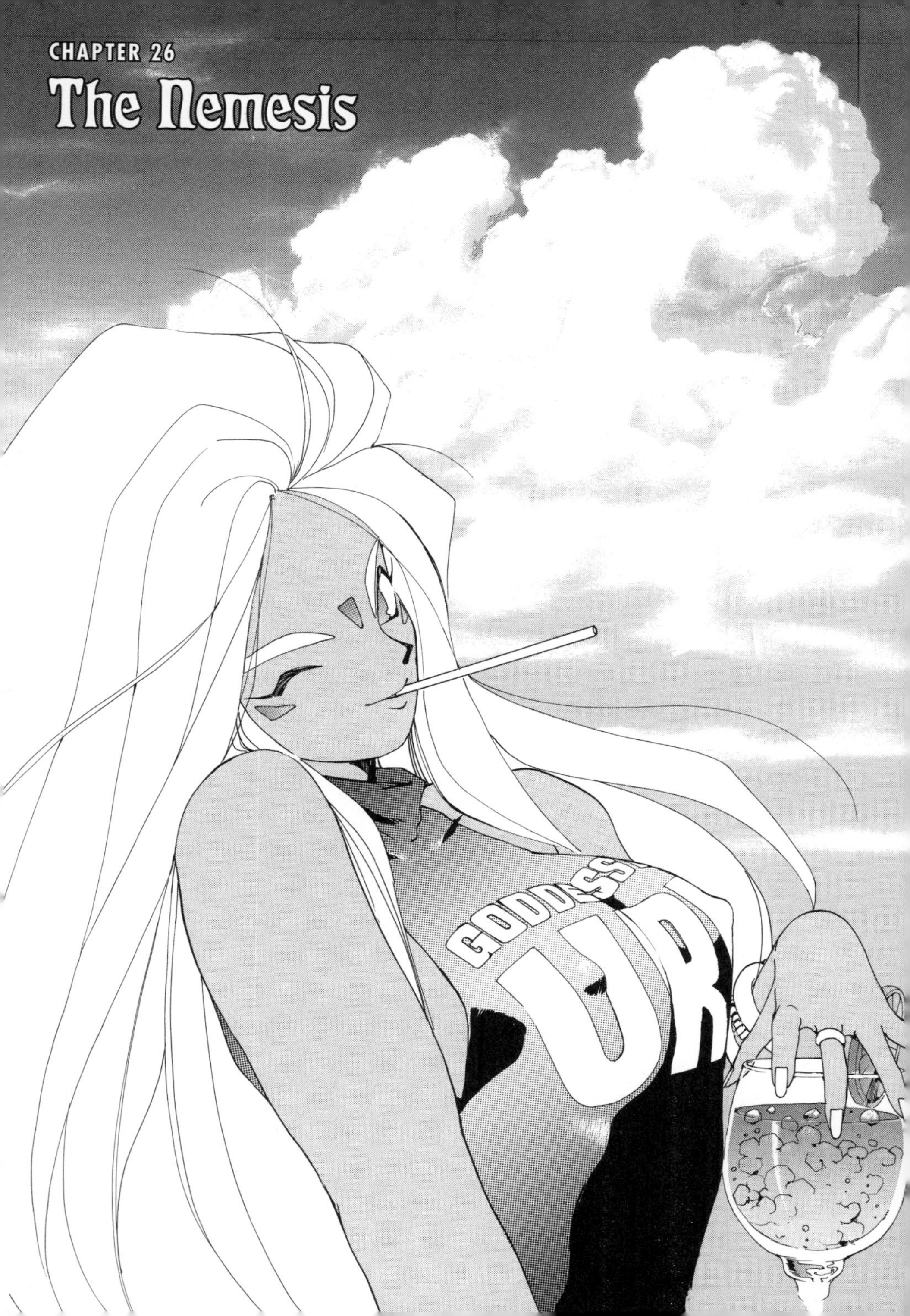

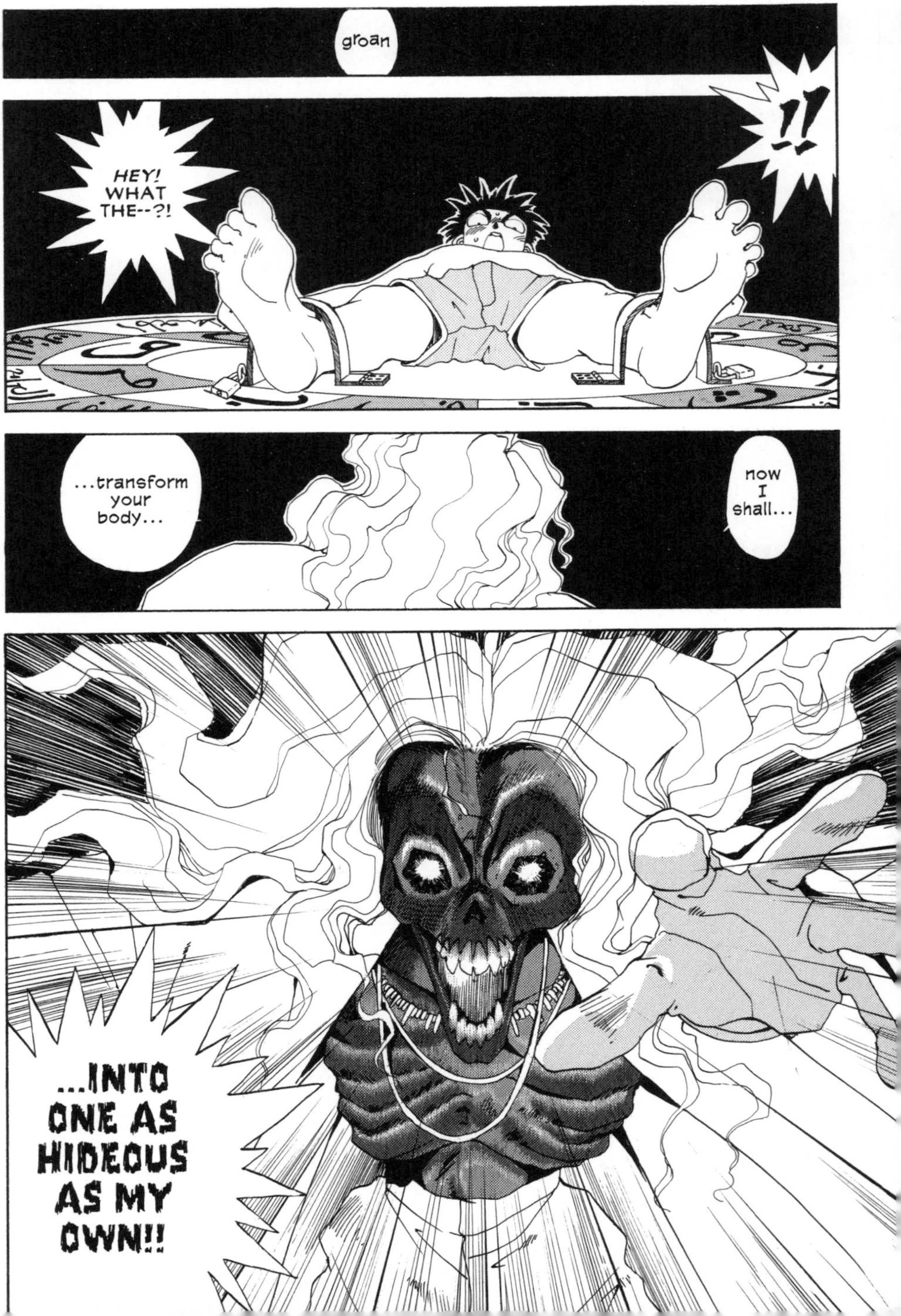
groan
!!
HEY! WHAT THE--?!
now I shall...
...transform your body...
...INTO ONE AS HIDEOUS AS MY OWN!!

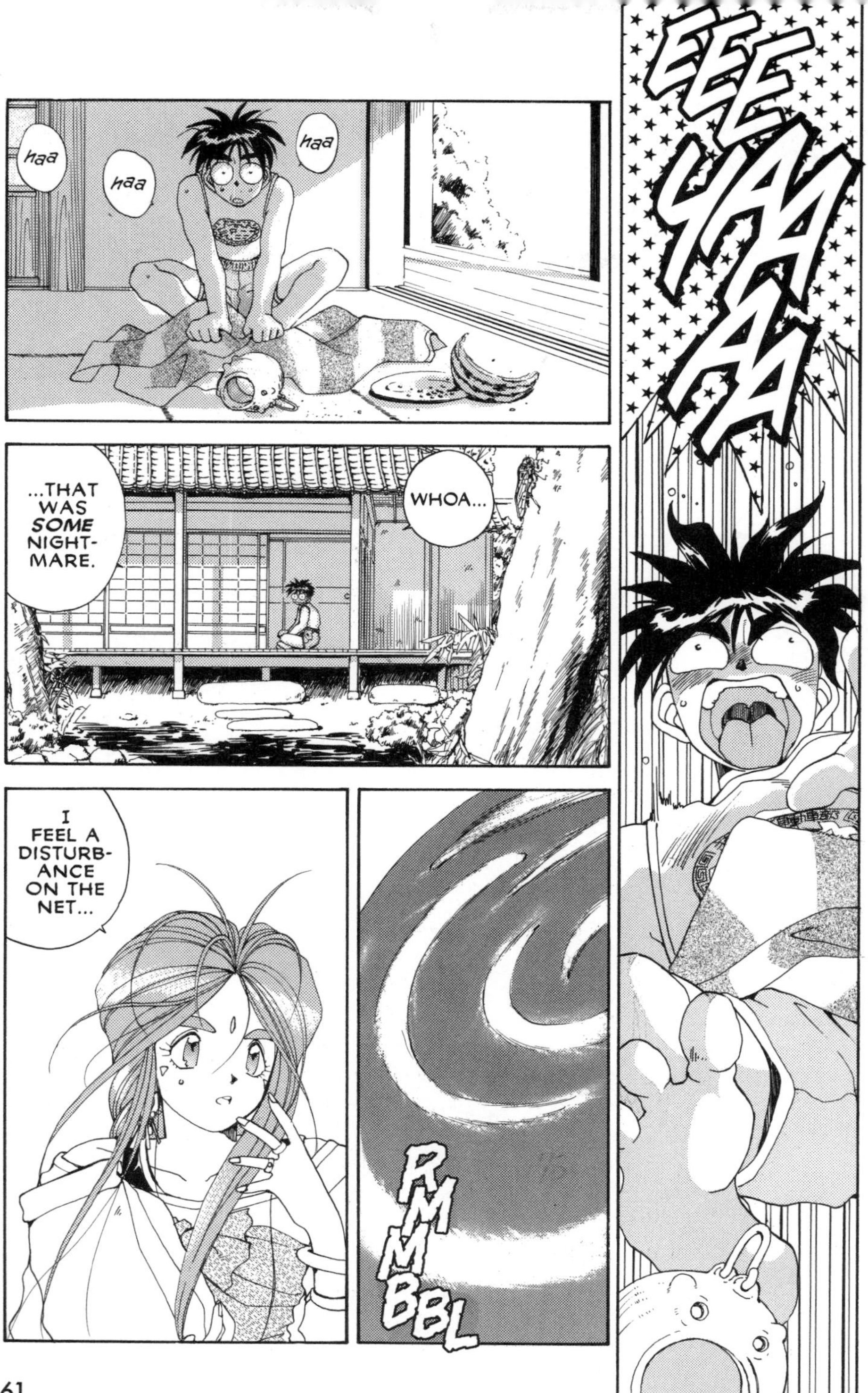
EEEYAAAAA
haa
haa
haa
WHOA...
...THAT WAS SOME NIGHTMARE.
RMMBBL
I FEEL A DISTURBANCE ON THE NET...

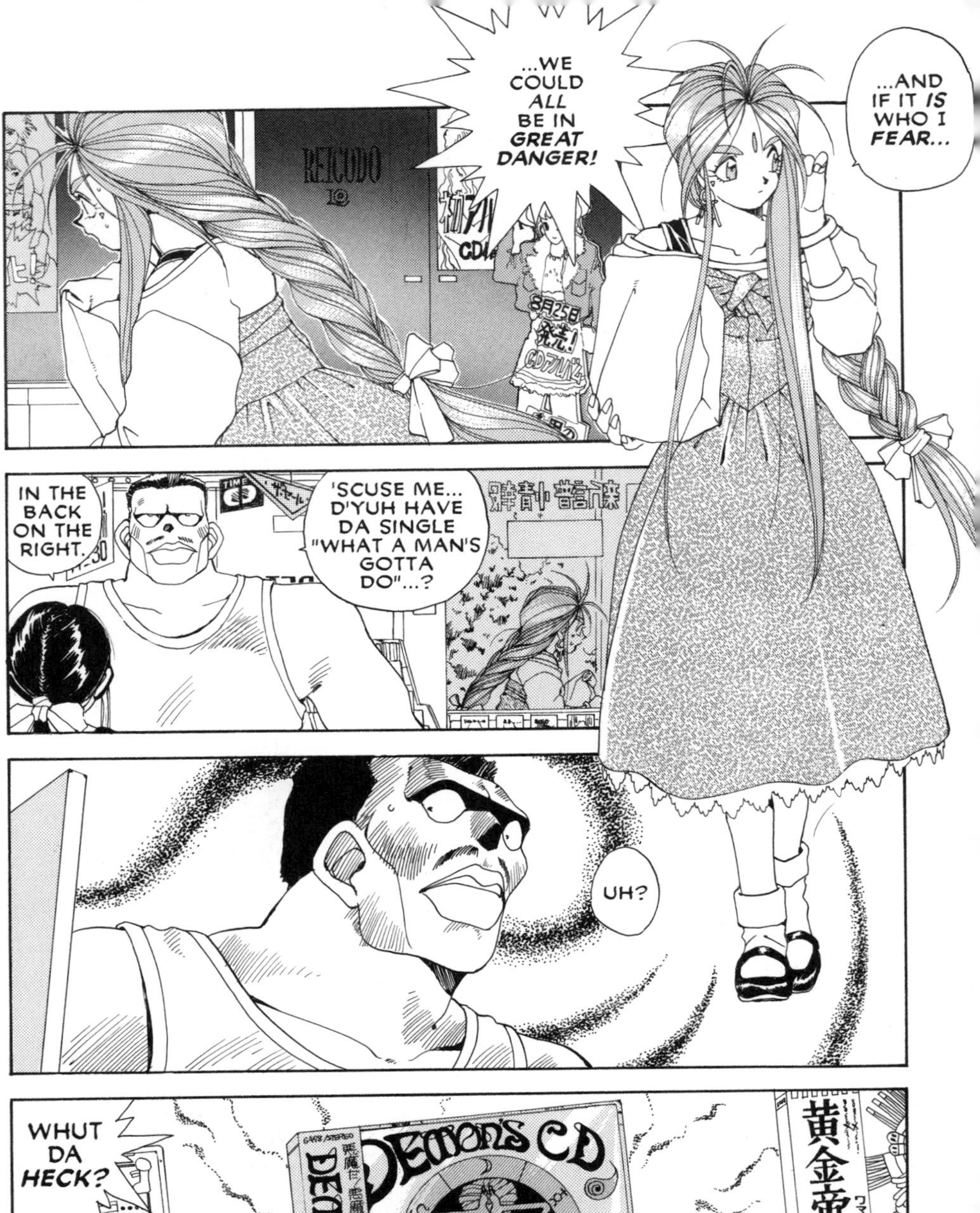
...AND IF IT *IS* WHO I *FEAR*...
...WE COULD *ALL* BE IN *GREAT DANGER!*
8月25日 発売!
'SCUSE ME... D'YUH HAVE DA SINGLE "WHAT A MAN'S GOTTA DO"...?
IN THE BACK ON THE RIGHT.
UH?
黄金帝国
2枚組 ¥4,800
DEMON'S CD
WHUT DA *HECK?*

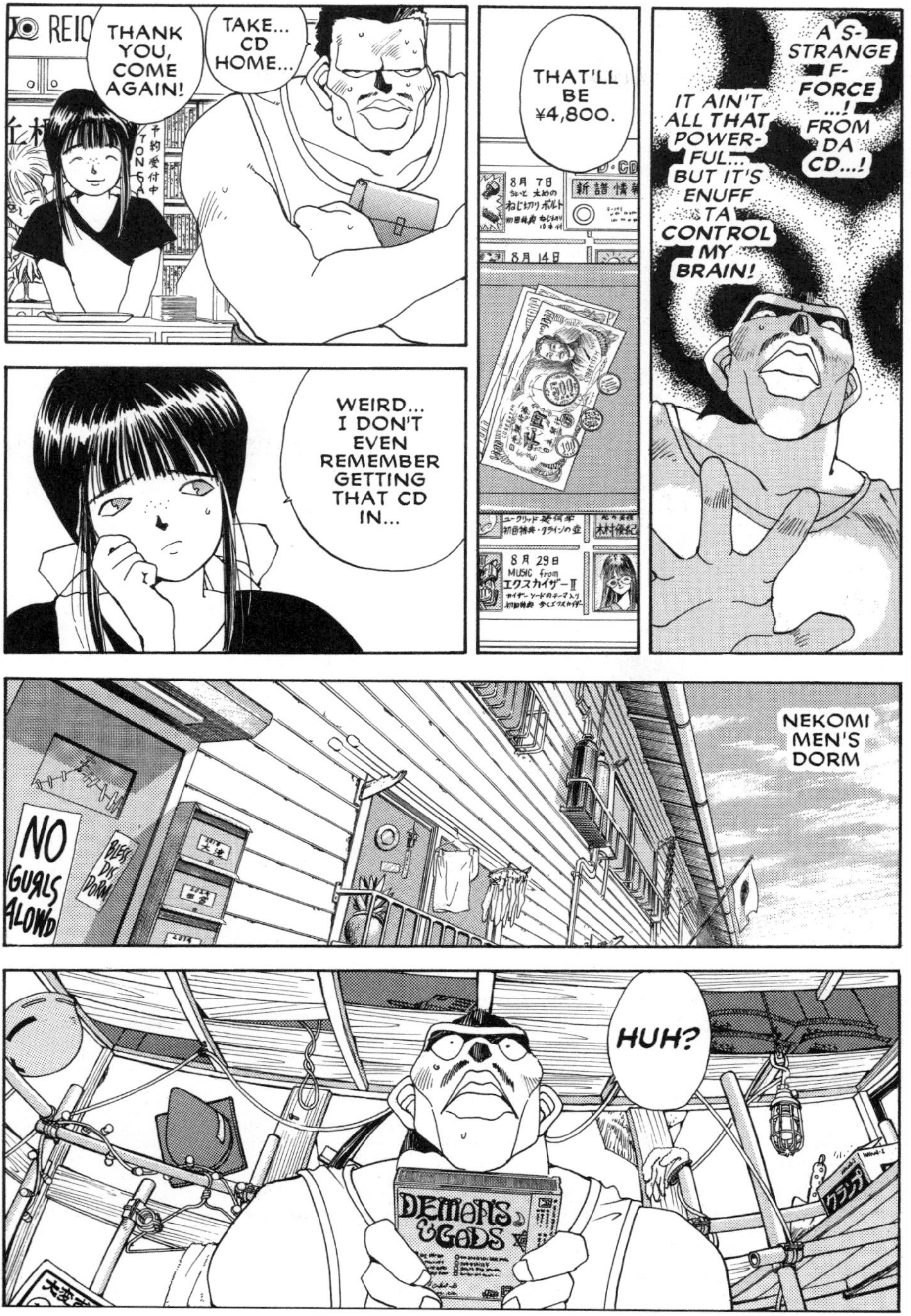
A S-STRANGE F-FORCE ...! FROM DA CD...!
IT AIN'T ALL THAT POWERFUL... BUT IT'S ENUFF TA CONTROL MY BRAIN!
THAT'LL BE ¥4,800.
TAKE... CD HOME...
THANK YOU, COME AGAIN!
REIO
WEIRD... I DON'T EVEN REMEMBER GETTING THAT CD IN...
NEKOMI MEN'S DORM
NO GURLS ALOWD
BLESS DIS DORM
HUH?
DEMONS & GODS

I DON'T REMEMBER BUYIN' IT!

WHUT'S *DIS*?!

BUT *HEY!*

I'LL PUT IT ON DA OL' *TURN-TABLE!* YA *NEVER* KNOW!

I DON'T REMEMBER HAVIN' A CD PLAYER, EITHER!

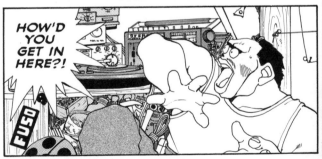

HOW'D YOU GET IN HERE?!

...INTO *COLLEGE,* I MEAN. TRYING TO PLAY A CD ON A RECORD PLAYER...WHAT ARE YOU, SOME KIND OF *LOW-BROWED MORON...?*

*oof*

I MEAN *HERE...*

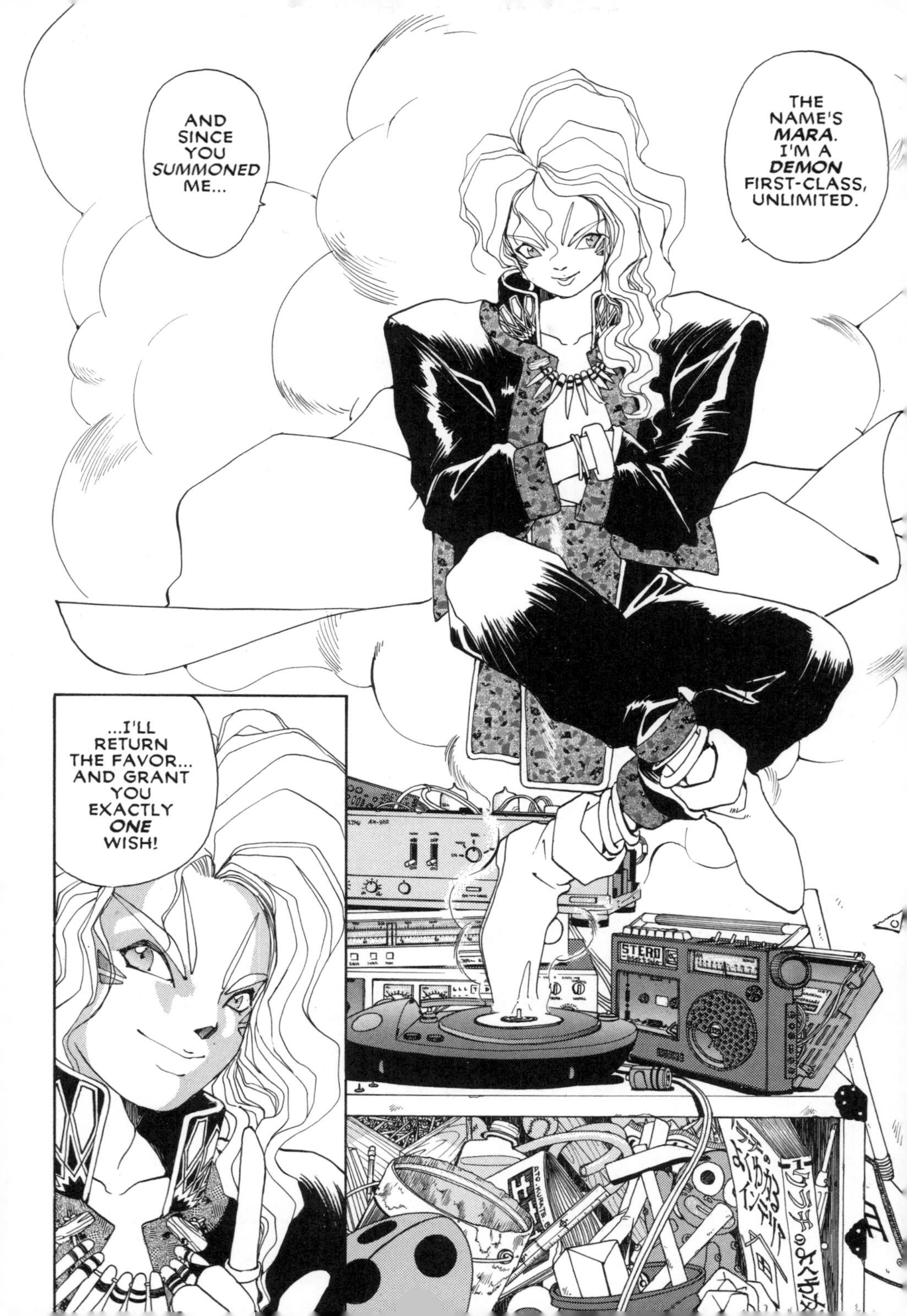
THE NAME'S *MARA*. I'M A *DEMON* FIRST-CLASS, UNLIMITED.
AND SINCE YOU *SUMMONED* ME...
...I'LL RETURN THE FAVOR... AND GRANT YOU EXACTLY *ONE* WISH!

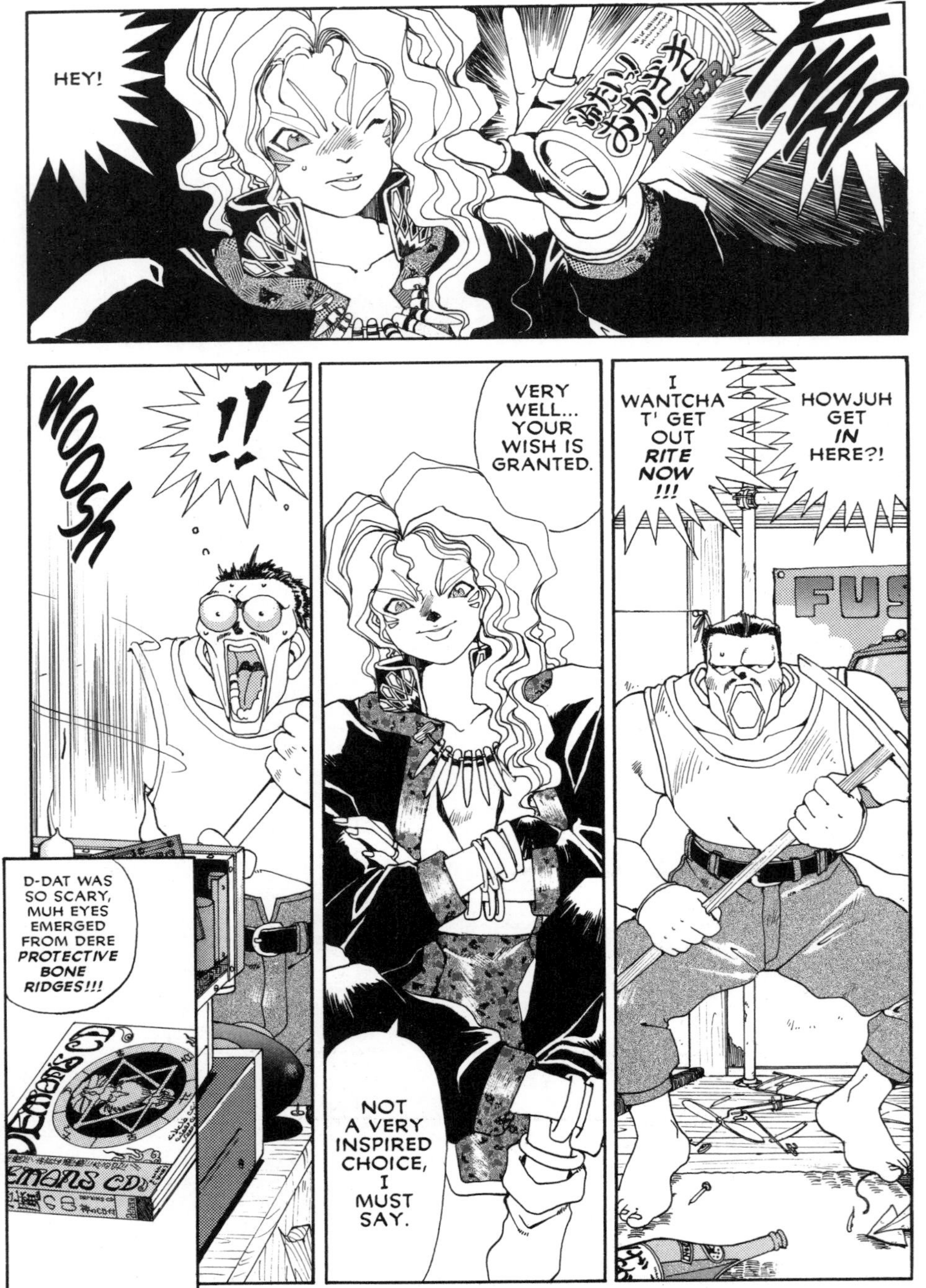
FWAP
HEY!
HOWJUH GET *IN* HERE?!
I WANTCHA T' GET OUT *RITE NOW* !!!
VERY WELL... YOUR WISH IS GRANTED.
NOT A VERY INSPIRED CHOICE, I MUST SAY.
!!
WOOSH
FUS
D-DAT WAS SO SCARY, MUH EYES EMERGED FROM DERE *PROTECTIVE BONE RIDGES!!!*
DEMONS CD

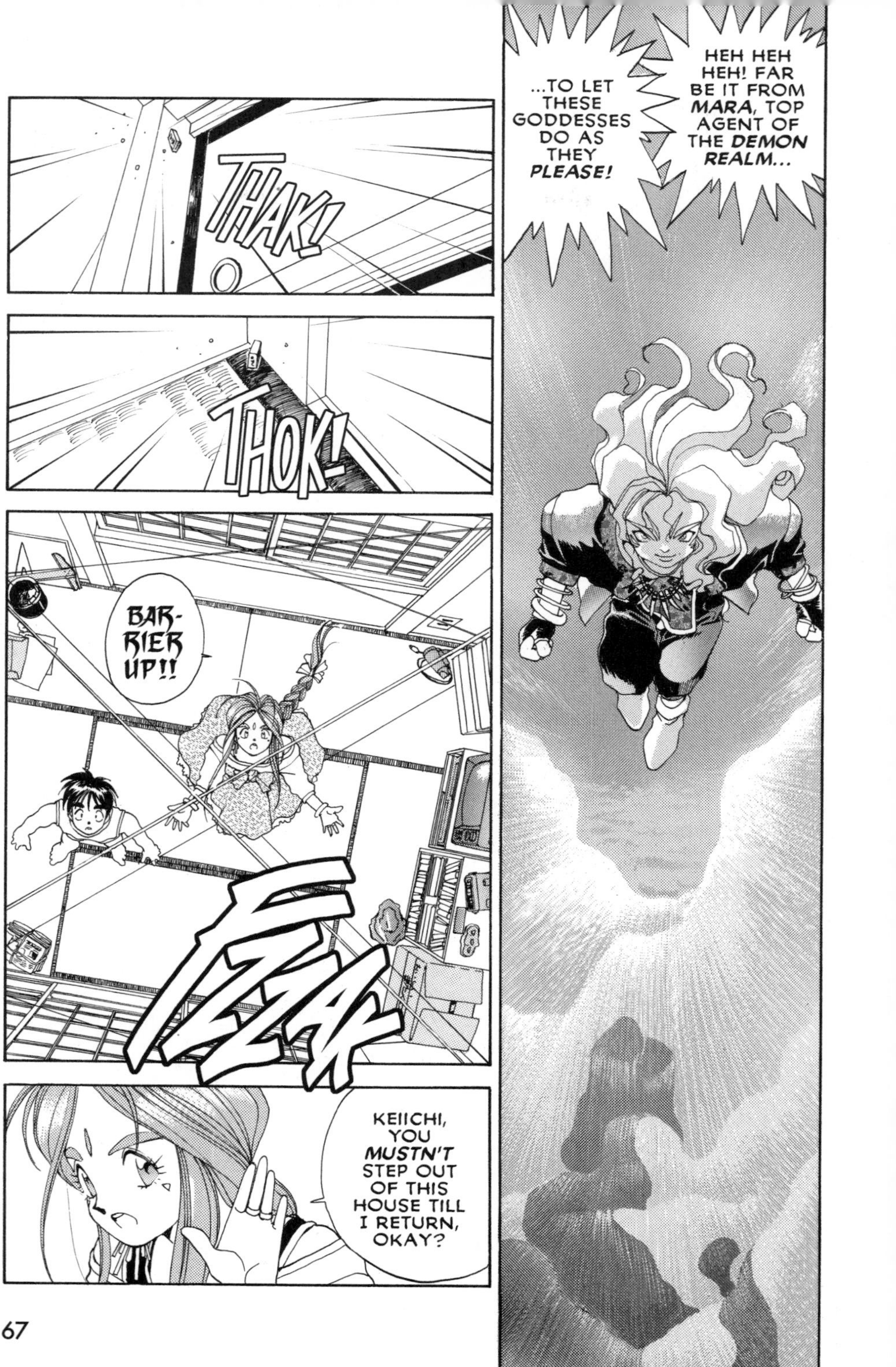
HEH HEH HEH! FAR BE IT FROM MARA, TOP AGENT OF THE DEMON REALM...
...TO LET THESE GODDESSES DO AS THEY PLEASE!
THAK!
THOK!
BAR-RIER UP!!
FZZAK
KEIICHI, YOU MUSTN'T STEP OUT OF THIS HOUSE TILL I RETURN, OKAY?

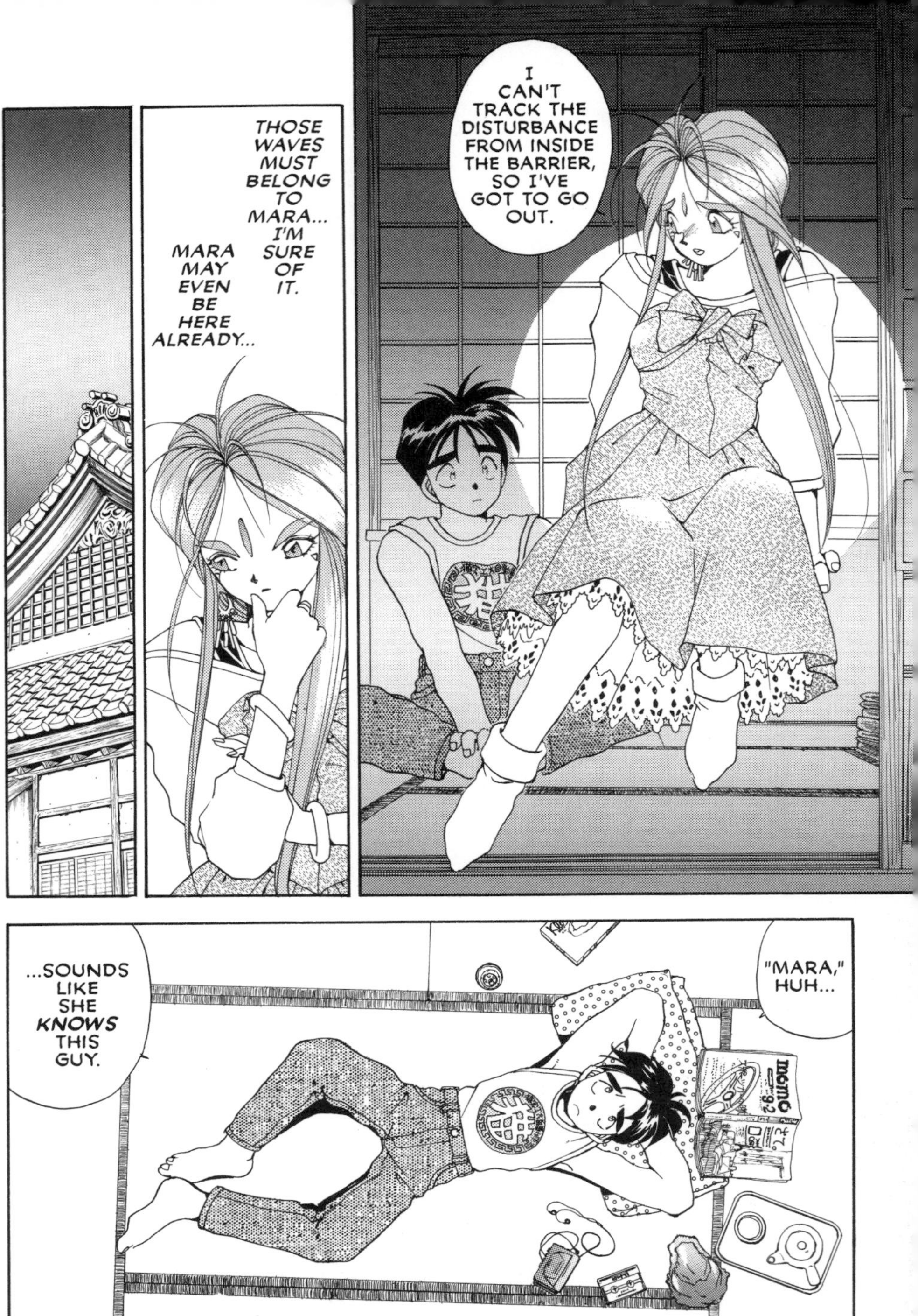
I CAN'T TRACK THE DISTURBANCE FROM INSIDE THE BARRIER, SO I'VE GOT TO GO OUT.
THOSE WAVES MUST BELONG TO MARA... I'M SURE OF IT.
MARA MAY EVEN BE HERE ALREADY...
"MARA," HUH...
...SOUNDS LIKE SHE *KNOWS* THIS GUY.

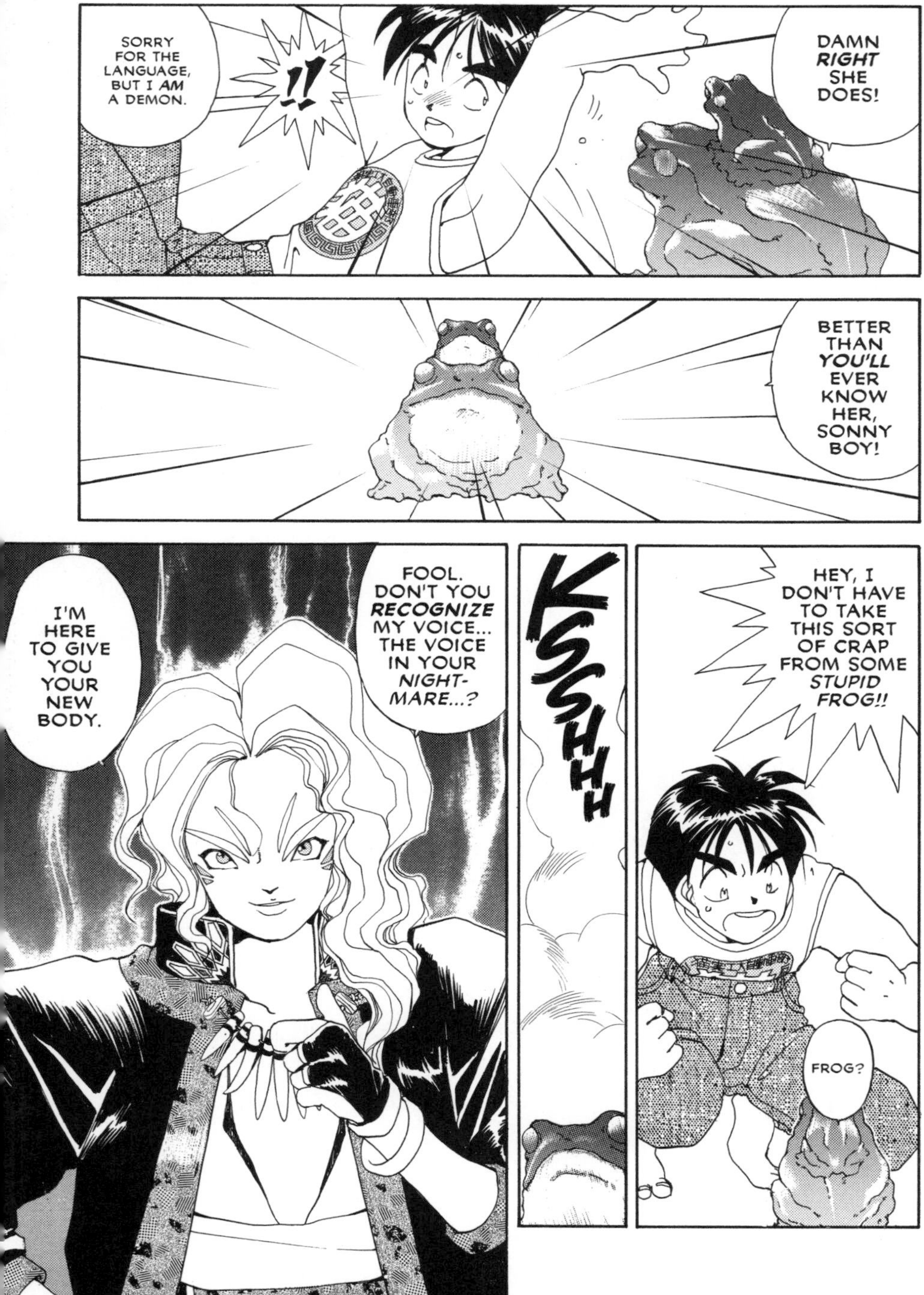
DAMN RIGHT SHE DOES!
!!
SORRY FOR THE LANGUAGE, BUT I AM A DEMON.
BETTER THAN YOU'LL EVER KNOW HER, SONNY BOY!
HEY, I DON'T HAVE TO TAKE THIS SORT OF CRAP FROM SOME STUPID FROG!!
FROG?
KSSHHH
FOOL. DON'T YOU RECOGNIZE MY VOICE... THE VOICE IN YOUR NIGHT-MARE...?
I'M HERE TO GIVE YOU YOUR NEW BODY.

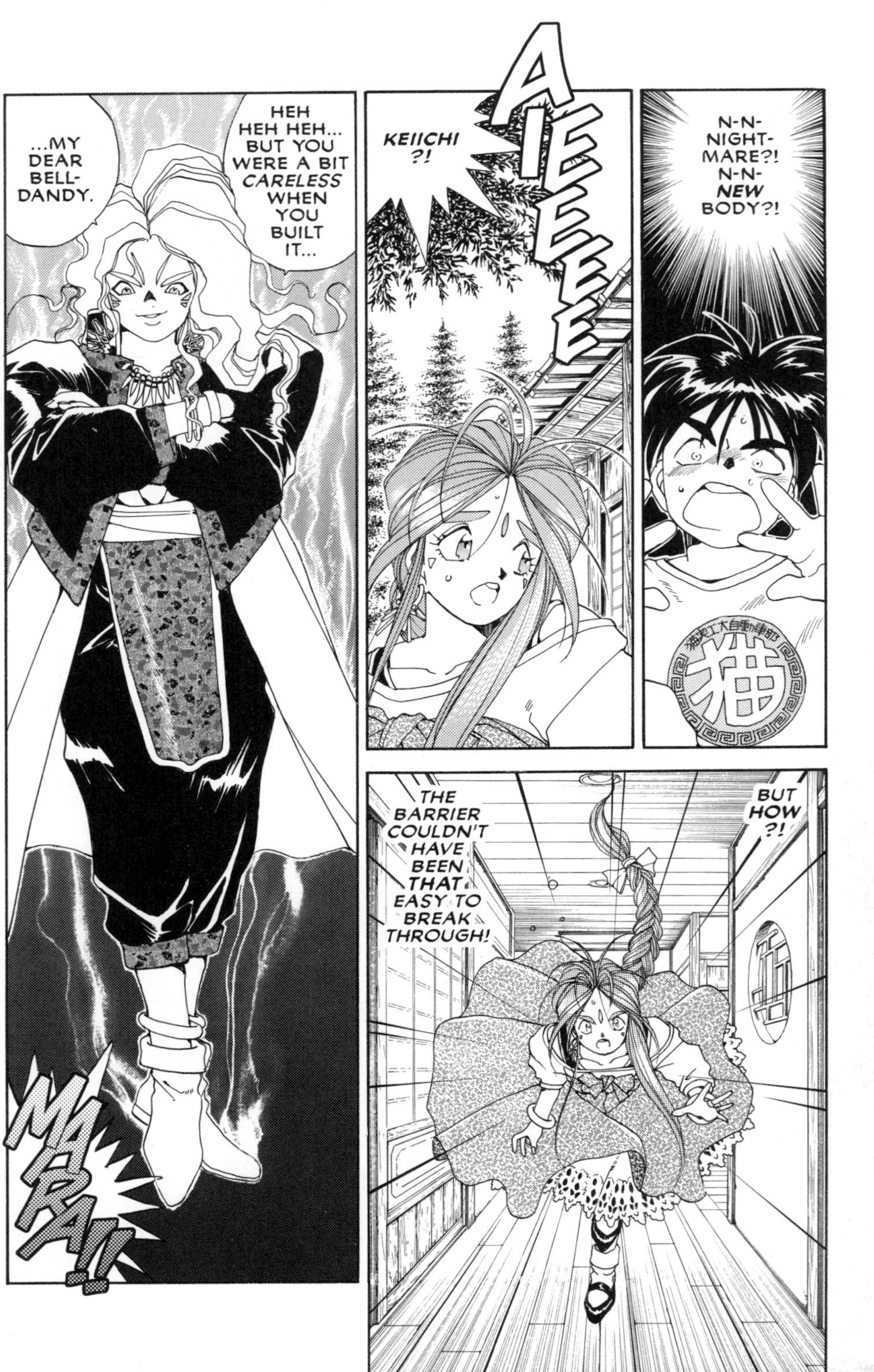
N-N-NIGHT-MARE?! N-N-NEW BODY?!
AIEEEEE
KEIICHI?!
BUT HOW?!
THE BARRIER COULDN'T HAVE BEEN THAT EASY TO BREAK THROUGH!
HEH HEH HEH... BUT YOU WERE A BIT CARELESS WHEN YOU BUILT IT...
...MY DEAR BELL-DANDY.
MARA!!

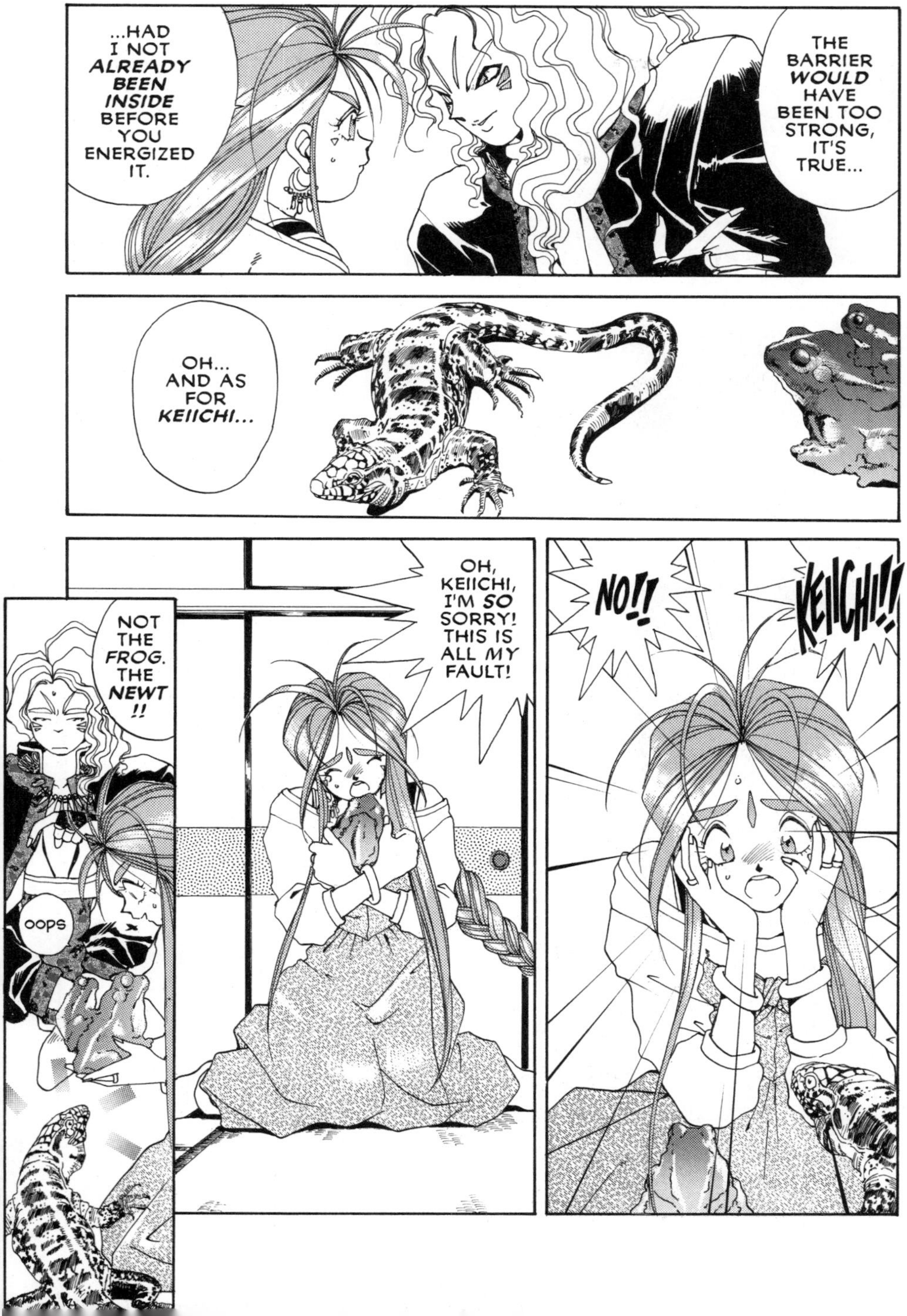
THE BARRIER *WOULD* HAVE BEEN TOO STRONG, IT'S TRUE...
...HAD I NOT *ALREADY BEEN INSIDE* BEFORE YOU ENERGIZED IT.
OH... AND AS FOR *KEIICHI...*
KEIICHI!!
NO!!
OH, KEIICHI, I'M *SO* SORRY! THIS IS ALL *MY* FAULT!
NOT THE *FROG*. THE *NEWT* !!
oops

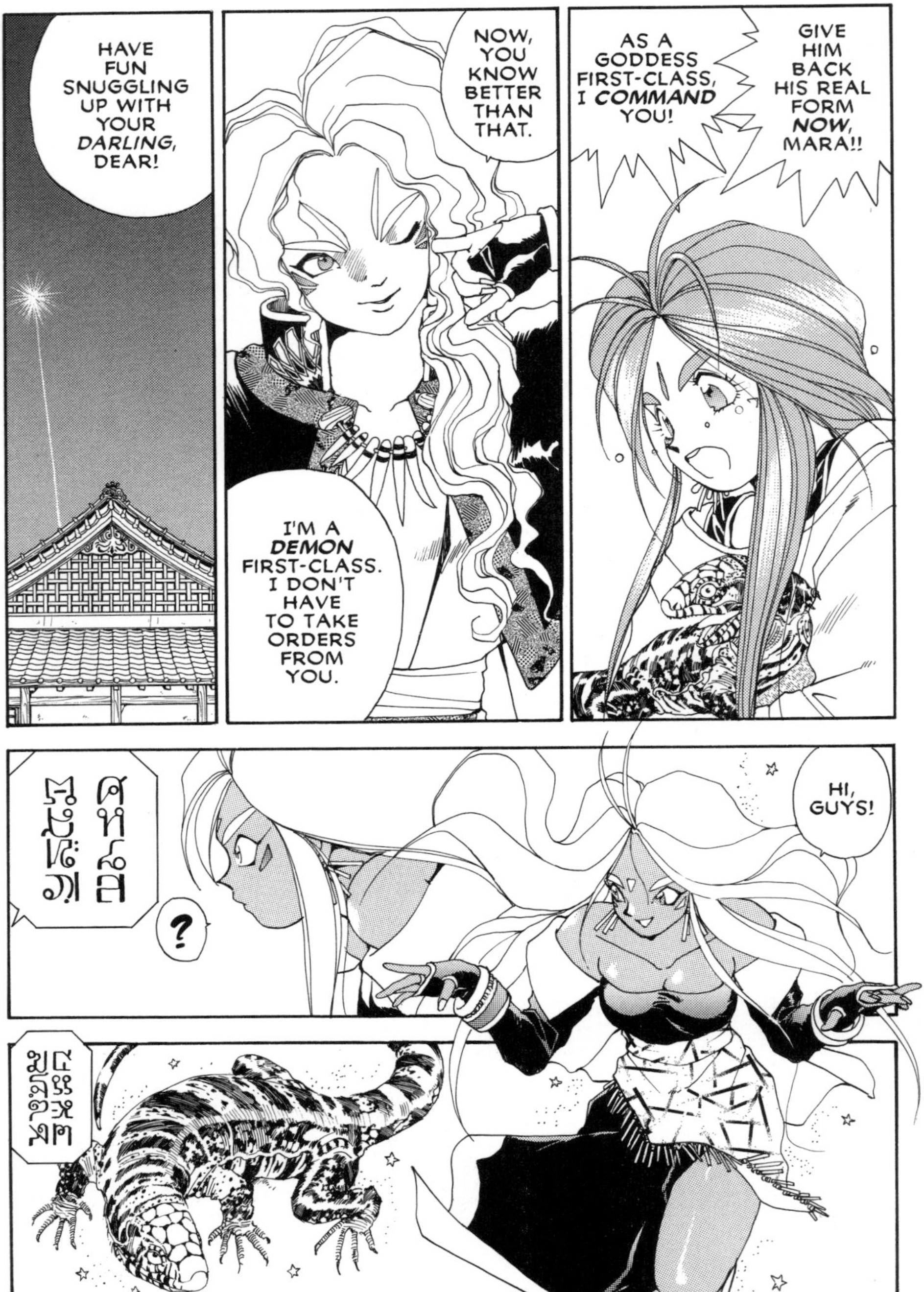
GIVE HIM BACK HIS REAL FORM *NOW*, MARA!!
AS A GODDESS FIRST-CLASS, I *COMMAND* YOU!
NOW, YOU KNOW BETTER THAN THAT.
I'M A *DEMON* FIRST-CLASS. I DON'T HAVE TO TAKE ORDERS FROM YOU.
HAVE FUN SNUGGLING UP WITH YOUR *DARLING*, DEAR!
HI, GUYS!
?

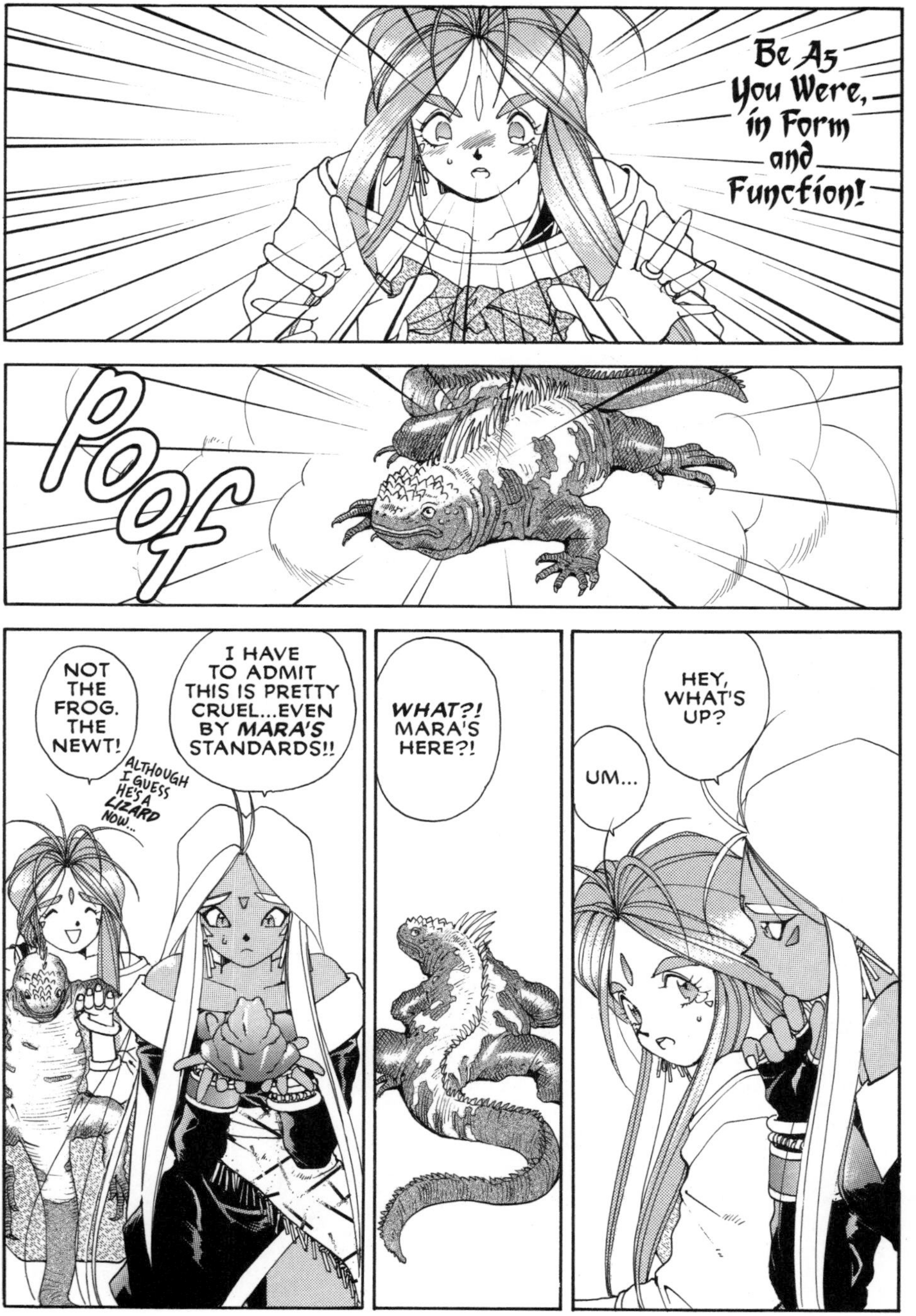
Be As You Were, in Form and Function!
poof
HEY, WHAT'S UP?
UM...
WHAT?! MARA'S HERE?!
I HAVE TO ADMIT THIS IS PRETTY CRUEL...EVEN BY MARA'S STANDARDS!!
NOT THE FROG. THE NEWT!
ALTHOUGH I GUESS HE'S A LIZARD NOW...

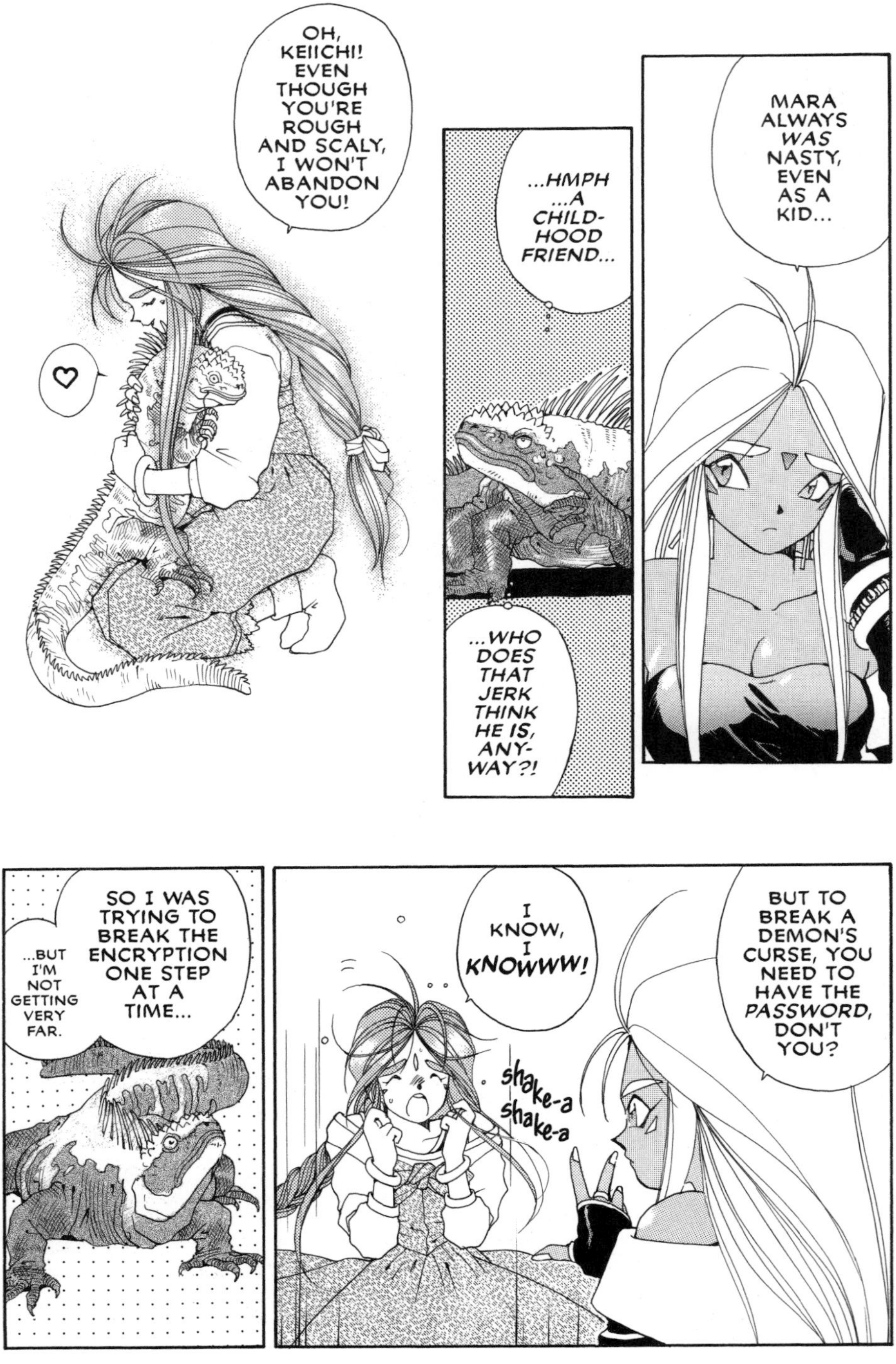
MARA ALWAYS *WAS* NASTY, EVEN AS A KID...
*...HMPH ...A CHILDHOOD FRIEND...*
*...WHO DOES THAT JERK THINK HE IS, ANYWAY?!*
OH, KEIICHI! EVEN THOUGH YOU'RE ROUGH AND SCALY, I WON'T ABANDON YOU!
♡
BUT TO BREAK A DEMON'S CURSE, YOU NEED TO HAVE THE *PASSWORD*, DON'T YOU?
I KNOW, I ***KNOWWW!***
shake-a shake-a
SO I WAS TRYING TO BREAK THE ENCRYPTION ONE STEP AT A TIME...
...BUT I'M NOT GETTING VERY FAR.

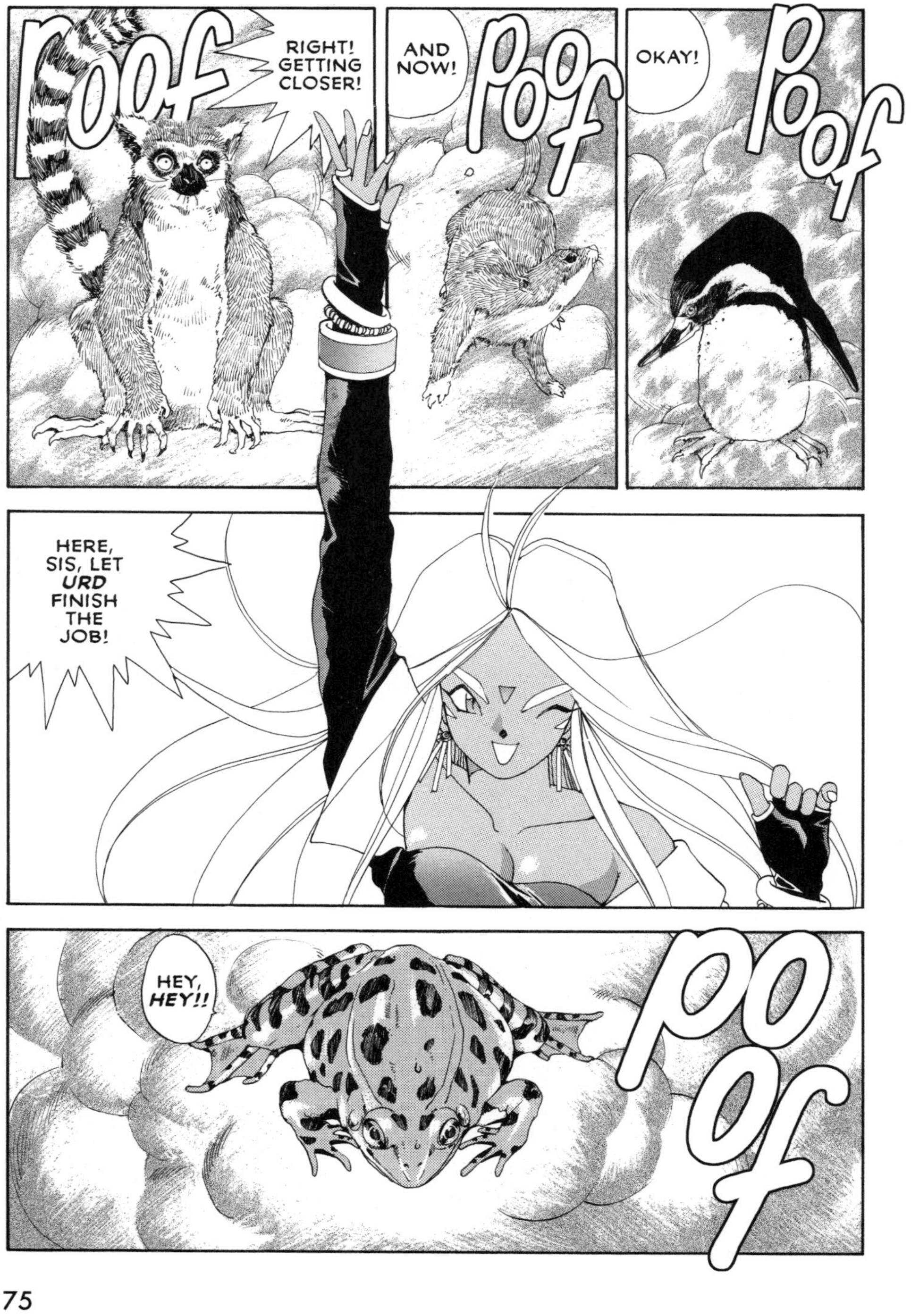
poof
OKAY!
poof
AND NOW!
RIGHT! GETTING CLOSER!
poof
HERE, SIS, LET URD FINISH THE JOB!
poof
HEY, HEY!!

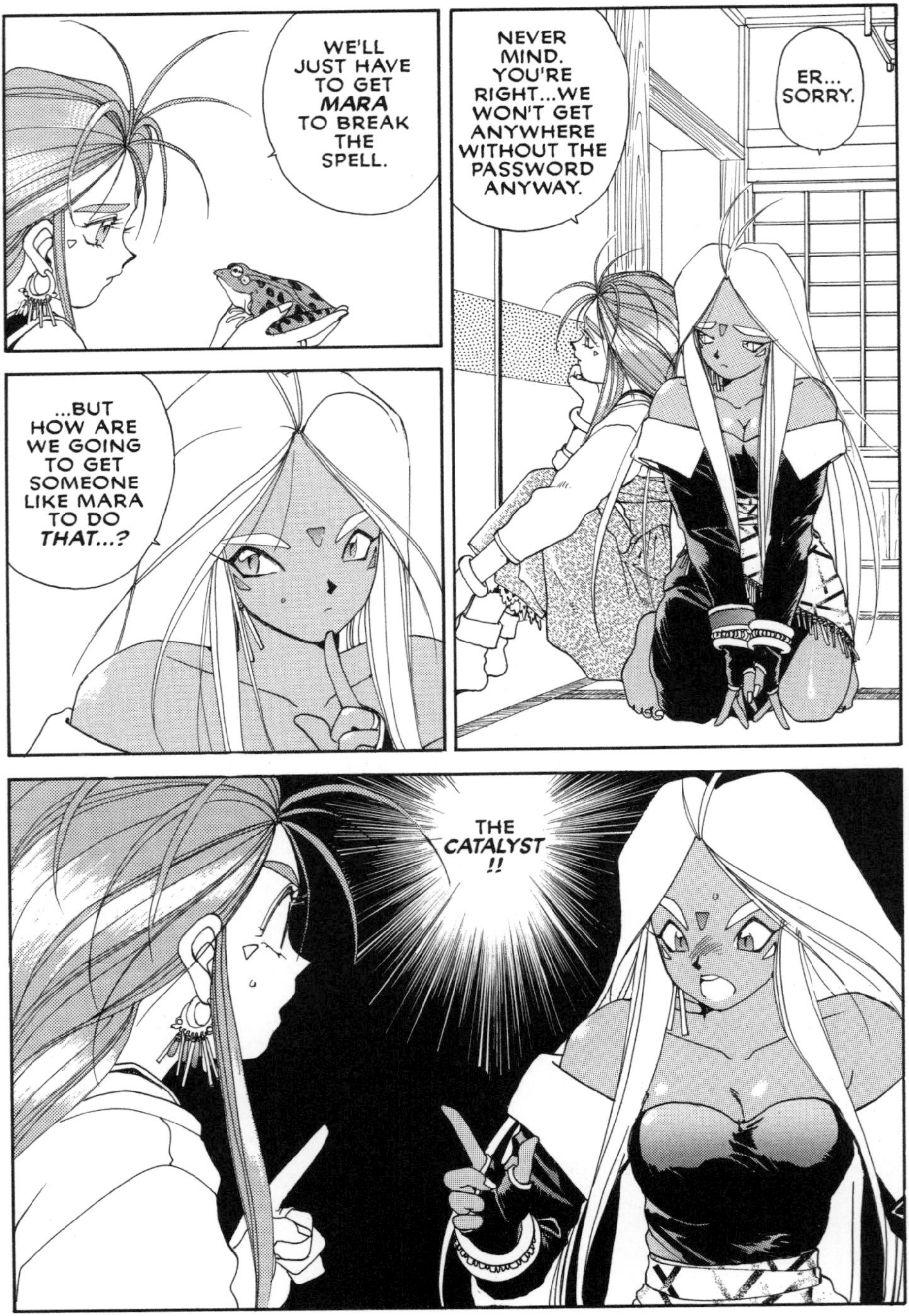
ER... SORRY.
NEVER MIND. YOU'RE RIGHT...WE WON'T GET ANYWHERE WITHOUT THE PASSWORD ANYWAY.
WE'LL JUST HAVE TO GET *MARA* TO BREAK THE SPELL.
...BUT HOW ARE WE GOING TO GET SOMEONE LIKE MARA TO DO *THAT...?*
THE *CATALYST* !!

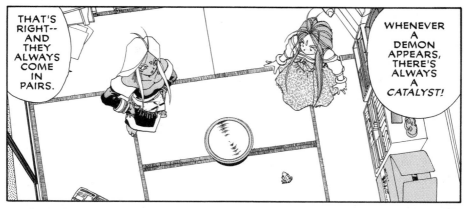

WHENEVER A DEMON APPEARS, THERE'S ALWAYS A *CATALYST!*
THAT'S RIGHT-- AND THEY ALWAYS COME IN PAIRS.
Eyes of Heaven, Eyes of Earth, Eyes of Sea...
...Show Us Where the Catalyst of Mara Be!
WELL ...?
*OH!*
IT'S CLOSE... AND IT'S GETTING ***CLOSER!***

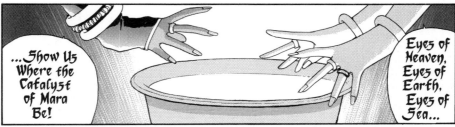

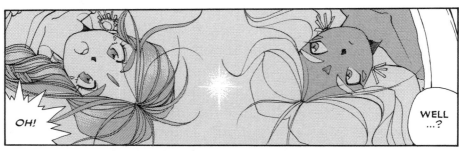

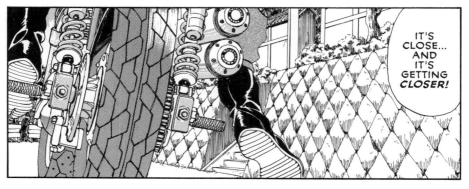

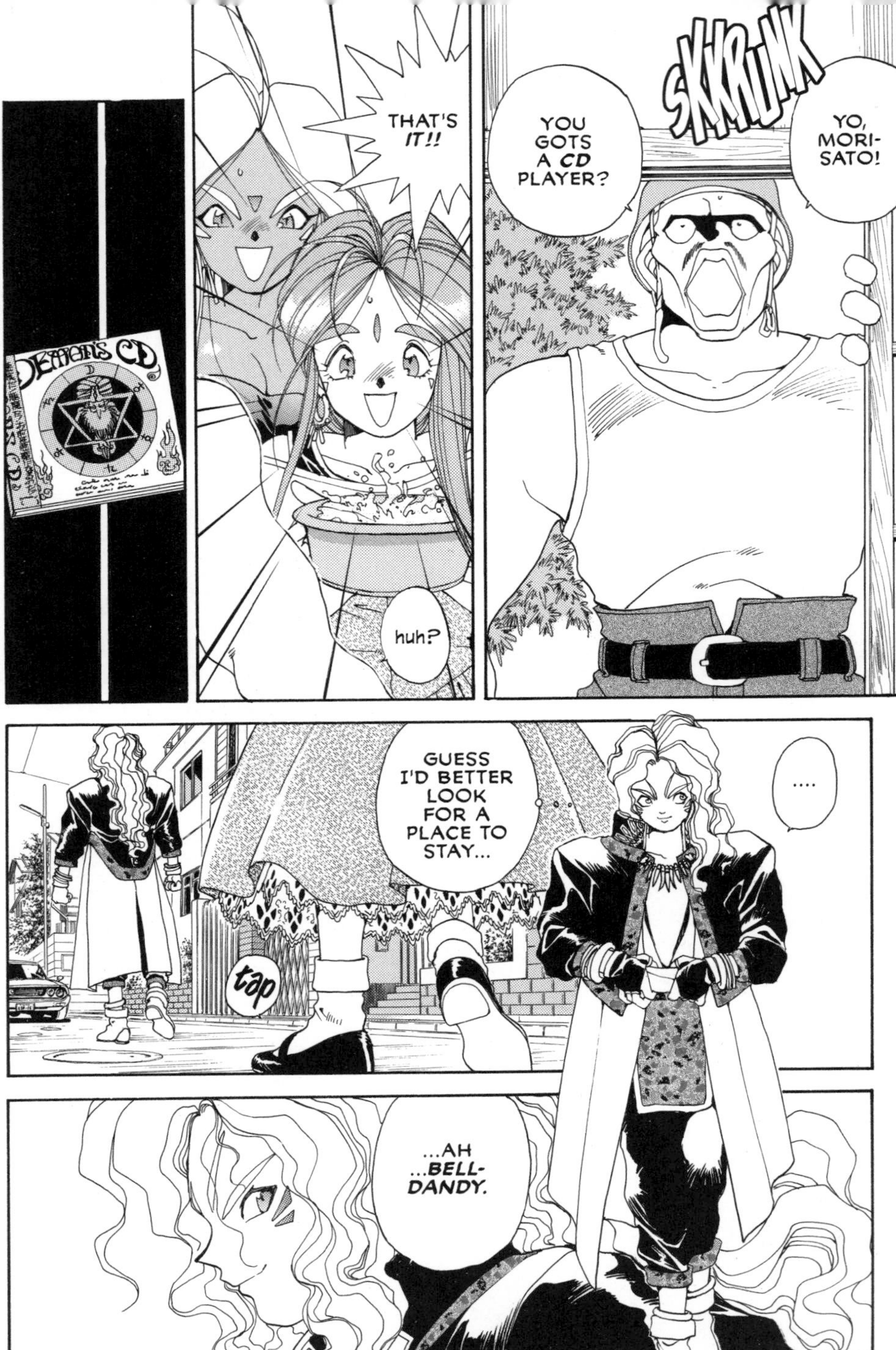
YO, MORI-SATO!
SKKRUNK
YOU GOTS A CD PLAYER?
THAT'S IT!!
huh?
DEMON'S CD
....
GUESS I'D BETTER LOOK FOR A PLACE TO STAY...
tap
...AH ...BELL-DANDY.

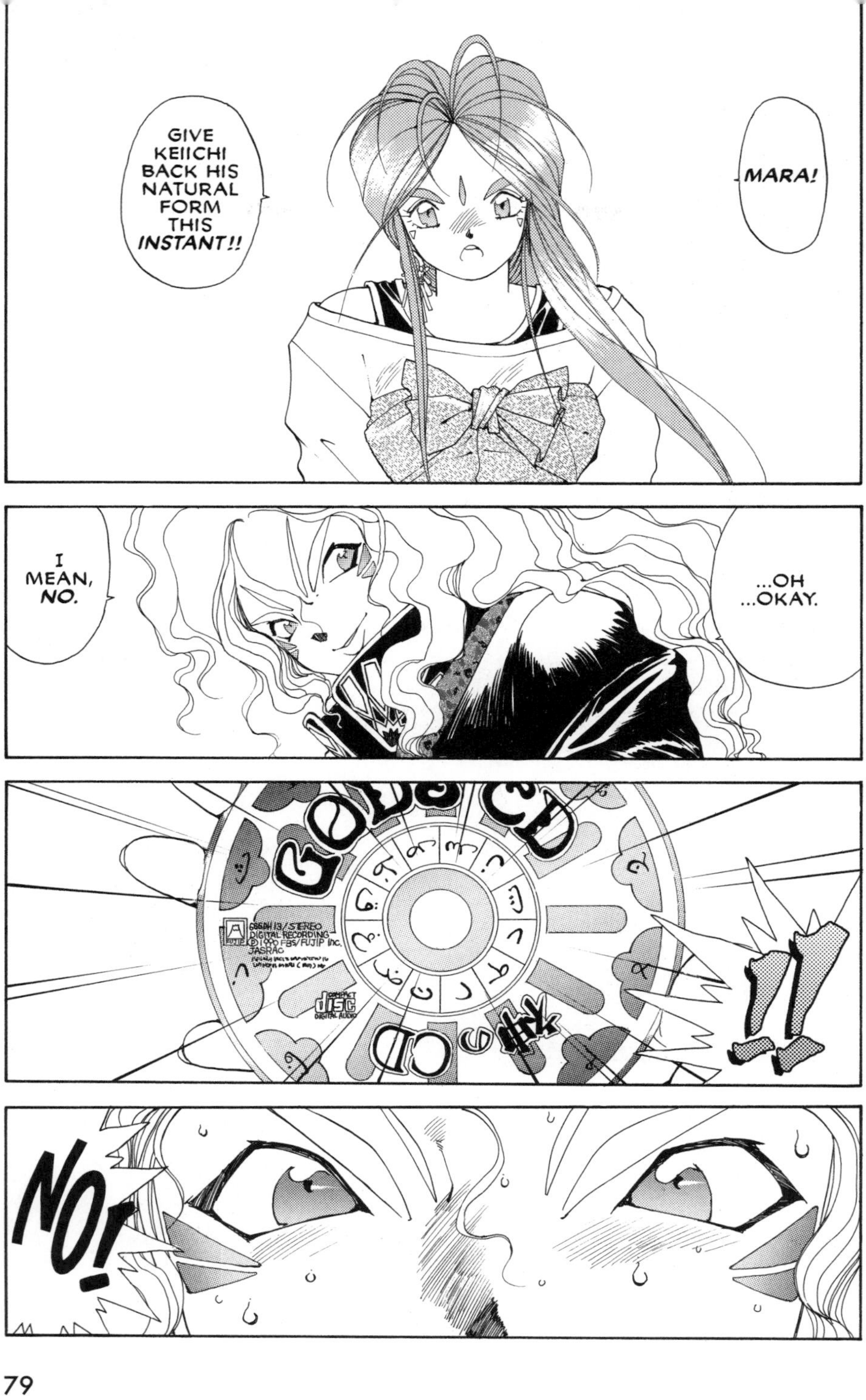
MARA!
GIVE KEIICHI BACK HIS NATURAL FORM THIS INSTANT!!
...OH ...OKAY.
I MEAN, NO.
!!
DIGITAL RECORDING
JASRAC
COMPACT disc DIGITAL AUDIO
NO!

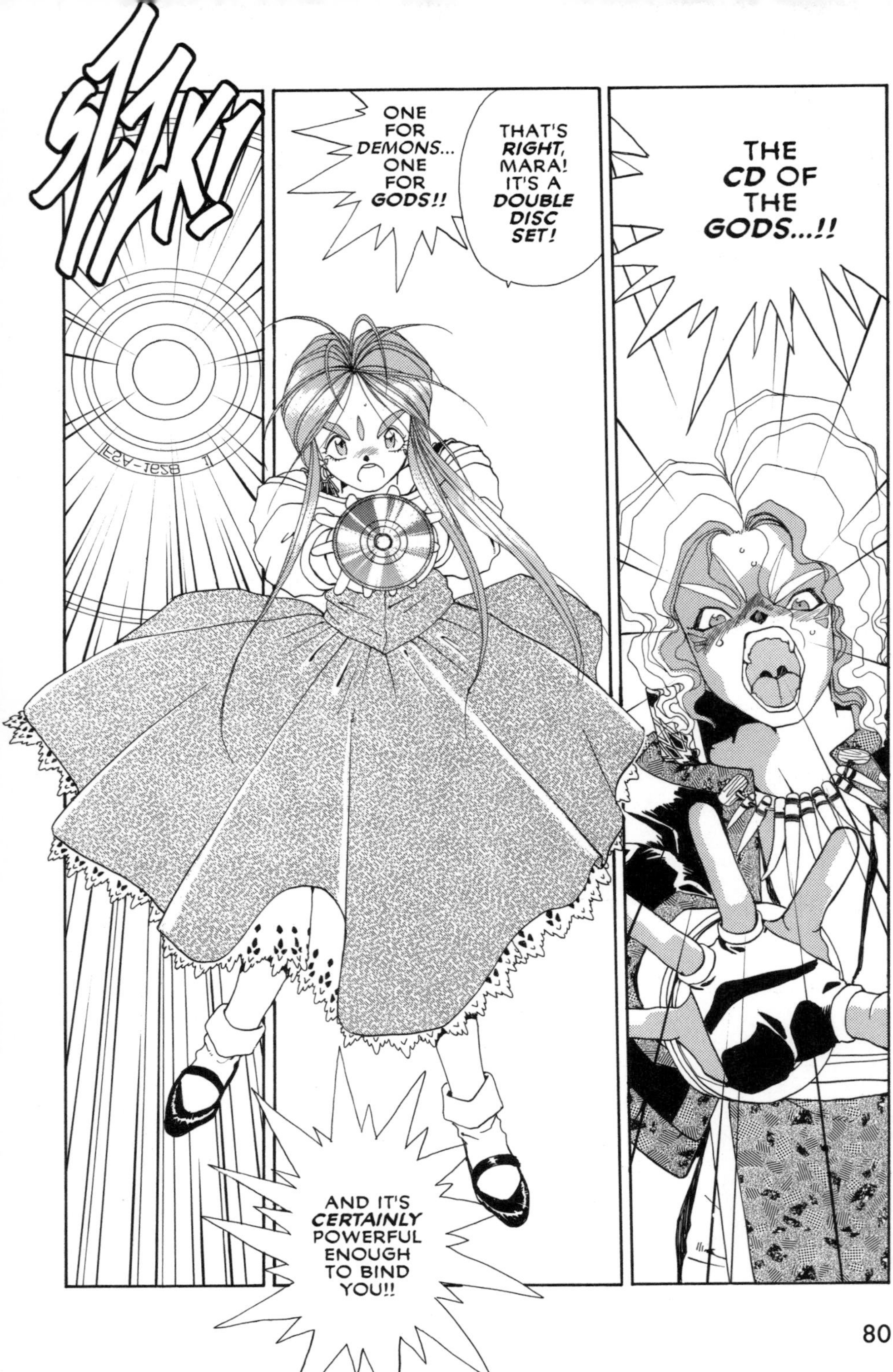
THE CD OF THE GODS...!!
ONE FOR DEMONS... ONE FOR GODS!!
THAT'S RIGHT, MARA! IT'S A DOUBLE DISC SET!
AND IT'S CERTAINLY POWERFUL ENOUGH TO BIND YOU!!

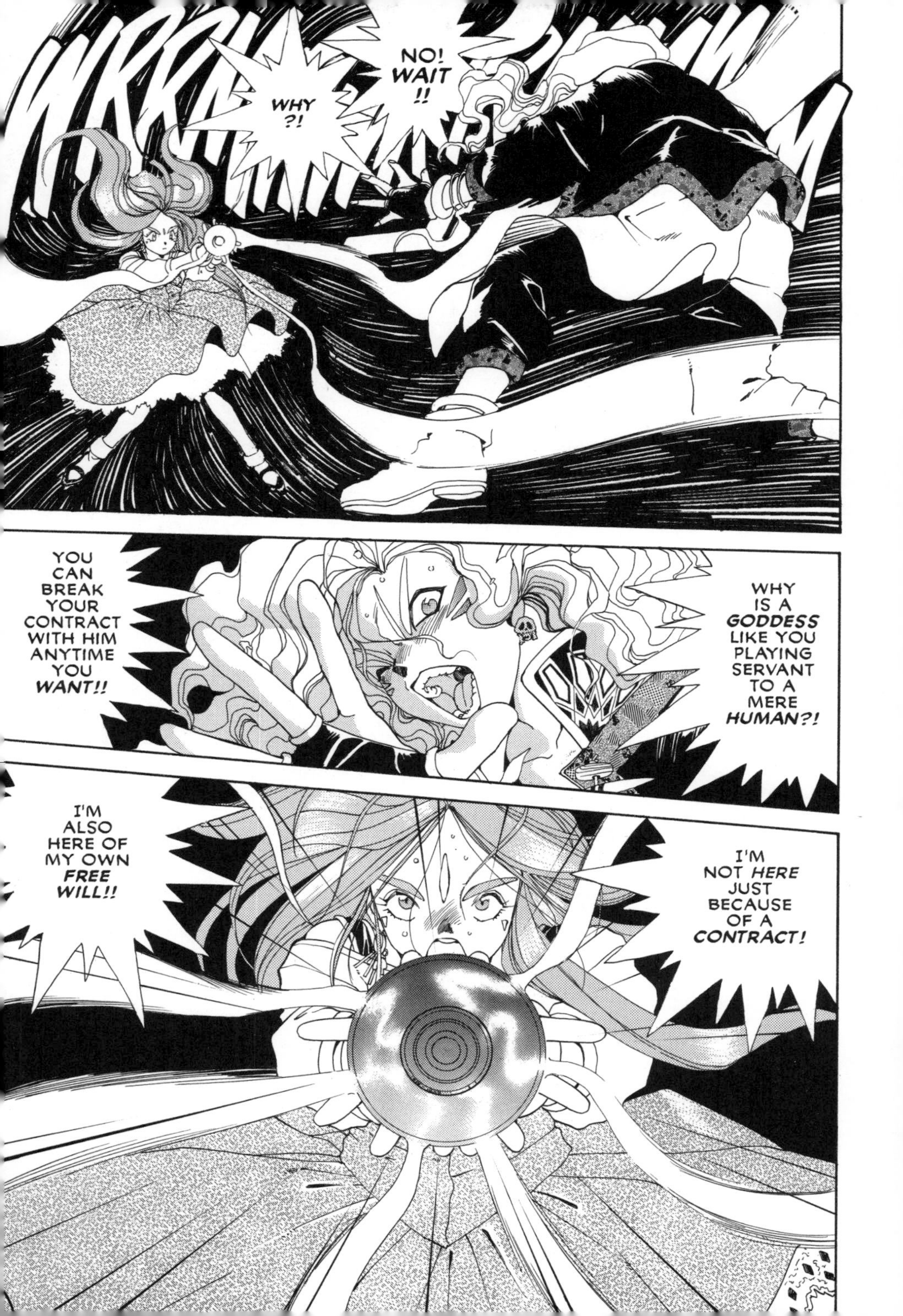
NO! WAIT!!
WHY?!
WHY IS A GODDESS LIKE YOU PLAYING SERVANT TO A MERE HUMAN?!
YOU CAN BREAK YOUR CONTRACT WITH HIM ANYTIME YOU WANT!!
I'M NOT HERE JUST BECAUSE OF A CONTRACT!
I'M ALSO HERE OF MY OWN FREE WILL!!

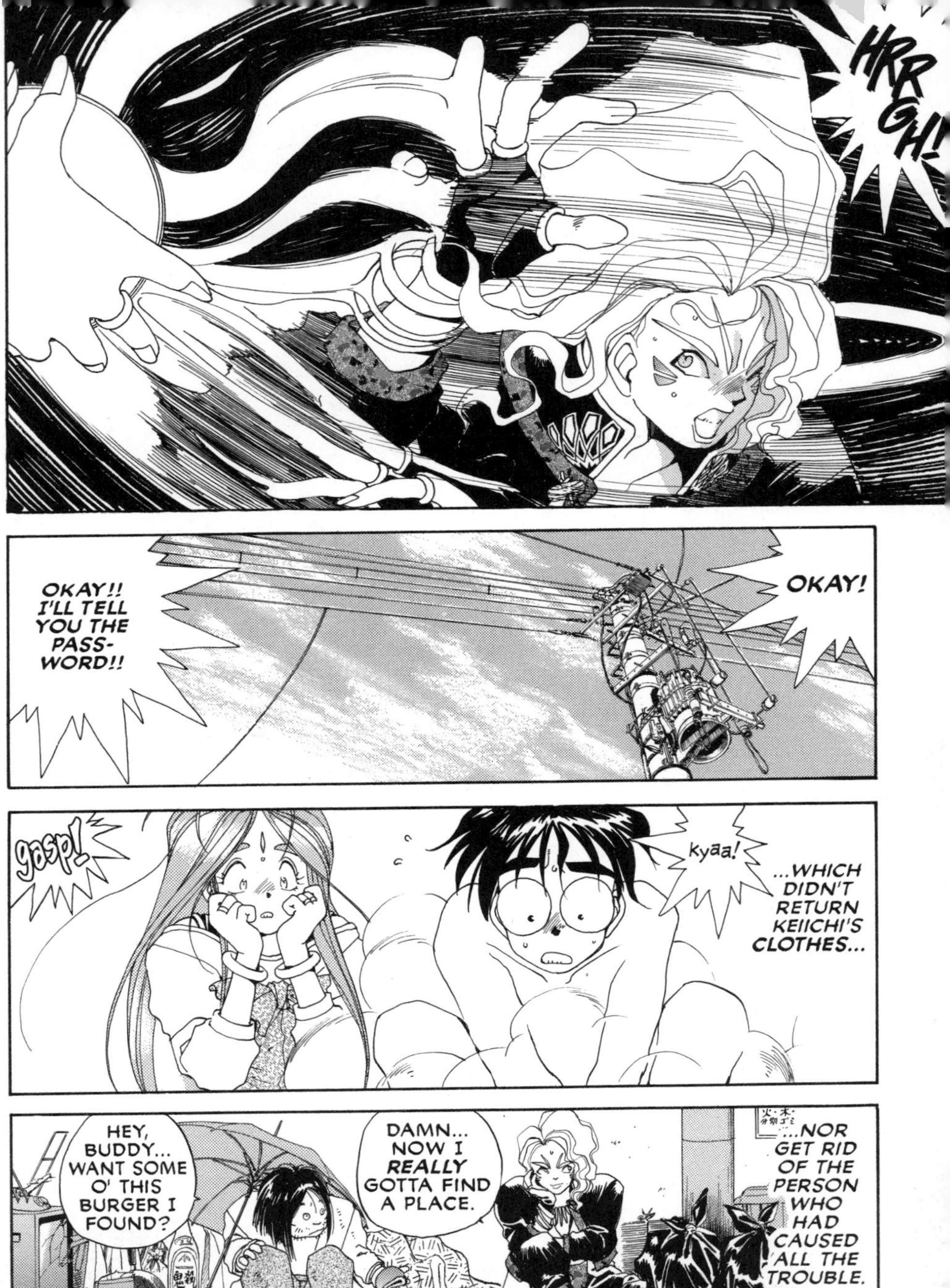
HRRGH!
OKAY!
OKAY!! I'LL TELL YOU THE PASS-WORD!!
...WHICH DIDN'T RETURN KEIICHI'S CLOTHES...
Kyaa!
gasp!
...NOR GET RID OF THE PERSON WHO HAD CAUSED ALL THE TROUBLE.
DAMN... NOW I REALLY GOTTA FIND A PLACE.
HEY, BUDDY... WANT SOME O' THIS BURGER I FOUND?

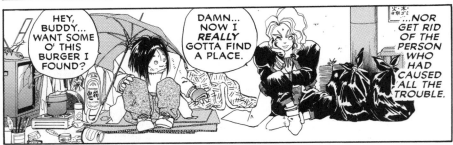

CHAPTER 27

# Mara's Counterattack

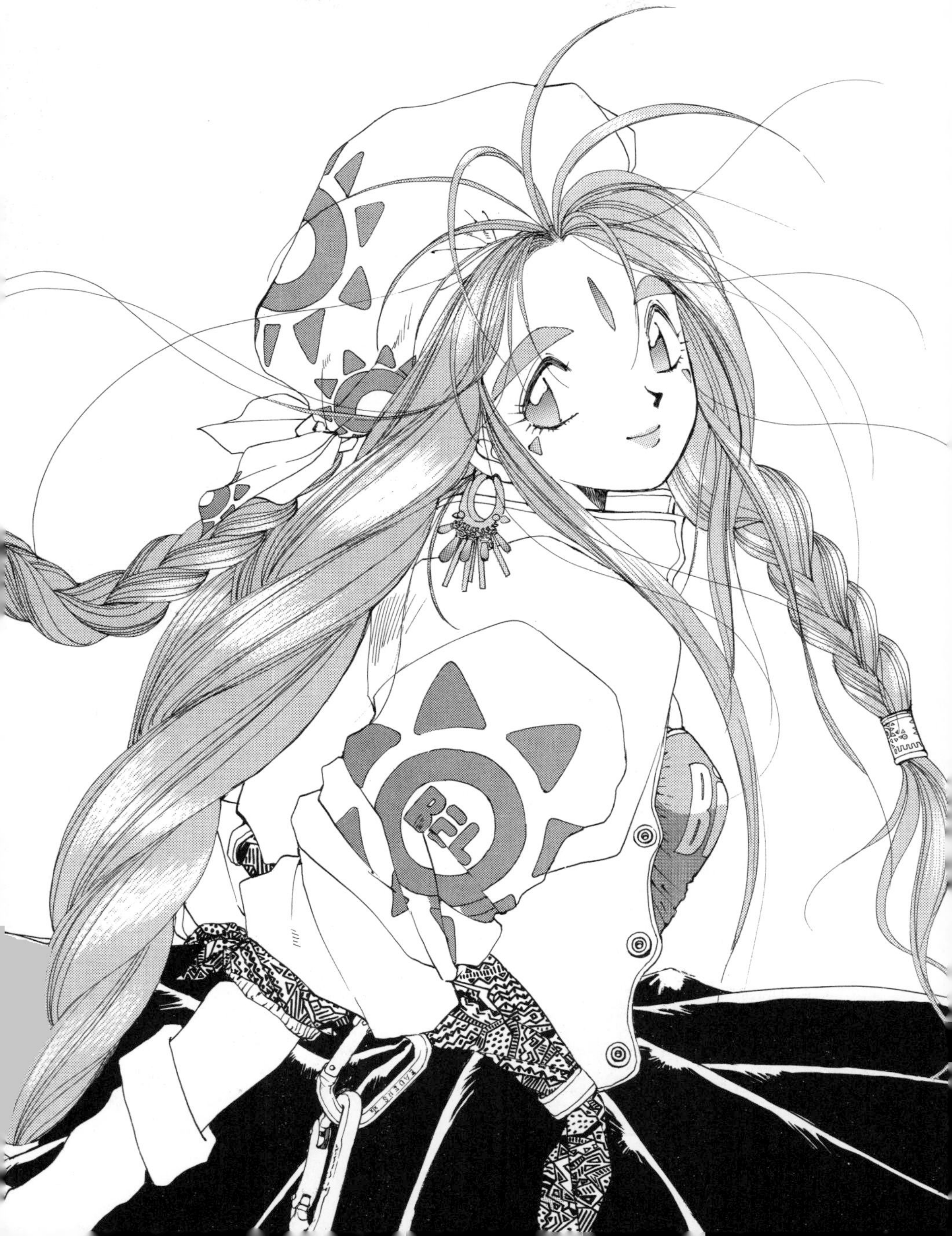

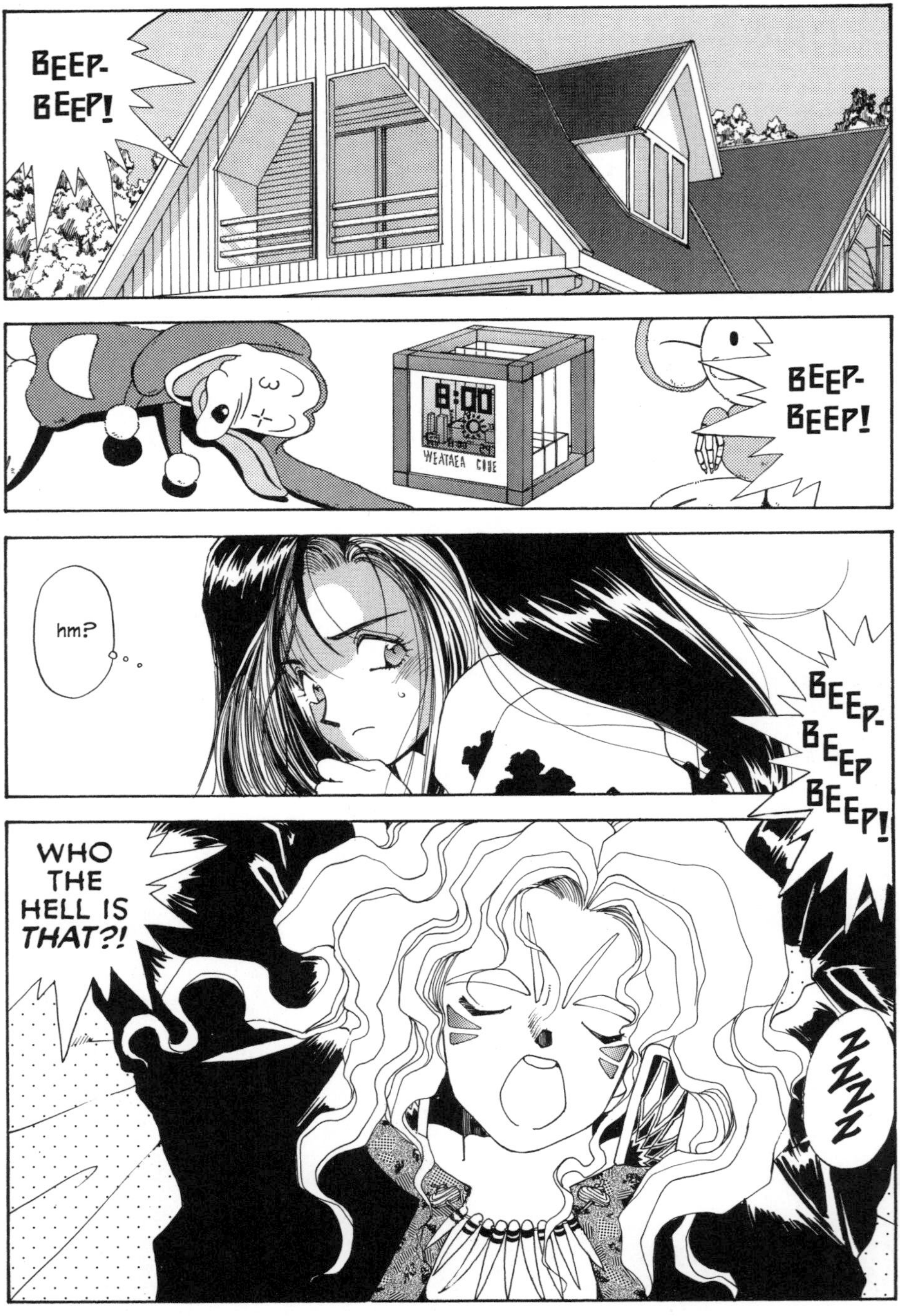
BEEP-BEEP!
BEEP-BEEP!
BEEP-BEEP BEEP BEEP!
hm?
ZZZZ
WHO THE HELL IS *THAT?!*

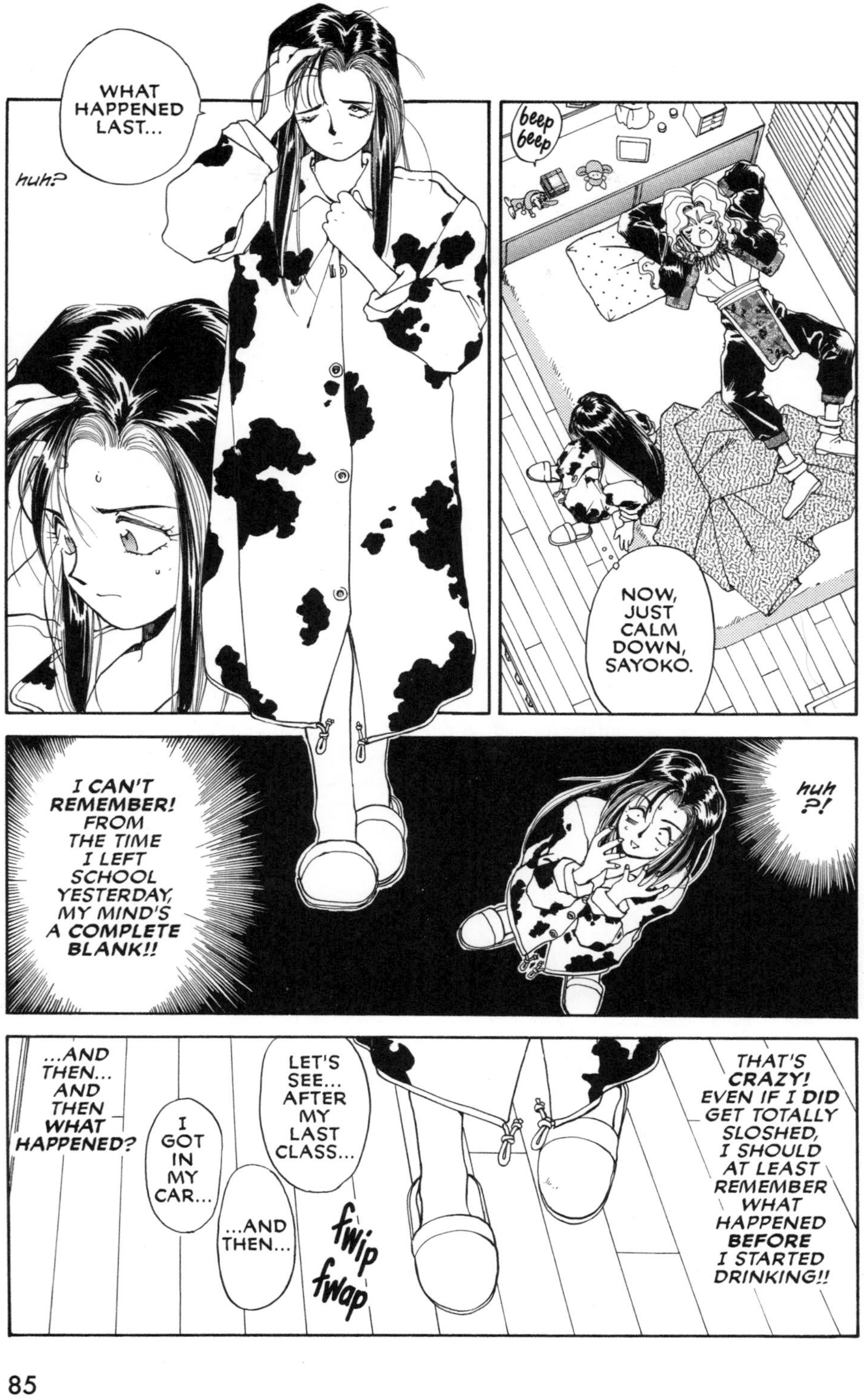
beep beep
NOW, JUST CALM DOWN, SAYOKO.
WHAT HAPPENED LAST...
huh?
huh?!
I CAN'T REMEMBER! FROM THE TIME I LEFT SCHOOL YESTERDAY, MY MIND'S A COMPLETE BLANK!!
THAT'S CRAZY! EVEN IF I DID GET TOTALLY SLOSHED, I SHOULD AT LEAST REMEMBER WHAT HAPPENED BEFORE I STARTED DRINKING!!
fwip fwap
LET'S SEE... AFTER MY LAST CLASS...
I GOT IN MY CAR...
...AND THEN...
...AND THEN... AND THEN WHAT HAPPENED?

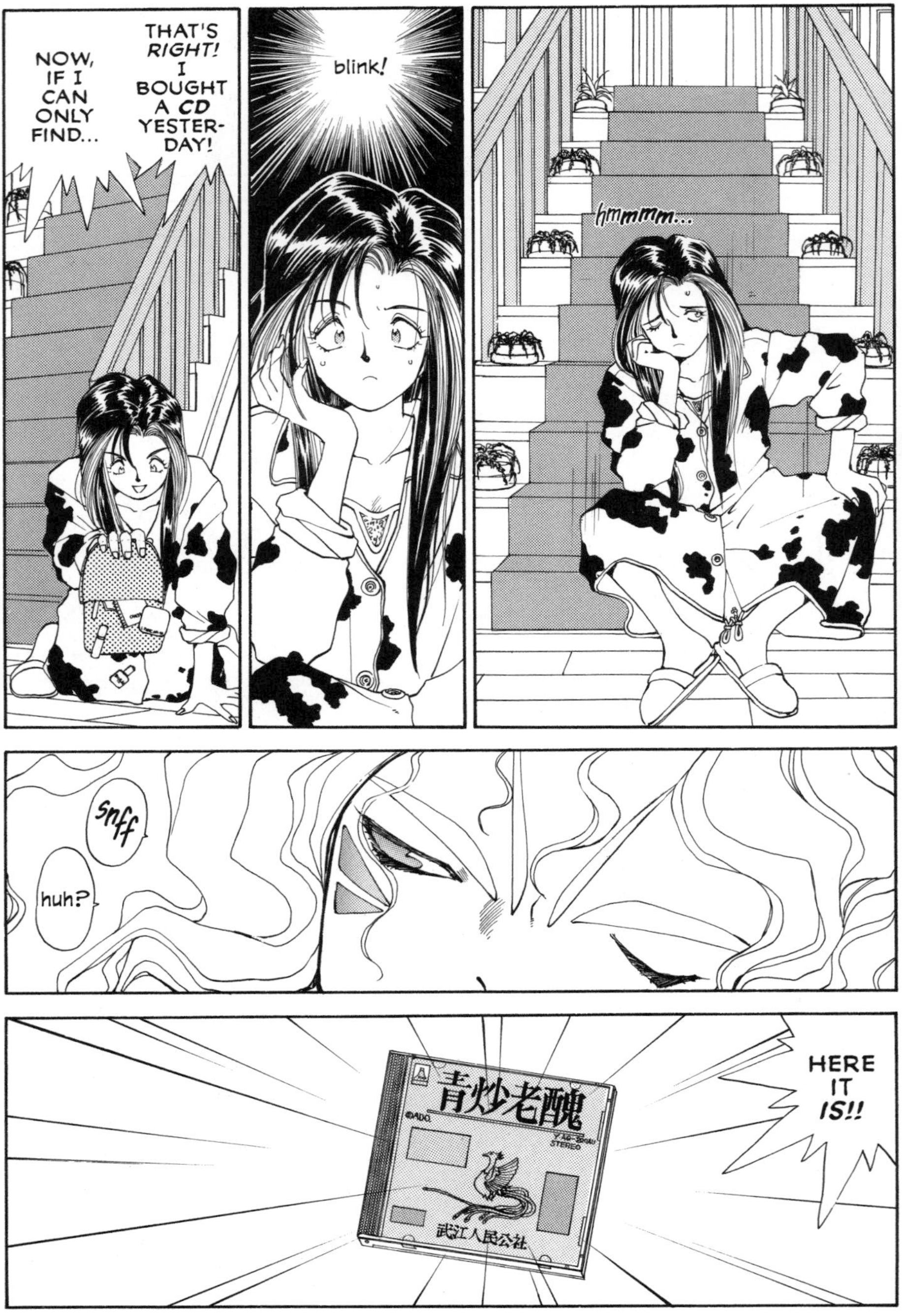
hmmmm...
blink!
THAT'S RIGHT! I BOUGHT A CD YESTER-DAY!
NOW, IF I CAN ONLY FIND...
snff
huh?
青炒老醜
STEREO
武江人民公社
HERE IT IS!!

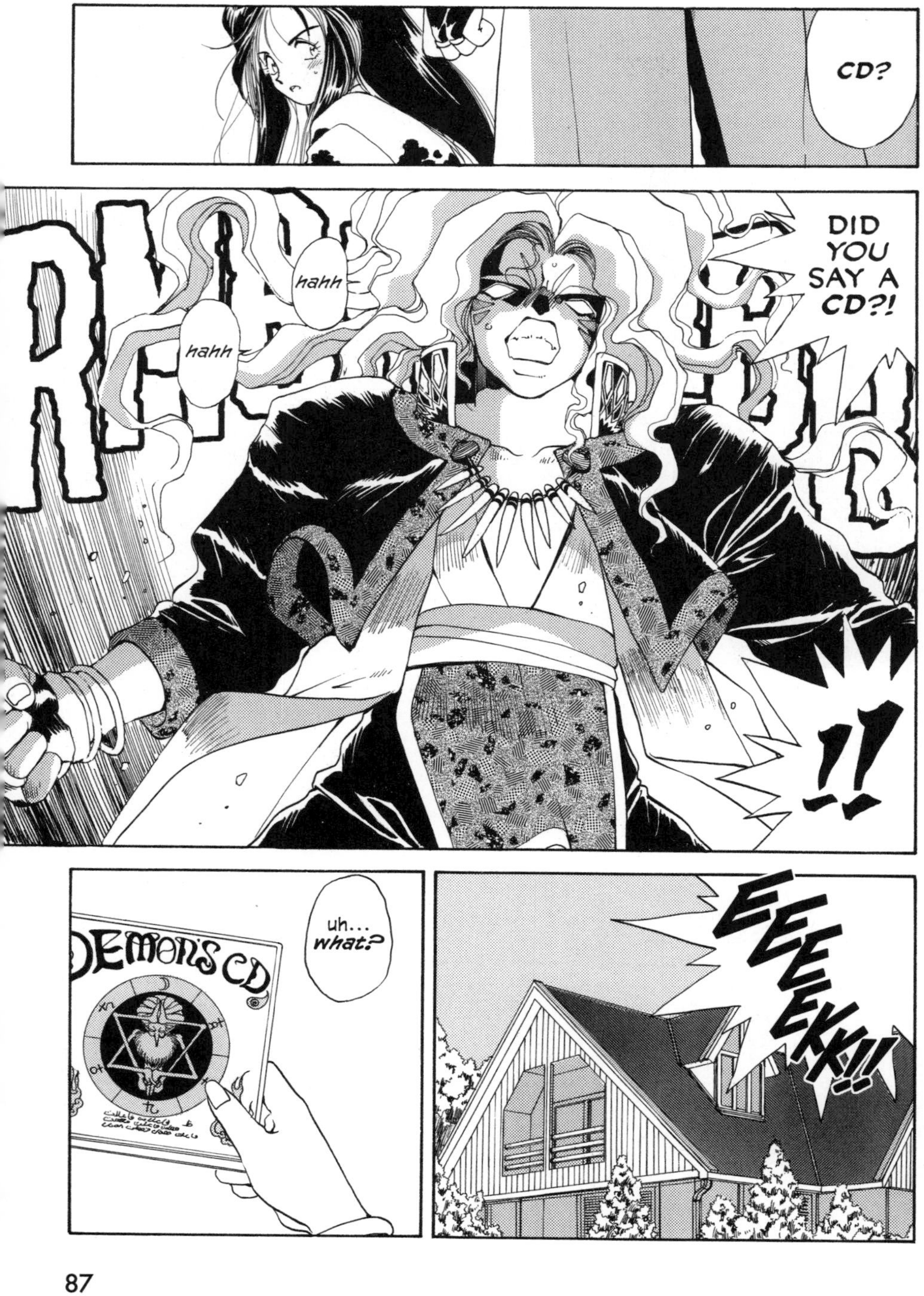
CD?
DID YOU SAY A CD?!
hahh
hahh
!!
EEEEEKK!!
uh... what?
DEMON'S CD

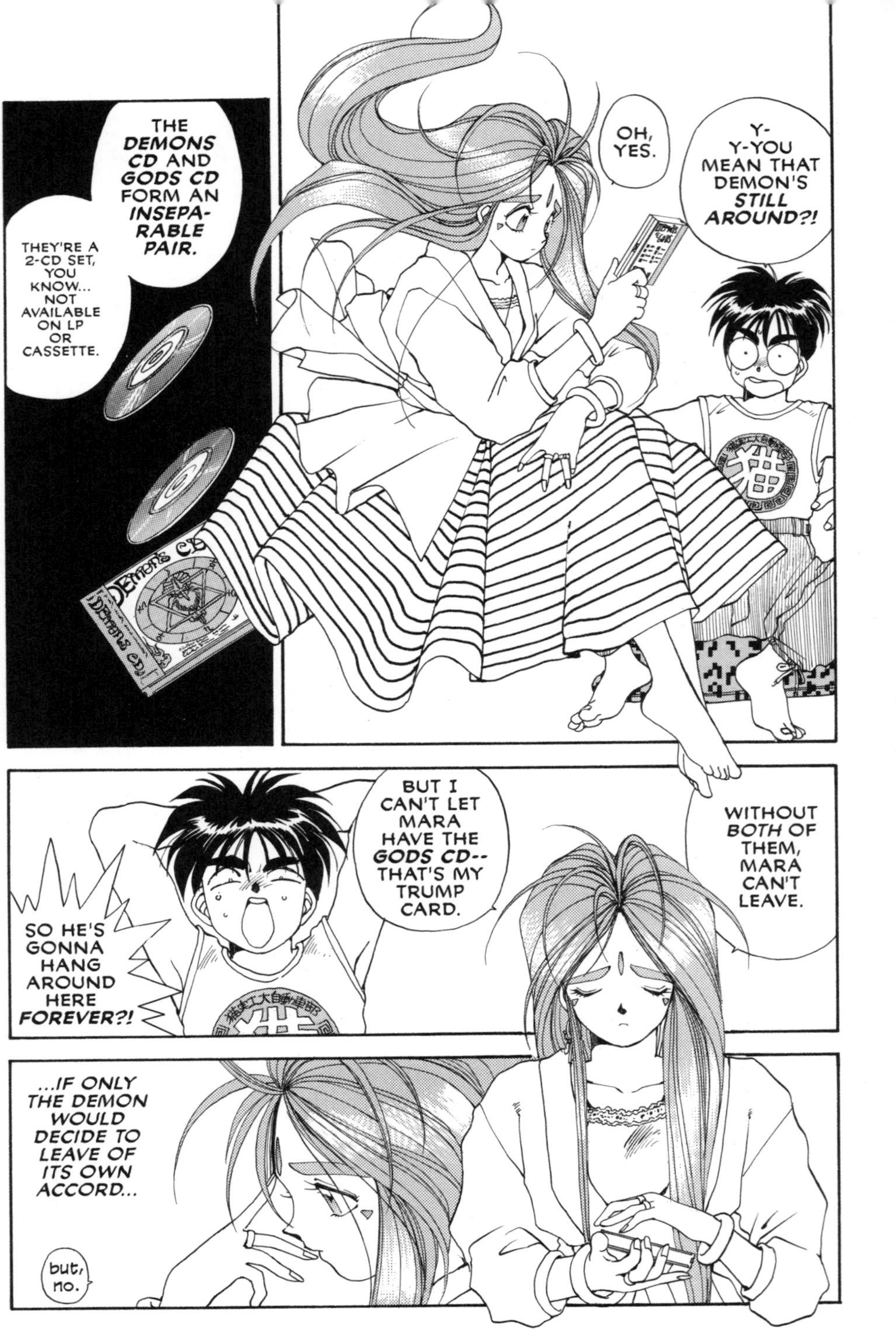
Y- Y-YOU MEAN THAT DEMON'S STILL AROUND?!
OH, YES.
THE DEMONS CD AND GODS CD FORM AN INSEPARABLE PAIR.
THEY'RE A 2-CD SET, YOU KNOW... NOT AVAILABLE ON LP OR CASSETTE.
WITHOUT BOTH OF THEM, MARA CAN'T LEAVE.
BUT I CAN'T LET MARA HAVE THE GODS CD--THAT'S MY TRUMP CARD.
SO HE'S GONNA HANG AROUND HERE FOREVER?!
...IF ONLY THE DEMON WOULD DECIDE TO LEAVE OF ITS OWN ACCORD...
but, no.

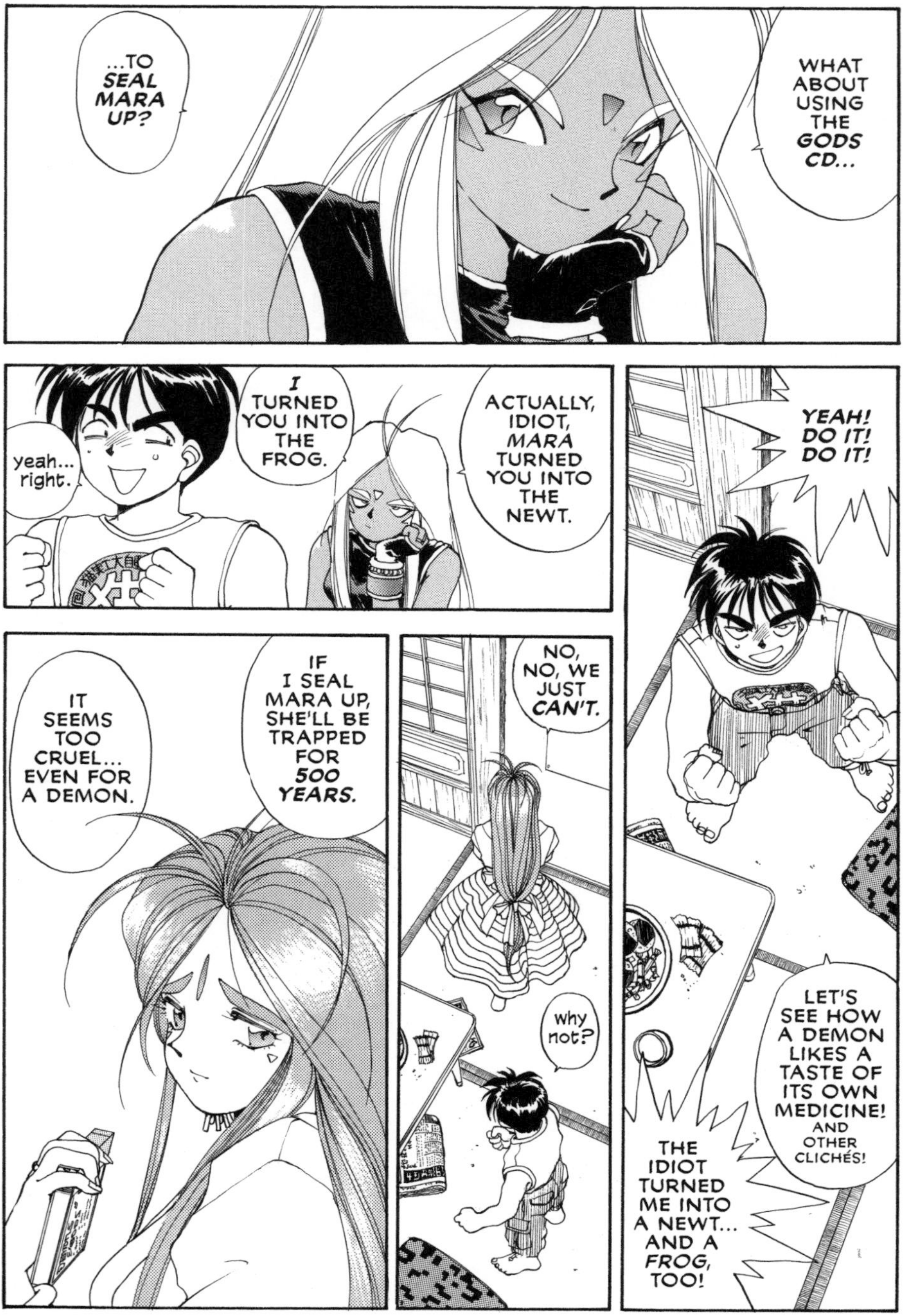
WHAT ABOUT USING THE GODS CD...
...TO SEAL MARA UP?
YEAH! DO IT! DO IT!
LET'S SEE HOW A DEMON LIKES A TASTE OF ITS OWN MEDICINE!
AND OTHER CLICHÉS!
THE IDIOT TURNED ME INTO A NEWT... AND A FROG, TOO!
ACTUALLY, IDIOT, MARA TURNED YOU INTO THE NEWT.
I TURNED YOU INTO THE FROG.
yeah... right.
NO, NO, WE JUST CAN'T.
why not?
IF I SEAL MARA UP, SHE'LL BE TRAPPED FOR 500 YEARS.
IT SEEMS TOO CRUEL... EVEN FOR A DEMON.

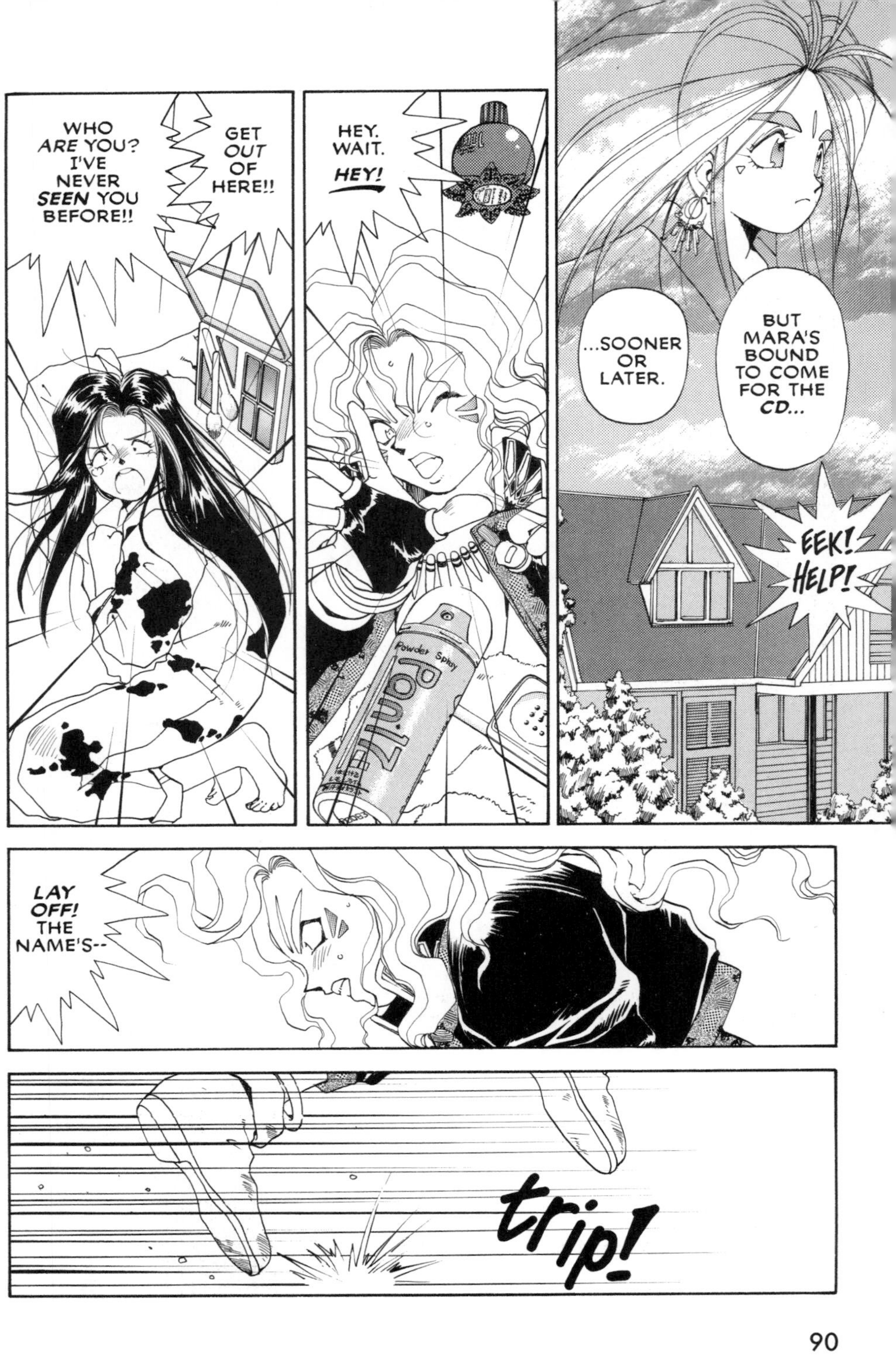
BUT MARA'S BOUND TO COME FOR THE CD...
...SOONER OR LATER.
EEK! HELP!
HEY. WAIT. HEY!
GET OUT OF HERE!!
WHO ARE YOU? I'VE NEVER SEEN YOU BEFORE!!
LAY OFF! THE NAME'S--
trip!

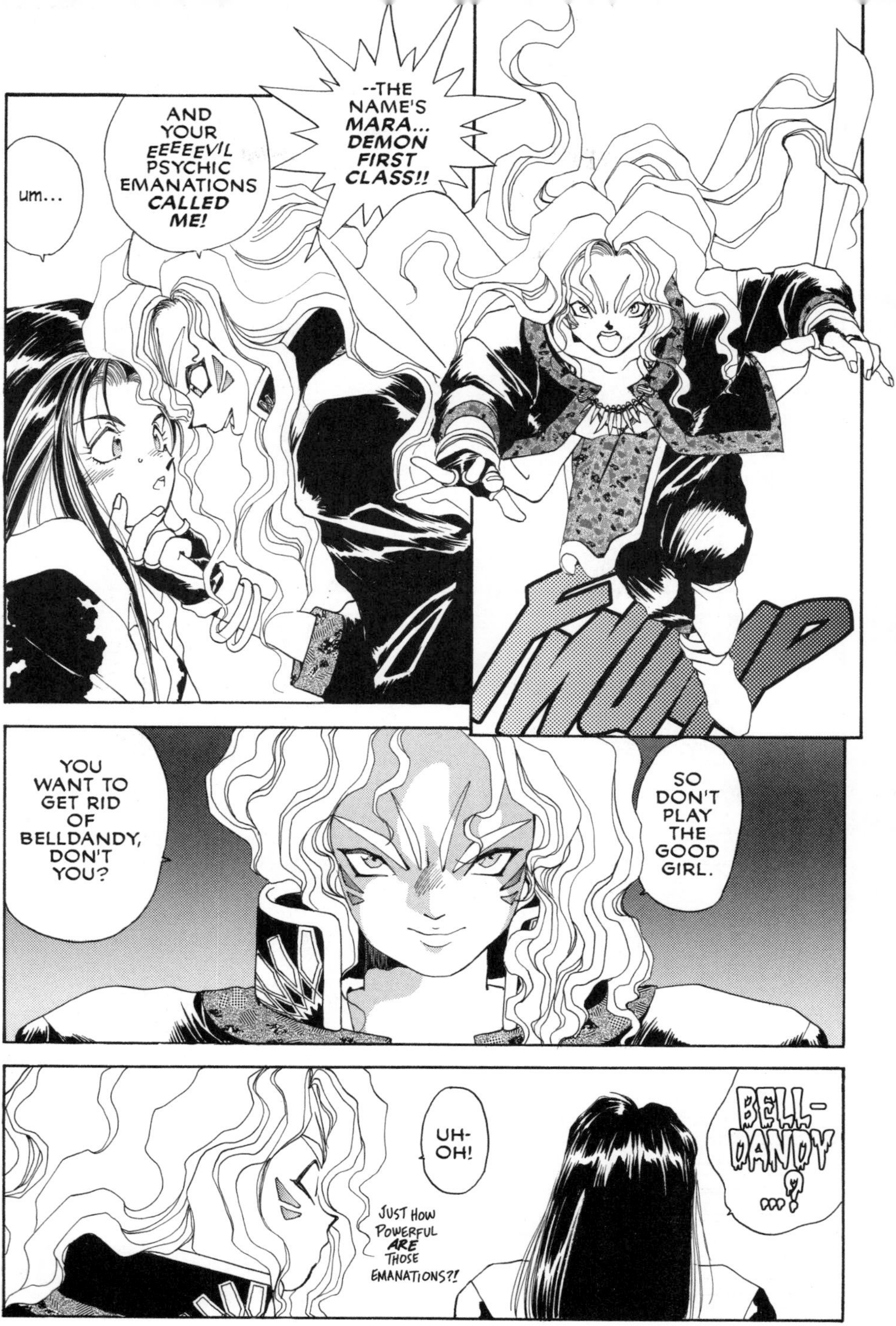
--THE NAME'S MARA... DEMON FIRST CLASS!!
AND YOUR EEEEEVIL PSYCHIC EMANATIONS CALLED ME!
um...
YOU WANT TO GET RID OF BELLDANDY, DON'T YOU?
SO DON'T PLAY THE GOOD GIRL.
BELL-DANDY...?!
UH-OH!
JUST HOW POWERFUL ARE THOSE EMANATIONS?!

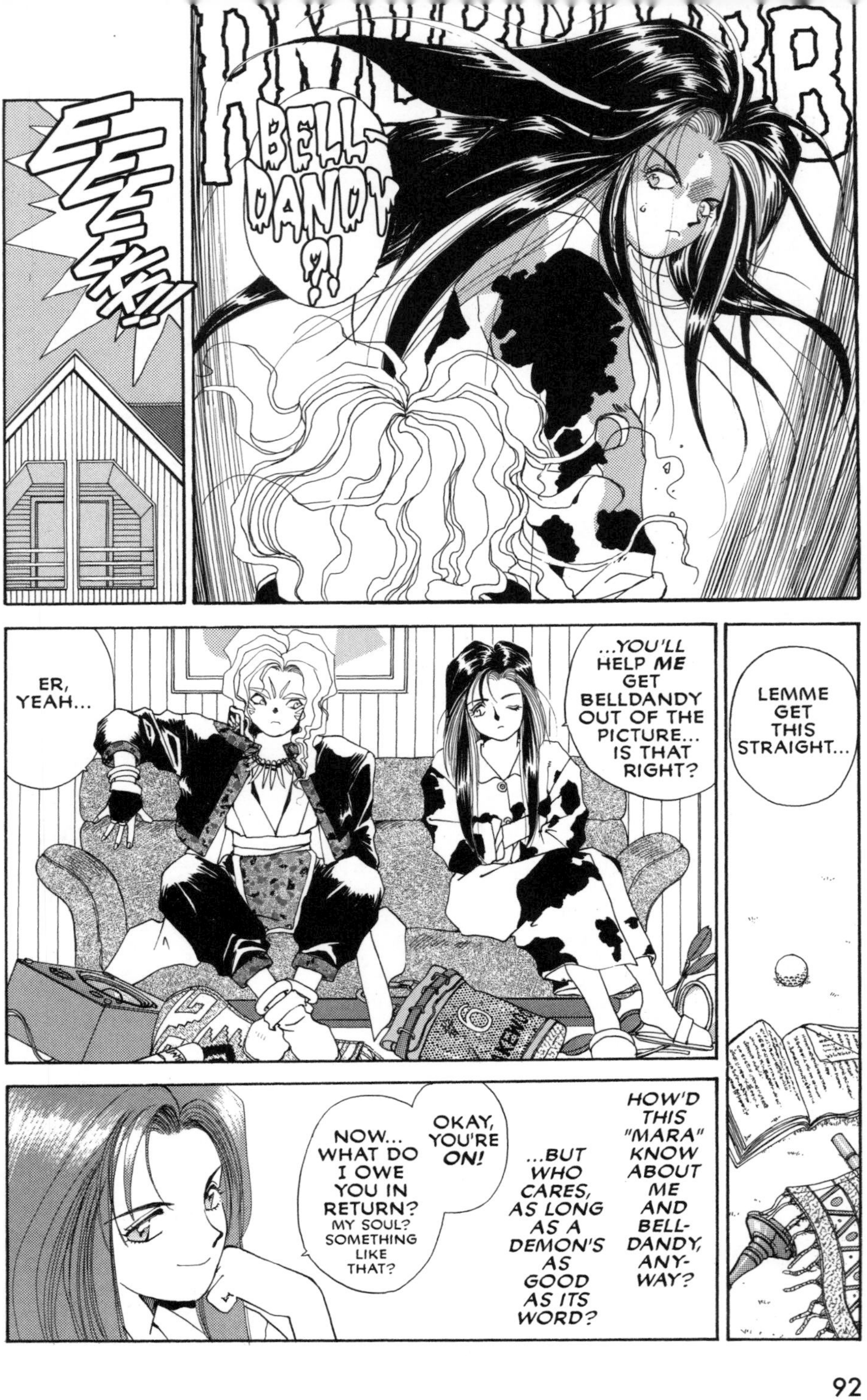
BELL-DANDY ?!
EEEEEK!!
LEMME GET THIS STRAIGHT...
...YOU'LL HELP ME GET BELLDANDY OUT OF THE PICTURE... IS THAT RIGHT?
ER, YEAH...
HOW'D THIS "MARA" KNOW ABOUT ME AND BELL-DANDY, ANY-WAY?
...BUT WHO CARES, AS LONG AS A DEMON'S AS GOOD AS ITS WORD?
OKAY, YOU'RE ON!
NOW... WHAT DO I OWE YOU IN RETURN? MY SOUL? SOMETHING LIKE THAT?

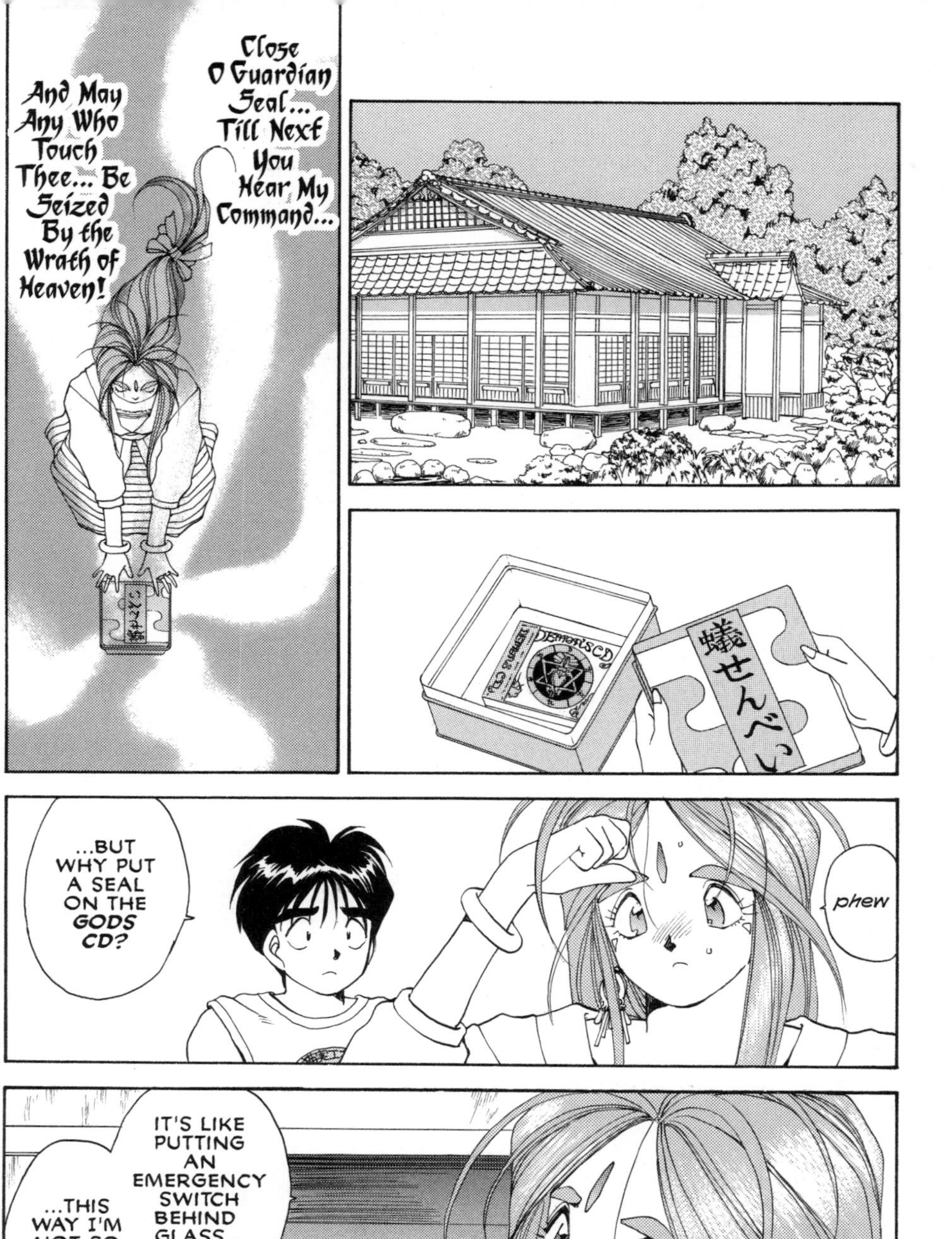
DEMONS CD
蟻せんべい
Close O Guardian Seal... Till Next You Hear My Command...
And May Any Who Touch Thee... Be Seized By the Wrath of Heaven!
phew
...BUT WHY PUT A SEAL ON THE *GODS CD*?
IT'S LIKE PUTTING AN EMERGENCY SWITCH BEHIND GLASS...
...THIS WAY I'M NOT SO TEMPTED TO SIMPLY *USE* IT.

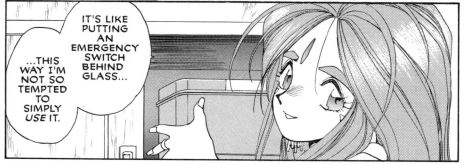

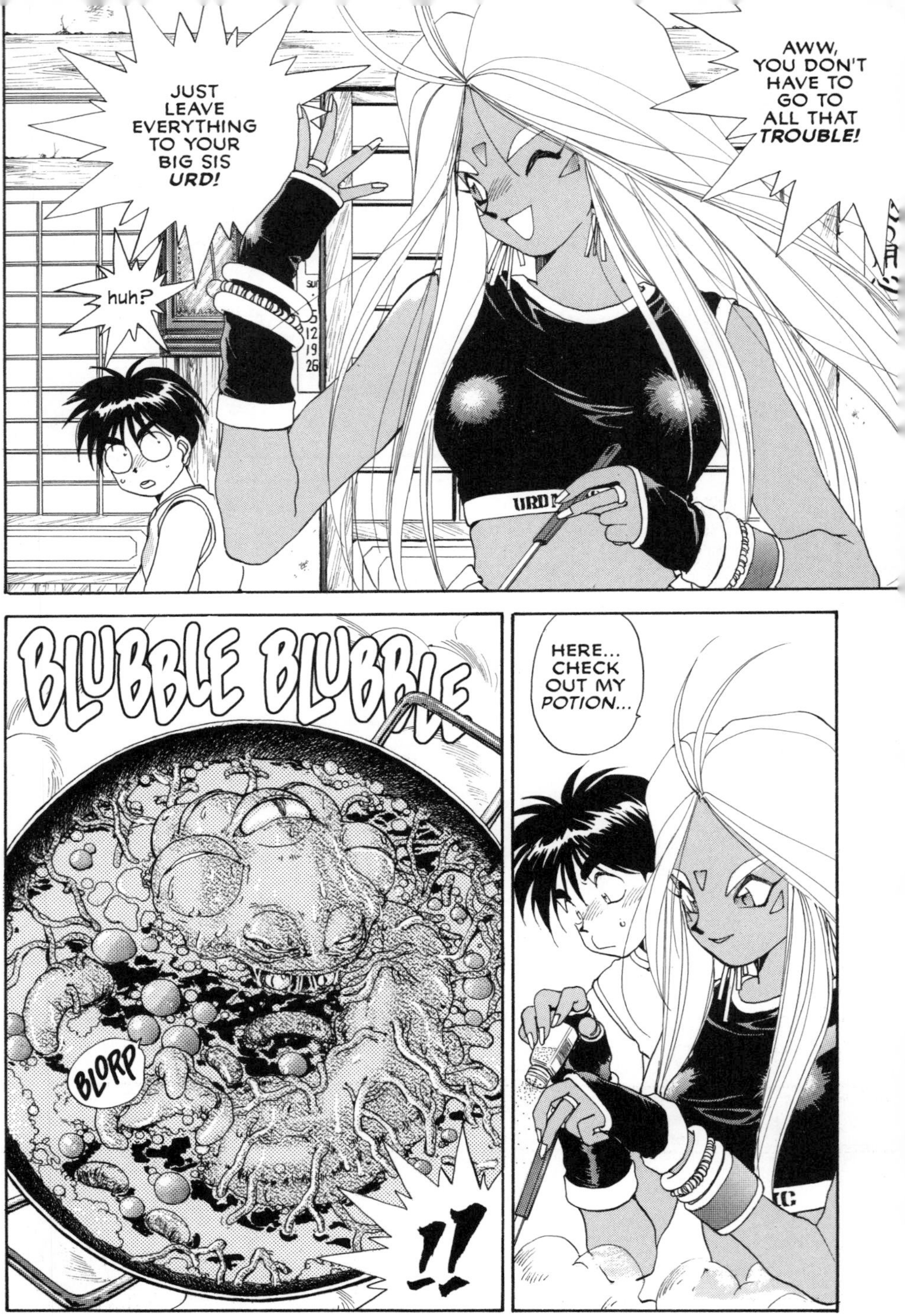
AWW, YOU DON'T HAVE TO GO TO ALL THAT *TROUBLE!*
JUST LEAVE EVERYTHING TO YOUR BIG SIS *URD!*
huh?
HERE... CHECK OUT MY *POTION*...
BLUBBLE BLUBBLE
BLORP
!!

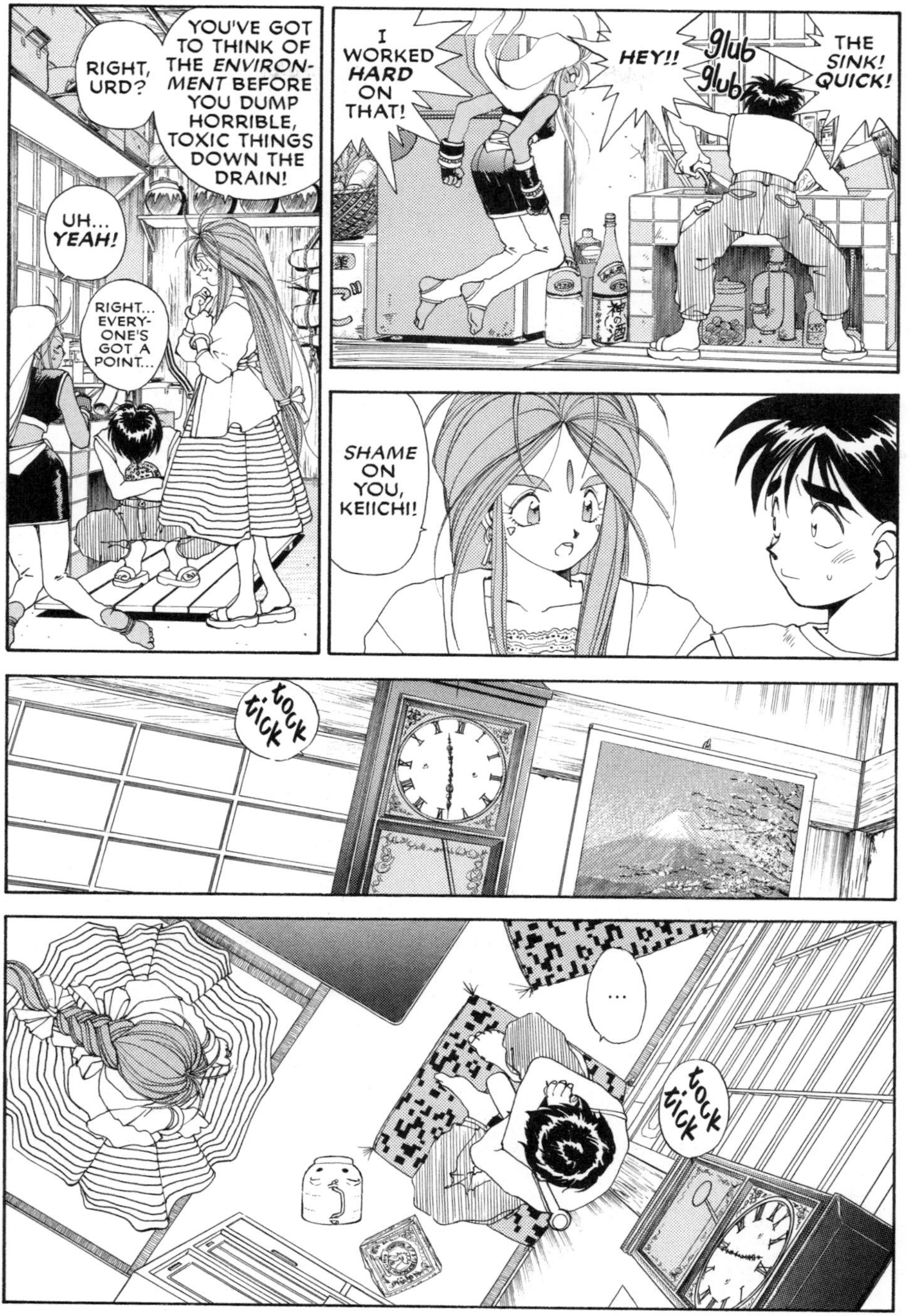
THE SINK! QUICK!
glub glub
HEY!!
I WORKED HARD ON THAT!
SHAME ON YOU, KEIICHI!
YOU'VE GOT TO THINK OF THE ENVIRONMENT BEFORE YOU DUMP HORRIBLE, TOXIC THINGS DOWN THE DRAIN!
RIGHT, URD?
UH... YEAH!
RIGHT... EVERYONE'S GOT A POINT...
tock tick
...
tock tick

...I'M READY.

I'VE GOT MY BASEBALL BAT...

...THE DISTURBANCE IS GETTING STRONGER! WE *MUST* BE VIGILANT!

MARA'S COMING...

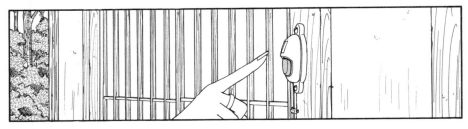

Ding-Dong!
AH!
hnf?
OKAY... THIS IS IT... STRIKE WITHOUT MERCY!!
KILL!! KILL!!
OH, HI...
URD MAGIC
....it's sayoko.

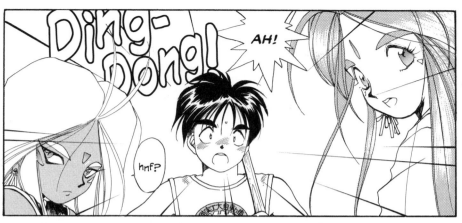

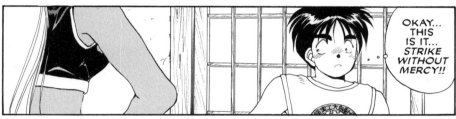

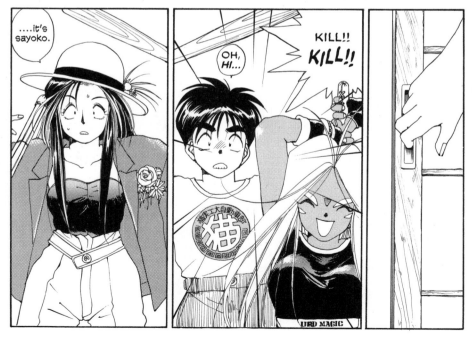

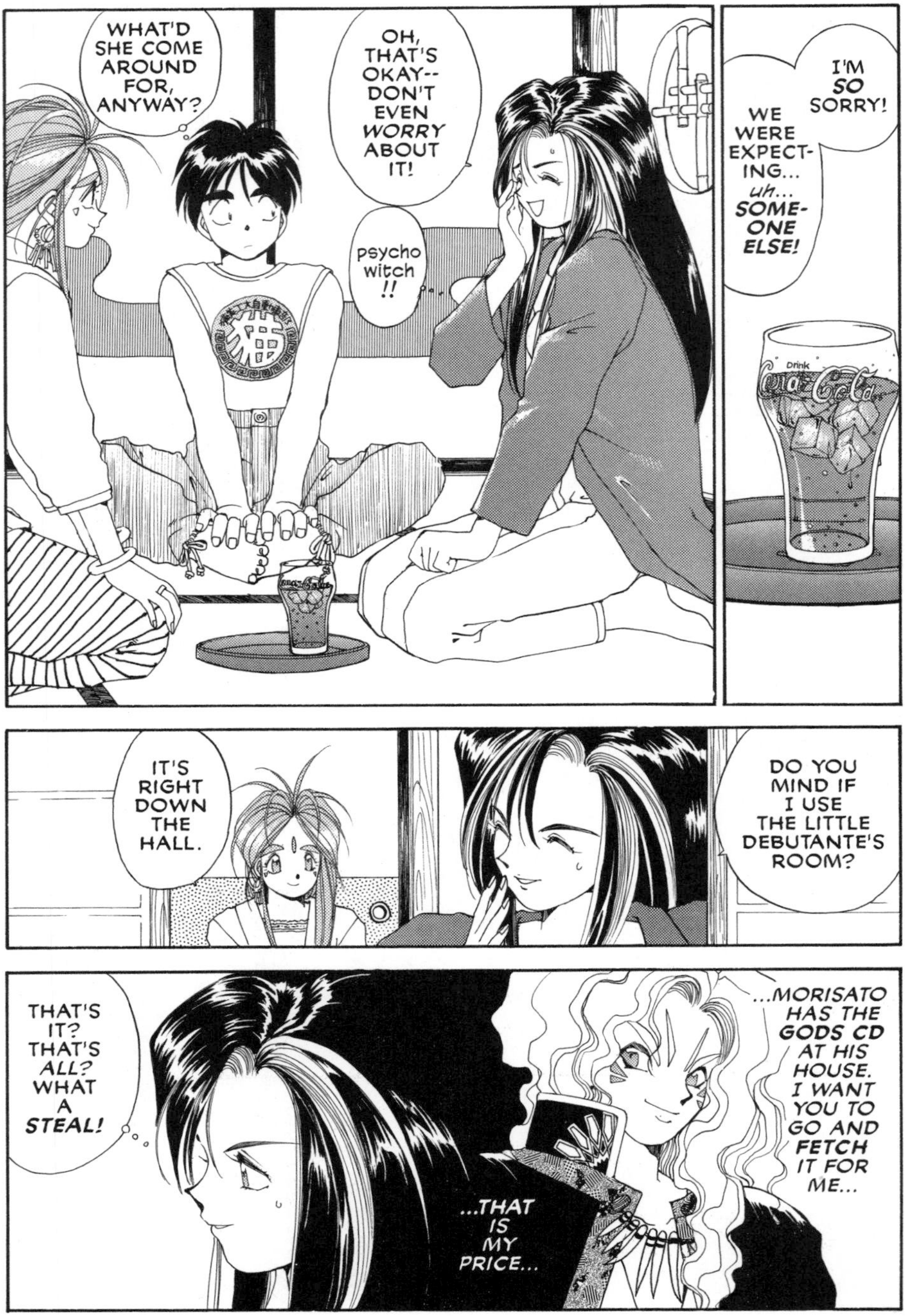
I'M SO SORRY! WE WERE EXPECTING... uh... SOMEONE ELSE!
OH, THAT'S OKAY-- DON'T EVEN WORRY ABOUT IT!
psycho witch !!
WHAT'D SHE COME AROUND FOR, ANYWAY?
DO YOU MIND IF I USE THE LITTLE DEBUTANTE'S ROOM?
IT'S RIGHT DOWN THE HALL.
...MORISATO HAS THE GODS CD AT HIS HOUSE. I WANT YOU TO GO AND FETCH IT FOR ME...
...THAT IS MY PRICE...
THAT'S IT? THAT'S ALL? WHAT A STEAL!

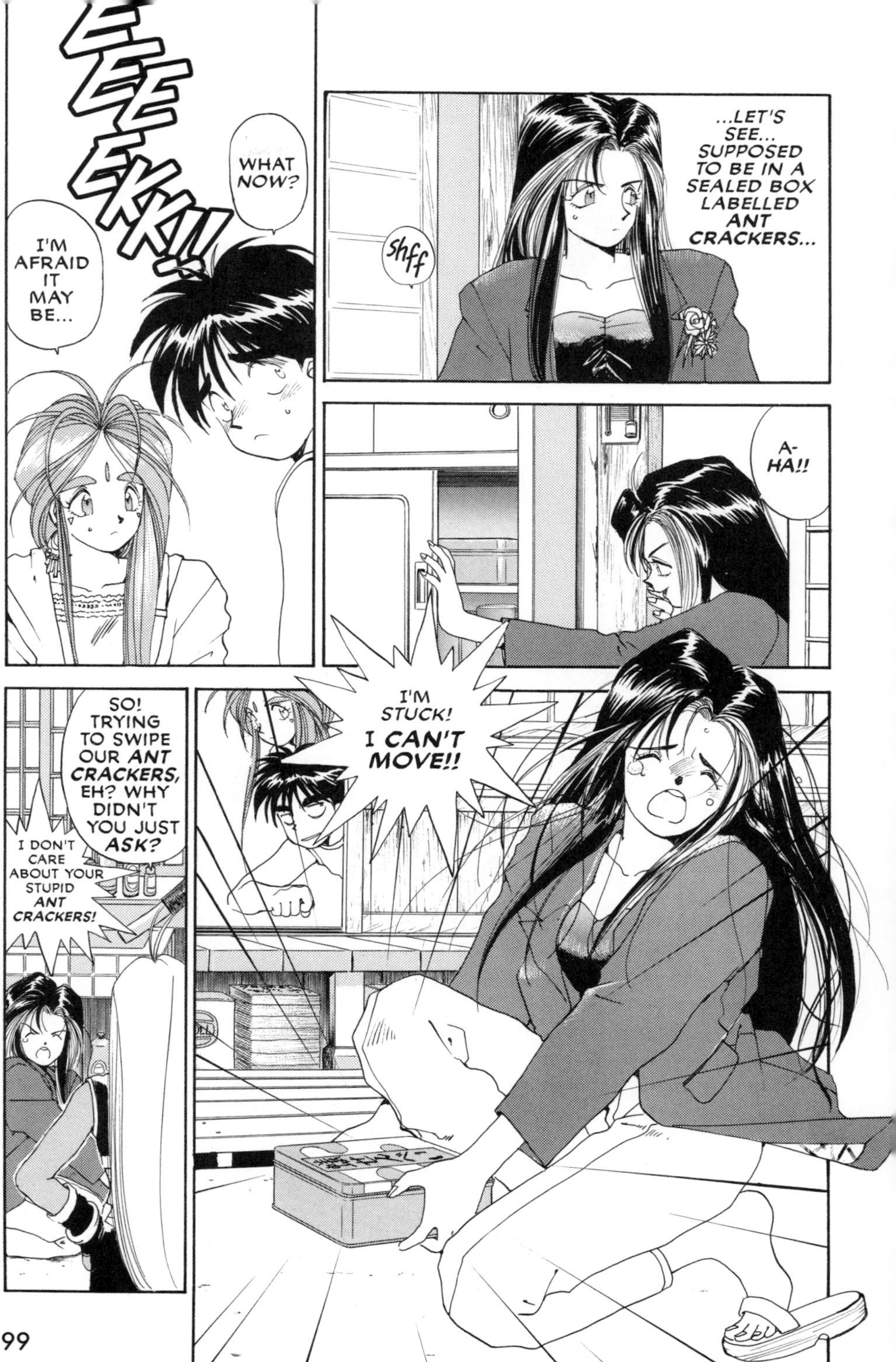
...LET'S SEE... SUPPOSED TO BE IN A SEALED BOX LABELLED ANT CRACKERS...
shff
A-HA!!
EEEEKK!!!
WHAT NOW?
I'M AFRAID IT MAY BE...
I'M STUCK! I CAN'T MOVE!!
SO! TRYING TO SWIPE OUR ANT CRACKERS, EH? WHY DIDN'T YOU JUST ASK?
I DON'T CARE ABOUT YOUR STUPID ANT CRACKERS!

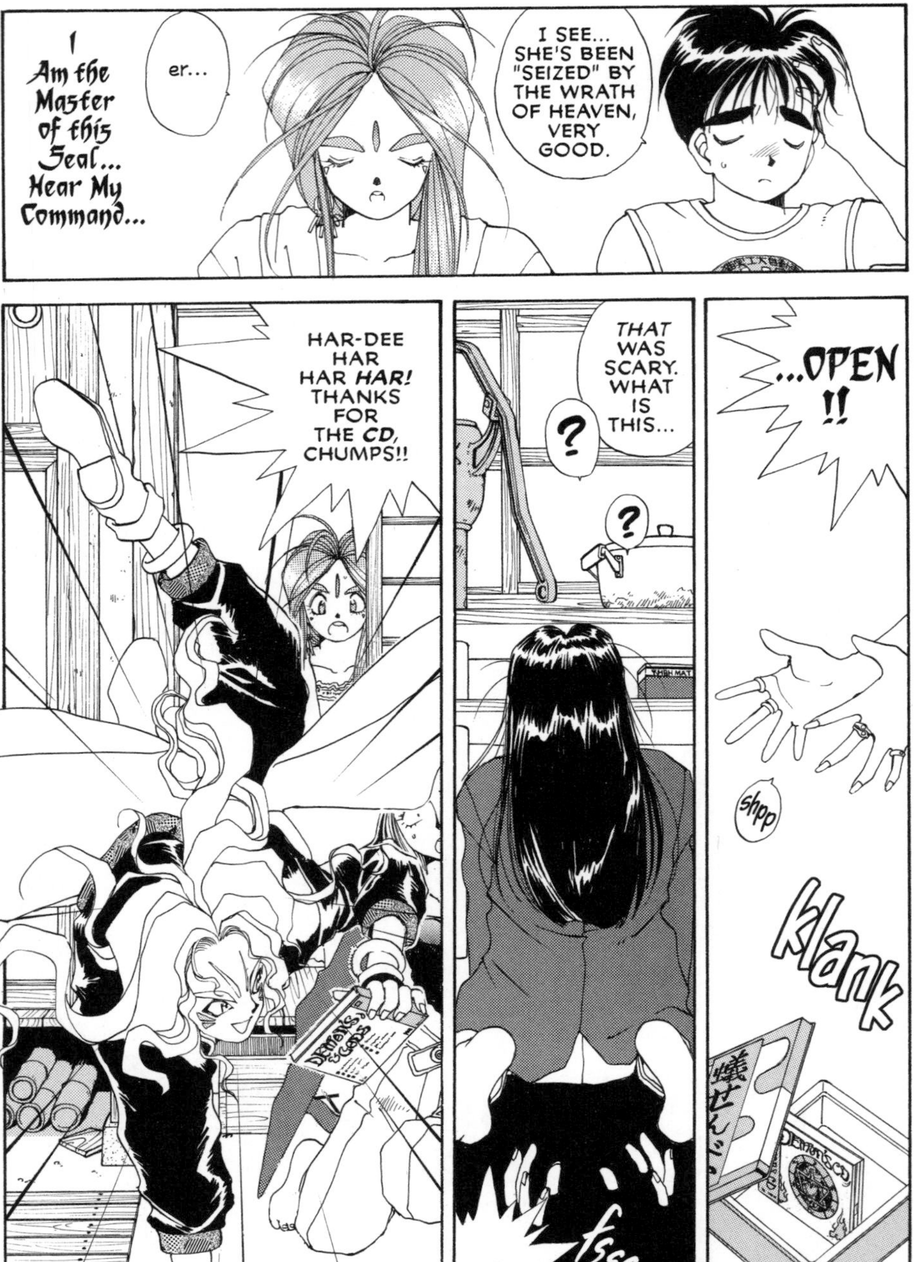
I SEE... SHE'S BEEN "SEIZED" BY THE WRATH OF HEAVEN, VERY GOOD.
er...
I Am the Master of this Seal... Hear My Command...
...OPEN !!
shpp
klank
THAT WAS SCARY. WHAT IS THIS...
?
?
NOW!
fssshh
HAR-DEE HAR HAR HAR! THANKS FOR THE CD, CHUMPS!!

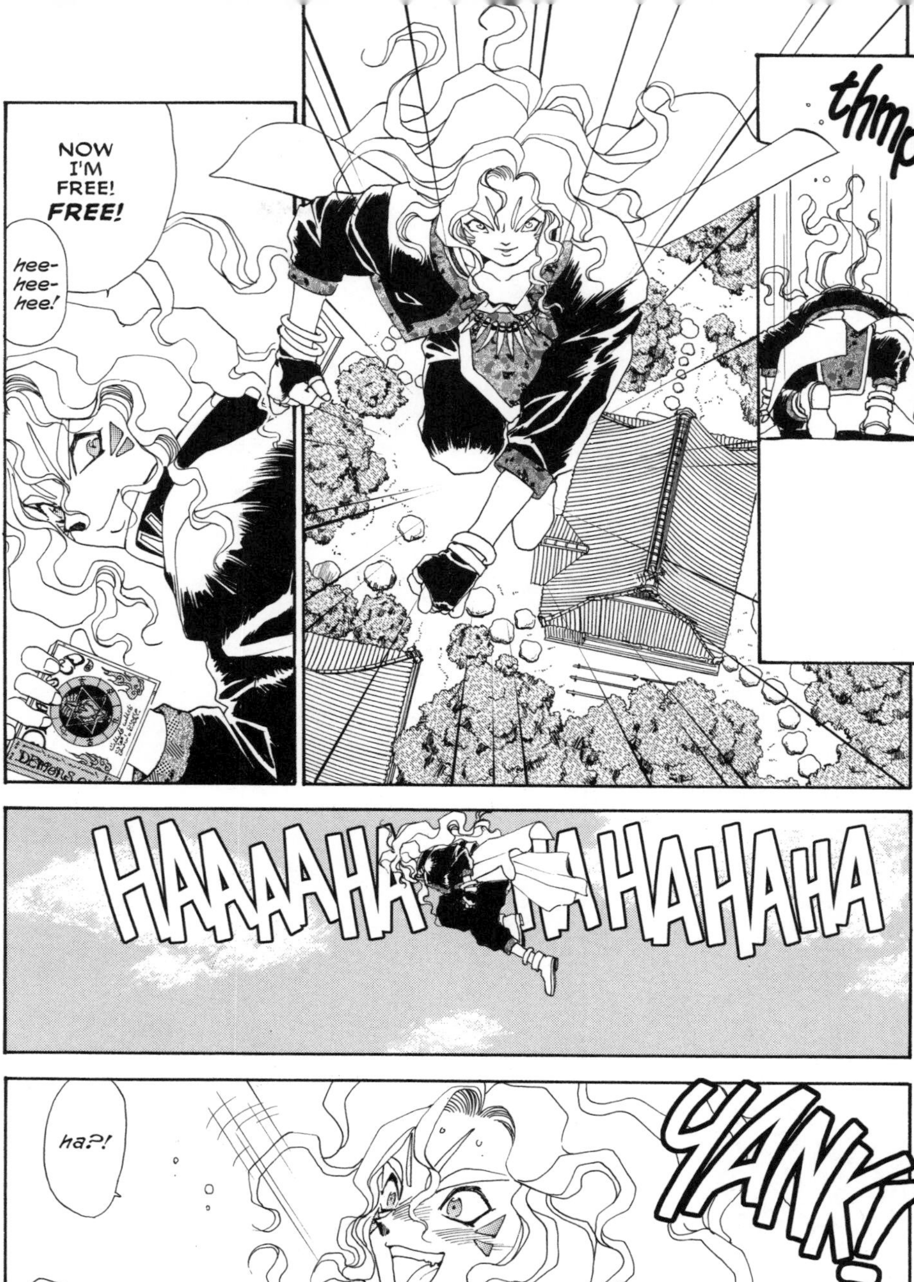
thmp
NOW I'M FREE! FREE!
hee-hee-hee!
HAAAAHAHAHAHAHAHA
YANK!
ha?!

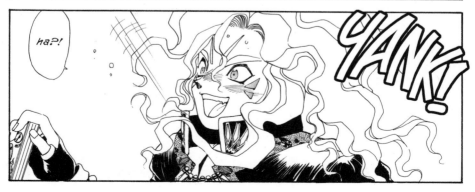

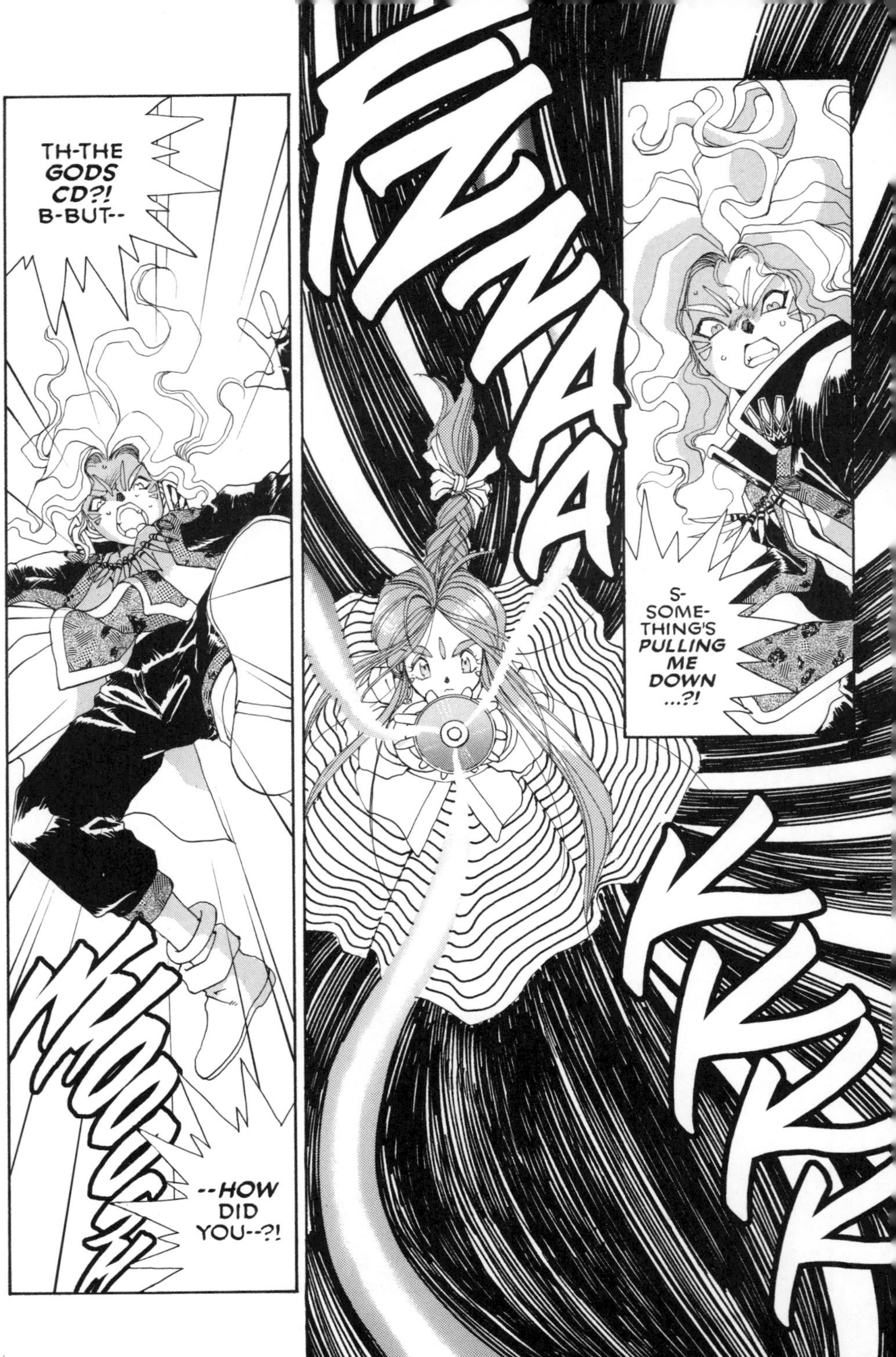
S-SOMETHING'S PULLING ME DOWN ...?!
TH-THE GODS CD?! B-BUT--
--HOW DID YOU--?!

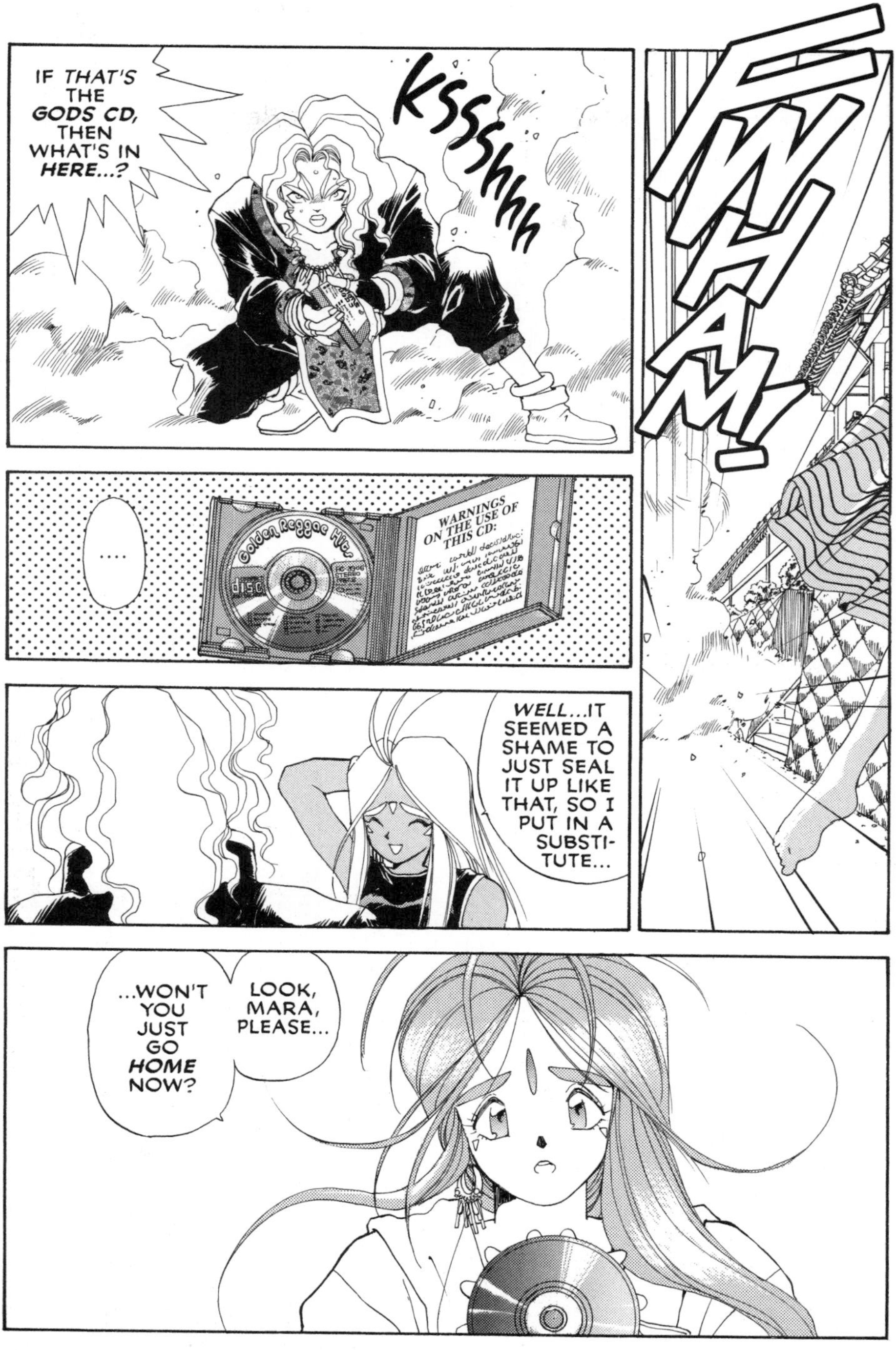
FWHAM!
KSSSHHH
IF THAT'S THE GODS CD, THEN WHAT'S IN HERE...?
....
WARNINGS ON THE USE OF THIS CD:
Golden Reggae Hits
disc
WELL...IT SEEMED A SHAME TO JUST SEAL IT UP LIKE THAT, SO I PUT IN A SUBSTITUTE...
LOOK, MARA, PLEASE...
...WON'T YOU JUST GO HOME NOW?

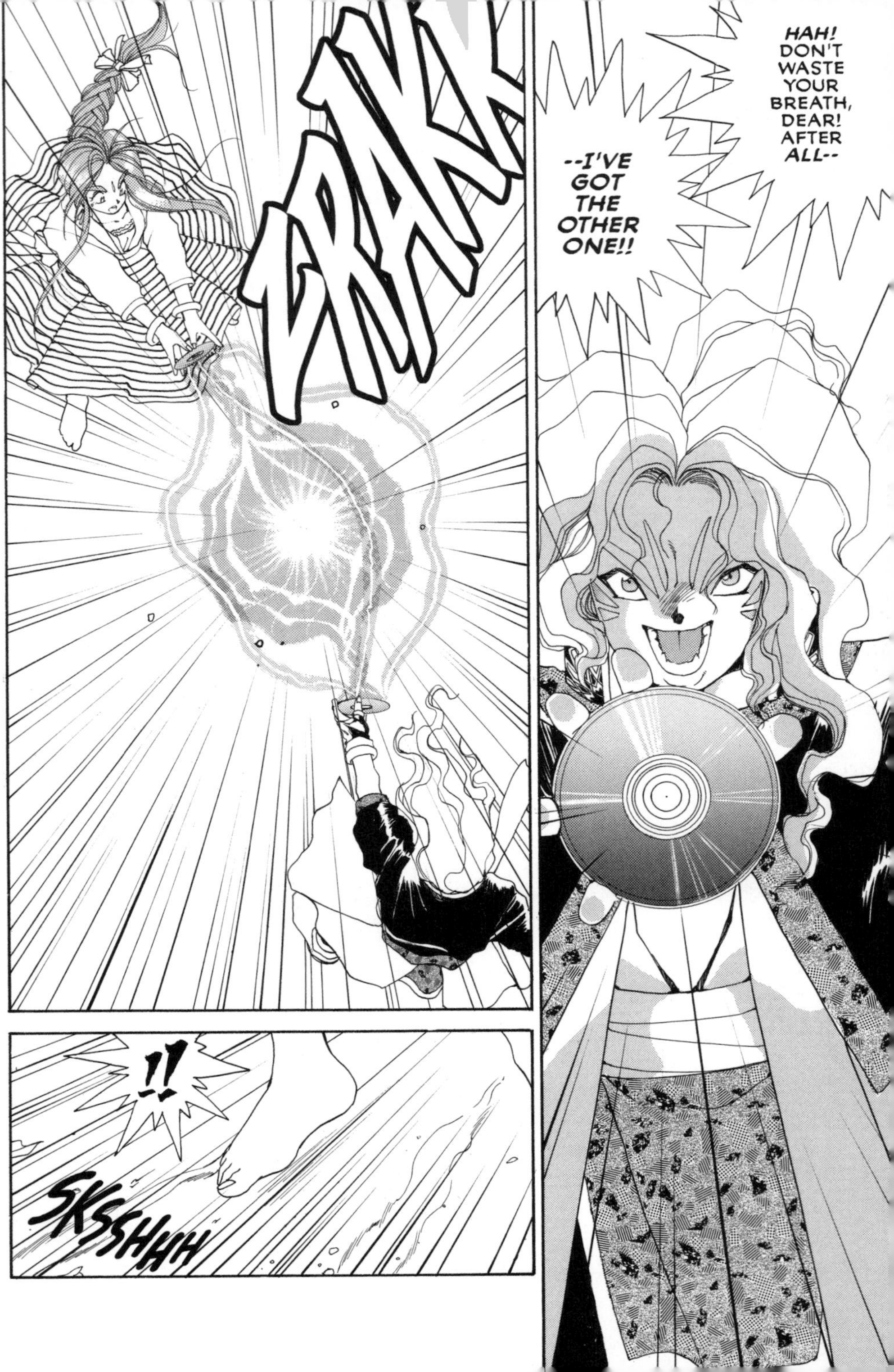
HAH! DON'T WASTE YOUR BREATH, DEAR! AFTER ALL--
--I'VE GOT THE OTHER ONE!!
CRAK
!!
SKSSHHH

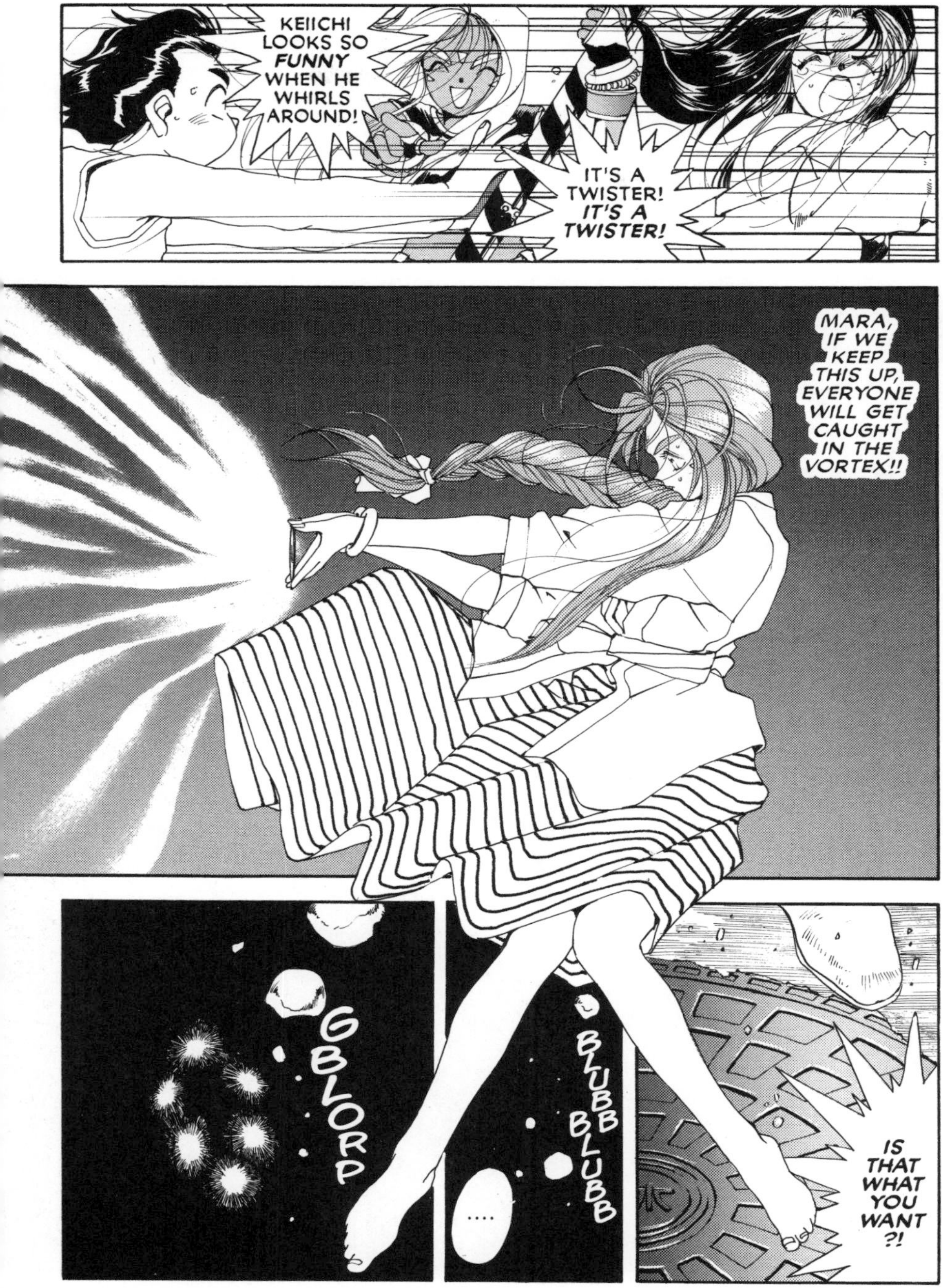
IT'S A TWISTER! IT'S A TWISTER!
KEIICHI LOOKS SO FUNNY WHEN HE WHIRLS AROUND!
MARA, IF WE KEEP THIS UP, EVERYONE WILL GET CAUGHT IN THE VORTEX!!
IS THAT WHAT YOU WANT?!
BLUBB BLUBB
....
GBLORP

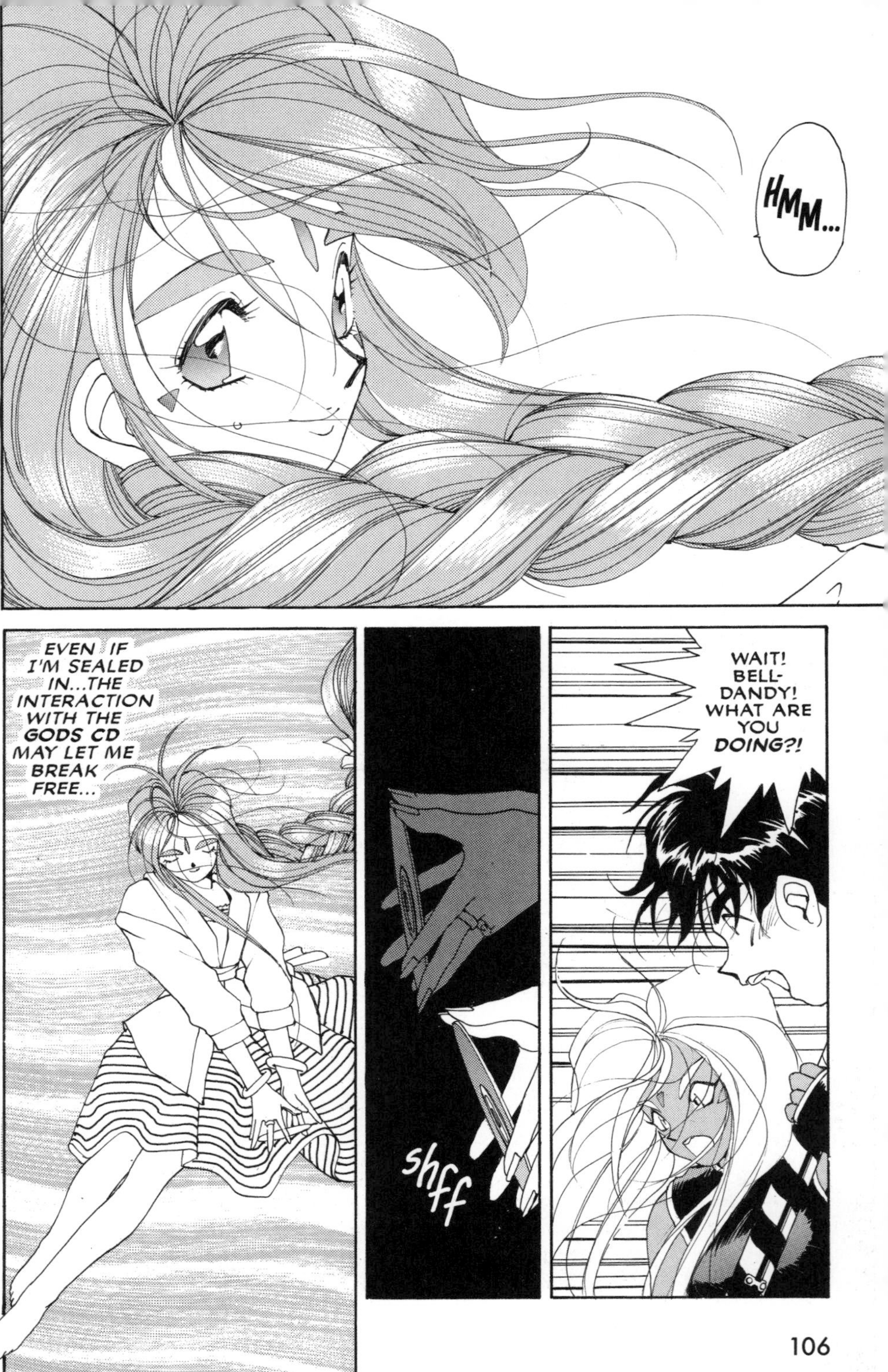
HMM...
WAIT! BELL-DANDY! WHAT ARE YOU DOING?!
shff
EVEN IF I'M SEALED IN...THE INTERACTION WITH THE GODS CD MAY LET ME BREAK FREE...

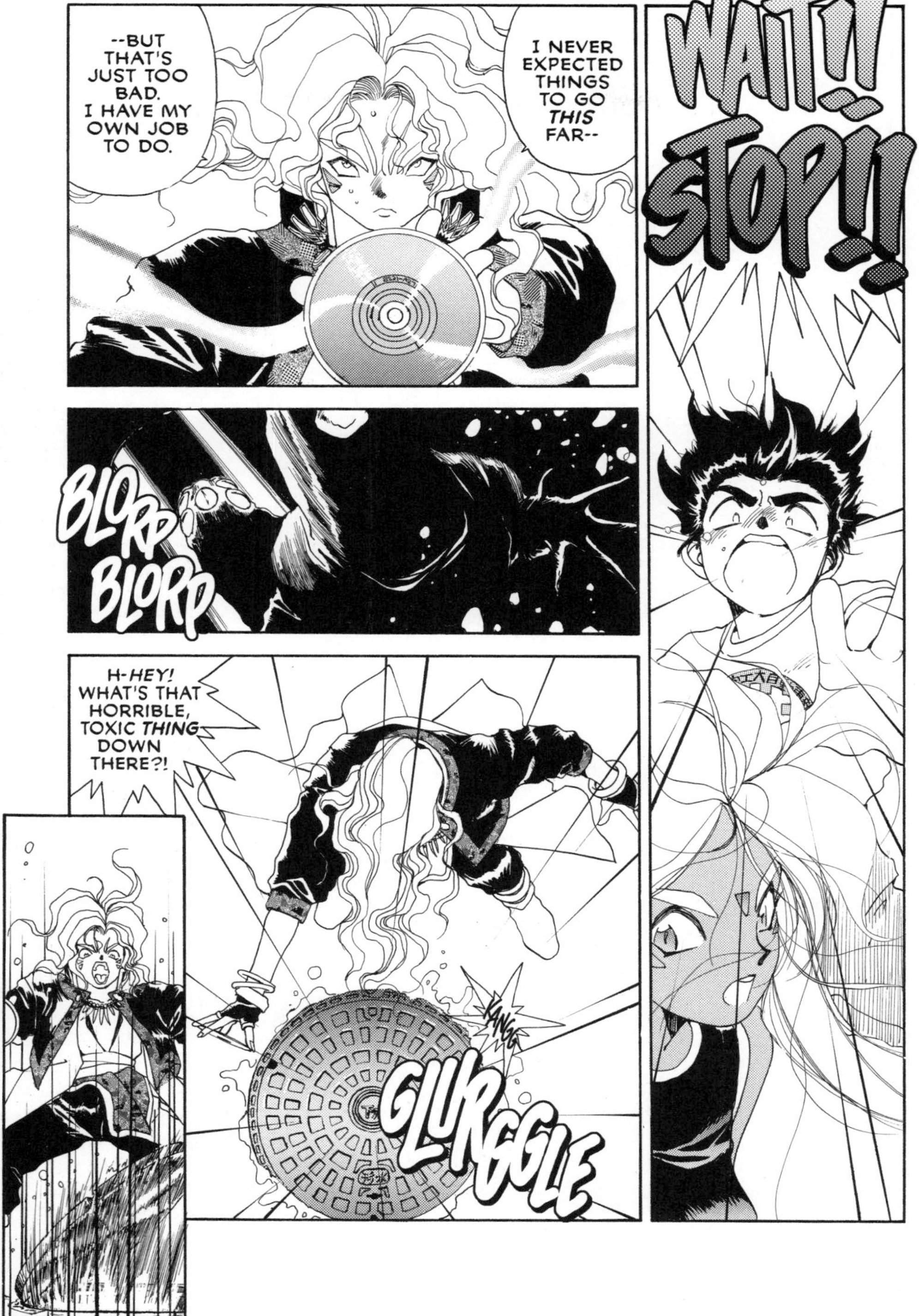
WAIT!! STOP!!
I NEVER EXPECTED THINGS TO GO *THIS* FAR--
--BUT THAT'S JUST TOO BAD. I HAVE MY OWN JOB TO DO.
BLORP BLORP
H-*HEY!* WHAT'S THAT HORRIBLE, TOXIC *THING* DOWN THERE?!
KANGG
GLURGGLE

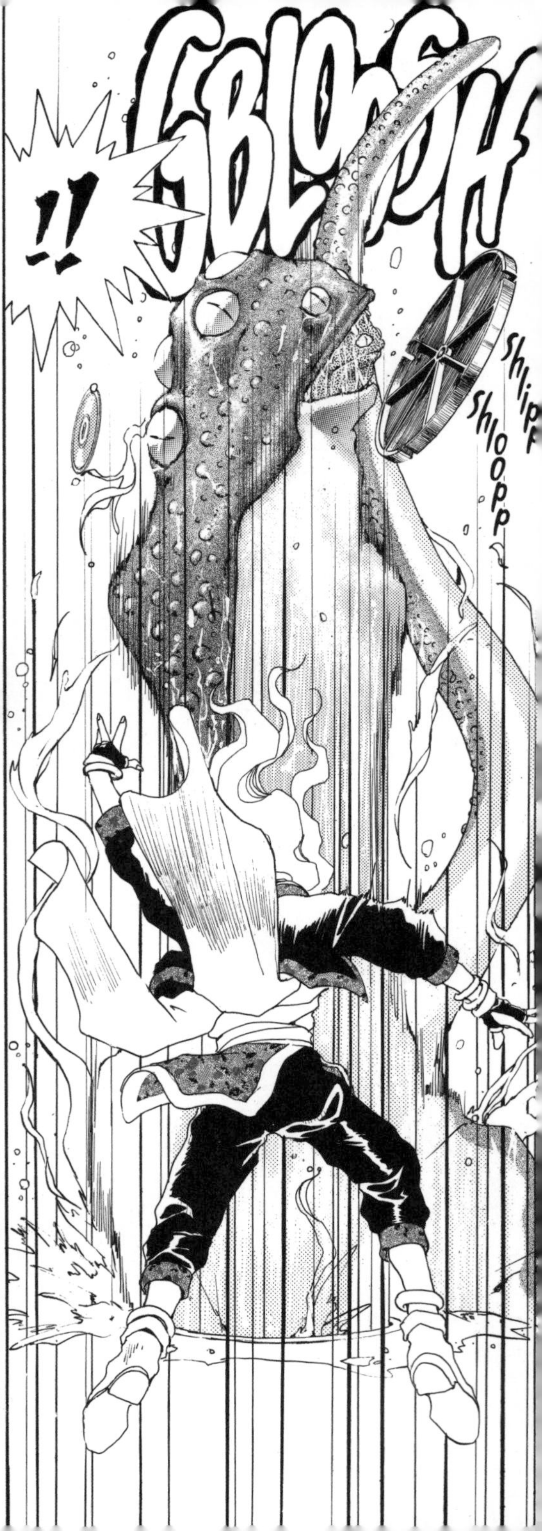
!!
GBLOOSH
Shlipp
Shlooopp

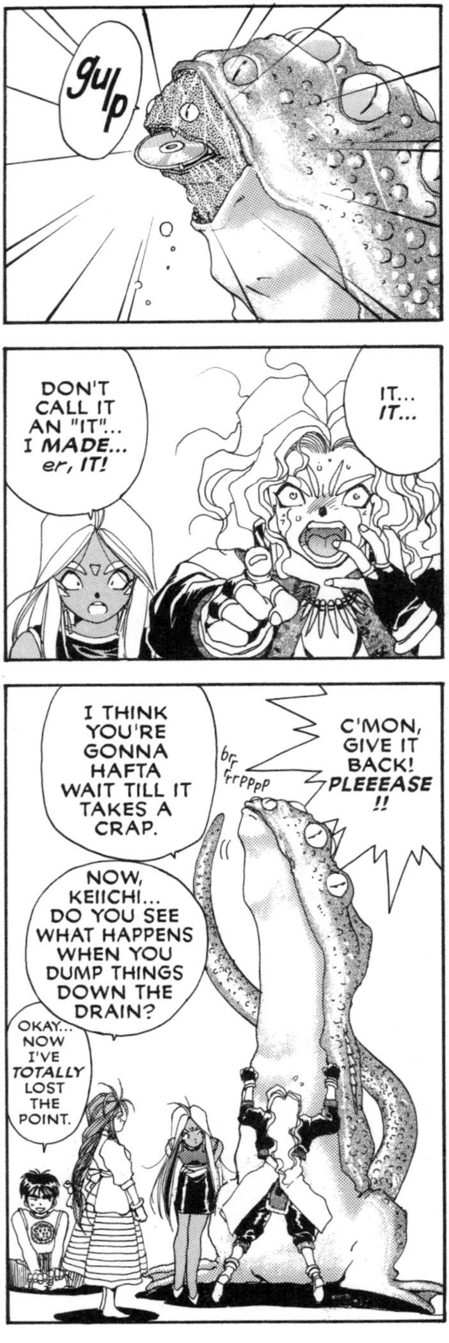
gulp
IT... *IT*...
DON'T CALL IT AN "IT"... I ***MADE...*** *er, **IT!***
C'MON, GIVE IT BACK! ***PLEEEASE !!***
brr rrrpppP
I THINK YOU'RE GONNA HAFTA WAIT TILL IT TAKES A CRAP.
NOW, KEIICHI... DO YOU SEE WHAT HAPPENS WHEN YOU DUMP THINGS DOWN THE DRAIN?
OKAY... NOW I'VE ***TOTALLY*** LOST THE POINT.

CHAPTER 28

# Balance-Ball Amour

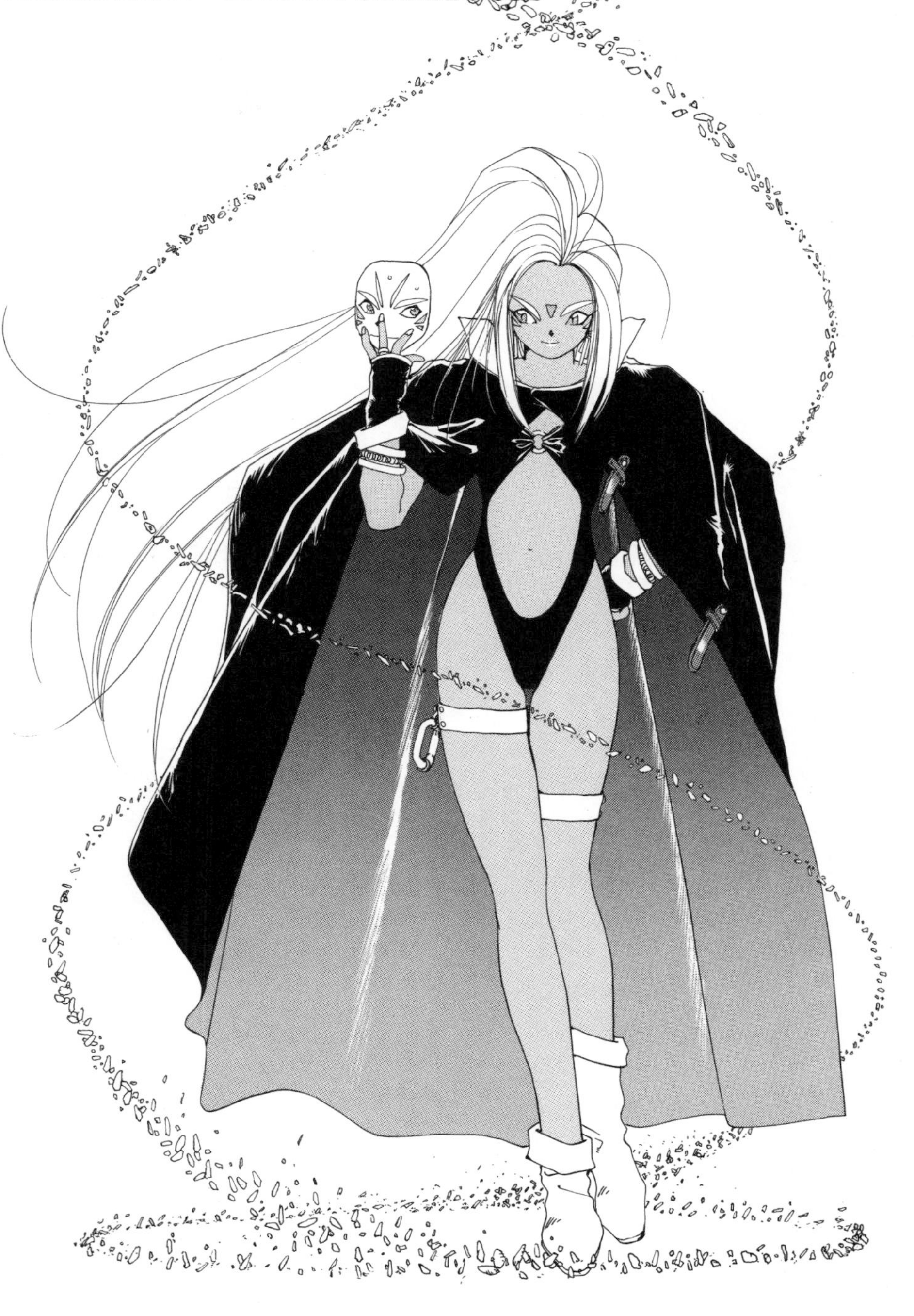

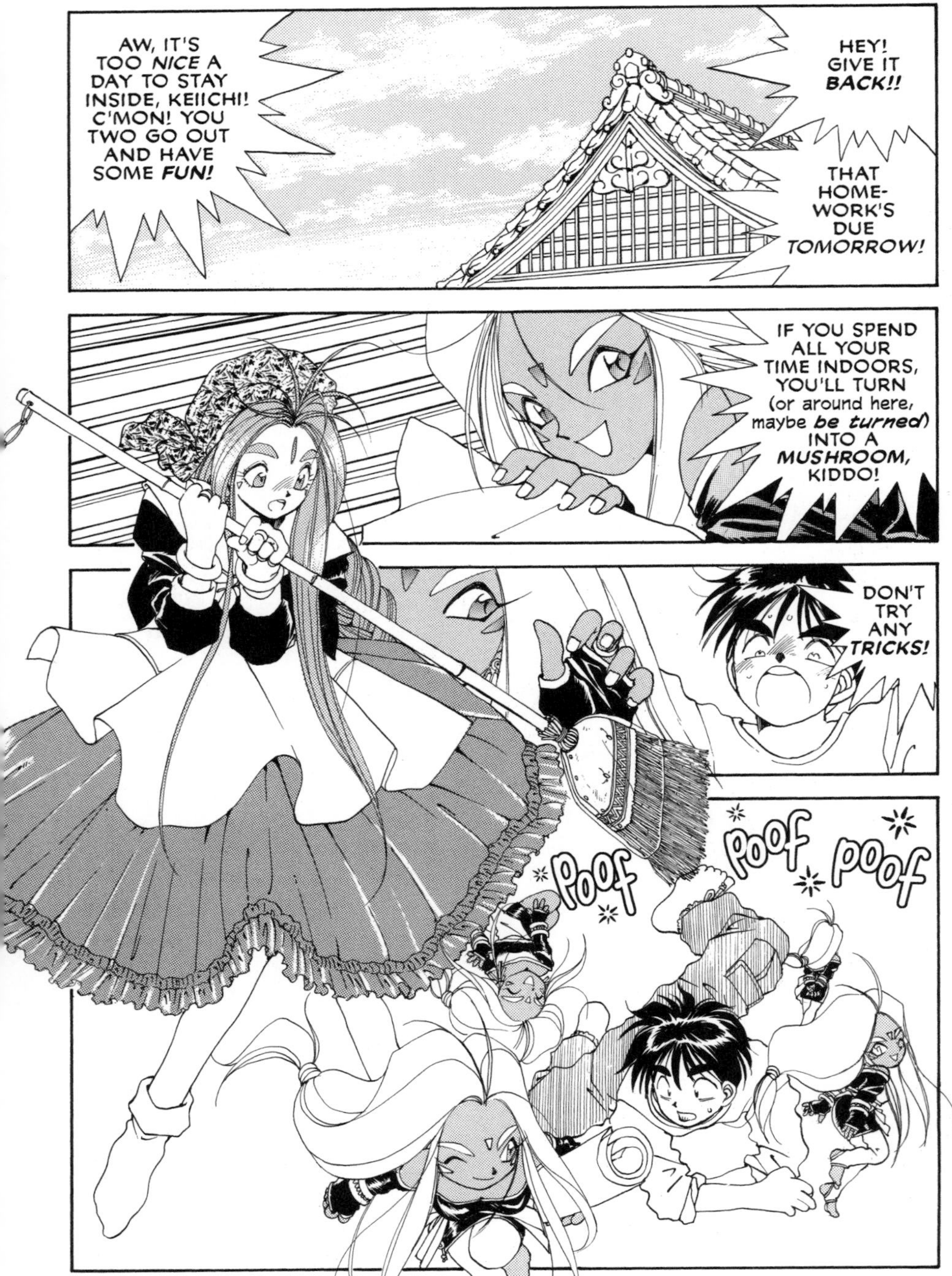
HEY! GIVE IT BACK!!
THAT HOME-WORK'S DUE TOMORROW!
AW, IT'S TOO NICE A DAY TO STAY INSIDE, KEIICHI! C'MON! YOU TWO GO OUT AND HAVE SOME FUN!
IF YOU SPEND ALL YOUR TIME INDOORS, YOU'LL TURN (or around here, maybe be turned) INTO A MUSHROOM, KIDDO!
DON'T TRY ANY TRICKS!
poof
poof
poof

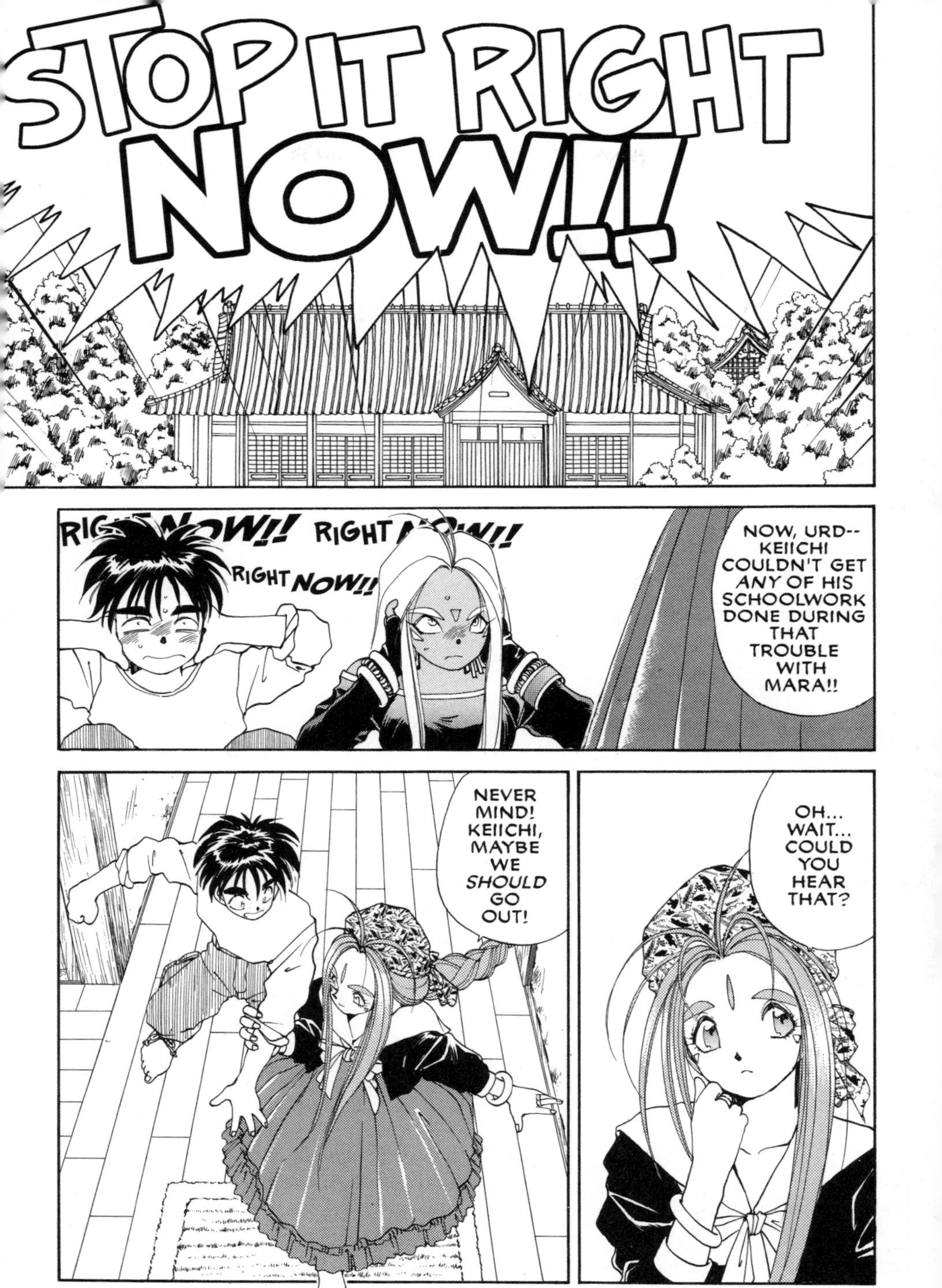
STOP IT RIGHT NOW!!
NOW, URD-- KEIICHI COULDN'T GET *ANY* OF HIS SCHOOLWORK DONE DURING THAT TROUBLE WITH MARA!!
RIGHT NOW!!
OH... WAIT... COULD YOU HEAR THAT?
NEVER MIND! KEIICHI, MAYBE WE *SHOULD* GO OUT!

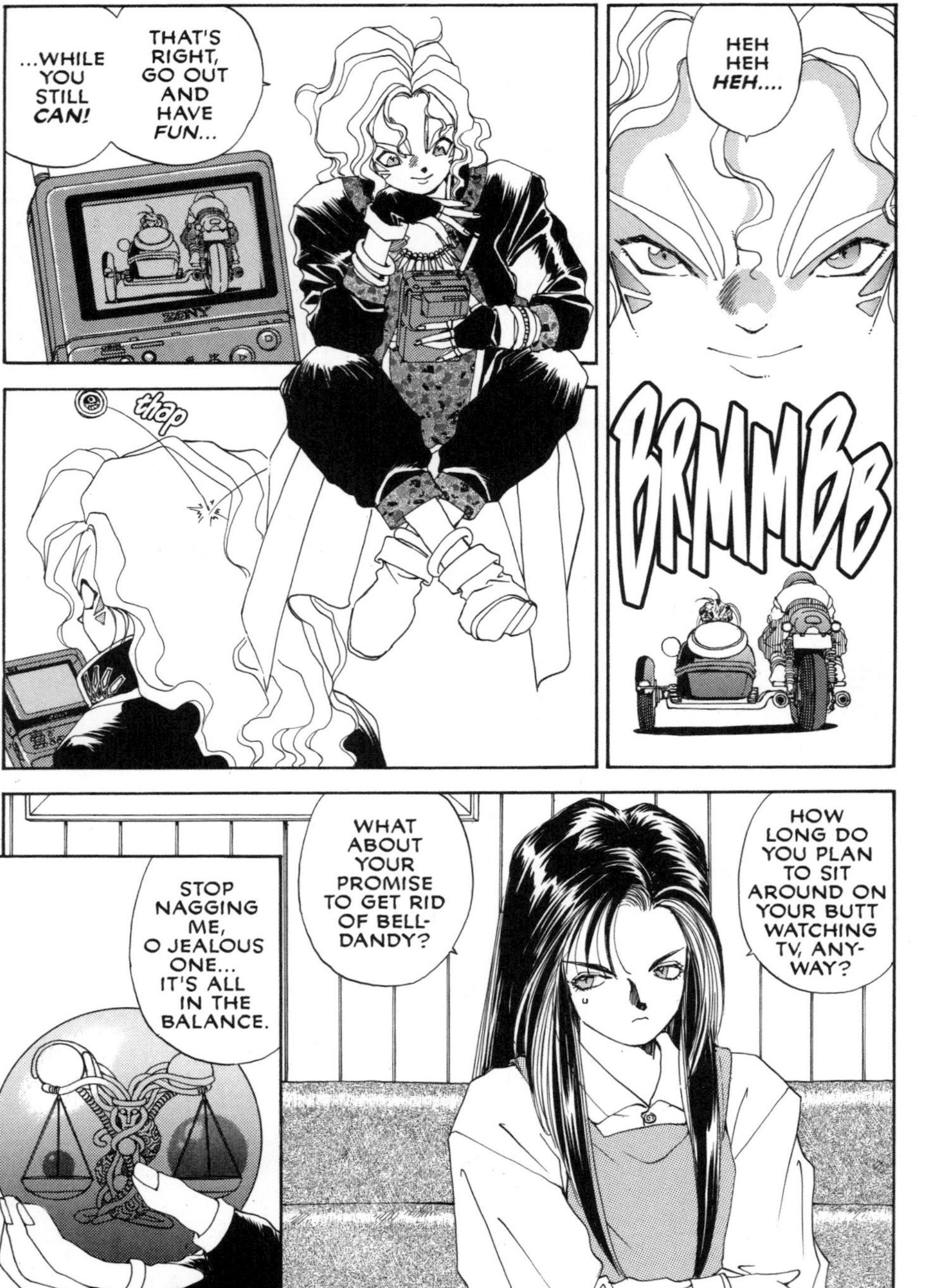
HEH HEH *HEH*....
BRMMBB
THAT'S RIGHT, GO OUT AND HAVE *FUN*...
...WHILE YOU STILL *CAN!*
thap
HOW LONG DO YOU PLAN TO SIT AROUND ON YOUR BUTT WATCHING TV, ANY-WAY?
WHAT ABOUT YOUR PROMISE TO GET RID OF BELL-DANDY?
STOP NAGGING ME, O JEALOUS ONE... IT'S ALL IN THE BALANCE.

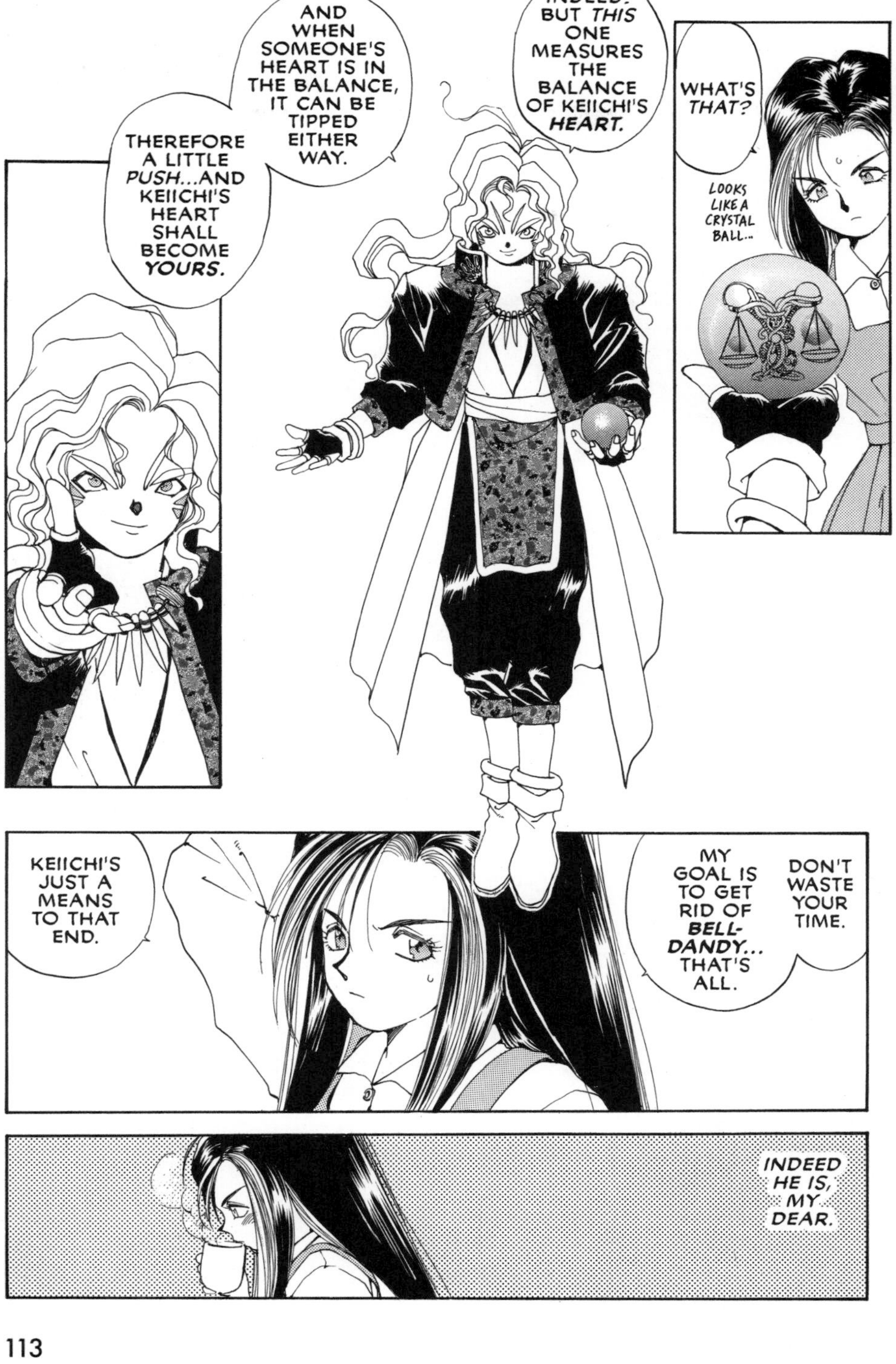
WHAT'S THAT?
LOOKS LIKE A CRYSTAL BALL...
INDEED! BUT THIS ONE MEASURES THE BALANCE OF KEIICHI'S HEART.
AND WHEN SOMEONE'S HEART IS IN THE BALANCE, IT CAN BE TIPPED EITHER WAY.
THEREFORE A LITTLE PUSH...AND KEIICHI'S HEART SHALL BECOME YOURS.
DON'T WASTE YOUR TIME.
MY GOAL IS TO GET RID OF BELL-DANDY... THAT'S ALL.
KEIICHI'S JUST A MEANS TO THAT END.
INDEED HE IS, MY DEAR.

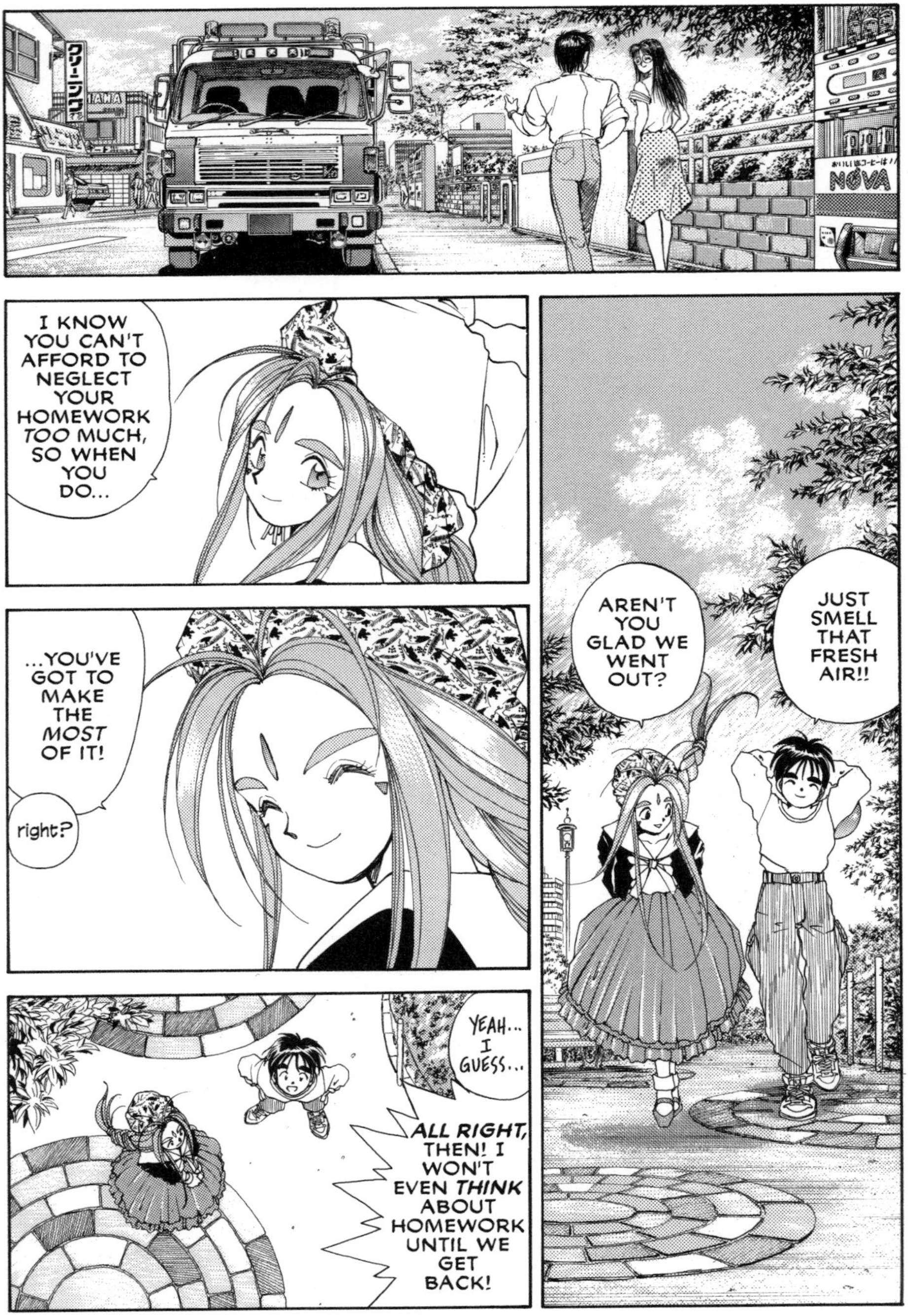
クリーニング
NOVA
JUST SMELL THAT FRESH AIR!!
AREN'T YOU GLAD WE WENT OUT?
I KNOW YOU CAN'T AFFORD TO NEGLECT YOUR HOMEWORK *TOO* MUCH, SO WHEN YOU DO...
...YOU'VE GOT TO MAKE THE *MOST* OF IT!
right?
YEAH... I GUESS...
***ALL RIGHT,*** THEN! I WON'T EVEN ***THINK*** ABOUT HOMEWORK UNTIL WE GET BACK!

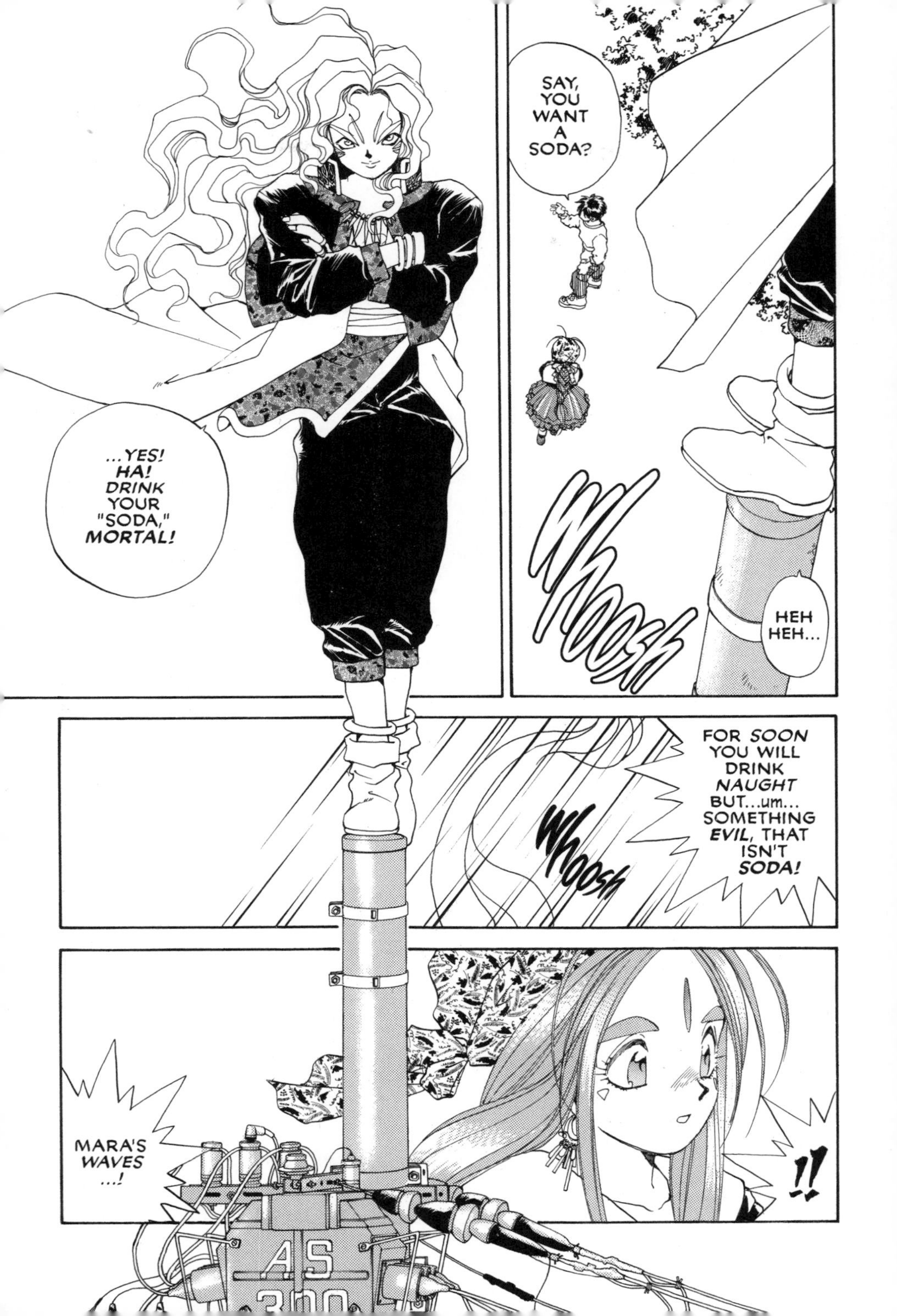
SAY, YOU WANT A SODA?
HEH HEH...
WHOOSH
...YES! HA! DRINK YOUR "SODA," MORTAL!
FOR SOON YOU WILL DRINK NAUGHT BUT...um... SOMETHING EVIL, THAT ISN'T SODA!
WHOOSH
!!
MARA'S WAVES ...!
AS 300

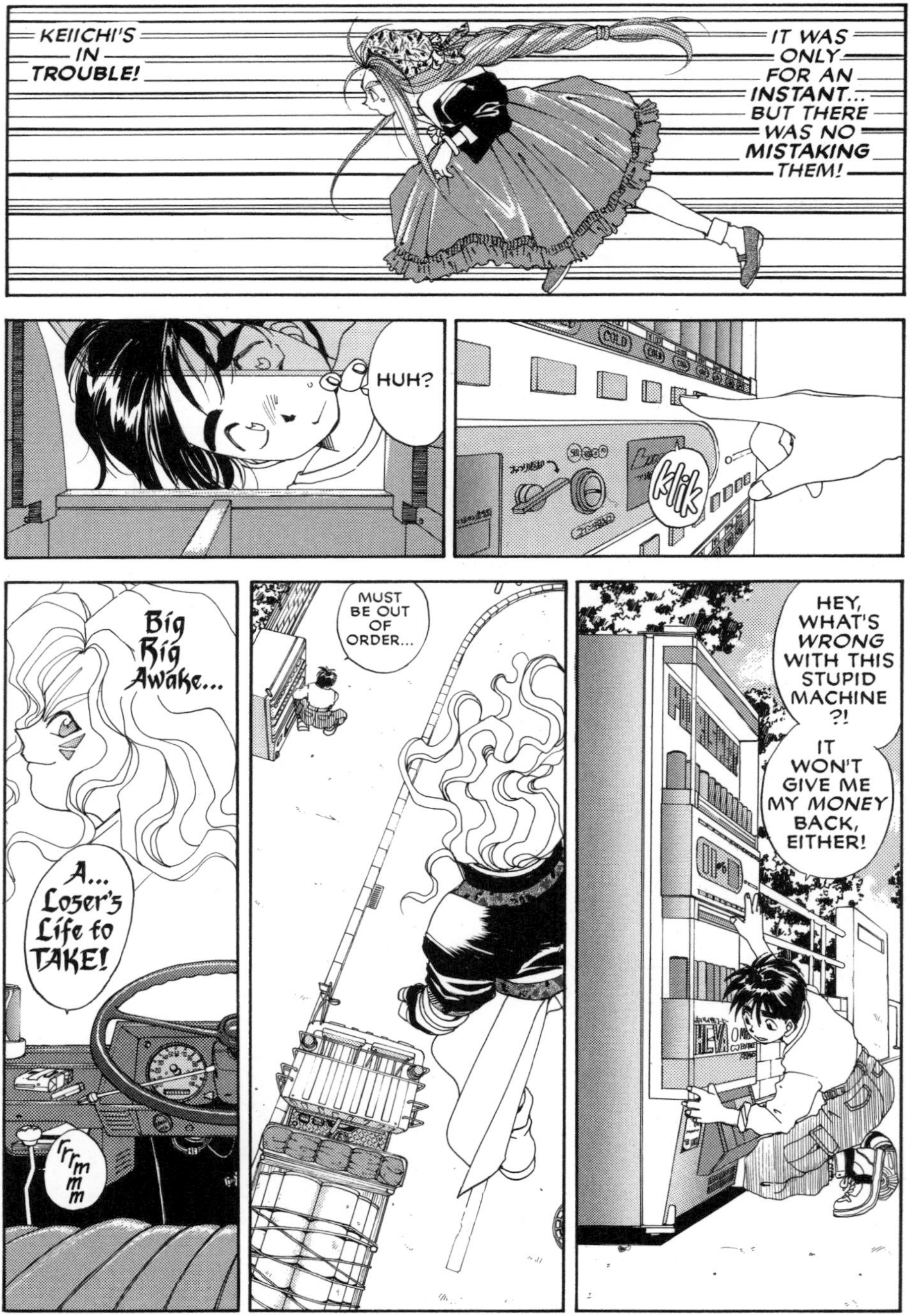
IT WAS ONLY FOR AN INSTANT... BUT THERE WAS NO MISTAKING THEM!
KEIICHI'S IN TROUBLE!
klik
HUH?
HEY, WHAT'S WRONG WITH THIS STUPID MACHINE?!
IT WON'T GIVE ME MY MONEY BACK, EITHER!
MUST BE OUT OF ORDER...
Big Rig Awake...
A... Loser's Life to TAKE!
rrrmmm

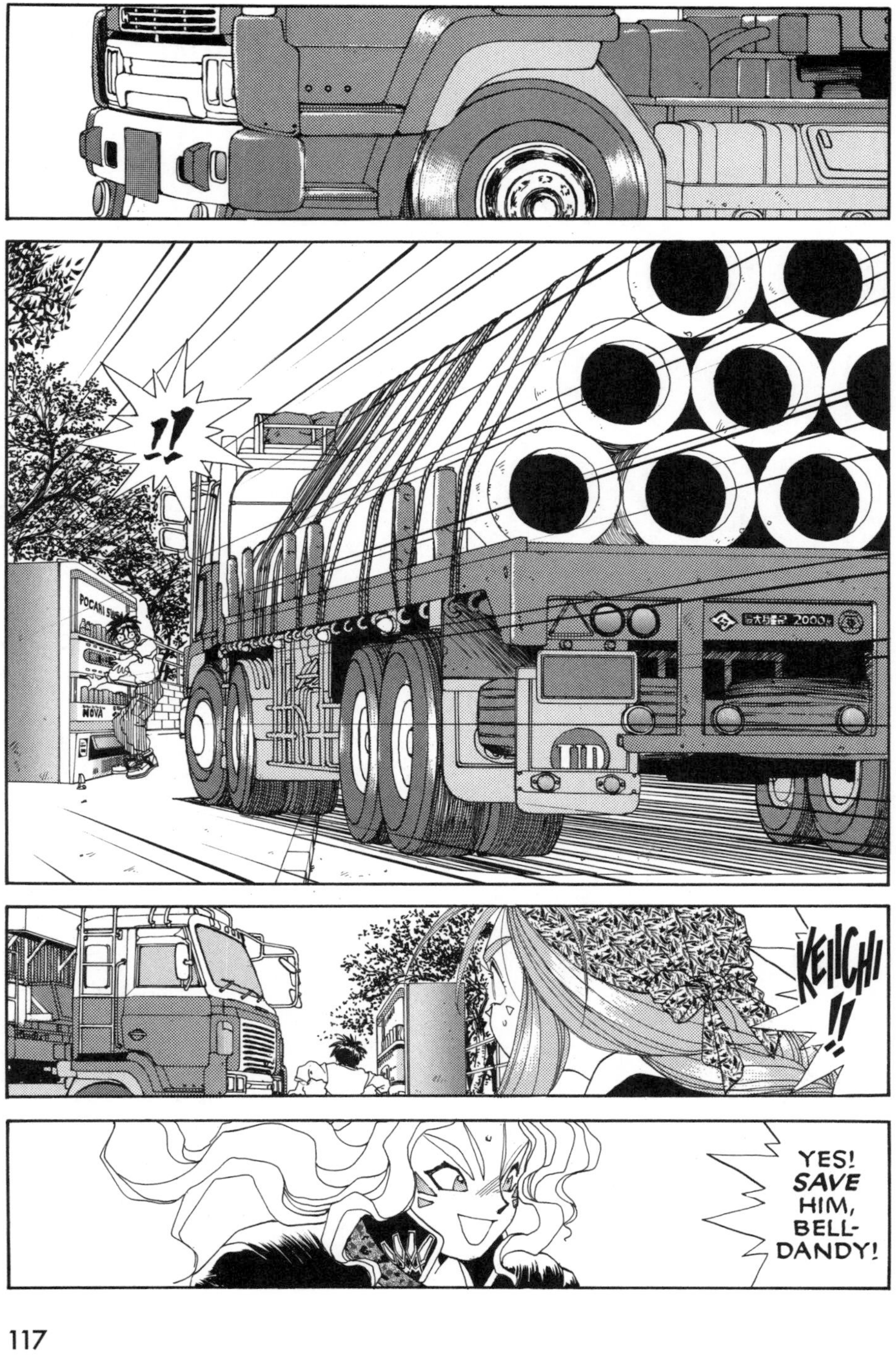
!!
NOVA
KEIICHI!!
YES! *SAVE* HIM, BELL-DANDY!

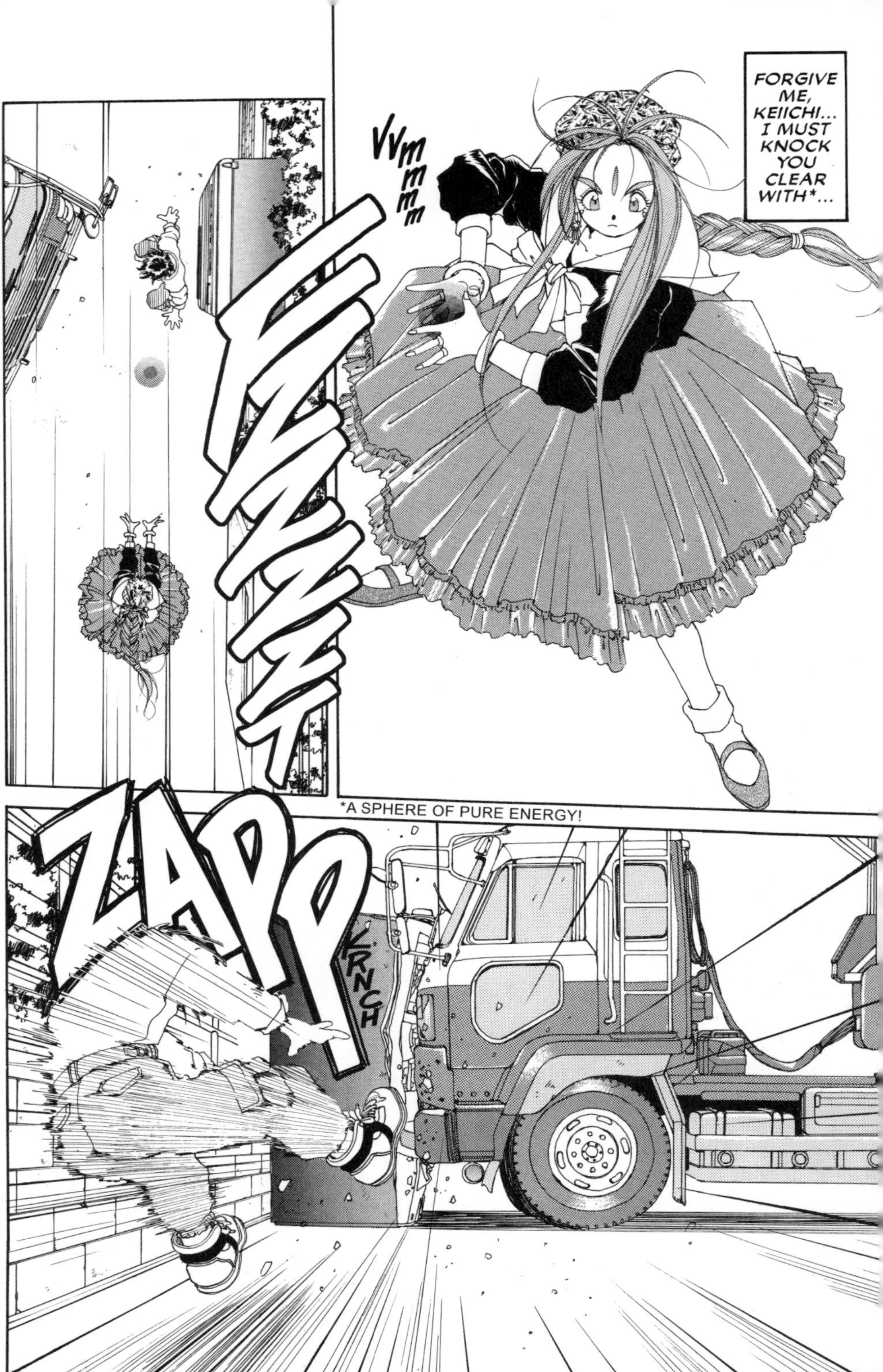
FORGIVE ME, KEIICHI... I MUST KNOCK YOU CLEAR WITH*...
Vvmmmmm
VNNNNNK
*A SPHERE OF PURE ENERGY!
ZAPP
KRNCH

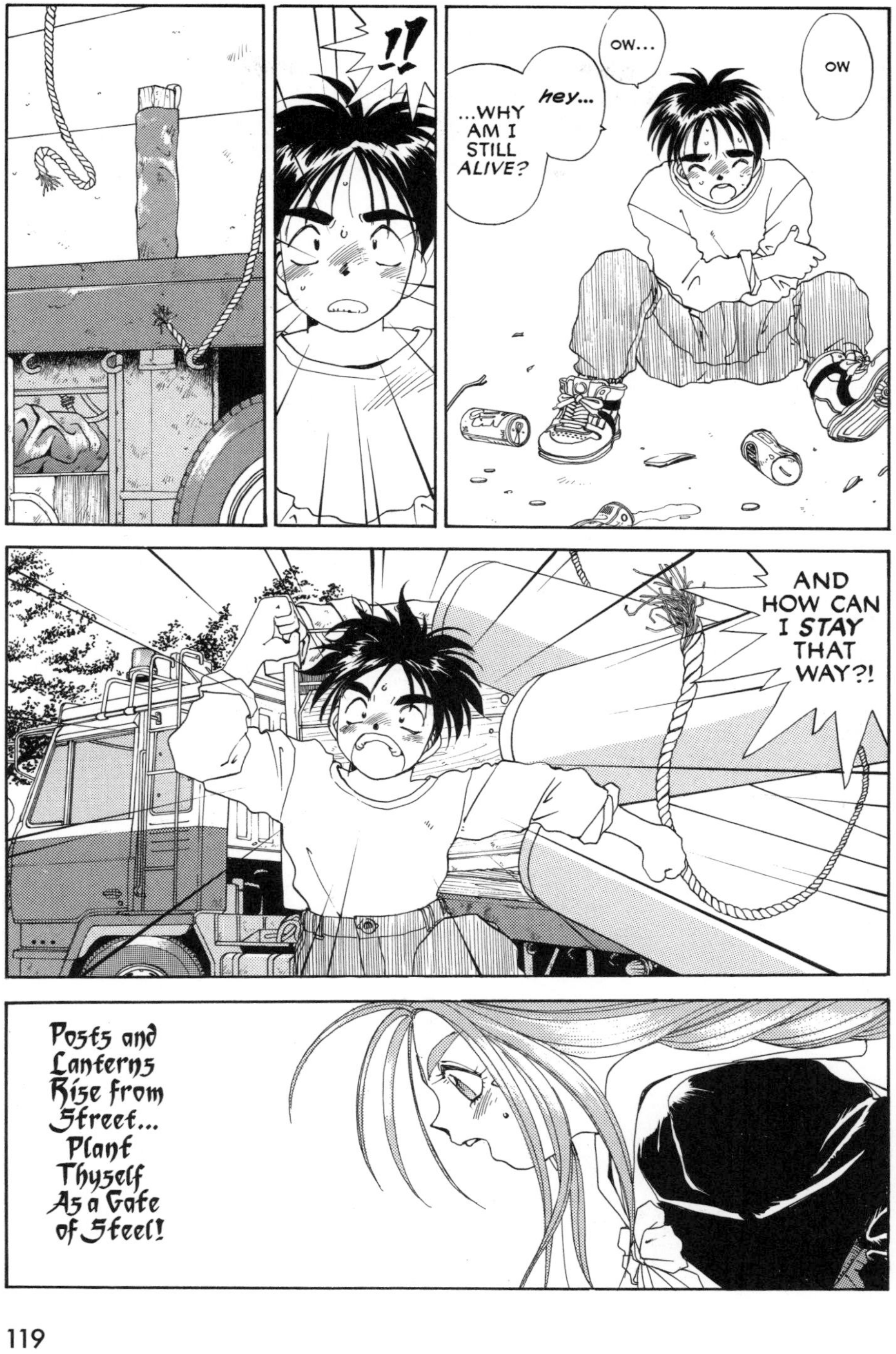
OW
OW...
hey...
...WHY AM I STILL ALIVE?
!!
AND HOW CAN I STAY THAT WAY?!
Posts and Lanterns Rise from Street... Plant Thyself As a Gate of Steel!

VWHIPPP
TONGGG
TONGGG
ALL RIGHT, MARA!! I KNOW YOU'RE THERE!!
wobble
AND I WON'T TOLERATE ANY MORE OF... OF YOUR...

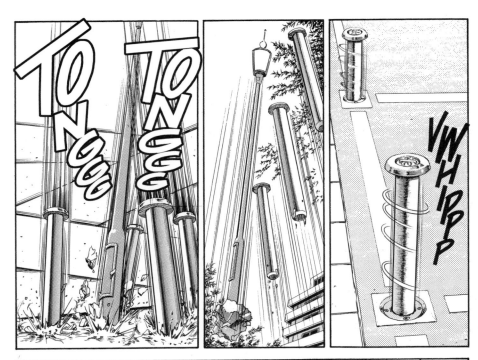

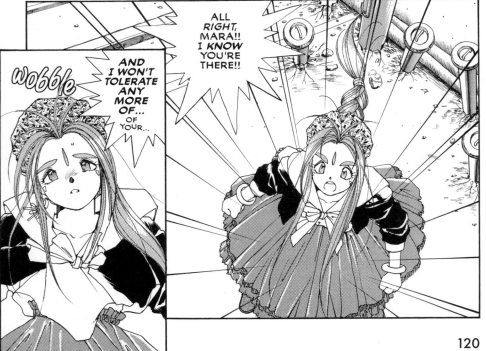

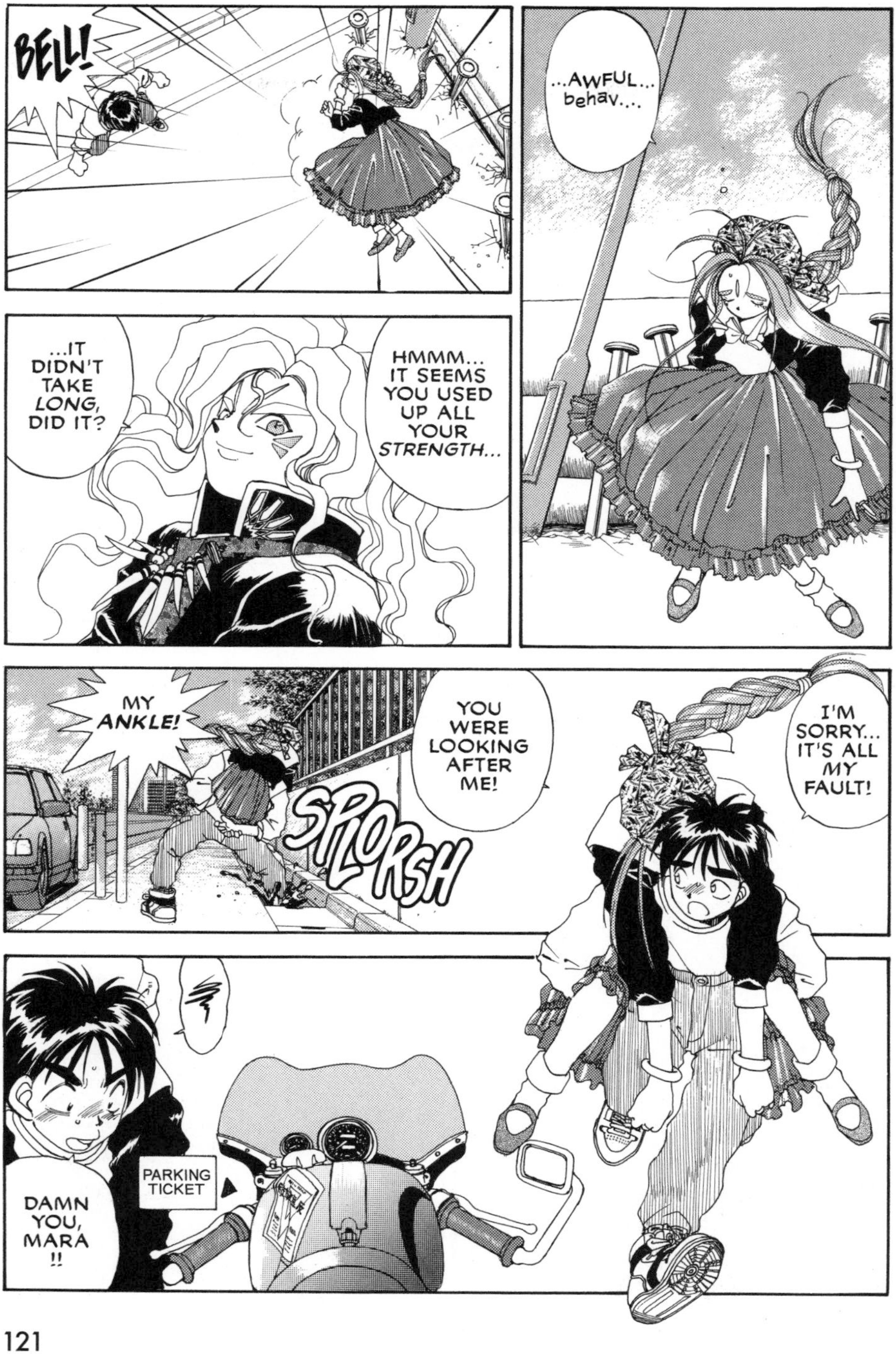
BELL!
...AWFUL... behav...
HMMM... IT SEEMS YOU USED UP ALL YOUR STRENGTH...
...IT DIDN'T TAKE LONG, DID IT?
MY ANKLE!
SPLORSH
YOU WERE LOOKING AFTER ME!
I'M SORRY... IT'S ALL MY FAULT!
PARKING TICKET
DAMN YOU, MARA !!

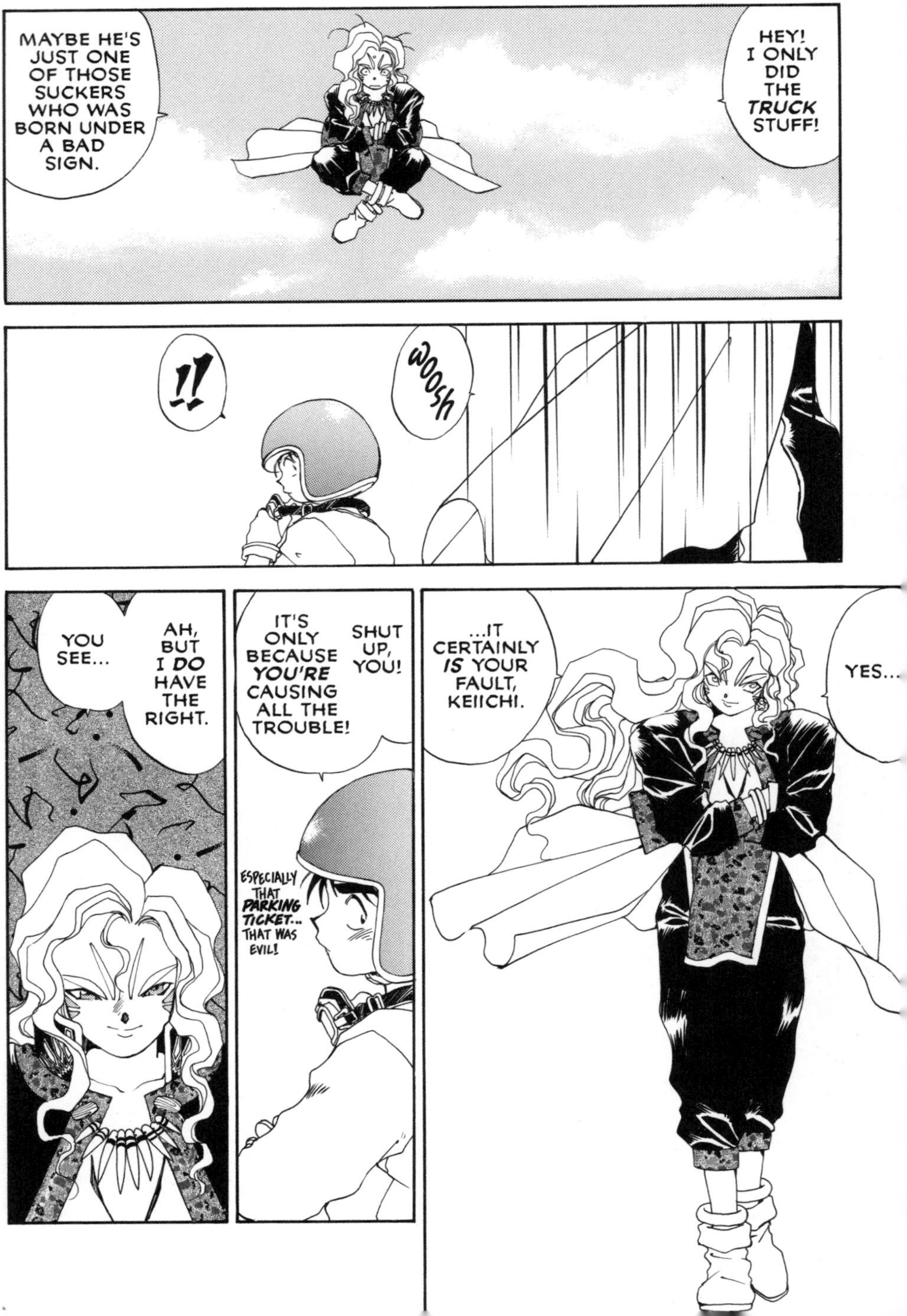
HEY! I ONLY DID THE TRUCK STUFF!
MAYBE HE'S JUST ONE OF THOSE SUCKERS WHO WAS BORN UNDER A BAD SIGN.
WOOSH
!!
YES...
...IT CERTAINLY IS YOUR FAULT, KEIICHI.
SHUT UP, YOU!
IT'S ONLY BECAUSE YOU'RE CAUSING ALL THE TROUBLE!
ESPECIALLY THAT PARKING TICKET... THAT WAS EVIL!
AH, BUT I DO HAVE THE RIGHT.
YOU SEE...

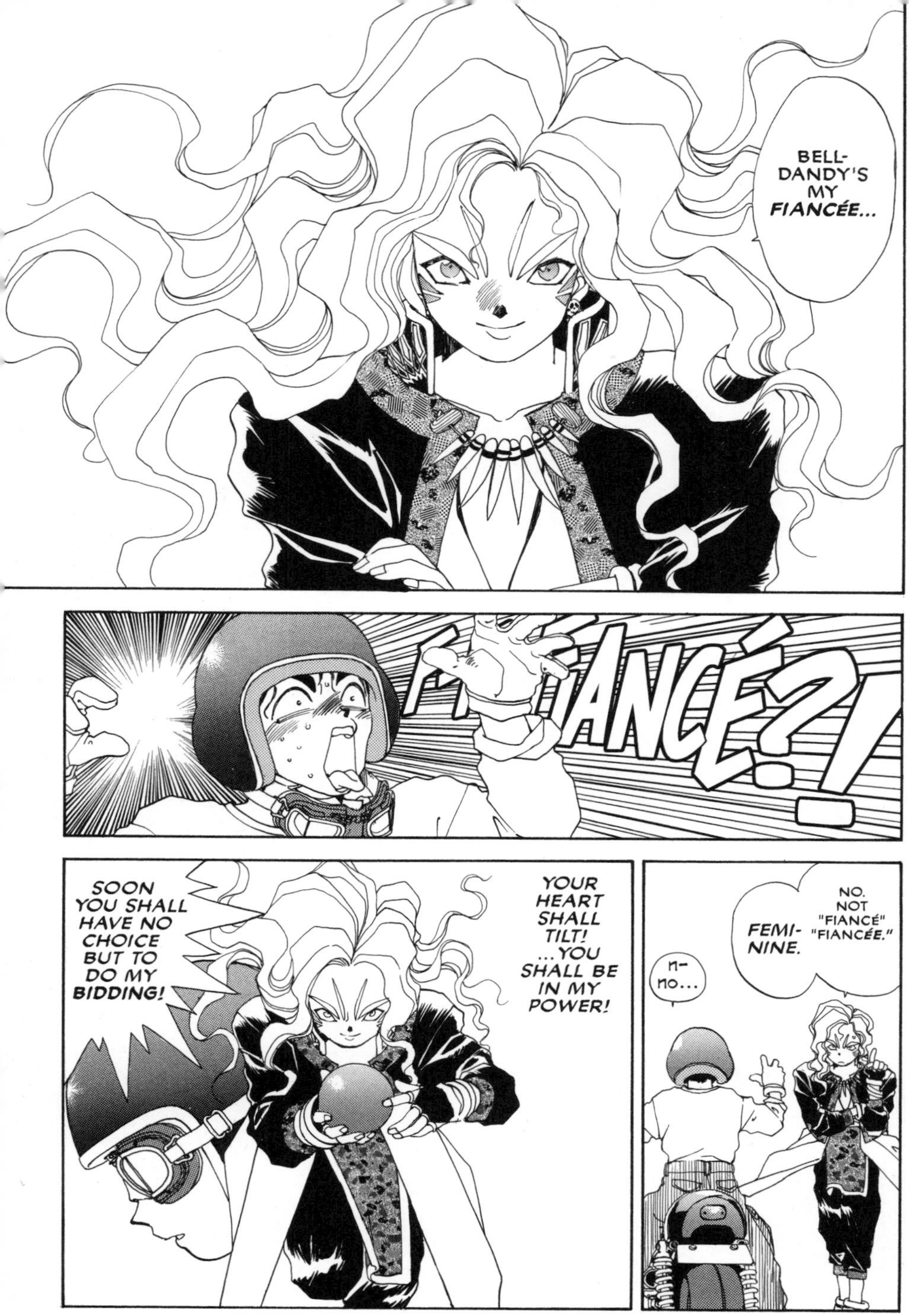
BELL-DANDY'S MY *FIANCÉE...*
IANCÉ?!
NO. NOT "FIANCÉ" FEMI-NINE. "FIANCÉE."
n-no...
YOUR HEART SHALL TILT! ...YOU SHALL BE IN MY POWER!
SOON YOU SHALL HAVE NO CHOICE BUT TO DO MY BIDDING!

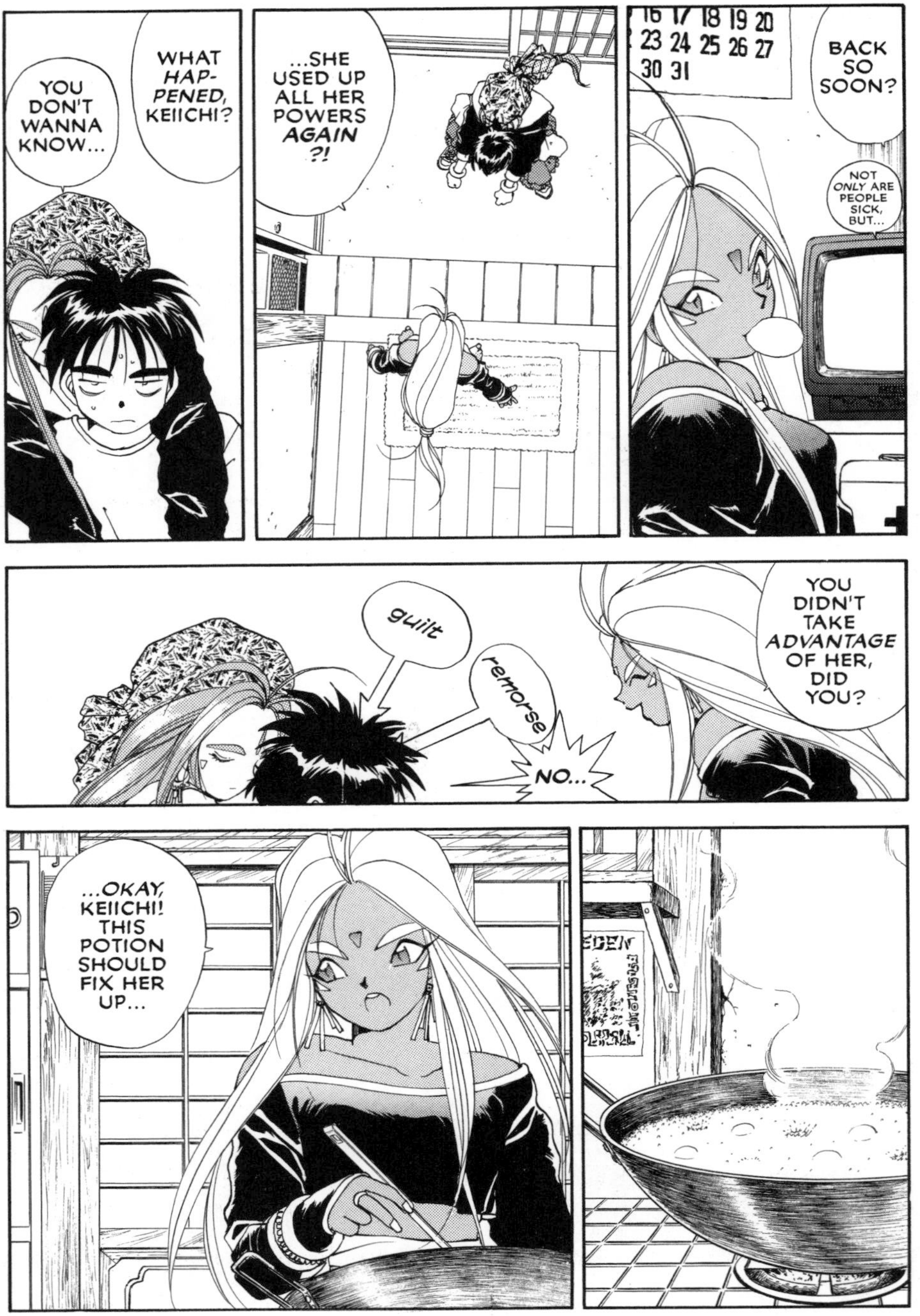
16 17 18 19 20
23 24 25 26 27
30 31
BACK SO SOON?
NOT *ONLY* ARE PEOPLE SICK, BUT...
...SHE USED UP ALL HER POWERS *AGAIN* ?!
WHAT *HAP-PENED,* KEIICHI?
YOU DON'T WANNA KNOW...
YOU DIDN'T TAKE *ADVANTAGE* OF HER, DID YOU?
guilt
remorse
NO...
EDEN
...OKAY, KEIICHI! THIS POTION SHOULD FIX HER UP...

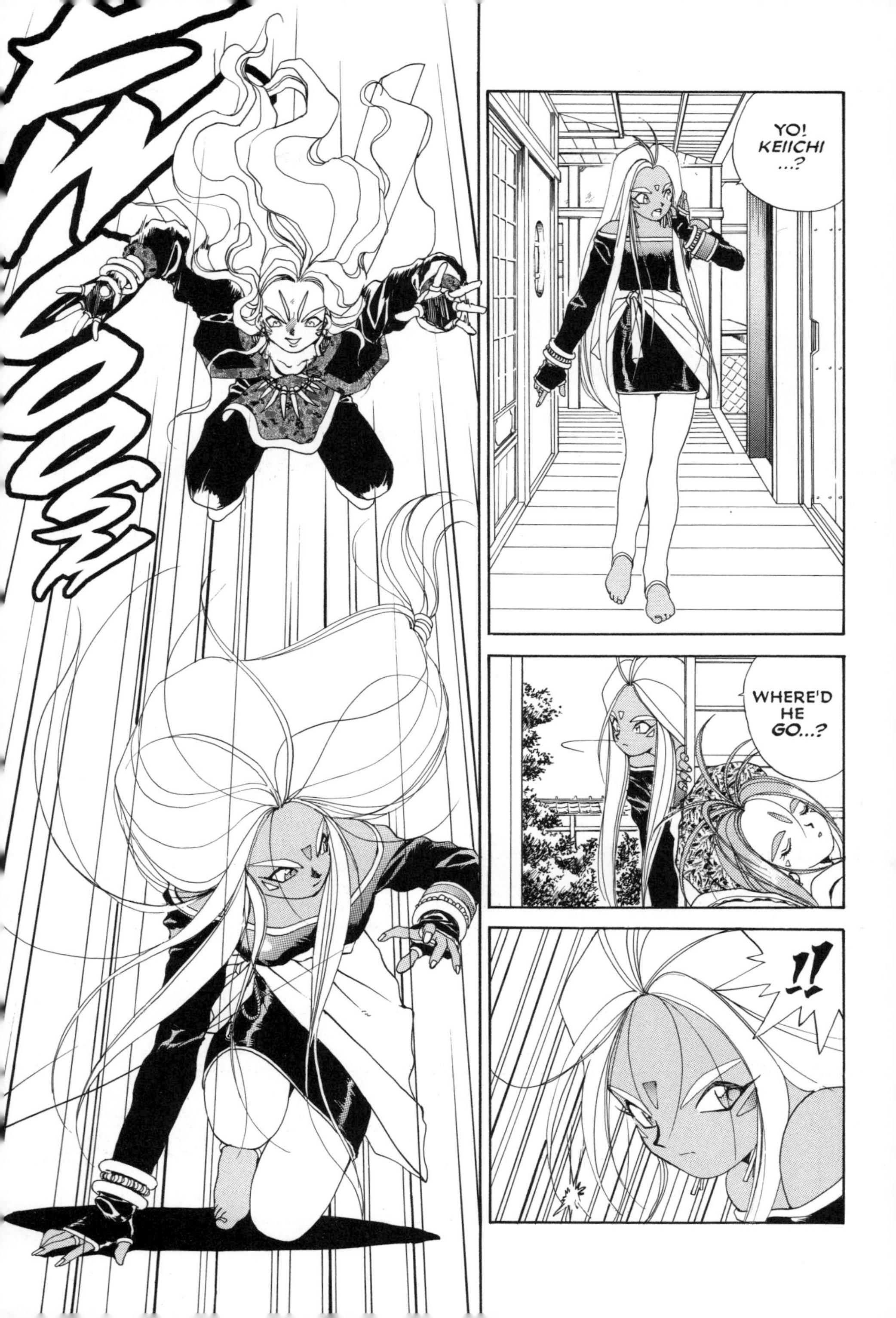
YO! KEIICHI ...?
WHERE'D HE GO...?
!!

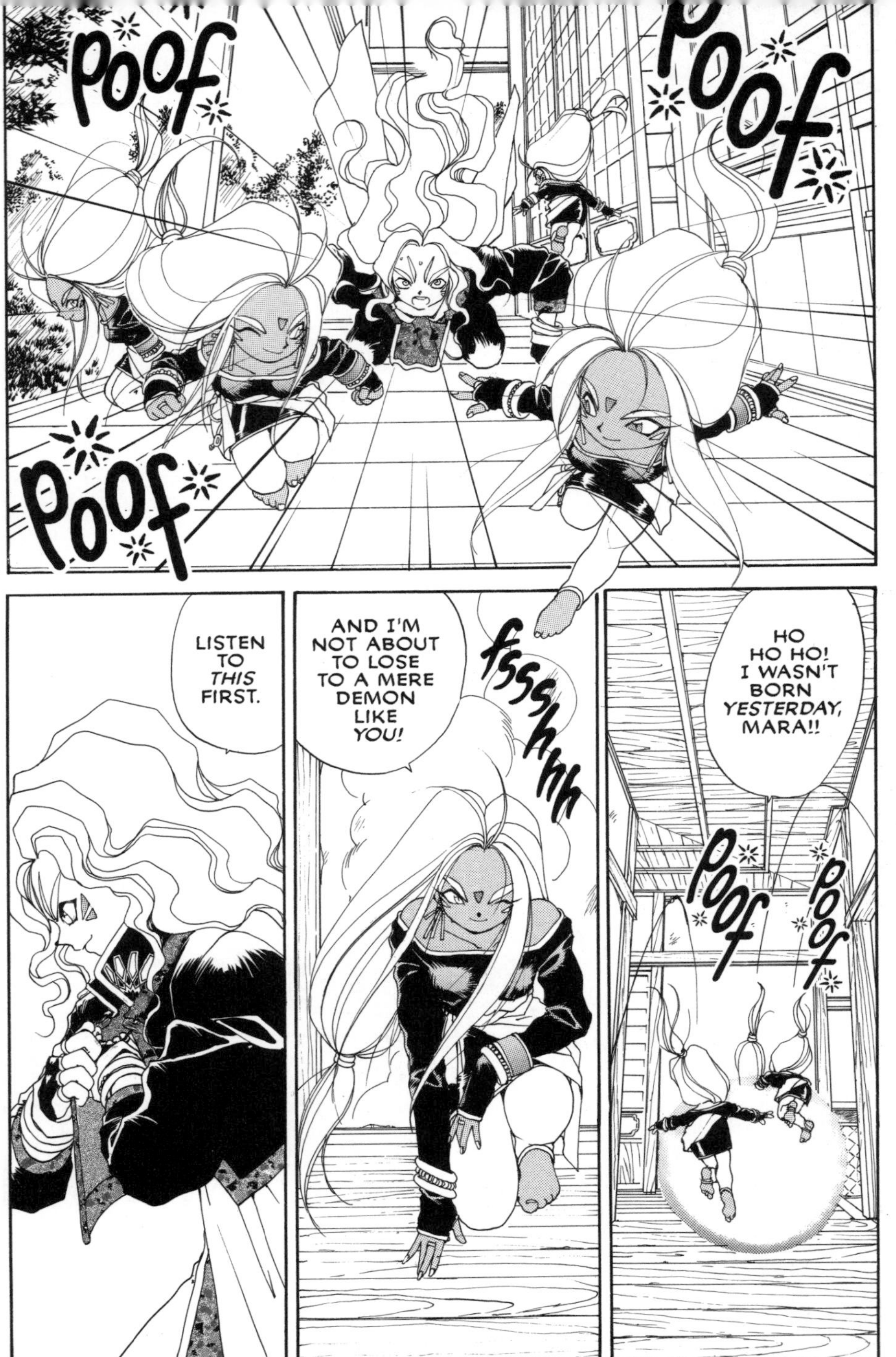
POOF
POOF
POOF
HO HO HO! I WASN'T BORN *YESTERDAY*, MARA!!
POOF
POOF
AND I'M NOT ABOUT TO LOSE TO A MERE DEMON LIKE *YOU!*
FSSSHHHH
LISTEN TO *THIS* FIRST.

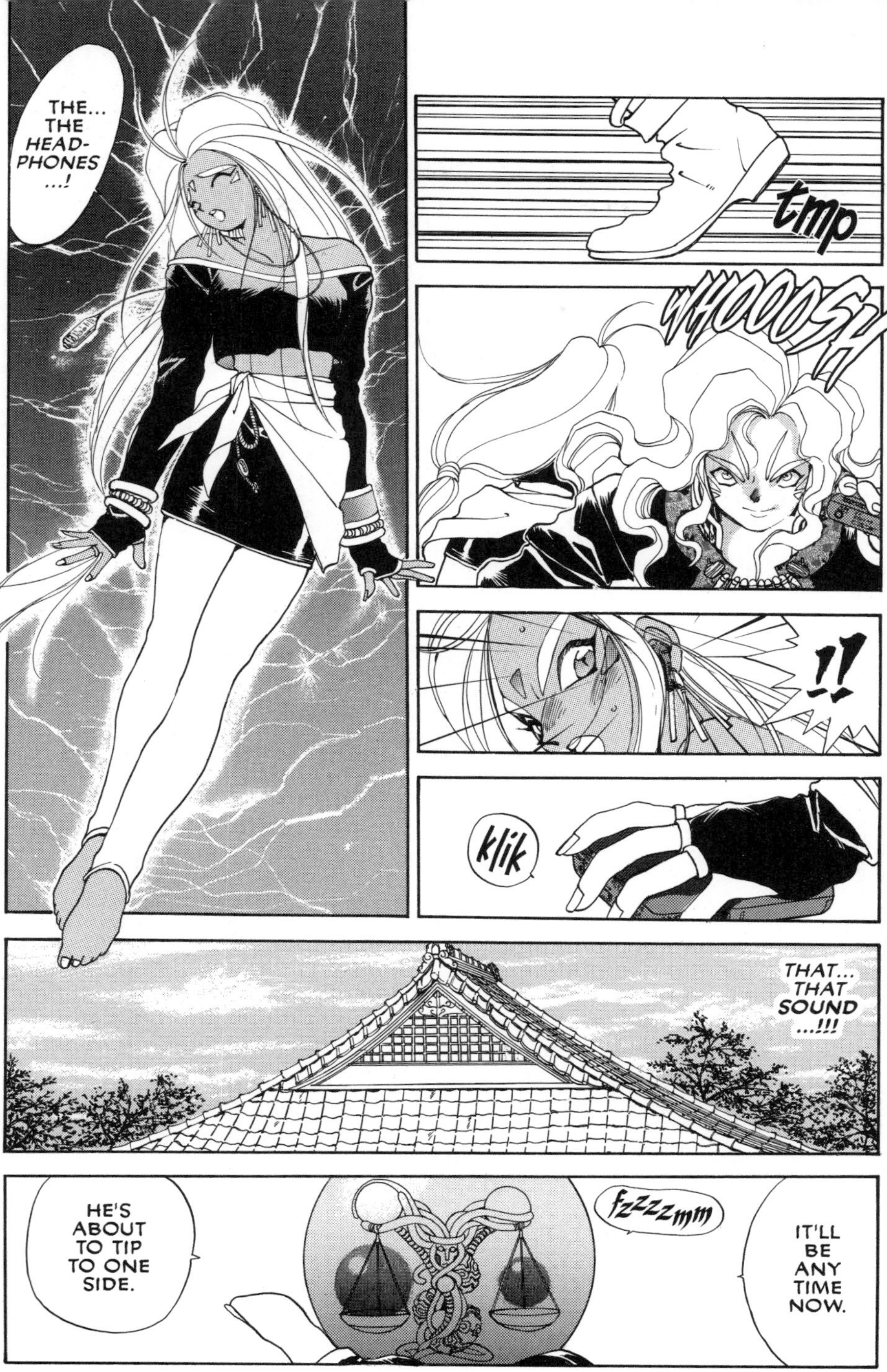
tmp
WHOOOSH
!!
klik
THE... THE HEAD-PHONES ...!
THAT... THAT SOUND ...!!!
IT'LL BE ANY TIME NOW.
fzzzzmm
HE'S ABOUT TO TIP TO ONE SIDE.

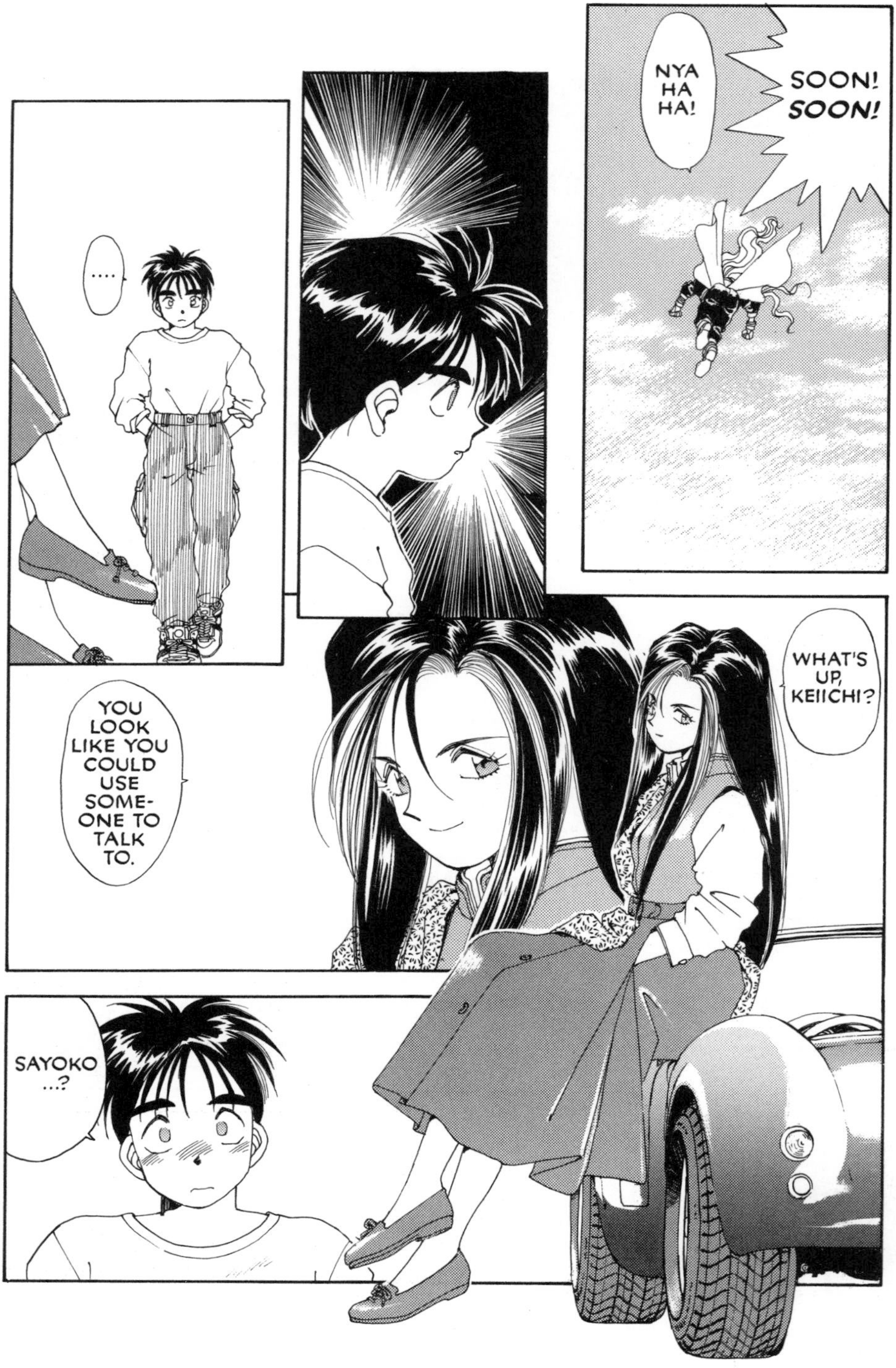
SOON! SOON!
NYA HA HA!
....
WHAT'S UP, KEIICHI?
YOU LOOK LIKE YOU COULD USE SOME-ONE TO TALK TO.
SAYOKO ...?

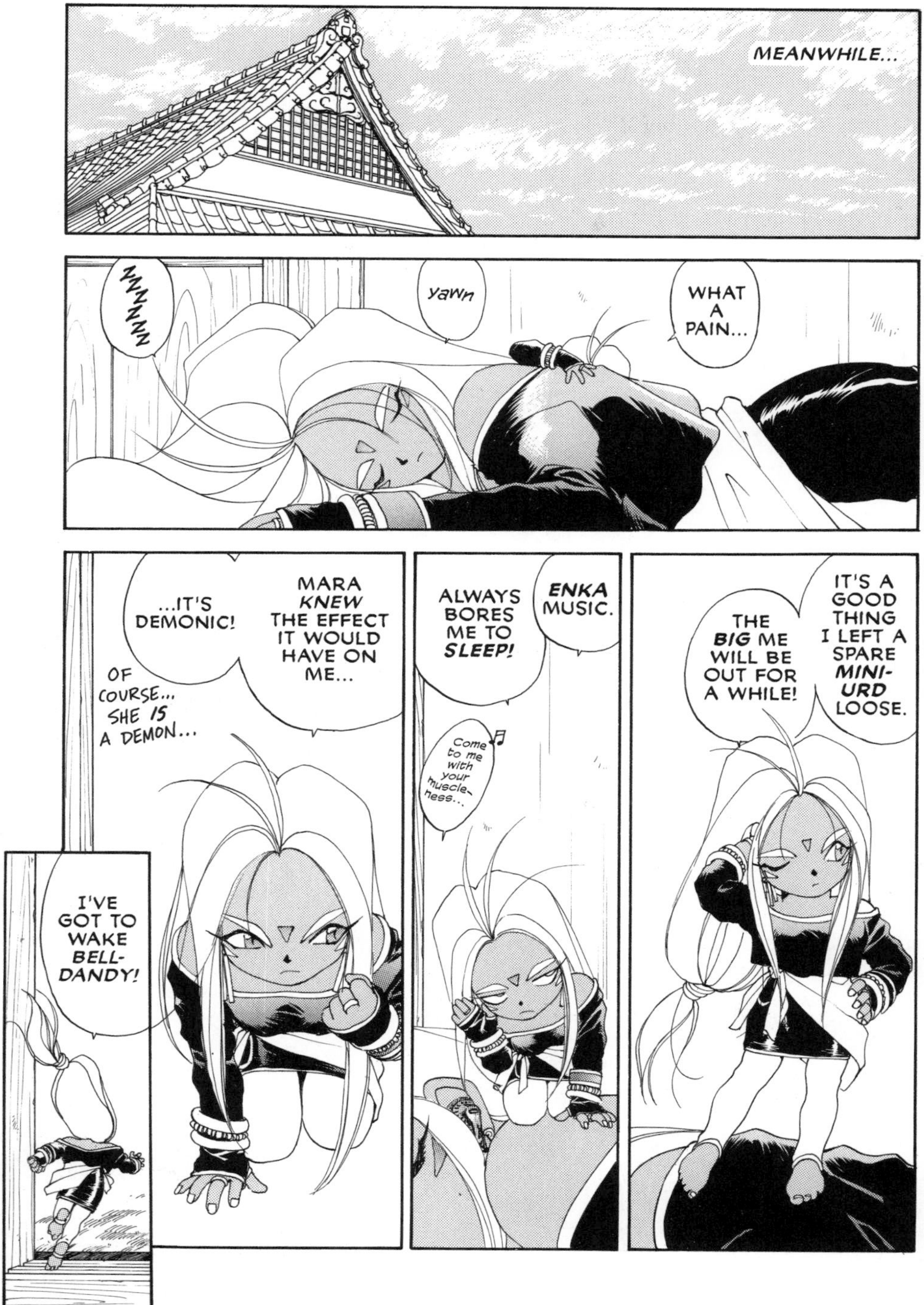
MEANWHILE...
WHAT A PAIN...
yawn
ZZZZZZ
IT'S A GOOD THING I LEFT A SPARE MINI-URD LOOSE.
THE BIG ME WILL BE OUT FOR A WHILE!
ENKA MUSIC.
ALWAYS BORES ME TO SLEEP!
Come to me with your muscle-ness...
MARA KNEW THE EFFECT IT WOULD HAVE ON ME...
...IT'S DEMONIC!
OF COURSE... SHE IS A DEMON...
I'VE GOT TO WAKE BELL-DANDY!

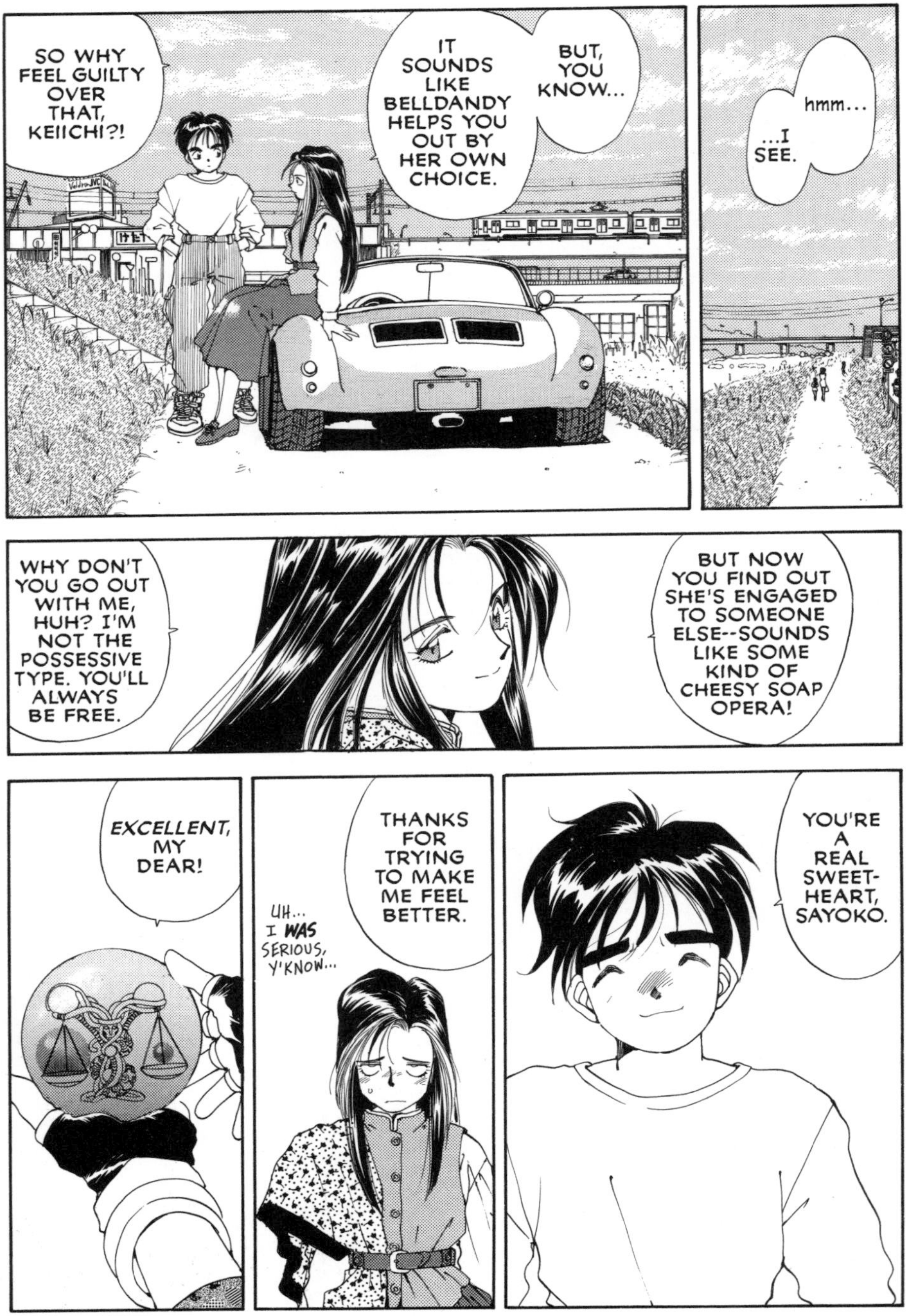
hmm...
...I SEE.
BUT, YOU KNOW...
IT SOUNDS LIKE BELLDANDY HELPS YOU OUT BY HER OWN CHOICE.
SO WHY FEEL GUILTY OVER THAT, KEIICHI?!
BUT NOW YOU FIND OUT SHE'S ENGAGED TO SOMEONE ELSE--SOUNDS LIKE SOME KIND OF CHEESY SOAP OPERA!
WHY DON'T YOU GO OUT WITH ME, HUH? I'M NOT THE POSSESSIVE TYPE. YOU'LL ALWAYS BE FREE.
YOU'RE A REAL SWEET-HEART, SAYOKO.
THANKS FOR TRYING TO MAKE ME FEEL BETTER.
UH... I **WAS** SERIOUS, Y'KNOW...
*EXCELLENT*, MY DEAR!

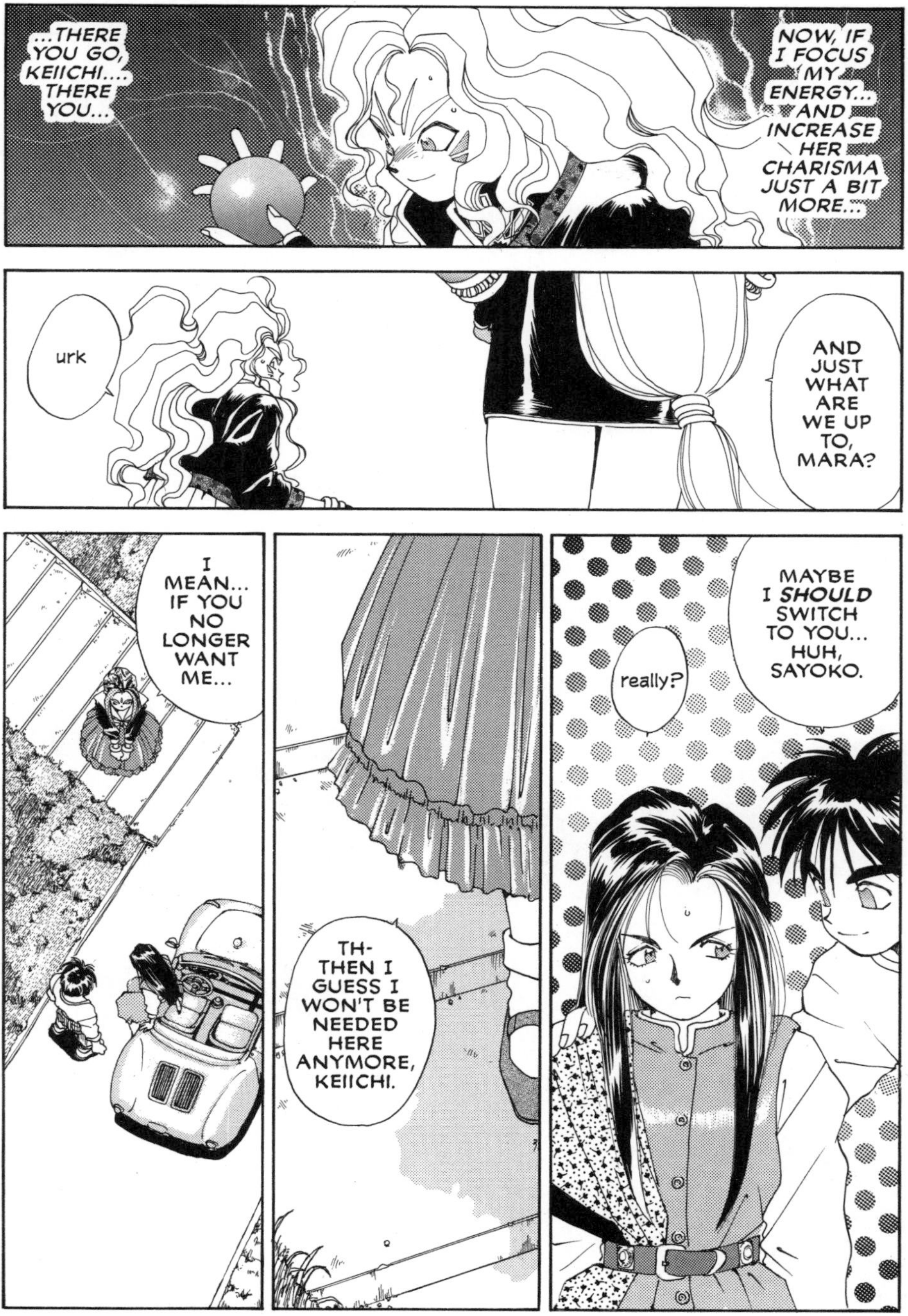

...THERE YOU GO, KEIICHI.... THERE YOU...
NOW, IF I FOCUS MY ENERGY... AND INCREASE HER CHARISMA JUST A BIT MORE...
urk
AND JUST WHAT ARE WE UP TO, MARA?
I MEAN... IF YOU NO LONGER WANT ME...
TH-THEN I GUESS I WON'T BE NEEDED HERE ANYMORE, KEIICHI.
MAYBE I ***SHOULD*** SWITCH TO YOU... HUH, SAYOKO.
really?

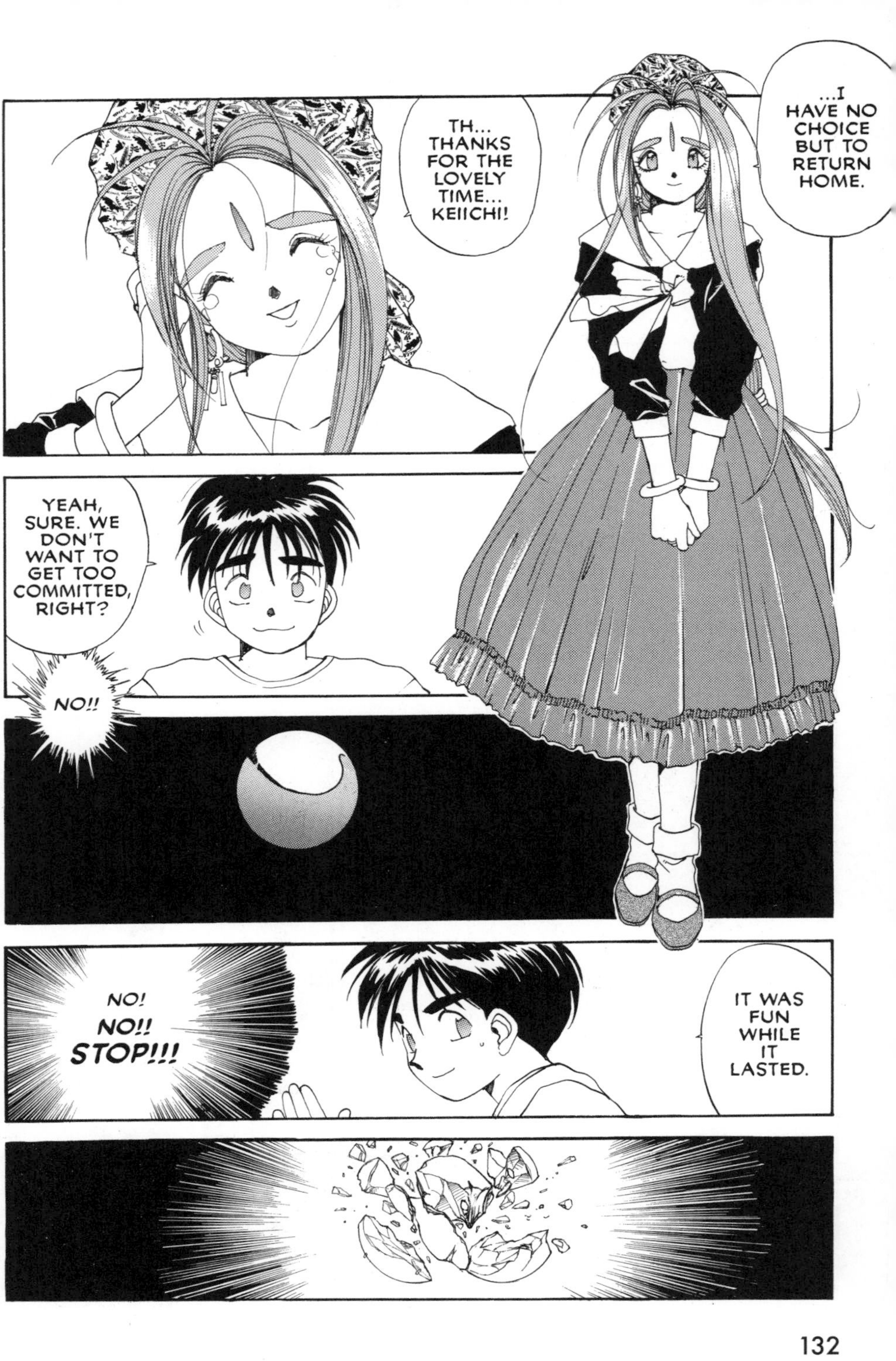

...I HAVE NO CHOICE BUT TO RETURN HOME.
TH... THANKS FOR THE LOVELY TIME... KEIICHI!
YEAH, SURE. WE DON'T WANT TO GET TOO COMMITTED, RIGHT?
NO!!
IT WAS FUN WHILE IT LASTED.
NO!
NO!!
STOP!!!

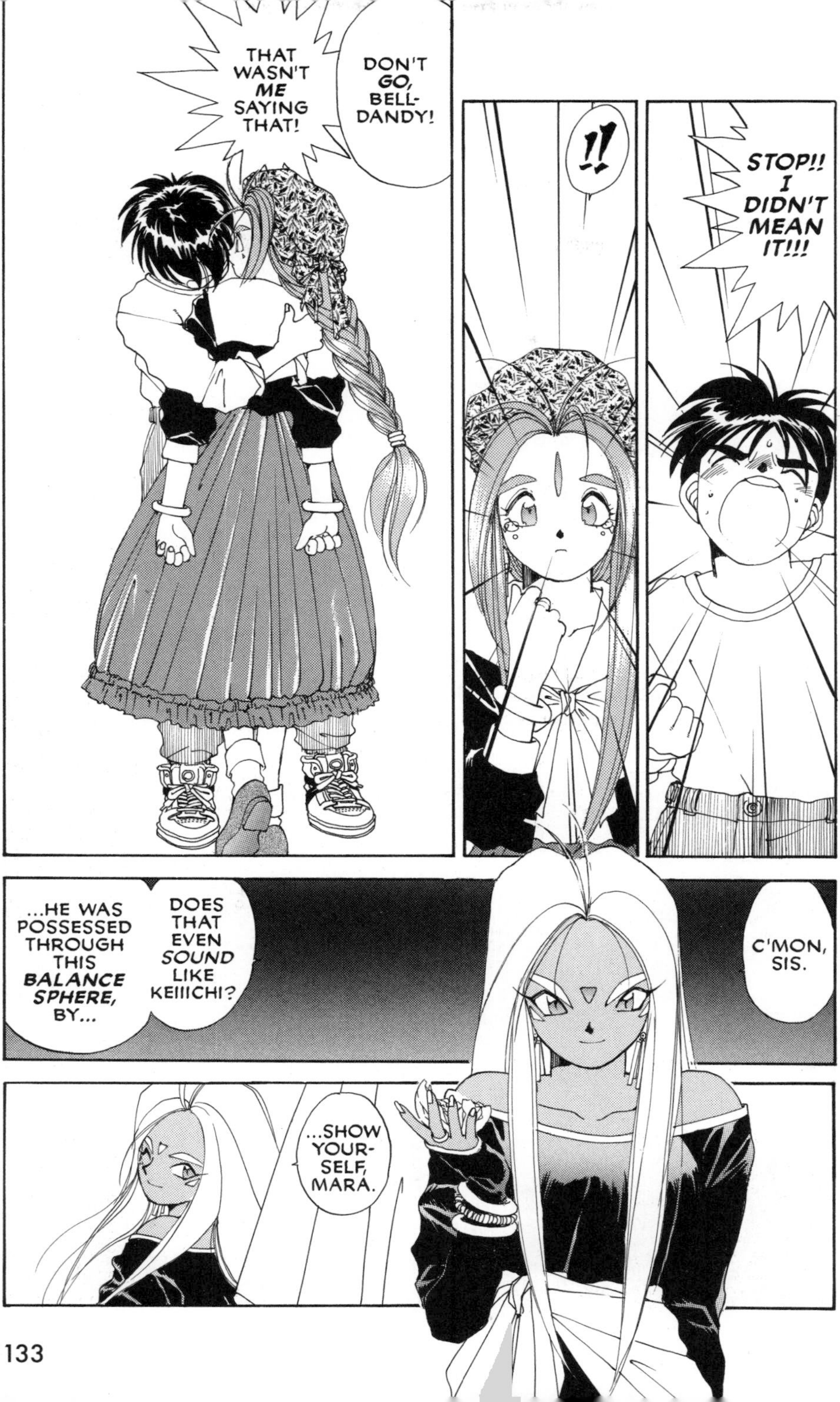
STOP!! I DIDN'T MEAN IT!!!
!!
DON'T GO, BELL-DANDY!
THAT WASN'T ME SAYING THAT!
C'MON, SIS.
DOES THAT EVEN SOUND LIKE KEIICHI?
...HE WAS POSSESSED THROUGH THIS BALANCE SPHERE, BY...
...SHOW YOURSELF, MARA.

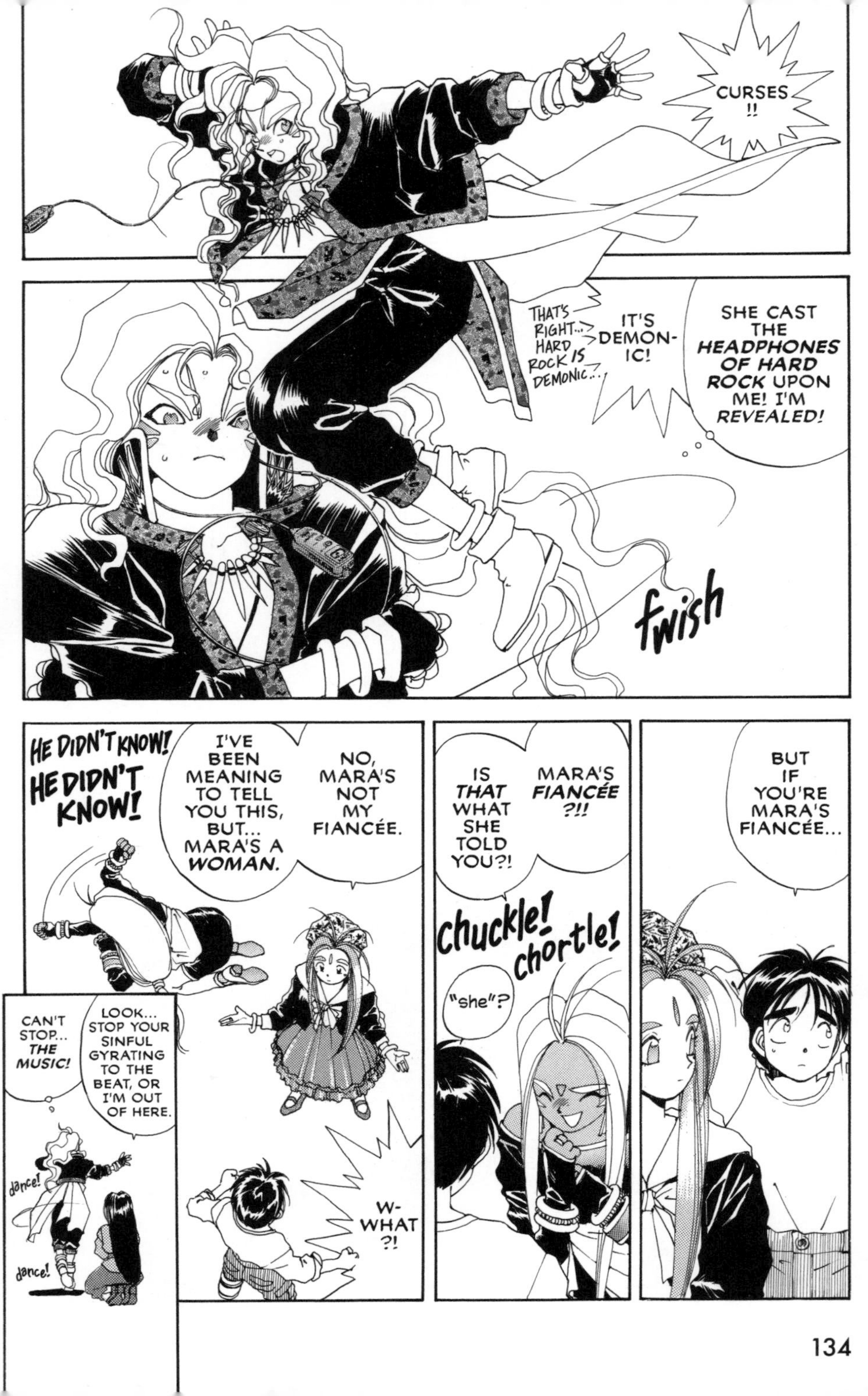
CURSES!!
SHE CAST THE *HEADPHONES OF HARD ROCK* UPON ME! I'M *REVEALED!*
IT'S DEMONIC!
THAT'S RIGHT... HARD ROCK *IS* DEMONIC...
fwish
BUT IF YOU'RE MARA'S FIANCÉE...
MARA'S *FIANCÉE* ?!!
IS *THAT* WHAT SHE TOLD YOU?!
chuckle! chortle!
"she"?
NO, MARA'S NOT MY FIANCÉE.
I'VE BEEN MEANING TO TELL YOU THIS, BUT... MARA'S A *WOMAN.*
HE DIDN'T KNOW! HE DIDN'T KNOW!
W-WHAT ?!
LOOK... STOP YOUR SINFUL GYRATING TO THE BEAT, OR I'M OUT OF HERE.
CAN'T STOP... *THE MUSIC!*
dance!
dance!

CHAPTER 29

# The Worst Day of a Demon

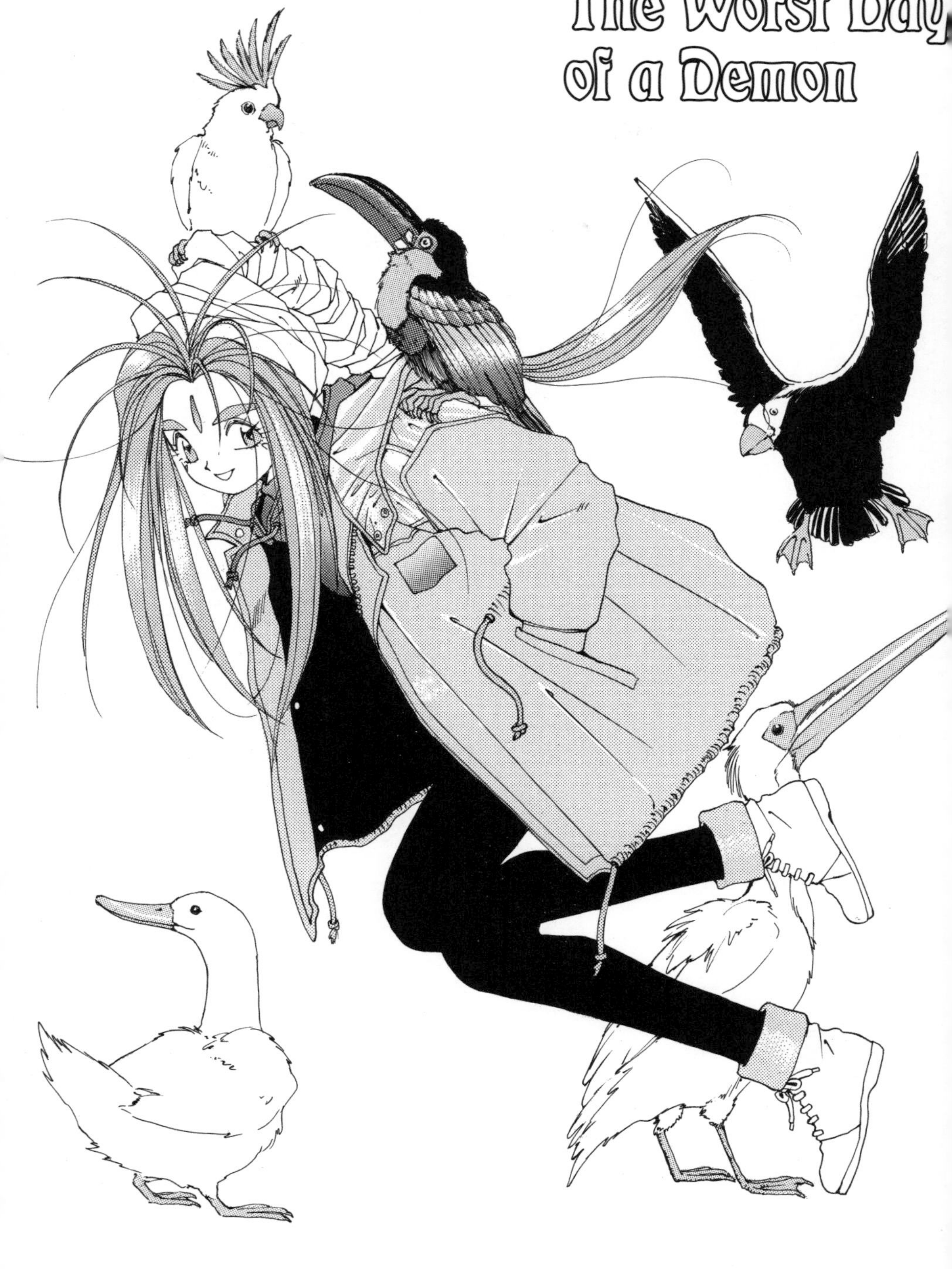

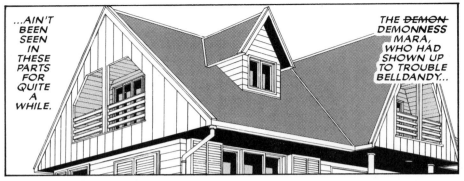

THE ~~DEMON~~ DEMONNESS MARA, WHO HAD SHOWN UP TO TROUBLE BELLDANDY...
...AIN'T BEEN SEEN IN THESE PARTS FOR QUITE A WHILE.
THAT'S 'CAUSE SHE WAS PLUMB TUCKERED OUT, AND RECKONED SHE NEEDED TO REST.
ALL THAT ~~GODLESS~~ GODDESS DANCING URD MADE HER DO.
KREEEK
urg
klunk
hahn
hahn

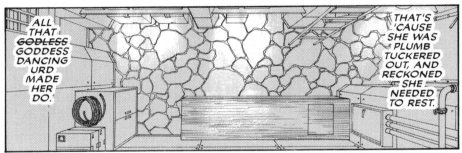

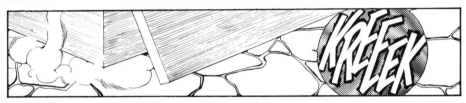

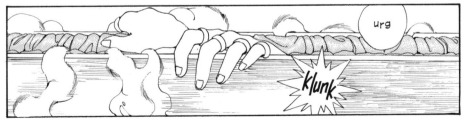

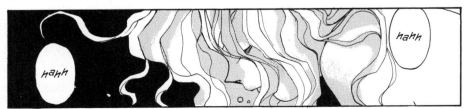

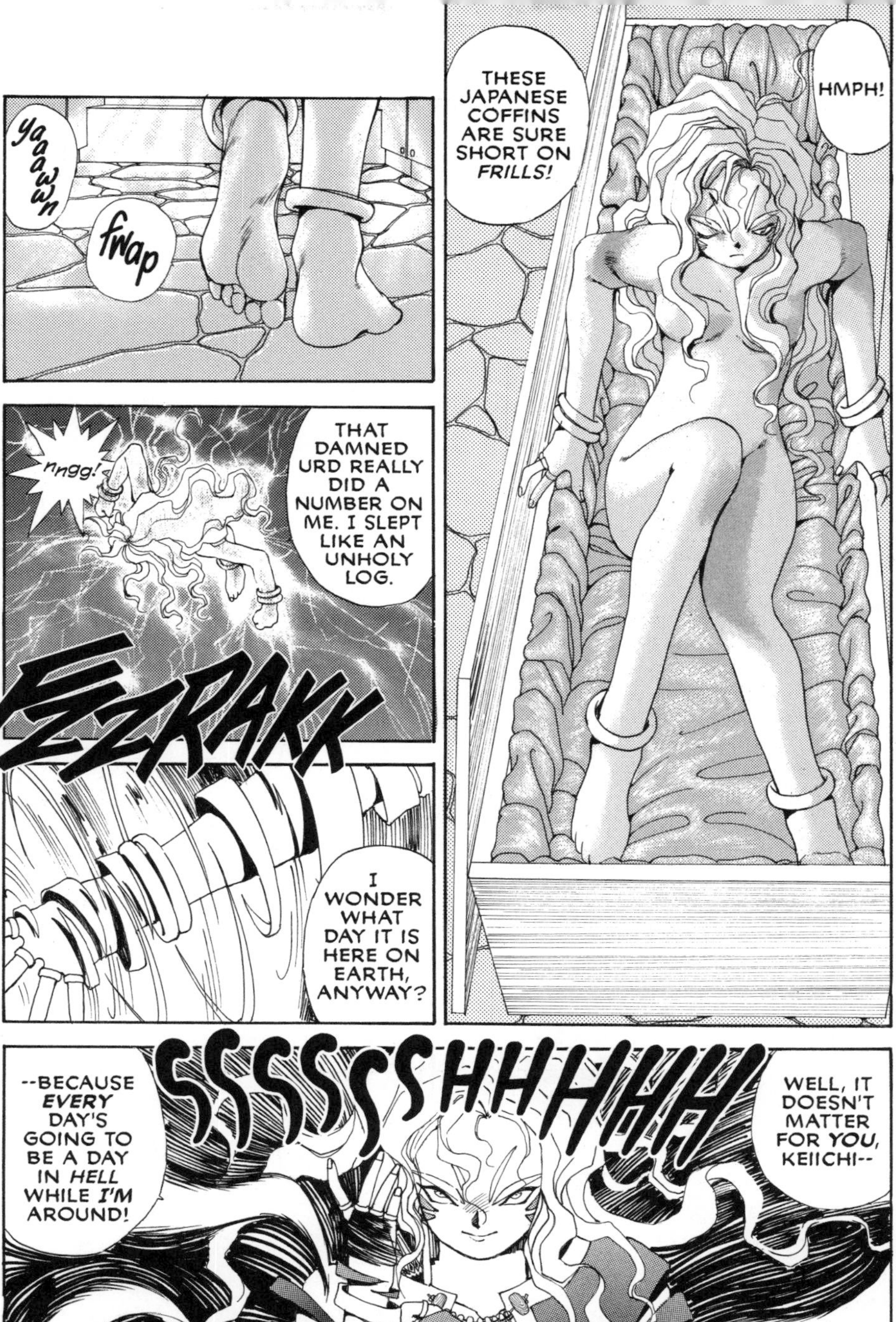
HMPH!
THESE JAPANESE COFFINS ARE SURE SHORT ON *FRILLS!*
yaaawn
fwap
nngg!
THAT DAMNED URD REALLY DID A NUMBER ON ME. I SLEPT LIKE AN UNHOLY LOG.
FZZRAKK
I WONDER WHAT DAY IT IS HERE ON EARTH, ANYWAY?
WELL, IT DOESN'T MATTER FOR *YOU*, KEIICHI--
SSSSSSHHHHHH
--BECAUSE *EVERY* DAY'S GOING TO BE A DAY IN *HELL* WHILE *I'M* AROUND!

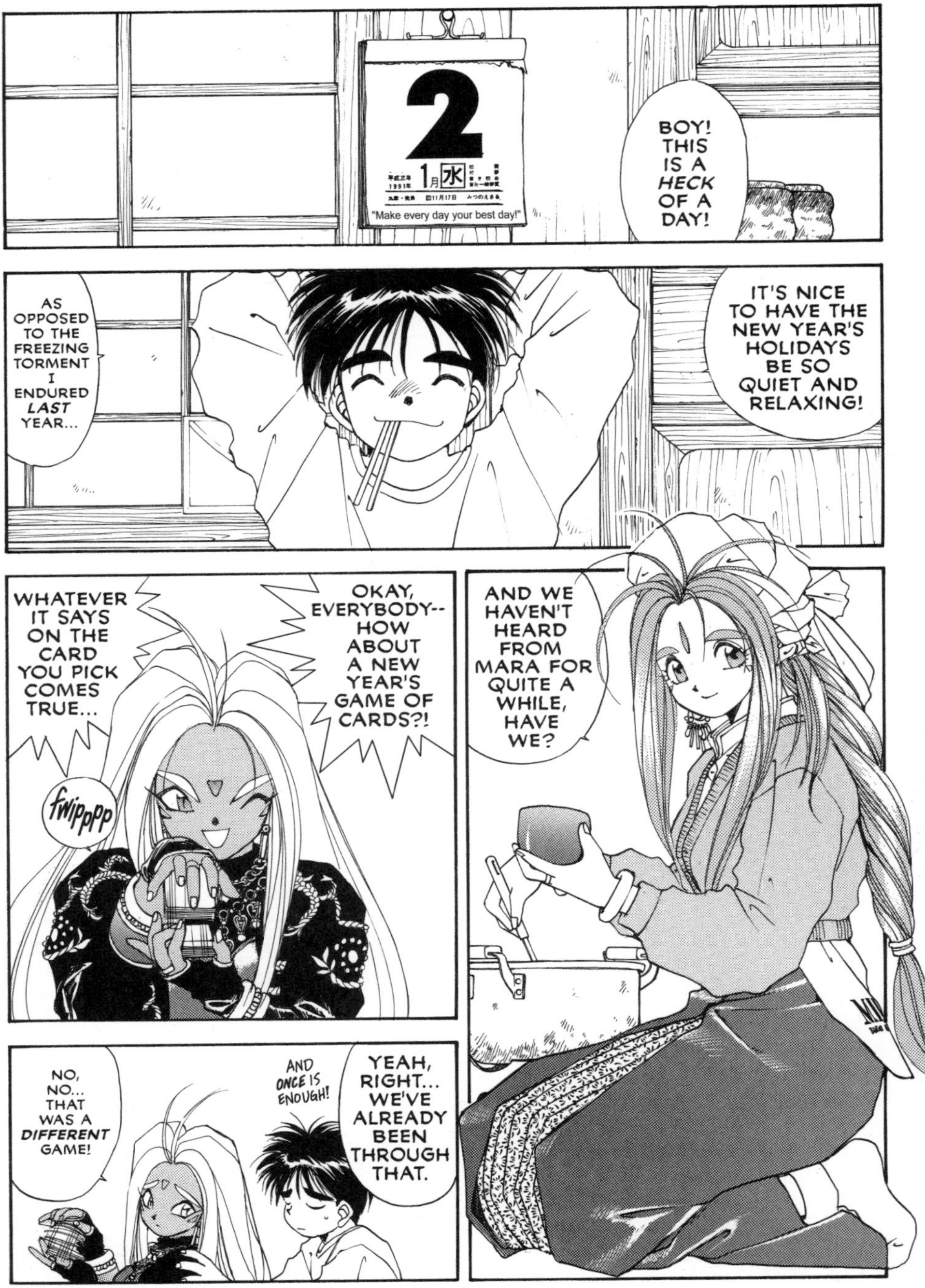
2
1月
水
"Make every day your best day!"
BOY! THIS IS A HECK OF A DAY!
IT'S NICE TO HAVE THE NEW YEAR'S HOLIDAYS BE SO QUIET AND RELAXING!
AS OPPOSED TO THE FREEZING TORMENT I ENDURED LAST YEAR...
AND WE HAVEN'T HEARD FROM MARA FOR QUITE A WHILE, HAVE WE?
OKAY, EVERYBODY-- HOW ABOUT A NEW YEAR'S GAME OF CARDS?!
WHATEVER IT SAYS ON THE CARD YOU PICK COMES TRUE...
fwipppp
YEAH, RIGHT... WE'VE ALREADY BEEN THROUGH THAT.
AND ONCE IS ENOUGH!
NO, NO... THAT WAS A DIFFERENT GAME!

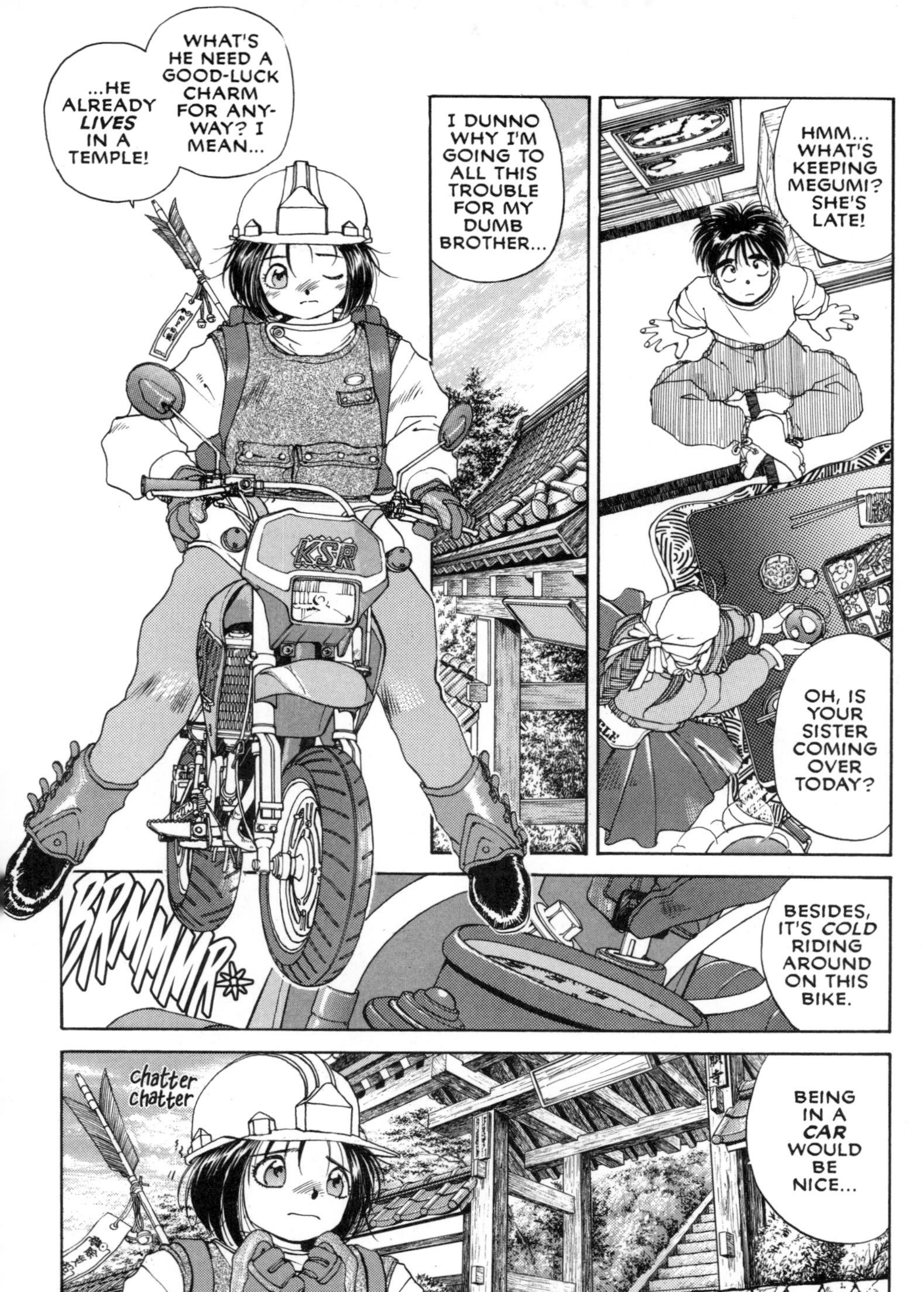
HMM... WHAT'S KEEPING MEGUMI? SHE'S LATE!
OH, IS YOUR SISTER COMING OVER TODAY?
I DUNNO WHY I'M GOING TO ALL THIS TROUBLE FOR MY DUMB BROTHER...
WHAT'S HE NEED A GOOD-LUCK CHARM FOR ANY-WAY? I MEAN...
...HE ALREADY *LIVES* IN A TEMPLE!
BESIDES, IT'S *COLD* RIDING AROUND ON THIS BIKE.
BRMMMMR
KSR
BEING IN A *CAR* WOULD BE NICE...
chatter chatter

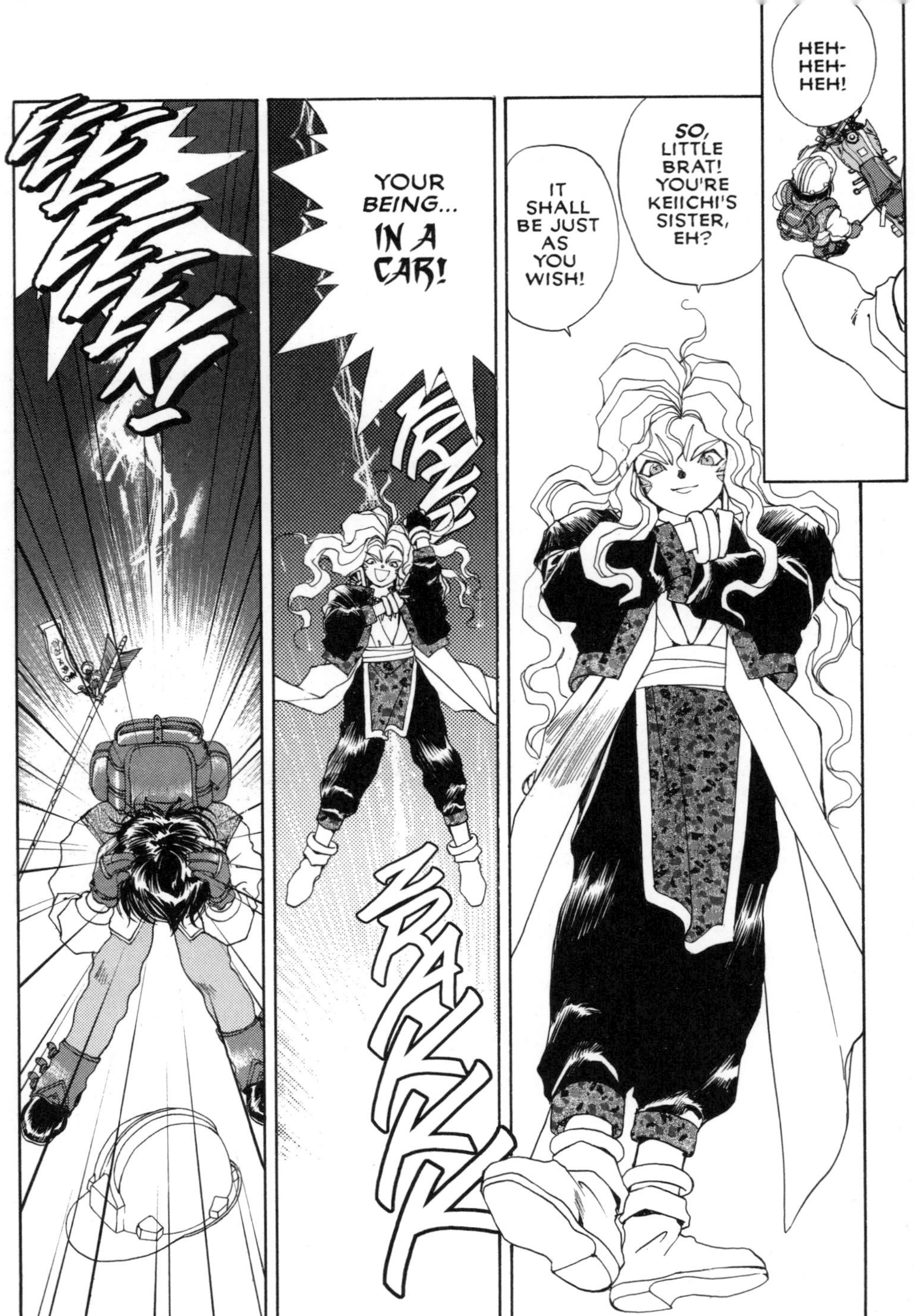
HEH-HEH-HEH!
SO, LITTLE BRAT! YOU'RE KEIICHI'S SISTER, EH?
IT SHALL BE JUST AS YOU WISH!
YOUR BEING... IN A CAR!

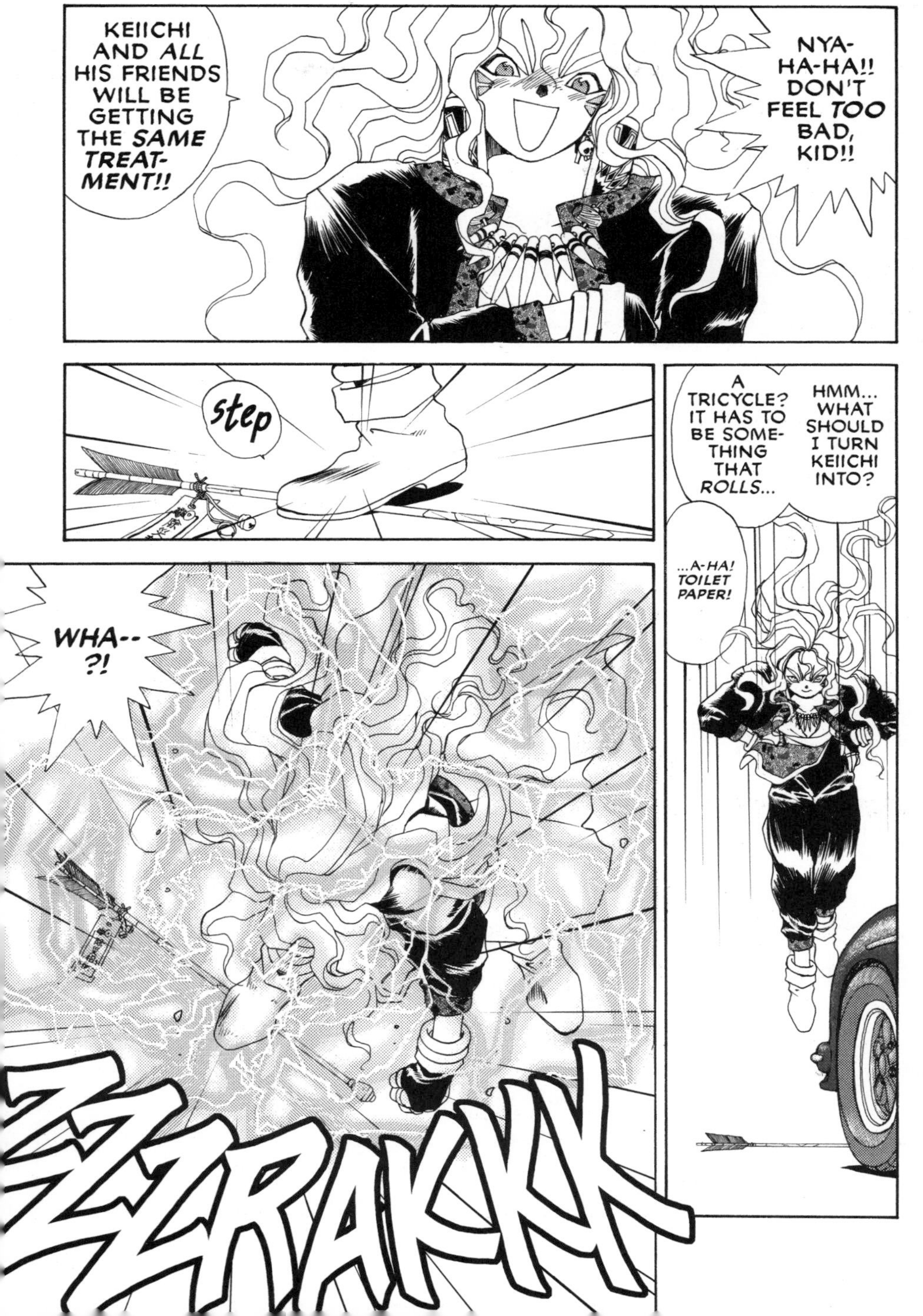
NYA-HA-HA!! DON'T FEEL *TOO* BAD, KID!!
KEIICHI AND *ALL* HIS FRIENDS WILL BE GETTING THE *SAME TREATMENT!!*
HMM... WHAT SHOULD I TURN KEIICHI INTO?
A TRICYCLE? IT HAS TO BE SOMETHING THAT *ROLLS*...
...A-HA! *TOILET PAPER!*
step
*WHA-- ?!*
ZZRAKKK

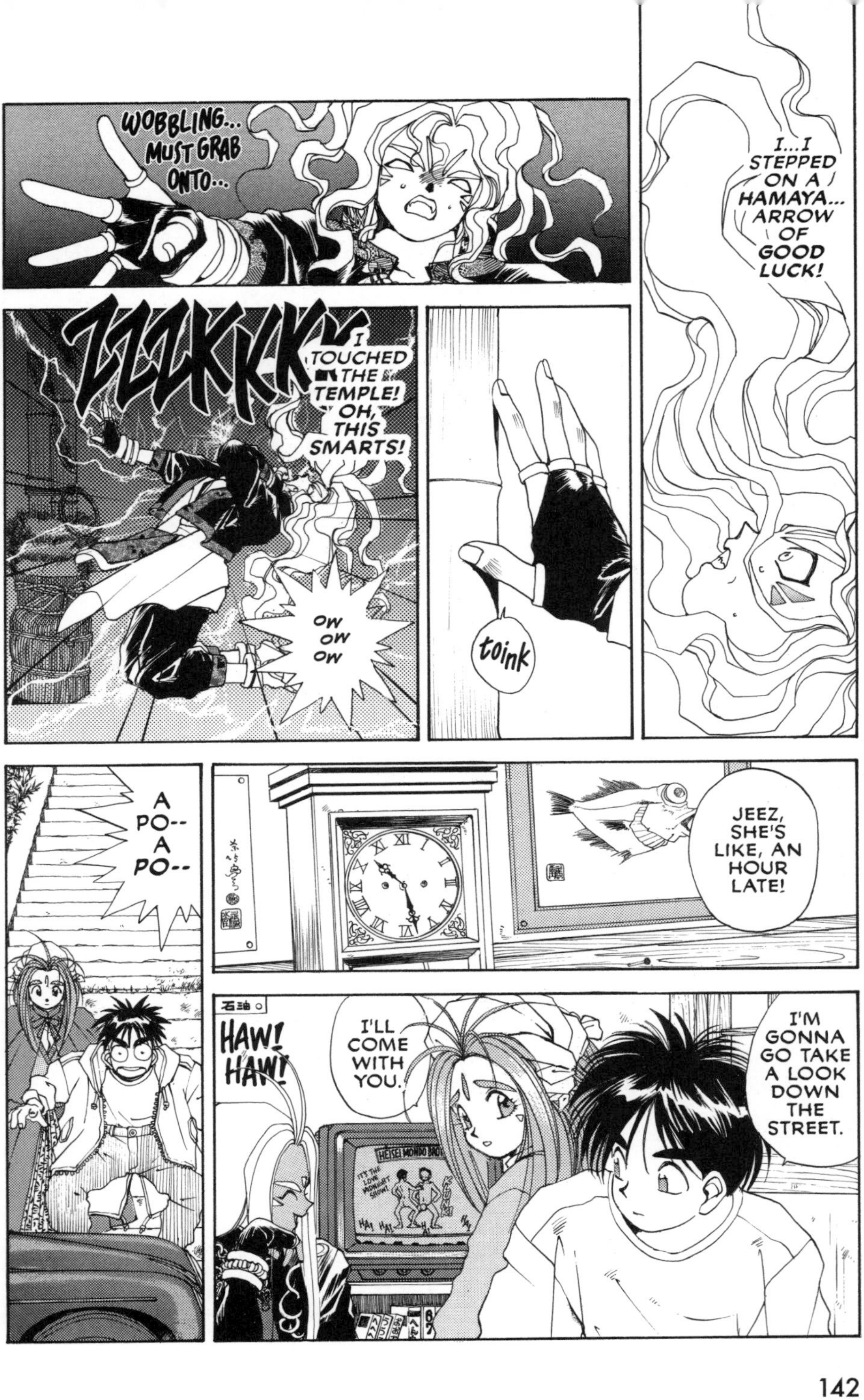
I...I STEPPED ON A HAMAYA... ARROW OF GOOD LUCK!
WOBBLING... MUST GRAB ONTO...
toink
ZZZKKKK
I TOUCHED THE TEMPLE! OH, THIS SMARTS!
OW OW OW
JEEZ, SHE'S LIKE, AN HOUR LATE!
I'M GONNA GO TAKE A LOOK DOWN THE STREET.
I'LL COME WITH YOU.
HAW! HAW!
A PO-- A PO--

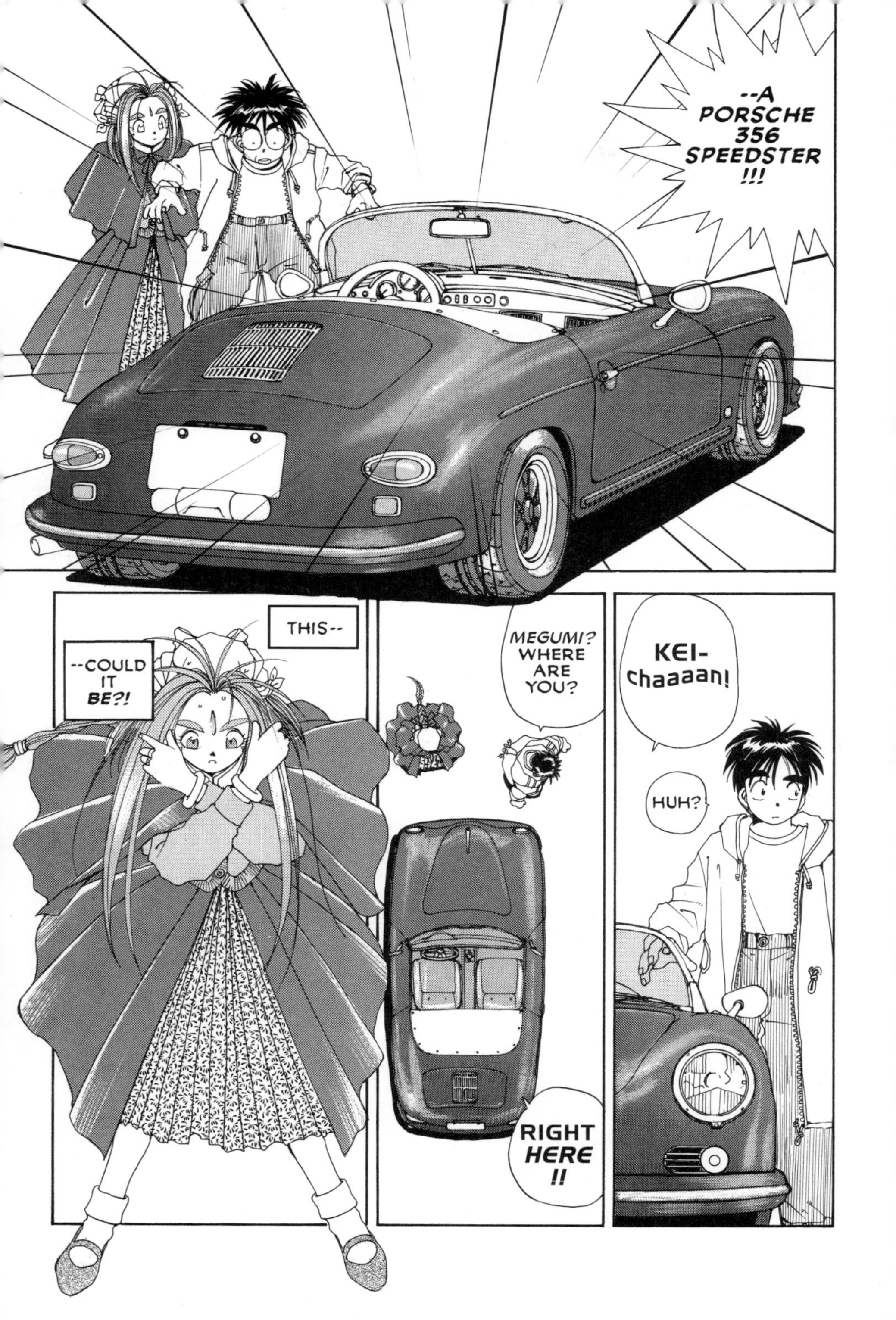
--A PORSCHE 356 SPEEDSTER !!!
KEI-chaaaan!
HUH?
MEGUMI? WHERE ARE YOU?
RIGHT HERE !!
THIS--
--COULD IT BE?!

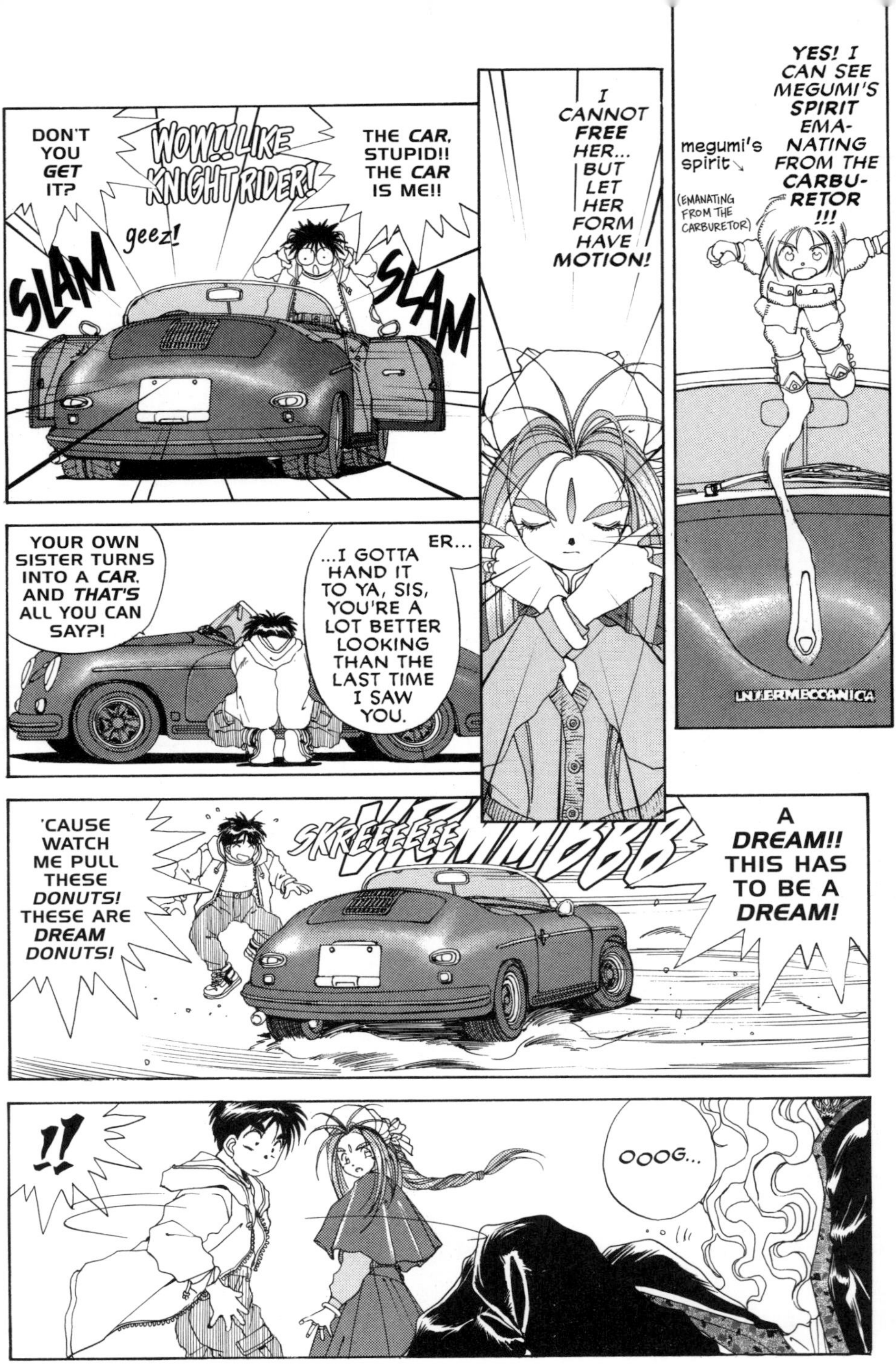
YES! I CAN SEE MEGUMI'S SPIRIT EMANATING FROM THE CARBURETOR !!!
megumi's spirit
(EMANATING FROM THE CARBURETOR)
UNIERMECCANICA
I CANNOT FREE HER... BUT LET HER FORM HAVE MOTION!
THE CAR, STUPID!! THE CAR IS ME!!
WOW!! LIKE KNIGHT RIDER!
DON'T YOU GET IT?
SLAM
geez!
SLAM
ER...
...I GOTTA HAND IT TO YA, SIS, YOU'RE A LOT BETTER LOOKING THAN THE LAST TIME I SAW YOU.
YOUR OWN SISTER TURNS INTO A CAR. AND THAT'S ALL YOU CAN SAY?!
A DREAM!! THIS HAS TO BE A DREAM!
VRMMMBBB
SKREEEEEEE
'CAUSE WATCH ME PULL THESE DONUTS! THESE ARE DREAM DONUTS!
OOOG...
!!

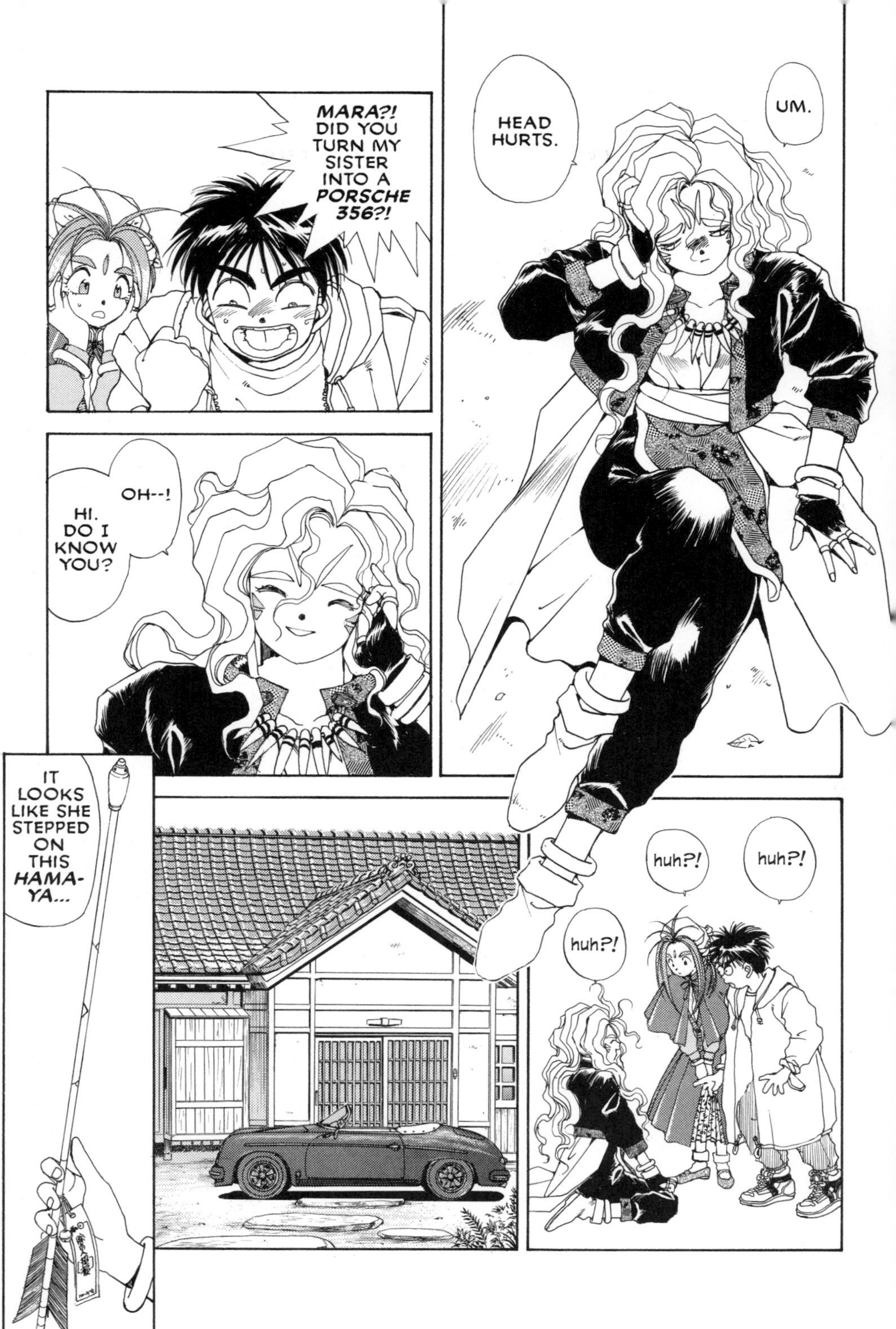
UM.
HEAD HURTS.
*MARA?!* DID YOU TURN MY SISTER INTO A *PORSCHE 356?!*
OH--!
HI. DO I KNOW YOU?
huh?!
huh?!
huh?!
IT LOOKS LIKE SHE STEPPED ON THIS *HAMA-YA...*

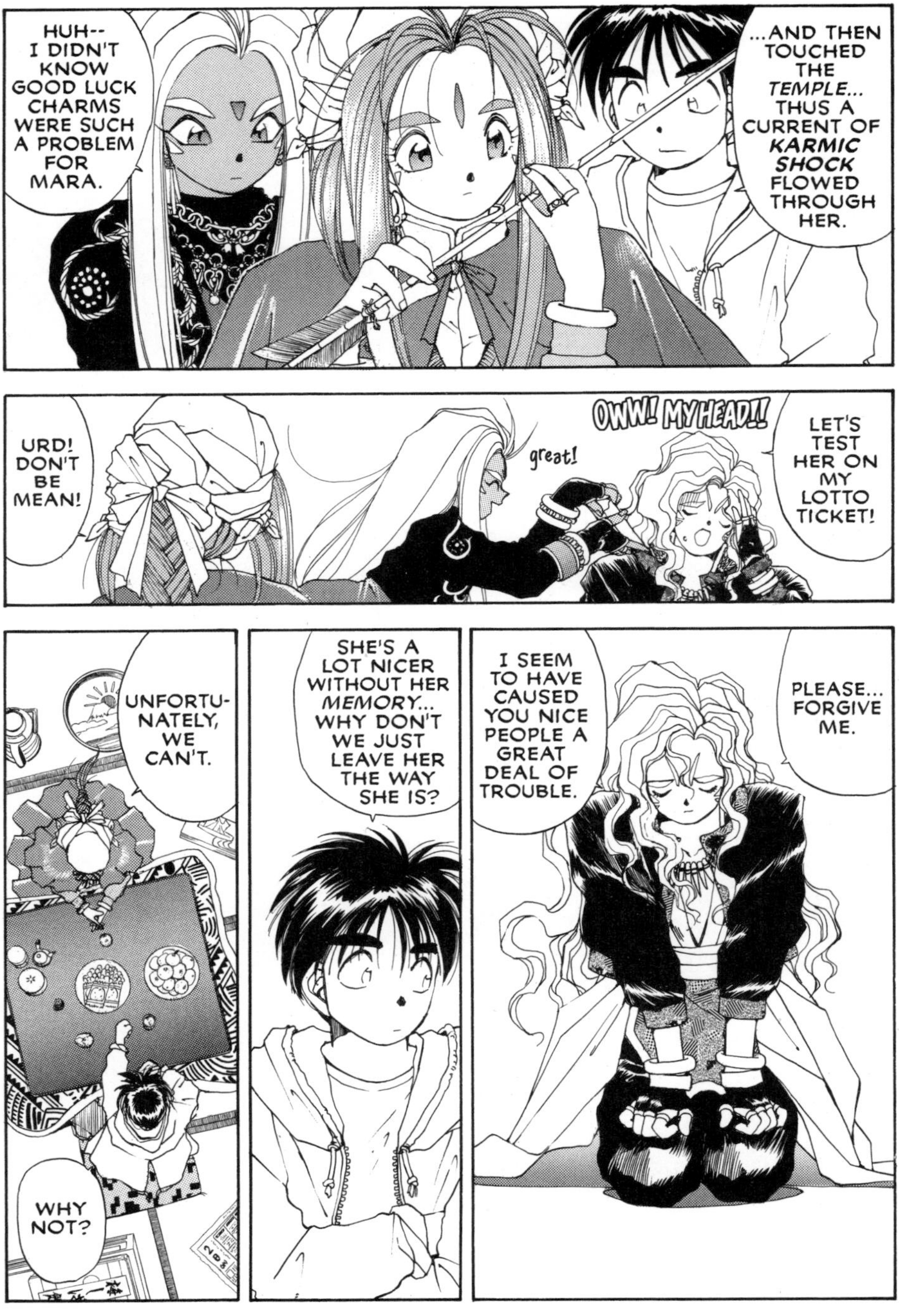
...AND THEN TOUCHED THE *TEMPLE*... THUS A CURRENT OF ***KARMIC SHOCK*** FLOWED THROUGH HER.
HUH-- I DIDN'T KNOW GOOD LUCK CHARMS WERE SUCH A PROBLEM FOR MARA.
LET'S TEST HER ON MY LOTTO TICKET!
OWW! MY HEAD!!
great!
URD! DON'T BE MEAN!
PLEASE... FORGIVE ME.
I SEEM TO HAVE CAUSED YOU NICE PEOPLE A GREAT DEAL OF TROUBLE.
SHE'S A LOT NICER WITHOUT HER *MEMORY*... WHY DON'T WE JUST LEAVE HER THE WAY SHE IS?
UNFORTUNATELY, WE CAN'T.
WHY NOT?

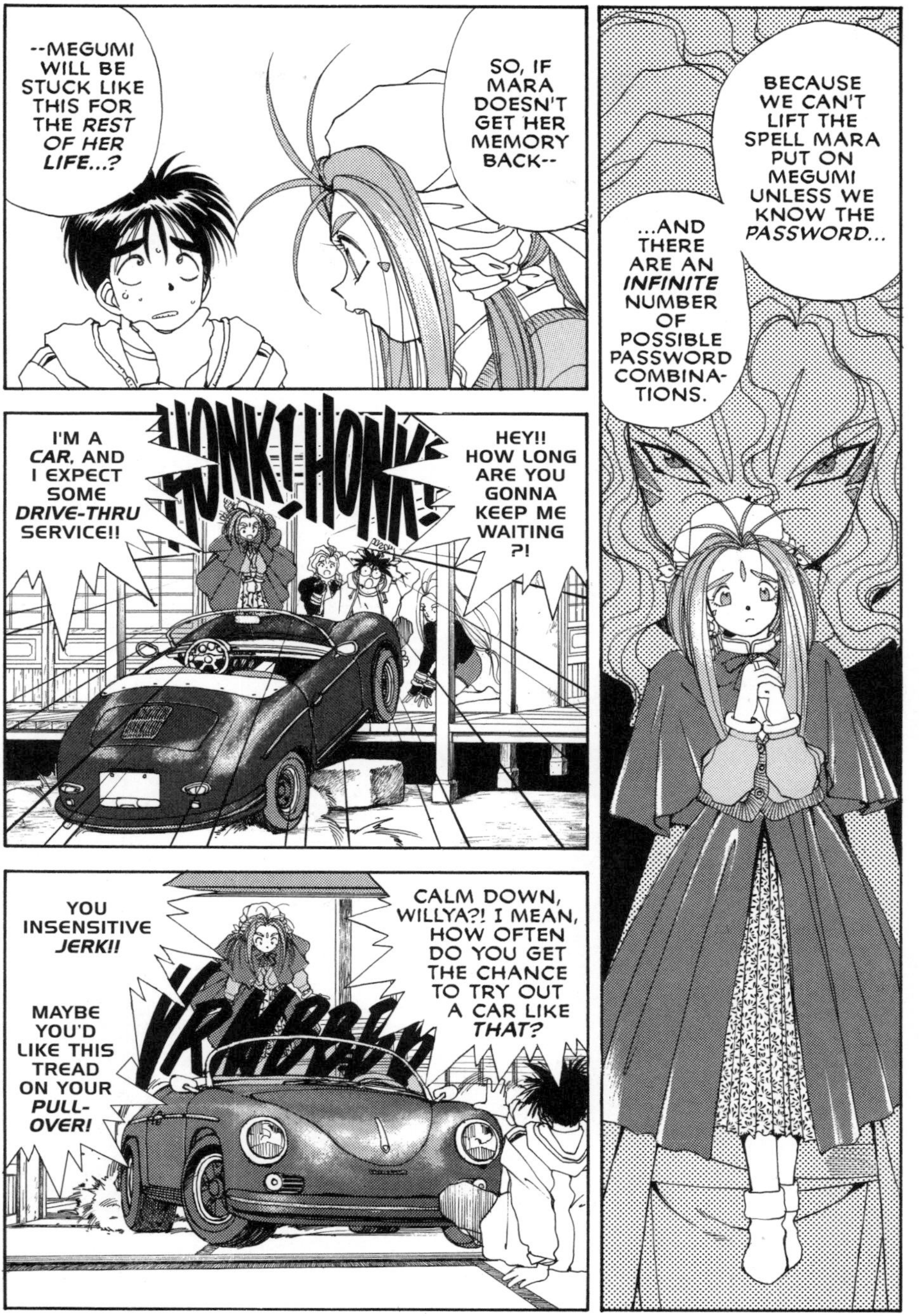
BECAUSE WE CAN'T LIFT THE SPELL MARA PUT ON MEGUMI UNLESS WE KNOW THE *PASSWORD...*
...AND THERE ARE AN *INFINITE* NUMBER OF POSSIBLE PASSWORD COMBINATIONS.
SO, IF MARA DOESN'T GET HER MEMORY BACK--
--MEGUMI WILL BE STUCK LIKE THIS FOR THE *REST OF HER LIFE...?*
HONK! HONK!
HEY!! HOW LONG ARE YOU GONNA KEEP ME WAITING ?!
I'M A *CAR*, AND I EXPECT SOME *DRIVE-THRU* SERVICE!!
CALM DOWN, WILLYA?! I MEAN, HOW OFTEN DO YOU GET THE CHANCE TO TRY OUT A CAR LIKE *THAT?*
YOU INSENSITIVE *JERK!!*
MAYBE YOU'D LIKE THIS TREAD ON YOUR *PULL-OVER!*

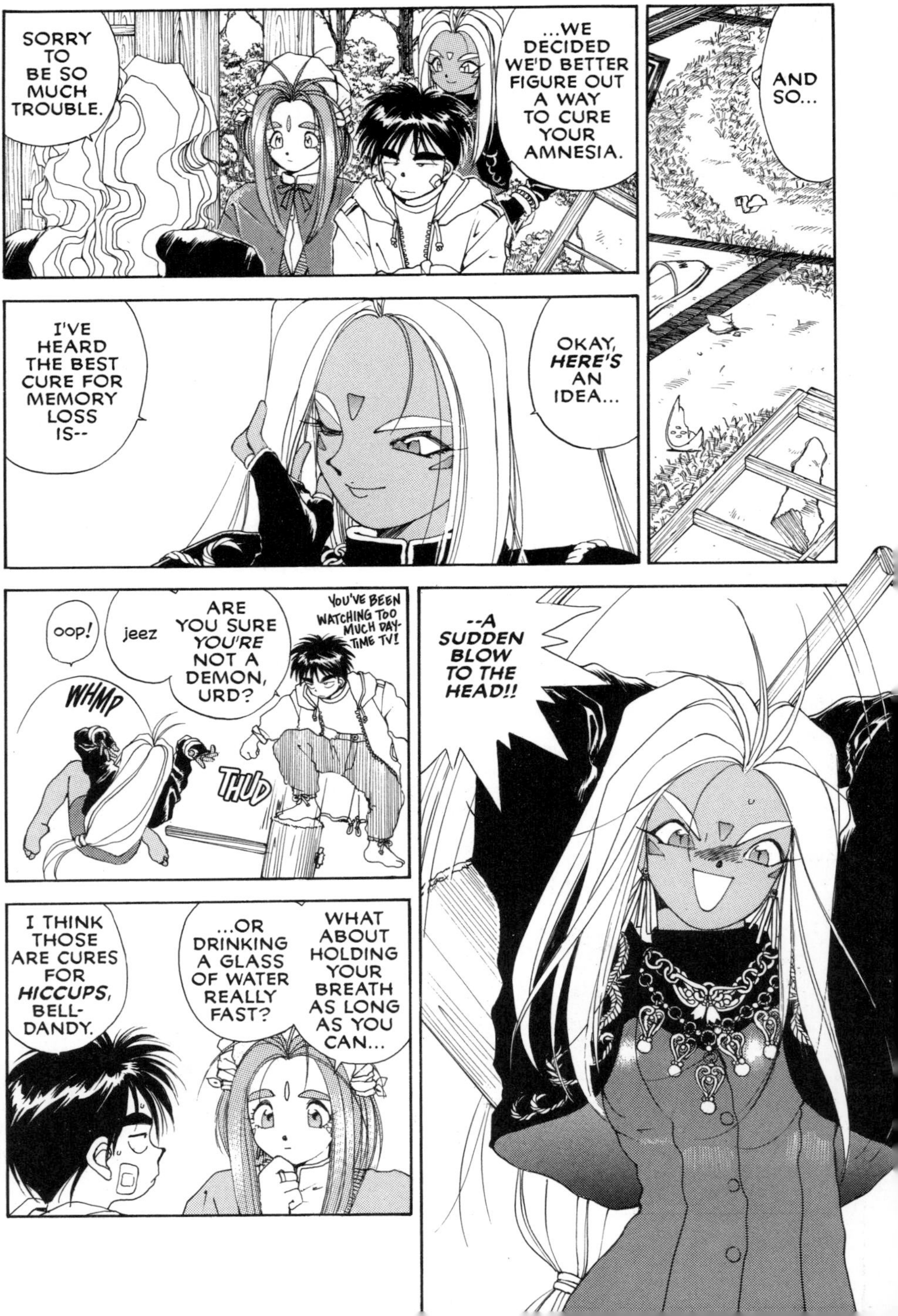
AND SO...
...WE DECIDED WE'D BETTER FIGURE OUT A WAY TO CURE YOUR AMNESIA.
SORRY TO BE SO MUCH TROUBLE.
OKAY, HERE'S AN IDEA...
I'VE HEARD THE BEST CURE FOR MEMORY LOSS IS--
--A SUDDEN BLOW TO THE HEAD!!
YOU'VE BEEN WATCHING TOO MUCH DAY-TIME TV!
ARE YOU SURE YOU'RE NOT A DEMON, URD?
jeez
oop!
WHMP
THUD
WHAT ABOUT HOLDING YOUR BREATH AS LONG AS YOU CAN...
...OR DRINKING A GLASS OF WATER REALLY FAST?
I THINK THOSE ARE CURES FOR HICCUPS, BELL-DANDY.

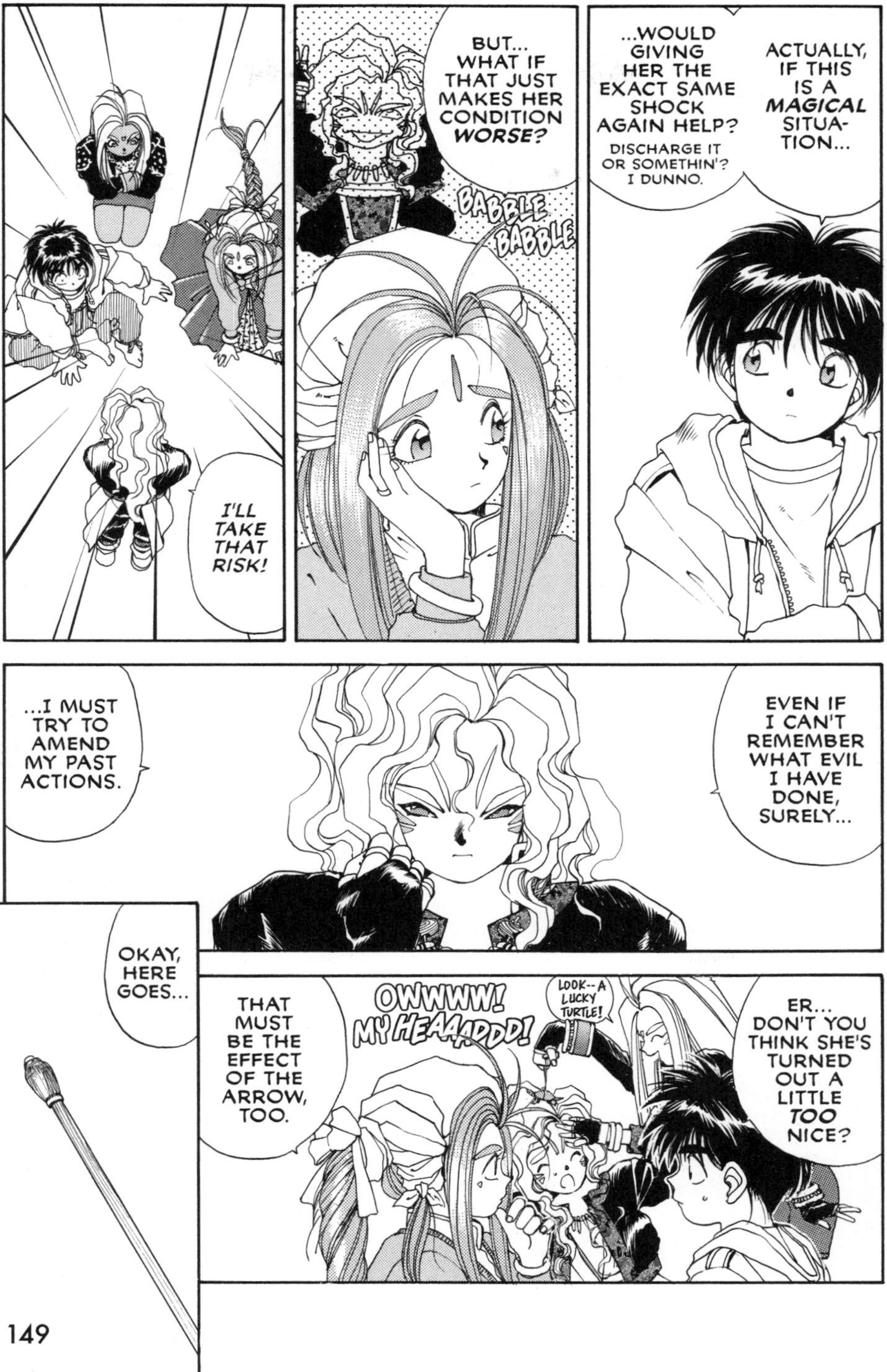
ACTUALLY, IF THIS IS A *MAGICAL* SITUATION...
...WOULD GIVING HER THE EXACT SAME SHOCK AGAIN HELP?
DISCHARGE IT OR SOMETHIN'? I DUNNO.
BUT... WHAT IF THAT JUST MAKES HER CONDITION ***WORSE?***
BABBLE BABBLE
*I'LL TAKE THAT RISK!*
EVEN IF I CAN'T REMEMBER WHAT EVIL I HAVE DONE, SURELY...
...I MUST TRY TO AMEND MY PAST ACTIONS.
ER... DON'T YOU THINK SHE'S TURNED OUT A LITTLE ***TOO*** NICE?
LOOK--A LUCKY TURTLE!
OWWWW! MY HEAAADDD!
THAT MUST BE THE EFFECT OF THE ARROW, TOO.
OKAY, HERE GOES...

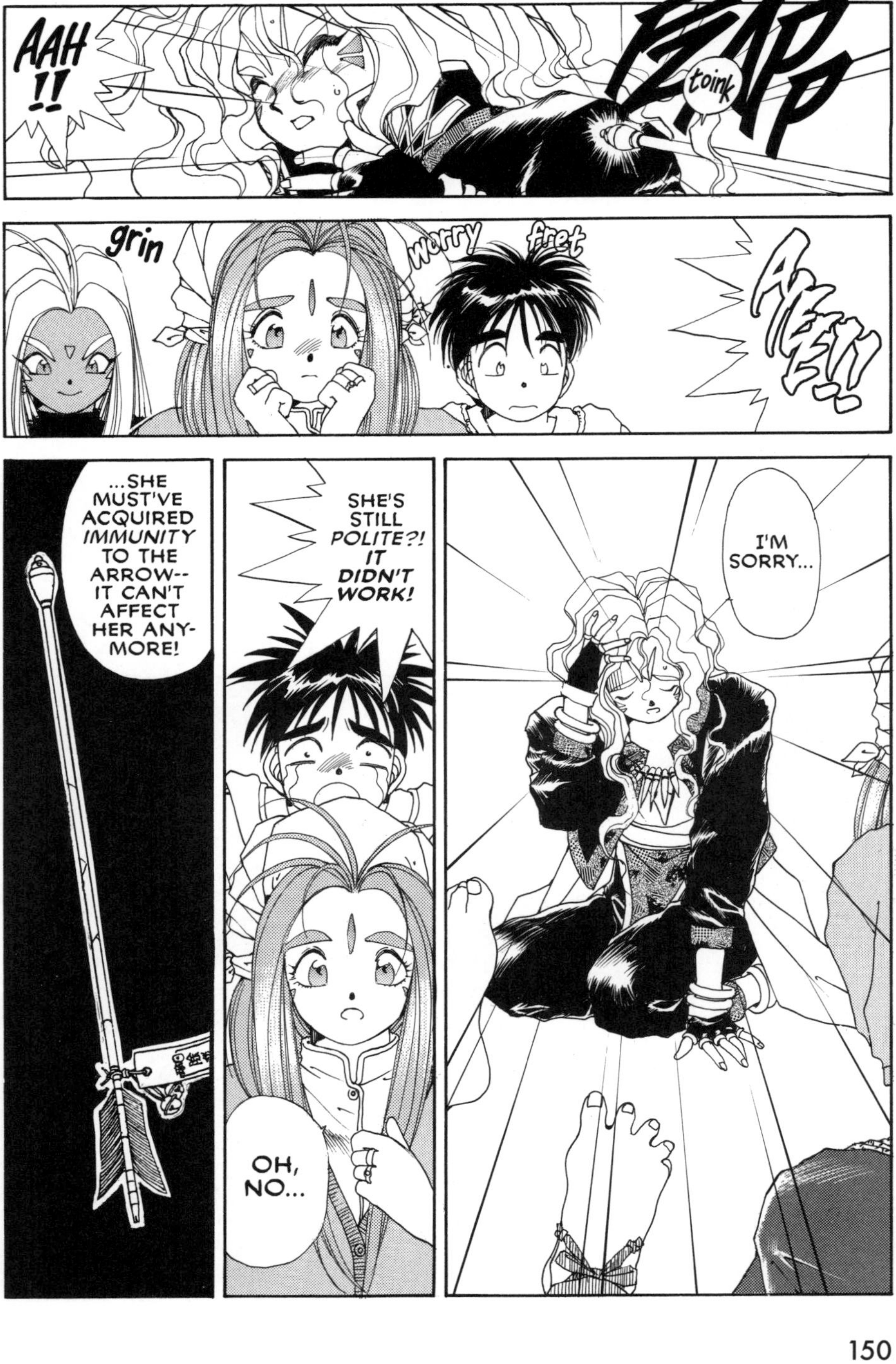
FZAPP
toink
AAH !!
AIEE!!
fret
worry
grin
I'M SORRY...
SHE'S STILL POLITE?! IT DIDN'T WORK!
OH, NO...
...SHE MUST'VE ACQUIRED IMMUNITY TO THE ARROW-- IT CAN'T AFFECT HER ANY-MORE!

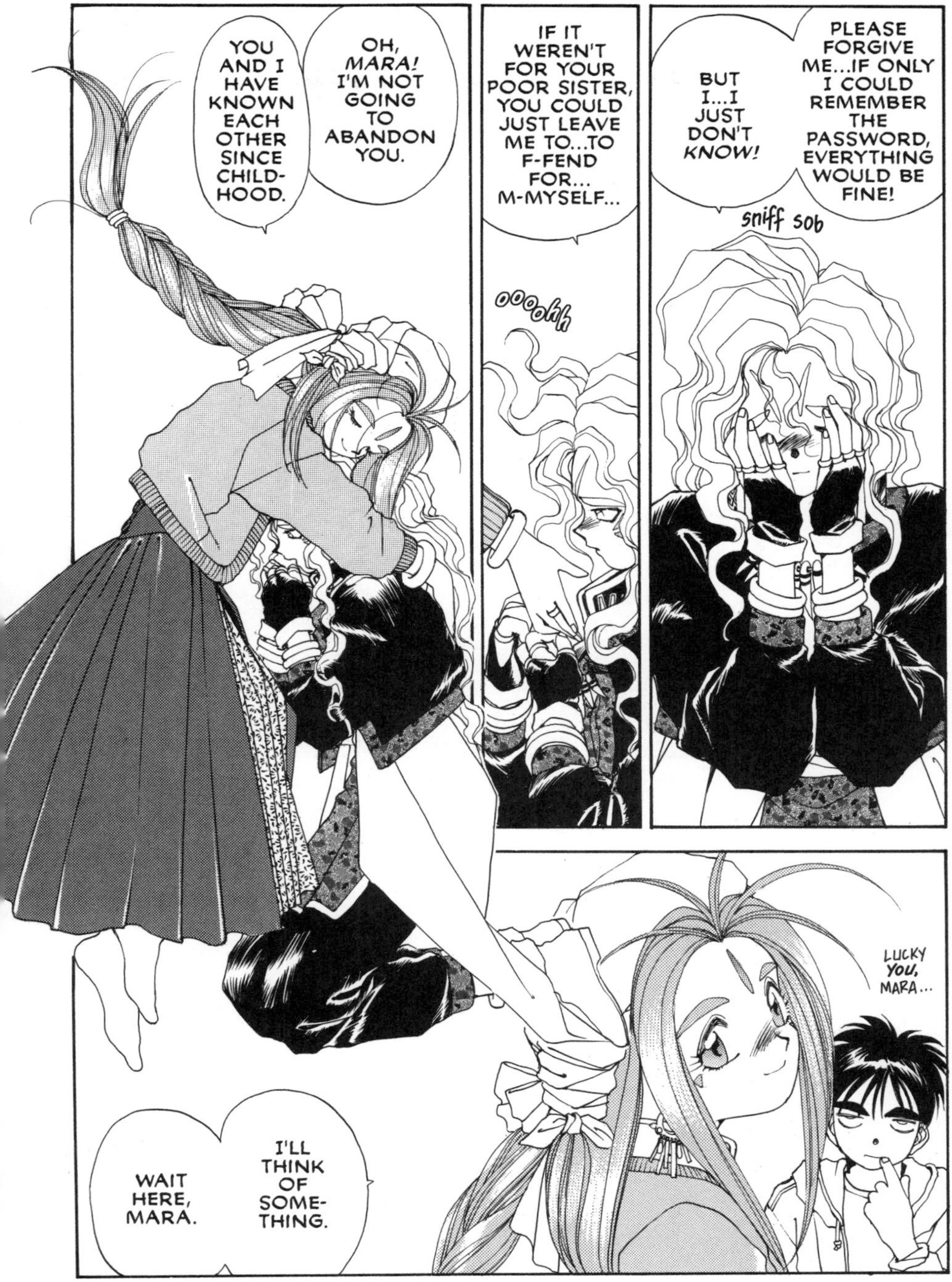

PLEASE FORGIVE ME...IF ONLY I COULD REMEMBER THE PASSWORD, EVERYTHING WOULD BE FINE!
BUT I...I JUST DON'T *KNOW!*
sniff sob
IF IT WEREN'T FOR YOUR POOR SISTER, YOU COULD JUST LEAVE ME TO...TO F-FEND FOR... M-MYSELF...
ooohh
OH, *MARA!* I'M NOT GOING TO ABANDON YOU.
YOU AND I HAVE KNOWN EACH OTHER SINCE CHILD-HOOD.
LUCKY *YOU,* MARA...
I'LL THINK OF SOME-THING.
WAIT HERE, MARA.

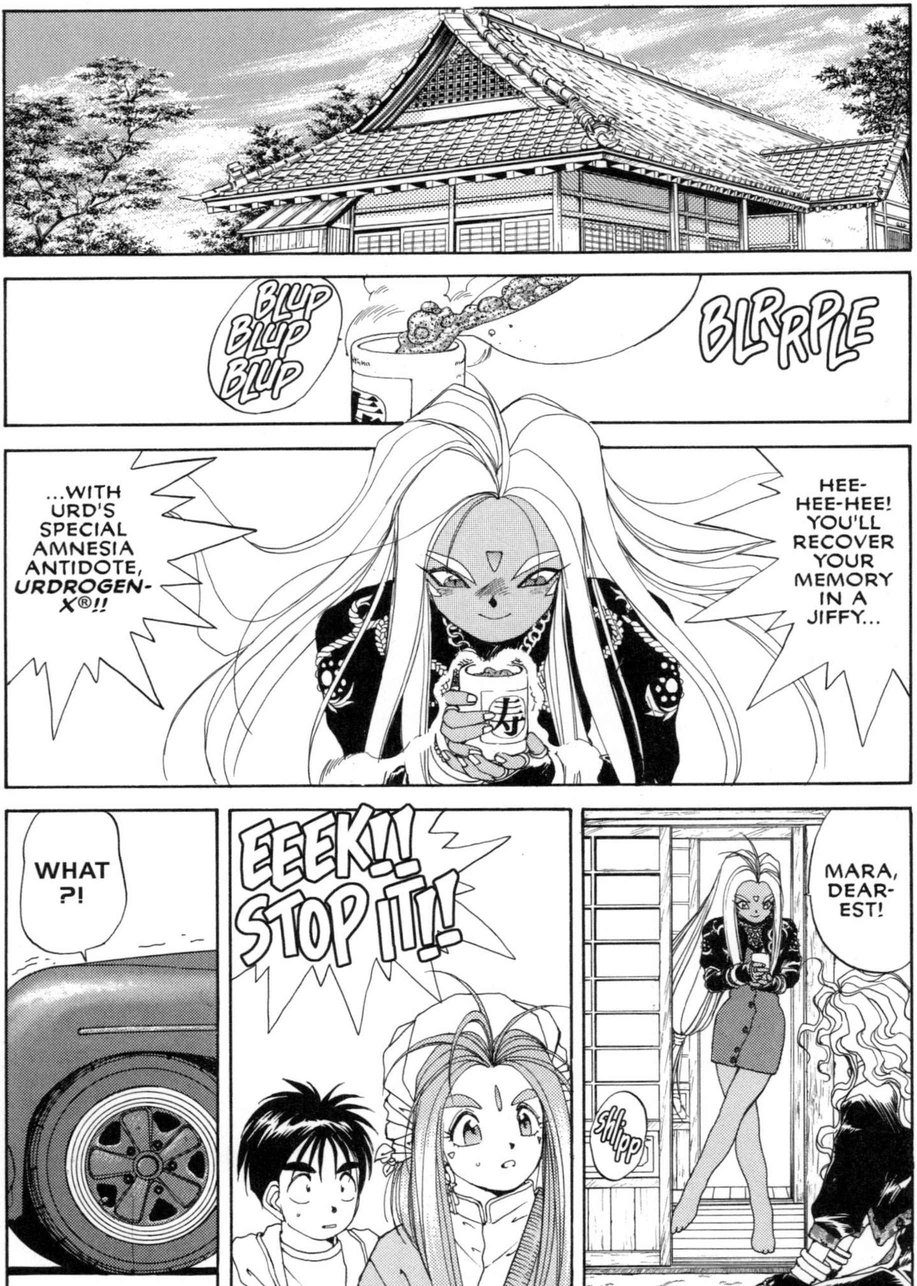
BLRRPLE
BLUP BLUP BLUP
HEE-HEE-HEE! YOU'LL RECOVER YOUR MEMORY IN A JIFFY...
...WITH URD'S SPECIAL AMNESIA ANTIDOTE, URDROGEN-X®!!
MARA, DEAREST!
SHIPP
EEEK!! STOP IT!!
WHAT ?!

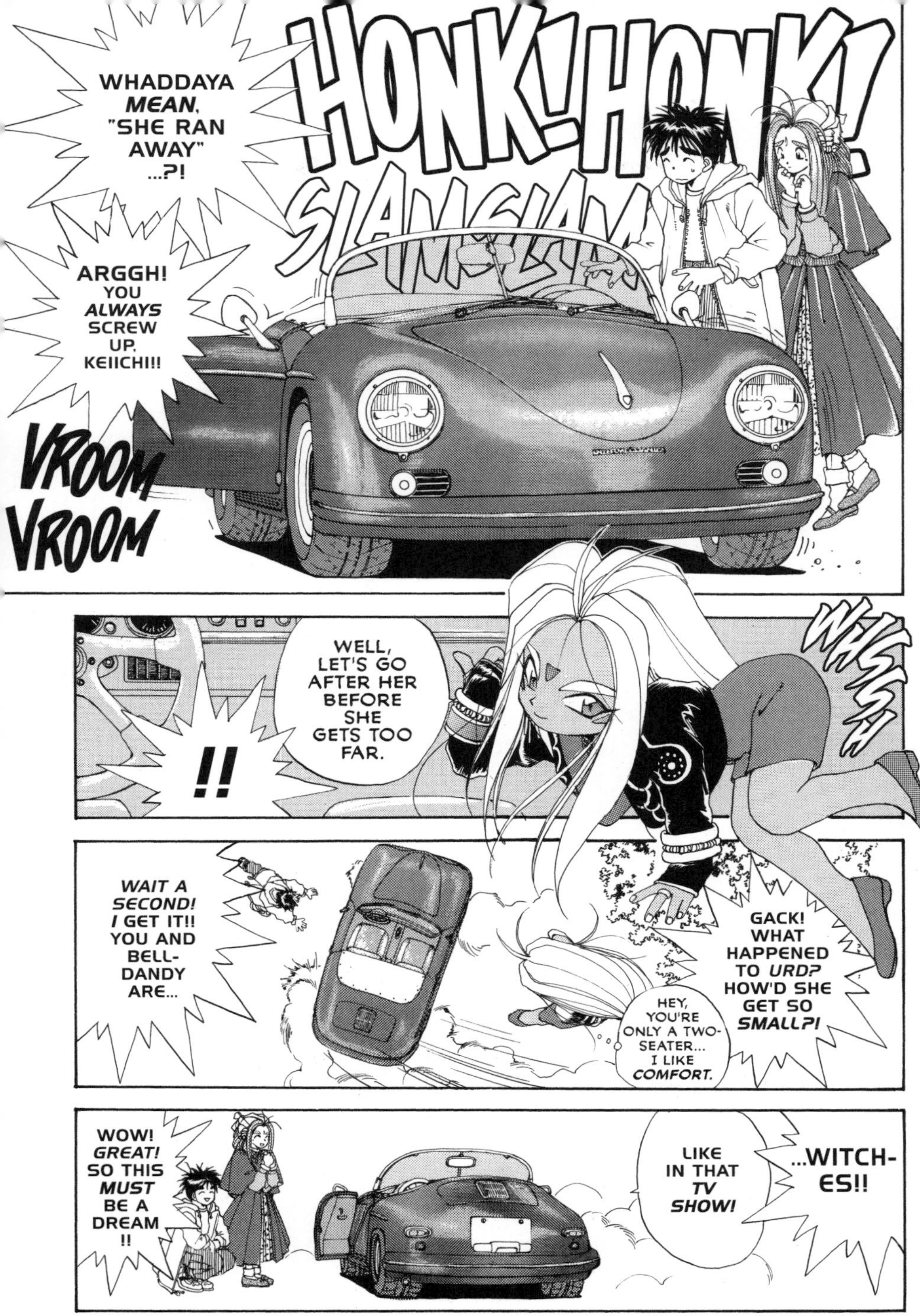

HONK! HONK!
SLAM SLAM
WHADDAYA MEAN, "SHE RAN AWAY" ...?!
ARGGH! YOU ALWAYS SCREW UP, KEIICHI!!
VROOM VROOM
WHSSSH
WELL, LET'S GO AFTER HER BEFORE SHE GETS TOO FAR.
!!
GACK! WHAT HAPPENED TO URD? HOW'D SHE GET SO SMALL?!
HEY, YOU'RE ONLY A TWO-SEATER... I LIKE COMFORT.
WAIT A SECOND! I GET IT!! YOU AND BELL-DANDY ARE...
...WITCH-ES!!
LIKE IN THAT TV SHOW!
WOW! GREAT! SO THIS MUST BE A DREAM !!

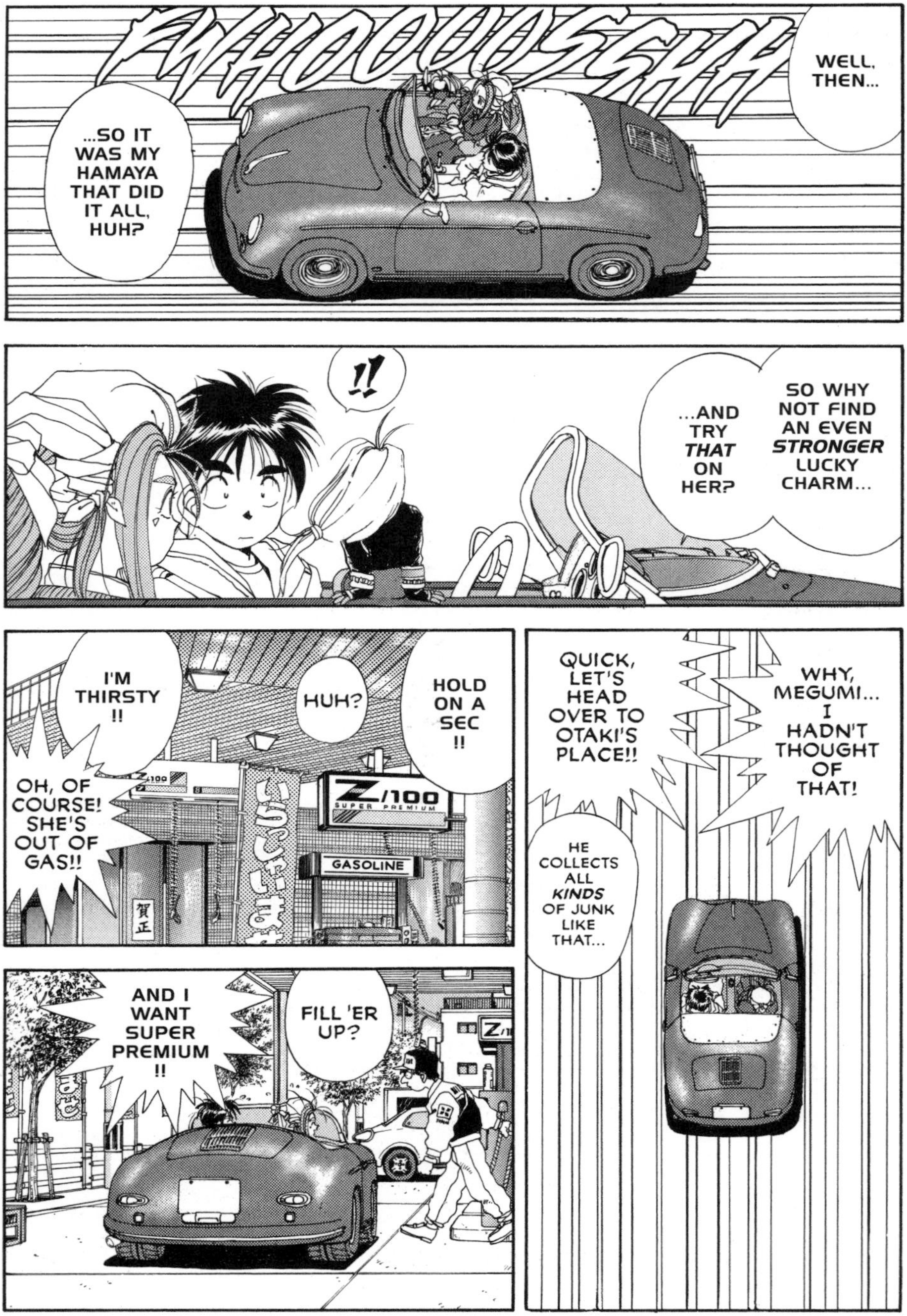
WELL, THEN...
FWHOOOOSSHH
...SO IT WAS MY HAMAYA THAT DID IT ALL, HUH?
SO WHY NOT FIND AN EVEN *STRONGER* LUCKY CHARM...
...AND TRY *THAT* ON HER?
!!
WHY, MEGUMI... I HADN'T THOUGHT OF THAT!
QUICK, LET'S HEAD OVER TO OTAKI'S PLACE!!
HE COLLECTS ALL *KINDS* OF JUNK LIKE THAT...
HOLD ON A SEC !!
HUH?
I'M THIRSTY !!
OH, OF COURSE! SHE'S OUT OF GAS!!
Z/100 SUPER PREMIUM
GASOLINE
FILL 'ER UP?
AND I WANT SUPER PREMIUM !!

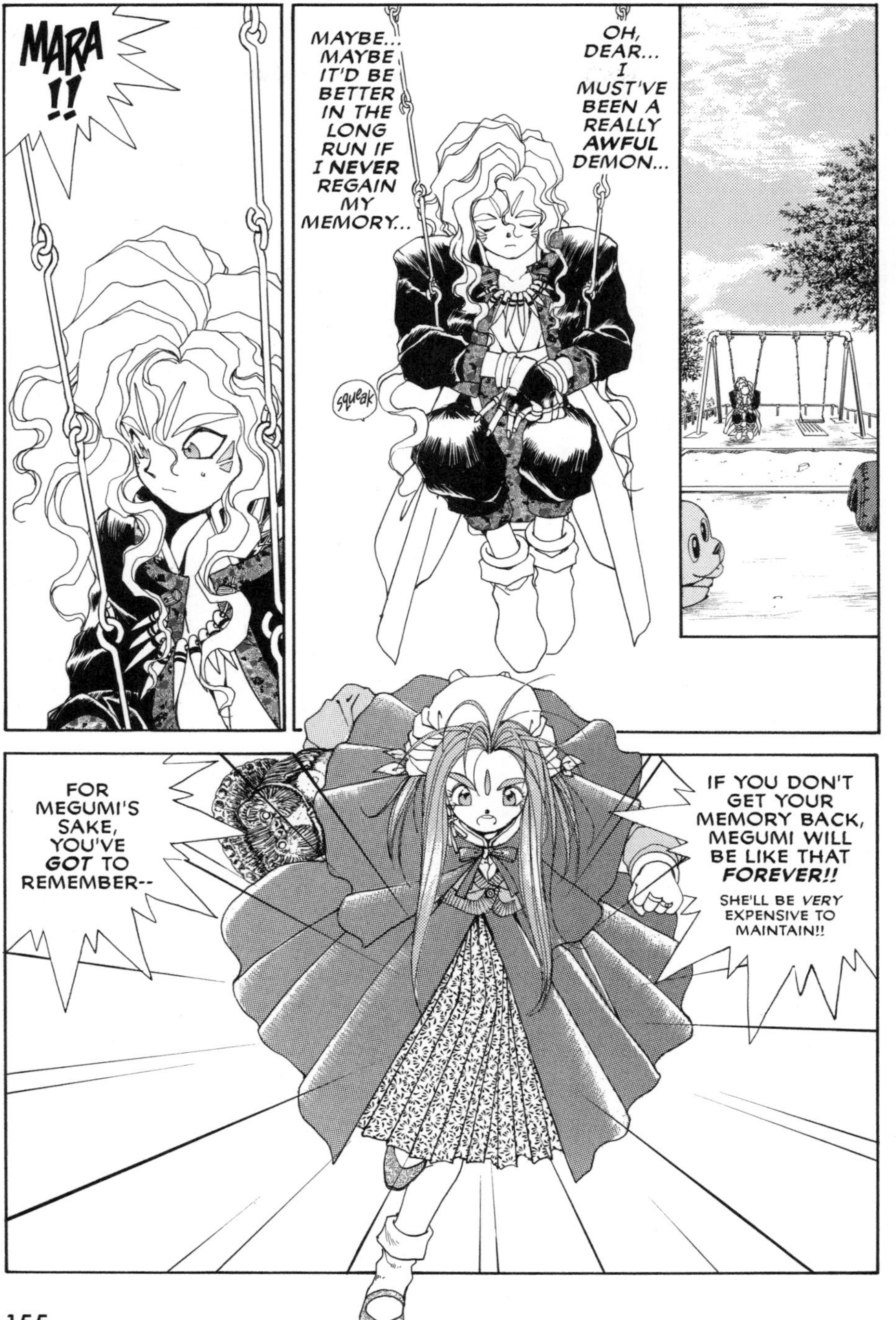
OH, DEAR... I MUST'VE BEEN A REALLY AWFUL DEMON...
MAYBE... MAYBE IT'D BE BETTER IN THE LONG RUN IF I NEVER REGAIN MY MEMORY...
squeak
MARA!!
IF YOU DON'T GET YOUR MEMORY BACK, MEGUMI WILL BE LIKE THAT FOREVER!!
SHE'LL BE VERY EXPENSIVE TO MAINTAIN!!
FOR MEGUMI'S SAKE, YOU'VE GOT TO REMEMBER--

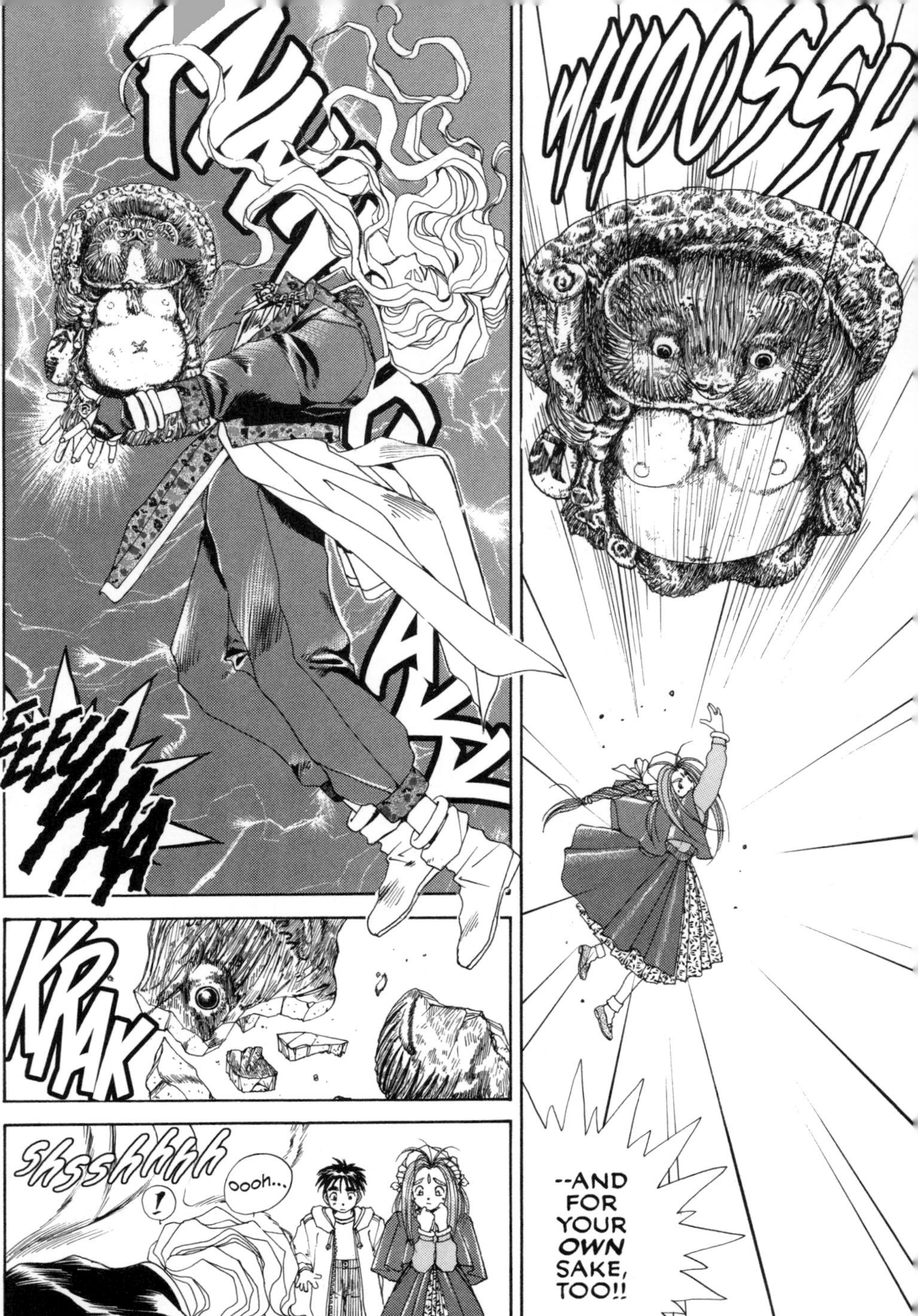
WHOOSSH
--AND FOR YOUR *OWN* SAKE, TOO!!
KRAK
Shsshhhh
!
oooh...

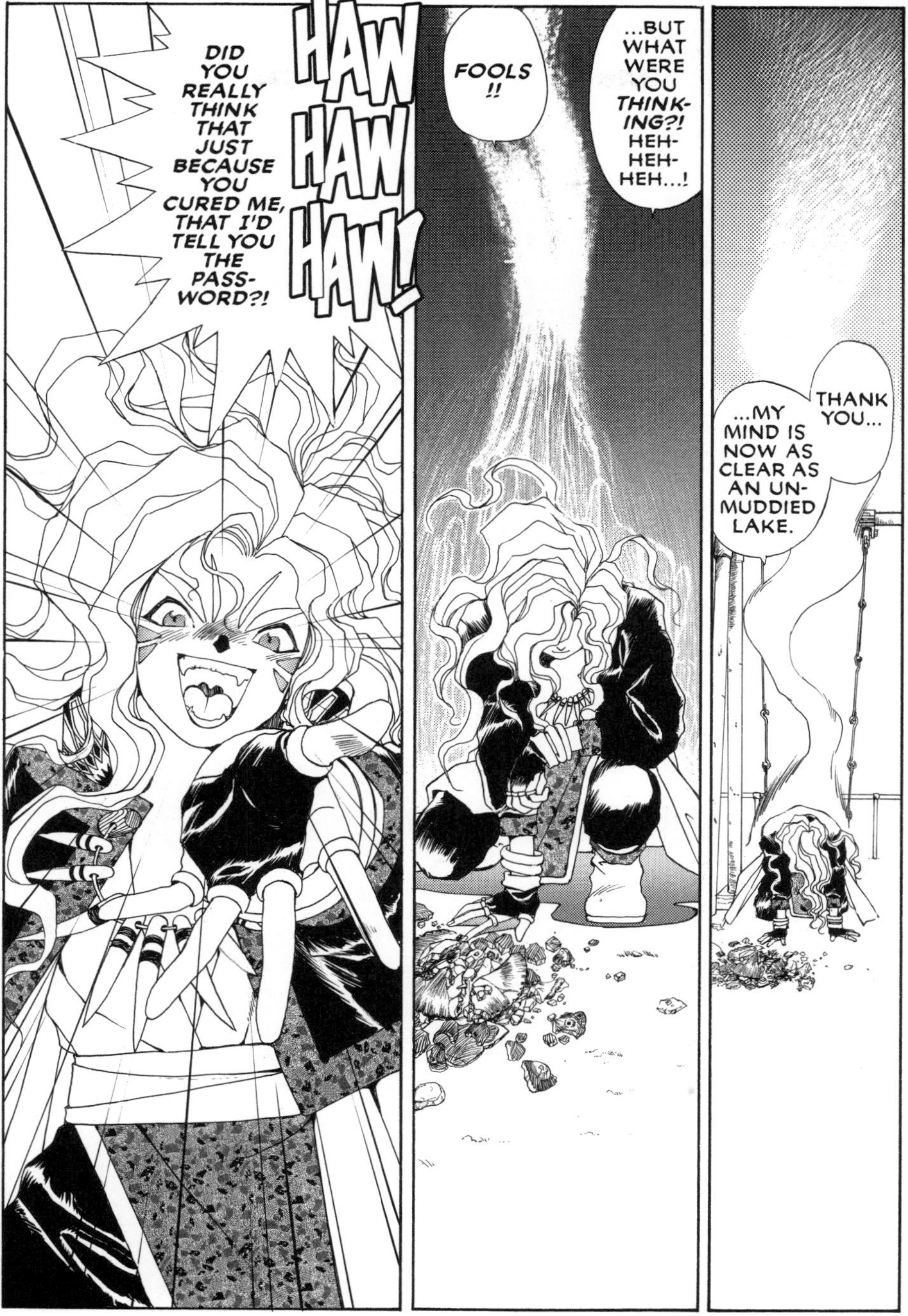
THANK YOU...
...MY MIND IS NOW AS CLEAR AS AN UN-MUDDIED LAKE.
...BUT WHAT WERE YOU THINKING?! HEH-HEH-HEH...!
FOOLS!!
HAW HAW HAW!
DID YOU REALLY THINK THAT JUST BECAUSE YOU CURED ME, THAT I'D TELL YOU THE PASS-WORD?!

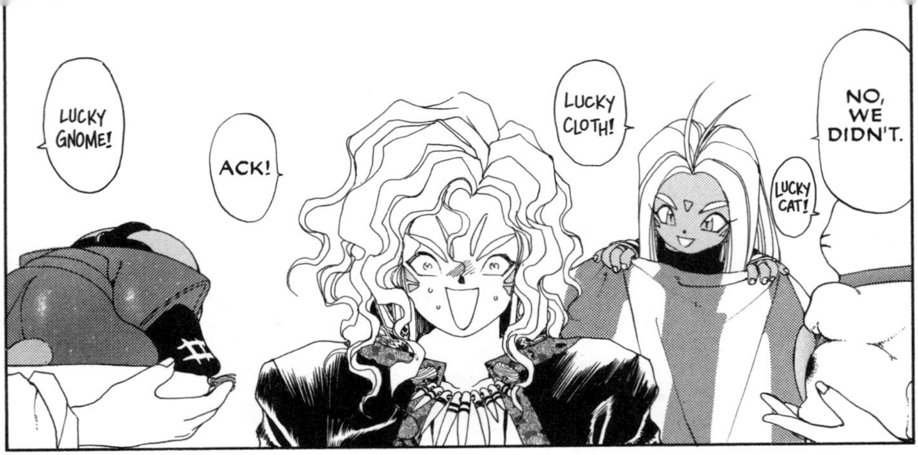
NO, WE DIDN'T.
LUCKY CAT!
LUCKY CLOTH!
ACK!
LUCKY GNOME!

ONE PASSWORD LATER

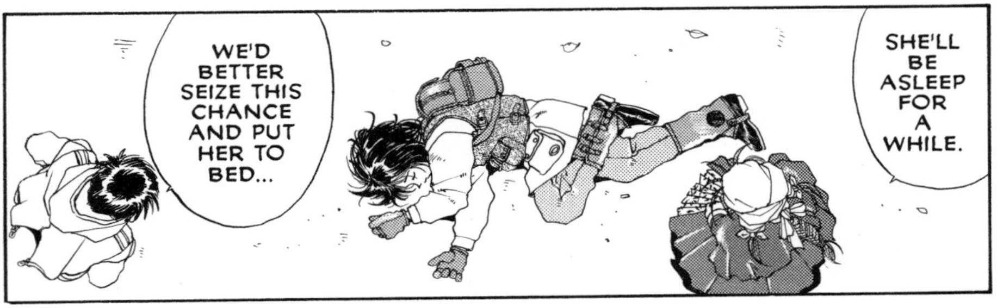
SHE'LL BE ASLEEP FOR A WHILE.
WE'D BETTER SEIZE THIS CHANCE AND PUT HER TO BED...

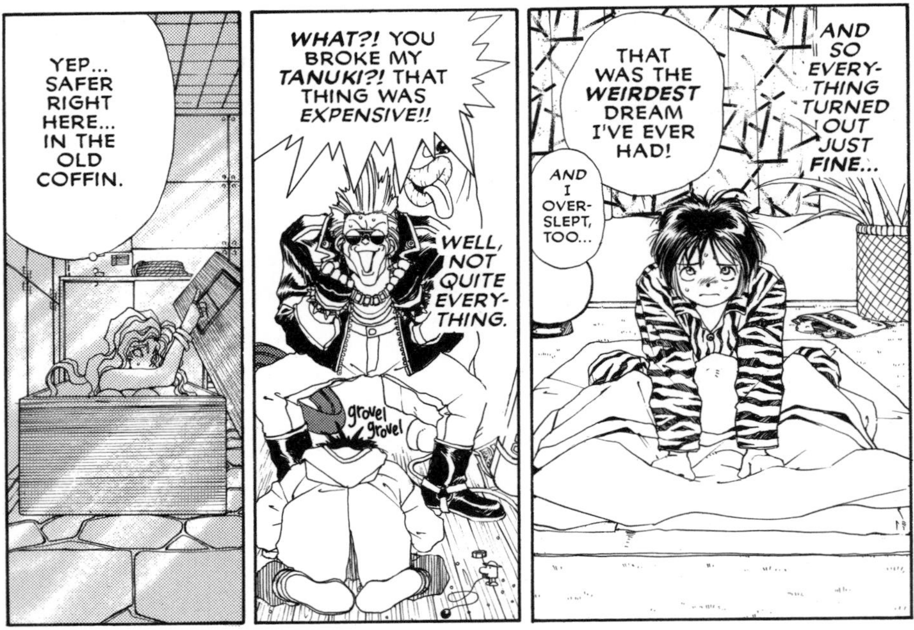
AND SO EVERY-THING TURNED OUT JUST *FINE*...
THAT WAS THE *WEIRDEST* DREAM I'VE EVER HAD!
AND I OVER-SLEPT, TOO...
*WHAT?!* YOU BROKE MY *TANUKI?!* THAT THING WAS *EXPENSIVE!!*
*WELL, NOT QUITE EVERY-THING.*
grovel grovel
YEP... SAFER RIGHT HERE... IN THE OLD COFFIN.

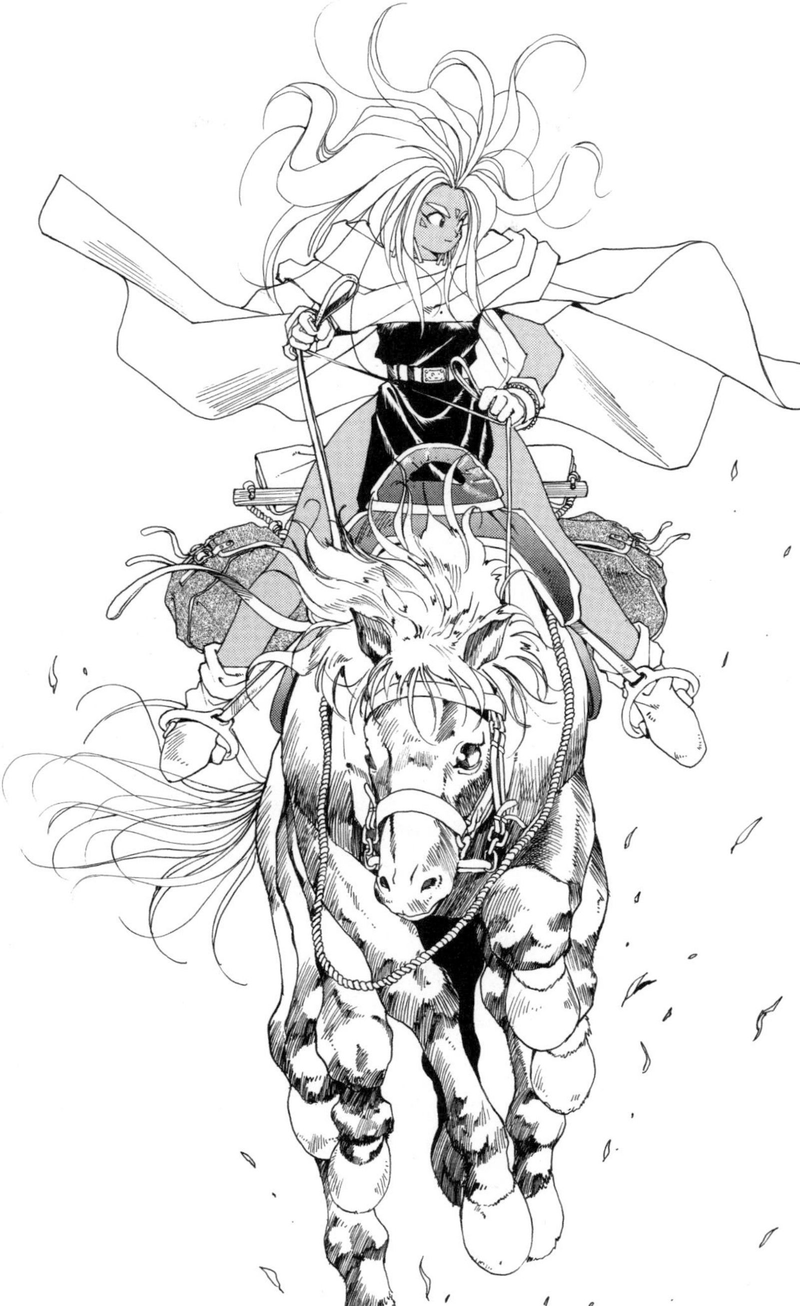

CHAPTER 30

# Engine o' Mystery

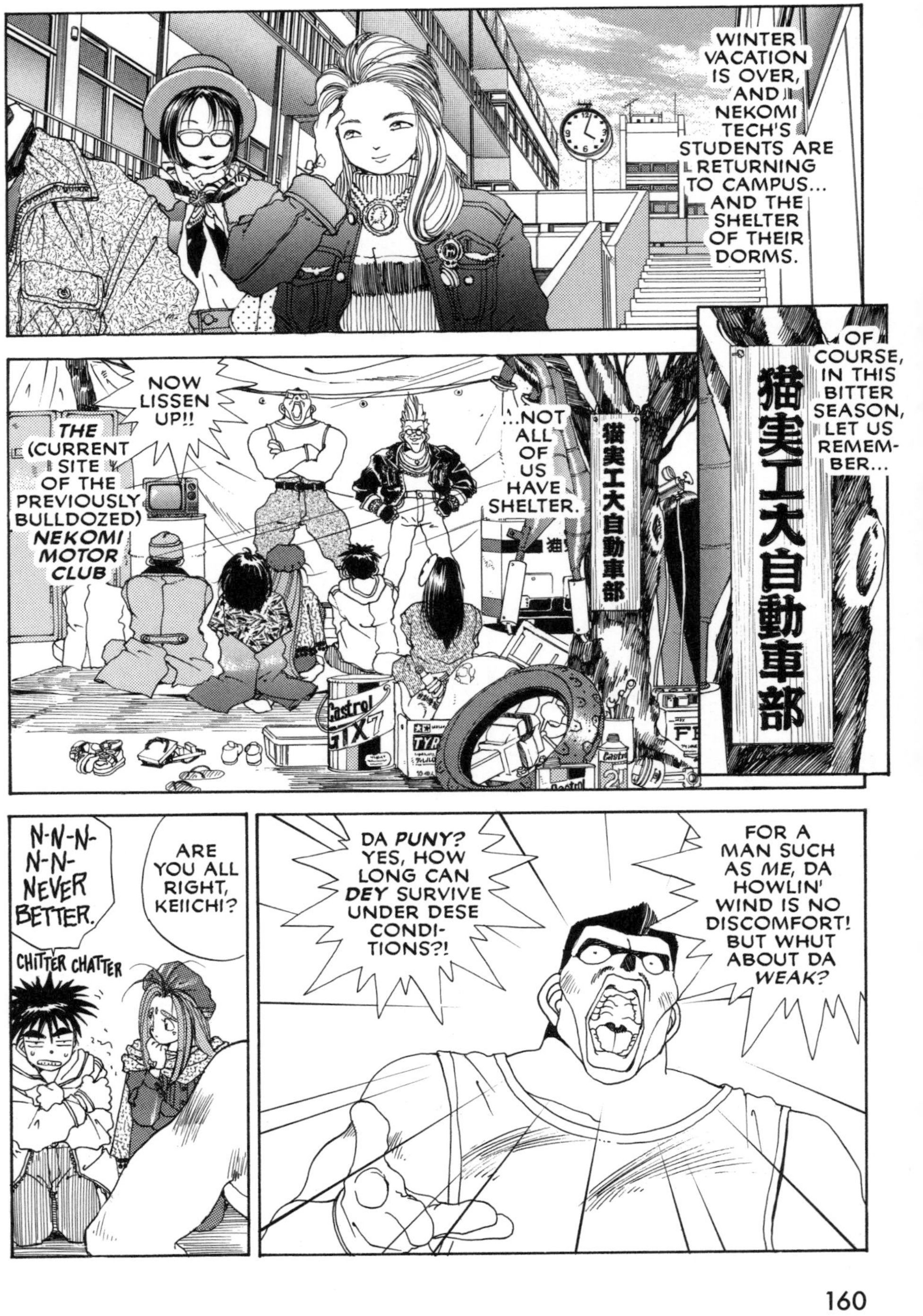
WINTER VACATION IS OVER, AND NEKOMI TECH'S STUDENTS ARE RETURNING TO CAMPUS... AND THE SHELTER OF THEIR DORMS.
OF COURSE, IN THIS BITTER SEASON, LET US REMEMBER...
猫実工大自動車部
...NOT ALL OF US HAVE SHELTER.
NOW LISSEN UP!!
THE (CURRENT SITE OF THE PREVIOUSLY BULLDOZED) NEKOMI MOTOR CLUB
猫実工大自動車部
FOR A MAN SUCH AS ME, DA HOWLIN' WIND IS NO DISCOMFORT! BUT WHUT ABOUT DA WEAK?
DA PUNY? YES, HOW LONG CAN DEY SURVIVE UNDER DESE CONDITIONS?!
ARE YOU ALL RIGHT, KEIICHI?
N-N-N-N-N-NEVER BETTER.
CHITTER CHATTER

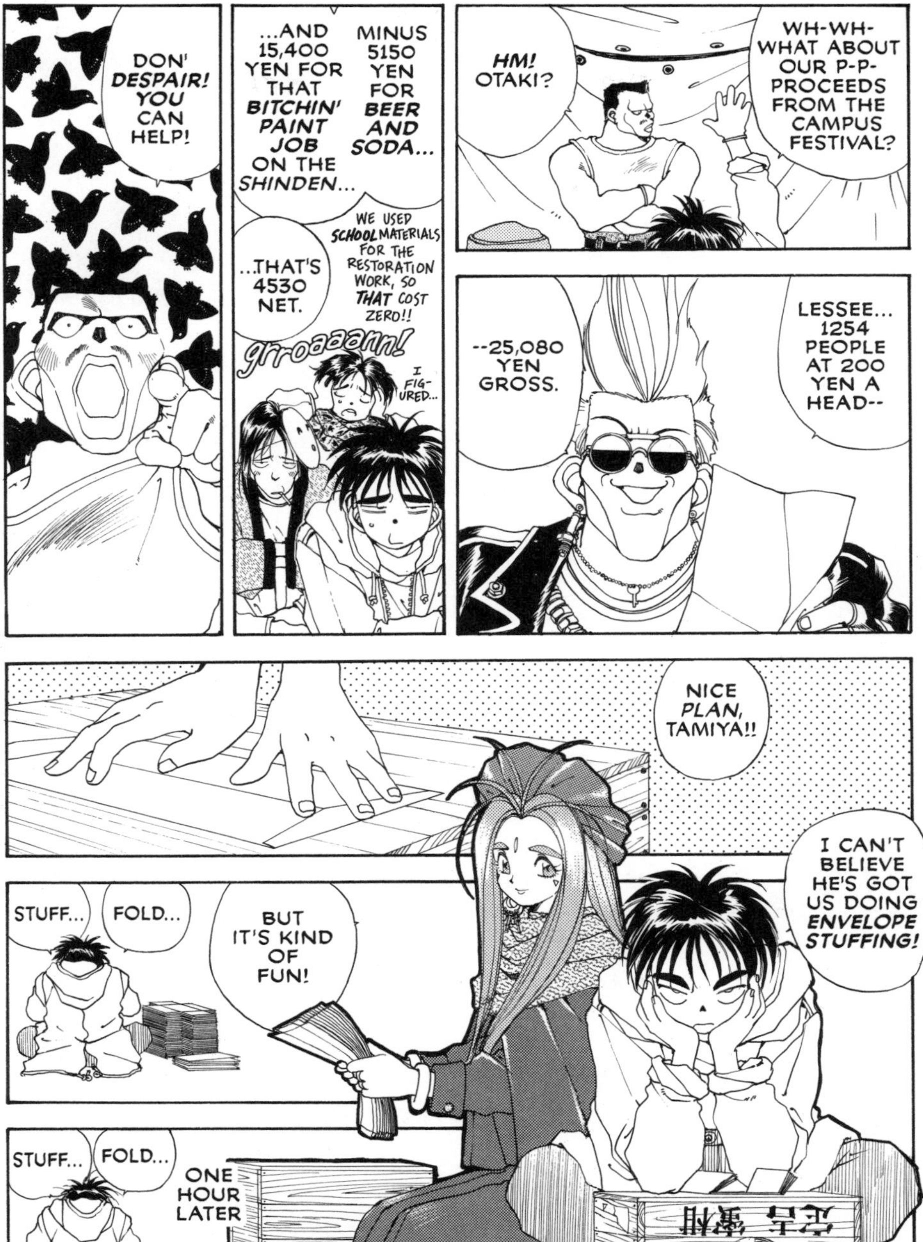
WH-WH-WHAT ABOUT OUR P-P-PROCEEDS FROM THE CAMPUS FESTIVAL?
HM! OTAKI?
LESSEE... 1254 PEOPLE AT 200 YEN A HEAD--
--25,080 YEN GROSS.
MINUS 5150 YEN FOR BEER AND SODA...
...AND 15,400 YEN FOR THAT BITCHIN' PAINT JOB ON THE SHINDEN...
WE USED SCHOOL MATERIALS FOR THE RESTORATION WORK, SO THAT COST ZERO!!
...THAT'S 4530 NET.
grroaaann!
I FIGURED...
DON' DESPAIR! YOU CAN HELP!
NICE PLAN, TAMIYA!!
I CAN'T BELIEVE HE'S GOT US DOING ENVELOPE STUFFING!
BUT IT'S KIND OF FUN!
FOLD...
STUFF...
ONE HOUR LATER
FOLD...
STUFF...

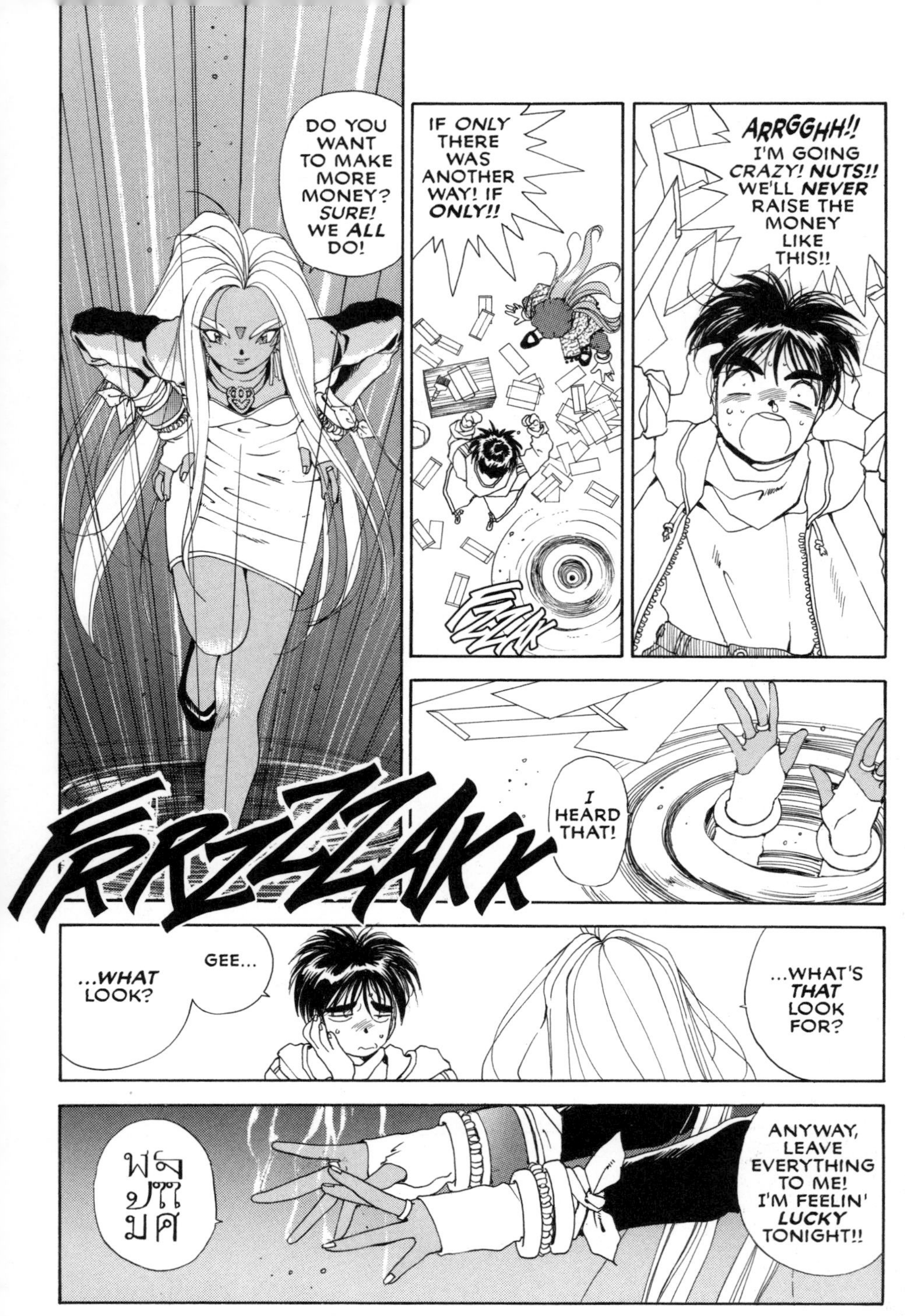
ARRGGHH!! I'M GOING CRAZY! NUTS!! WE'LL NEVER RAISE THE MONEY LIKE THIS!!
IF ONLY THERE WAS ANOTHER WAY! IF ONLY!!
I HEARD THAT!
DO YOU WANT TO MAKE MORE MONEY? SURE! WE ALL DO!
FRRZZZAKK
...WHAT'S THAT LOOK FOR?
GEE...
...WHAT LOOK?
ANYWAY, LEAVE EVERYTHING TO ME! I'M FEELIN' LUCKY TONIGHT!!

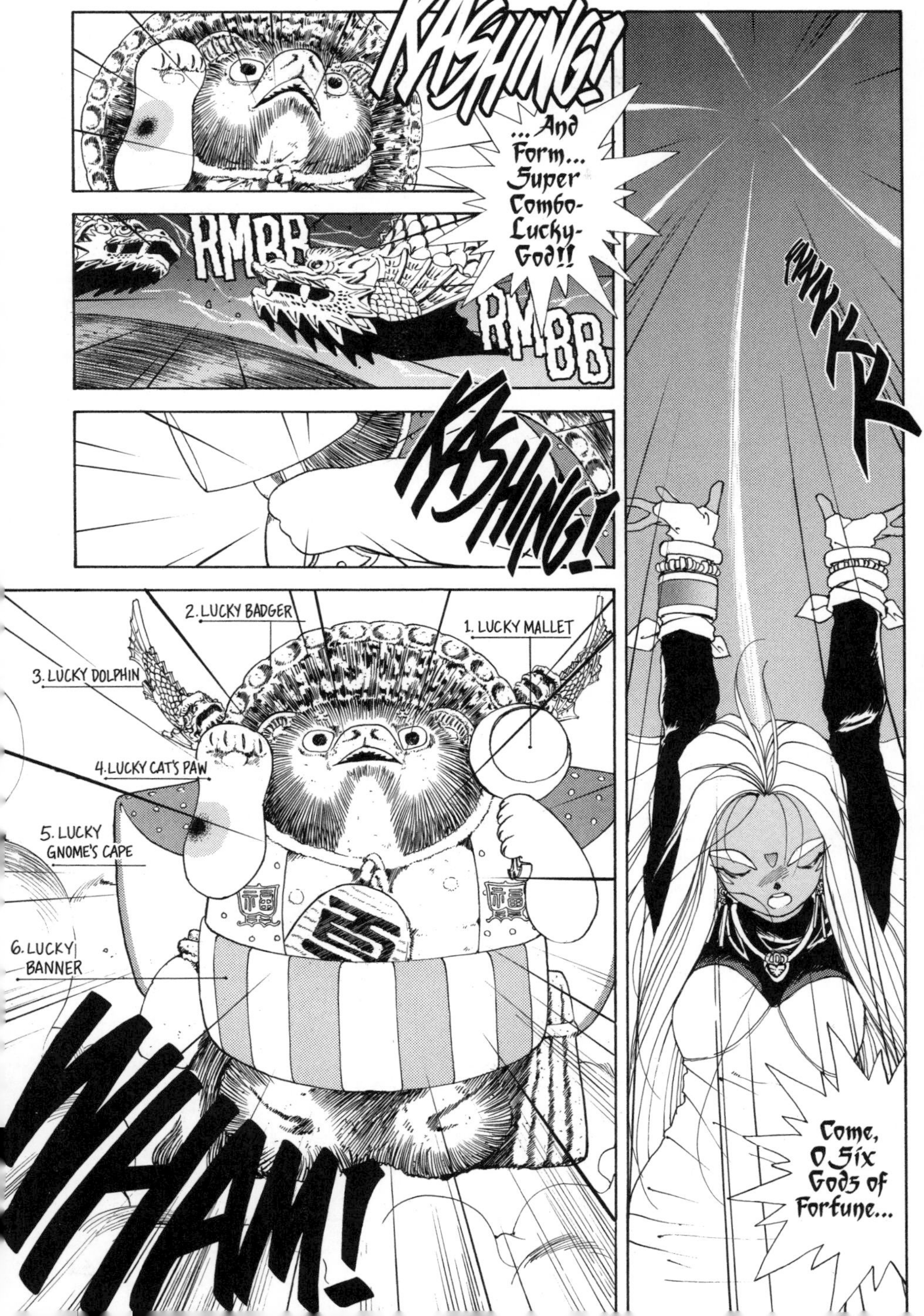
INNN KRR
Come, O Six Gods of Fortune...
KASHING!
...And Form... Super Combo-Lucky-God!!
RMBB
RMBB
KASHING!
1. LUCKY MALLET
2. LUCKY BADGER
3. LUCKY DOLPHIN
4. LUCKY CAT'S PAW
5. LUCKY GNOME'S CAPE
6. LUCKY BANNER
WHAM!

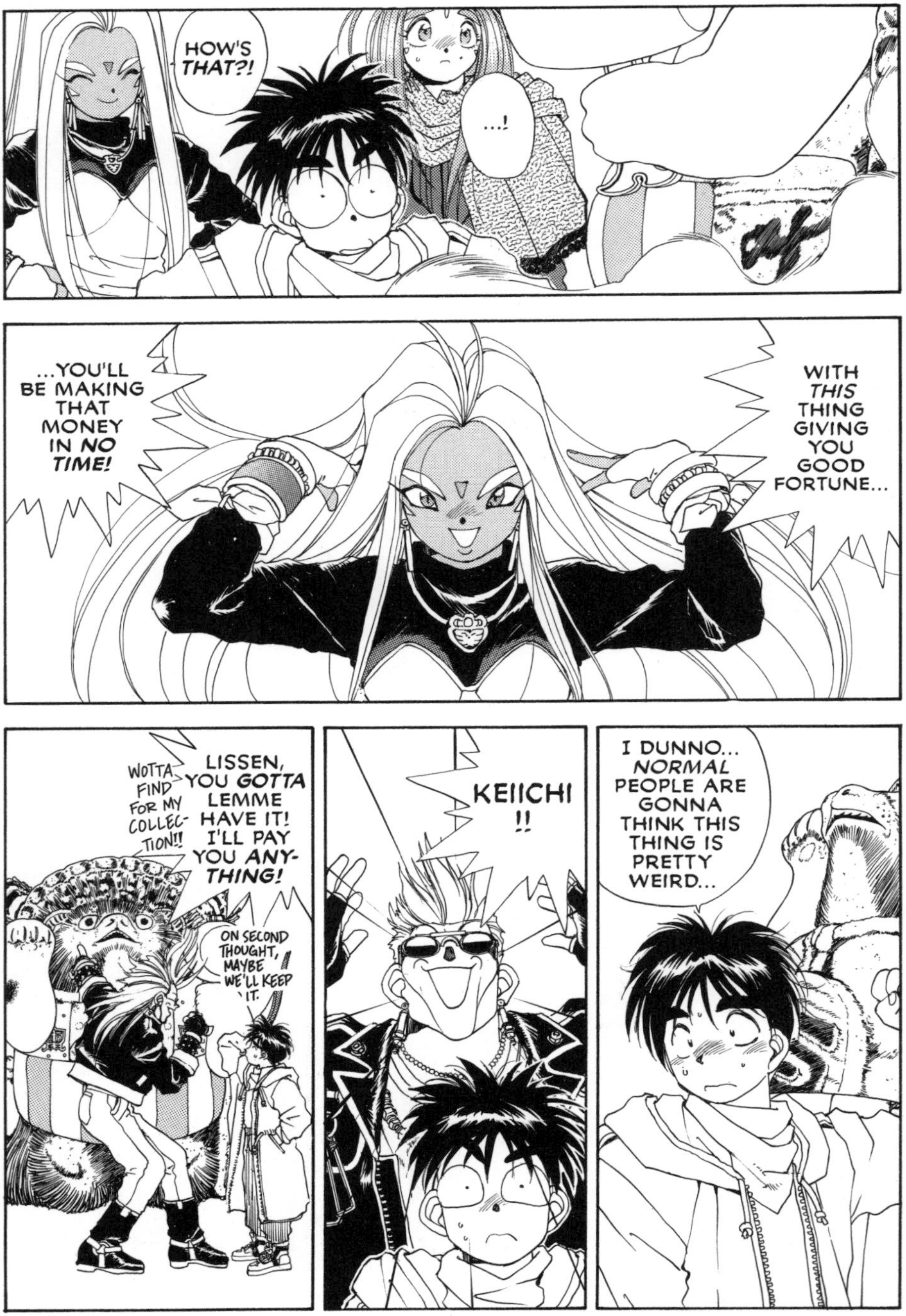
...!
HOW'S THAT?!
WITH THIS THING GIVING YOU GOOD FORTUNE...
...YOU'LL BE MAKING THAT MONEY IN NO TIME!
I DUNNO... NORMAL PEOPLE ARE GONNA THINK THIS THING IS PRETTY WEIRD...
KEIICHI!!
LISSEN, YOU GOTTA LEMME HAVE IT! I'LL PAY YOU ANYTHING!
WOTTA FIND FOR MY COLLECTION!!
ON SECOND THOUGHT, MAYBE WE'LL KEEP IT.

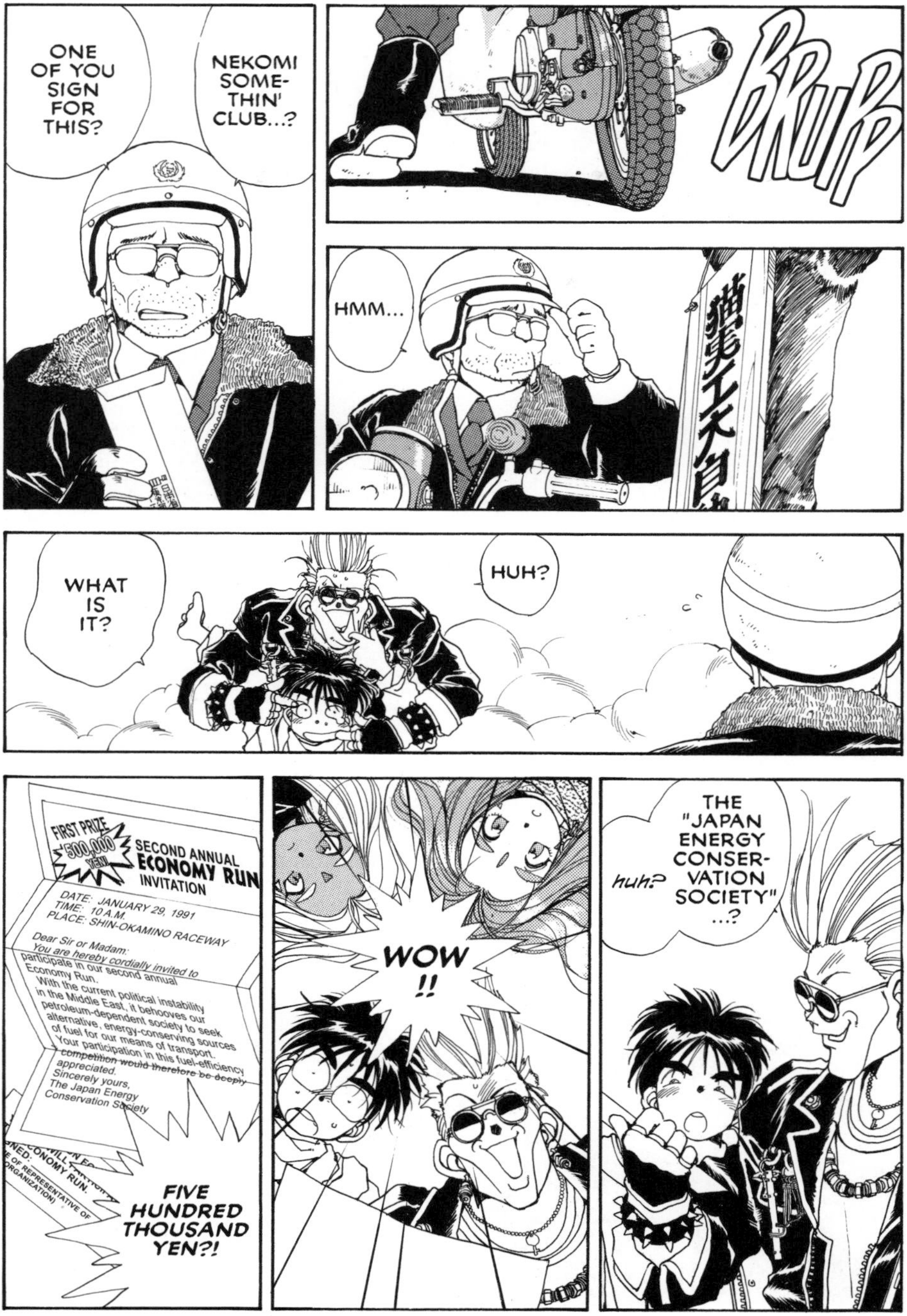
BRUB
HMM...
NEKOMI SOMETHIN' CLUB...?
ONE OF YOU SIGN FOR THIS?
HUH?
WHAT IS IT?
THE "JAPAN ENERGY CONSERVATION SOCIETY"...?
huh?
WOW!!
FIRST PRIZE 500,000 YEN
SECOND ANNUAL ECONOMY RUN INVITATION
DATE: JANUARY 29, 1991
TIME: 10 A.M.
PLACE: SHIN-OKAMINO RACEWAY
Dear Sir or Madam:
You are hereby cordially invited to participate in our second annual Economy Run.
With the current political instability in the Middle East, it behooves our petroleum-dependent society to seek alternative, energy-conserving sources of fuel for our means of transport.
Your participation in this fuel-efficiency competition would therefore be deeply appreciated.
Sincerely yours,
The Japan Energy Conservation Society
FIVE HUNDRED THOUSAND YEN?!

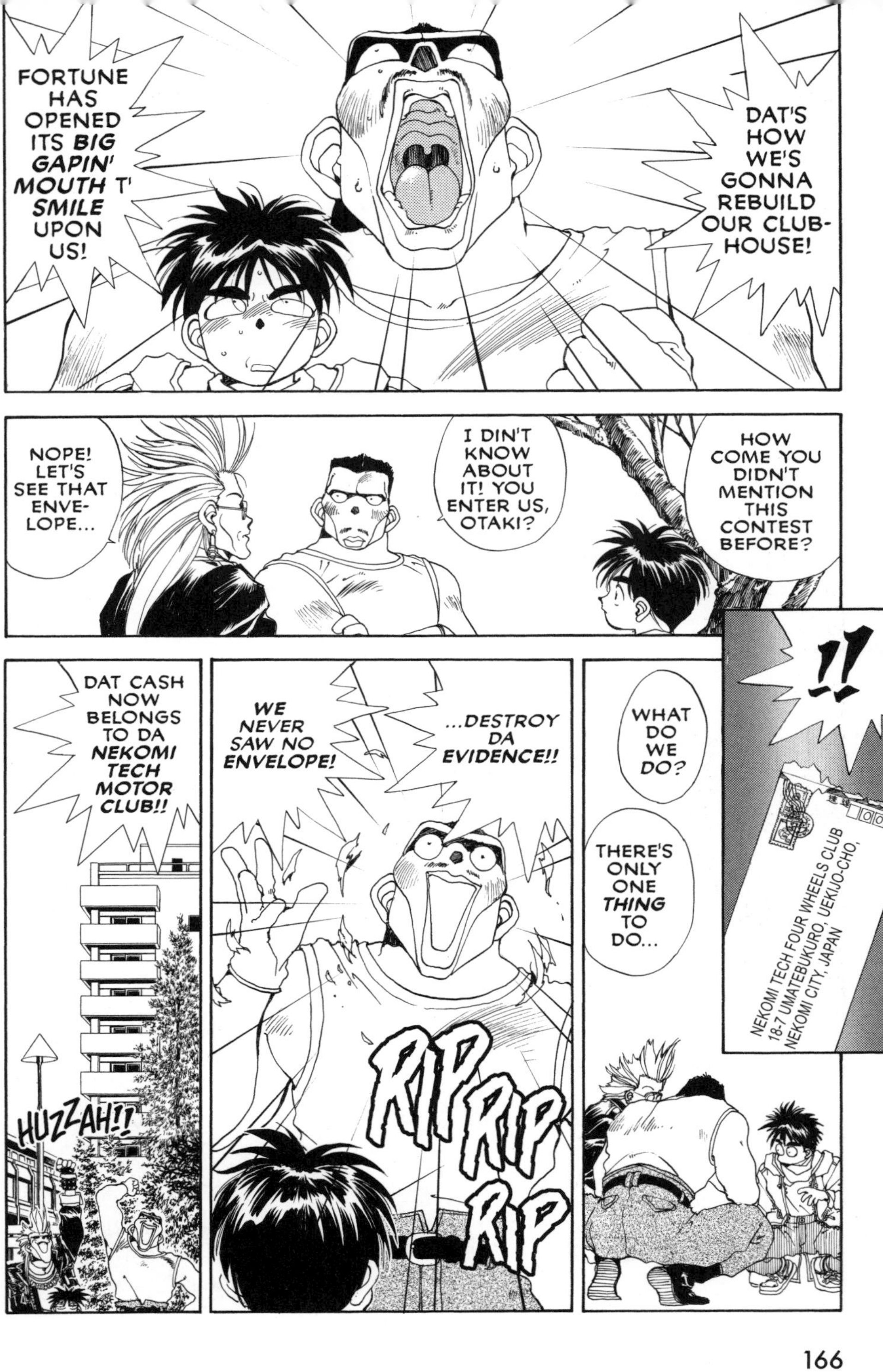
FORTUNE HAS OPENED ITS BIG GAPIN' MOUTH T' SMILE UPON US!
DAT'S HOW WE'S GONNA REBUILD OUR CLUB-HOUSE!
HOW COME YOU DIDN'T MENTION THIS CONTEST BEFORE?
I DIN'T KNOW ABOUT IT! YOU ENTER US, OTAKI?
NOPE! LET'S SEE THAT ENVE-LOPE...
!!
NEKOMI TECH FOUR WHEELS CLUB
18-7 UMATEBUKURO, UEKIJO-CHO,
NEKOMI CITY, JAPAN
WHAT DO WE DO?
THERE'S ONLY ONE THING TO DO...
...DESTROY DA EVIDENCE!!
WE NEVER SAW NO ENVELOPE!
RIP RIP RIP RIP
DAT CASH NOW BELONGS TO DA NEKOMI TECH MOTOR CLUB!!
HUZZAH!!

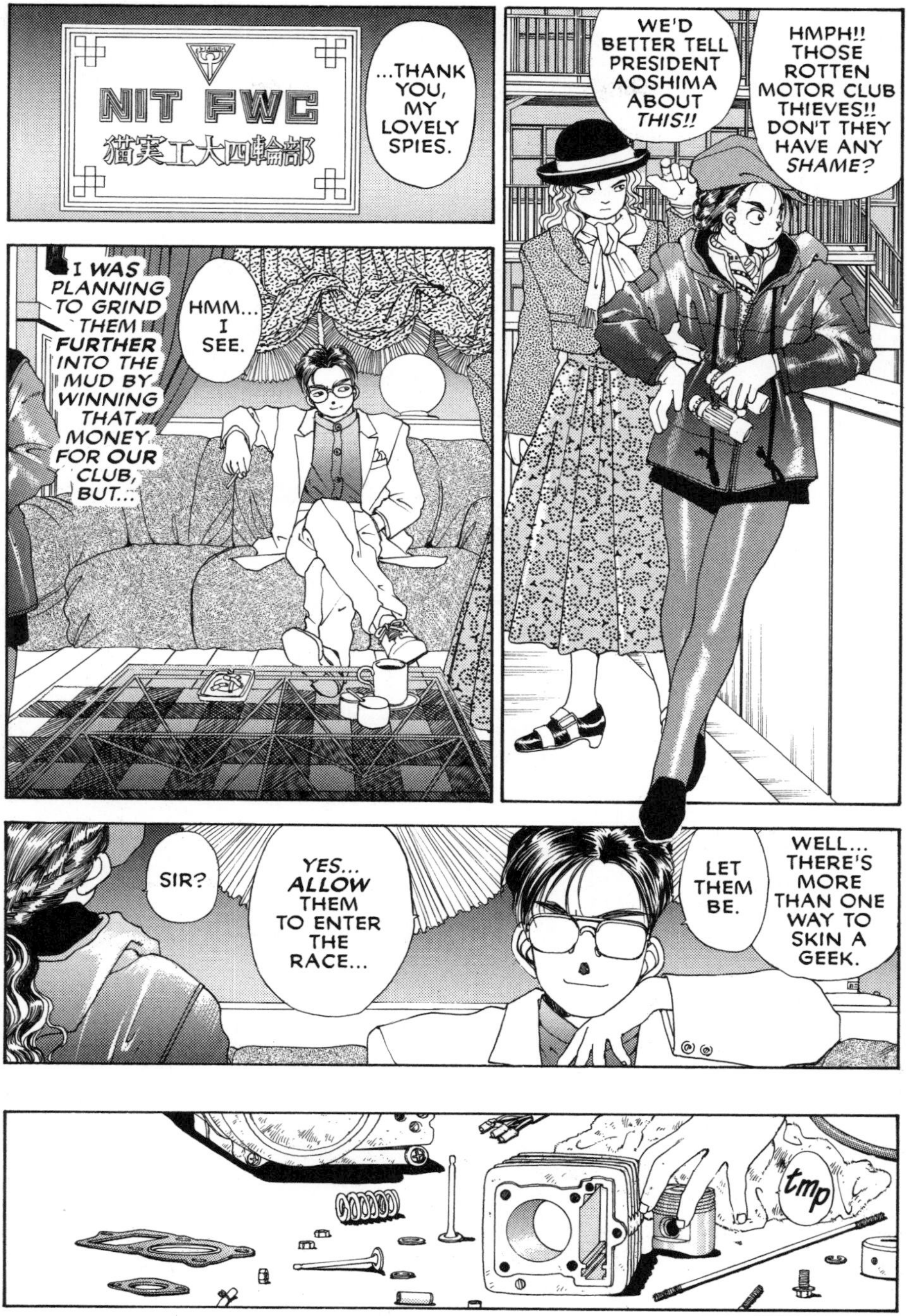
HMPH!! THOSE ROTTEN MOTOR CLUB THIEVES!! DON'T THEY HAVE ANY SHAME?
WE'D BETTER TELL PRESIDENT AOSHIMA ABOUT THIS!!
...THANK YOU, MY LOVELY SPIES.
NIT FWC
猫実工大四輪部
HMM... I SEE.
I WAS PLANNING TO GRIND THEM FURTHER INTO THE MUD BY WINNING THAT MONEY FOR OUR CLUB, BUT...
WELL... THERE'S MORE THAN ONE WAY TO SKIN A GEEK.
LET THEM BE.
YES... ALLOW THEM TO ENTER THE RACE...
SIR?
tmp

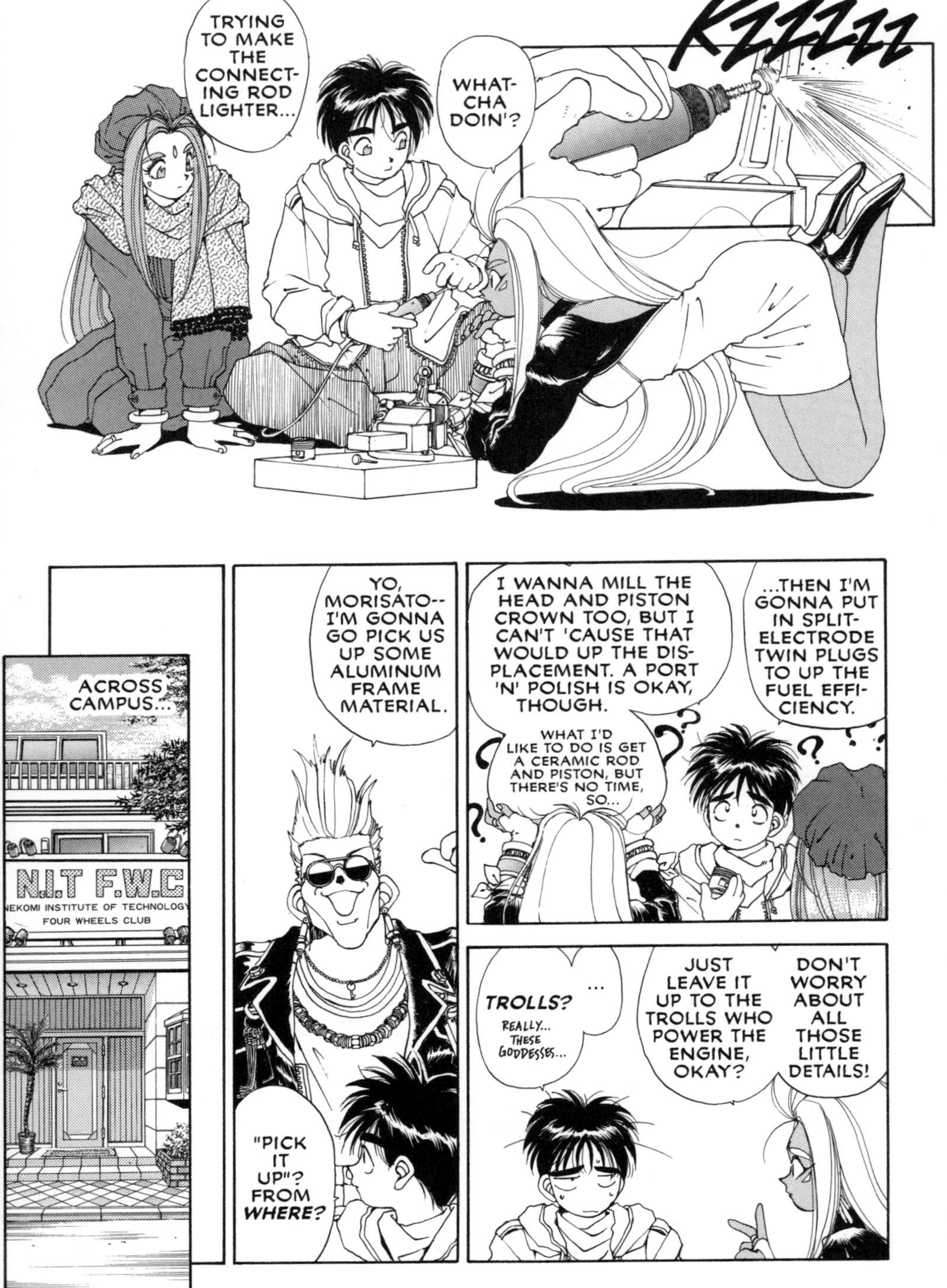

TRYING TO MAKE THE CONNECT-ING ROD LIGHTER...
WHAT-CHA DOIN'?
KZZZZZZ
ACROSS CAMPUS...
N.I.T F.W.C
NEKOMI INSTITUTE OF TECHNOLOGY
FOUR WHEELS CLUB
YO, MORISATO-- I'M GONNA GO PICK US UP SOME ALUMINUM FRAME MATERIAL.
"PICK IT UP"? FROM WHERE?
I WANNA MILL THE HEAD AND PISTON CROWN TOO, BUT I CAN'T 'CAUSE THAT WOULD UP THE DIS-PLACEMENT. A PORT 'N' POLISH IS OKAY, THOUGH.
WHAT I'D LIKE TO DO IS GET A CERAMIC ROD AND PISTON, BUT THERE'S NO TIME, SO...
...THEN I'M GONNA PUT IN SPLIT-ELECTRODE TWIN PLUGS TO UP THE FUEL EFFI-CIENCY.
DON'T WORRY ABOUT ALL THOSE LITTLE DETAILS!
JUST LEAVE IT UP TO THE TROLLS WHO POWER THE ENGINE, OKAY?
...
TROLLS?
REALLY... THESE GODDESSES...

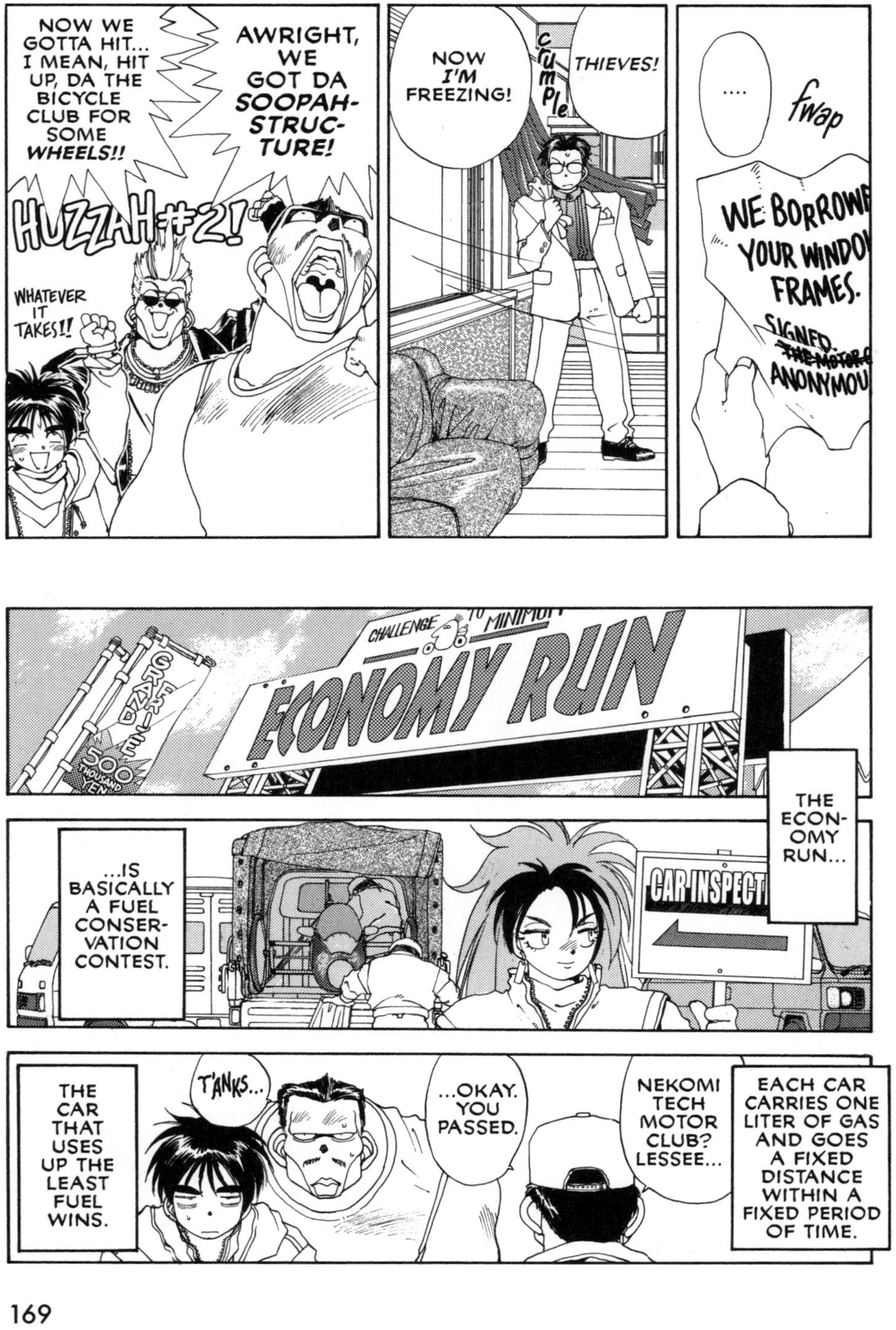
....
fwap
WE BORROWE
YOUR WINDOW
FRAMES.
SIGNED,
THE MOTOR C
ANONYMOU
THIEVES!
crumple
NOW I'M FREEZING!
AWRIGHT, WE GOT DA SOOPAH-STRUCTURE!
NOW WE GOTTA HIT... I MEAN, HIT UP, DA THE BICYCLE CLUB FOR SOME WHEELS!!
HUZZAH #2!
WHATEVER IT TAKES!!
THE ECONOMY RUN...
CHALLENGE
ECONOMY RUN
500 THOUSAND YEN
CAR INSPECTI
...IS BASICALLY A FUEL CONSERVATION CONTEST.
EACH CAR CARRIES ONE LITER OF GAS AND GOES A FIXED DISTANCE WITHIN A FIXED PERIOD OF TIME.
NEKOMI TECH MOTOR CLUB? LESSEE...
...OKAY. YOU PASSED.
T'ANKS...
THE CAR THAT USES UP THE LEAST FUEL WINS.

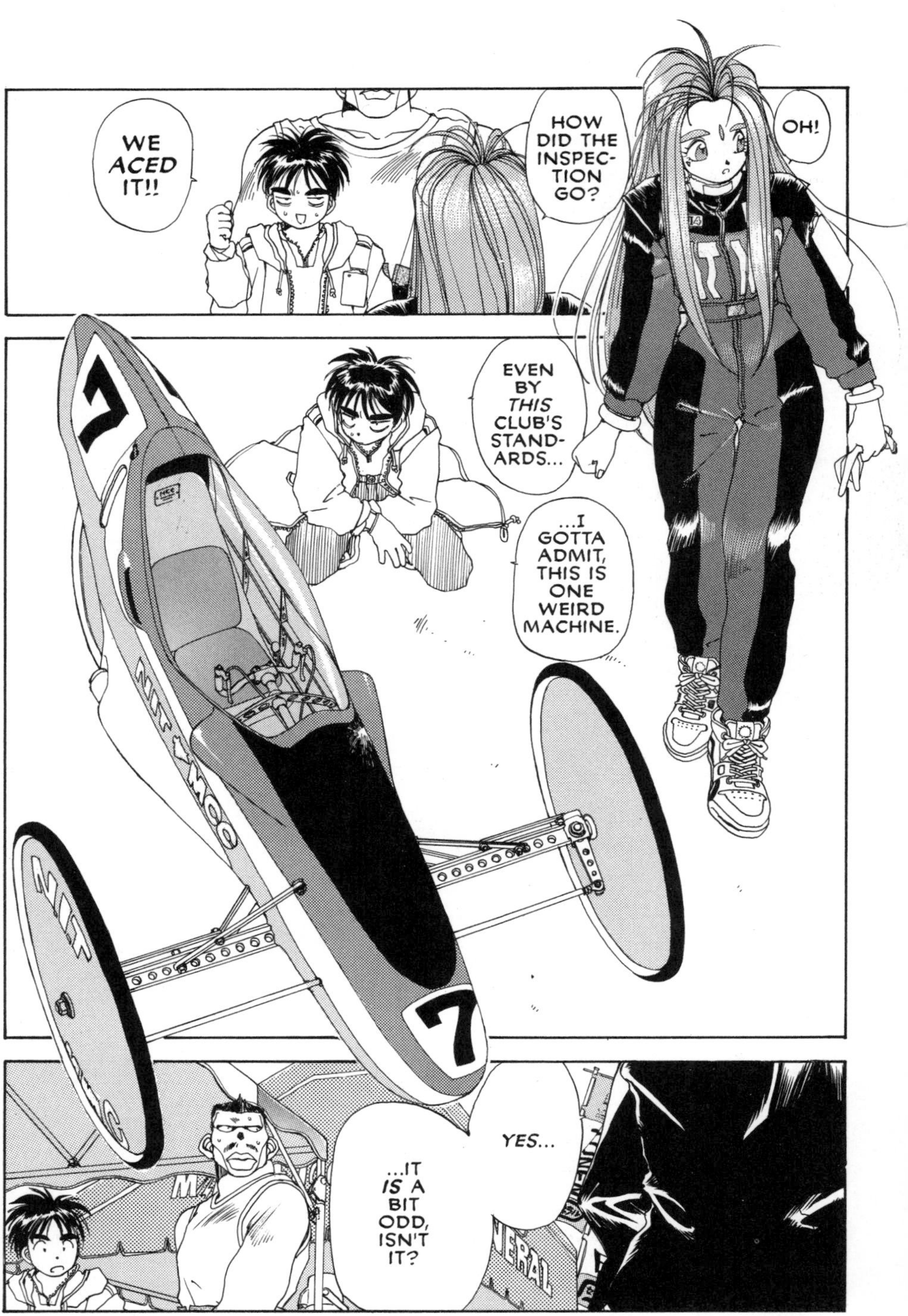
OH!
HOW DID THE INSPECTION GO?
WE ACED IT!!
EVEN BY THIS CLUB'S STANDARDS...
...I GOTTA ADMIT, THIS IS ONE WEIRD MACHINE.
YES...
...IT IS A BIT ODD, ISN'T IT?

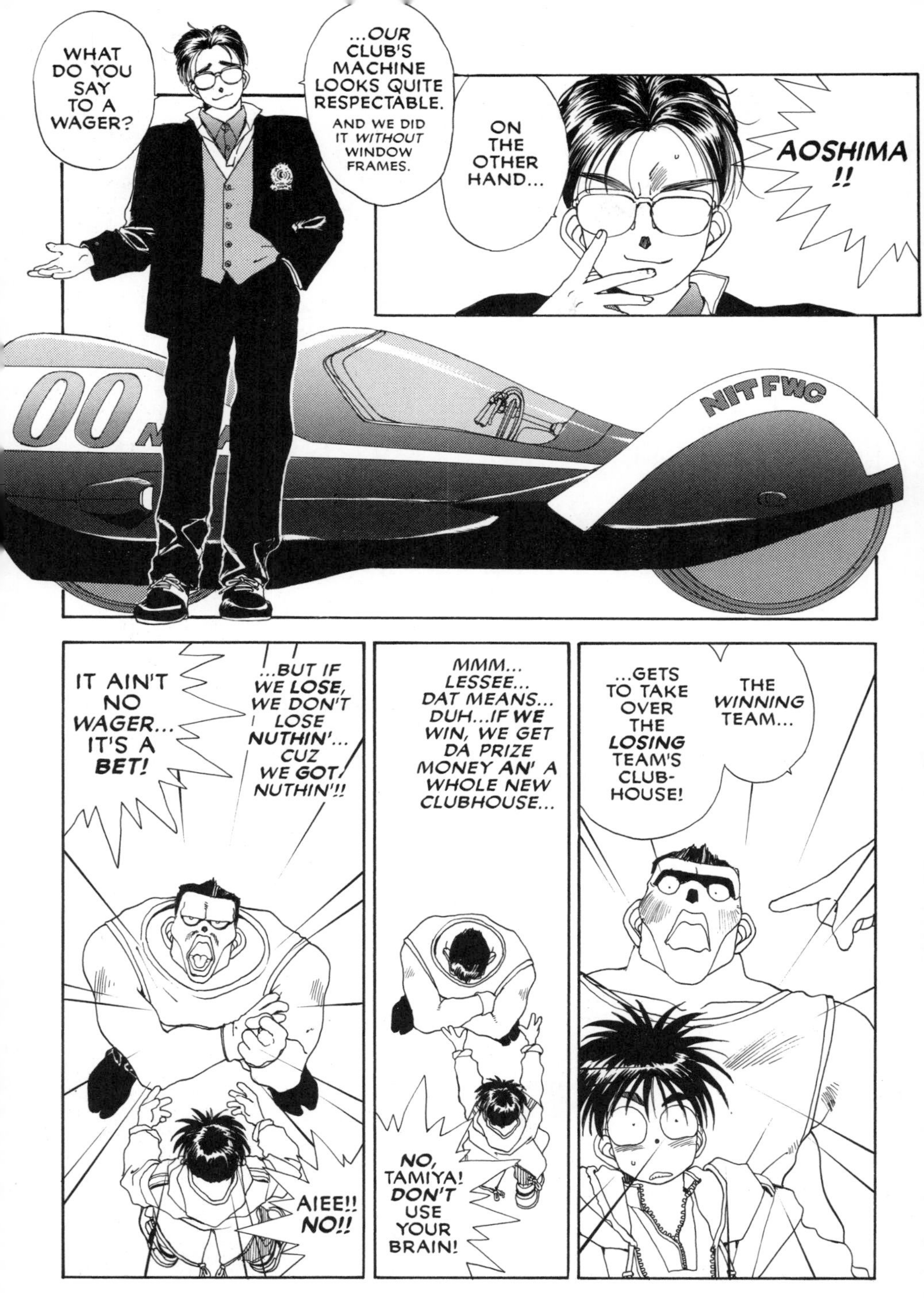
AOSHIMA !!
ON THE OTHER HAND...
...OUR CLUB'S MACHINE LOOKS QUITE RESPECTABLE.
AND WE DID IT WITHOUT WINDOW FRAMES.
WHAT DO YOU SAY TO A WAGER?
NIT FWC
00
THE WINNING TEAM...
...GETS TO TAKE OVER THE LOSING TEAM'S CLUB-HOUSE!
MMM... LESSEE... DAT MEANS... DUH...IF WE WIN, WE GET DA PRIZE MONEY AN' A WHOLE NEW CLUBHOUSE...
NO, TAMIYA! DON'T USE YOUR BRAIN!
...BUT IF WE LOSE, WE DON'T LOSE NUTHIN'... CUZ WE GOT NUTHIN'!!
IT AIN'T NO WAGER... IT'S A BET!
AIEE!! NO!!

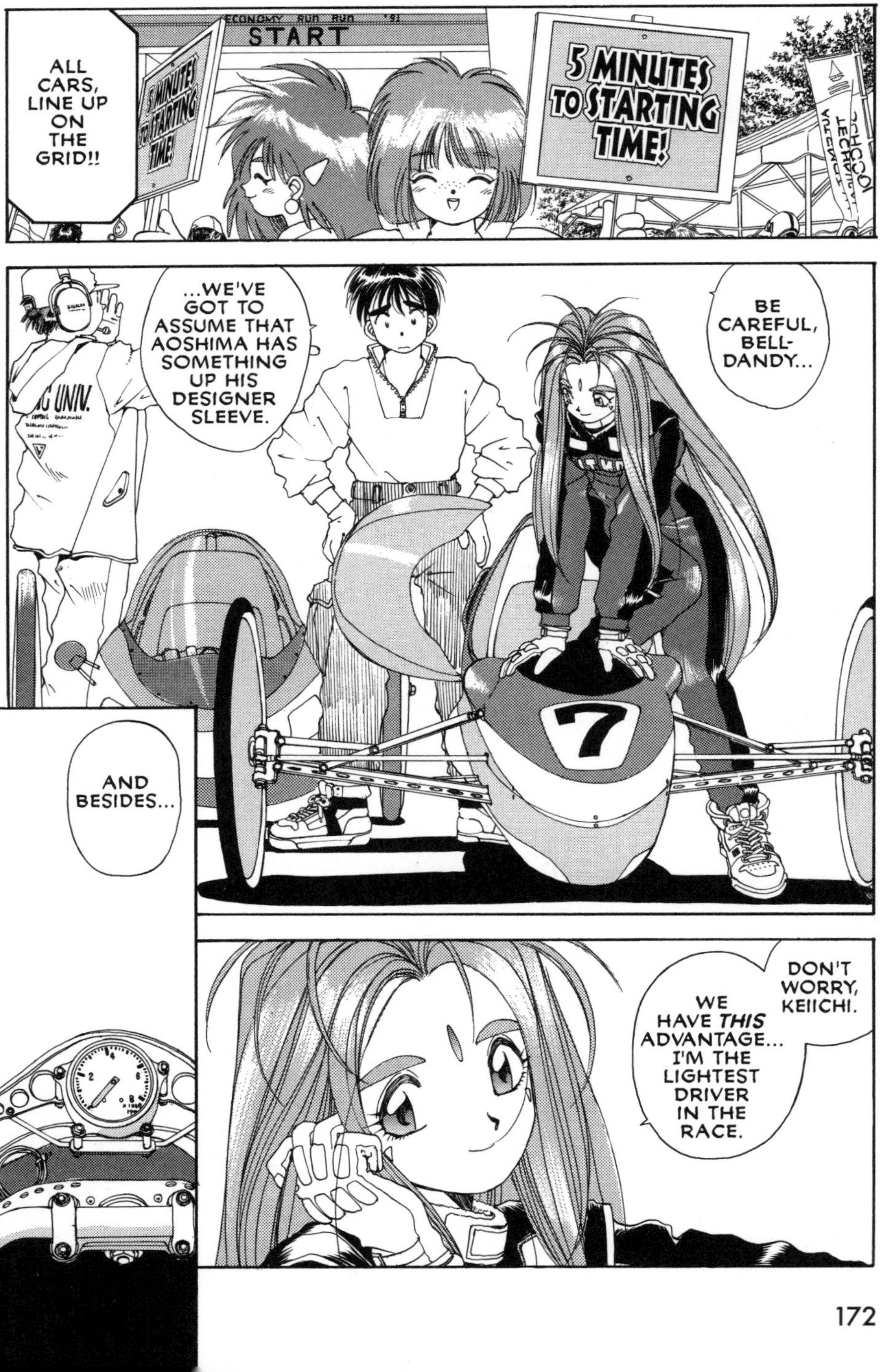
ECONOMY RUN RUN '91
START
ALL CARS, LINE UP ON THE GRID!!
5 MINUTES TO STARTING TIME!
5 MINUTES TO STARTING TIME!
BE CAREFUL, BELL-DANDY...
...WE'VE GOT TO ASSUME THAT AOSHIMA HAS SOMETHING UP HIS DESIGNER SLEEVE.
AND BESIDES...
DON'T WORRY, KEIICHI.
WE HAVE *THIS* ADVANTAGE... I'M THE LIGHTEST DRIVER IN THE RACE.

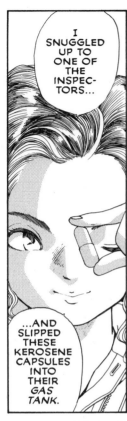

...WE ASSEMBLED THIS CAR OUR-SELVES... PART BY PART.
EVERY LAST COMPONENT IS LIKE A FRIEND TO ME.
ATTENTION--NEKOMI TECH MOTOR CLUB, TO THE STARTING GRID!!
HOW COULD THEY POSSIBLY HOPE TO BEAT OUR EXPENSIVE TITANIUM AND CARBON-FIBER RACER?!
DID YOU DO AS INSTRUCT-ED?
YES, SIR!
I SNUGGLED UP TO ONE OF THE INSPEC-TORS...
...AND SLIPPED THESE KEROSENE CAPSULES INTO THEIR GAS TANK.
bloop
C-5!!
DAMN! A DIRECT HIT!!

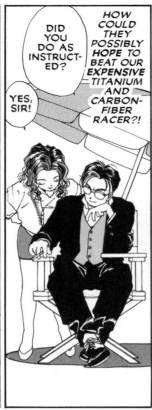

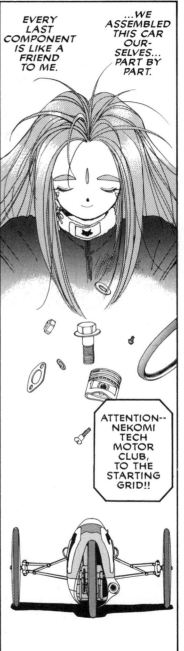

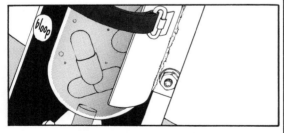

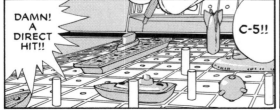

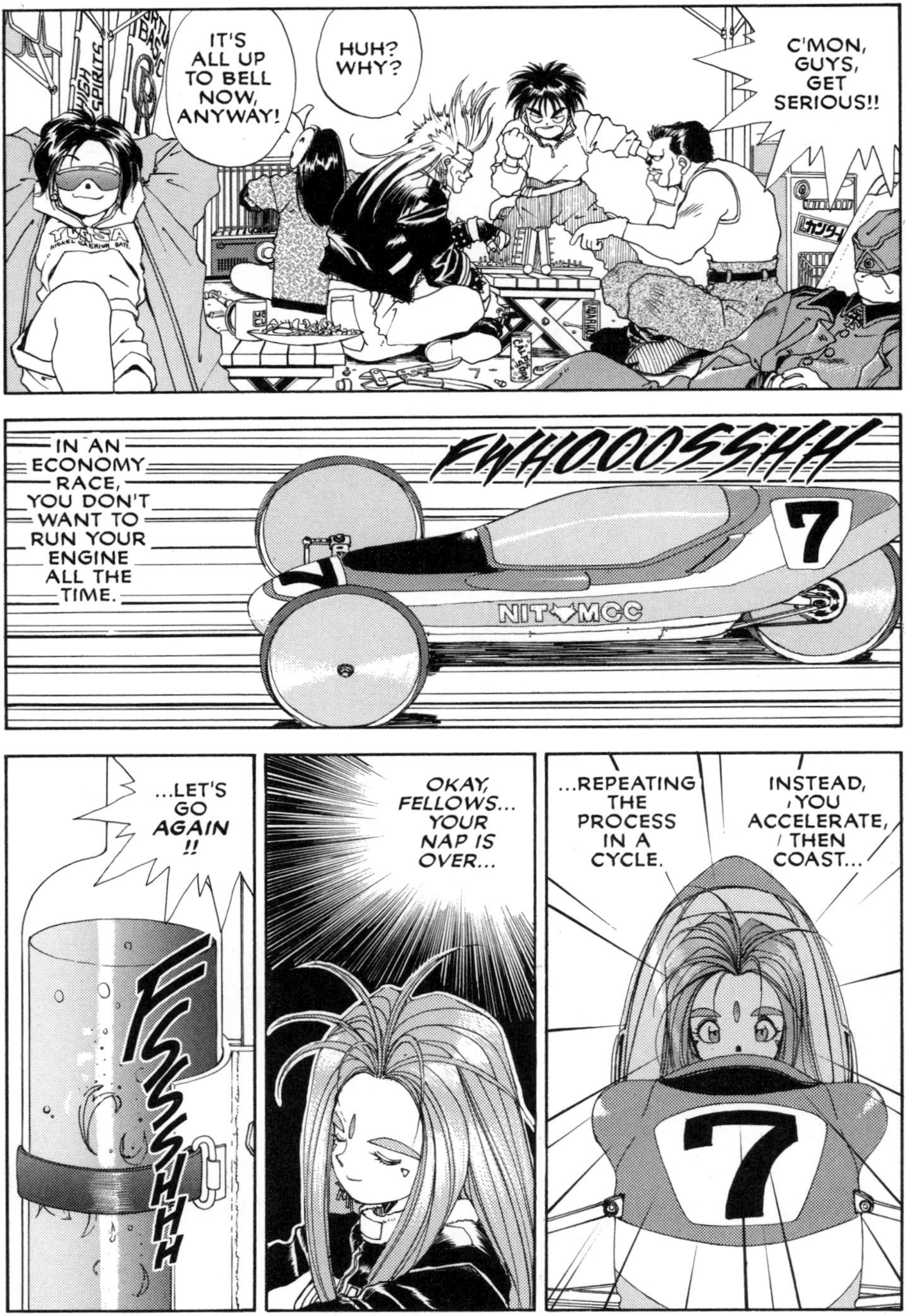
C'MON, GUYS, GET SERIOUS!!
HUH? WHY?
IT'S ALL UP TO BELL NOW, ANYWAY!
FWHOOOSSHH
IN AN ECONOMY RACE, YOU DON'T WANT TO RUN YOUR ENGINE ALL THE TIME.
7
NIT MCC
INSTEAD, YOU ACCELERATE, THEN COAST...
...REPEATING THE PROCESS IN A CYCLE.
7
OKAY, FELLOWS... YOUR NAP IS OVER...
...LET'S GO AGAIN !!
FSSSHHHH

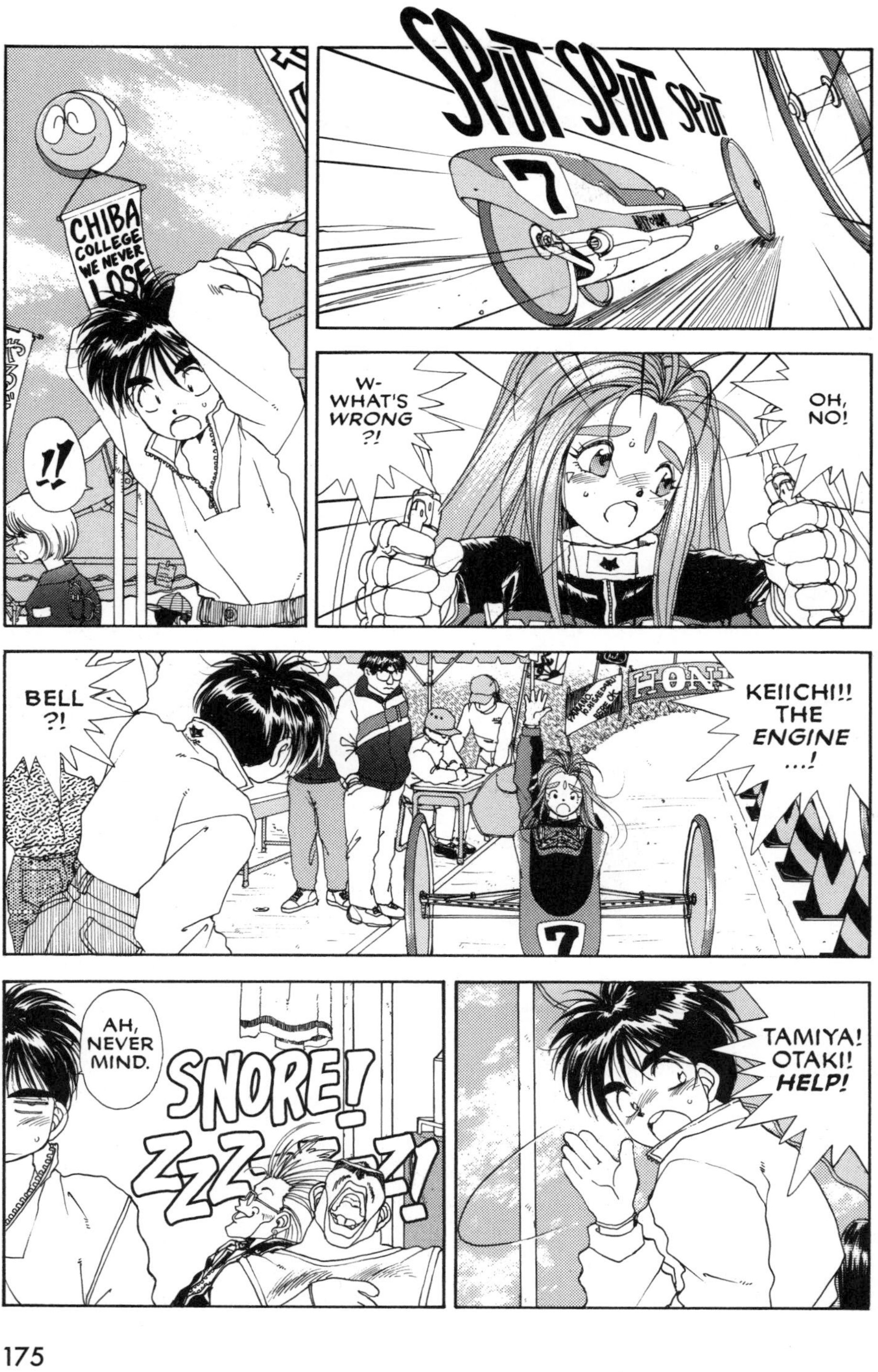
SPUT SPUT SPUT
OH, NO!
W-WHAT'S WRONG?!
CHIBA COLLEGE WE NEVER LOSE
!!
KEIICHI!!! THE ENGINE...!
BELL?!
TAMIYA! OTAKI! HELP!
AH, NEVER MIND.
SNORE!
ZZZ---Z!

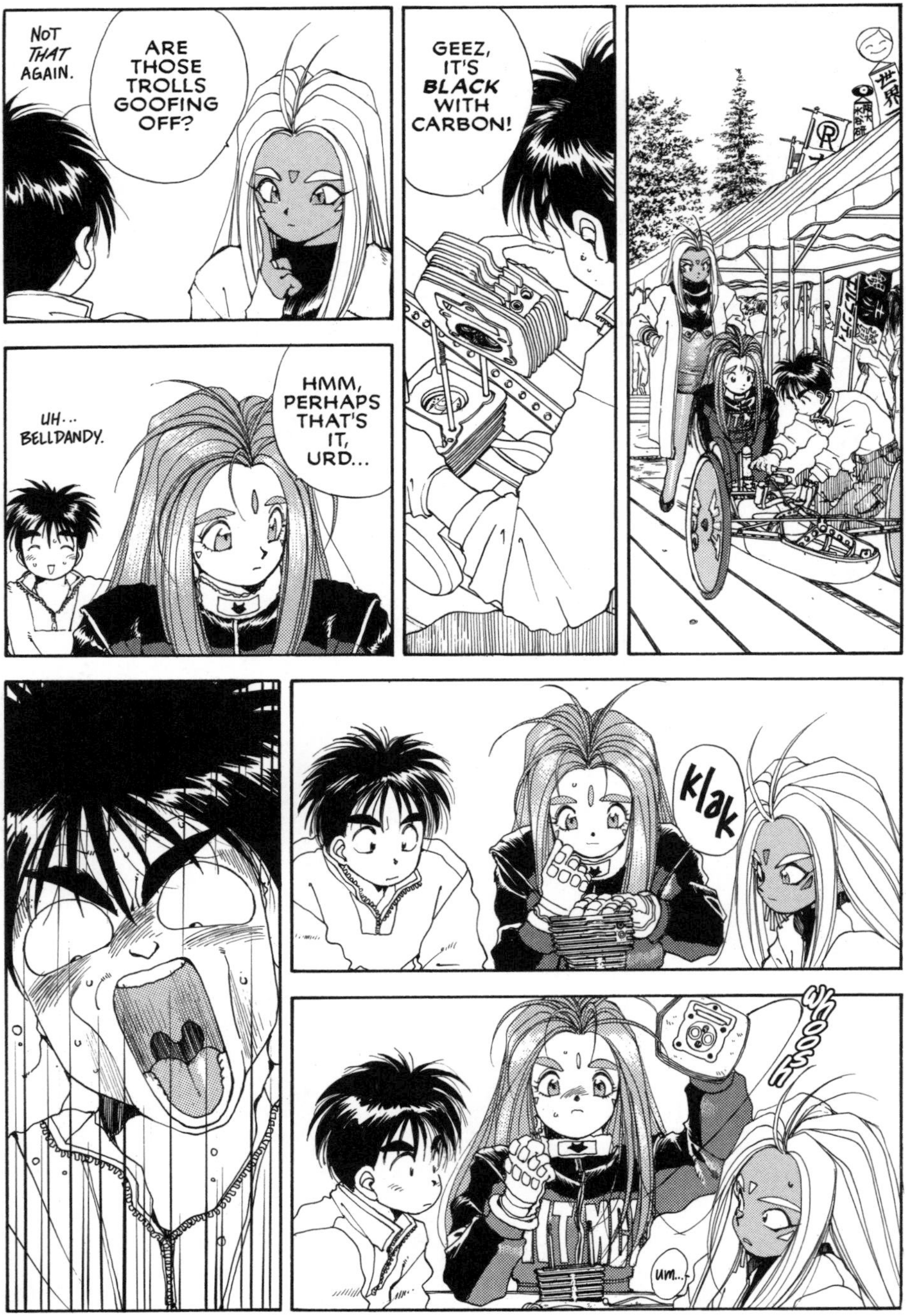
GEEZ, IT'S BLACK WITH CARBON!
ARE THOSE TROLLS GOOFING OFF?
NOT THAT AGAIN.
HMM, PERHAPS THAT'S IT, URD...
UH... BELLDANDY.
klak
WHOOSH
um...

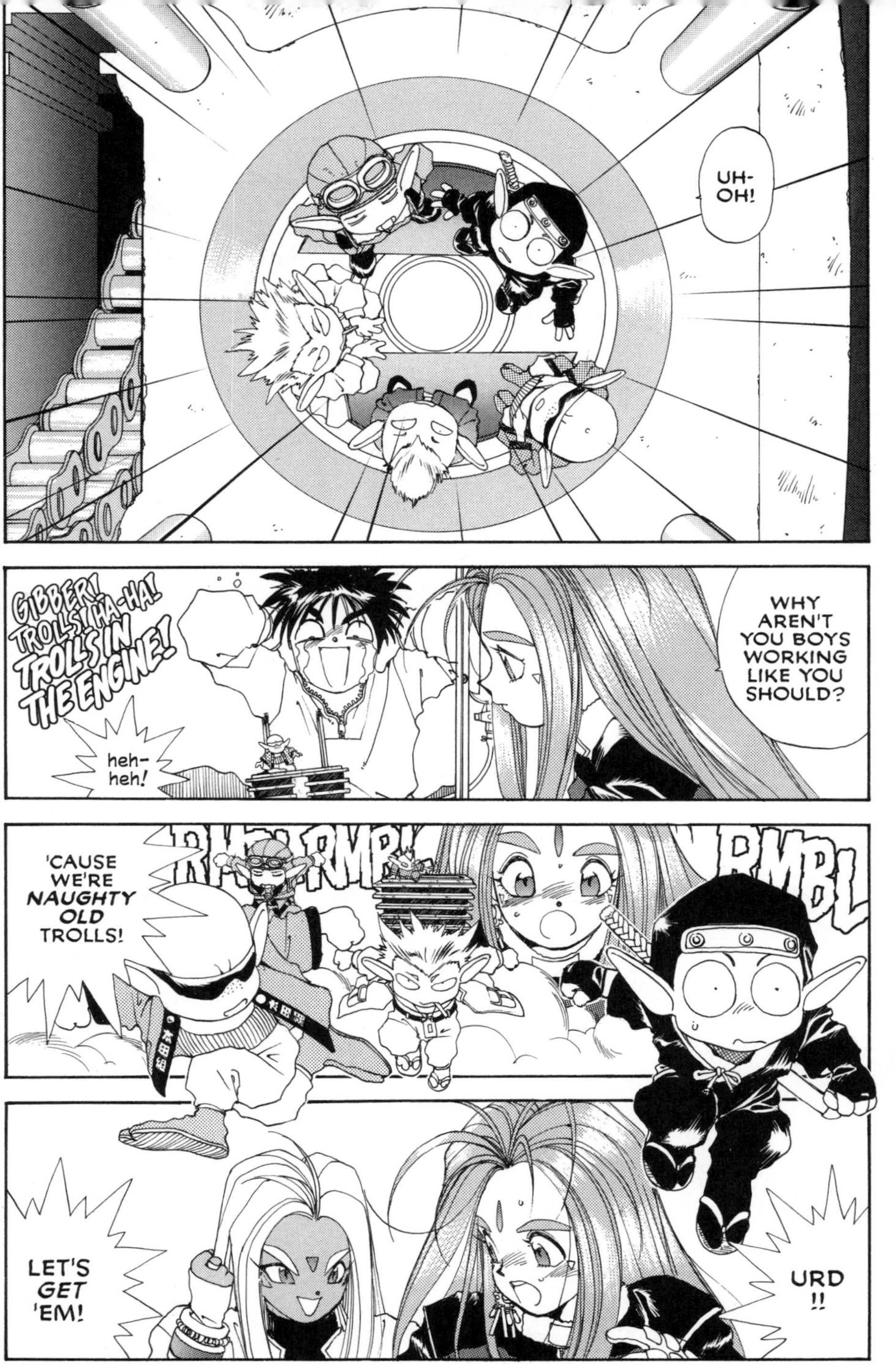
UH-OH!
WHY AREN'T YOU BOYS WORKING LIKE YOU SHOULD?
GIBBER! TROLLS! HA-HA! TROLLS IN THE ENGINE!
heh-heh!
RMBL
'CAUSE WE'RE NAUGHTY OLD TROLLS!
URD !!
LET'S GET 'EM!

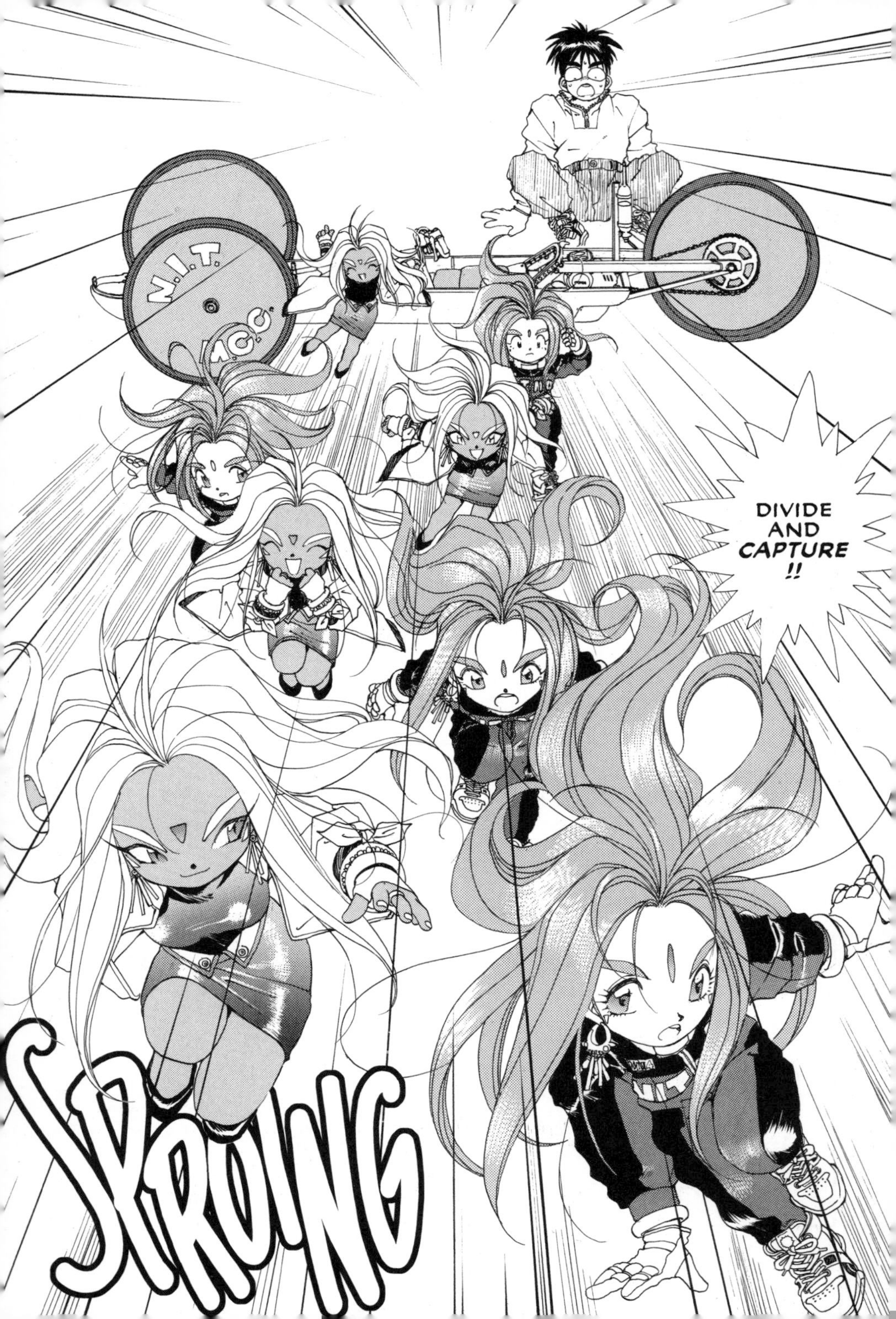
DIVIDE AND CAPTURE !!
SPROING
N.I.T.
M.C.C.

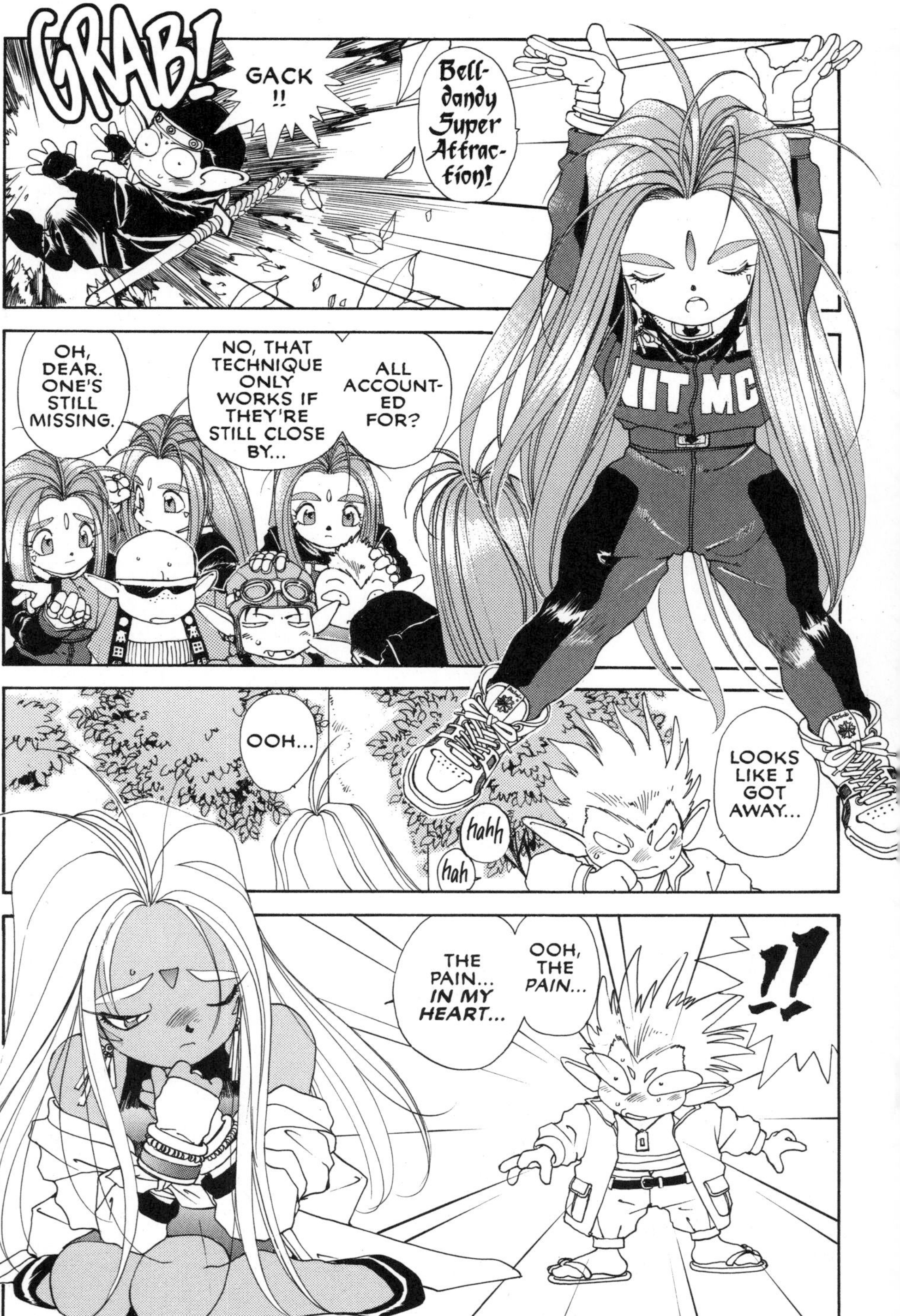
Bell-dandy Super Attraction!
GRAB!
GACK !!
ALL ACCOUNT-ED FOR?
NO, THAT TECHNIQUE ONLY WORKS IF THEY'RE STILL CLOSE BY...
OH, DEAR. ONE'S STILL MISSING.
LOOKS LIKE I GOT AWAY...
hahh
hah
OOH...
!!
OOH, THE PAIN...
THE PAIN... *IN MY HEART...*

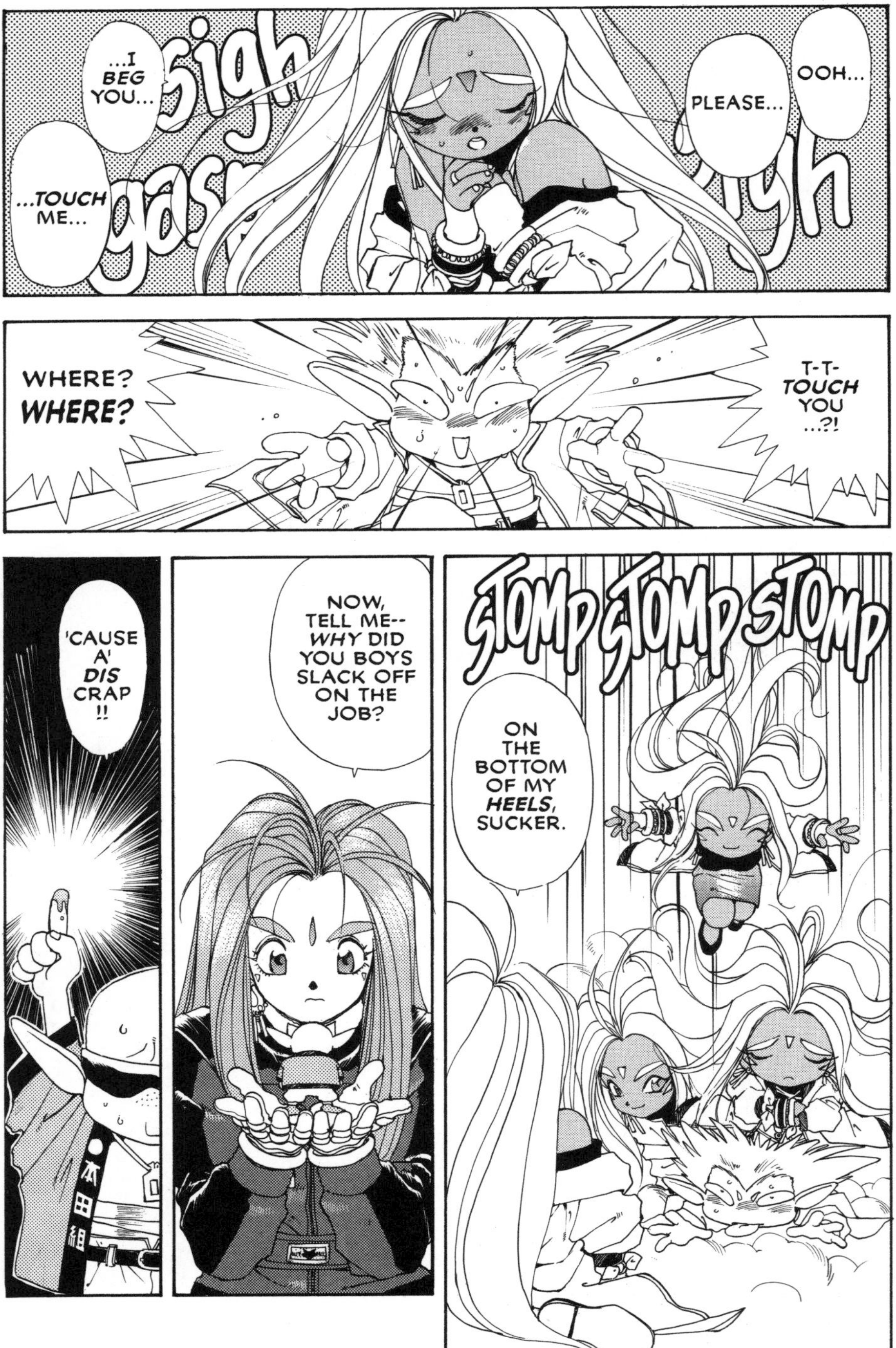
OOH...
PLEASE...
...I BEG YOU...
sigh
...TOUCH ME...
T-T-*TOUCH* YOU ...?!
WHERE? **WHERE?**
STOMP STOMP STOMP
ON THE BOTTOM OF MY *HEELS*, SUCKER.
NOW, TELL ME-- *WHY* DID YOU BOYS SLACK OFF ON THE JOB?
'CAUSE A' *DIS* CRAP !!
本田組

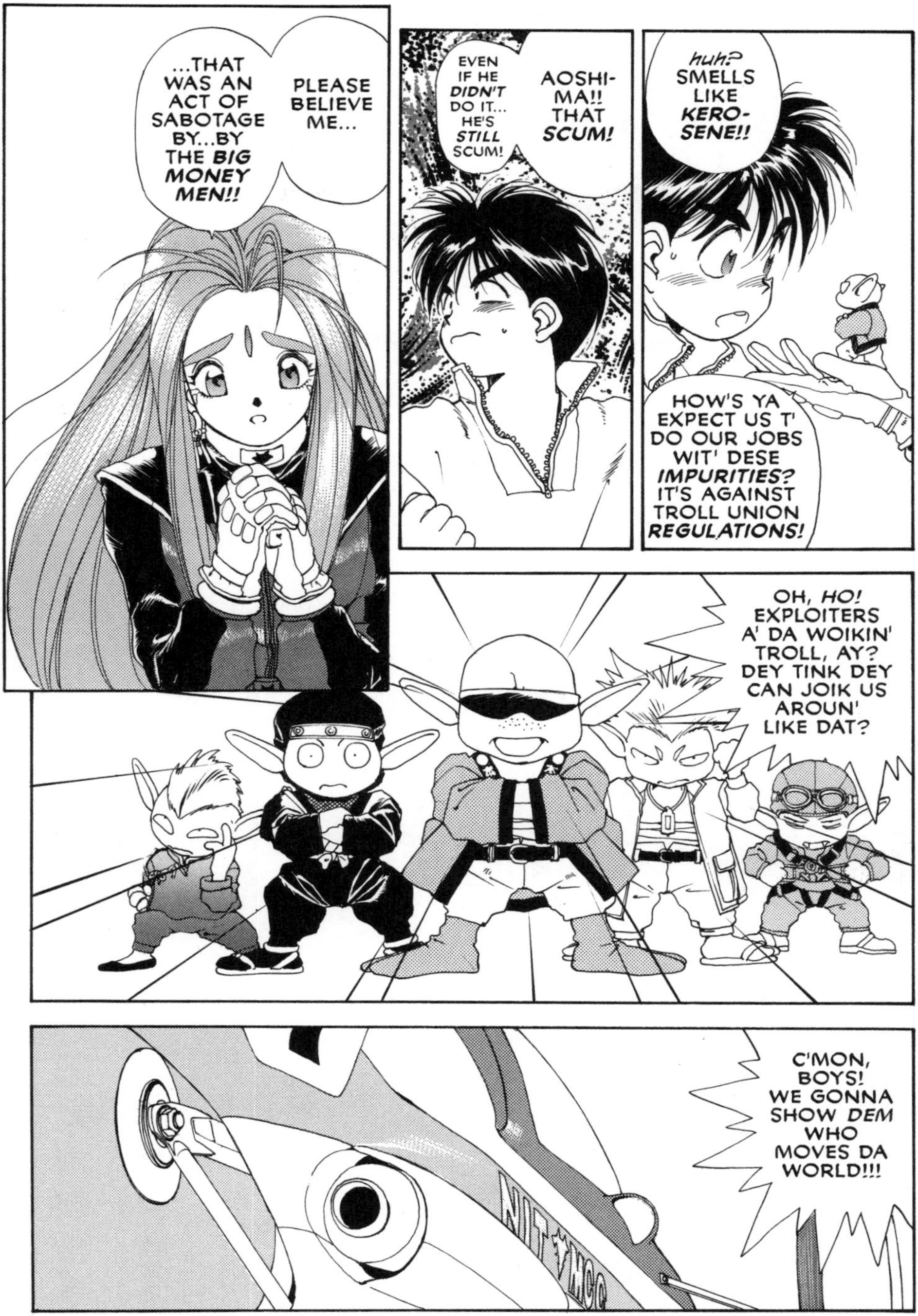
huh? SMELLS LIKE KERO-SENE!!
HOW'S YA EXPECT US T' DO OUR JOBS WIT' DESE IMPURITIES? IT'S AGAINST TROLL UNION REGULATIONS!
AOSHIMA!! THAT SCUM!
EVEN IF HE DIDN'T DO IT... HE'S STILL SCUM!
PLEASE BELIEVE ME...
...THAT WAS AN ACT OF SABOTAGE BY...BY THE BIG MONEY MEN!!
OH, HO! EXPLOITERS A' DA WOIKIN' TROLL, AY? DEY TINK DEY CAN JOIK US AROUN' LIKE DAT?
C'MON, BOYS! WE GONNA SHOW DEM WHO MOVES DA WORLD!!!
NIT*MCC

FWHOOOSSHH
7
NIT MCC
DAT'S IT! WOIK IT, BOYS!!
DA GAS IS RUNNIN' OUT, SO WE'S GOTTA MAKE UP FOR IT!!
COMPRESSION
mmph...
SHAKK
EXPANSION
HYAH !!
BOOM!
EXHAUST
gasp!
INTAKE
huff!

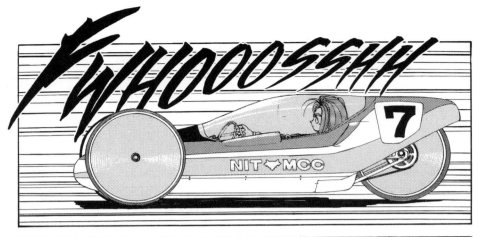

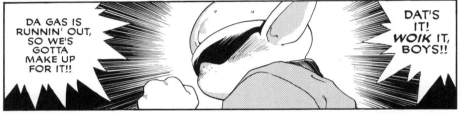

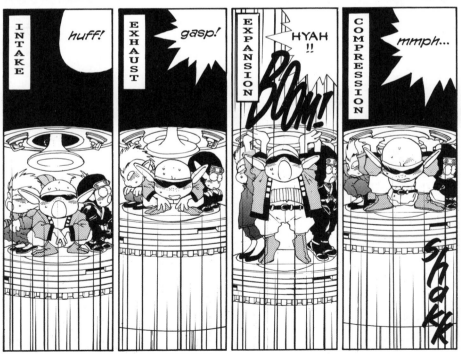

(REPEAT 1500 TIMES PER MINUTE = 3000RPM)

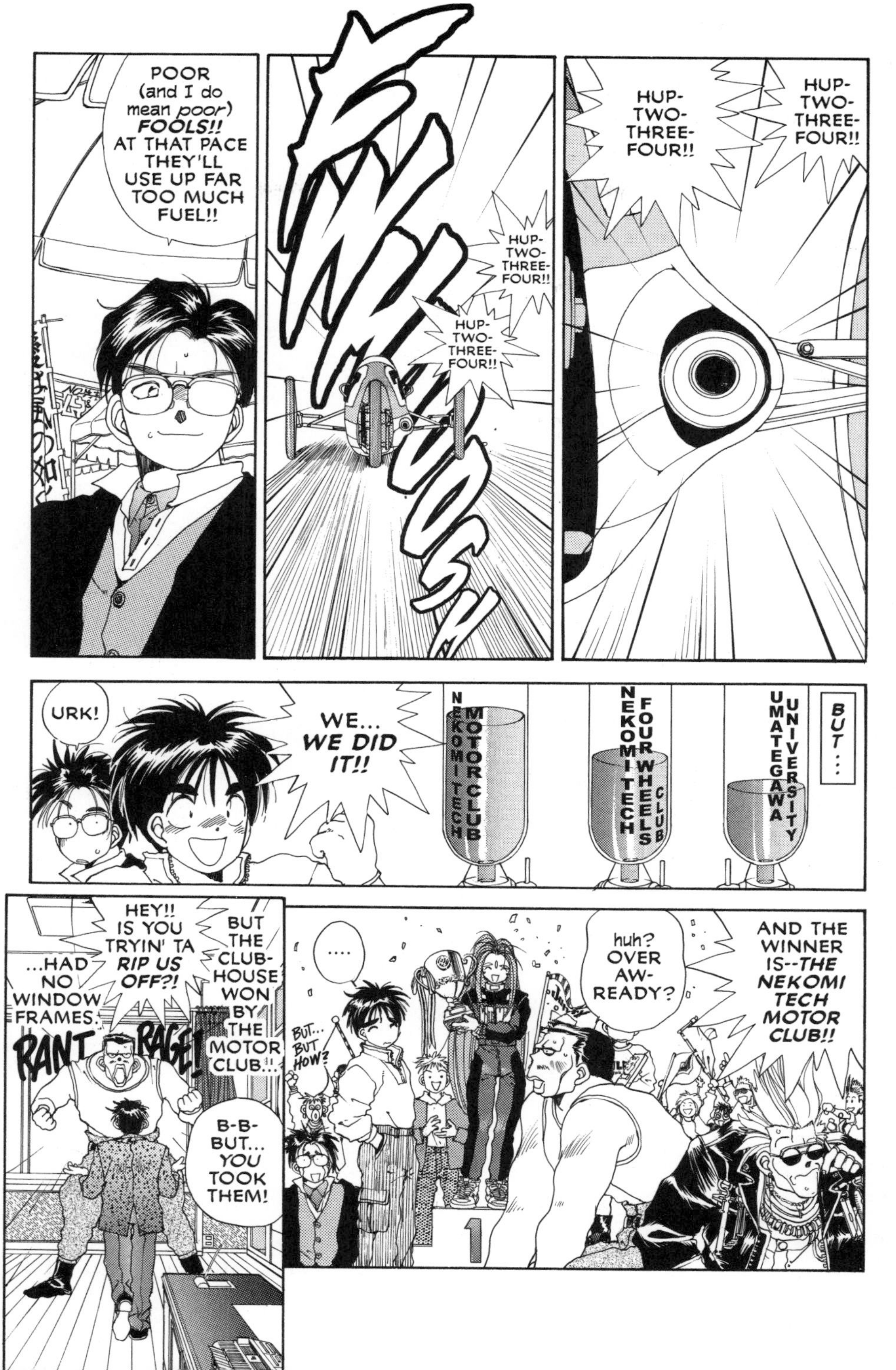
HUP-TWO-THREE-FOUR!!
HUP-TWO-THREE-FOUR!!
HUP-TWO-THREE-FOUR!!
HUP-TWO-THREE-FOUR!!
POOR (and I do mean *poor*) **FOOLS!!** AT THAT PACE THEY'LL USE UP FAR TOO MUCH FUEL!!
BUT...
UMATEGAWA UNIVERSITY
NEKOMI TECH FOUR WHEELS CLUB
NEKOMI TECH MOTOR CLUB
WE... **WE DID IT!!**
URK!
AND THE WINNER IS--*THE NEKOMI TECH MOTOR CLUB!!*
huh? OVER AW-READY?
....
BUT... BUT HOW?
BUT THE CLUB-HOUSE WON BY THE MOTOR CLUB...
HEY!! IS YOU TRYIN' TA *RIP US OFF?!*
...HAD NO WINDOW FRAMES.
RANT RAGE!
B-B-BUT... *YOU* TOOK THEM!

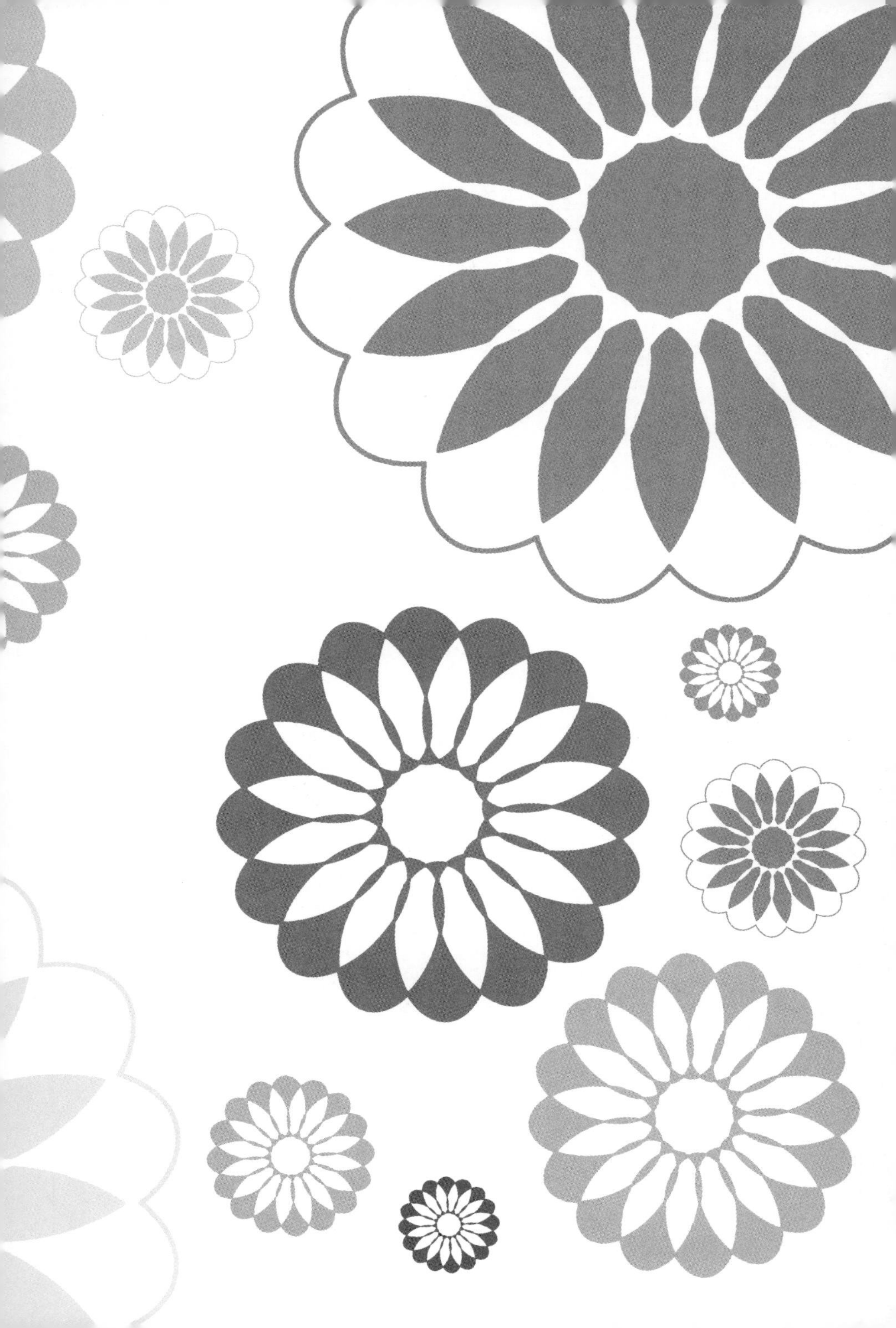

CHAPTER 31

# Valentine Capriccio

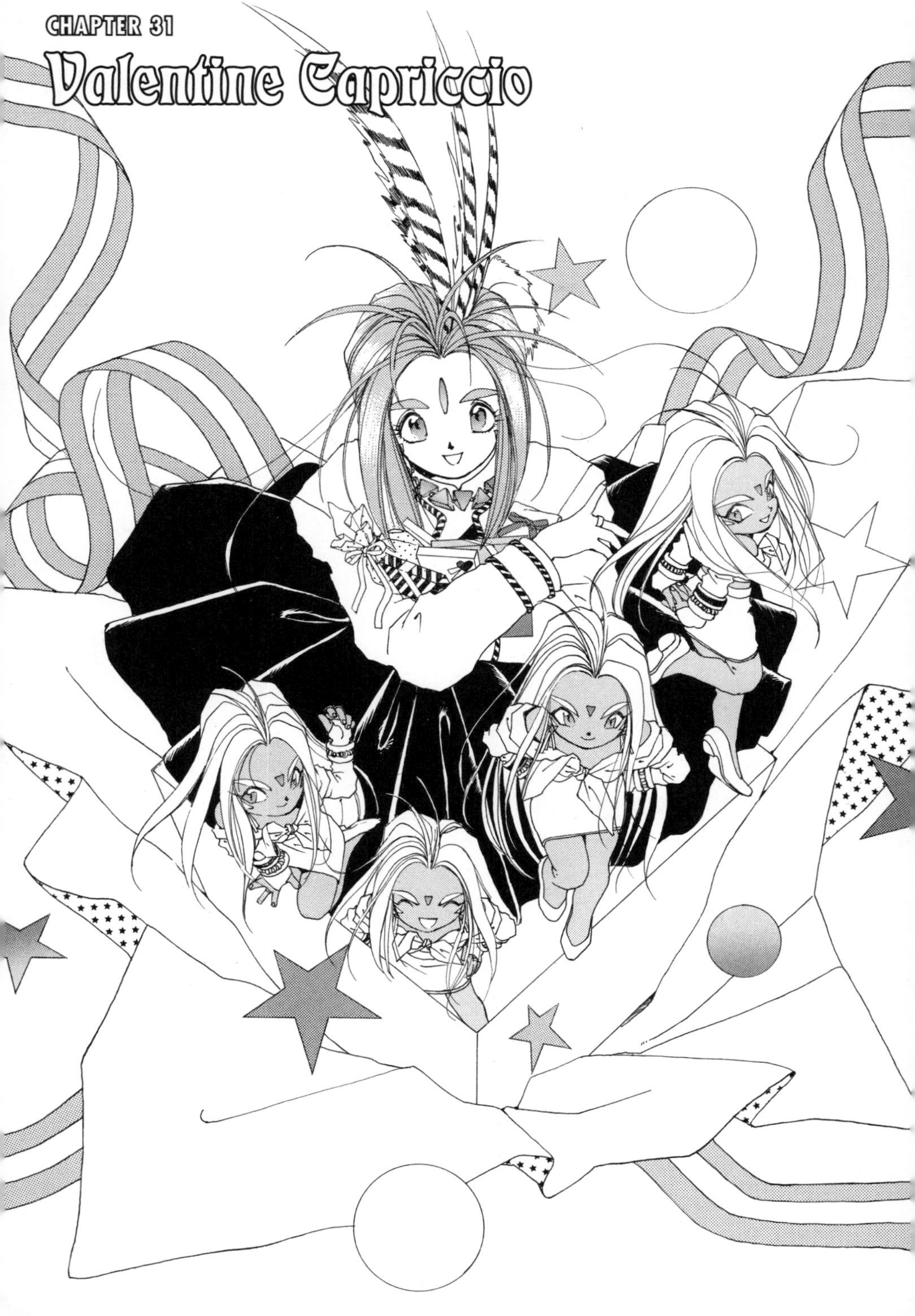

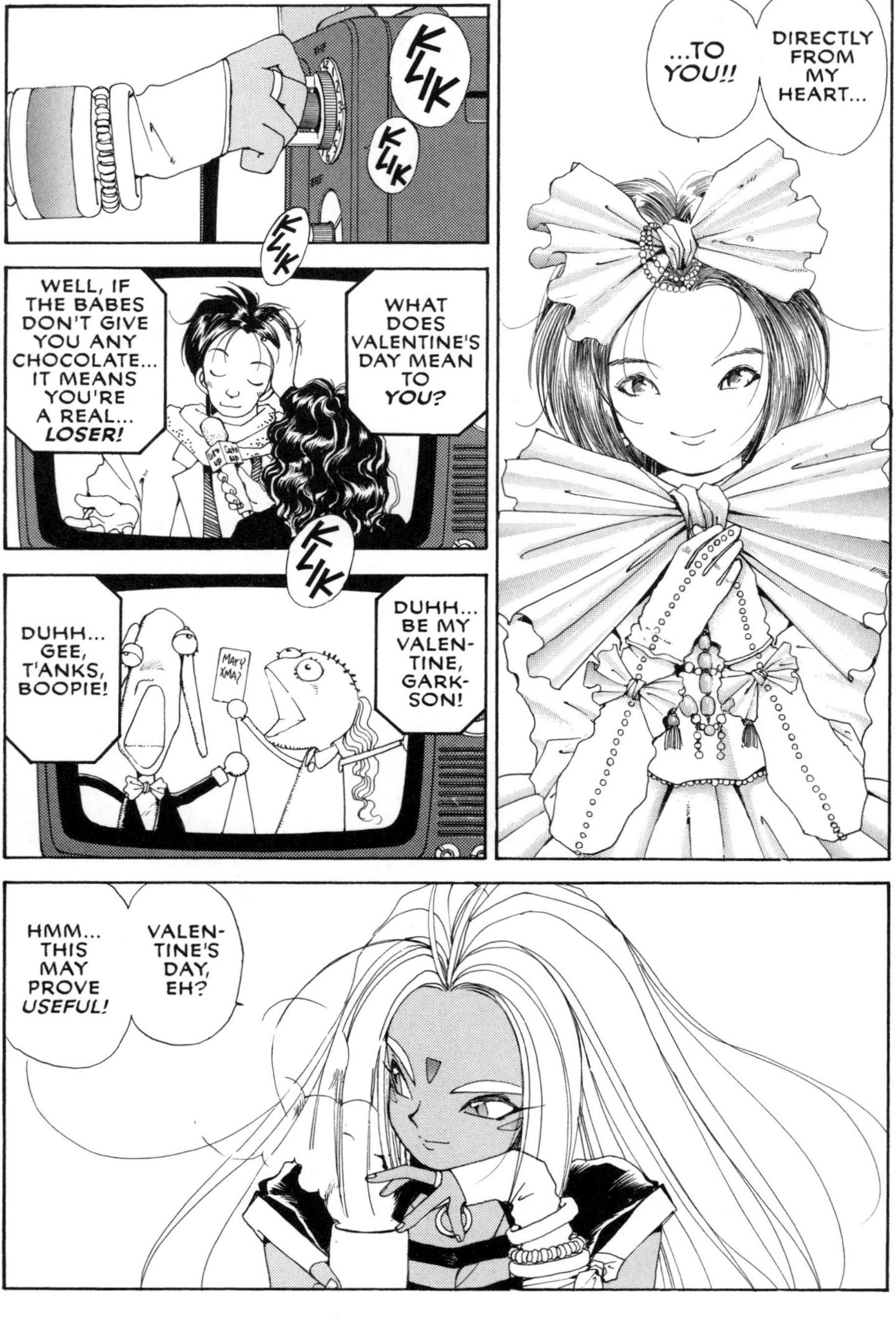
DIRECTLY FROM MY HEART...
...TO YOU!!
KLIK
KLIK
KLIK
WHAT DOES VALENTINE'S DAY MEAN TO YOU?
WELL, IF THE BABES DON'T GIVE YOU ANY CHOCOLATE... IT MEANS YOU'RE A REAL... LOSER!
KLIK
DUHH... BE MY VALENTINE, GARKSON!
DUHH... GEE, T'ANKS, BOOPIE!
VALENTINE'S DAY, EH?
HMM... THIS MAY PROVE USEFUL!

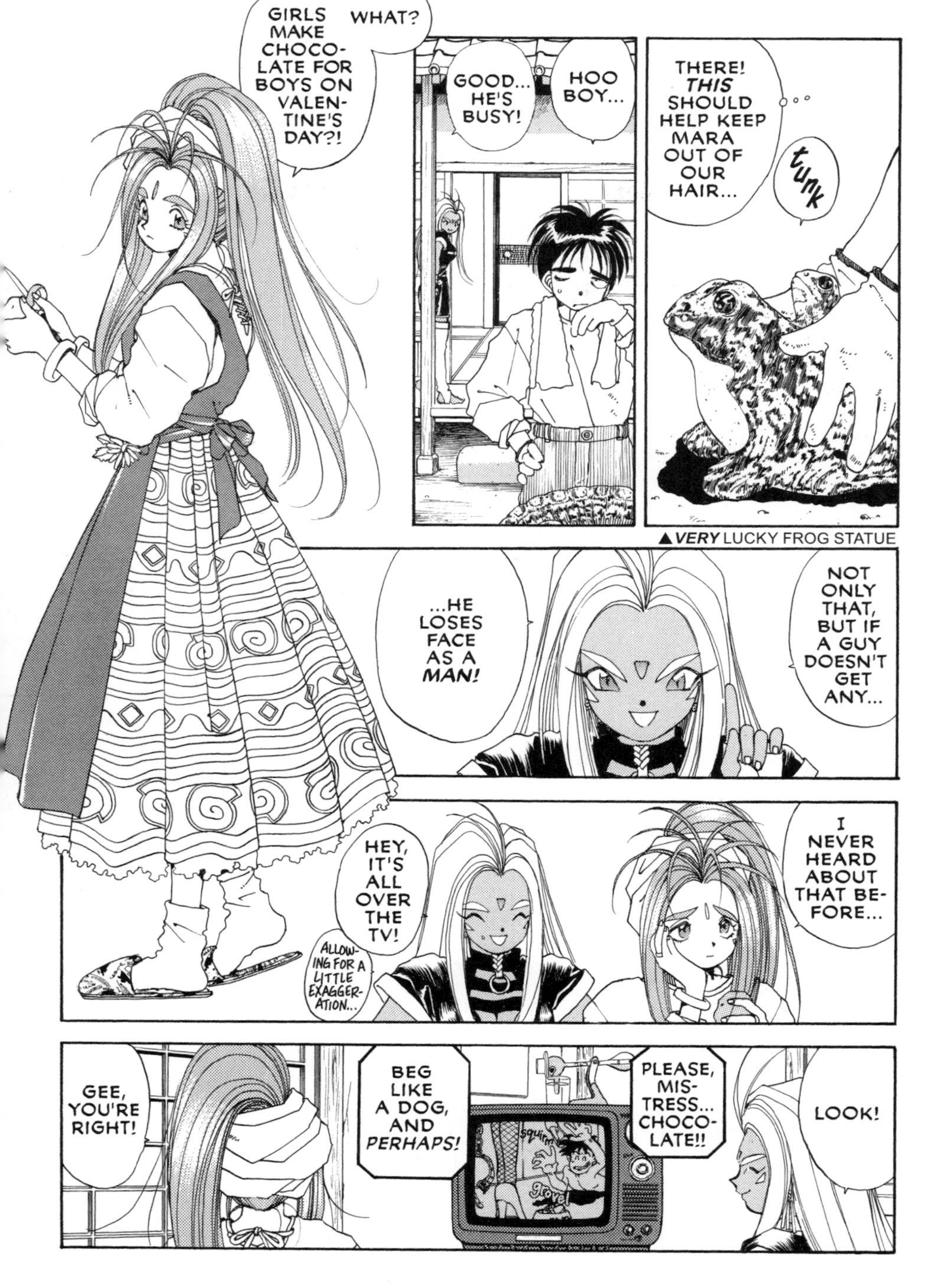
THERE! *THIS* SHOULD HELP KEEP MARA OUT OF OUR HAIR...
tunk
HOO BOY...
GOOD... HE'S BUSY!
WHAT?
GIRLS MAKE CHOCOLATE FOR BOYS ON VALENTINE'S DAY?!
▲*VERY* LUCKY FROG STATUE
NOT ONLY THAT, BUT IF A GUY DOESN'T GET ANY...
...HE LOSES FACE AS A *MAN!*
I NEVER HEARD ABOUT THAT BEFORE...
HEY, IT'S ALL OVER THE TV!
ALLOWING FOR A LITTLE EXAGGERATION...
LOOK!
PLEASE, MISTRESS... CHOCOLATE!!
squirm
grovel
BEG LIKE A DOG, AND *PERHAPS!*
GEE, YOU'RE RIGHT!

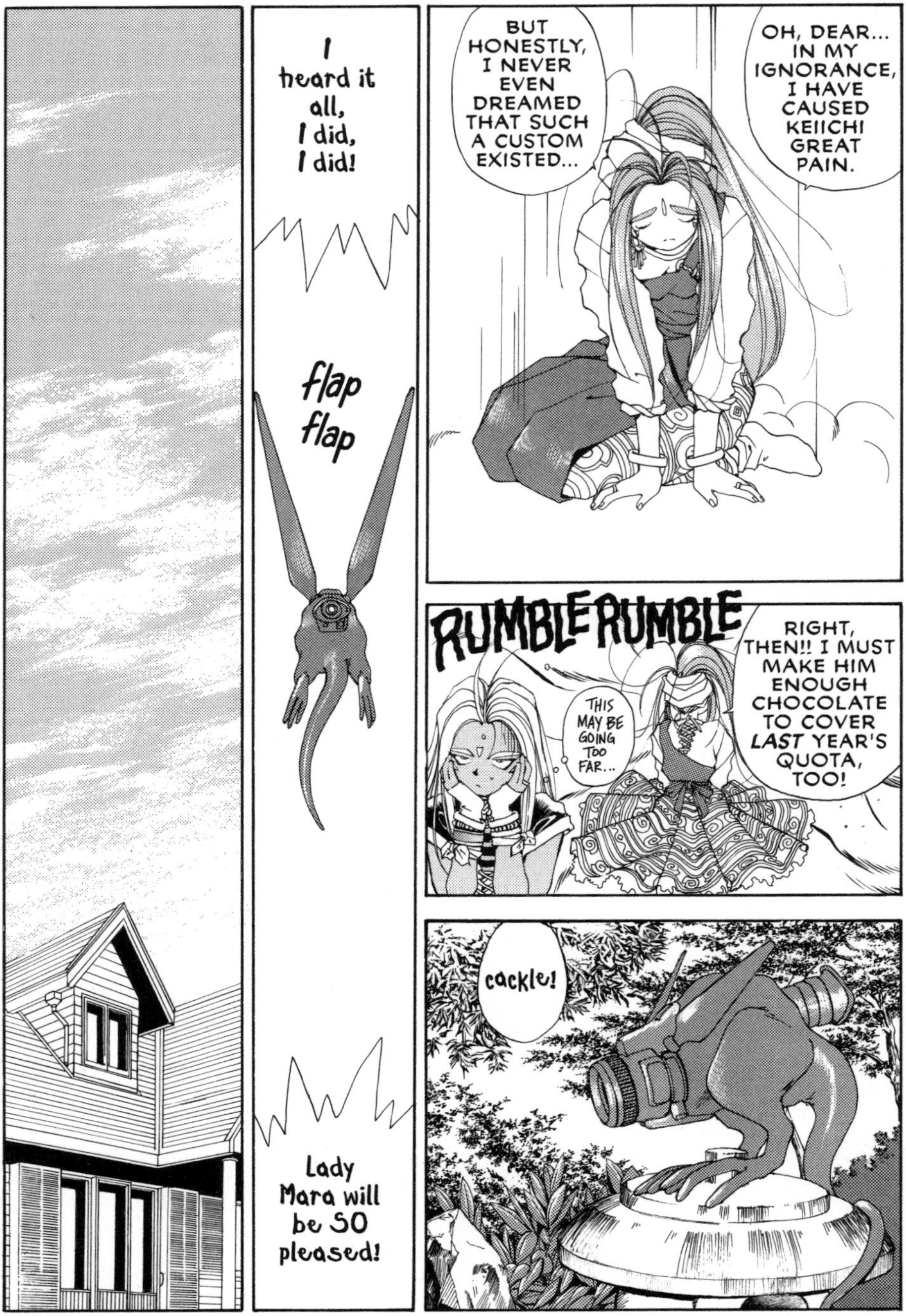
OH, DEAR... IN MY IGNORANCE, I HAVE CAUSED KEIICHI GREAT PAIN.
BUT HONESTLY, I NEVER EVEN DREAMED THAT SUCH A CUSTOM EXISTED...
RIGHT, THEN!! I MUST MAKE HIM ENOUGH CHOCOLATE TO COVER LAST YEAR'S QUOTA, TOO!
RUMBLE RUMBLE
THIS MAY BE GOING TOO FAR...
cackle!
I heard it all, I did, I did!
flap flap
Lady Mara will be SO pleased!

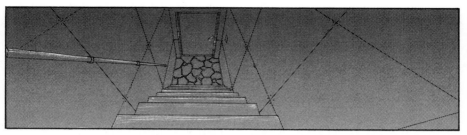

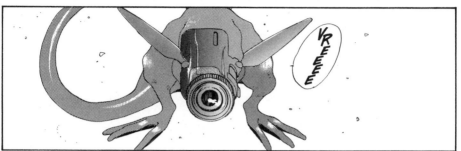

VREEEE
OH, *HO!*
CHOCO-LATE... *EH?*
MARA DOWNLOADS THE SPY FOOTAGE VIA THE TAIL.
KEIICHI'S TRYING TO KEEP ME AWAY WITH CHARMS, BUT SORRY, PAL...
...I NEVER FALL FOR THE SAME TRICK TWICE.
AND SO...

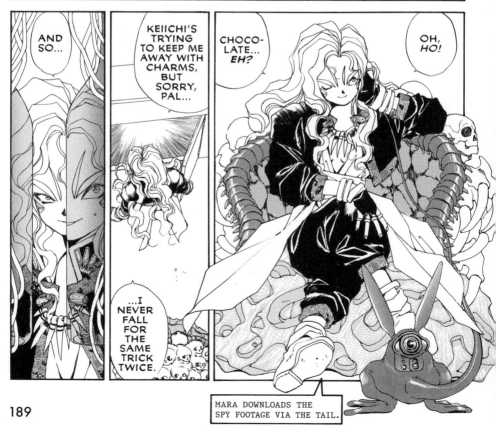

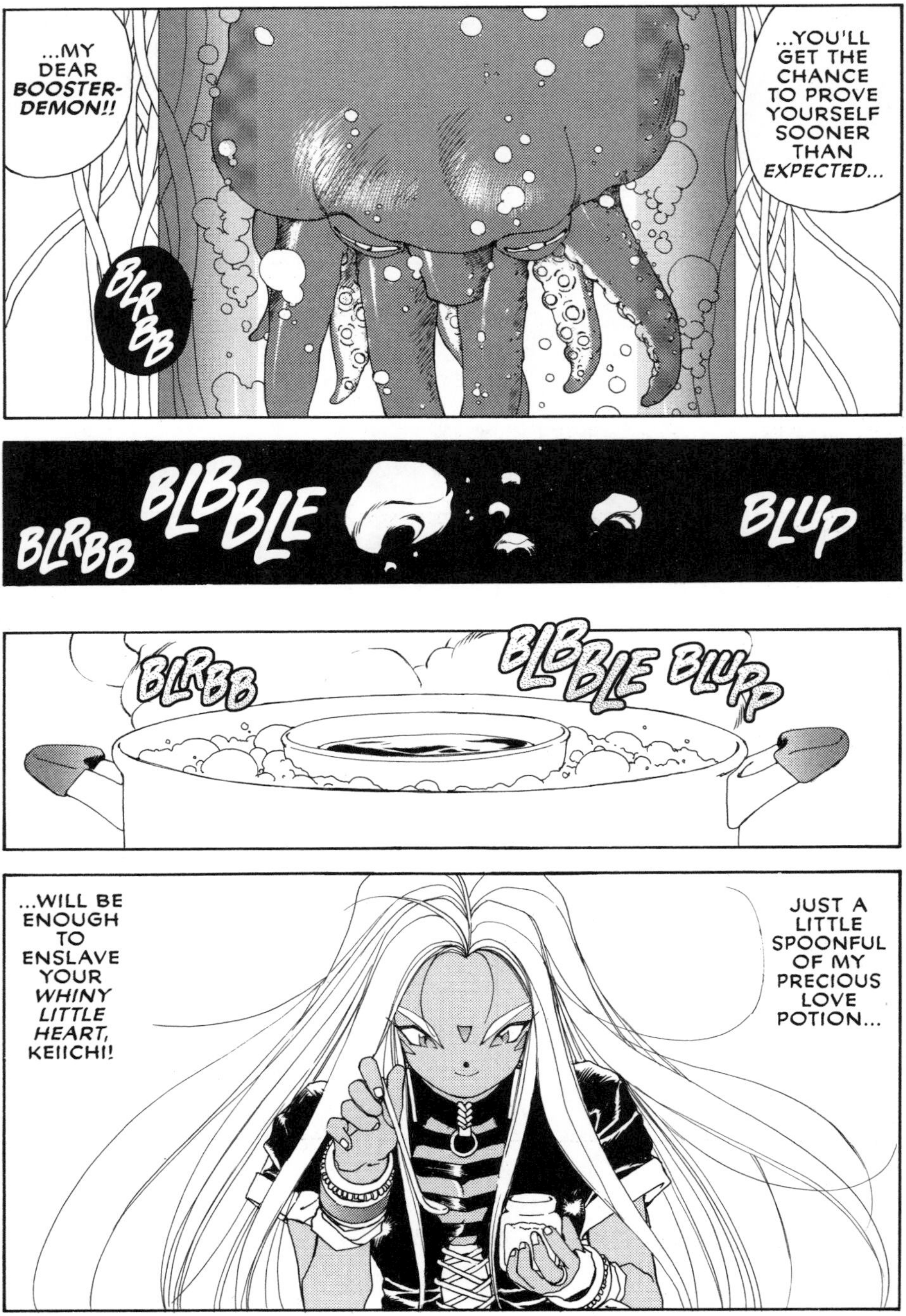
...YOU'LL GET THE CHANCE TO PROVE YOURSELF SOONER THAN *EXPECTED...*
...MY DEAR ***BOOSTER-DEMON!!***
BLRBB
BLUP
BLBBLE
BLRBB
BLBBLE BLUPP
BLRBB
JUST A LITTLE SPOONFUL OF MY PRECIOUS LOVE POTION...
...WILL BE ENOUGH TO ENSLAVE YOUR *WHINY LITTLE* HEART, KEIICHI!

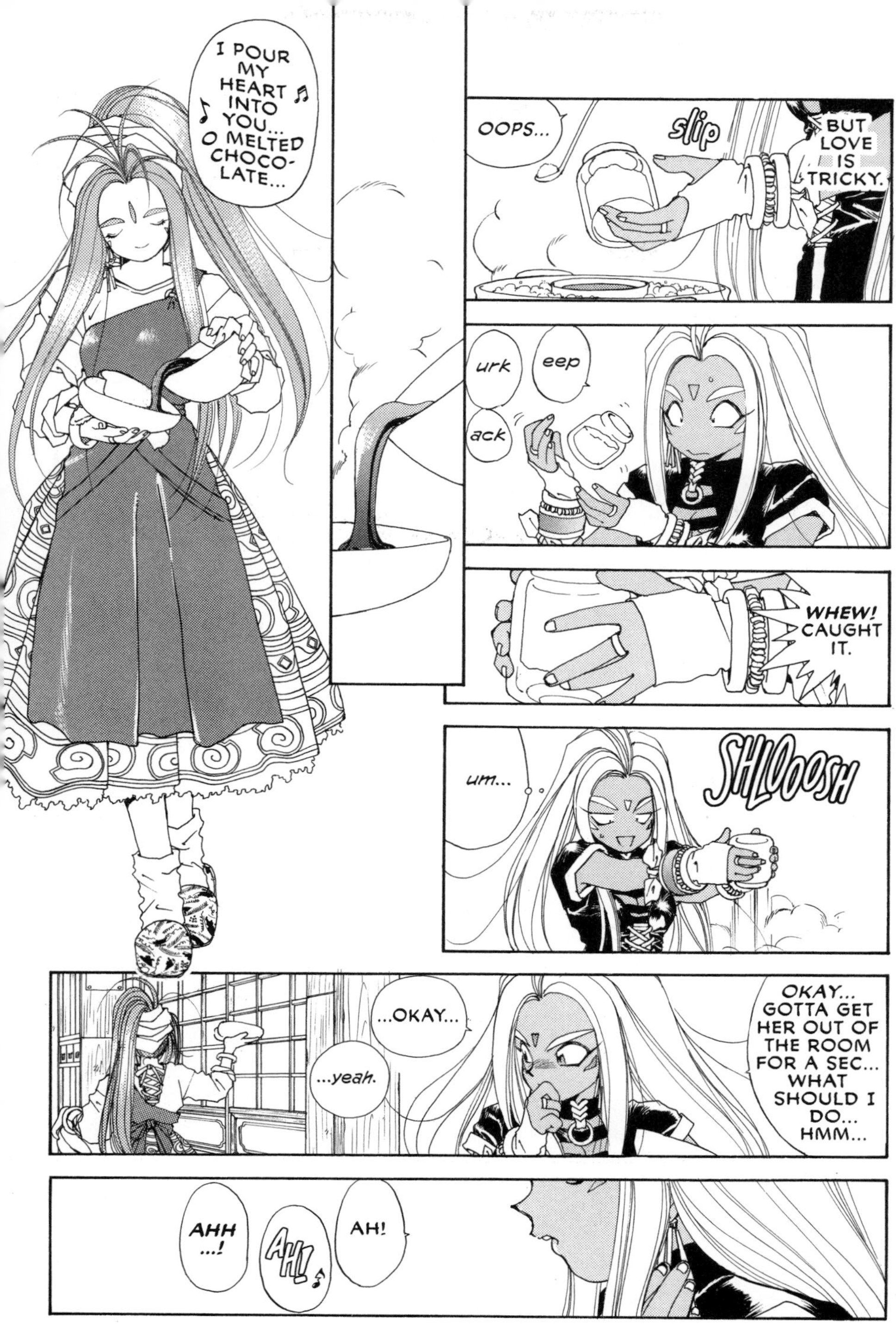
I POUR MY HEART ♫ ♪ INTO YOU... O MELTED CHOCO-LATE...
BUT LOVE IS TRICKY.
slip
OOPS...
eep
urk
ack
WHEW! CAUGHT IT.
SHLOOOSH
um...
OKAY... GOTTA GET HER OUT OF THE ROOM FOR A SEC... WHAT SHOULD I DO... HMM...
...OKAY...
...yeah.
AH!
AH!
AHH ...!

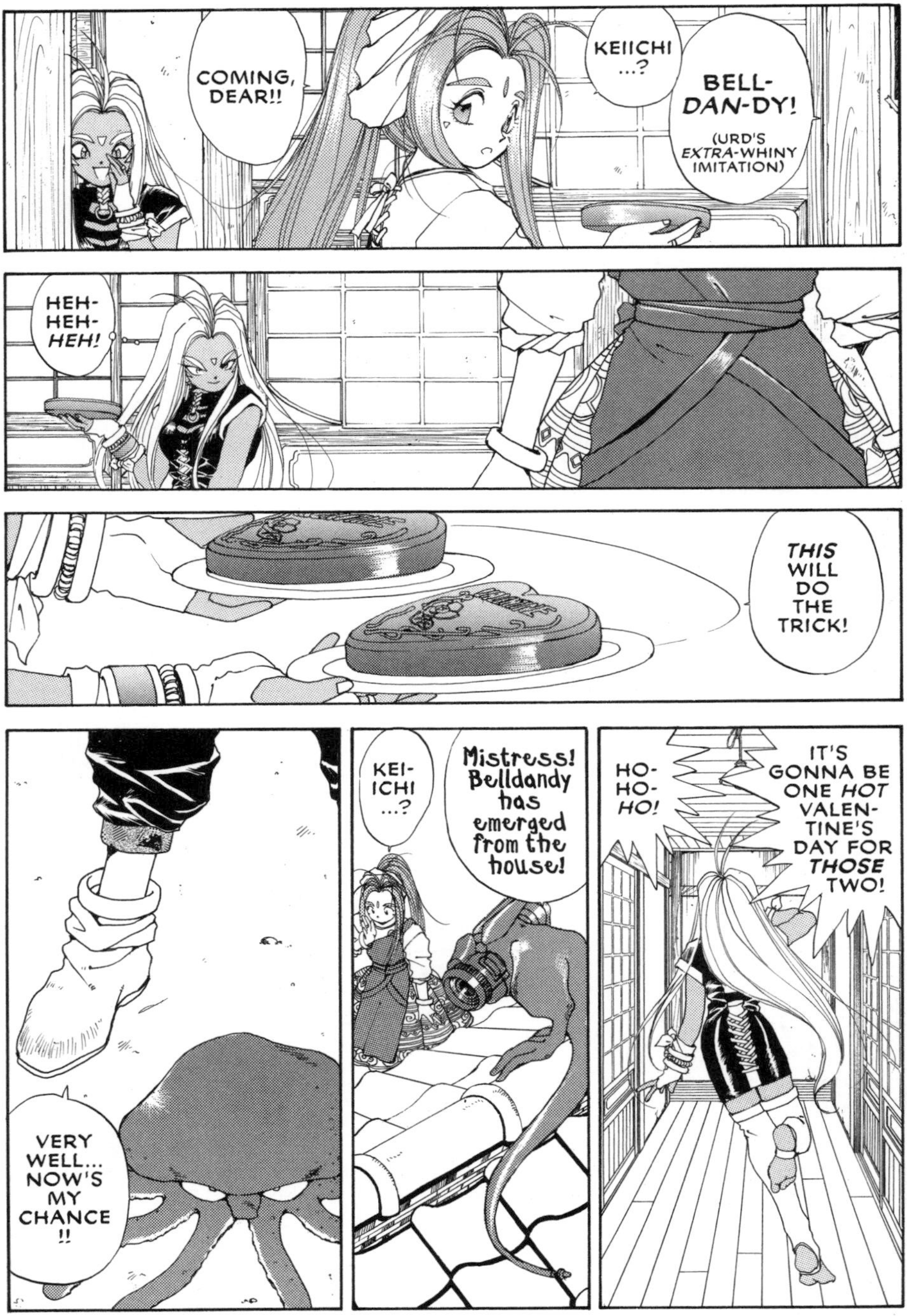
BELL-DAN-DY!
(URD'S EXTRA-WHINY IMITATION)
KEIICHI ...?
COMING, DEAR!!
HEH-HEH-HEH!
THIS WILL DO THE TRICK!
IT'S GONNA BE ONE HOT VALENTINE'S DAY FOR THOSE TWO!
HO-HO-HO!
Mistress! Belldandy has emerged from the house!
KEI-ICHI ...?
VERY WELL... NOW'S MY CHANCE !!

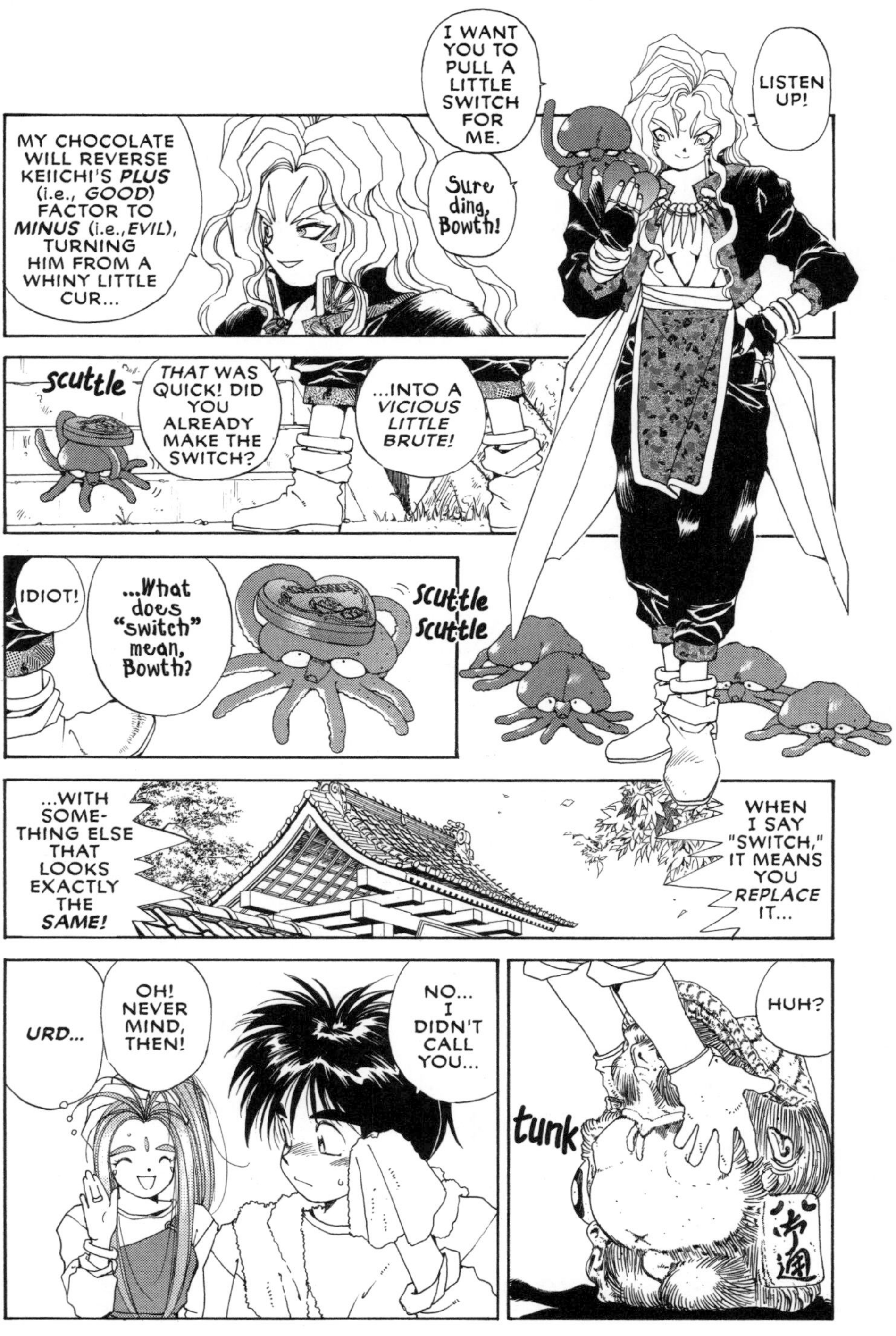
LISTEN UP!
I WANT YOU TO PULL A LITTLE SWITCH FOR ME.
Sure ding, Bowth!
scuttle scuttle
MY CHOCOLATE WILL REVERSE KEIICHI'S PLUS (i.e., GOOD) FACTOR TO MINUS (i.e., EVIL), TURNING HIM FROM A WHINY LITTLE CUR...
...INTO A VICIOUS LITTLE BRUTE!
THAT WAS QUICK! DID YOU ALREADY MAKE THE SWITCH?
scuttle
...What does "switch" mean, Bowth?
IDIOT!
WHEN I SAY "SWITCH," IT MEANS YOU REPLACE IT...
...WITH SOMETHING ELSE THAT LOOKS EXACTLY THE SAME!
HUH?
tunk
NO... I DIDN'T CALL YOU...
OH! NEVER MIND, THEN!
URD...

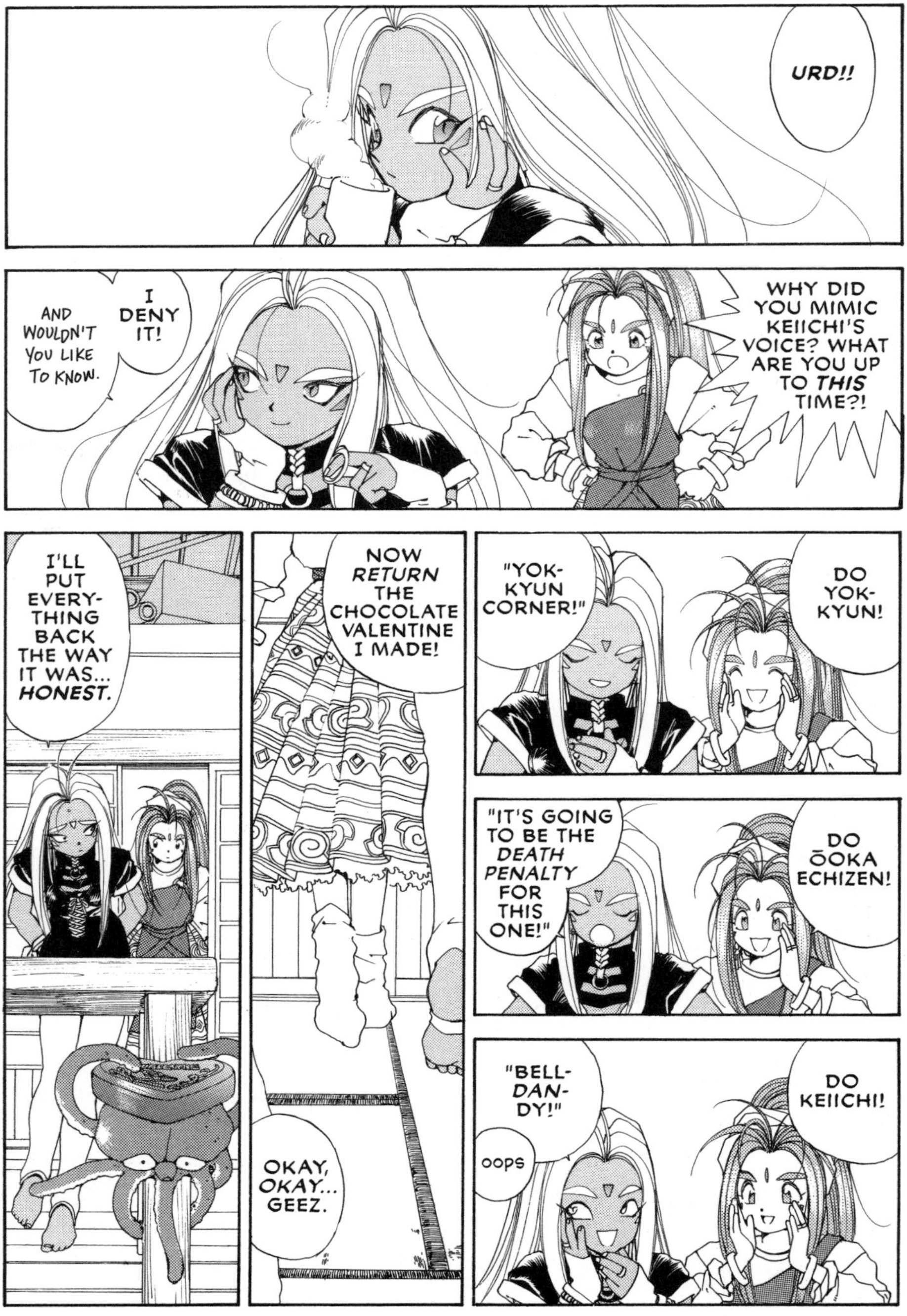
URD!!
WHY DID YOU MIMIC KEIICHI'S VOICE? WHAT ARE YOU UP TO *THIS* TIME?!
I DENY IT!
AND WOULDN'T YOU LIKE TO KNOW.
DO YOK-KYUN!
"YOK-KYUN CORNER!"
DO ŌOKA ECHIZEN!
"IT'S GOING TO BE THE *DEATH PENALTY* FOR THIS ONE!"
DO KEIICHI!
"BELL-*DAN*-DY!"
oops
NOW *RETURN* THE CHOCOLATE VALENTINE I MADE!
OKAY, *OKAY*... GEEZ.
I'LL PUT EVERY-THING BACK THE WAY IT WAS... *HONEST*.

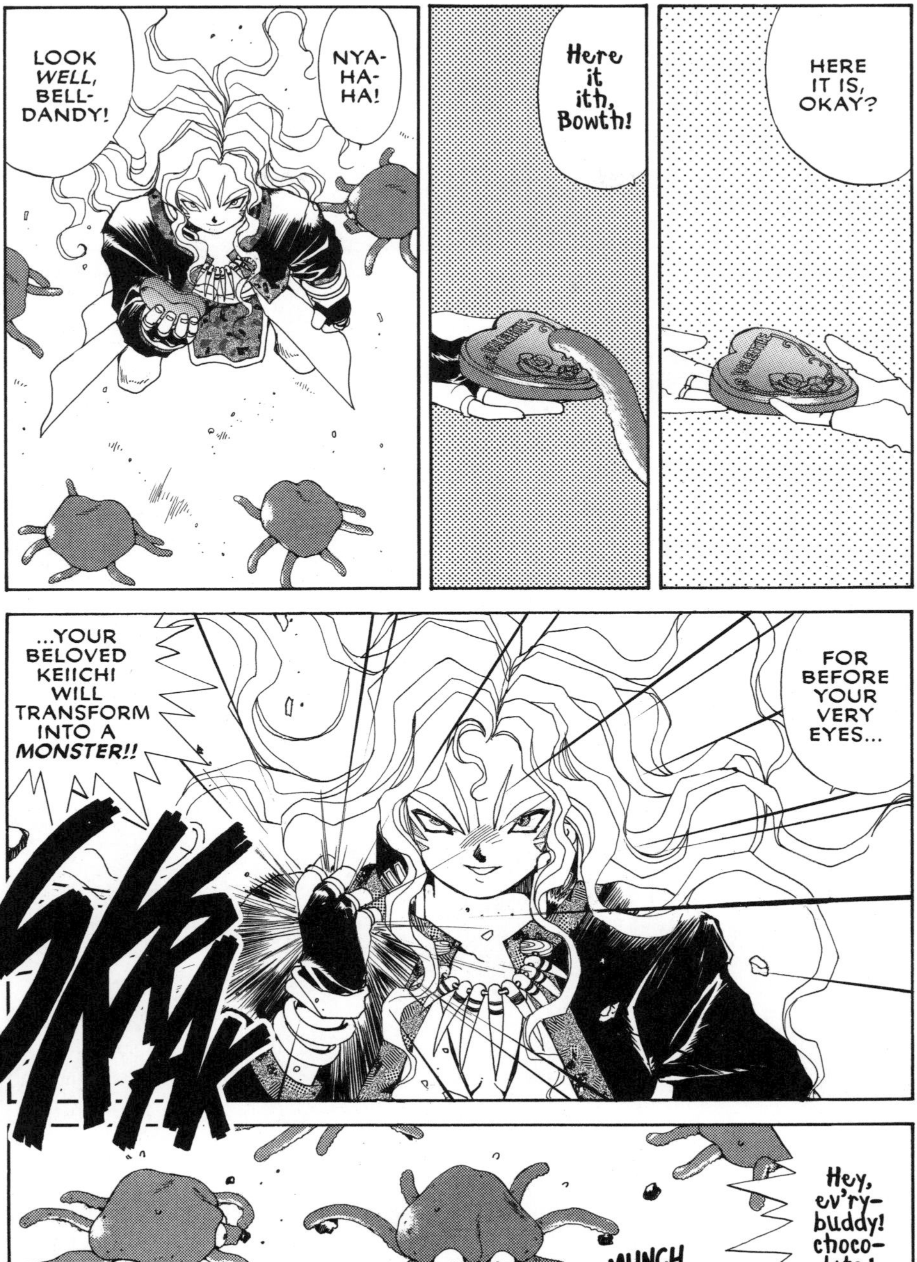
HERE IT IS, OKAY?
Here it ith, Bowth!
NYA-HA-HA!
LOOK *WELL*, BELL-DANDY!
FOR BEFORE YOUR VERY EYES...
...YOUR BELOVED KEIICHI WILL TRANSFORM INTO A *MONSTER!!*
Hey, ev'ry-buddy! chocolate!
MUNCH
GULP

AND NOW-- STAND BY... BA-BA-BOOSTERS!!

Yeth, Bowth!

THAT MEANS STOP EATING, IDIOTS!

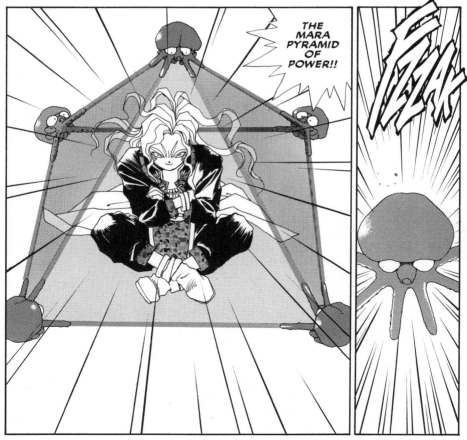

THE MARA PYRAMID OF POWER!!

FFZZAK

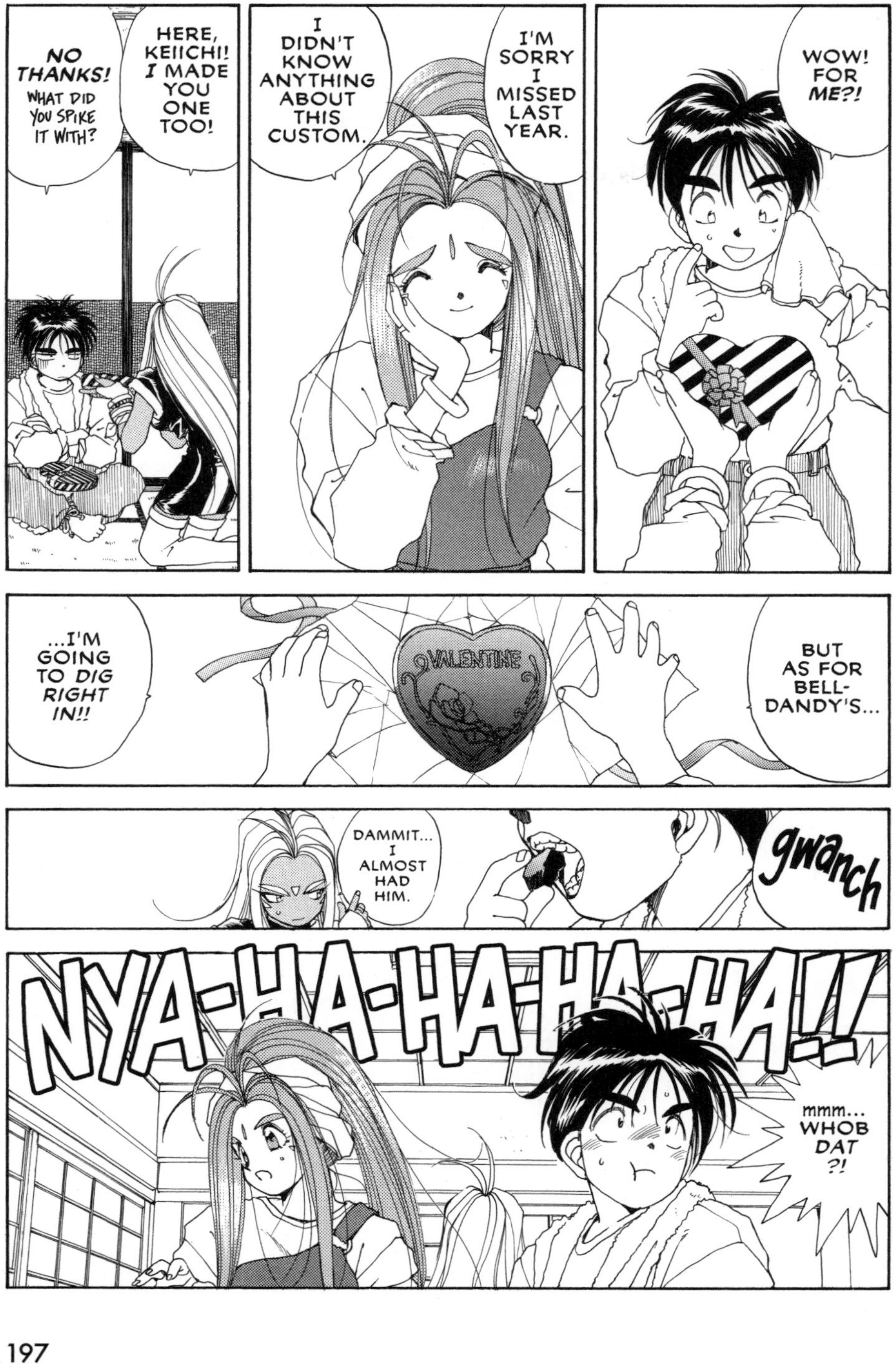
WOW! FOR *ME?!*
I'M SORRY I MISSED LAST YEAR.
I DIDN'T KNOW ANYTHING ABOUT THIS CUSTOM.
HERE, KEIICHI! *I* MADE YOU ONE TOO!
*NO THANKS!* WHAT DID YOU SPIKE IT WITH?
BUT AS FOR BELL-DANDY'S...
VALENTINE
...I'M GOING TO *DIG RIGHT IN!!*
gwanch
DAMMIT... I ALMOST HAD HIM.
NYA-HA-HA-HA-HA!!
mmm... WHOB *DAT ?!*

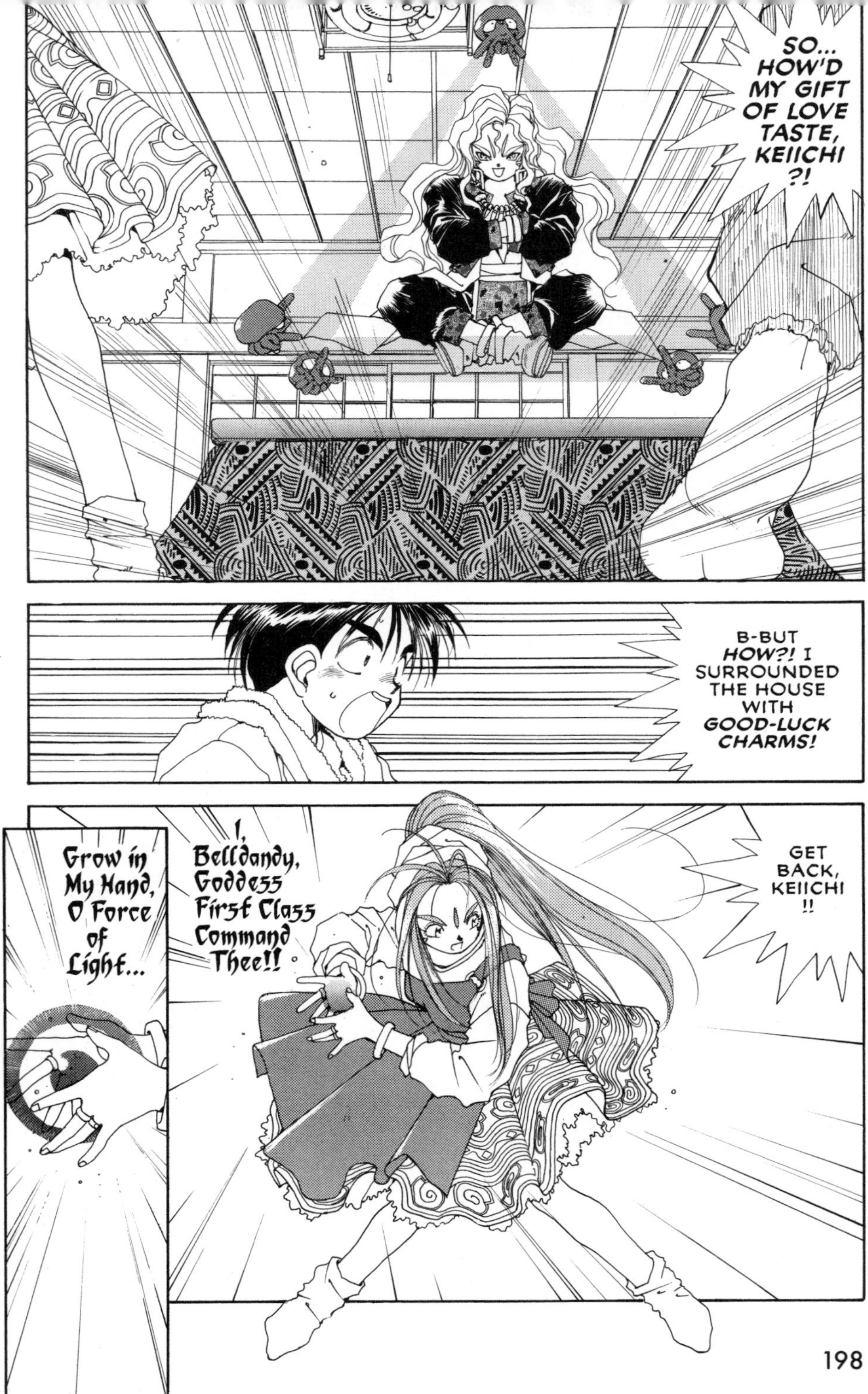
SO... HOW'D MY GIFT OF LOVE TASTE, KEIICHI ?!
B-BUT HOW?! I SURROUNDED THE HOUSE WITH GOOD-LUCK CHARMS!
GET BACK, KEIICHI !!
I, Belldandy, Goddess First Class Command Thee!!
Grow in My Hand, O Force of Light...

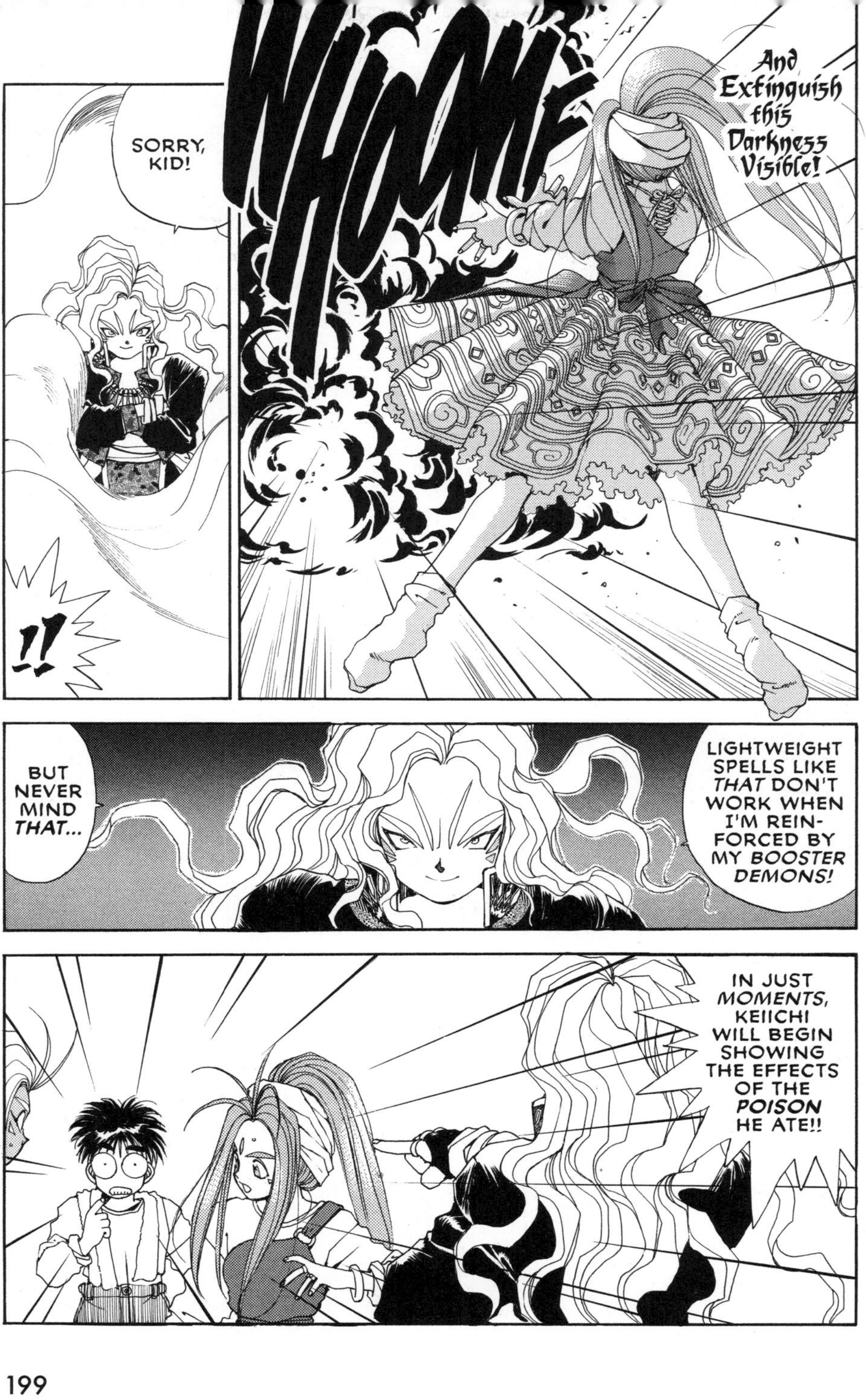
And Extinguish this Darkness Visible!
WHOOMF
SORRY, KID!
!!
LIGHTWEIGHT SPELLS LIKE *THAT* DON'T WORK WHEN I'M REIN-FORCED BY MY *BOOSTER DEMONS!*
BUT NEVER MIND *THAT*...
IN JUST *MOMENTS*, KEIICHI WILL BEGIN SHOWING THE EFFECTS OF THE *POISON* HE ATE!!

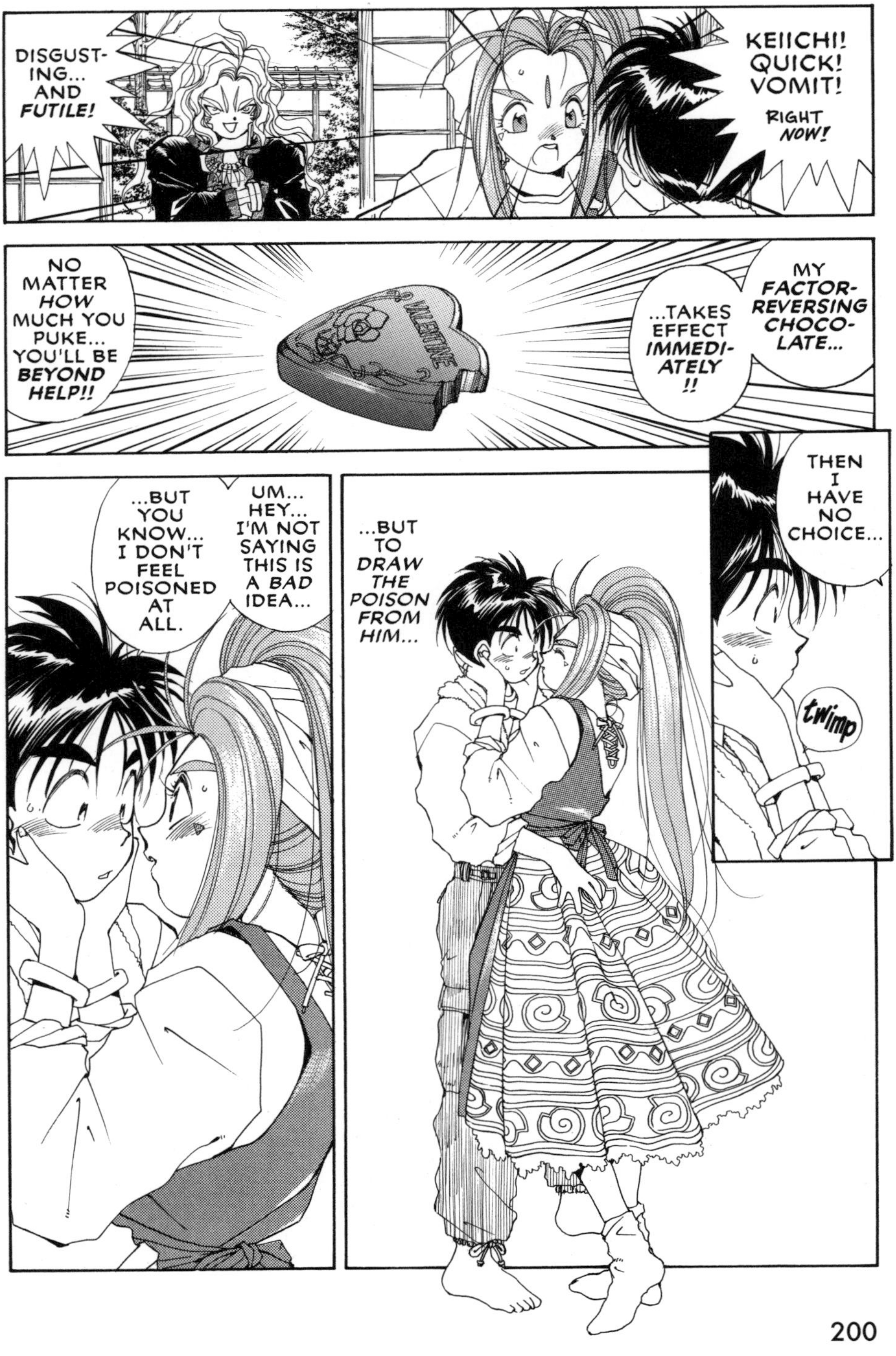
KEIICHI! QUICK! VOMIT!
RIGHT NOW!
DISGUSTING... AND FUTILE!
MY FACTOR-REVERSING CHOCOLATE...
...TAKES EFFECT IMMEDIATELY!!
VALENTINE
NO MATTER HOW MUCH YOU PUKE... YOU'LL BE BEYOND HELP!!
THEN I HAVE NO CHOICE...
twimp
...BUT TO DRAW THE POISON FROM HIM...
UM... HEY... I'M NOT SAYING THIS IS A BAD IDEA...
...BUT YOU KNOW... I DON'T FEEL POISONED AT ALL.

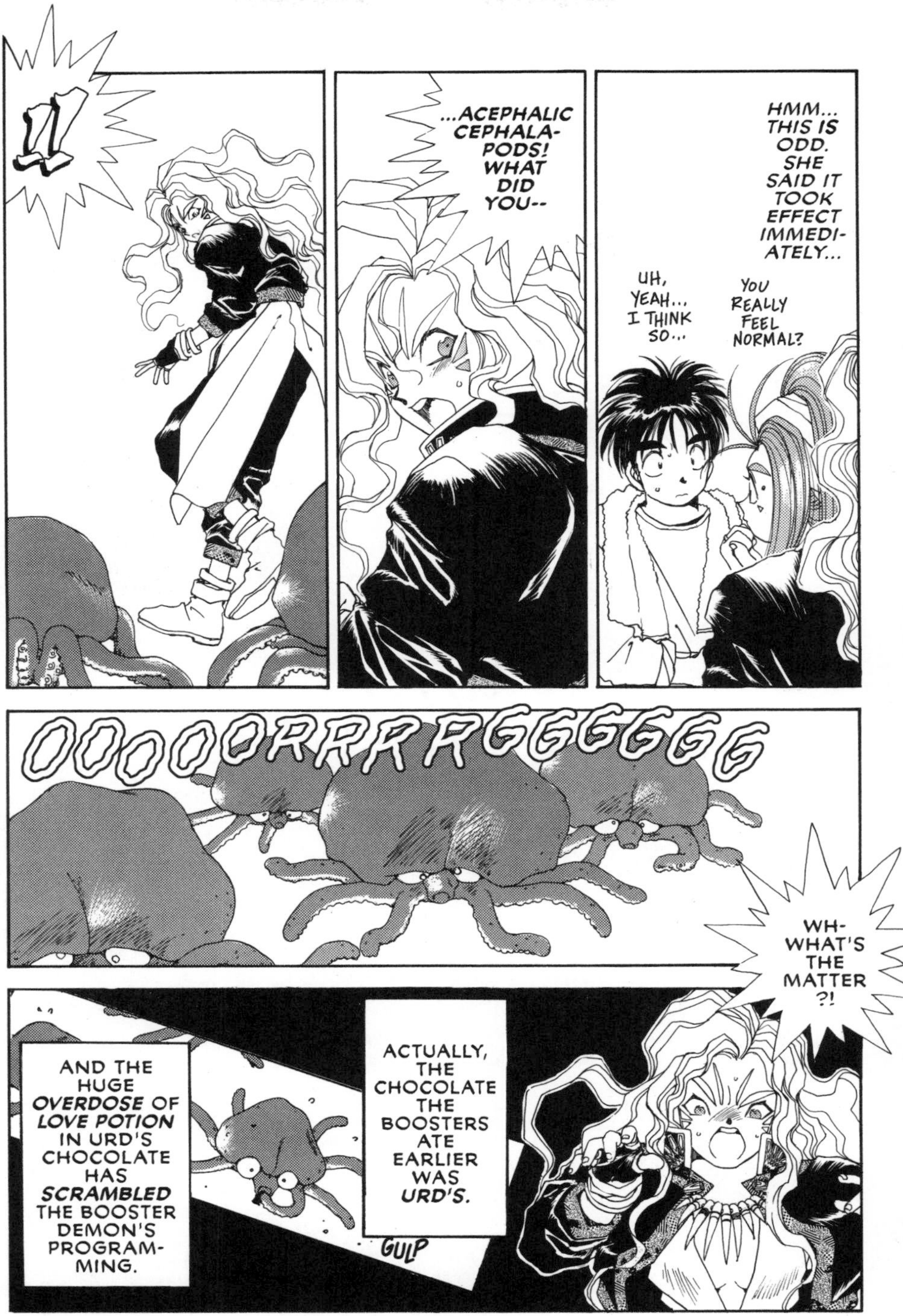
HMM... THIS IS ODD. SHE SAID IT TOOK EFFECT IMMEDIATELY...
YOU REALLY FEEL NORMAL?
UH, YEAH... I THINK SO...
...ACEPHALIC CEPHALAPODS! WHAT DID YOU--
OOOOORRRRGGGGGG
WH-WHAT'S THE MATTER?!
ACTUALLY, THE CHOCOLATE THE BOOSTERS ATE EARLIER WAS URD'S.
AND THE HUGE OVERDOSE OF LOVE POTION IN URD'S CHOCOLATE HAS SCRAMBLED THE BOOSTER DEMON'S PROGRAMMING.
GULP

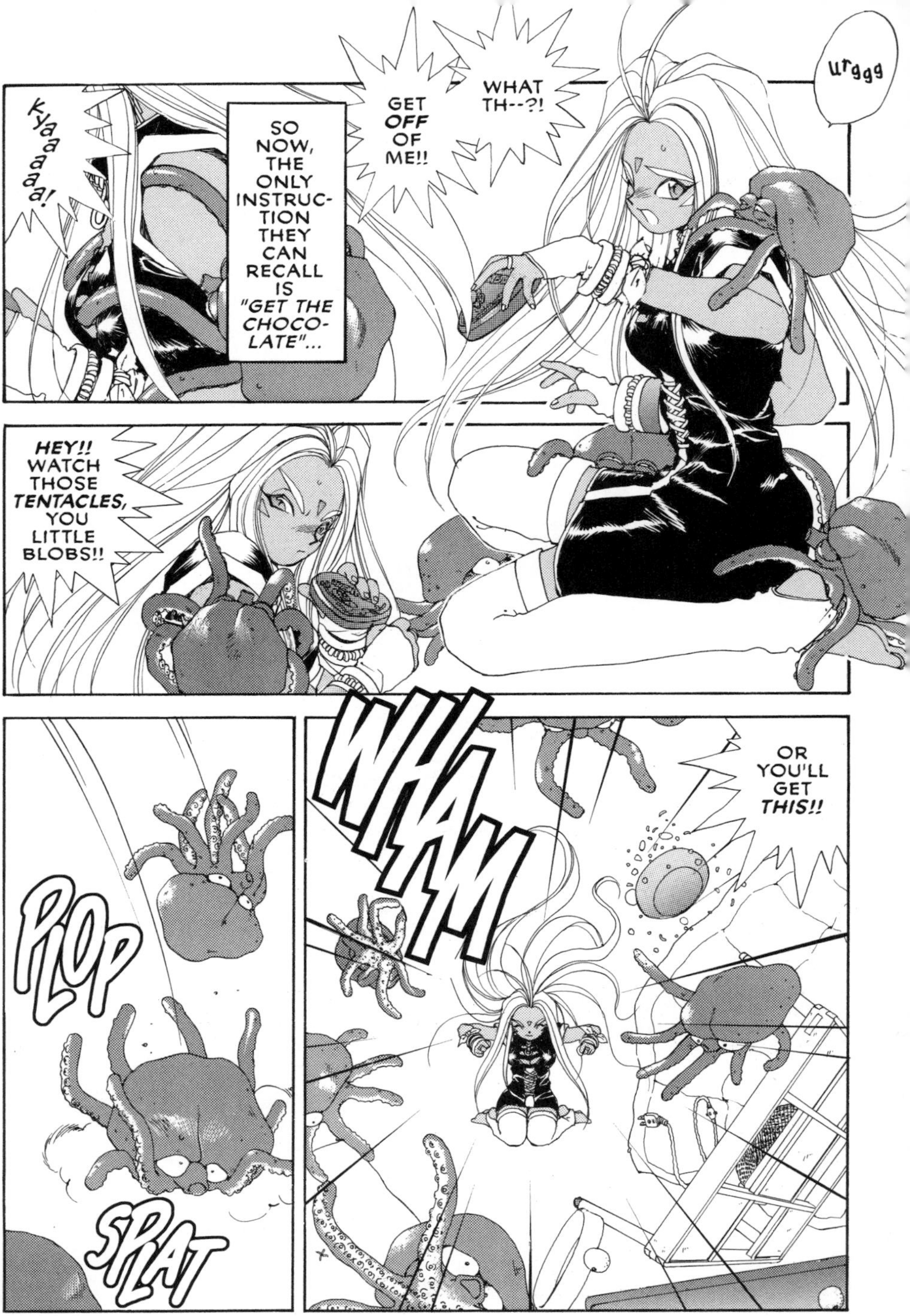

Urggg
WHAT TH--?!
GET OFF OF ME!!
SO NOW, THE ONLY INSTRUCTION THEY CAN RECALL IS "GET THE CHOCOLATE"...
kyaaaaaa!
HEY!! WATCH THOSE TENTACLES, YOU LITTLE BLOBS!!
OR YOU'LL GET THIS!!
WHAM
PLOP
SPLAT

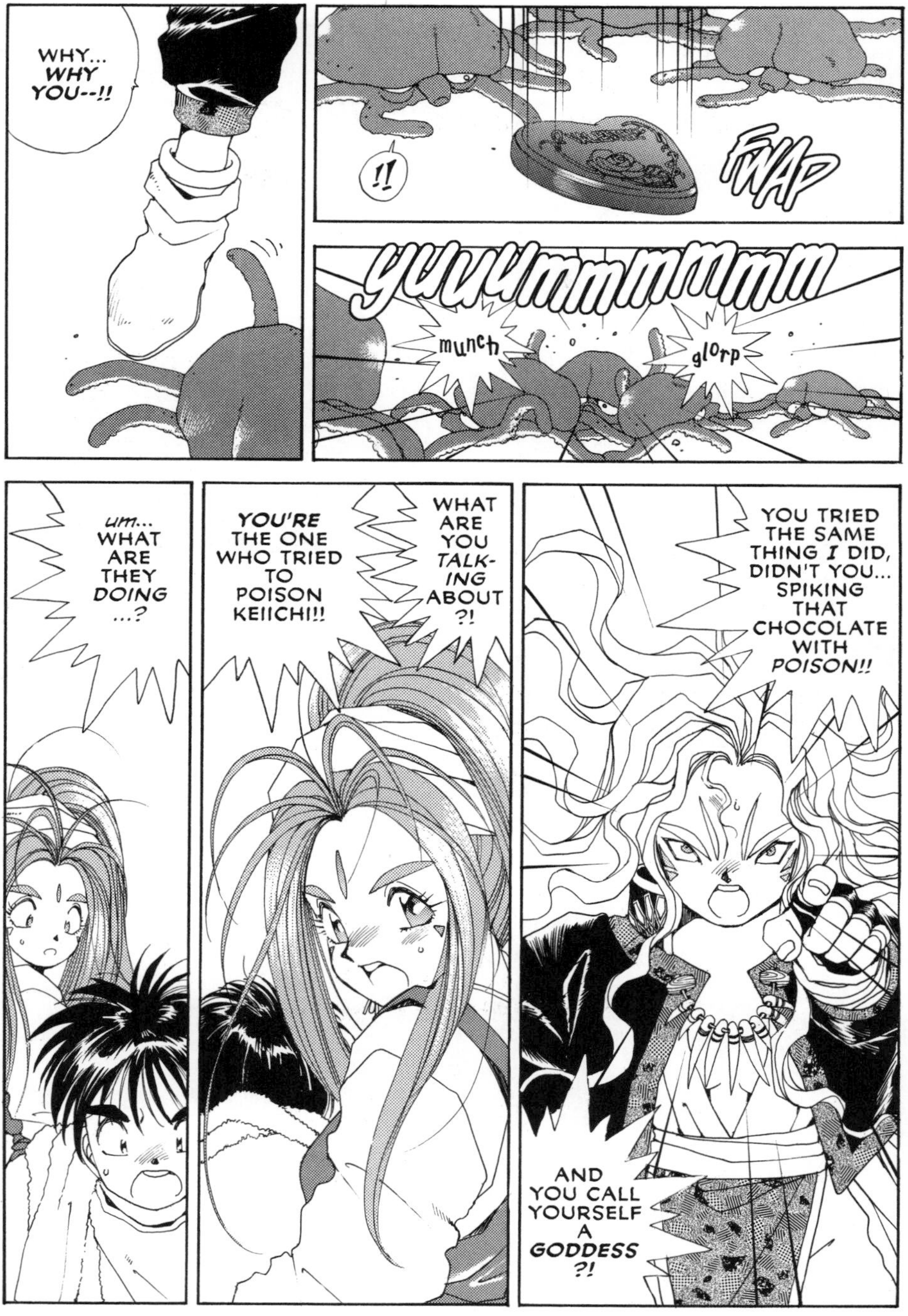
FWAP
!!
yuuummmmmmm
glorp
munch
WHY... WHY YOU--!!
YOU TRIED THE SAME THING I DID, DIDN'T YOU... SPIKING THAT CHOCOLATE WITH POISON!!
AND YOU CALL YOURSELF A GODDESS ?!
WHAT ARE YOU TALKING ABOUT ?!
YOU'RE THE ONE WHO TRIED TO POISON KEIICHI!!
um... WHAT ARE THEY DOING ...?

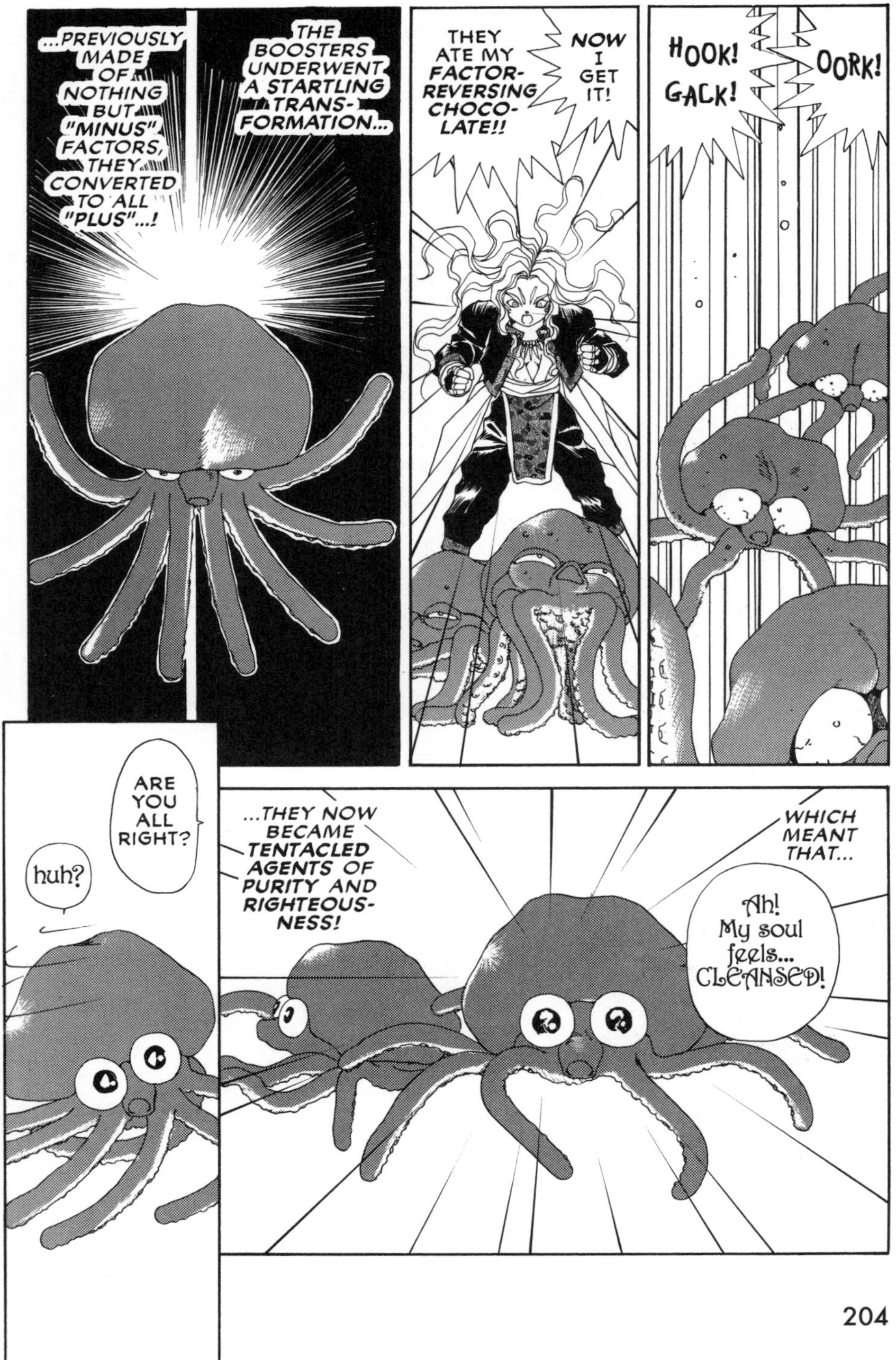
OORK!
HOOK! GACK!
NOW I GET IT!
THEY ATE MY FACTOR-REVERSING CHOCOLATE!!
THE BOOSTERS UNDERWENT A STARTLING TRANSFORMATION...
...PREVIOUSLY MADE OF NOTHING BUT "MINUS" FACTORS, THEY CONVERTED TO ALL "PLUS"...!
WHICH MEANT THAT...
...THEY NOW BECAME TENTACLED AGENTS OF PURITY AND RIGHTEOUSNESS!
Ah! My soul feels... CLEANSED!
ARE YOU ALL RIGHT?
huh?

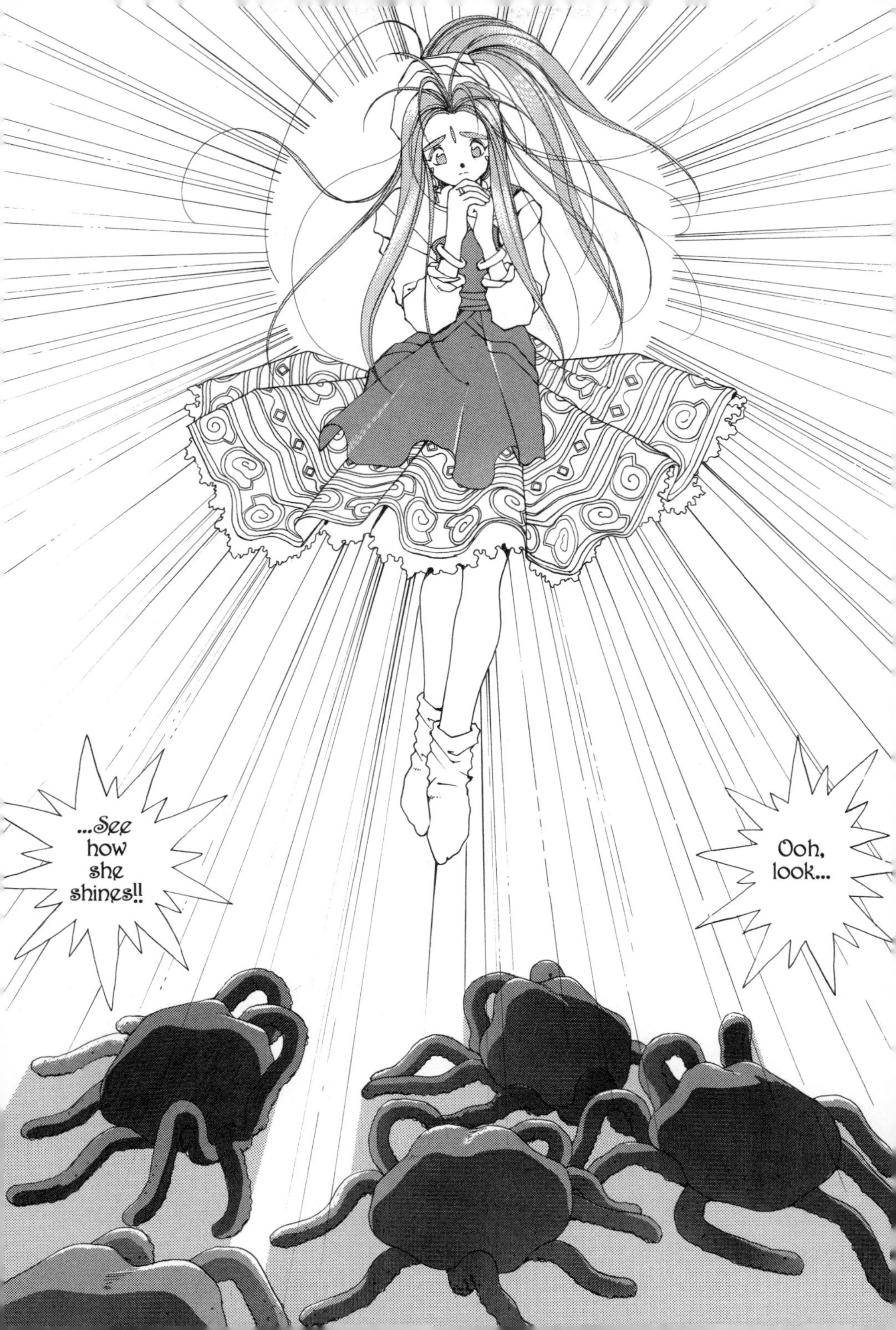
Ooh, look...
...See how she shines!!

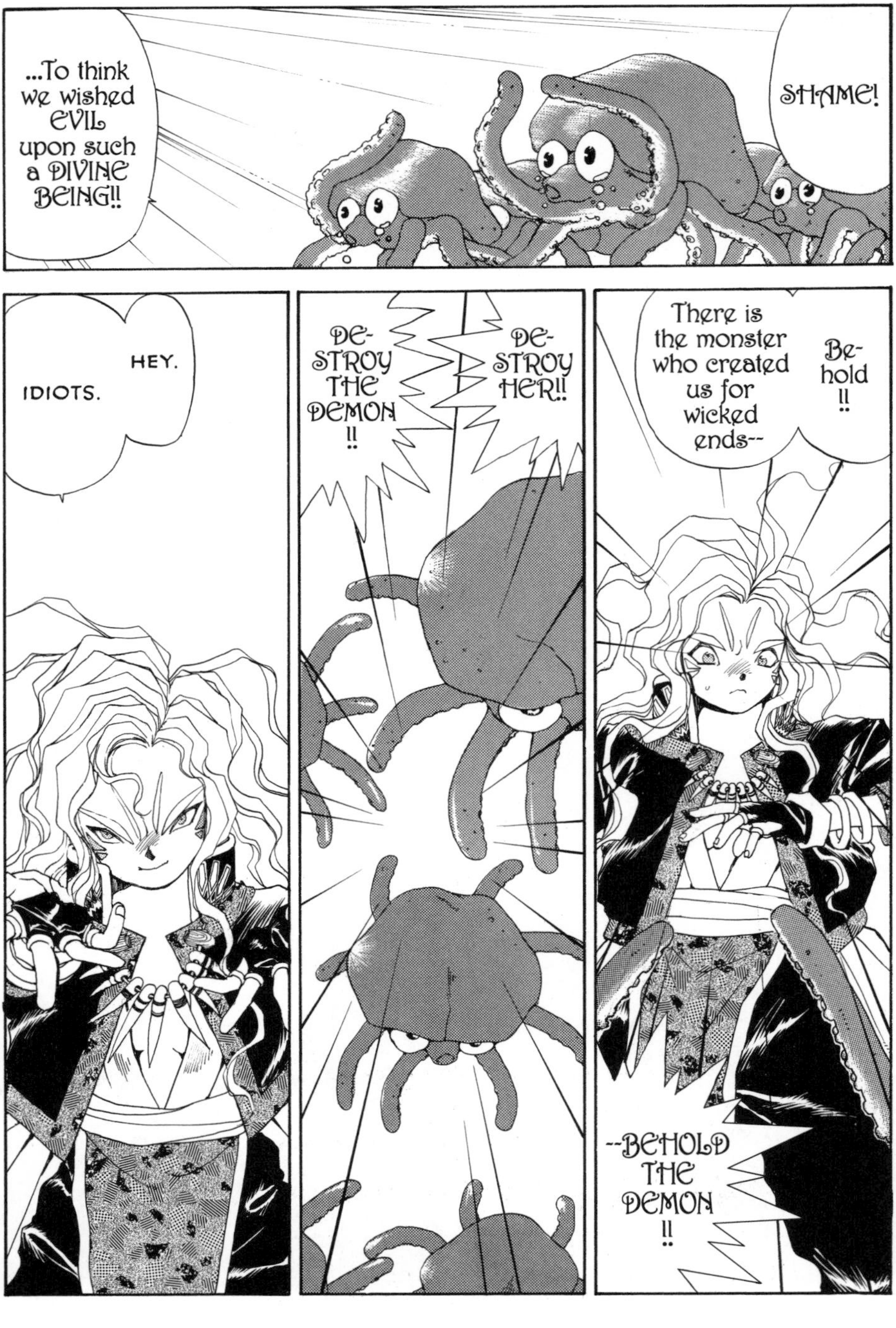
SHAME!
...To think we wished EVIL upon such a DIVINE BEING!!
Be-hold!!
There is the monster who created us for wicked ends--
--BEHOLD THE DEMON!!
DE-STROY HER!!
DE-STROY THE DEMON!!
HEY.
IDIOTS.

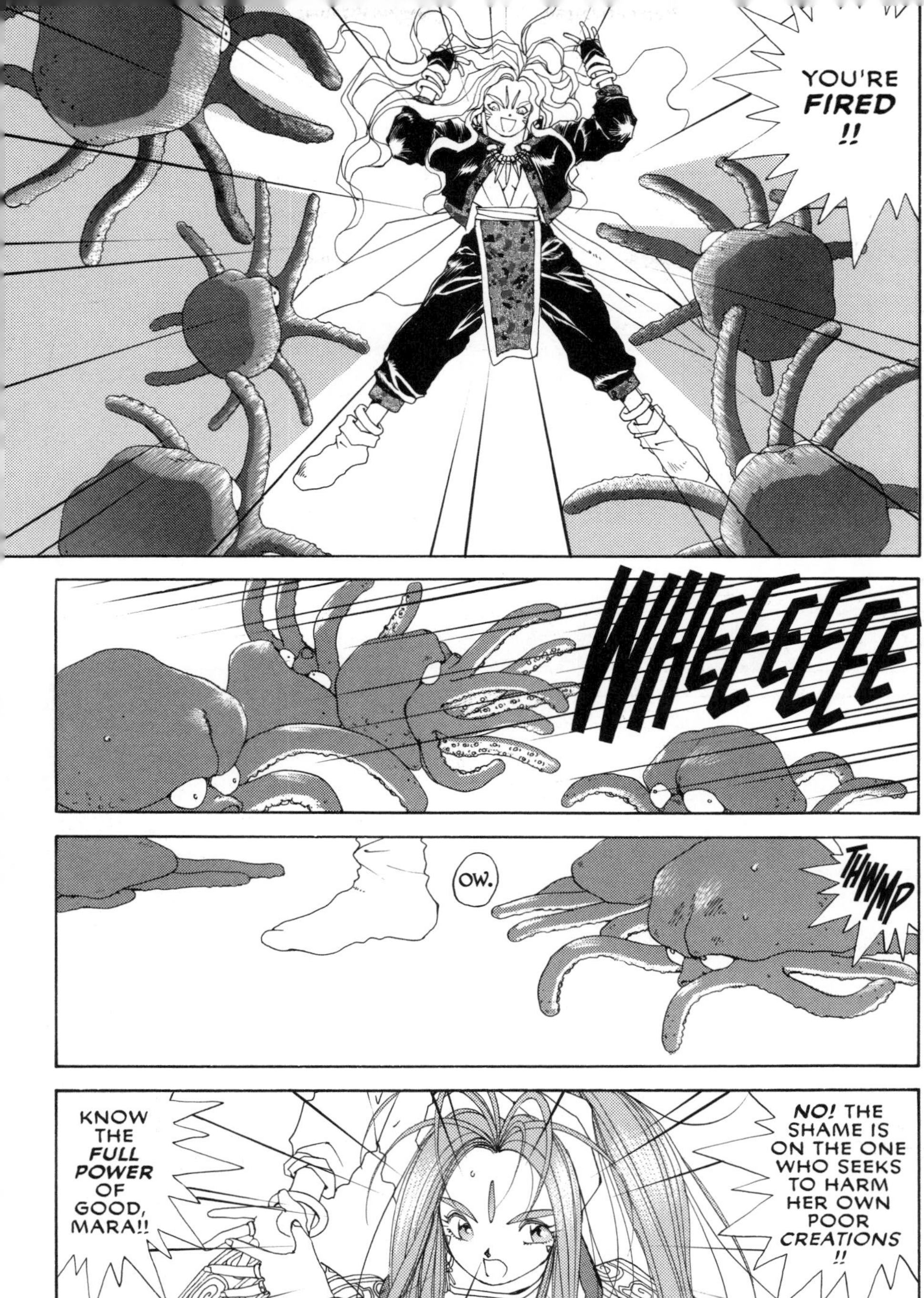
YOU'RE *FIRED* !!
WHEEEEEE
THWMP
OW.
*NO!* THE SHAME IS ON THE ONE WHO SEEKS TO HARM HER OWN POOR *CREATIONS* !!
KNOW THE *FULL POWER* OF GOOD, MARA!!

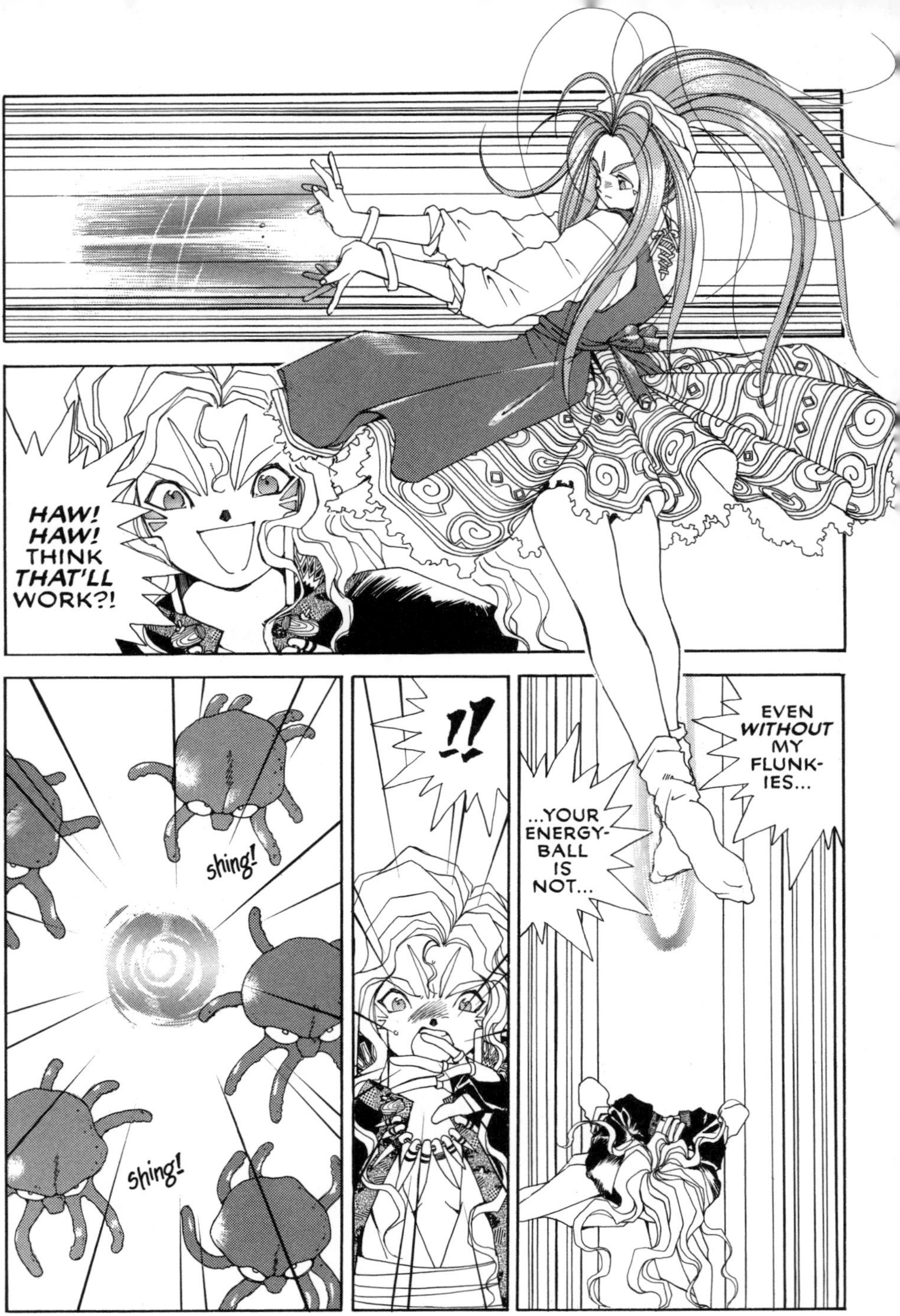
HAW! HAW! THINK THAT'LL WORK?!
EVEN WITHOUT MY FLUNK-IES...
...YOUR ENERGY-BALL IS NOT...
!!
shing!
shing!

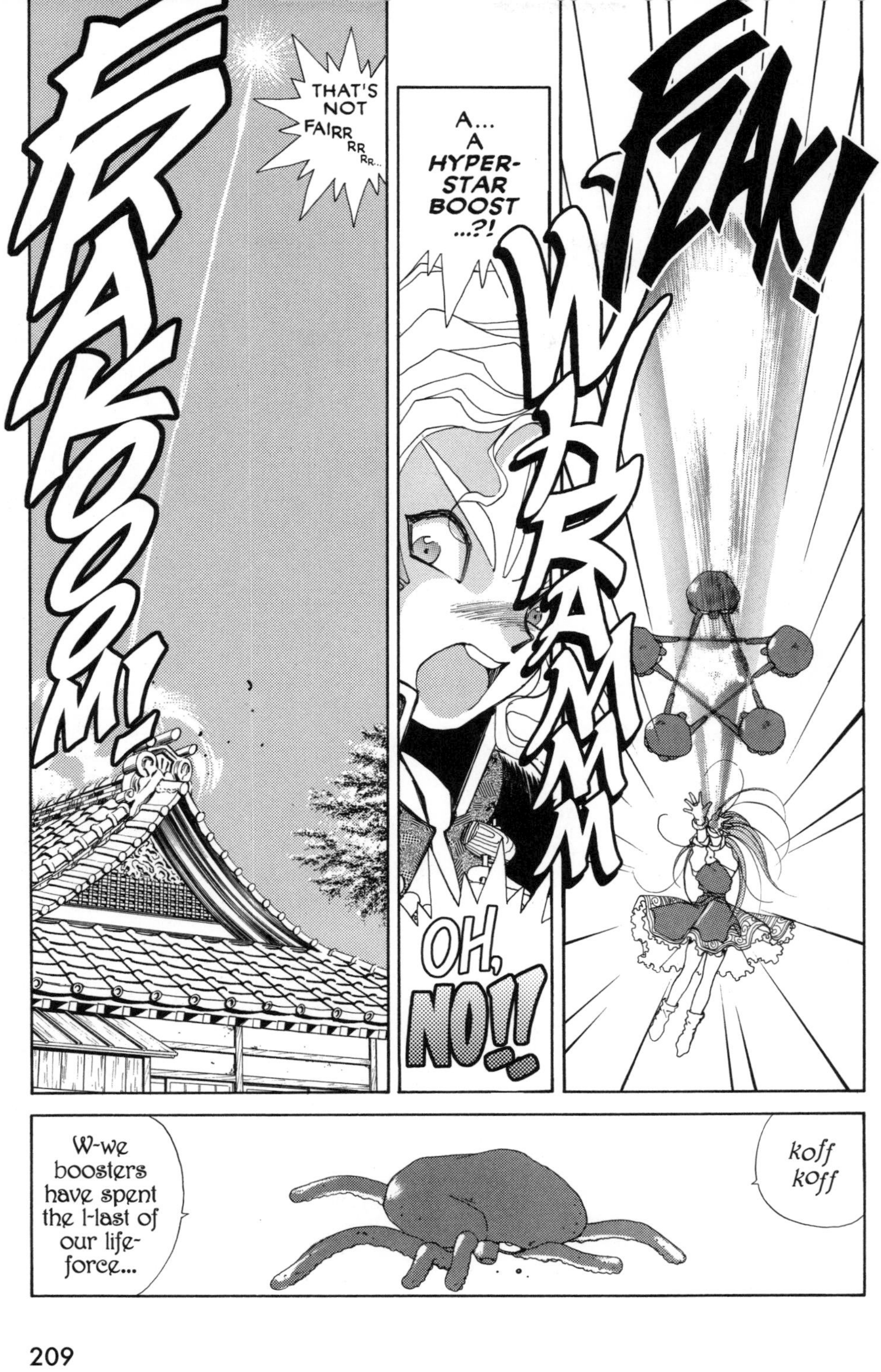
FZAK!
WHRAMMMM
A... A HYPER-STAR BOOST ...?!
OH, NO!!
THAT'S NOT FAIRRRRRR...
KRAKOOOM!
koff koff
W-we boosters have spent the l-last of our life-force...

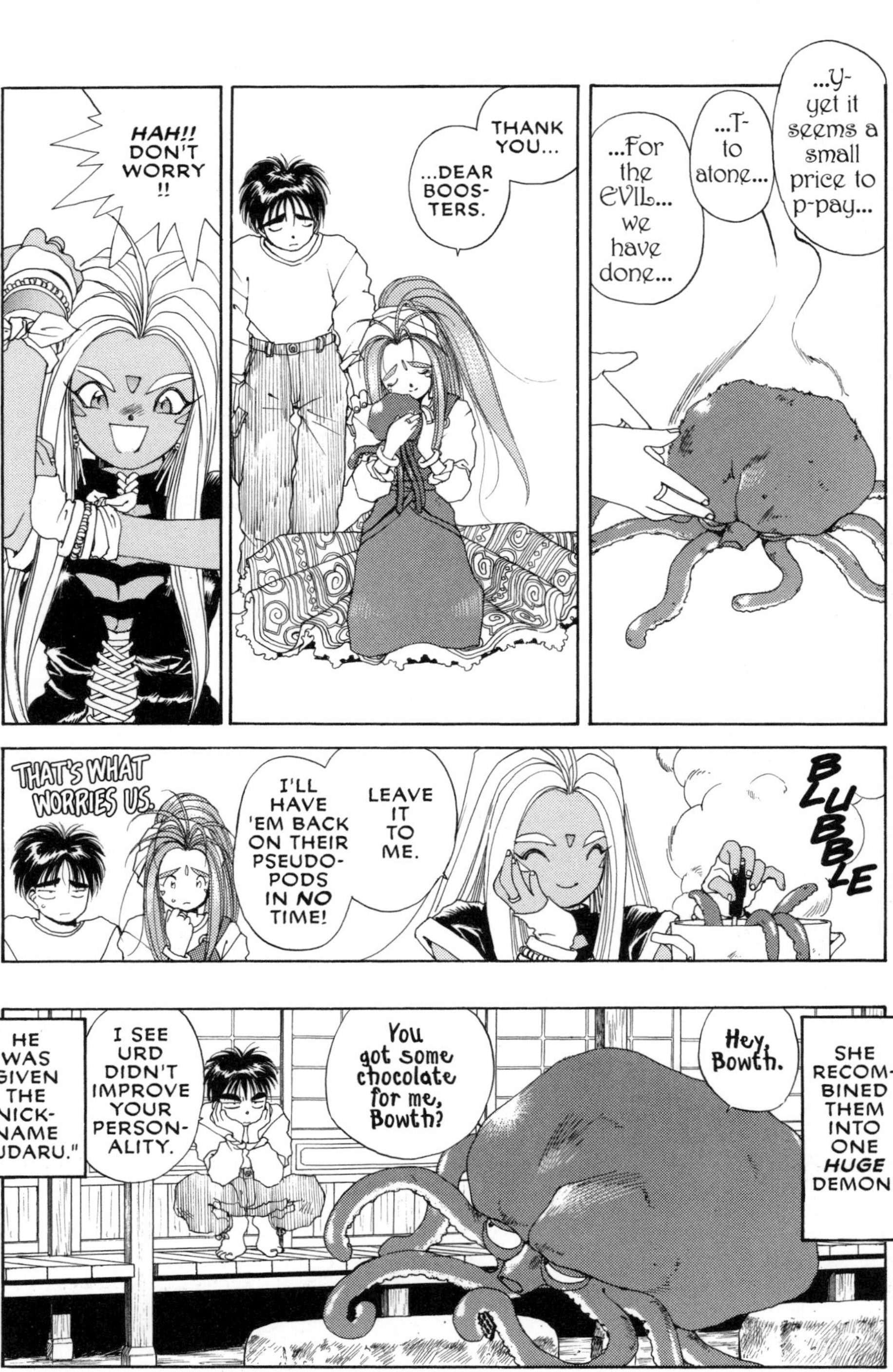
...Y-yet it seems a small price to p-pay...
...T-to atone...
...For the EVIL... we have done...
THANK YOU...
...DEAR BOOSTERS.
HAH!! DON'T WORRY!!
BLUBBLE
LEAVE IT TO ME.
I'LL HAVE 'EM BACK ON THEIR PSEUDOPODS IN NO TIME!
THAT'S WHAT WORRIES US.
SHE RECOMBINED THEM INTO ONE HUGE DEMON.
Hey, Bowth.
You got some chocolate for me, Bowth?
I SEE URD DIDN'T IMPROVE YOUR PERSONALITY.
HE WAS GIVEN THE NICKNAME "SUDARU."

# The Adventures of Mini-Urd

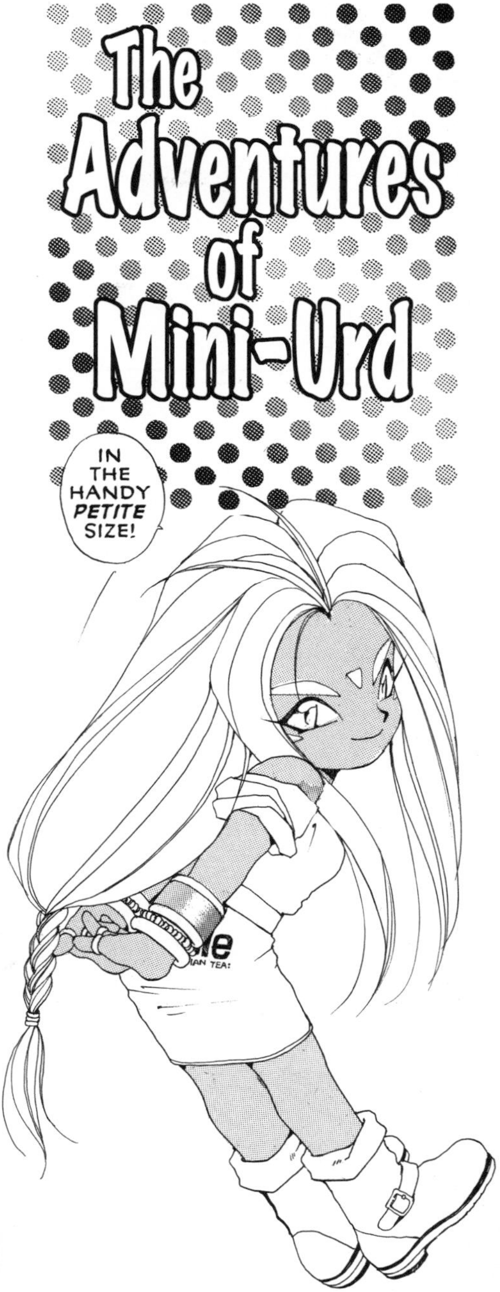
IN THE HANDY *PETITE* SIZE!

## ◆ CUP O' URD ◆

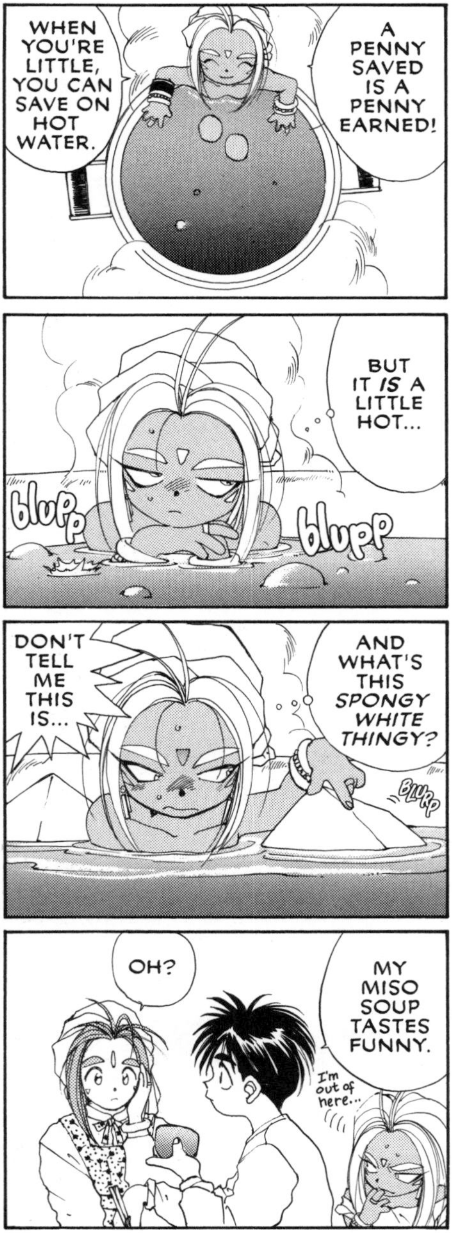
A PENNY SAVED IS A PENNY EARNED!
WHEN YOU'RE LITTLE, YOU CAN SAVE ON HOT WATER.
BUT IT *IS* A LITTLE HOT...
blupp
bluPP
AND WHAT'S THIS *SPONGY WHITE THINGY?*
DON'T TELL ME THIS IS...
BLURP
MY MISO SOUP TASTES FUNNY.
OH?
I'm out of here...

## THE BIKE MECHANIC AND THE ELVES

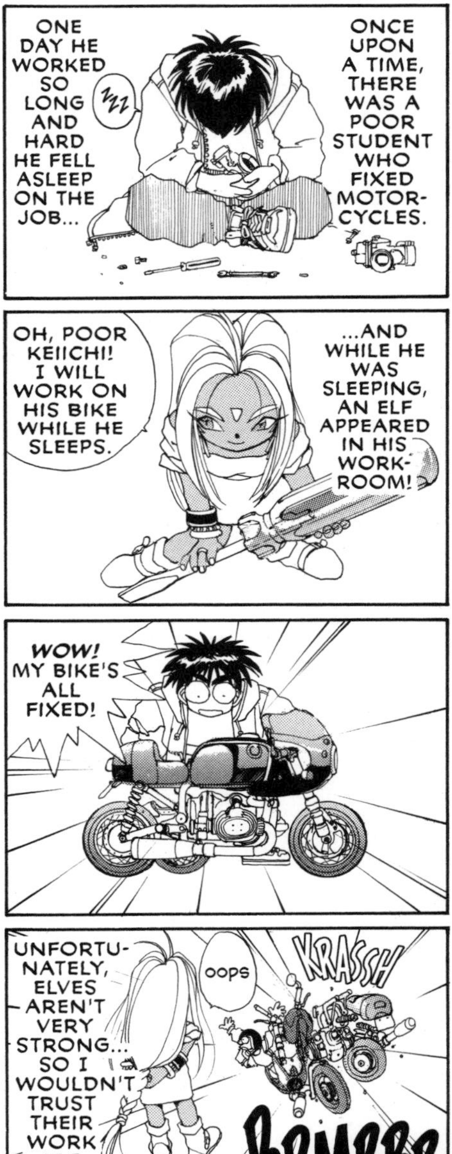
ONCE UPON A TIME, THERE WAS A POOR STUDENT WHO FIXED MOTOR-CYCLES.
ONE DAY HE WORKED SO LONG AND HARD HE FELL ASLEEP ON THE JOB...
ZZZ
...AND WHILE HE WAS SLEEPING, AN ELF APPEARED IN HIS WORK-ROOM!
OH, POOR KEIICHI! I WILL WORK ON HIS BIKE WHILE HE SLEEPS.
WOW! MY BIKE'S ALL FIXED!
KRASSH
oops
UNFORTU-NATELY, ELVES AREN'T VERY STRONG... SO I WOULDN'T TRUST THEIR WORK IF I WERE YOU.
BRMBBB

## TASTY

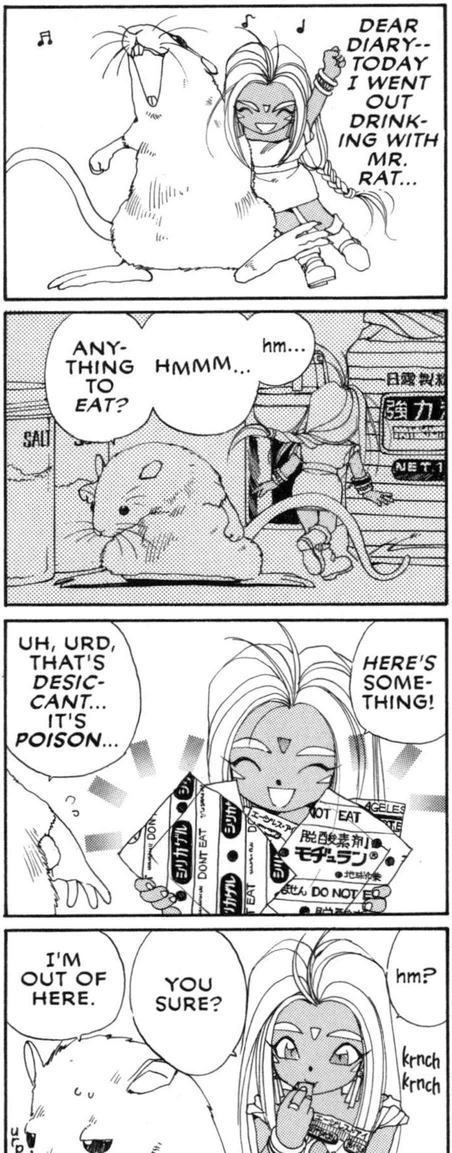
DEAR DIARY-- TODAY I WENT OUT DRINK-ING WITH MR. RAT...
hm...
HMMM...
ANY-THING TO EAT?
HERE'S SOME-THING!
UH, URD, THAT'S DESIC-CANT... IT'S POISON...
脱酸素剤
モヂュラン
DO NOT EAT
hm?
krnch krnch
YOU SURE?
I'M OUT OF HERE.
urp

WARNING: ***DON'T DO*** WHAT MINI-URD ***DOES.***

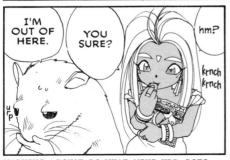

## CELL DIVISION

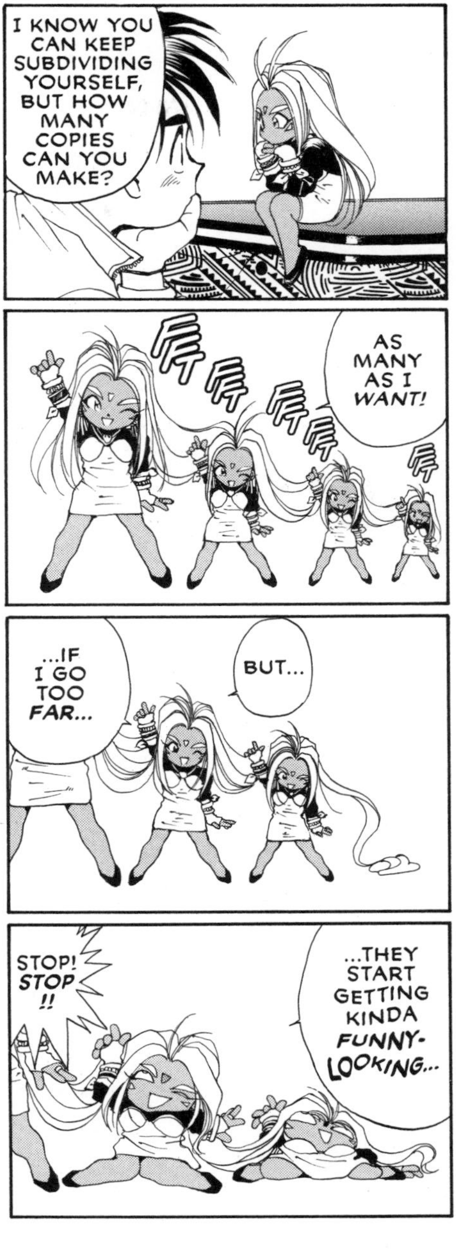
I KNOW YOU CAN KEEP SUBDIVIDING YOURSELF, BUT HOW MANY COPIES CAN YOU MAKE?
AS MANY AS I *WANT!*
BUT...
...IF I GO TOO *FAR...*
...THEY START GETTING KINDA *FUNNY-LOOKING...*
STOP! *STOP !!*

## LOST AND FOUND

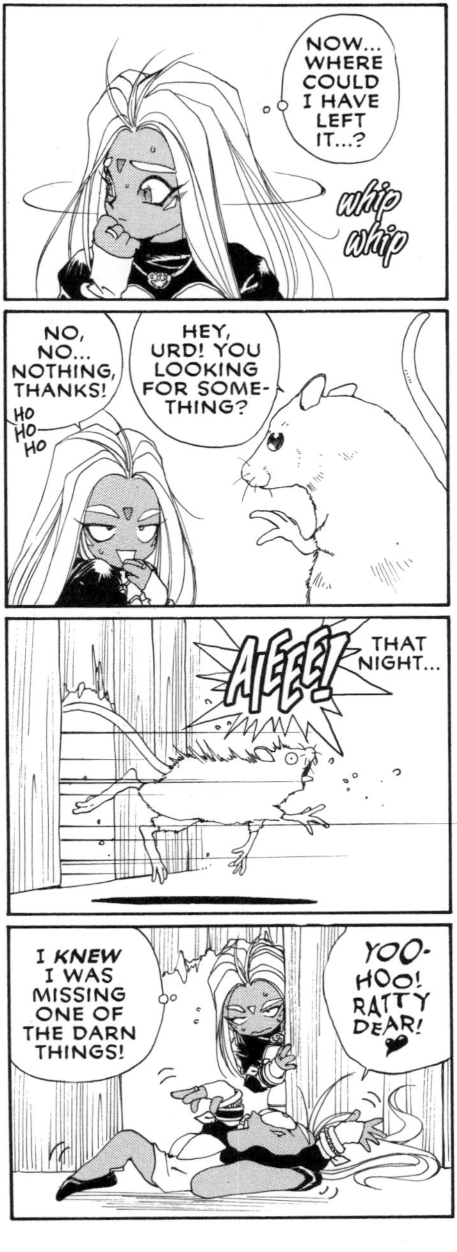
NOW... WHERE COULD I HAVE LEFT IT...?
whip whip
HEY, URD! YOU LOOKING FOR SOME-THING?
NO, NO... NOTHING, THANKS!
HO HO HO
THAT NIGHT...
AIEEE!
YOO-HOO! RATTY DEAR!
I *KNEW* I WAS MISSING ONE OF THE DARN THINGS!

## IT'S THE THOUGHT THAT COUNTS

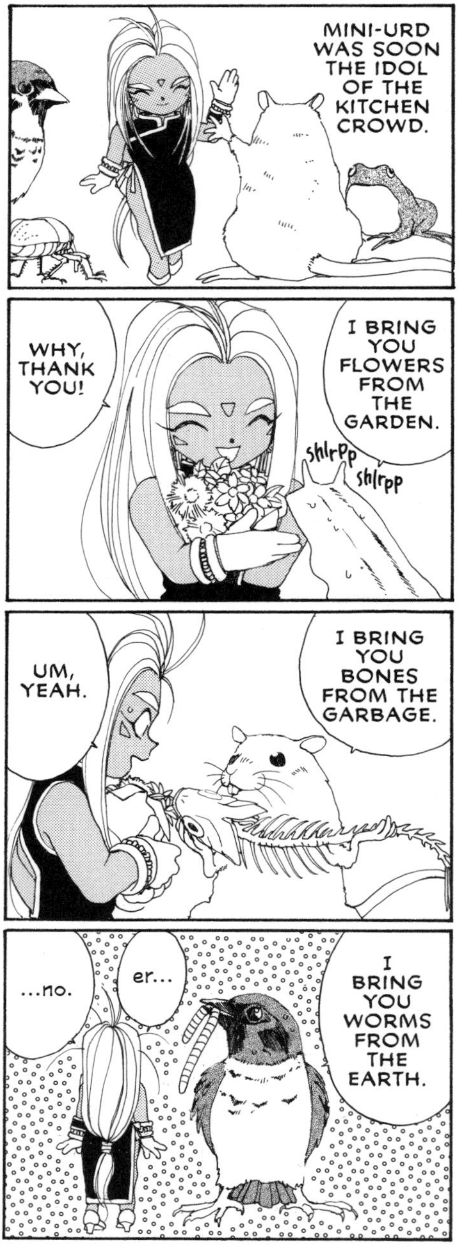
MINI-URD WAS SOON THE IDOL OF THE KITCHEN CROWD.
I BRING YOU FLOWERS FROM THE GARDEN.
shlrpp
shlrpp
WHY, THANK YOU!
I BRING YOU BONES FROM THE GARBAGE.
UM, YEAH.
I BRING YOU WORMS FROM THE EARTH.
er...
...no.

## FAMILY

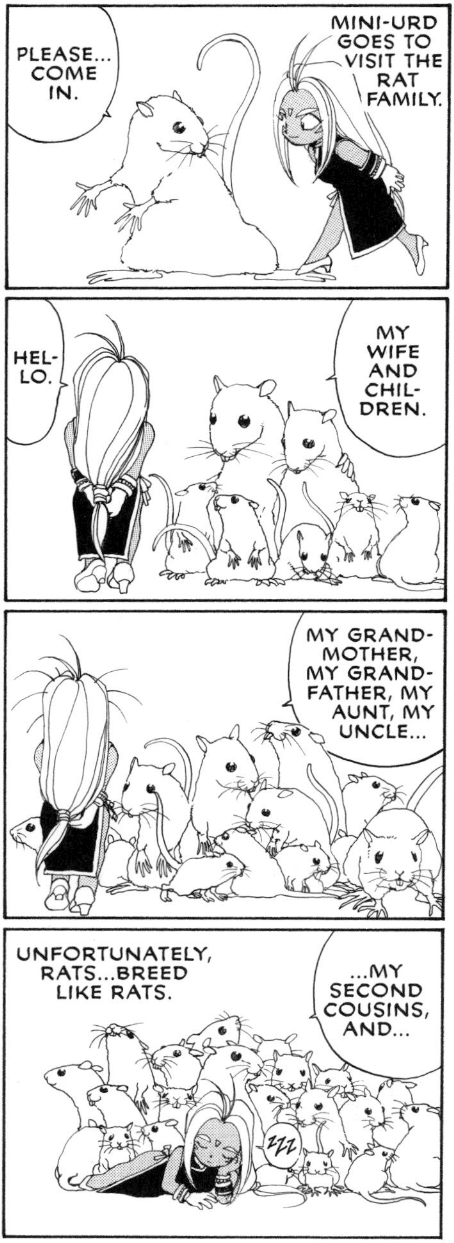
MINI-URD GOES TO VISIT THE RAT FAMILY.
PLEASE... COME IN.
MY WIFE AND CHIL-DREN.
HEL-LO.
MY GRAND-MOTHER, MY GRAND-FATHER, MY AUNT, MY UNCLE...
...MY SECOND COUSINS, AND...
UNFORTUNATELY, RATS...BREED LIKE RATS.
zzz

## ◆ TRUST ME! ◆

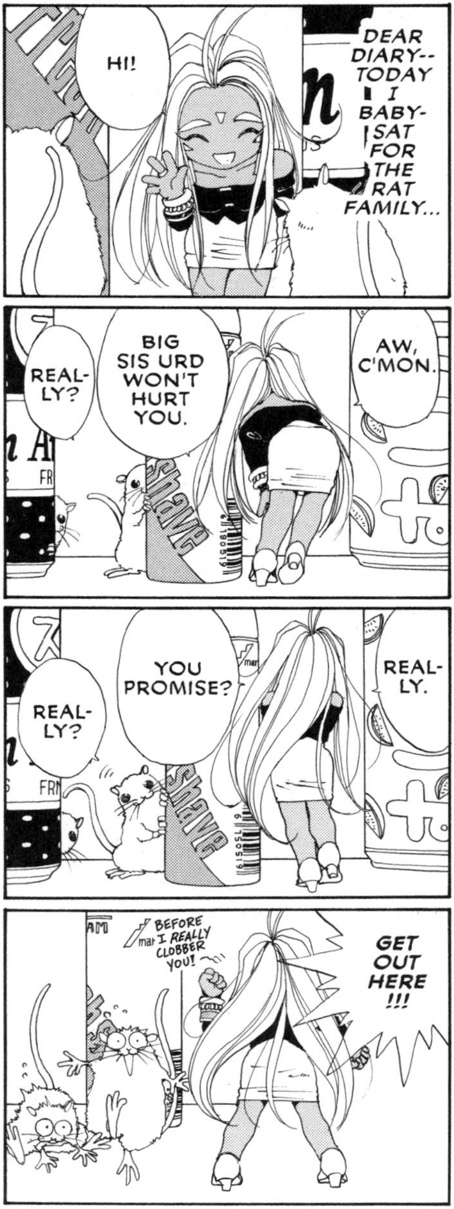
DEAR DIARY-- TODAY I BABY-SAT FOR THE RAT FAMILY...
HI!
AW, C'MON.
BIG SIS URD WON'T HURT YOU.
REAL-LY?
REAL-LY.
YOU PROMISE?
REAL-LY?
GET OUT HERE !!!
BEFORE I REALLY CLOBBER YOU!

## ◆ GOD OF GAMBLERS ◆

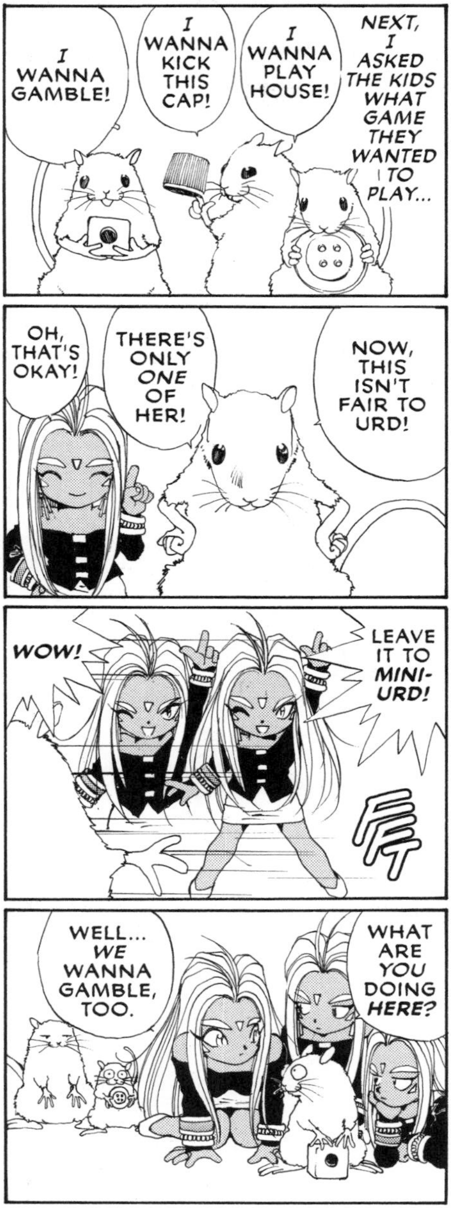
NEXT, I ASKED THE KIDS WHAT GAME THEY WANTED TO PLAY...
I WANNA PLAY HOUSE!
I WANNA KICK THIS CAP!
I WANNA GAMBLE!
NOW, THIS ISN'T FAIR TO URD!
THERE'S ONLY ONE OF HER!
OH, THAT'S OKAY!
LEAVE IT TO MINI-URD!
FFT
WOW!
WHAT ARE YOU DOING HERE?
WELL... WE WANNA GAMBLE, TOO.

## AMAZING!
## ◆ THE CARDS NEVER LIE! ◆

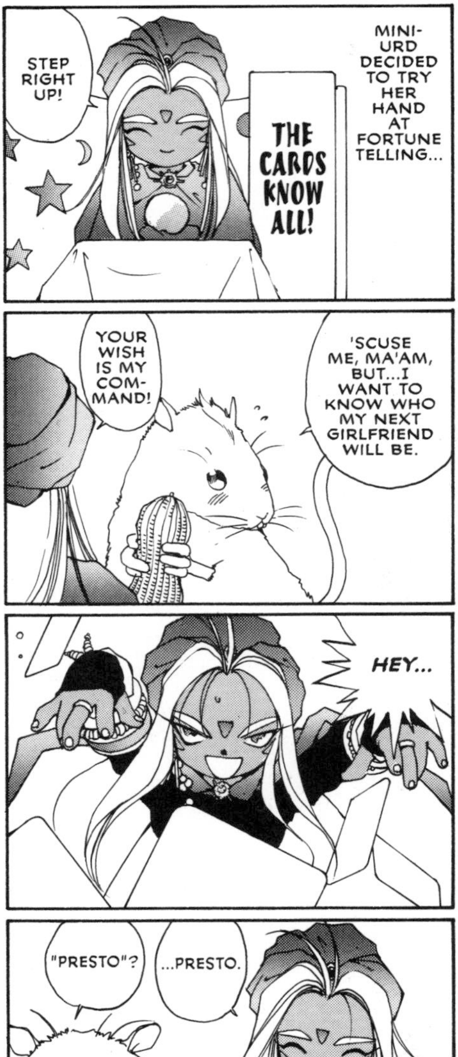
MINI-URD DECIDED TO TRY HER HAND AT FORTUNE TELLING...
THE CARDS KNOW ALL!
STEP RIGHT UP!
'SCUSE ME, MA'AM, BUT...I WANT TO KNOW WHO MY NEXT GIRLFRIEND WILL BE.
YOUR WISH IS MY COM-MAND!
HEY...
...PRESTO.
"PRESTO"?
A
TEA
POT

## YOU'RE COVERED!
## ◆ URD'S WARRANTY SERVICE ◆

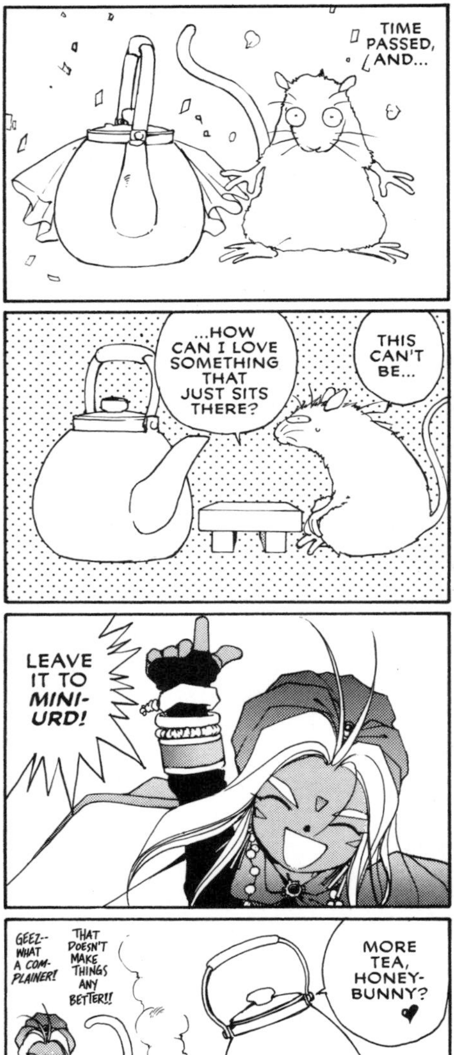
TIME PASSED, AND...
THIS CAN'T BE...
...HOW CAN I LOVE SOMETHING THAT JUST SITS THERE?
LEAVE IT TO MINI-URD!
MORE TEA, HONEY-BUNNY?
THAT DOESN'T MAKE THINGS ANY BETTER!!
GEEZ-- WHAT A COM-PLAINER!

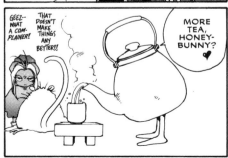

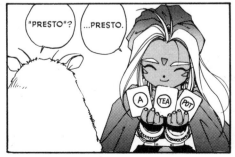

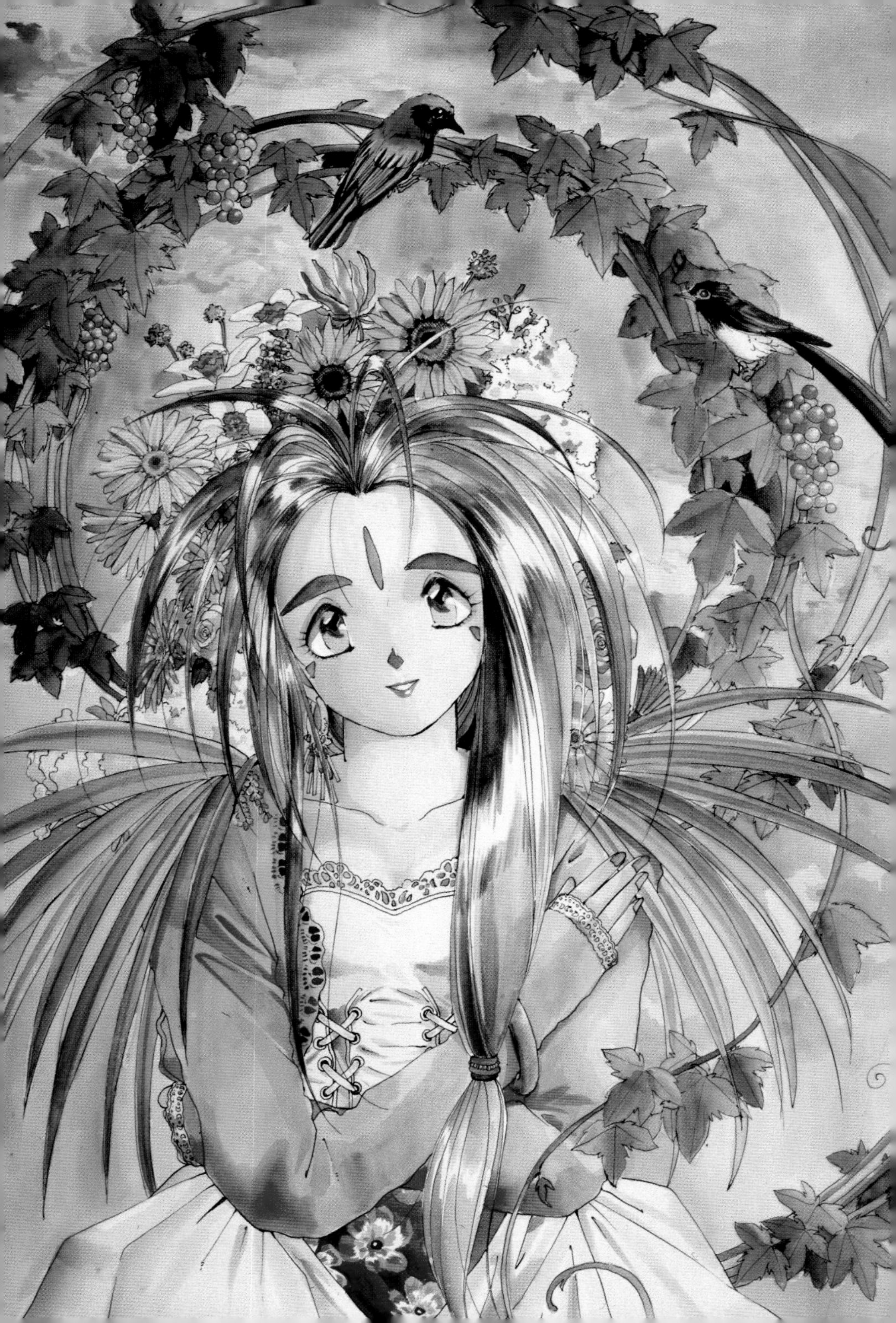

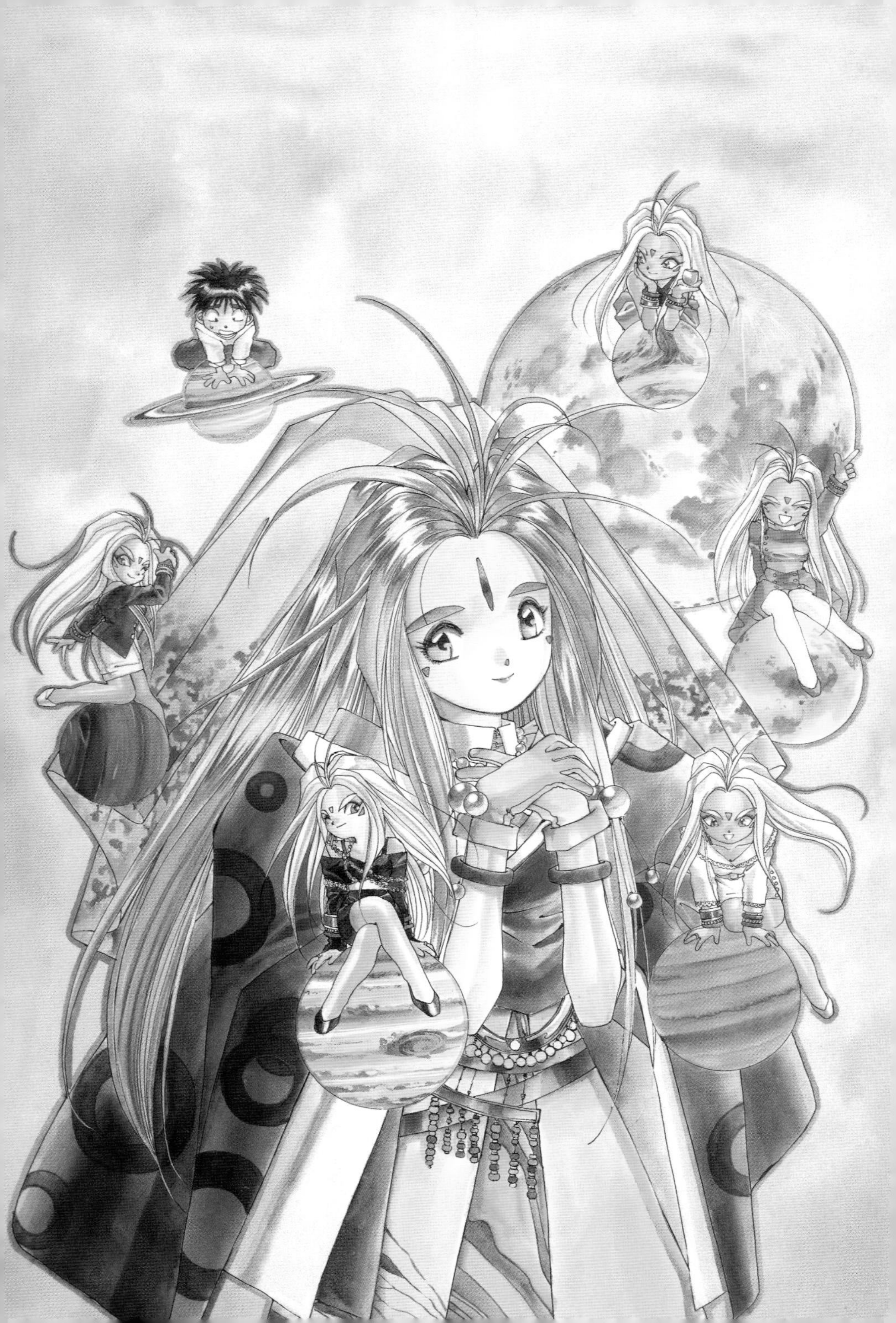

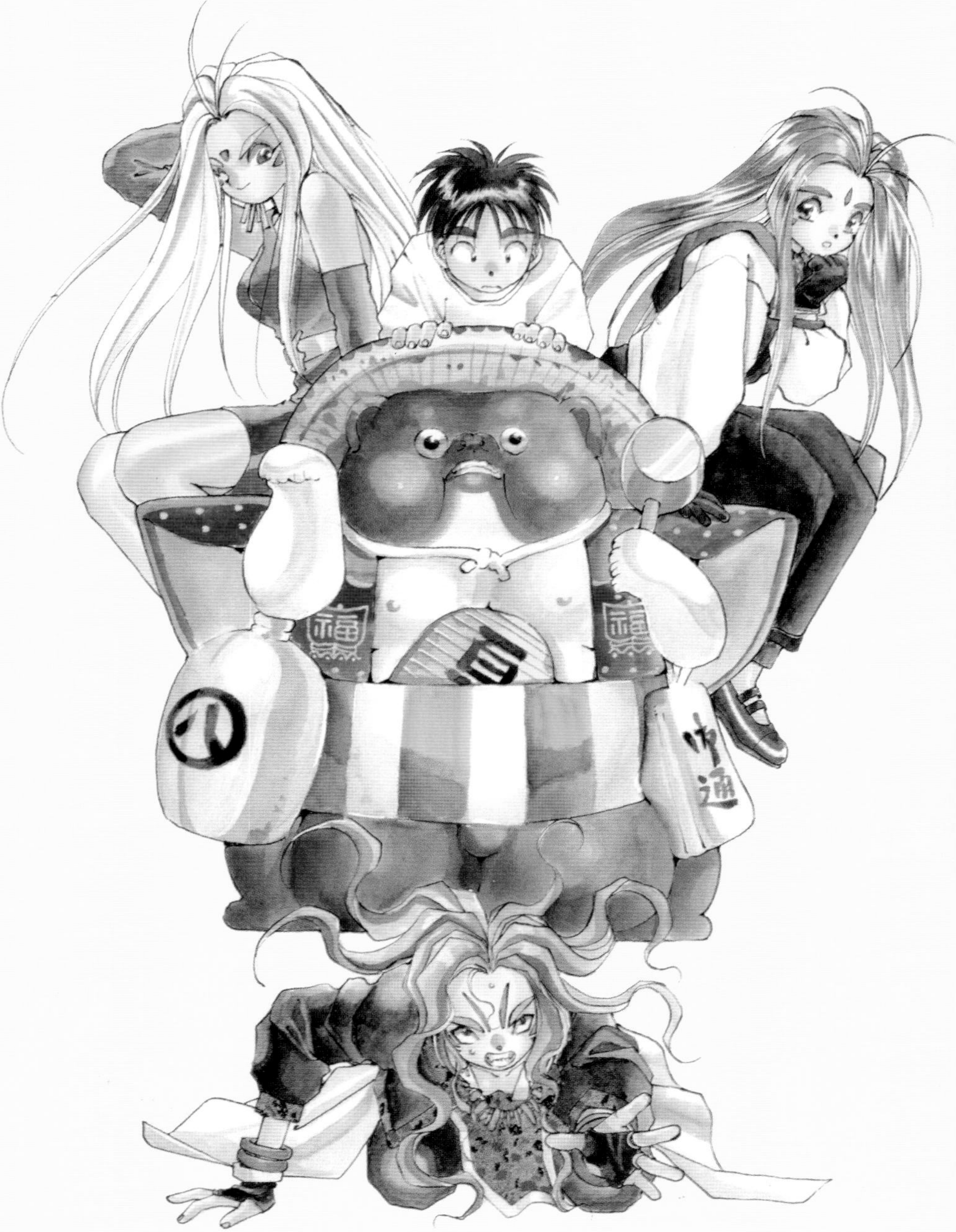
福
福

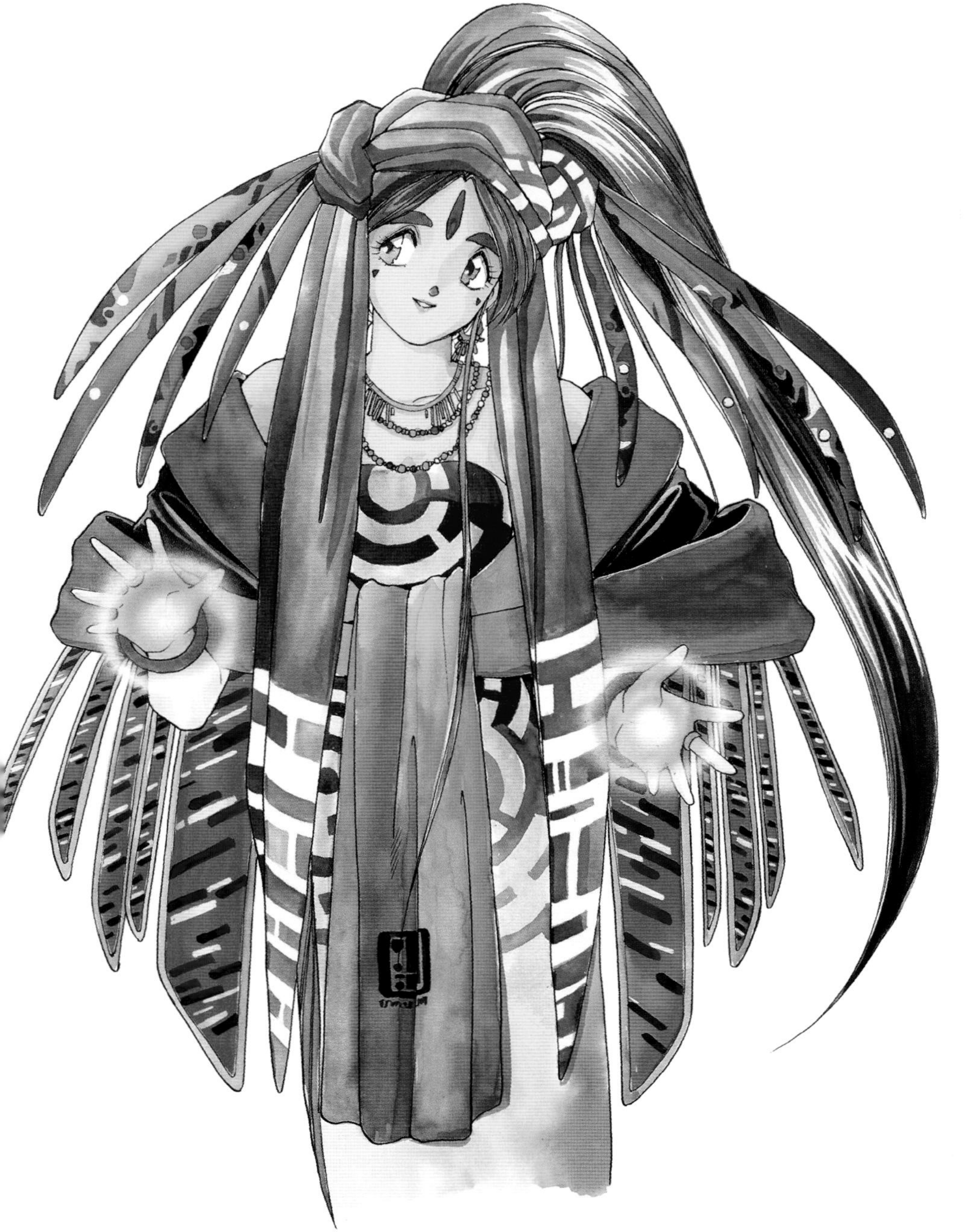

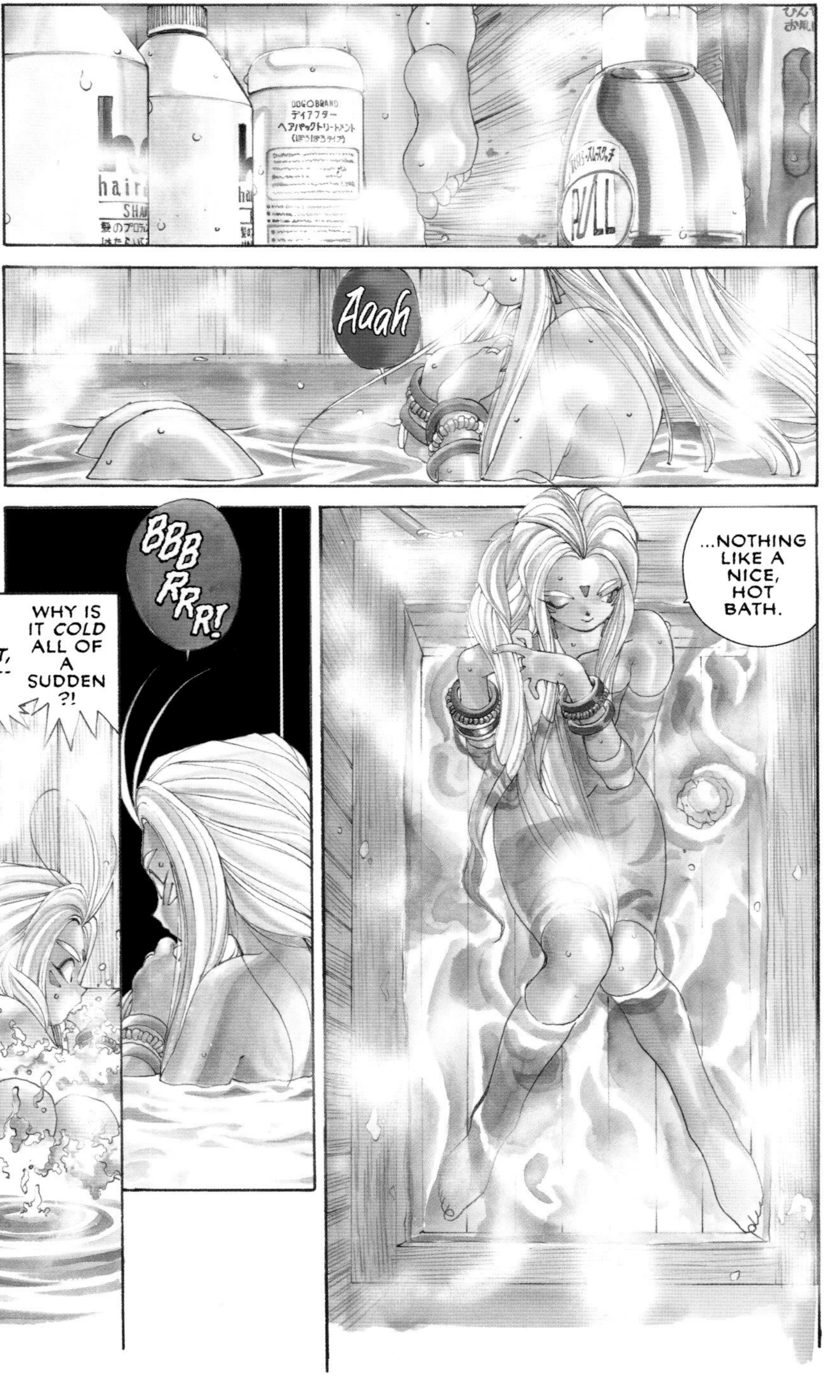
DOGO BRAND
PULL
Aaah
...NOTHING LIKE A NICE, HOT BATH.
BBBRRRR!
WHY IS IT COLD ALL OF A SUDDEN?!
AL-RIGHT, WHO--

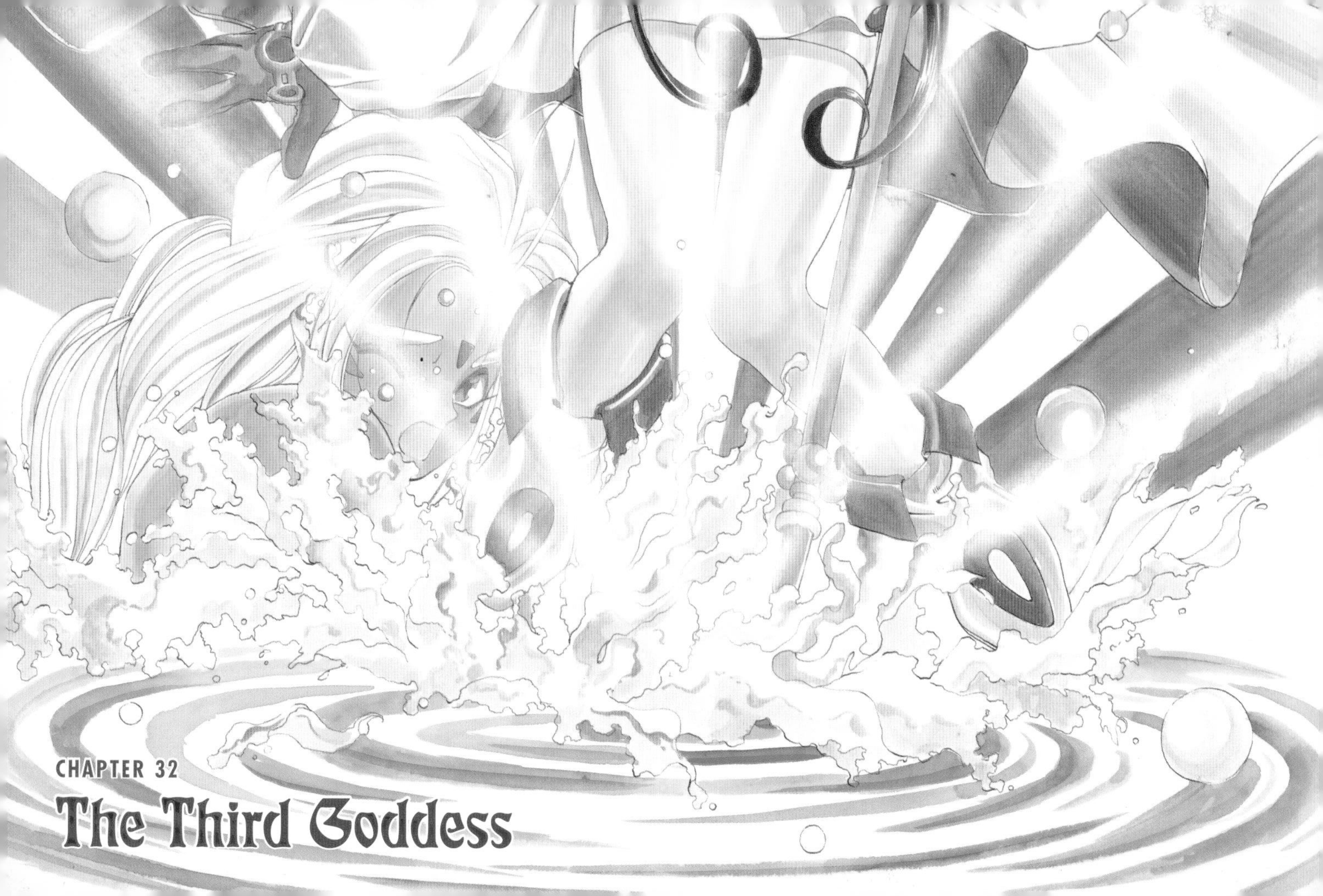
CHAPTER 32
The Third Goddess

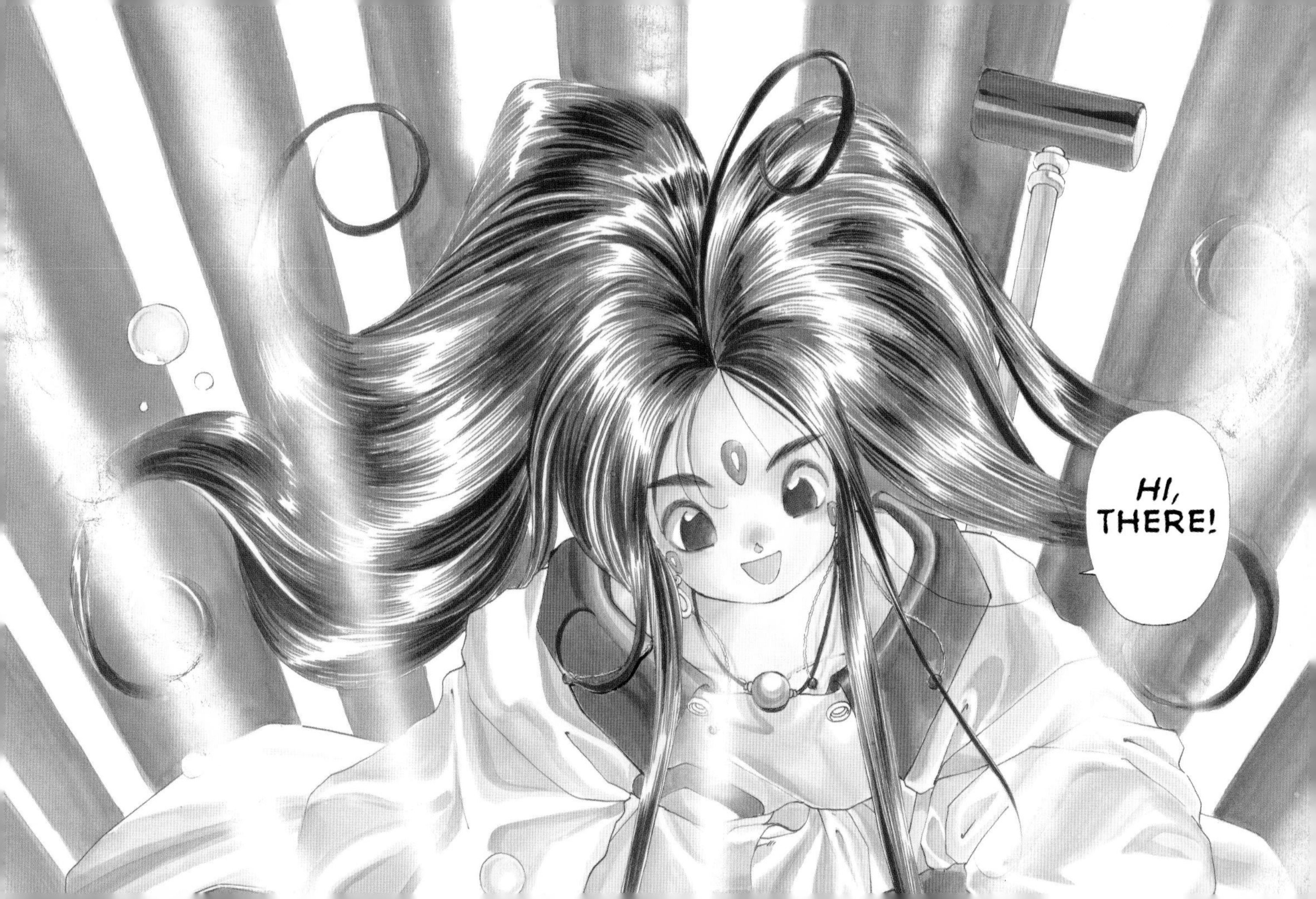
HI, THERE!

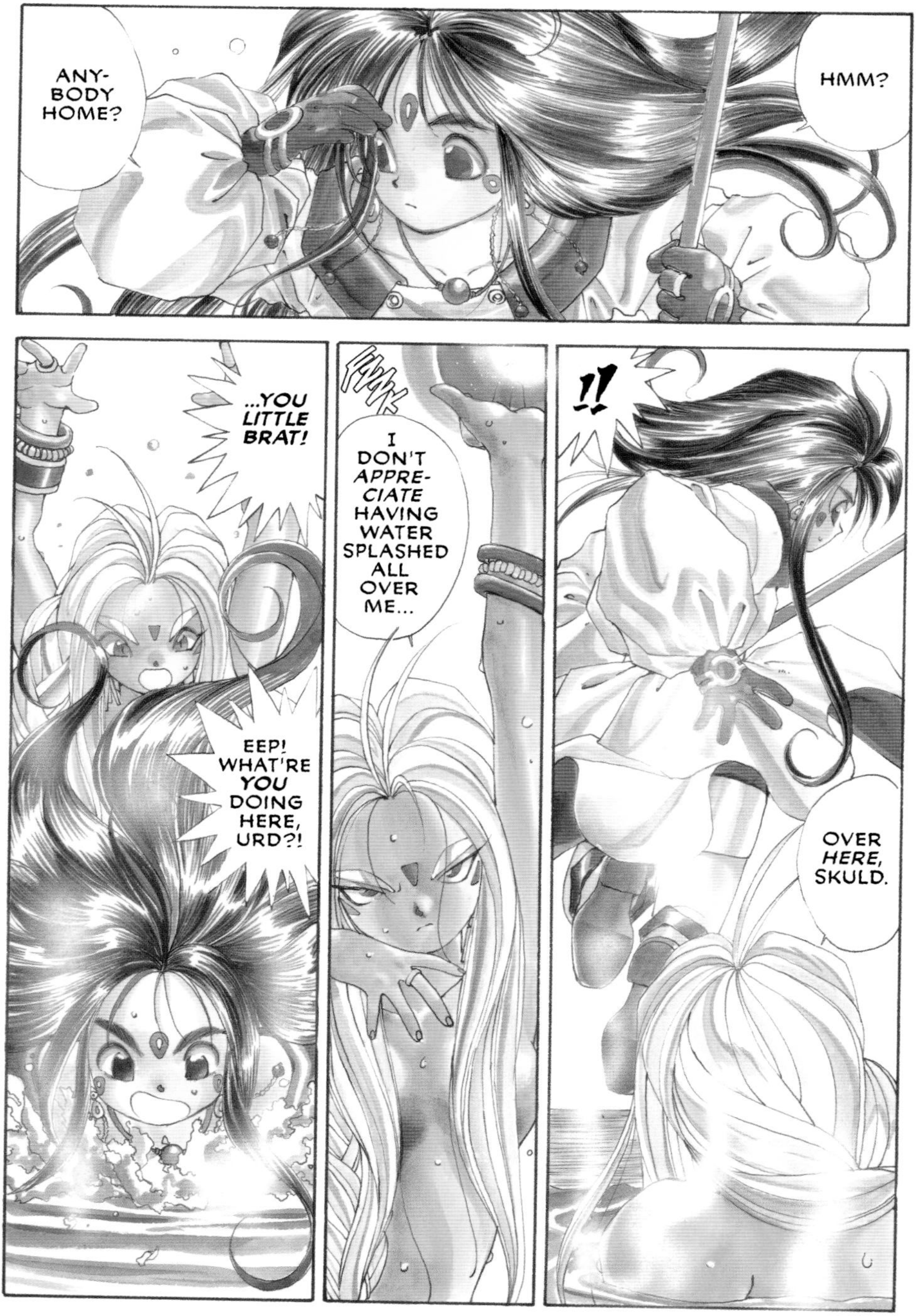
HMM?
ANY-BODY HOME?
!!
OVER HERE, SKULD.
I DON'T APPRECIATE HAVING WATER SPLASHED ALL OVER ME...
...YOU LITTLE BRAT!
EEP! WHAT'RE YOU DOING HERE, URD?!

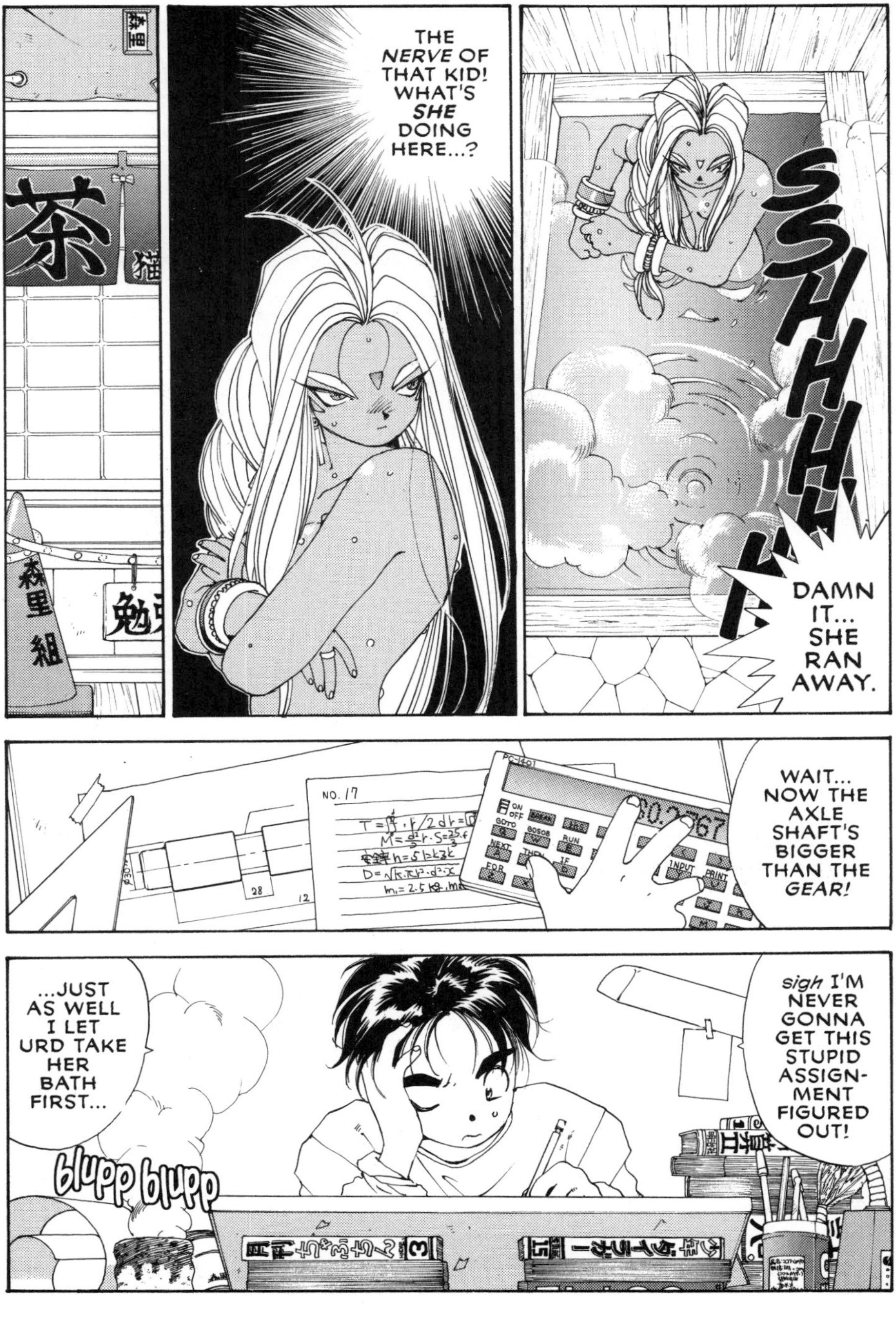
SHHHHH
DAMN IT... SHE RAN AWAY.
THE NERVE OF THAT KID! WHAT'S SHE DOING HERE...?
茶
森里組
WAIT... NOW THE AXLE SHAFT'S BIGGER THAN THE GEAR!
sigh I'M NEVER GONNA GET THIS STUPID ASSIGNMENT FIGURED OUT!
...JUST AS WELL I LET URD TAKE HER BATH FIRST...
blupp blupp

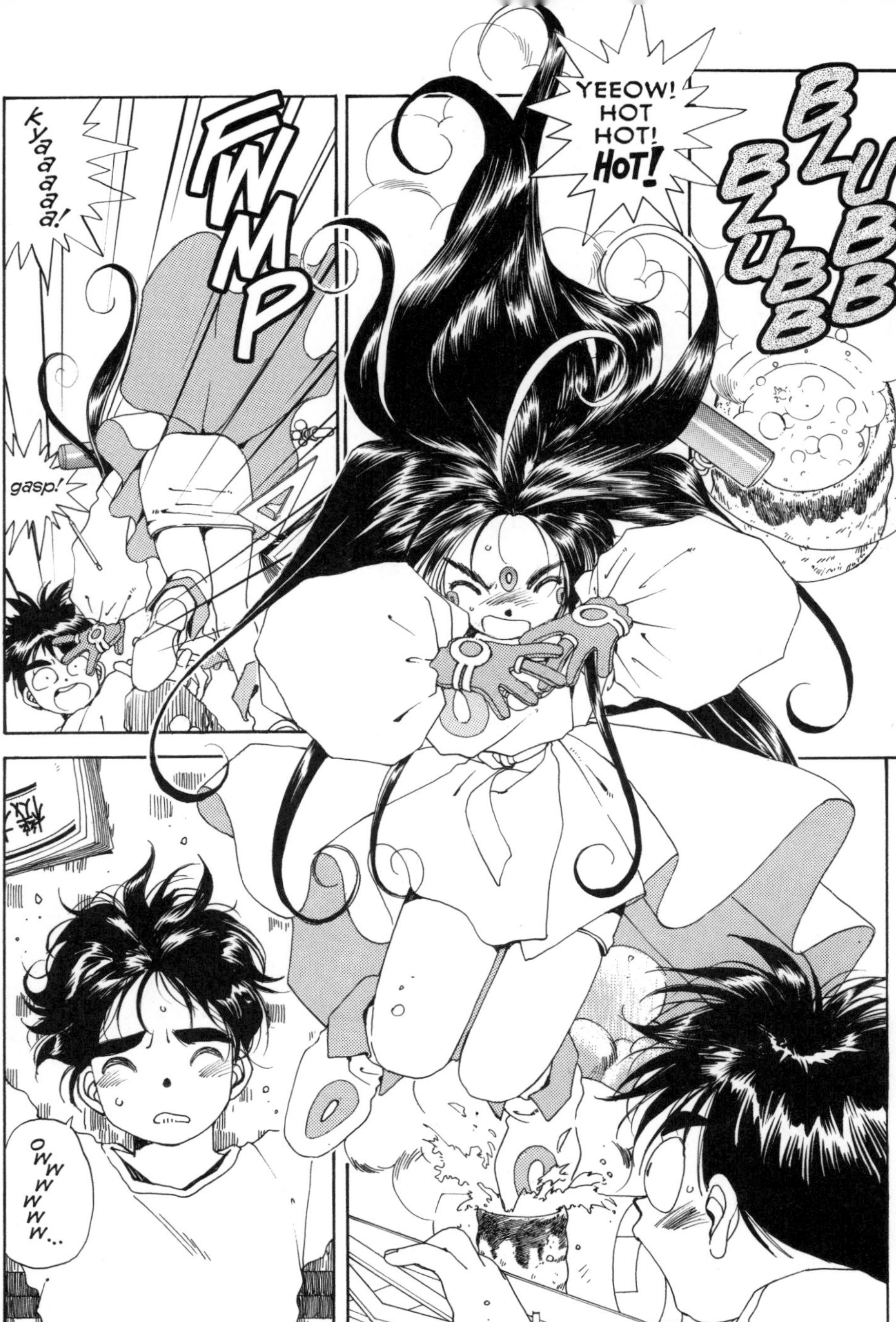

BLUBB
BLUBB
YEEOW! HOT HOT! HOT!
FWMP
Kyaaaaaa!
gasp!
owwwwwww...

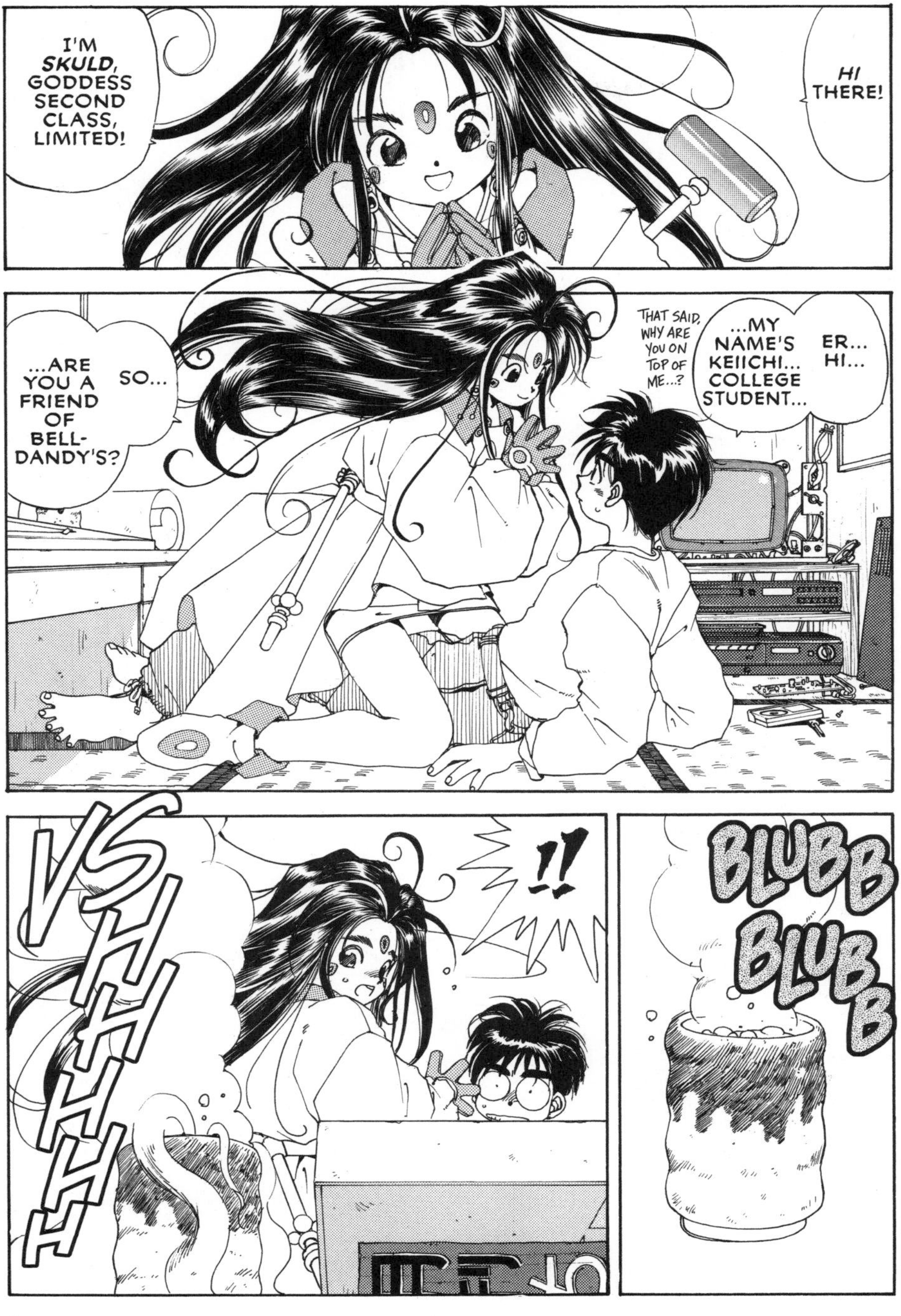
HI THERE!
I'M SKULD, GODDESS SECOND CLASS, LIMITED!
ER... HI...
...MY NAME'S KEIICHI... COLLEGE STUDENT...
THAT SAID, WHY ARE YOU ON TOP OF ME...?
SO...
...ARE YOU A FRIEND OF BELL-DANDY'S?
BLUBB BLUBB
!!
VSHHHHHH

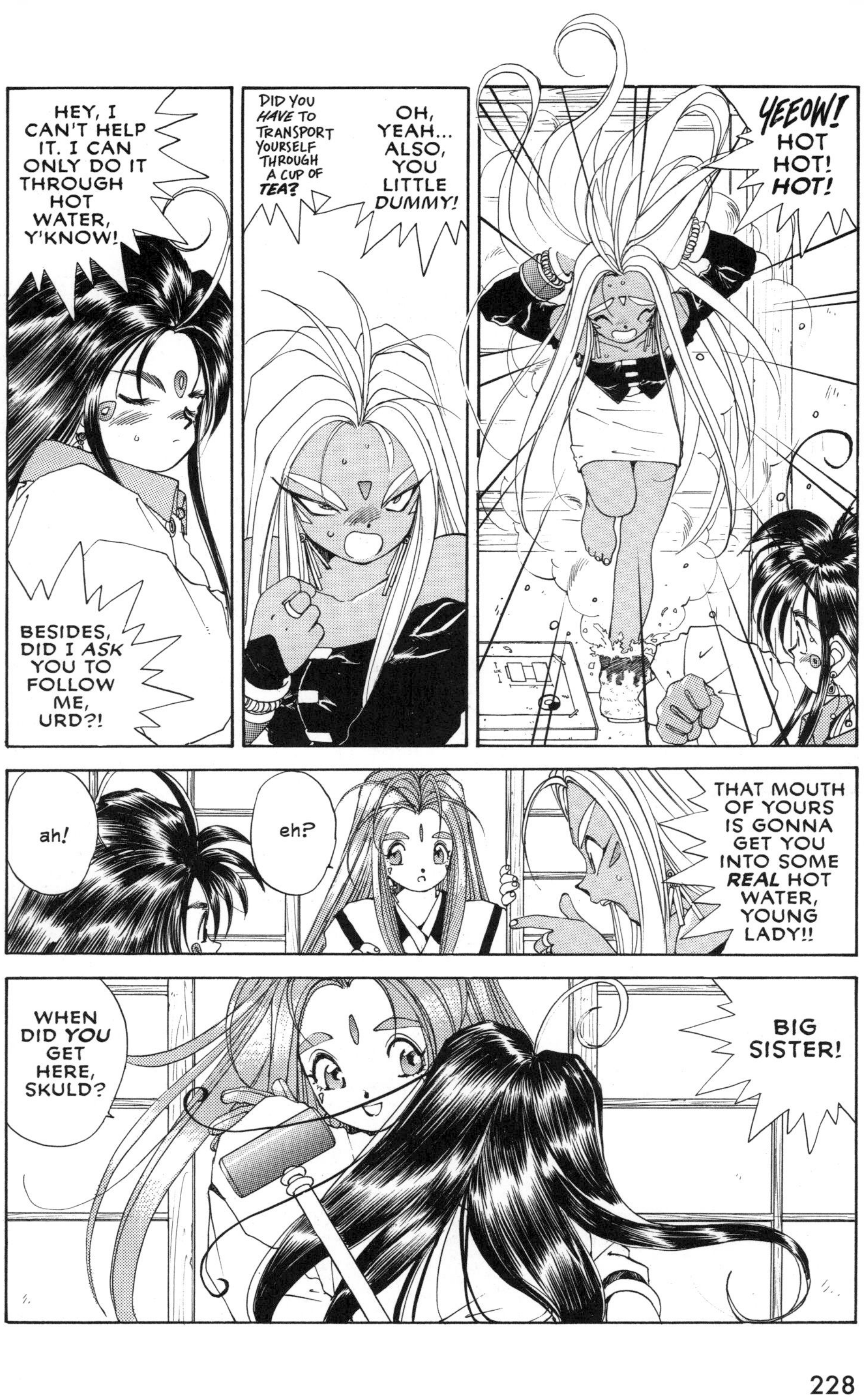
YEEOW! HOT HOT! HOT!
DID YOU HAVE TO TRANSPORT YOURSELF THROUGH A CUP OF TEA?
OH, YEAH... ALSO, YOU LITTLE DUMMY!
HEY, I CAN'T HELP IT. I CAN ONLY DO IT THROUGH HOT WATER, Y'KNOW!
BESIDES, DID I ASK YOU TO FOLLOW ME, URD?!
THAT MOUTH OF YOURS IS GONNA GET YOU INTO SOME REAL HOT WATER, YOUNG LADY!!
eh?
ah!
BIG SISTER!
WHEN DID YOU GET HERE, SKULD?

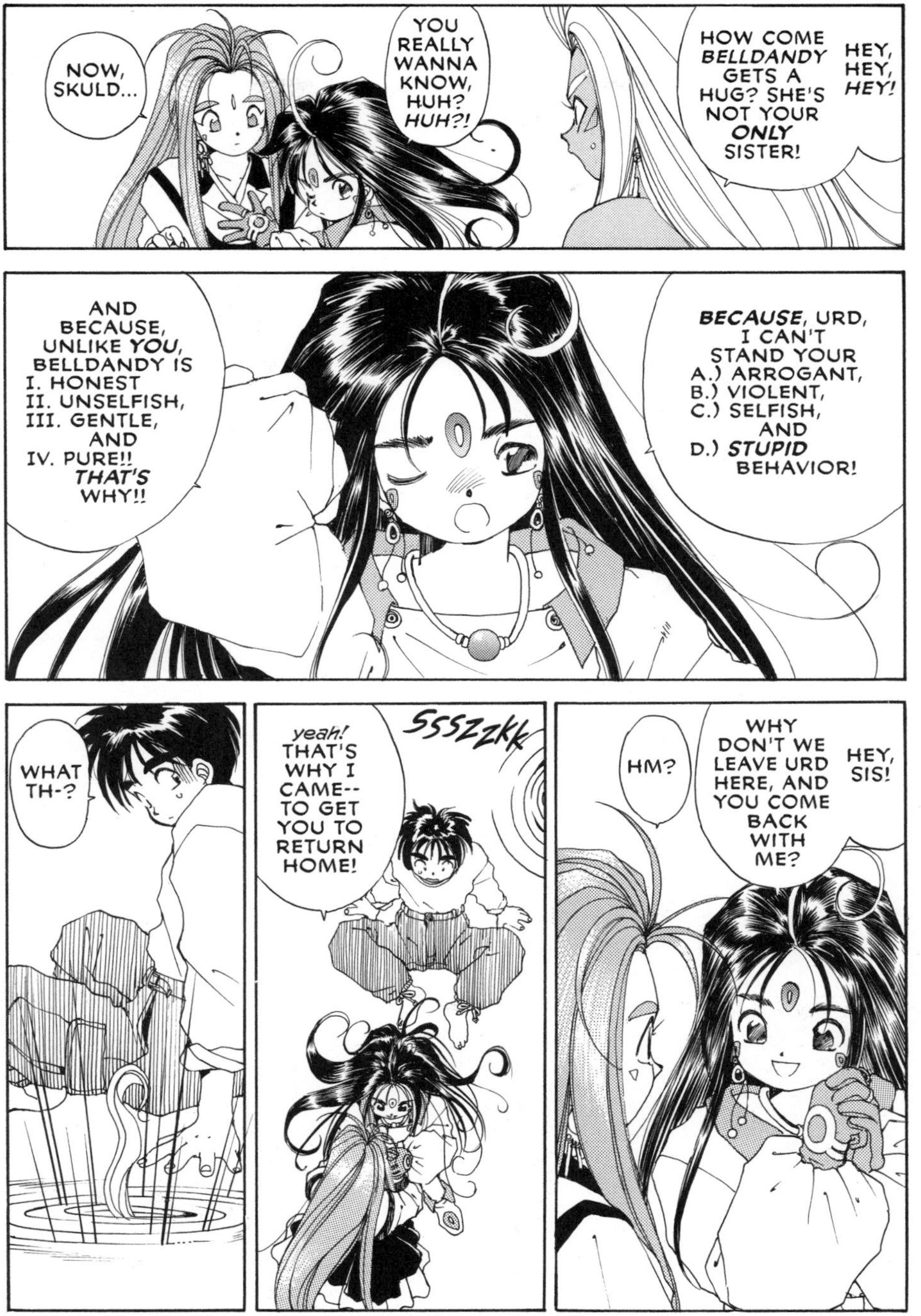
HEY, HEY, HEY!
HOW COME BELLDANDY GETS A HUG? SHE'S NOT YOUR ONLY SISTER!
YOU REALLY WANNA KNOW, HUH? HUH?!
NOW, SKULD...
BECAUSE, URD, I CAN'T STAND YOUR A.) ARROGANT, B.) VIOLENT, C.) SELFISH, AND D.) STUPID BEHAVIOR!
AND BECAUSE, UNLIKE YOU, BELLDANDY IS I. HONEST II. UNSELFISH, III. GENTLE, AND IV. PURE!! THAT'S WHY!!
HEY, SIS!
WHY DON'T WE LEAVE URD HERE, AND YOU COME BACK WITH ME?
HM?
SSSZZKK
yeah! THAT'S WHY I CAME-- TO GET YOU TO RETURN HOME!
WHAT TH-?

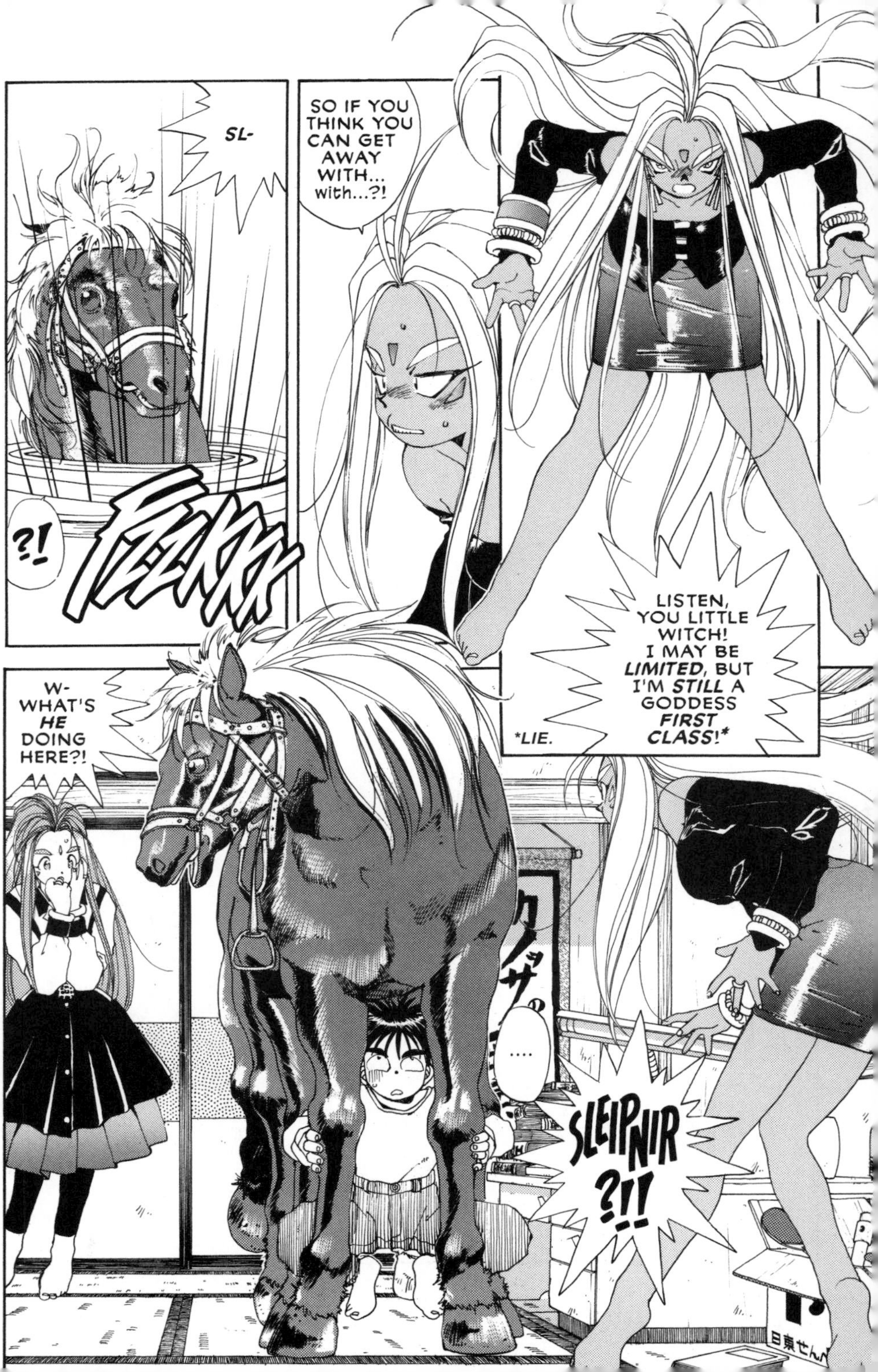
LISTEN, YOU LITTLE WITCH! I MAY BE *LIMITED*, BUT I'M *STILL* A GODDESS *FIRST CLASS*!*
*LIE.
SO IF YOU THINK YOU CAN GET AWAY WITH... with...?!
SL-
FZZKKK
?!
SLEIPNIR ?!!
....
W-WHAT'S *HE* DOING HERE?!

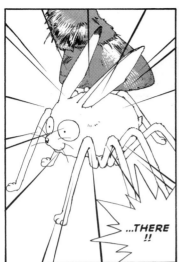

...THERE!!

? ? blink blink

OH, NO! I'M TOO LATE!!

AND THAT MEANS...

SLEIP-NIR!

FWAK

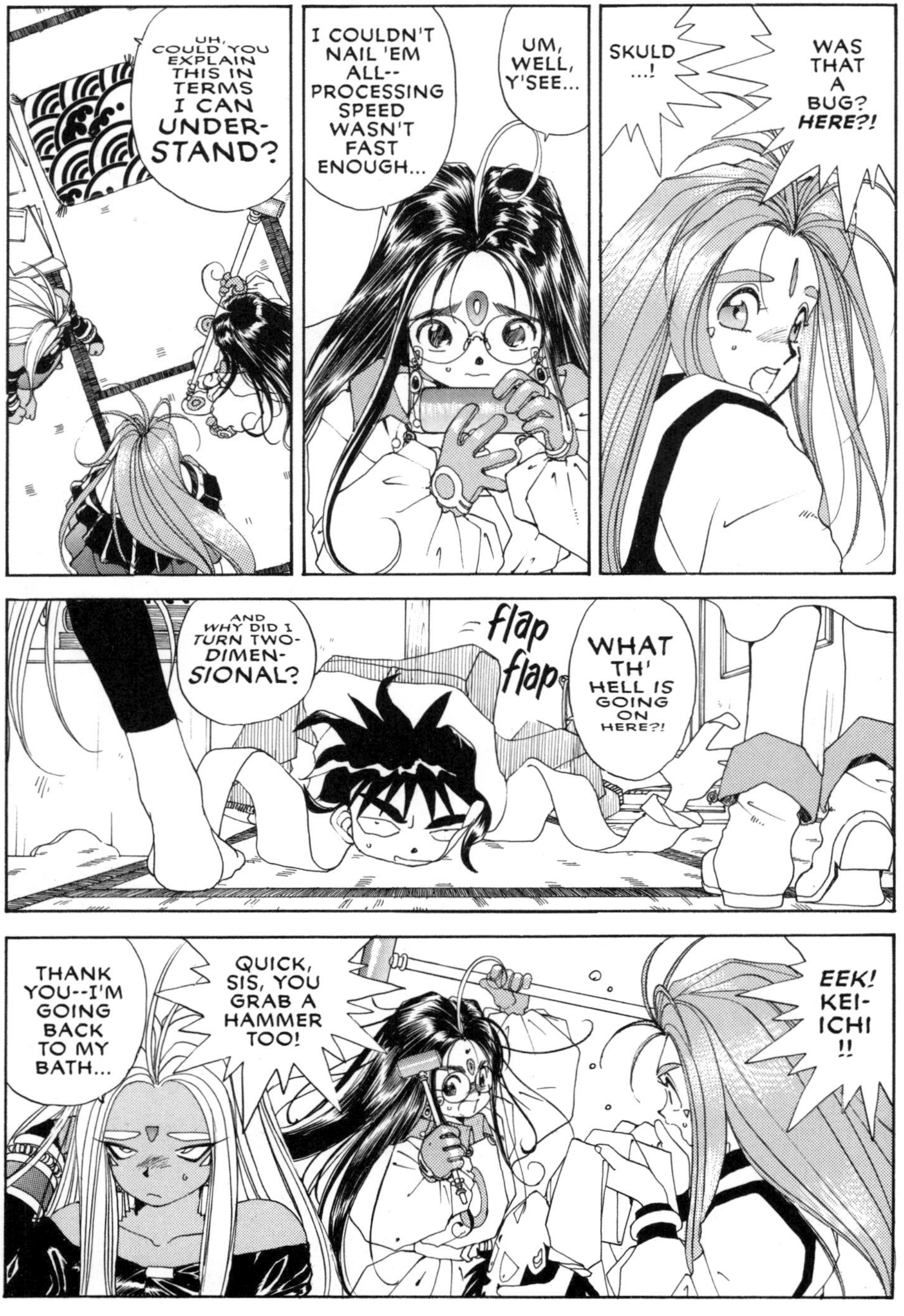
WAS THAT A BUG? HERE?!
SKULD ...!
UM, WELL, Y'SEE...
I COULDN'T NAIL 'EM ALL-- PROCESSING SPEED WASN'T FAST ENOUGH...
UH, COULD YOU EXPLAIN THIS IN TERMS I CAN UNDER-STAND?
WHAT TH' HELL IS GOING ON HERE?!
flap flap
AND WHY DID I TURN TWO-DIMEN-SIONAL?
EEK! KEI-ICHI !!
QUICK, SIS, YOU GRAB A HAMMER TOO!
THANK YOU--I'M GOING BACK TO MY BATH...

SO, YOU SEE...
...BUGS ARE PROLIFERATING OUT OF CONTROL IN THE YGGDRASIL SYSTEM META-PROGRAM.
WITHOUT CONSTANT DEBUGGING, THEY'LL GO INTO A LOOP STATE...
...IN WHICH THE BUGS WILL ENDLESSLY REPRODUCE THEM-SELVES.
AND IF *THAT* HAPPENS, A QUASI-DIFFERENTIAL WILL OCCUR BETWEEN THE EXISTENCE PROBABILITIES OF NORMALLY EQUIVALENT SPACES...
...CAUSING FLUCTUATIONS IN THE LOCUS OF SPACE A, OR THE COMPLETE DISAPPEAR-ANCE OF SPACE B, FOR EXAMPLE.
B
A
A
C
B DISAPPEARS FROM LOCUS β
γ
β
CHANGE OVER TIME
α
OR AN ENTIRELY DIFFERENT SPACE--"C"--MAY SUDDENLY MATERIALIZE, JUST LIKE SLEIPNIR DID A MOMENT AGO.
YOU MEAN, IN ADDITION TO BEING FLATTENED, I MIGHT SUDDENLY FLY OFF--
KEIICHI!
fffttt

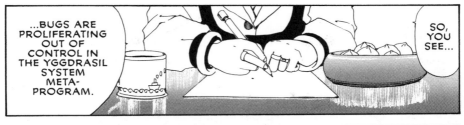

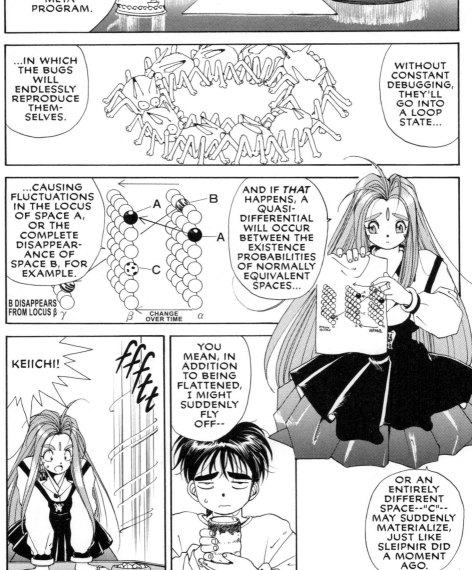

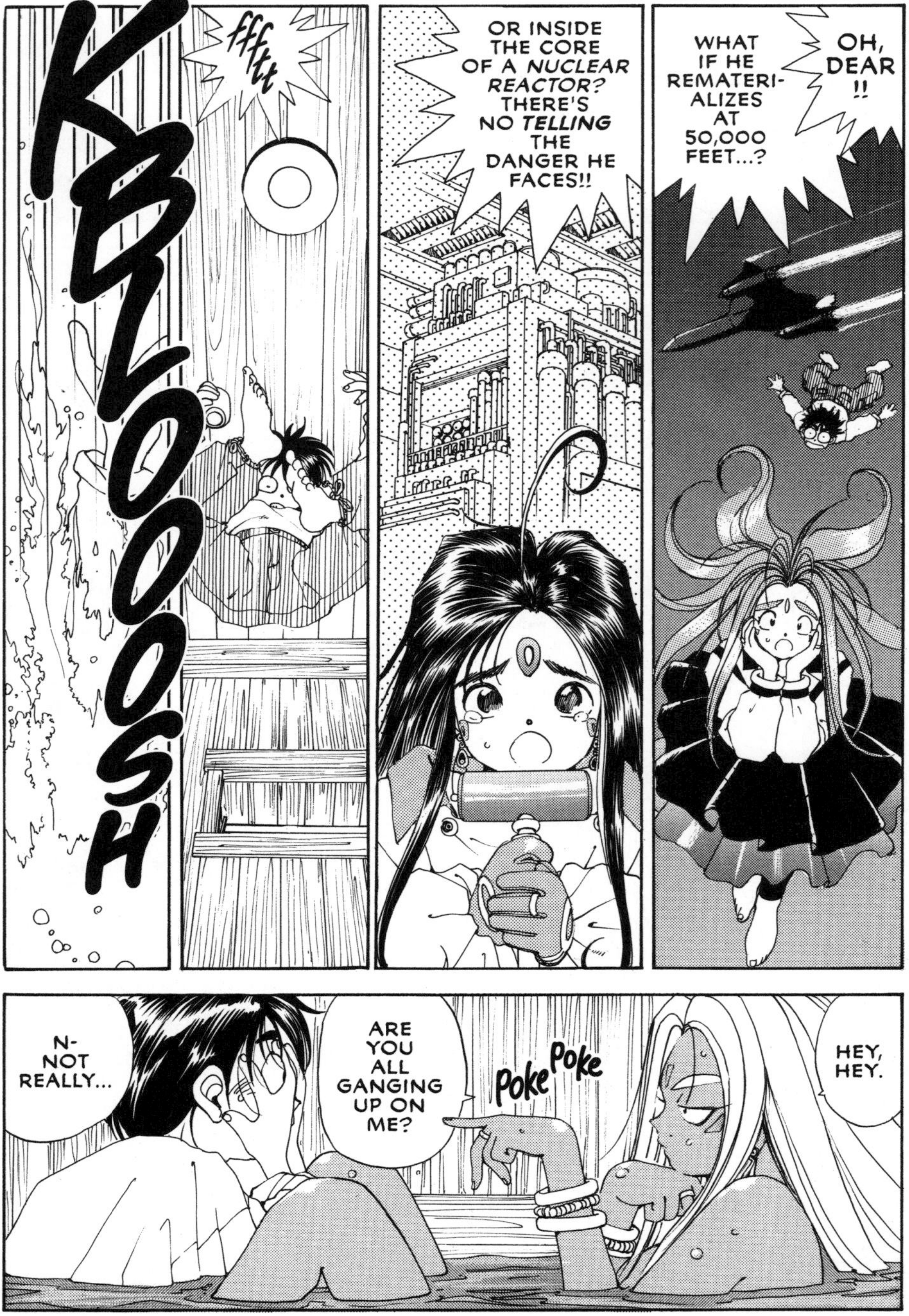
OH, DEAR!!
WHAT IF HE REMATERIALIZES AT 50,000 FEET...?
OR INSIDE THE CORE OF A *NUCLEAR REACTOR?* THERE'S NO *TELLING* THE DANGER HE FACES!!
ffftt
KBLOOOSH
HEY, HEY.
Poke Poke
ARE YOU ALL GANGING UP ON ME?
N-NOT REALLY...

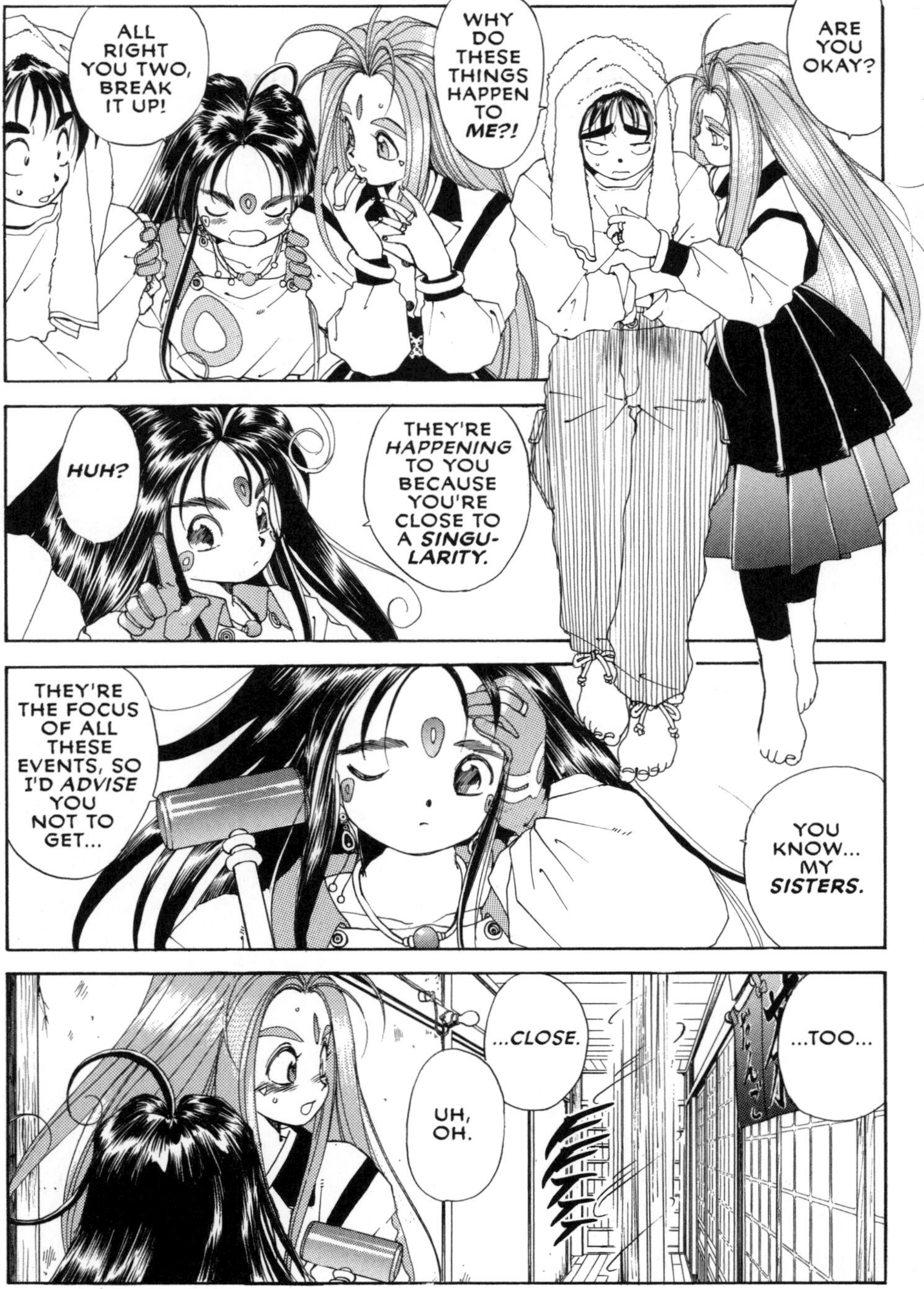
ARE YOU OKAY?
WHY DO THESE THINGS HAPPEN TO *ME?!*
ALL RIGHT YOU TWO, BREAK IT UP!
THEY'RE *HAPPENING* TO YOU BECAUSE YOU'RE CLOSE TO A *SINGULARITY.*
*HUH?*
YOU KNOW... MY *SISTERS.*
THEY'RE THE FOCUS OF ALL THESE EVENTS, SO I'D *ADVISE* YOU NOT TO GET...
...TOO...
*...CLOSE.*
UH, OH.

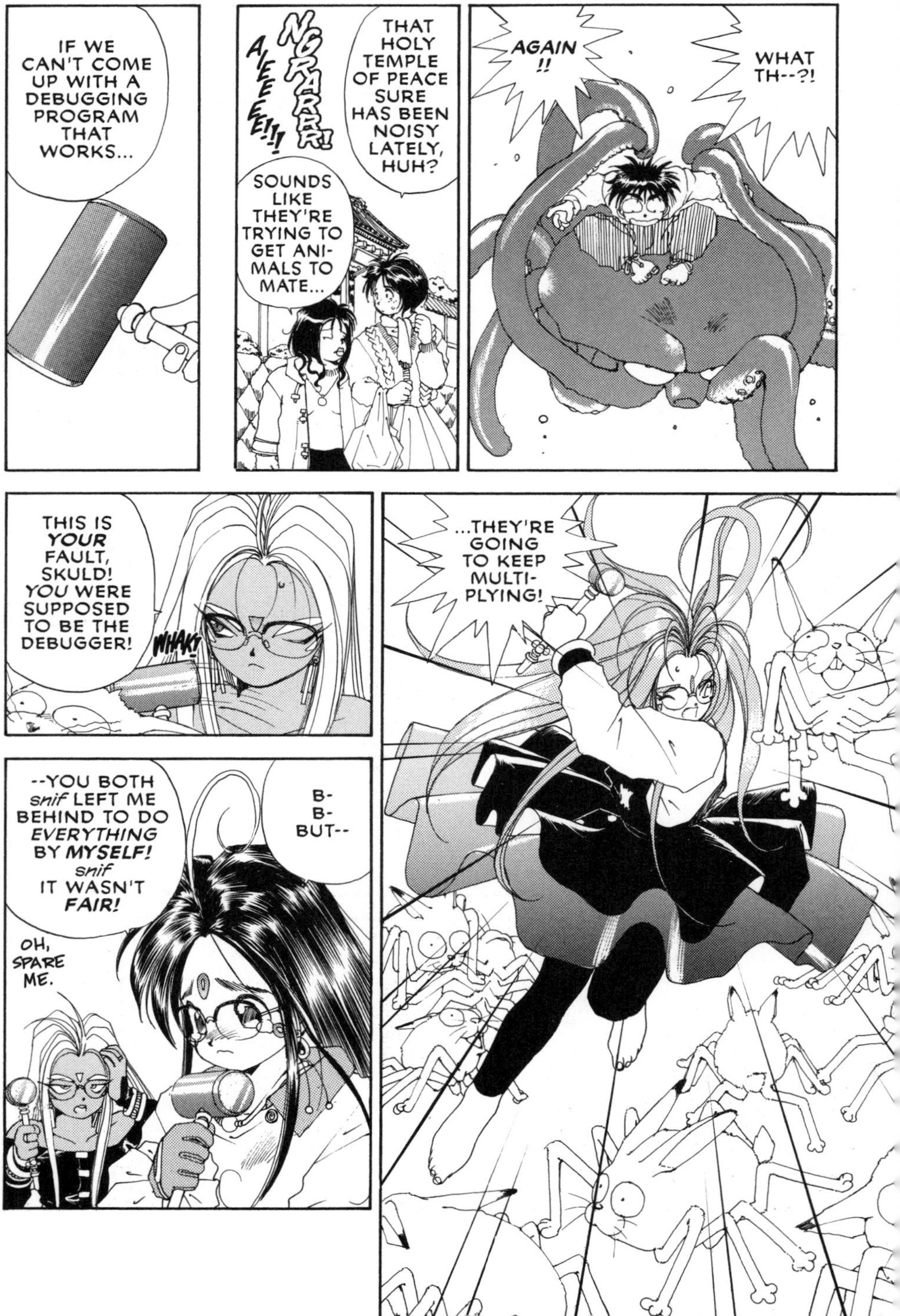
WHAT TH--?!
AGAIN !!
THAT HOLY TEMPLE OF PEACE SURE HAS BEEN NOISY LATELY, HUH?
NGRARARR!
AIEEEE!!!
SOUNDS LIKE THEY'RE TRYING TO GET ANI-MALS TO MATE...
IF WE CAN'T COME UP WITH A DEBUGGING PROGRAM THAT WORKS...
...THEY'RE GOING TO KEEP MULTI-PLYING!
THIS IS **YOUR** FAULT, SKULD! *YOU* WERE SUPPOSED TO BE THE DEBUGGER!
WHAK!
B- B- BUT--
--YOU BOTH *snif* LEFT ME BEHIND TO DO *EVERYTHING* BY ***MYSELF!*** *snif* IT WASN'T ***FAIR!***
OH, SPARE ME.

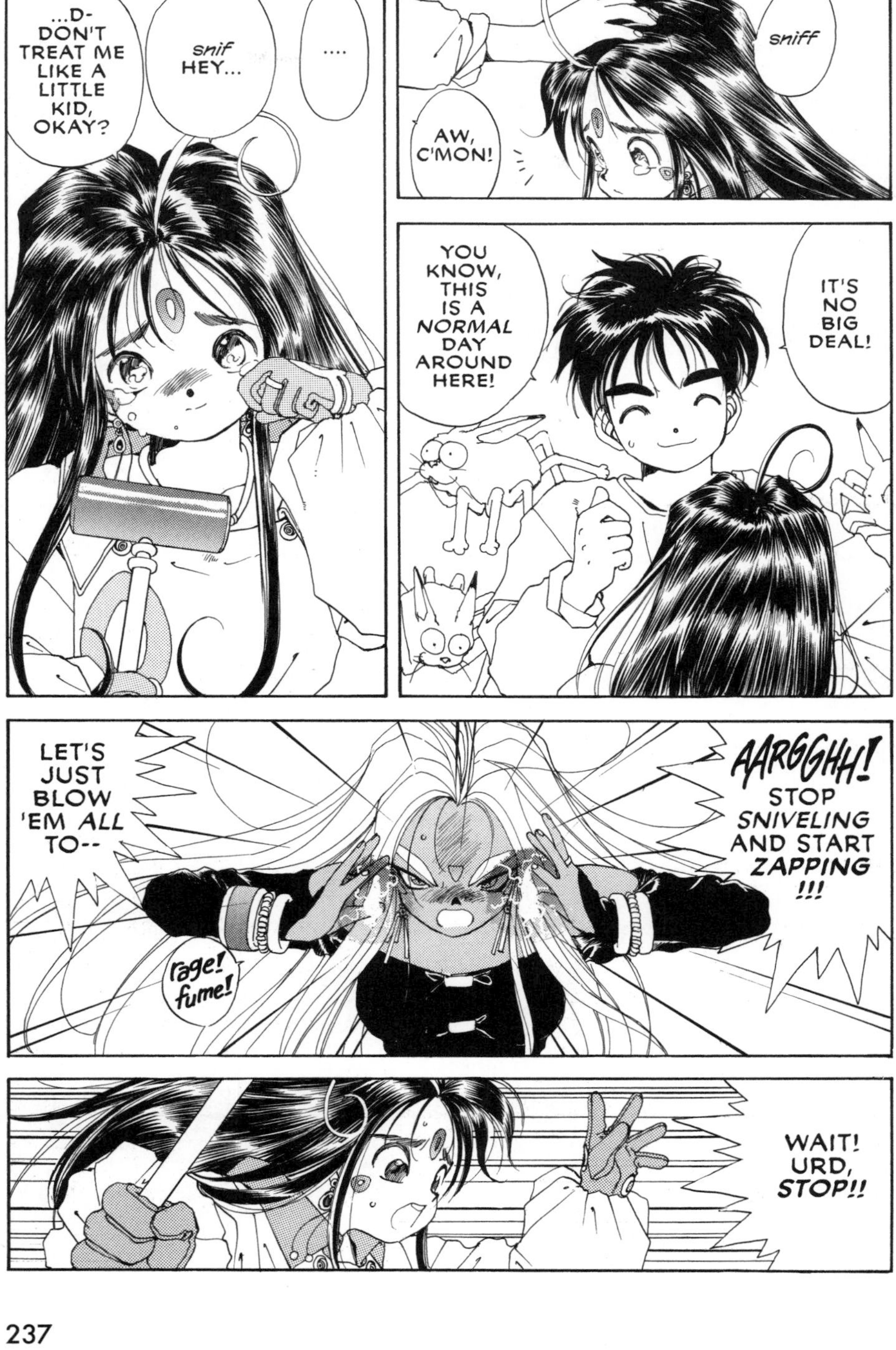
sniff
AW, C'MON!
IT'S NO BIG DEAL!
YOU KNOW, THIS IS A NORMAL DAY AROUND HERE!
....
snif HEY...
...D-DON'T TREAT ME LIKE A LITTLE KID, OKAY?
AARGGHH! STOP SNIVELING AND START ZAPPING!!!
rage! fume!
LET'S JUST BLOW 'EM ALL TO--
WAIT! URD, STOP!!

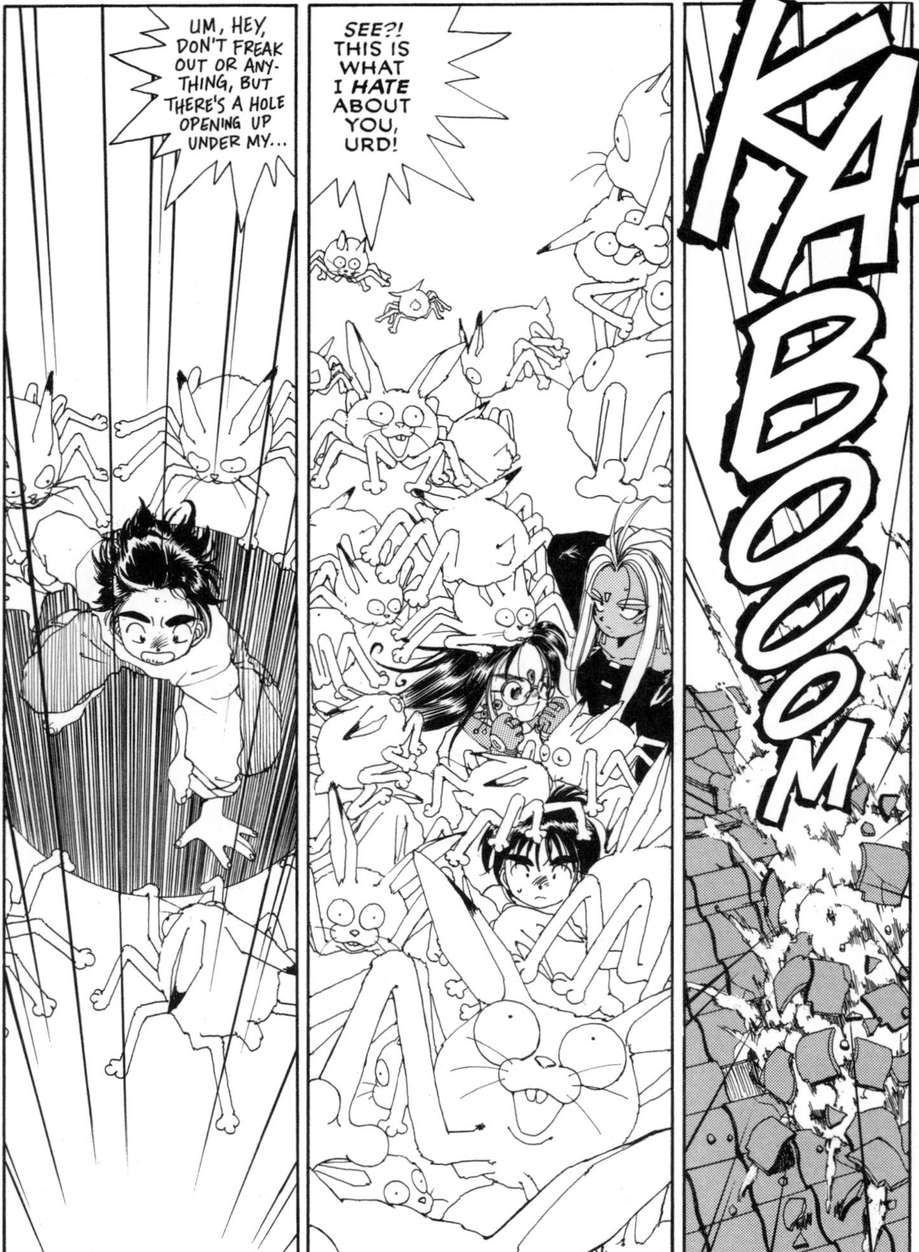
KA-BOOOOM!
SEE?! THIS IS WHAT I *HATE* ABOUT YOU, URD!
UM, HEY, DON'T FREAK OUT OR ANY-THING, BUT THERE'S A HOLE OPENING UP UNDER MY...

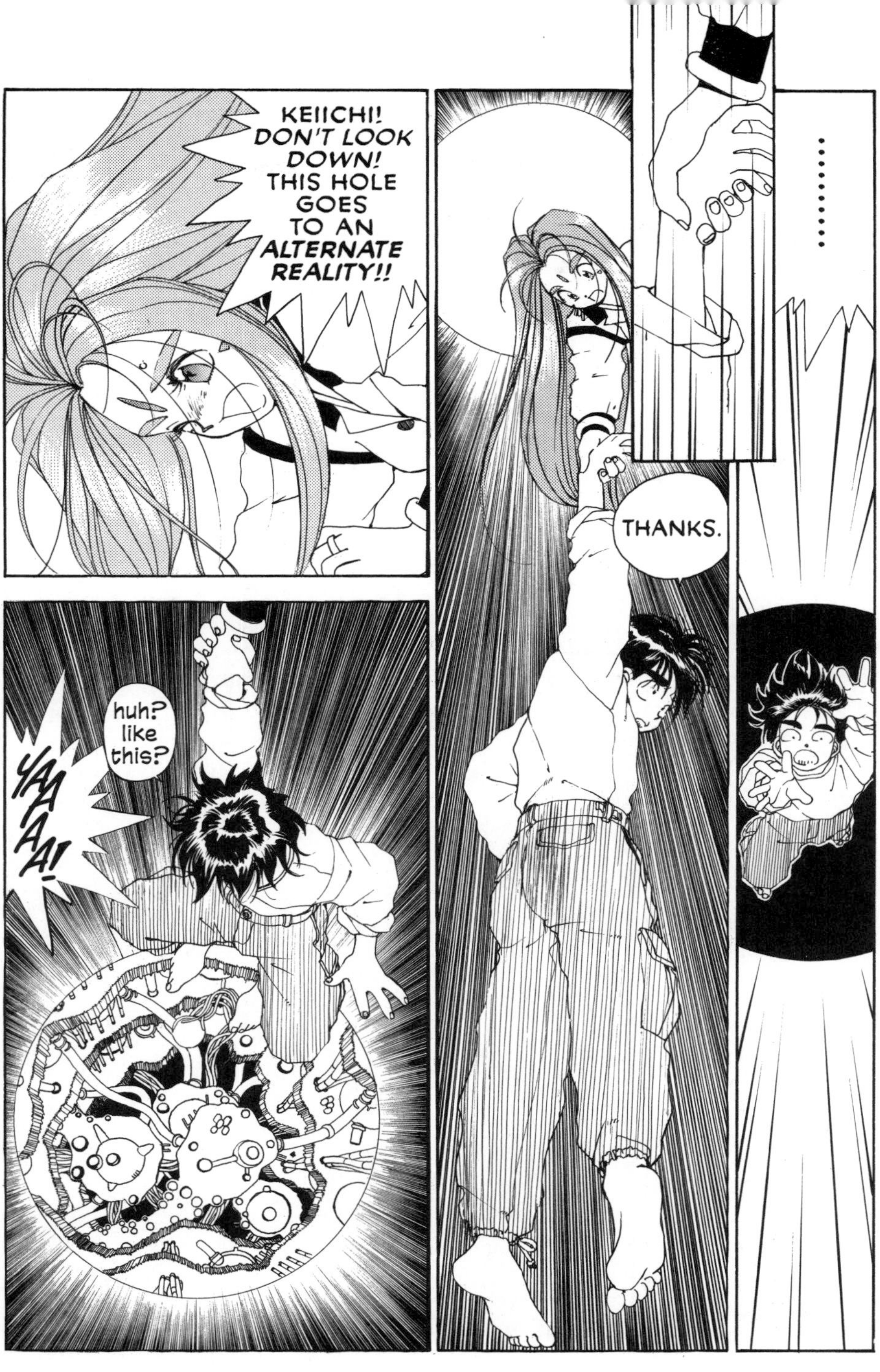
......
THANKS.
KEIICHI! DON'T LOOK DOWN! THIS HOLE GOES TO AN ALTERNATE REALITY!!
huh? like this?
YAAAAA!

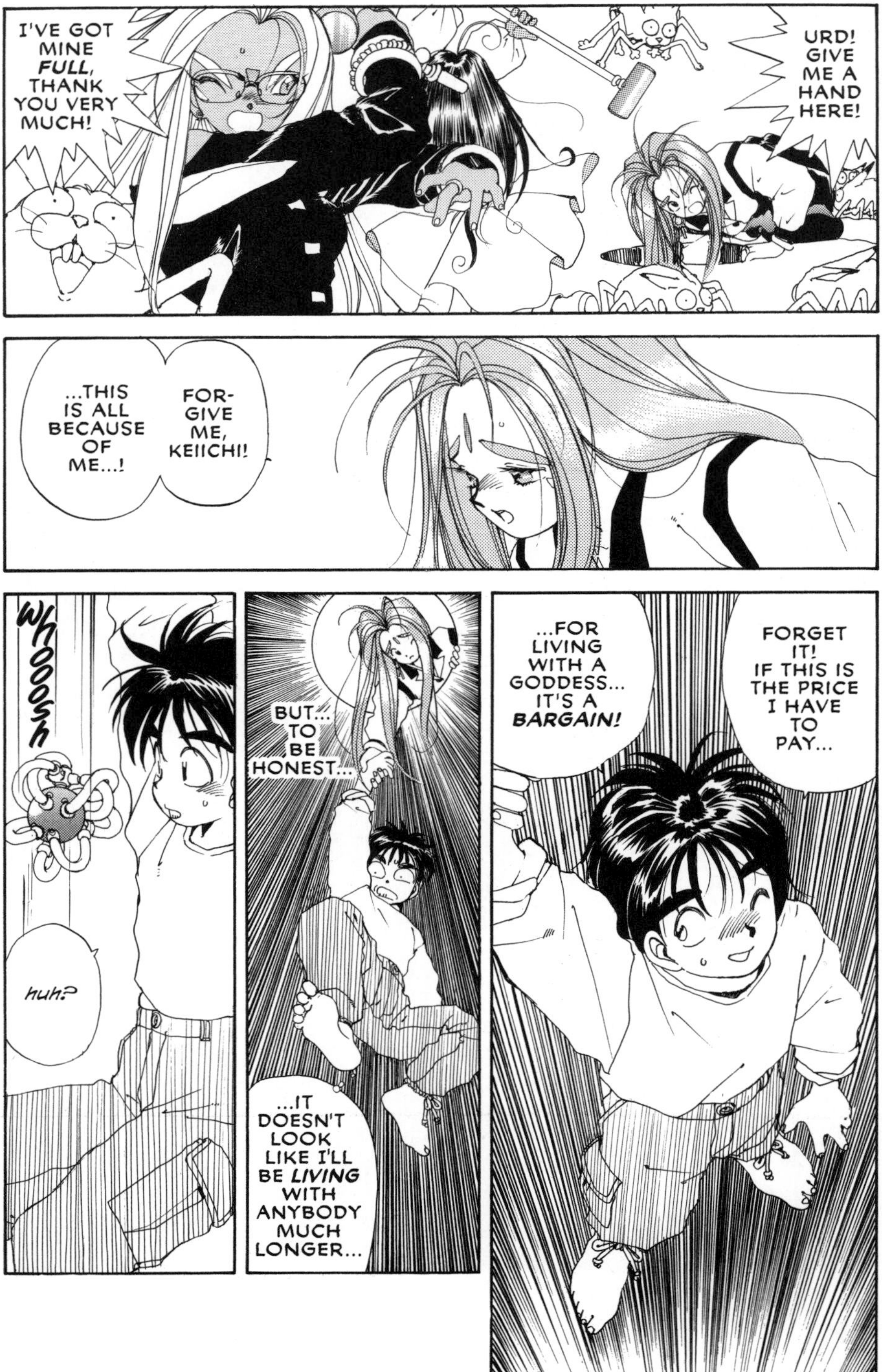
URD! GIVE ME A HAND HERE!
I'VE GOT MINE FULL, THANK YOU VERY MUCH!
FOR-GIVE ME, KEIICHI!
...THIS IS ALL BECAUSE OF ME...!
FORGET IT! IF THIS IS THE PRICE I HAVE TO PAY...
...FOR LIVING WITH A GODDESS... IT'S A BARGAIN!
BUT... TO BE HONEST...
...IT DOESN'T LOOK LIKE I'LL BE LIVING WITH ANYBODY MUCH LONGER...
WHOOOSH
huh?

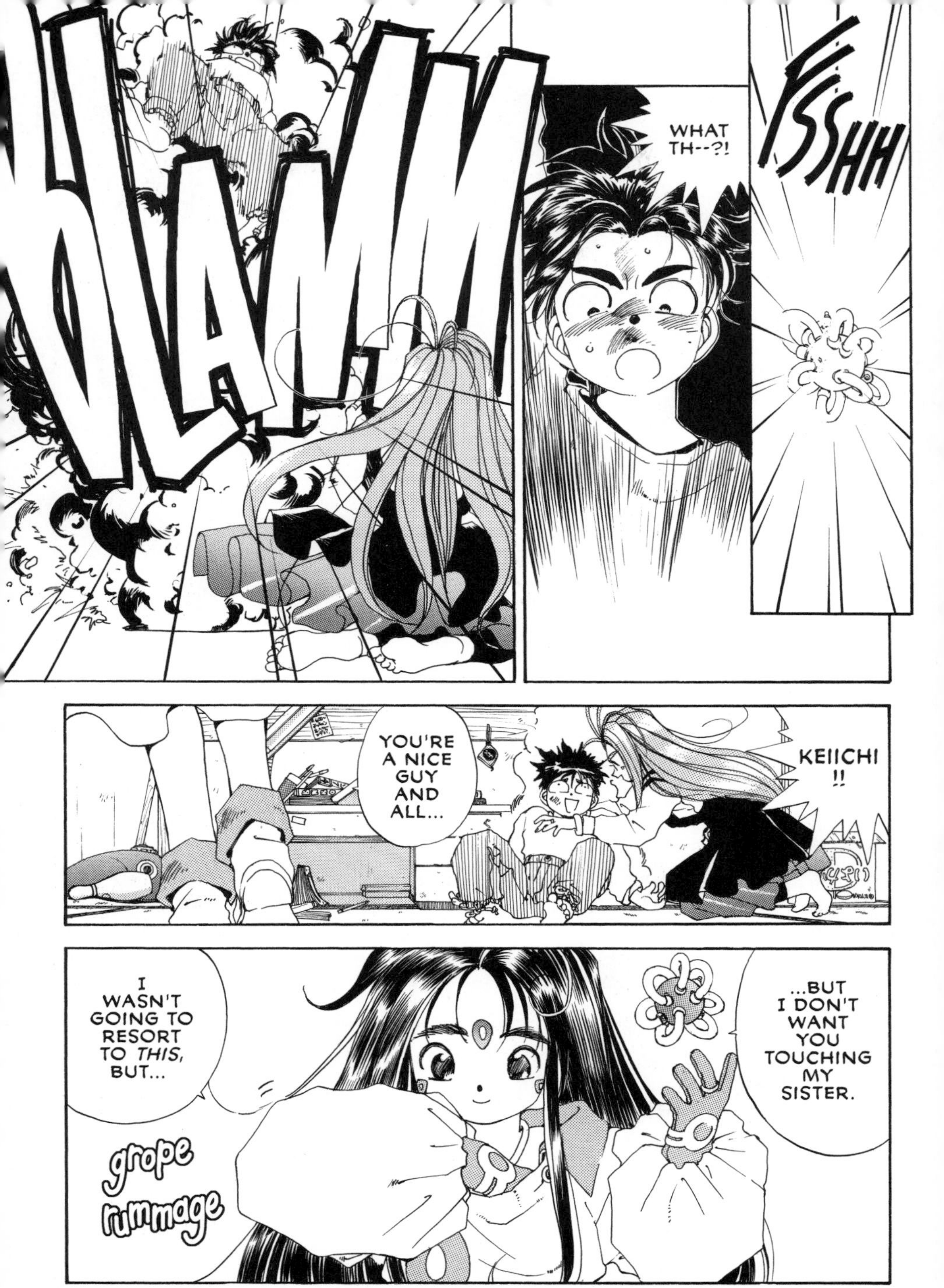
FSSHH
WHAT TH--?!
KEIICHI !!
YOU'RE A NICE GUY AND ALL...
...BUT I DON'T WANT YOU TOUCHING MY SISTER.
I WASN'T GOING TO RESORT TO *THIS*, BUT...
grope rummage

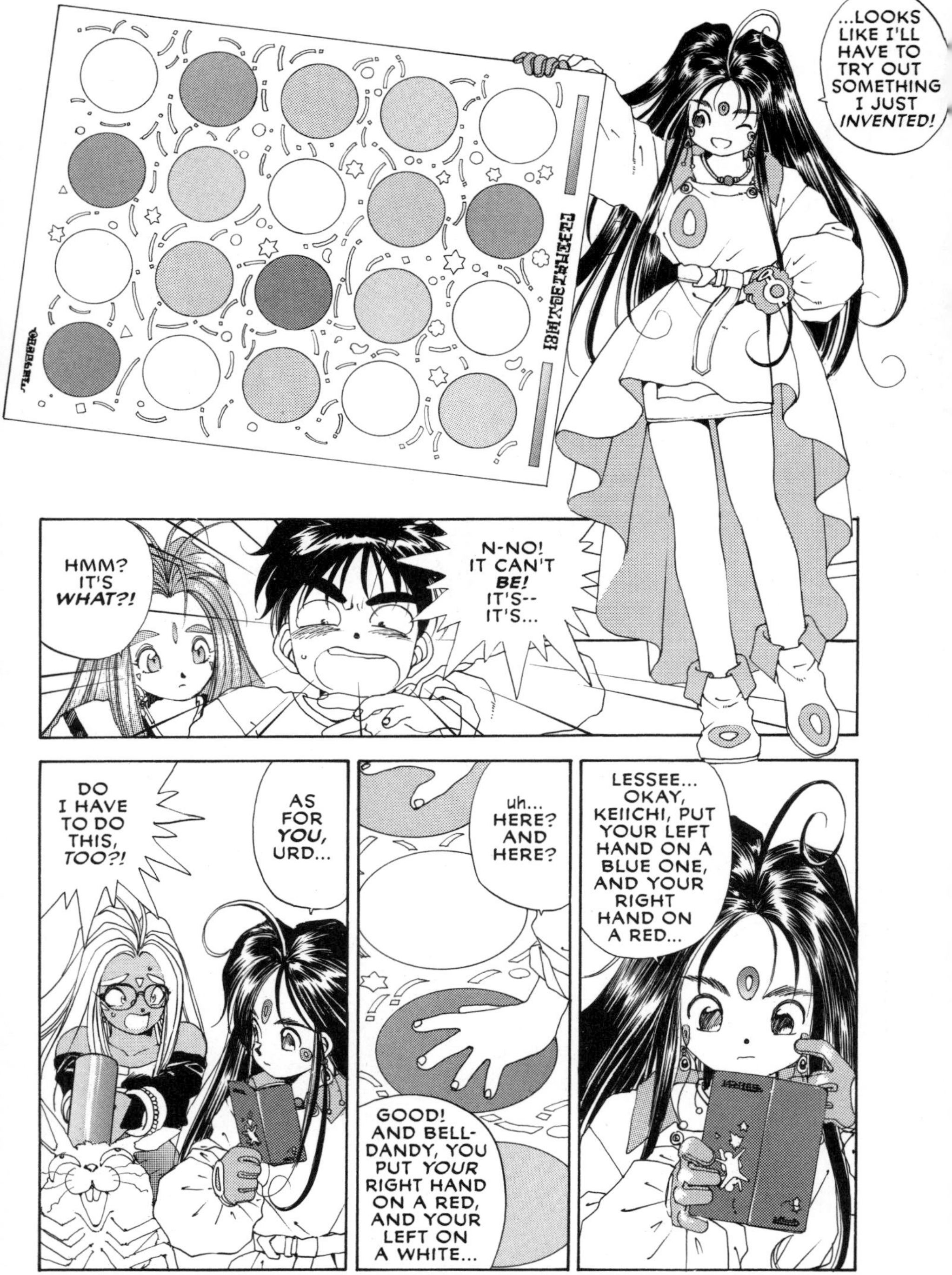
...LOOKS LIKE I'LL HAVE TO TRY OUT SOMETHING I JUST *INVENTED!*
N-NO! IT CAN'T *BE!* IT'S-- IT'S...
HMM? IT'S *WHAT?!*
LESSEE... OKAY, KEIICHI, PUT YOUR LEFT HAND ON A BLUE ONE, AND YOUR RIGHT HAND ON A RED...
uh... HERE? AND HERE?
GOOD! AND BELL-DANDY, YOU PUT *YOUR* RIGHT HAND ON A RED, AND YOUR LEFT ON A WHITE...
AS FOR *YOU,* URD...
DO I HAVE TO DO THIS, *TOO?!*

...OVER HERE ...?
HERE, MAY-BE?
JEEZ... C'MON, SIS...
HEY! MOVE YER *FOOT*, KIDDO!
YOU KNOW...
...I'M GETTING TO *LIKE* THIS GAME...
!!

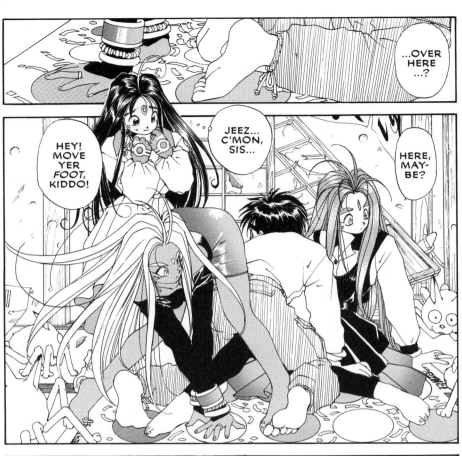

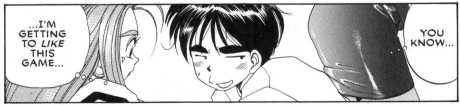

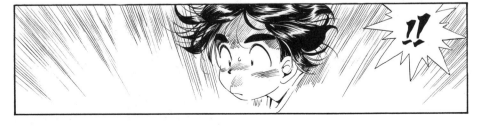

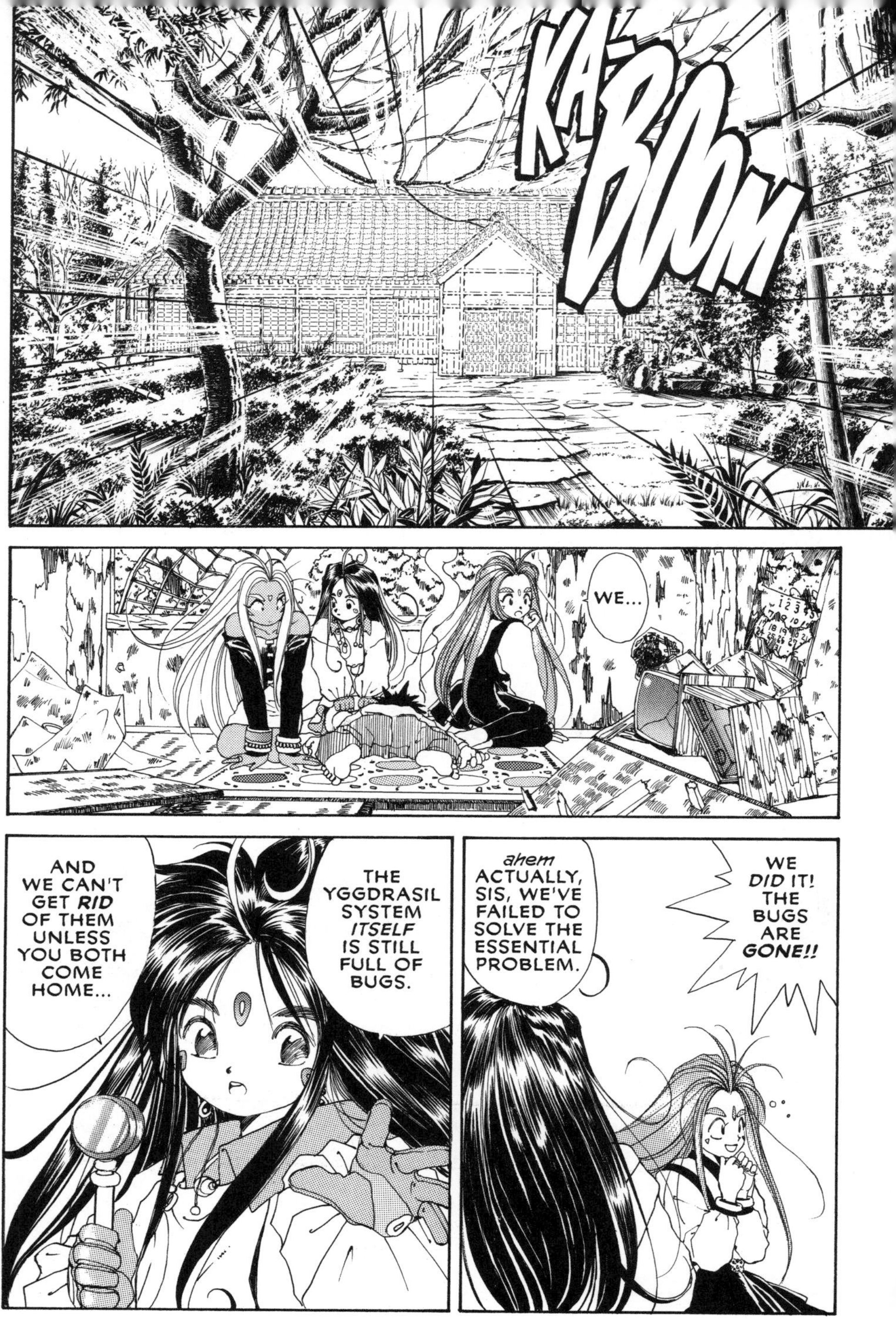
KA-BOOM
WE...
WE *DID* IT! THE BUGS ARE *GONE!!*
*ahem* ACTUALLY, SIS, WE'VE FAILED TO SOLVE THE ESSENTIAL PROBLEM.
THE YGGDRASIL SYSTEM *ITSELF* IS STILL FULL OF BUGS.
AND WE CAN'T GET *RID* OF THEM UNLESS YOU BOTH COME HOME...

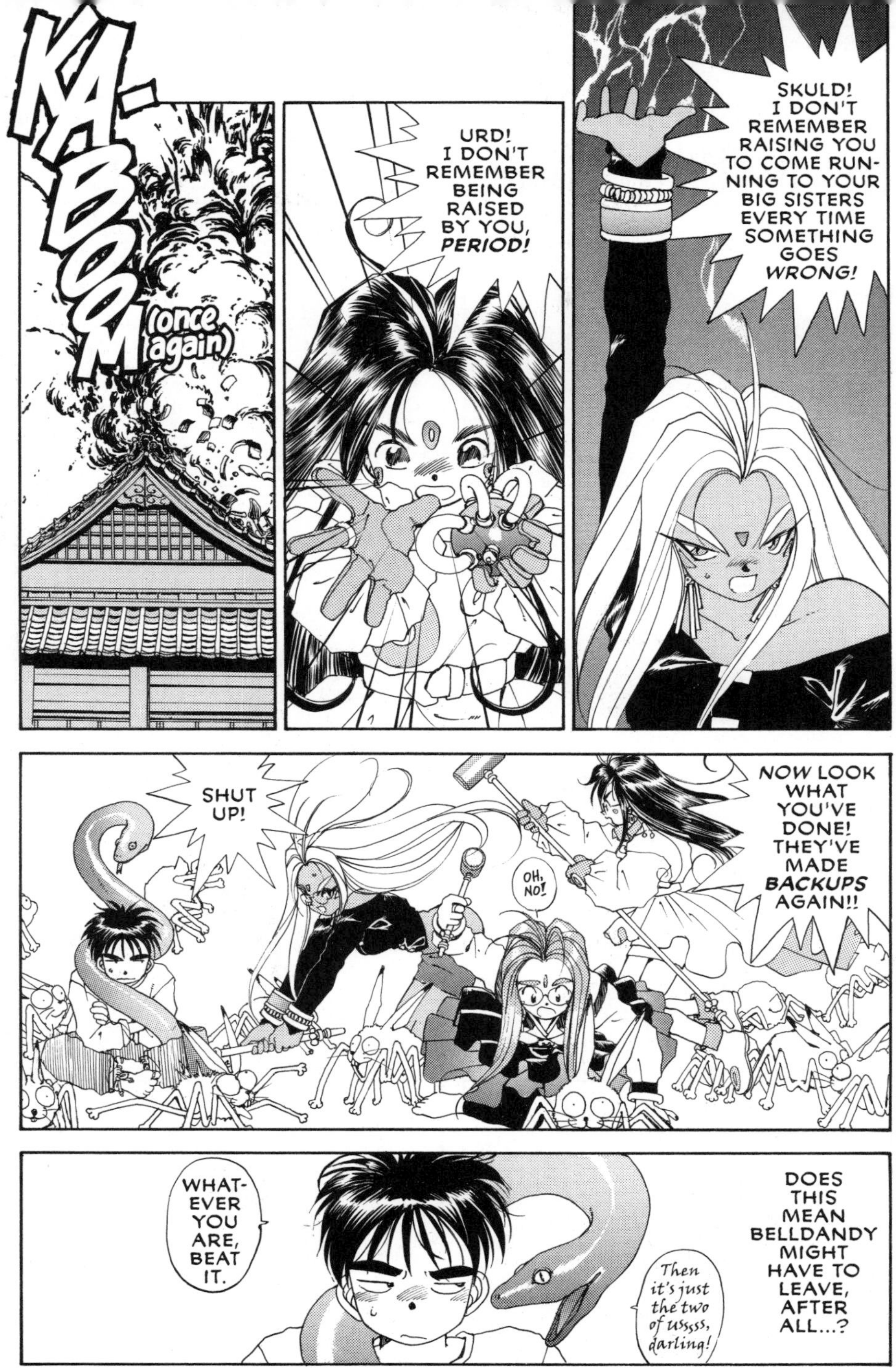
SKULD! I DON'T REMEMBER RAISING YOU TO COME RUNNING TO YOUR BIG SISTERS EVERY TIME SOMETHING GOES *WRONG!*
URD! I DON'T REMEMBER BEING RAISED BY YOU, *PERIOD!*
KA-BOOOM (once again)
*NOW* LOOK WHAT YOU'VE DONE! THEY'VE MADE *BACKUPS* AGAIN!!
OH, NO!
SHUT UP!
DOES THIS MEAN BELLDANDY MIGHT HAVE TO LEAVE, AFTER ALL...?
Then it's just the two of usssss, darling!
WHAT-EVER YOU ARE, BEAT IT.

# THE ADVENTURES OF MINI-URD

introducing MINI-SKULD!!

## ◆ A CASUAL BET ◆

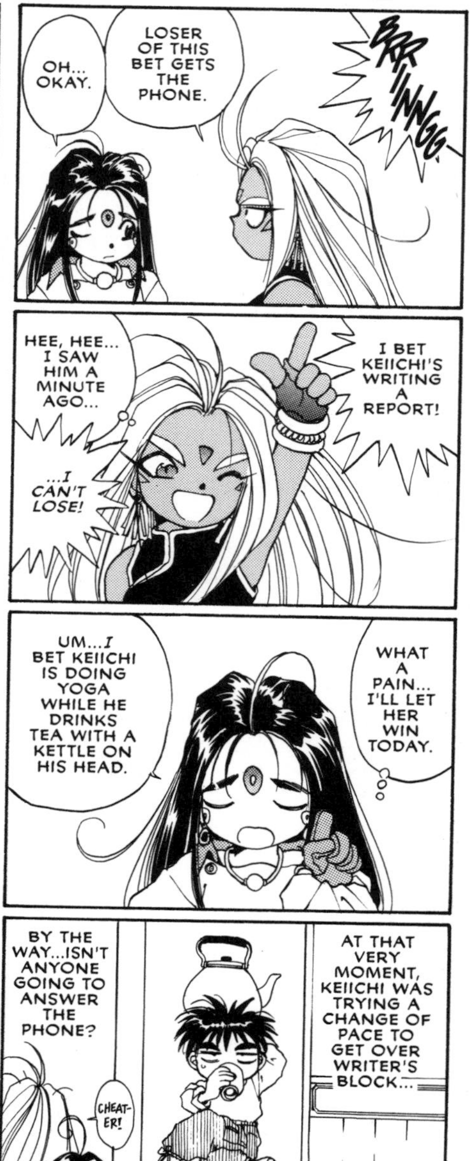
BRRIIINNGG-
LOSER OF THIS BET GETS THE PHONE.
OH... OKAY.
I BET KEIICHI'S WRITING A REPORT!
HEE, HEE... I SAW HIM A MINUTE AGO...
...I CAN'T LOSE!
WHAT A PAIN... I'LL LET HER WIN TODAY.
UM...I BET KEIICHI IS DOING YOGA WHILE HE DRINKS TEA WITH A KETTLE ON HIS HEAD.
AT THAT VERY MOMENT, KEIICHI WAS TRYING A CHANGE OF PACE TO GET OVER WRITER'S BLOCK...
BY THE WAY...ISN'T ANYONE GOING TO ANSWER THE PHONE?
CHEATER!

## CAN YOU EAT THIS?! ◆THE ULTIMATE GOURMAND!◆

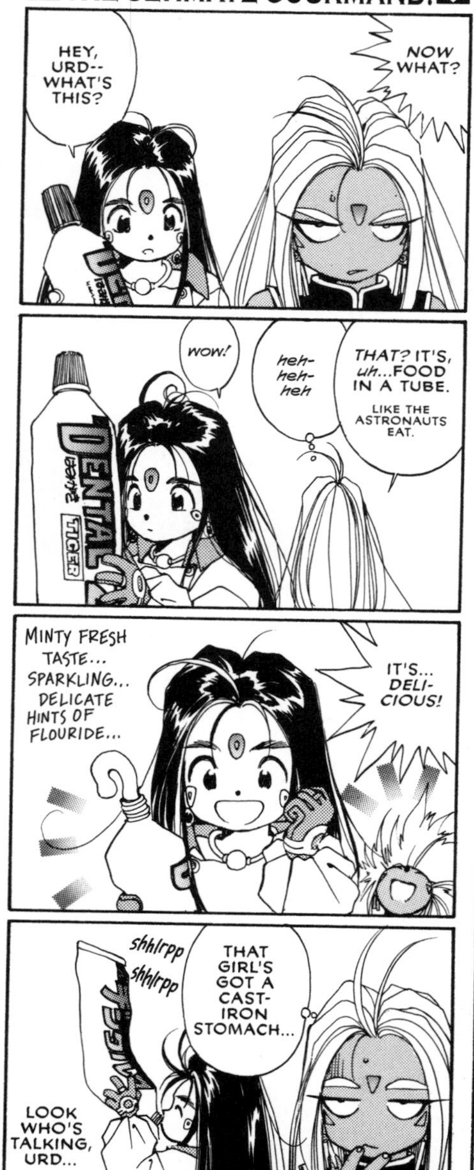
NOW WHAT?
HEY, URD-- WHAT'S THIS?
THAT? IT'S, uh...FOOD IN A TUBE.
LIKE THE ASTRONAUTS EAT.
heh-heh-heh
wow!
DENTAL
TIGER
IT'S... DELICIOUS!
MINTY FRESH TASTE... SPARKLING... DELICATE HINTS OF FLOURIDE...
THAT GIRL'S GOT A CAST-IRON STOMACH...
shhlrpp
shhlrpp
LOOK WHO'S TALKING, URD...

CHAPTER 33

# The Goddesses' Greatest Danger

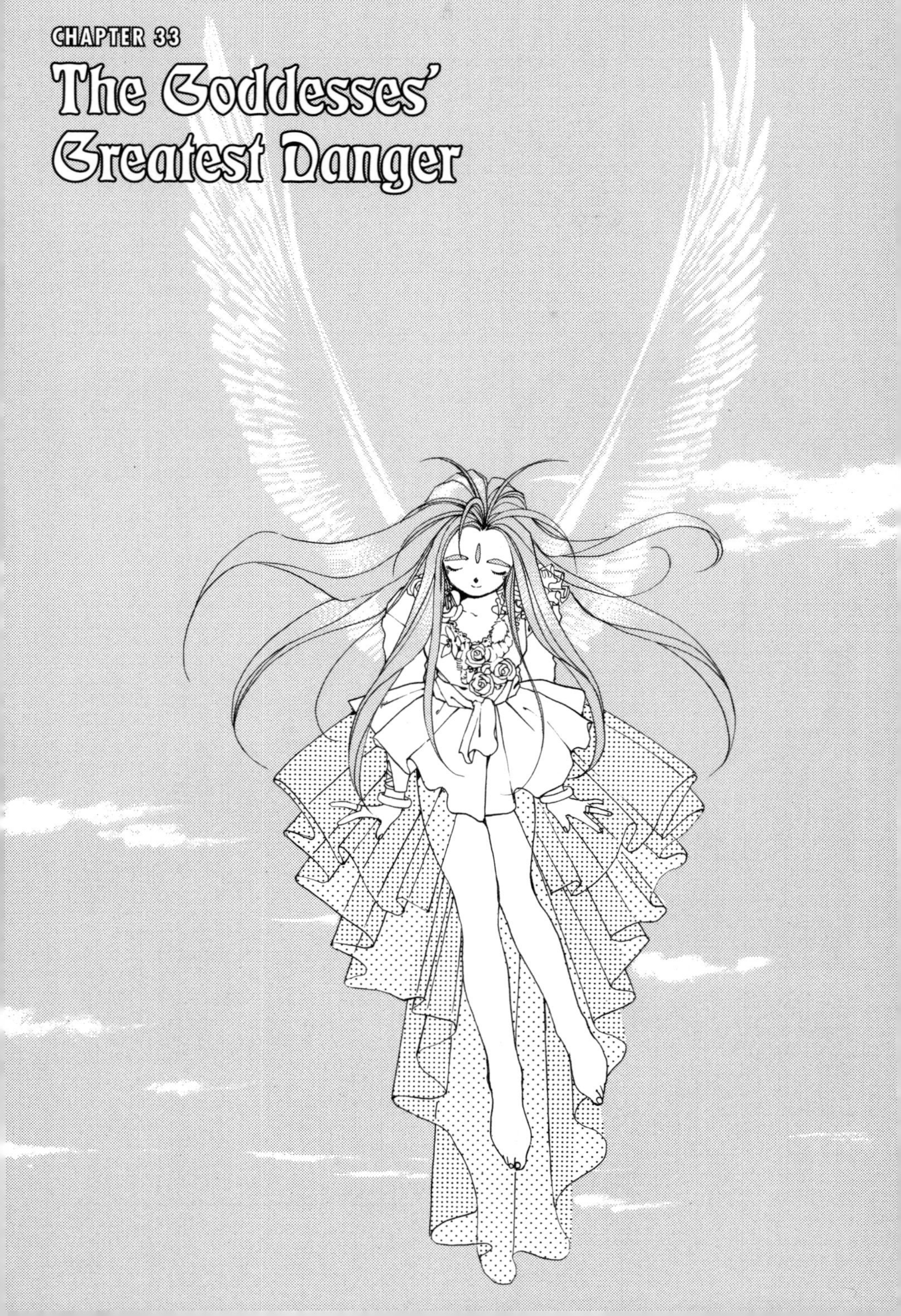

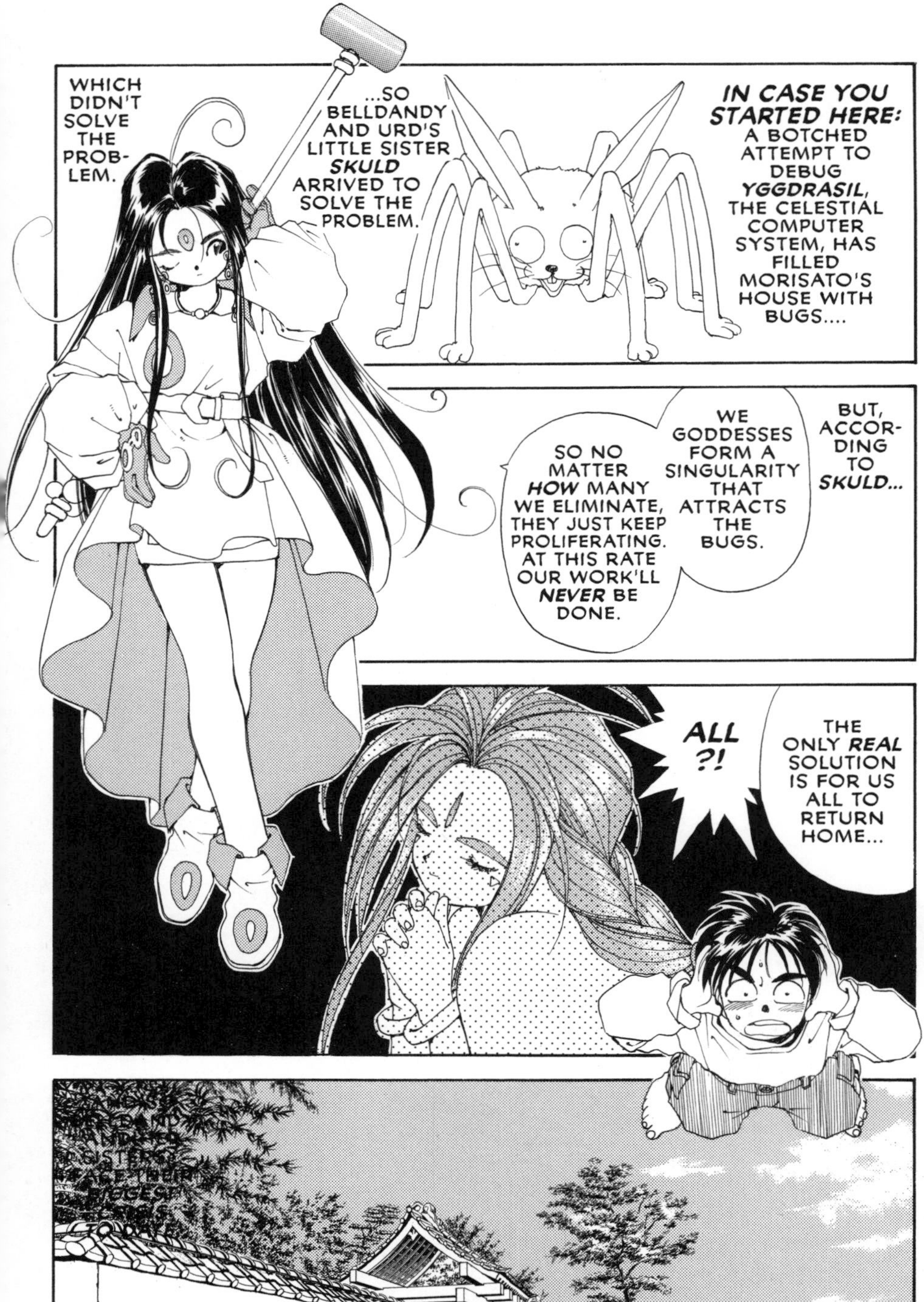
IN CASE YOU STARTED HERE: A BOTCHED ATTEMPT TO DEBUG YGGDRASIL, THE CELESTIAL COMPUTER SYSTEM, HAS FILLED MORISATO'S HOUSE WITH BUGS....
...SO BELLDANDY AND URD'S LITTLE SISTER SKULD ARRIVED TO SOLVE THE PROBLEM.
WHICH DIDN'T SOLVE THE PROB-LEM.
BUT, ACCORD-ING TO SKULD...
WE GODDESSES FORM A SINGULARITY THAT ATTRACTS THE BUGS.
SO NO MATTER HOW MANY WE ELIMINATE, THEY JUST KEEP PROLIFERATING. AT THIS RATE OUR WORK'LL NEVER BE DONE.
THE ONLY REAL SOLUTION IS FOR US ALL TO RETURN HOME...
ALL ?!

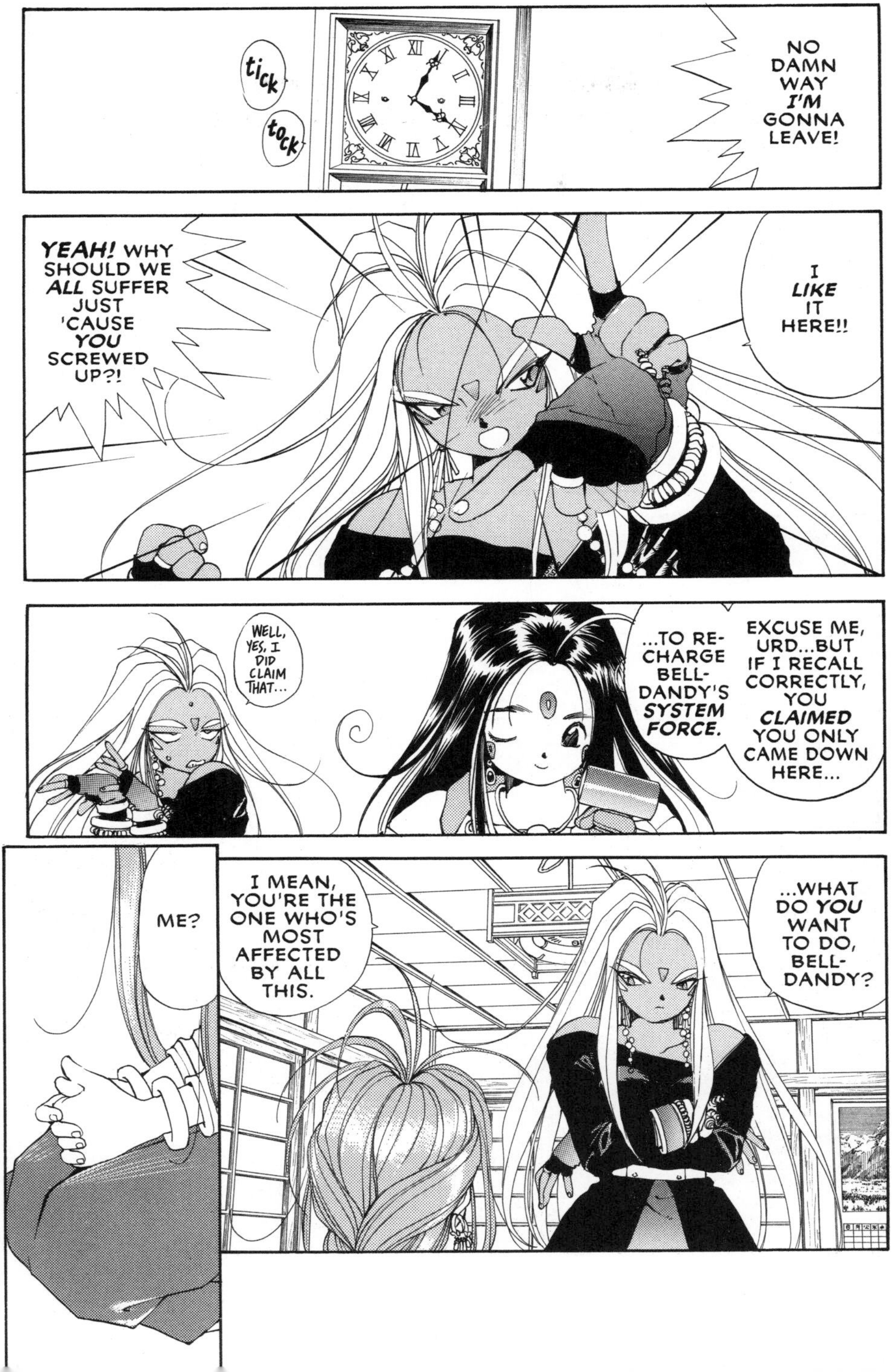
NO DAMN WAY I'M GONNA LEAVE!
tick
tock
I LIKE IT HERE!!
YEAH! WHY SHOULD WE ALL SUFFER JUST 'CAUSE YOU SCREWED UP?!
EXCUSE ME, URD...BUT IF I RECALL CORRECTLY, YOU CLAIMED YOU ONLY CAME DOWN HERE...
...TO RE-CHARGE BELL-DANDY'S SYSTEM FORCE.
WELL, YES, I DID CLAIM THAT...
...WHAT DO YOU WANT TO DO, BELL-DANDY?
I MEAN, YOU'RE THE ONE WHO'S MOST AFFECTED BY ALL THIS.
ME?

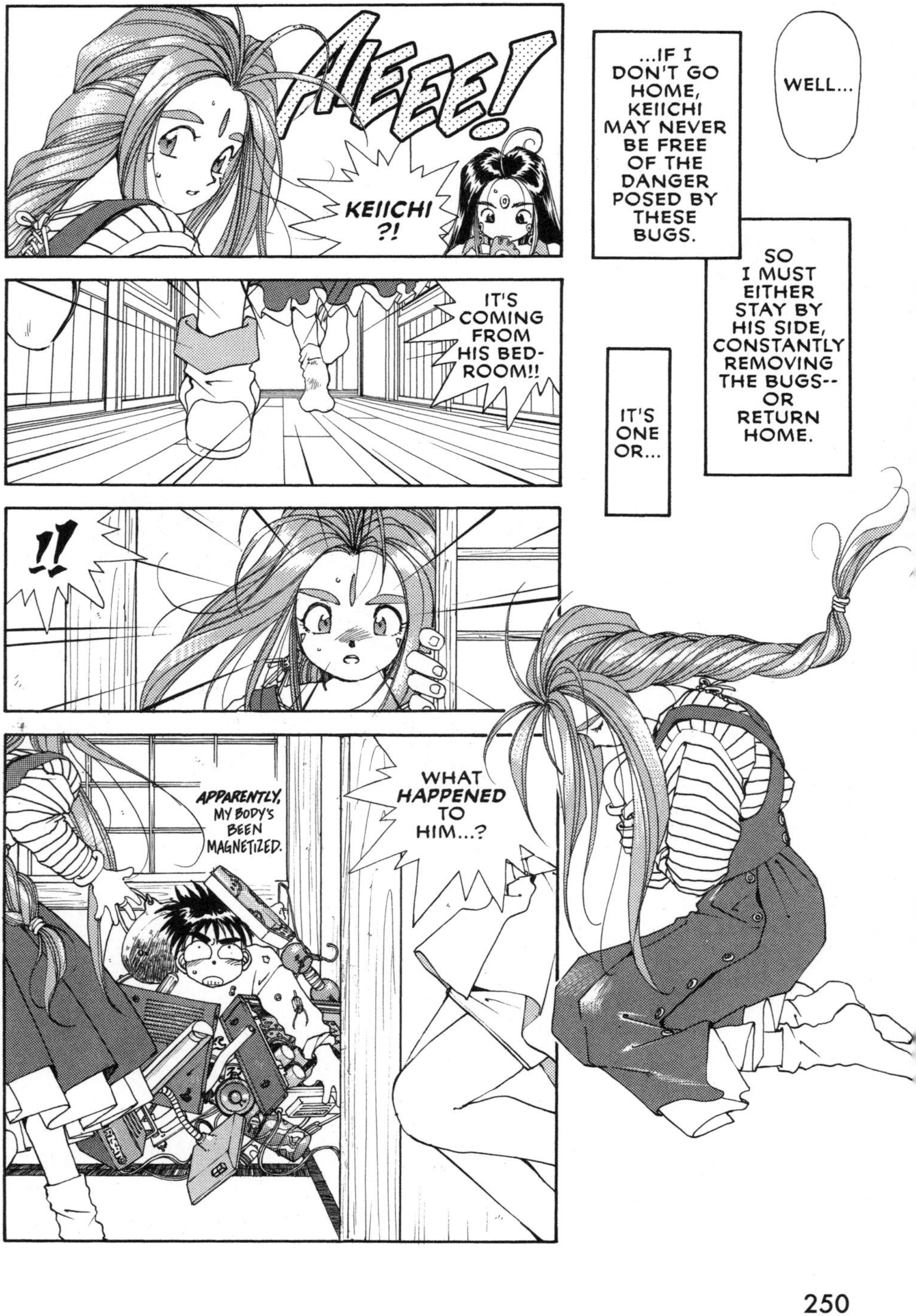
WELL...
...IF I DON'T GO HOME, KEIICHI MAY NEVER BE FREE OF THE DANGER POSED BY THESE BUGS.
SO I MUST EITHER STAY BY HIS SIDE, CONSTANTLY REMOVING THE BUGS-- OR RETURN HOME.
IT'S ONE OR...
AIEEE!
KEIICHI ?!
IT'S COMING FROM HIS BED-ROOM!!
!!
WHAT HAPPENED TO HIM...?
APPARENTLY, MY BODY'S BEEN MAGNETIZED.

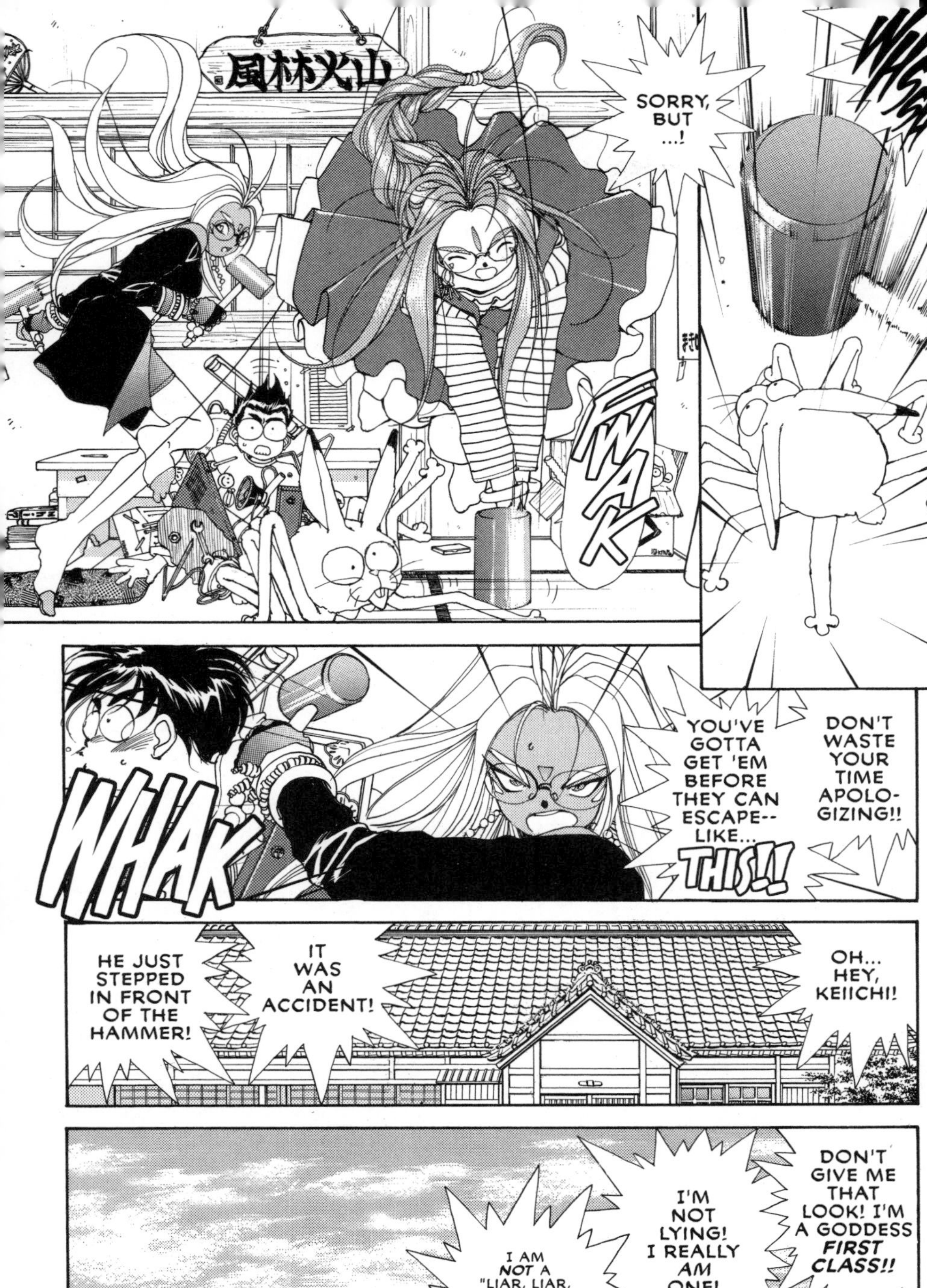
WHSSH
SORRY, BUT ...!
WHAK
DON'T WASTE YOUR TIME APOLOGIZING!!
YOU'VE GOTTA GET 'EM BEFORE THEY CAN ESCAPE-- LIKE... THIS!!
WHAK
OH... HEY, KEIICHI!
IT WAS AN ACCIDENT!
HE JUST STEPPED IN FRONT OF THE HAMMER!
DON'T GIVE ME THAT LOOK! I'M A GODDESS *FIRST CLASS!!*
I'M NOT LYING! I REALLY *AM* ONE!
I AM *NOT* A "LIAR, LIAR, PANTS ON FIRE!"

_groan_

NO... IT'S OKAY...

...IS THE SUN TOO BRIGHT FOR YOU?

I'M SORRY...

...I PROMISE TO COME BACK.

.....

?

KEI-ICHI...

I...

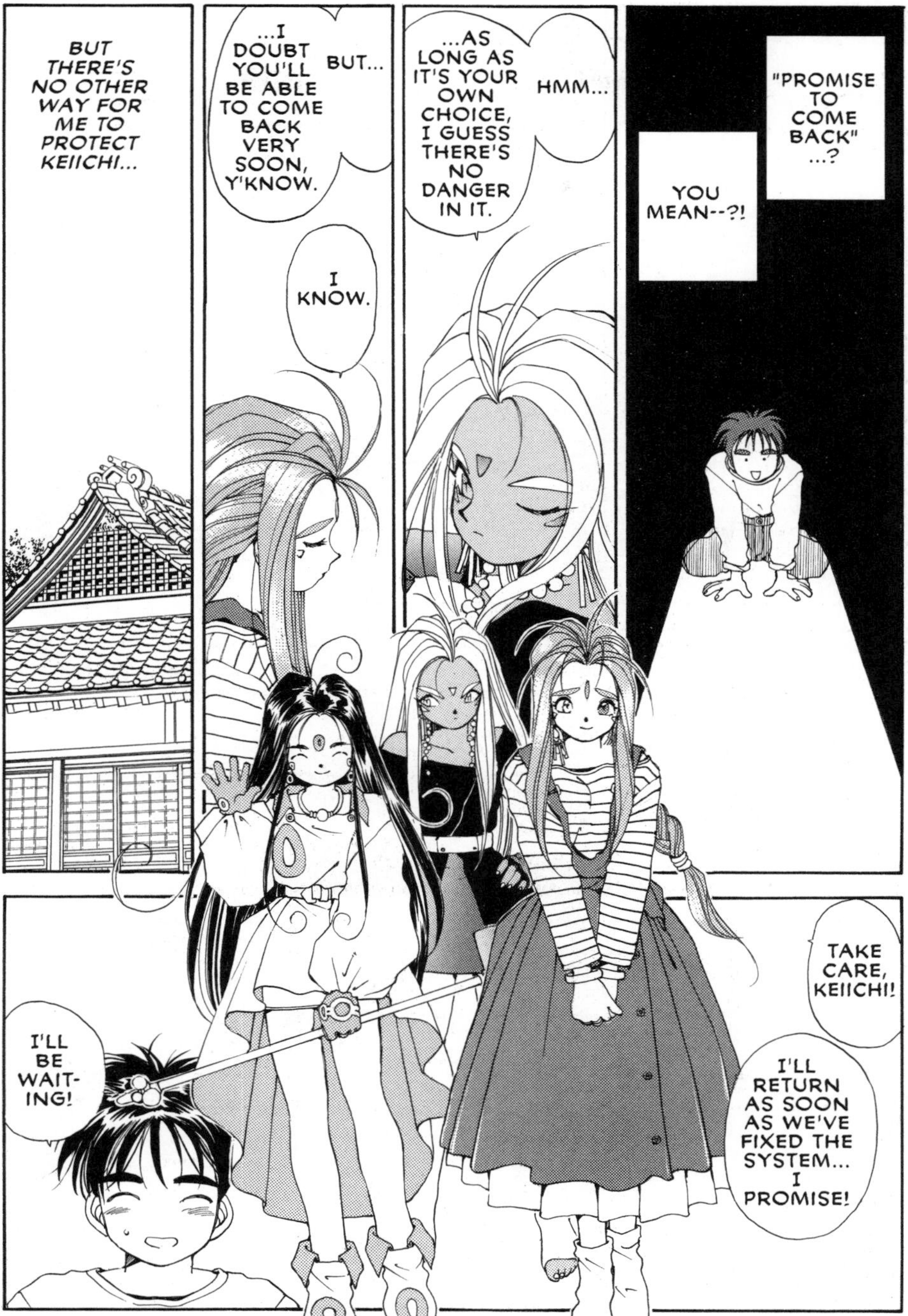
"PROMISE TO COME BACK" ...?
YOU MEAN--?!
HMM...
...AS LONG AS IT'S YOUR OWN CHOICE, I GUESS THERE'S NO DANGER IN IT.
BUT...
...I DOUBT YOU'LL BE ABLE TO COME BACK VERY SOON, Y'KNOW.
I KNOW.
BUT THERE'S NO OTHER WAY FOR ME TO PROTECT KEIICHI...
TAKE CARE, KEIICHI!
I'LL RETURN AS SOON AS WE'VE FIXED THE SYSTEM... I PROMISE!
I'LL BE WAIT-ING!

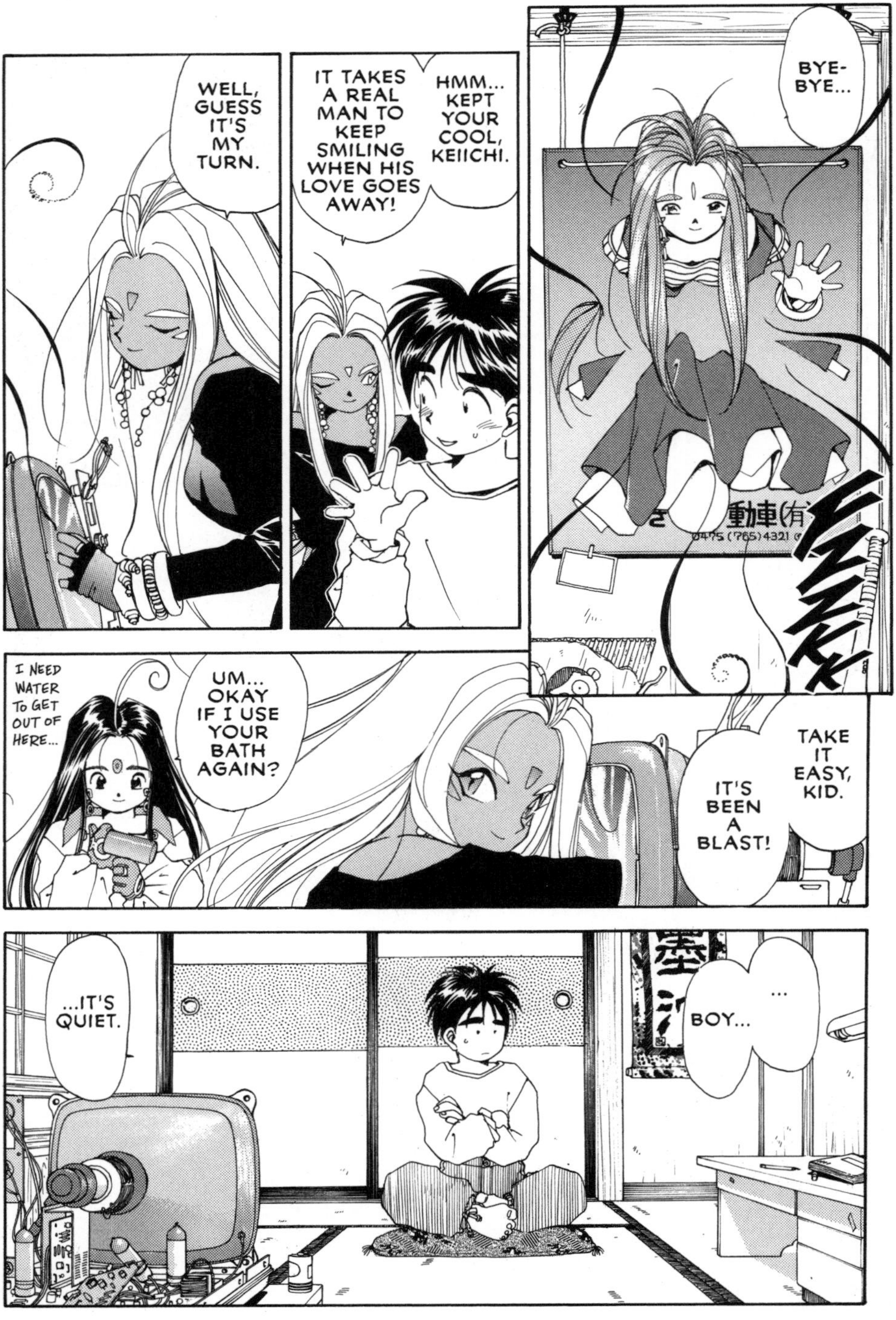
BYE-BYE...
HMM... KEPT YOUR COOL, KEIICHI.
IT TAKES A REAL MAN TO KEEP SMILING WHEN HIS LOVE GOES AWAY!
WELL, GUESS IT'S MY TURN.
TAKE IT EASY, KID.
IT'S BEEN A BLAST!
UM... OKAY IF I USE YOUR BATH AGAIN?
I NEED WATER TO GET OUT OF HERE...
BOY...
...
...IT'S QUIET.

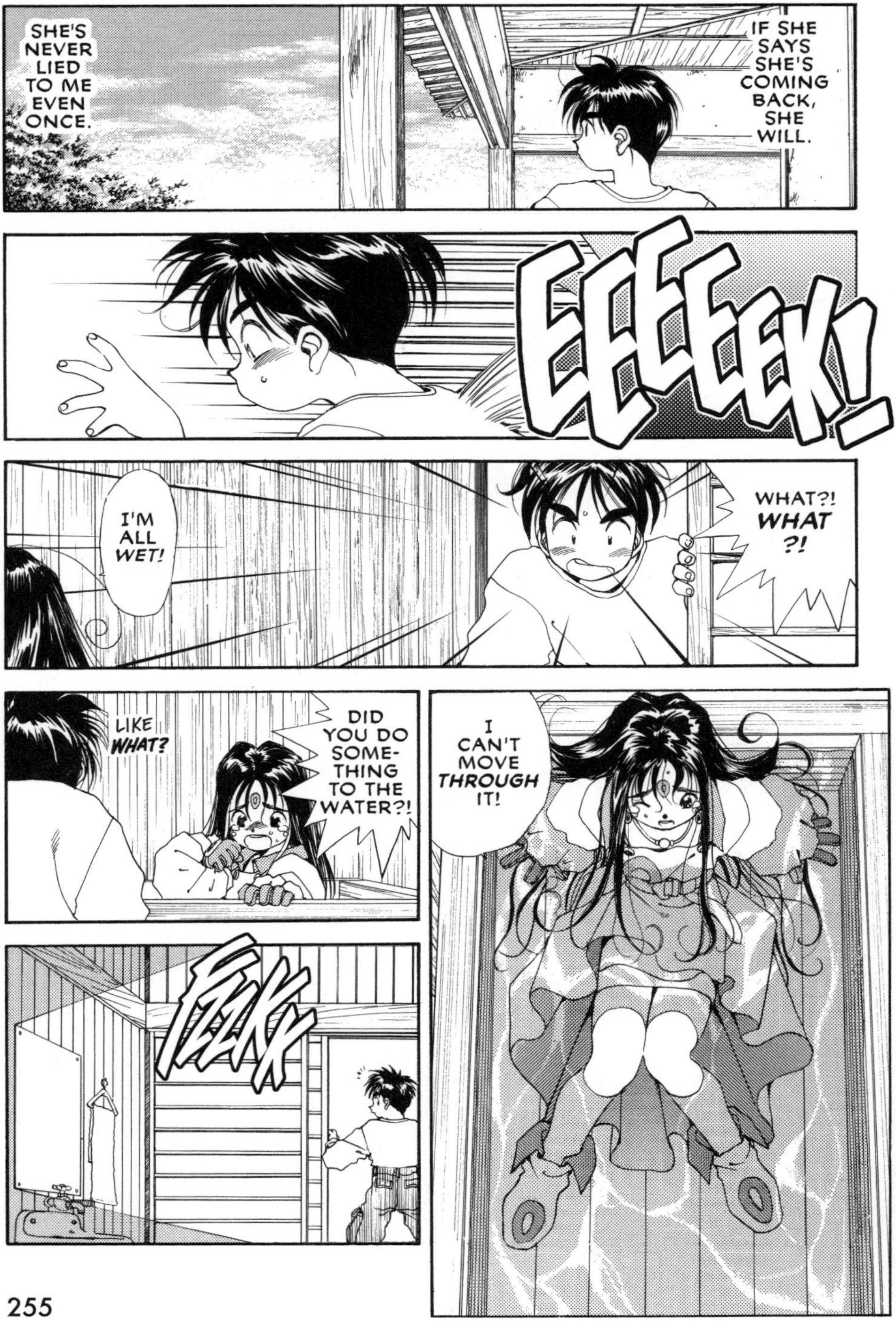
IF SHE SAYS SHE'S COMING BACK, SHE WILL.
SHE'S NEVER LIED TO ME EVEN ONCE.
EEEEEK!
WHAT?! *WHAT* ?!
I'M ALL *WET!*
I CAN'T MOVE *THROUGH* IT!
DID YOU DO SOME-THING TO THE WATER?!
LIKE *WHAT?*
FZKK

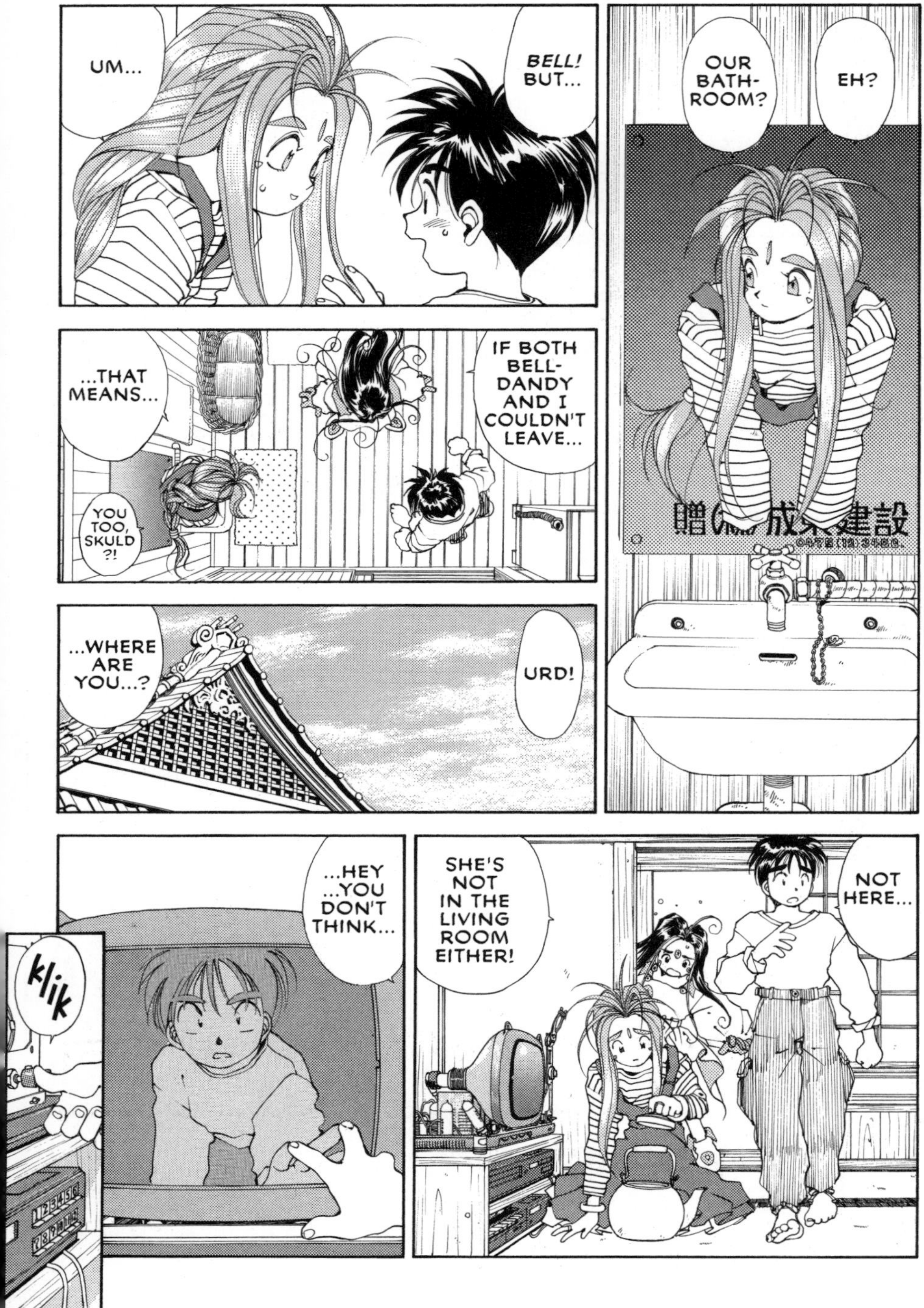
EH?
OUR BATH-ROOM?
BELL! BUT...
UM...
IF BOTH BELL-DANDY AND I COULDN'T LEAVE...
...THAT MEANS...
YOU TOO, SKULD?!
URD!
...WHERE ARE YOU...?
NOT HERE...
SHE'S NOT IN THE LIVING ROOM EITHER!
...HEY ...YOU DON'T THINK...
klik

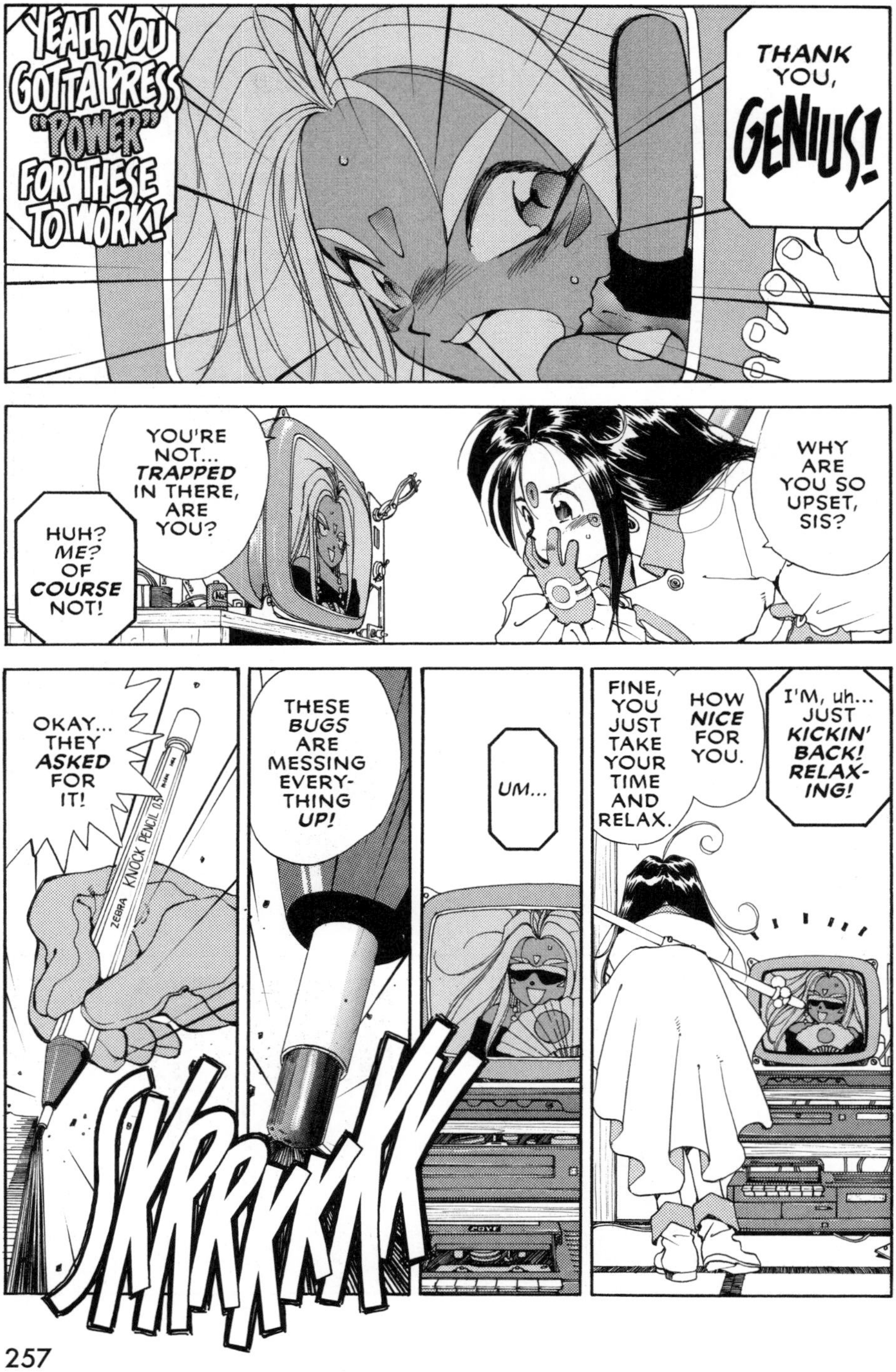

THANK YOU, GENIUS!
YEAH, YOU GOTTA PRESS "POWER" FOR THESE TO WORK!
WHY ARE YOU SO UPSET, SIS?
YOU'RE NOT... TRAPPED IN THERE, ARE YOU?
HUH? ME? OF COURSE NOT!
I'M, uh... JUST KICKIN' BACK! RELAXING!
HOW NICE FOR YOU.
FINE, YOU JUST TAKE YOUR TIME AND RELAX.
UM...
THESE BUGS ARE MESSING EVERYTHING UP!
OKAY... THEY ASKED FOR IT!
ZEBRA KNOCK PENCIL 0.5
SKRRKKKK

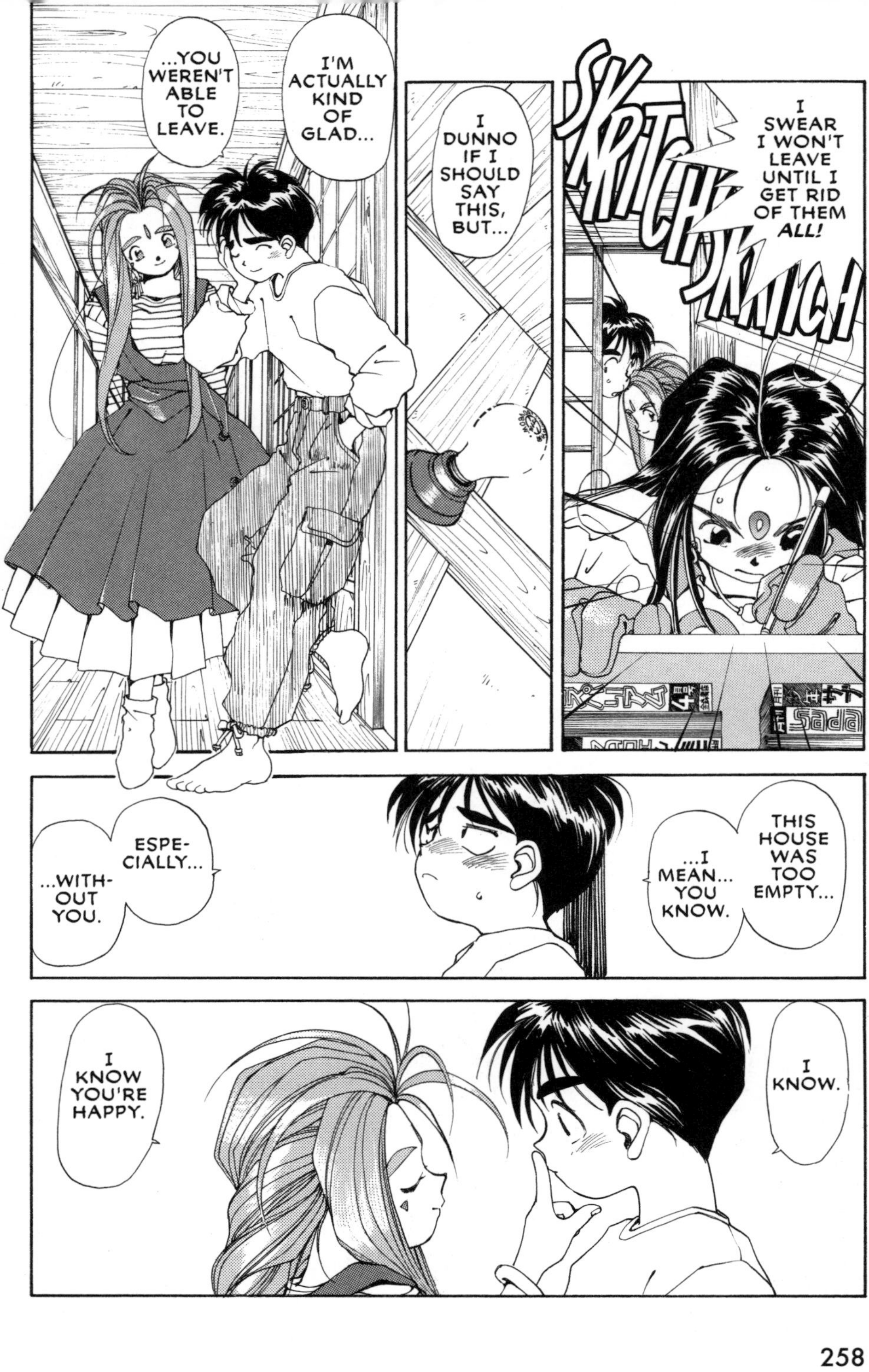
SKRITCH
SKRITCH
I SWEAR I WON'T LEAVE UNTIL I GET RID OF THEM *ALL!*
I DUNNO IF I SHOULD SAY THIS, BUT...
I'M ACTUALLY KIND OF GLAD...
...YOU WEREN'T ABLE TO LEAVE.
THIS HOUSE WAS TOO EMPTY...
...I MEAN... YOU KNOW.
ESPE-CIALLY...
...WITH-OUT YOU.
I KNOW.
I KNOW YOU'RE HAPPY.

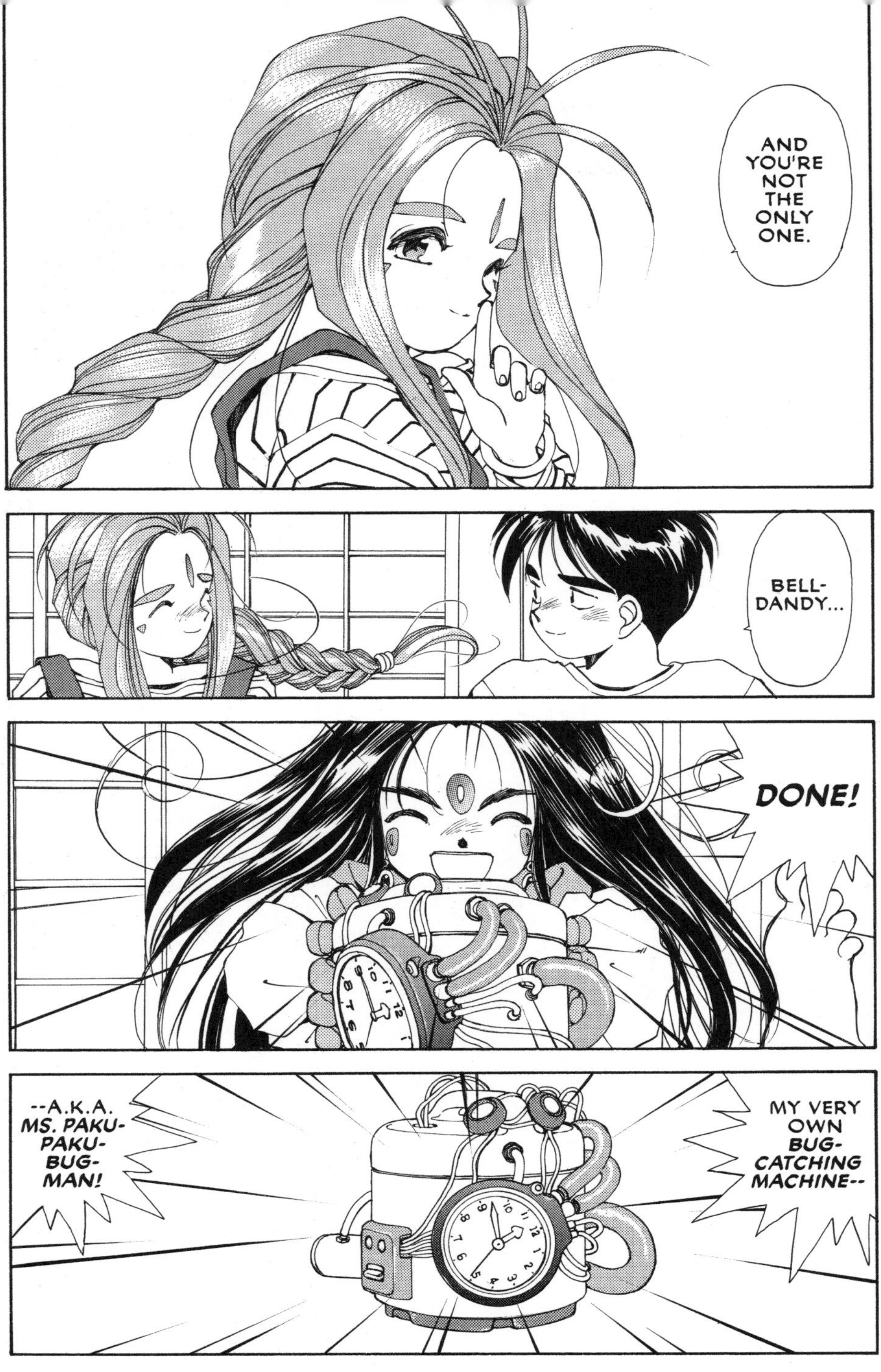
AND YOU'RE NOT THE ONLY ONE.
BELL-DANDY...
DONE!
MY VERY OWN BUG-CATCHING MACHINE--
--A.K.A. MS. PAKU-PAKU-BUG-MAN!

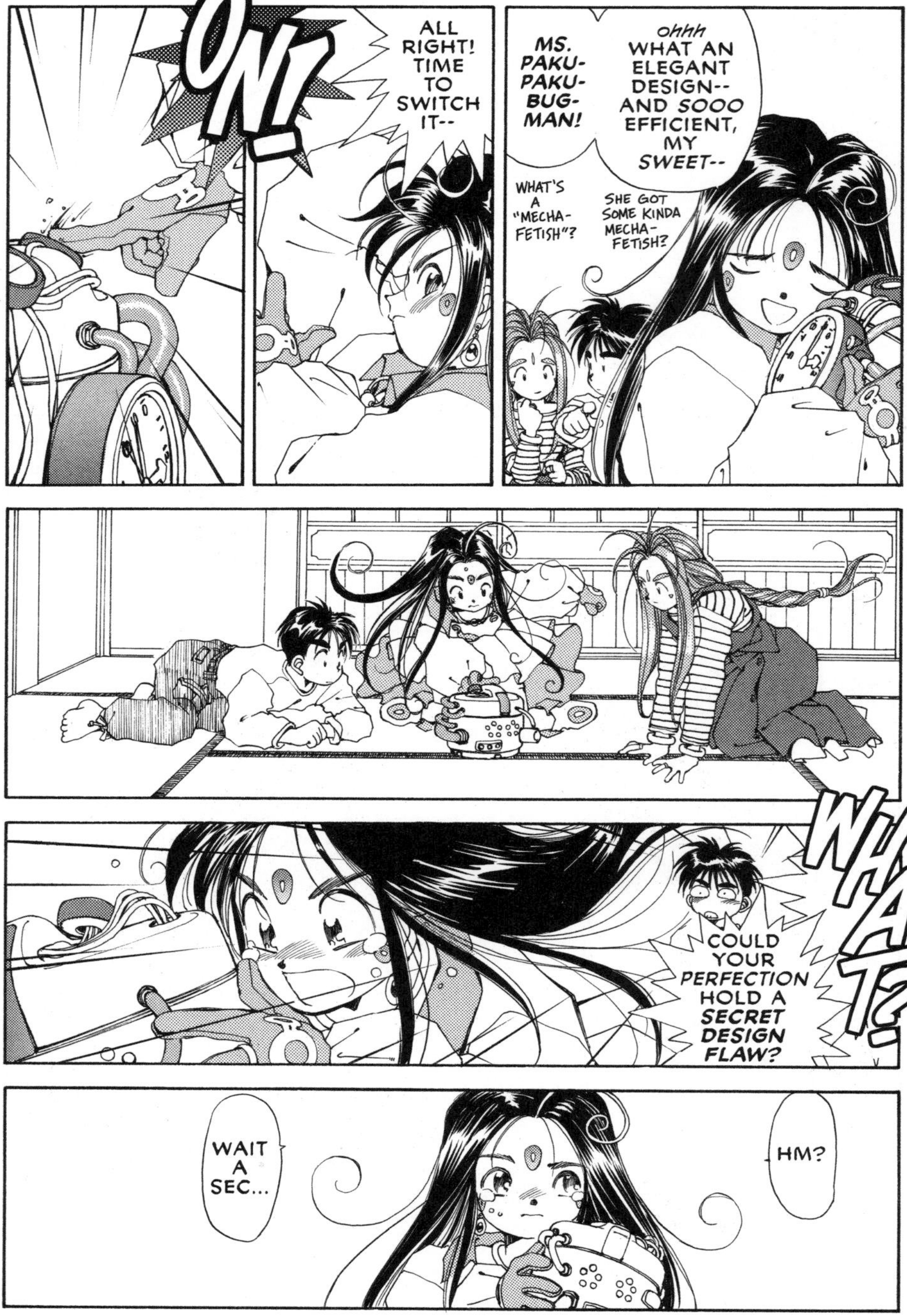
ohhh WHAT AN ELEGANT DESIGN-- AND SOOO EFFICIENT, MY SWEET--
MS. PAKU-PAKU-BUG-MAN!
SHE GOT SOME KINDA MECHA-FETISH?
WHAT'S A "MECHA-FETISH"?
ALL RIGHT! TIME TO SWITCH IT--
ON!
WHAT?
COULD YOUR PERFECTION HOLD A SECRET DESIGN FLAW?
HM?
WAIT A SEC...

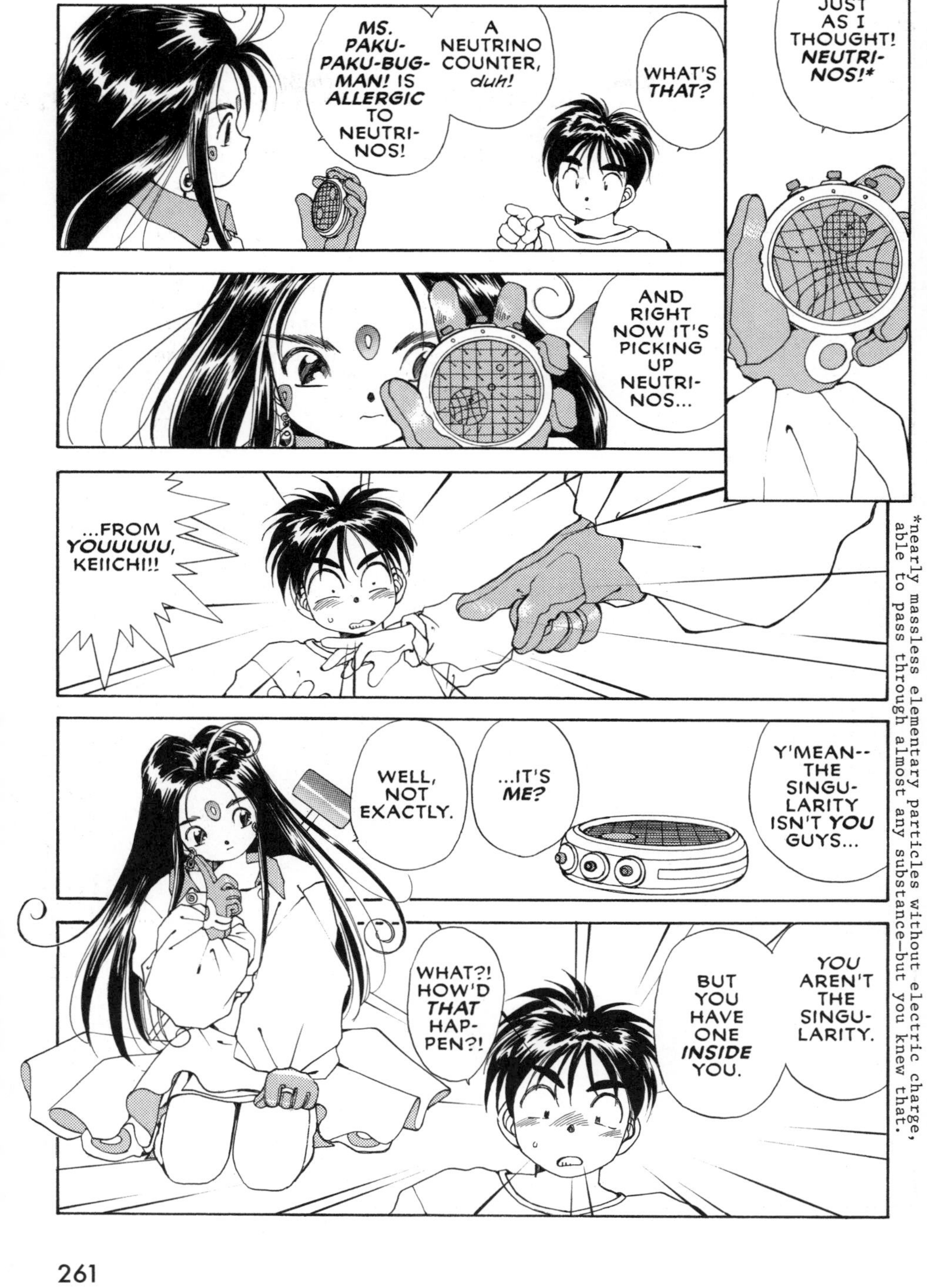
JUST AS I THOUGHT! *NEUTRINOS!**
WHAT'S *THAT?*
A NEUTRINO COUNTER, *duh!*
*MS. PAKU-PAKU-BUG-MAN!* IS *ALLERGIC* TO NEUTRINOS!
AND RIGHT NOW IT'S PICKING UP NEUTRINOS...
...FROM *YOUUUUU,* KEIICHI!!
Y'MEAN-- THE SINGULARITY ISN'T *YOU* GUYS...
...IT'S *ME?*
WELL, NOT EXACTLY.
*YOU* AREN'T THE SINGULARITY.
BUT YOU HAVE ONE *INSIDE* YOU.
WHAT?! HOW'D *THAT* HAPPEN?!

*nearly massless elementary particles without electric charge, able to pass through almost any substance—but you knew that.

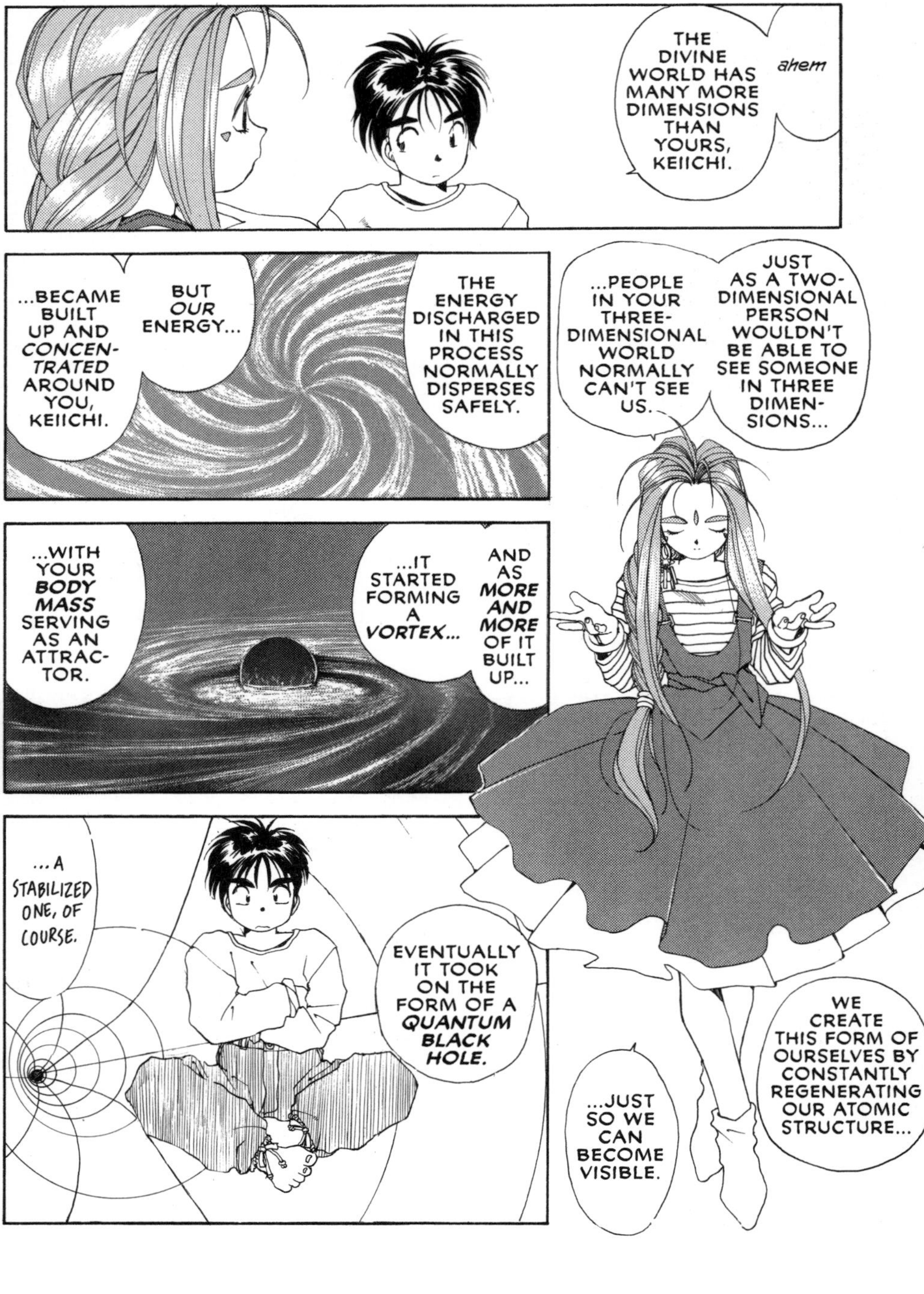
ahem
THE DIVINE WORLD HAS MANY MORE DIMENSIONS THAN YOURS, KEIICHI.
JUST AS A TWO-DIMENSIONAL PERSON WOULDN'T BE ABLE TO SEE SOMEONE IN THREE DIMENSIONS...
...PEOPLE IN YOUR THREE-DIMENSIONAL WORLD NORMALLY CAN'T SEE US.
WE CREATE THIS FORM OF OURSELVES BY CONSTANTLY REGENERATING OUR ATOMIC STRUCTURE...
...JUST SO WE CAN BECOME VISIBLE.
THE ENERGY DISCHARGED IN THIS PROCESS NORMALLY DISPERSES SAFELY.
BUT *OUR* ENERGY...
...BECAME BUILT UP AND *CONCENTRATED* AROUND YOU, KEIICHI.
AND AS ***MORE AND MORE*** OF IT BUILT UP...
...IT STARTED FORMING A ***VORTEX...***
...WITH YOUR ***BODY MASS*** SERVING AS AN ATTRACTOR.
EVENTUALLY IT TOOK ON THE FORM OF A ***QUANTUM BLACK HOLE.***
...A STABILIZED ONE, OF COURSE.

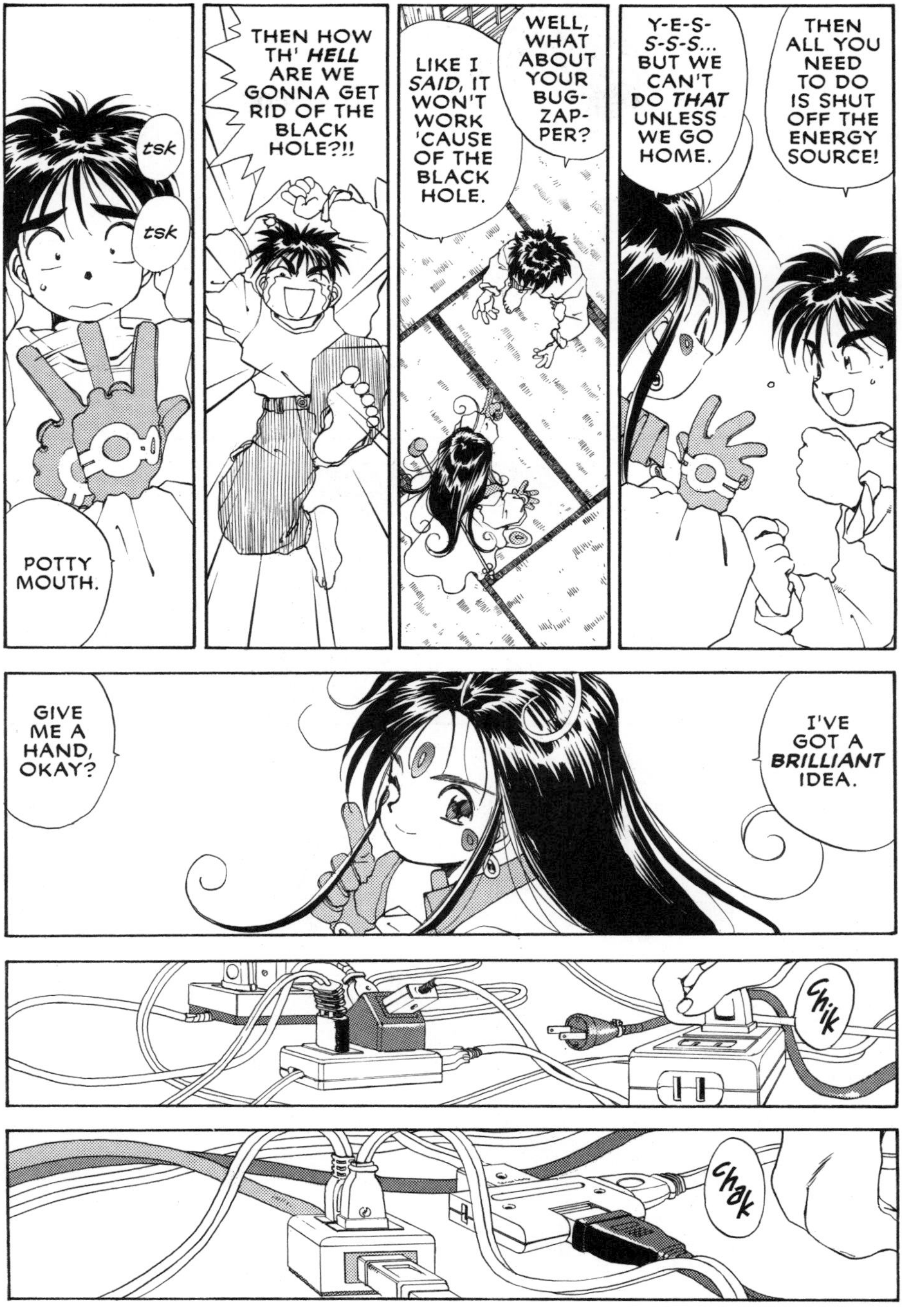
THEN ALL YOU NEED TO DO IS SHUT OFF THE ENERGY SOURCE!
Y-E-S-S-S-S... BUT WE CAN'T DO *THAT* UNLESS WE GO HOME.
WELL, WHAT ABOUT YOUR BUG-ZAPPER?
LIKE I *SAID*, IT WON'T WORK 'CAUSE OF THE BLACK HOLE.
THEN HOW TH' *HELL* ARE WE GONNA GET RID OF THE BLACK HOLE?!!
tsk
tsk
POTTY MOUTH.
I'VE GOT A *BRILLIANT* IDEA.
GIVE ME A HAND, OKAY?
Chik
Chak

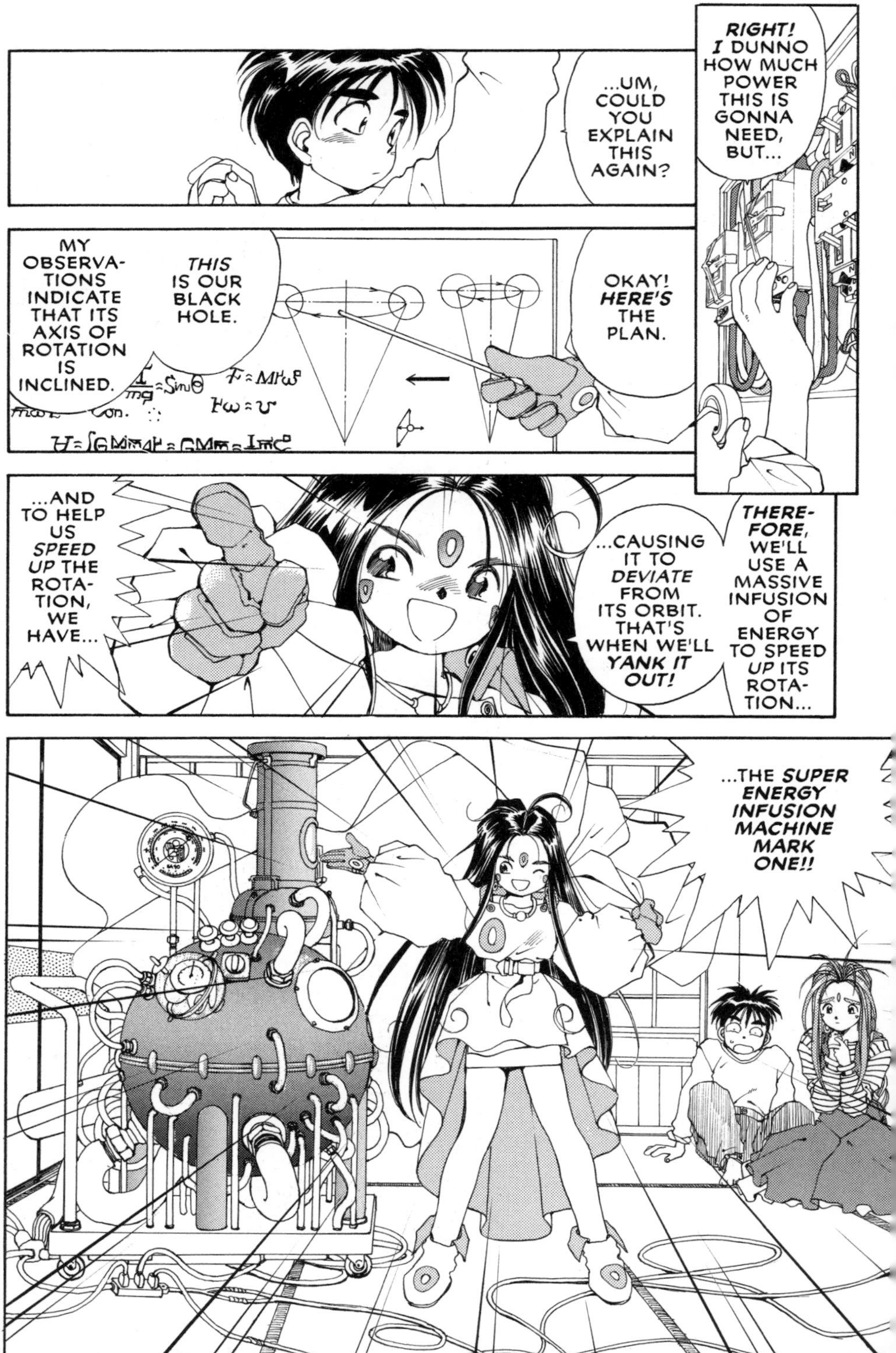
RIGHT! I DUNNO HOW MUCH POWER THIS IS GONNA NEED, BUT...
...UM, COULD YOU EXPLAIN THIS AGAIN?
OKAY! HERE'S THE PLAN.
THIS IS OUR BLACK HOLE.
MY OBSERVATIONS INDICATE THAT ITS AXIS OF ROTATION IS INCLINED.
THEREFORE, WE'LL USE A MASSIVE INFUSION OF ENERGY TO SPEED UP ITS ROTATION...
...CAUSING IT TO DEVIATE FROM ITS ORBIT. THAT'S WHEN WE'LL YANK IT OUT!
...AND TO HELP US SPEED UP THE ROTATION, WE HAVE...
...THE SUPER ENERGY INFUSION MACHINE MARK ONE!!

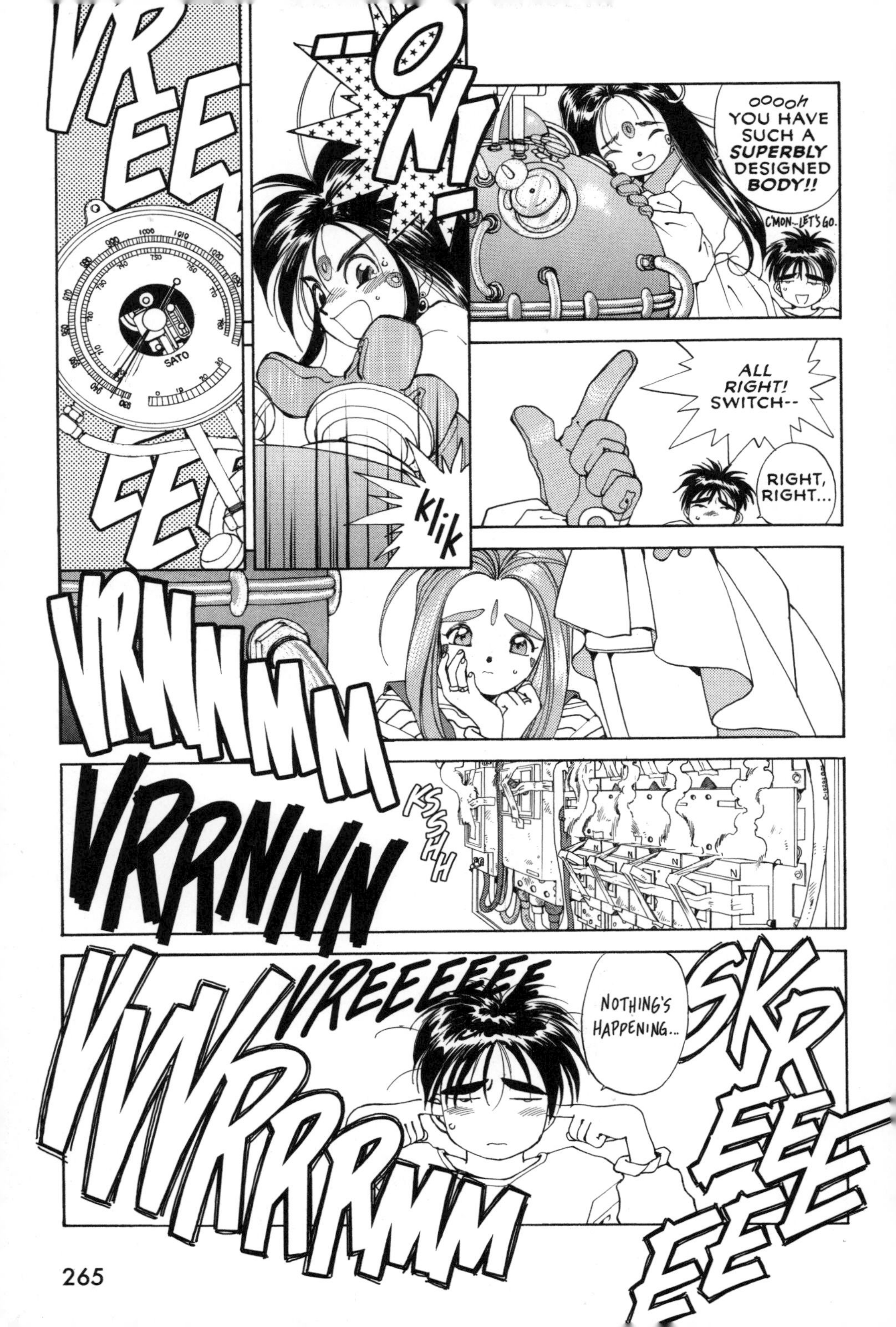
oooh YOU HAVE SUCH A SUPERBLY DESIGNED BODY!!
C'MON.. LET'S GO.
ALL RIGHT! SWITCH--
RIGHT, RIGHT...
..ON!
klik
VREEEEE
VRNNMMM
VRRNNNN
KSSHH
SKREEEEEE
NOTHING'S HAPPENING...
VREEEEEE
VVVRRRMM

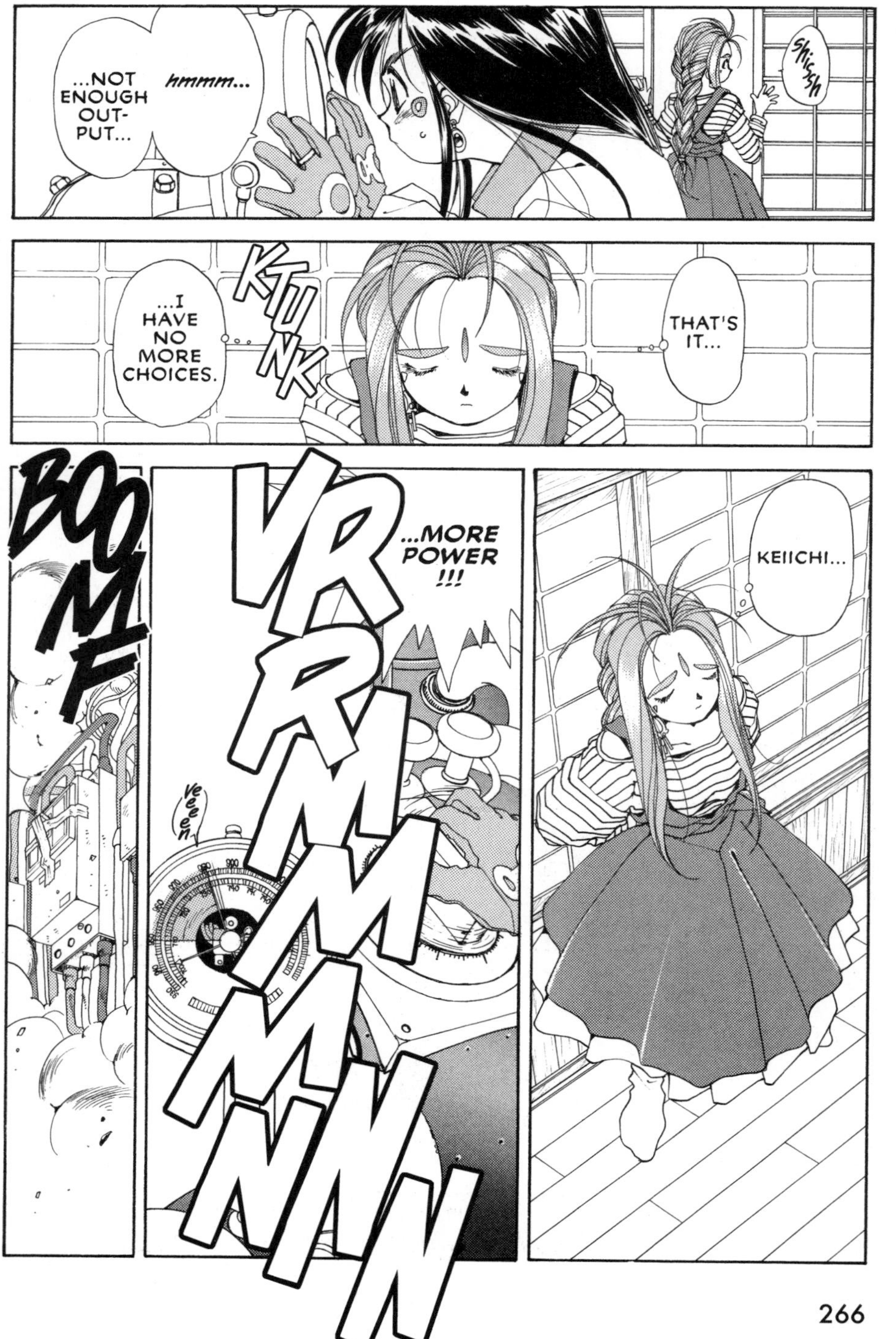
Shissh
hmmm...
...NOT ENOUGH OUT-PUT...
THAT'S IT...
KTUNK
...I HAVE NO MORE CHOICES.
KEIICHI...
...MORE POWER !!!
VRRMMMMMMN
veeeen
BOOMF

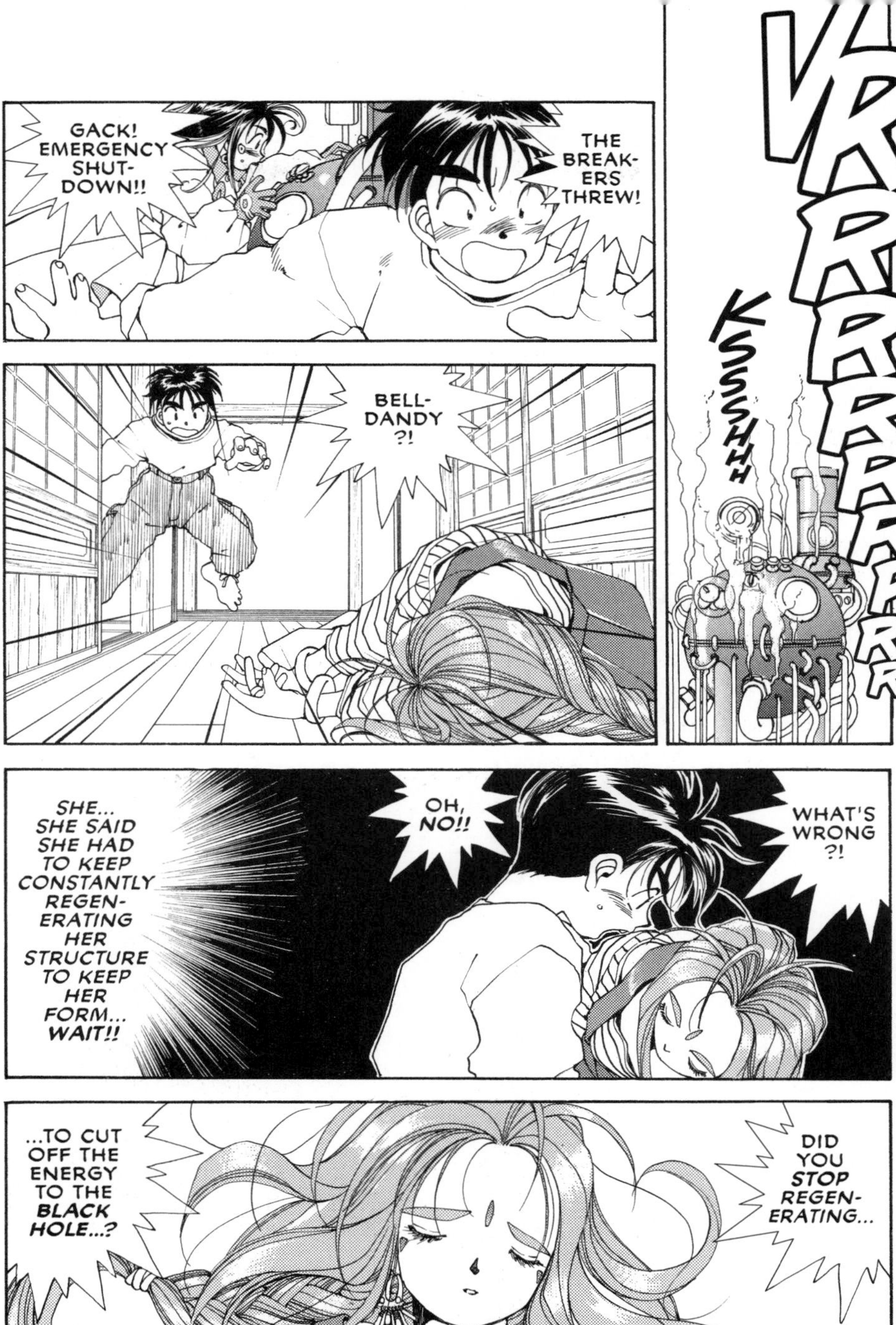
VRRRRRRRRRRR
KSSSSHHH
THE BREAKERS THREW!
GACK! EMERGENCY SHUTDOWN!!
BELLDANDY ?!
WHAT'S WRONG ?!
OH, NO!!
SHE... SHE SAID SHE HAD TO KEEP CONSTANTLY REGENERATING HER STRUCTURE TO KEEP HER FORM... WAIT!!
DID YOU STOP REGENERATING...
...TO CUT OFF THE ENERGY TO THE BLACK HOLE...?

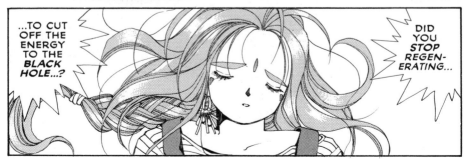

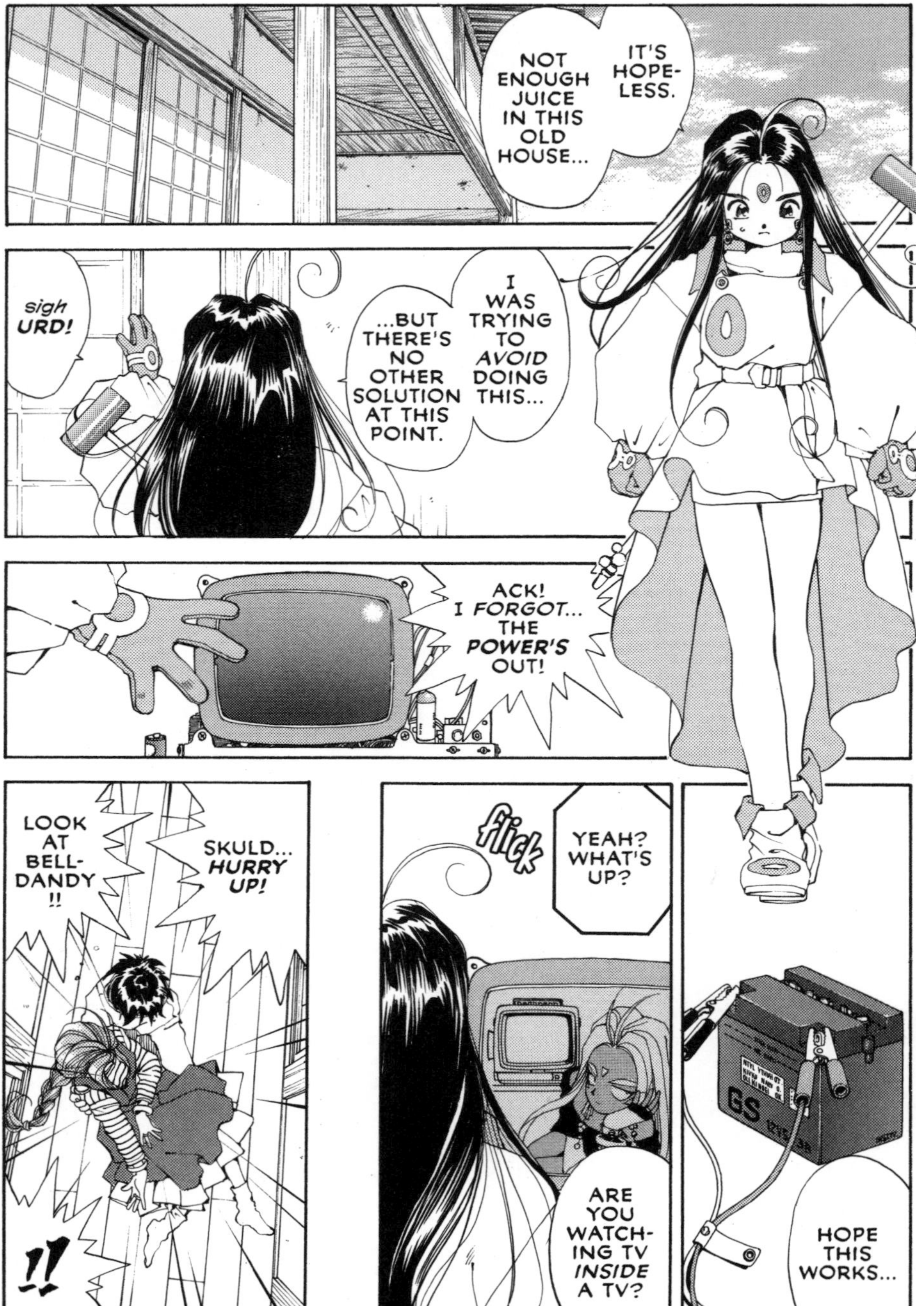
IT'S HOPE-LESS.
NOT ENOUGH JUICE IN THIS OLD HOUSE...
I WAS TRYING TO *AVOID* DOING THIS...
...BUT THERE'S NO OTHER SOLUTION AT THIS POINT.
*sigh* **URD!**
ACK! I *FORGOT*... THE ***POWER'S*** OUT!
HOPE THIS WORKS...
flick
YEAH? WHAT'S UP?
ARE YOU WATCHING TV *INSIDE* A TV?
SKULD... ***HURRY UP!***
LOOK AT BELL-DANDY !!
!!

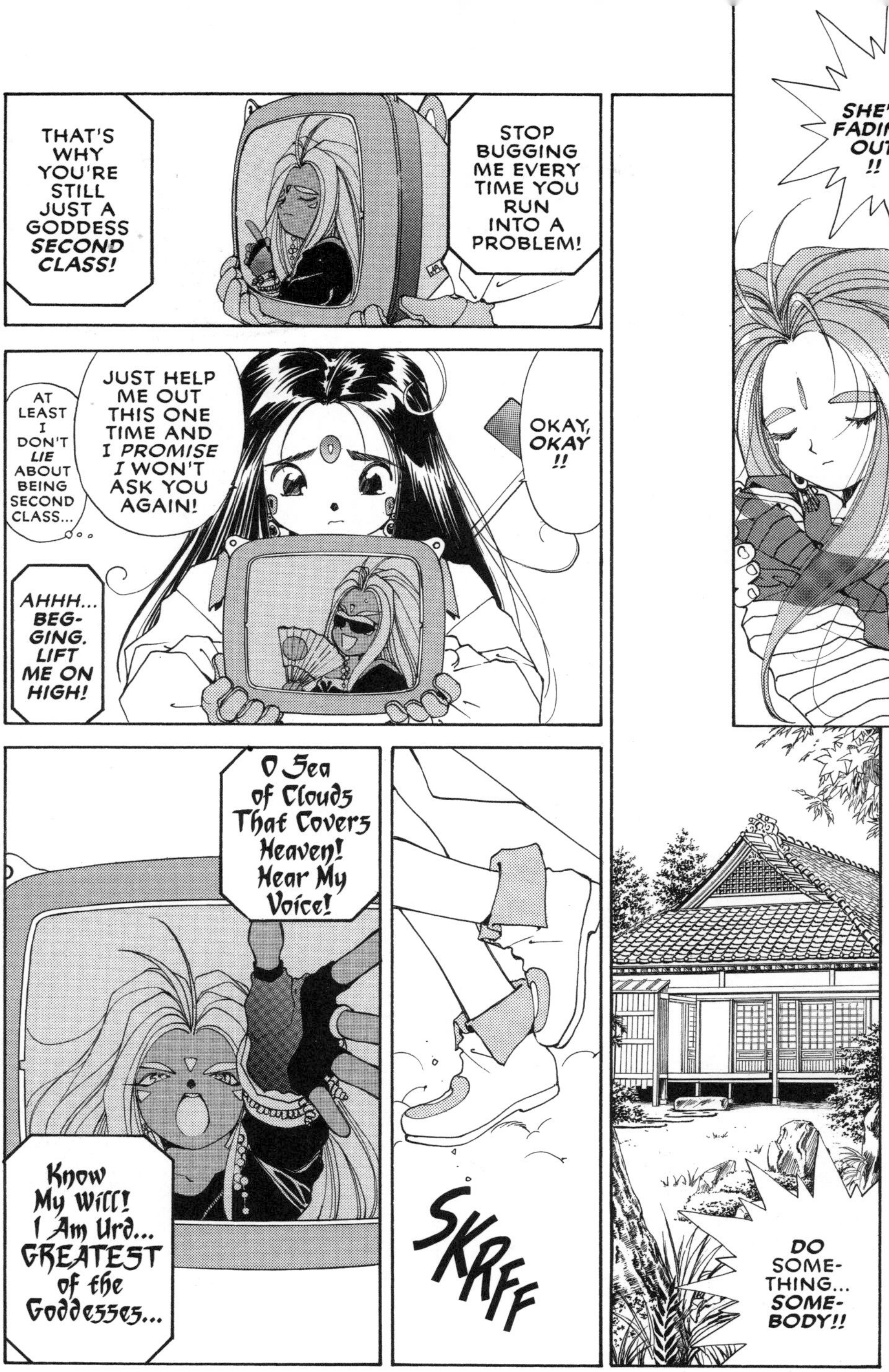
SHE'S FADING OUT !!
STOP BUGGING ME EVERY TIME YOU RUN INTO A PROBLEM!
THAT'S WHY YOU'RE STILL JUST A GODDESS *SECOND CLASS!*
OKAY, *OKAY !!*
JUST HELP ME OUT THIS ONE TIME AND I *PROMISE I* WON'T ASK YOU AGAIN!
AT LEAST I DON'T *LIE* ABOUT BEING SECOND CLASS...
AHHH... BEG-GING. LIFT ME ON HIGH!
DO SOME-THING... SOME-BODY!!
SKRFF
O Sea of Clouds That Covers Heaven! Hear My Voice!
Know My Will! I Am Urd... GREATEST of the Goddesses...

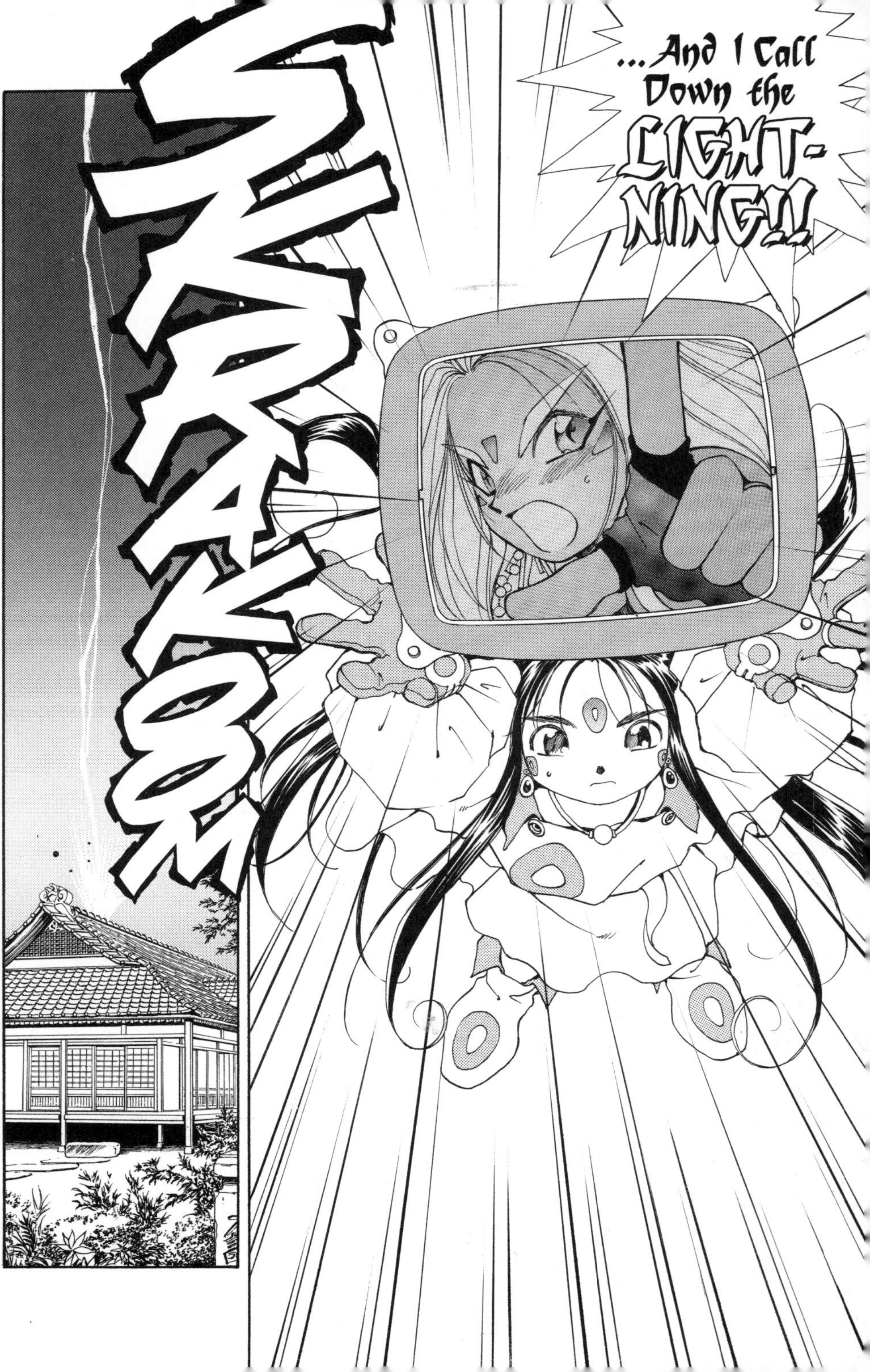
...And I Call Down the LIGHT-NING!!

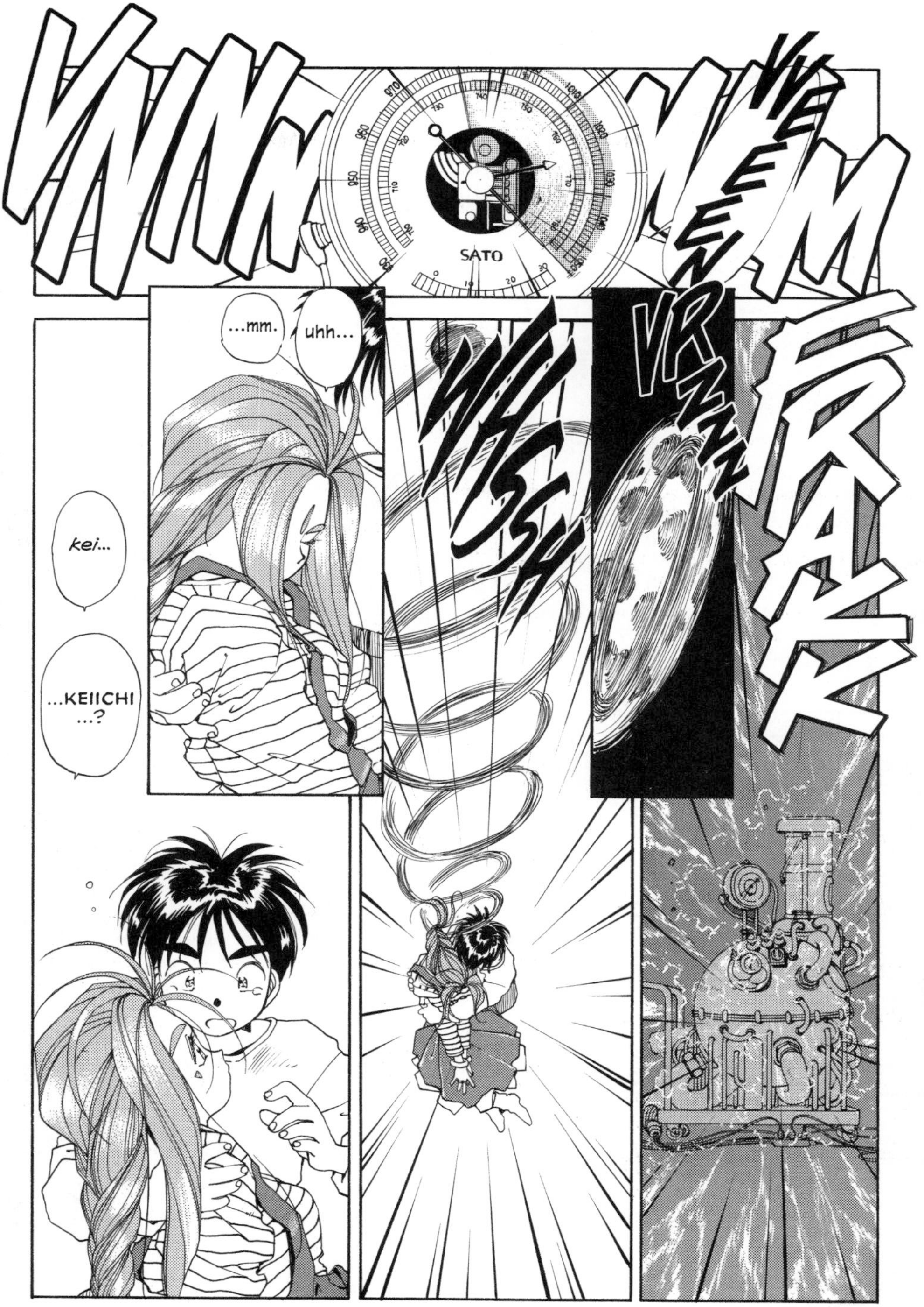
SATO
FRAKK
VRZZZ
WHSSH
uhh...
...mm.
kei...
...KEIICHI ...?

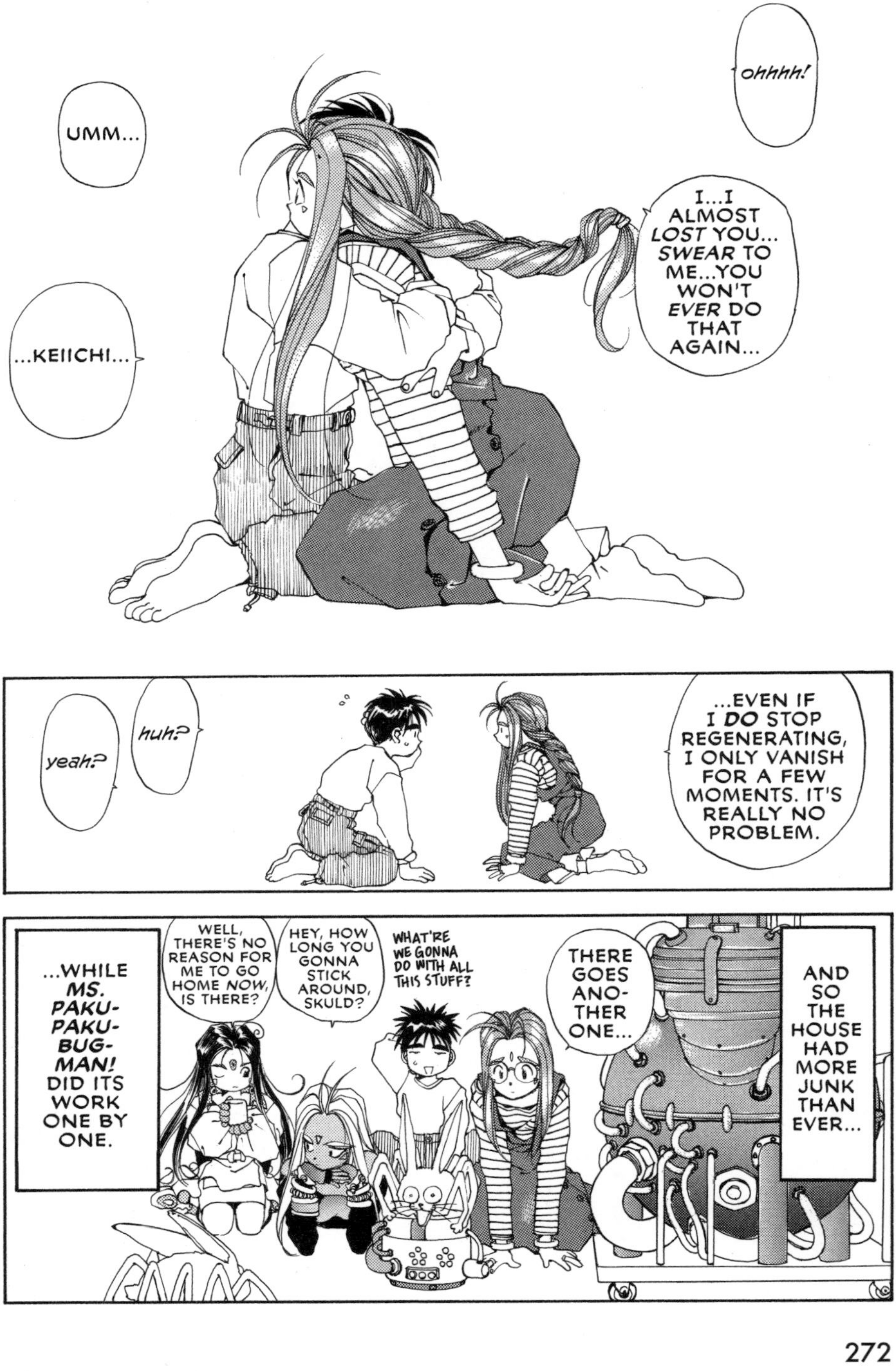
ohhhh!
I...I ALMOST LOST YOU... SWEAR TO ME...YOU WON'T EVER DO THAT AGAIN...
UMM...
...KEIICHI...
...EVEN IF I DO STOP REGENERATING, I ONLY VANISH FOR A FEW MOMENTS. IT'S REALLY NO PROBLEM.
huh?
yeah?
AND SO THE HOUSE HAD MORE JUNK THAN EVER...
THERE GOES ANO-THER ONE...
WHAT'RE WE GONNA DO WITH ALL THIS STUFF?
HEY, HOW LONG YOU GONNA STICK AROUND, SKULD?
WELL, THERE'S NO REASON FOR ME TO GO HOME NOW, IS THERE?
...WHILE MS. PAKU-PAKU-BUG-MAN! DID ITS WORK ONE BY ONE.

CHAPTER 34

# Urd Goes Wild

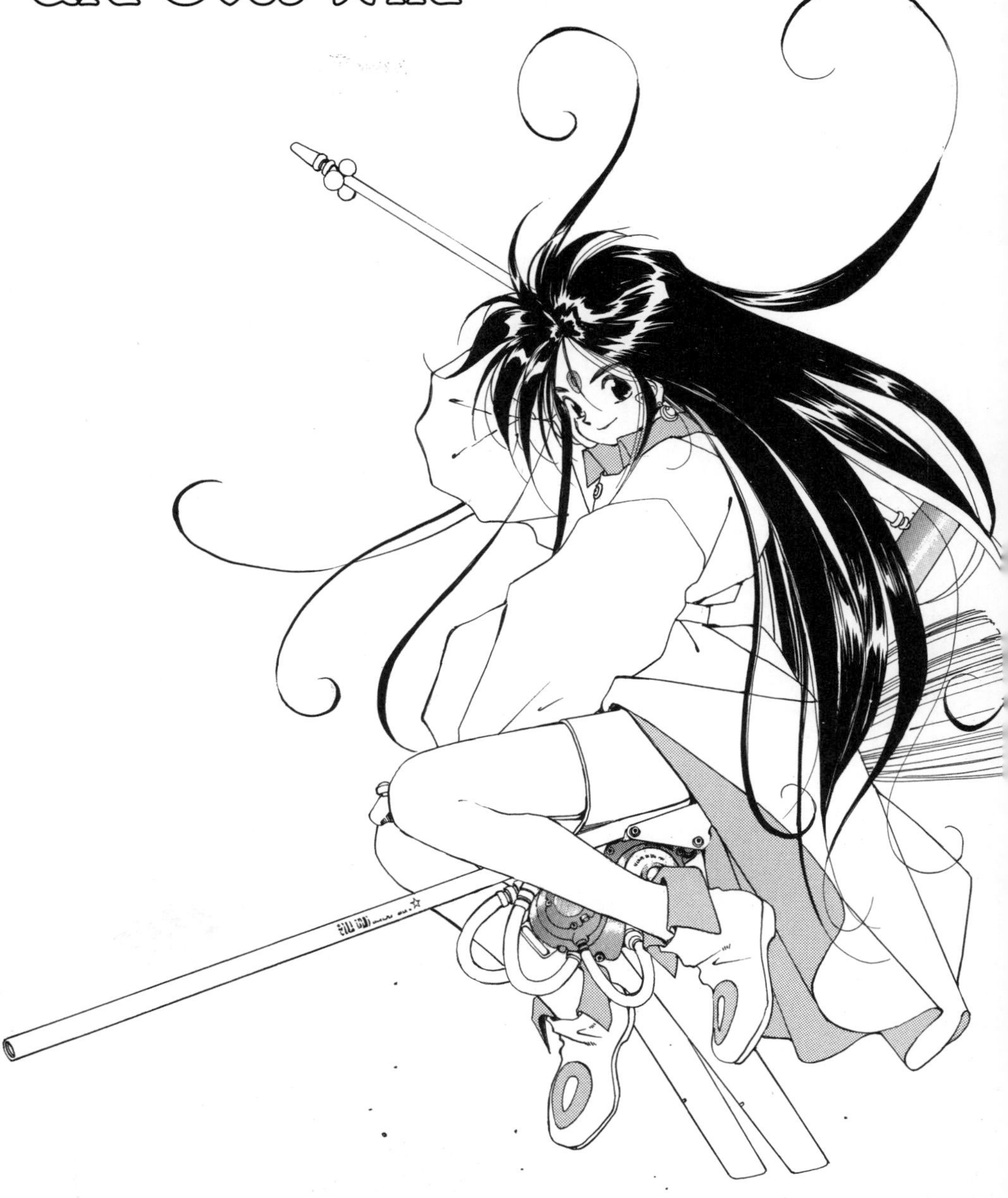

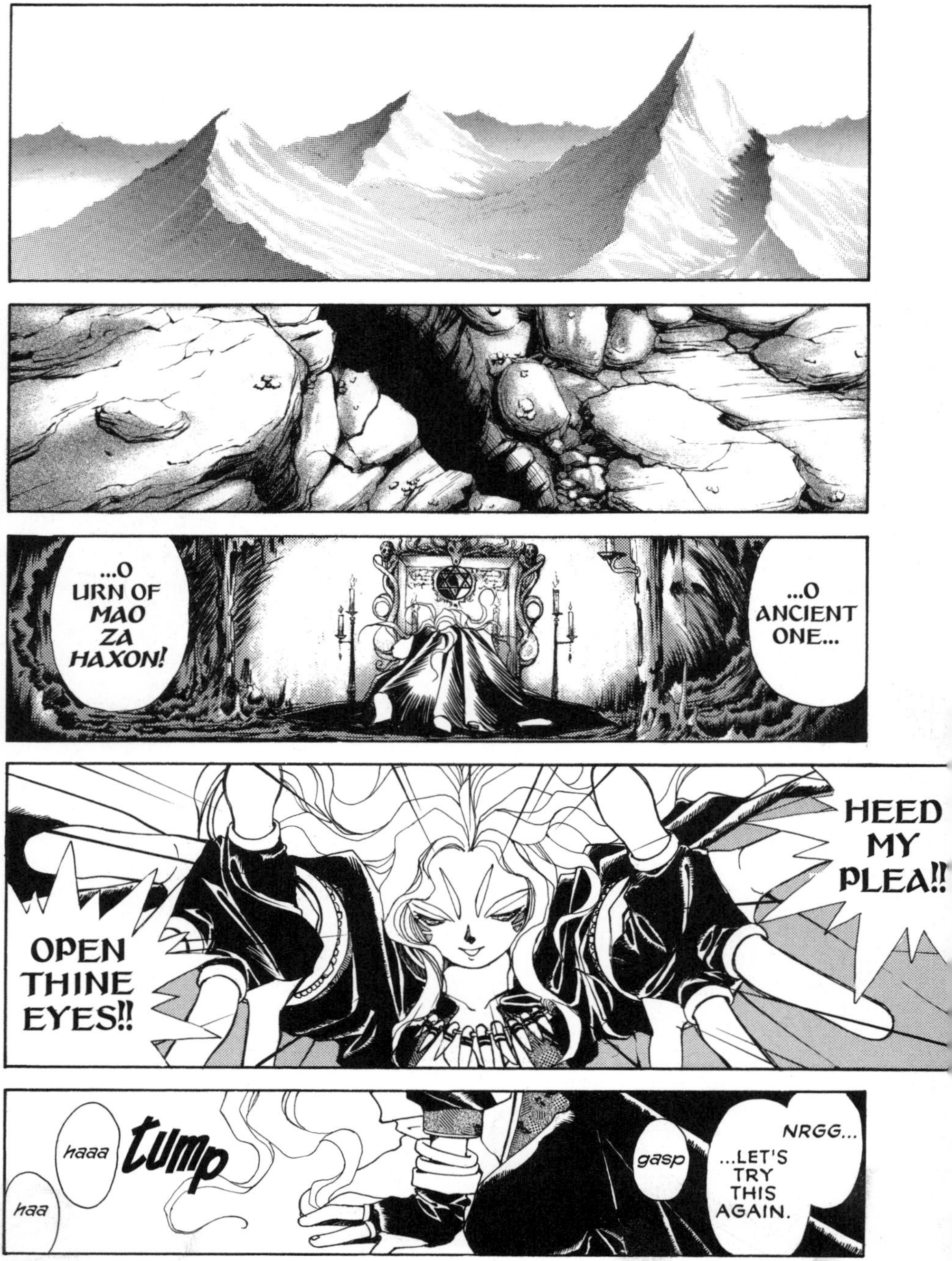
...O ANCIENT ONE...
...O URN OF MAO ZA HAXON!
HEED MY PLEA!!
OPEN THINE EYES!!
NRGG... ...LET'S TRY THIS AGAIN.
gasp
tump
haaa
haa

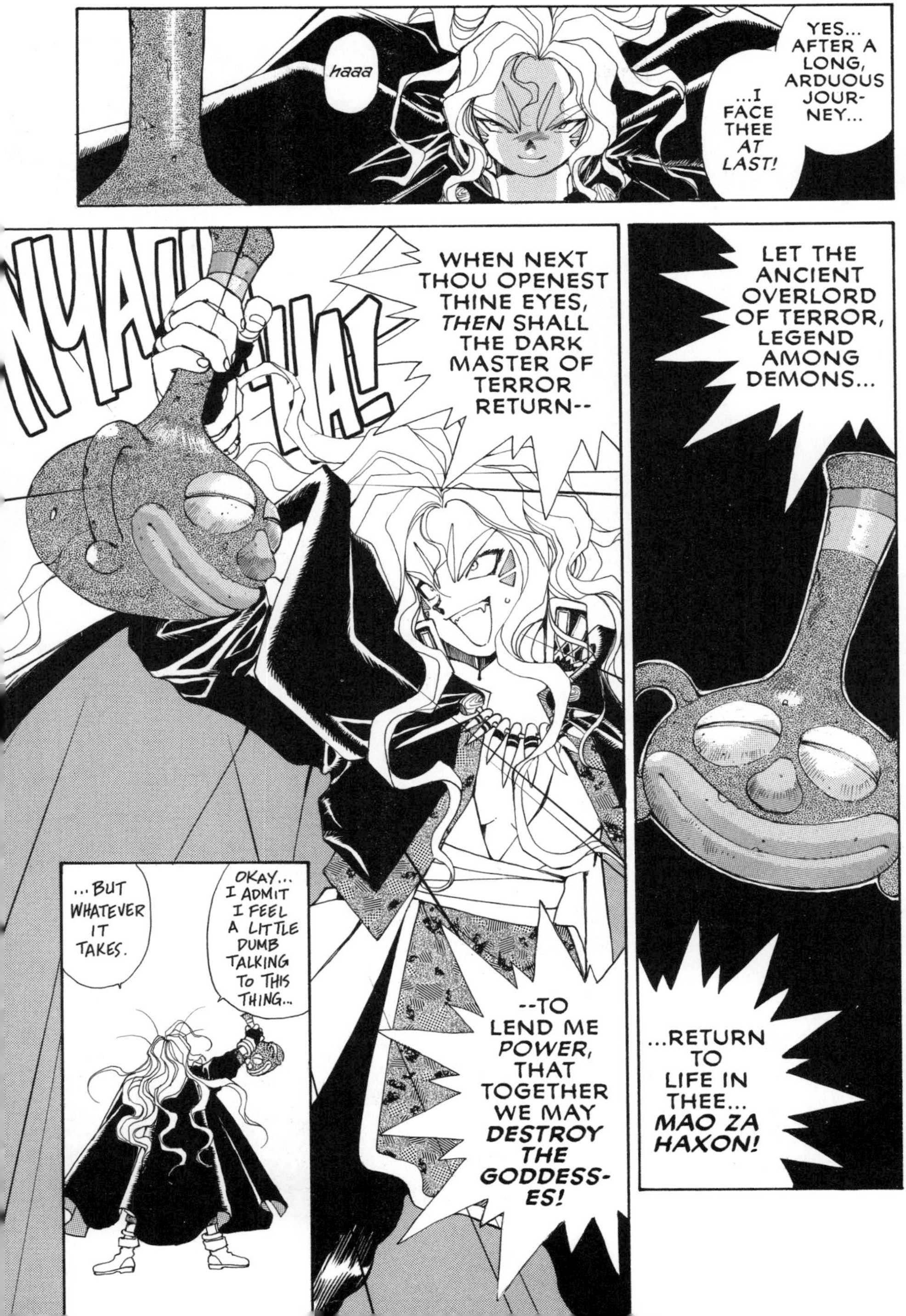
YES... AFTER A LONG, ARDUOUS JOURNEY...
...I FACE THEE AT LAST!
haaa
LET THE ANCIENT OVERLORD OF TERROR, LEGEND AMONG DEMONS...
...RETURN TO LIFE IN THEE... MAO ZA HAXON!
WHEN NEXT THOU OPENEST THINE EYES, THEN SHALL THE DARK MASTER OF TERROR RETURN--
--TO LEND ME POWER, THAT TOGETHER WE MAY DESTROY THE GODDESS-ES!
OKAY... I ADMIT I FEEL A LITTLE DUMB TALKING TO THIS THING...
...BUT WHATEVER IT TAKES.

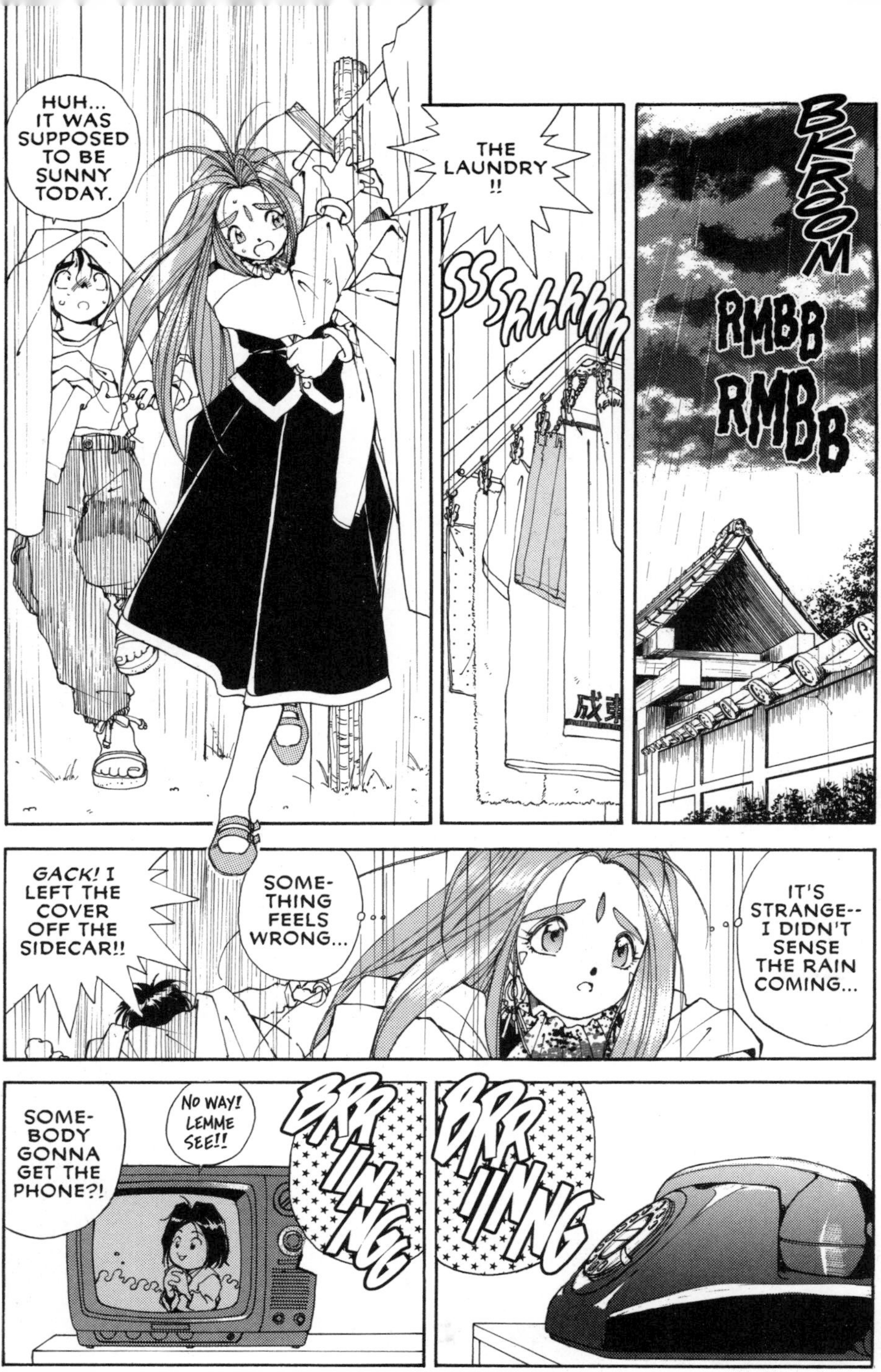
BKROOM
RMBB RMBB
SSShhhhhh
THE LAUNDRY!!
HUH... IT WAS SUPPOSED TO BE SUNNY TODAY.
IT'S STRANGE-- I DIDN'T SENSE THE RAIN COMING...
SOME-THING FEELS WRONG...
GACK! I LEFT THE COVER OFF THE SIDECAR!!
BRRIINNG
BRRIINNGG
NO WAY! LEMME SEE!!
SOME-BODY GONNA GET THE PHONE?!

WHY DON'T YOU GET IT *YOURSELF*, URD?
BECAUSE TODAY'S AN UNLUCKY DAY FOR BIG SISTERS TO PICK UP THE PHONE.
KEEP LYING LIKE *THAT* AND YOU'LL HAVE YOUR LICENSE SUSPENDED FOR ***SURE!***
*hmph!*
SMART-MOUTH LITTLE BRAT...
...IT'S STILL RING-ING.
OKAY, LET'S USE THIS TO DECIDE.
YOU THINK YOU CAN BEAT THE GODDESS OF GAMBLING AT HER OWN GAME, EH?!
*ha!*
*RIGHT...*
...I'LL GO FIRST.
FIRST ONE TO PULL THE DETONATOR HAS TO GET THE PHONE, OKAY?

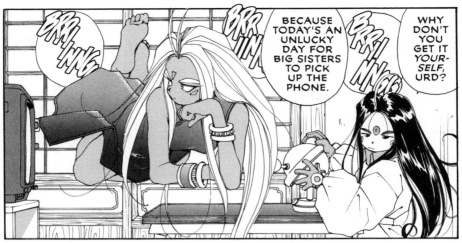

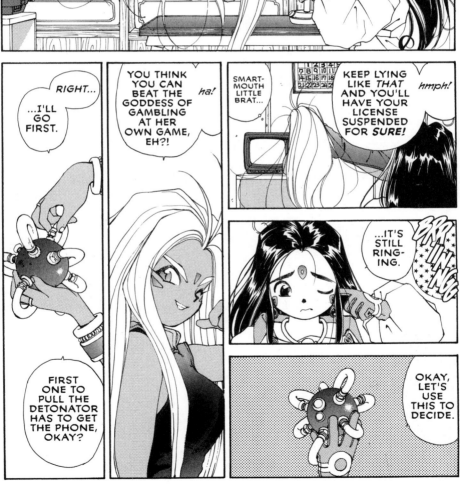

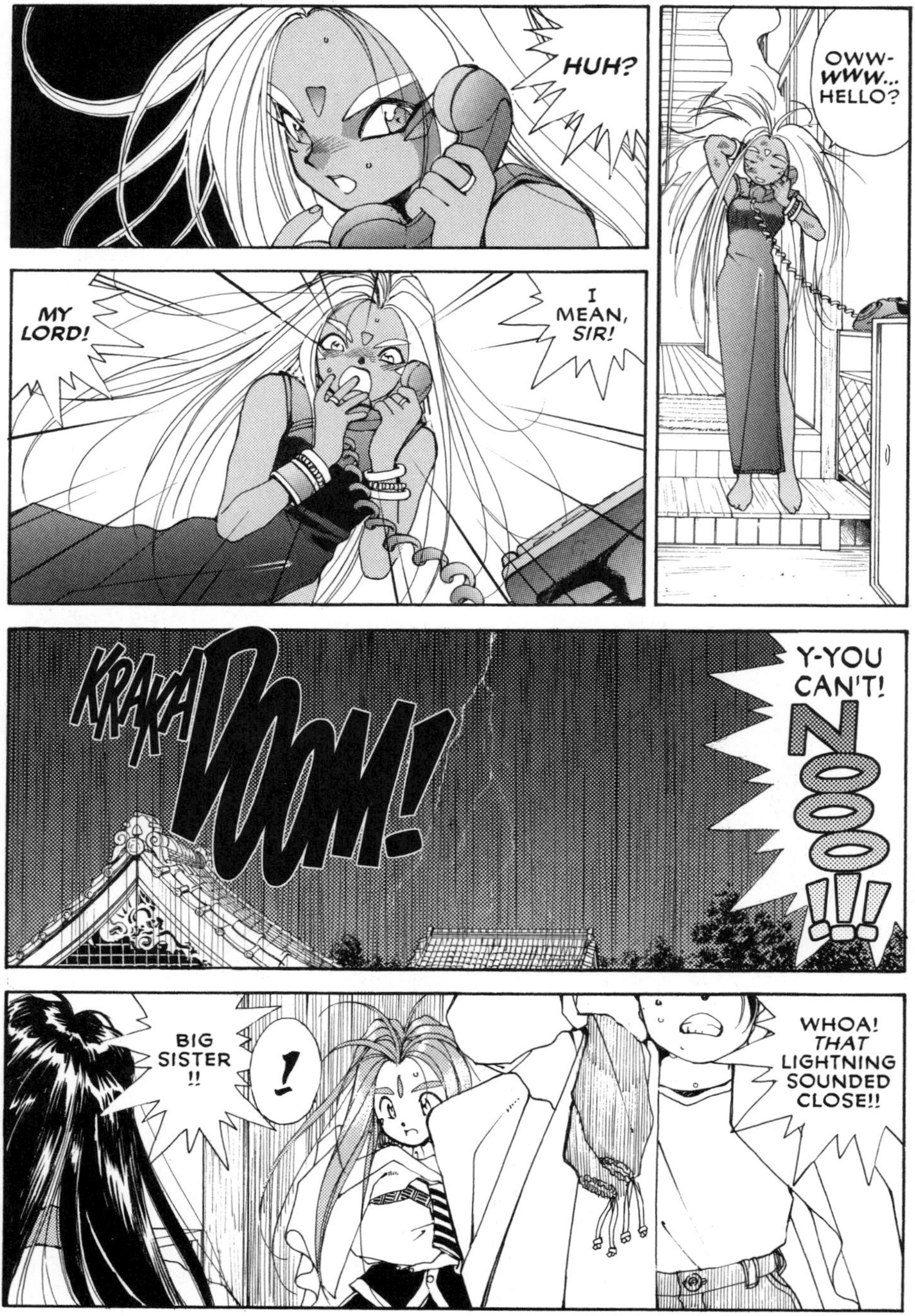
OWW-WWW... HELLO?
HUH?
I MEAN, *SIR!*
MY LORD!
Y-YOU CAN'T!
NOOO!!!
KRAKADOOM!
WHOA! *THAT* LIGHTNING SOUNDED CLOSE!!
!
BIG SISTER!!

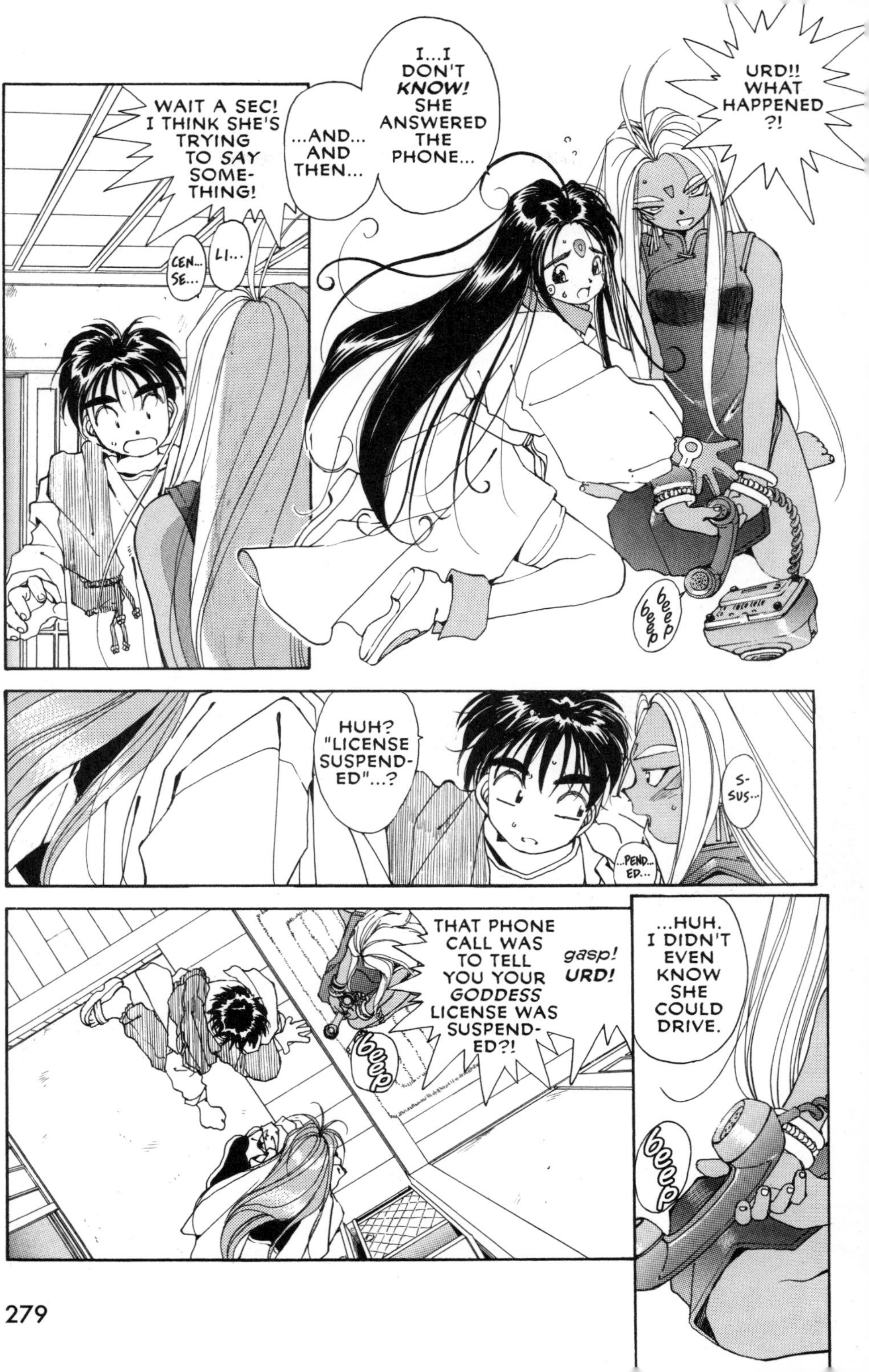
URD!! WHAT HAPPENED ?!
I...I DON'T *KNOW!* SHE ANSWERED THE PHONE...
...AND... AND THEN...
beep beep
WAIT A SEC! I THINK SHE'S TRYING TO *SAY* SOME-THING!
LI...
CEN... SE...
S-SUS...
...PEND... ED...
HUH? "LICENSE SUSPEND-ED"...?
...HUH. I DIDN'T EVEN KNOW SHE COULD DRIVE.
beep
*gasp!* ***URD!***
THAT PHONE CALL WAS TO TELL YOU YOUR *GODDESS* LICENSE WAS SUSPEND-ED?!
beep

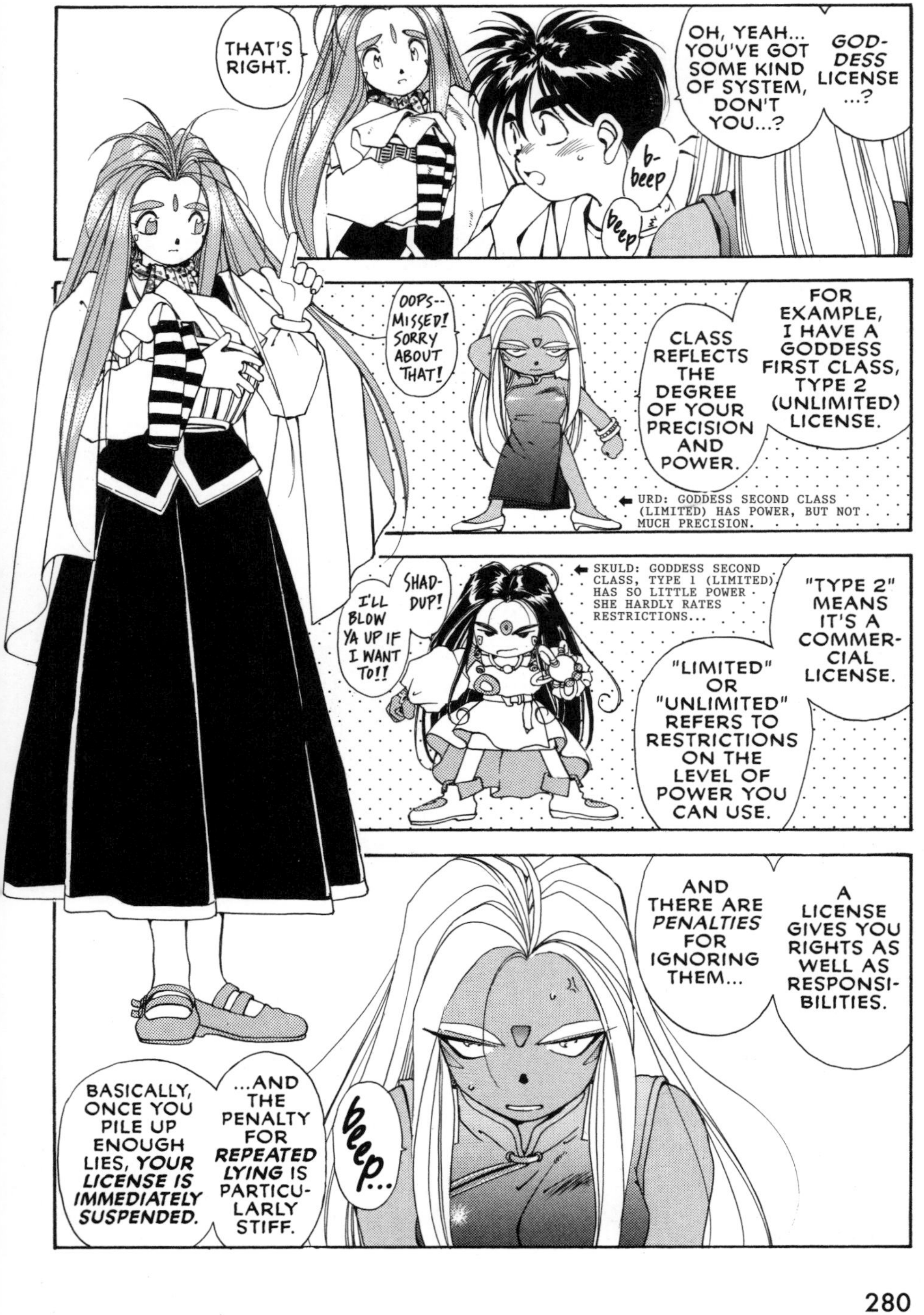
GODDESS LICENSE ...?
OH, YEAH... YOU'VE GOT SOME KIND OF SYSTEM, DON'T YOU...?
b-beep
beep
THAT'S RIGHT.
FOR EXAMPLE, I HAVE A GODDESS FIRST CLASS, TYPE 2 (UNLIMITED) LICENSE.
CLASS REFLECTS THE DEGREE OF YOUR PRECISION AND POWER.
URD: GODDESS SECOND CLASS (LIMITED) HAS POWER, BUT NOT MUCH PRECISION.
OOPS-- MISSED! SORRY ABOUT THAT!
"TYPE 2" MEANS IT'S A COMMERCIAL LICENSE.
"LIMITED" OR "UNLIMITED" REFERS TO RESTRICTIONS ON THE LEVEL OF POWER YOU CAN USE.
SKULD: GODDESS SECOND CLASS, TYPE 1 (LIMITED) HAS SO LITTLE POWER SHE HARDLY RATES RESTRICTIONS...
SHAD-DUP!
I'LL BLOW YA UP IF I WANT TO!!
A LICENSE GIVES YOU RIGHTS AS WELL AS RESPONSIBILITIES.
AND THERE ARE *PENALTIES* FOR IGNORING THEM...
beep...
...AND THE PENALTY FOR ***REPEATED LYING*** IS PARTICULARLY STIFF.
BASICALLY, ONCE YOU PILE UP ENOUGH LIES, ***YOUR LICENSE IS IMMEDIATELY SUSPENDED.***

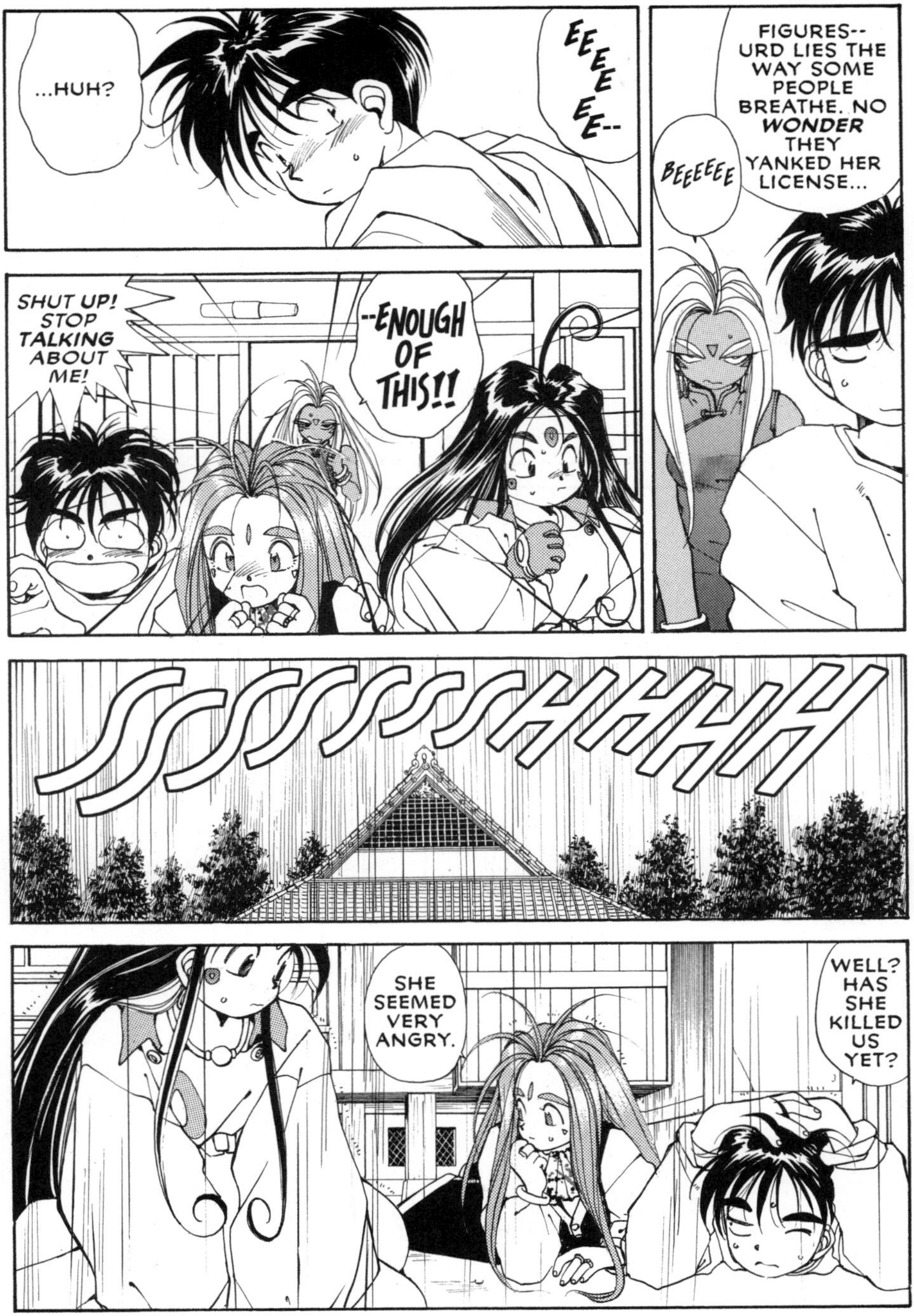

FIGURES-- URD LIES THE WAY SOME PEOPLE BREATHE. NO **WONDER** THEY YANKED HER LICENSE...
BEEEEEE
EEEEEE--
...HUH?
--ENOUGH OF THIS!!
SHUT UP! STOP TALKING ABOUT ME!
SSSSSSHHHHH
WELL? HAS SHE KILLED US YET?
SHE SEEMED VERY ANGRY.

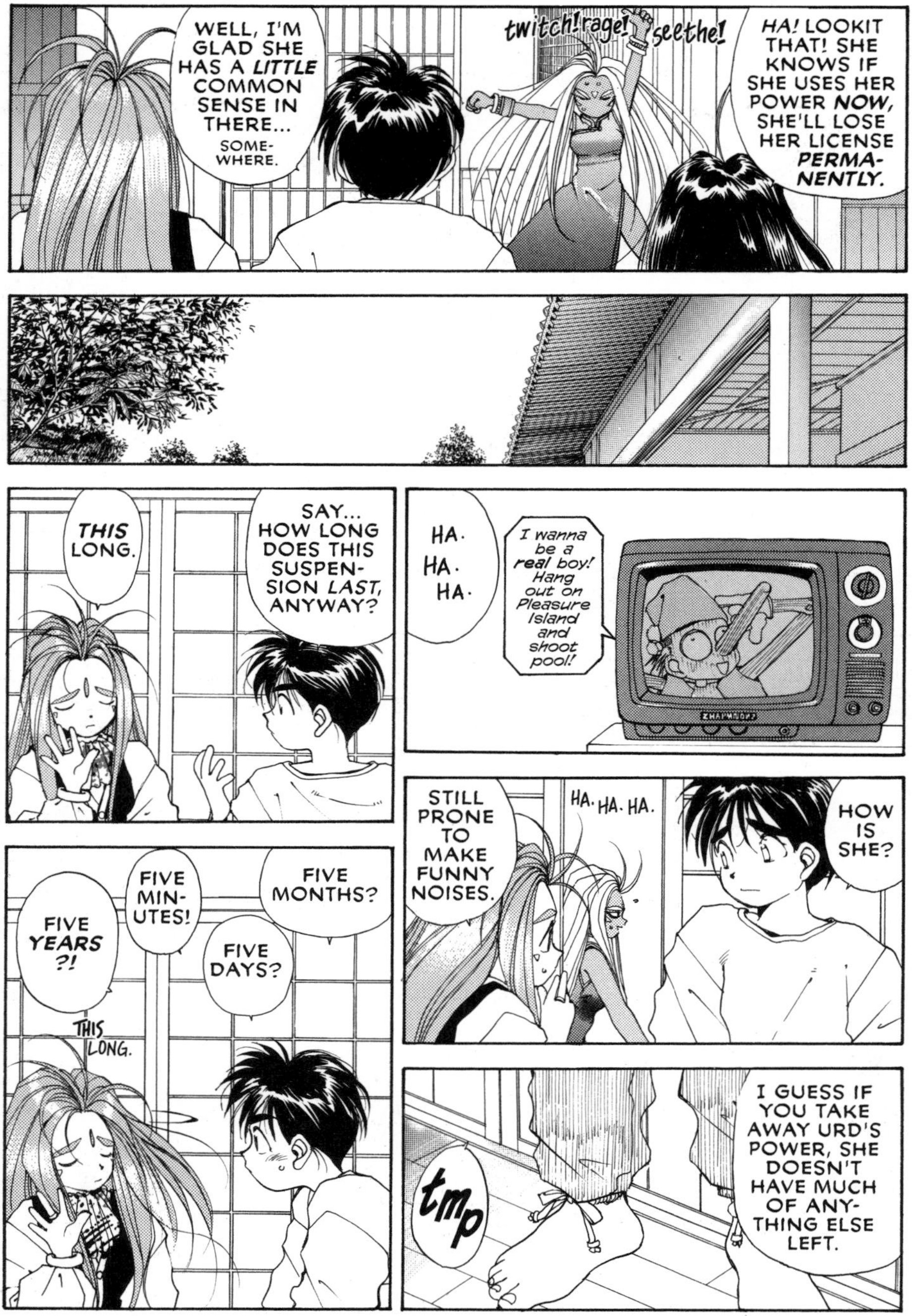
HA! LOOKIT THAT! SHE KNOWS IF SHE USES HER POWER NOW, SHE'LL LOSE HER LICENSE PERMANENTLY.
twitch! rage! seethe!
WELL, I'M GLAD SHE HAS A LITTLE COMMON SENSE IN THERE... SOME-WHERE.
I wanna be a real boy! Hang out on Pleasure Island and shoot pool!
HA. HA. HA.
HOW IS SHE?
HA. HA. HA.
STILL PRONE TO MAKE FUNNY NOISES.
I GUESS IF YOU TAKE AWAY URD'S POWER, SHE DOESN'T HAVE MUCH OF ANY-THING ELSE LEFT.
tmp
SAY... HOW LONG DOES THIS SUSPEN-SION LAST, ANYWAY?
THIS LONG.
FIVE MONTHS?
FIVE MIN-UTES!
FIVE DAYS?
FIVE YEARS?!
THIS LONG.

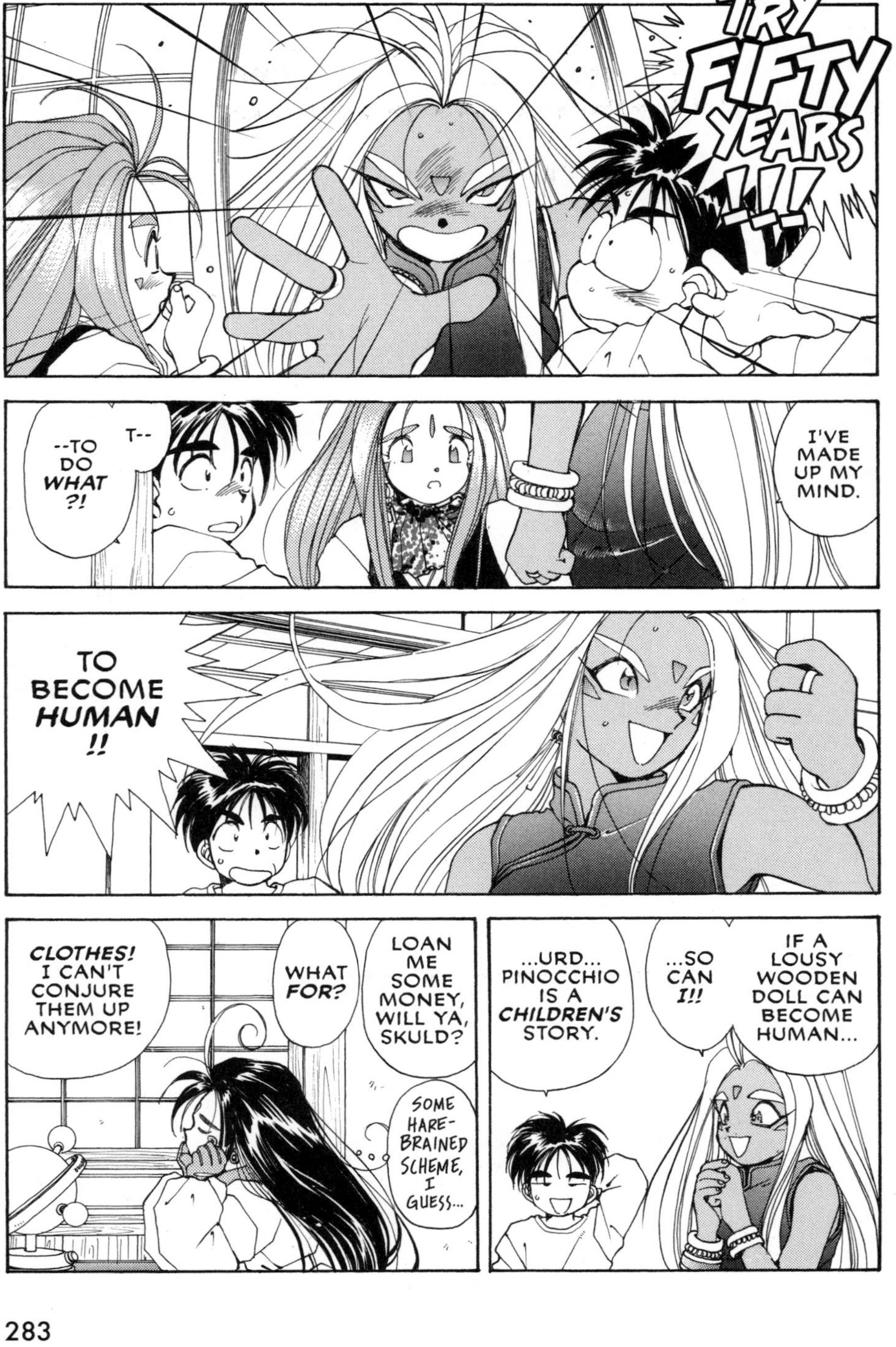
TRY FIFTY YEARS!!!
I'VE MADE UP MY MIND.
T--
--TO DO WHAT?!
TO BECOME HUMAN!!
IF A LOUSY WOODEN DOLL CAN BECOME HUMAN...
...SO CAN I!!
...URD... PINOCCHIO IS A CHILDREN'S STORY.
LOAN ME SOME MONEY, WILL YA, SKULD?
WHAT FOR?
CLOTHES! I CAN'T CONJURE THEM UP ANYMORE!
SOME HARE-BRAINED SCHEME, I GUESS...

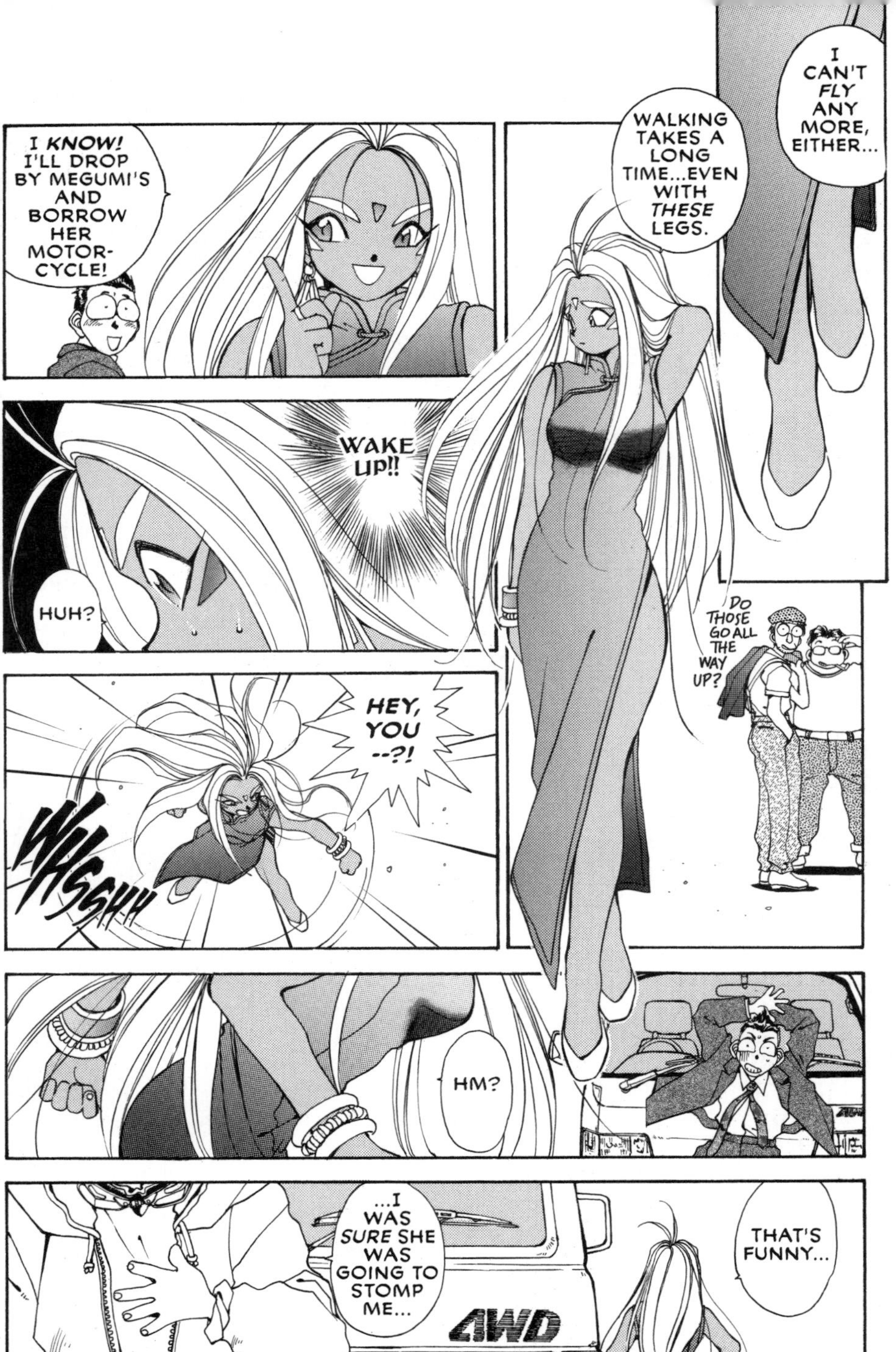
I CAN'T FLY ANY MORE, EITHER...
WALKING TAKES A LONG TIME...EVEN WITH THESE LEGS.
DO THOSE GO ALL THE WAY UP?
I KNOW! I'LL DROP BY MEGUMI'S AND BORROW HER MOTOR-CYCLE!
WAKE UP!!
HUH?
HEY, YOU --?!
WHSSHH
HM?
THAT'S FUNNY...
...I WAS SURE SHE WAS GOING TO STOMP ME...
4WD

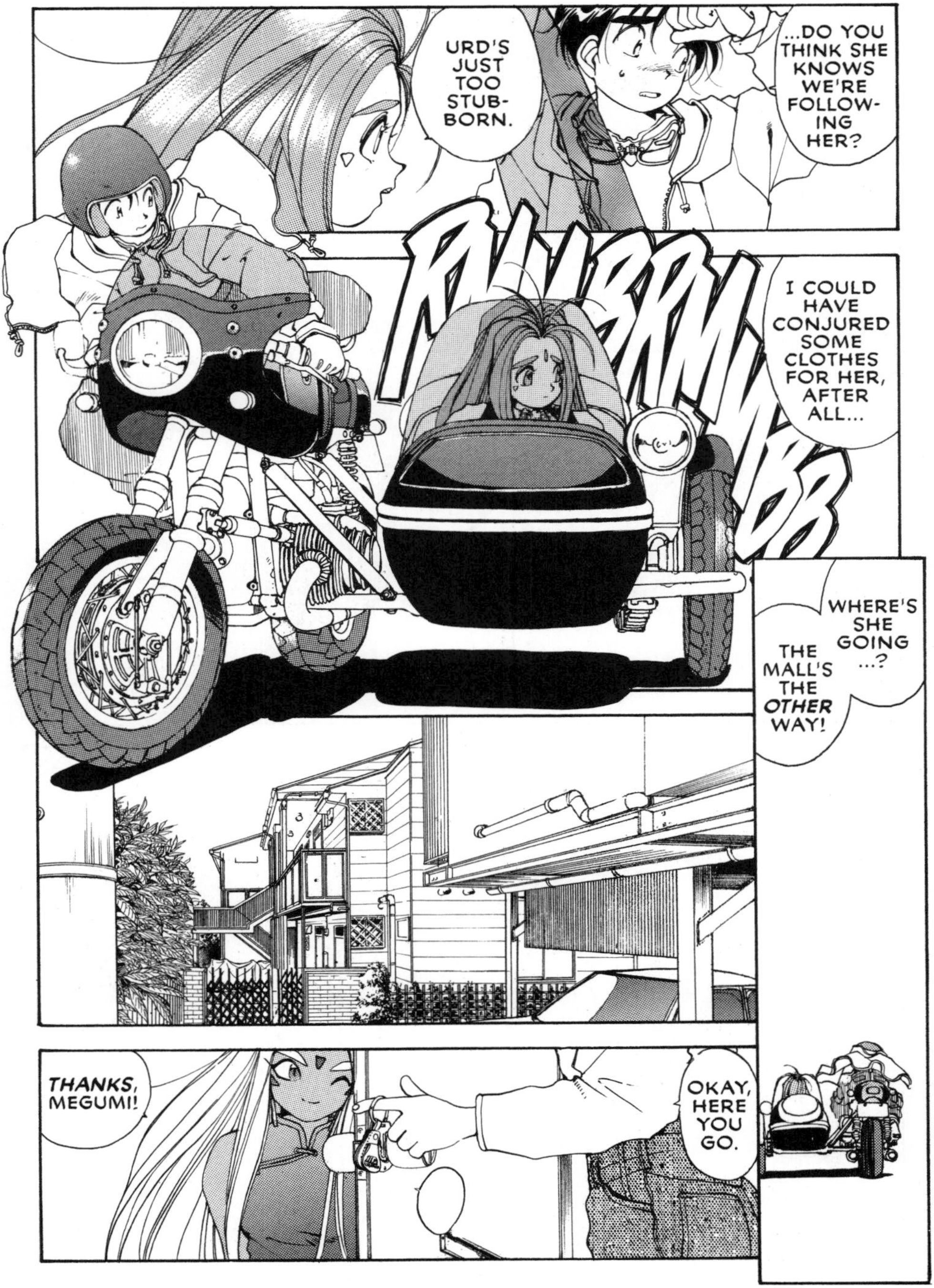
...DO YOU THINK SHE KNOWS WE'RE FOLLOW-ING HER?
URD'S JUST TOO STUB-BORN.
I COULD HAVE CONJURED SOME CLOTHES FOR HER, AFTER ALL...
WHERE'S SHE GOING ...?
THE MALL'S THE *OTHER* WAY!
OKAY, HERE YOU GO.
*THANKS*, MEGUMI!

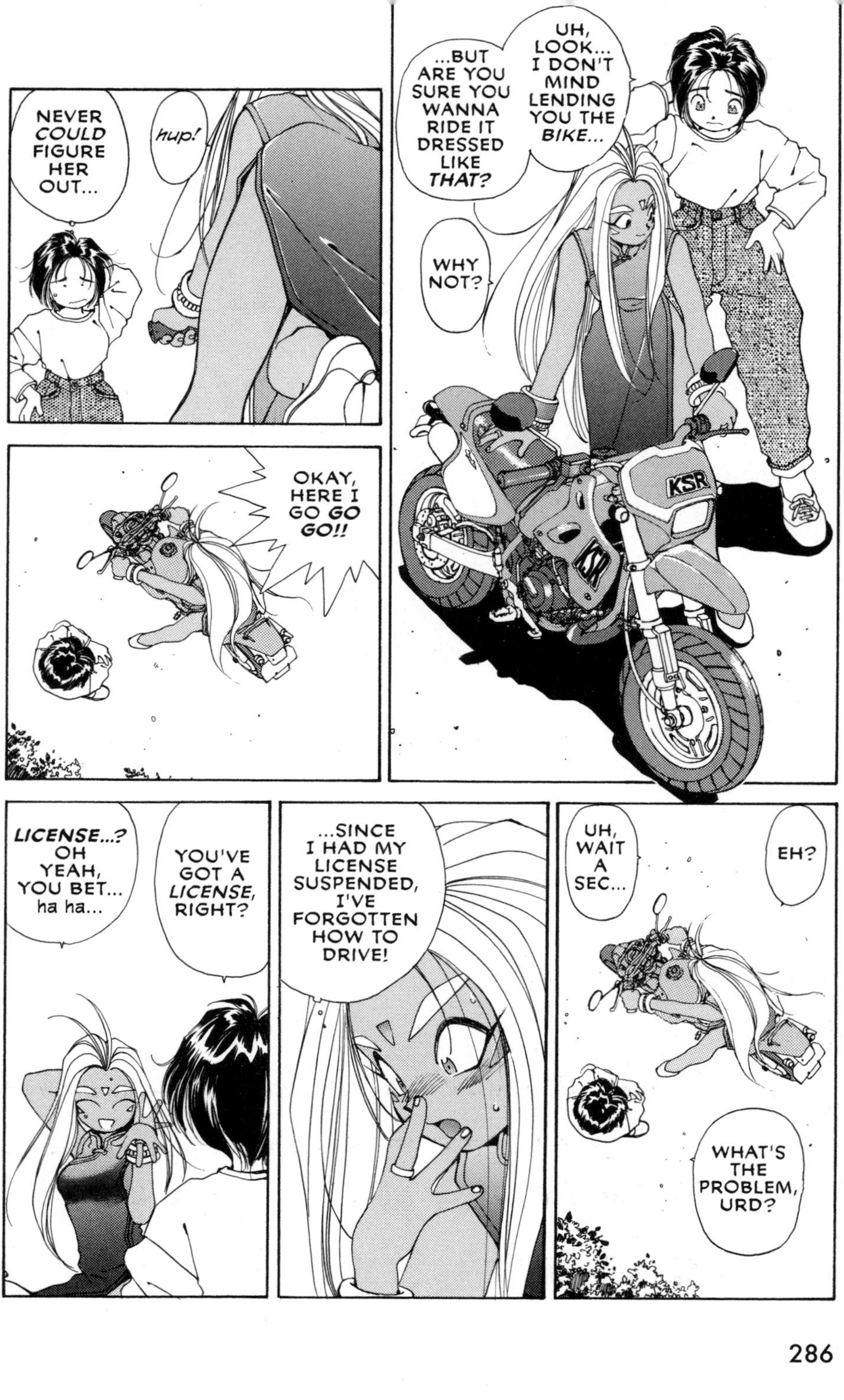
UH, LOOK... I DON'T MIND LENDING YOU THE *BIKE*...
...BUT ARE YOU SURE YOU WANNA RIDE IT DRESSED LIKE *THAT?*
WHY NOT?
KSR
*hup!*
NEVER *COULD* FIGURE HER OUT...
OKAY, HERE I GO *GO GO!!*
EH?
UH, WAIT A SEC...
WHAT'S THE PROBLEM, URD?
...SINCE I HAD MY LICENSE SUSPENDED, I'VE FORGOTTEN HOW TO DRIVE!
YOU'VE GOT A *LICENSE*, RIGHT?
*LICENSE...?* OH YEAH, YOU BET... ha ha...

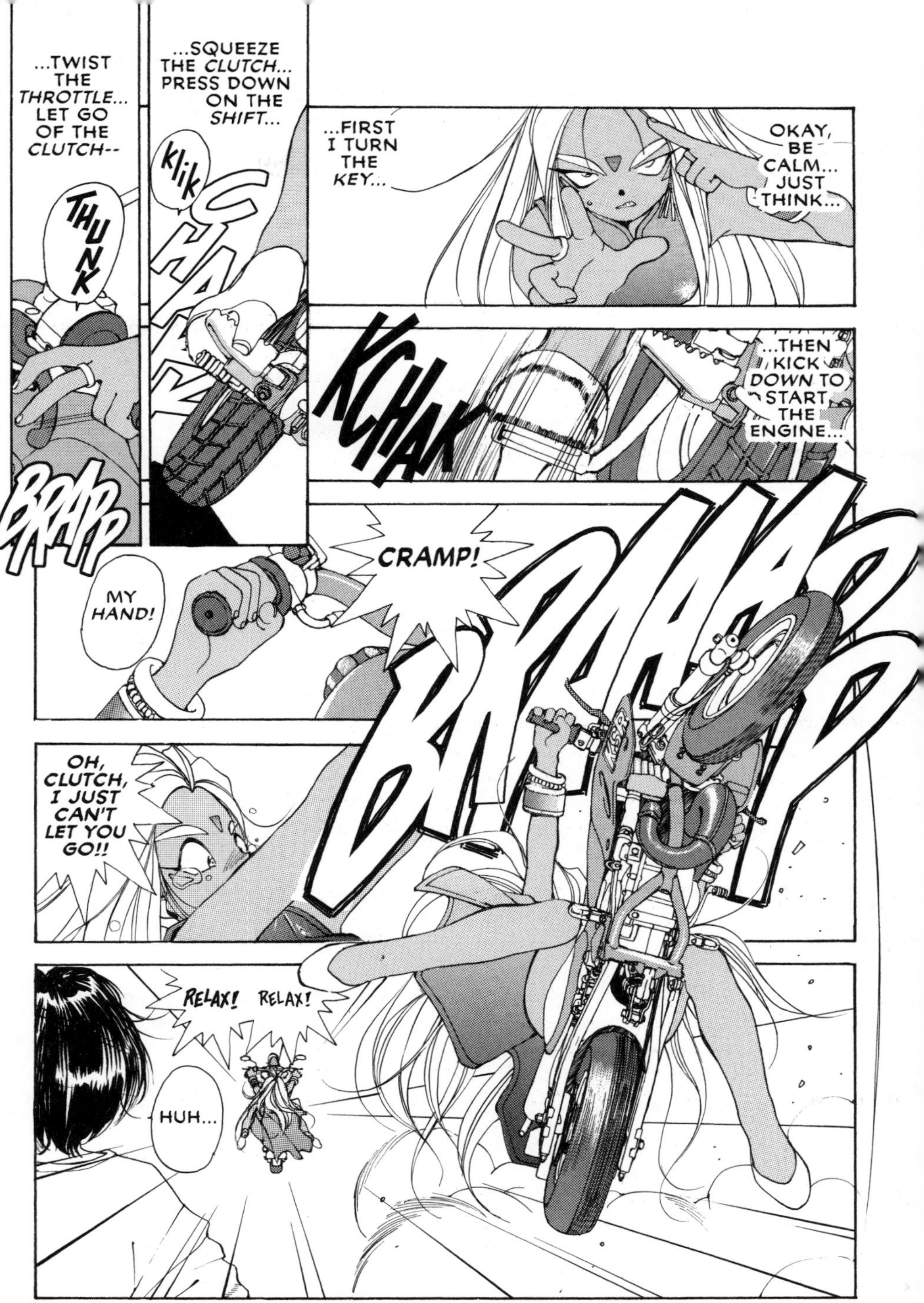
OKAY, BE CALM... JUST THINK...
...FIRST I TURN THE KEY...
...THEN KICK DOWN TO START THE ENGINE...
KCHAK
...SQUEEZE THE CLUTCH... PRESS DOWN ON THE SHIFT...
KLIK
CHAK
...TWIST THE THROTTLE... LET GO OF THE CLUTCH--
THUNK
BRAPP
MY HAND!
CRAMP!
OH, CLUTCH, I JUST CAN'T LET YOU GO!!
RELAX! RELAX!
HUH...

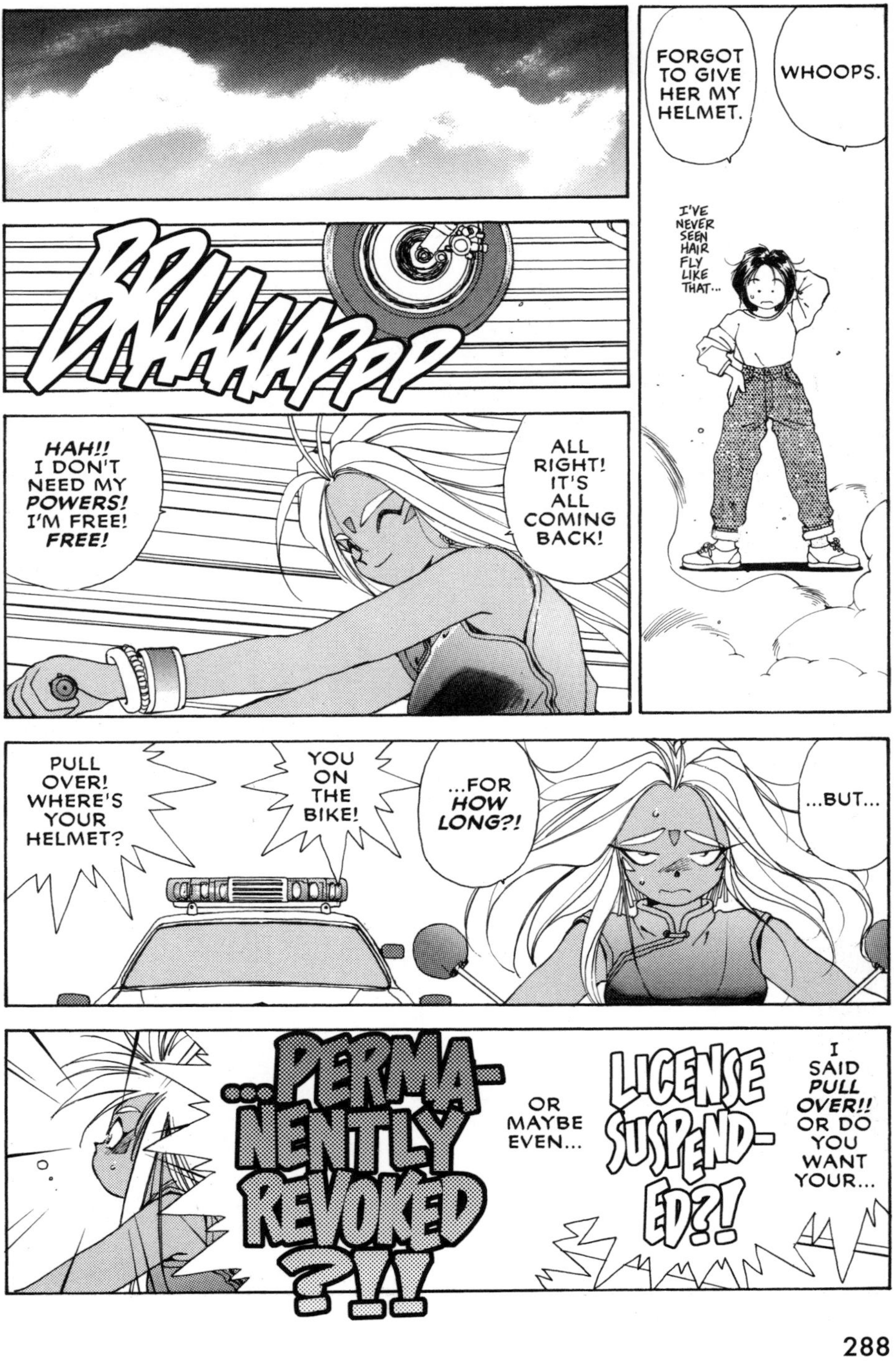
WHOOPS.
FORGOT TO GIVE HER MY HELMET.
I'VE NEVER SEEN HAIR FLY LIKE THAT...
BRAAAAAPPPP
ALL RIGHT! IT'S ALL COMING BACK!
HAH!! I DON'T NEED MY *POWERS!* I'M FREE! *FREE!*
...BUT...
...FOR *HOW LONG?!*
YOU ON THE BIKE!
PULL OVER! WHERE'S YOUR HELMET?
I SAID *PULL OVER!!* OR DO YOU WANT YOUR...
LICENSE SUSPEND-ED?!
OR MAYBE EVEN...
...PERMA-NENTLY REVOKED ?!!

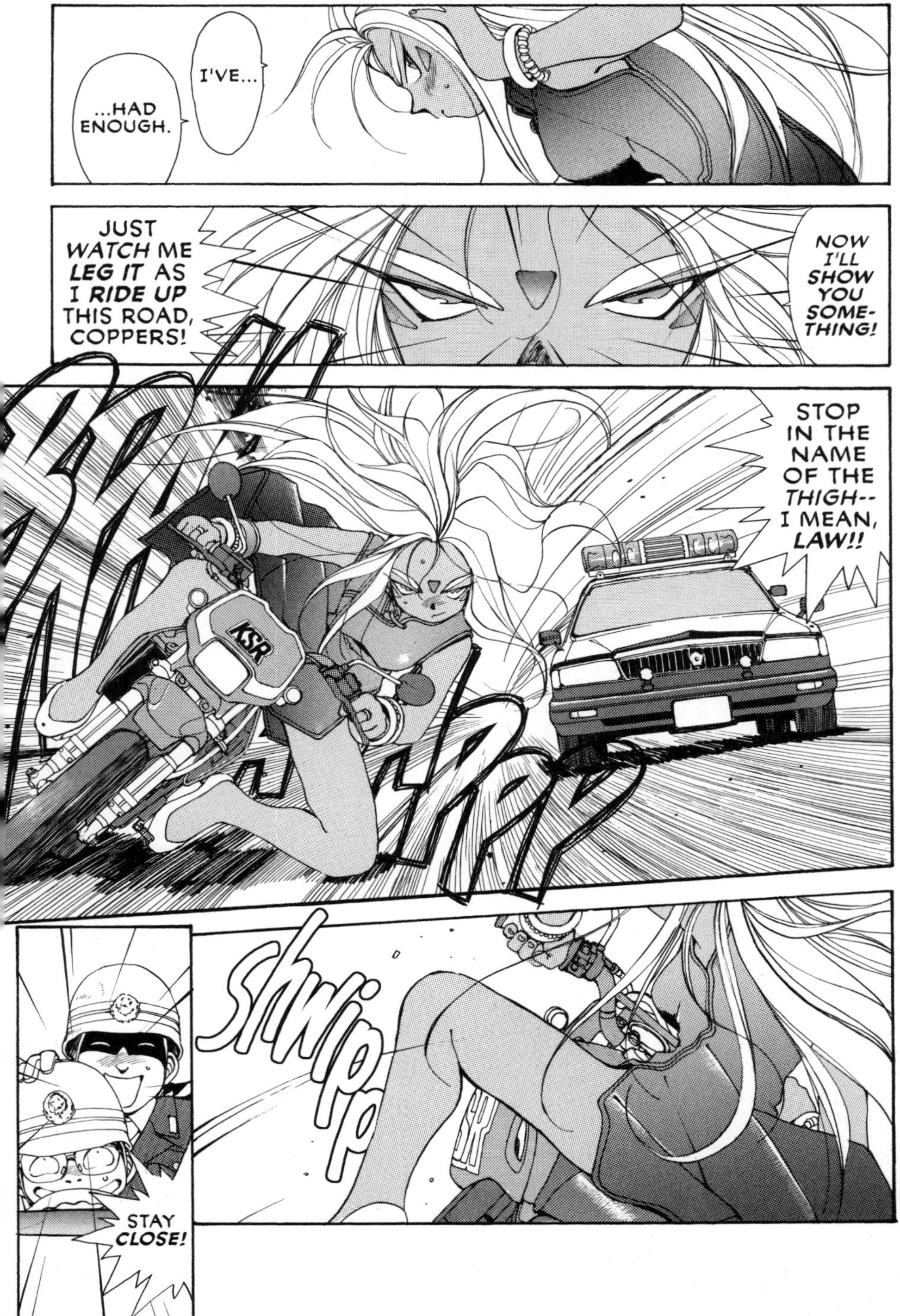
I'VE...
...HAD ENOUGH.
NOW I'LL SHOW YOU SOME-THING!
JUST WATCH ME LEG IT AS I RIDE UP THIS ROAD, COPPERS!
STOP IN THE NAME OF THE THIGH-- I MEAN, LAW!!
SHWIPP
STAY CLOSE!

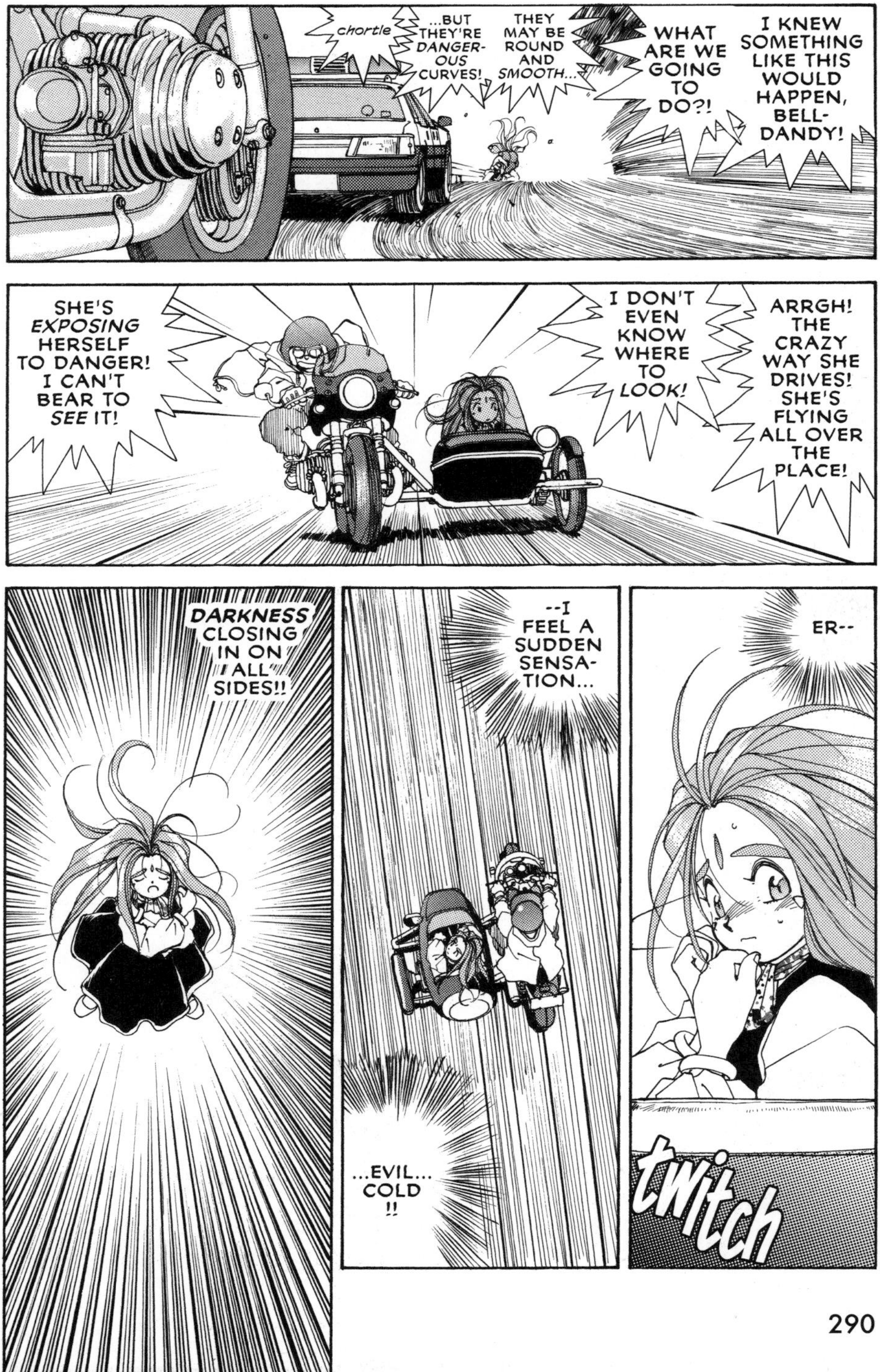
I KNEW SOMETHING LIKE THIS WOULD HAPPEN, BELL-DANDY!
WHAT ARE WE GOING TO DO?!
THEY MAY BE ROUND AND *SMOOTH*...
...BUT THEY'RE *DANGER-OUS CURVES!*
*chortle*
ARRGH! THE CRAZY WAY SHE DRIVES! SHE'S FLYING ALL OVER THE PLACE!
I DON'T EVEN KNOW WHERE TO *LOOK!*
SHE'S *EXPOSING* HERSELF TO DANGER! I CAN'T BEAR TO *SEE* IT!
ER--
twitch
--I FEEL A SUDDEN SENSA-TION...
...EVIL... COLD !!
*DARKNESS* CLOSING IN ON ALL SIDES!!

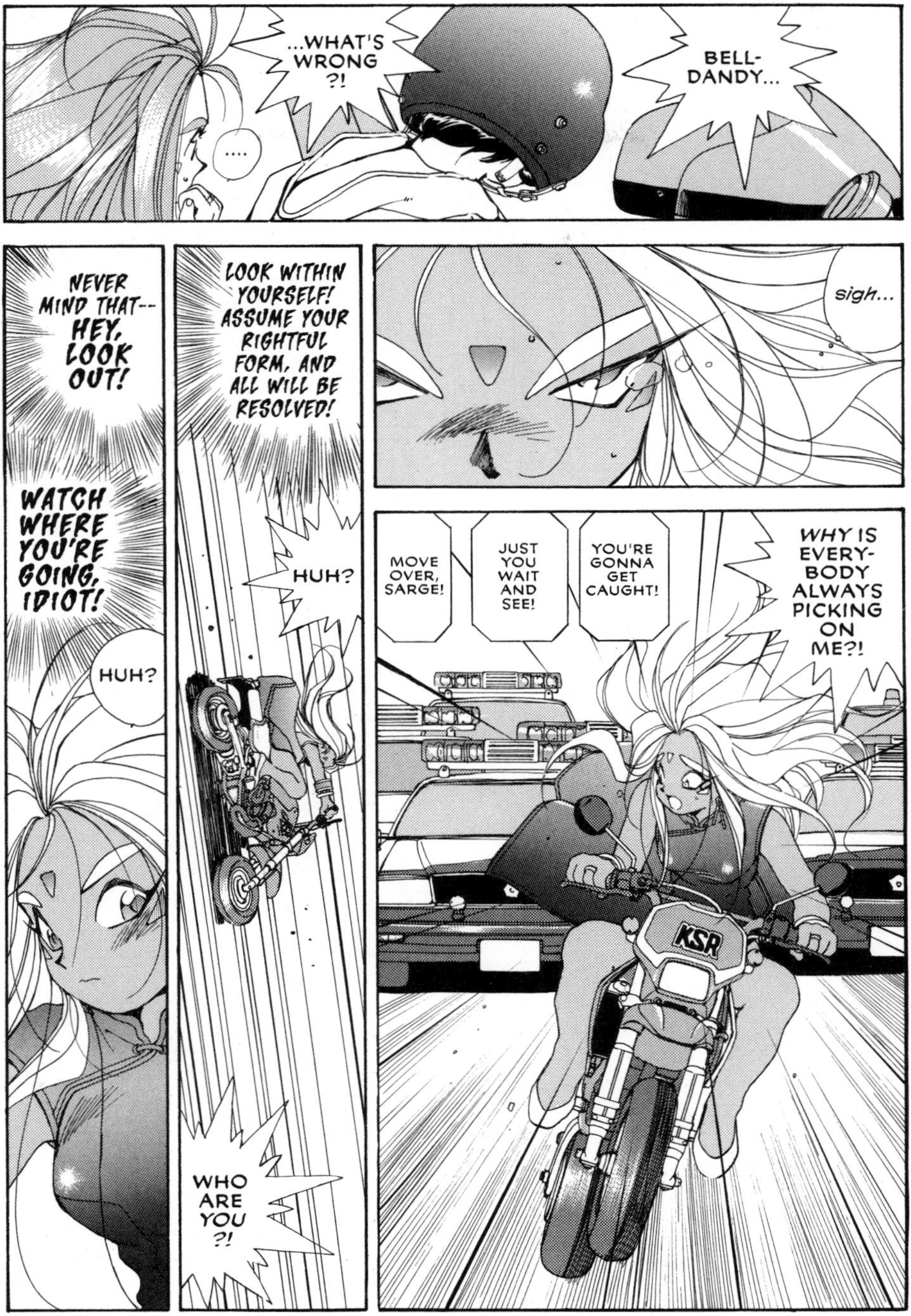
BELL-DANDY...
...WHAT'S WRONG ?!
....
sigh...
*WHY* IS EVERY-BODY ALWAYS PICKING ON ME?!
YOU'RE GONNA GET CAUGHT!
JUST YOU WAIT AND SEE!
MOVE OVER, SARGE!
LOOK WITHIN YOURSELF! ASSUME YOUR RIGHTFUL FORM, AND ALL WILL BE RESOLVED!
HUH?
WHO ARE *YOU* ?!
NEVER MIND THAT-- **HEY, LOOK OUT!**
WATCH WHERE YOU'RE GOING, IDIOT!
HUH?

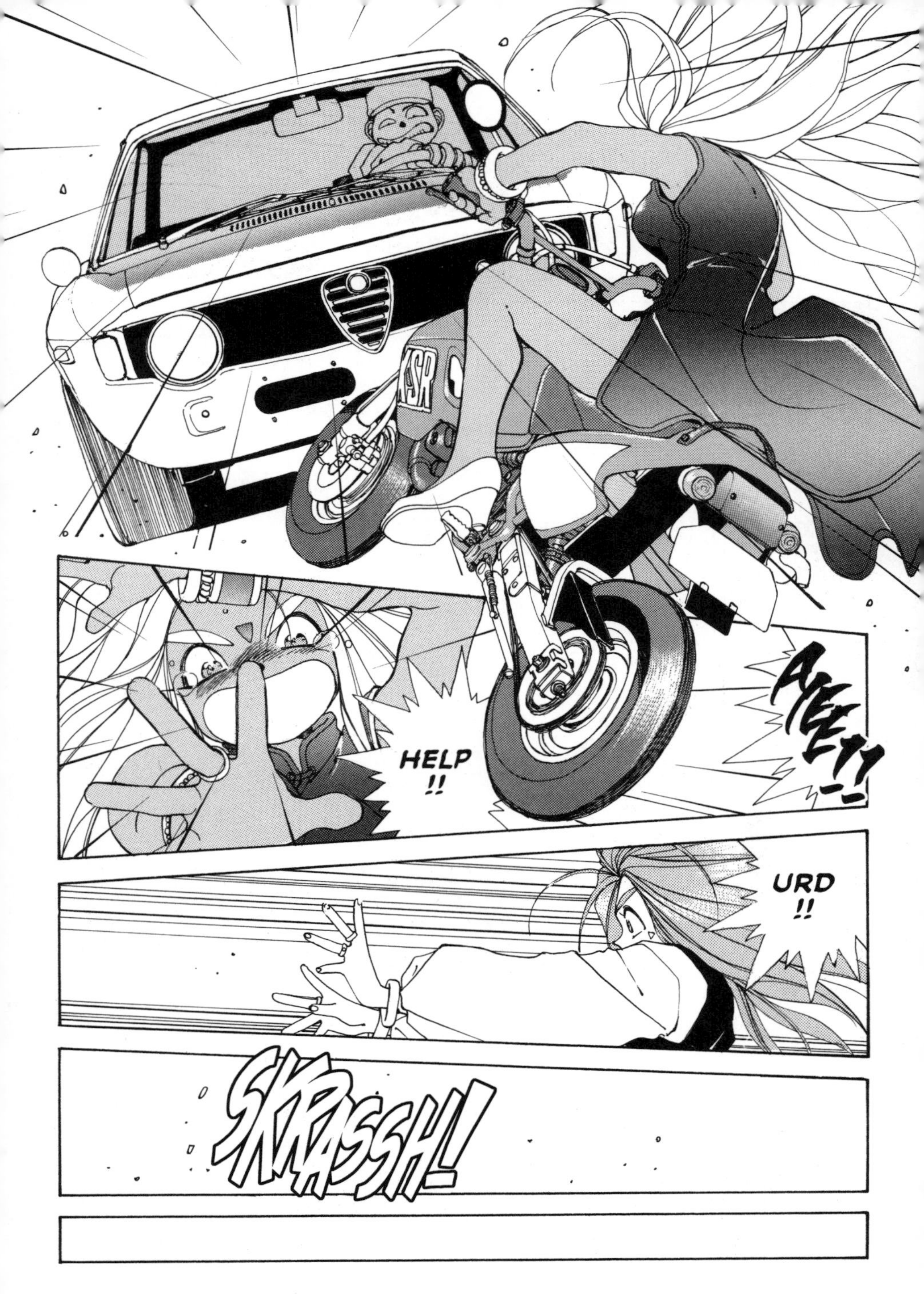
AIEEE!!
HELP !!
URD !!
SKRASSH!

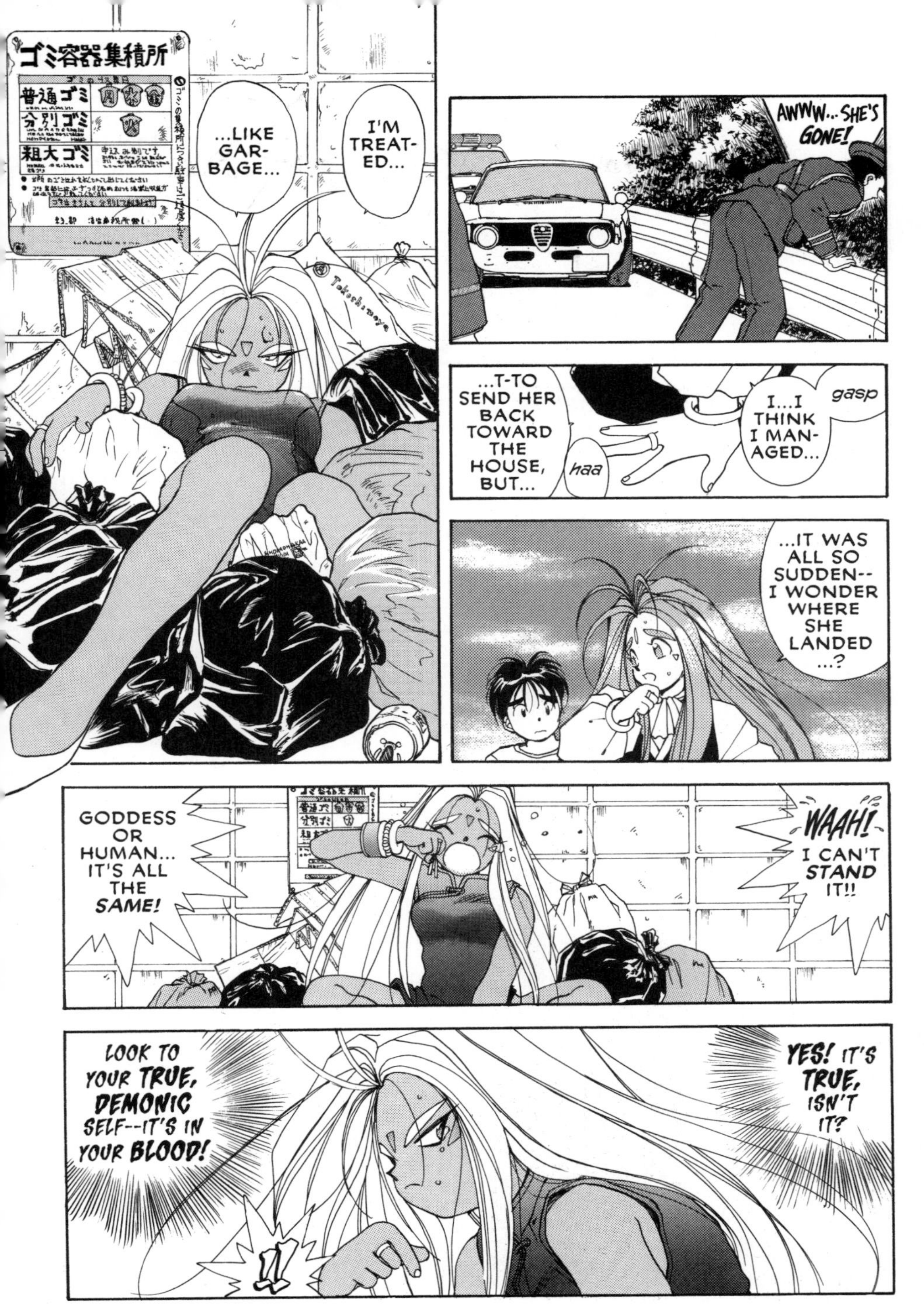
AWWW... SHE'S GONE!
gasp
I...I THINK I MAN-AGED...
haa
...T-TO SEND HER BACK TOWARD THE HOUSE, BUT...
...IT WAS ALL SO SUDDEN-- I WONDER WHERE SHE LANDED ...?
ゴミ容器集積所
普通ゴミ
分別ゴミ
粗大ゴミ
I'M TREAT-ED...
...LIKE GAR-BAGE...
WAAH! I CAN'T STAND IT!!
GODDESS OR HUMAN... IT'S ALL THE SAME!
YES! IT'S TRUE, ISN'T IT?
LOOK TO YOUR TRUE, DEMONIC SELF--IT'S IN YOUR BLOOD!

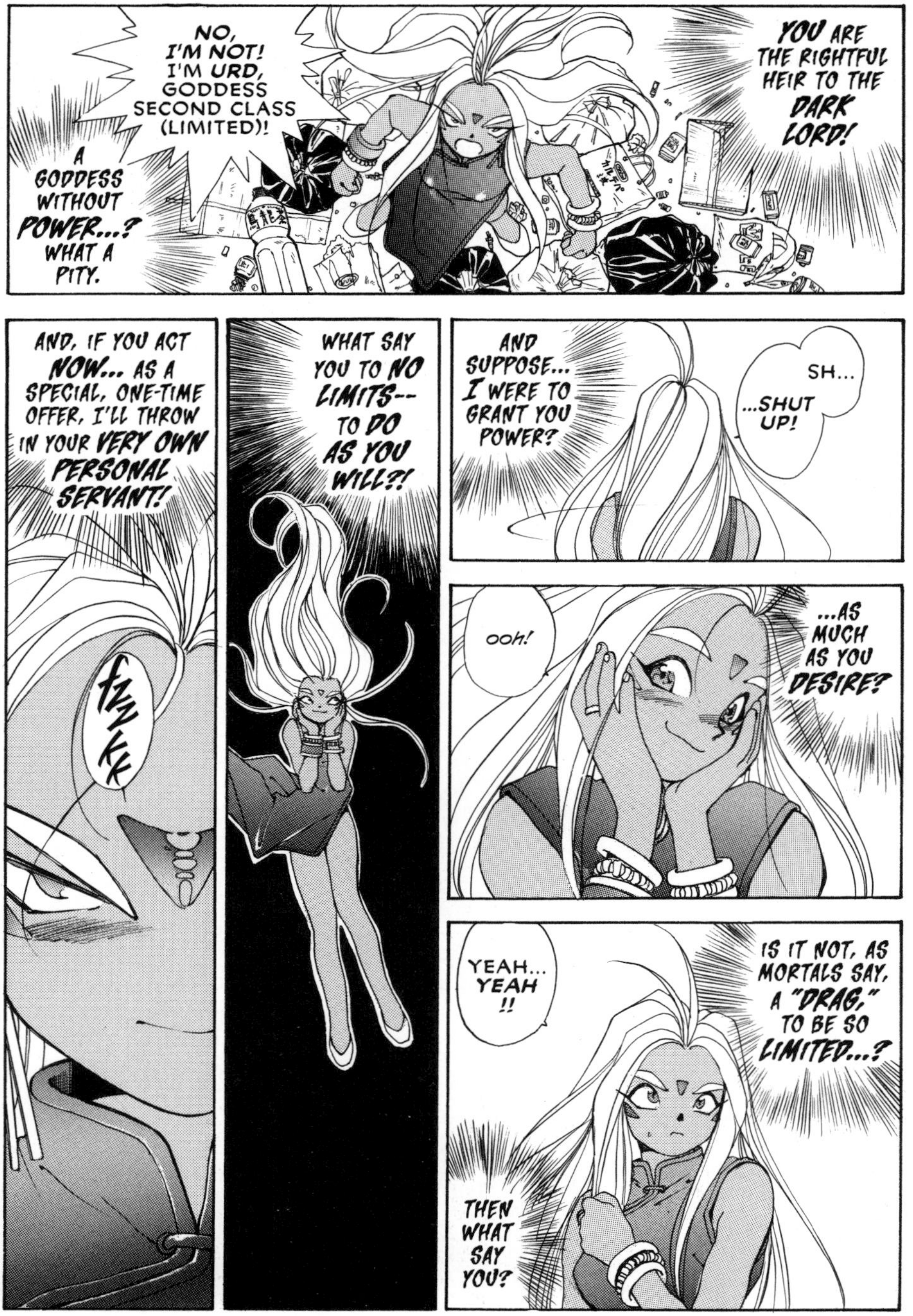
YOU ARE THE RIGHTFUL HEIR TO THE DARK LORD!
NO, I'M NOT! I'M URD, GODDESS SECOND CLASS (LIMITED)!
A GODDESS WITHOUT POWER...? WHAT A PITY.
SH... ...SHUT UP!
AND SUPPOSE... I WERE TO GRANT YOU POWER?
...AS MUCH AS YOU DESIRE?
ooh!
IS IT NOT, AS MORTALS SAY, A "DRAG," TO BE SO LIMITED...?
YEAH... YEAH !!
THEN WHAT SAY YOU?
WHAT SAY YOU TO NO LIMITS-- TO DO AS YOU WILL?!
AND, IF YOU ACT NOW... AS A SPECIAL, ONE-TIME OFFER, I'LL THROW IN YOUR VERY OWN PERSONAL SERVANT!
FZZKK

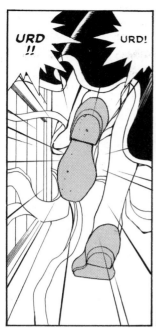

URD!!

URD!

THESE VAPORS!

...I'VE SEEN THEM BEFORE...

KKSSHH!!

U...URD...?

I NO LONGER ANSWER TO MY OLD NAME.

SISTER...

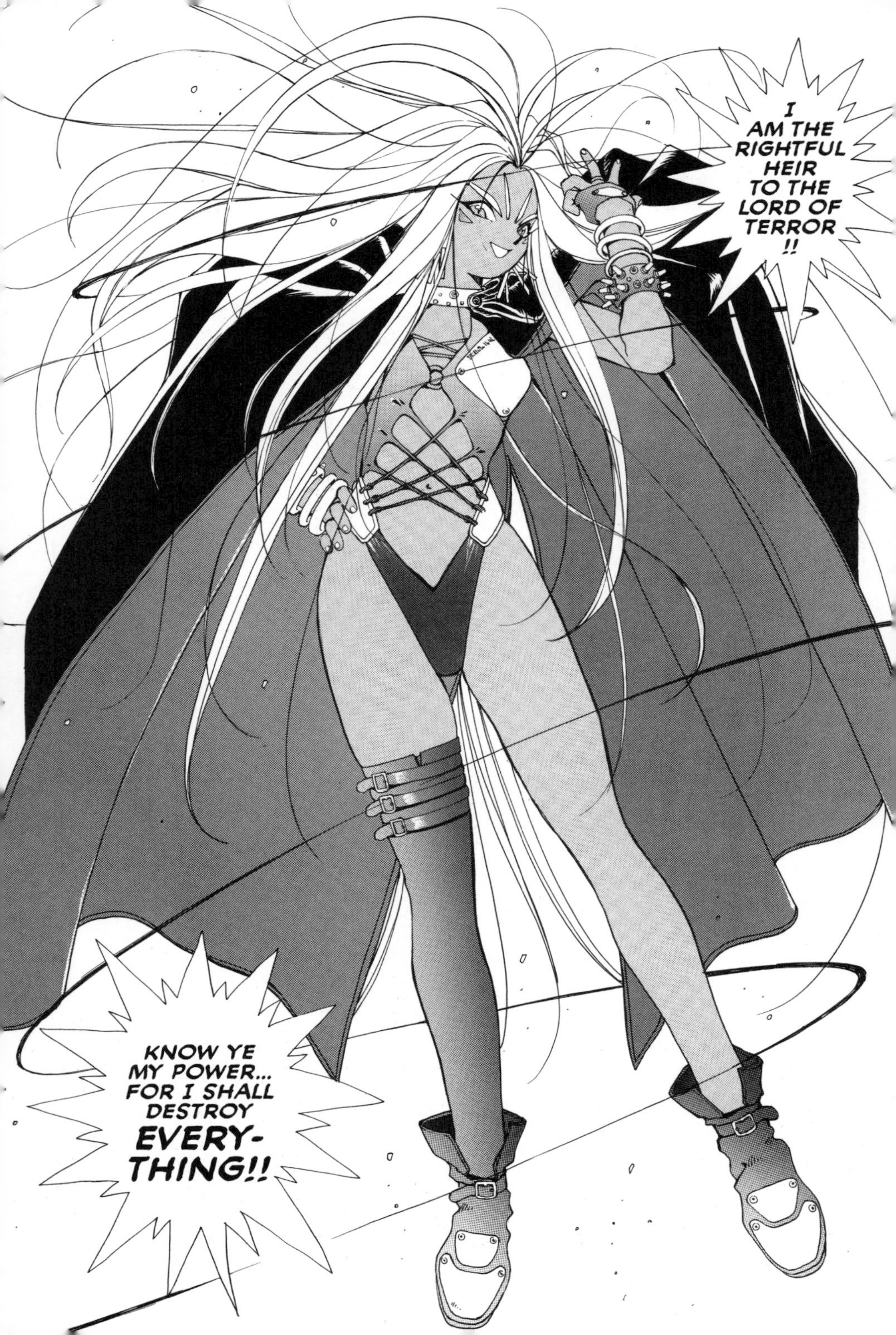
I AM THE RIGHTFUL HEIR TO THE LORD OF TERROR !!
KNOW YE MY POWER... FOR I SHALL DESTROY EVERY-THING!!

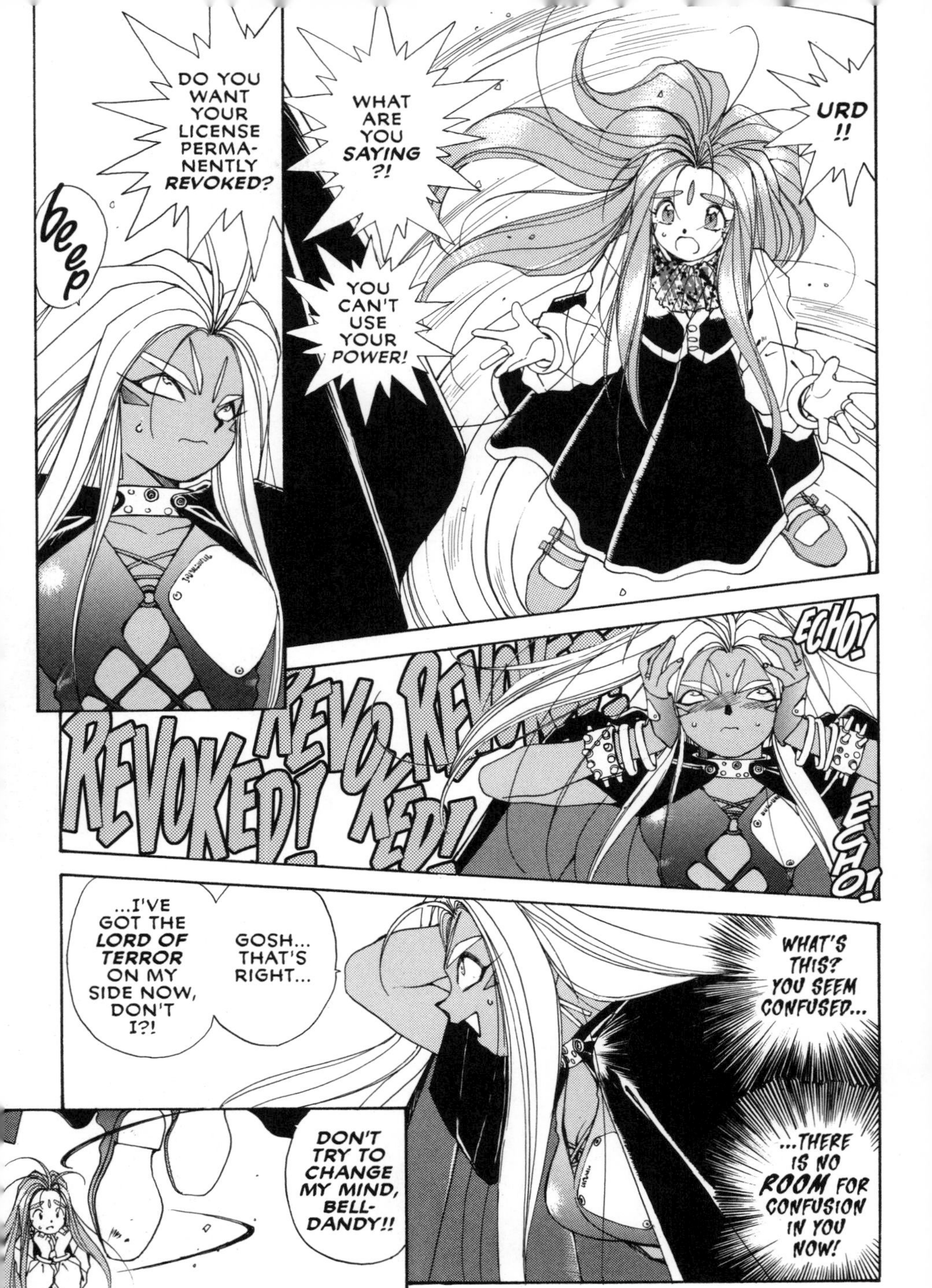

URD !!
WHAT ARE YOU SAYING ?!
YOU CAN'T USE YOUR POWER!
DO YOU WANT YOUR LICENSE PERMANENTLY REVOKED?
beep
ECHO!
REVO KED!
REVOKED!
ECHO!
WHAT'S THIS? YOU SEEM CONFUSED...
GOSH... THAT'S RIGHT...
...I'VE GOT THE LORD OF TERROR ON MY SIDE NOW, DON'T I?!
...THERE IS NO ROOM FOR CONFUSION IN YOU NOW!
DON'T TRY TO CHANGE MY MIND, BELL-DANDY!!

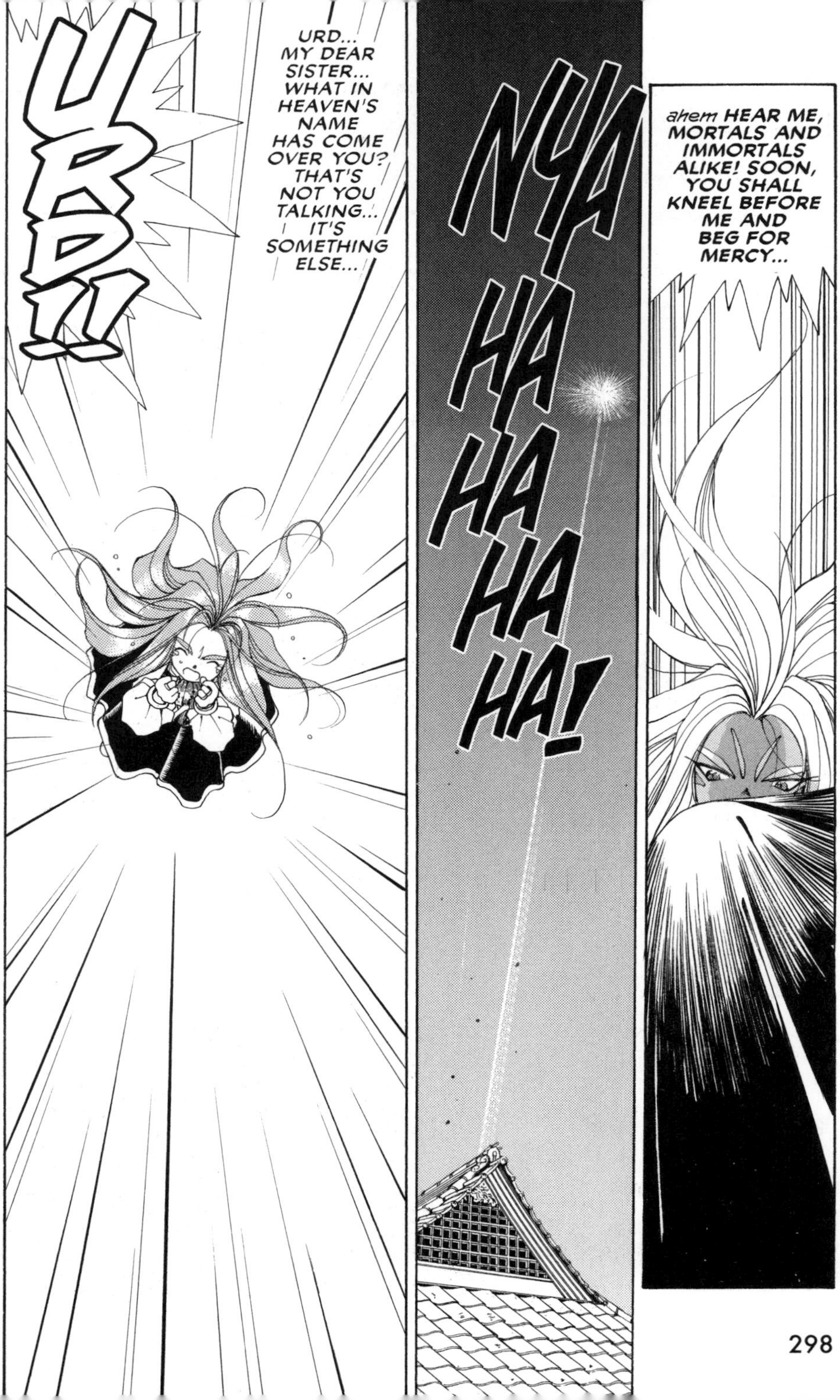
ahem HEAR ME, MORTALS AND IMMORTALS ALIKE! SOON, YOU SHALL KNEEL BEFORE ME AND BEG FOR MERCY...
NYA HA HA HA HA HA!
URD... MY DEAR SISTER... WHAT IN HEAVEN'S NAME HAS COME OVER YOU? THAT'S NOT YOU TALKING... IT'S SOMETHING ELSE...
URD!!

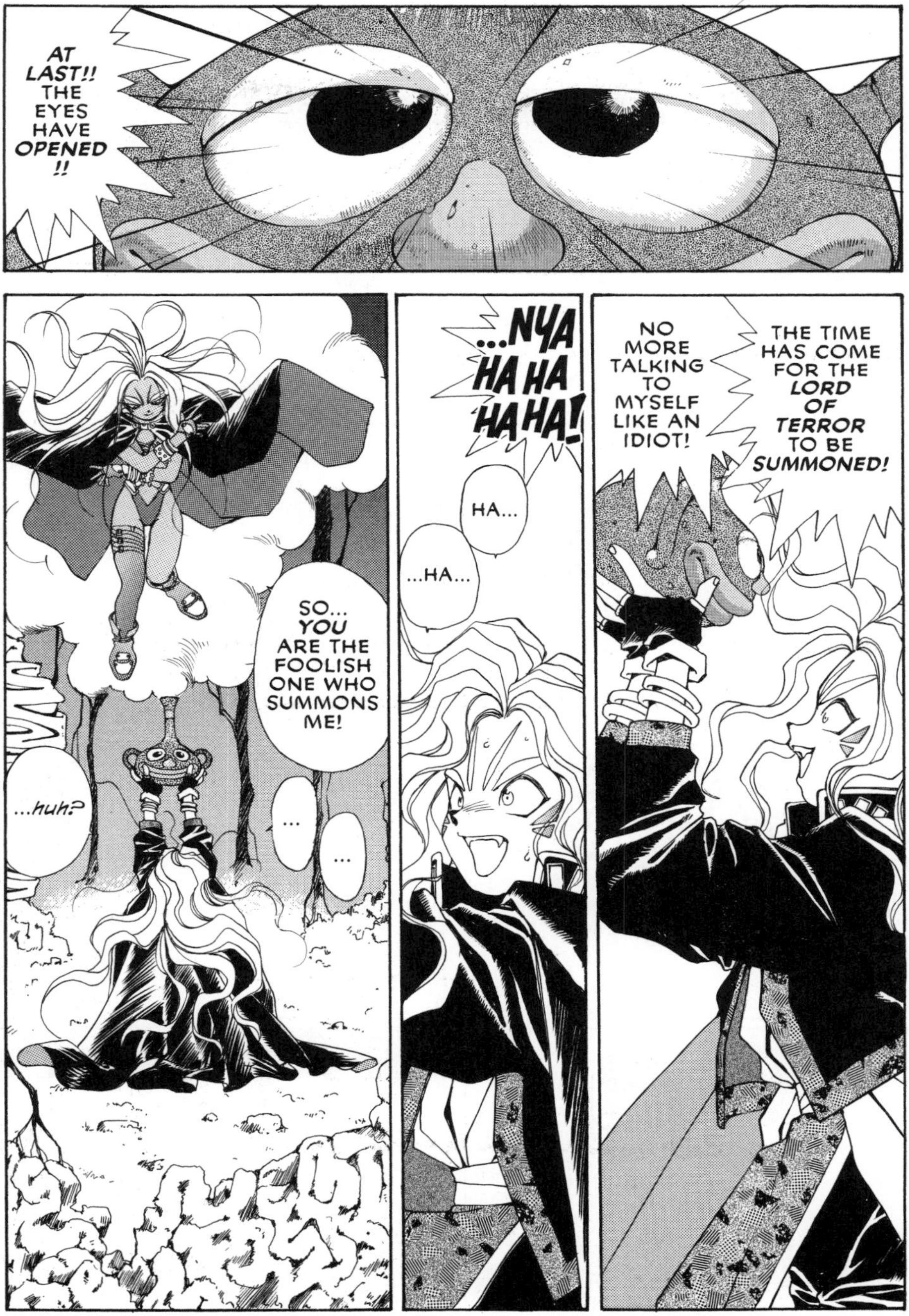
AT LAST!! THE EYES HAVE OPENED !!
THE TIME HAS COME FOR THE LORD OF TERROR TO BE SUMMONED!
NO MORE TALKING TO MYSELF LIKE AN IDIOT!
...NYA HA HA HA HA!
HA...
...HA...
SO... YOU ARE THE FOOLISH ONE WHO SUMMONS ME!
...
...
...huh?

# THE ADVENTURES OF MINI-URD

## ◆ WAKE-UP CALL ◆

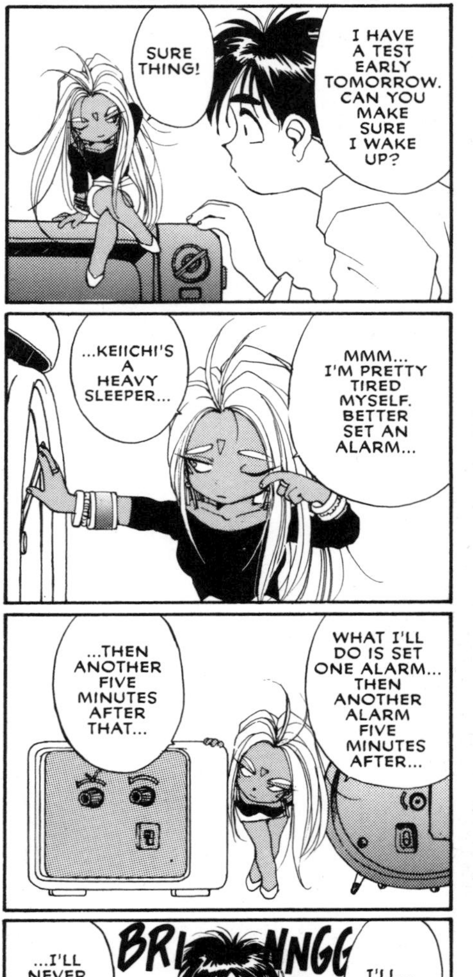
I HAVE A TEST EARLY TOMORROW. CAN YOU MAKE SURE I WAKE UP?
SURE THING!
MMM... I'M PRETTY TIRED MYSELF. BETTER SET AN ALARM...
...KEIICHI'S A HEAVY SLEEPER...
WHAT I'LL DO IS SET ONE ALARM... THEN ANOTHER ALARM FIVE MINUTES AFTER...
...THEN ANOTHER FIVE MINUTES AFTER THAT...
I'LL...
BING-BONG
BRI NNGG
BEEP BEEP
...I'LL NEVER FIND THEM ALL.

## ◆ JUST ONE OF THOSE DAYS ◆

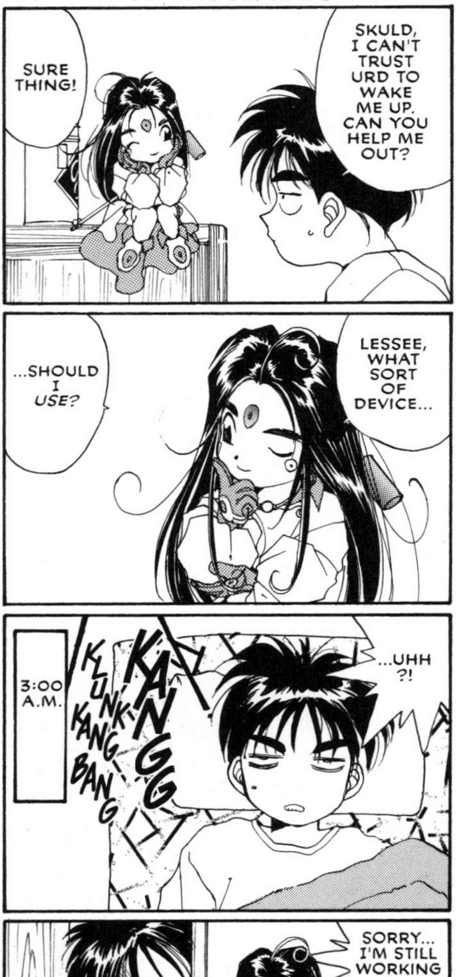
SKULD, I CAN'T TRUST URD TO WAKE ME UP. CAN YOU HELP ME OUT?
SURE THING!
LESSEE, WHAT SORT OF DEVICE...
...SHOULD I *USE?*
...UHH ?!
KANGG
KLUNK-KANG-BANG
3:00 A.M.
SORRY... I'M STILL WORKING ON IT.
tik
tok

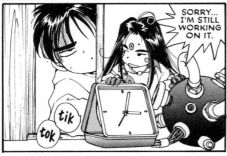

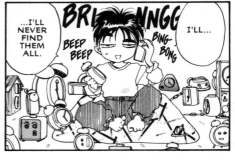

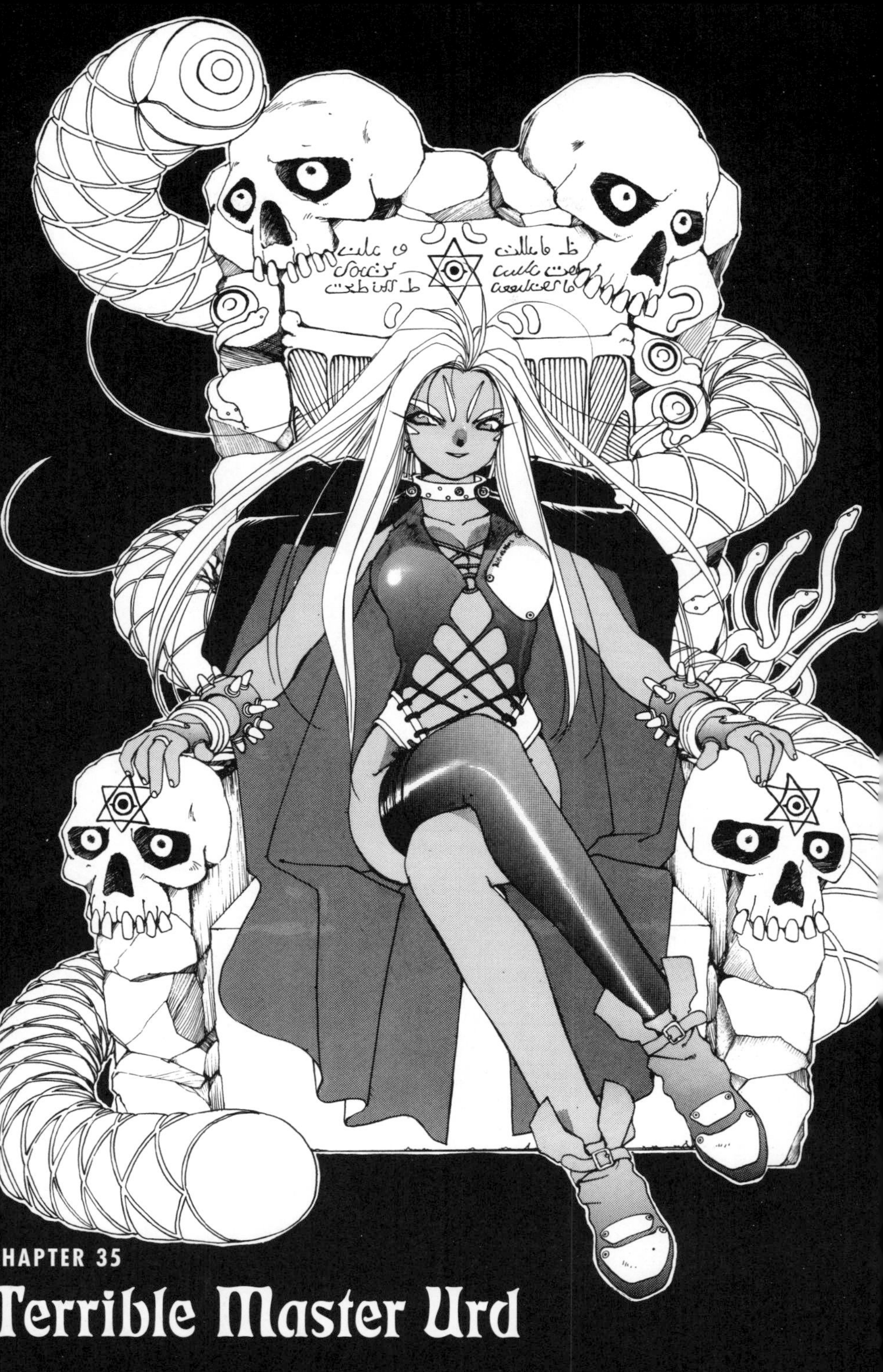

CHAPTER 35

# Terrible Master Urd

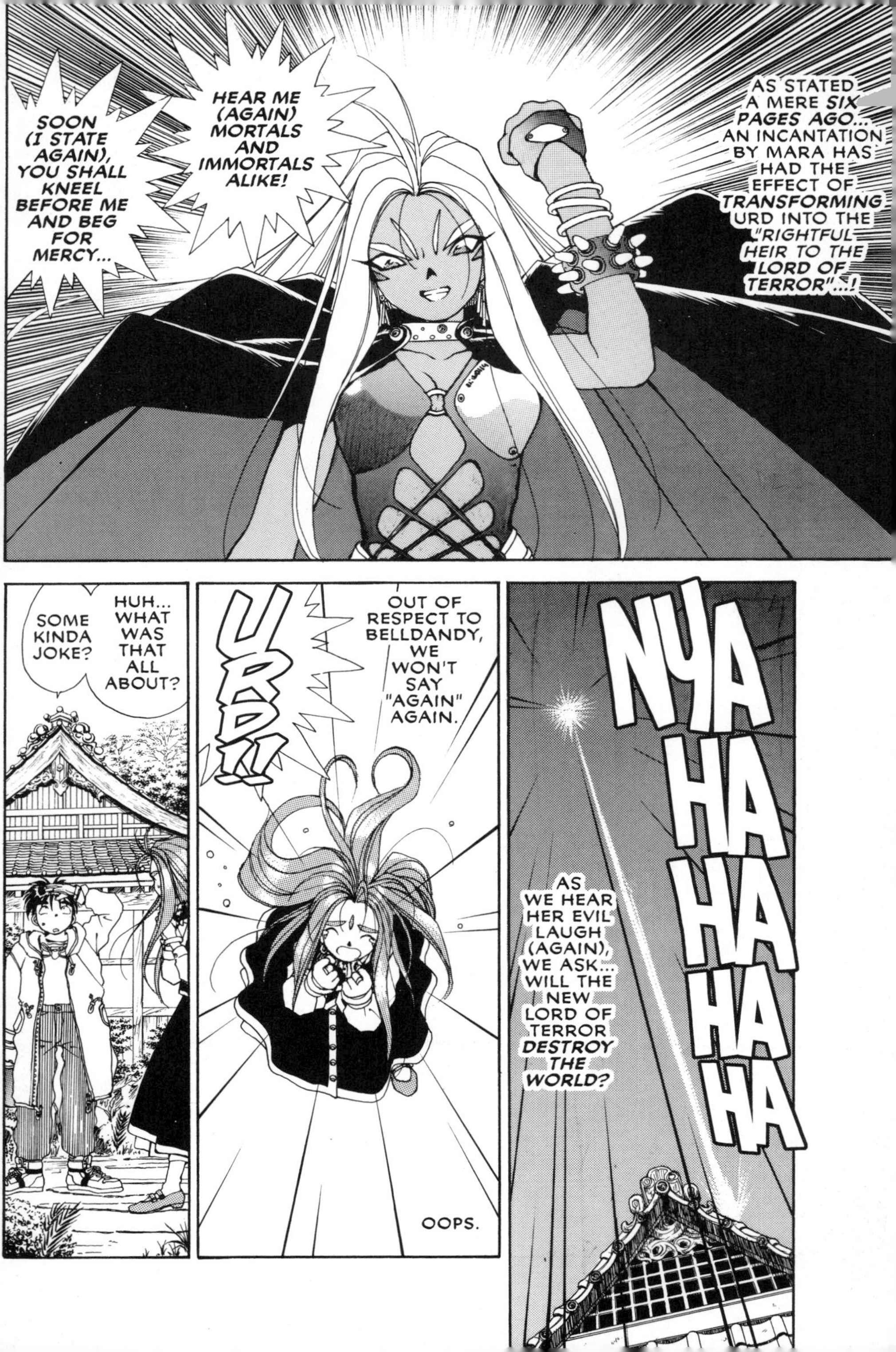
AS STATED A MERE SIX PAGES AGO... AN INCANTATION BY MARA HAS HAD THE EFFECT OF TRANSFORMING URD INTO THE "RIGHTFUL HEIR TO THE LORD OF TERROR"...!
HEAR ME (AGAIN) MORTALS AND IMMORTALS ALIKE!
SOON (I STATE AGAIN), YOU SHALL KNEEL BEFORE ME AND BEG FOR MERCY...
NYAHAHAHAHAHAHAHA
AS WE HEAR HER EVIL LAUGH (AGAIN), WE ASK... WILL THE NEW LORD OF TERROR DESTROY THE WORLD?
OUT OF RESPECT TO BELLDANDY, WE WON'T SAY "AGAIN" AGAIN.
URD!!
OOPS.
HUH... WHAT WAS THAT ALL ABOUT?
SOME KINDA JOKE?

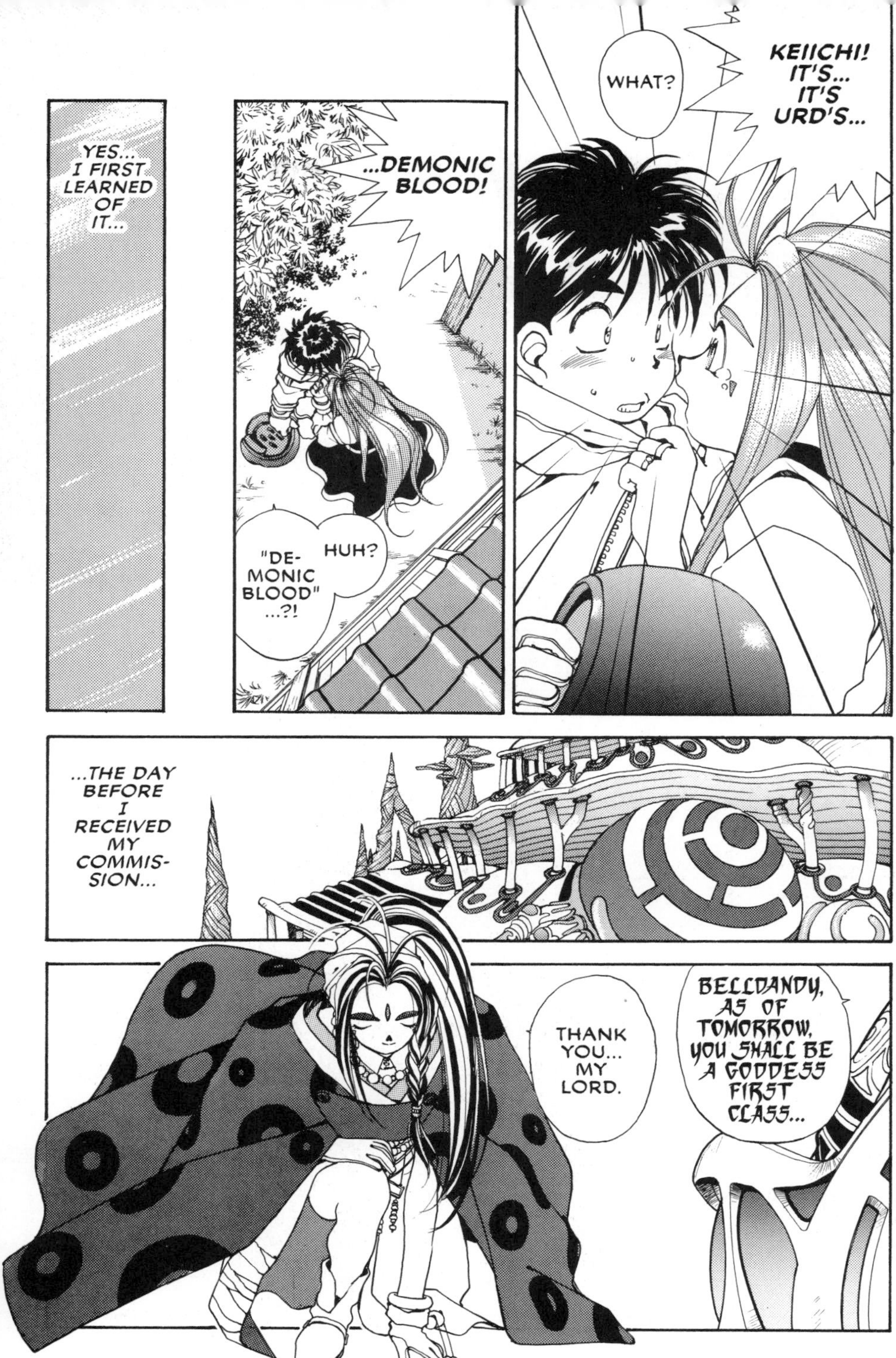
KEIICHI! IT'S... IT'S URD'S...
WHAT?
...DEMONIC BLOOD!
HUH?
"DE-MONIC BLOOD" ...?!
YES... I FIRST LEARNED OF IT...
...THE DAY BEFORE I RECEIVED MY COMMIS-SION...
BELLDANDY, AS OF TOMORROW, YOU SHALL BE A GODDESS FIRST CLASS...
THANK YOU... MY LORD.

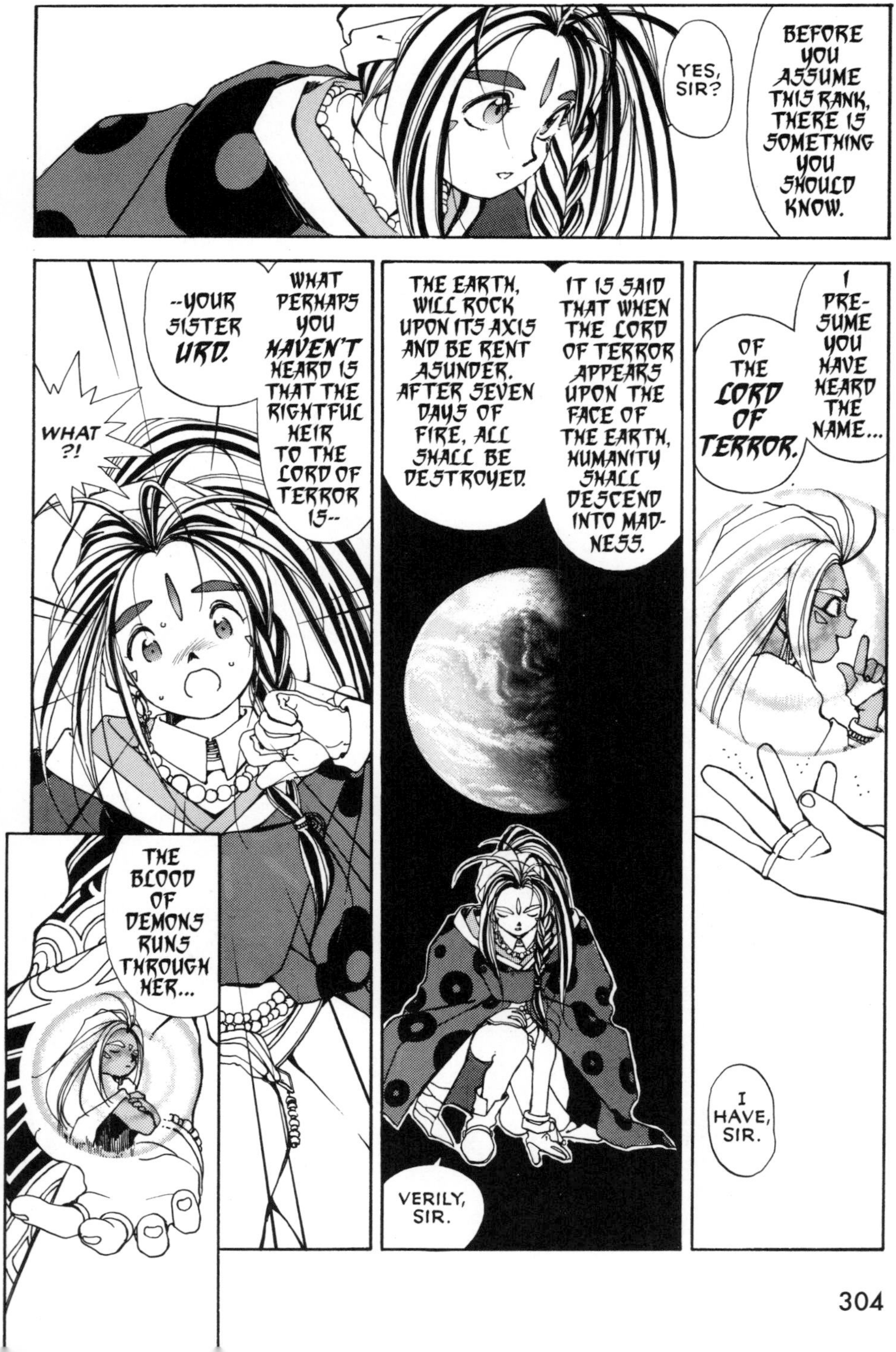
BEFORE YOU ASSUME THIS RANK, THERE IS SOMETHING YOU SHOULD KNOW.
YES, SIR?
I PRESUME YOU HAVE HEARD THE NAME...
OF THE LORD OF TERROR.
I HAVE, SIR.
IT IS SAID THAT WHEN THE LORD OF TERROR APPEARS UPON THE FACE OF THE EARTH, HUMANITY SHALL DESCEND INTO MADNESS.
THE EARTH, WILL ROCK UPON ITS AXIS AND BE RENT ASUNDER. AFTER SEVEN DAYS OF FIRE, ALL SHALL BE DESTROYED.
VERILY, SIR.
WHAT PERHAPS YOU HAVEN'T HEARD IS THAT THE RIGHTFUL HEIR TO THE LORD OF TERROR IS--
--YOUR SISTER URD.
WHAT?!
THE BLOOD OF DEMONS RUNS THROUGH HER...

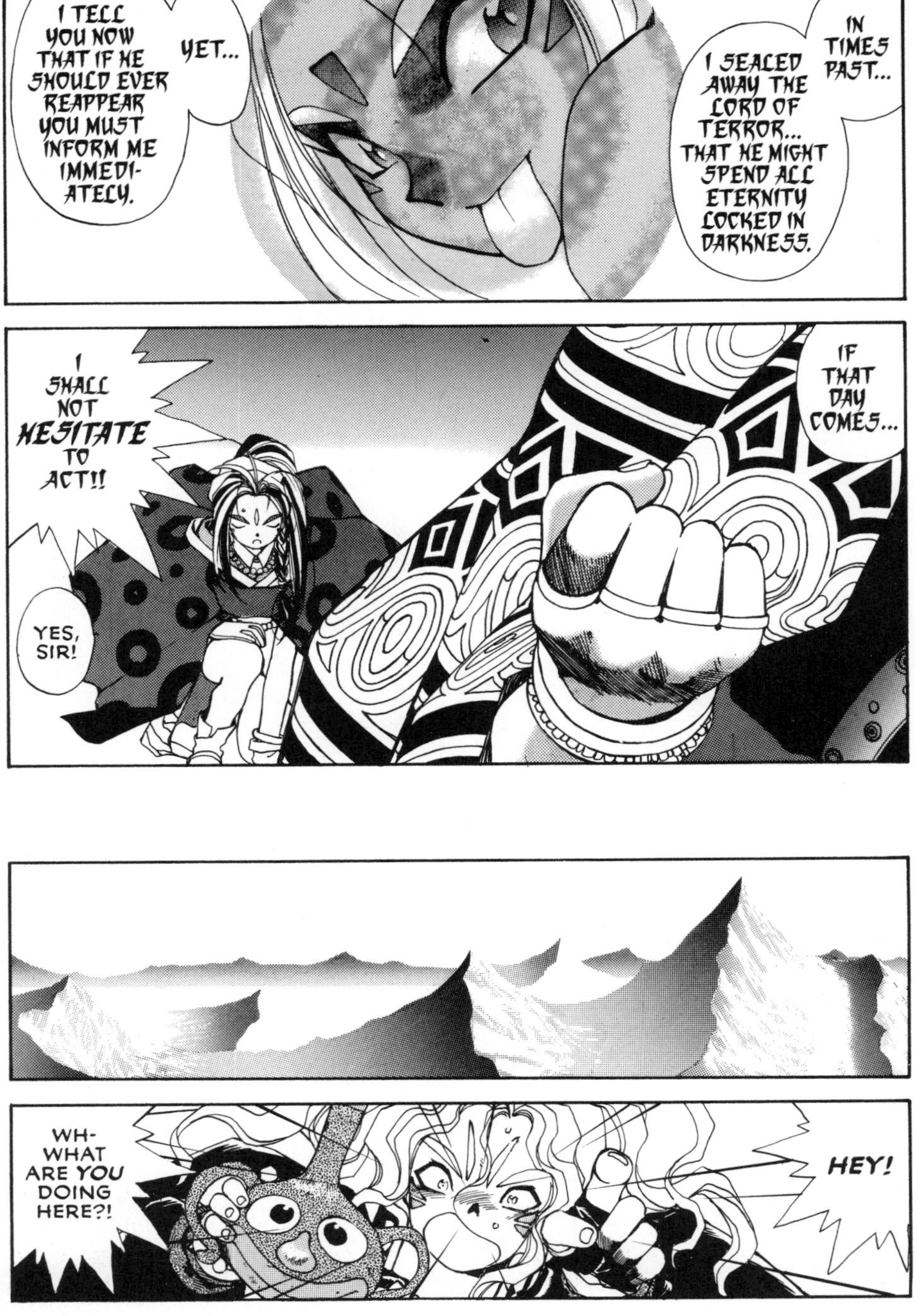
IN TIMES PAST...
I SEALED AWAY THE LORD OF TERROR... THAT HE MIGHT SPEND ALL ETERNITY LOCKED IN DARKNESS.
YET...
I TELL YOU NOW THAT IF HE SHOULD EVER REAPPEAR YOU MUST INFORM ME IMMEDI-ATELY.
IF THAT DAY COMES...
I SHALL NOT HESITATE TO ACT!!
YES, SIR!
HEY!
WH-WHAT ARE YOU DOING HERE?!

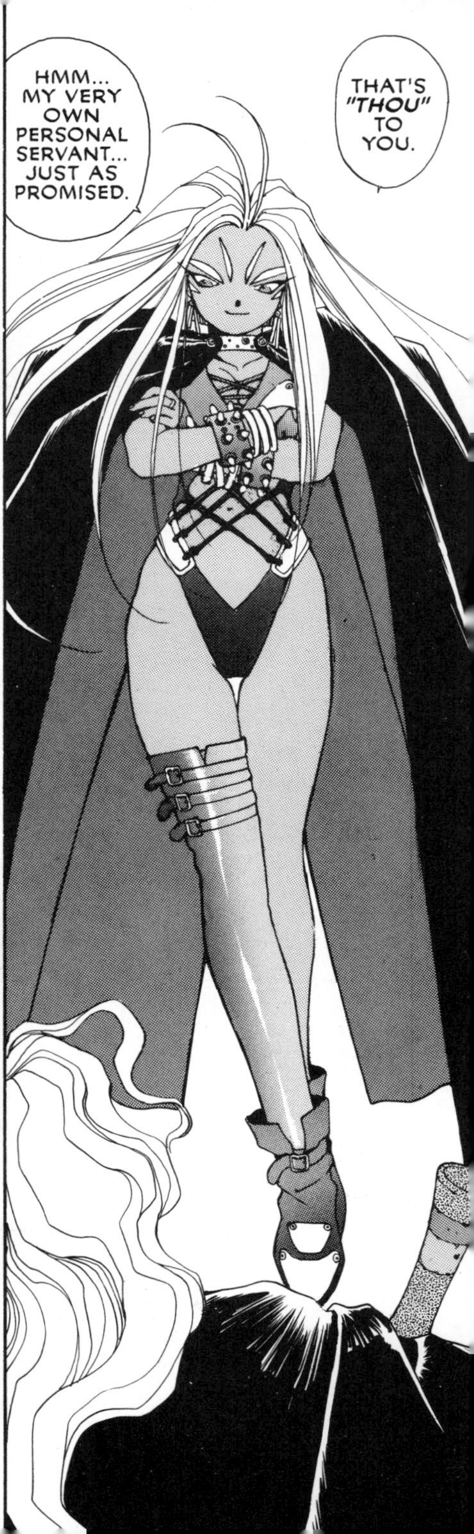
THAT'S "THOU" TO YOU.
HMM... MY VERY OWN PERSONAL SERVANT... JUST AS PROMISED.

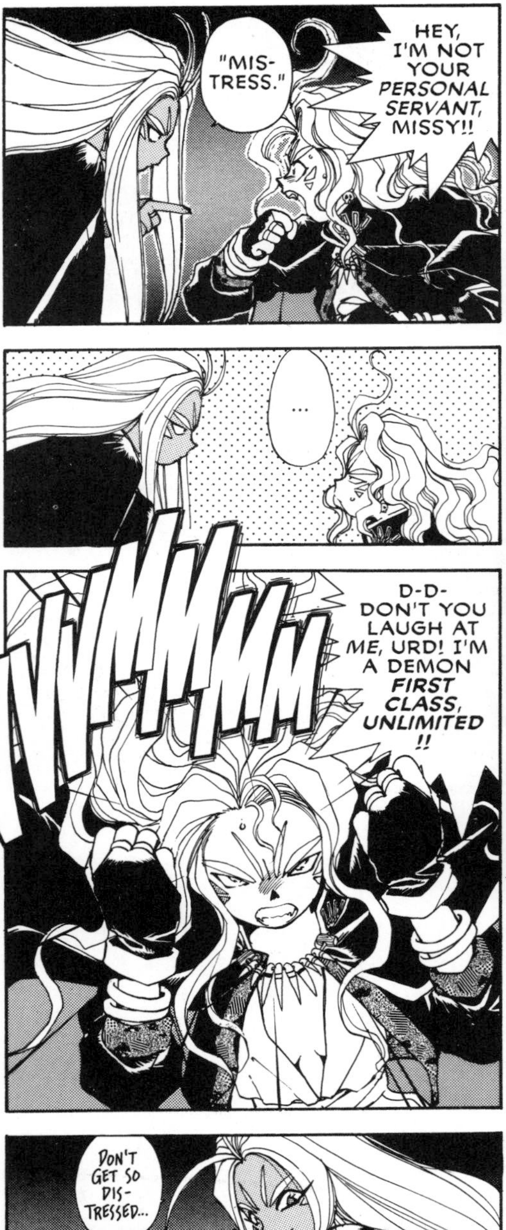
HEY, I'M NOT YOUR PERSONAL SERVANT, MISSY!!
"MIS-TRESS."
...
D-D-DON'T YOU LAUGH AT ME, URD! I'M A DEMON FIRST CLASS, UNLIMITED!!
VVVMMMMMM
DON'T GET SO DIS-TRESSED...

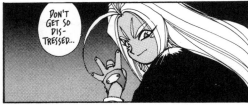

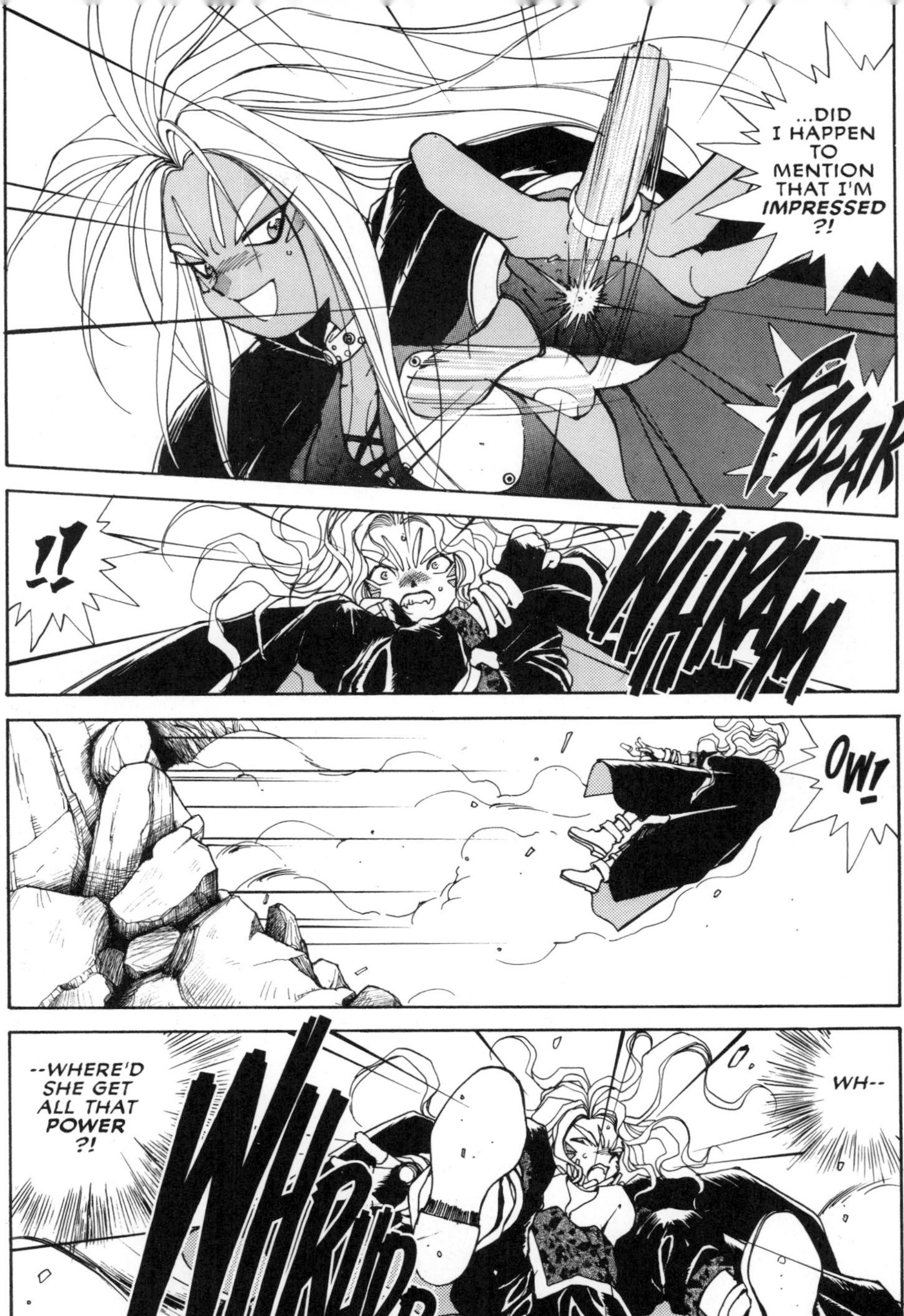
...DID I HAPPEN TO MENTION THAT I'M *IMPRESSED* ?!
FZZAK
WHRAM
!!
OW!
WH--
--WHERE'D SHE GET ALL THAT POWER ?!
WHRUDD

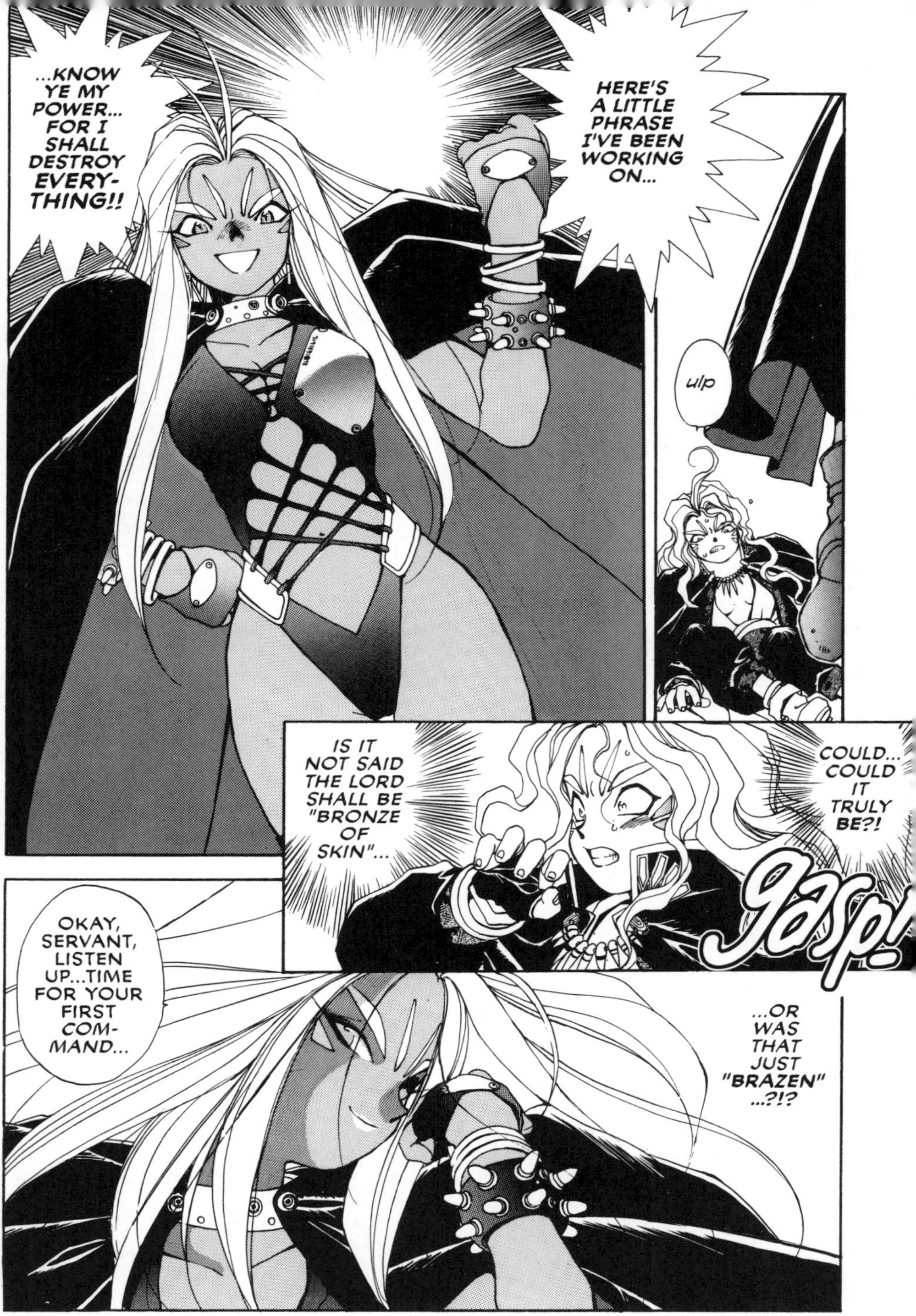
ulp
COULD... COULD IT TRULY BE?!
IS IT NOT SAID THE LORD SHALL BE "BRONZE OF SKIN"...
gasp!
HERE'S A LITTLE PHRASE I'VE BEEN WORKING ON...
...KNOW YE MY POWER... FOR I SHALL DESTROY EVERY-THING!!
...OR WAS THAT JUST "BRAZEN" ...?!?
OKAY, SERVANT, LISTEN UP...TIME FOR YOUR FIRST COM-MAND...

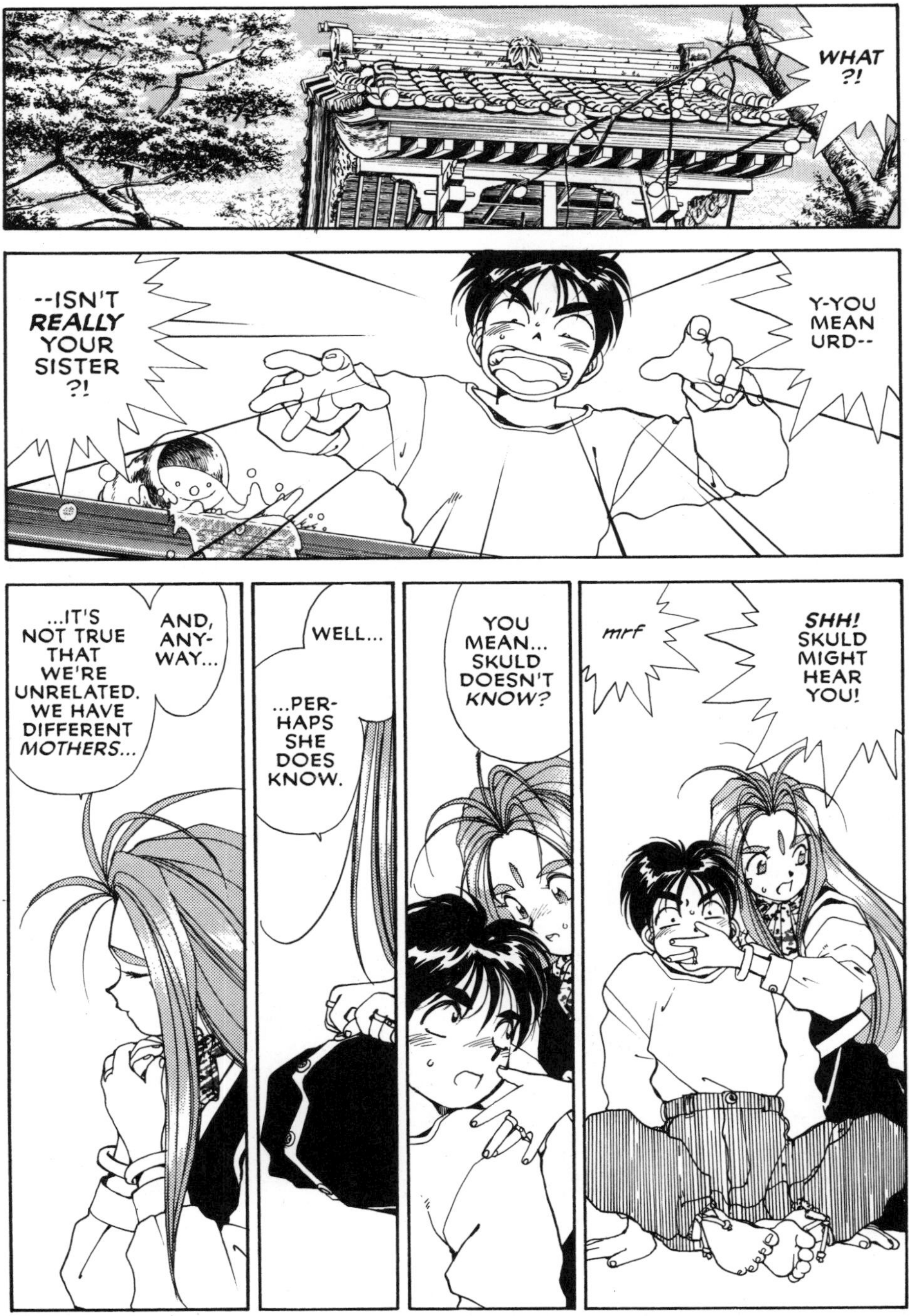
WHAT ?!
Y-YOU MEAN URD--
--ISN'T **REALLY** YOUR SISTER ?!
**SHH!** SKULD MIGHT HEAR YOU!
*mrf*
YOU MEAN... SKULD DOESN'T *KNOW?*
WELL...
...PER-HAPS SHE DOES KNOW.
AND, ANY-WAY...
...IT'S NOT TRUE THAT WE'RE UNRELATED. WE HAVE DIFFERENT *MOTHERS...*

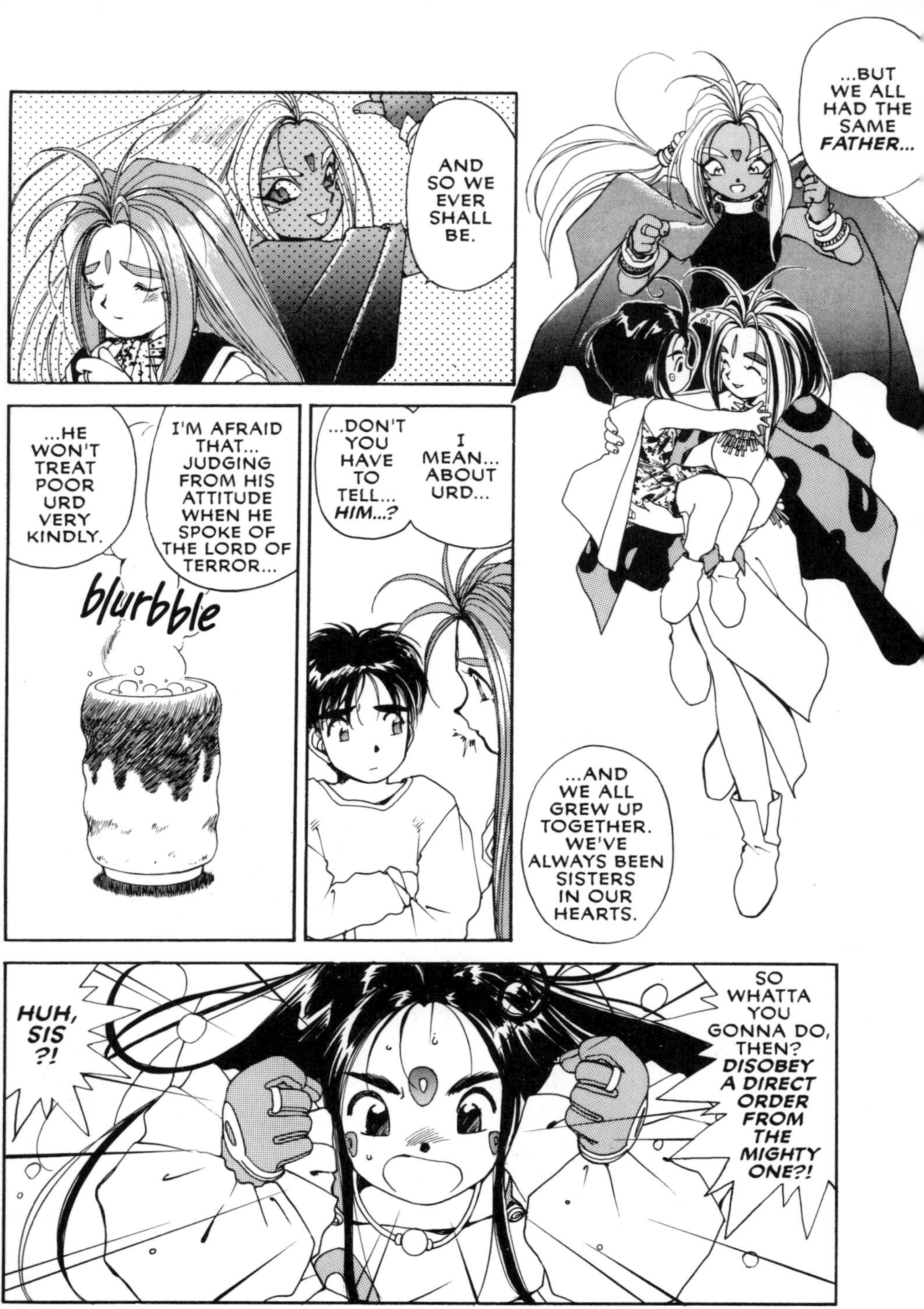
...BUT WE ALL HAD THE SAME *FATHER...*
...AND WE ALL GREW UP TOGETHER. WE'VE ALWAYS BEEN SISTERS IN OUR HEARTS.
AND SO WE EVER SHALL BE.
...DON'T YOU HAVE TO TELL... *HIM...?*
I MEAN... ABOUT URD...
I'M AFRAID THAT... JUDGING FROM HIS ATTITUDE WHEN HE SPOKE OF THE LORD OF TERROR...
...HE WON'T TREAT POOR URD VERY KINDLY.
blurbble
SO WHATTA YOU GONNA DO, THEN? ***DISOBEY A DIRECT ORDER FROM THE MIGHTY ONE?!***
***HUH, SIS?!***

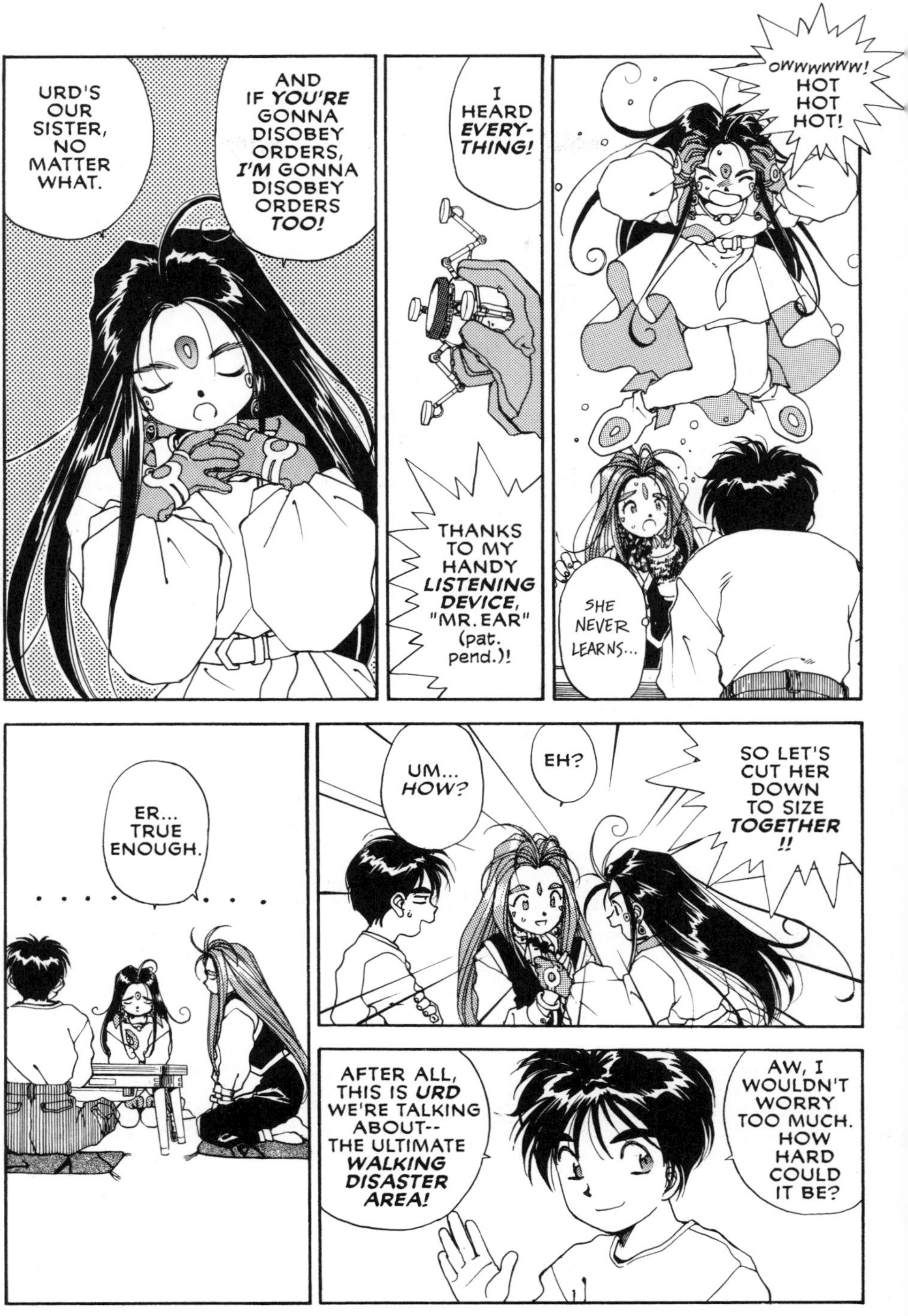
OWWWWWWW! HOT HOT HOT!
SHE NEVER LEARNS...
I HEARD EVERYTHING!
THANKS TO MY HANDY LISTENING DEVICE, "MR. EAR" (pat. pend.)!
AND IF YOU'RE GONNA DISOBEY ORDERS, I'M GONNA DISOBEY ORDERS TOO!
URD'S OUR SISTER, NO MATTER WHAT.
SO LET'S CUT HER DOWN TO SIZE TOGETHER !!
EH?
UM... HOW?
AW, I WOULDN'T WORRY TOO MUCH. HOW HARD COULD IT BE?
AFTER ALL, THIS IS URD WE'RE TALKING ABOUT-- THE ULTIMATE WALKING DISASTER AREA!
ER... TRUE ENOUGH.

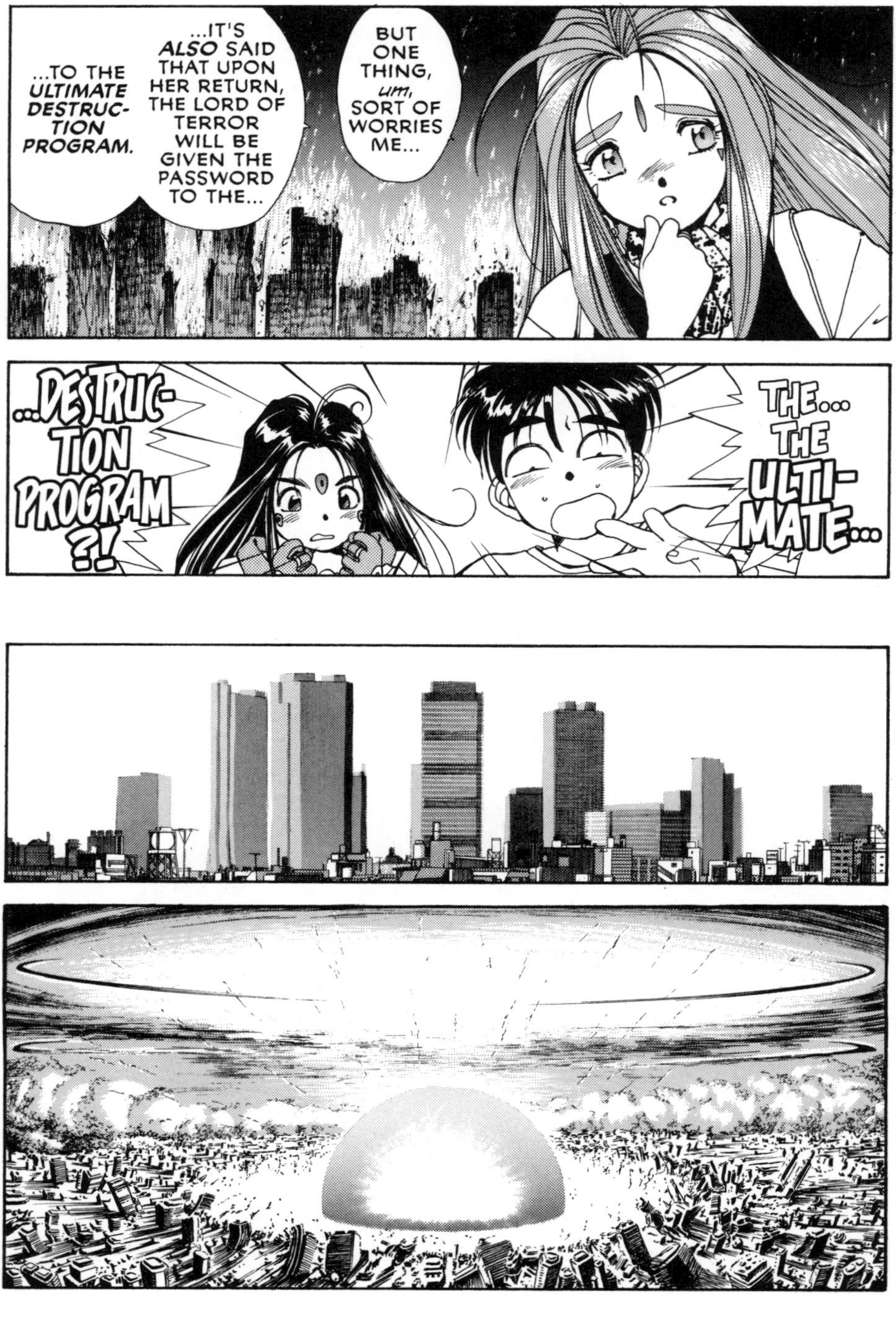
BUT ONE THING, *um*, SORT OF WORRIES ME...
...IT'S *ALSO* SAID THAT UPON HER RETURN, THE LORD OF TERROR WILL BE GIVEN THE PASSWORD TO THE...
...TO THE *ULTIMATE DESTRUCTION PROGRAM.*
THE... THE ULTIMATE...
...DESTRUCTION PROGRAM?!

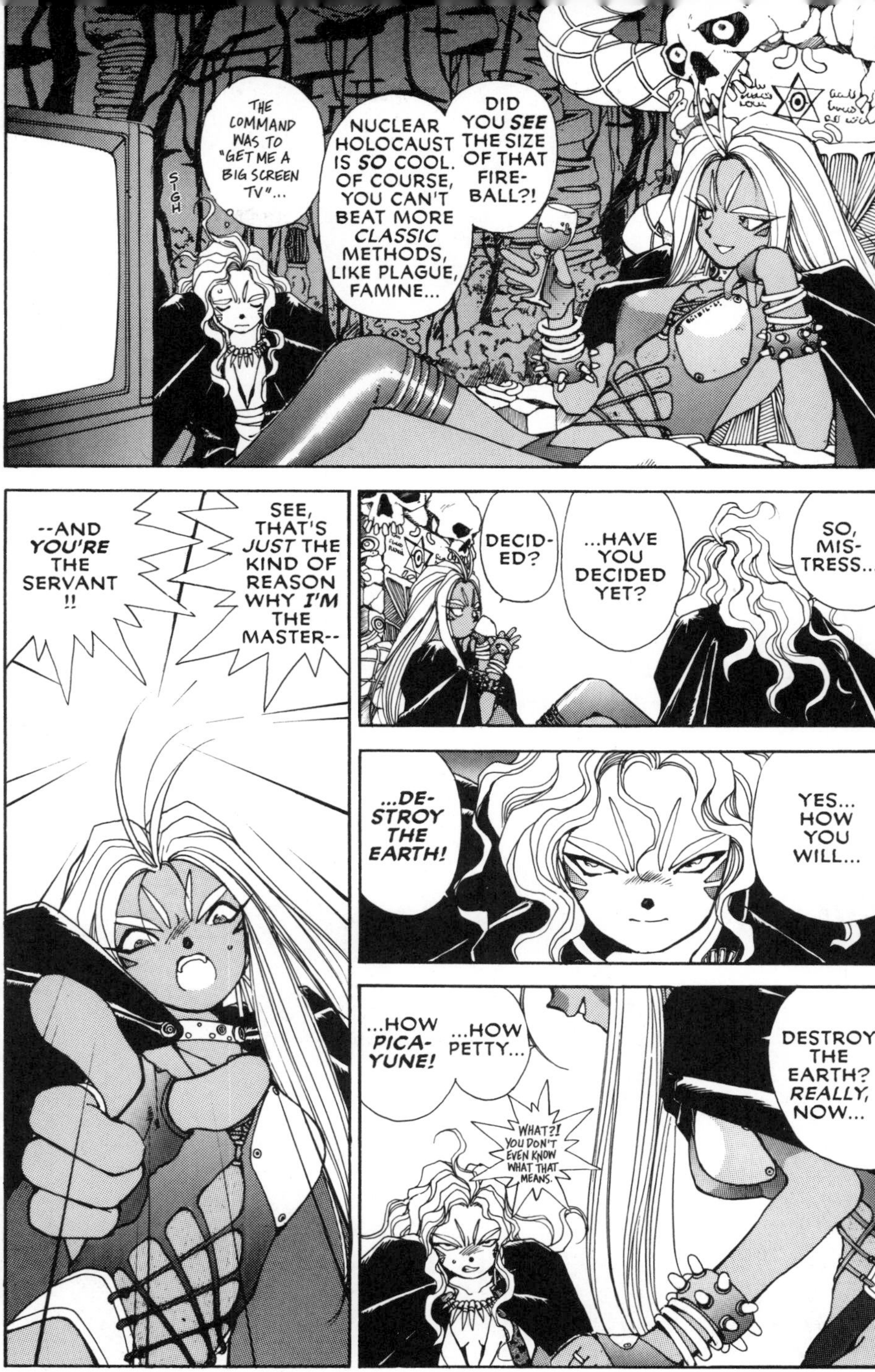
DID YOU SEE THE SIZE OF THAT FIRE-BALL?!
NUCLEAR HOLOCAUST IS SO COOL. OF COURSE, YOU CAN'T BEAT MORE CLASSIC METHODS, LIKE PLAGUE, FAMINE...
THE COMMAND WAS TO "GET ME A BIG SCREEN TV"...
SIGH
SO, MIS-TRESS...
...HAVE YOU DECIDED YET?
DECID-ED?
YES... HOW YOU WILL...
...DE-STROY THE EARTH!
DESTROY THE EARTH? REALLY, NOW...
...HOW PETTY...
...HOW PICA-YUNE!
WHAT?! YOU DON'T EVEN KNOW WHAT THAT MEANS.
SEE, THAT'S JUST THE KIND OF REASON WHY I'M THE MASTER--
--AND YOU'RE THE SERVANT !!

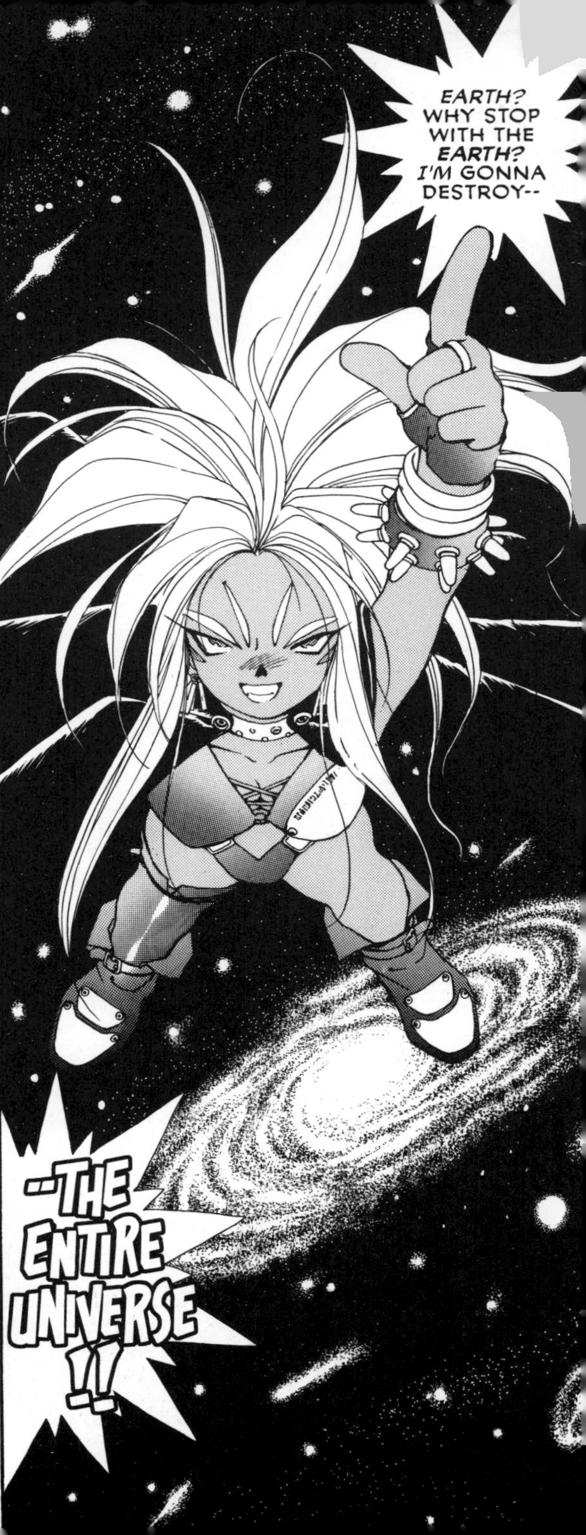
EARTH? WHY STOP WITH THE EARTH? I'M GONNA DESTROY--
--THE ENTIRE UNIVERSE!!

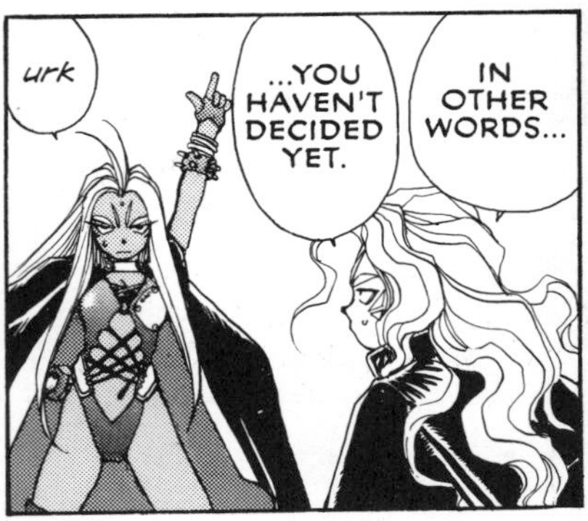
IN OTHER WORDS...
...YOU HAVEN'T DECIDED YET.
urk

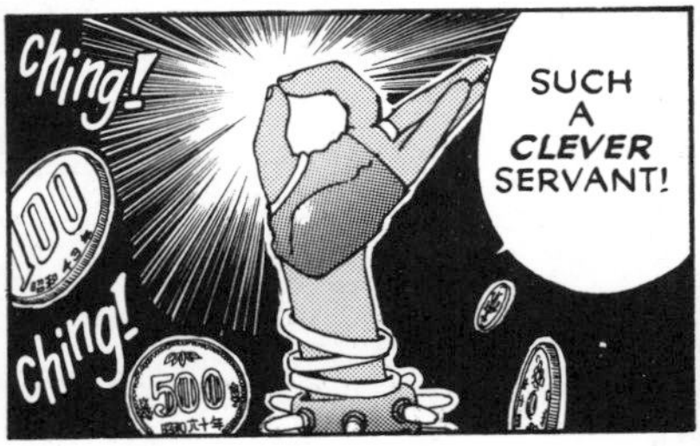
SUCH A CLEVER SERVANT!
ching!
ching!

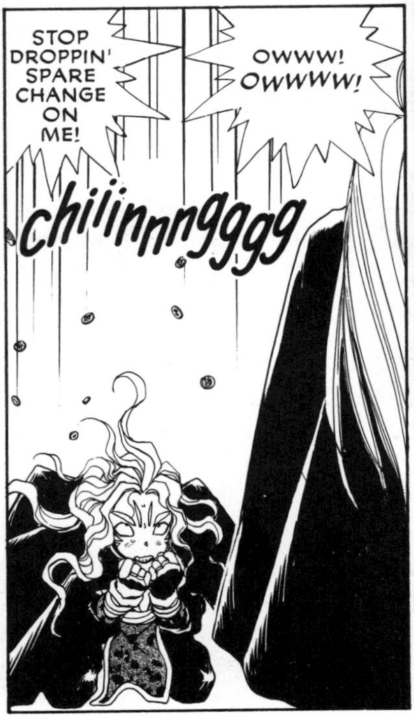
OWWW! OWWWW!
STOP DROPPIN' SPARE CHANGE ON ME!
chiiinnngggg

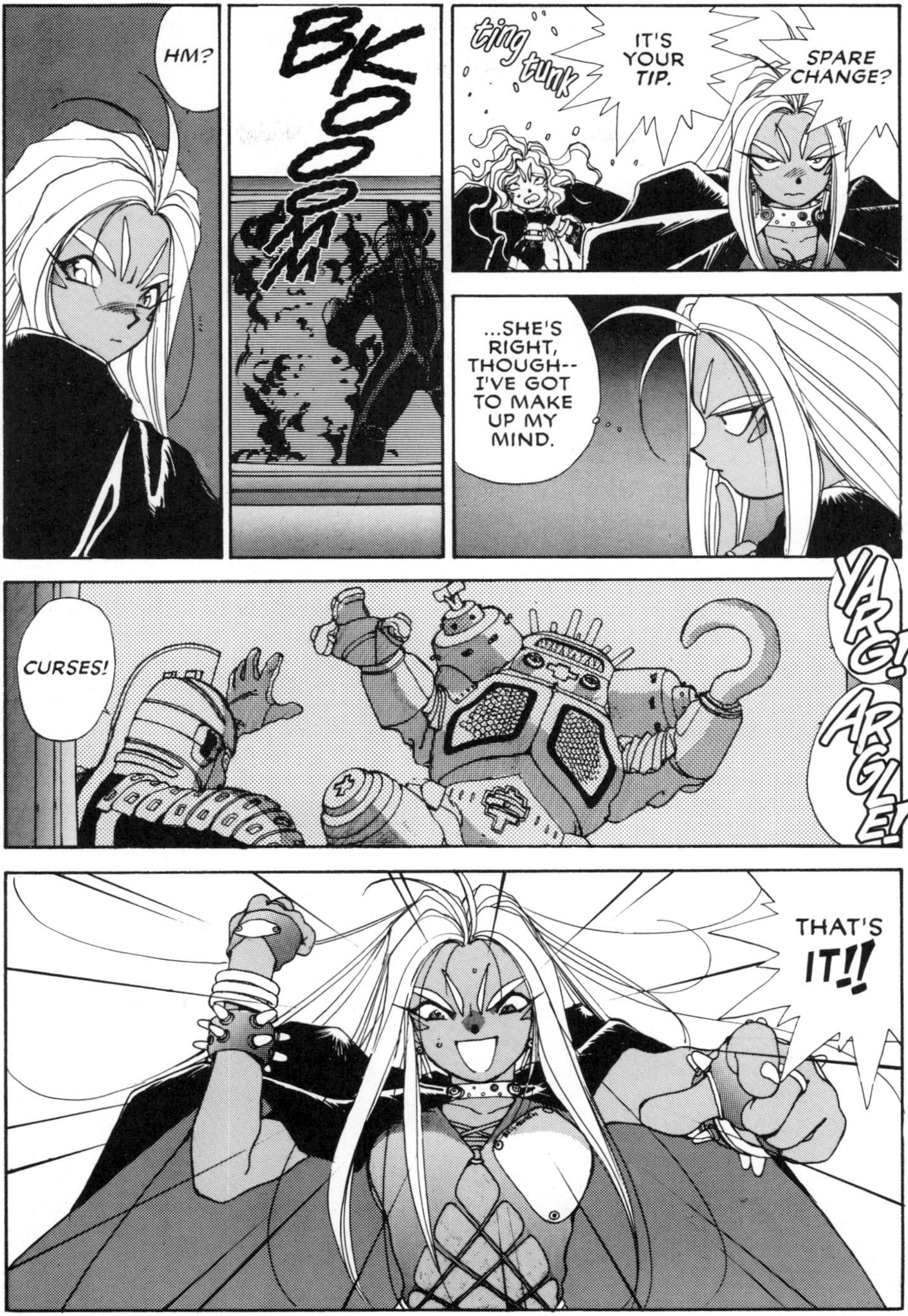
SPARE CHANGE?
IT'S YOUR TIP.
ting tunk
...SHE'S RIGHT, THOUGH-- I'VE GOT TO MAKE UP MY MIND.
BKOOOOM
HM?
YARG! ARGLE!
CURSES!
THAT'S IT!!

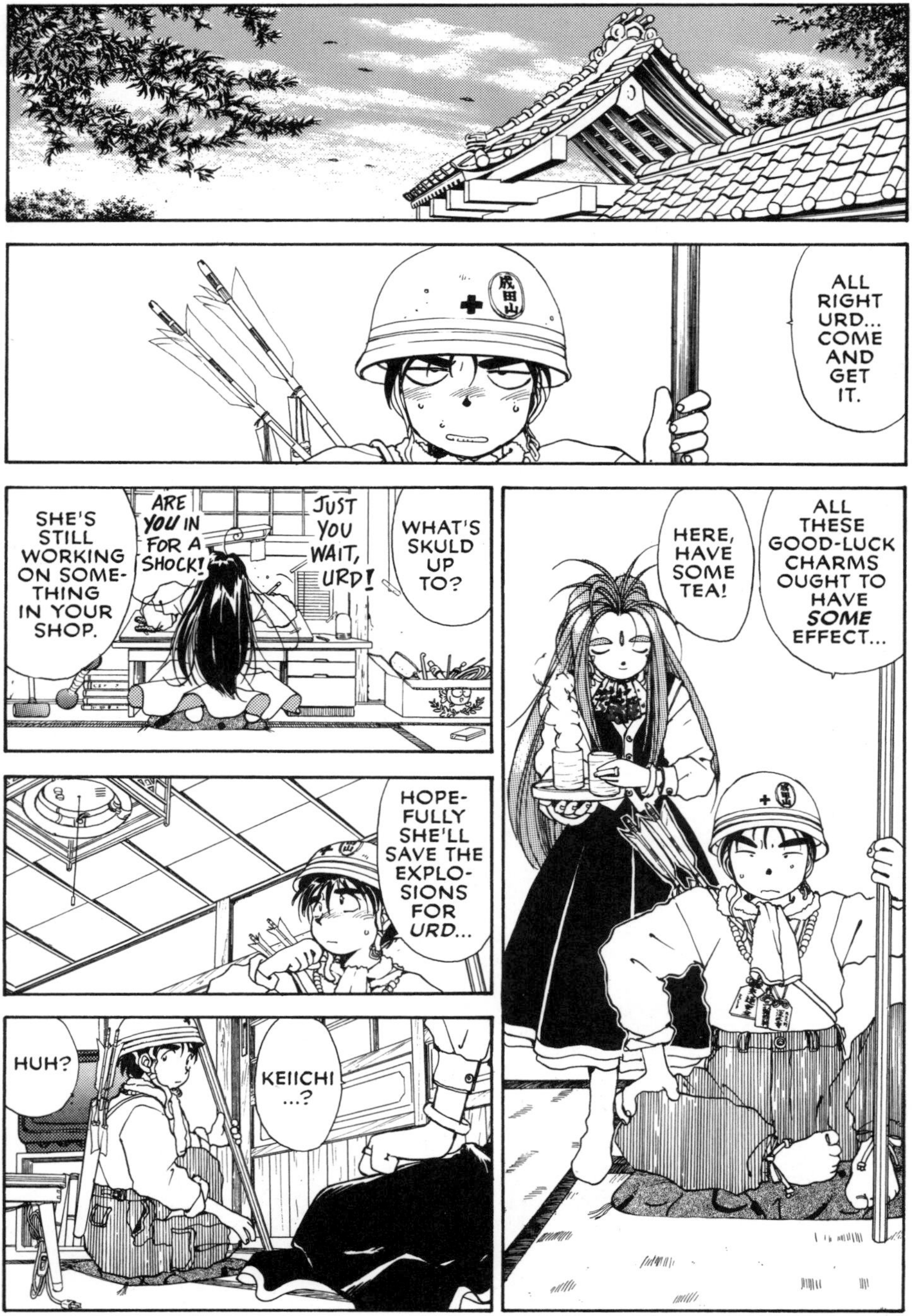
ALL RIGHT URD... COME AND GET IT.
ALL THESE GOOD-LUCK CHARMS OUGHT TO HAVE *SOME* EFFECT...
HERE, HAVE SOME TEA!
WHAT'S SKULD UP TO?
JUST YOU WAIT, URD!
ARE *YOU* IN FOR A SHOCK!
SHE'S STILL WORKING ON SOMETHING IN YOUR SHOP.
HOPEFULLY SHE'LL SAVE THE EXPLOSIONS FOR *URD*...
KEIICHI ...?
HUH?

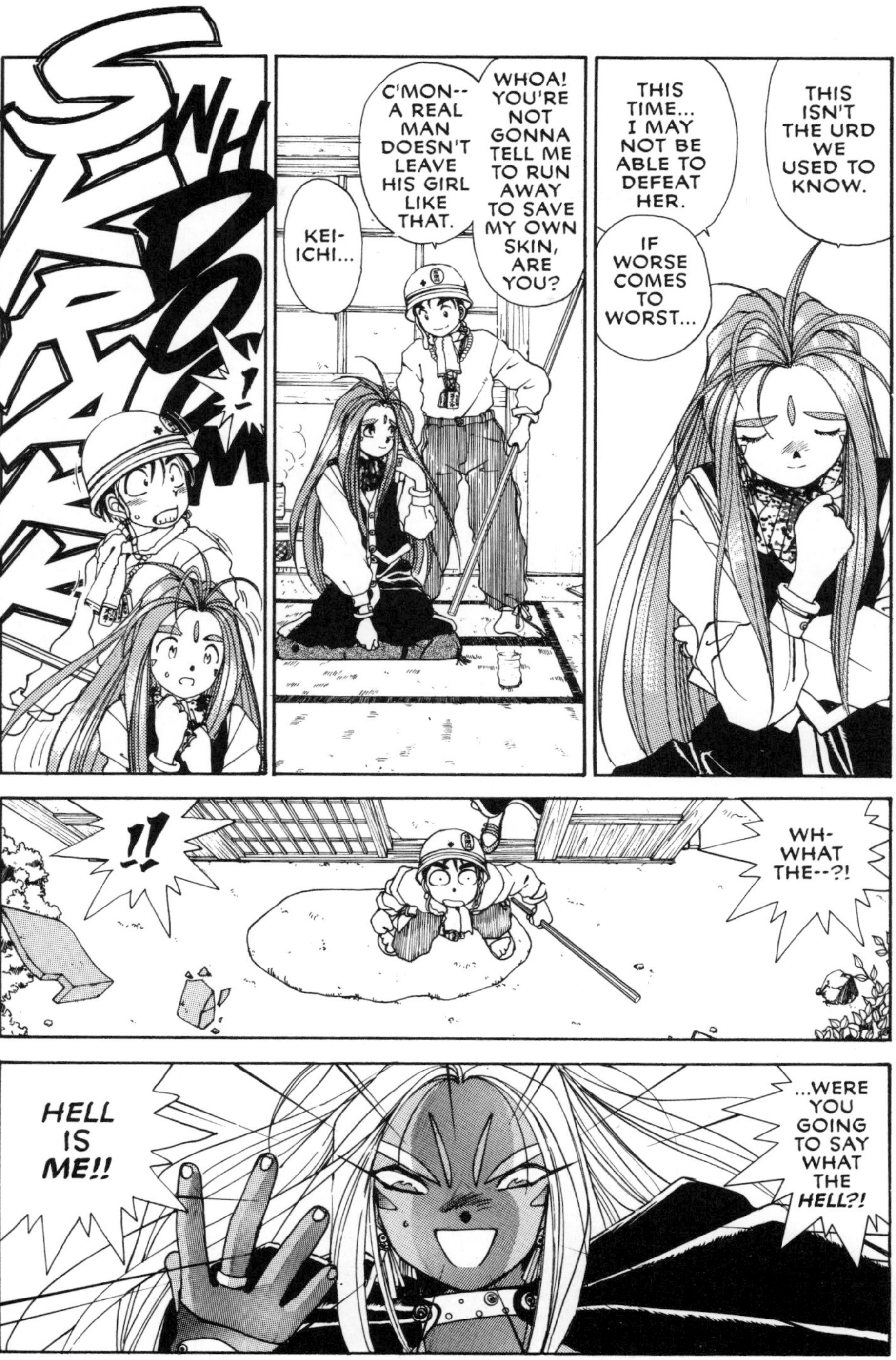
THIS ISN'T THE URD WE USED TO KNOW.
THIS TIME... I MAY NOT BE ABLE TO DEFEAT HER.
IF WORSE COMES TO WORST...
WHOA! YOU'RE NOT GONNA TELL ME TO RUN AWAY TO SAVE MY OWN SKIN, ARE YOU?
C'MON-- A REAL MAN DOESN'T LEAVE HIS GIRL LIKE THAT.
KEI-ICHI...
WH-WHAT THE--?!
!!
...WERE YOU GOING TO SAY WHAT THE HELL?!
HELL IS ME!!

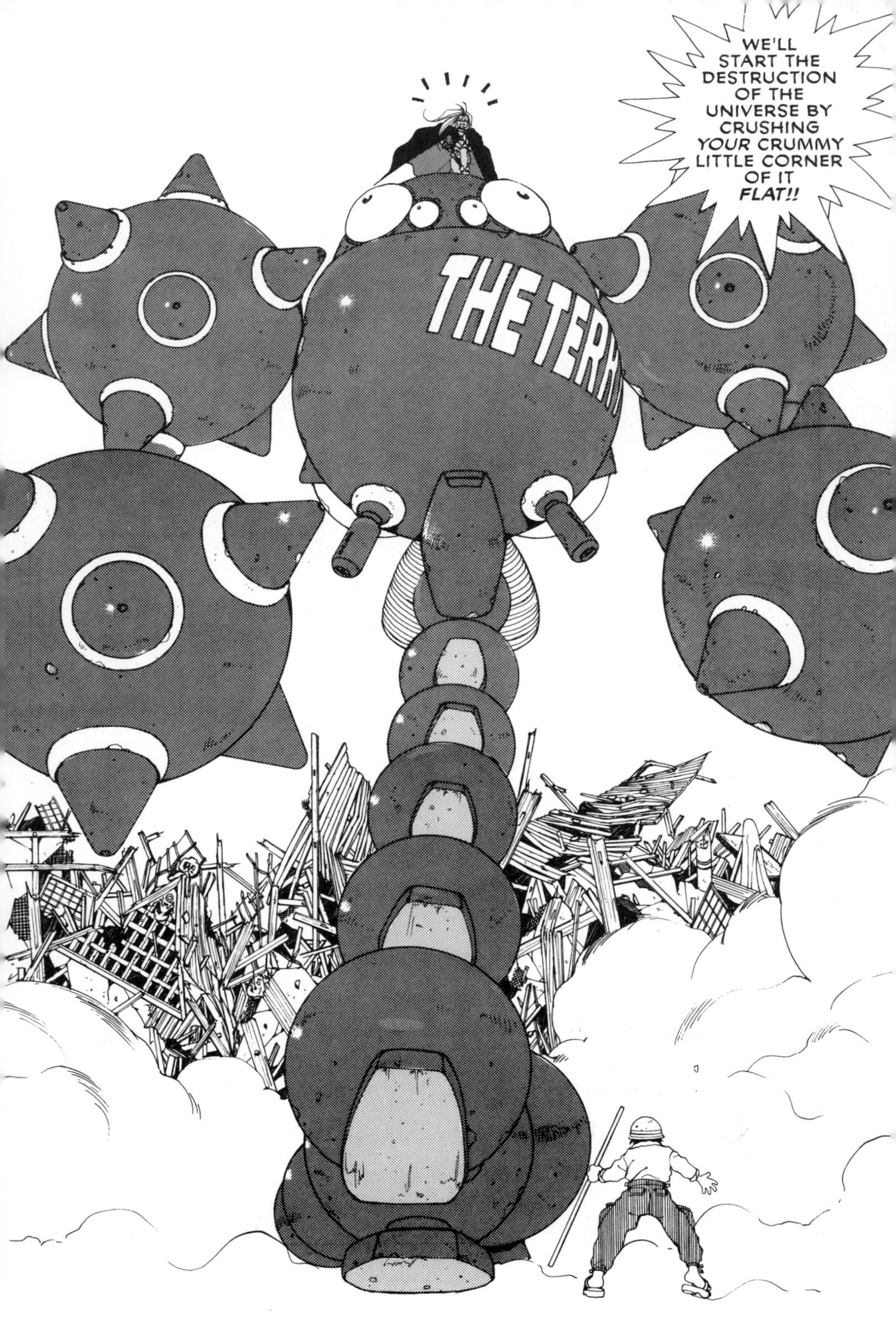
WE'LL START THE DESTRUCTION OF THE UNIVERSE BY CRUSHING *YOUR* CRUMMY LITTLE CORNER OF IT ***FLAT!!***
THE TERR

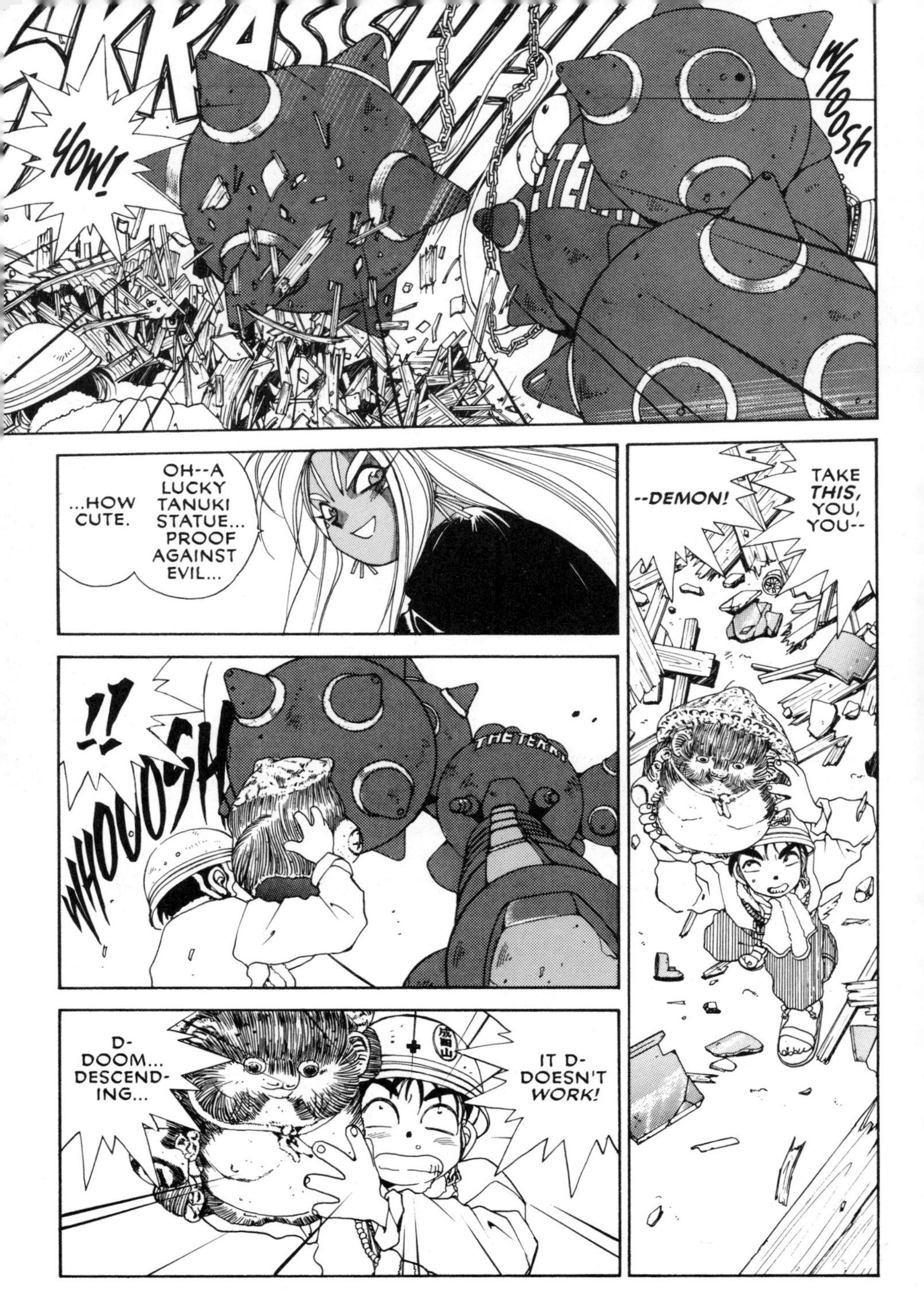
WHOOSH
KRASSSH
YOW!
TAKE *THIS,* YOU, YOU--
--*DEMON!*
OH--A LUCKY TANUKI STATUE... PROOF AGAINST EVIL...
...HOW CUTE.
!!
WHOOOSH
IT D-DOESN'T *WORK!*
D-DOOM... DESCEND-ING...

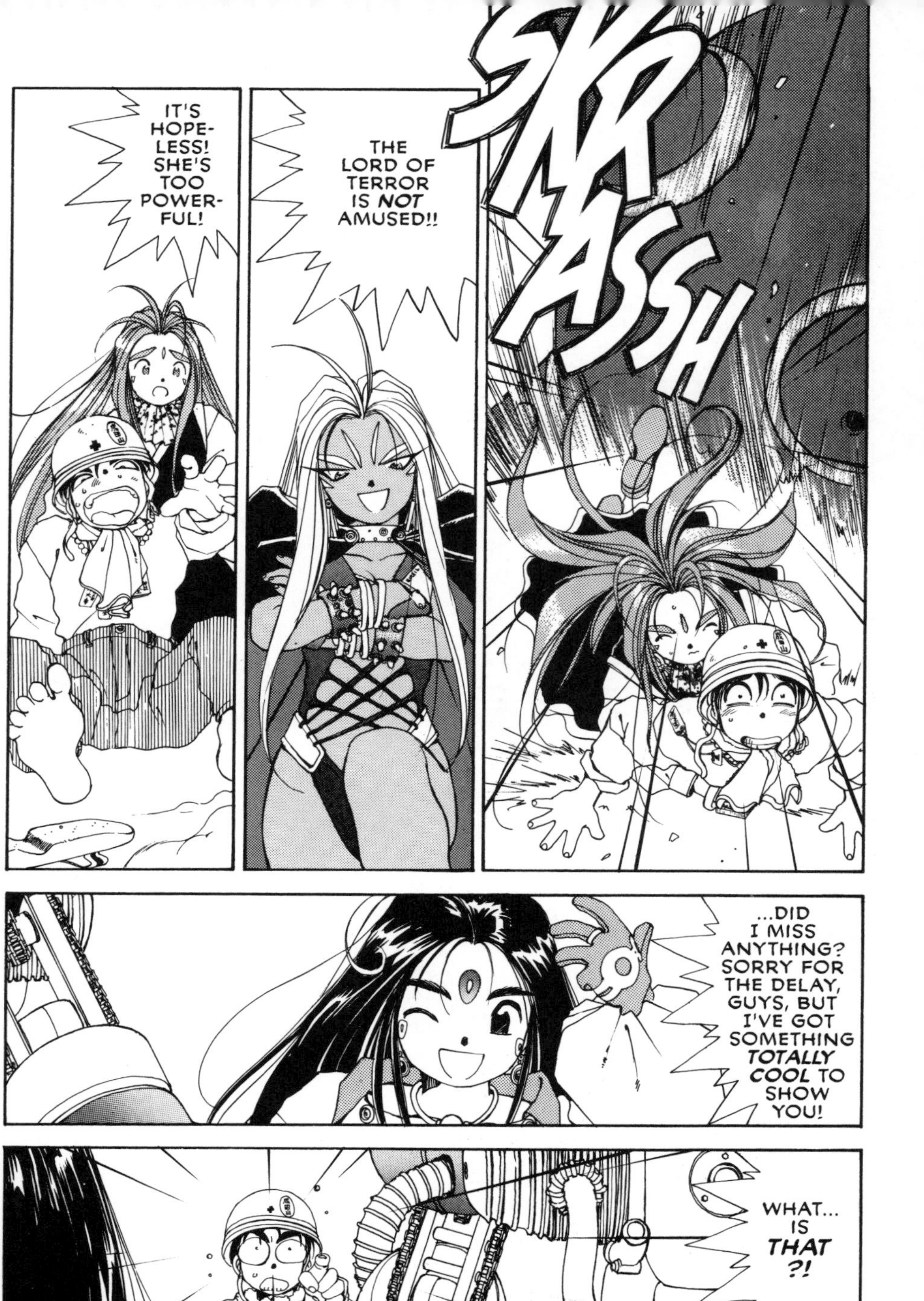
SKRASH
THE LORD OF TERROR IS *NOT* AMUSED!!
IT'S HOPE-LESS! SHE'S TOO POWER-FUL!
...DID I MISS ANYTHING? SORRY FOR THE DELAY, GUYS, BUT I'VE GOT SOMETHING ***TOTALLY COOL*** TO SHOW YOU!
WHAT... IS ***THAT*** ?!

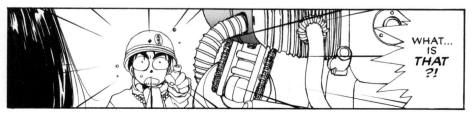

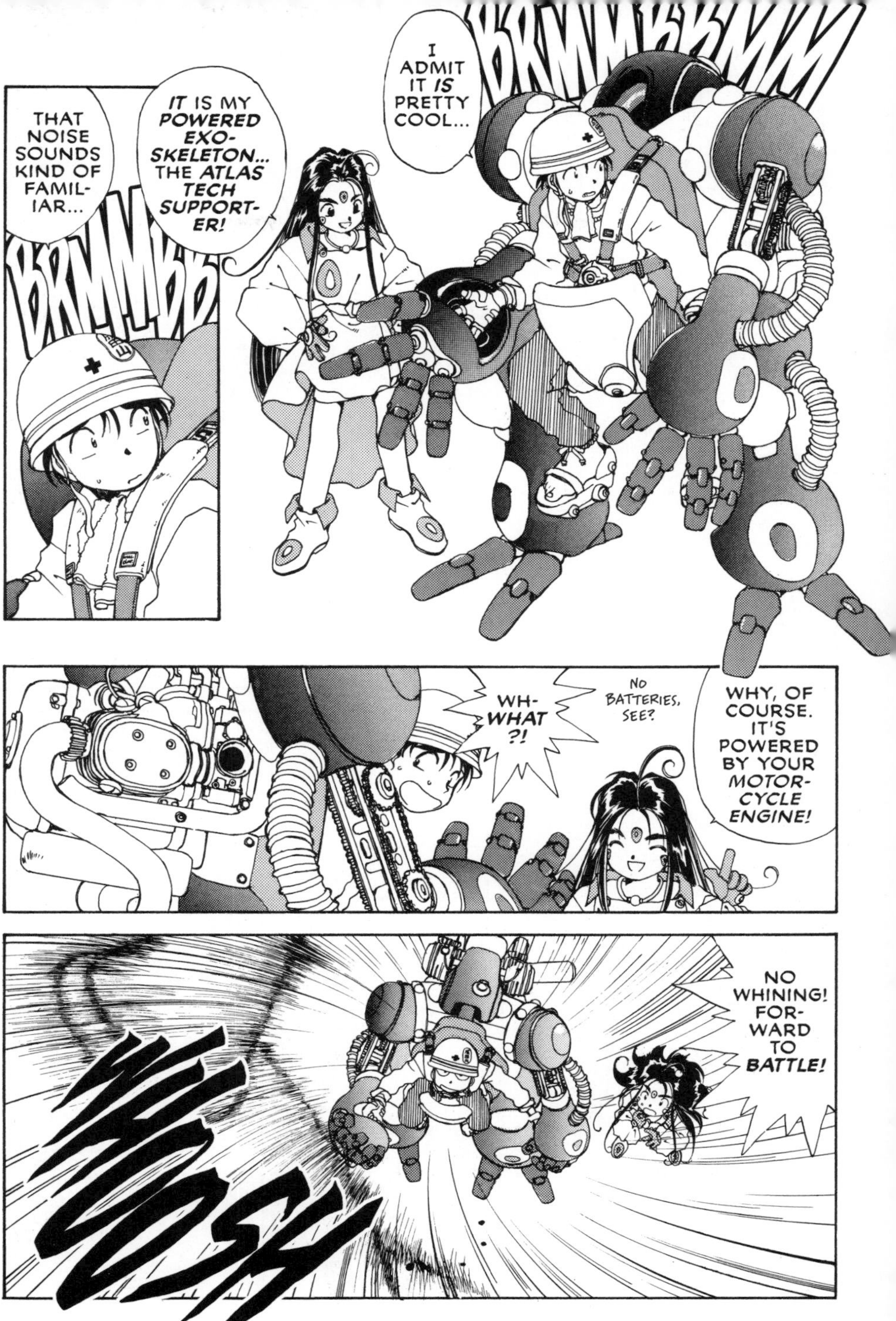
BRMMBMM
I ADMIT IT *IS* PRETTY COOL...
*IT* IS MY *POWERED EXO-SKELETON*... THE *ATLAS TECH SUPPORTER!*
THAT NOISE SOUNDS KIND OF FAMILIAR...
BRMMBB
WHY, OF COURSE. IT'S POWERED BY YOUR *MOTORCYCLE ENGINE!*
NO BATTERIES, SEE?
WH-*WHAT*?!
NO WHINING! FORWARD TO *BATTLE!*
WHOOSH

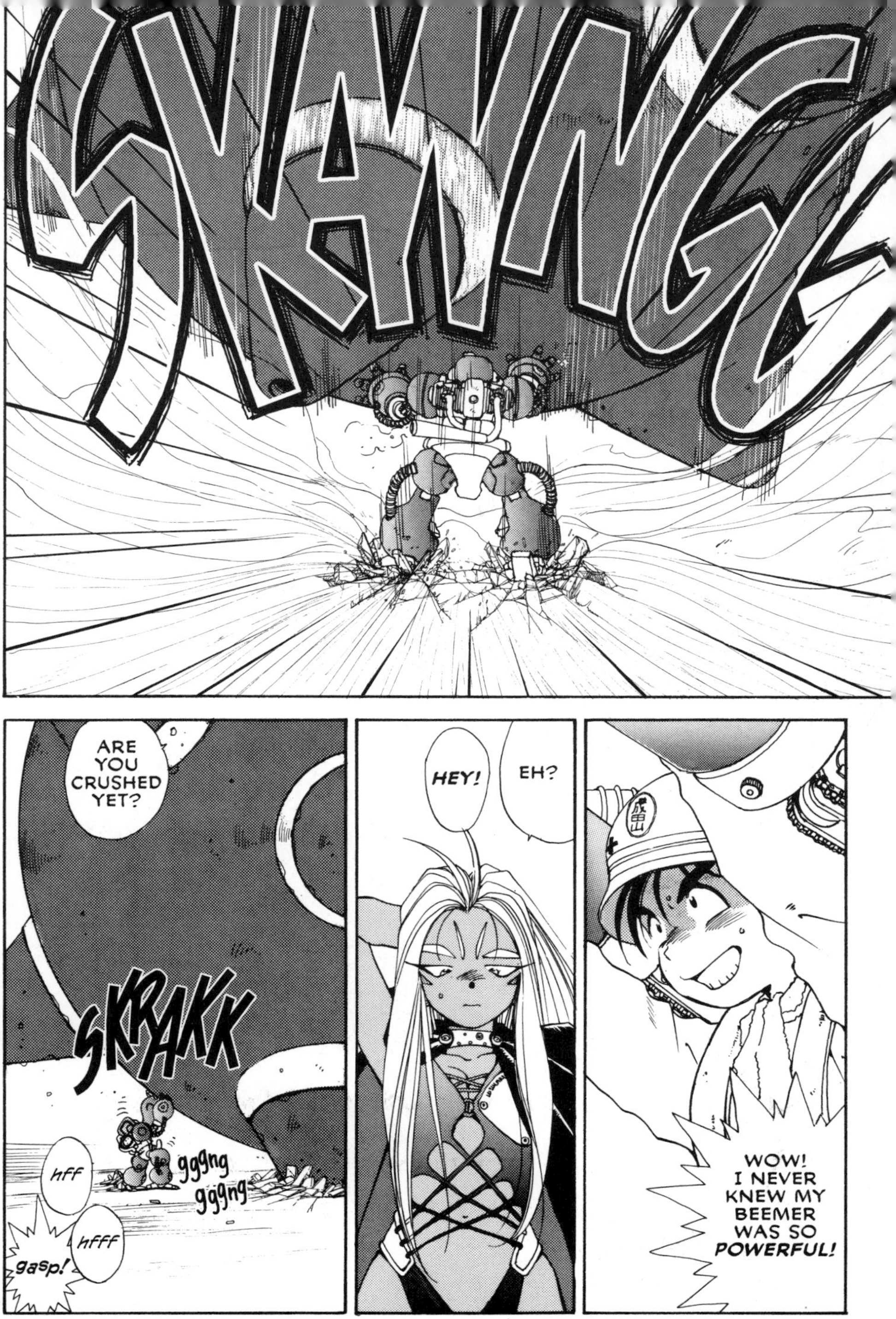
WOW! I NEVER KNEW MY BEEMER WAS SO POWERFUL!
EH?
HEY!
ARE YOU CRUSHED YET?
SKRAKK
gggng
gggng
hff
hfff
gasp!

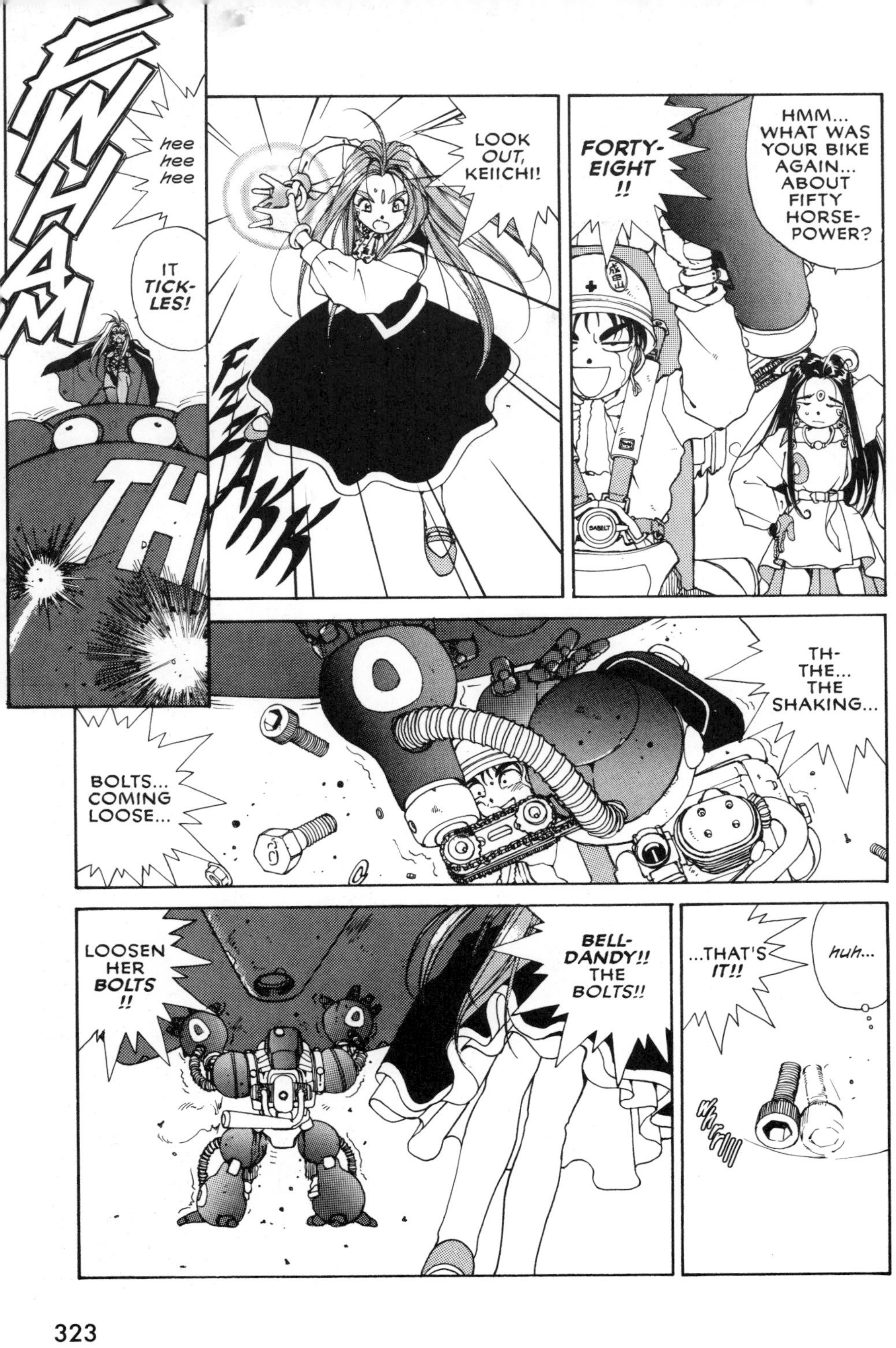
HMM... WHAT WAS YOUR BIKE AGAIN... ABOUT FIFTY HORSE-POWER?
FORTY-EIGHT !!
LOOK OUT, KEIICHI!
FWHAM
hee hee hee
IT TICKLES!
TH
TH-THE... THE SHAKING...
BOLTS... COMING LOOSE...
huh...
...THAT'S IT!!
BELL-DANDY!! THE BOLTS!!
LOOSEN HER BOLTS !!

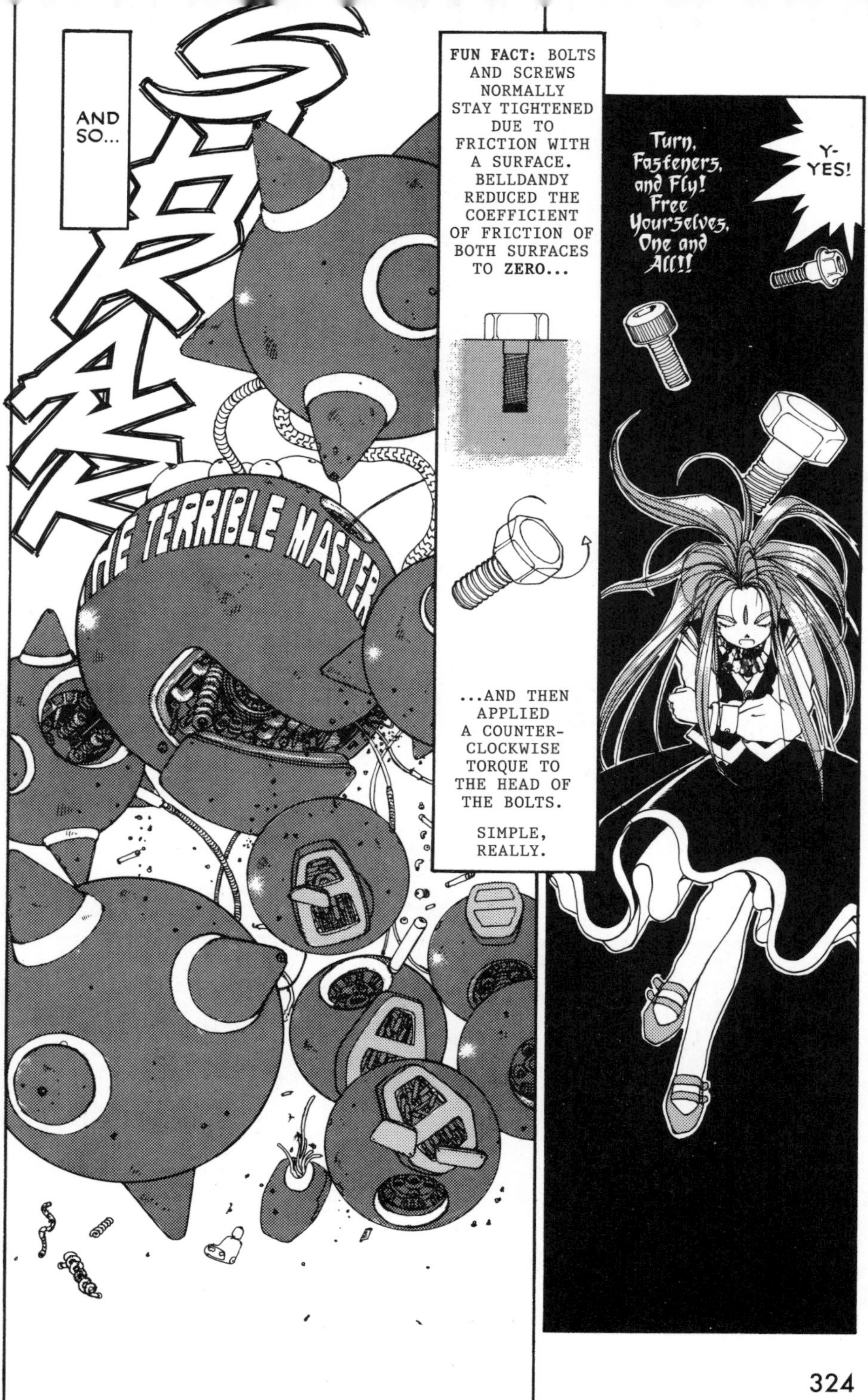
Turn, Fasteners, and Fly! Free Yourselves, One and All!!
Y-YES!
FUN FACT: BOLTS AND SCREWS NORMALLY STAY TIGHTENED DUE TO FRICTION WITH A SURFACE. BELLDANDY REDUCED THE COEFFICIENT OF FRICTION OF BOTH SURFACES TO ZERO...
...AND THEN APPLIED A COUNTER-CLOCKWISE TORQUE TO THE HEAD OF THE BOLTS.
SIMPLE, REALLY.
AND SO...
THE TERRIBLE MASTER

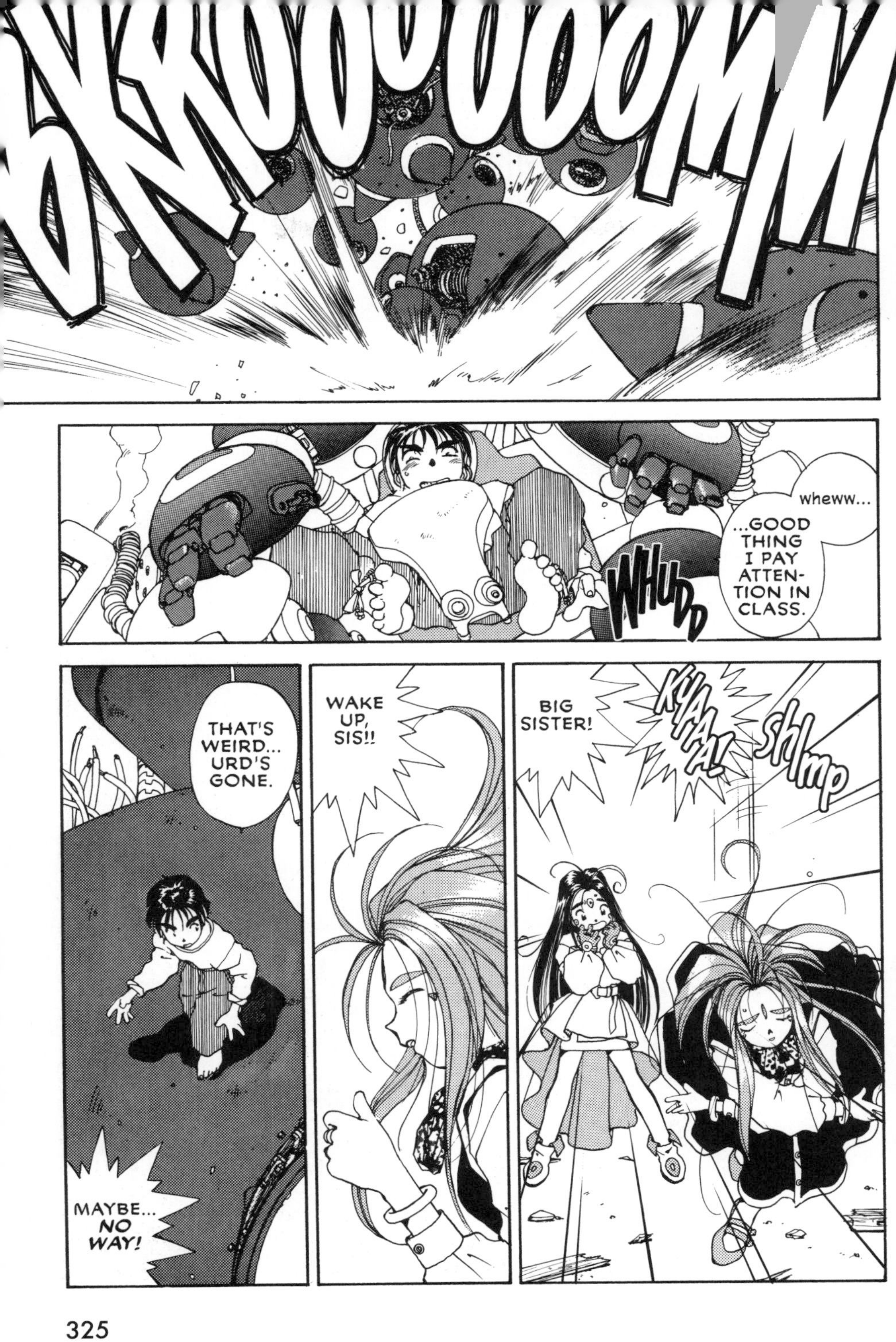

WHUDD
wheww...
...GOOD THING I PAY ATTEN-TION IN CLASS.
KYAAA!
shlmp
BIG SISTER!
WAKE UP, SIS!!
THAT'S WEIRD... URD'S GONE.
MAYBE... NO WAY!

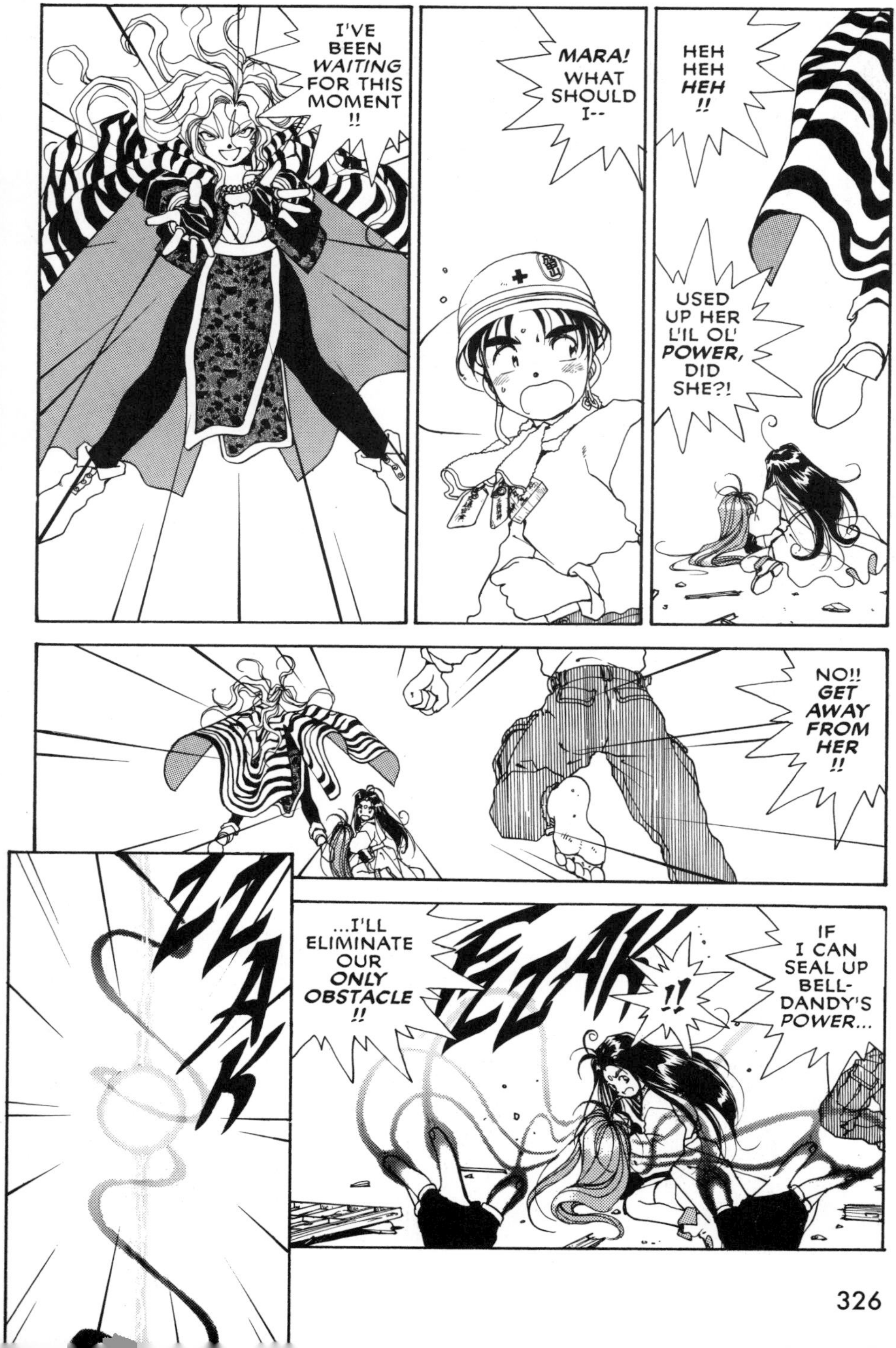
HEH HEH HEH !!
USED UP HER L'IL OL' POWER, DID SHE?!
MARA! WHAT SHOULD I--
I'VE BEEN WAITING FOR THIS MOMENT !!
NO!! GET AWAY FROM HER !!
IF I CAN SEAL UP BELL-DANDY'S POWER...
ZZAK
!!
...I'LL ELIMINATE OUR ONLY OBSTACLE !!
ZZAK

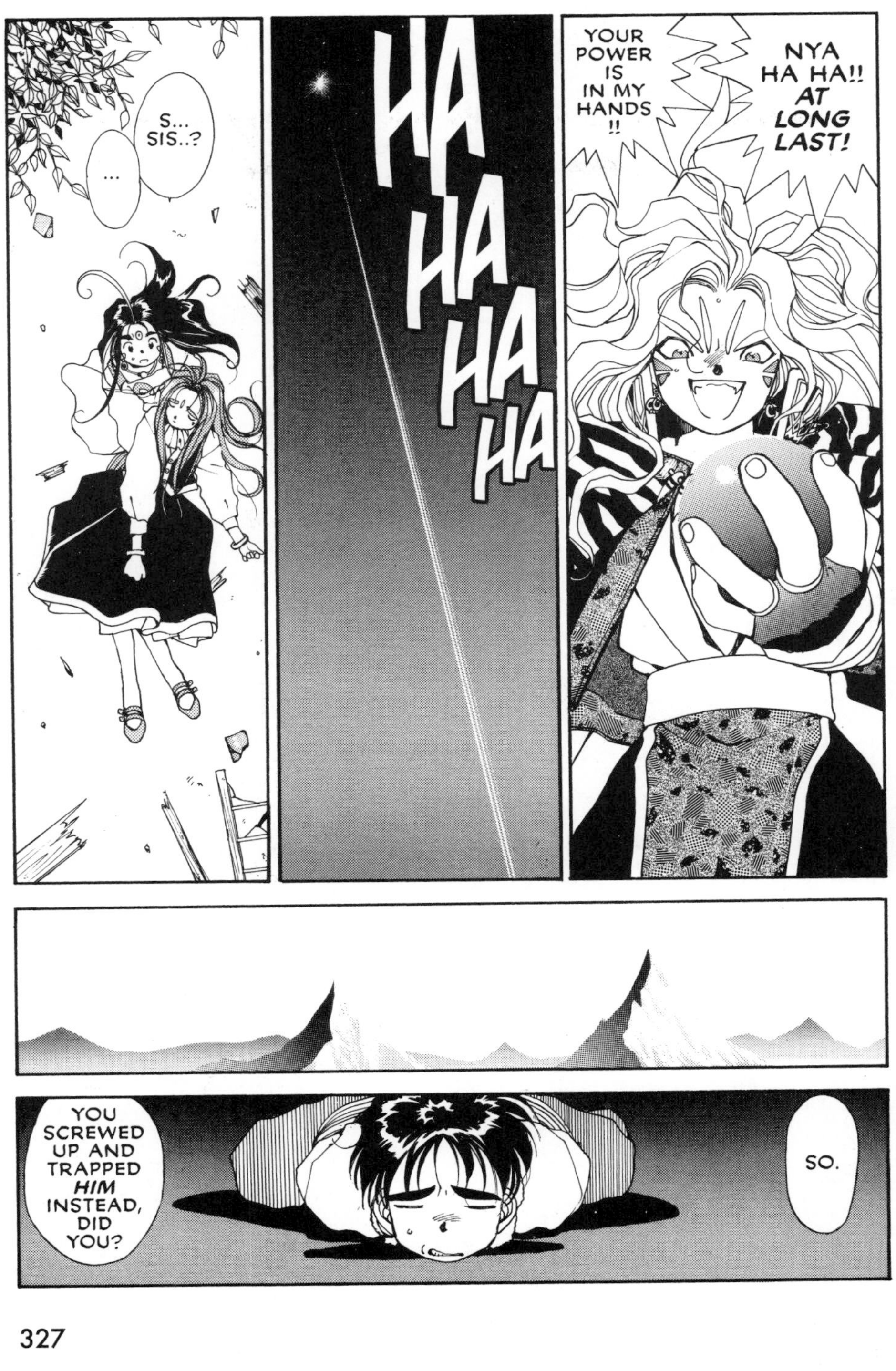
NYA HA HA!! AT LONG LAST!
YOUR POWER IS IN MY HANDS !!
HA HA HA HA HA
S... SIS..?
...
SO.
YOU SCREWED UP AND TRAPPED HIM INSTEAD, DID YOU?

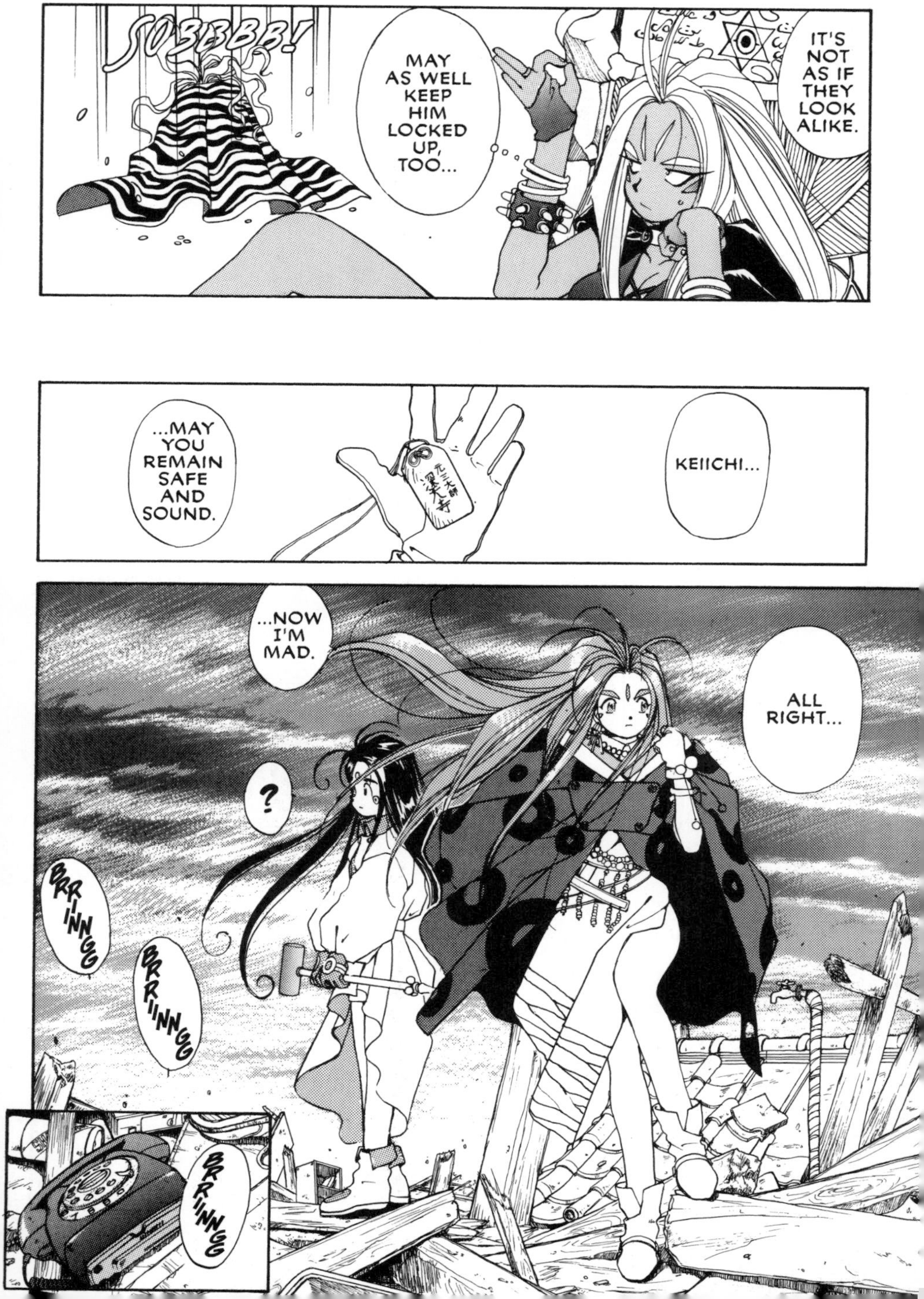
IT'S NOT AS IF THEY LOOK ALIKE.
MAY AS WELL KEEP HIM LOCKED UP, TOO...
SOBBBB!
KEIICHI...
...MAY YOU REMAIN SAFE AND SOUND.
ALL RIGHT...
...NOW I'M MAD.
?
BRRIINNGG
BRRIINNGG
BRRIINNGG

CHAPTER 36

# The Ultimate Destruction Program

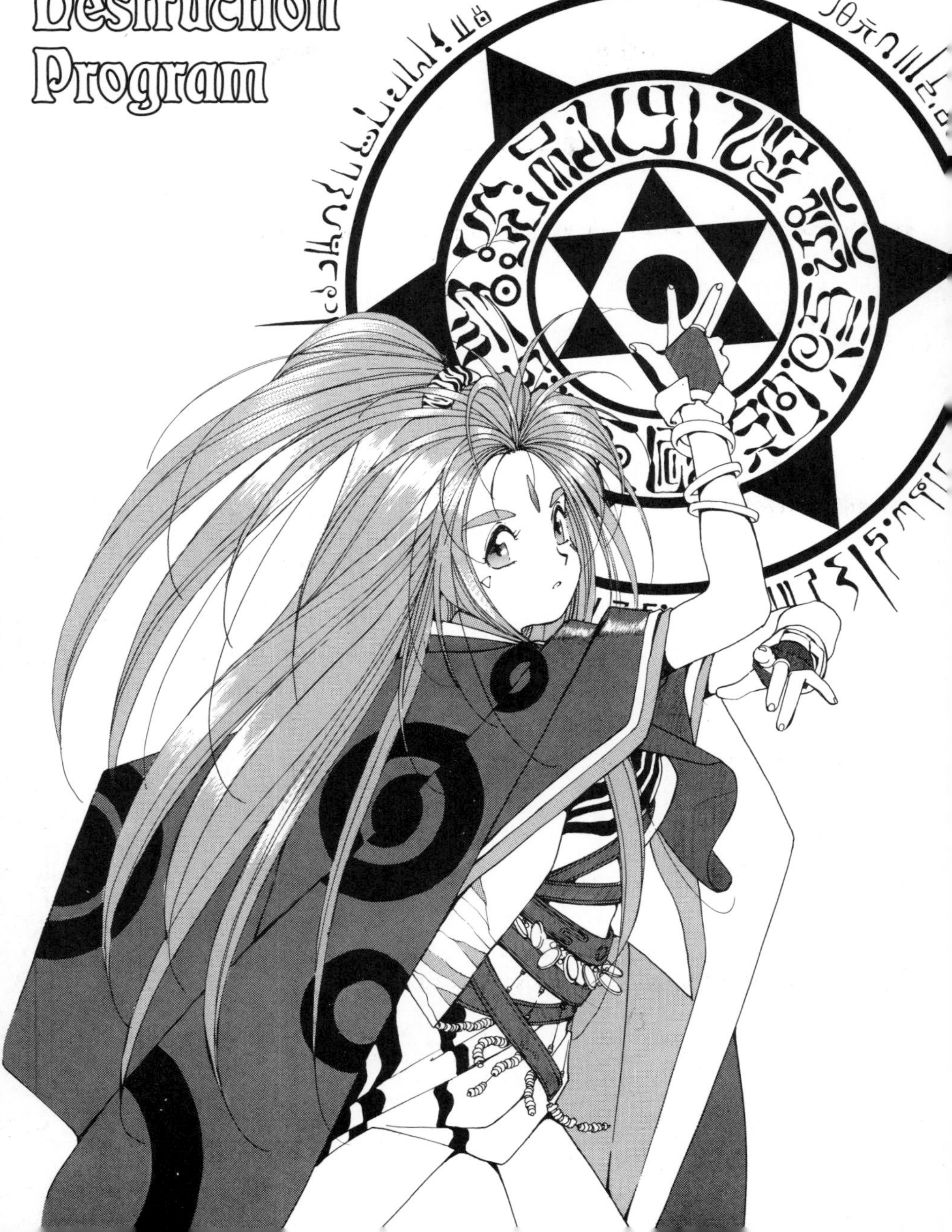

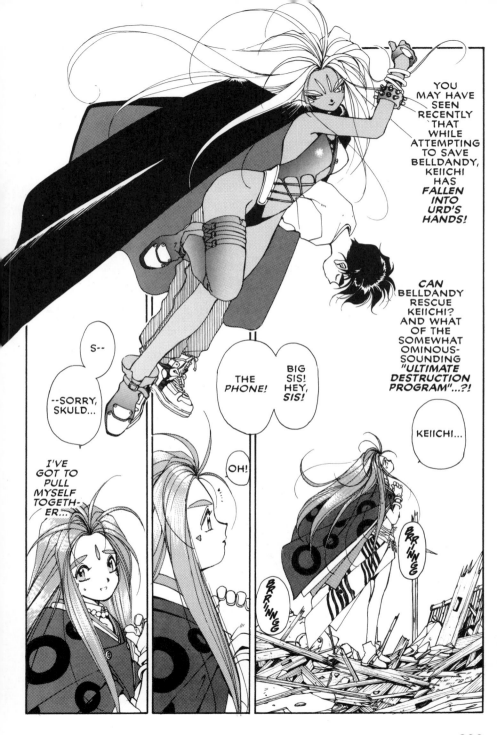

YOU MAY HAVE SEEN RECENTLY THAT WHILE ATTEMPTING TO SAVE BELLDANDY, KEIICHI HAS *FALLEN INTO URD'S HANDS!*

*CAN BELLDANDY RESCUE KEIICHI? AND WHAT OF THE SOMEWHAT OMINOUS-SOUNDING "ULTIMATE DESTRUCTION PROGRAM"...?!*

S--

--SORRY, SKULD...

THE *PHONE!*

BIG SIS! HEY, *SIS!*

KEIICHI...

*I'VE GOT TO PULL MYSELF TOGETH- ER...*

OH!

BRRIINNGG

BRRIINNGG

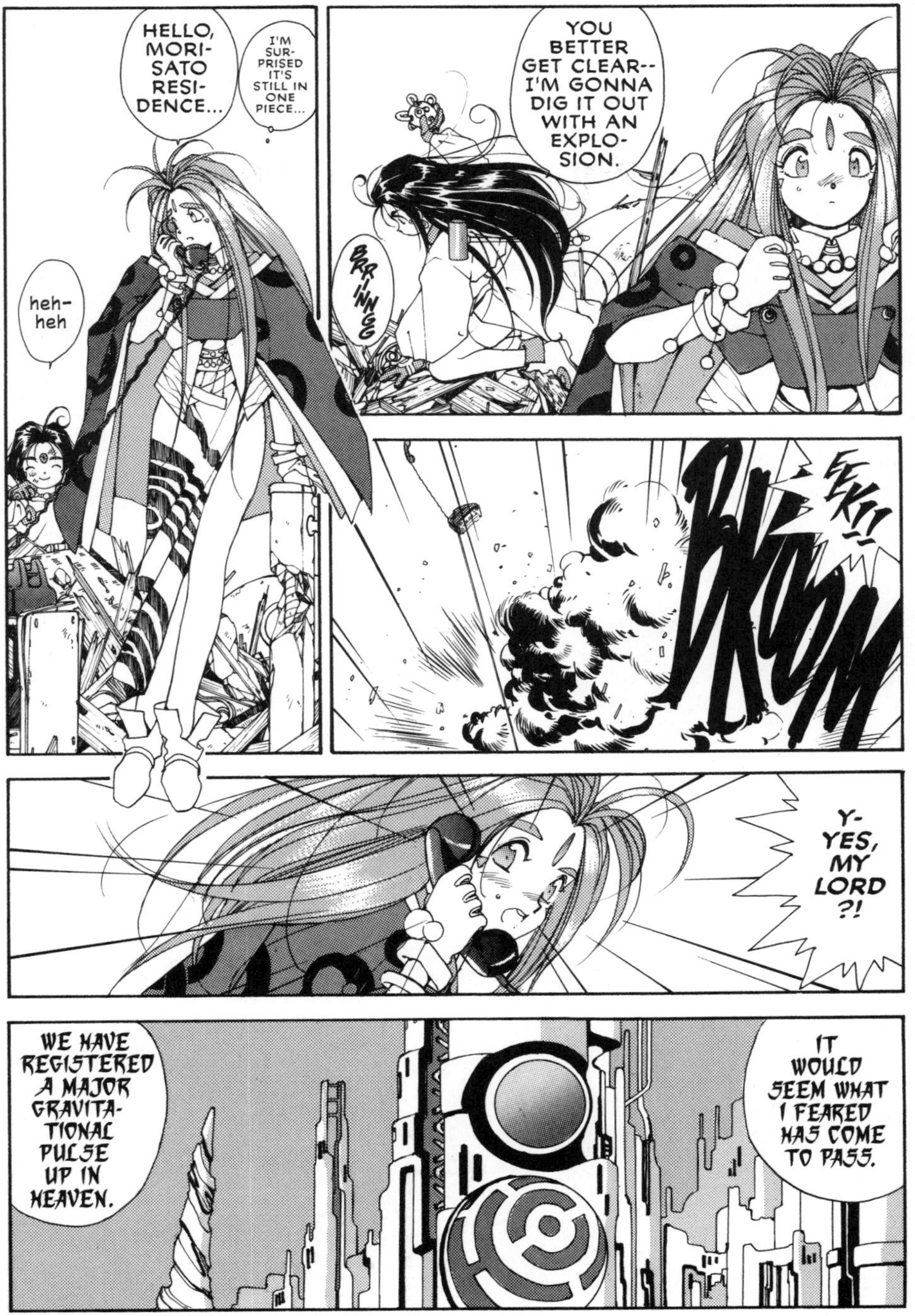

YOU BETTER GET CLEAR-- I'M GONNA DIG IT OUT WITH AN EXPLOSION.
BRRIINNGG
EEK!!
BKOOM
I'M SURPRISED IT'S STILL IN ONE PIECE...
HELLO, MORISATO RESIDENCE...
heh-heh
Y-YES, MY LORD?!
IT WOULD SEEM WHAT I FEARED HAS COME TO PASS.
WE HAVE REGISTERED A MAJOR GRAVITATIONAL PULSE UP IN HEAVEN.

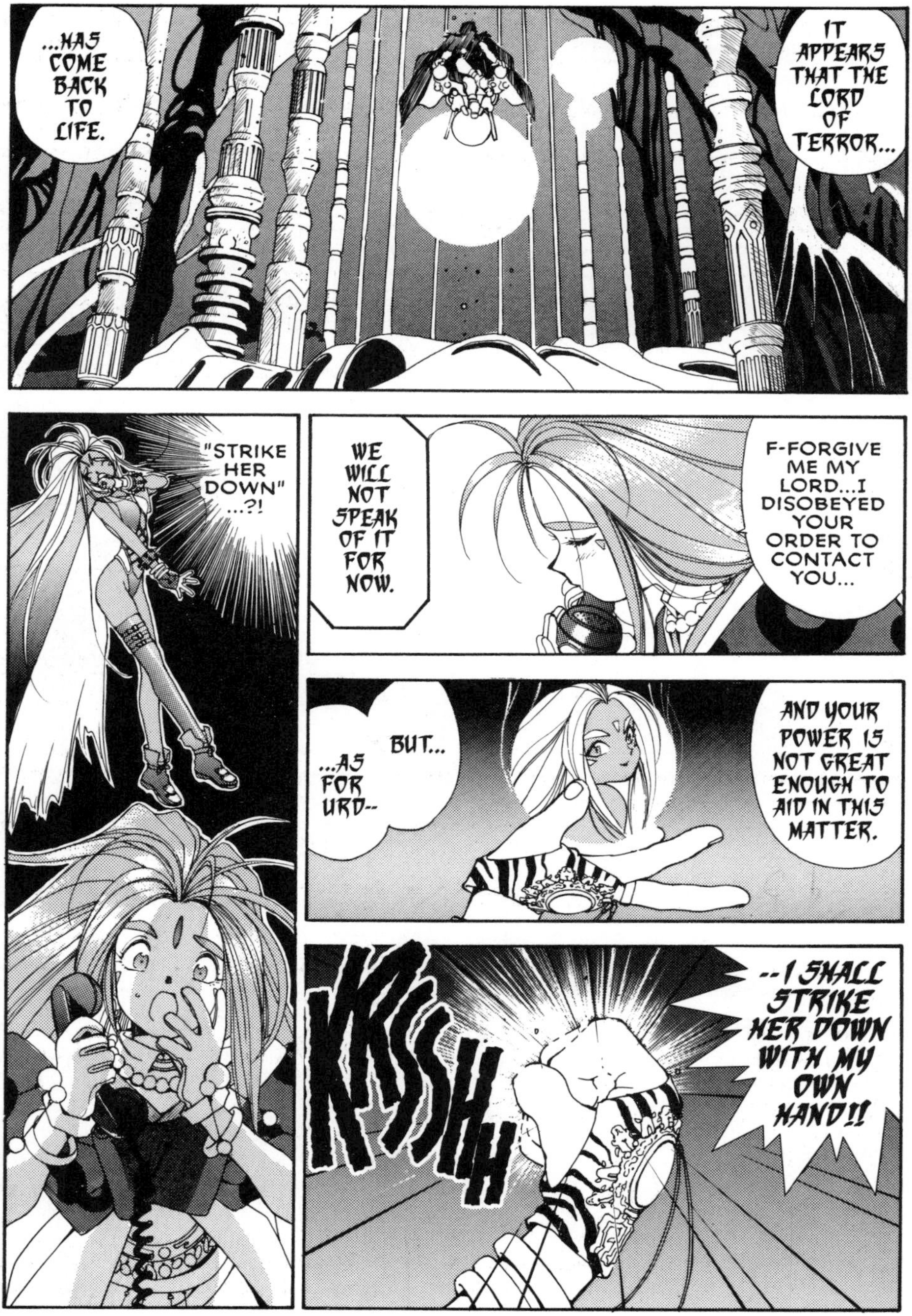
IT APPEARS THAT THE LORD OF TERROR...
...HAS COME BACK TO LIFE.
F-FORGIVE ME MY LORD...I DISOBEYED YOUR ORDER TO CONTACT YOU...
WE WILL NOT SPEAK OF IT FOR NOW.
AND YOUR POWER IS NOT GREAT ENOUGH TO AID IN THIS MATTER.
BUT... ...AS FOR URD--
--I SHALL STRIKE HER DOWN WITH MY OWN HAND!!
KASHHH
"STRIKE HER DOWN" ...?!

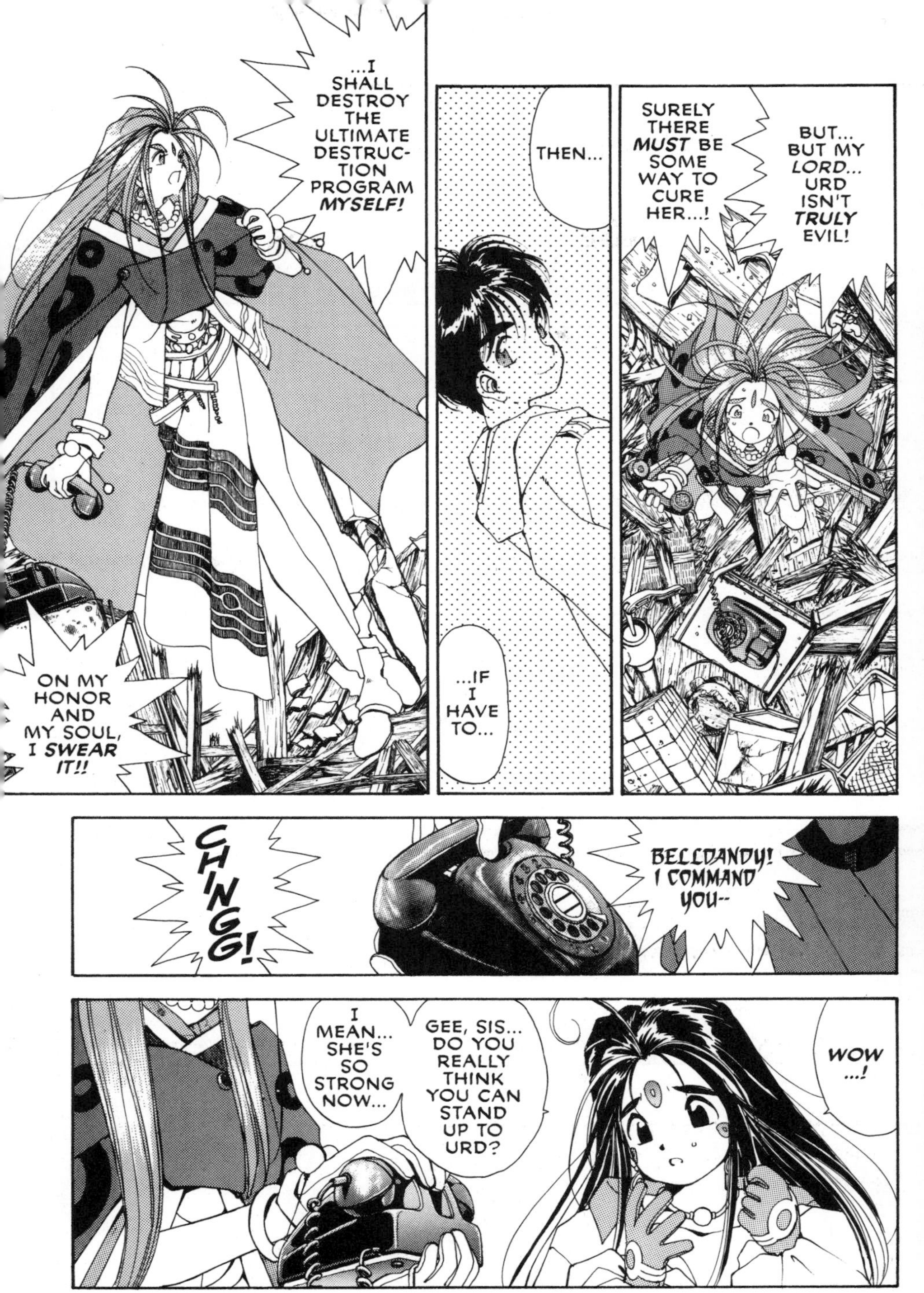
BUT... BUT MY *LORD*... URD ISN'T *TRULY* EVIL!
SURELY THERE *MUST* BE SOME WAY TO CURE HER...!
THEN...
...IF I HAVE TO...
...I SHALL DESTROY THE ULTIMATE DESTRUCTION PROGRAM *MYSELF!*
ON MY HONOR AND MY SOUL, I *SWEAR IT!!*
BELLDANDY! I COMMAND YOU--
CHINGG!
WOW ...!
GEE, SIS... DO YOU REALLY THINK YOU CAN STAND UP TO URD?
I MEAN... SHE'S SO STRONG NOW...

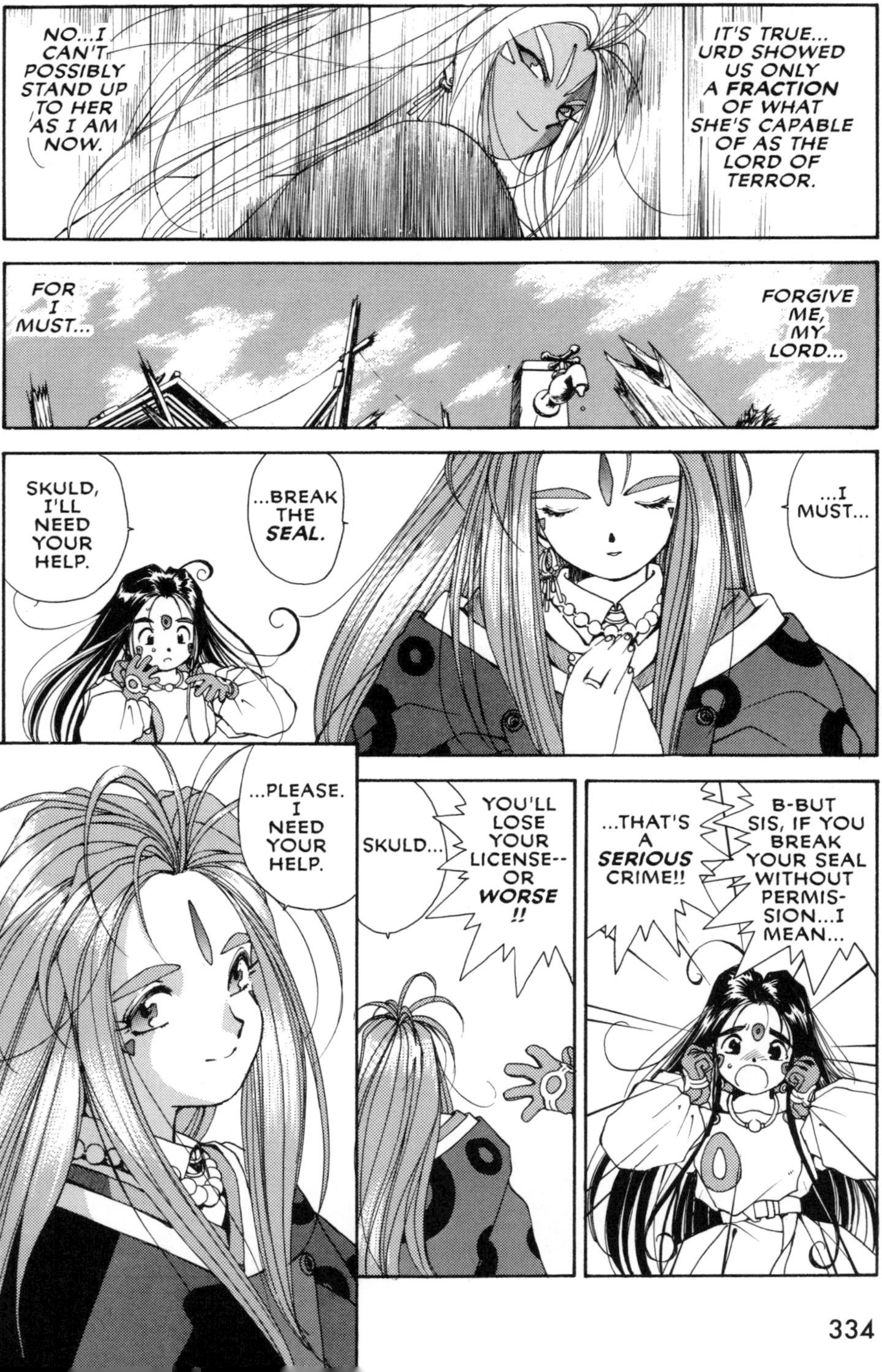
IT'S TRUE... URD SHOWED US ONLY A FRACTION OF WHAT SHE'S CAPABLE OF AS THE LORD OF TERROR.
NO...I CAN'T POSSIBLY STAND UP TO HER AS I AM NOW.
FORGIVE ME, MY LORD...
FOR I MUST...
...I MUST...
...BREAK THE SEAL.
SKULD, I'LL NEED YOUR HELP.
B-BUT SIS, IF YOU BREAK YOUR SEAL WITHOUT PERMISSION...I MEAN...
...THAT'S A SERIOUS CRIME!!
YOU'LL LOSE YOUR LICENSE--OR WORSE!!
SKULD...
...PLEASE. I NEED YOUR HELP.

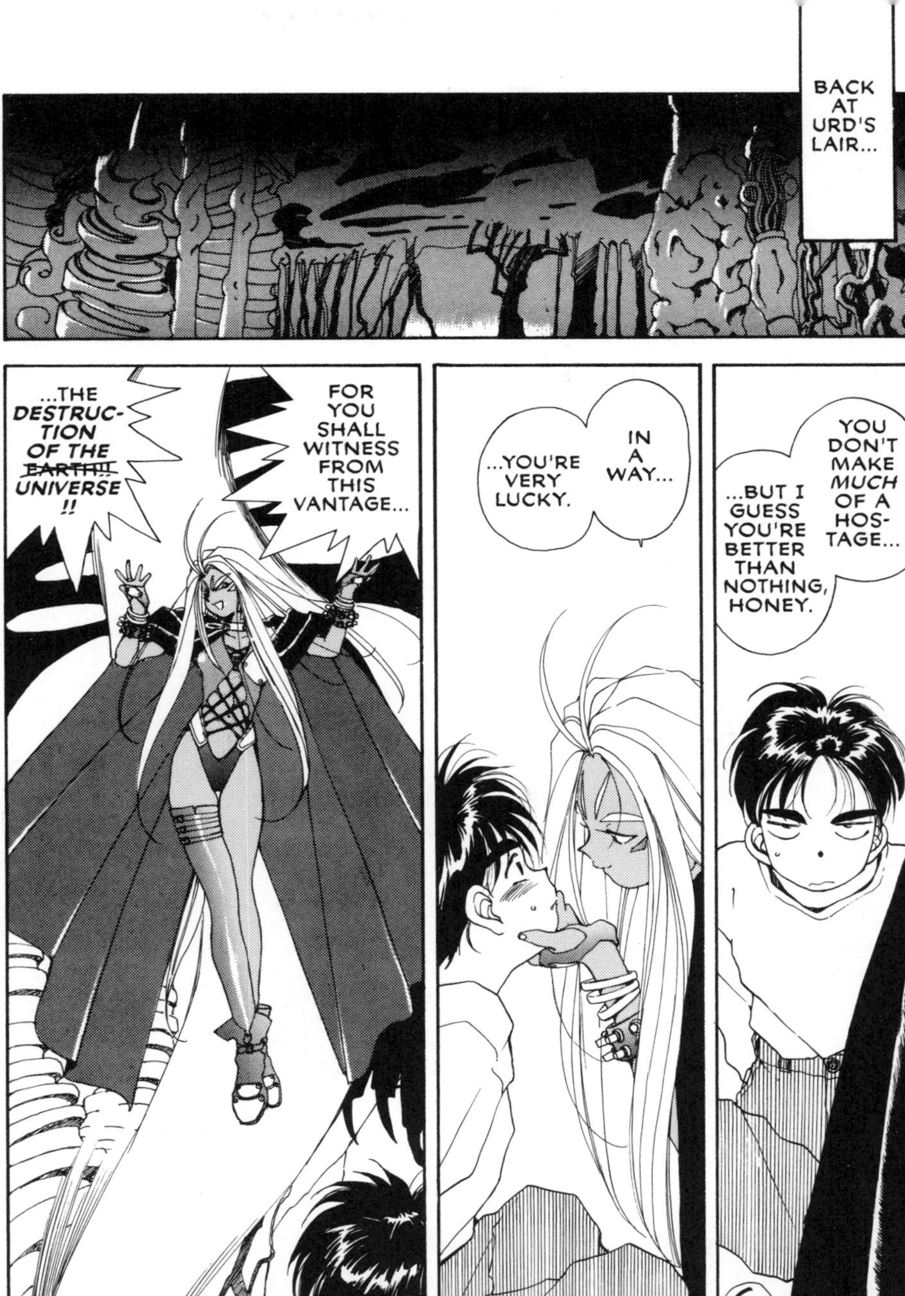
BACK AT URD'S LAIR...
YOU DON'T MAKE *MUCH* OF A HOSTAGE...
...BUT I GUESS YOU'RE BETTER THAN NOTHING, HONEY.
SWSHH
IN A WAY...
...YOU'RE VERY LUCKY.
FOR YOU SHALL WITNESS FROM THIS VANTAGE...
...THE *DESTRUCTION OF THE ~~EARTH!!~~ UNIVERSE!!*

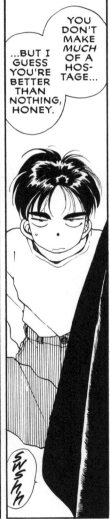

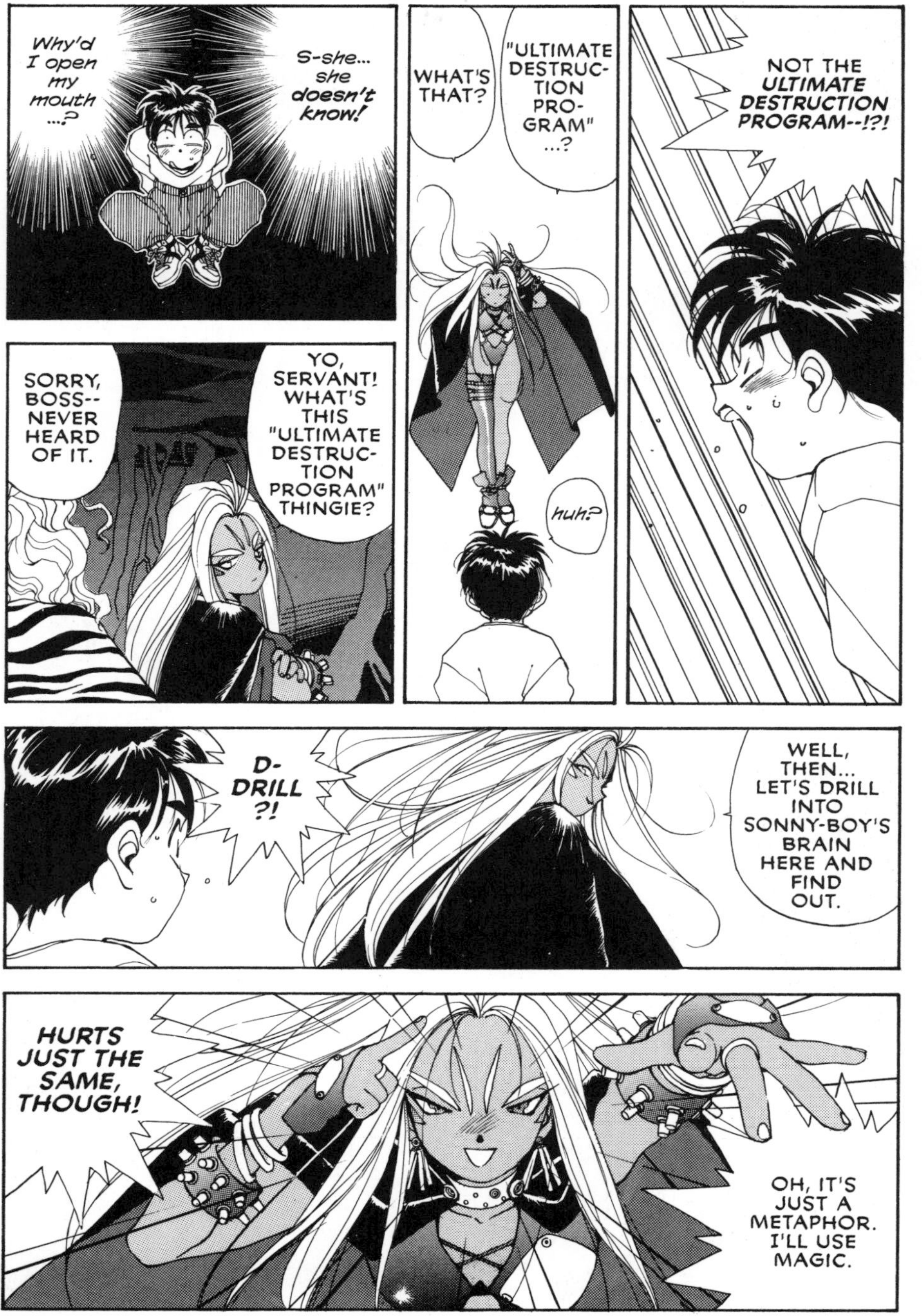
NOT THE *ULTIMATE DESTRUCTION PROGRAM--!?!*
"ULTIMATE DESTRUCTION PROGRAM" ...?
WHAT'S THAT?
*huh?*
*S-she... she **doesn't know!***
*Why'd I open my mouth ...?*
YO, SERVANT! WHAT'S THIS "ULTIMATE DESTRUCTION PROGRAM" THINGIE?
SORRY, BOSS-- NEVER HEARD OF IT.
WELL, THEN... LET'S DRILL INTO SONNY-BOY'S BRAIN HERE AND FIND OUT.
***D-DRILL ?!***
OH, IT'S JUST A METAPHOR. I'LL USE MAGIC.
***HURTS JUST THE SAME, THOUGH!***

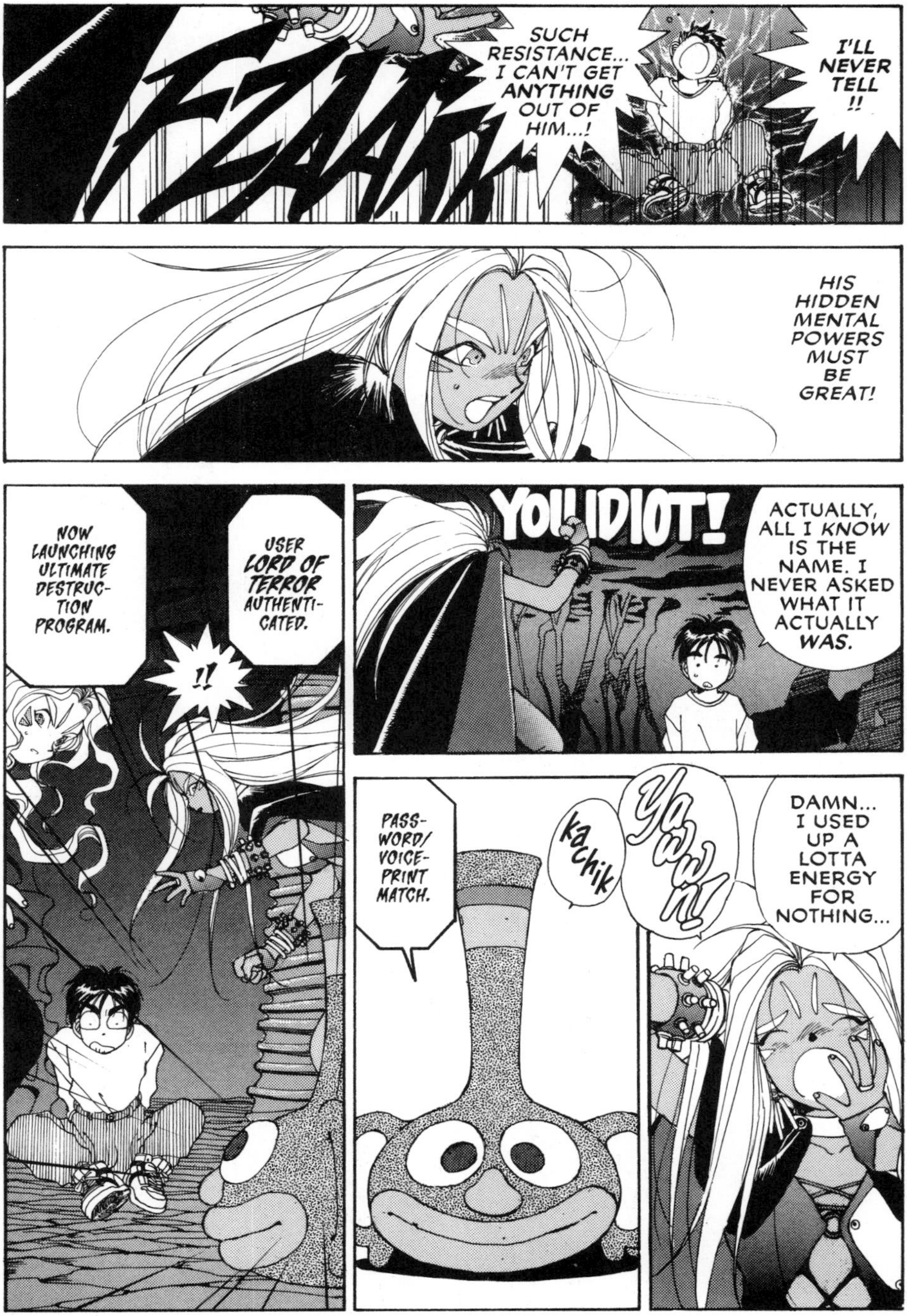
I'LL NEVER TELL !!
SUCH RESISTANCE... I CAN'T GET ANYTHING OUT OF HIM...!
FZAAK
HIS HIDDEN MENTAL POWERS MUST BE GREAT!
ACTUALLY, ALL I KNOW IS THE NAME. I NEVER ASKED WHAT IT ACTUALLY WAS.
YOU IDIOT!
DAMN... I USED UP A LOTTA ENERGY FOR NOTHING...
Yawwn!
kachik
PASS-WORD/ VOICE-PRINT MATCH.
USER LORD OF TERROR AUTHENTI-CATED.
NOW LAUNCHING ULTIMATE DESTRUC-TION PROGRAM.
!!

HELLO. WELCOME TO THE ULTIMATE DESTRUCTION PROGRAM TUTORIAL.
LESSON 1...
FZZK
THANK YOU, SKULD.
HEY, A PROMISE IS A PROMISE, SIS.
I'LL STICK WITH YOU TO THE BITTER END!
FZZK
FZZK
THERE-- THAT SHOULD DO IT.

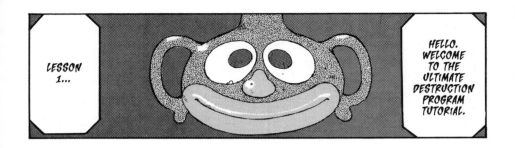

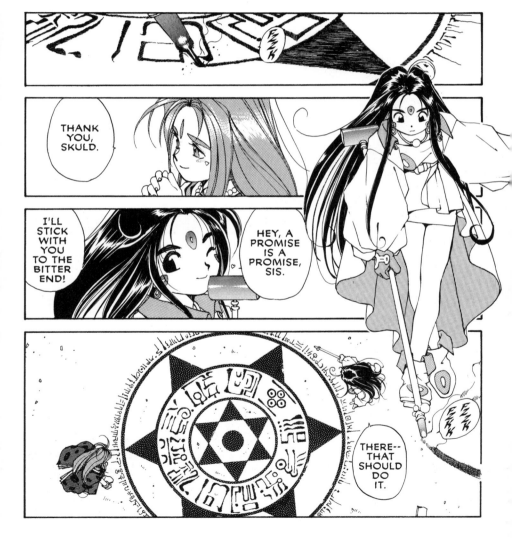

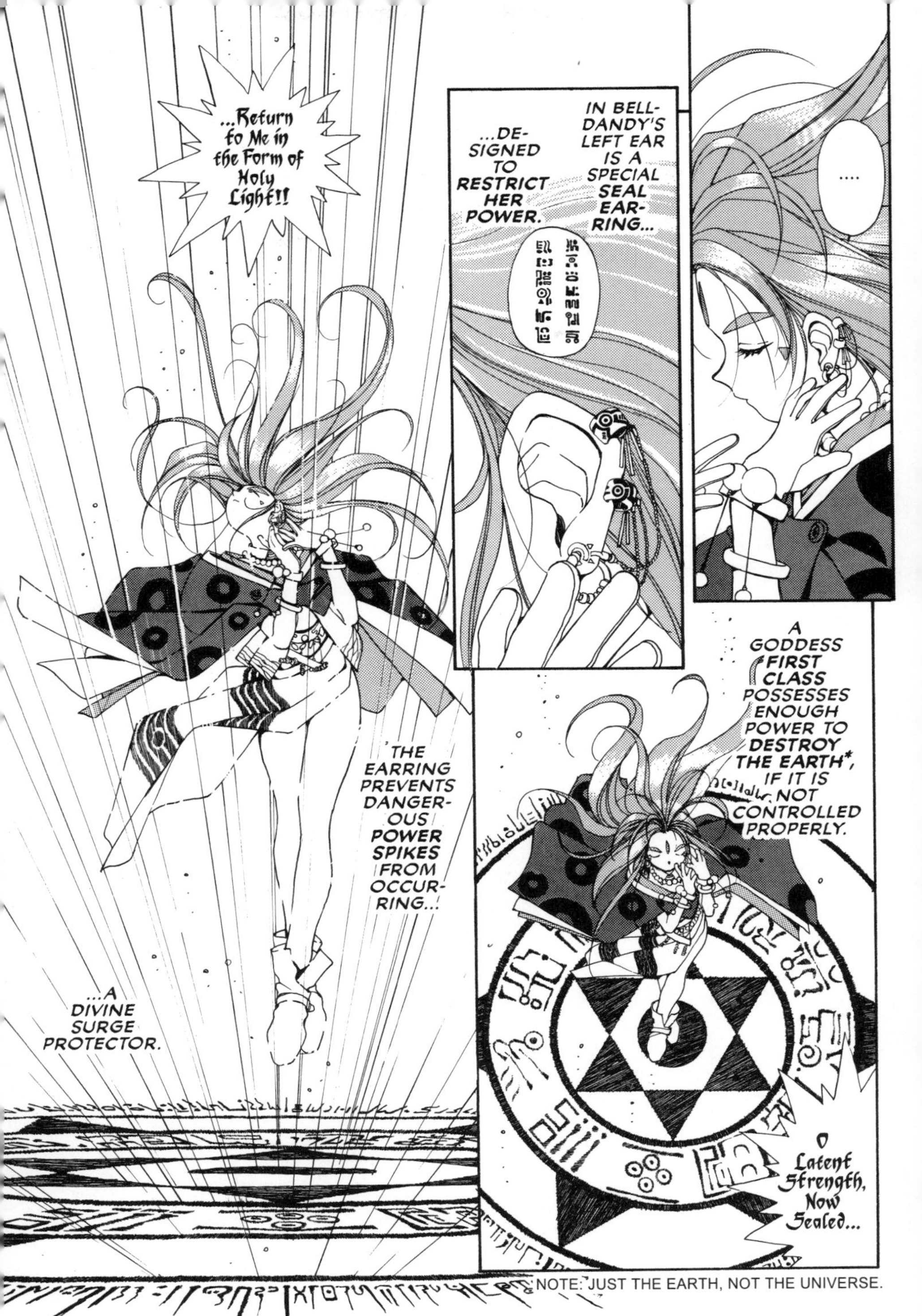
....
IN BELL-DANDY'S LEFT EAR IS A SPECIAL SEAL EAR-RING...
...DE-SIGNED TO RESTRICT HER POWER.
A GODDESS FIRST CLASS POSSESSES ENOUGH POWER TO DESTROY THE EARTH*, IF IT IS NOT CONTROLLED PROPERLY.
O Latent Strength, Now Sealed...
...Return to Me in the Form of Holy Light!!
THE EARRING PREVENTS DANGER-OUS POWER SPIKES FROM OCCUR-RING...
...A DIVINE SURGE PROTECTOR.

NOTE: JUST THE EARTH, NOT THE UNIVERSE.

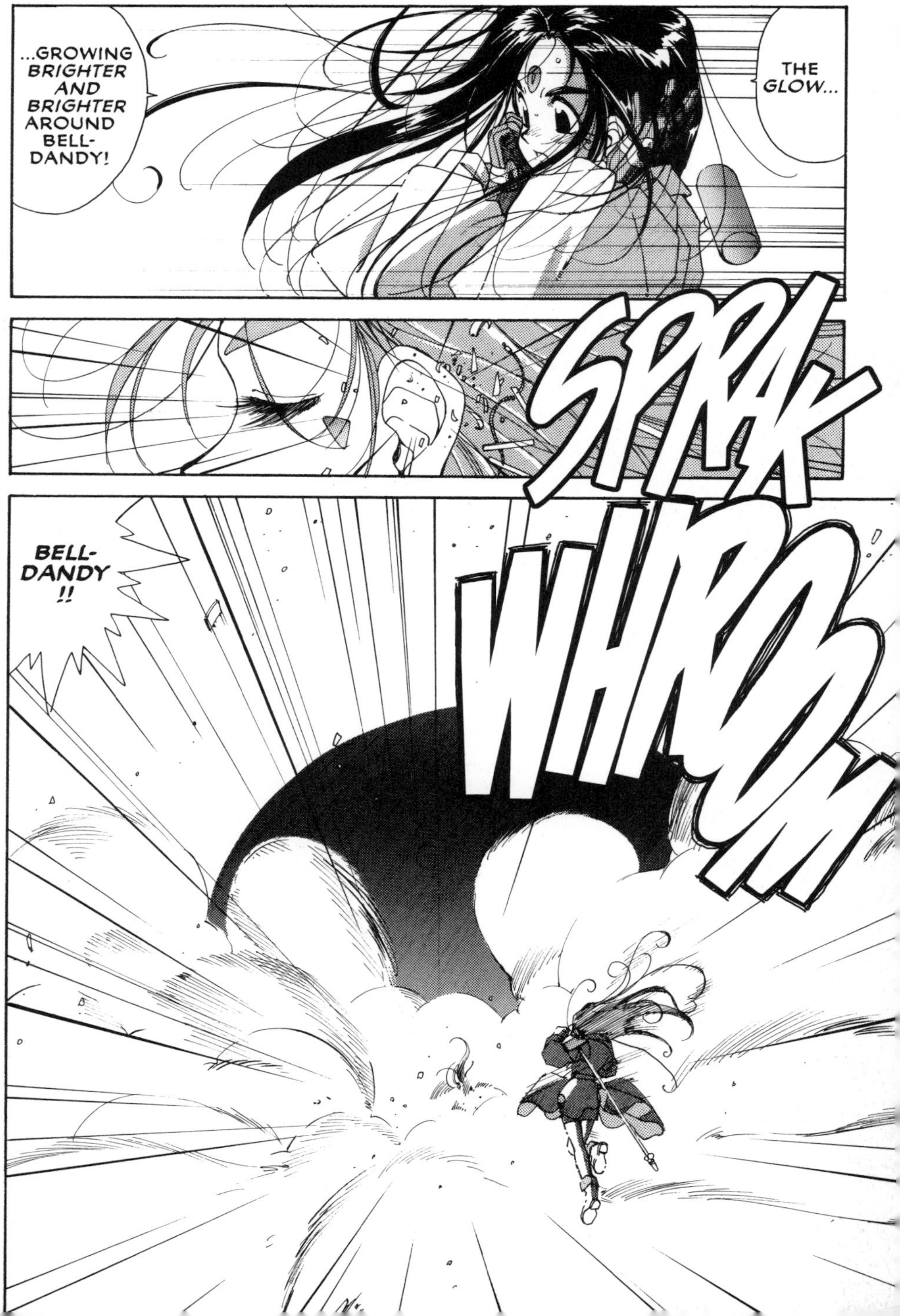
THE GLOW...
...GROWING BRIGHTER AND BRIGHTER AROUND BELL-DANDY!
SPRAK
WHROOM
BELL-DANDY!!

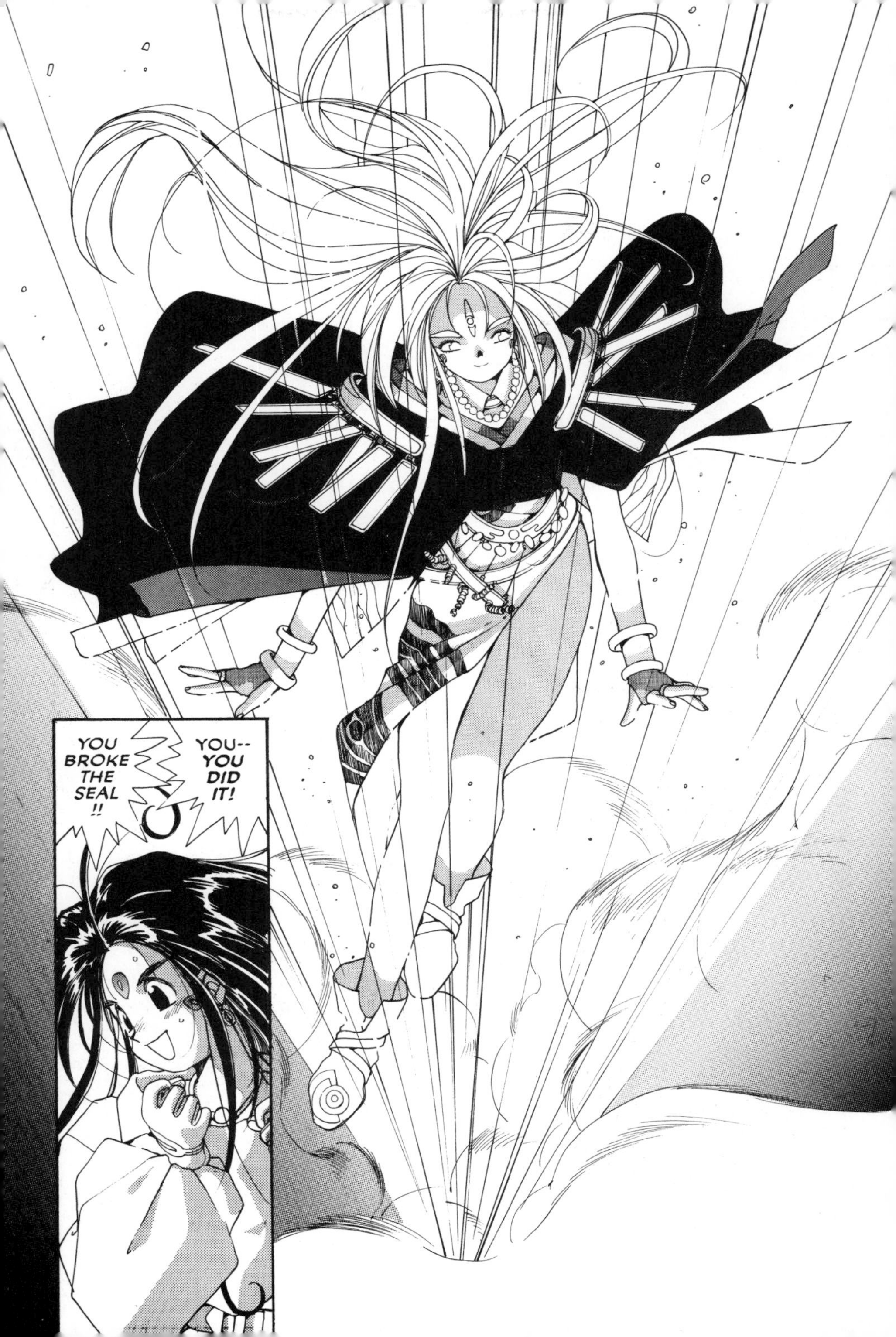
YOU-- YOU DID IT!
YOU BROKE THE SEAL !!

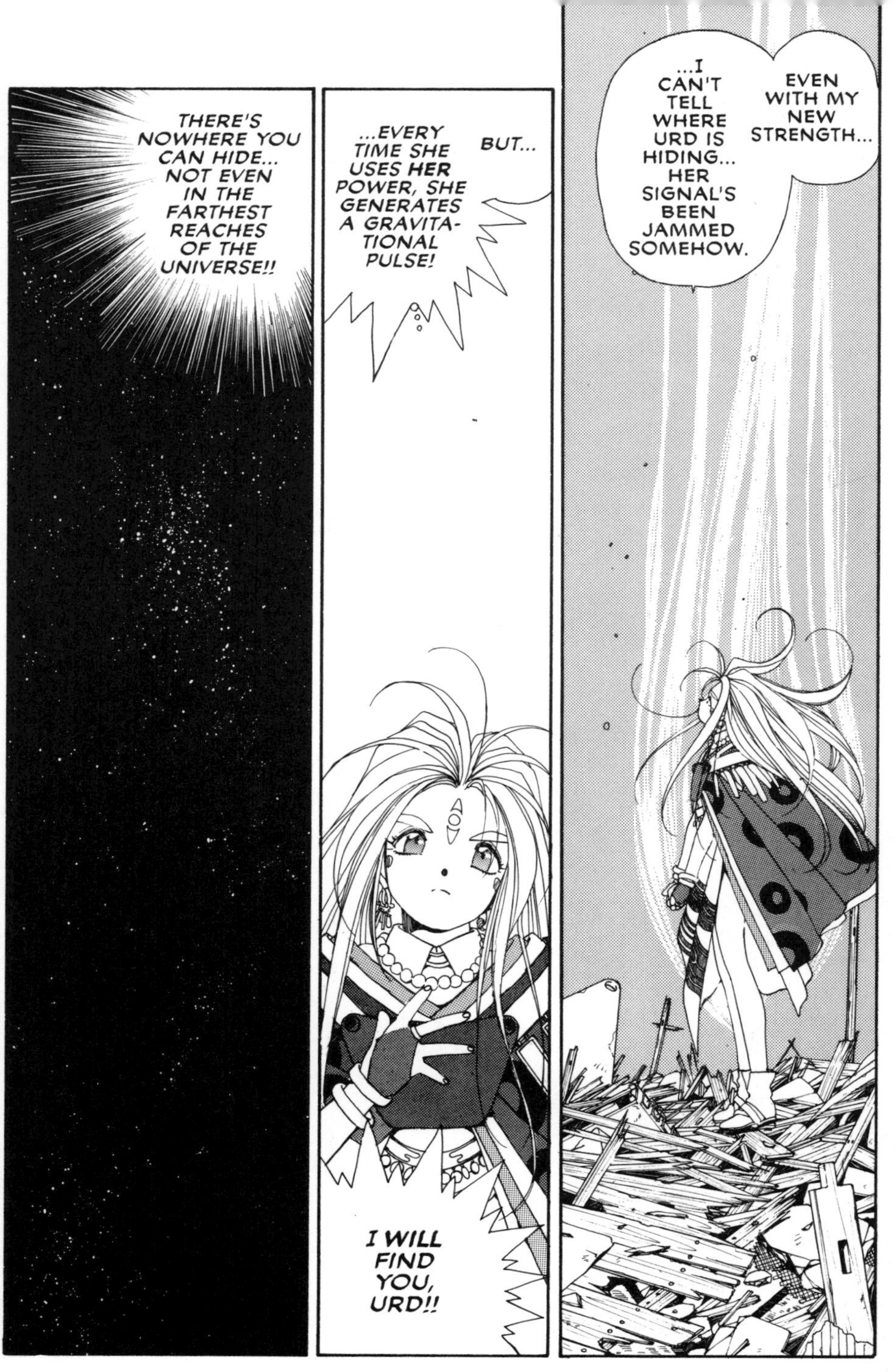

EVEN WITH MY NEW STRENGTH...
...I CAN'T TELL WHERE URD IS HIDING... HER SIGNAL'S BEEN JAMMED SOMEHOW.
BUT...
...EVERY TIME SHE USES **HER** POWER, SHE GENERATES A GRAVITATIONAL PULSE!
I WILL FIND YOU, URD!!
THERE'S NOWHERE YOU CAN HIDE... NOT EVEN IN THE FARTHEST REACHES OF THE UNIVERSE!!

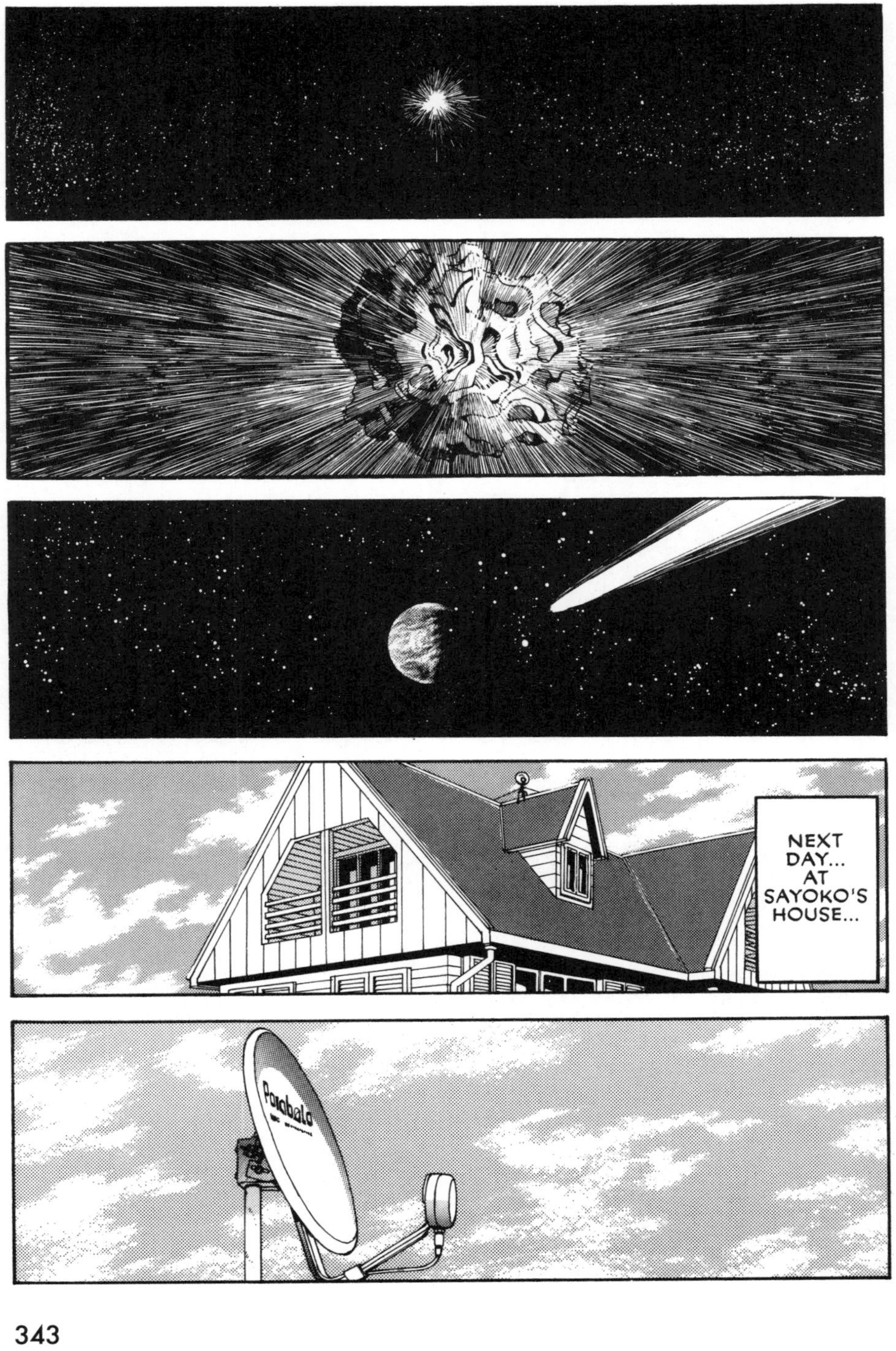
NEXT DAY... AT SAYOKO'S HOUSE...

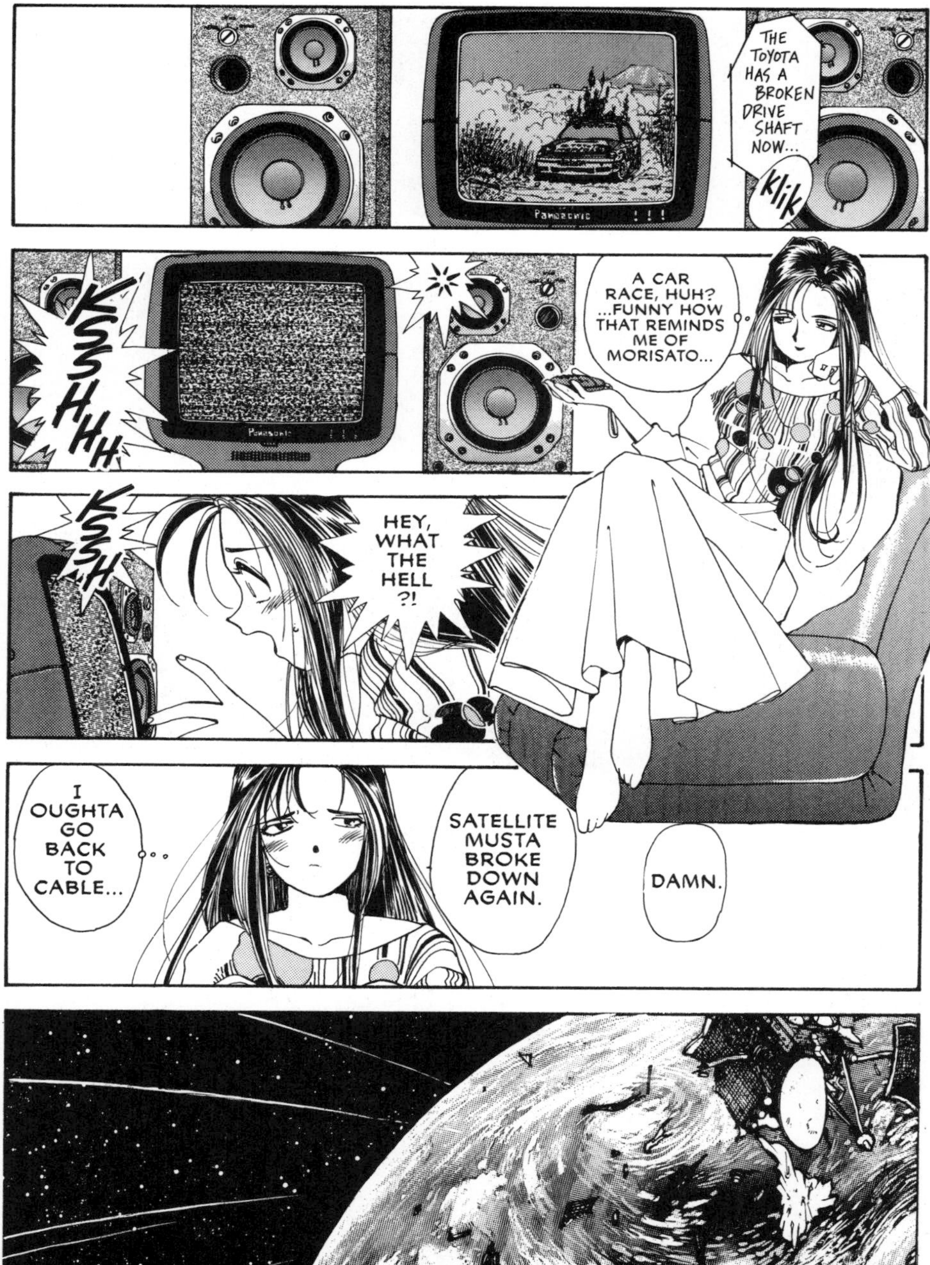
THE TOYOTA HAS A BROKEN DRIVE SHAFT NOW...
Klik
A CAR RACE, HUH? ...FUNNY HOW THAT REMINDS ME OF MORISATO...
KSSHHHH
HEY, WHAT THE HELL ?!
KSSH
DAMN.
SATELLITE MUSTA BROKE DOWN AGAIN.
I OUGHTA GO BACK TO CABLE...

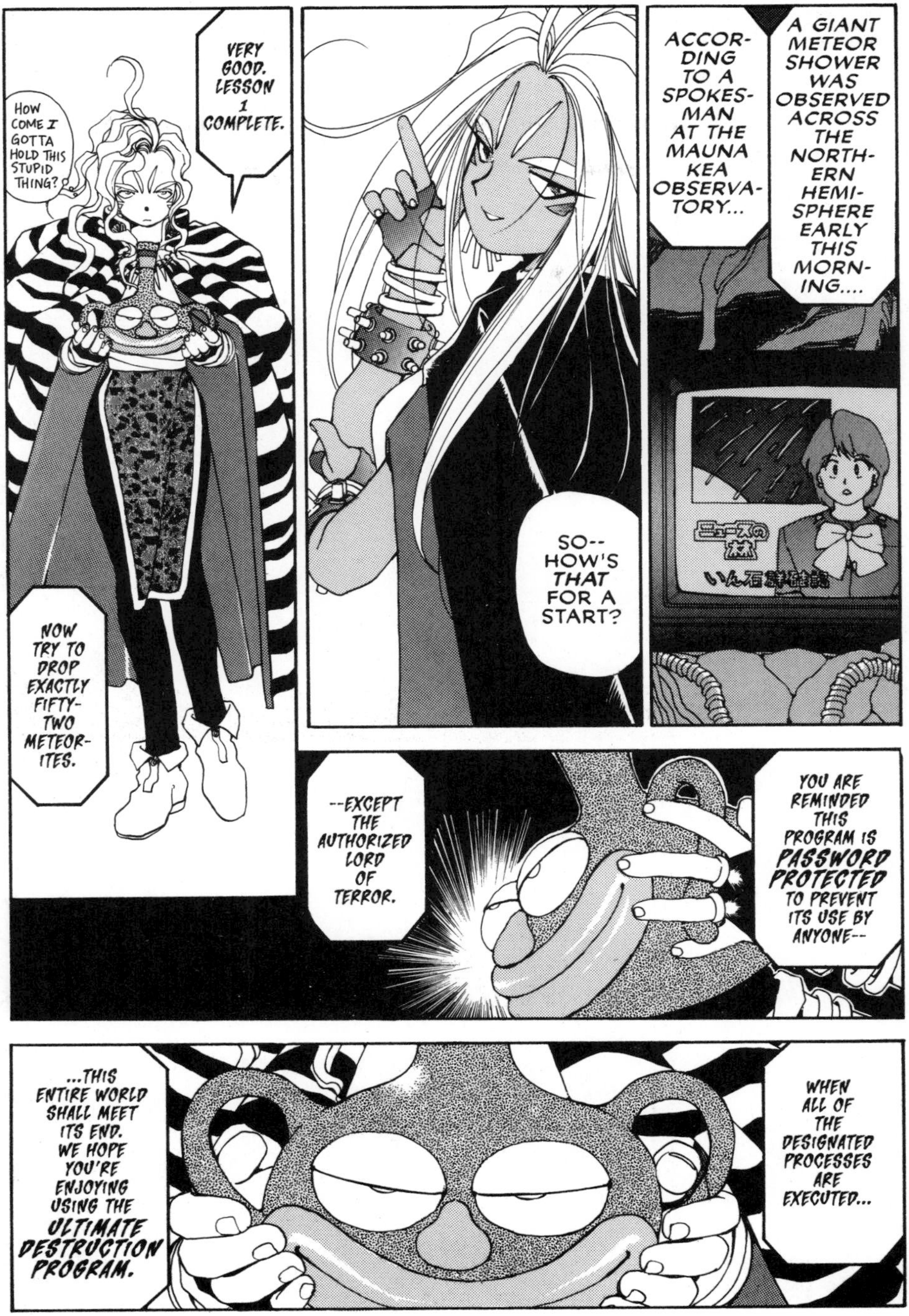
A GIANT METEOR SHOWER WAS OBSERVED ACROSS THE NORTHERN HEMISPHERE EARLY THIS MORNING....
ACCORDING TO A SPOKESMAN AT THE MAUNA KEA OBSERVATORY...
SO--HOW'S *THAT* FOR A START?
YOU ARE REMINDED THIS PROGRAM IS **PASSWORD PROTECTED** TO PREVENT ITS USE BY ANYONE--
--EXCEPT THE AUTHORIZED LORD OF TERROR.
VERY GOOD. LESSON 1 COMPLETE.
HOW COME I GOTTA HOLD THIS STUPID THING?
NOW TRY TO DROP EXACTLY FIFTY-TWO METEORITES.
WHEN ALL OF THE DESIGNATED PROCESSES ARE EXECUTED...
...THIS ENTIRE WORLD SHALL MEET ITS END. WE HOPE YOU'RE ENJOYING USING THE **ULTIMATE DESTRUCTION PROGRAM.**

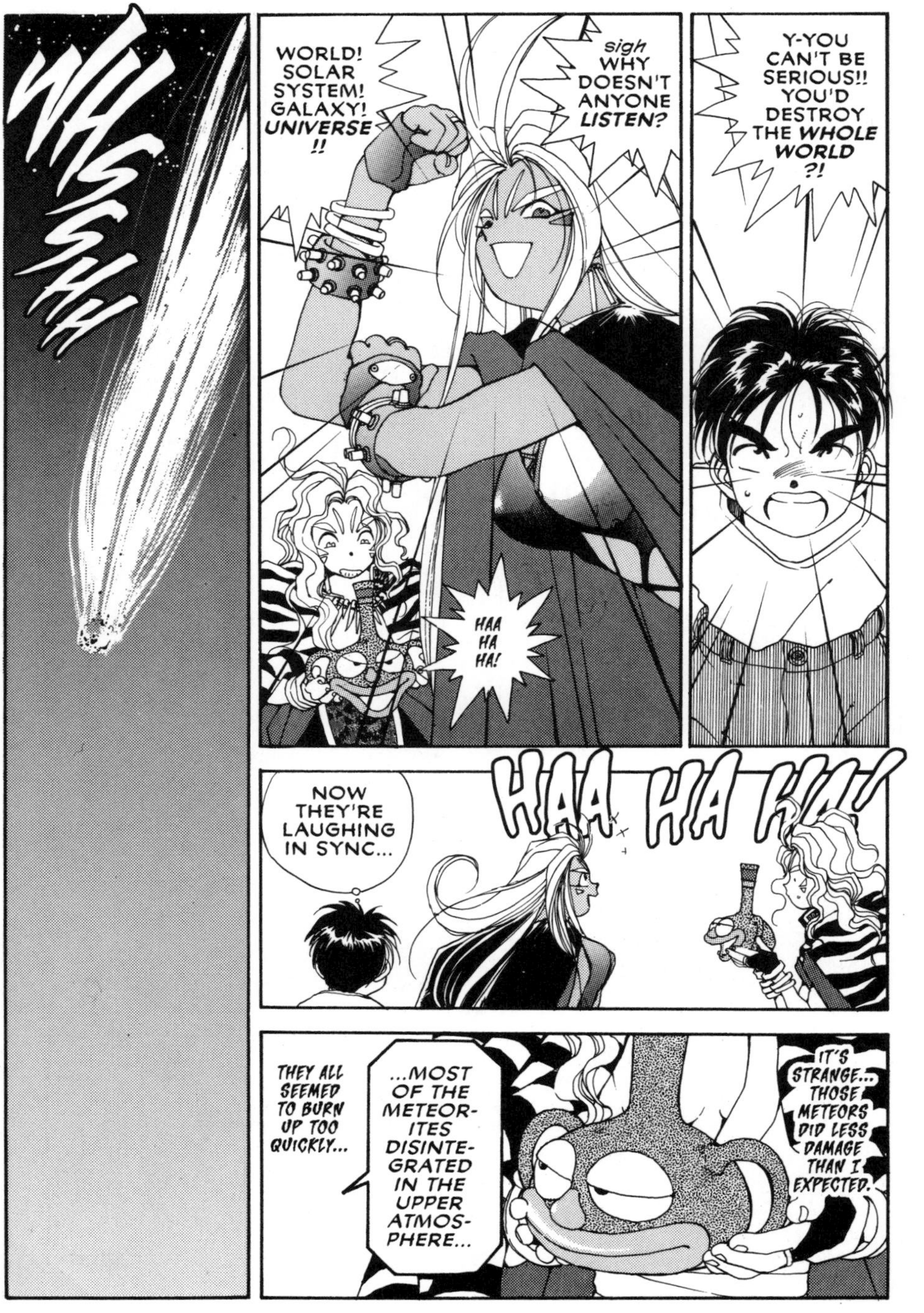
Y-YOU CAN'T BE SERIOUS!! YOU'D DESTROY THE WHOLE WORLD ?!
sigh WHY DOESN'T ANYONE LISTEN?
WORLD! SOLAR SYSTEM! GALAXY! UNIVERSE !!
HAA HA HA!
HAA HA HA!
NOW THEY'RE LAUGHING IN SYNC...
IT'S STRANGE... THOSE METEORS DID LESS DAMAGE THAN I EXPECTED.
...MOST OF THE METEOR-ITES DISINTE-GRATED IN THE UPPER ATMOS-PHERE...
THEY ALL SEEMED TO BURN UP TOO QUICKLY...
WHSSHH

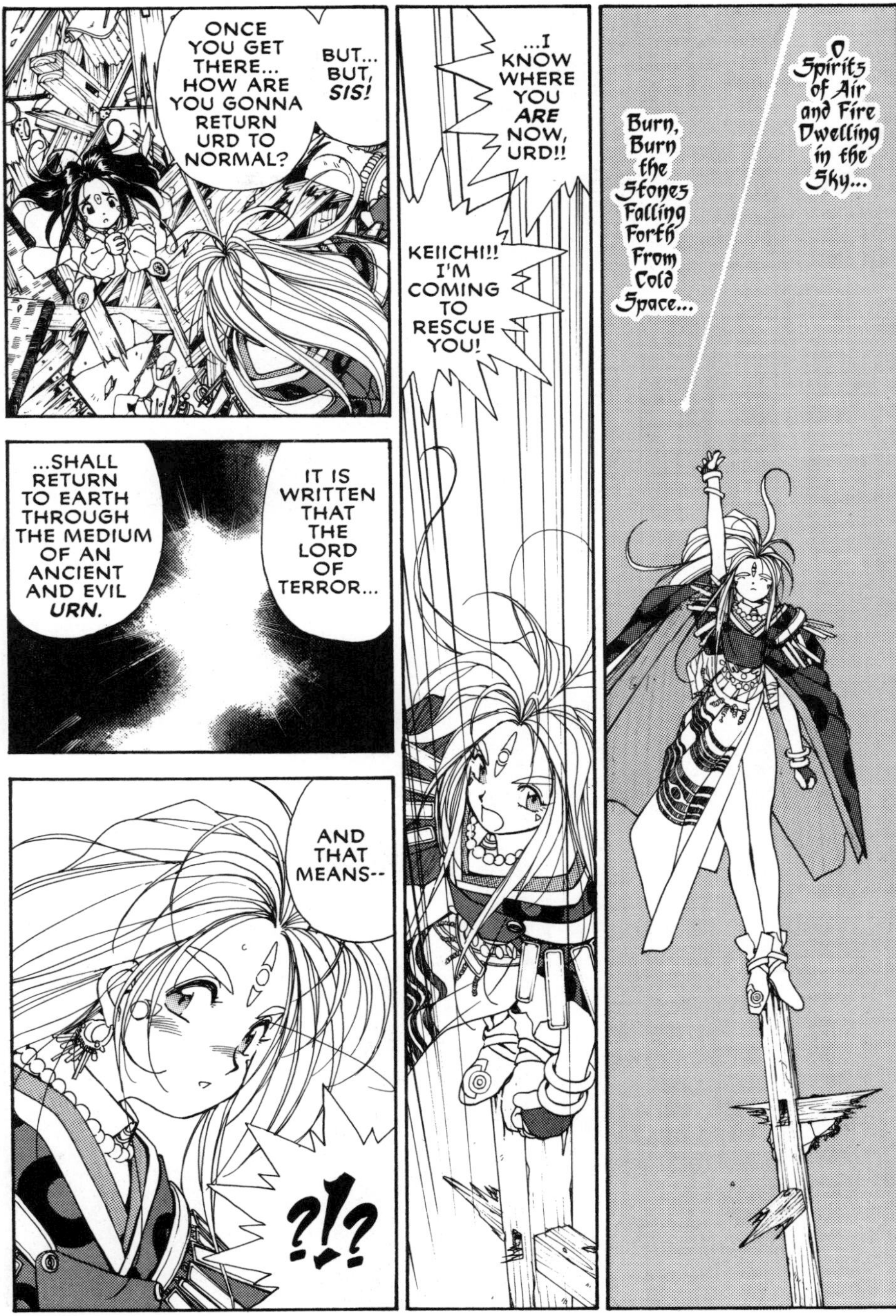
O Spirits of Air and Fire Dwelling in the Sky...
Burn, Burn the Stones Falling Forth From Cold Space...
...I KNOW WHERE YOU *ARE* NOW, URD!!
KEIICHI!!! I'M COMING TO RESCUE YOU!
BUT... BUT, *SIS!*
ONCE YOU GET THERE... HOW ARE YOU GONNA RETURN URD TO NORMAL?
IT IS WRITTEN THAT THE LORD OF TERROR...
...SHALL RETURN TO EARTH THROUGH THE MEDIUM OF AN ANCIENT AND EVIL *URN.*
AND THAT MEANS--
?!?

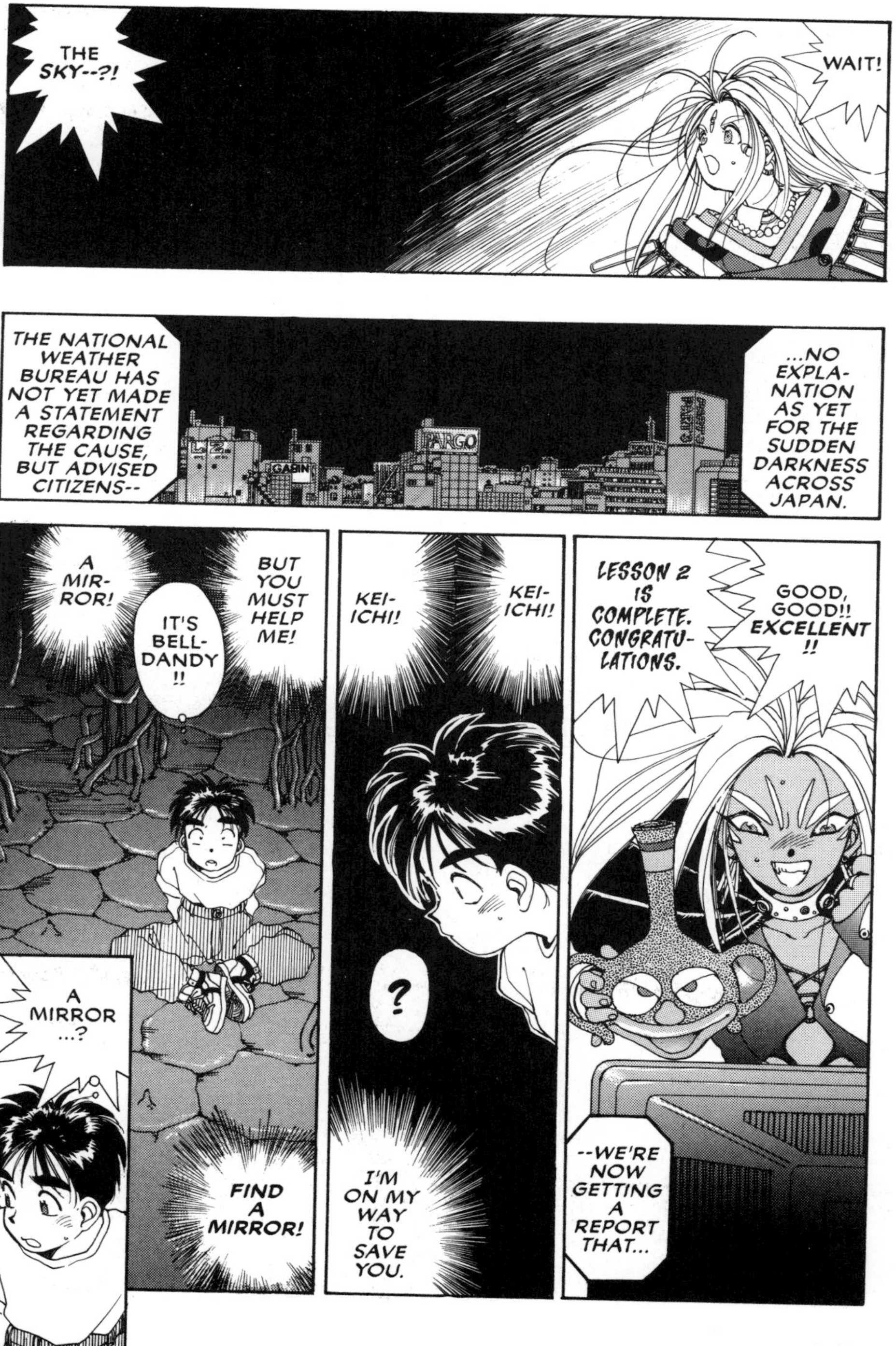
WAIT!
THE SKY--?!
...NO EXPLANATION AS YET FOR THE SUDDEN DARKNESS ACROSS JAPAN.
THE NATIONAL WEATHER BUREAU HAS NOT YET MADE A STATEMENT REGARDING THE CAUSE, BUT ADVISED CITIZENS--
PARGO
GOOD, GOOD!! EXCELLENT !!
LESSON 2 IS COMPLETE. CONGRATULATIONS.
--WE'RE NOW GETTING A REPORT THAT...
KEI-ICHI!
KEI-ICHI!
?
I'M ON MY WAY TO SAVE YOU.
BUT YOU MUST HELP ME!
A MIR-ROR!
IT'S BELL-DANDY !!
FIND A MIRROR!
A MIRROR ...?

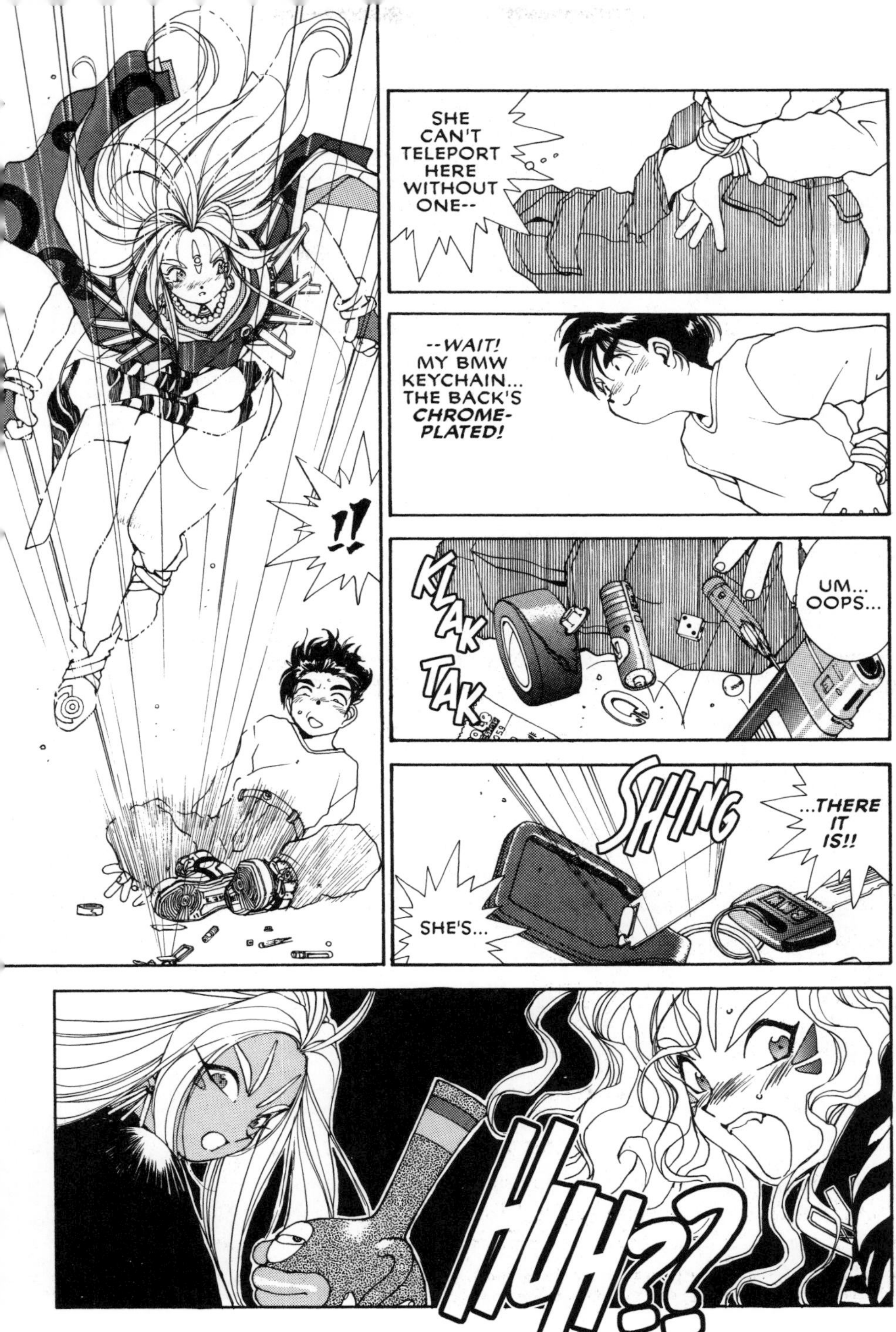
SHE CAN'T TELEPORT HERE WITHOUT ONE--
--WAIT! MY BMW KEYCHAIN... THE BACK'S CHROME-PLATED!
UM... OOPS...
KLAK
TAK
...THERE IT IS!!
SHING
SHE'S...
!!
HUH??

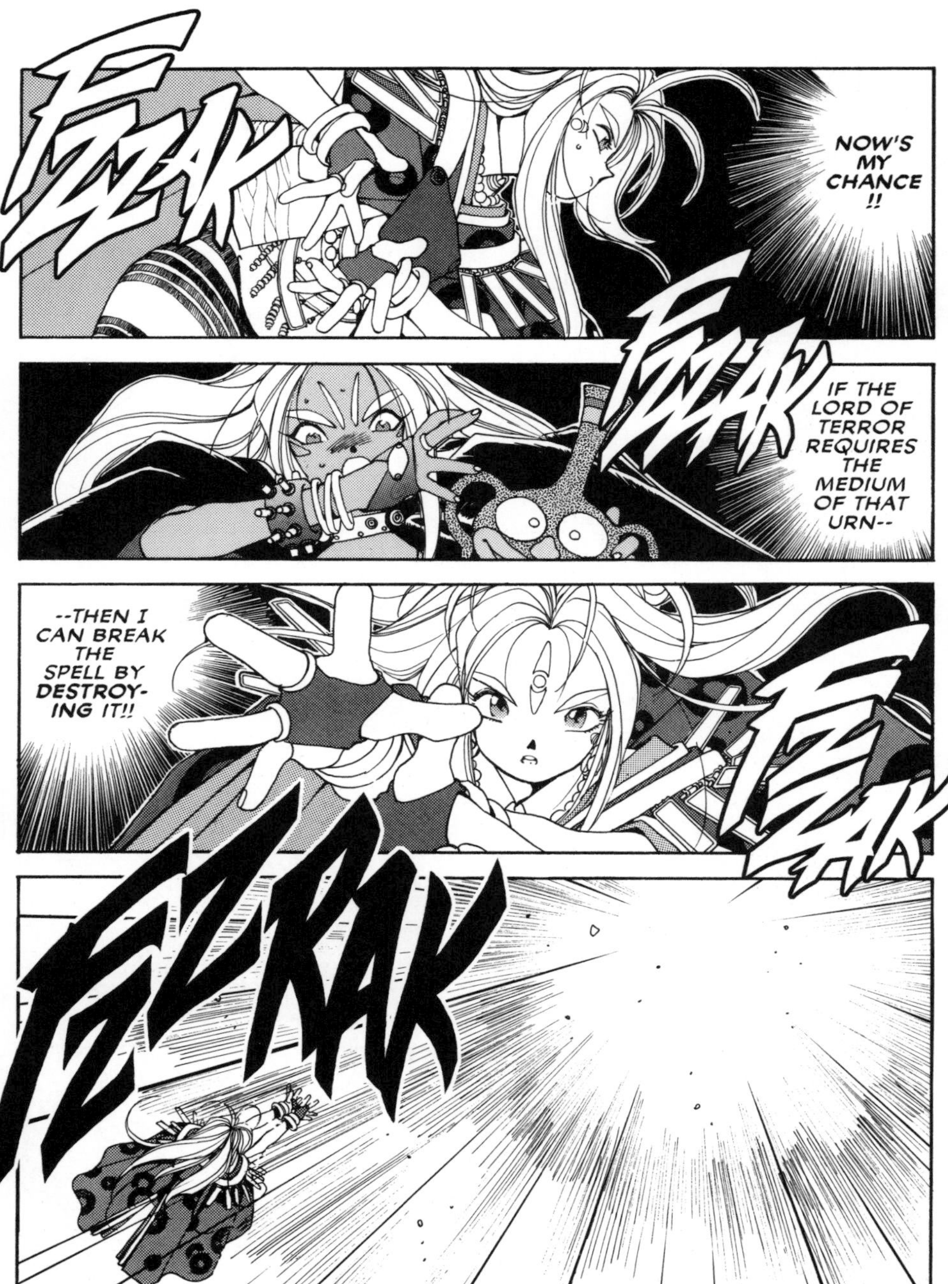
FZZAK
NOW'S MY CHANCE !!
FZZAK
IF THE LORD OF TERROR REQUIRES THE MEDIUM OF THAT URN--
--THEN I CAN BREAK THE SPELL BY DESTROYING IT!!
FZZAK
FZZKRAK

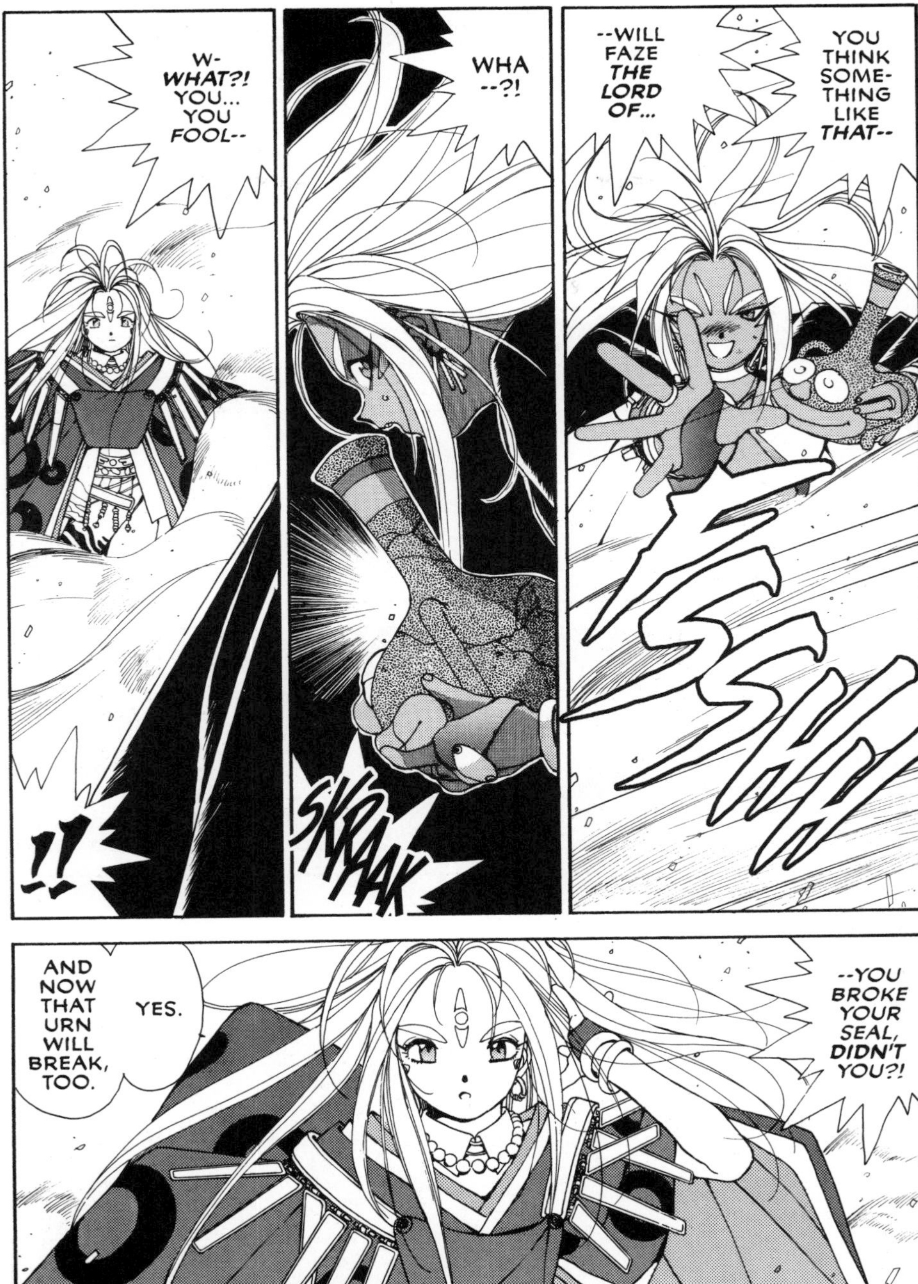
YOU THINK SOMETHING LIKE THAT--
--WILL FAZE THE LORD OF...
SSHH
WHA --?!
SKRAAK
W- WHAT?! YOU... YOU FOOL--
!!
--YOU BROKE YOUR SEAL, DIDN'T YOU?!
YES.
AND NOW THAT URN WILL BREAK, TOO.

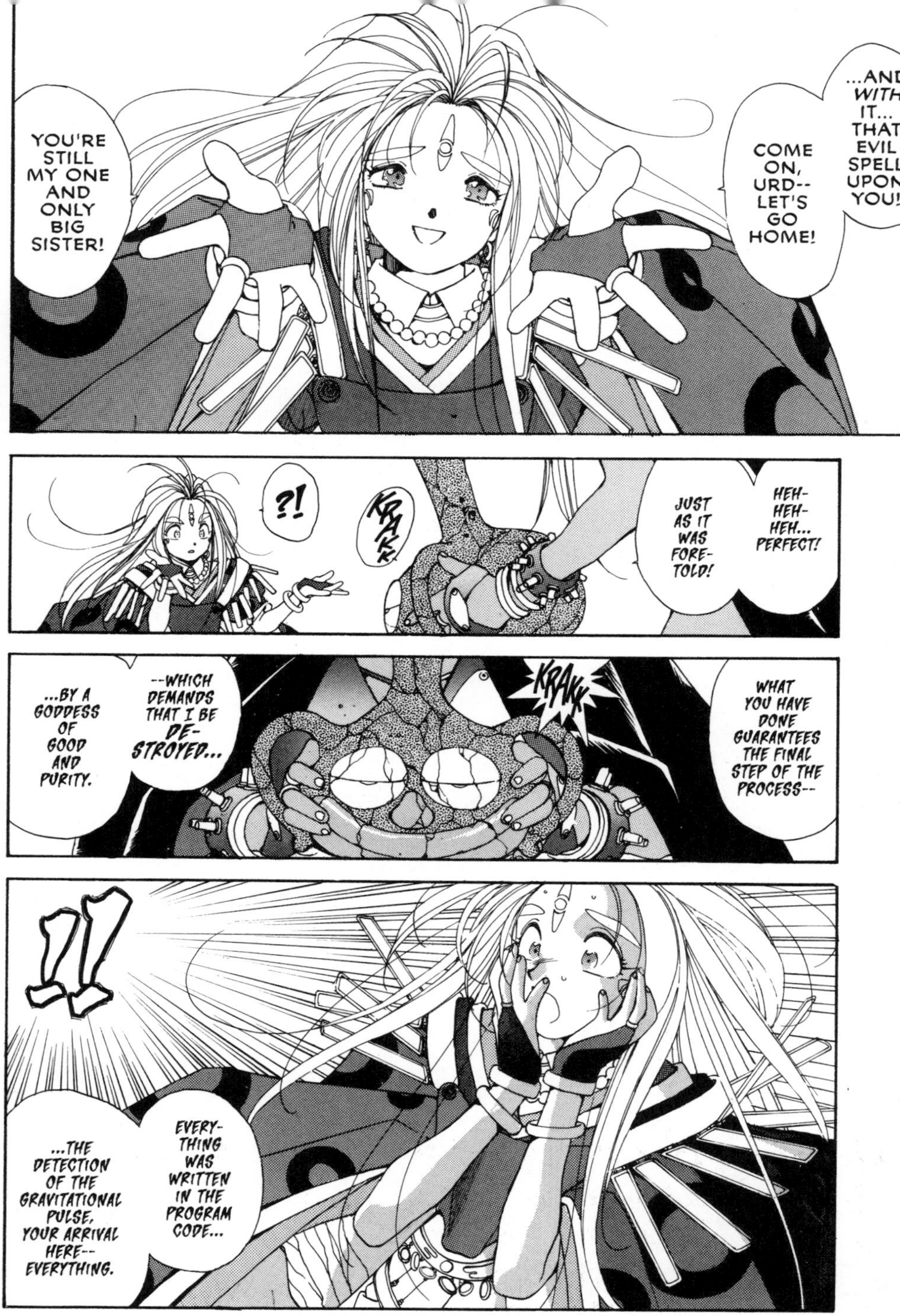
...AND WITH IT... THAT EVIL SPELL UPON YOU!
COME ON, URD--LET'S GO HOME!
YOU'RE STILL MY ONE AND ONLY BIG SISTER!
HEH-HEH-HEH... PERFECT!
JUST AS IT WAS FORETOLD!
KRAKK
?!
WHAT YOU HAVE DONE GUARANTEES THE FINAL STEP OF THE PROCESS--
KRAKK
--WHICH DEMANDS THAT I BE DESTROYED...
...BY A GODDESS OF GOOD AND PURITY.
!!
EVERYTHING WAS WRITTEN IN THE PROGRAM CODE...
...THE DETECTION OF THE GRAVITATIONAL PULSE, YOUR ARRIVAL HERE--EVERYTHING.

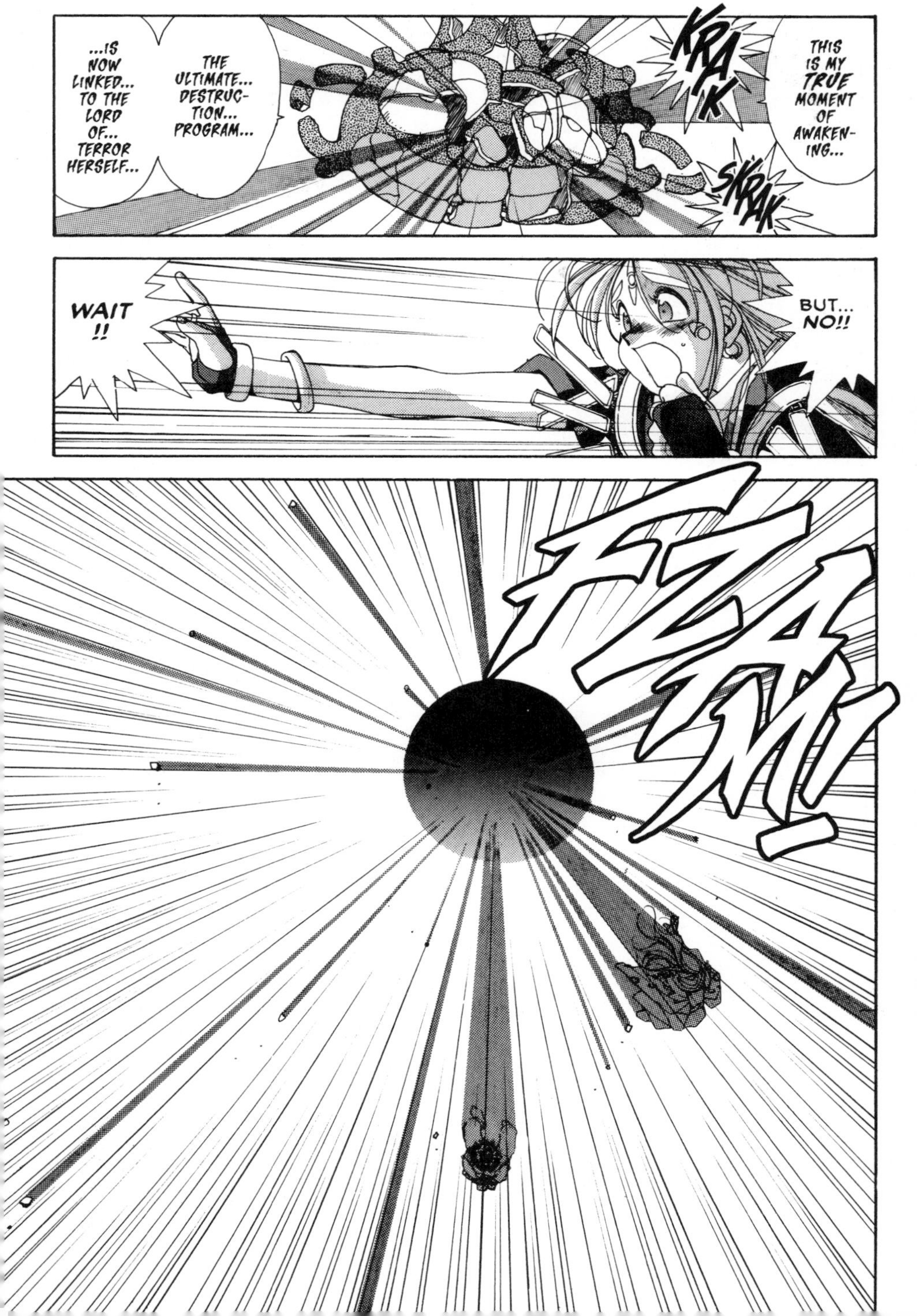
THIS IS MY TRUE MOMENT OF AWAKENING...
KRAK
SKRAK
THE ULTIMATE... DESTRUCTION... PROGRAM...
...IS NOW LINKED... TO THE LORD OF... TERROR HERSELF...
BUT... NO!!
WAIT!!
FZAM!

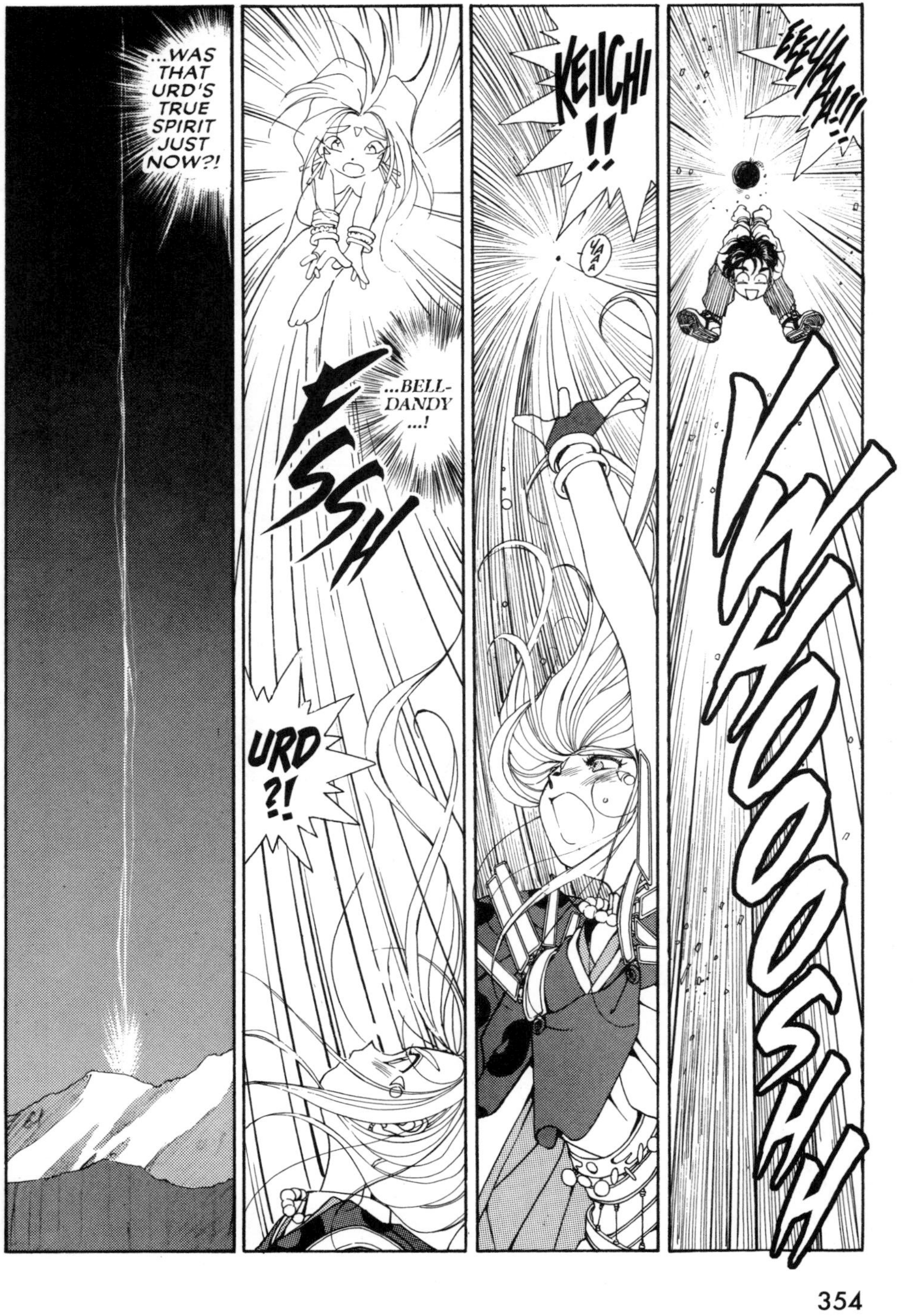
EEEYAAA!!!
VWHOOOOSHHH
KEIICHI!!
YAAA
URD?!
...BELL-DANDY...!
FSSH
...WAS THAT URD'S TRUE SPIRIT JUST NOW?!

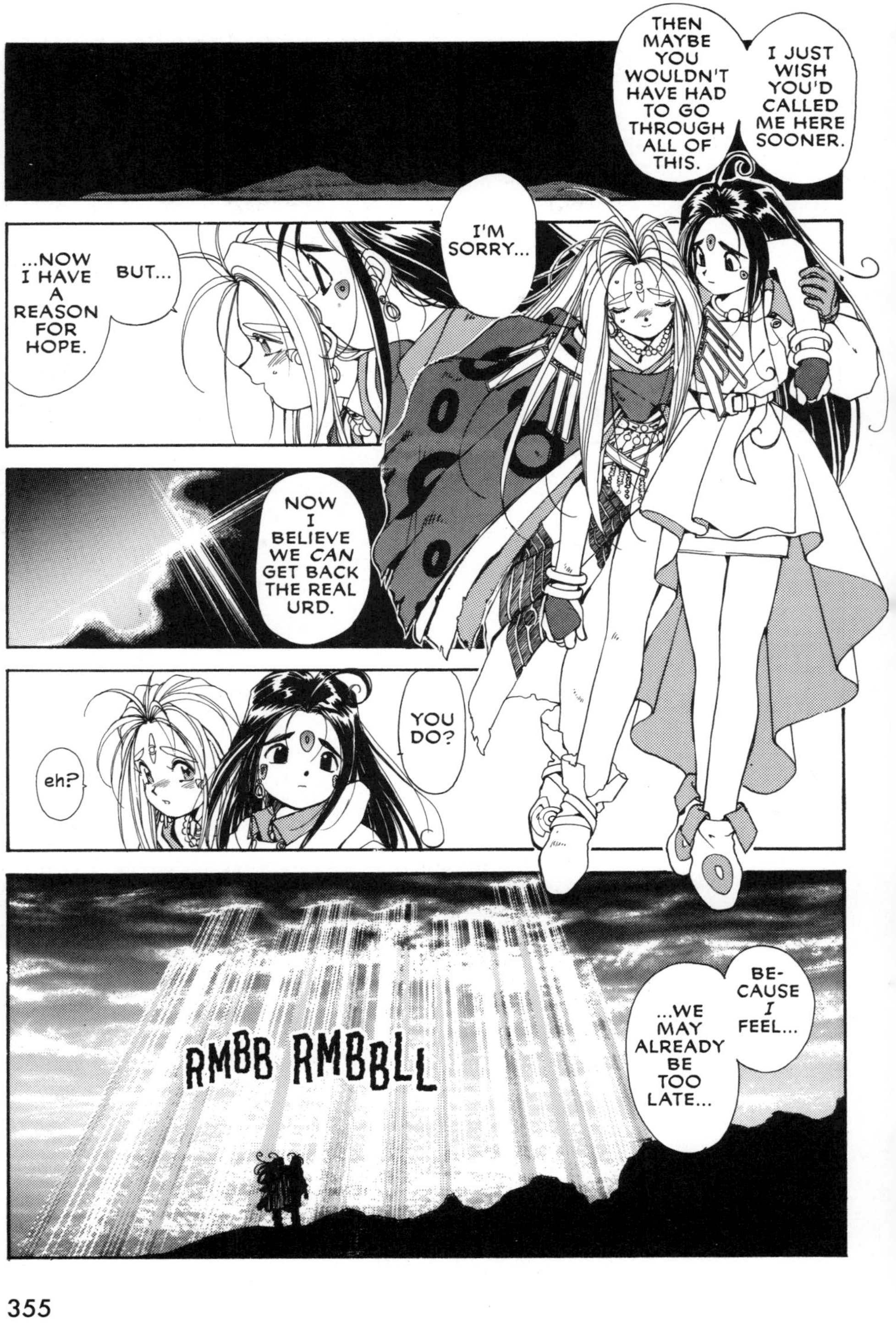
I JUST WISH YOU'D CALLED ME HERE SOONER.
THEN MAYBE YOU WOULDN'T HAVE HAD TO GO THROUGH ALL OF THIS.
I'M SORRY...
BUT...
...NOW I HAVE A REASON FOR HOPE.
NOW I BELIEVE WE *CAN* GET BACK THE REAL URD.
YOU DO?
eh?
BE-CAUSE *I* FEEL...
...WE MAY ALREADY BE TOO LATE...
RMBB RMBBLL

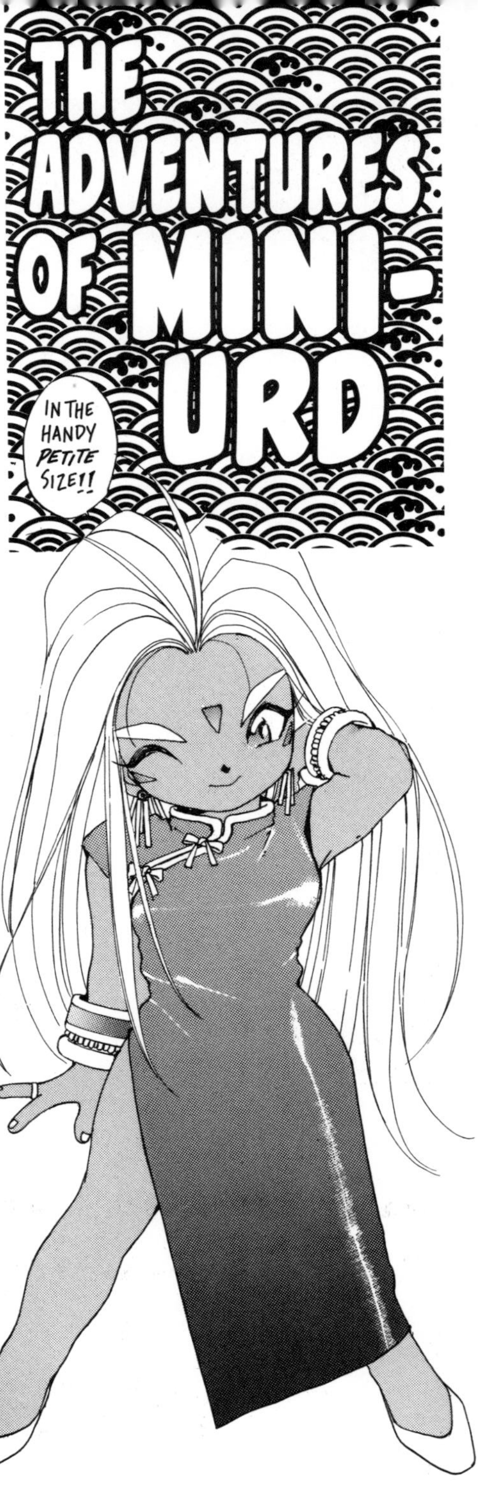
THE ADVENTURES OF MINI-URD
IN THE HANDY PETITE SIZE!!

## HEALTH CARE

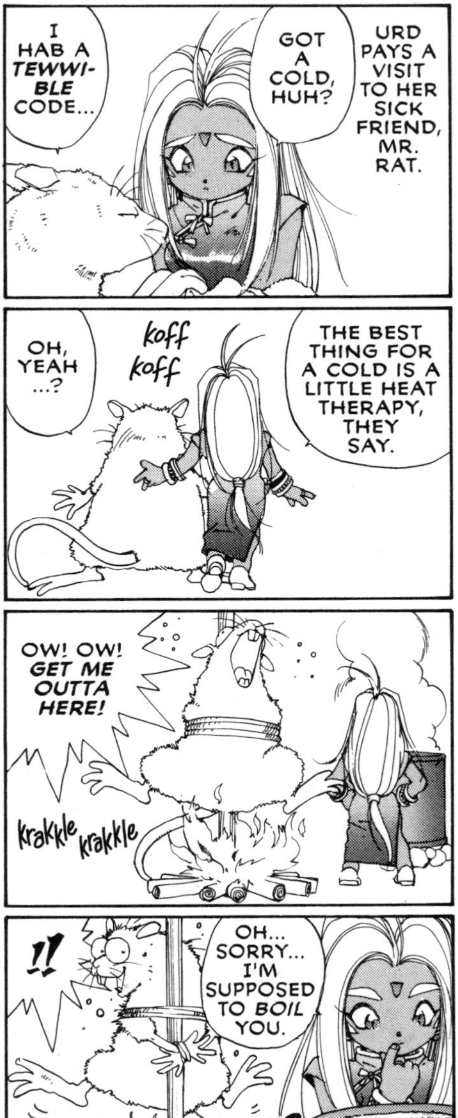
URD PAYS A VISIT TO HER SICK FRIEND, MR. RAT.
GOT A COLD, HUH?
I HAB A *TEWWIBLE* CODE...
THE BEST THING FOR A COLD IS A LITTLE HEAT THERAPY, THEY SAY.
koff koff
OH, YEAH ...?
OW! OW! *GET ME OUTTA HERE!*
krakkle krakkle
OH... SORRY... I'M SUPPOSED TO *BOIL* YOU.
!!
BLUBBLE BLURP

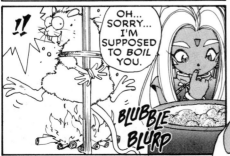

## ◆ COLD MEDICINE ◆

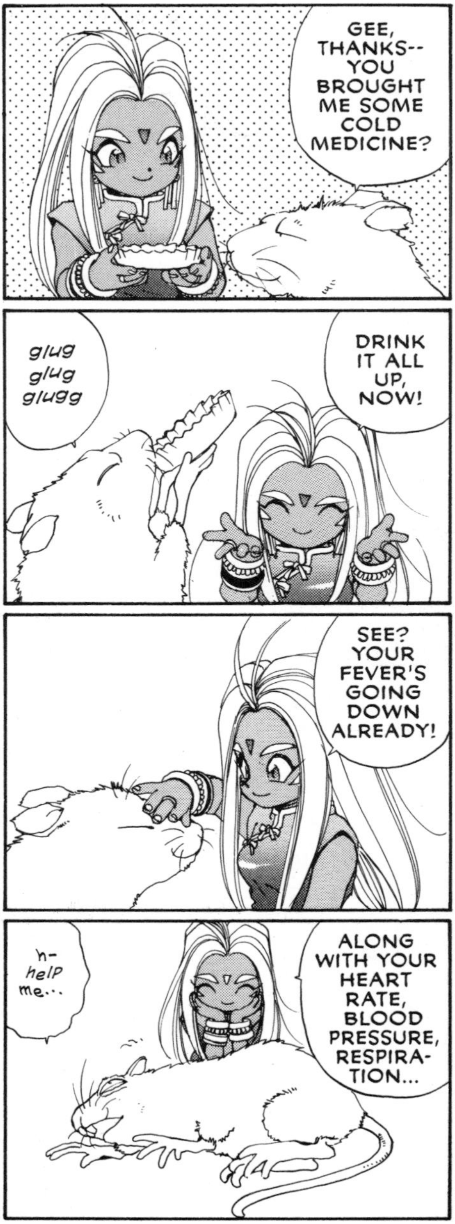
GEE, THANKS-- YOU BROUGHT ME SOME COLD MEDICINE?
DRINK IT ALL UP, NOW!
glug glug glugg
SEE? YOUR FEVER'S GOING DOWN ALREADY!
ALONG WITH YOUR HEART RATE, BLOOD PRESSURE, RESPIRATION...
h-help me...

## ◆ STOMACH MEDICINE ◆

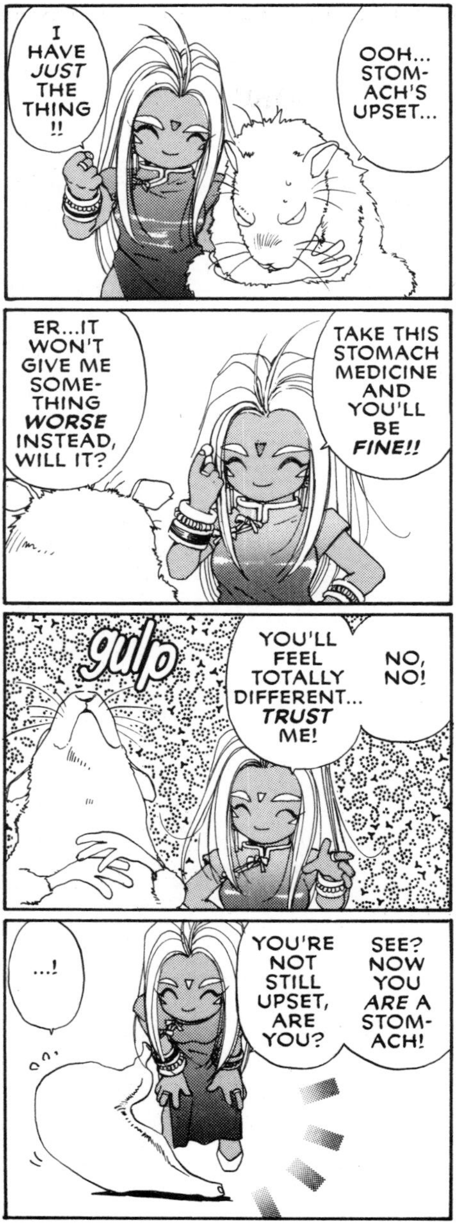
OOH... STOMACH'S UPSET...
I HAVE *JUST* THE THING!!
TAKE THIS STOMACH MEDICINE AND YOU'LL BE ***FINE!!***
ER...IT WON'T GIVE ME SOMETHING **WORSE** INSTEAD, WILL IT?
NO, NO!
YOU'LL FEEL TOTALLY DIFFERENT... ***TRUST*** ME!
gulp
SEE? NOW YOU *ARE* A STOMACH!
YOU'RE NOT STILL UPSET, ARE YOU?
...!

## ◆ THE GREAT SLUG RACE ◆

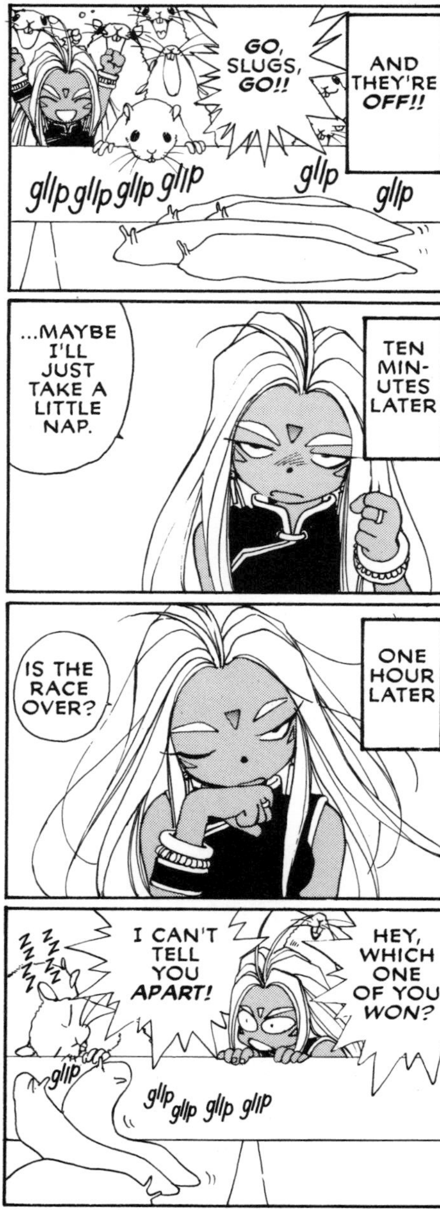
AND THEY'RE OFF!!
GO, SLUGS, GO!!
gllp gllp gllp gllp gllp gllp
TEN MIN-UTES LATER
...MAYBE I'LL JUST TAKE A LITTLE NAP.
ONE HOUR LATER
IS THE RACE OVER?
HEY, WHICH ONE OF YOU WON?
I CAN'T TELL YOU APART!
Z Z Z Z Z Z
gllp
gllp gllp gllp gllp

## ◆ THE GREAT CRICKET RACE ◆

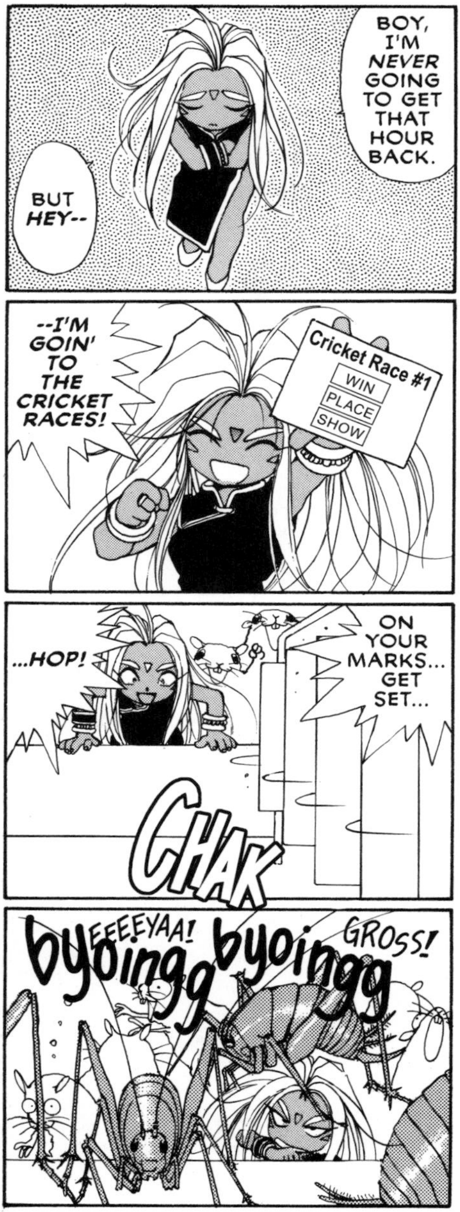
BOY, I'M NEVER GOING TO GET THAT HOUR BACK.
BUT HEY--
Cricket Race #1
WIN
PLACE
SHOW
--I'M GOIN' TO THE CRICKET RACES!
ON YOUR MARKS... GET SET...
...HOP!
CHAK
GROSS!
EEEEYAA!
byoingg byoingg

# Oh My Goddess!

ああっ女神さまっ

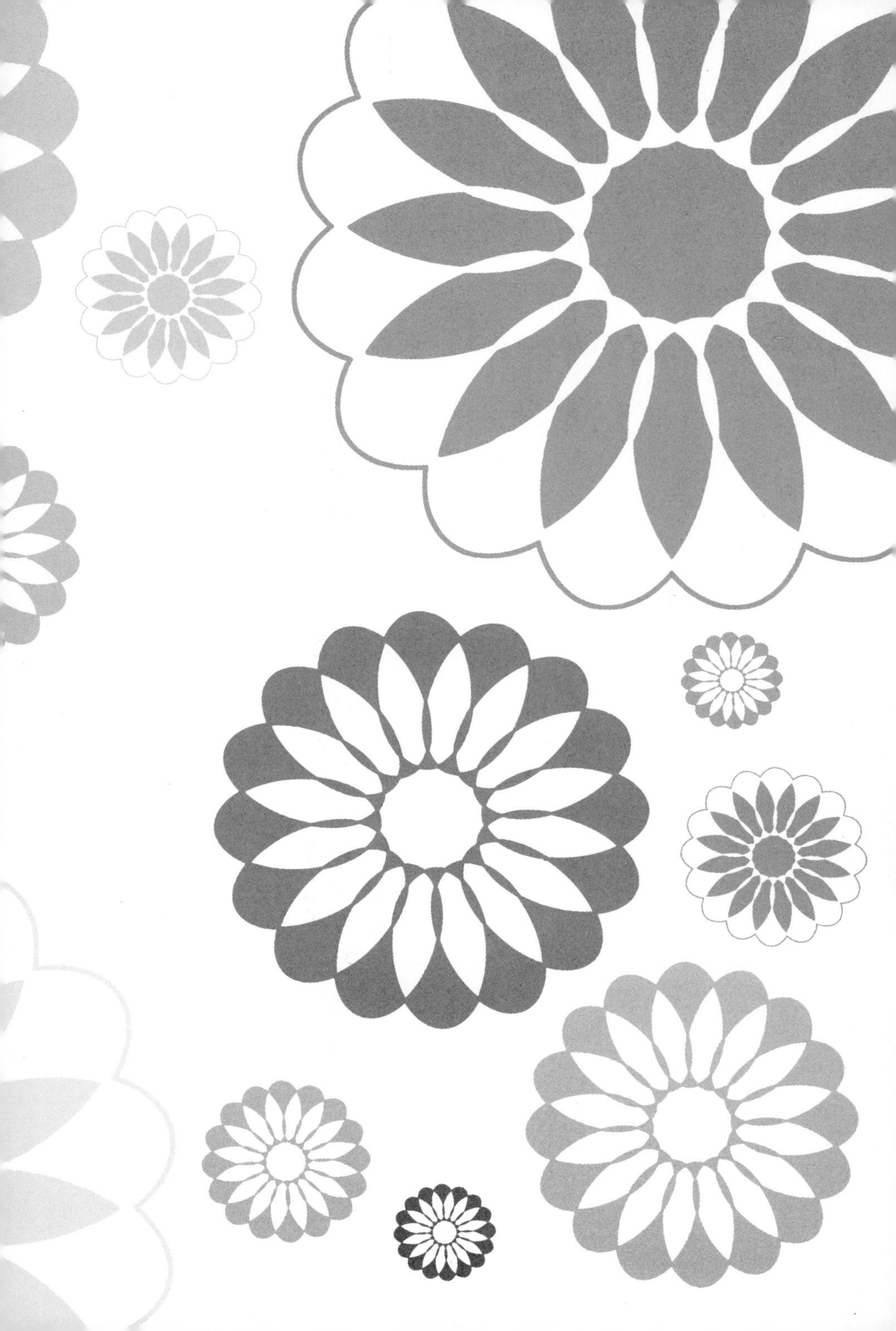

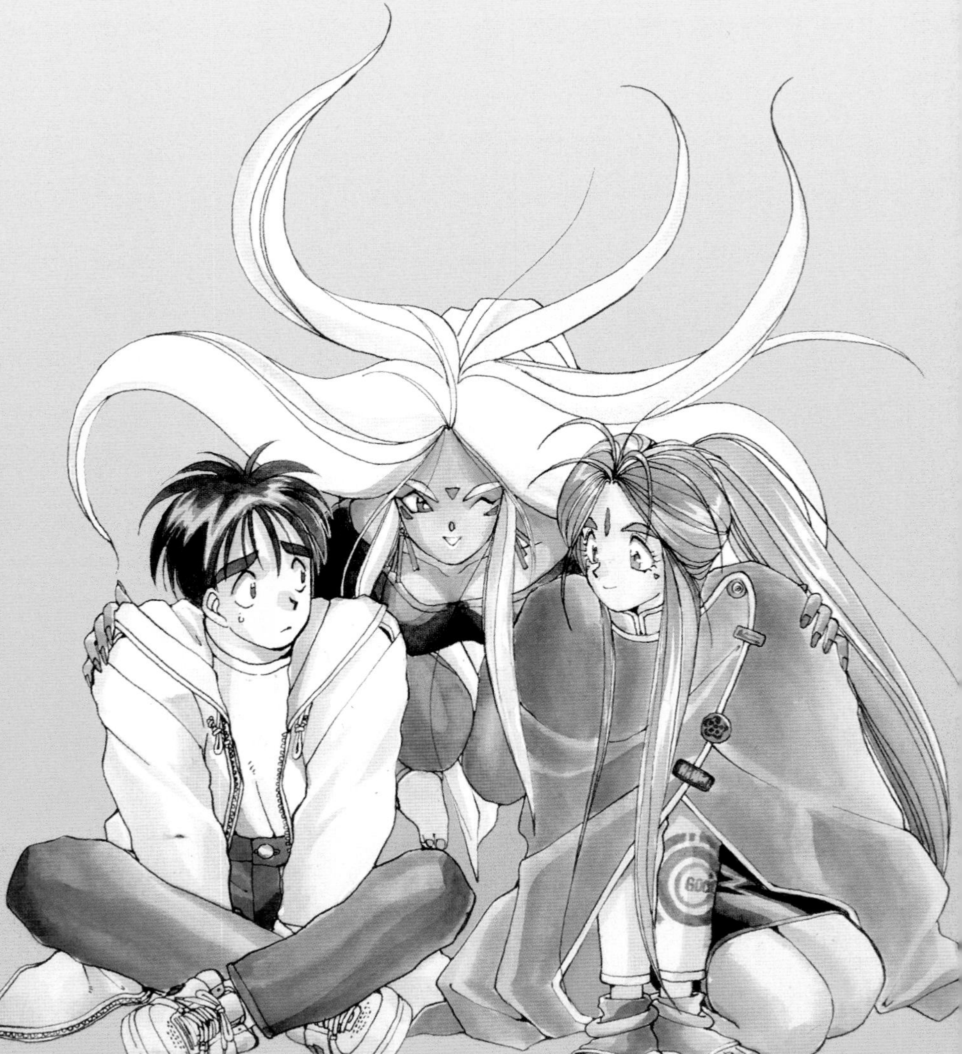

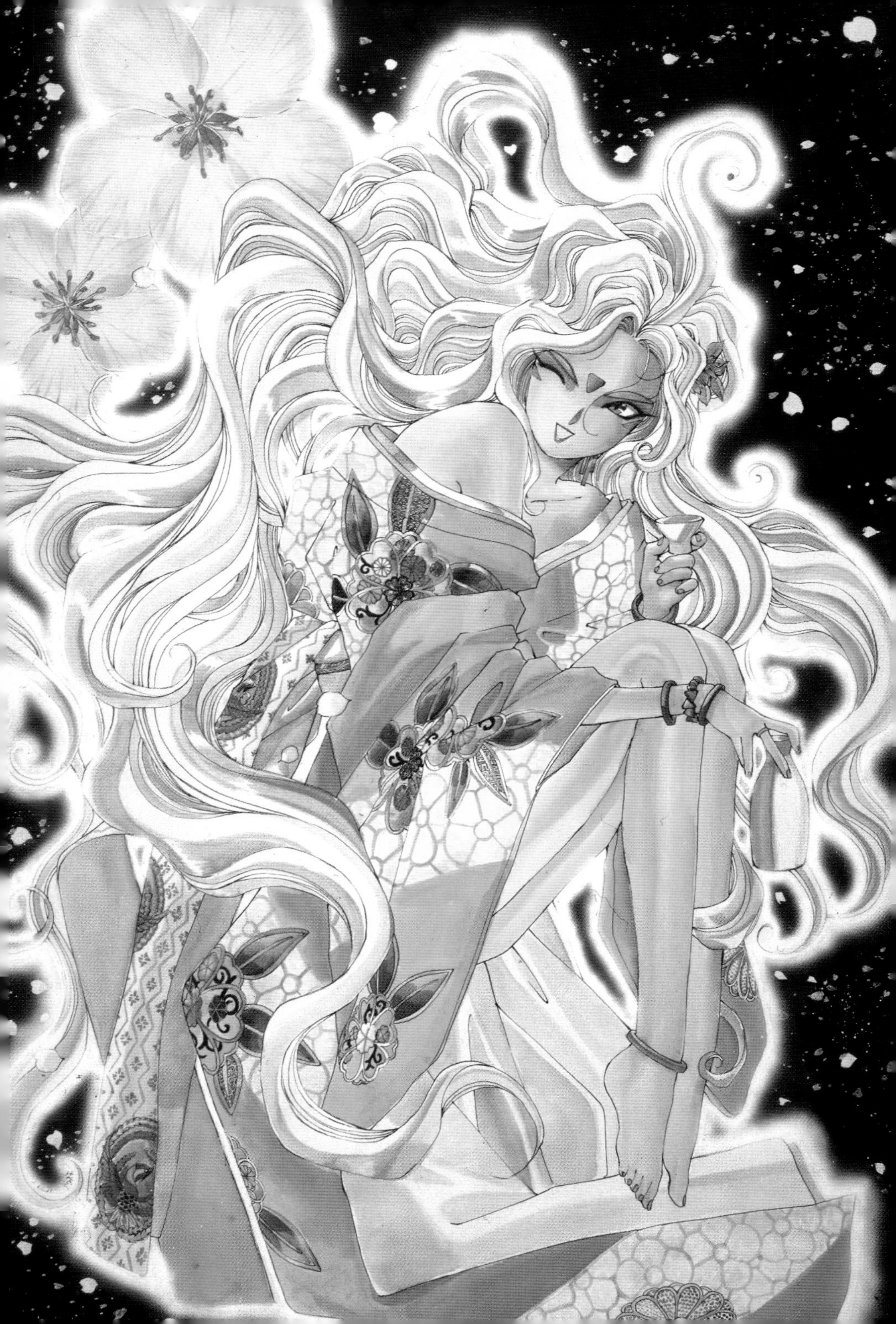

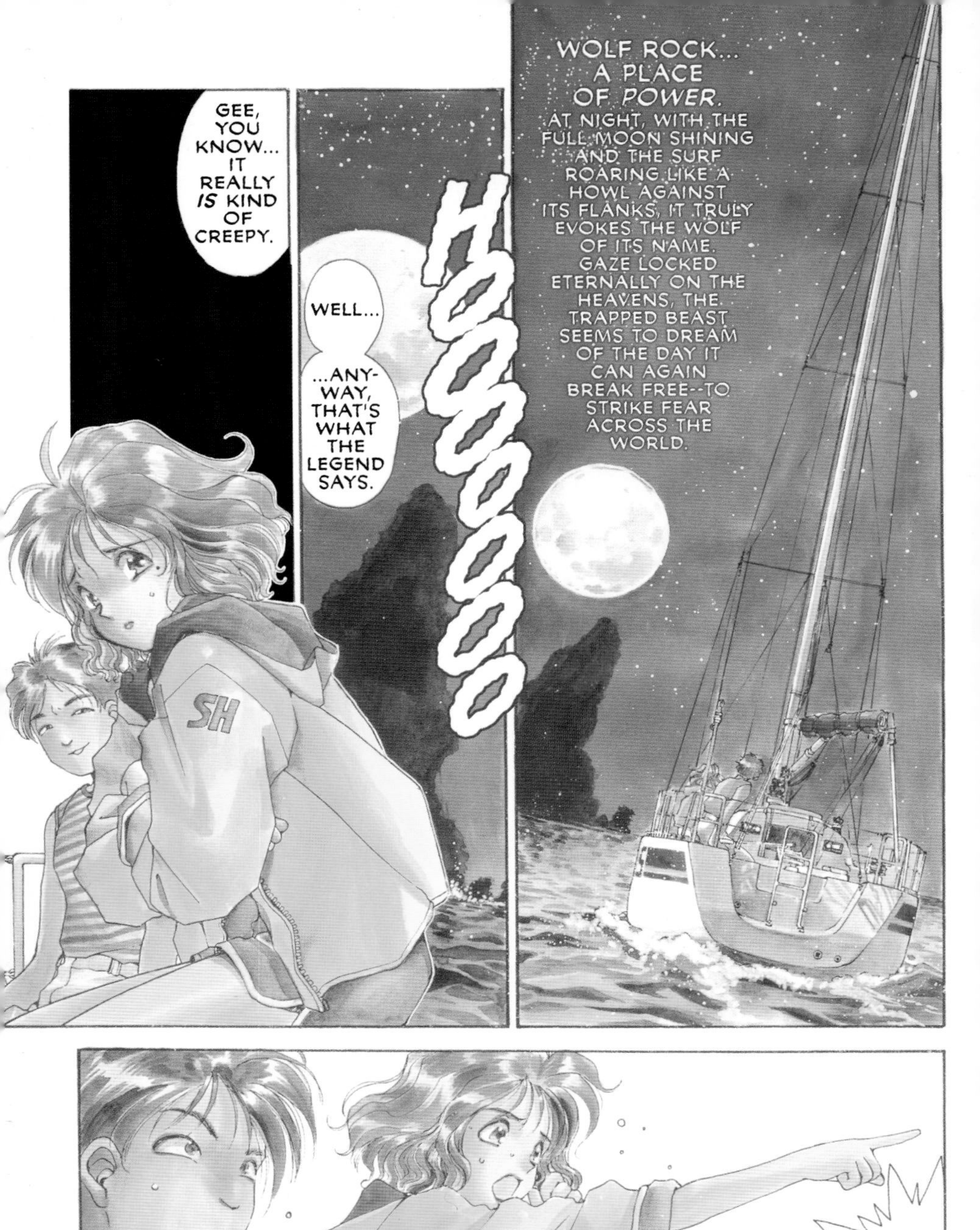
WOLF ROCK... A PLACE OF *POWER*. AT NIGHT, WITH THE FULL MOON SHINING AND THE SURF ROARING LIKE A HOWL AGAINST ITS FLANKS, IT TRULY EVOKES THE WOLF OF ITS NAME. GAZE LOCKED ETERNALLY ON THE HEAVENS, THE TRAPPED BEAST SEEMS TO DREAM OF THE DAY IT CAN AGAIN BREAK FREE--TO STRIKE FEAR ACROSS THE WORLD.
HOOOOOOO
WELL...
...ANYWAY, THAT'S WHAT THE LEGEND SAYS.
GEE, YOU KNOW... IT REALLY *IS* KIND OF CREEPY.
HEY!! WHAT'S *THAT?!*

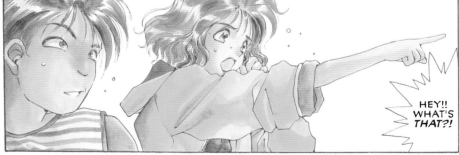

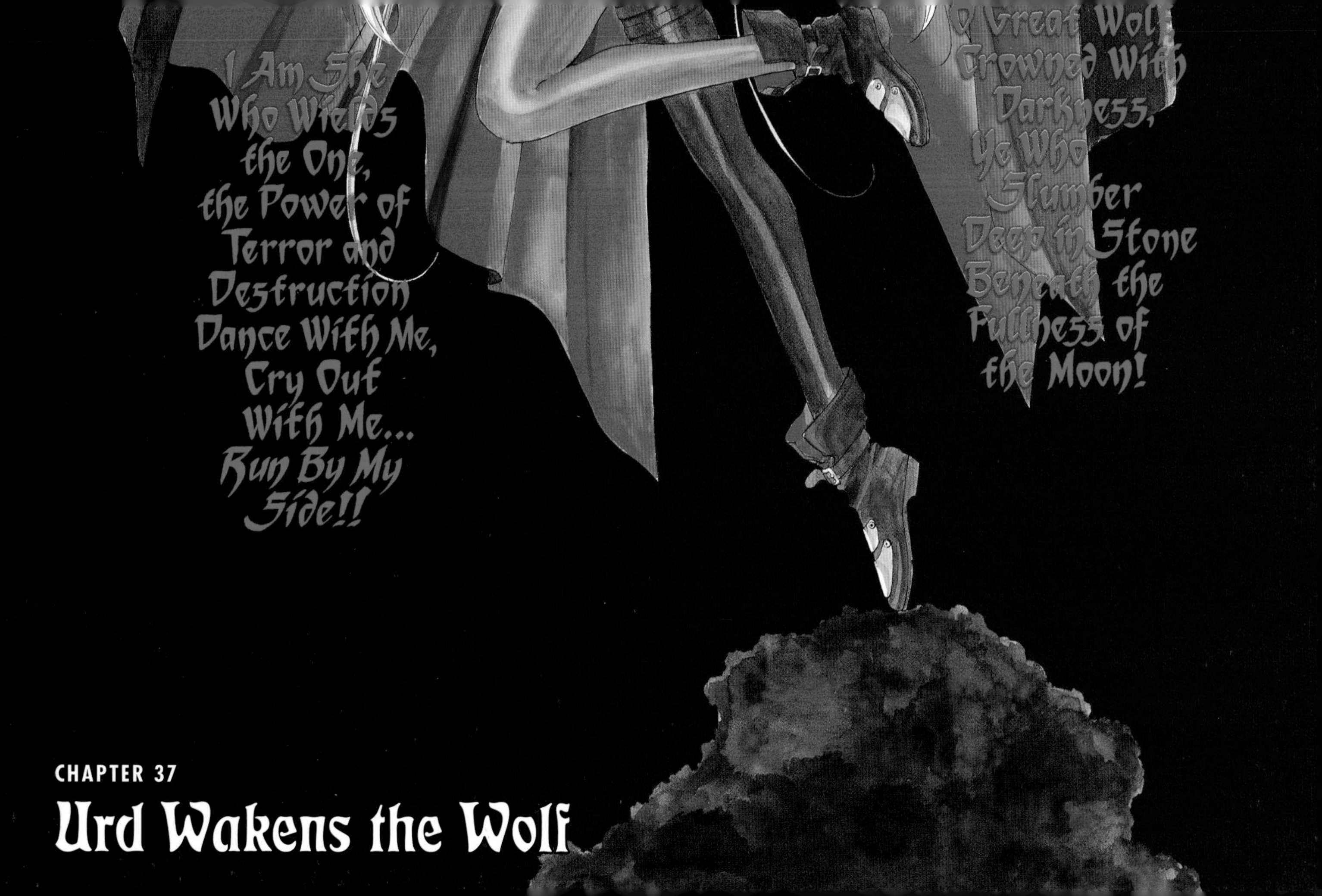
O Great Wolf Crowned With Darkness, Ye Who Slumber Deep in Stone Beneath the Fullness of the Moon!
I Am She Who Wields the One, the Power of Terror and Destruction Dance With Me, Cry Out With Me... Run By My Side!!

CHAPTER 37

# Urd Wakens the Wolf

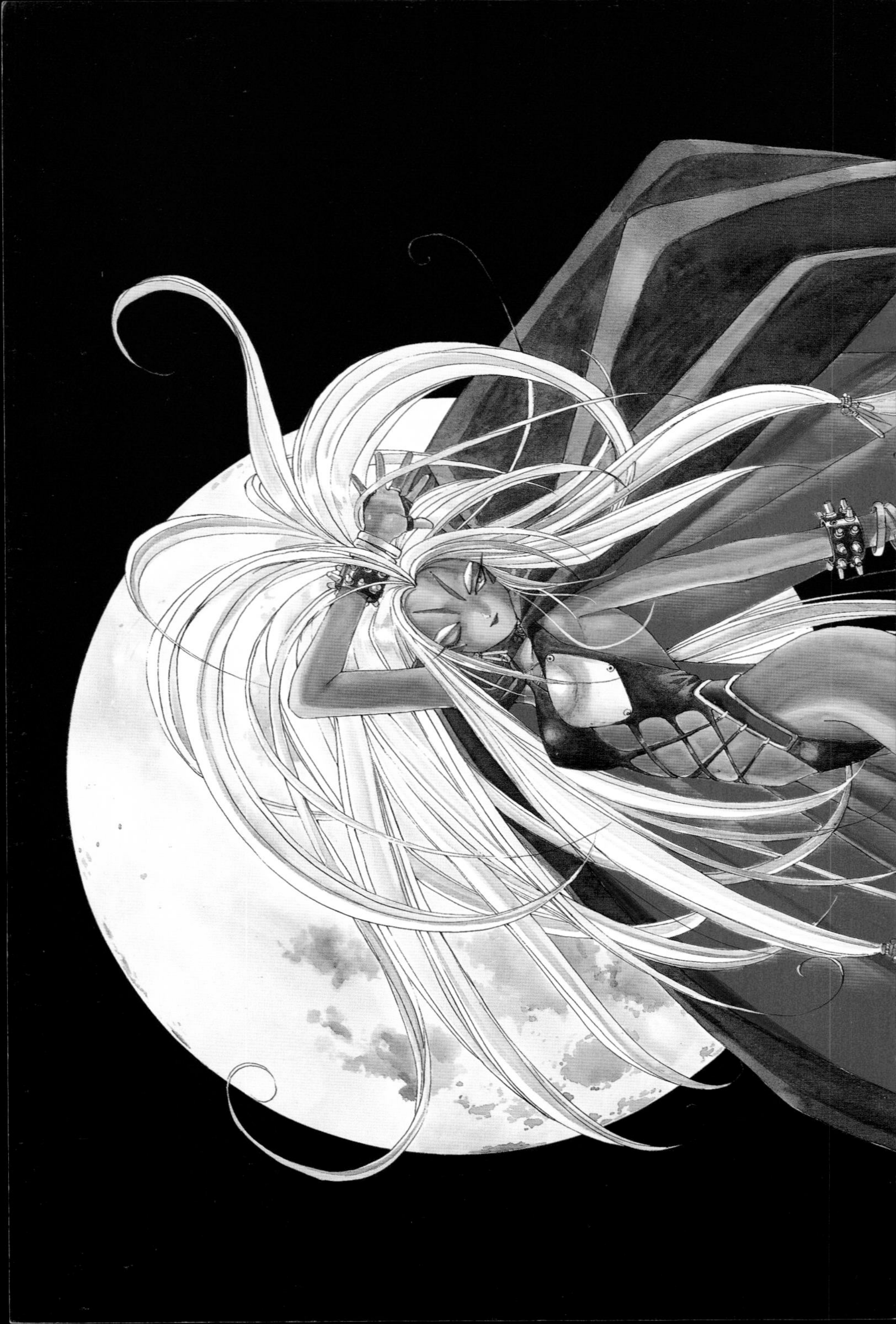

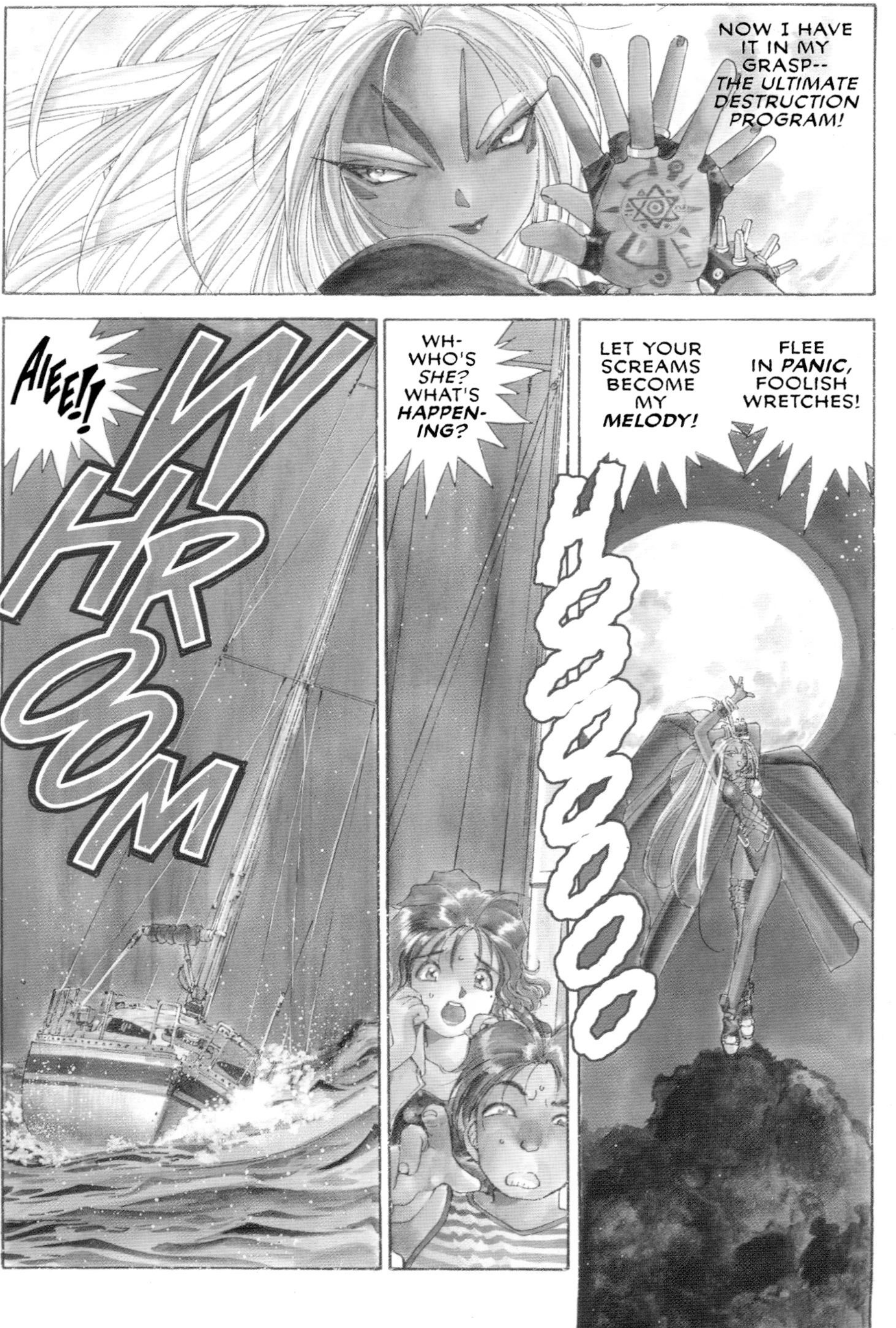
NOW I HAVE IT IN MY GRASP-- *THE ULTIMATE DESTRUCTION PROGRAM!*
FLEE IN *PANIC,* FOOLISH WRETCHES!
LET YOUR SCREAMS BECOME MY *MELODY!*
HOOOOOOO
WH-WHO'S *SHE?* WHAT'S *HAPPEN-ING?*
AIEE!!
WHROOM

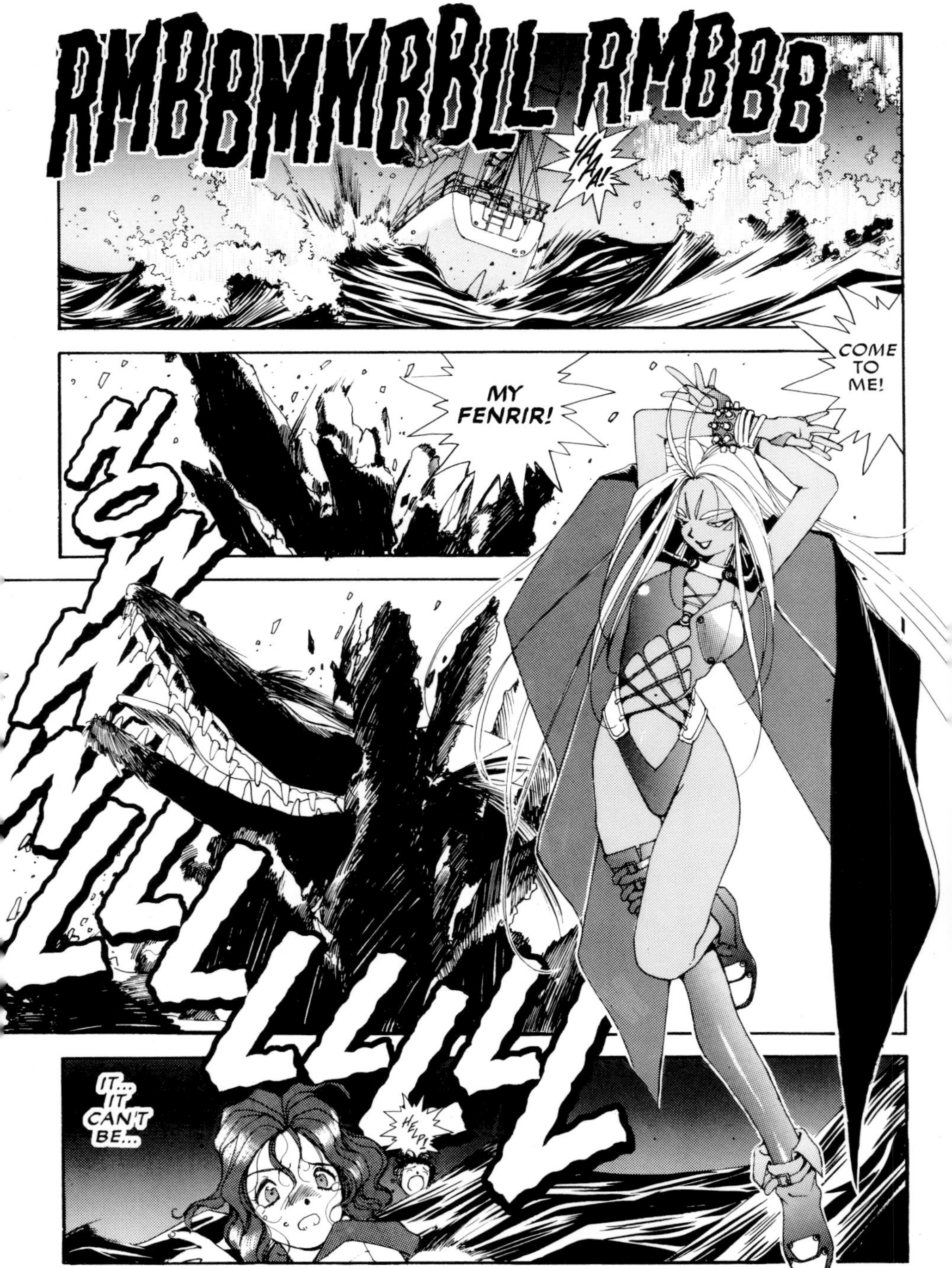
RMBBMMRBLL RMBBB
YAAA!
COME TO ME!
MY FENRIR!
HOWWLLLLL
IT... IT CAN'T BE...
HELP!

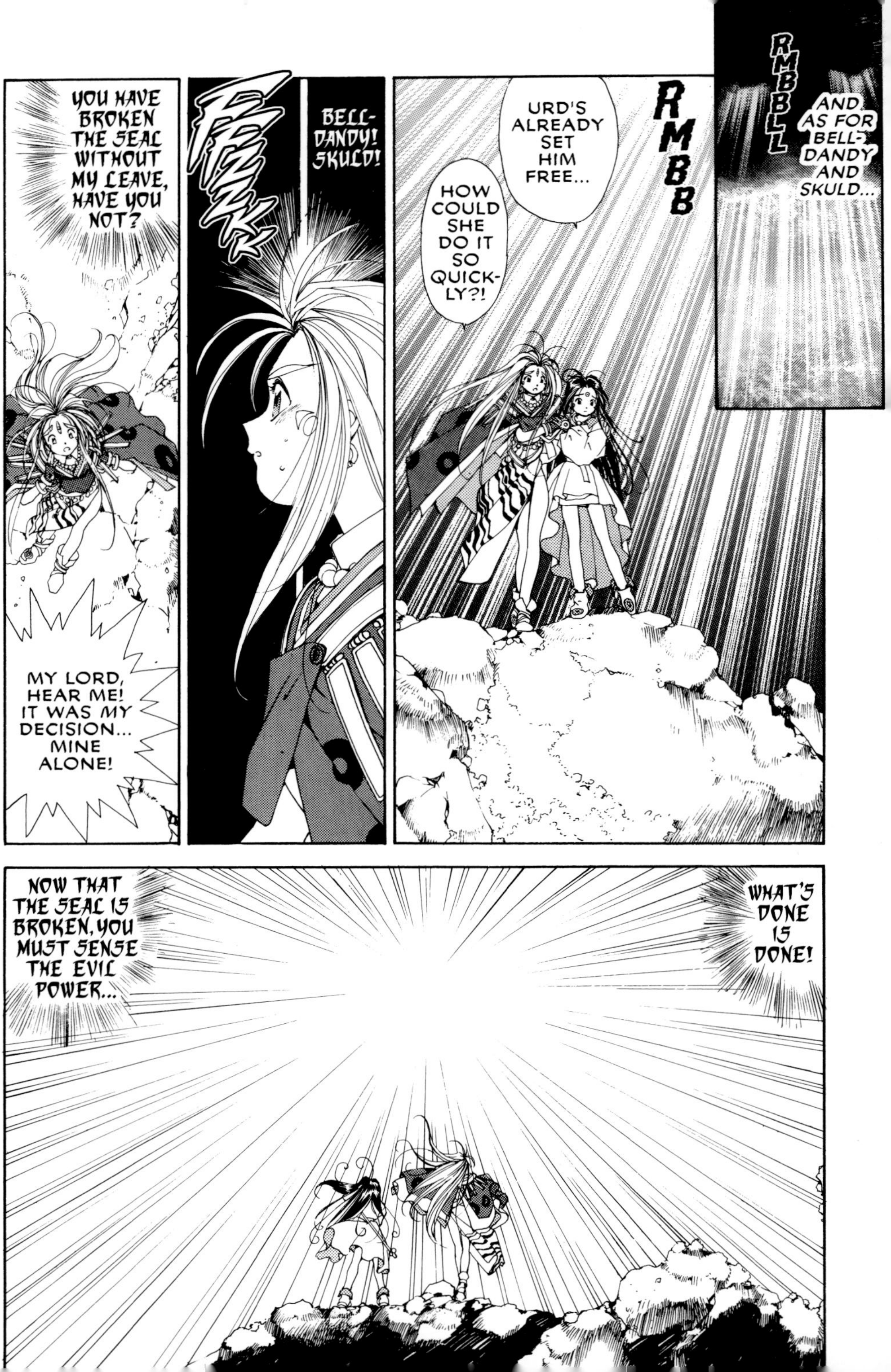
RMBBLL
AND AS FOR BELL-DANDY AND SKULD...
RMBB
URD'S ALREADY SET HIM FREE...
HOW COULD SHE DO IT SO QUICKLY?!
BELL-DANDY! SKULD!
YOU HAVE BROKEN THE SEAL WITHOUT MY LEAVE, HAVE YOU NOT?
MY LORD, HEAR ME! IT WAS MY DECISION... MINE ALONE!
WHAT'S DONE IS DONE!
NOW THAT THE SEAL IS BROKEN, YOU MUST SENSE THE EVIL POWER...

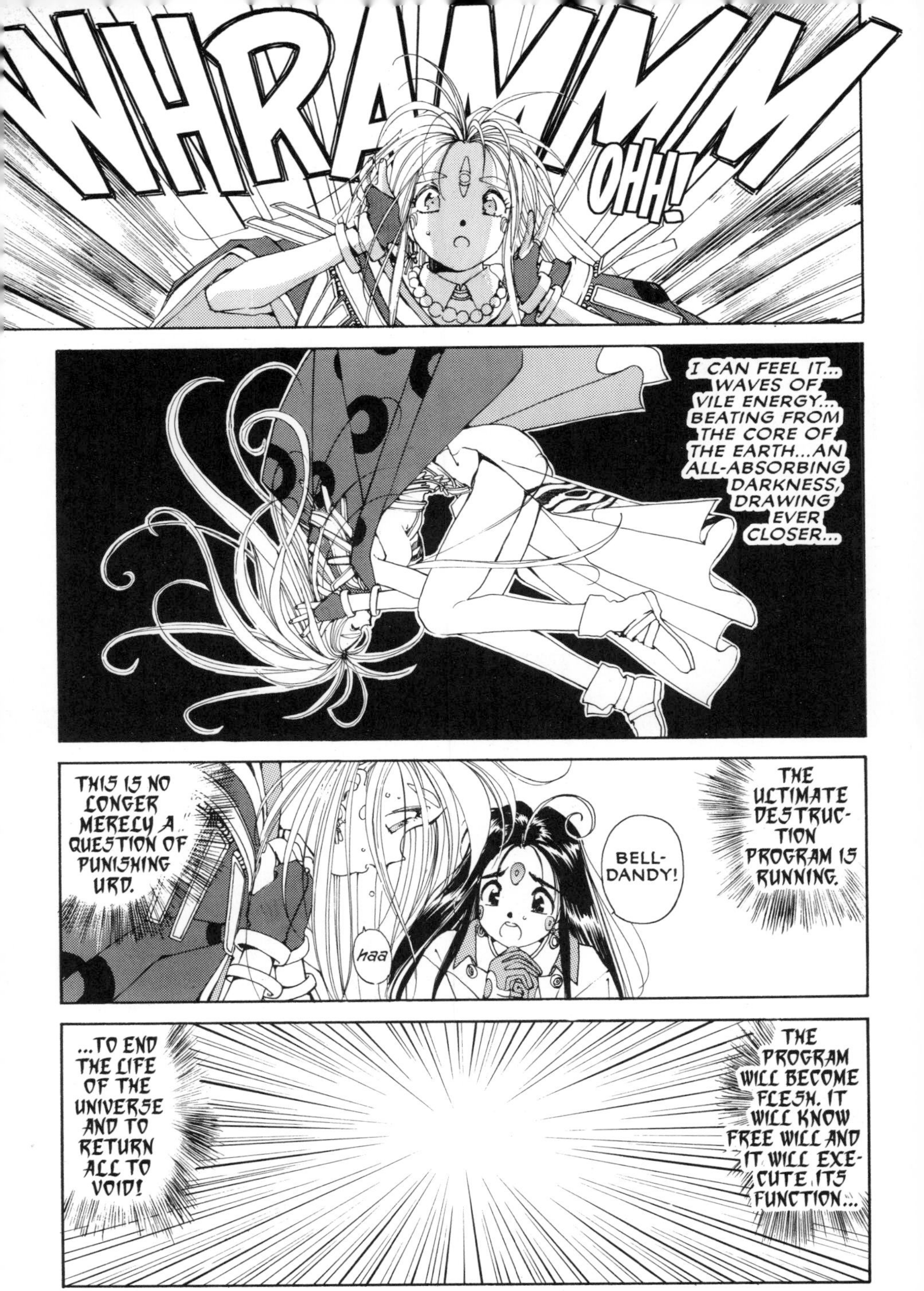
WHRAMMM
OHH!
I CAN FEEL IT... WAVES OF VILE ENERGY... BEATING FROM THE CORE OF THE EARTH...AN ALL-ABSORBING DARKNESS, DRAWING EVER CLOSER...
THE ULTIMATE DESTRUCTION PROGRAM IS RUNNING.
BELL-DANDY!
THIS IS NO LONGER MERELY A QUESTION OF PUNISHING URD.
haa
THE PROGRAM WILL BECOME FLESH. IT WILL KNOW FREE WILL AND IT WILL EXECUTE ITS FUNCTION...
...TO END THE LIFE OF THE UNIVERSE AND TO RETURN ALL TO VOID!

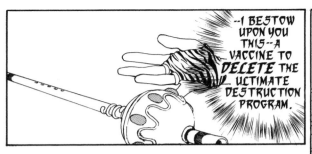

I MUST CONSERVE MY STRENGTH TO PROTECT YGGDRASIL ITSELF!
THERE-FORE I SHALL RELY UPON YOU, BELL-DANDY--
--YOU WHO DARED TO BREAK THE SEAL MUST NOW DARE PROTECT THE WORLD BELOW.
--I BESTOW UPON YOU THIS--A VACCINE TO DELETE THE ULTIMATE DESTRUCTION PROGRAM.
IT HAS ONLY ONE DOSE--
THERE-FORE USE IT WISELY.
Chingg!
AND READ THE MANUAL FIRST... FARE-WELL!
GEE, Y'THINK THIS SILLY THING REALLY WORKS? LEMME TRY IT...
Sip
I SAID READ THE MANUAL!

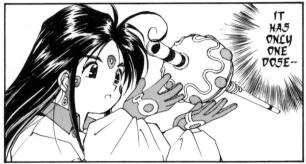

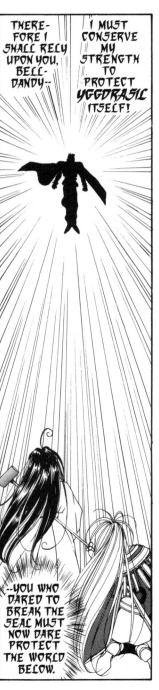

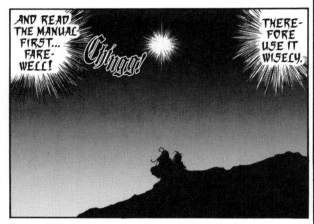

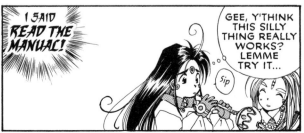

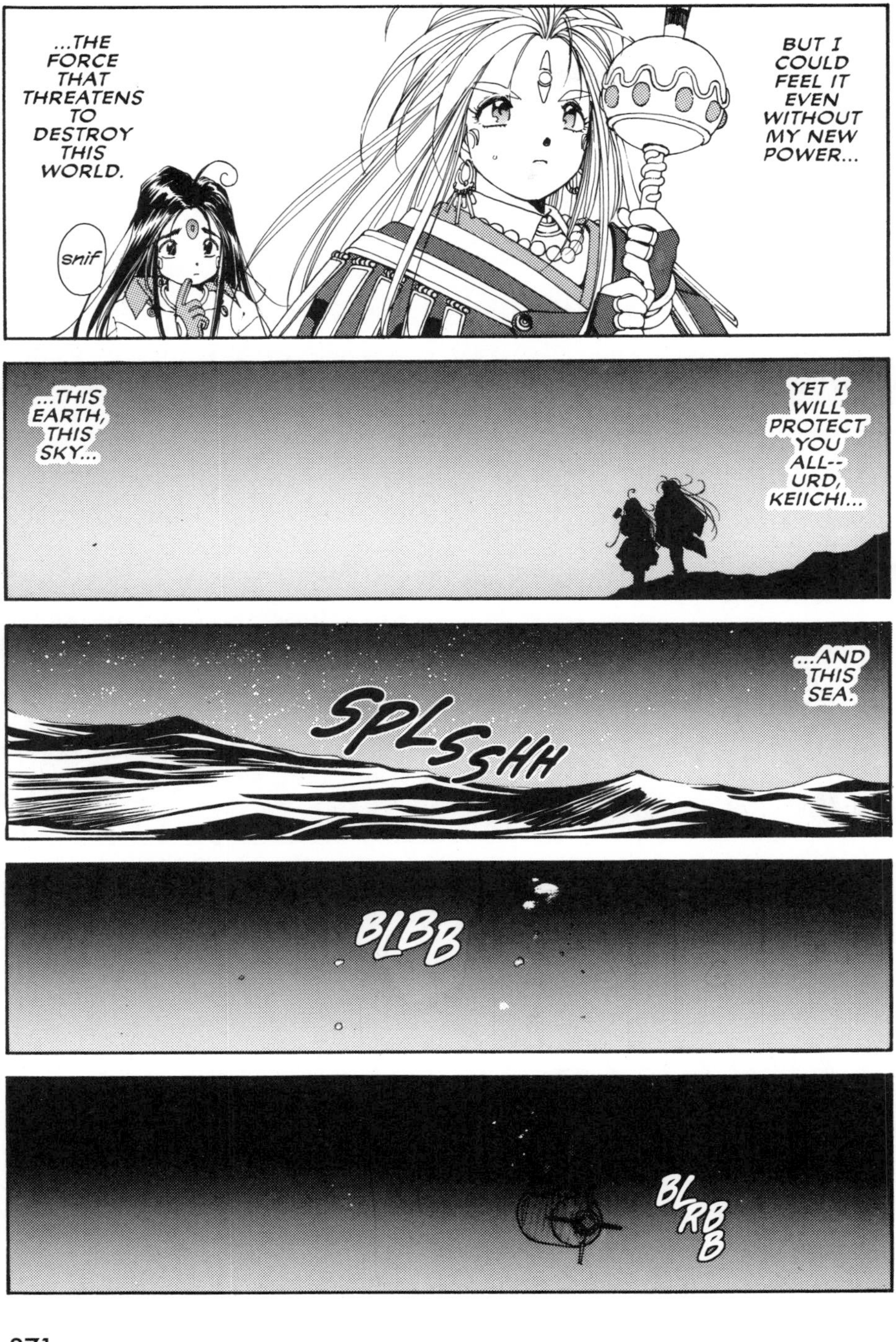
BUT I COULD FEEL IT EVEN WITHOUT MY NEW POWER...
...THE FORCE THAT THREATENS TO DESTROY THIS WORLD.
snif
YET I WILL PROTECT YOU ALL-- URD, KEIICHI...
...THIS EARTH, THIS SKY...
...AND THIS SEA.
SPLSSHH
BLBB
BLRBB

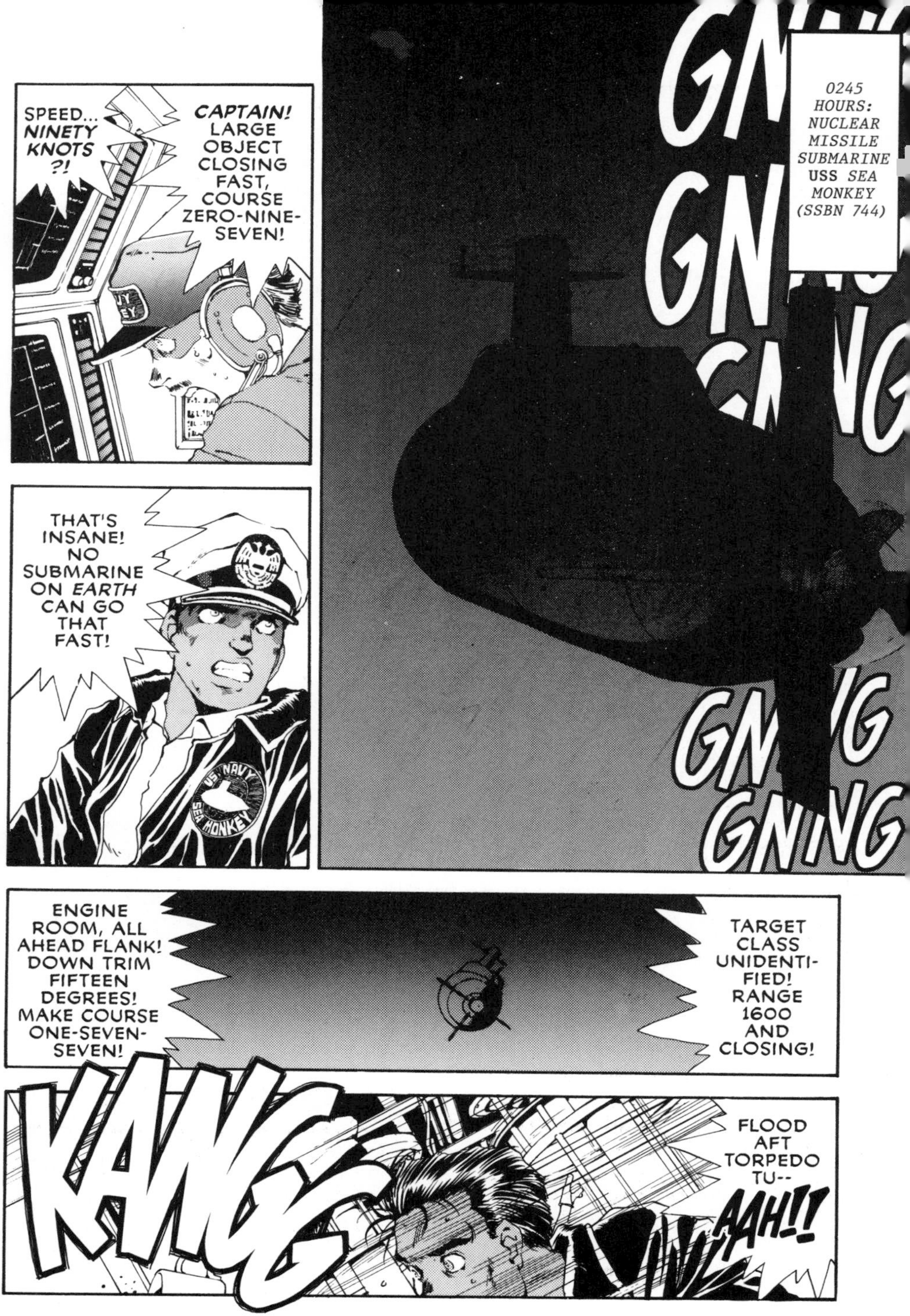
0245 HOURS: NUCLEAR MISSILE SUBMARINE USS SEA MONKEY (SSBN 744)
GNING
GNING
CAPTAIN! LARGE OBJECT CLOSING FAST, COURSE ZERO-NINE-SEVEN!
SPEED... NINETY KNOTS ?!
THAT'S INSANE! NO SUBMARINE ON EARTH CAN GO THAT FAST!
US NAVY SEA MONKEY
TARGET CLASS UNIDENTIFIED! RANGE 1600 AND CLOSING!
ENGINE ROOM, ALL AHEAD FLANK! DOWN TRIM FIFTEEN DEGREES! MAKE COURSE ONE-SEVEN-SEVEN!
FLOOD AFT TORPEDO TU-- AAH!!!
KANG

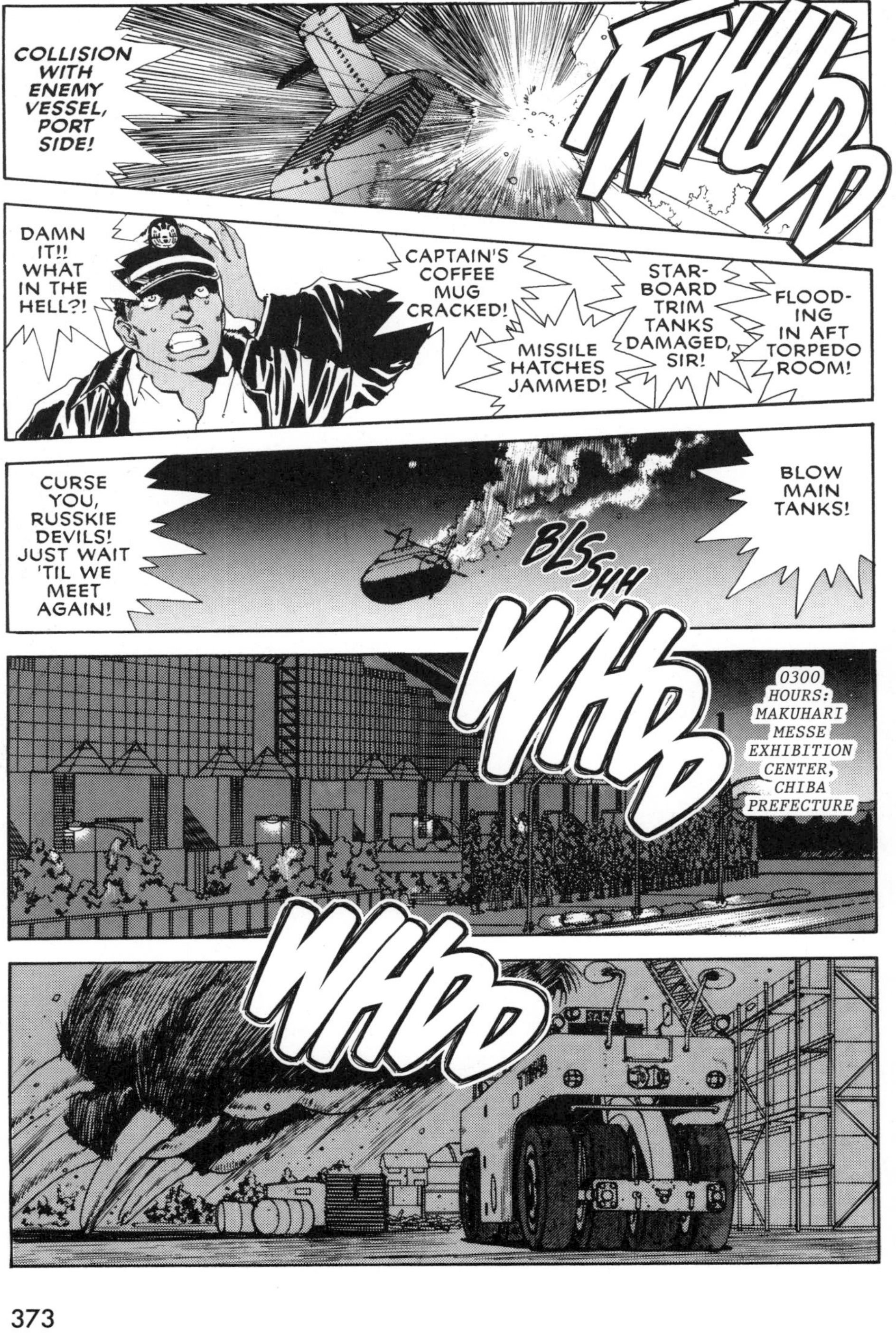
FWHUDD
COLLISION WITH ENEMY VESSEL, PORT SIDE!
FLOODING IN AFT TORPEDO ROOM!
STARBOARD TRIM TANKS DAMAGED, SIR!
MISSILE HATCHES JAMMED!
CAPTAIN'S COFFEE MUG CRACKED!
DAMN IT!! WHAT IN THE HELL?!
BLOW MAIN TANKS!
BLSSHH
CURSE YOU, RUSSKIE DEVILS! JUST WAIT 'TIL WE MEET AGAIN!
0300 HOURS: MAKUHARI MESSE EXHIBITION CENTER, CHIBA PREFECTURE
WHOD
WHOD

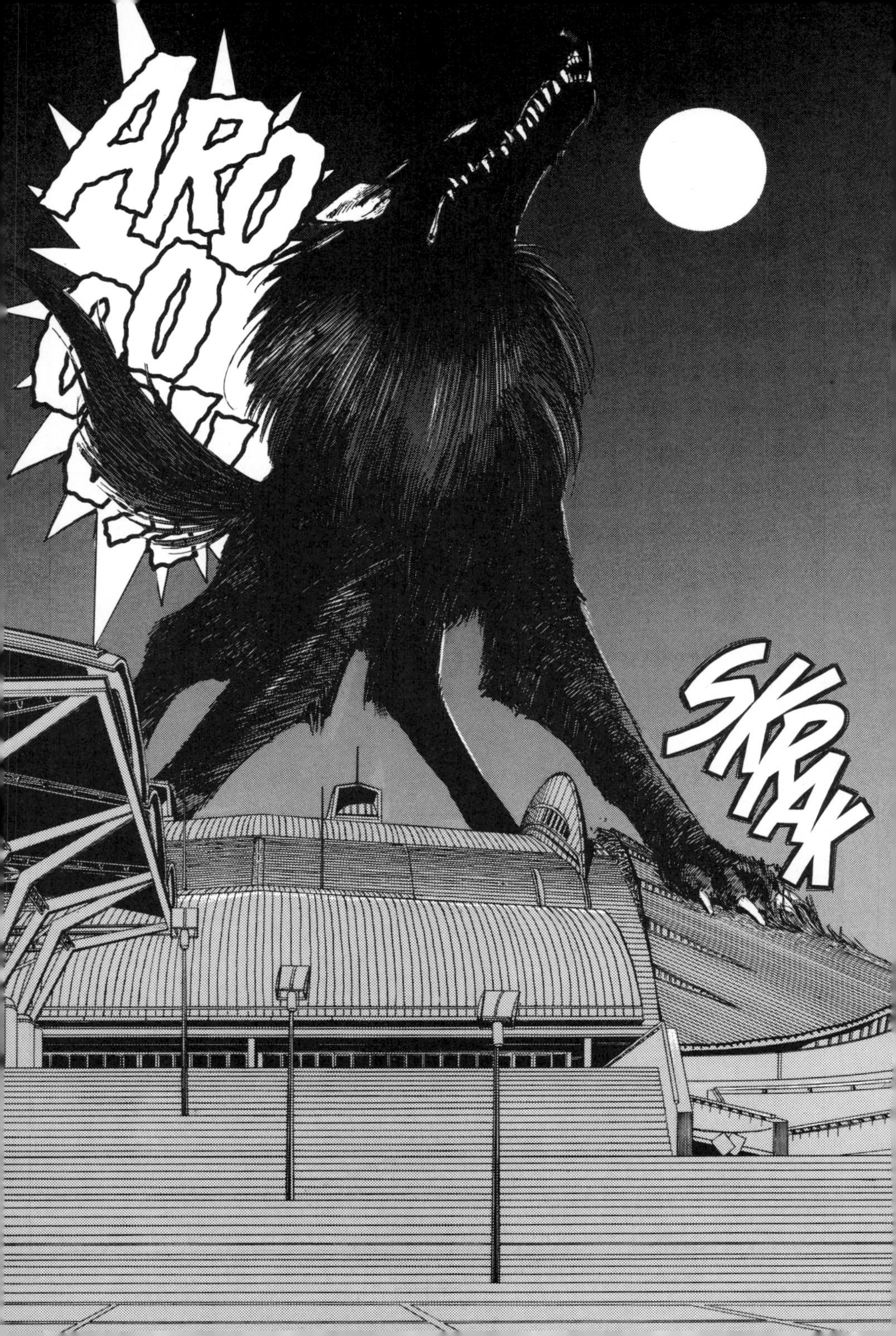
ARO
SKRAK

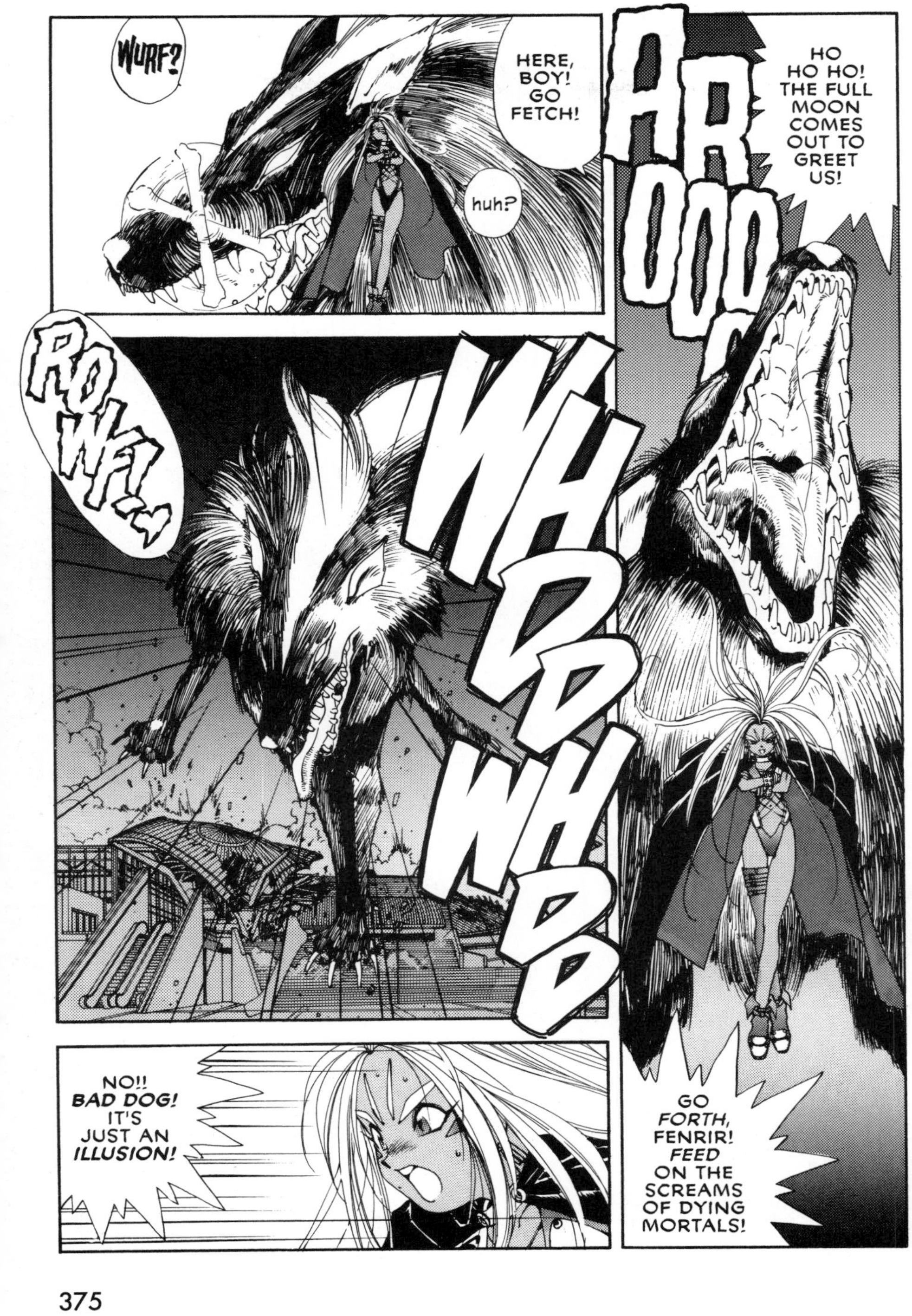
HO HO HO! THE FULL MOON COMES OUT TO GREET US!
AROOOO
GO *FORTH*, FENRIR! *FEED* ON THE SCREAMS OF DYING MORTALS!
HERE, BOY! GO FETCH!
huh?
WURF?
WHDD WHDD
ROWF!..
NO!! ***BAD DOG!*** IT'S JUST AN ***ILLUSION!***

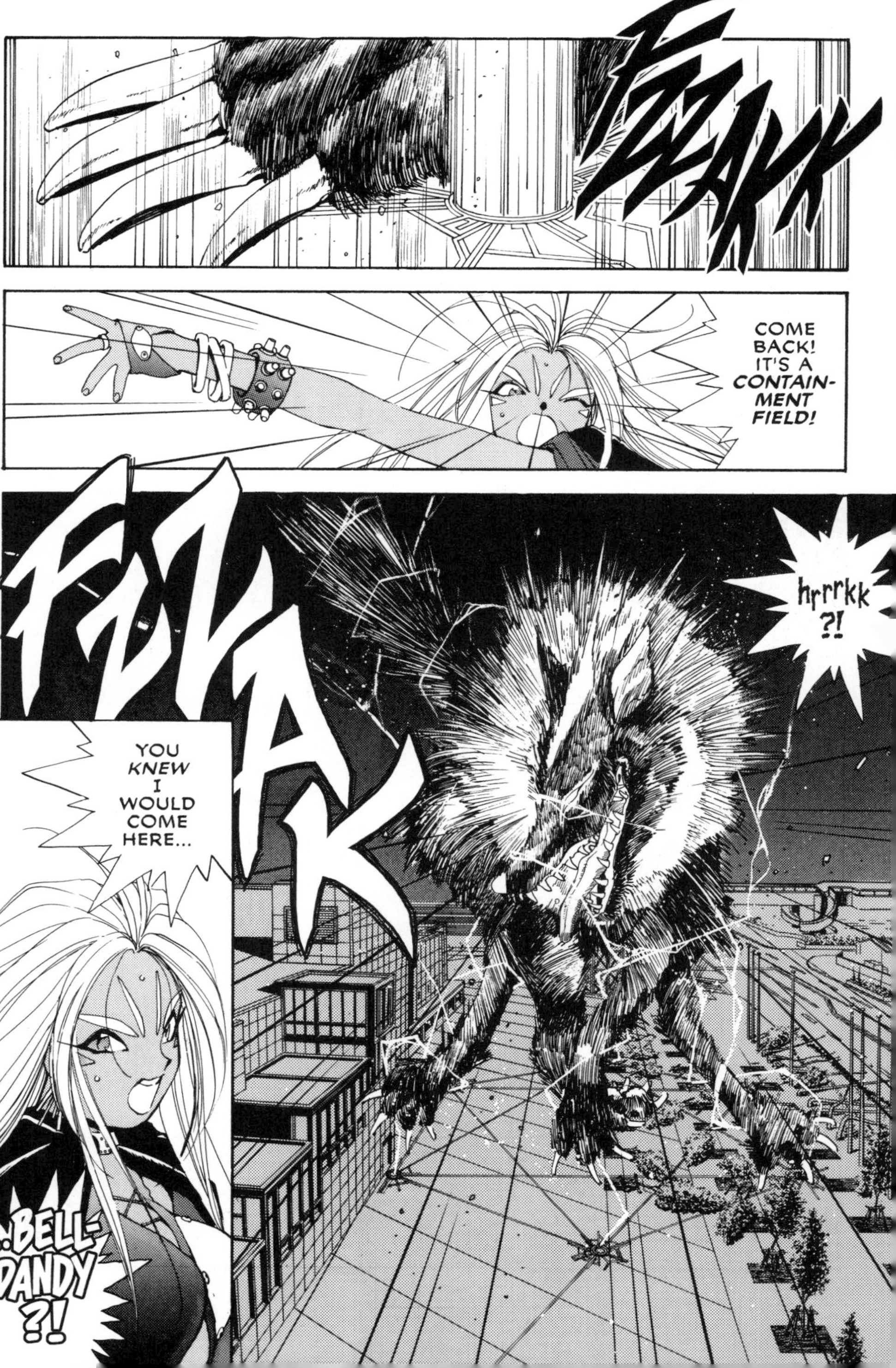
FZZAKK
COME BACK! IT'S A *CONTAINMENT FIELD!*
hrrrkk ?!
FZZAK
YOU *KNEW* I WOULD COME HERE...
...BELL-DANDY ?!

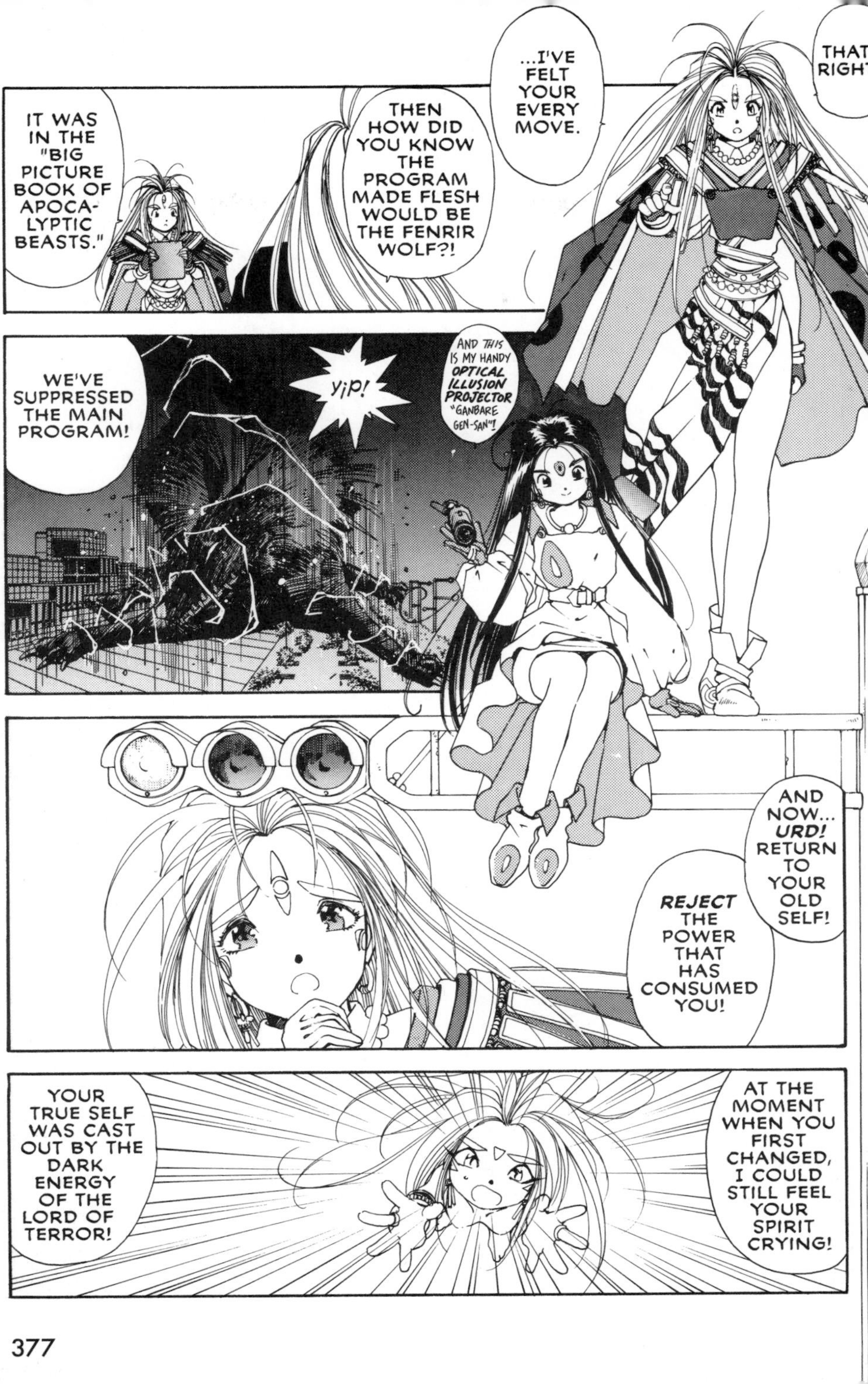
THAT'S RIGHT...
...I'VE FELT YOUR EVERY MOVE.
THEN HOW DID YOU KNOW THE PROGRAM MADE FLESH WOULD BE THE FENRIR WOLF?!
IT WAS IN THE "BIG PICTURE BOOK OF APOCA-LYPTIC BEASTS."
AND THIS IS MY HANDY OPTICAL ILLUSION PROJECTOR "GANBARE GEN-SAN"!
yip!
WE'VE SUPPRESSED THE MAIN PROGRAM!
AND NOW... URD! RETURN TO YOUR OLD SELF!
REJECT THE POWER THAT HAS CONSUMED YOU!
AT THE MOMENT WHEN YOU FIRST CHANGED, I COULD STILL FEEL YOUR SPIRIT CRYING!
YOUR TRUE SELF WAS CAST OUT BY THE DARK ENERGY OF THE LORD OF TERROR!

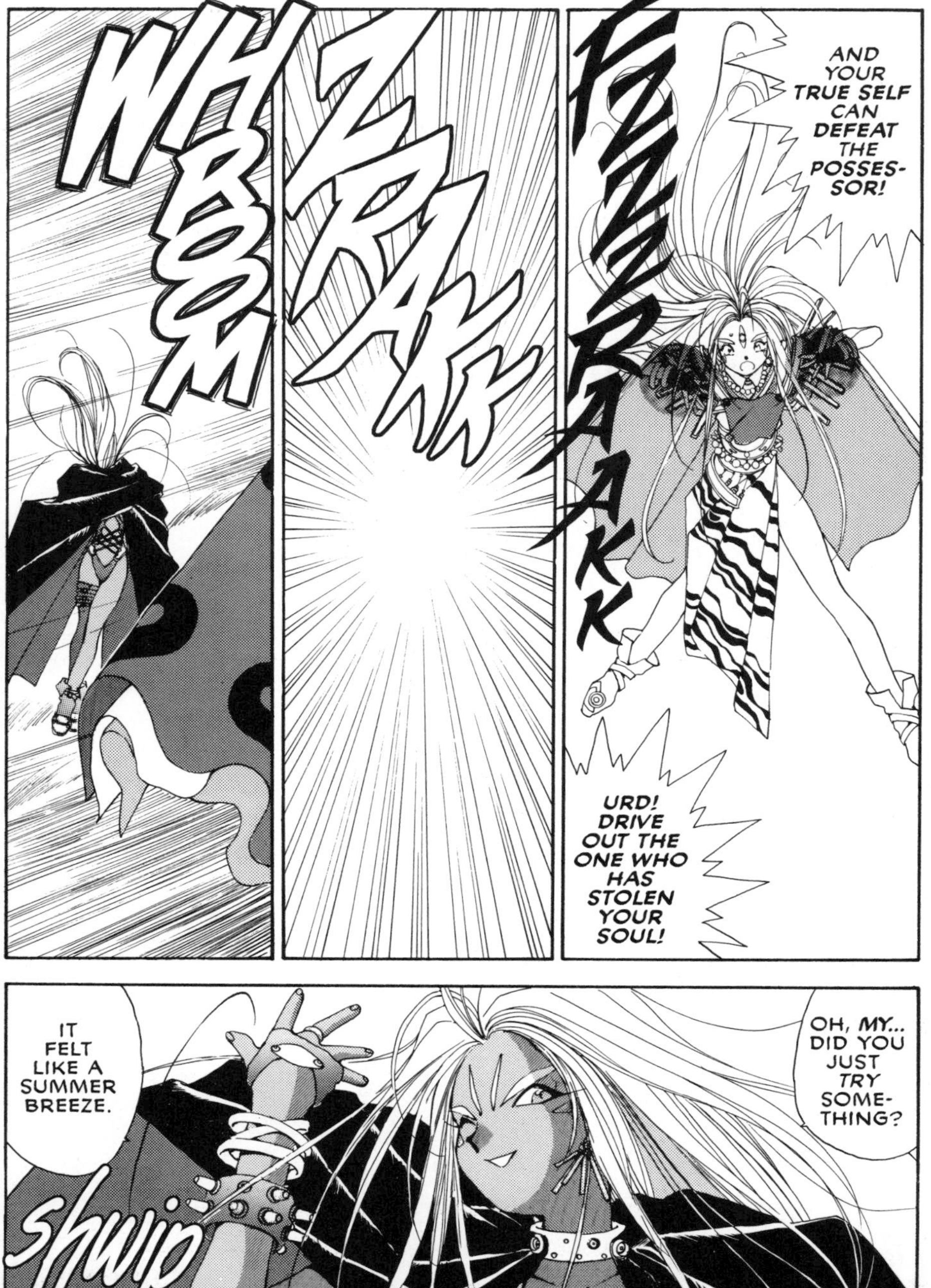
AND YOUR TRUE SELF CAN DEFEAT THE POSSES-SOR!
URD! DRIVE OUT THE ONE WHO HAS STOLEN YOUR SOUL!
ZRAKK
WHBOOM
OH, MY... DID YOU JUST TRY SOME-THING?
IT FELT LIKE A SUMMER BREEZE.
shwip

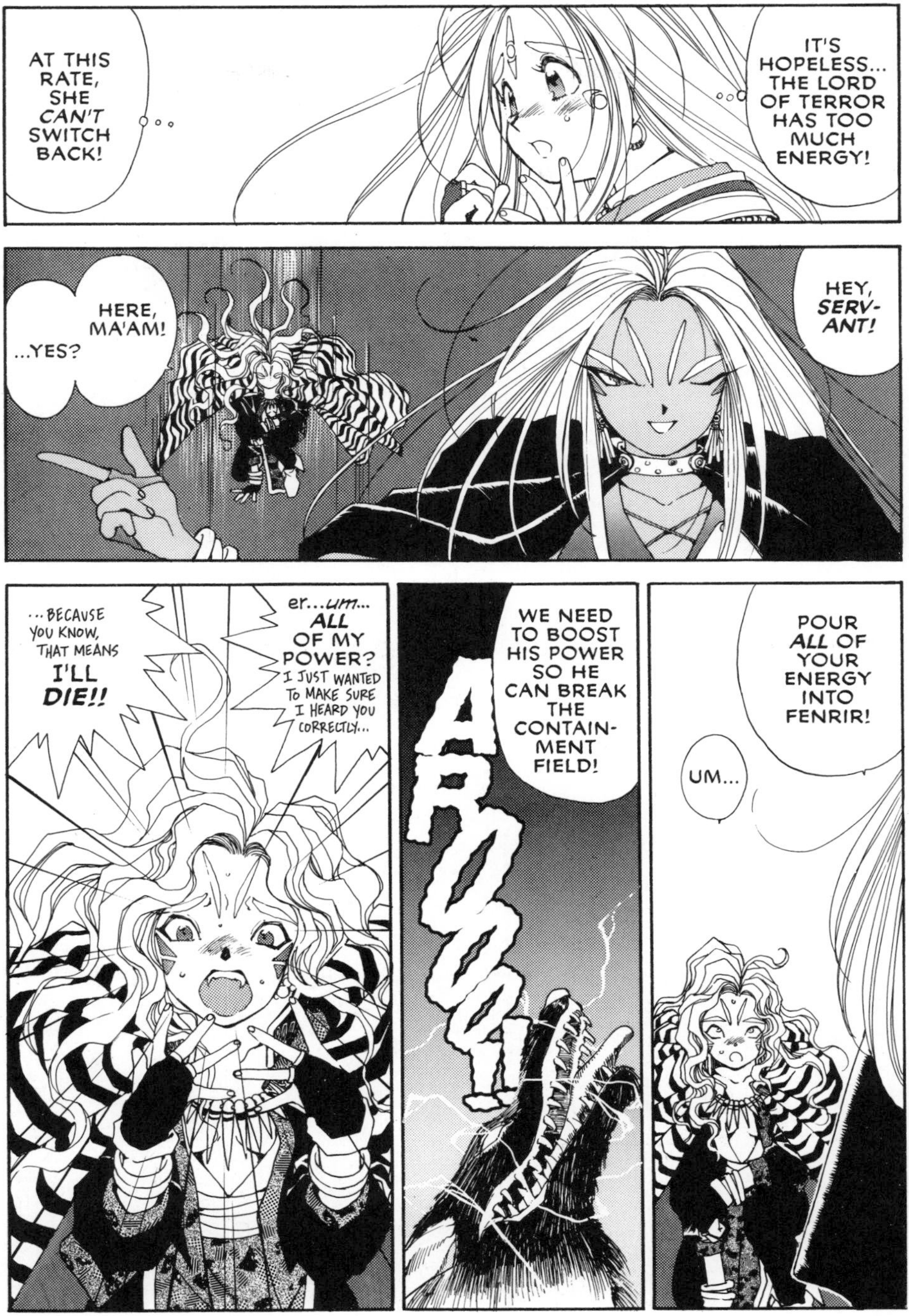
IT'S HOPELESS... THE LORD OF TERROR HAS TOO MUCH ENERGY!
AT THIS RATE, SHE CAN'T SWITCH BACK!
HEY, SERVANT!
HERE, MA'AM!
...YES?
POUR ALL OF YOUR ENERGY INTO FENRIR!
UM...
WE NEED TO BOOST HIS POWER SO HE CAN BREAK THE CONTAINMENT FIELD!
AROOO!
er...um... ALL OF MY POWER? I JUST WANTED TO MAKE SURE I HEARD YOU CORRECTLY...
...BECAUSE YOU KNOW, THAT MEANS I'LL DIE!!

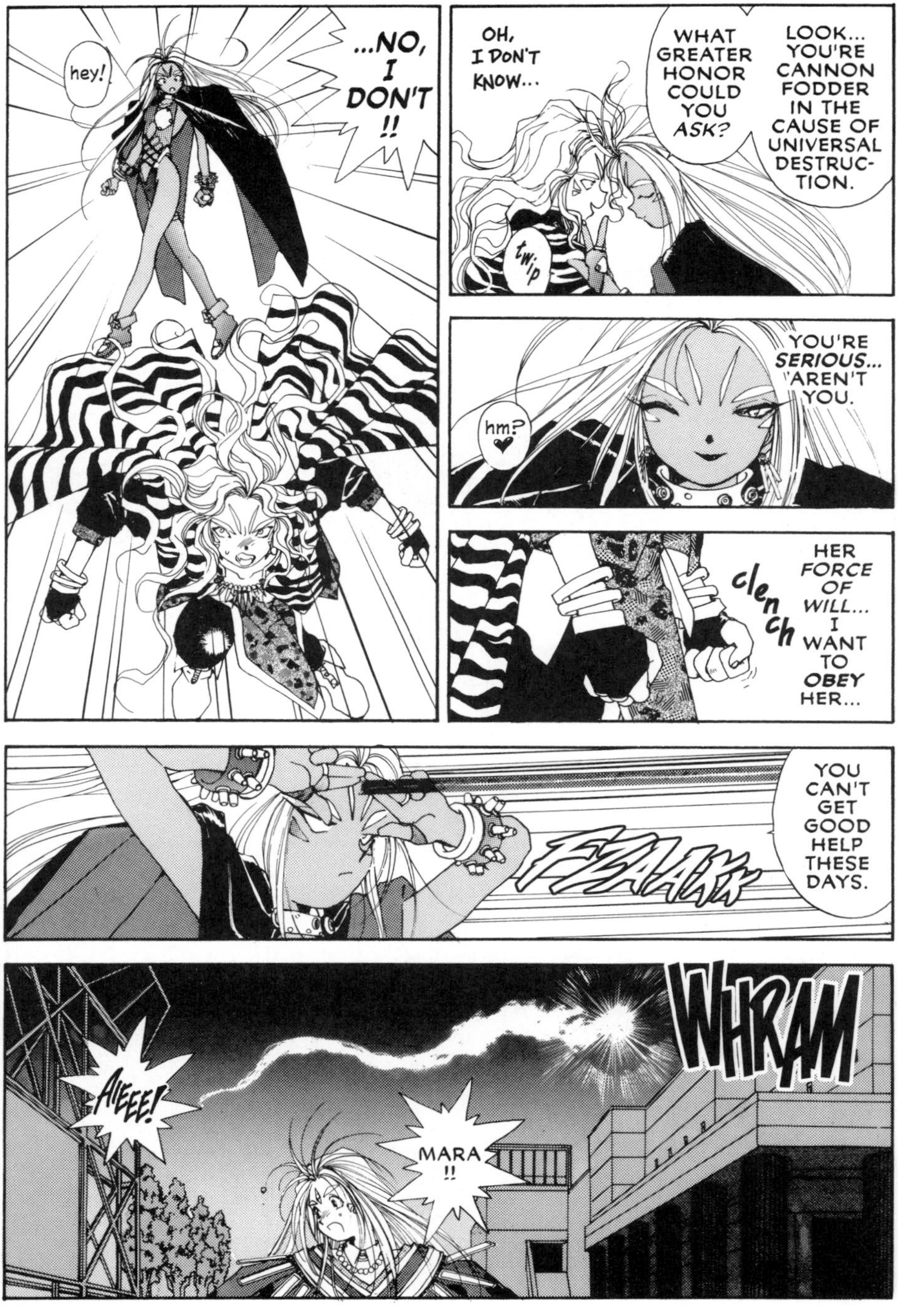
LOOK... YOU'RE CANNON FODDER IN THE CAUSE OF UNIVERSAL DESTRUCTION.
WHAT GREATER HONOR COULD YOU ASK?
OH, I DON'T KNOW...
twip
YOU'RE SERIOUS... AREN'T YOU.
hm? ♥
HER FORCE OF WILL... I WANT TO OBEY HER...
clench
...NO, I DON'T !!
hey!
YOU CAN'T GET GOOD HELP THESE DAYS.
FZAAKK
WHRAM
MARA !!
AIEEE!

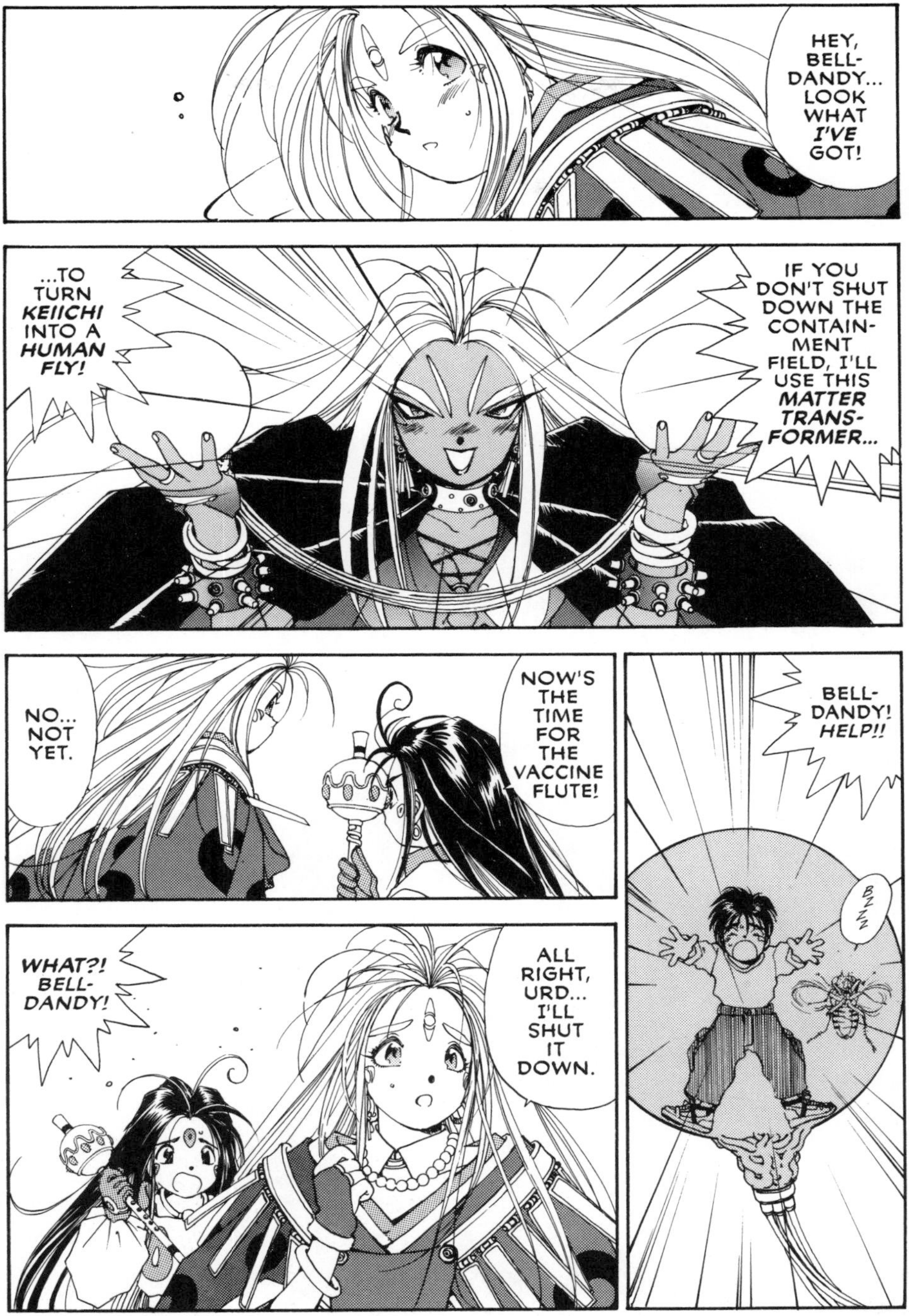
HEY, BELL-DANDY... LOOK WHAT *I'VE* GOT!
IF YOU DON'T SHUT DOWN THE CONTAIN-MENT FIELD, I'LL USE THIS *MATTER TRANS-FORMER...*
...TO TURN *KEIICHI* INTO A *HUMAN FLY!*
BELL-DANDY! *HELP!!*
BZZZ
NOW'S THE TIME FOR THE VACCINE FLUTE!
NO... NOT YET.
ALL RIGHT, URD... I'LL SHUT IT DOWN.
*WHAT?! BELL-DANDY!*

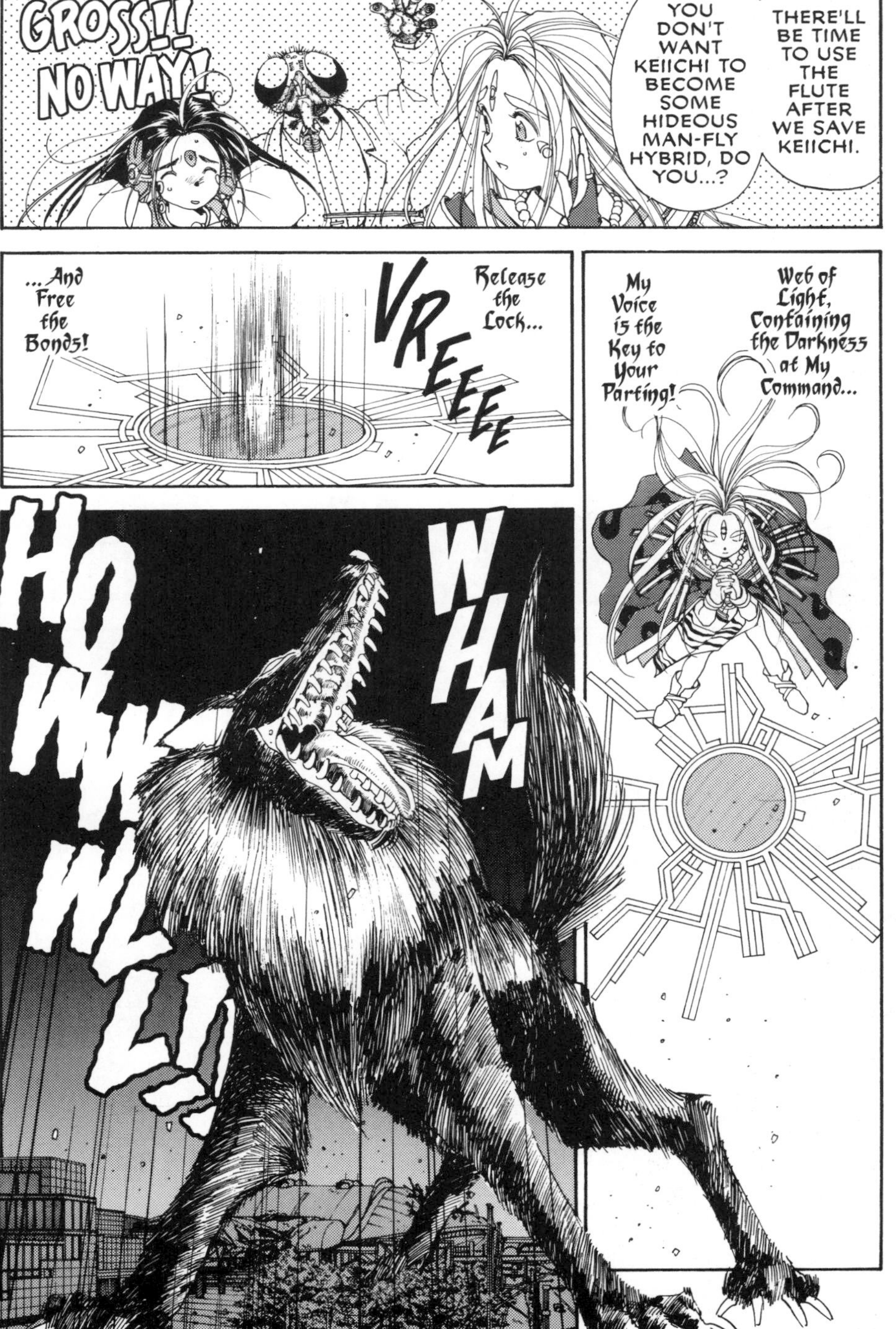

THERE'LL BE TIME TO USE THE FLUTE AFTER WE SAVE KEIICHI.
YOU DON'T WANT KEIICHI TO BECOME SOME HIDEOUS MAN-FLY HYBRID, DO YOU...?
GROSS!! NO WAY!
Web of Light, Containing the Darkness at My Command...
My Voice is the Key to Your Parting!
Release the Lock...
VREEEEE
...And Free the Bonds!
WHAM
HOWWWLL!!

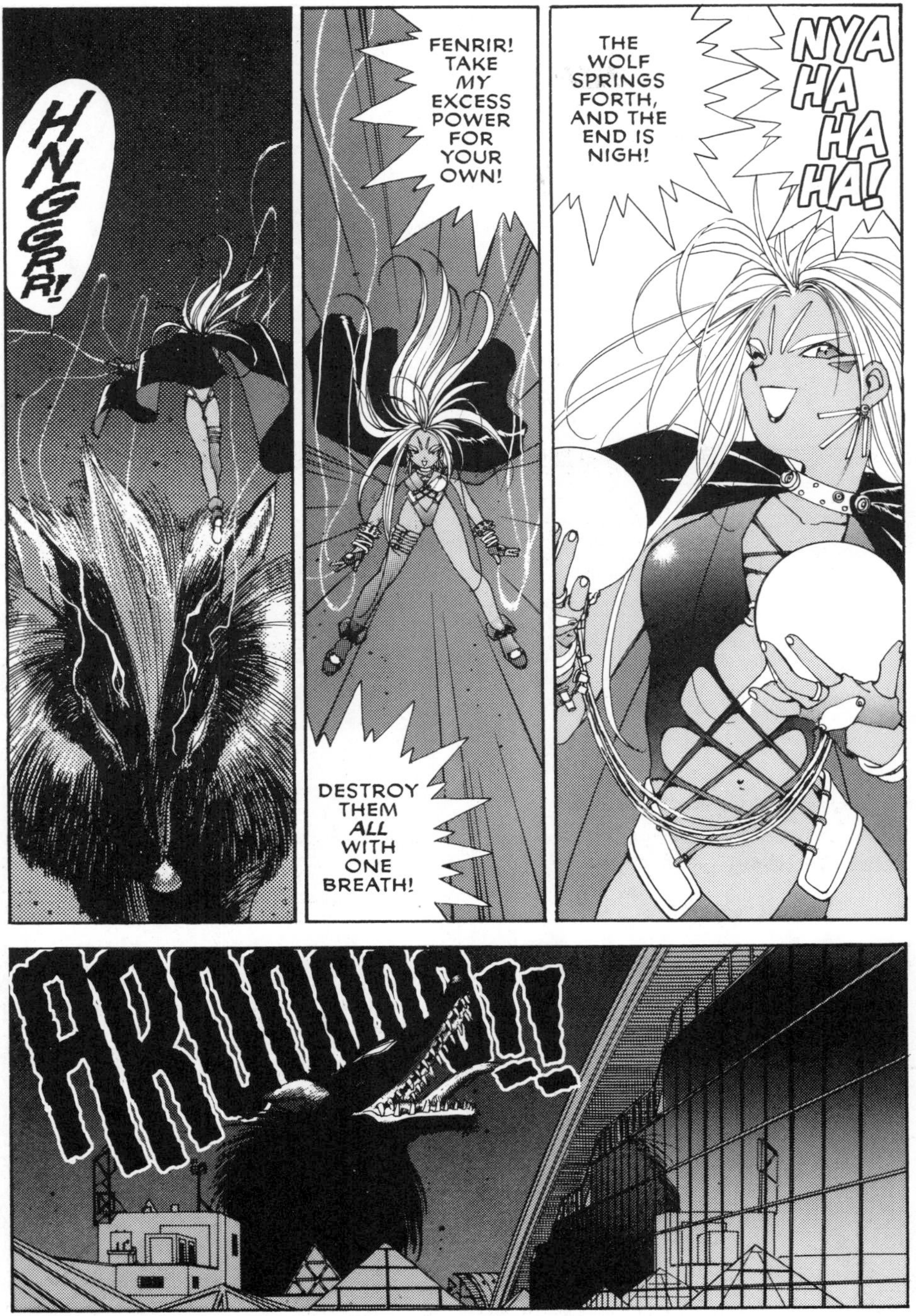
NYA HA HA HA HA!
THE WOLF SPRINGS FORTH, AND THE END IS NIGH!
FENRIR! TAKE MY EXCESS POWER FOR YOUR OWN!
DESTROY THEM ALL WITH ONE BREATH!
HNGGRR!

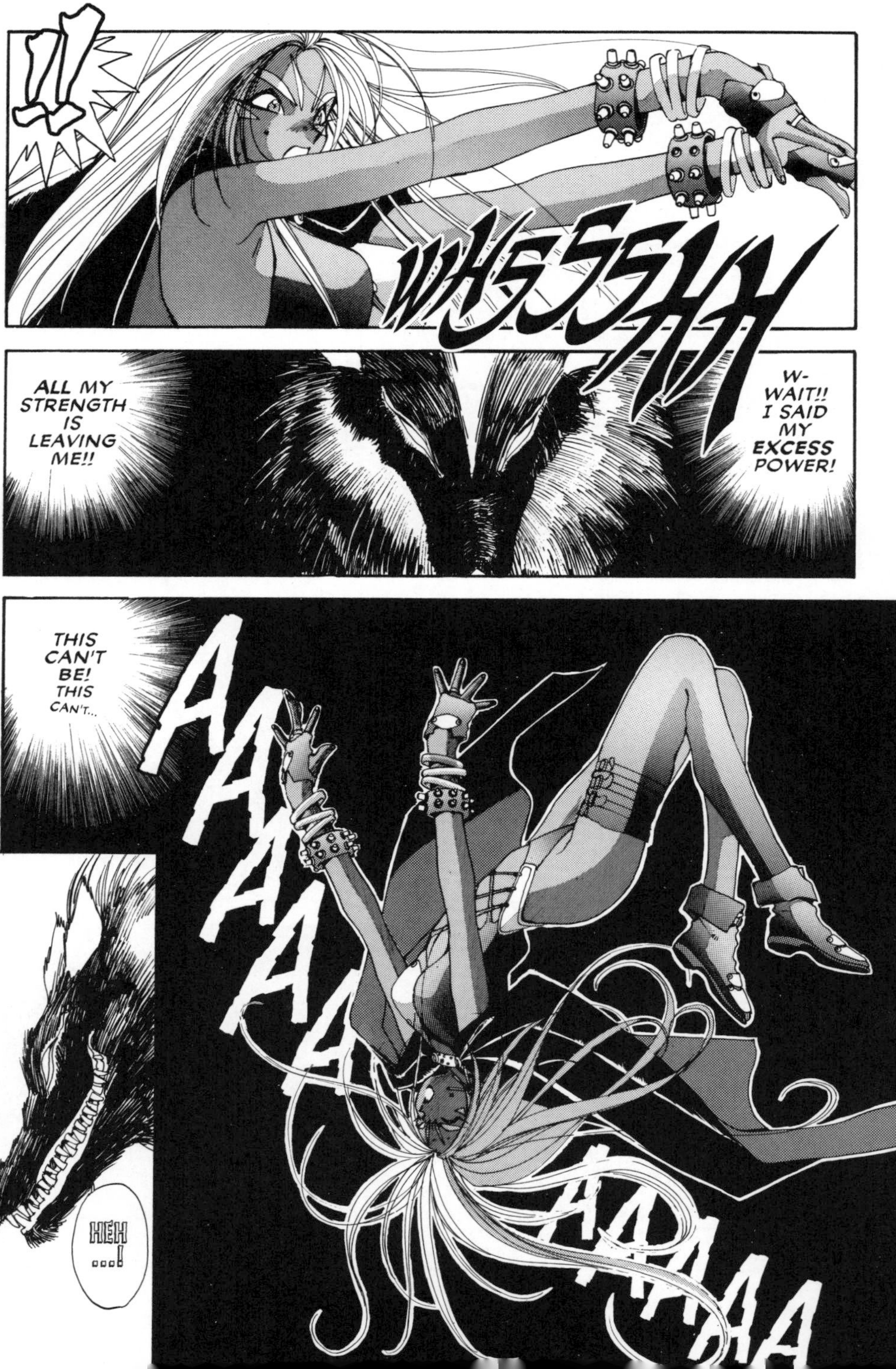
!!
WHSSSH
W-WAIT!! I SAID MY EXCESS POWER!
ALL MY STRENGTH IS LEAVING ME!!
THIS CAN'T BE! THIS CAN'T...
AAAAAAAAAAAA
HEH ...!

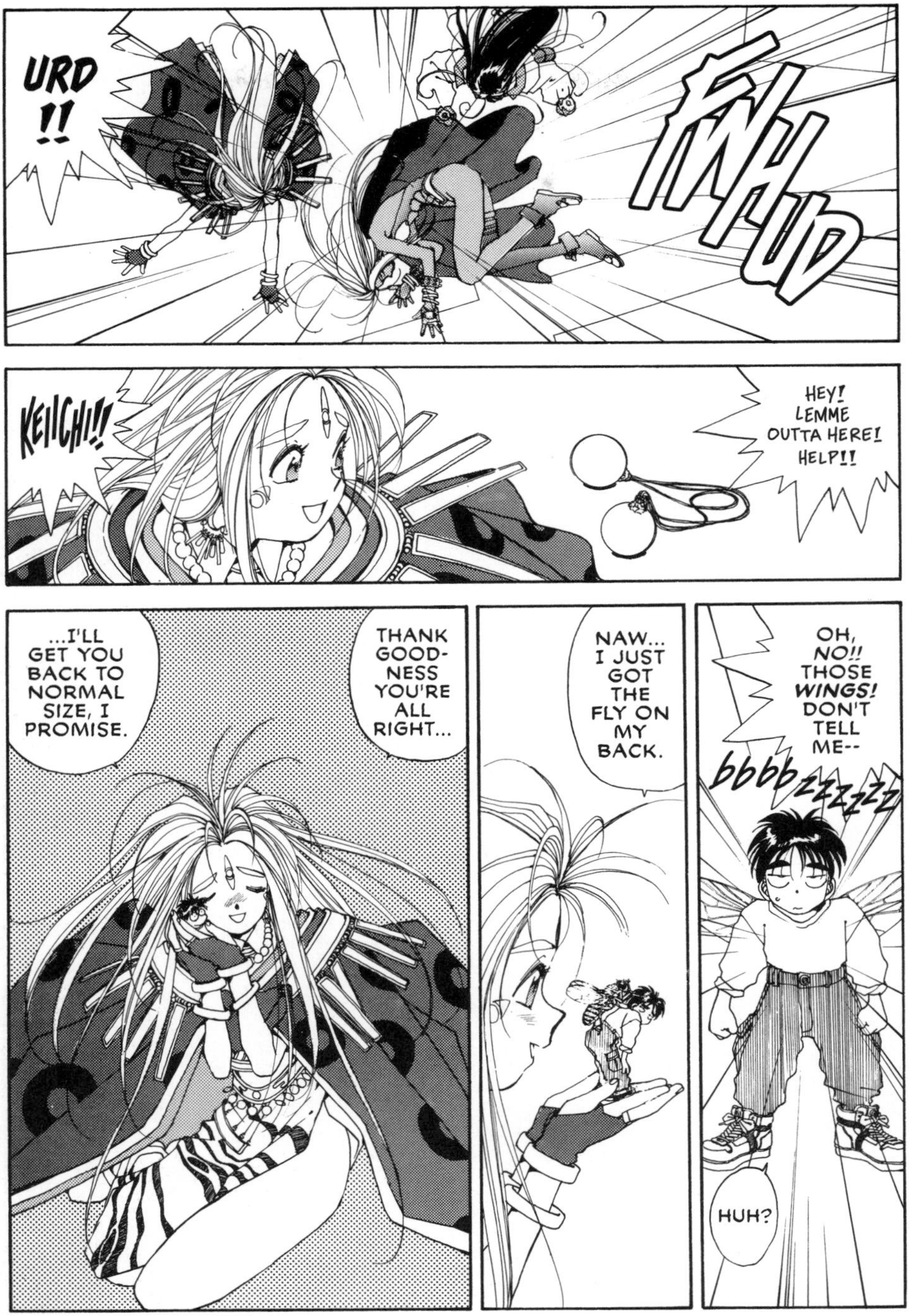
FWHUD
URD !!
HEY! LEMME OUTTA HERE! HELP!!
KEIICHI!!!
OH, NO!! THOSE WINGS! DON'T TELL ME--
bbbbzzzzzzz
HUH?
NAW... I JUST GOT THE FLY ON MY BACK.
THANK GOODNESS YOU'RE ALL RIGHT...
...I'LL GET YOU BACK TO NORMAL SIZE, I PROMISE.

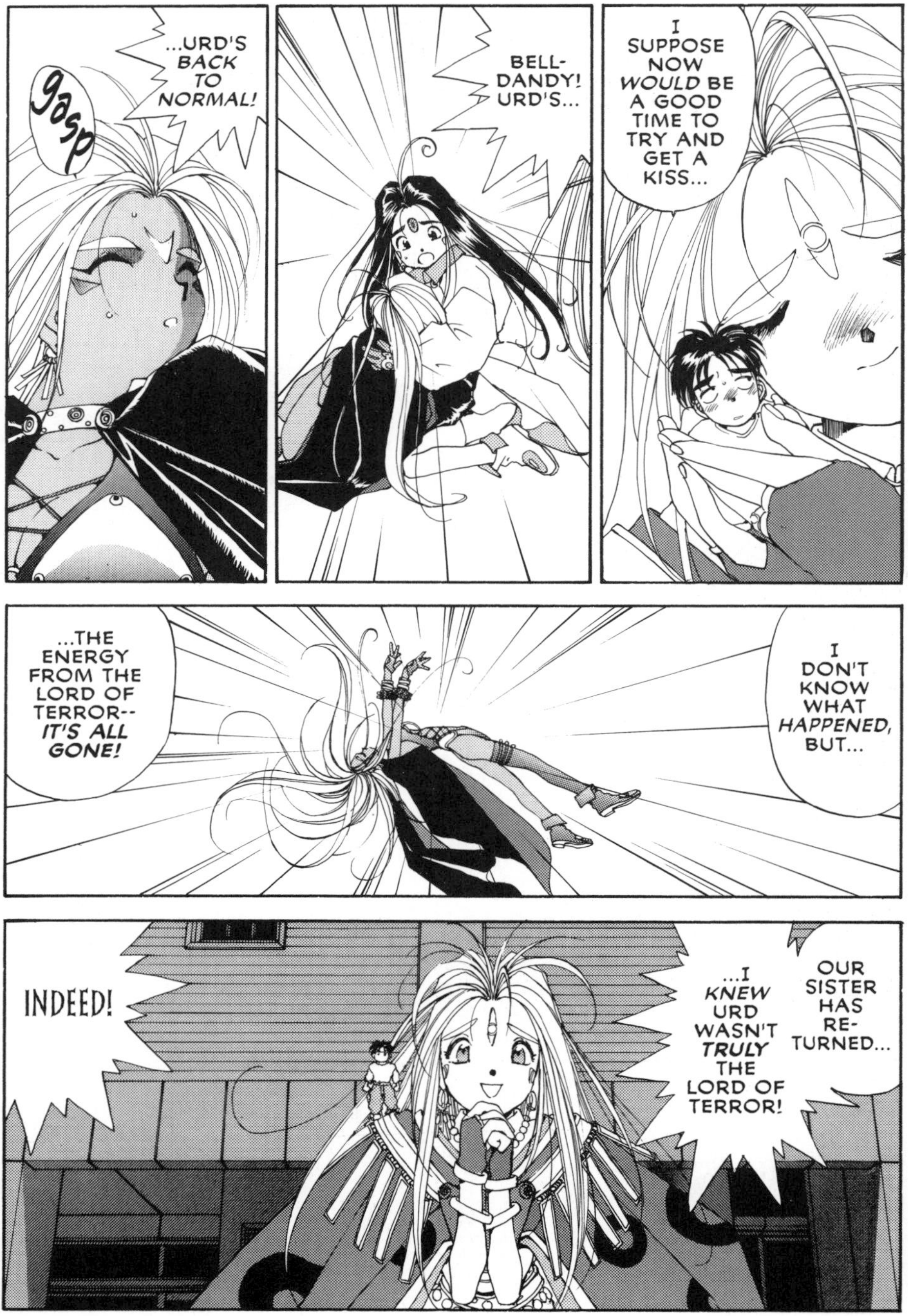
I SUPPOSE NOW *WOULD* BE A GOOD TIME TO TRY AND GET A KISS...
BELL-DANDY! URD'S...
...URD'S *BACK TO* NORMAL!
gasp
I DON'T KNOW WHAT *HAPPENED,* BUT...
...THE ENERGY FROM THE LORD OF TERROR-- *IT'S ALL GONE!*
OUR SISTER HAS RE-TURNED...
...I *KNEW* URD WASN'T *TRULY* THE LORD OF TERROR!
INDEED!

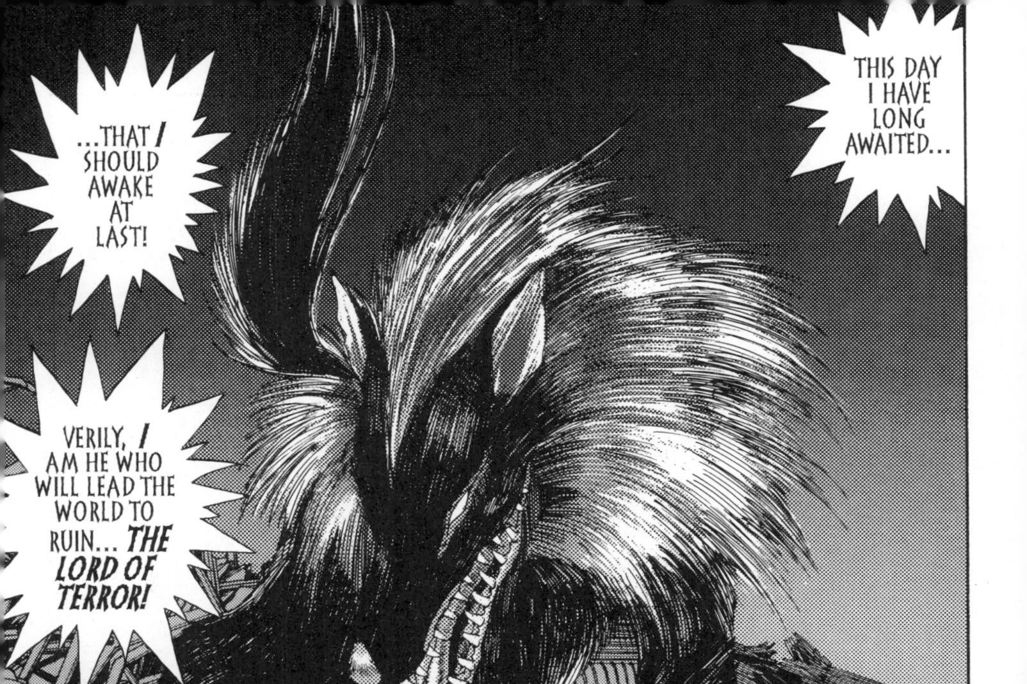
THIS DAY I HAVE LONG AWAITED...
...THAT *I* SHOULD AWAKE AT LAST!
VERILY, *I* AM HE WHO WILL LEAD THE WORLD TO RUIN... ***THE LORD OF TERROR!***

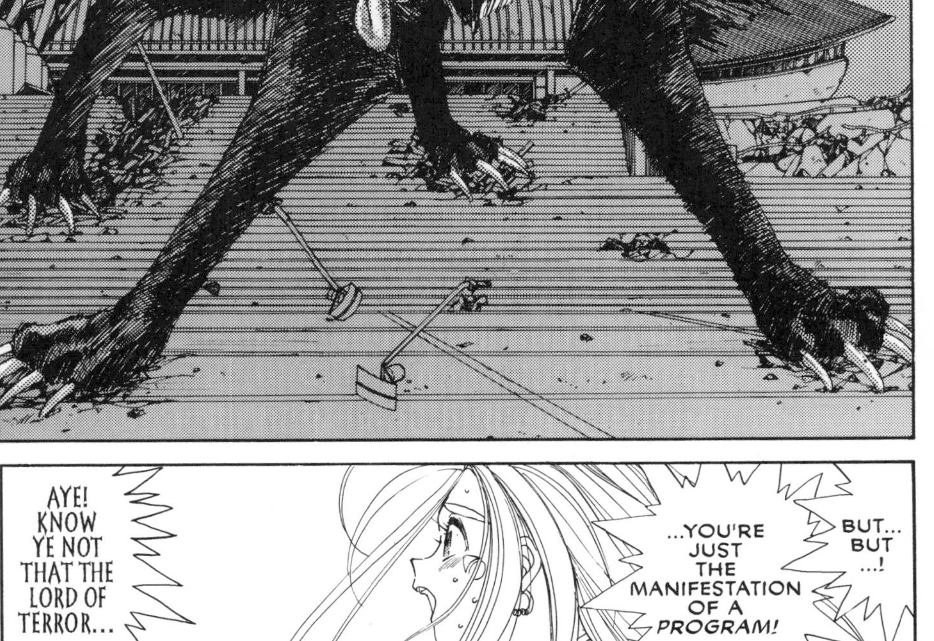
BUT... BUT ...!
...YOU'RE JUST THE MANIFESTATION OF A *PROGRAM!*
AYE! KNOW YE NOT THAT THE LORD OF TERROR...

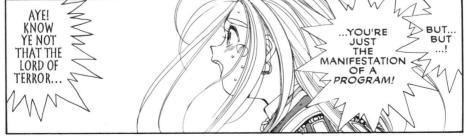

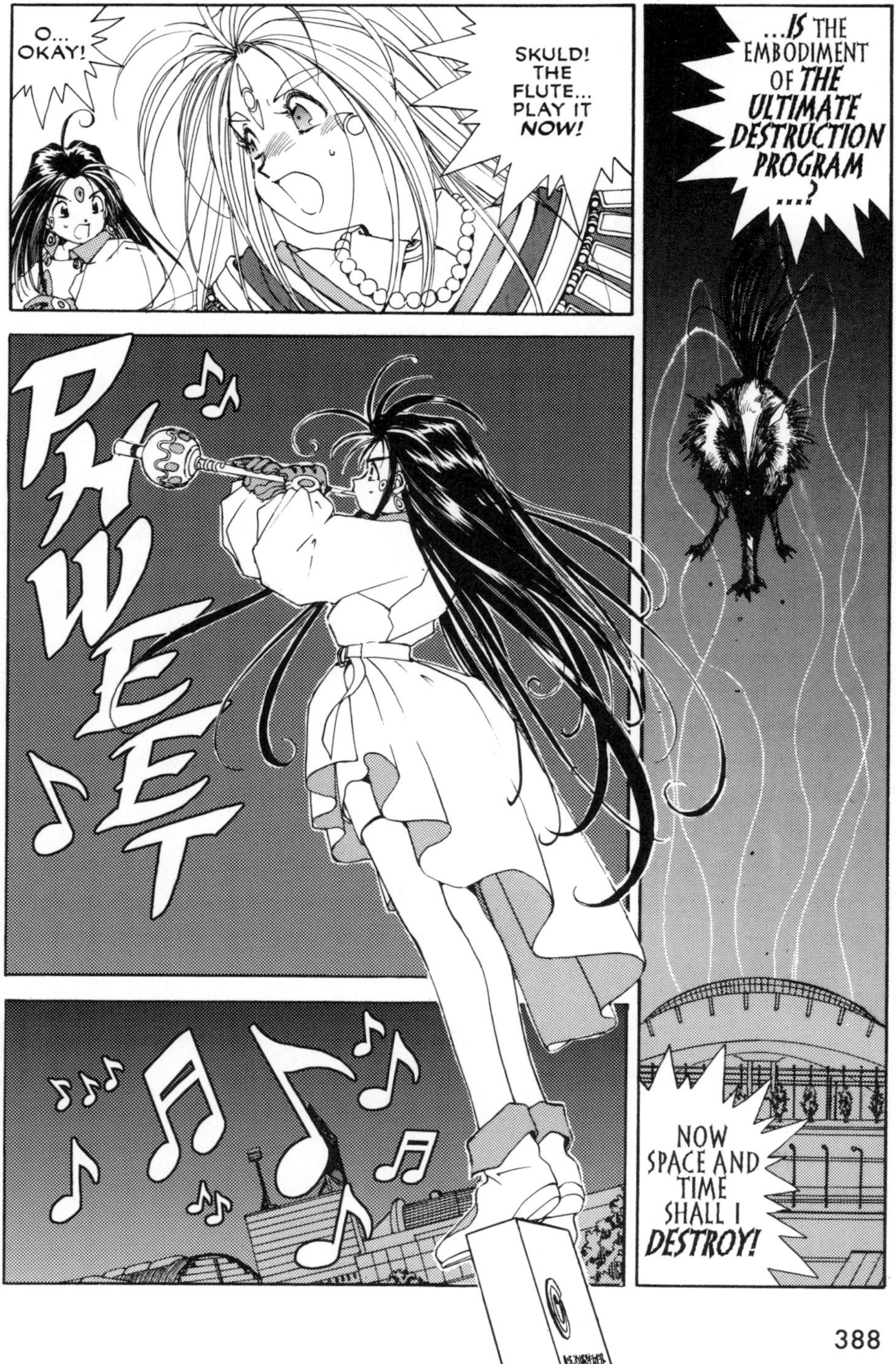
...IS THE EMBODIMENT OF THE ULTIMATE DESTRUCTION PROGRAM ...?
NOW SPACE AND TIME SHALL I DESTROY!
SKULD! THE FLUTE... PLAY IT NOW!
O... OKAY!
PWEET

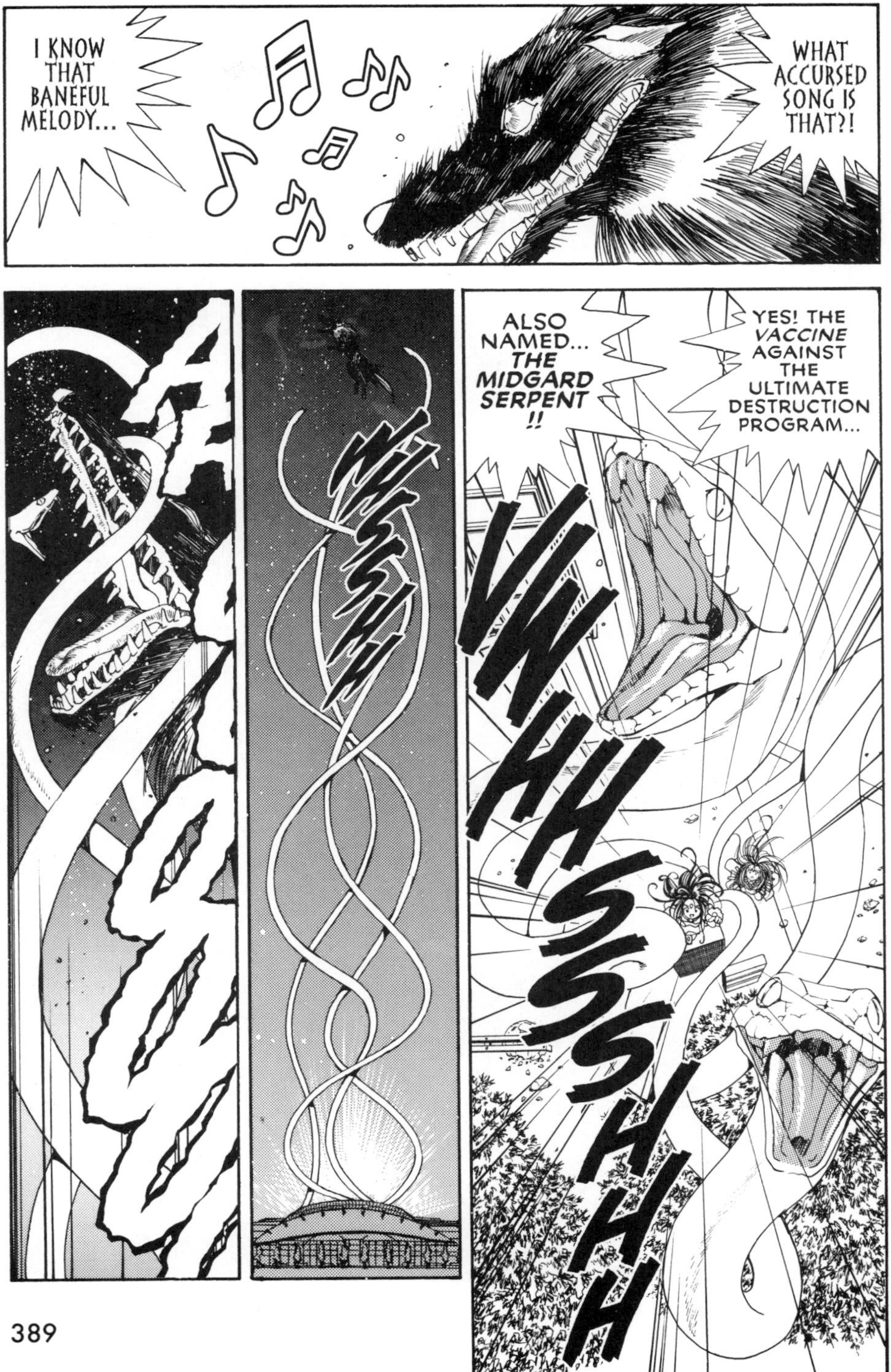
WHAT ACCURSED SONG IS THAT?!
I KNOW THAT BANEFUL MELODY...
YES! THE *VACCINE* AGAINST THE ULTIMATE DESTRUCTION PROGRAM...
ALSO NAMED... ***THE MIDGARD SERPENT*** !!
VWHHSSSHHH

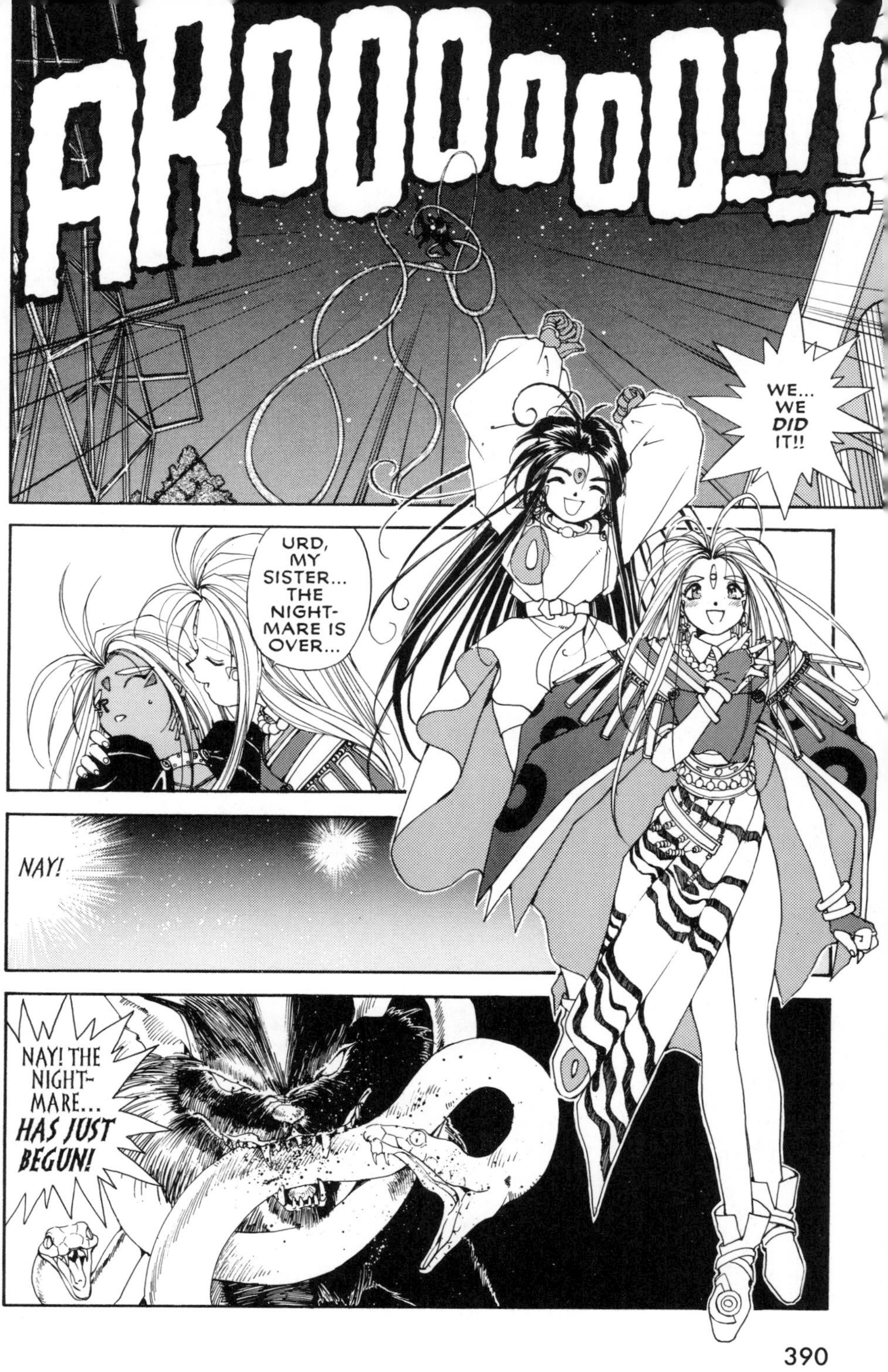
AROOOOOOO!!!
WE... WE *DID* IT!!
URD, MY SISTER... THE NIGHT-MARE IS OVER...
NAY!
NAY! THE NIGHT-MARE... **HAS JUST BEGUN!**

CHAPTER 38

# The Secret of the Lord of Terror

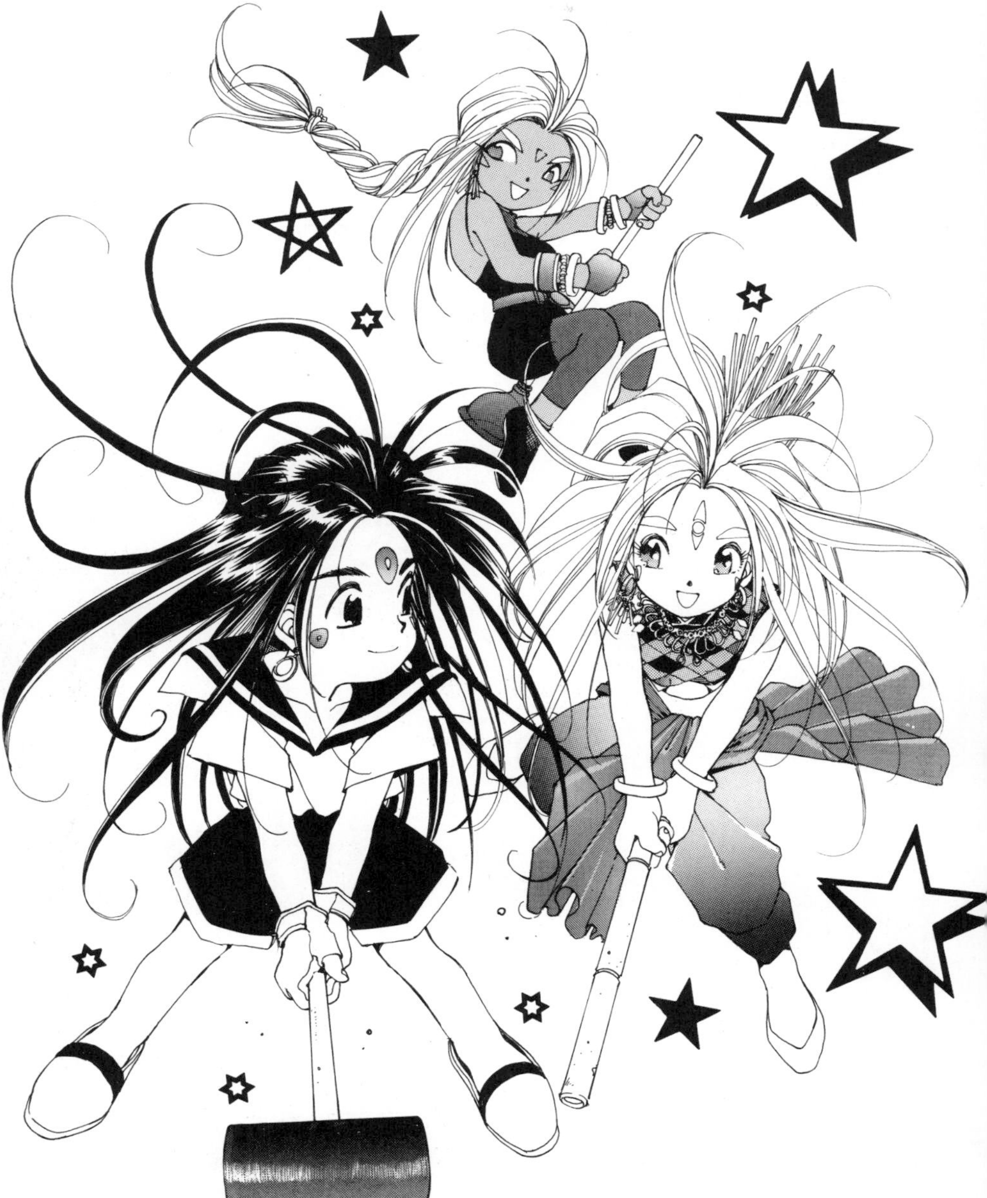

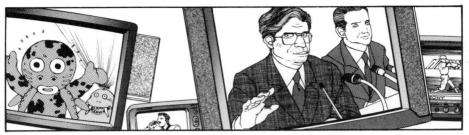

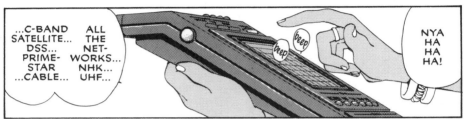

NYA HA HA HA!
beep
beep
ALL THE NETWORKS... NHK... UHF...
...C-BAND SATELLITE... DSS... PRIME-STAR ...CABLE...
...NOW I CAN WATCH EVERY TV SHOW IN THE WORLD!!
PARADISE!!
HAA HA HA HA HA!

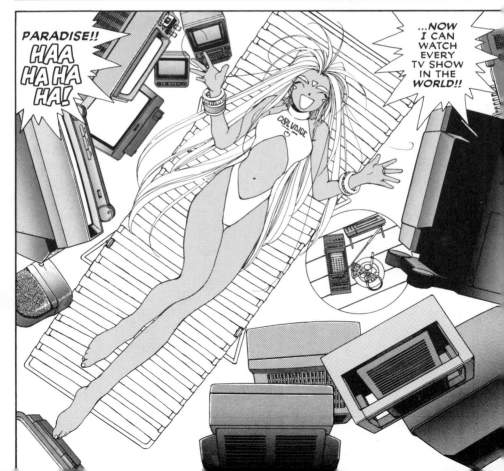

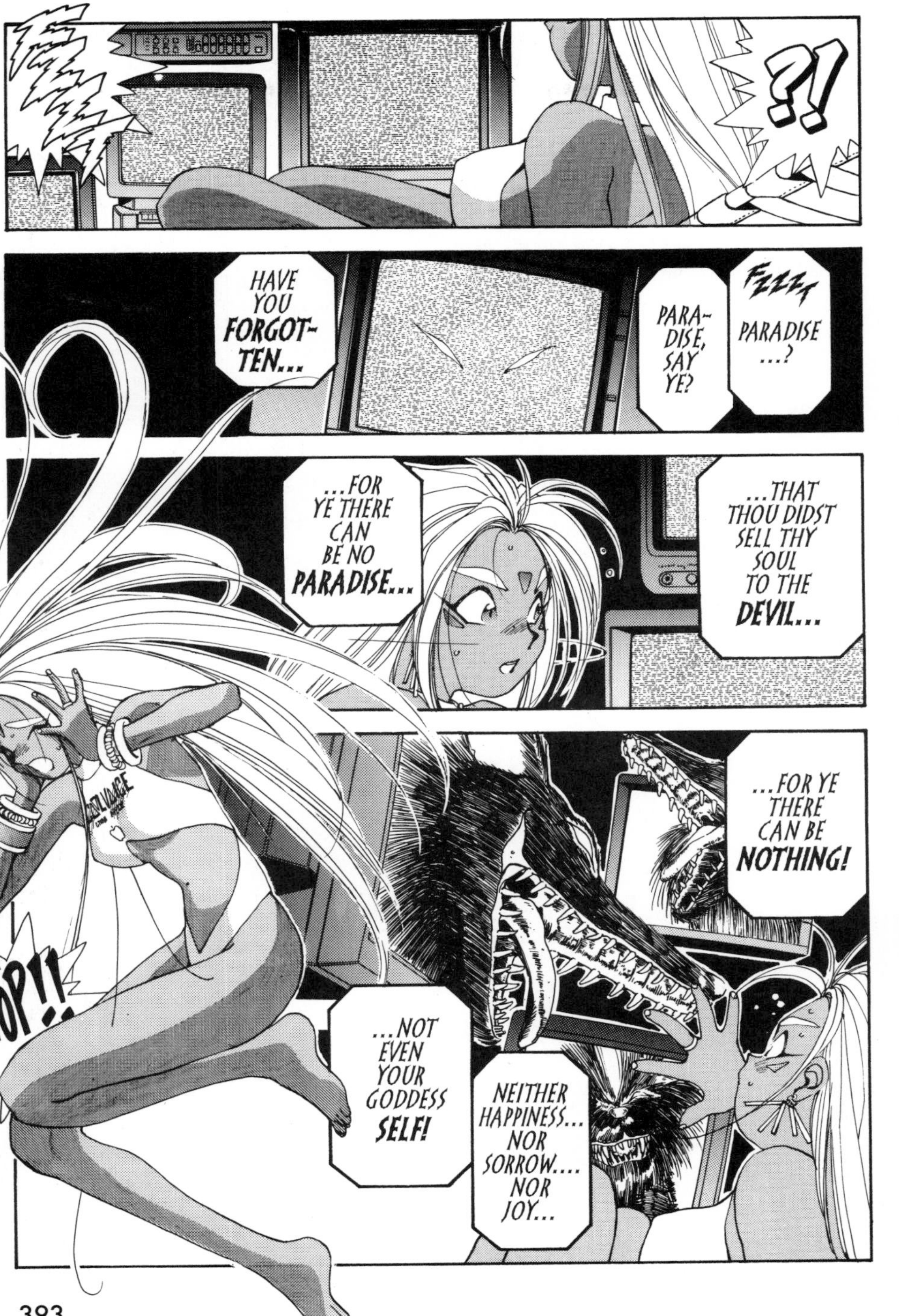
?!
FZZZZ
PARADISE ...?
PARA-DISE, SAY YE?
HAVE YOU FORGOT-TEN...
...THAT THOU DIDST SELL THY SOUL TO THE DEVIL...
...FOR YE THERE CAN BE NO PARADISE...
...FOR YE THERE CAN BE NOTHING!
NEITHER HAPPINESS... NOR SORROW.... NOR JOY...
...NOT EVEN YOUR GODDESS SELF!
STOP!!

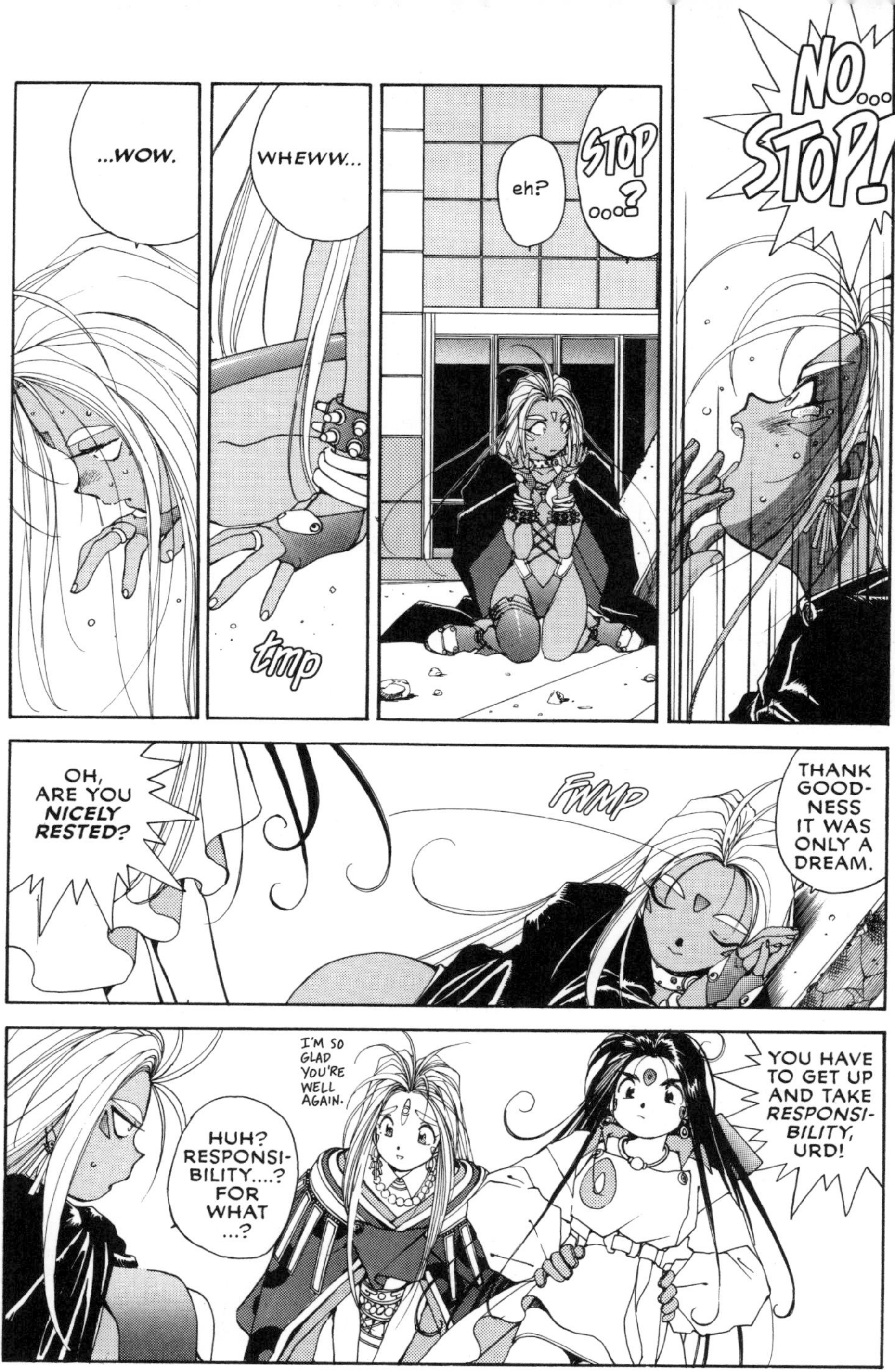
NO... STOP!
STOP...?
eh?
WHEWW...
tmp
...WOW.
THANK GOODNESS IT WAS ONLY A DREAM.
FWMP
OH, ARE YOU *NICELY RESTED?*
YOU HAVE TO GET UP AND TAKE *RESPONSIBILITY*, URD!
I'M SO GLAD YOU'RE WELL AGAIN.
HUH? RESPONSIBILITY....? FOR WHAT...?

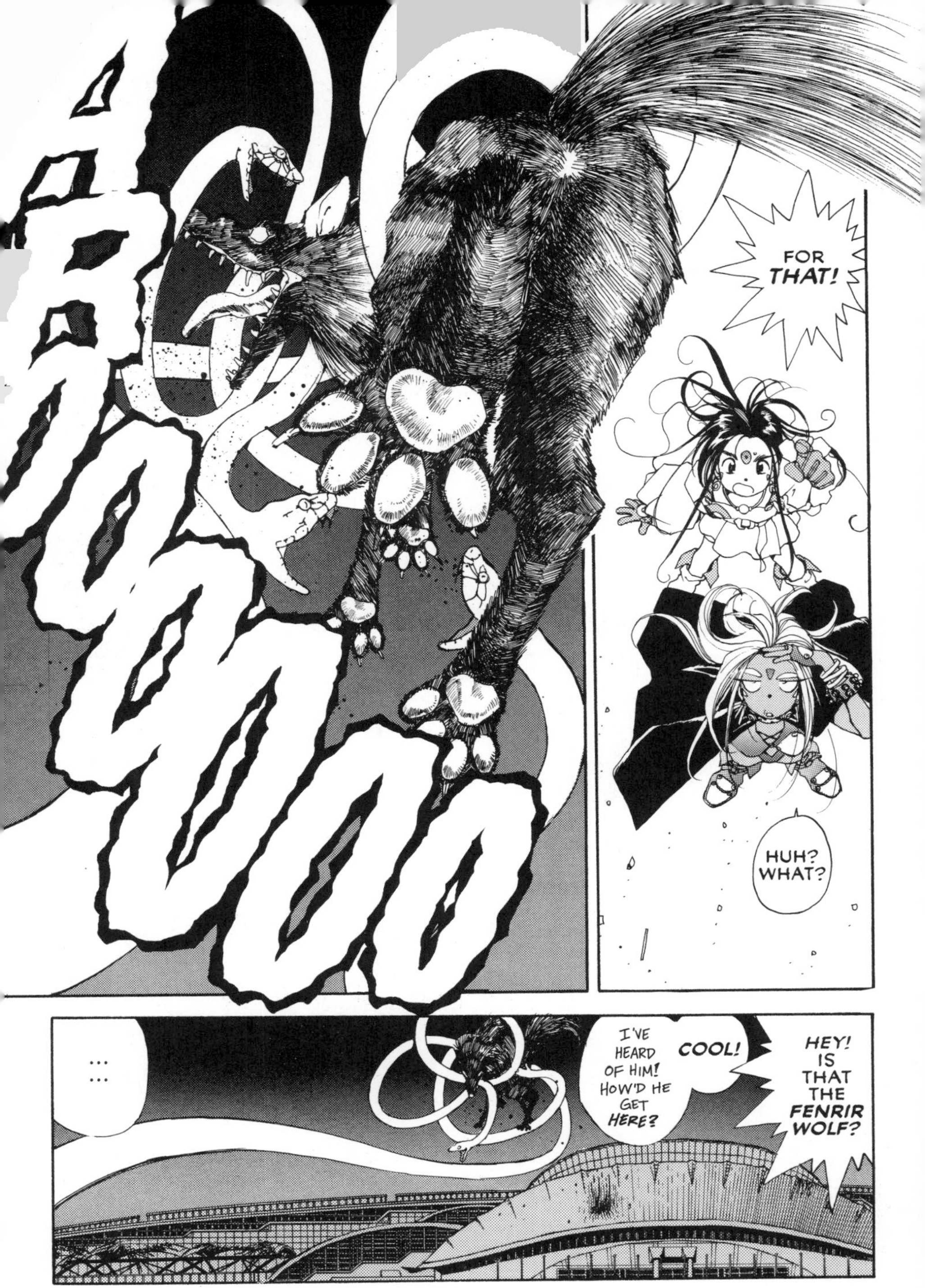
FOR THAT!
HUH? WHAT?
HEY! IS THAT THE FENRIR WOLF?
COOL!
I'VE HEARD OF HIM! HOW'D HE GET HERE?
... ...

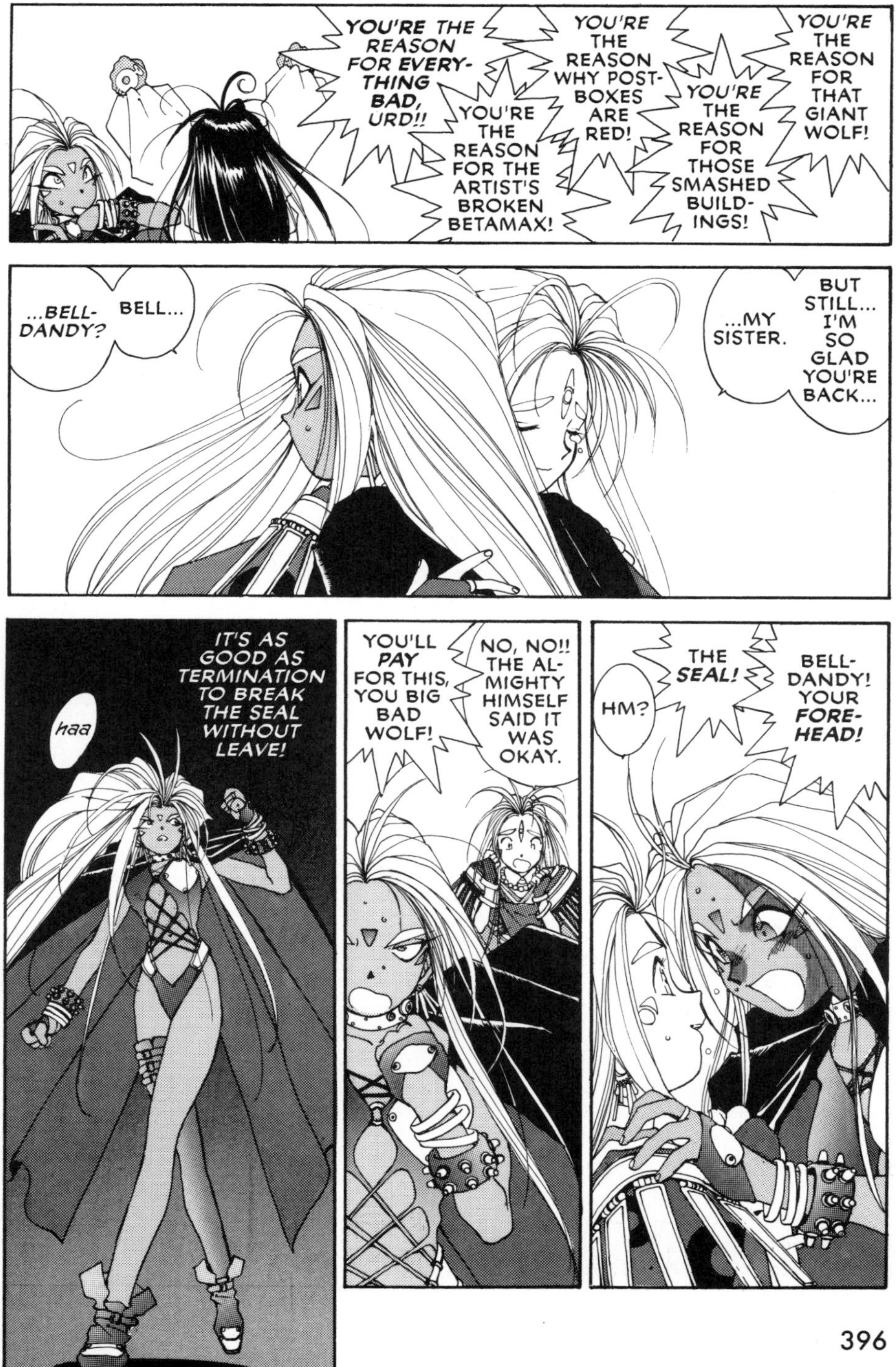

YOU'RE THE REASON FOR THAT GIANT WOLF!
YOU'RE THE REASON FOR THOSE SMASHED BUILDINGS!
YOU'RE THE REASON WHY POST-BOXES ARE RED!
YOU'RE THE REASON FOR THE ARTIST'S BROKEN BETAMAX!
*YOU'RE* THE REASON FOR *EVERYTHING BAD, URD!!*
BUT STILL... I'M SO GLAD YOU'RE BACK...
...MY SISTER.
BELL...
...BELL-DANDY?
BELL-DANDY! YOUR *FOREHEAD!*
THE *SEAL!*
HM?
NO, NO!! THE ALMIGHTY HIMSELF SAID IT WAS OKAY.
YOU'LL *PAY* FOR THIS, YOU BIG BAD WOLF!
*IT'S AS GOOD AS TERMINATION TO BREAK THE SEAL WITHOUT LEAVE!*
*haa*

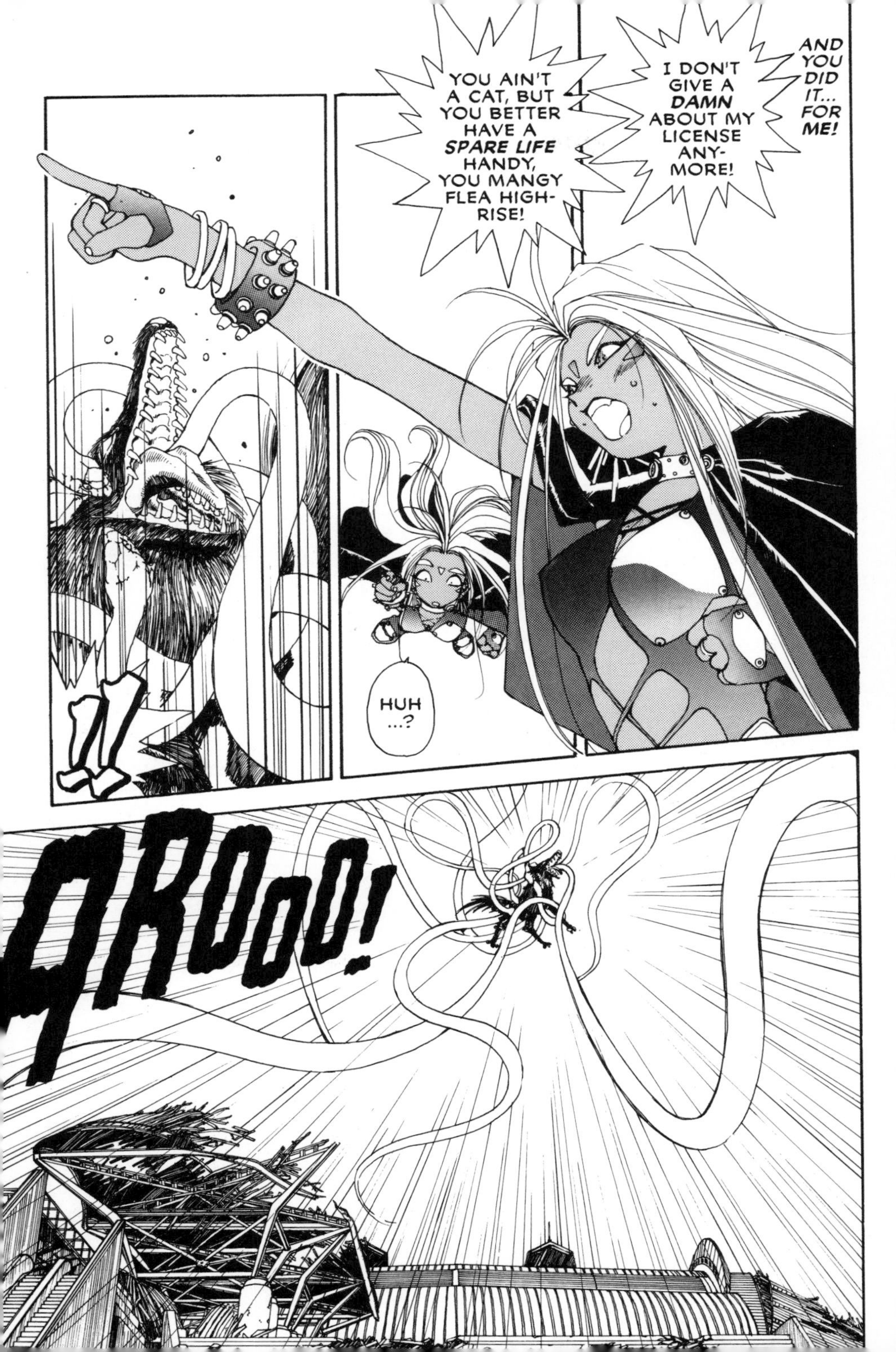
AND YOU DID IT... FOR ME!
I DON'T GIVE A DAMN ABOUT MY LICENSE ANY-MORE!
YOU AIN'T A CAT, BUT YOU BETTER HAVE A SPARE LIFE HANDY, YOU MANGY FLEA HIGH-RISE!
HUH ...?
AROOOO!

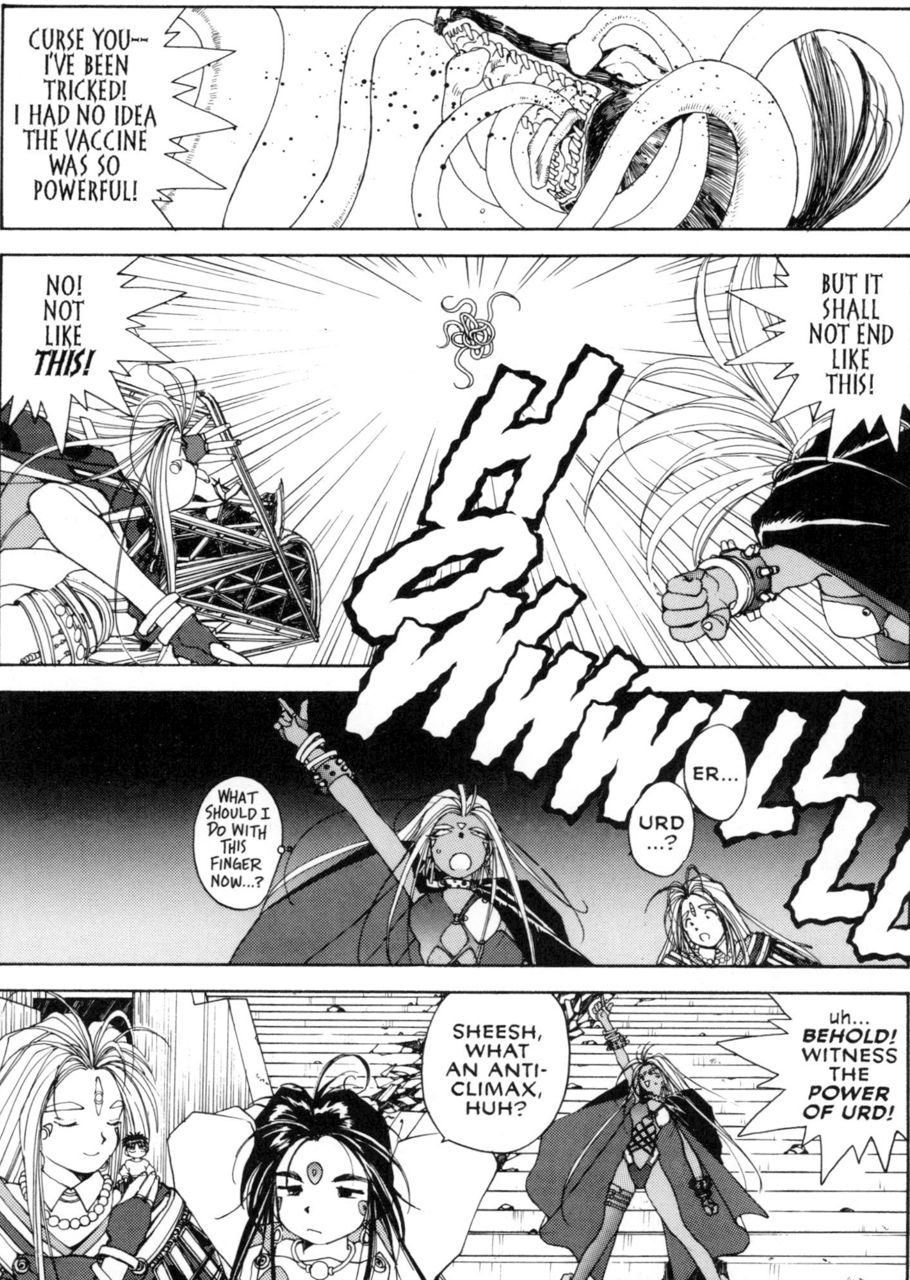
CURSE YOU-- I'VE BEEN TRICKED! I HAD NO IDEA THE VACCINE WAS SO POWERFUL!
BUT IT SHALL NOT END LIKE THIS!
NO! NOT LIKE *THIS!*
HOWWLLLL
ER...
URD ...?
WHAT SHOULD I DO WITH THIS FINGER NOW...?
uh... ***BEHOLD!*** WITNESS THE ***POWER OF URD!***
SHEESH, WHAT AN ANTI-CLIMAX, HUH?

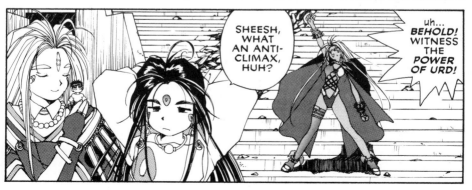

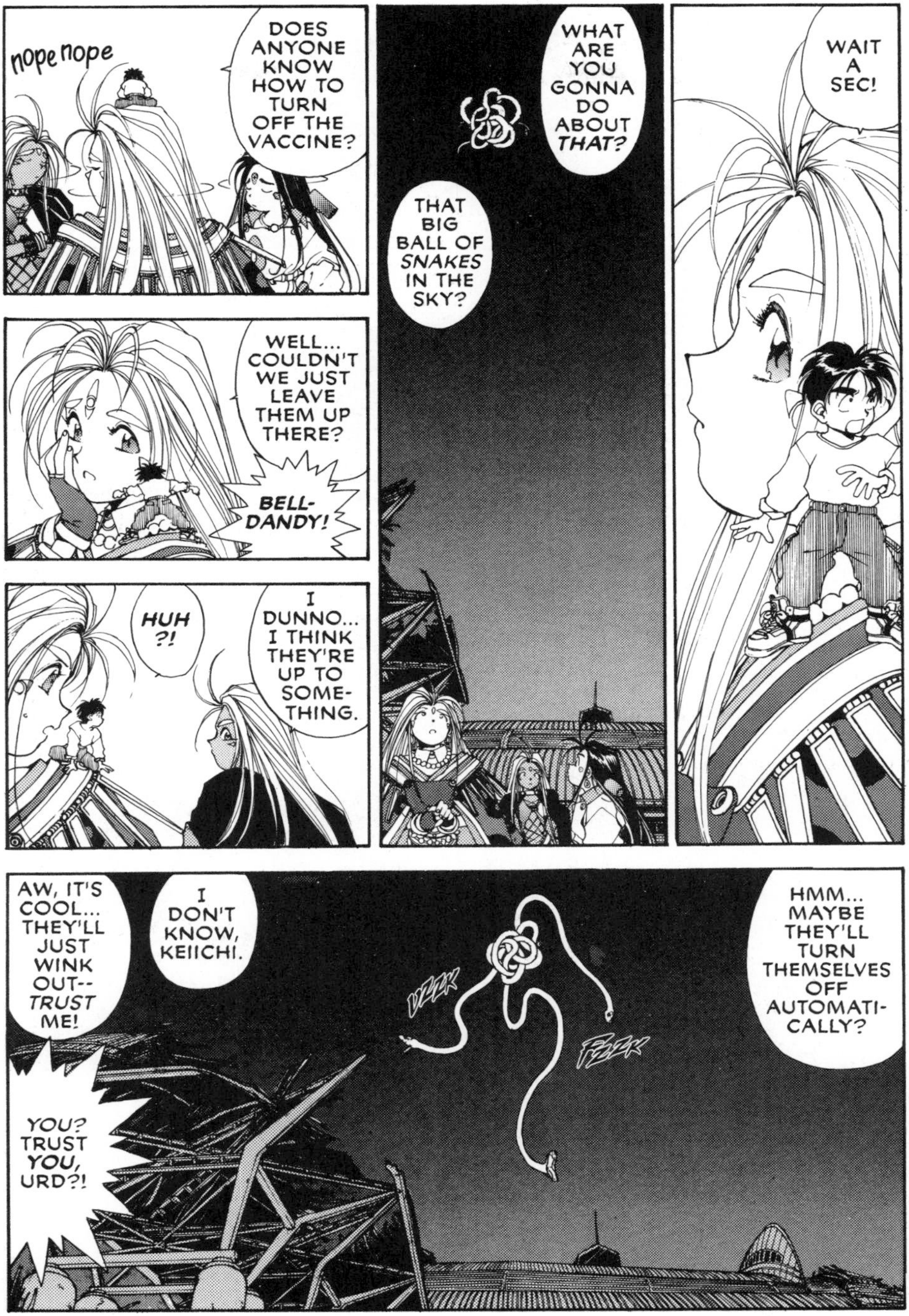
WAIT A SEC!
WHAT ARE YOU GONNA DO ABOUT THAT?
THAT BIG BALL OF SNAKES IN THE SKY?
DOES ANYONE KNOW HOW TO TURN OFF THE VACCINE?
nope nope
WELL... COULDN'T WE JUST LEAVE THEM UP THERE?
BELL-DANDY!
I DUNNO... I THINK THEY'RE UP TO SOME-THING.
HUH?!
HMM... MAYBE THEY'LL TURN THEMSELVES OFF AUTOMATI-CALLY?
I DON'T KNOW, KEIICHI.
AW, IT'S COOL... THEY'LL JUST WINK OUT-- TRUST ME!
YOU? TRUST YOU, URD?!

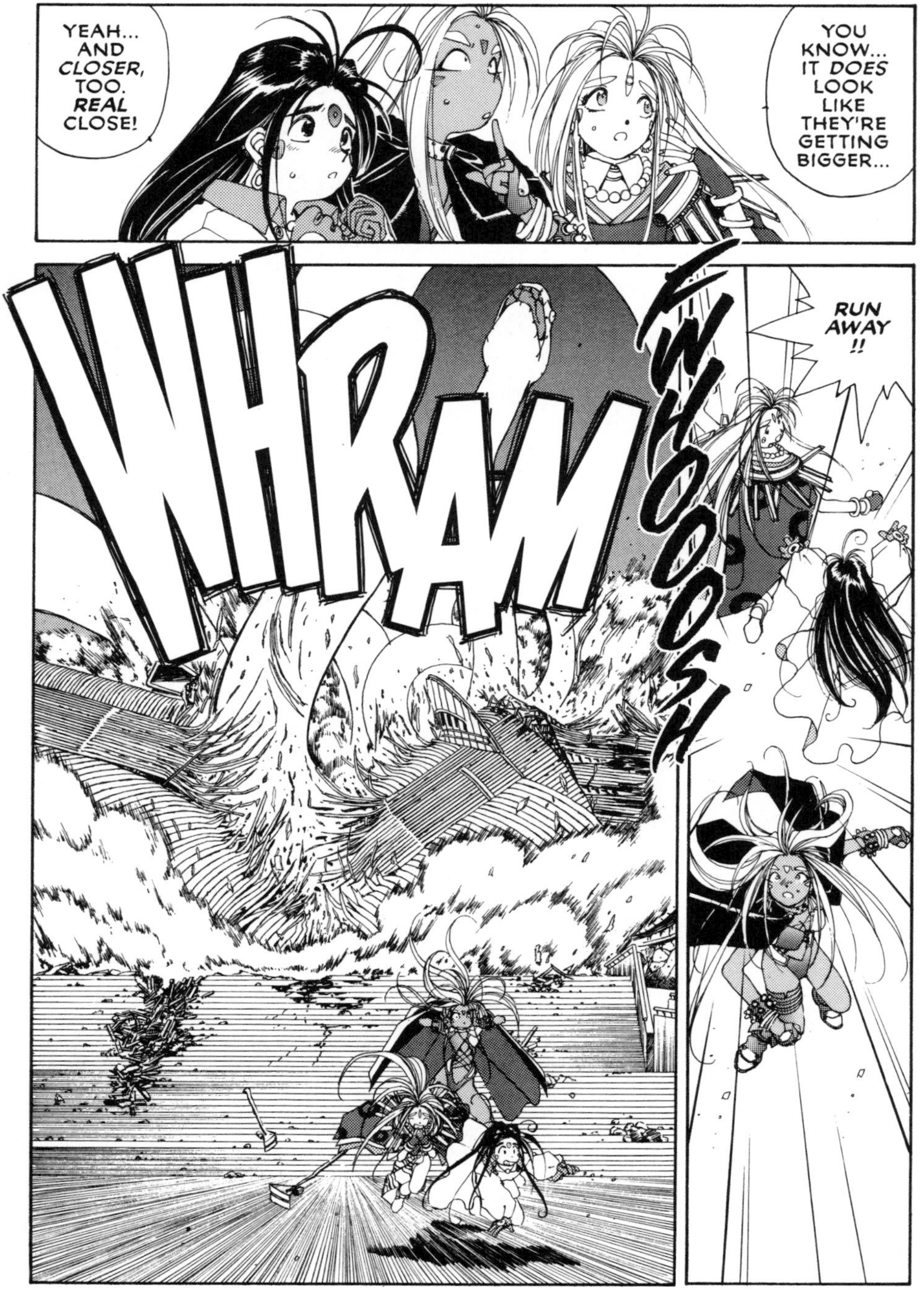
YOU KNOW... IT *DOES* LOOK LIKE THEY'RE GETTING BIGGER...
YEAH... AND *CLOSER*, TOO. *REAL* CLOSE!
*RUN AWAY !!*
FWHOOOOSH
WHRAM

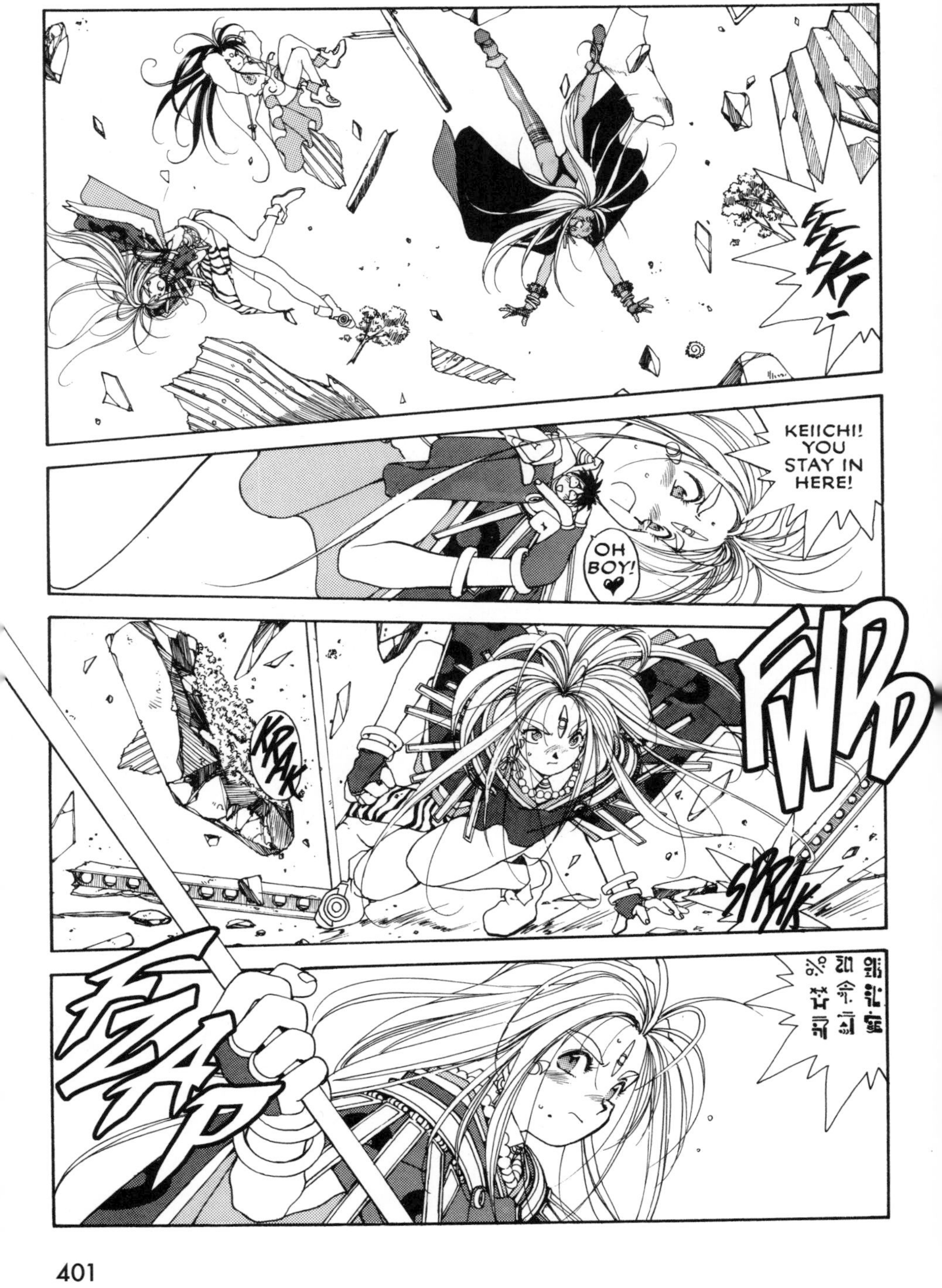
EEK!
KEIICHI! YOU STAY IN HERE!
OH BOY!
FWBD
KRAK
SPRAK
FZAP

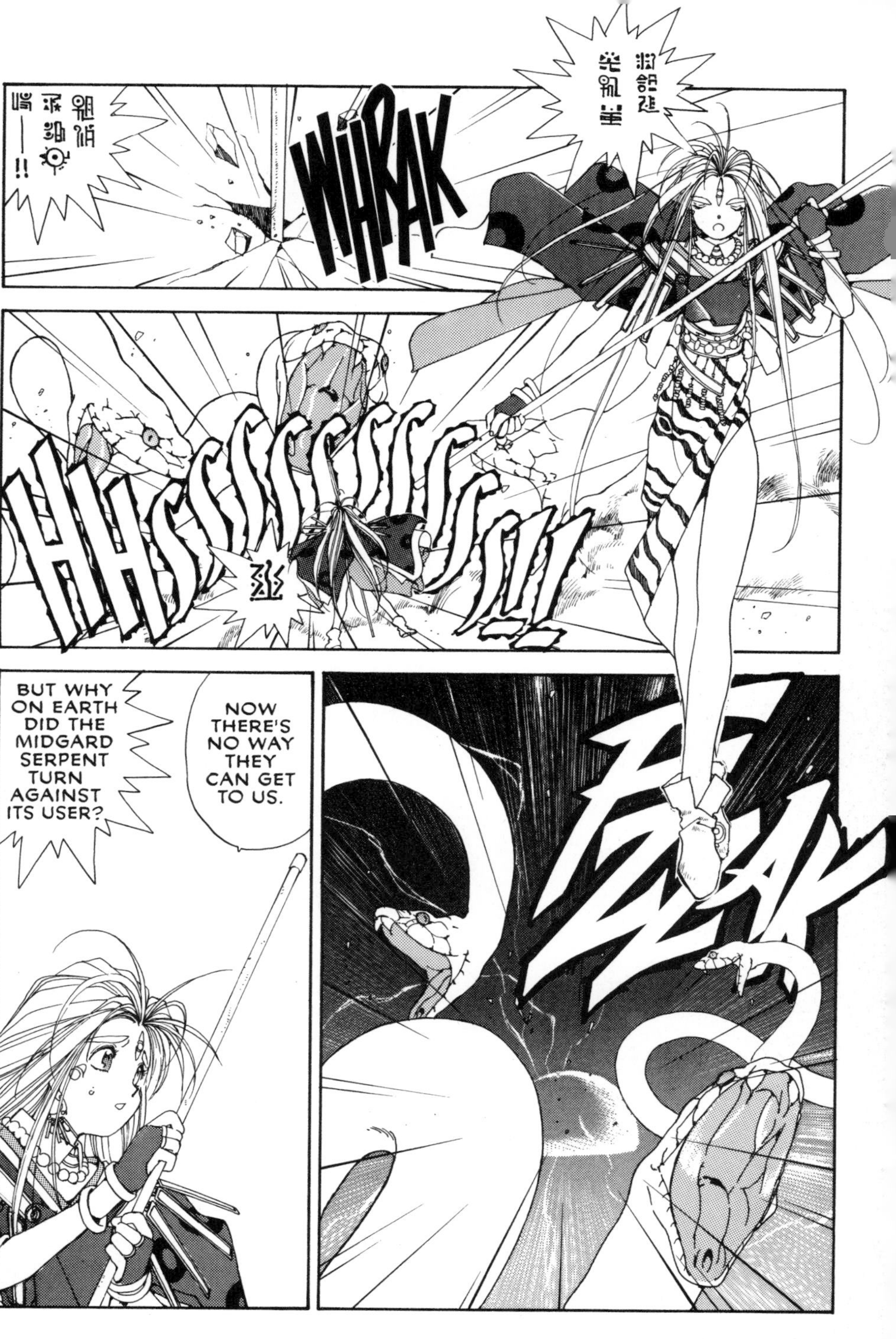
WHRAK
NOW THERE'S NO WAY THEY CAN GET TO US.
BUT WHY ON EARTH DID THE MIDGARD SERPENT TURN AGAINST ITS USER?

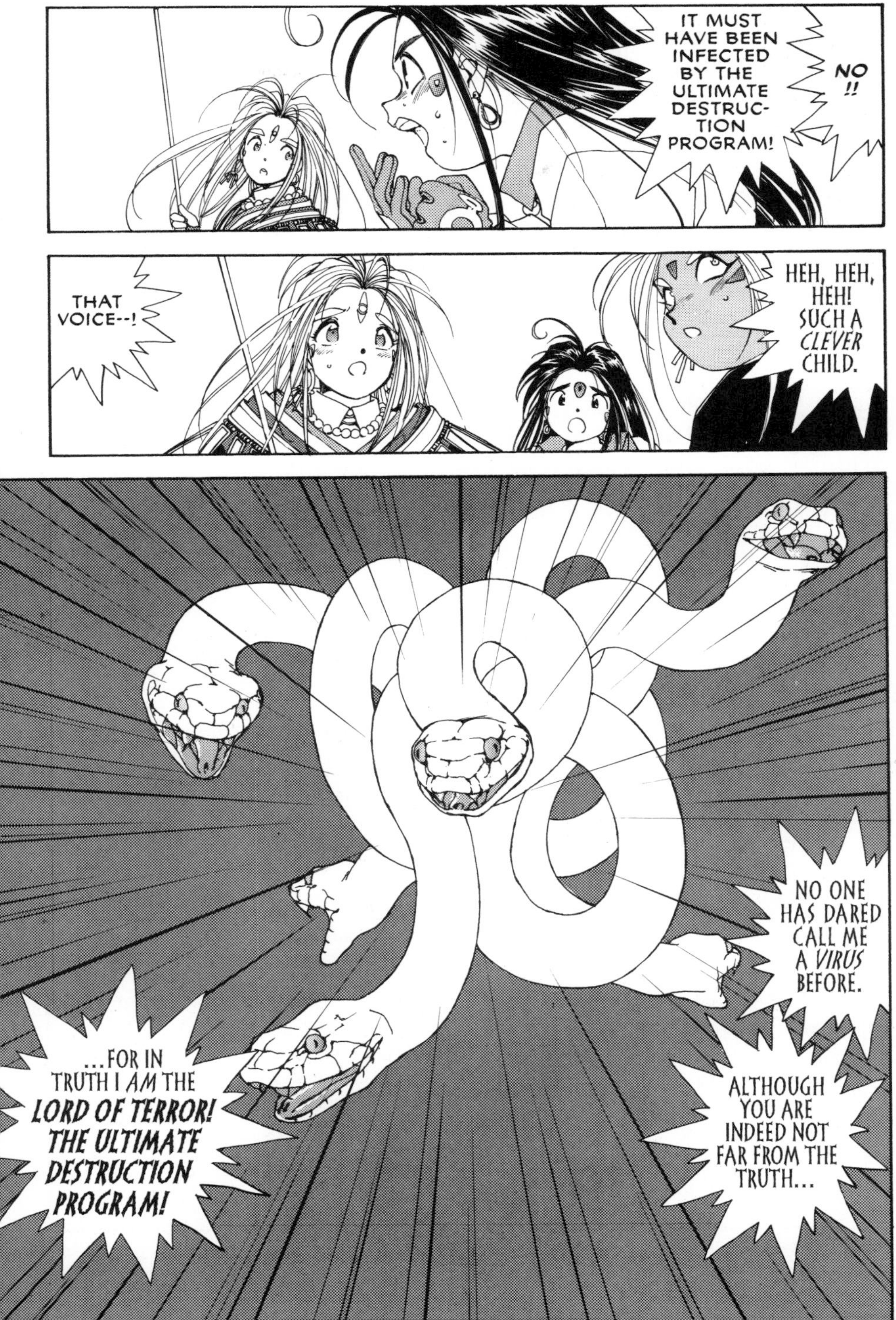
IT MUST HAVE BEEN INFECTED BY THE ULTIMATE DESTRUCTION PROGRAM!
NO !!
HEH, HEH, HEH! SUCH A *CLEVER* CHILD.
THAT VOICE--!
NO ONE HAS DARED CALL ME A *VIRUS* BEFORE.
ALTHOUGH YOU ARE INDEED NOT FAR FROM THE TRUTH...
...FOR IN TRUTH I *AM* THE **LORD OF TERROR! THE ULTIMATE DESTRUCTION PROGRAM!**

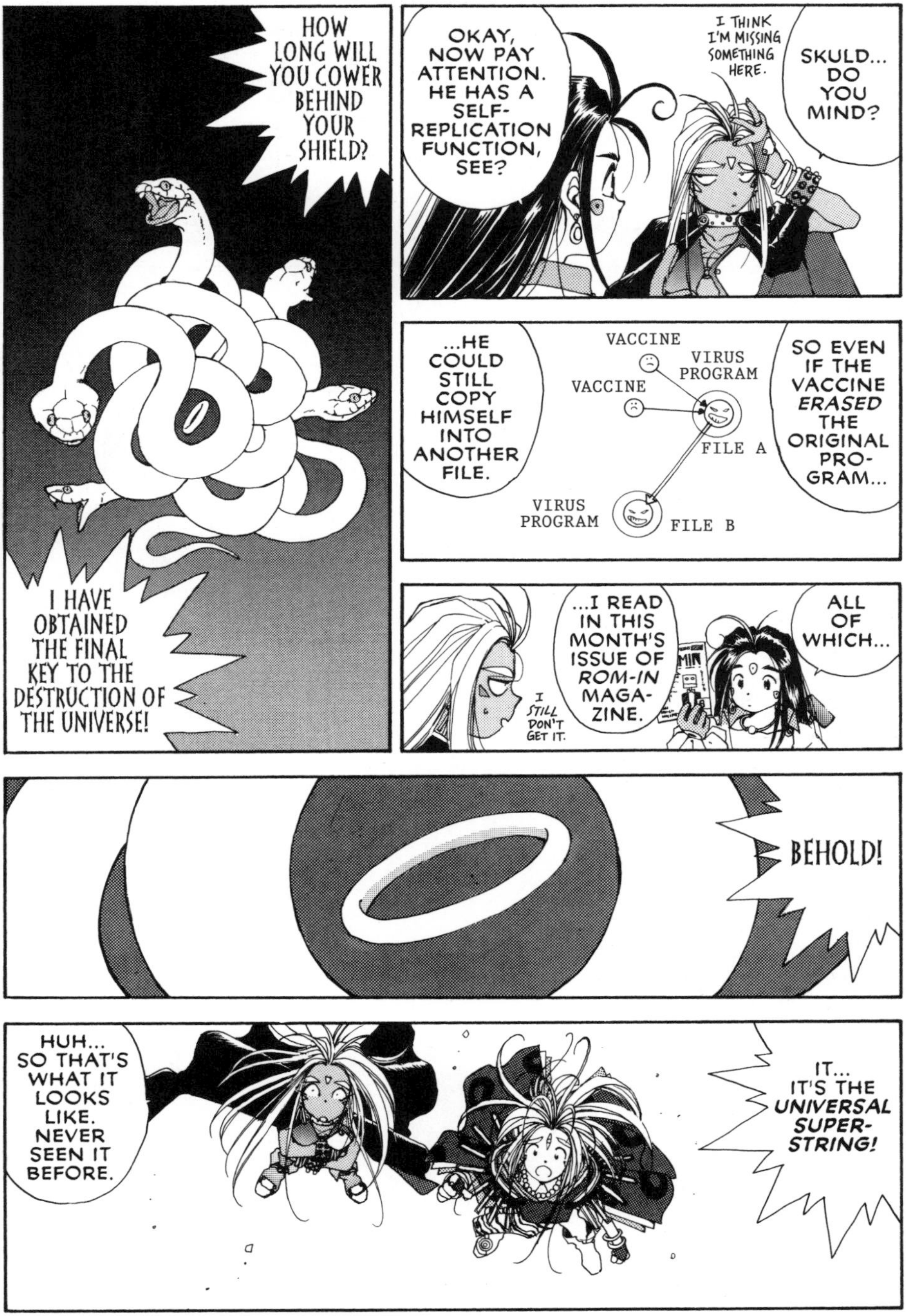
SKULD... DO YOU MIND?
I THINK I'M MISSING SOMETHING HERE.
OKAY, NOW PAY ATTENTION. HE HAS A SELF-REPLICATION FUNCTION, SEE?
SO EVEN IF THE VACCINE *ERASED* THE ORIGINAL PROGRAM...
VACCINE
VIRUS PROGRAM
VACCINE
FILE A
VIRUS PROGRAM
FILE B
...HE COULD STILL COPY HIMSELF INTO ANOTHER FILE.
ALL OF WHICH...
...I READ IN THIS MONTH'S ISSUE OF *ROM-IN* MAGAZINE.
I STILL DON'T GET IT.
HOW LONG WILL YOU COWER BEHIND YOUR SHIELD?
I HAVE OBTAINED THE FINAL KEY TO THE DESTRUCTION OF THE UNIVERSE!
BEHOLD!
IT... IT'S THE *UNIVERSAL SUPER-STRING!*
HUH... SO THAT'S WHAT IT LOOKS LIKE. NEVER SEEN IT BEFORE.

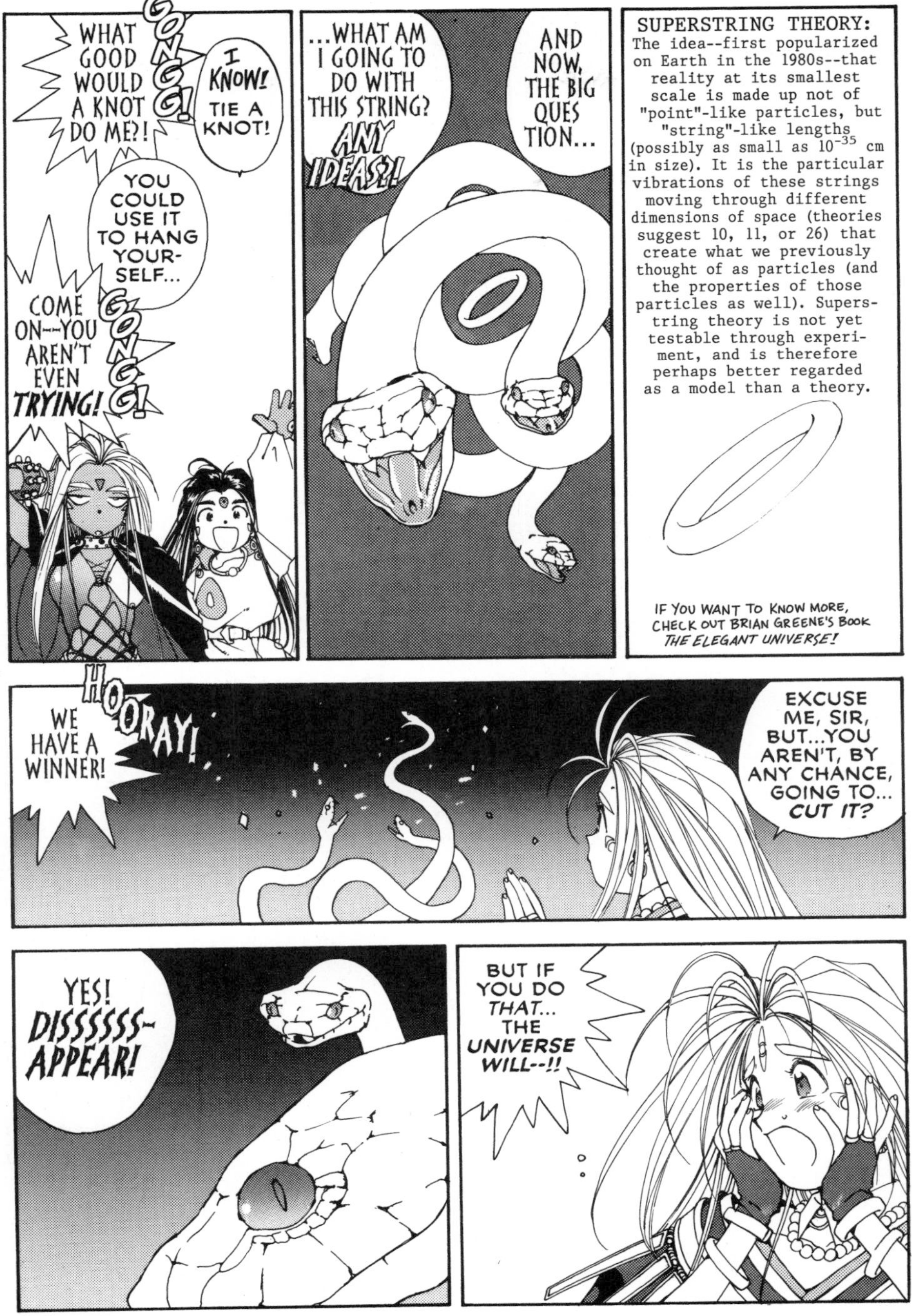
SUPERSTRING THEORY:
The idea--first popularized on Earth in the 1980s--that reality at its smallest scale is made up not of "point"-like particles, but "string"-like lengths (possibly as small as $10^{-35}$ cm in size). It is the particular vibrations of these strings moving through different dimensions of space (theories suggest 10, 11, or 26) that create what we previously thought of as particles (and the properties of those particles as well). Superstring theory is not yet testable through experiment, and is therefore perhaps better regarded as a model than a theory.
IF YOU WANT TO KNOW MORE, CHECK OUT BRIAN GREENE'S BOOK *THE ELEGANT UNIVERSE!*
AND NOW, THE BIG QUESTION...
...WHAT AM I GOING TO DO WITH THIS STRING? ANY IDEAS?!
I KNOW! TIE A KNOT!
GONGG!
WHAT GOOD WOULD A KNOT DO ME?!
YOU COULD USE IT TO HANG YOURSELF...
GONGG!
COME ON--YOU AREN'T EVEN *TRYING!*
EXCUSE ME, SIR, BUT...YOU AREN'T, BY ANY CHANCE, GOING TO... *CUT IT?*
HOORAY!
WE HAVE A WINNER!
BUT IF YOU DO *THAT*... THE *UNIVERSE WILL--!!*
YES! *DISSSSSS-APPEAR!*

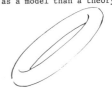

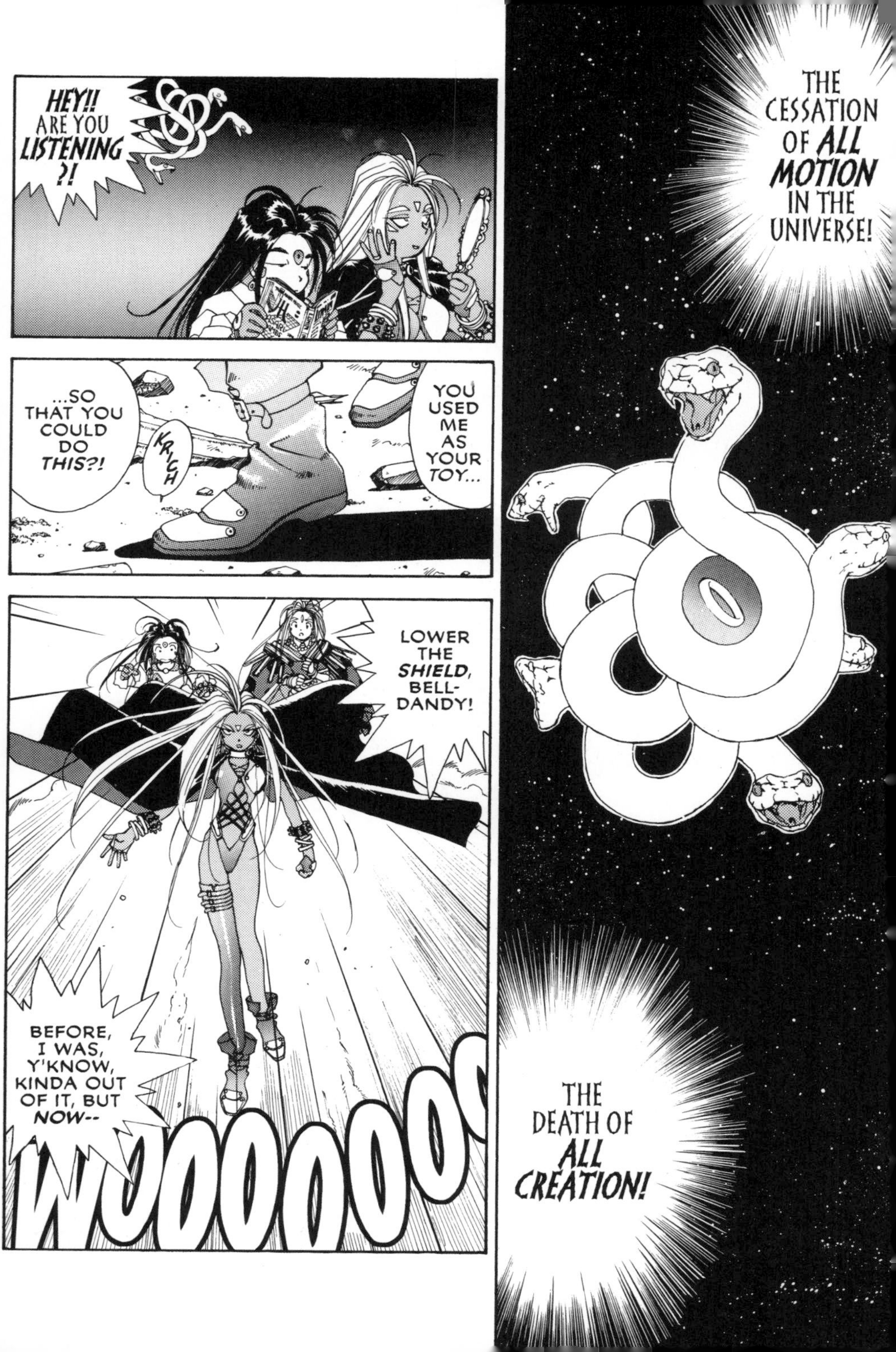

THE CESSATION OF *ALL MOTION* IN THE UNIVERSE!
THE DEATH OF *ALL CREATION!*
*HEY!!* ARE YOU *LISTENING* ?!
YOU USED ME AS YOUR *TOY*...
...SO THAT YOU COULD DO *THIS?!*
KRICH
LOWER THE *SHIELD*, BELL-DANDY!
BEFORE, I WAS, Y'KNOW, KINDA OUT OF IT, BUT *NOW--*
WOOOOOOOO

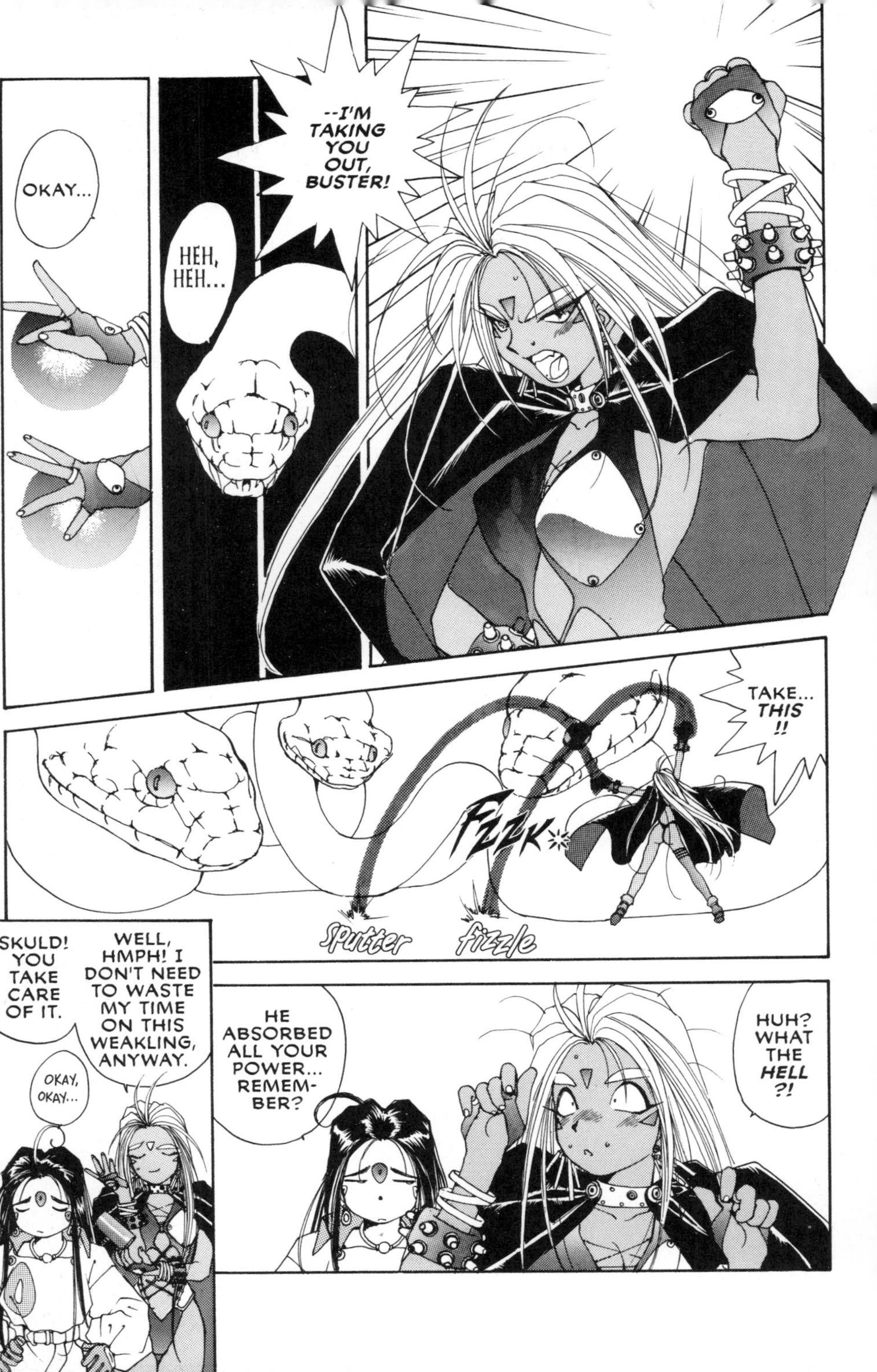
--I'M TAKING YOU OUT, BUSTER!
HEH, HEH...
OKAY...
TAKE... *THIS* !!
FZZK
sputter
fizzle
HUH? WHAT THE *HELL* ?!
HE ABSORBED ALL YOUR POWER... REMEMBER?
WELL, HMPH! I DON'T NEED TO WASTE MY TIME ON THIS WEAKLING, ANYWAY.
SKULD! YOU TAKE CARE OF IT.
OKAY, OKAY...

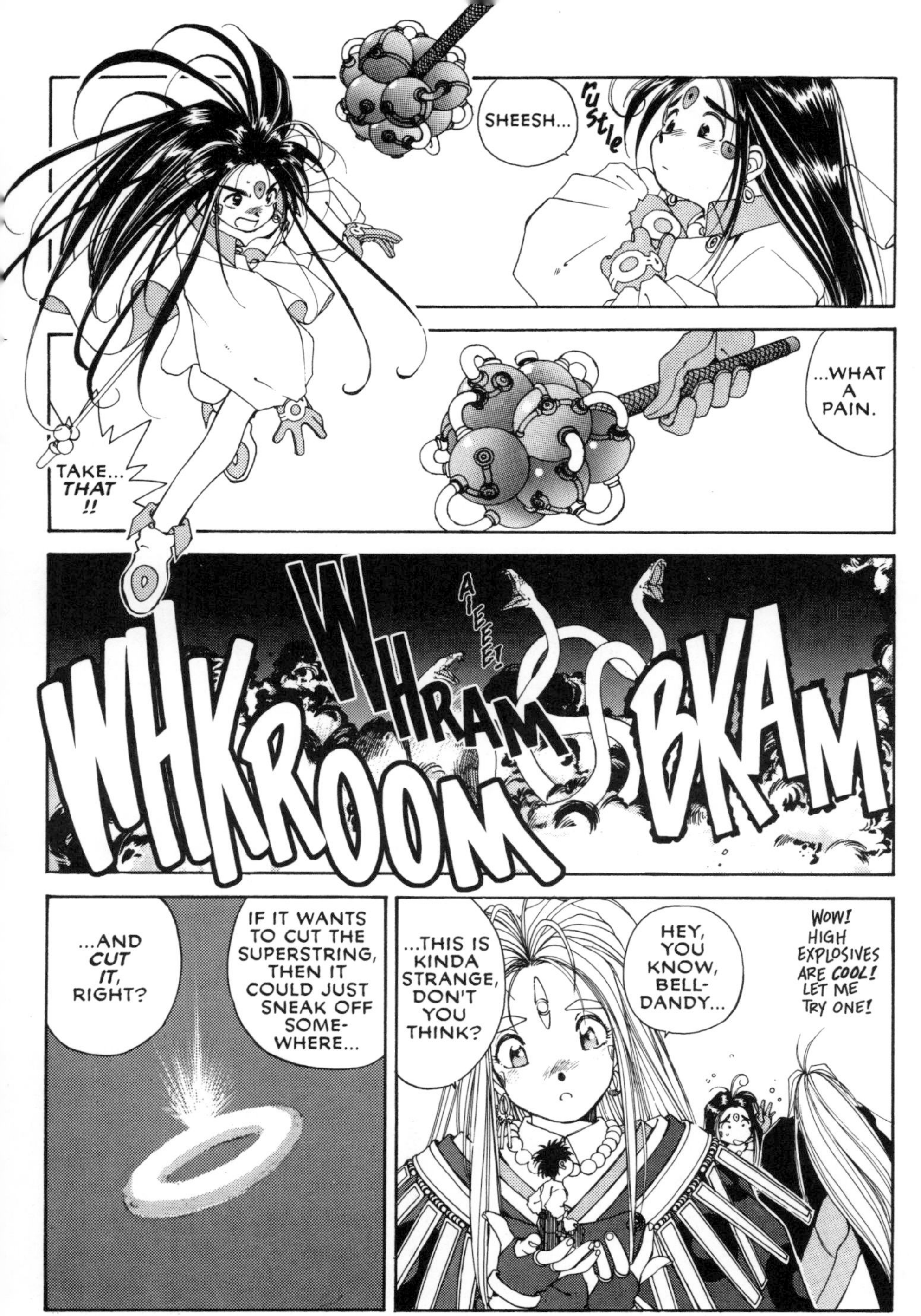
SHEESH...
rustle
...WHAT A PAIN.
TAKE... THAT!!
BKAM
WHHRAM
AIEEEE!
WHKROOM
WOW! HIGH EXPLOSIVES ARE COOL! LET ME TRY ONE!
HEY, YOU KNOW, BELL-DANDY...
...THIS IS KINDA STRANGE, DON'T YOU THINK?
IF IT WANTS TO CUT THE SUPERSTRING, THEN IT COULD JUST SNEAK OFF SOME-WHERE...
...AND CUT IT, RIGHT?

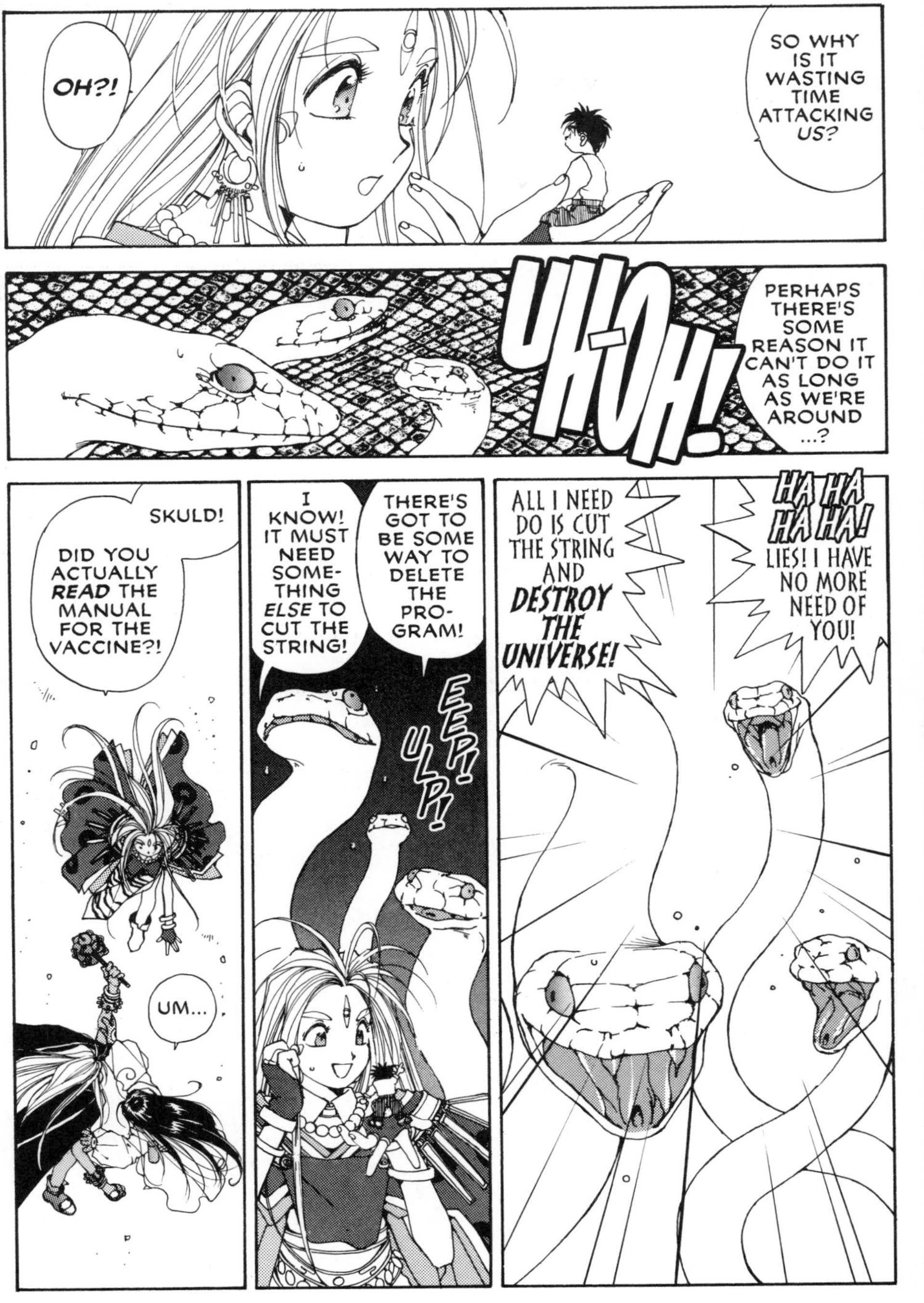
SO WHY IS IT WASTING TIME ATTACKING *US?*
*OH?!*
PERHAPS THERE'S SOME REASON IT CAN'T DO IT AS LONG AS WE'RE AROUND ...?
UH-OH!
HA HA HA HA!
LIES! I HAVE NO MORE NEED OF YOU!
ALL I NEED DO IS CUT THE STRING AND ***DESTROY THE UNIVERSE!***
THERE'S GOT TO BE SOME WAY TO DELETE THE PRO-GRAM!
I KNOW! IT MUST NEED SOME-THING *ELSE* TO CUT THE STRING!
EEP!
ULP!
SKULD!
DID YOU ACTUALLY ***READ*** THE MANUAL FOR THE VACCINE?!
UM...

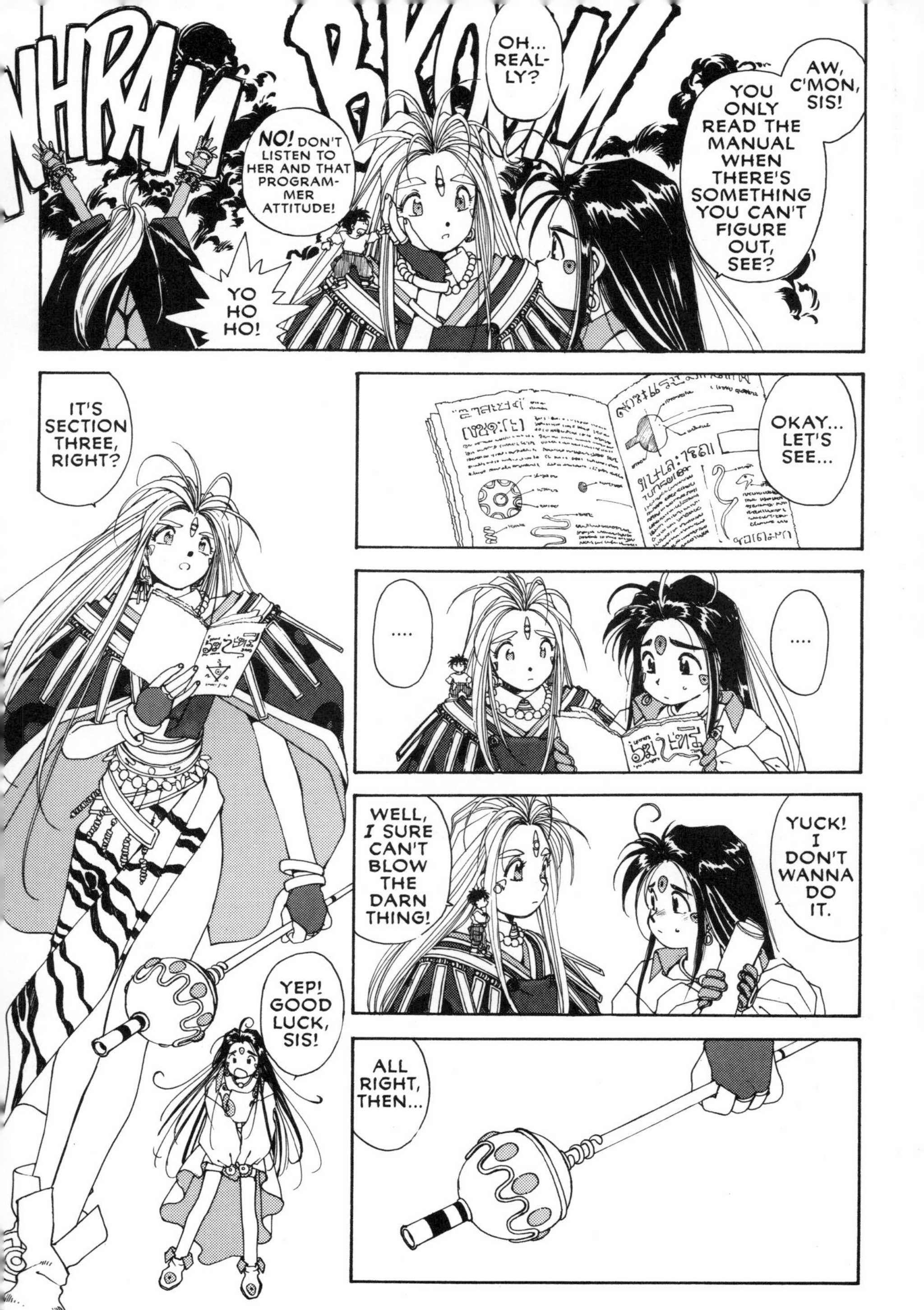
AW, C'MON, SIS!
YOU ONLY READ THE MANUAL WHEN THERE'S SOMETHING YOU CAN'T FIGURE OUT, SEE?
OH... REAL-LY?
BKOOM
NO! DON'T LISTEN TO HER AND THAT PROGRAM-MER ATTITUDE!
WHRAM
YO HO HO!
OKAY... LET'S SEE...
....
....
YUCK! I DON'T WANNA DO IT.
WELL, I SURE CAN'T BLOW THE DARN THING!
ALL RIGHT, THEN...
IT'S SECTION THREE, RIGHT?
YEP! GOOD LUCK, SIS!

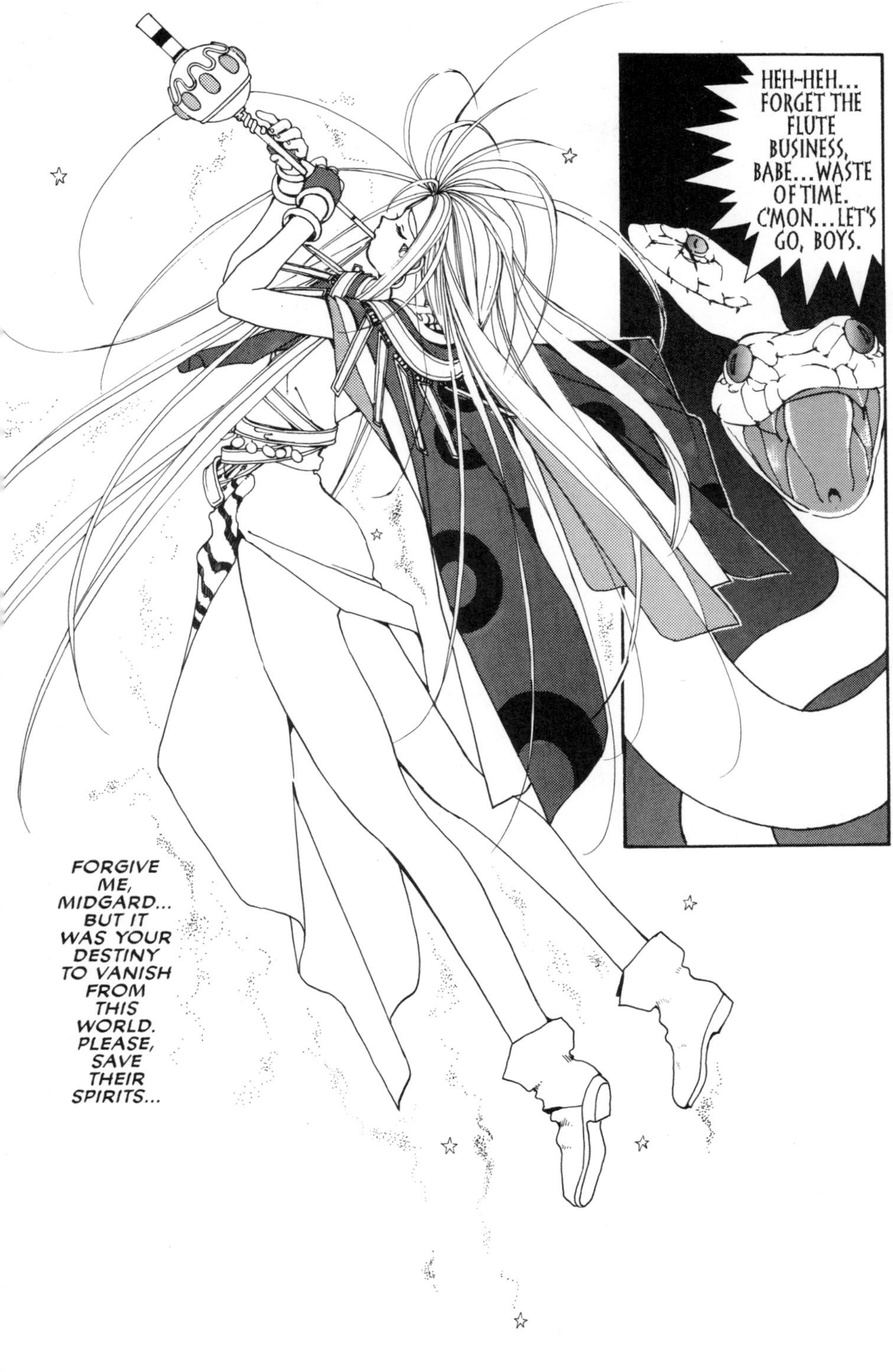
HEH-HEH... FORGET THE FLUTE BUSINESS, BABE... WASTE OF TIME. C'MON... LET'S GO, BOYS.
FORGIVE ME, MIDGARD... BUT IT WAS YOUR DESTINY TO VANISH FROM THIS WORLD. PLEASE, SAVE THEIR SPIRITS...

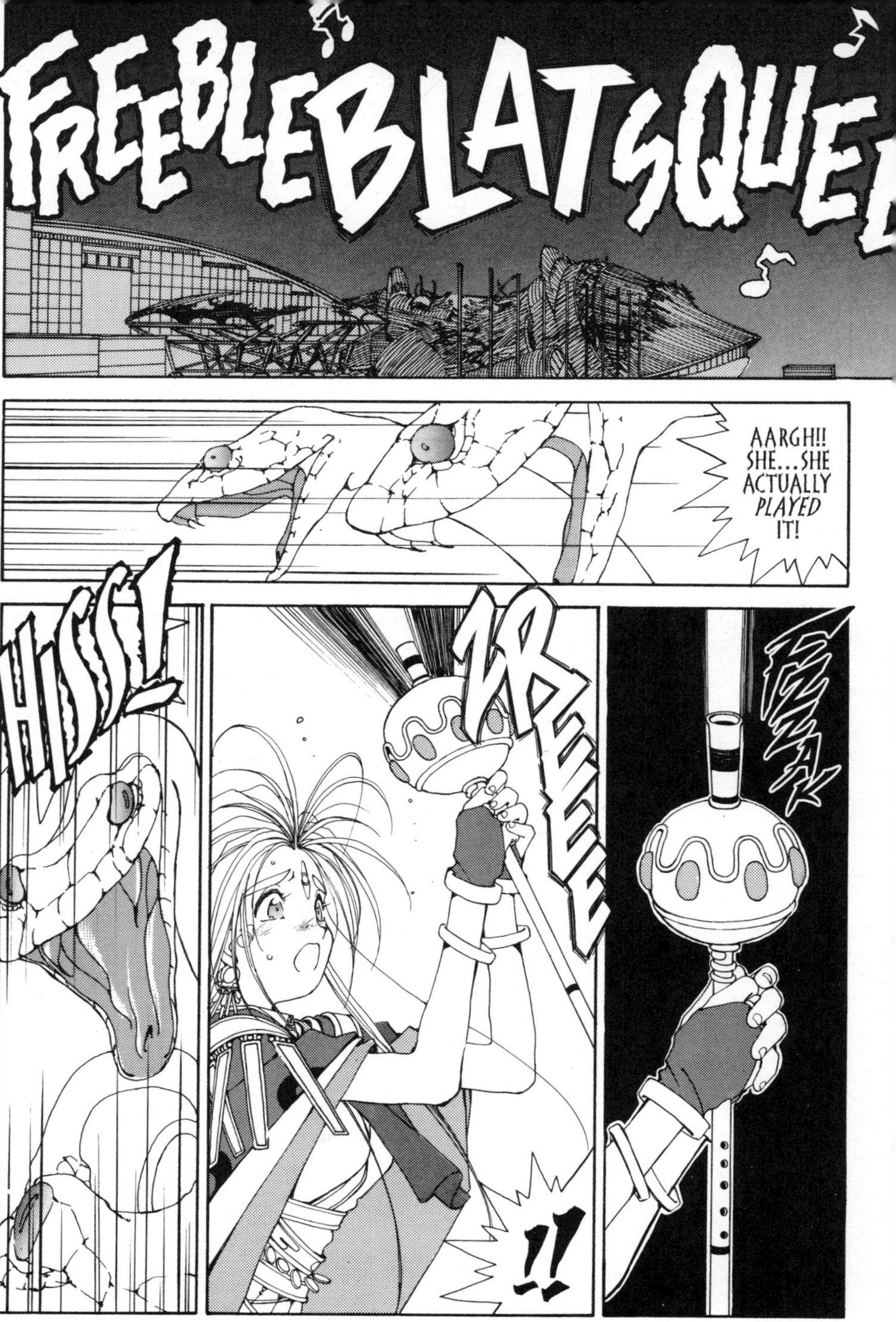
FREEBLEBLATSQUE
AARGH!! SHE...SHE ACTUALLY PLAYED IT!
ZREEEEE
!!
HISSS!

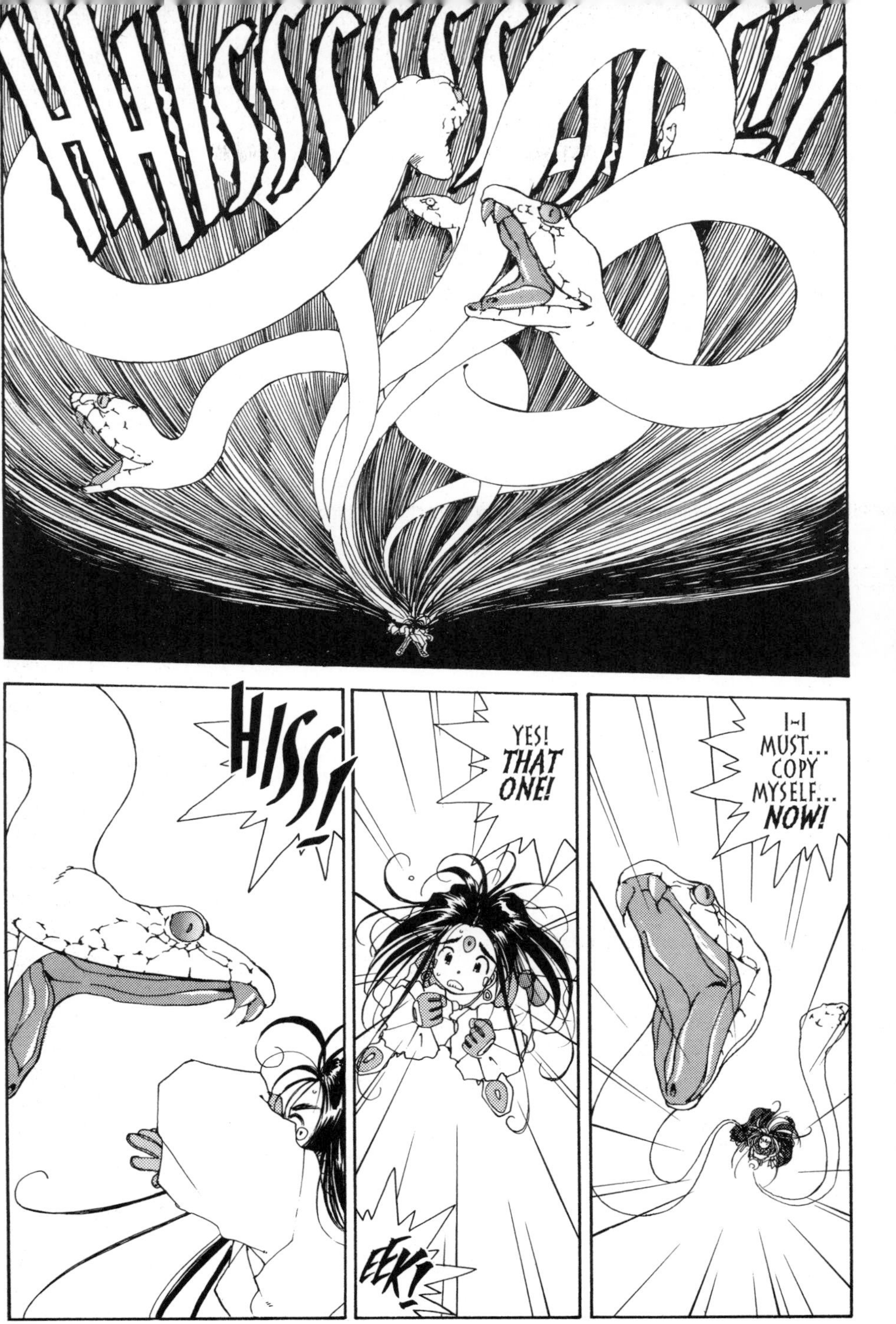
HHISSSSSSSSSSSS!
I-I MUST... COPY MYSELF... NOW!
YES! THAT ONE!
EEK!
HISS!

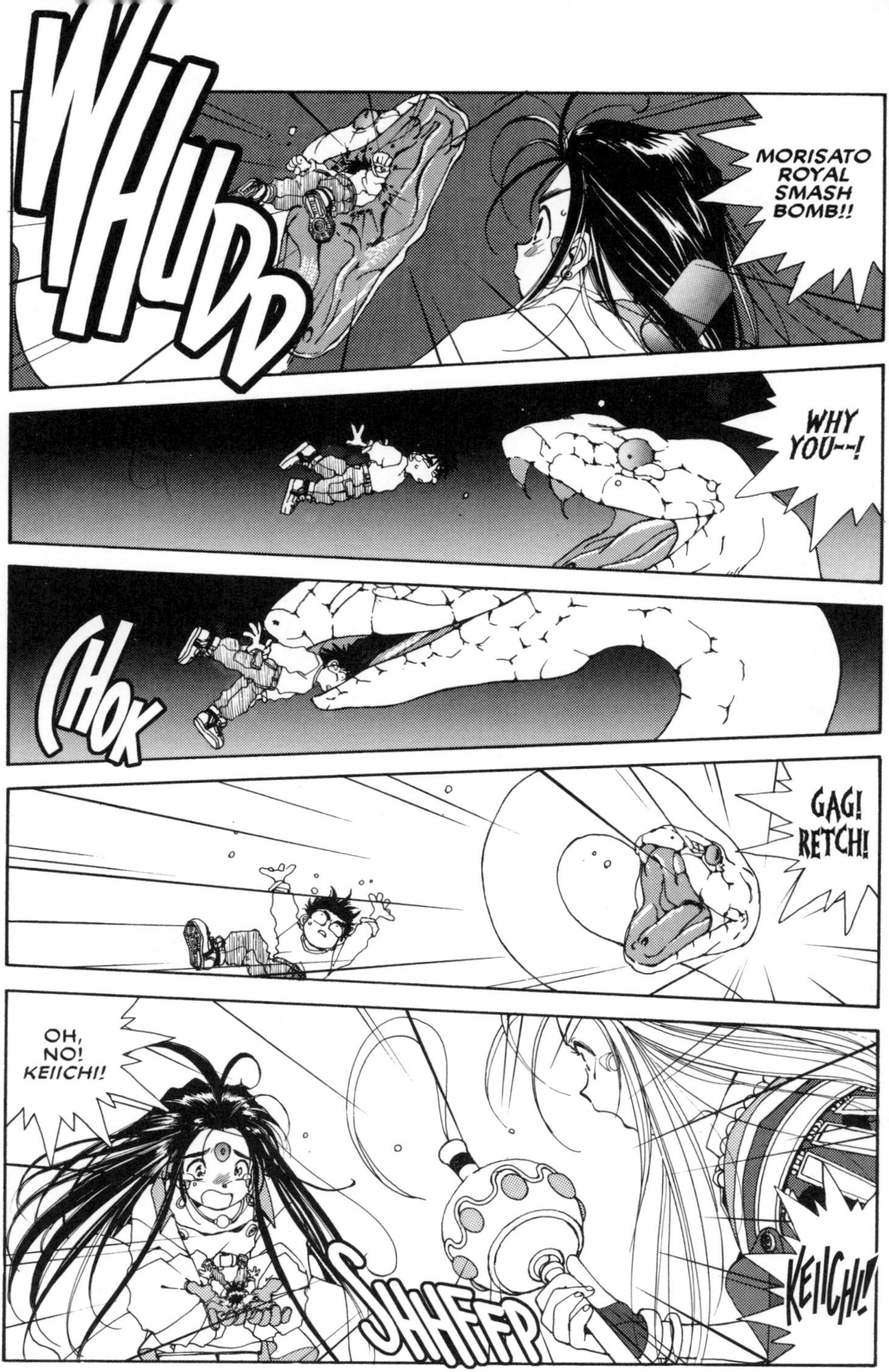
MORISATO ROYAL SMASH BOMB!!
WHUDD
WHY YOU--!
CHOK
GAG! RETCH!
KEIICHI!
SHHFFP
OH, NO! KEIICHI!

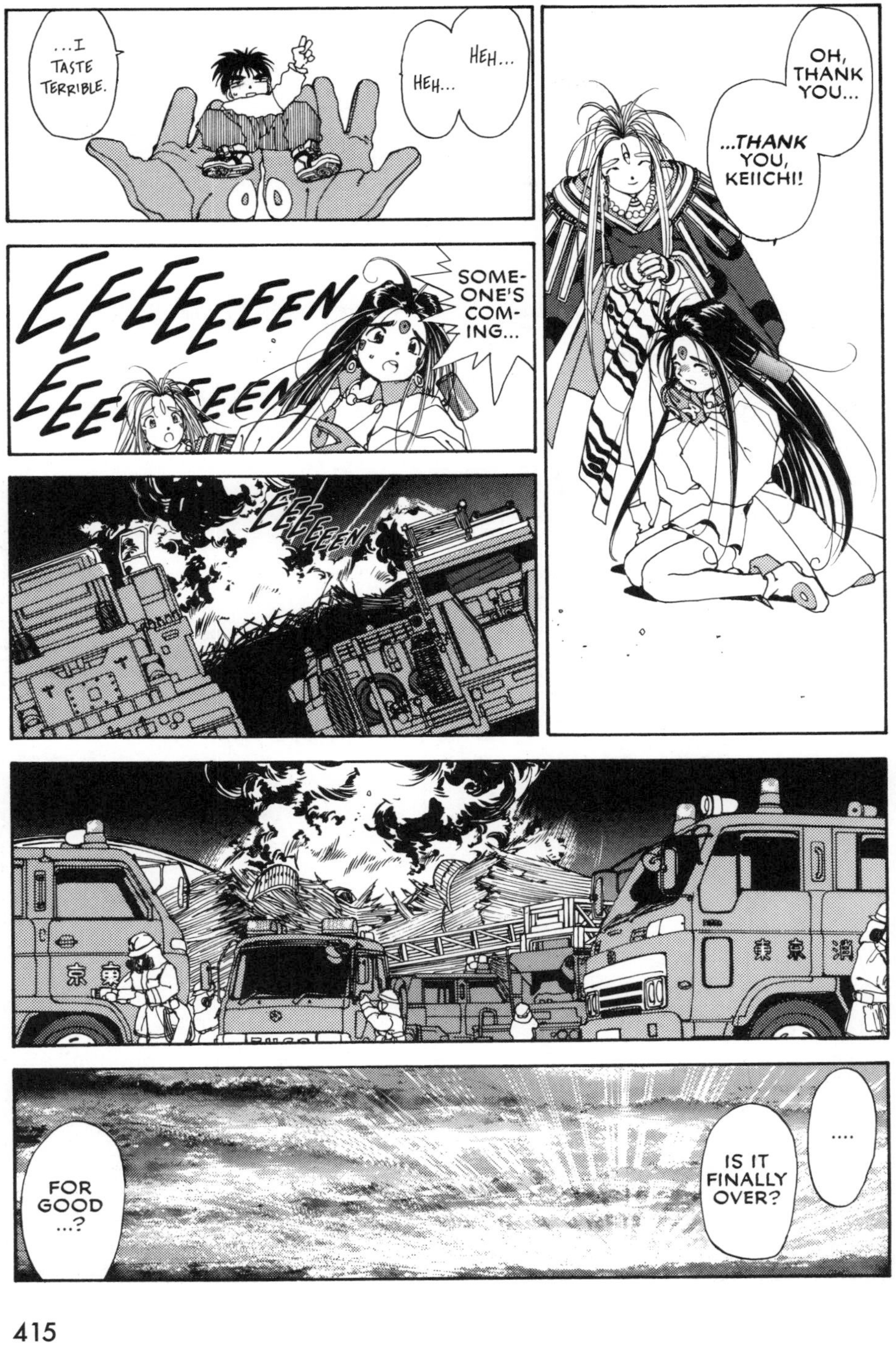
OH, THANK YOU...
...THANK YOU, KEIICHI!
HEH... HEH...
...I TASTE TERRIBLE.
SOME-ONE'S COM-ING...
EEEEEEEEN EEEEEEEEN
EEEEEEEN
....
IS IT FINALLY OVER?
FOR GOOD ...?

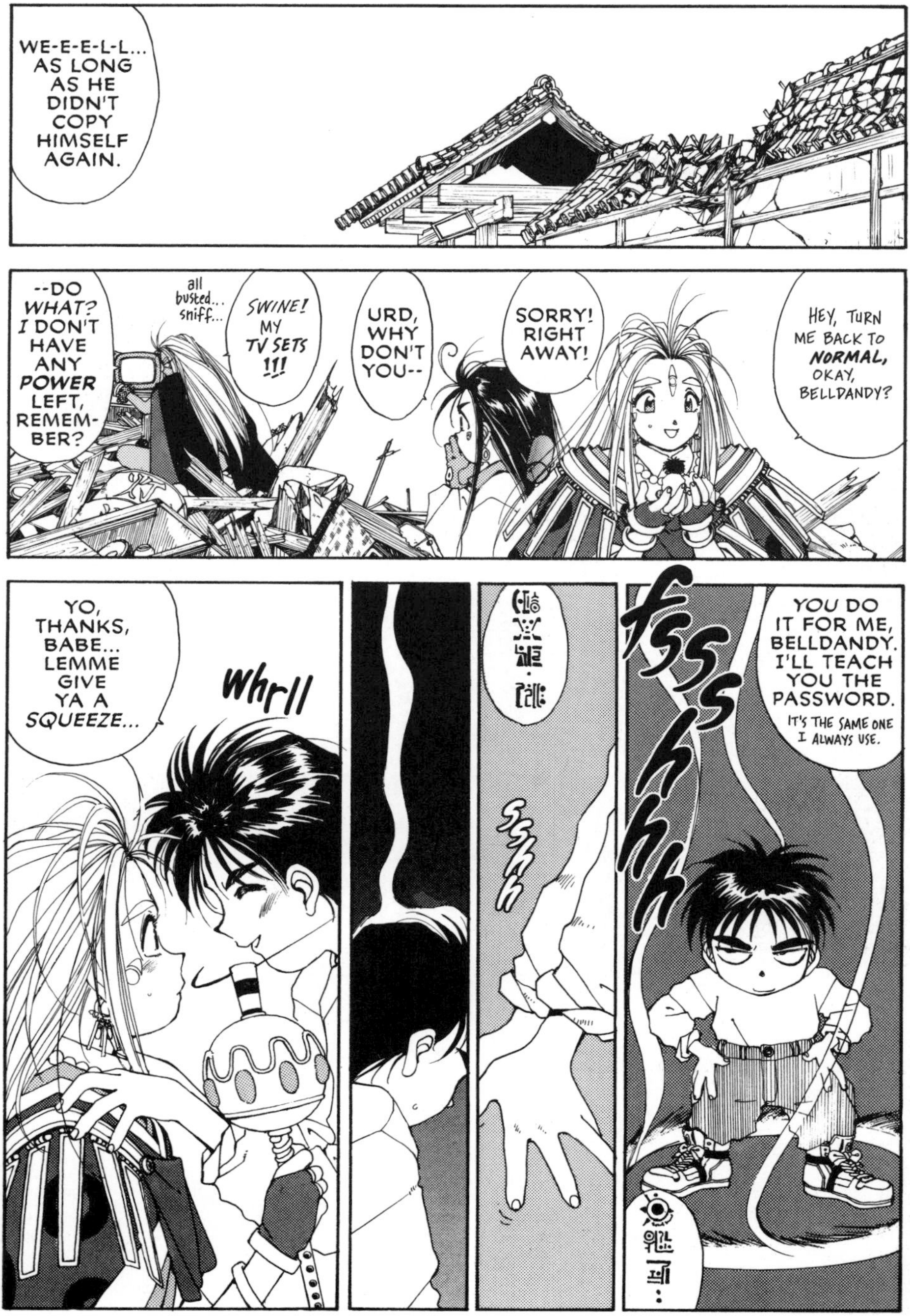
WE-E-E-L-L... AS LONG AS HE DIDN'T COPY HIMSELF AGAIN.
HEY, TURN ME BACK TO NORMAL, OKAY, BELLDANDY?
SORRY! RIGHT AWAY!
URD, WHY DON'T YOU--
SWINE! MY TV SETS !!!
all busted... sniff...
--DO WHAT? I DON'T HAVE ANY POWER LEFT, REMEMBER?
YOU DO IT FOR ME, BELLDANDY. I'LL TEACH YOU THE PASSWORD.
IT'S THE SAME ONE I ALWAYS USE.
fsssshhhh
sshhh
whrll
YO, THANKS, BABE... LEMME GIVE YA A SQUEEZE...

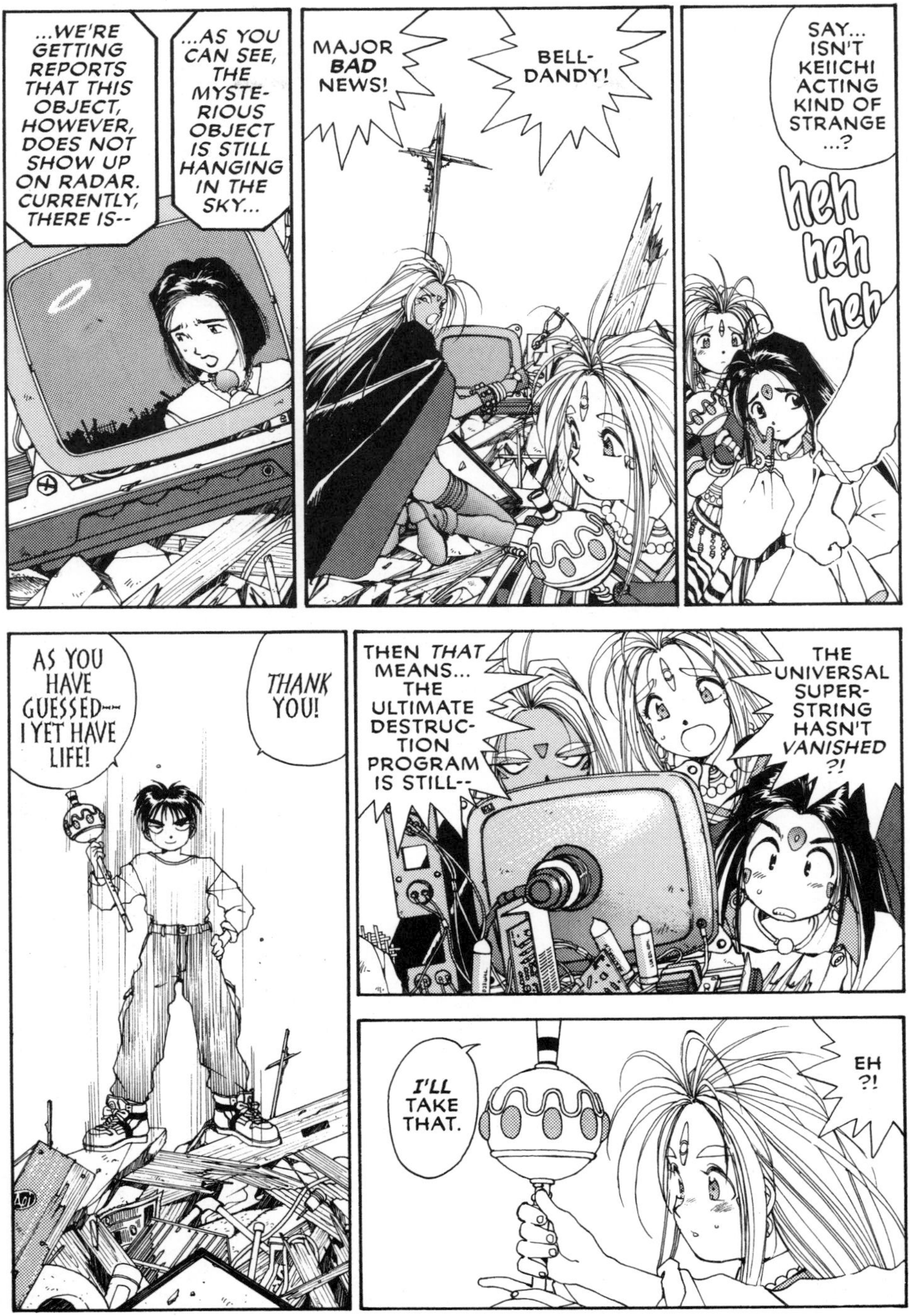
SAY... ISN'T KEIICHI ACTING KIND OF STRANGE ...?
heh heh heh
BELL-DANDY!
MAJOR BAD NEWS!
...AS YOU CAN SEE, THE MYSTERIOUS OBJECT IS STILL HANGING IN THE SKY...
...WE'RE GETTING REPORTS THAT THIS OBJECT, HOWEVER, DOES NOT SHOW UP ON RADAR. CURRENTLY, THERE IS--
THE UNIVERSAL SUPER-STRING HASN'T VANISHED ?!
THEN THAT MEANS... THE ULTIMATE DESTRUCTION PROGRAM IS STILL--
EH ?!
I'LL TAKE THAT.
THANK YOU!
AS YOU HAVE GUESSED-- I YET HAVE LIFE!

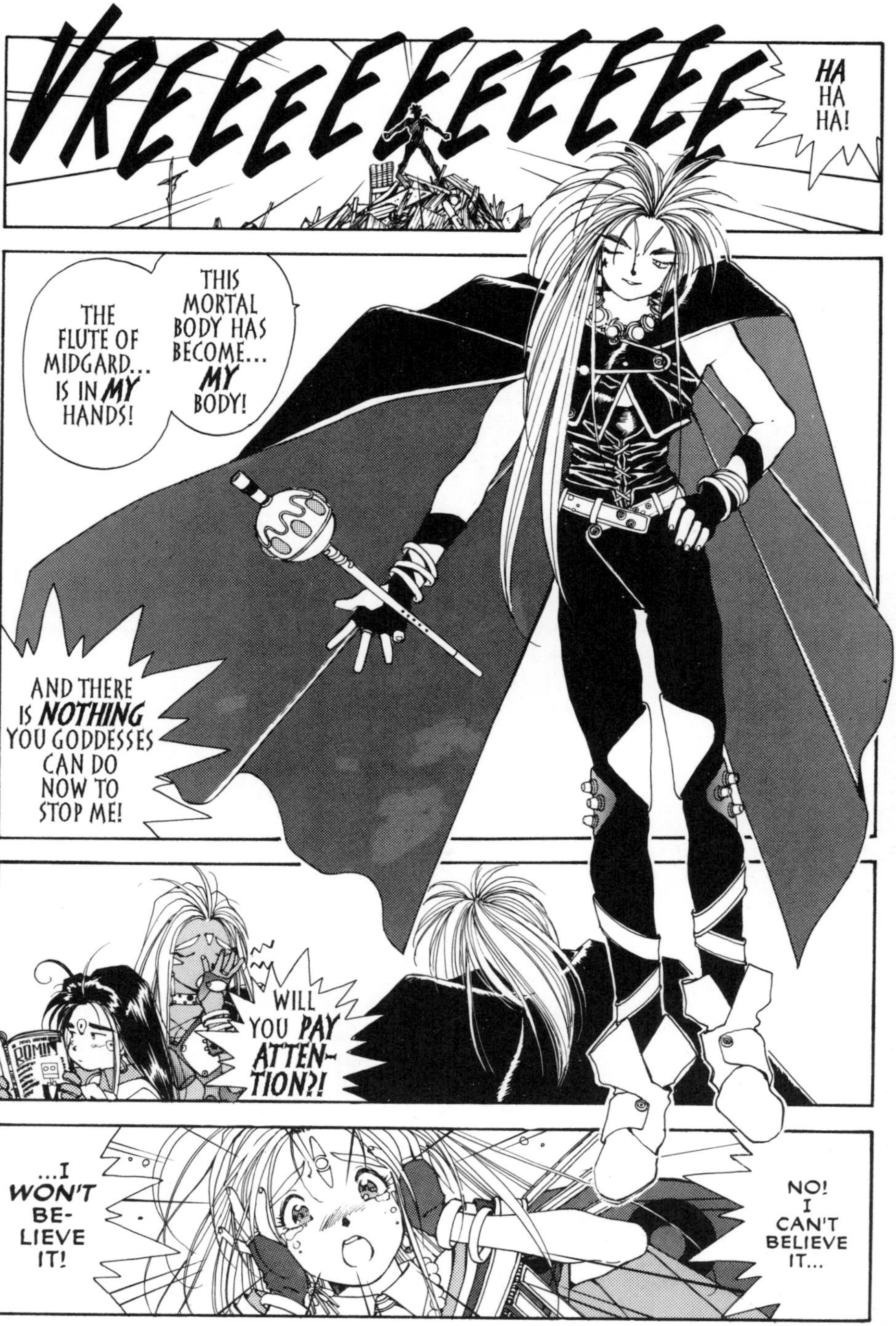

HA HA HA!
VREEEEEEEEEE
THIS MORTAL BODY HAS BECOME... MY BODY!
THE FLUTE OF MIDGARD... IS IN MY HANDS!
AND THERE IS NOTHING YOU GODDESSES CAN DO NOW TO STOP ME!
WILL YOU PAY ATTEN-TION?!
NO! I CAN'T BELIEVE IT...
...I WON'T BE-LIEVE IT!

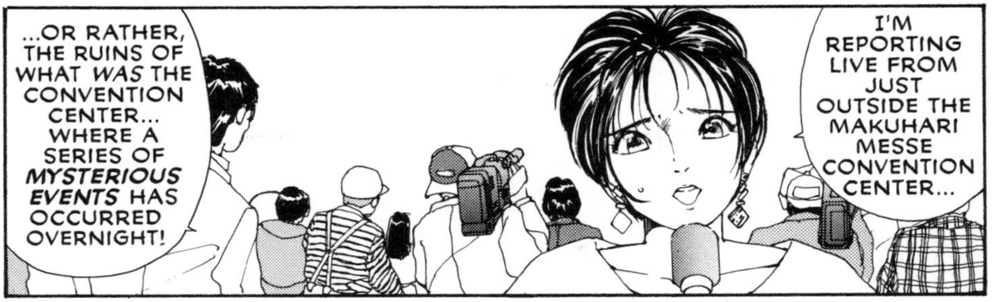
I'M REPORTING LIVE FROM JUST OUTSIDE THE MAKUHARI MESSE CONVENTION CENTER...
...OR RATHER, THE RUINS OF WHAT *WAS* THE CONVENTION CENTER... WHERE A SERIES OF ***MYSTERIOUS EVENTS*** HAS OCCURRED OVERNIGHT!

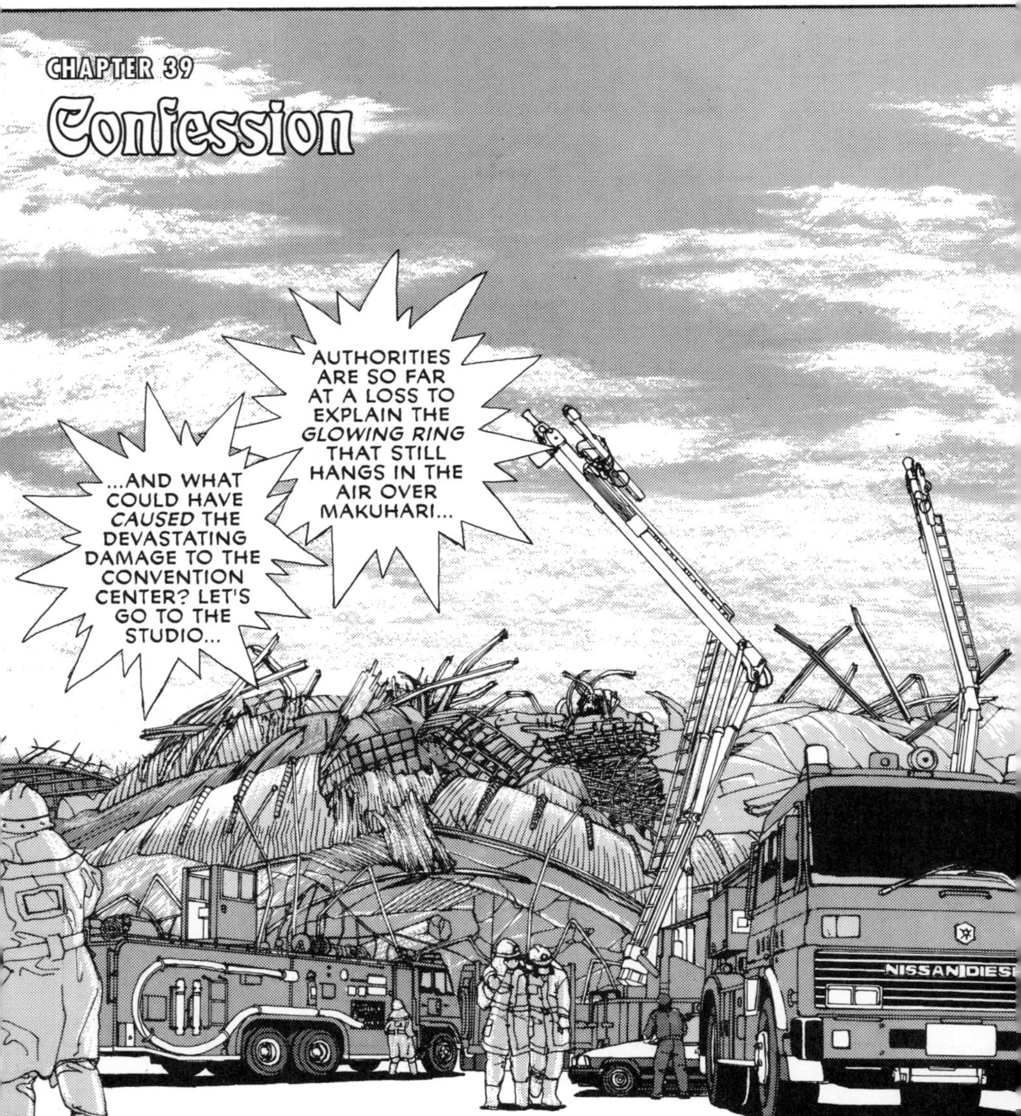
CHAPTER 39
Confession
AUTHORITIES ARE SO FAR AT A LOSS TO EXPLAIN THE *GLOWING RING* THAT STILL HANGS IN THE AIR OVER MAKUHARI...
...AND WHAT COULD HAVE *CAUSED* THE DEVASTATING DAMAGE TO THE CONVENTION CENTER? LET'S GO TO THE STUDIO...
NISSAN DIES

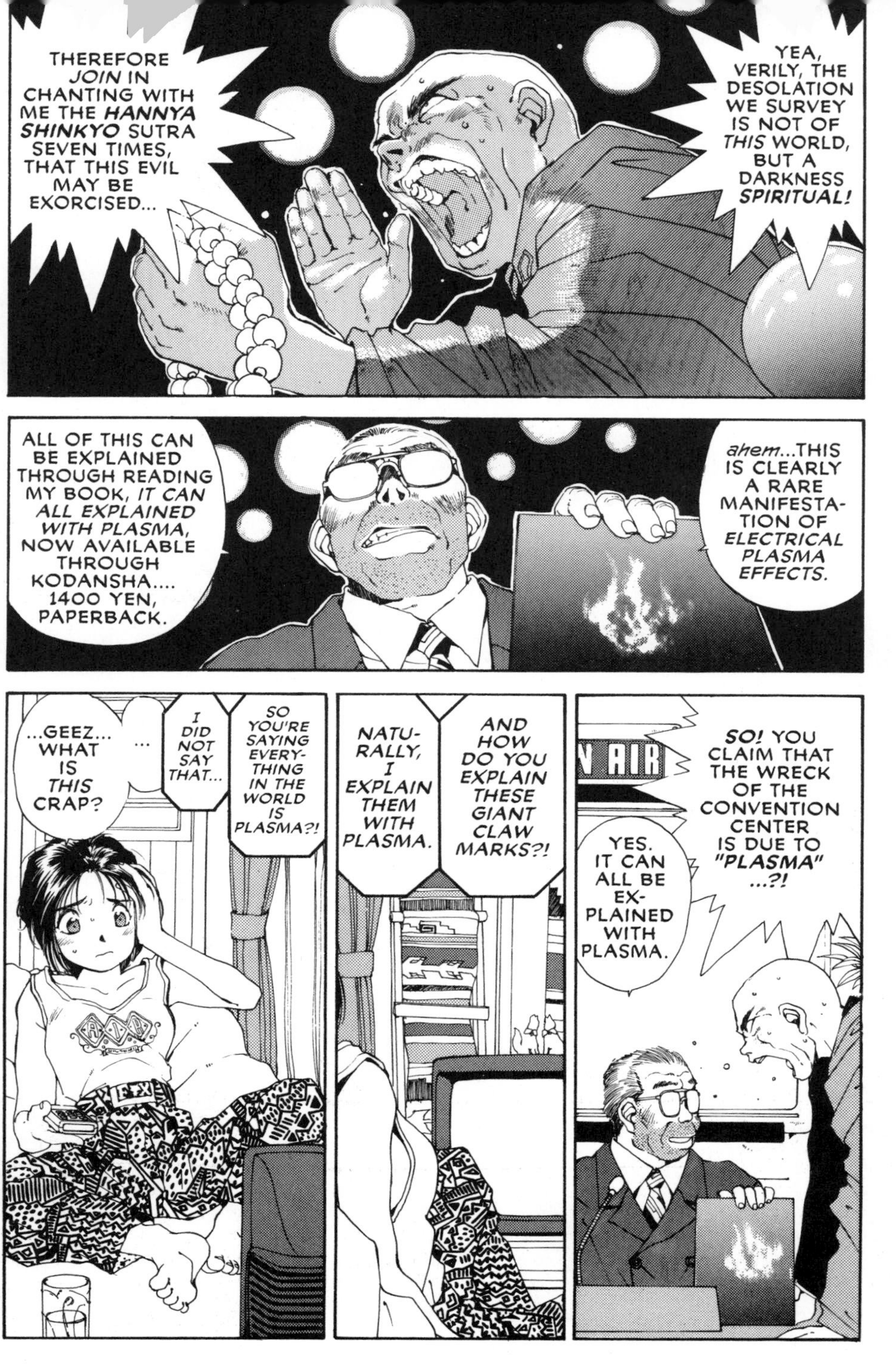
YEA, VERILY, THE DESOLATION WE SURVEY IS NOT OF *THIS* WORLD, BUT A DARKNESS *SPIRITUAL!*
THEREFORE *JOIN* IN CHANTING WITH ME THE *HANNYA SHINKYO* SUTRA SEVEN TIMES, THAT THIS EVIL MAY BE EXORCISED...
*ahem*...THIS IS CLEARLY A RARE MANIFESTATION OF *ELECTRICAL PLASMA EFFECTS.*
ALL OF THIS CAN BE EXPLAINED THROUGH READING MY BOOK, *IT CAN ALL EXPLAINED WITH PLASMA,* NOW AVAILABLE THROUGH KODANSHA.... 1400 YEN, PAPERBACK.
*SO!* YOU CLAIM THAT THE WRECK OF THE CONVENTION CENTER IS DUE TO *"PLASMA"* ...?!
YES. IT CAN ALL BE EXPLAINED WITH PLASMA.
AND HOW DO YOU EXPLAIN THESE GIANT CLAW MARKS?!
NATURALLY, I EXPLAIN THEM WITH PLASMA.
SO YOU'RE SAYING EVERYTHING IN THE WORLD IS PLASMA?!
I DID NOT SAY THAT...
...
...GEEZ... WHAT IS *THIS* CRAP?

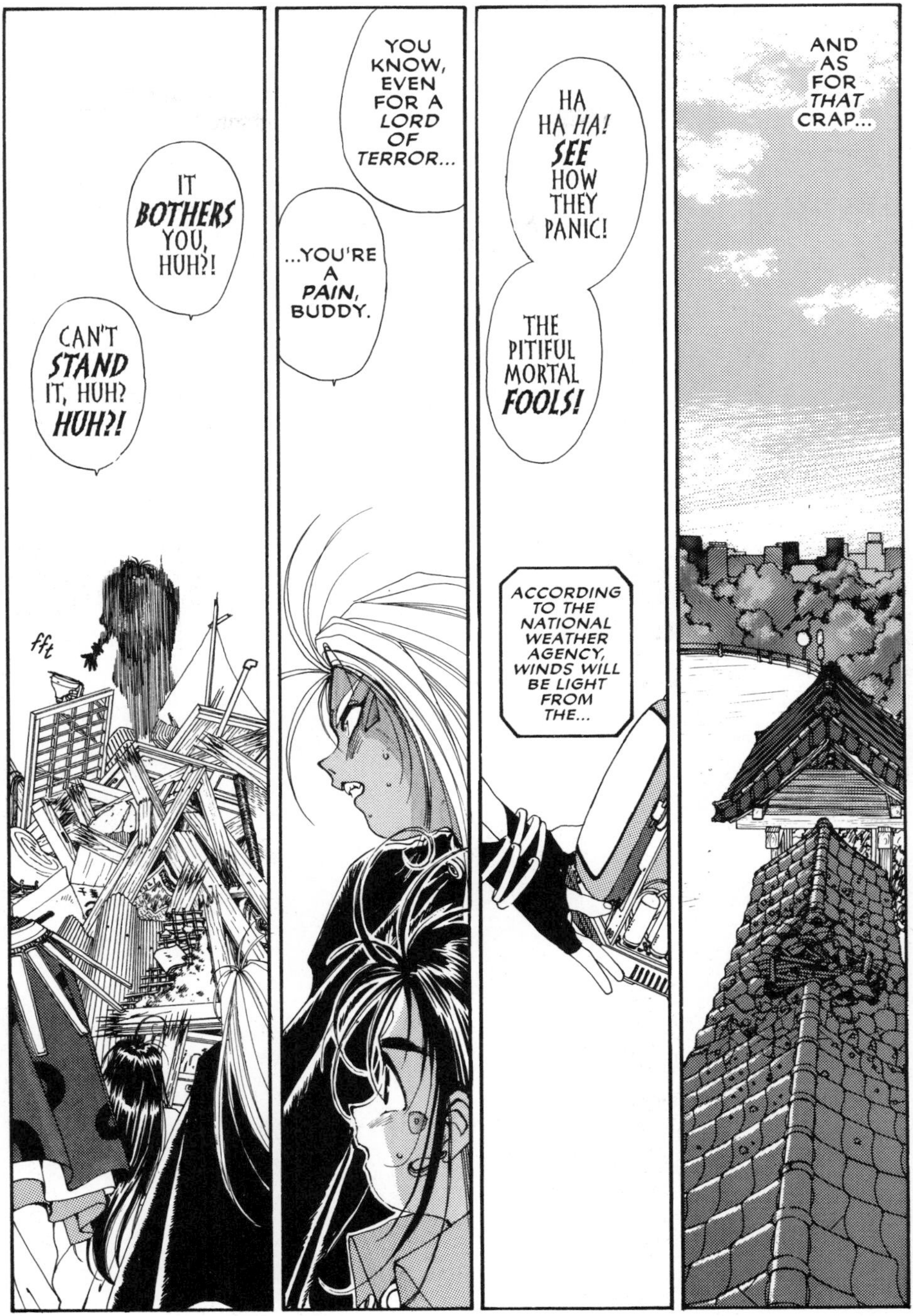
AND AS FOR THAT CRAP...
HA HA HA! SEE HOW THEY PANIC!
THE PITIFUL MORTAL FOOLS!
ACCORDING TO THE NATIONAL WEATHER AGENCY, WINDS WILL BE LIGHT FROM THE...
YOU KNOW, EVEN FOR A LORD OF TERROR...
...YOU'RE A PAIN, BUDDY.
IT BOTHERS YOU, HUH?!
CAN'T STAND IT, HUH? HUH?!
fft

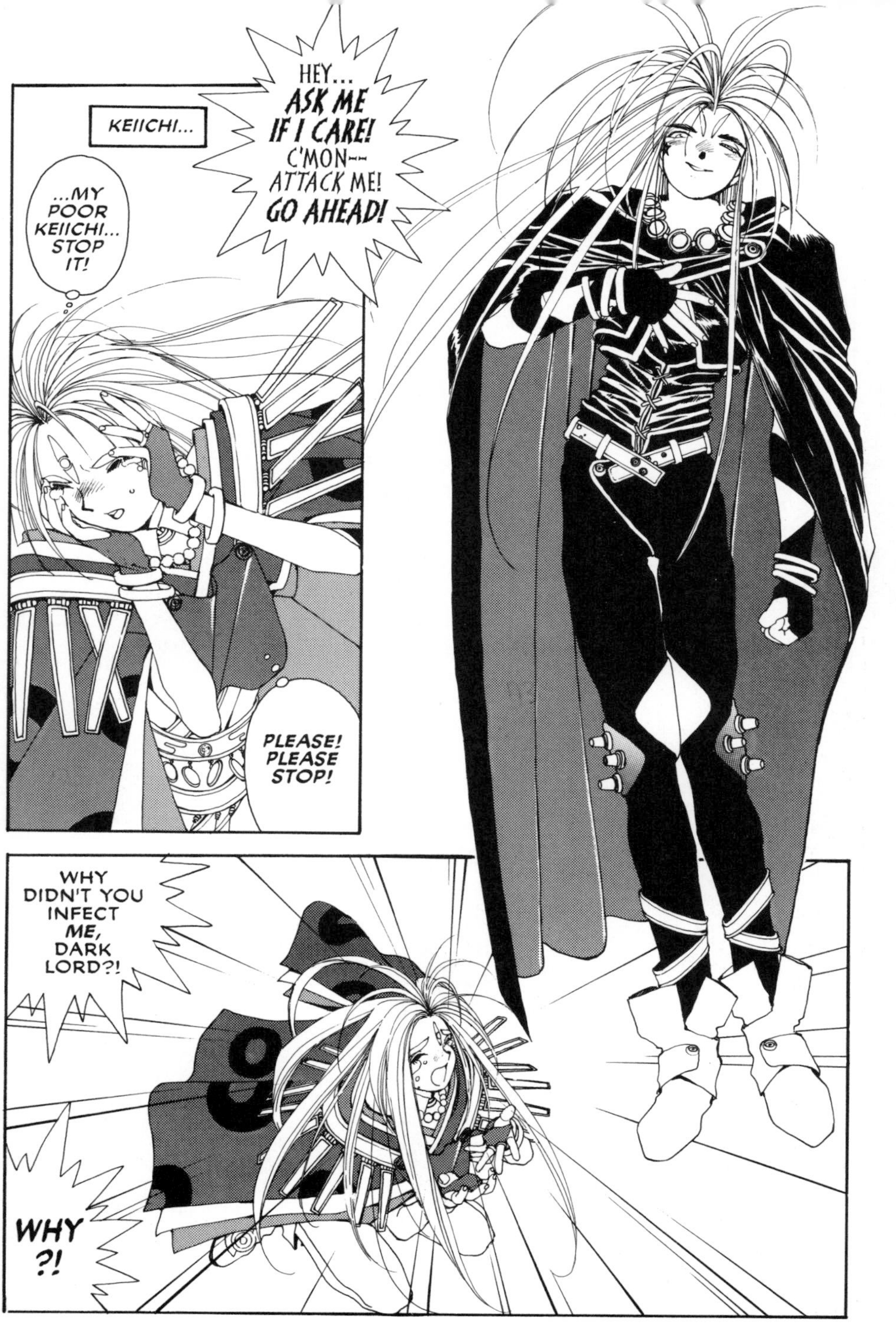
HEY... ASK ME IF I CARE! C'MON-- ATTACK ME! GO AHEAD!
KEIICHI...
...MY POOR KEIICHI... STOP IT!
PLEASE! PLEASE STOP!
WHY DIDN'T YOU INFECT ME, DARK LORD?!
WHY ?!

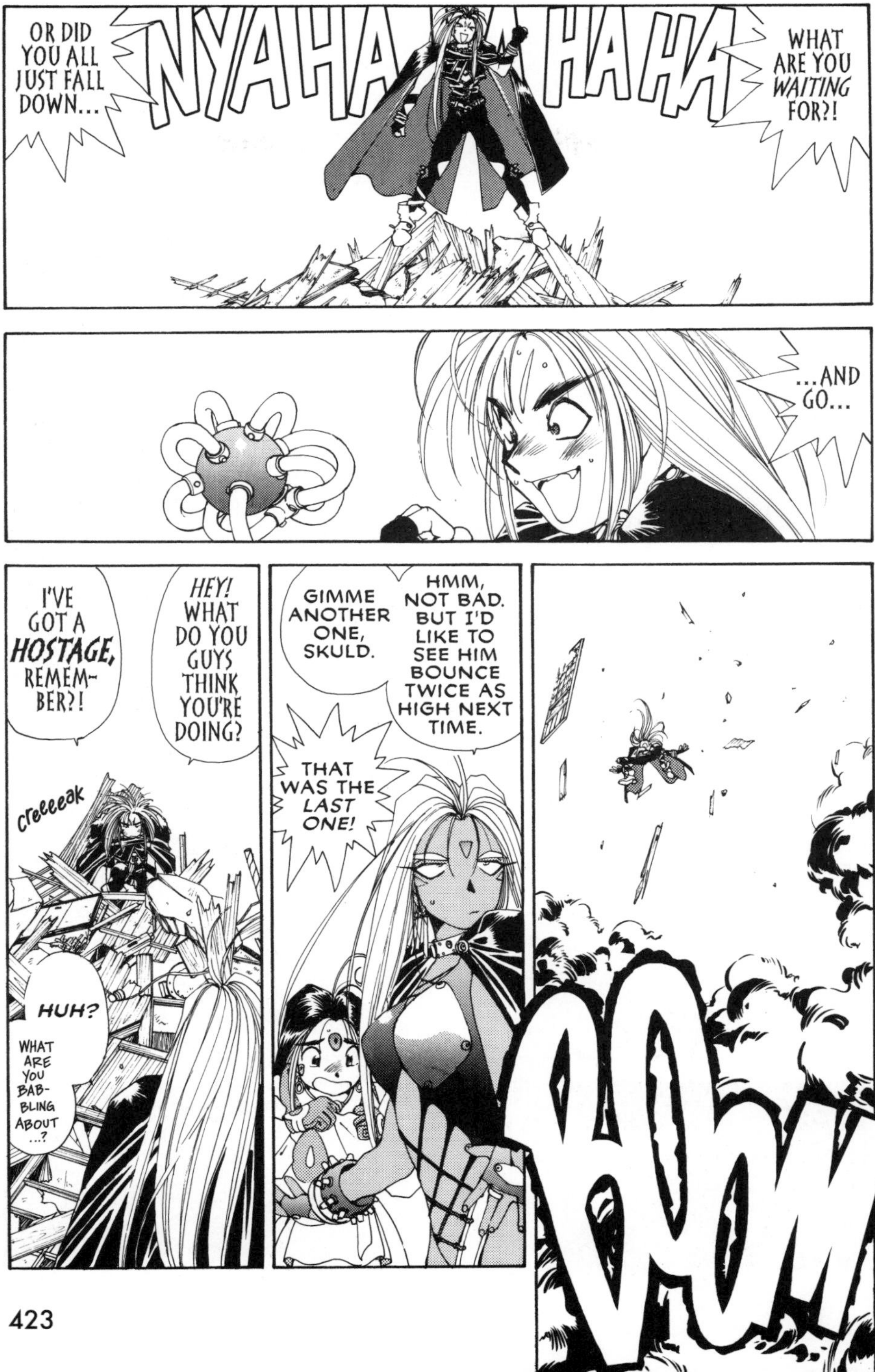
WHAT ARE YOU *WAITING* FOR?!
NYAHAHAHAHA
OR DID YOU ALL JUST FALL DOWN...
...AND GO...
BOOM
HMM, NOT BAD. BUT I'D LIKE TO SEE HIM BOUNCE TWICE AS HIGH NEXT TIME.
GIMME ANOTHER ONE, SKULD.
THAT WAS THE *LAST ONE!*
*HEY!* WHAT DO YOU GUYS THINK YOU'RE DOING?
I'VE GOT A ***HOSTAGE,*** REMEMBER?!
creeeeak
HUH?
WHAT ARE YOU BABBLING ABOUT...?

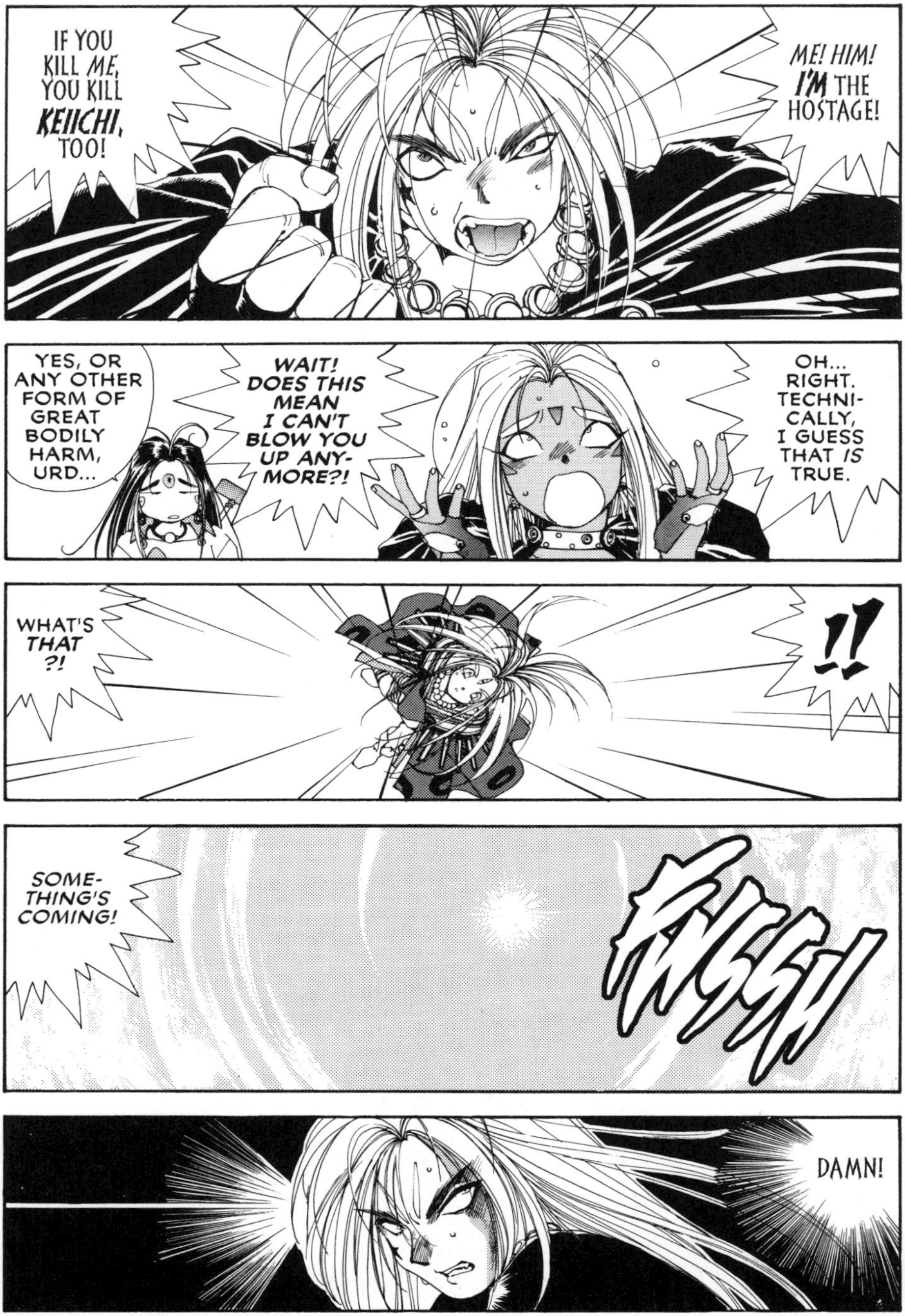
ME! HIM! *I'M* THE HOSTAGE!
IF YOU KILL *ME*, YOU KILL **KEIICHI**, TOO!
OH... RIGHT. TECHNICALLY, I GUESS THAT *IS* TRUE.
*WAIT! DOES THIS MEAN I CAN'T BLOW YOU UP ANYMORE?!*
YES, OR ANY OTHER FORM OF GREAT BODILY HARM, URD...
!!
WHAT'S *THAT* ?!
FWSSH
*SOMETHING'S COMING!*
DAMN!

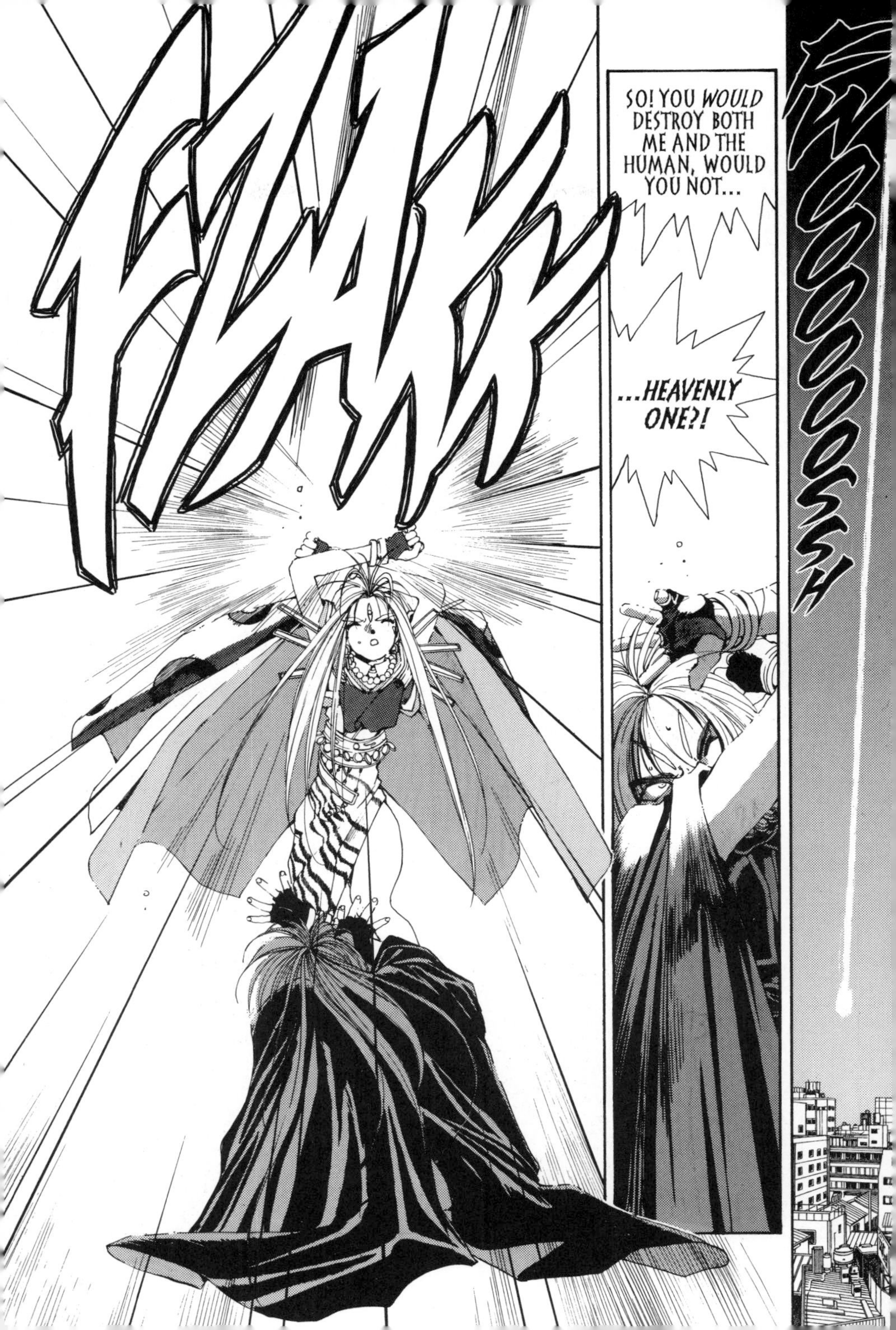
FWOOOOOOSSH
SO! YOU *WOULD* DESTROY BOTH ME AND THE HUMAN, WOULD YOU NOT...
...HEAVENLY ONE?!
FLASH

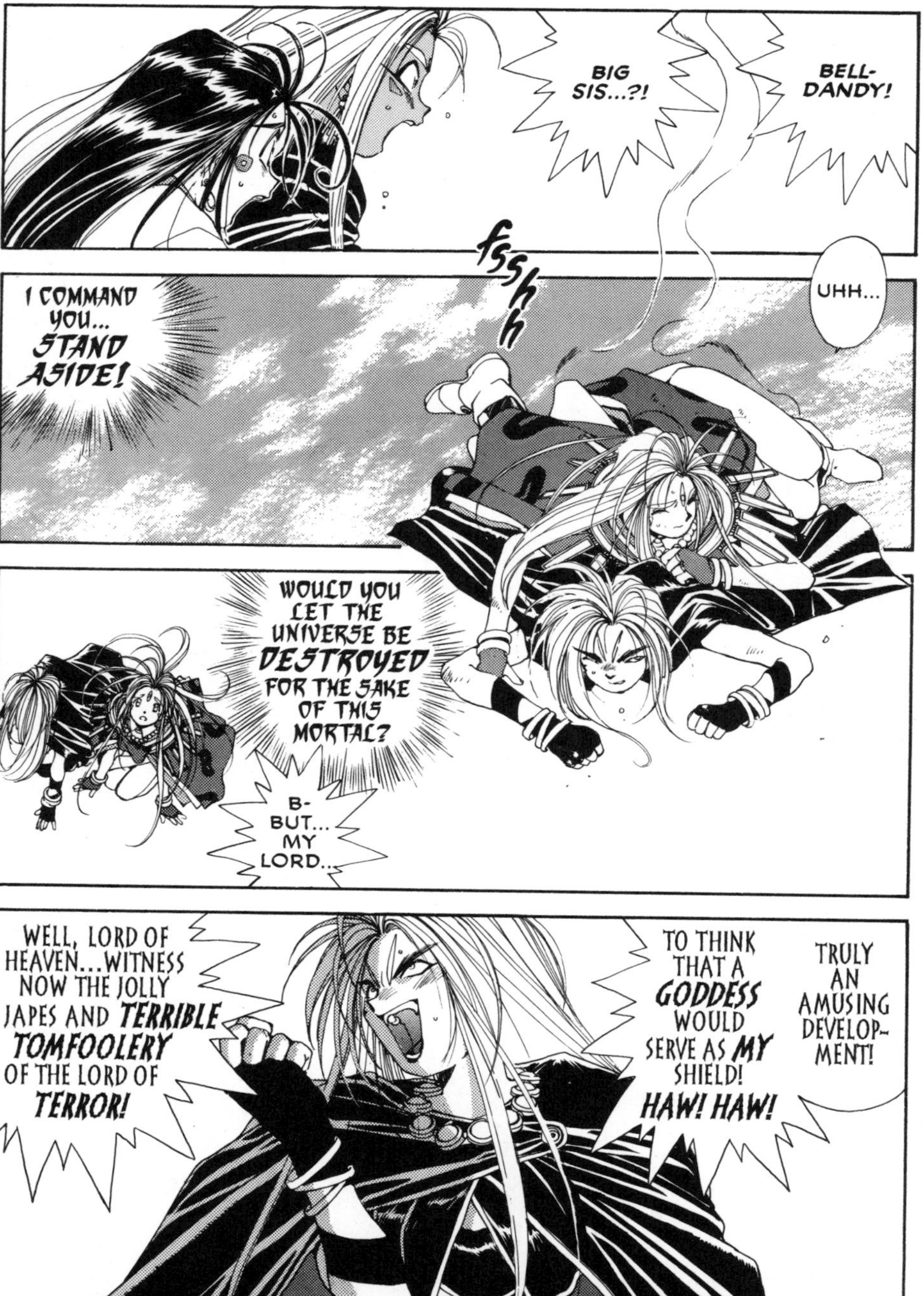
BELL-DANDY!
BIG SIS...?!
fsshh
UHH...
I COMMAND YOU... STAND ASIDE!
WOULD YOU LET THE UNIVERSE BE DESTROYED FOR THE SAKE OF THIS MORTAL?
B-BUT... MY LORD...
TRULY AN AMUSING DEVELOP-MENT!
TO THINK THAT A GODDESS WOULD SERVE AS MY SHIELD! HAW! HAW!
WELL, LORD OF HEAVEN...WITNESS NOW THE JOLLY JAPES AND TERRIBLE TOMFOOLERY OF THE LORD OF TERROR!

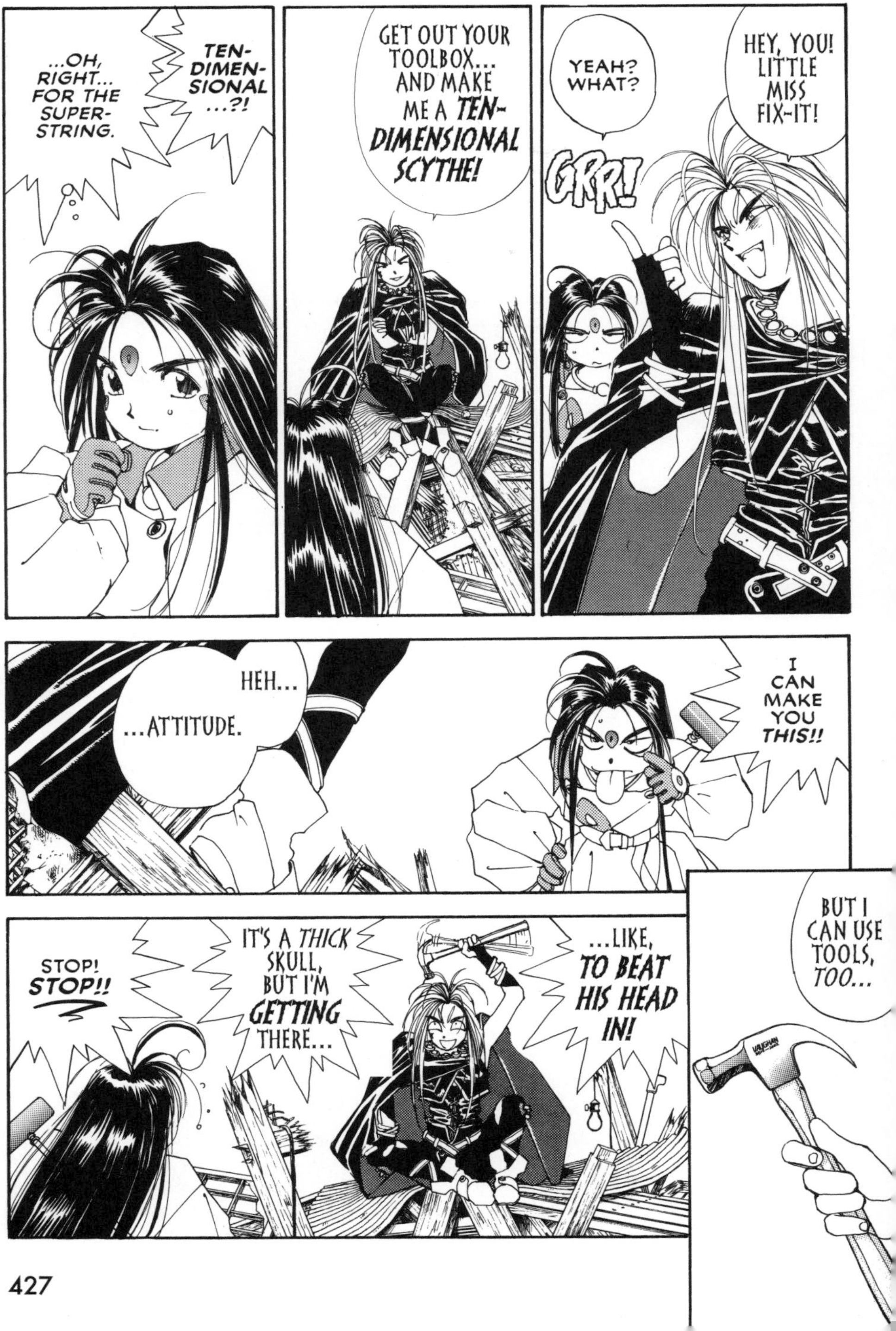
HEY, YOU! LITTLE MISS FIX-IT!
YEAH? WHAT?
GRR!
GET OUT YOUR TOOLBOX... AND MAKE ME A TEN-DIMENSIONAL SCYTHE!
TEN-DIMENSIONAL...?!
...OH, RIGHT... FOR THE SUPER-STRING.
I CAN MAKE YOU THIS!!
HEH...
...ATTITUDE.
BUT I CAN USE TOOLS, TOO...
...LIKE, TO BEAT HIS HEAD IN!
IT'S A THICK SKULL, BUT I'M GETTING THERE...
STOP! STOP!!

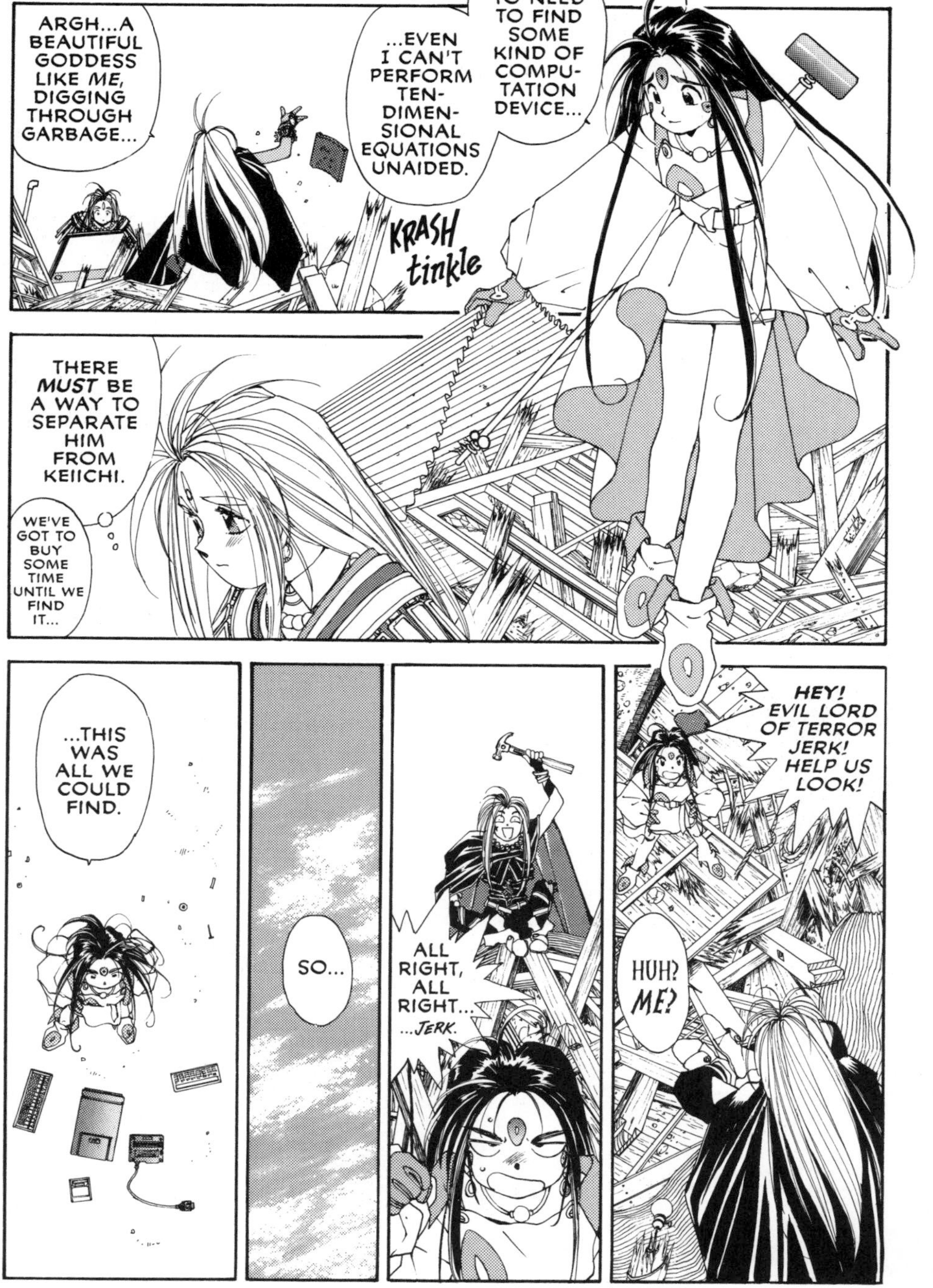
I'M GOING TO NEED TO FIND SOME KIND OF COMPU-TATION DEVICE...
...EVEN I CAN'T PERFORM TEN-DIMEN-SIONAL EQUATIONS UNAIDED.
KRASH
tinkle
ARGH...A BEAUTIFUL GODDESS LIKE *ME*, DIGGING THROUGH GARBAGE...
THERE *MUST* BE A WAY TO SEPARATE HIM FROM KEIICHI.
WE'VE GOT TO BUY SOME TIME UNTIL WE FIND IT...
HEY! EVIL LORD OF TERROR JERK! HELP US LOOK!
HUH? ME?
ALL RIGHT, ALL RIGHT... ...JERK.
SO...
...THIS WAS ALL WE COULD FIND.

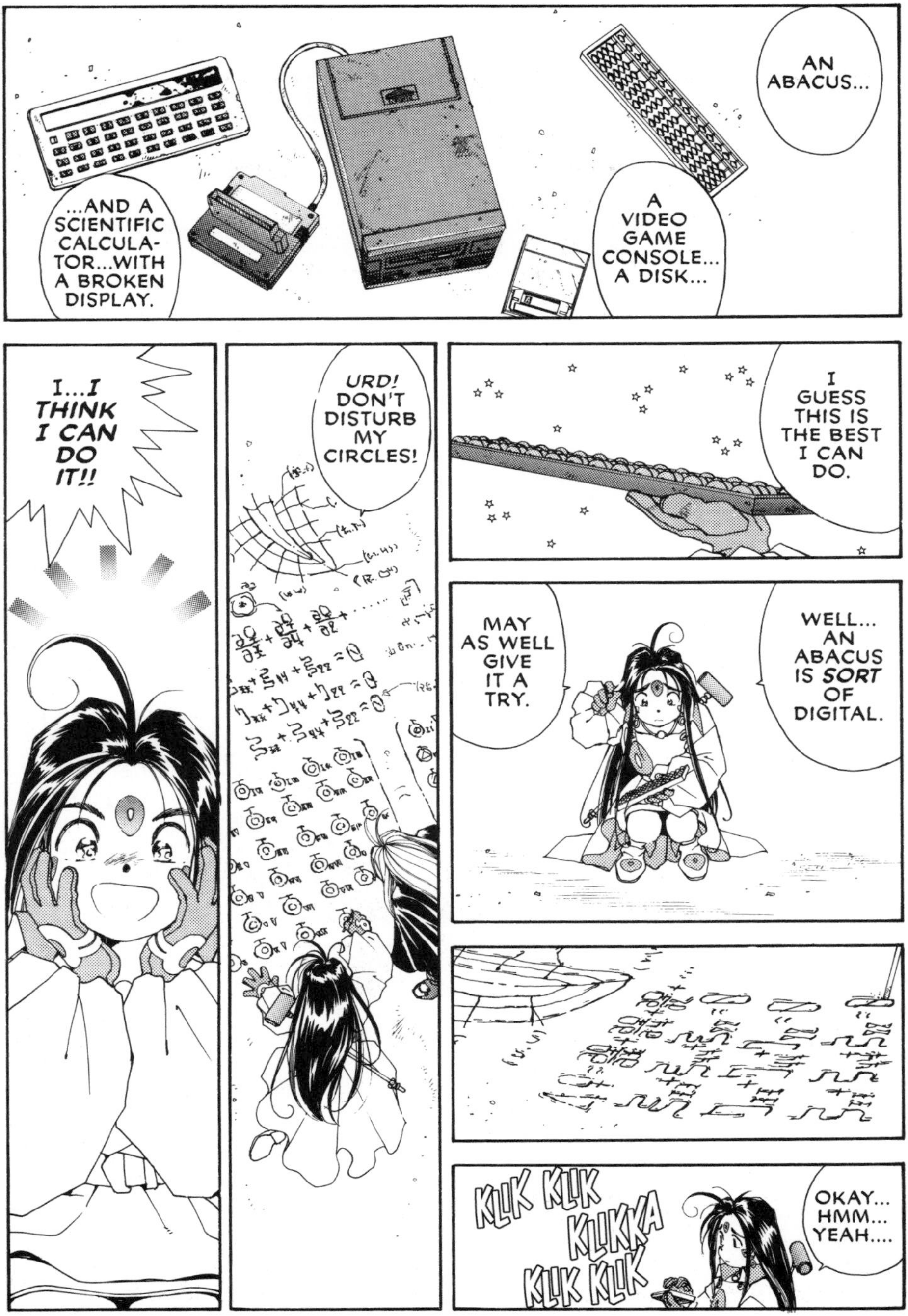
AN ABACUS...
A VIDEO GAME CONSOLE... A DISK...
...AND A SCIENTIFIC CALCULATOR...WITH A BROKEN DISPLAY.
I GUESS THIS IS THE BEST I CAN DO.
WELL... AN ABACUS IS *SORT* OF DIGITAL.
MAY AS WELL GIVE IT A TRY.
OKAY... HMM... YEAH....
KLIK KLIK KLIKKA KLIK KLIK
*URD!* DON'T DISTURB MY CIRCLES!
*I...I THINK I CAN DO IT!!*

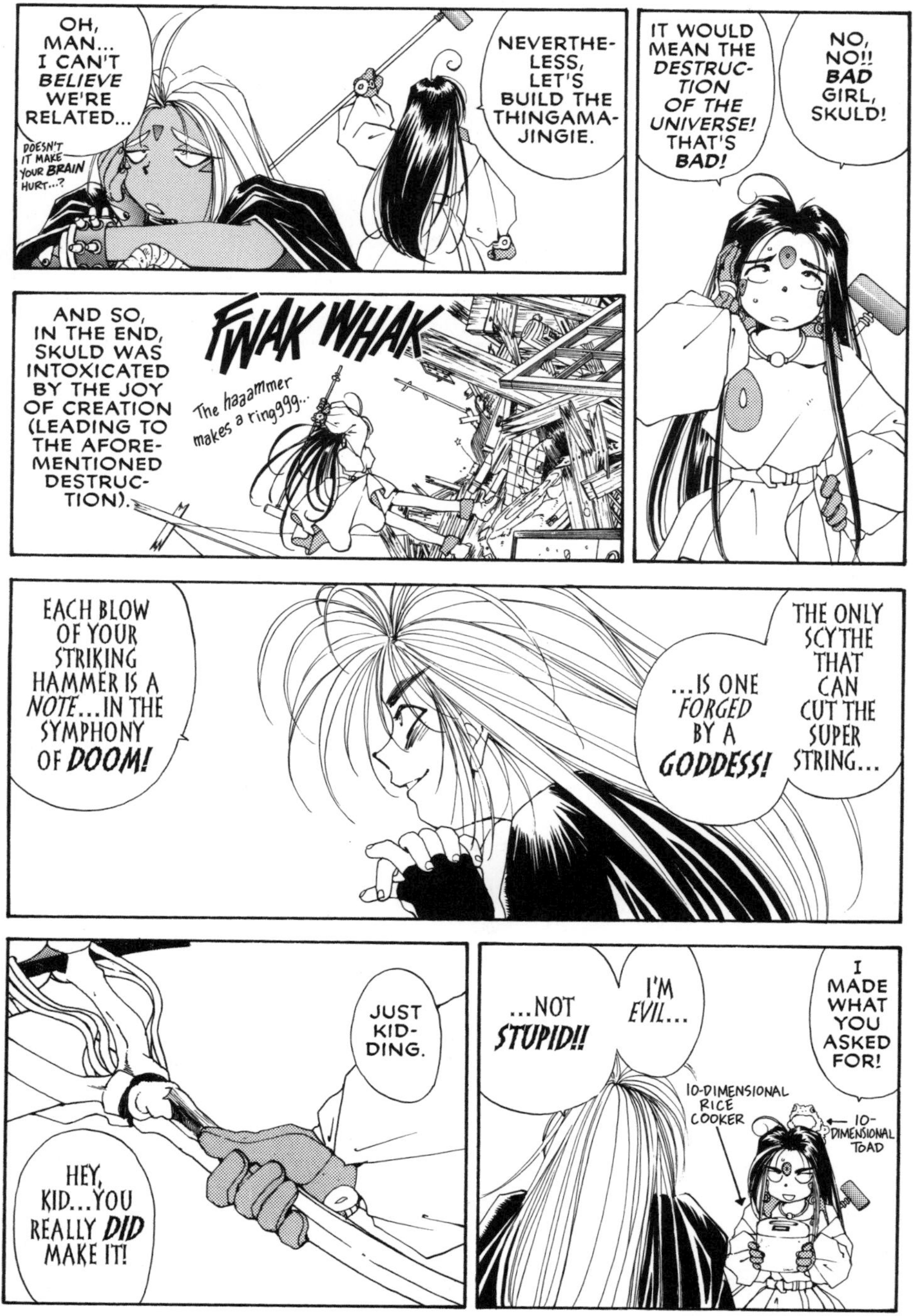
NO, NO!! BAD GIRL, SKULD!
IT WOULD MEAN THE DESTRUCTION OF THE UNIVERSE! THAT'S BAD!
NEVERTHELESS, LET'S BUILD THE THINGAMAJINGIE.
OH, MAN... I CAN'T BELIEVE WE'RE RELATED...
DOESN'T IT MAKE YOUR BRAIN HURT...?
FWAK WHAK
AND SO, IN THE END, SKULD WAS INTOXICATED BY THE JOY OF CREATION (LEADING TO THE AFOREMENTIONED DESTRUCTION).
The haaammer makes a ringggg...
THE ONLY SCYTHE THAT CAN CUT THE SUPER STRING...
...IS ONE FORGED BY A GODDESS!
EACH BLOW OF YOUR STRIKING HAMMER IS A NOTE...IN THE SYMPHONY OF DOOM!
I MADE WHAT YOU ASKED FOR!
I'M EVIL...
...NOT STUPID!!
10-DIMENSIONAL RICE COOKER
10-DIMENSIONAL TOAD
JUST KIDDING.
HEY, KID...YOU REALLY DID MAKE IT!

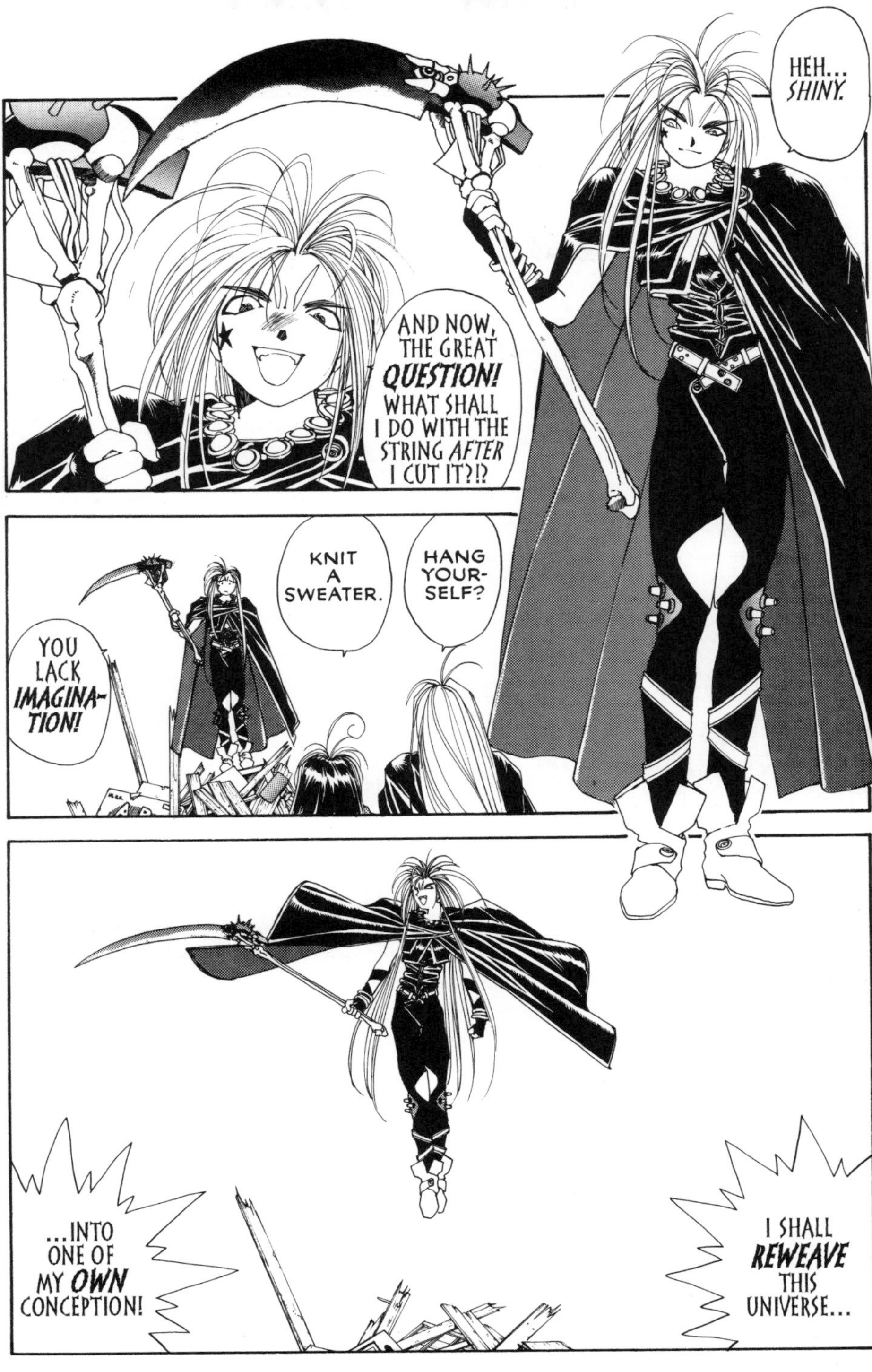
HEH... SHINY.
AND NOW, THE GREAT QUESTION! WHAT SHALL I DO WITH THE STRING AFTER I CUT IT?!?
HANG YOURSELF?
KNIT A SWEATER.
YOU LACK IMAGINATION!
I SHALL REWEAVE THIS UNIVERSE...
...INTO ONE OF MY OWN CONCEPTION!

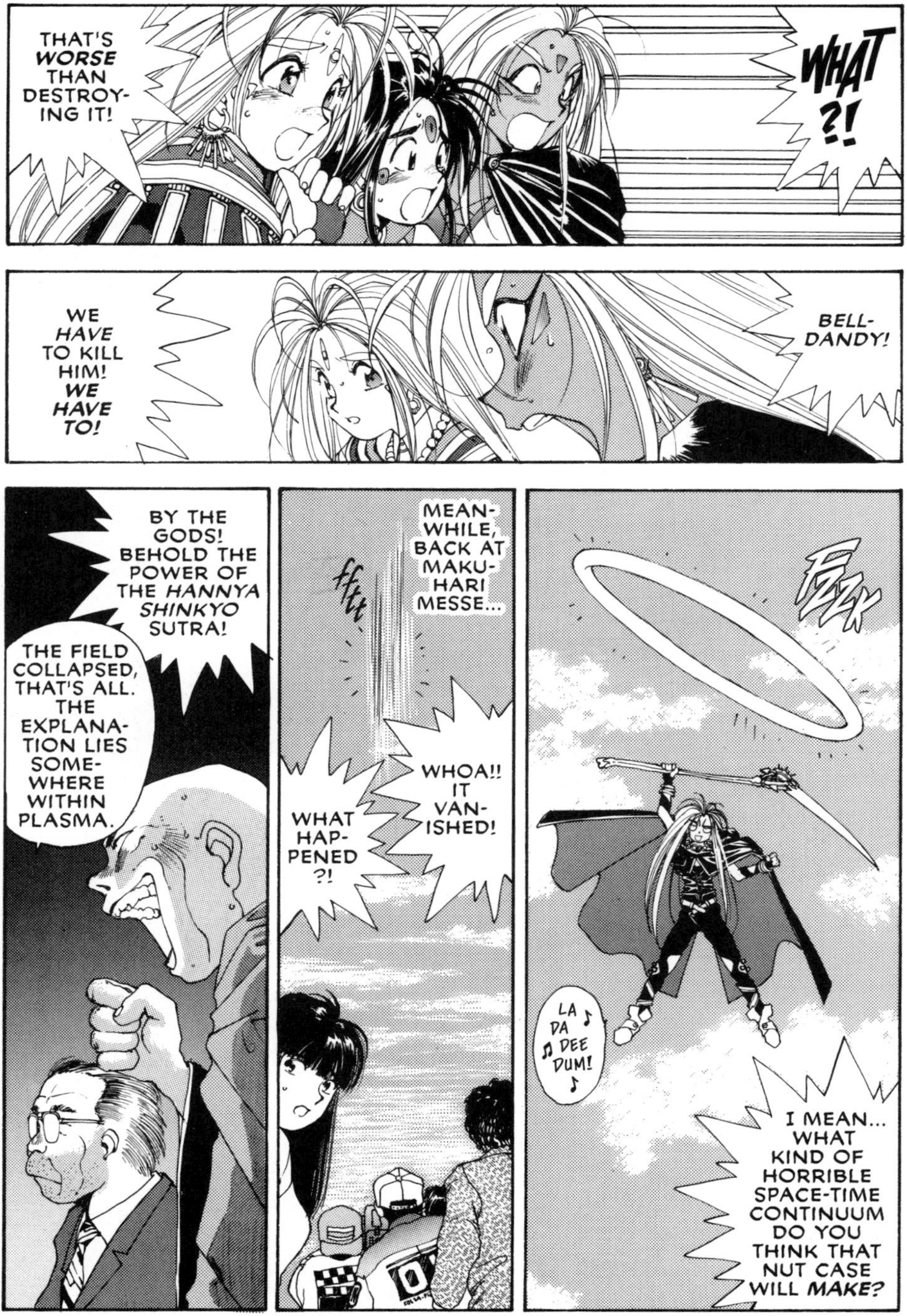
WHAT ?!
THAT'S WORSE THAN DESTROY-ING IT!
BELL-DANDY!
WE HAVE TO KILL HIM! WE HAVE TO!
FZZK
LA DA DEE DUM!
I MEAN... WHAT KIND OF HORRIBLE SPACE-TIME CONTINUUM DO YOU THINK THAT NUT CASE WILL MAKE?
MEAN-WHILE, BACK AT MAKU-HARI MESSE...
WHOA!! IT VAN-ISHED!
WHAT HAP-PENED ?!
BY THE GODS! BEHOLD THE POWER OF THE HANNYA SHINKYO SUTRA!
THE FIELD COLLAPSED, THAT'S ALL. THE EXPLANA-TION LIES SOME-WHERE WITHIN PLASMA.

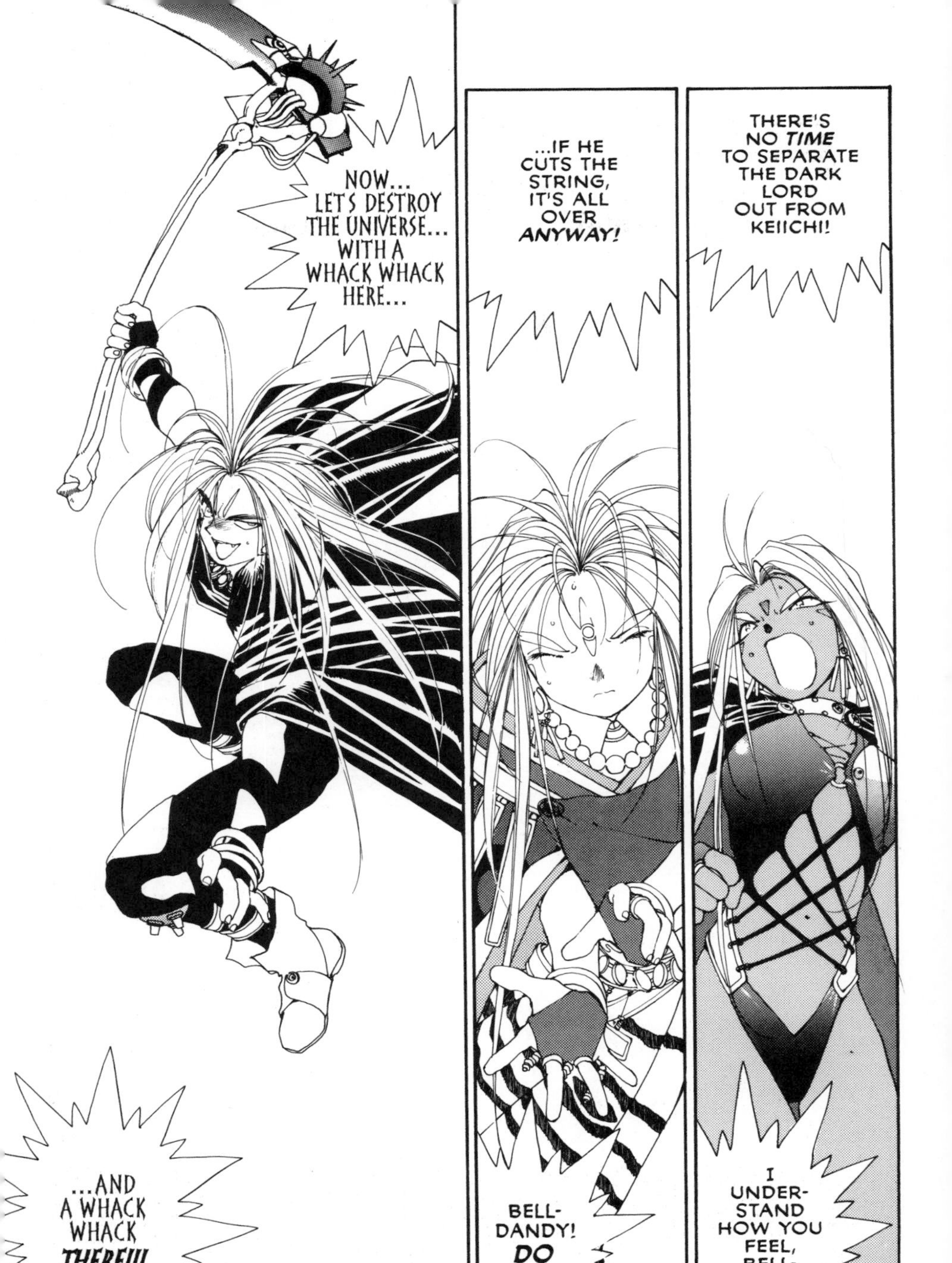
THERE'S NO *TIME* TO SEPARATE THE DARK LORD OUT FROM KEIICHI!
I UNDER-STAND HOW YOU FEEL, BELL-DANDY, BUT...
...IF HE CUTS THE STRING, IT'S ALL OVER *ANYWAY!*
BELL-DANDY! ***DO IT!!***
NOW... LET'S DESTROY THE UNIVERSE... WITH A WHACK WHACK HERE...
...AND A WHACK WHACK ***THERE!!!***

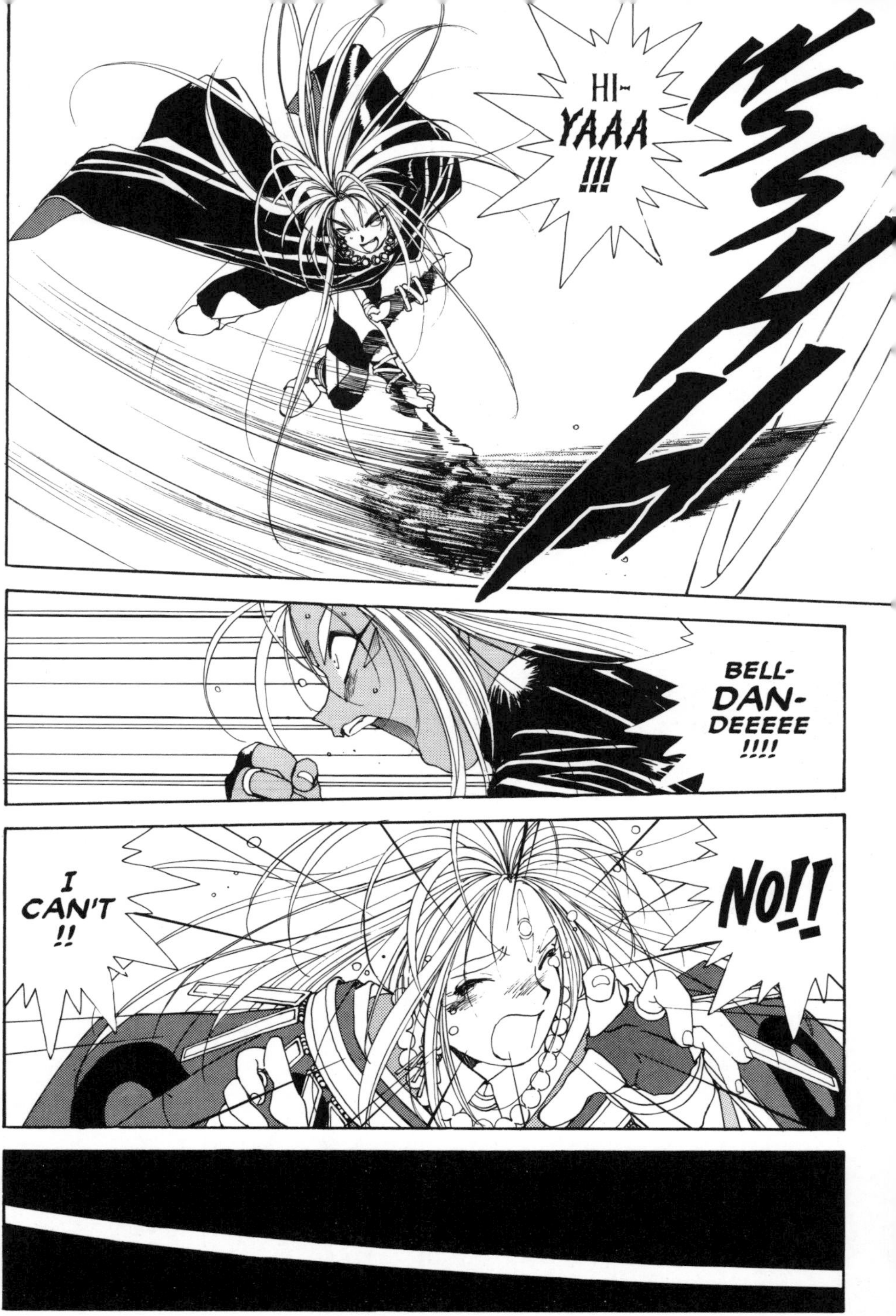
HI-YAAA!!!
BELL-DAN-DEEEEE!!!!
NO!!
I CAN'T!!

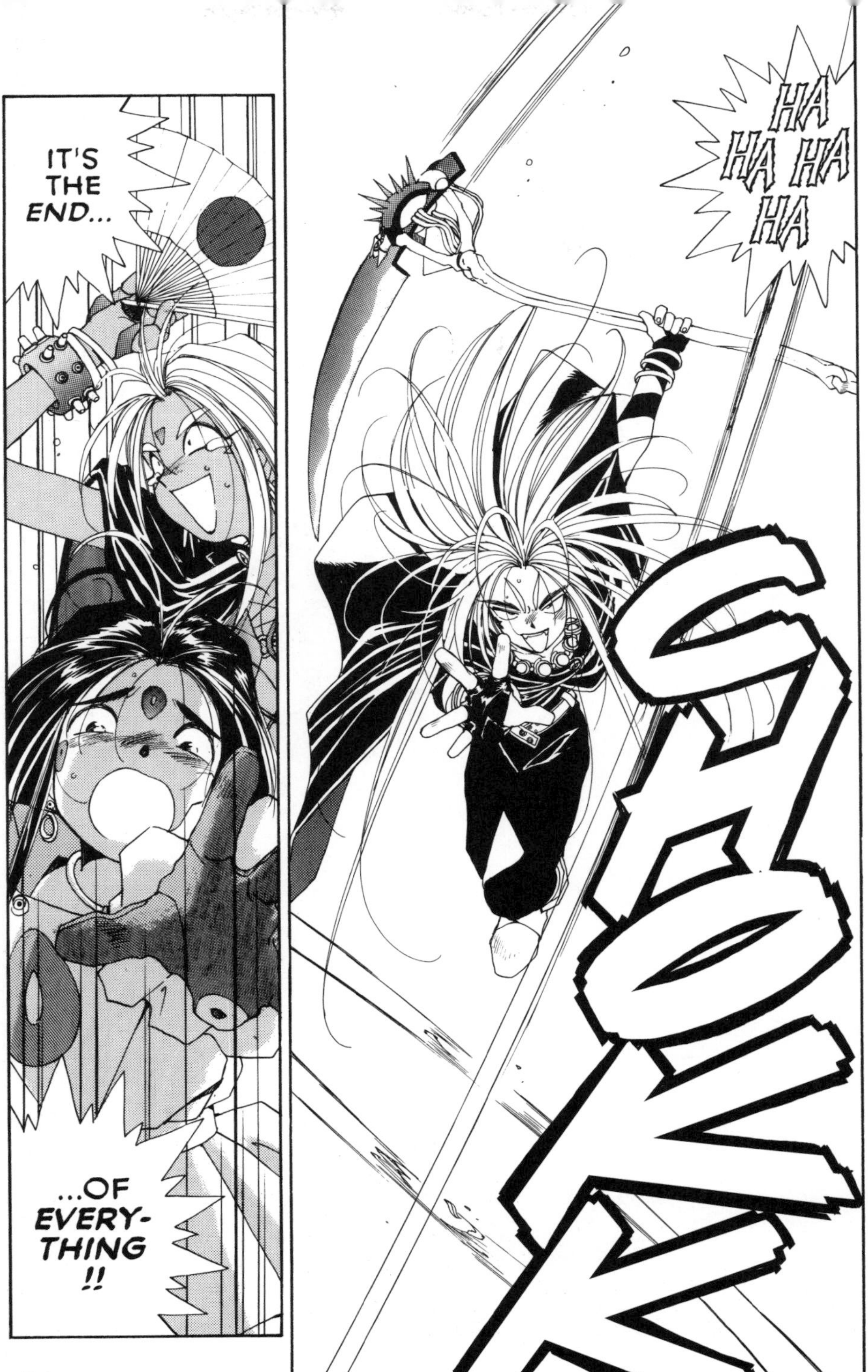
HA HA HA HA HA
IT'S THE END...
...OF EVERYTHING!!

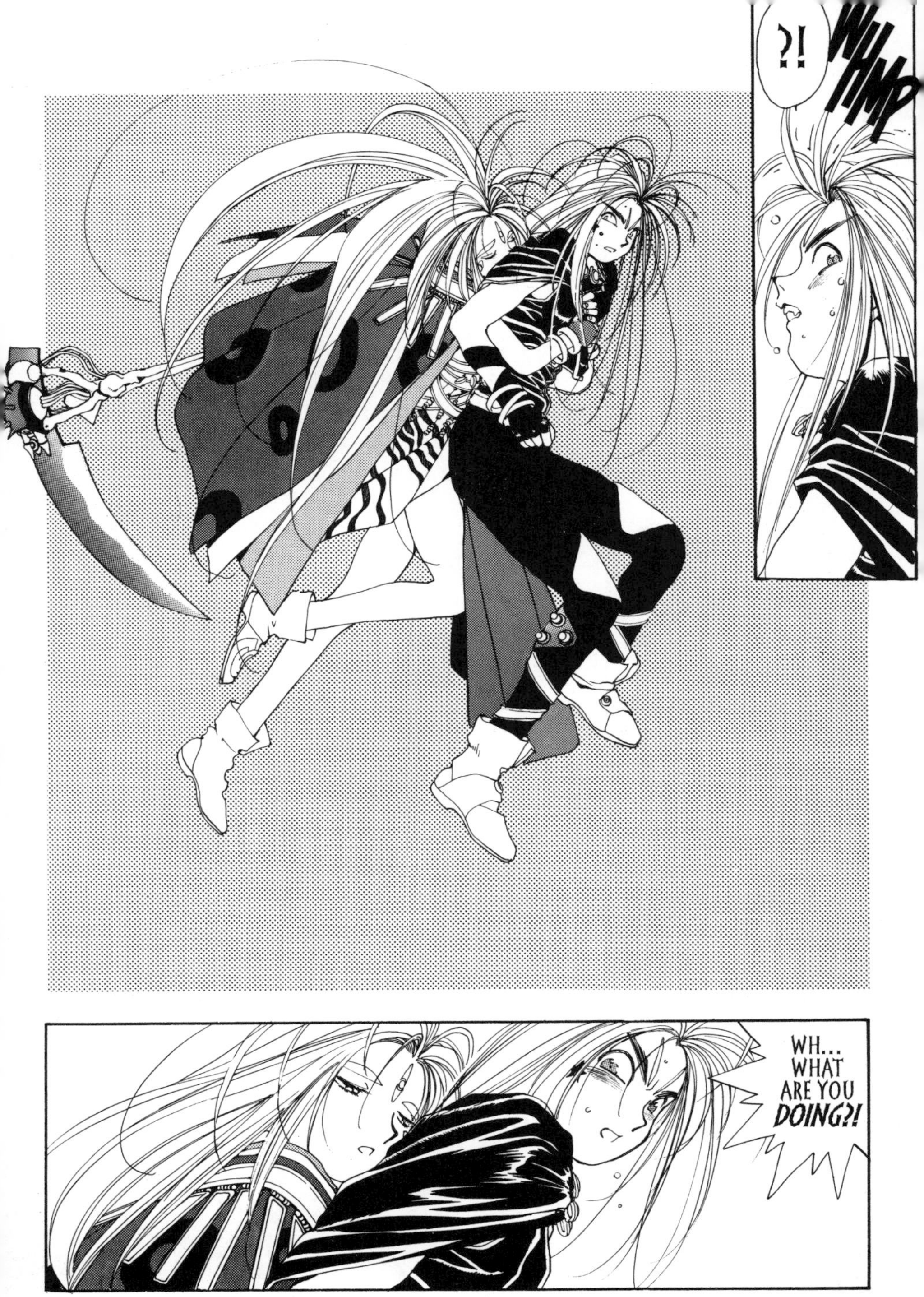
?!
WHMP
WH... WHAT ARE YOU DOING?!

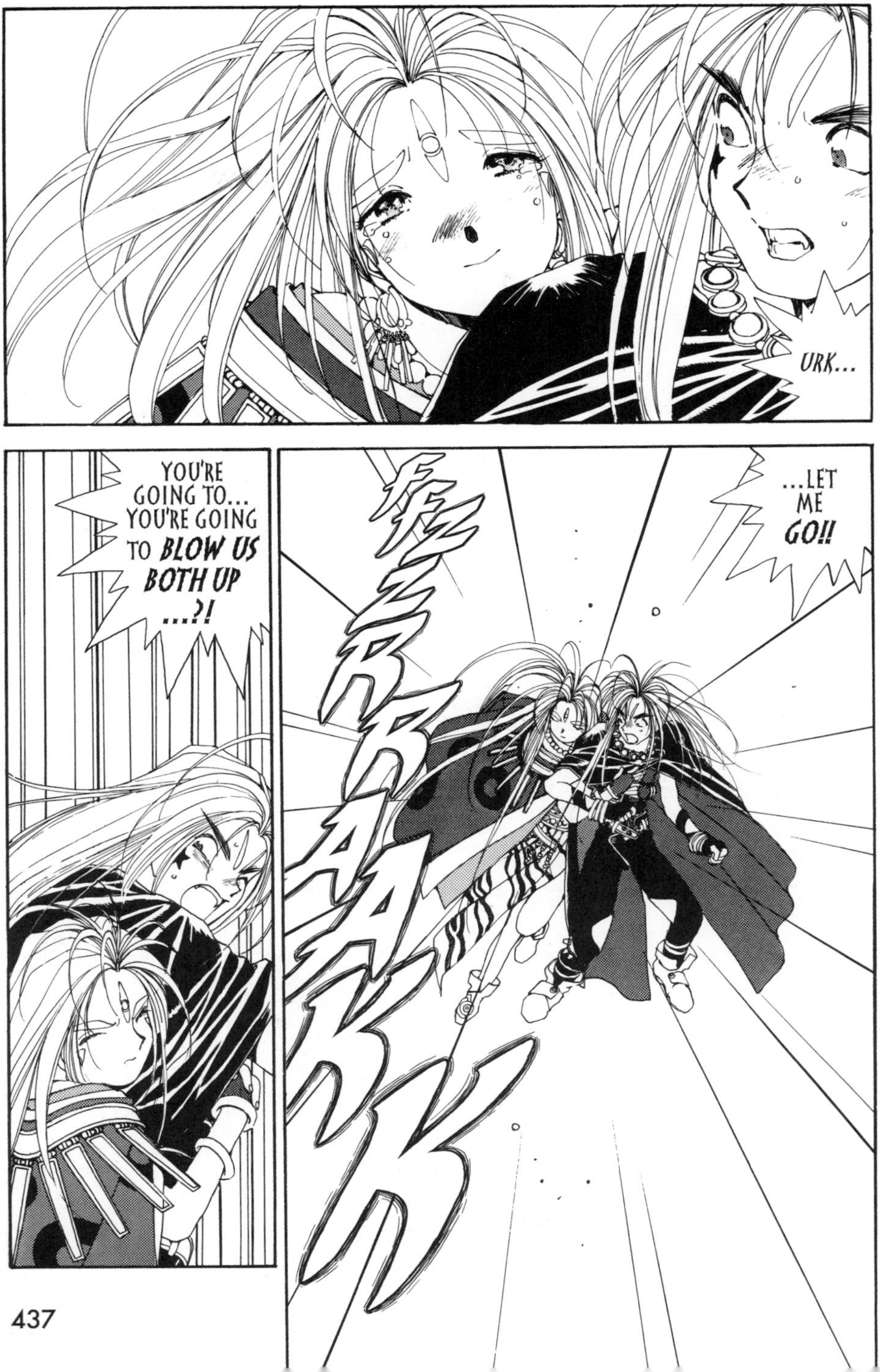
URK...
...LET ME GO!!
YOU'RE GOING TO... YOU'RE GOING TO BLOW US BOTH UP ...?!

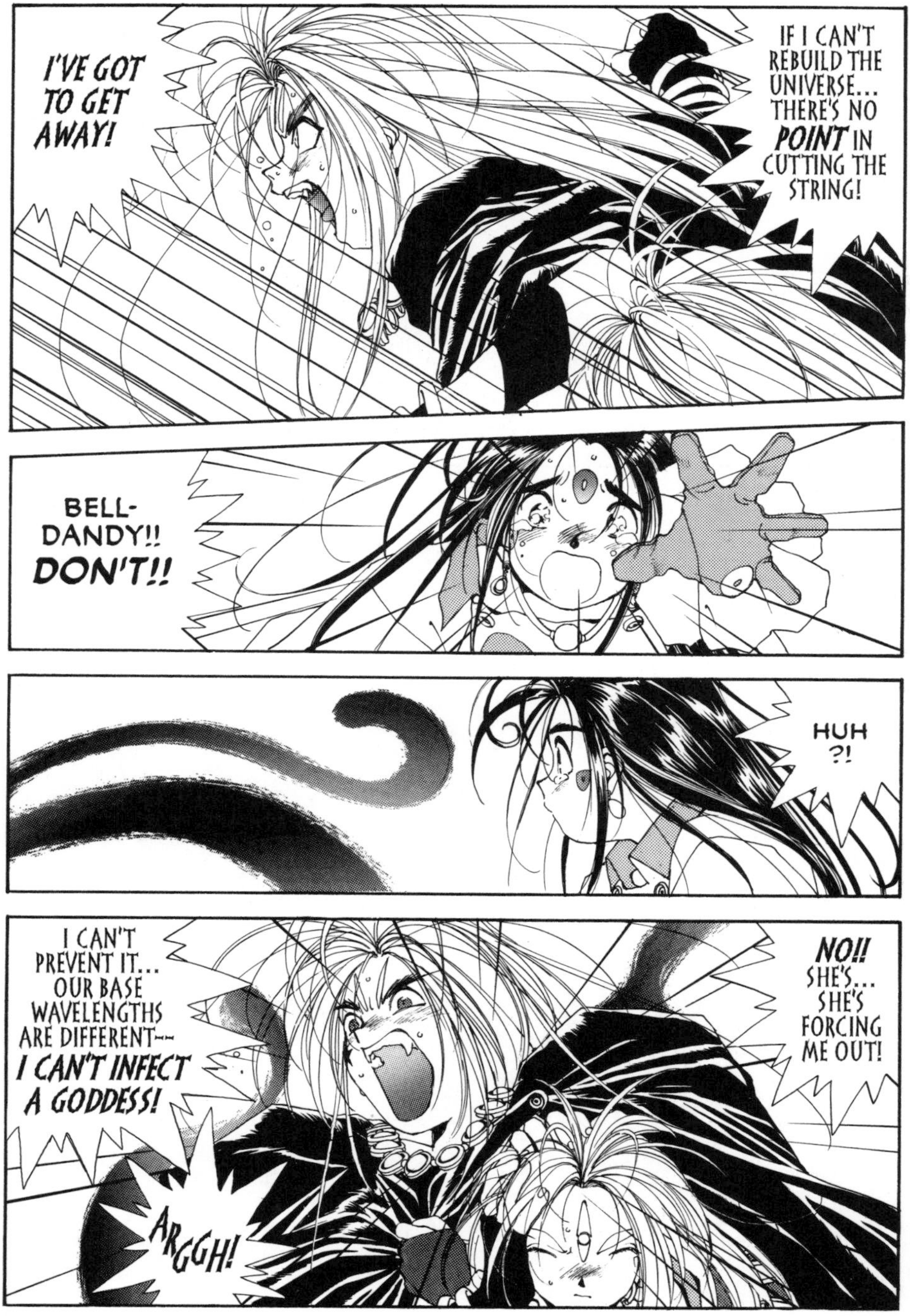
IF I CAN'T REBUILD THE UNIVERSE... THERE'S NO POINT IN CUTTING THE STRING!
I'VE GOT TO GET AWAY!
BELL-DANDY!! DON'T!!
HUH ?!
NO!! SHE'S... SHE'S FORCING ME OUT!
I CAN'T PREVENT IT... OUR BASE WAVELENGTHS ARE DIFFERENT-- I CAN'T INFECT A GODDESS!
ARGGH!

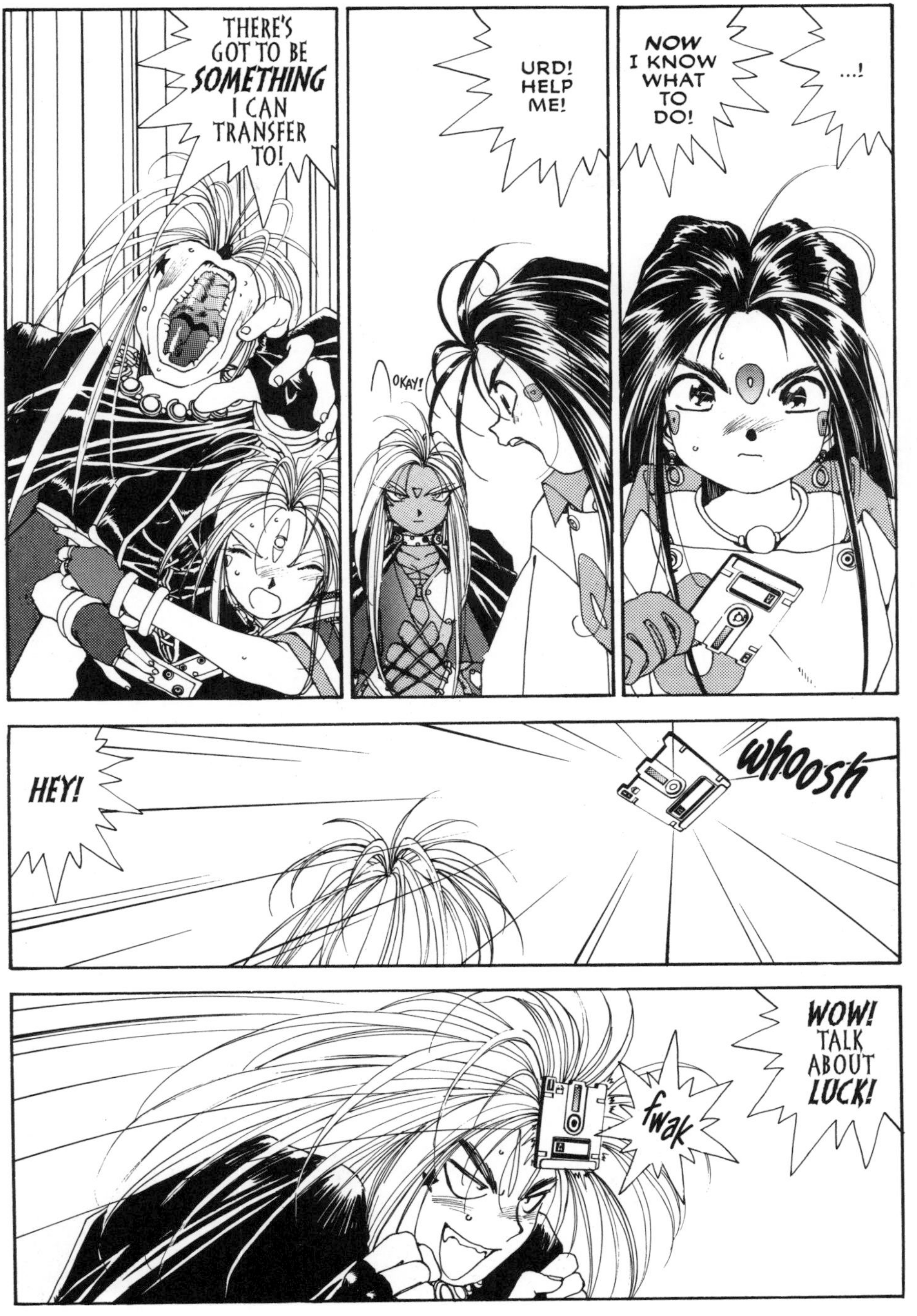
THERE'S GOT TO BE SOMETHING I CAN TRANSFER TO!
URD! HELP ME!
OKAY!
NOW I KNOW WHAT TO DO!
...!
HEY!
whoosh
fwak
WOW! TALK ABOUT LUCK!

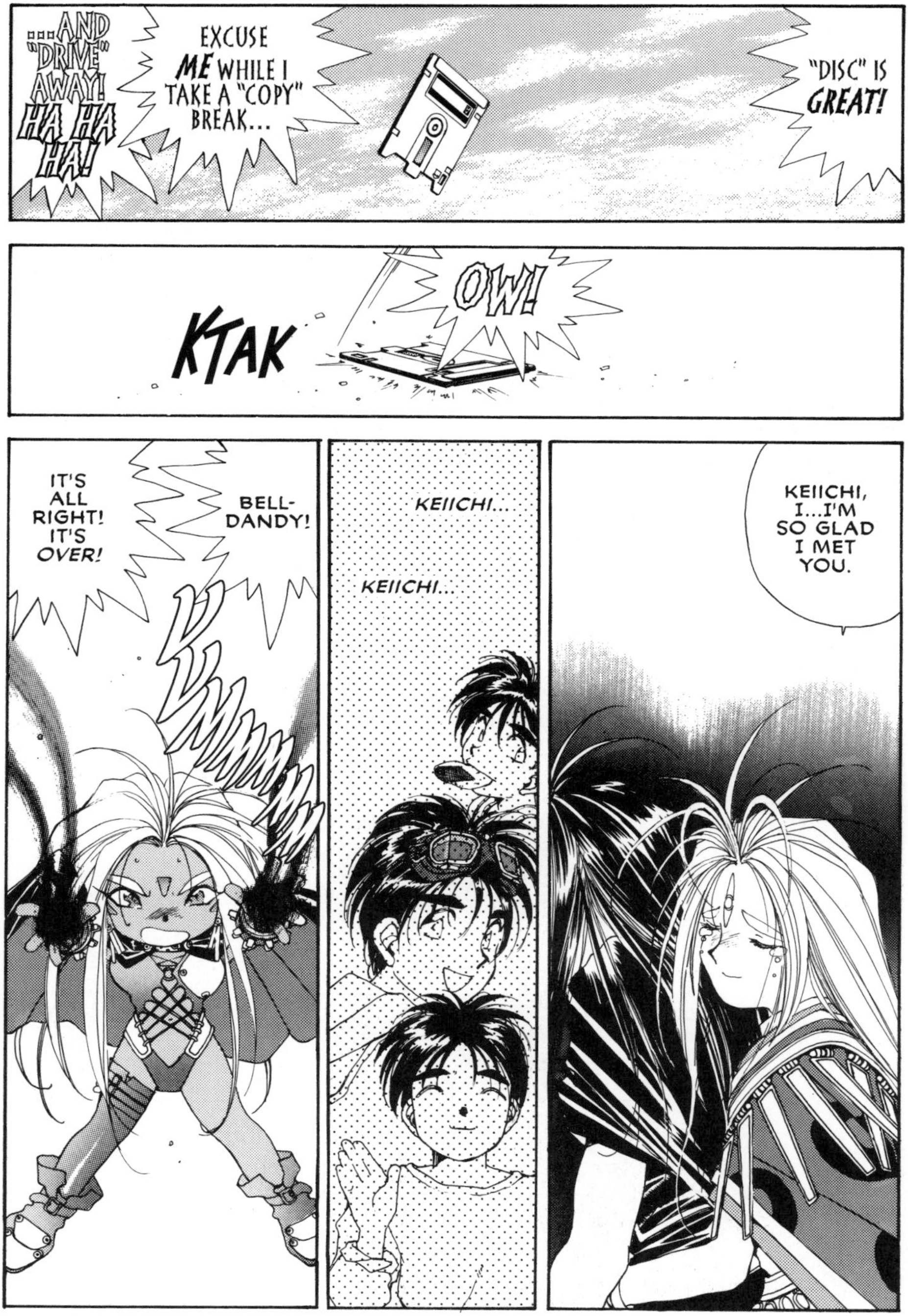
"DISC" IS GREAT!
EXCUSE ME WHILE I TAKE A "COPY" BREAK...
...AND "DRIVE" AWAY! HA HA HA!
OW!
KTAK
KEIICHI, I...I'M SO GLAD I MET YOU.
KEIICHI...
KEIICHI...
BELL-DANDY!
IT'S ALL RIGHT! IT'S OVER!

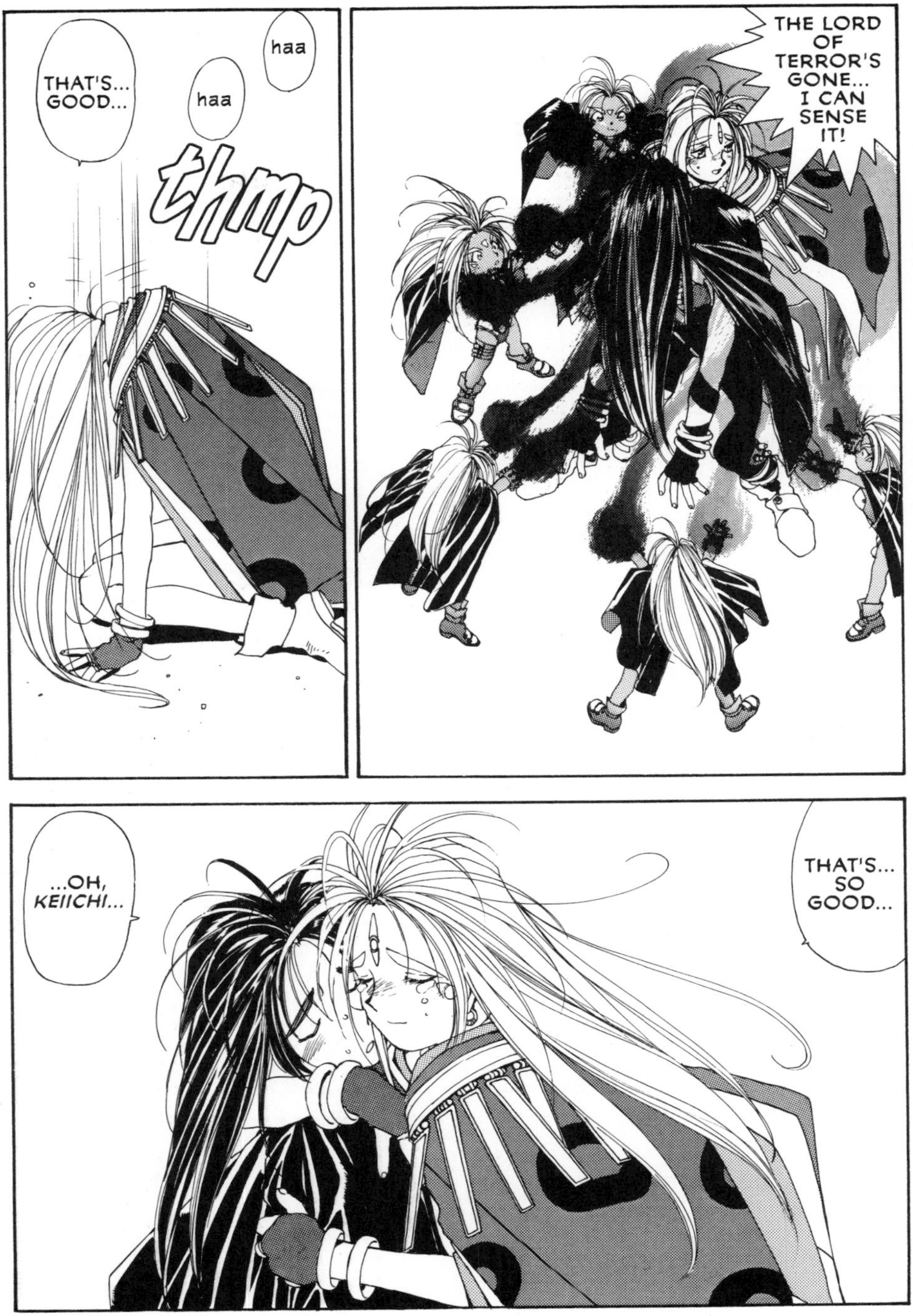
THE LORD OF TERROR'S GONE... I CAN SENSE IT!
haa
haa
THAT'S... GOOD...
thmp
THAT'S... SO GOOD...
...OH, *KEIICHI*...

NOW THEN, THE PROBLEM IS...
...WHO DO I INFECT NOW...?
tink
HEY!
SNAP
HEY! WHAT ARE YOU DOING?!
I'VE POPPED THE TAB.
YOU'RE A READ-ONLY FILE NOW!
NOOOOO!
AND NOW, A PROPOSED SCIENCE LESSON.
HERE I HAVE A POWERFUL MAGNET.
WHAT WOULD BE ITS EFFECT ON A MAGNETIC DISC?!
ER...
...I DUNNO.

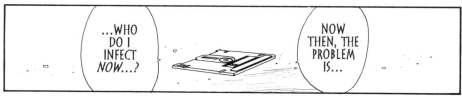

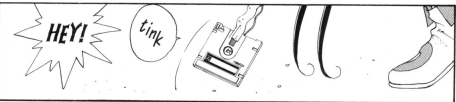

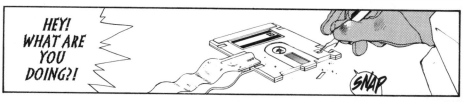

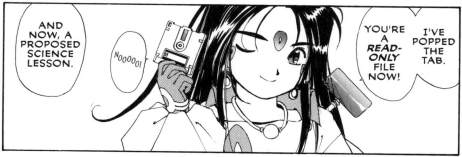

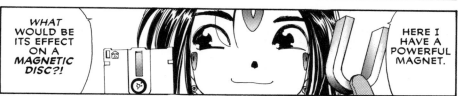

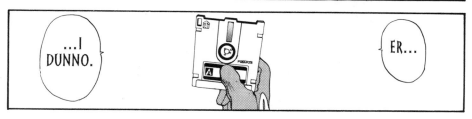

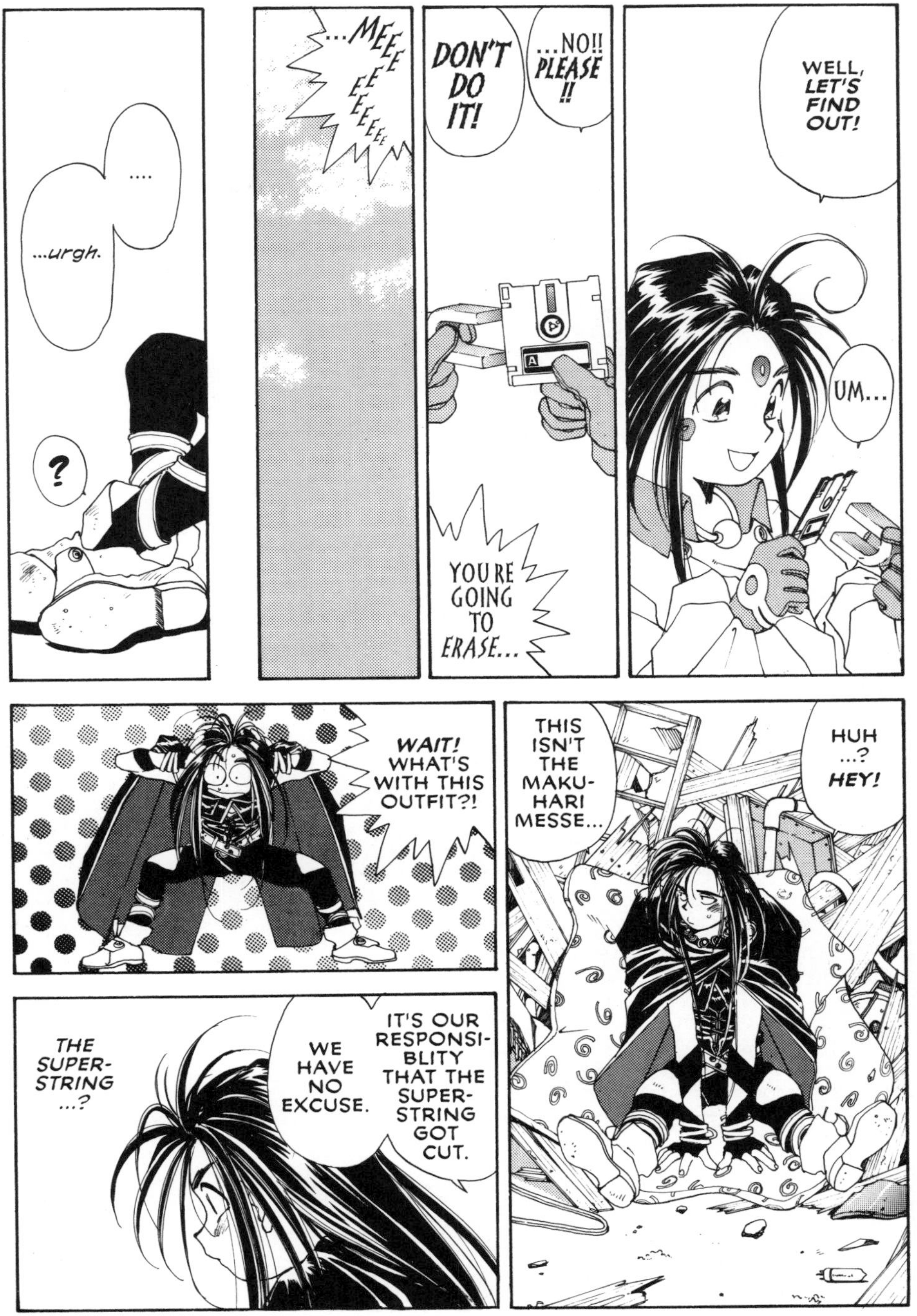
WELL, LET'S FIND OUT!
UM...
...NO!! PLEASE !!
DON'T DO IT!
YOU'RE GOING TO ERASE...
...MEEEEEEEEEE
....
...urgh.
?
HUH ...? HEY!
THIS ISN'T THE MAKU-HARI MESSE...
WAIT! WHAT'S WITH THIS OUTFIT?!
IT'S OUR RESPONSI-BLITY THAT THE SUPER-STRING GOT CUT.
WE HAVE NO EXCUSE.
THE SUPER-STRING ...?

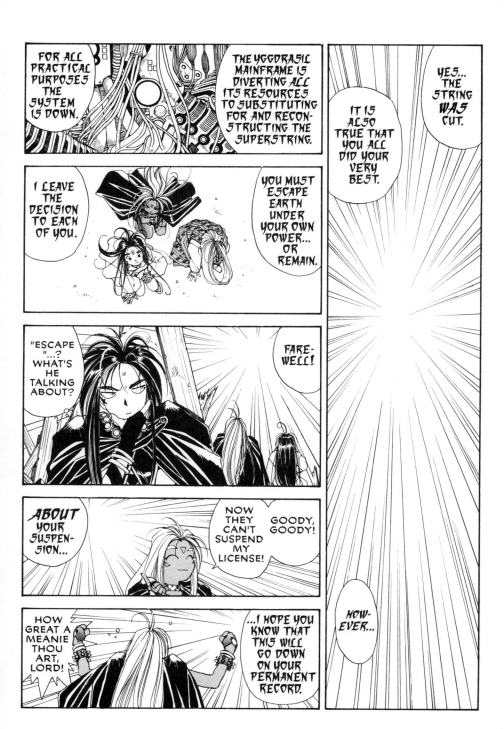

YES... THE STRING WAS CUT.
IT IS ALSO TRUE THAT YOU ALL DID YOUR VERY BEST.
HOW-EVER...
THE YGGDRASIL MAINFRAME IS DIVERTING ALL ITS RESOURCES TO SUBSTITUTING FOR AND RECON-STRUCTING THE SUPERSTRING.
FOR ALL PRACTICAL PURPOSES THE SYSTEM IS DOWN.
YOU MUST ESCAPE EARTH UNDER YOUR OWN POWER... OR REMAIN.
I LEAVE THE DECISION TO EACH OF YOU.
FARE-WELL!
"ESCAPE"...? WHAT'S HE TALKING ABOUT?
GOODY, GOODY!
NOW THEY CAN'T SUSPEND MY LICENSE!
ABOUT YOUR SUSPEN-SION...
...I HOPE YOU KNOW THAT THIS WILL GO DOWN ON YOUR PERMANENT RECORD.
HOW GREAT A MEANIE THOU ART, LORD!

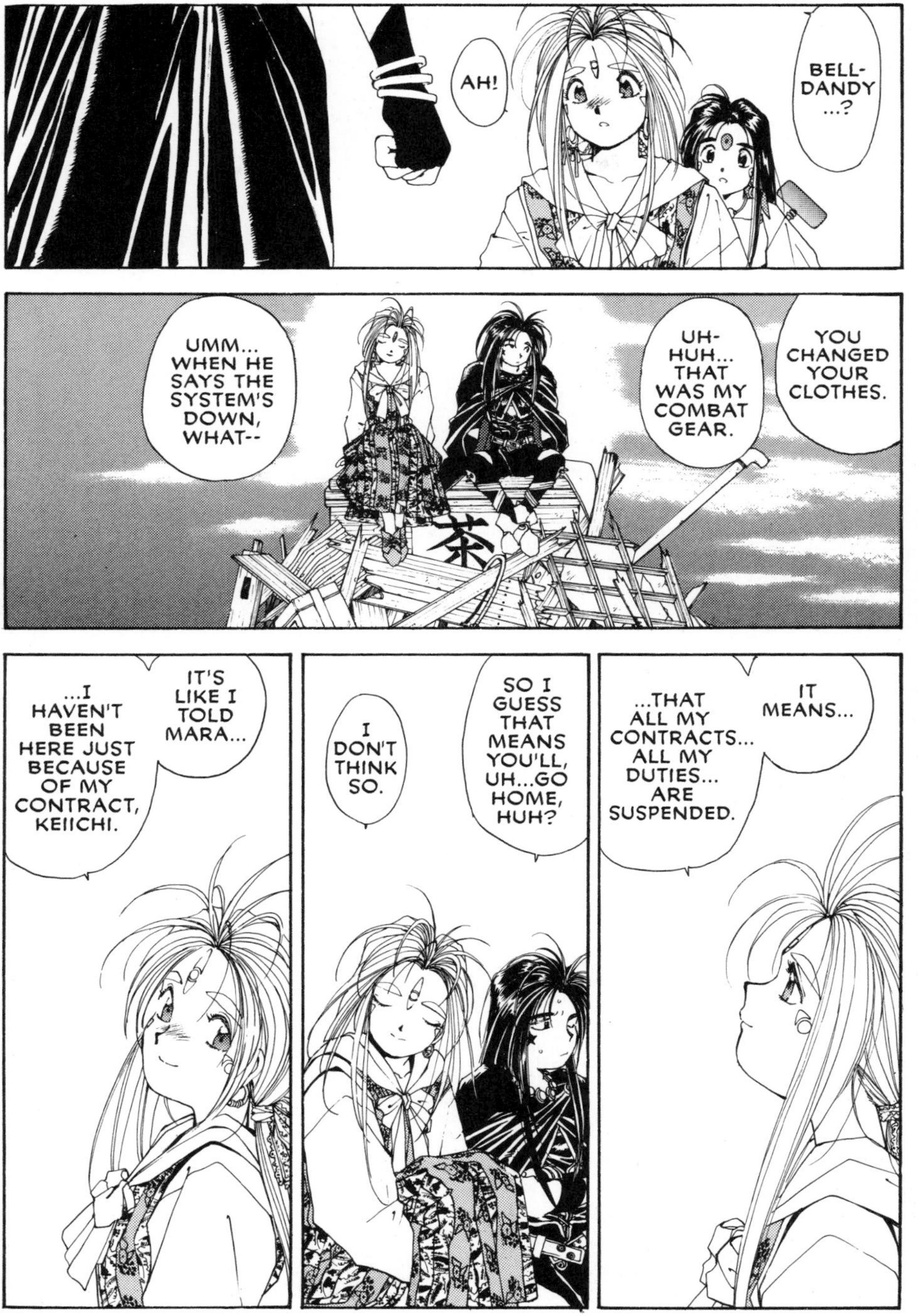
BELL-DANDY ...?
AH!
YOU CHANGED YOUR CLOTHES.
UH-HUH... THAT WAS MY COMBAT GEAR.
UMM... WHEN HE SAYS THE SYSTEM'S DOWN, WHAT--
IT MEANS...
...THAT ALL MY CONTRACTS... ALL MY DUTIES... ARE SUSPENDED.
SO I GUESS THAT MEANS YOU'LL, UH...GO HOME, HUH?
I DON'T THINK SO.
IT'S LIKE I TOLD MARA...
...I HAVEN'T BEEN HERE JUST BECAUSE OF MY CONTRACT, KEIICHI.

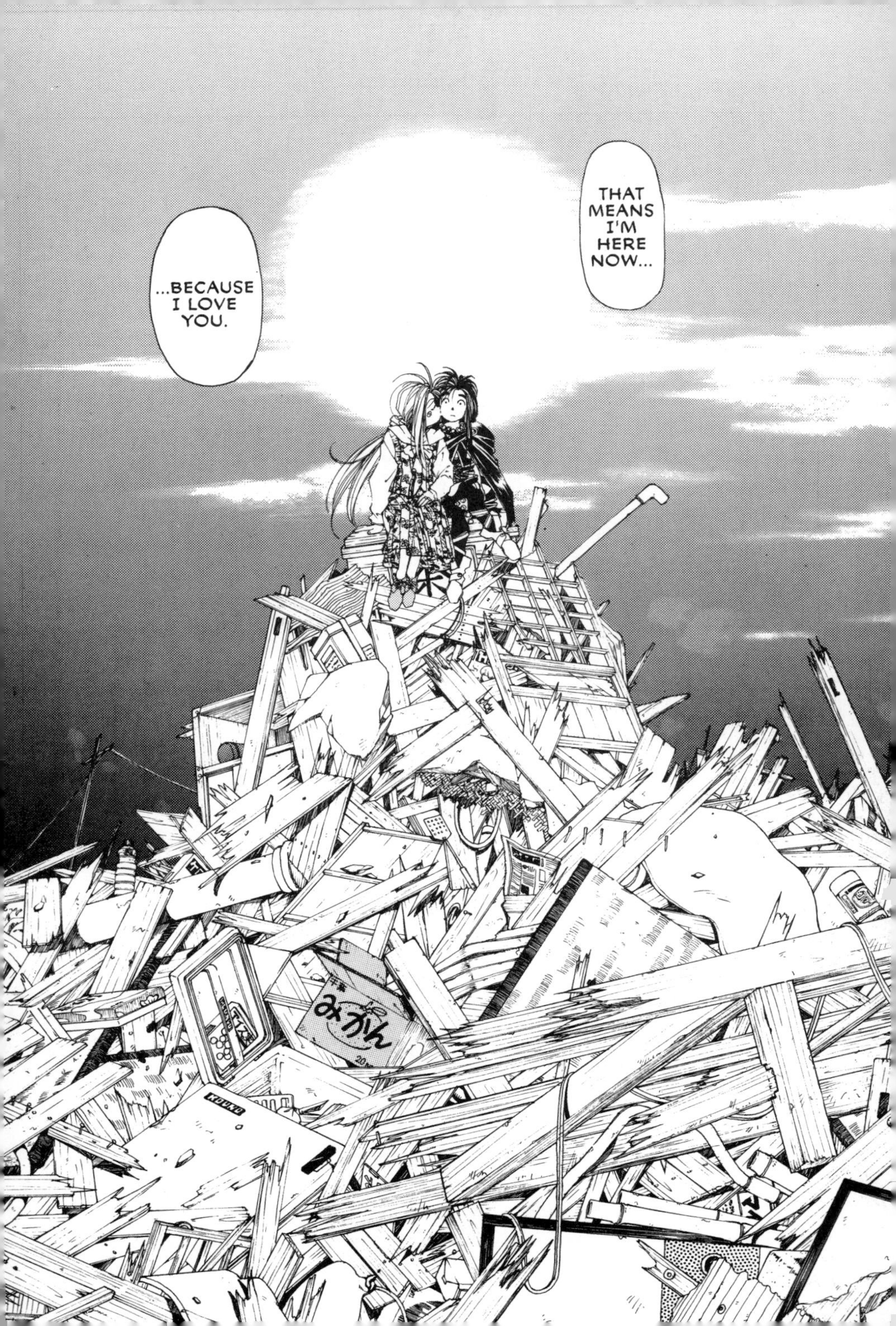
THAT MEANS I'M HERE NOW...
...BECAUSE I LOVE YOU.
みかん

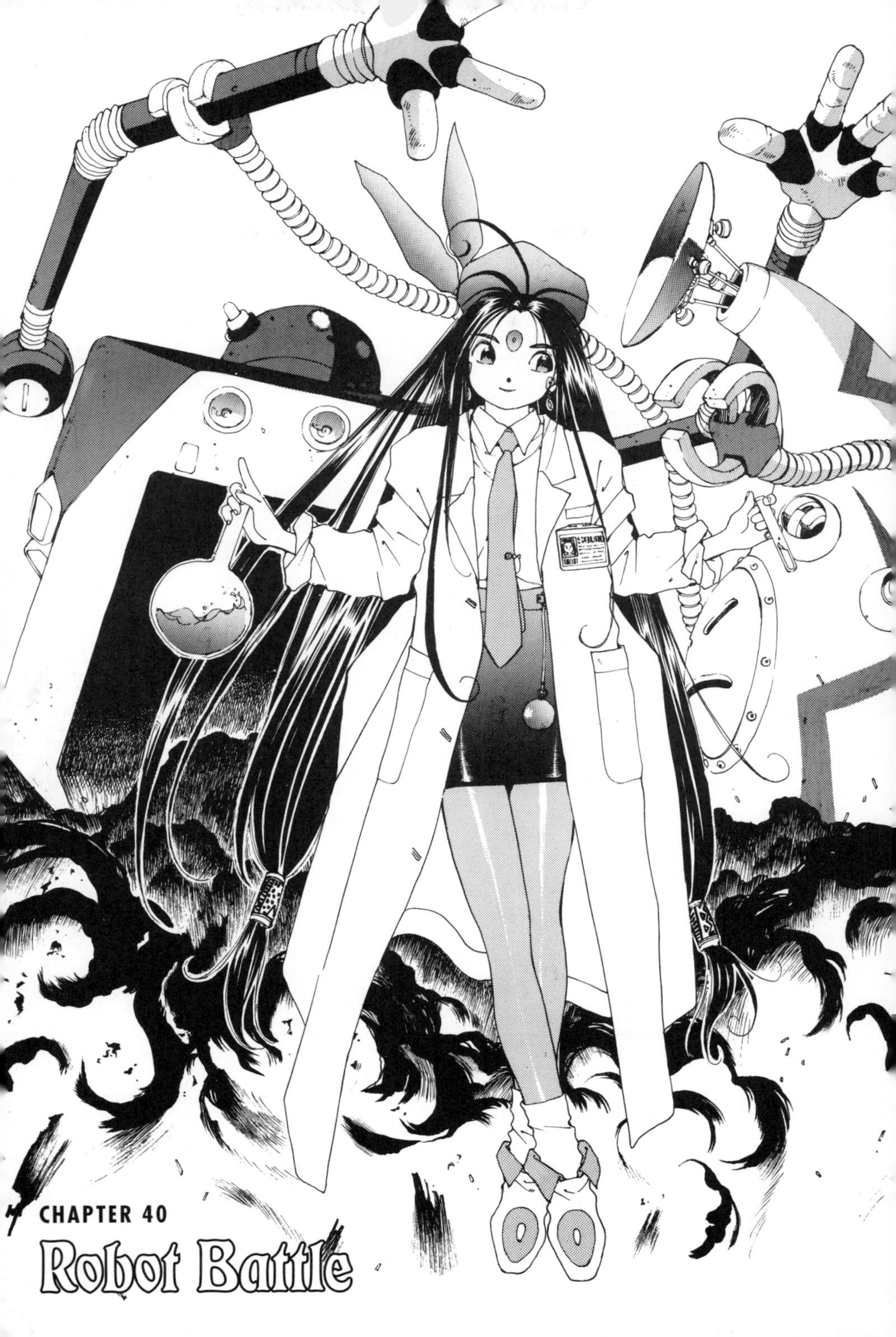

## CHAPTER 40

# Robot Battle

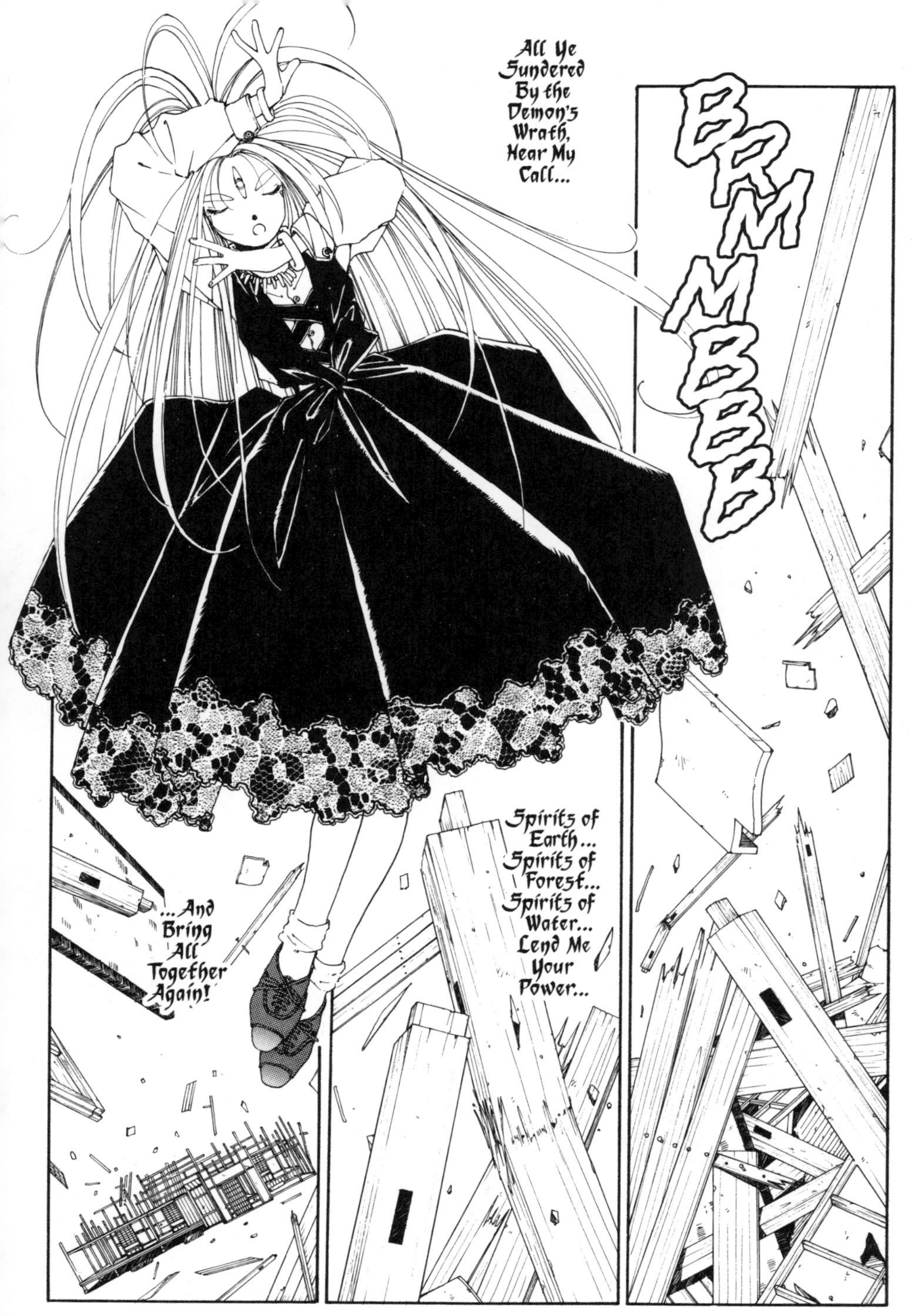
BRMMBBB
All Ye Sundered By the Demon's Wrath, Hear My Call...
Spirits of Earth... Spirits of Forest... Spirits of Water... Lend Me Your Power...
...And Bring All Together Again!

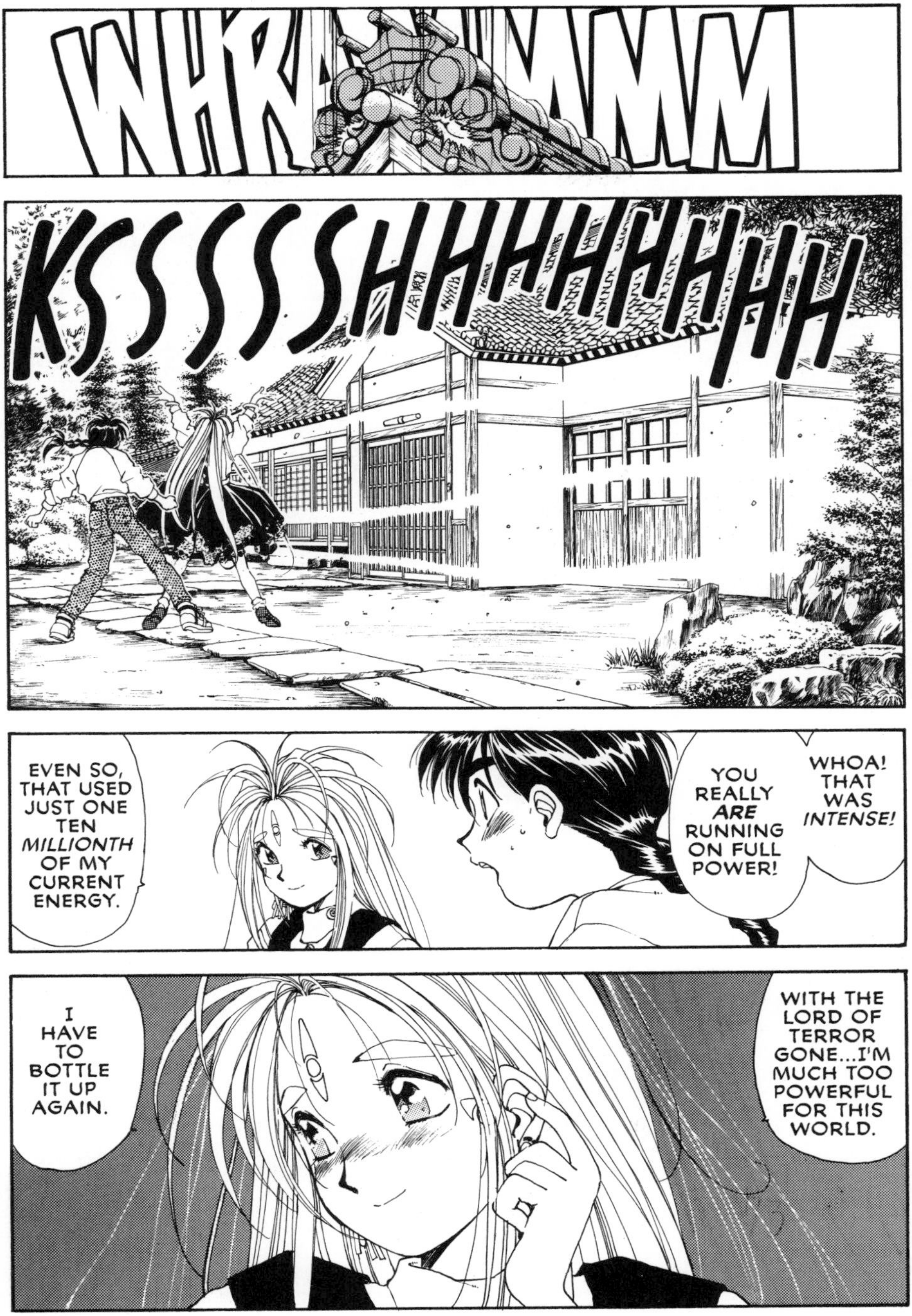
WHRAMMMM
KSSSSSHHHHHHHHH
WHOA! THAT WAS *INTENSE!*
YOU REALLY *ARE* RUNNING ON FULL POWER!
EVEN SO, THAT USED JUST ONE TEN *MILLIONTH* OF MY CURRENT ENERGY.
WITH THE LORD OF TERROR GONE...I'M MUCH TOO POWERFUL FOR THIS WORLD.
I HAVE TO BOTTLE IT UP AGAIN.

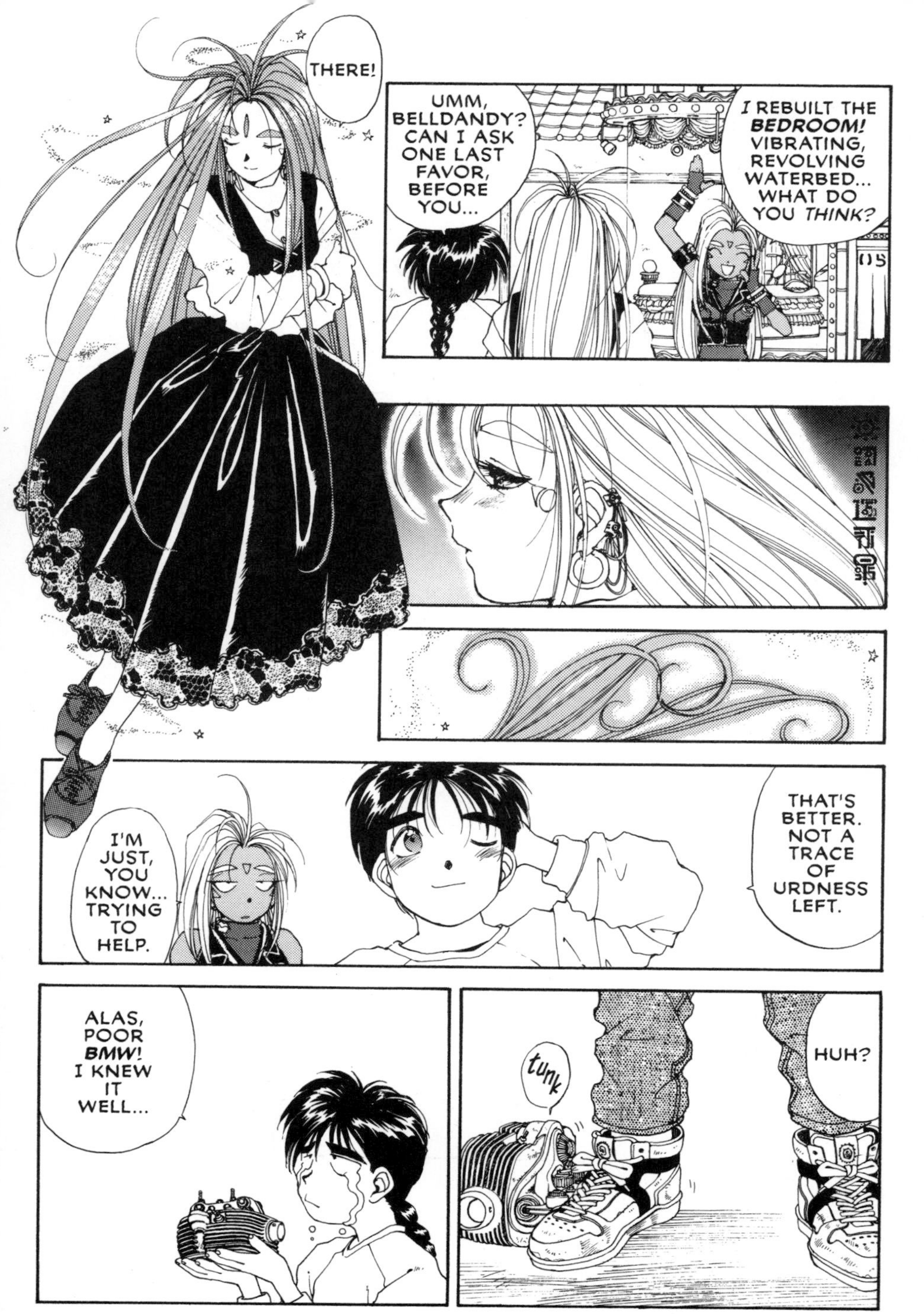
I REBUILT THE BEDROOM! VIBRATING, REVOLVING WATERBED... WHAT DO YOU THINK?
UMM, BELLDANDY? CAN I ASK ONE LAST FAVOR, BEFORE YOU...
THERE!
THAT'S BETTER. NOT A TRACE OF URDNESS LEFT.
I'M JUST, YOU KNOW... TRYING TO HELP.
HUH?
tunk
ALAS, POOR BMW! I KNEW IT WELL...

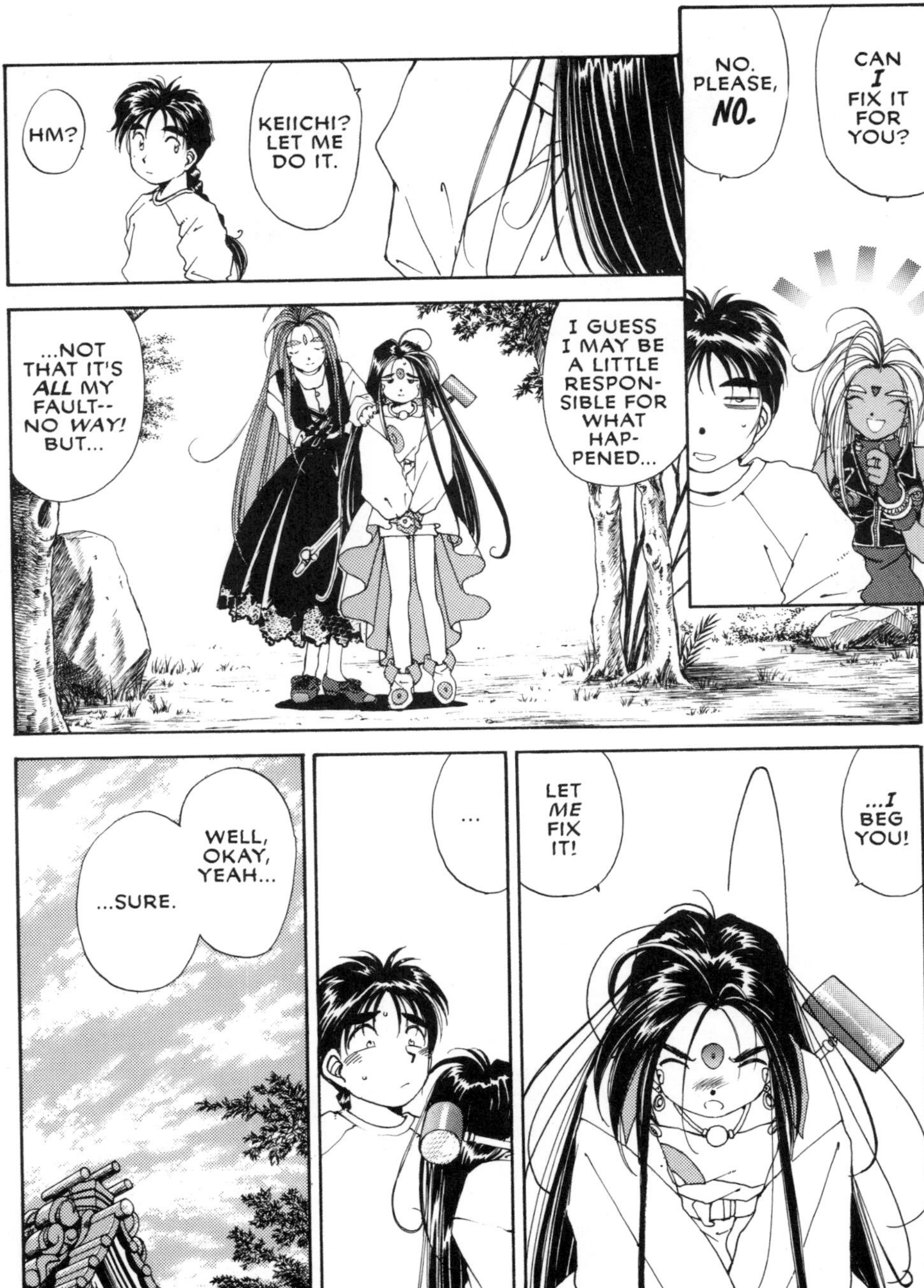
CAN *I* FIX IT FOR YOU?
NO. PLEASE, **NO.**
KEIICHI? LET ME DO IT.
HM?
I GUESS I MAY BE A LITTLE RESPONSIBLE FOR WHAT HAPPENED...
...NOT THAT IT'S ***ALL*** MY FAULT-- NO *WAY!* BUT...
...*I* BEG YOU!
LET *ME* FIX IT!
...
WELL, OKAY, YEAH...
...SURE.

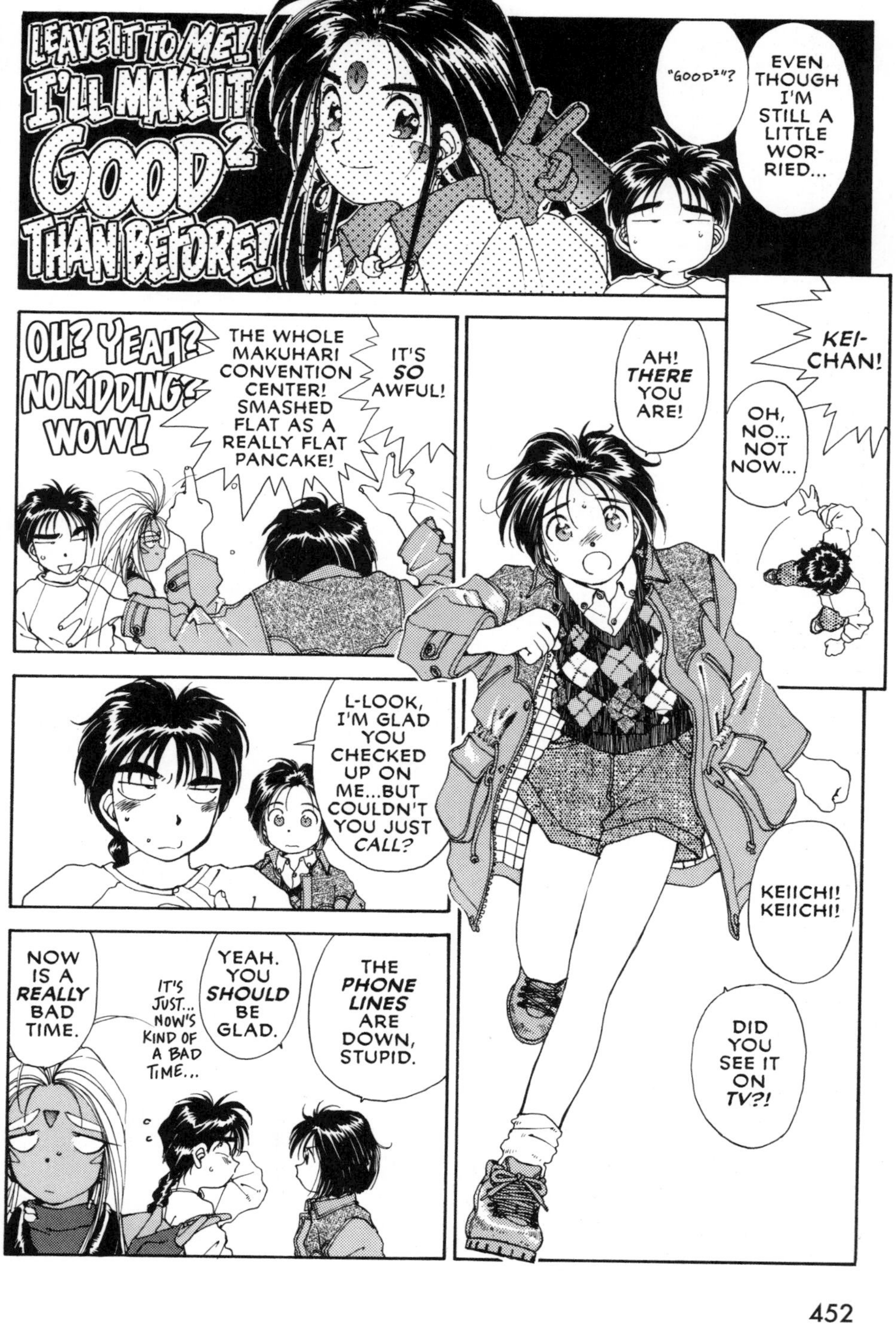
EVEN THOUGH I'M STILL A LITTLE WORRIED...
"GOOD$^2$"?
LEAVE IT TO ME! I'LL MAKE IT GOOD$^2$ THAN BEFORE!
KEI-CHAN!
OH, NO... NOT NOW...
AH! *THERE* YOU ARE!
KEIICHI! KEIICHI!
DID YOU SEE IT ON *TV*?!
IT'S *SO* AWFUL!
THE WHOLE MAKUHARI CONVENTION CENTER! SMASHED FLAT AS A REALLY FLAT PANCAKE!
OH? YEAH? NO KIDDING? WOW!
L-LOOK, I'M GLAD YOU CHECKED UP ON ME...BUT COULDN'T YOU JUST *CALL*?
THE *PHONE LINES* ARE DOWN, STUPID.
YEAH. YOU *SHOULD* BE GLAD.
IT'S JUST... NOW'S KIND OF A BAD TIME...
NOW IS A *REALLY* BAD TIME.

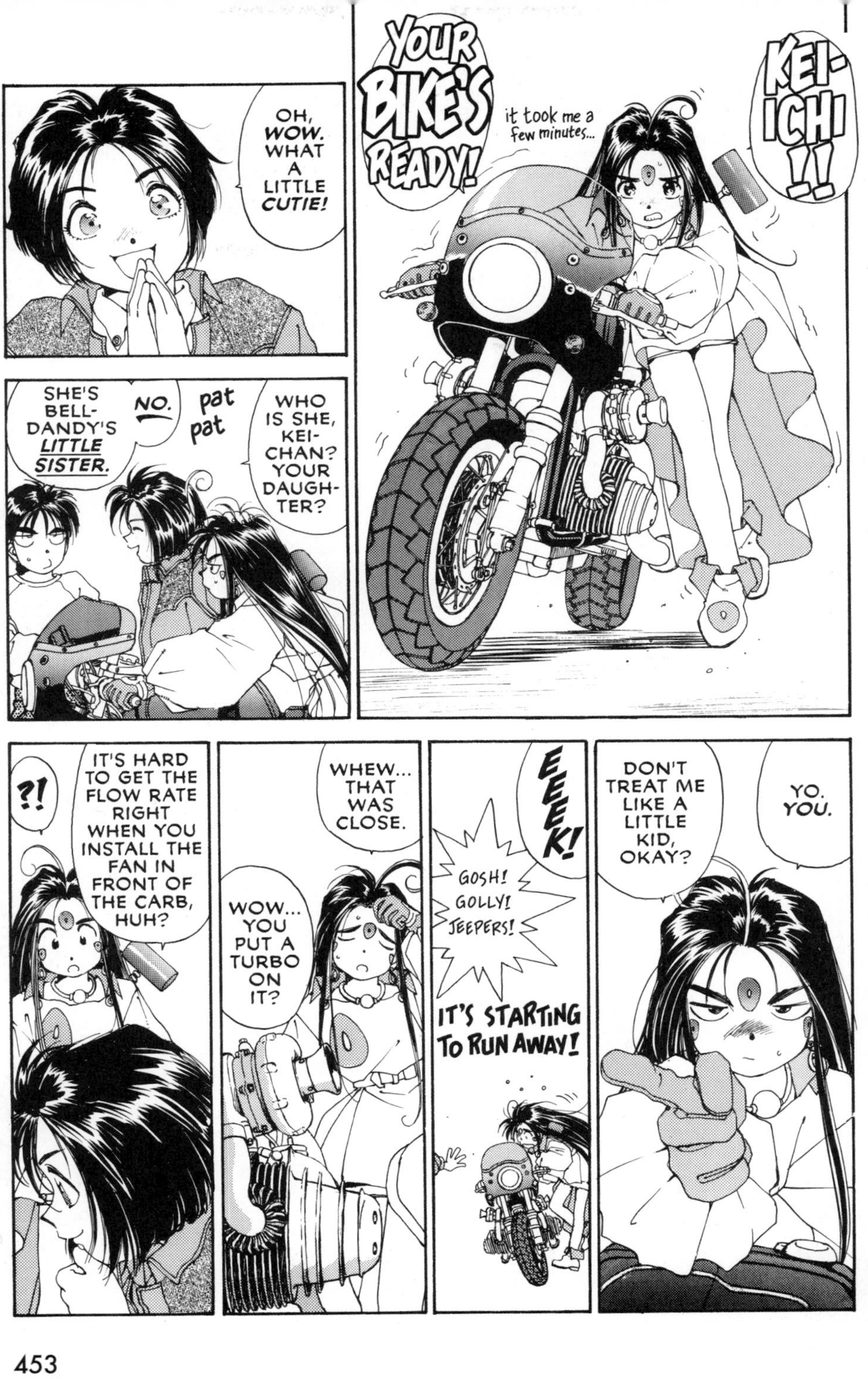
KEI-ICHI!!
it took me a few minutes...
YOUR BIKE'S READY!
OH, WOW. WHAT A LITTLE CUTIE!
WHO IS SHE, KEI-CHAN? YOUR DAUGHTER?
pat pat
NO.
SHE'S BELL-DANDY'S LITTLE SISTER.
YO. YOU.
DON'T TREAT ME LIKE A LITTLE KID, OKAY?
EEEK!
GOSH! GOLLY! JEEPERS!
IT'S STARTING TO RUN AWAY!
WHEW... THAT WAS CLOSE.
WOW... YOU PUT A TURBO ON IT?
IT'S HARD TO GET THE FLOW RATE RIGHT WHEN YOU INSTALL THE FAN IN FRONT OF THE CARB, HUH?
?!

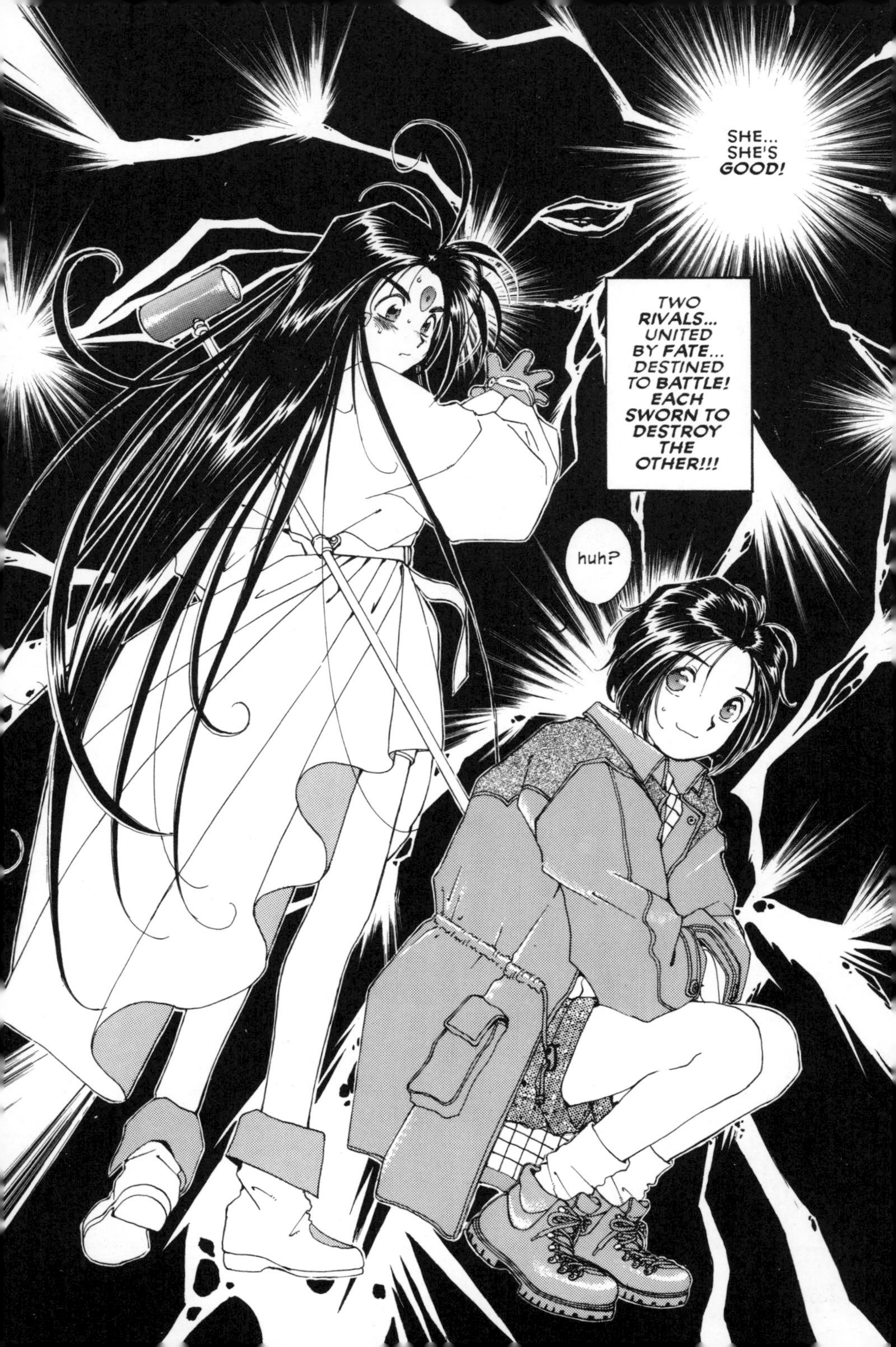
SHE... SHE'S GOOD!
TWO RIVALS... UNITED BY FATE... DESTINED TO BATTLE! EACH SWORN TO DESTROY THE OTHER!!!
huh?

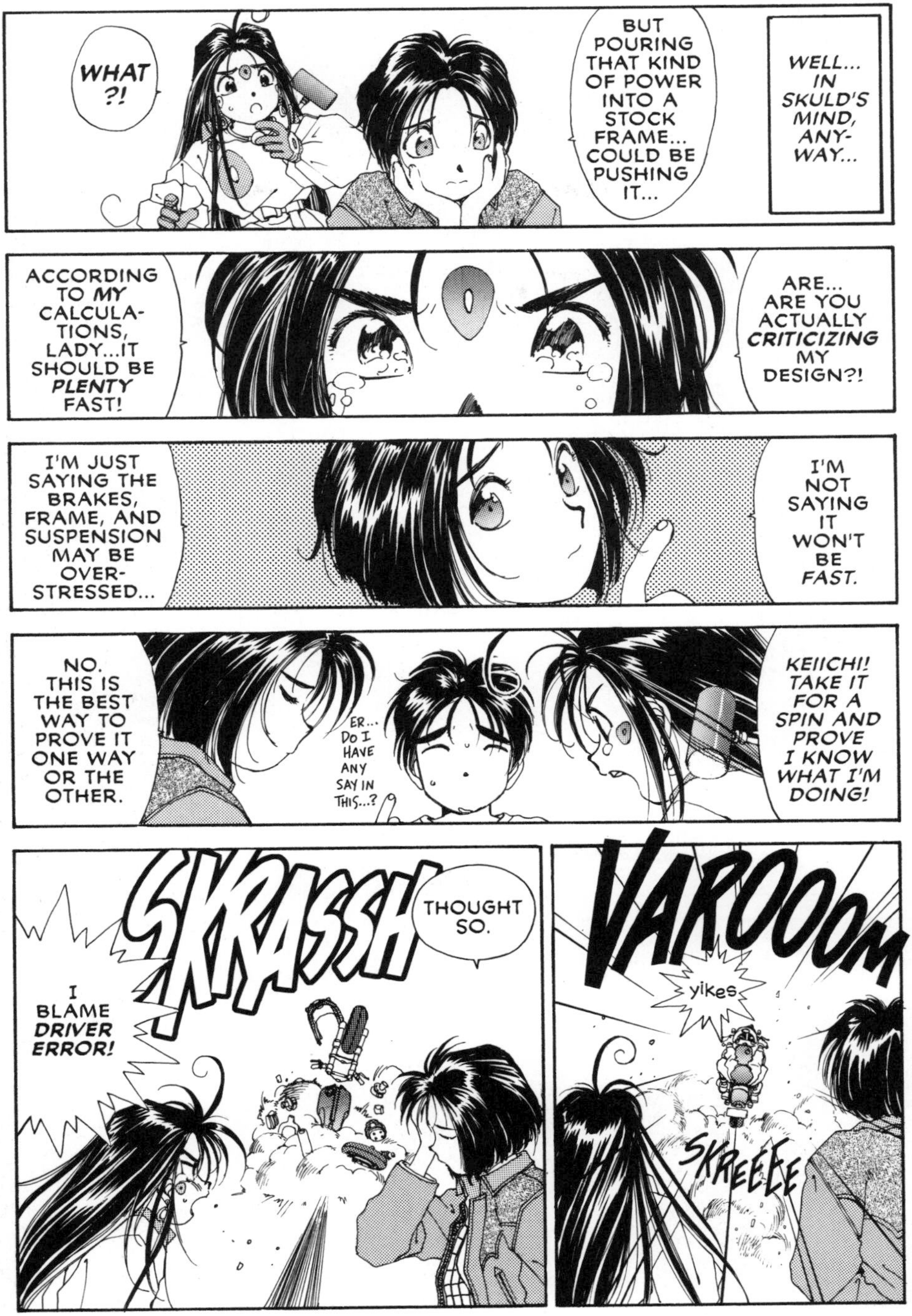

WELL... IN SKULD'S MIND, ANYWAY...
BUT POURING THAT KIND OF POWER INTO A STOCK FRAME... COULD BE PUSHING IT...
WHAT ?!
ARE... ARE YOU ACTUALLY CRITICIZING MY DESIGN?!
ACCORDING TO MY CALCULATIONS, LADY...IT SHOULD BE PLENTY FAST!
I'M NOT SAYING IT WON'T BE FAST.
I'M JUST SAYING THE BRAKES, FRAME, AND SUSPENSION MAY BE OVER-STRESSED...
KEIICHI! TAKE IT FOR A SPIN AND PROVE I KNOW WHAT I'M DOING!
ER... DO I HAVE ANY SAY IN THIS...?
NO. THIS IS THE BEST WAY TO PROVE IT ONE WAY OR THE OTHER.
VAROOOM
yikes
SKREEEE
SKRASSH
THOUGHT SO.
I BLAME DRIVER ERROR!

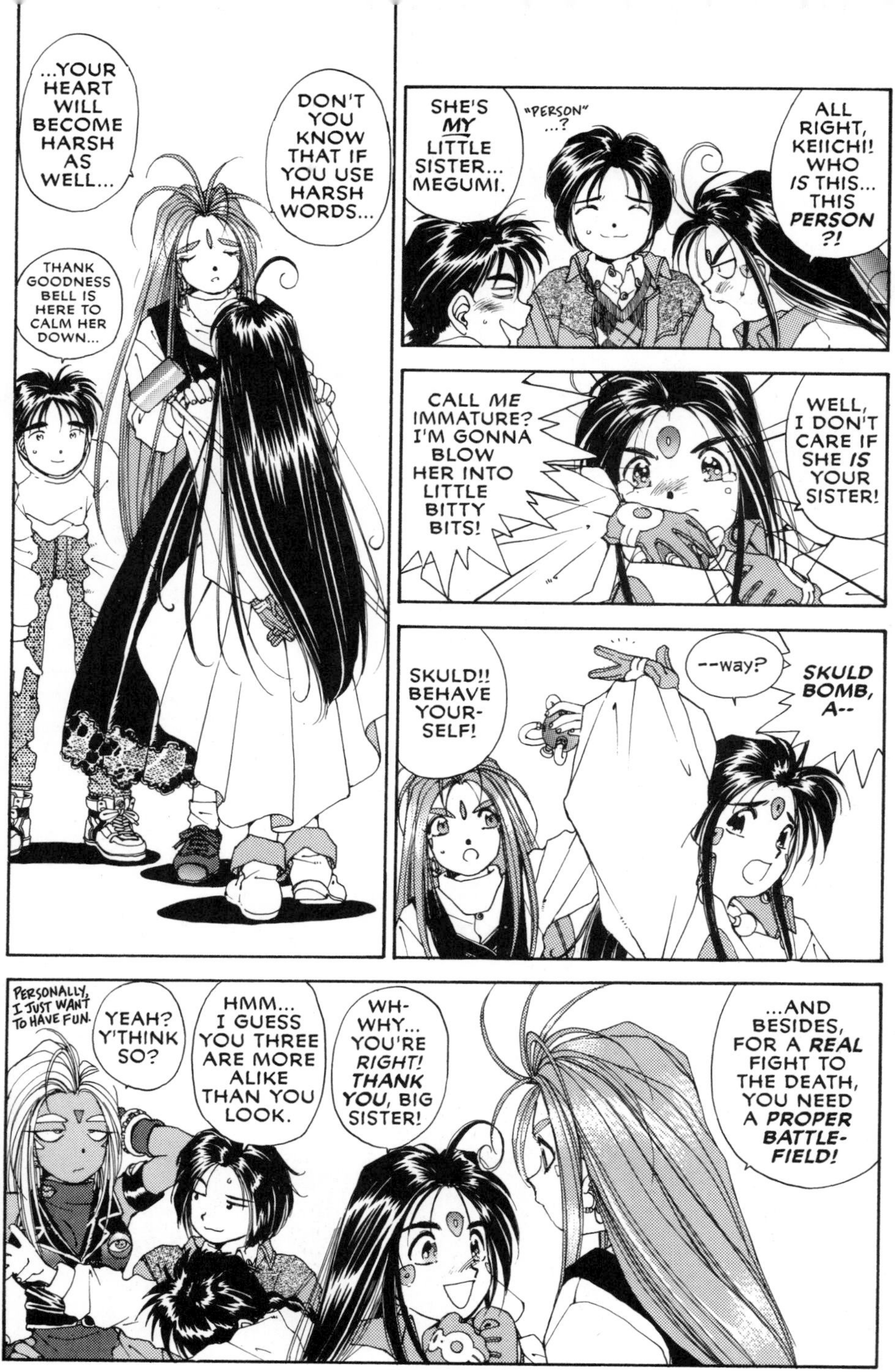
ALL RIGHT, KEIICHI! WHO IS THIS... THIS PERSON?!
"PERSON" ...?
SHE'S MY LITTLE SISTER... MEGUMI.
WELL, I DON'T CARE IF SHE IS YOUR SISTER!
CALL ME IMMATURE? I'M GONNA BLOW HER INTO LITTLE BITTY BITS!
SKULD BOMB, A--
--way?
SKULD!! BEHAVE YOUR-SELF!
DON'T YOU KNOW THAT IF YOU USE HARSH WORDS...
...YOUR HEART WILL BECOME HARSH AS WELL...
THANK GOODNESS BELL IS HERE TO CALM HER DOWN...
...AND BESIDES, FOR A REAL FIGHT TO THE DEATH, YOU NEED A PROPER BATTLE-FIELD!
WH-WHY... YOU'RE RIGHT! THANK YOU, BIG SISTER!
HMM... I GUESS YOU THREE ARE MORE ALIKE THAN YOU LOOK.
YEAH? Y'THINK SO?
PERSONALLY, I JUST WANT TO HAVE FUN.

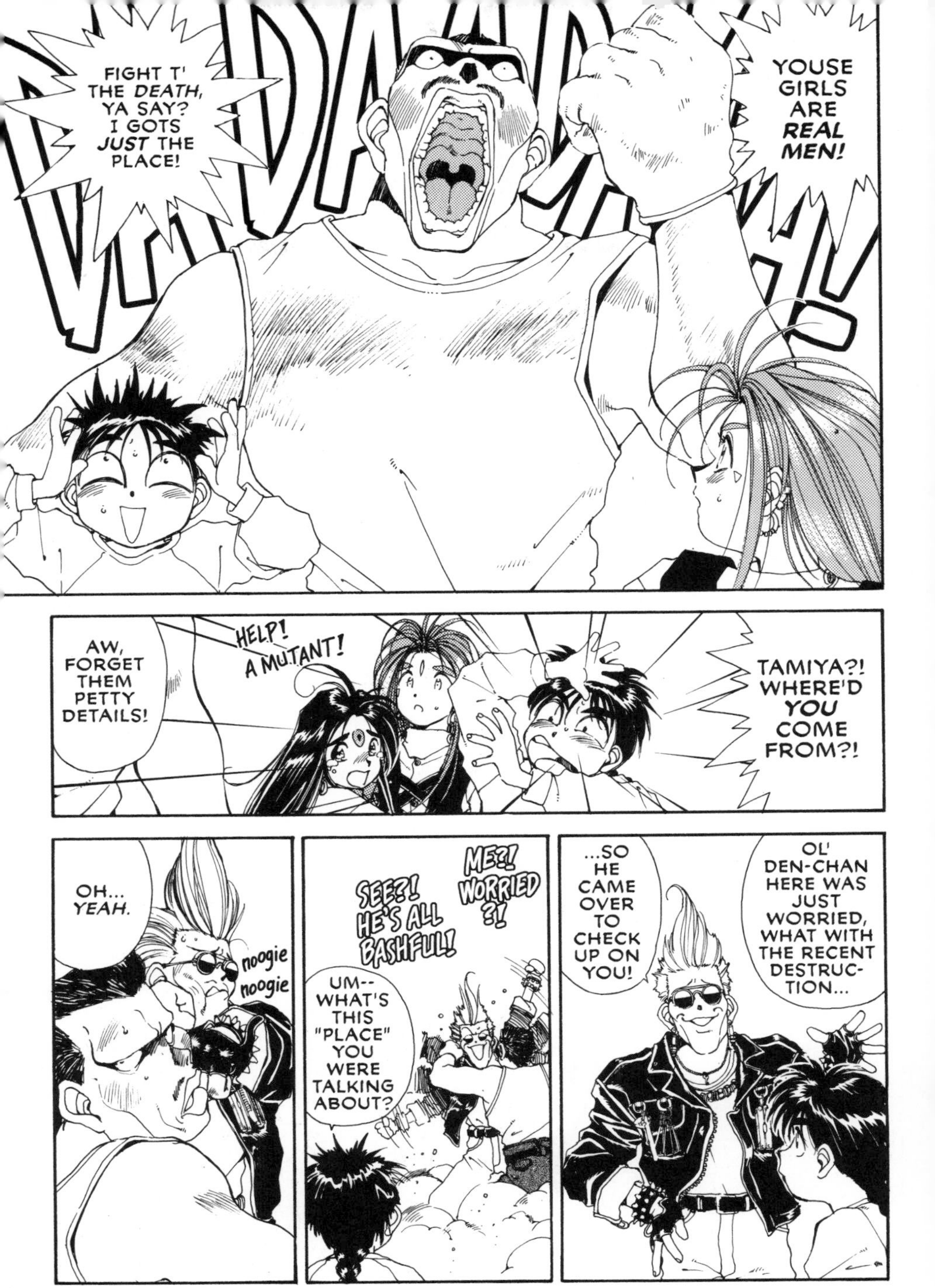
YOUSE GIRLS ARE *REAL MEN!*
FIGHT T' THE *DEATH,* YA SAY? I GOTS *JUST* THE PLACE!
TAMIYA?! WHERE'D **YOU** COME FROM?!
HELP! A MUTANT!
AW, FORGET THEM PETTY DETAILS!
OL' DEN-CHAN HERE WAS JUST WORRIED, WHAT WITH THE RECENT DESTRUC-TION...
...SO HE CAME OVER TO CHECK UP ON YOU!
ME?! WORRIED ?!
SEE?! HE'S ALL BASHFUL!
UM-- WHAT'S THIS "PLACE" YOU WERE TALKING ABOUT?
noogie noogie
OH... *YEAH.*

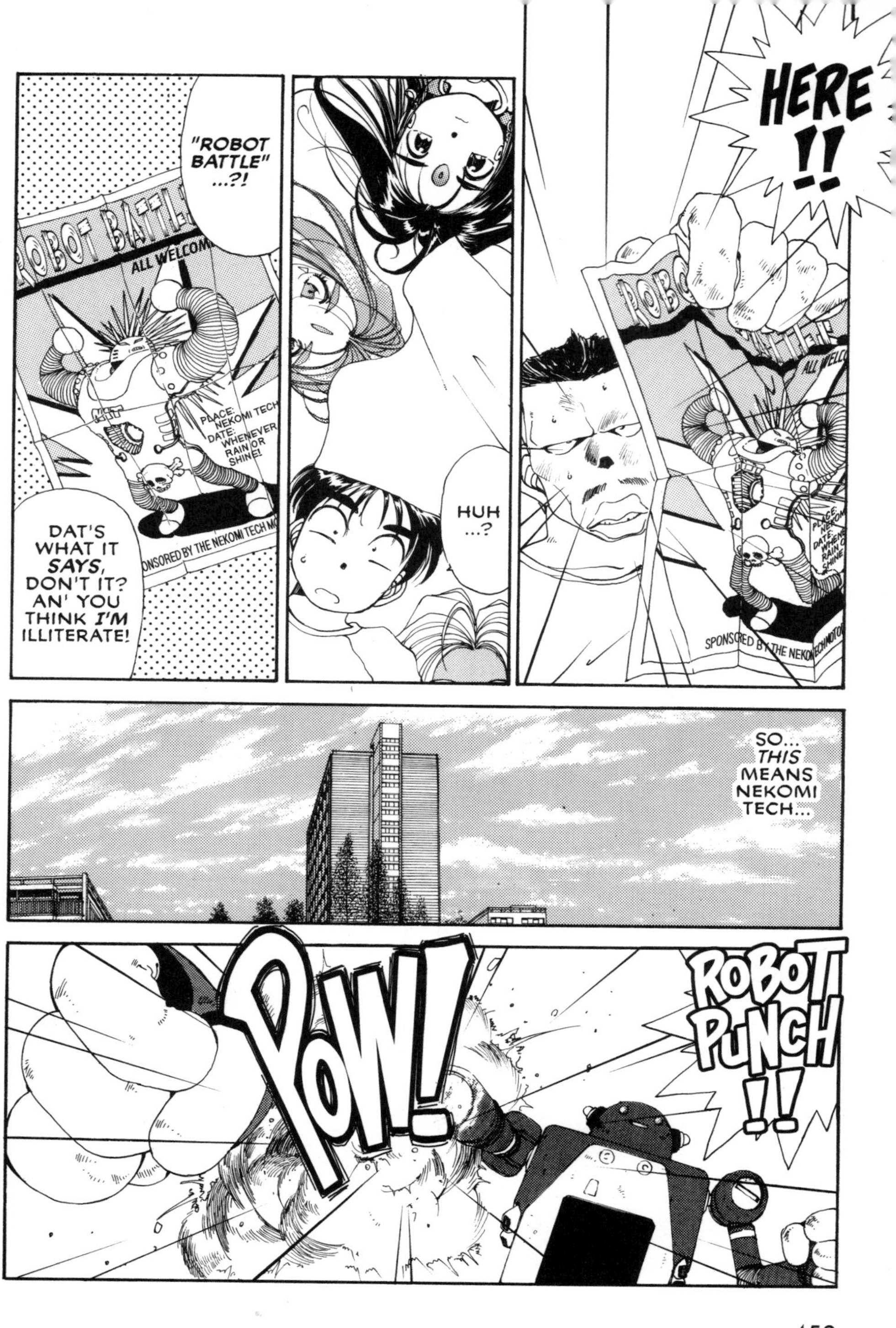
HERE!!
HUH ...?
"ROBOT BATTLE" ...?!
ROBOT BATTLE
ALL WELCOM
PLACE: NEKOMI TECH
DATE: WHENEVER RAIN OR SHINE!
SPONSORED BY THE NEKOMI TECH MO
DAT'S WHAT IT *SAYS*, DON'T IT? AN' YOU THINK *I'M* ILLITERATE!
SO... *THIS* MEANS NEKOMI TECH...
POW!
ROBOT PUNCH!!

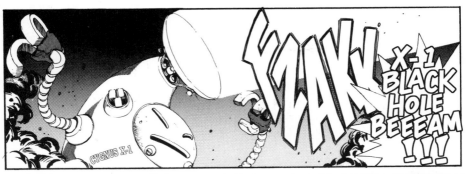

FZAKK
X-1 BLACK HOLE BEEEAM!!!
CYGNUS X-1
KLANKKLANK
KLUNK KLUNK
...WILL BECOME A WAR ZONE OF CLASHING METAL TITANS!
RIGHT?
WRONG.
SQUEE WHAM KRANG
OKAY... HERE'S DA LAYOUT.
WE GOT DIS RING, AN' IN DA RING IS A BUNCH A' EMPTY DRUMS.
DA ROBOTS FIGHT T'SEE WHO CAN GRAB DA MOST DRUMS, AN' DA ONE WIT' DA MOSTEST WINS!
RING
ROBOT A
ROBOT B

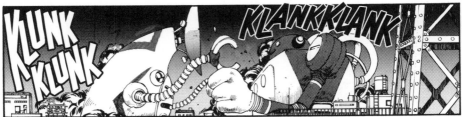

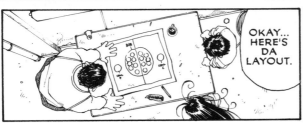

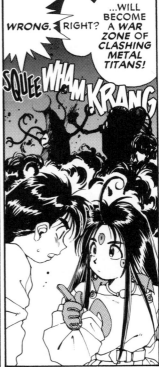

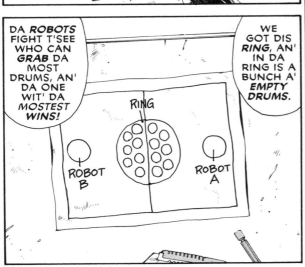

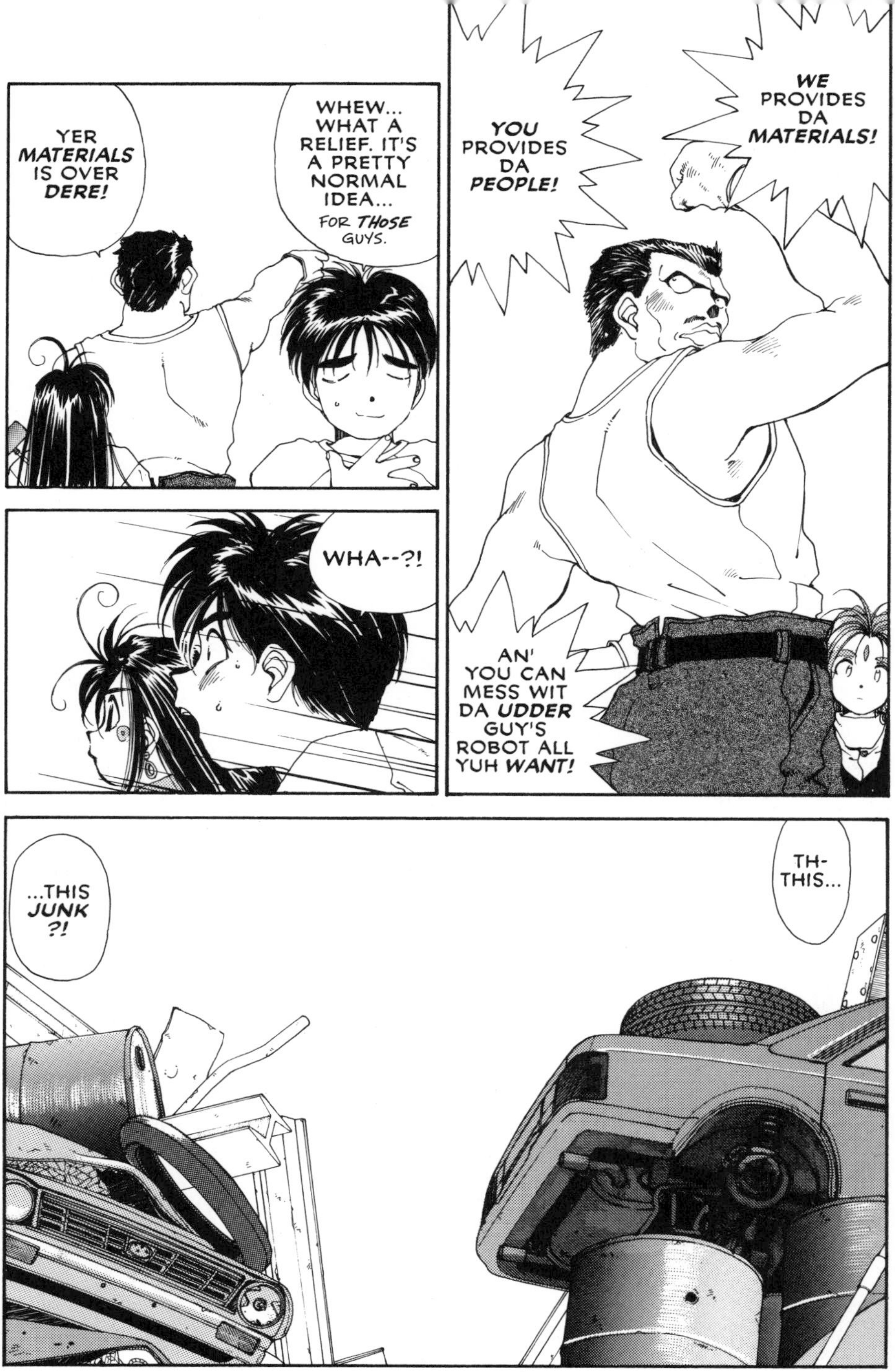
WE PROVIDES DA MATERIALS!
YOU PROVIDES DA PEOPLE!
AN' YOU CAN MESS WIT DA UDDER GUY'S ROBOT ALL YUH WANT!
WHEW... WHAT A RELIEF. IT'S A PRETTY NORMAL IDEA... FOR THOSE GUYS.
YER MATERIALS IS OVER DERE!
WHA--?!
TH- THIS...
...THIS JUNK ?!

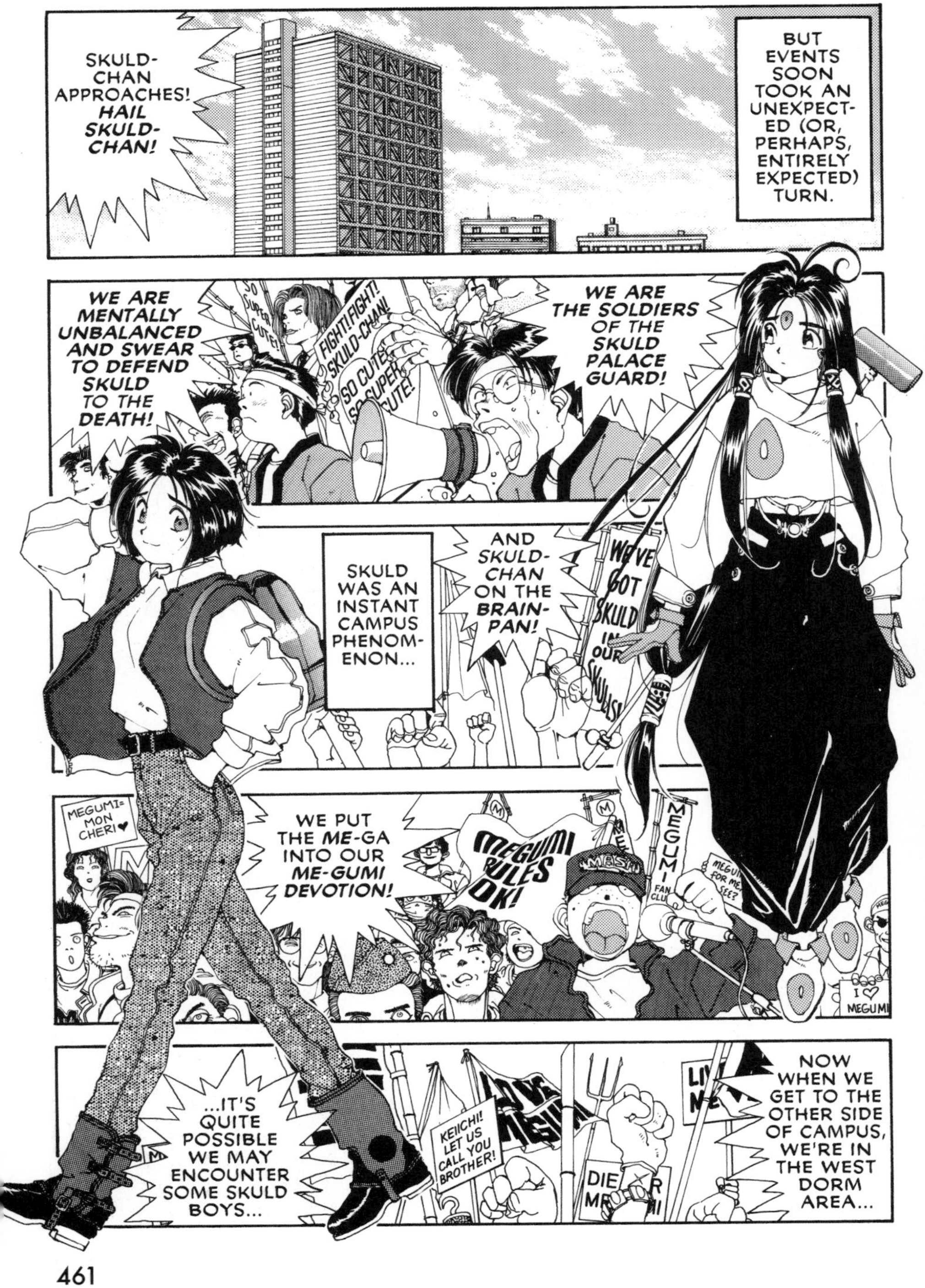

BUT EVENTS SOON TOOK AN UNEXPECTED (OR, PERHAPS, ENTIRELY EXPECTED) TURN.
SKULD-CHAN APPROACHES! HAIL SKULD-CHAN!
WE ARE THE SOLDIERS OF THE SKULD PALACE GUARD!
FIGHT! FIGHT! SKULD-CHAN!
SO CUTE! SO SUPER CUTE!
SO SUPER CUTE!
WE ARE MENTALLY UNBALANCED AND SWEAR TO DEFEND SKULD TO THE DEATH!
AND SKULD-CHAN ON THE BRAIN-PAN!
SKULD WAS AN INSTANT CAMPUS PHENOMENON...
I ♥ MEGUMI
MEGUMI FAN CLUB
MEGUMI RULES OK!
WE PUT THE ME-GA INTO OUR ME-GUMI DEVOTION!
MEGUMI= MON CHERI ♥
NOW WHEN WE GET TO THE OTHER SIDE OF CAMPUS, WE'RE IN THE WEST DORM AREA...
KEIICHI! LET US CALL YOU BROTHER!
...IT'S QUITE POSSIBLE WE MAY ENCOUNTER SOME SKULD BOYS...

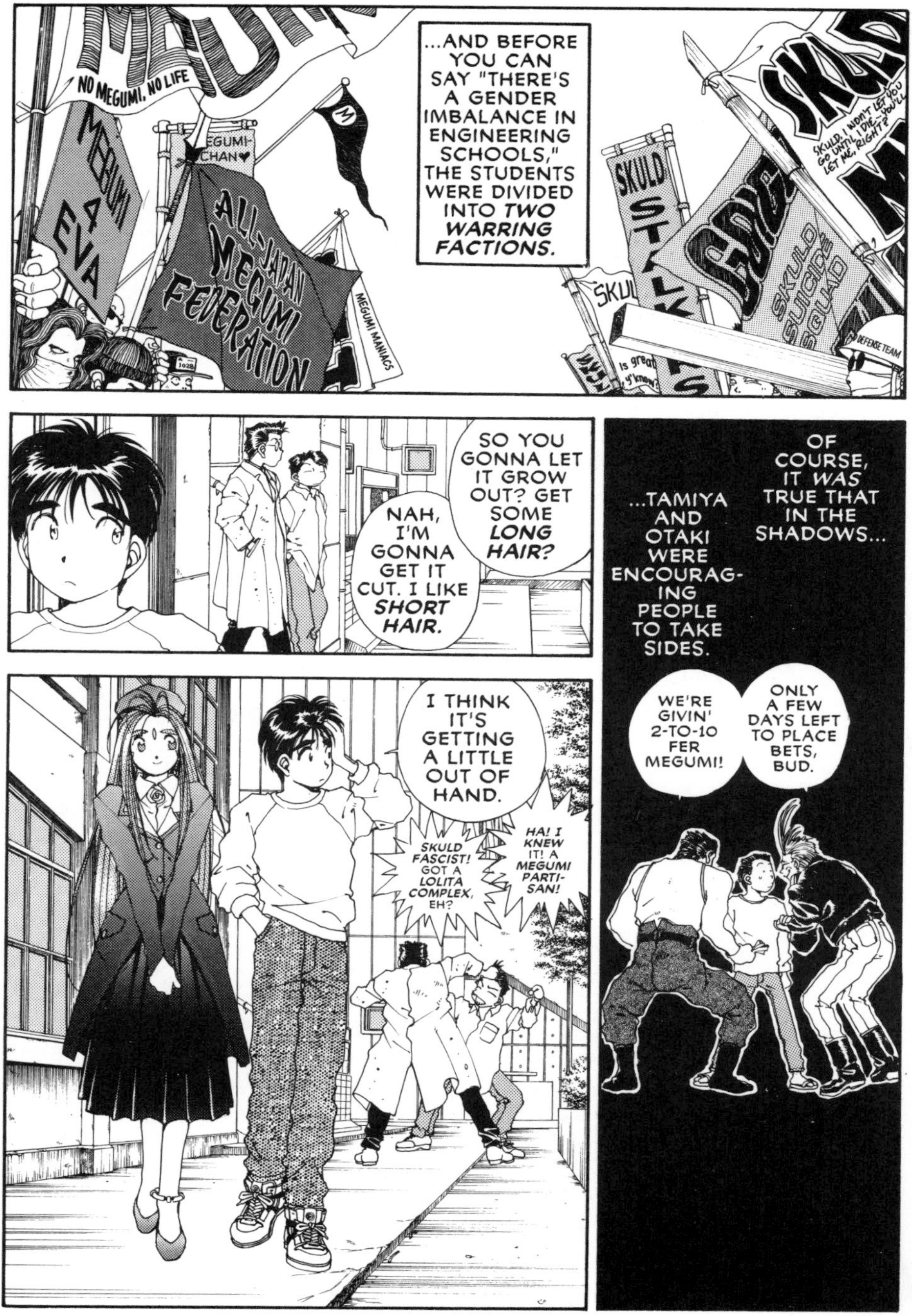
SKULD, I WON'T LET YOU GO UNTIL I DIE... YOU'LL LET ME, RIGHT?
SKULD SUICIDE SQUAD
DEFENSE TEAM
Is great, y'know?
...AND BEFORE YOU CAN SAY "THERE'S A GENDER IMBALANCE IN ENGINEERING SCHOOLS," THE STUDENTS WERE DIVIDED INTO *TWO WARRING FACTIONS*.
NO MEGUMI, NO LIFE
MEGUMI-CHAN♥
ALL-JAPAN MEGUMI FEDERATION
MEGUMI MANIACS
MEGUMI 4 EVA
OF COURSE, IT *WAS* TRUE THAT IN THE SHADOWS...
...TAMIYA AND OTAKI WERE ENCOURAGING PEOPLE TO TAKE SIDES.
ONLY A FEW DAYS LEFT TO PLACE BETS, BUD.
WE'RE GIVIN' 2-TO-10 FER MEGUMI!
SO YOU GONNA LET IT GROW OUT? GET SOME *LONG HAIR?*
NAH, I'M GONNA GET IT CUT. I LIKE *SHORT HAIR.*
I THINK IT'S GETTING A LITTLE OUT OF HAND.
HA! I KNEW IT! A MEGUMI PARTISAN!
SKULD FASCIST! GOT A LOLITA COMPLEX, EH?

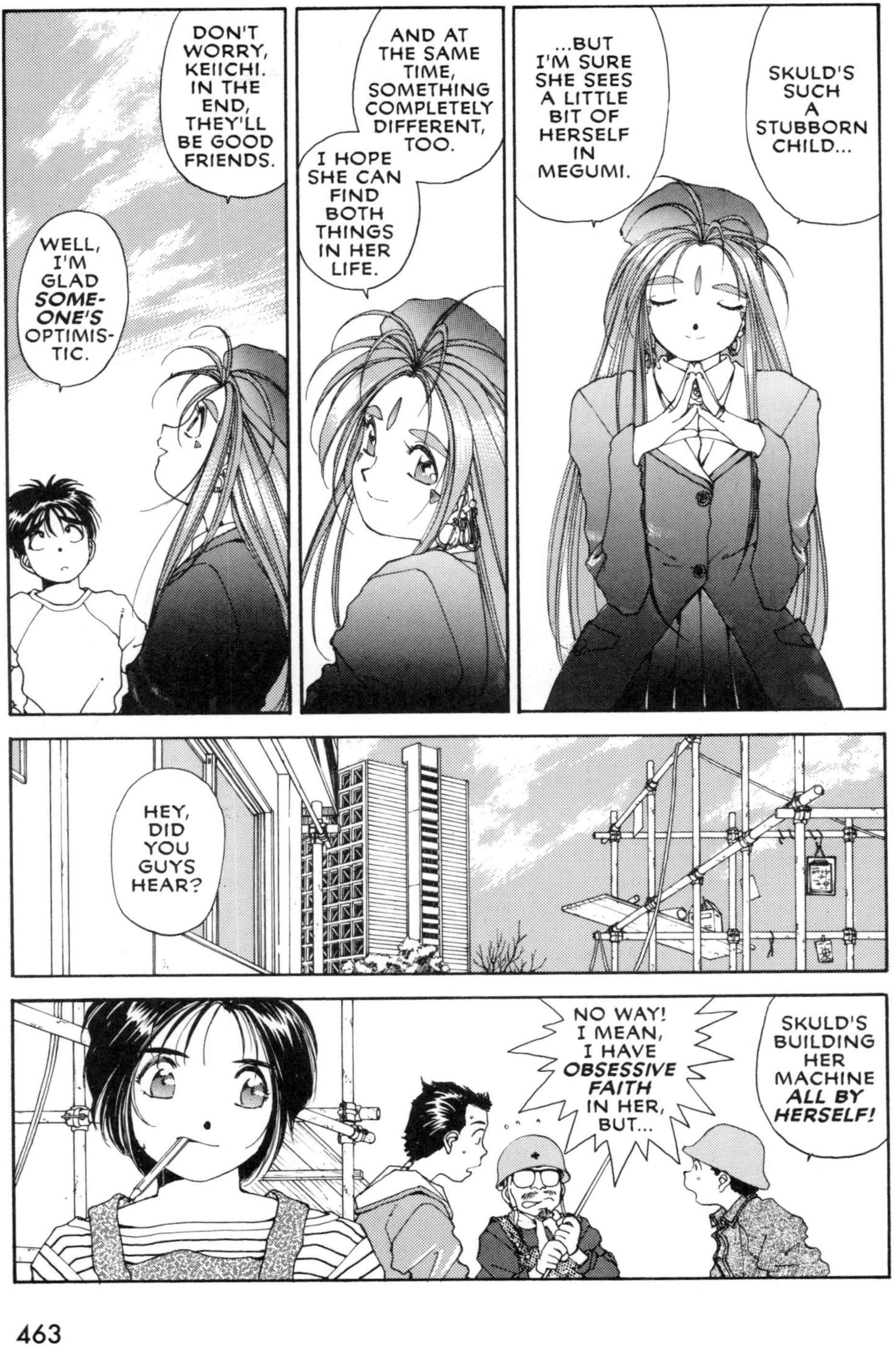
SKULD'S SUCH A STUBBORN CHILD...
...BUT I'M SURE SHE SEES A LITTLE BIT OF HERSELF IN MEGUMI.
AND AT THE SAME TIME, SOMETHING COMPLETELY DIFFERENT, TOO.
I HOPE SHE CAN FIND BOTH THINGS IN HER LIFE.
DON'T WORRY, KEIICHI. IN THE END, THEY'LL BE GOOD FRIENDS.
WELL, I'M GLAD ***SOME-ONE'S*** OPTIMIS-TIC.
HEY, DID YOU GUYS HEAR?
SKULD'S BUILDING HER MACHINE ***ALL BY HERSELF!***
NO WAY! I MEAN, I HAVE ***OBSESSIVE FAITH*** IN HER, BUT...

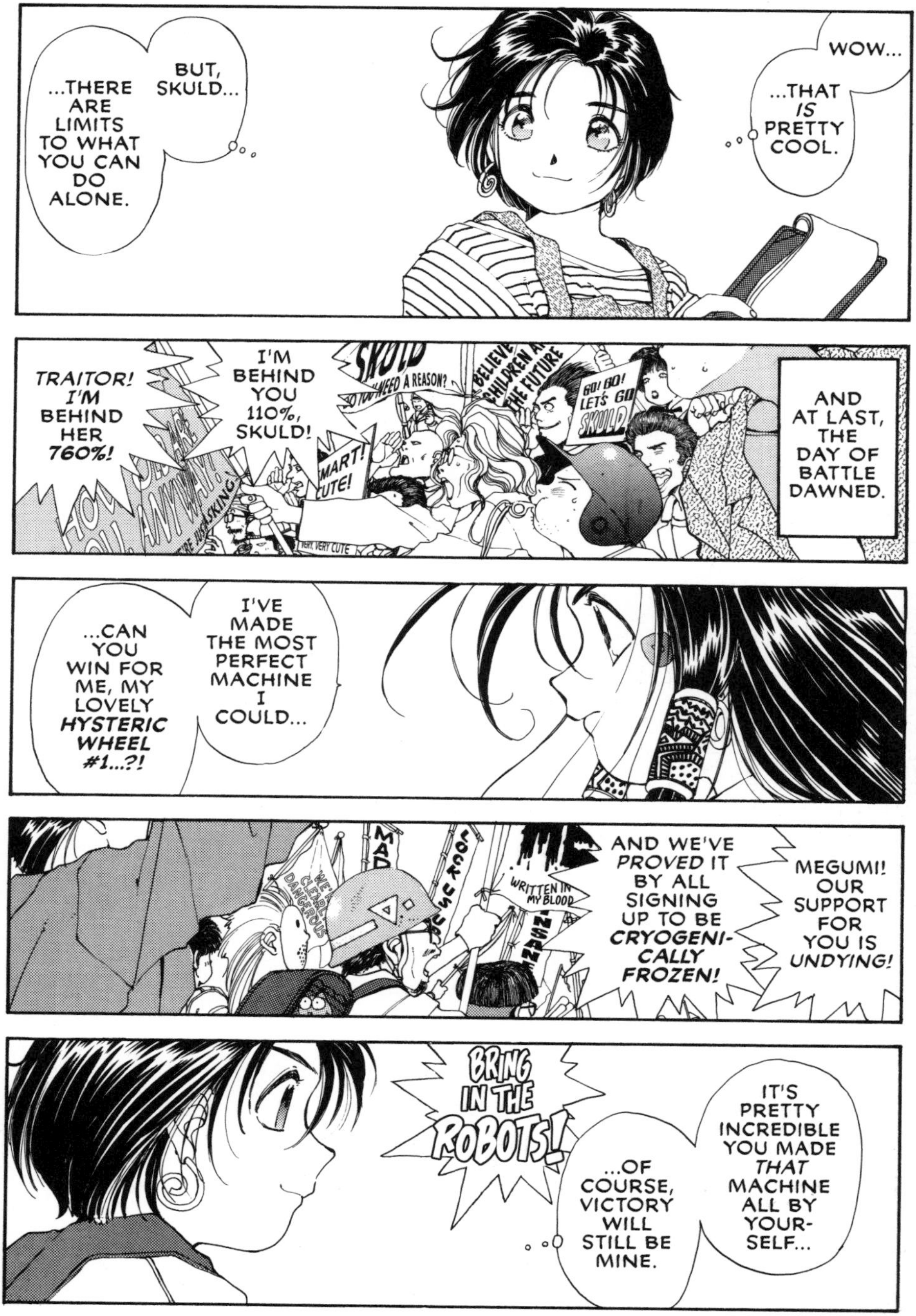
WOW... ...THAT *IS* PRETTY COOL.
BUT, SKULD... ...THERE ARE LIMITS TO WHAT YOU CAN DO ALONE.
AND AT LAST, THE DAY OF BATTLE DAWNED.
GO! GO! LET'S GO SKULD
I'M BEHIND YOU 110%, SKULD!
*TRAITOR! I'M* BEHIND HER *760%!*
VERY, VERY CUTE
I'VE MADE THE MOST PERFECT MACHINE I COULD...
...CAN YOU WIN FOR ME, MY LOVELY ***HYSTERIC WHEEL #1...?!***
MEGUMI! OUR SUPPORT FOR YOU IS *UNDYING!*
AND WE'VE *PROVED* IT BY ALL SIGNING UP TO BE ***CRYOGENICALLY FROZEN!***
WRITTEN IN MY BLOOD
IT'S PRETTY INCREDIBLE YOU MADE *THAT* MACHINE ALL BY YOURSELF...
...OF COURSE, VICTORY WILL STILL BE MINE.
BRING IN THE ROBOTS!

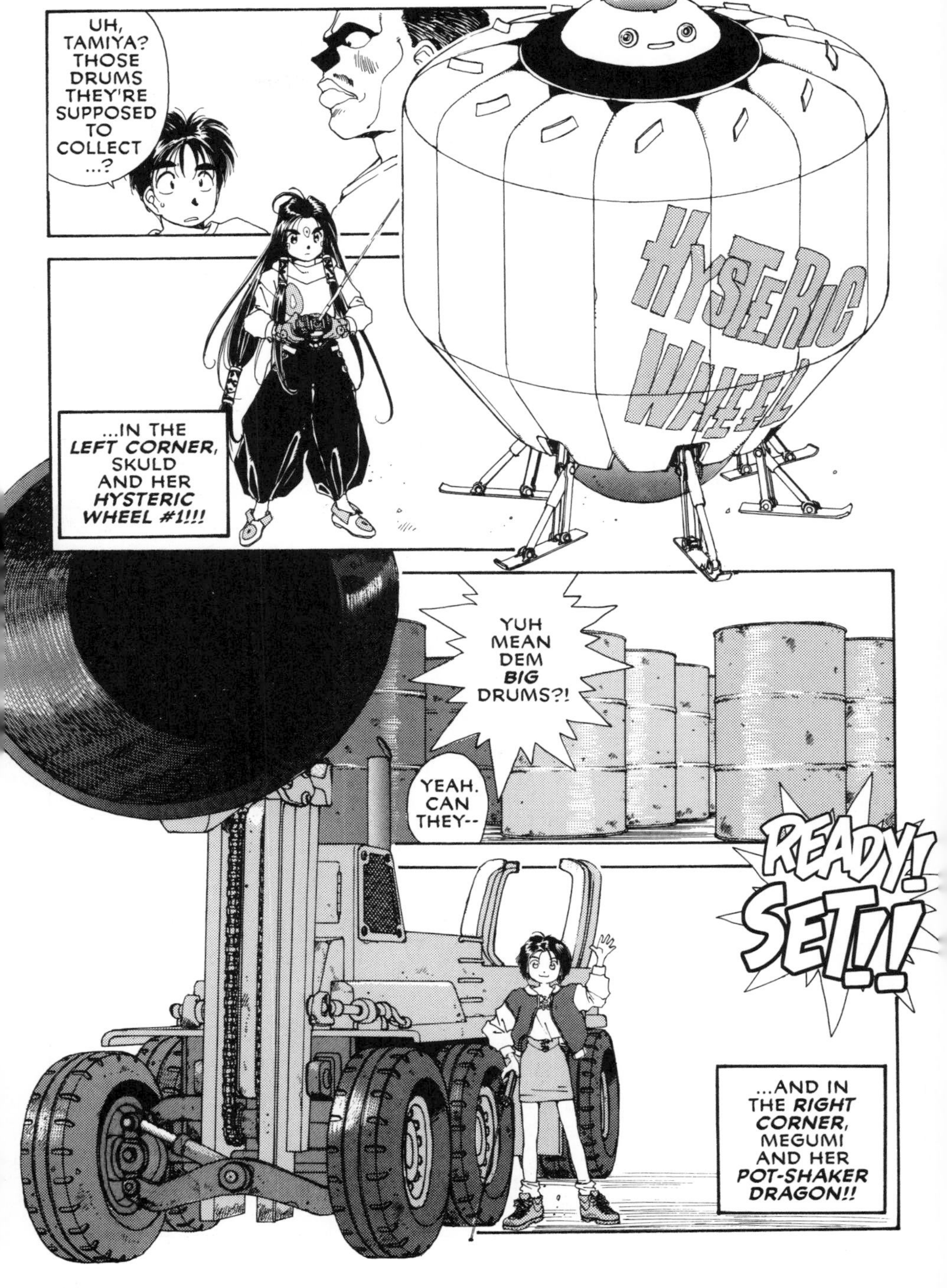
UH, TAMIYA? THOSE DRUMS THEY'RE SUPPOSED TO COLLECT ...?
HYSTERIC WHEEL
...IN THE *LEFT CORNER,* SKULD AND HER *HYSTERIC WHEEL #1!!!*
YUH MEAN DEM *BIG* DRUMS?!
YEAH. CAN THEY--
READY! SET!!
...AND IN THE *RIGHT CORNER,* MEGUMI AND HER *POT-SHAKER DRAGON!!*

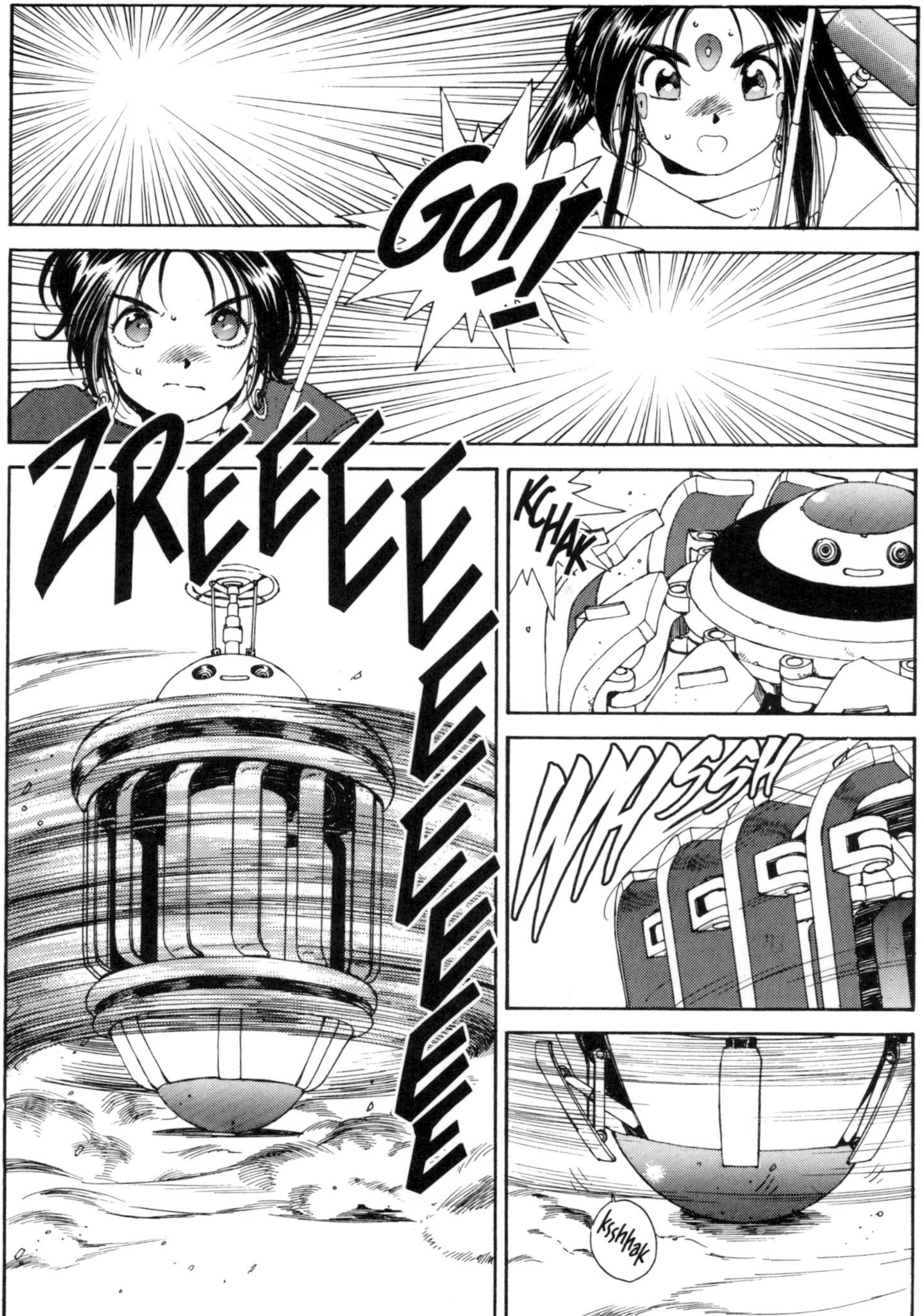
GO!!
ZREEEEEEEEEEEEE
KCHAK
WHISSH
ksshhak

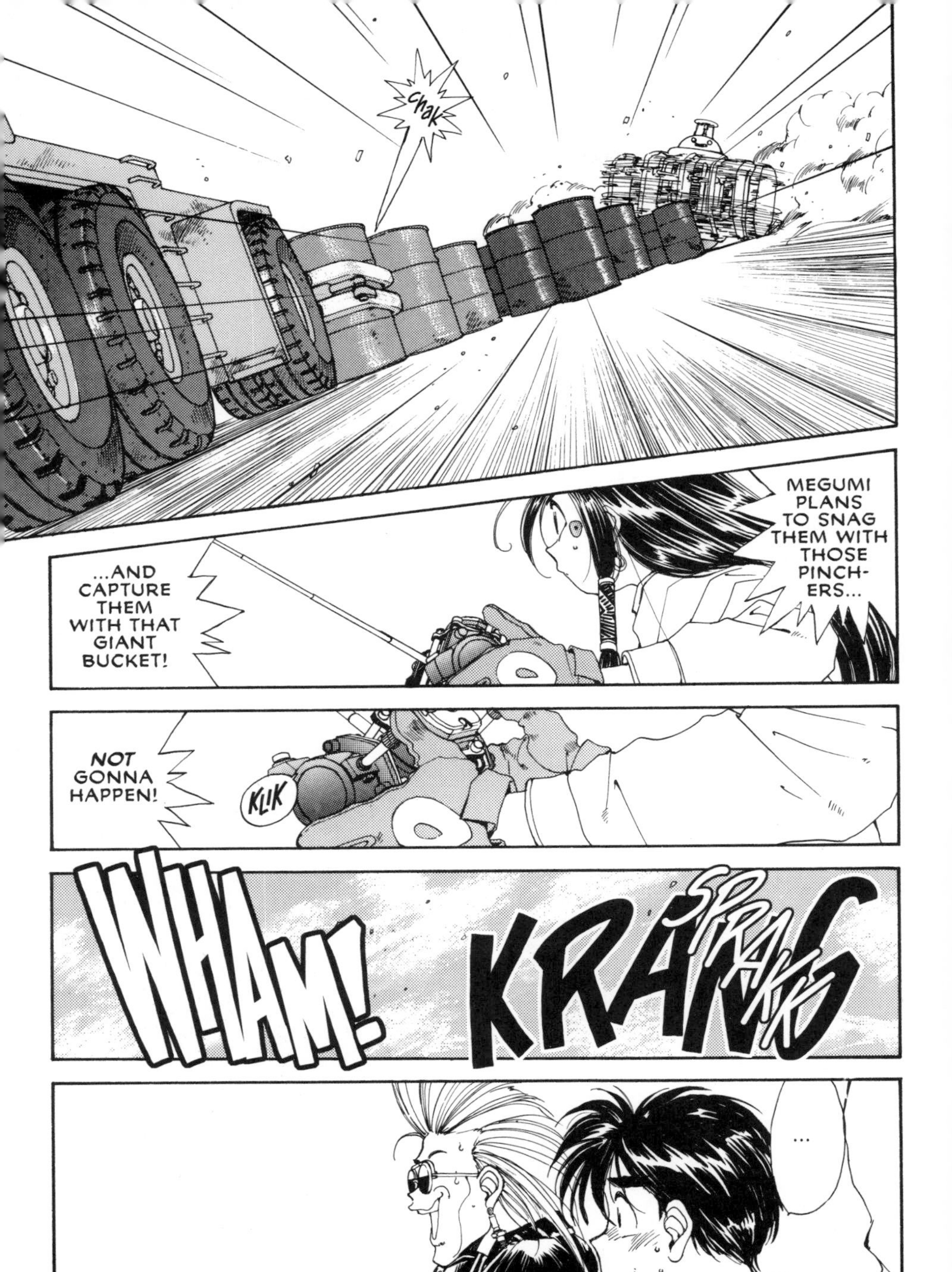
chak
MEGUMI PLANS TO SNAG THEM WITH THOSE PINCHERS...
...AND CAPTURE THEM WITH THAT GIANT BUCKET!
KLIK
NOT GONNA HAPPEN!
KRANG
SPRAKK
WHAM!
...

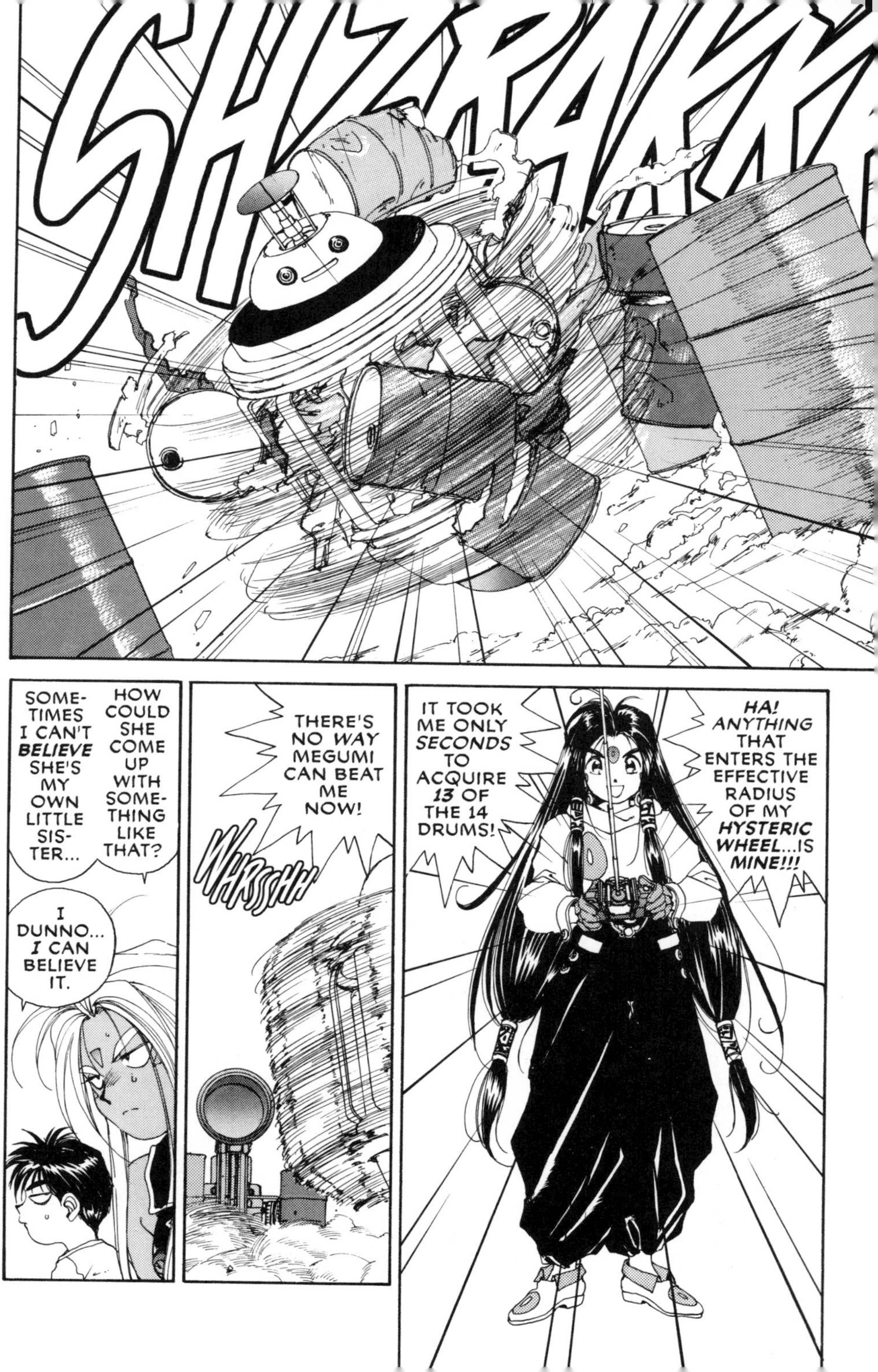
SHZRAKK
HA! ANYTHING THAT ENTERS THE EFFECTIVE RADIUS OF MY HYSTERIC WHEEL...IS MINE!!!
IT TOOK ME ONLY SECONDS TO ACQUIRE 13 OF THE 14 DRUMS!
THERE'S NO WAY MEGUMI CAN BEAT ME NOW!
WHRSSHH
HOW COULD SHE COME UP WITH SOMETHING LIKE THAT?
SOMETIMES I CAN'T BELIEVE SHE'S MY OWN LITTLE SISTER...
I DUNNO... I CAN BELIEVE IT.

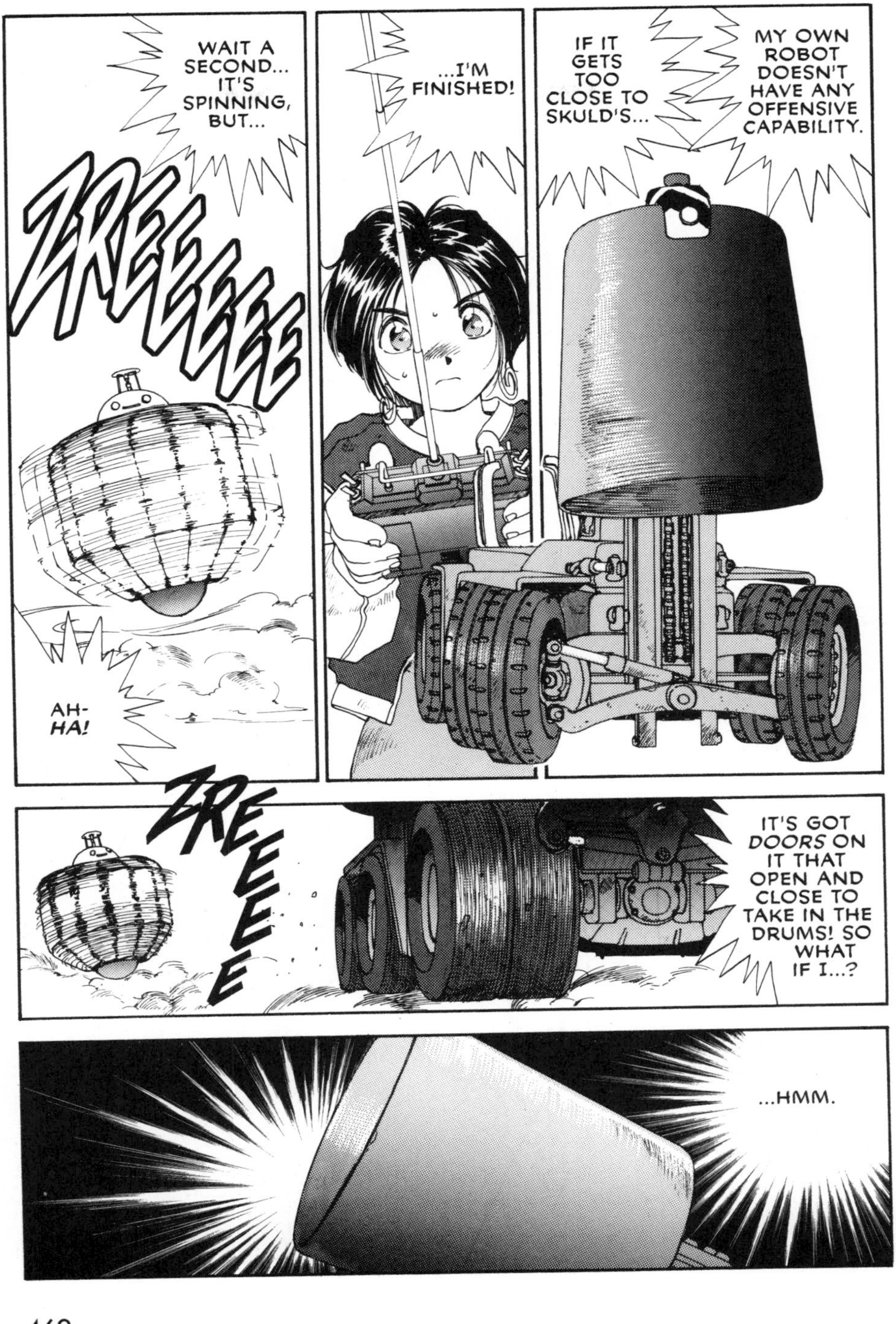
MY OWN ROBOT DOESN'T HAVE ANY OFFENSIVE CAPABILITY.
IF IT GETS TOO CLOSE TO SKULD'S...
...I'M FINISHED!
WAIT A SECOND... IT'S SPINNING, BUT...
ZREEEEE
AH-HA!
IT'S GOT *DOORS* ON IT THAT OPEN AND CLOSE TO TAKE IN THE DRUMS! SO WHAT IF I...?
ZREEEEE
...HMM.

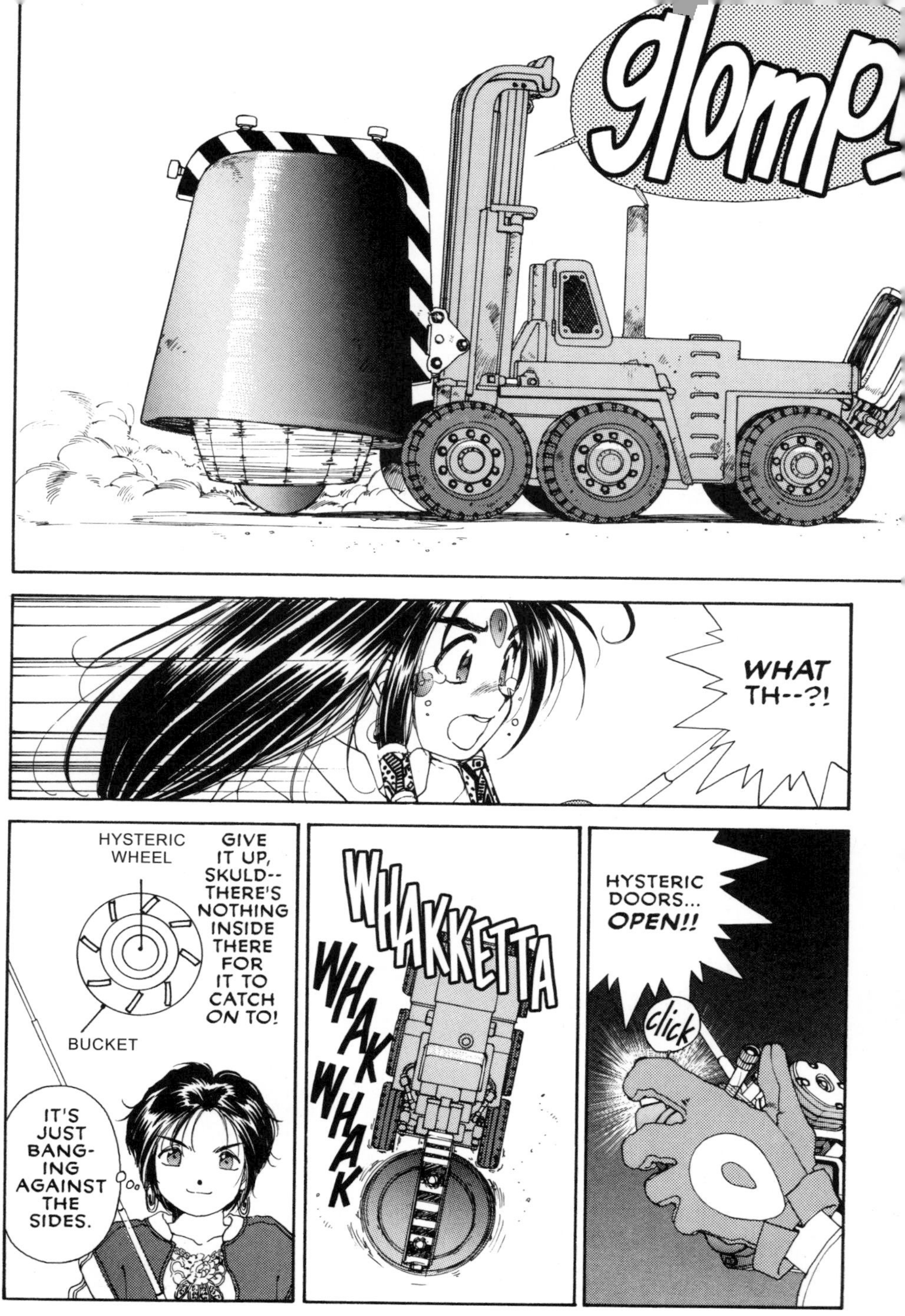
glomp
WHAT TH--?!
HYSTERIC DOORS... OPEN!!
click
WHAKKETTA
WHAK WHAK WHAK
GIVE IT UP, SKULD-- THERE'S NOTHING INSIDE THERE FOR IT TO CATCH ON TO!
HYSTERIC WHEEL
BUCKET
IT'S JUST BANGING AGAINST THE SIDES.

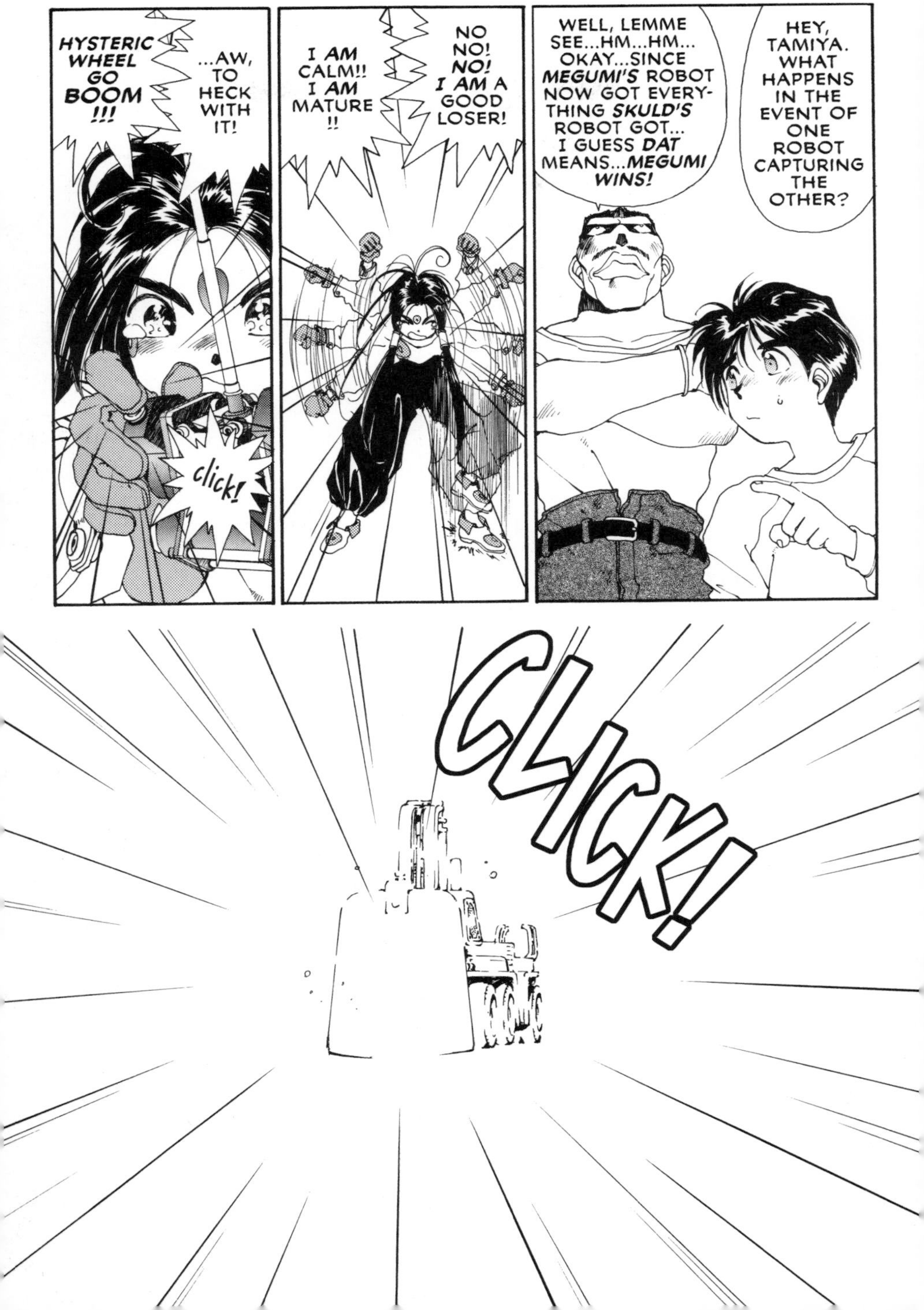
HEY, TAMIYA. WHAT HAPPENS IN THE EVENT OF ONE ROBOT CAPTURING THE OTHER?
WELL, LEMME SEE...HM...HM... OKAY...SINCE MEGUMI'S ROBOT NOW GOT EVERY-THING SKULD'S ROBOT GOT... I GUESS DAT MEANS...MEGUMI WINS!
NO NO! NO! I AM A GOOD LOSER!
I AM CALM!! I AM MATURE !!
...AW, TO HECK WITH IT!
HYSTERIC WHEEL GO BOOM !!!
click!
CLICK!

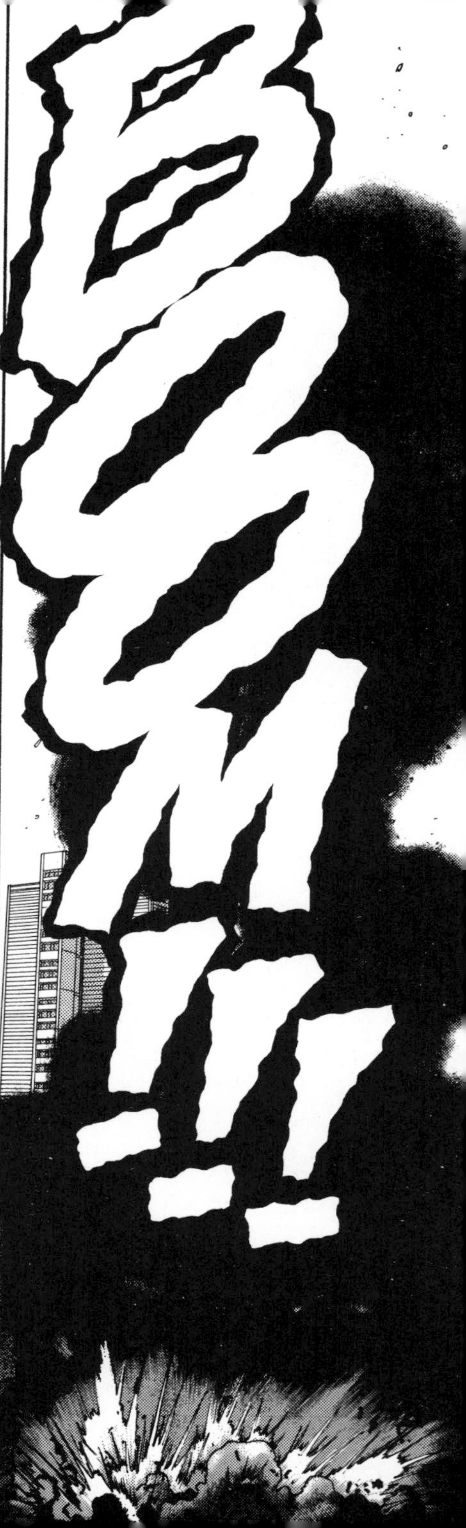

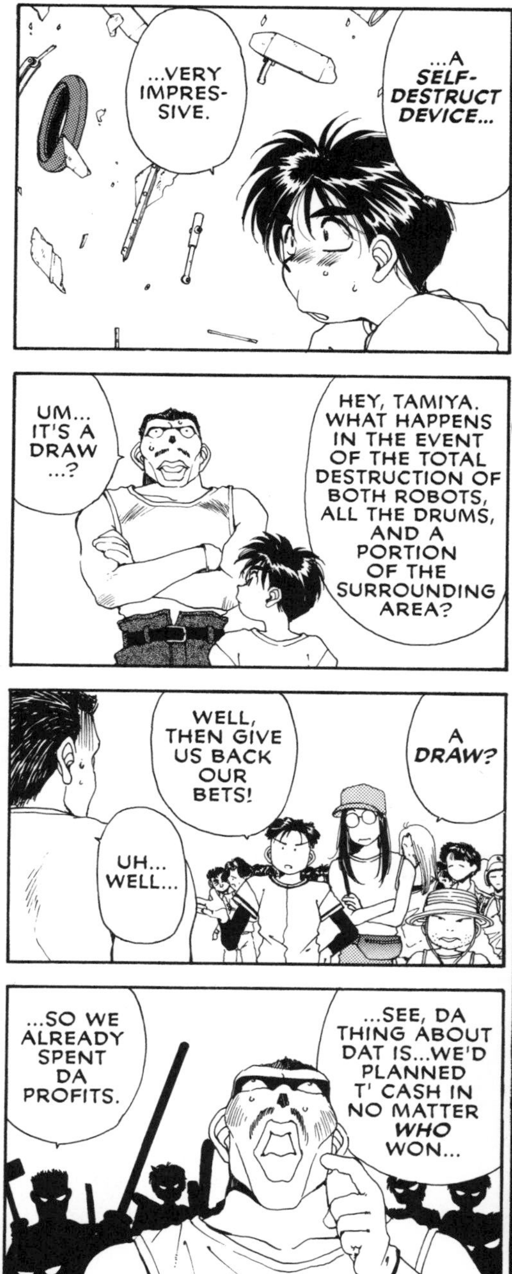
...A SELF-DESTRUCT DEVICE...
...VERY IMPRESSIVE.
HEY, TAMIYA. WHAT HAPPENS IN THE EVENT OF THE TOTAL DESTRUCTION OF BOTH ROBOTS, ALL THE DRUMS, AND A PORTION OF THE SURROUNDING AREA?
UM... IT'S A DRAW ...?
A DRAW?
WELL, THEN GIVE US BACK OUR BETS!
UH... WELL...
...SEE, DA THING ABOUT DAT IS...WE'D PLANNED T' CASH IN NO MATTER WHO WON...
...SO WE ALREADY SPENT DA PROFITS.

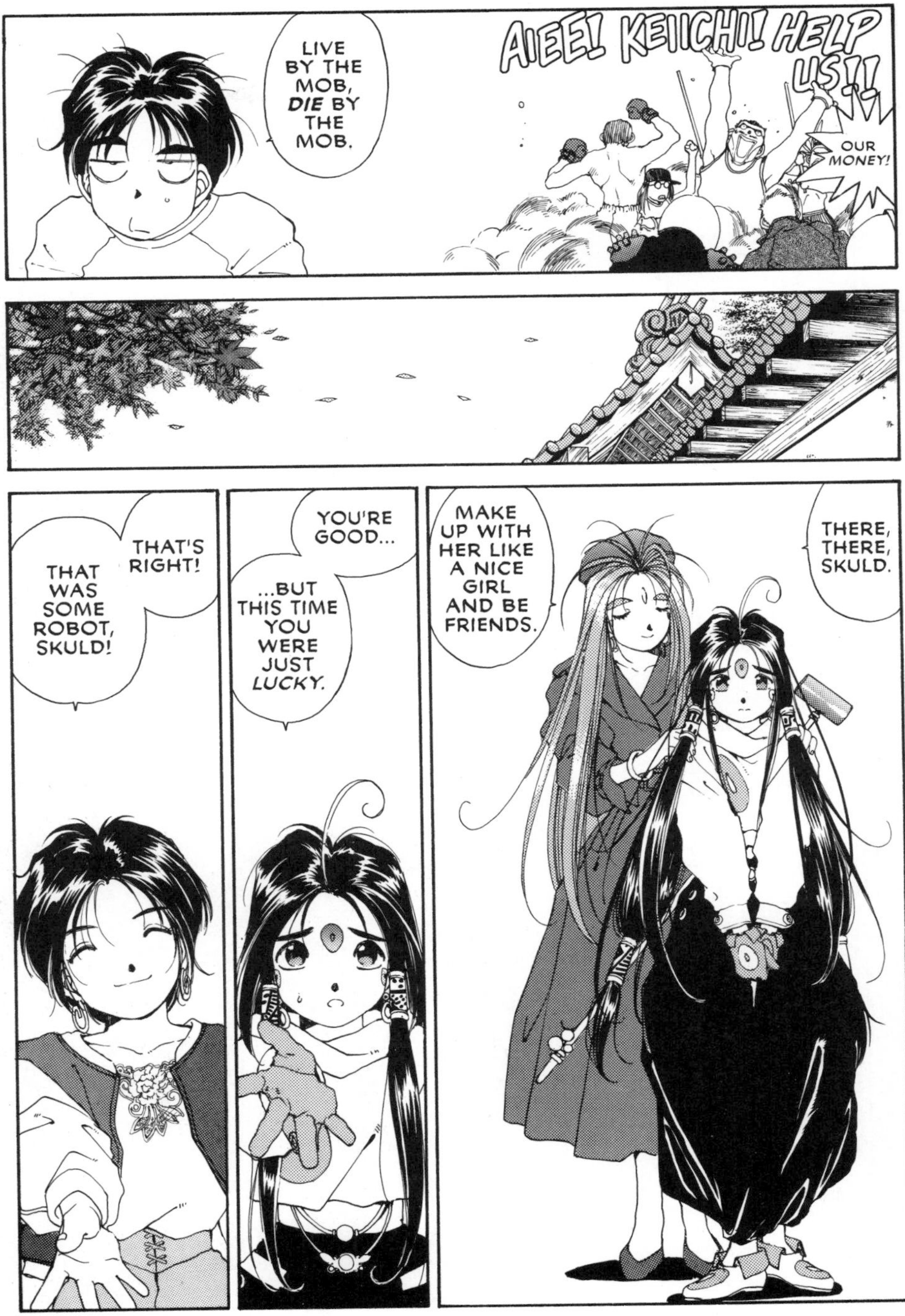
AIEEE! KEIICHI! HELP US!!
OUR MONEY!
LIVE BY THE MOB, DIE BY THE MOB.
THERE, THERE, SKULD.
MAKE UP WITH HER LIKE A NICE GIRL AND BE FRIENDS.
YOU'RE GOOD...
...BUT THIS TIME YOU WERE JUST LUCKY.
THAT'S RIGHT!
THAT WAS SOME ROBOT, SKULD!

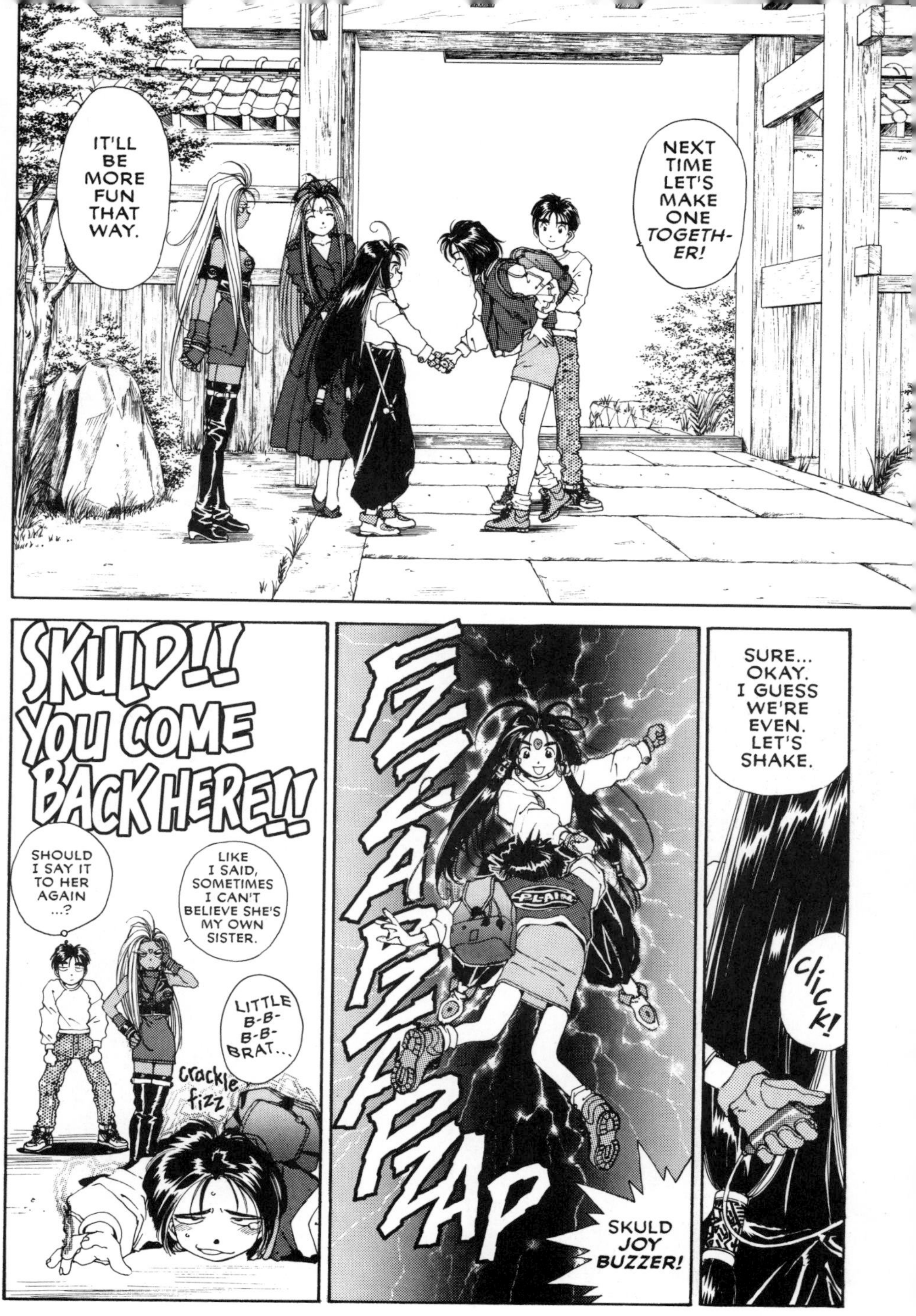
NEXT TIME LET'S MAKE ONE TOGETHER!
IT'LL BE MORE FUN THAT WAY.
SURE... OKAY. I GUESS WE'RE EVEN. LET'S SHAKE.
click!
FZZAZZFZZAP
SKULD JOY BUZZER!
SKULD!!! YOU COME BACK HERE!!!
LIKE I SAID, SOMETIMES I CAN'T BELIEVE SHE'S MY OWN SISTER.
SHOULD I SAY IT TO HER AGAIN ...?
LITTLE B-B-B-B-BRAT...
crackle fizz

CHAPTER 41

# The Trials of Morisato

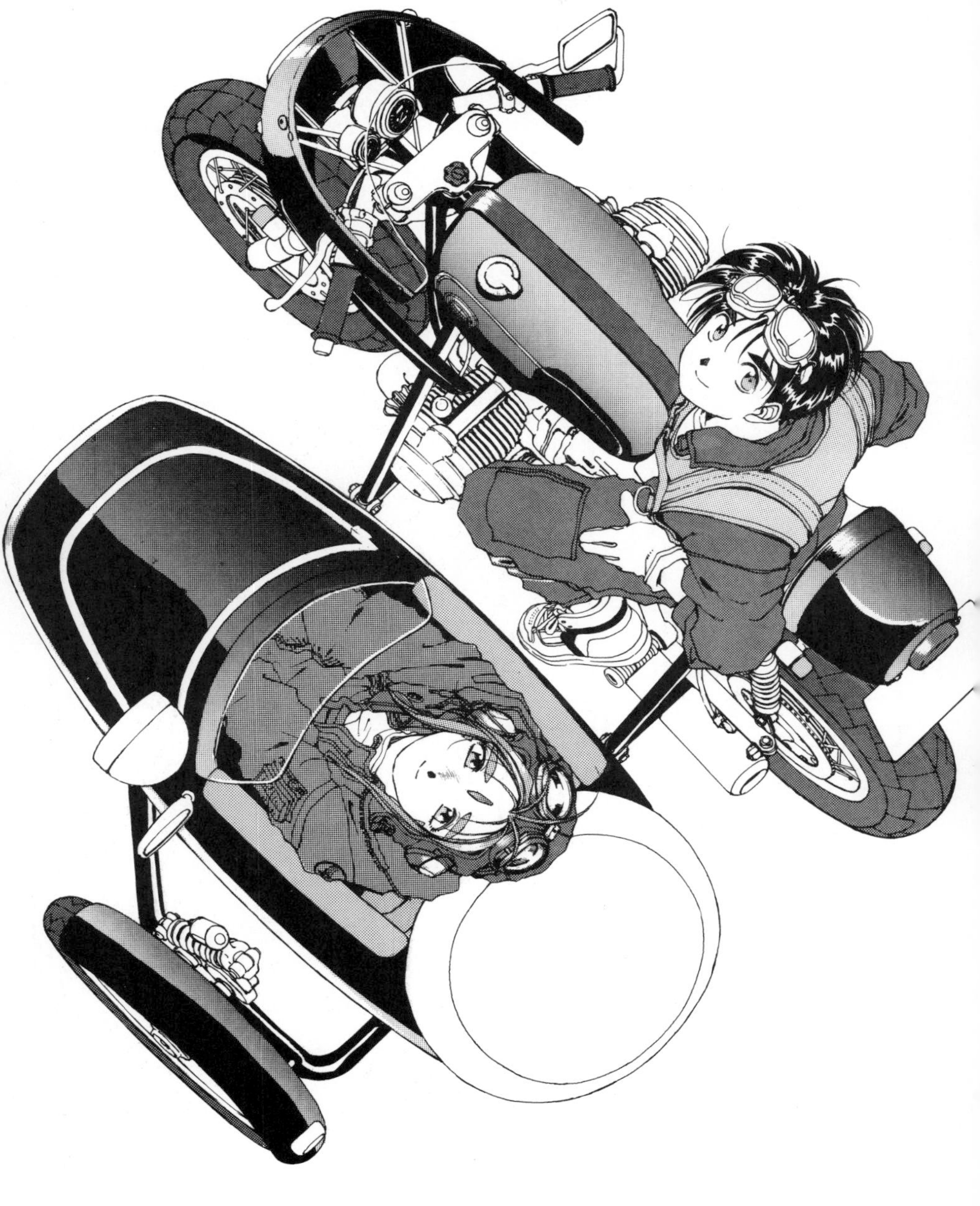

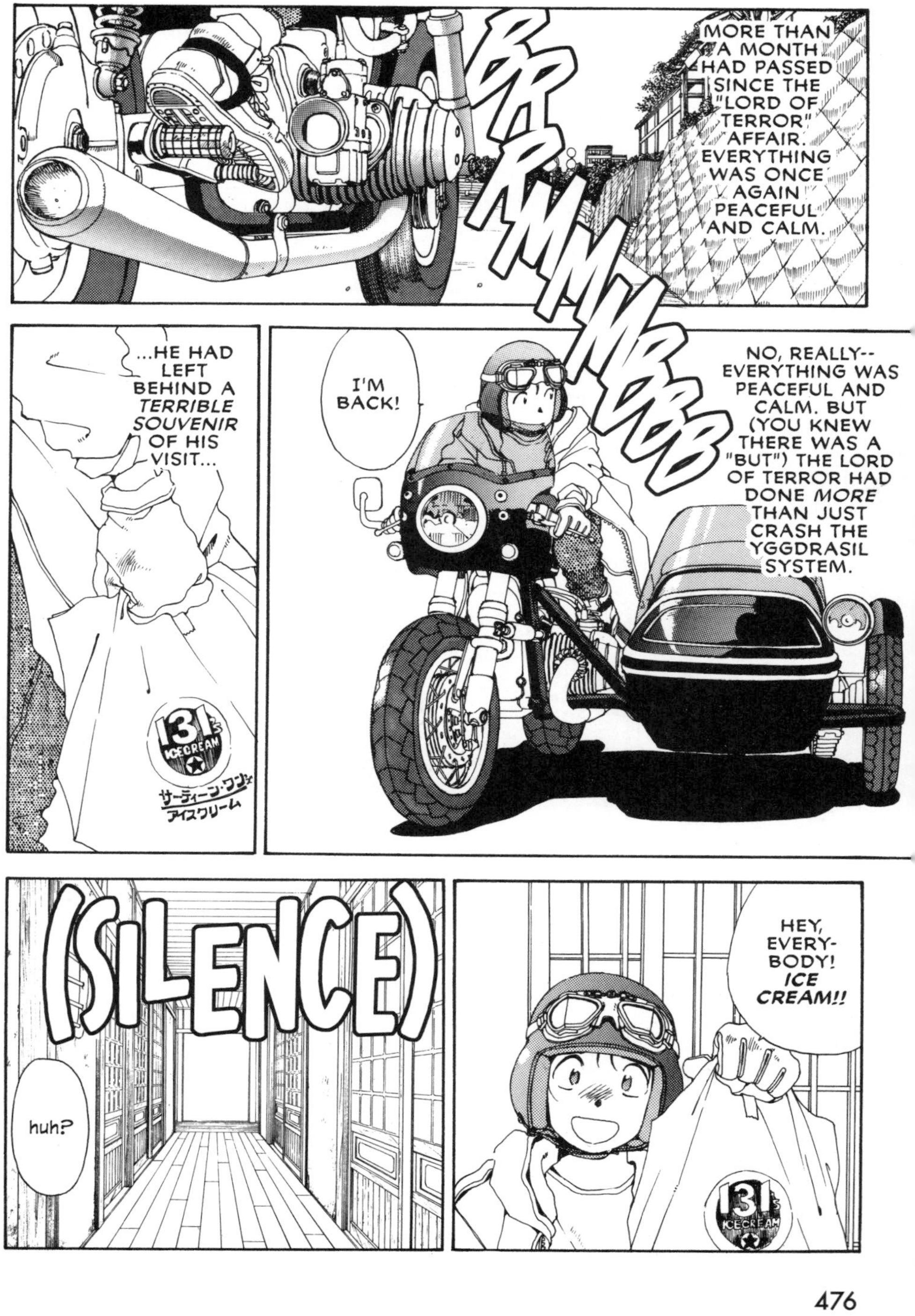
MORE THAN A MONTH HAD PASSED SINCE THE "LORD OF TERROR" AFFAIR. EVERYTHING WAS ONCE AGAIN PEACEFUL AND CALM.
BRRMMMMBOOB
NO, REALLY-- EVERYTHING WAS PEACEFUL AND CALM. BUT (YOU KNEW THERE WAS A "BUT") THE LORD OF TERROR HAD DONE *MORE* THAN JUST CRASH THE YGGDRASIL SYSTEM.
I'M BACK!
...HE HAD LEFT BEHIND A *TERRIBLE SOUVENIR* OF HIS VISIT...
131's ICECREAM
サーティーン・ワンズ アイスクリーム
HEY, EVERY-BODY! ***ICE CREAM!!***
131's ICECREAM
(SILENCE)
huh?

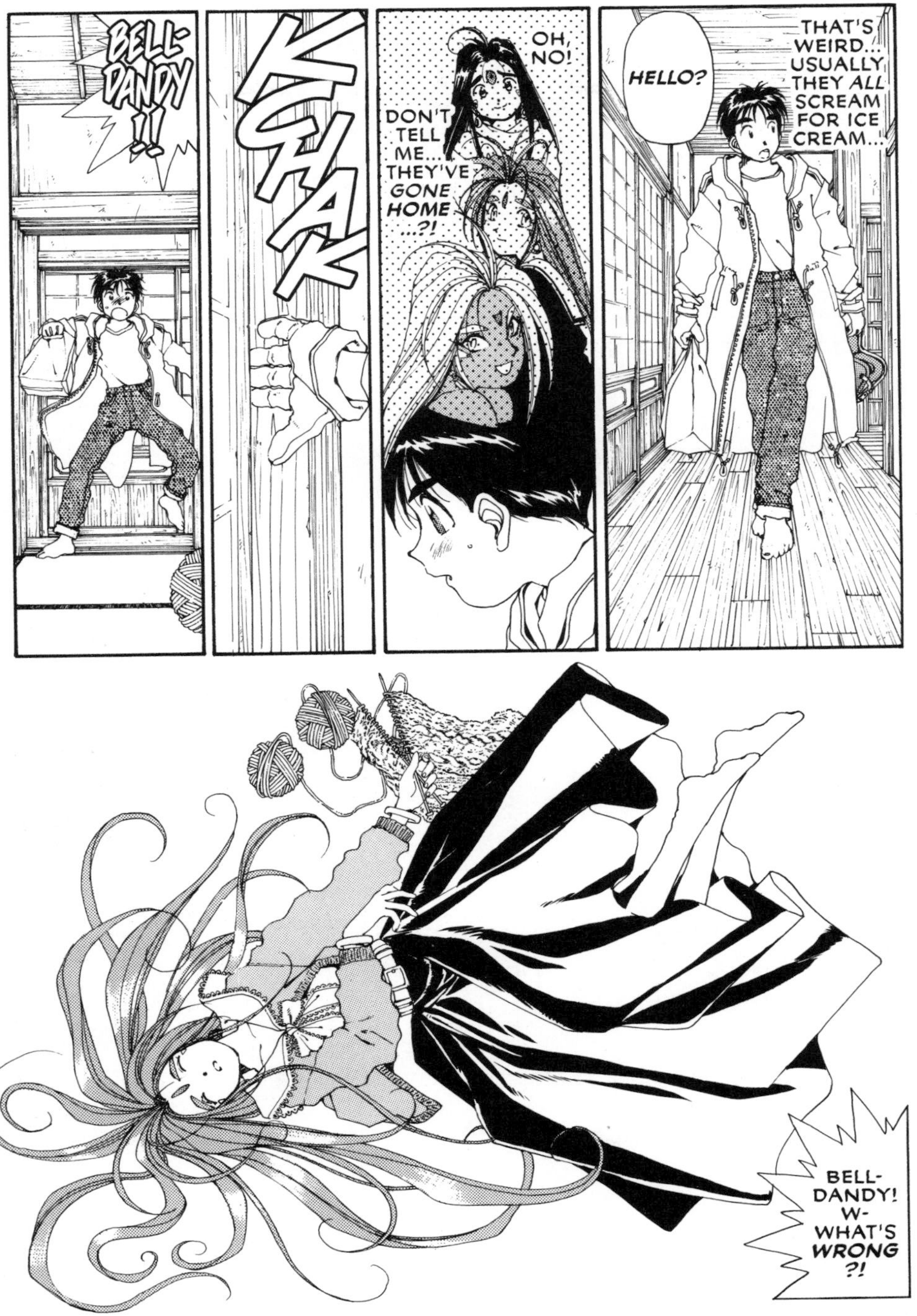
THAT'S WEIRD... USUALLY THEY *ALL* SCREAM FOR ICE CREAM...!
*HELLO?*
OH, NO!
DON'T TELL ME... THEY'VE *GONE* ***HOME*** ...?!
KCHAK
BELL-DANDY!!
BELL-DANDY! W-WHAT'S ***WRONG*** ?!

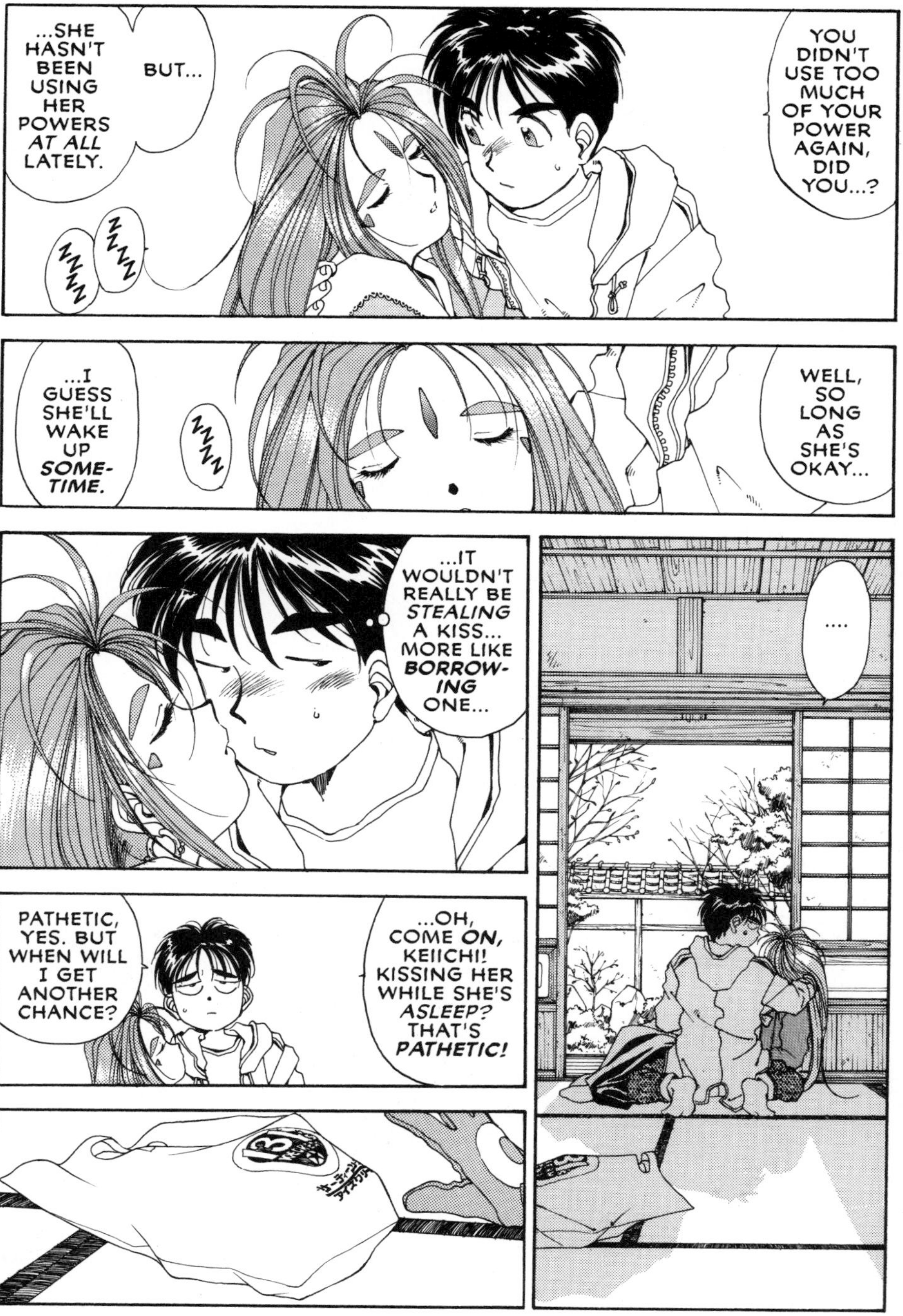
YOU DIDN'T USE TOO MUCH OF YOUR POWER AGAIN, DID YOU...?
BUT...
...SHE HASN'T BEEN USING HER POWERS *AT ALL* LATELY.
ZZZZ
ZZZZ
WELL, SO LONG AS SHE'S OKAY...
ZZZZ
...I GUESS SHE'LL WAKE UP *SOME-TIME.*
....
...IT WOULDN'T REALLY BE *STEALING* A KISS... MORE LIKE *BORROW-ING* ONE...
...OH, COME *ON,* KEIICHI! KISSING HER WHILE SHE'S *ASLEEP?* THAT'S *PATHETIC!*
PATHETIC, YES. BUT WHEN WILL I GET ANOTHER CHANCE?

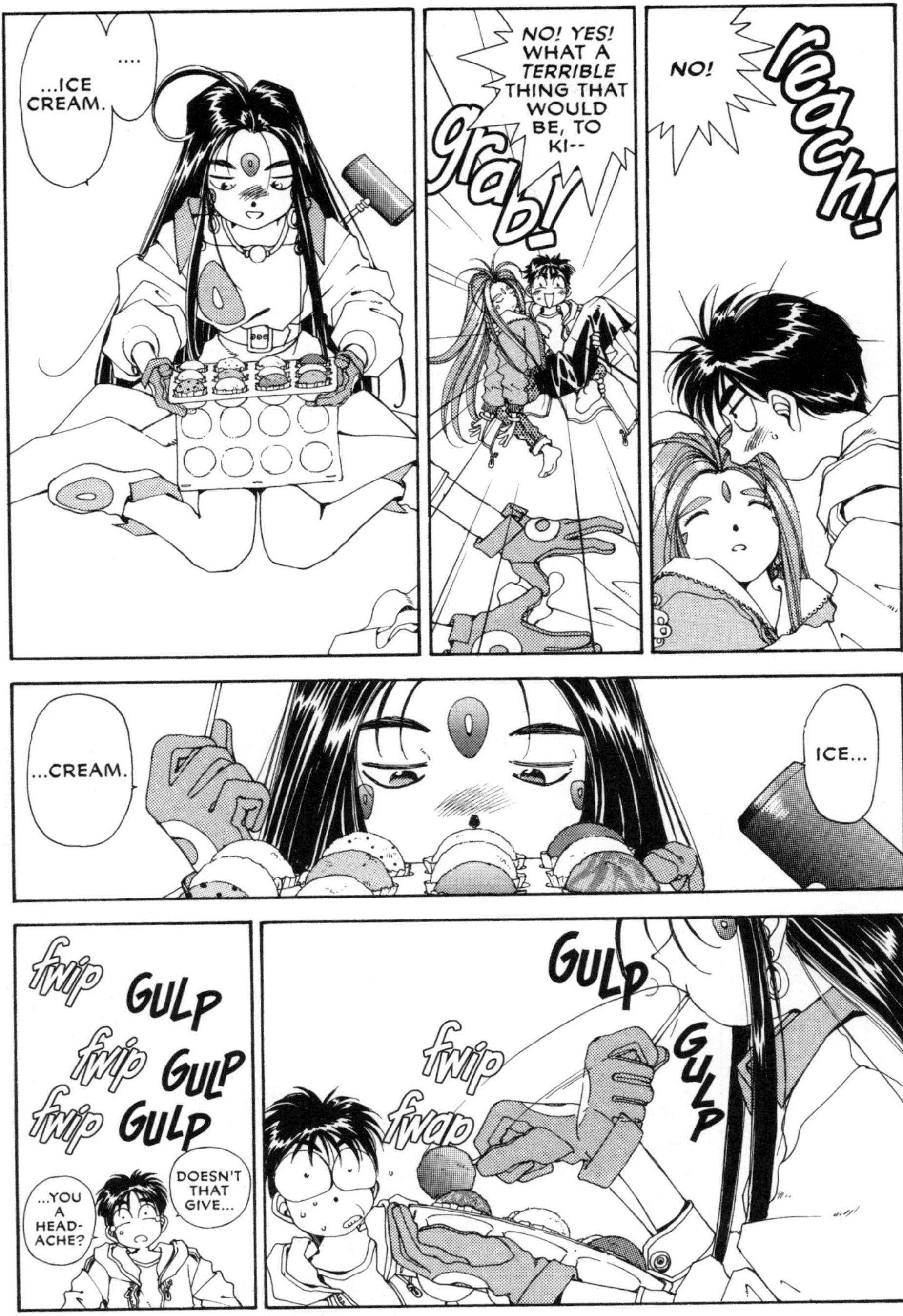
NO!
reach!
NO! YES! WHAT A TERRIBLE THING THAT WOULD BE, TO KI--
grab!
....
...ICE CREAM.
ICE...
...CREAM.
GULP
GULP
fwip
fwap
fwip GULP
fwip GULP
fwip GULP
DOESN'T THAT GIVE...
...YOU A HEAD-ACHE?

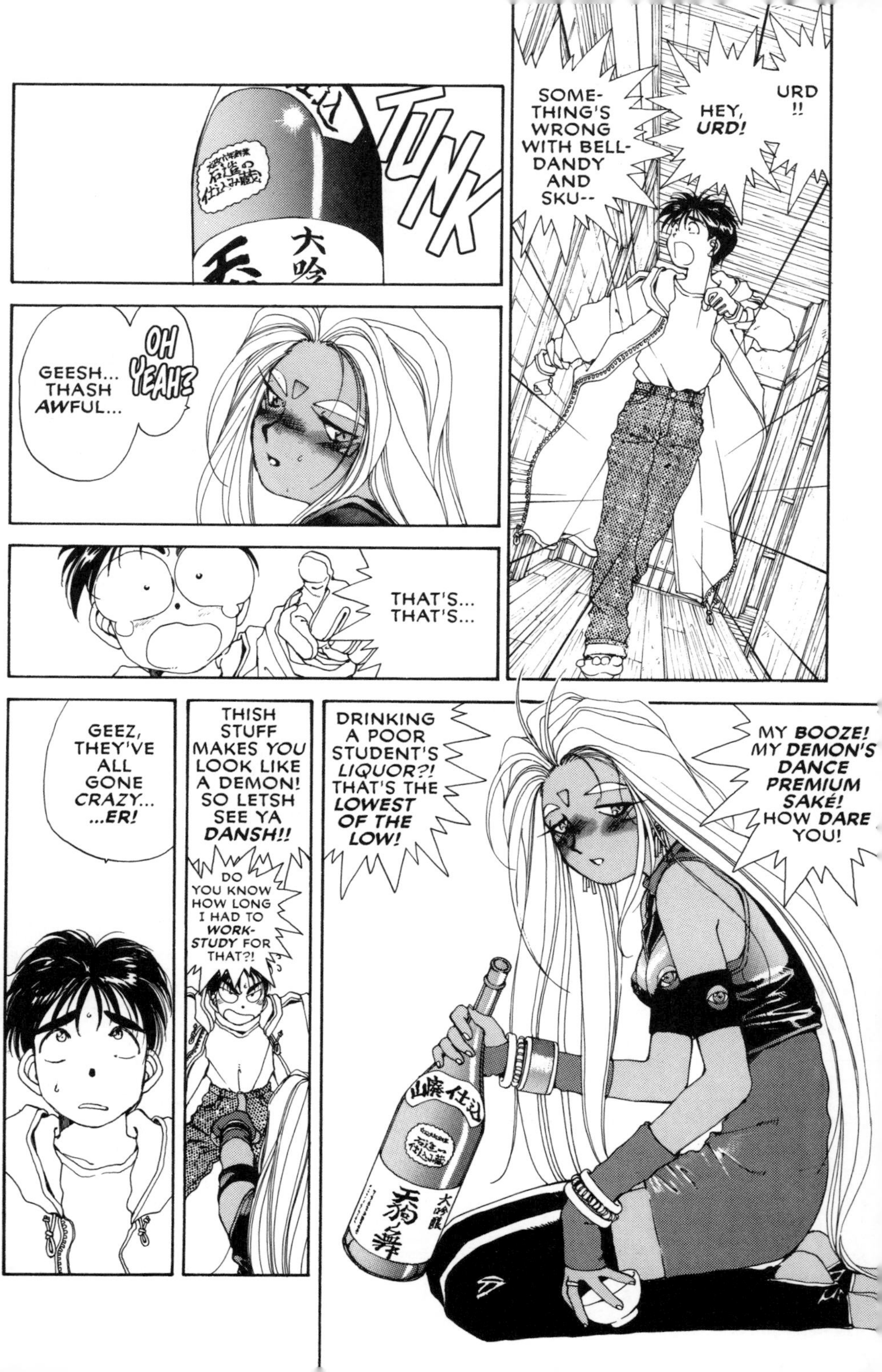
URD !!
HEY, URD!
SOME-THING'S WRONG WITH BELL-DANDY AND SKU--
TUNK
OH YEAH?
GEESH... THASH AWFUL...
THAT'S... THAT'S...
MY BOOZE! MY DEMON'S DANCE PREMIUM SAKÉ! HOW DARE YOU!
DRINKING A POOR STUDENT'S LIQUOR?! THAT'S THE LOWEST OF THE LOW!
THISH STUFF MAKES YOU LOOK LIKE A DEMON! SO LETSH SEE YA DANSH!!
DO YOU KNOW HOW LONG I HAD TO WORK-STUDY FOR THAT?!
GEEZ, THEY'VE ALL GONE CRAZY... ...ER!

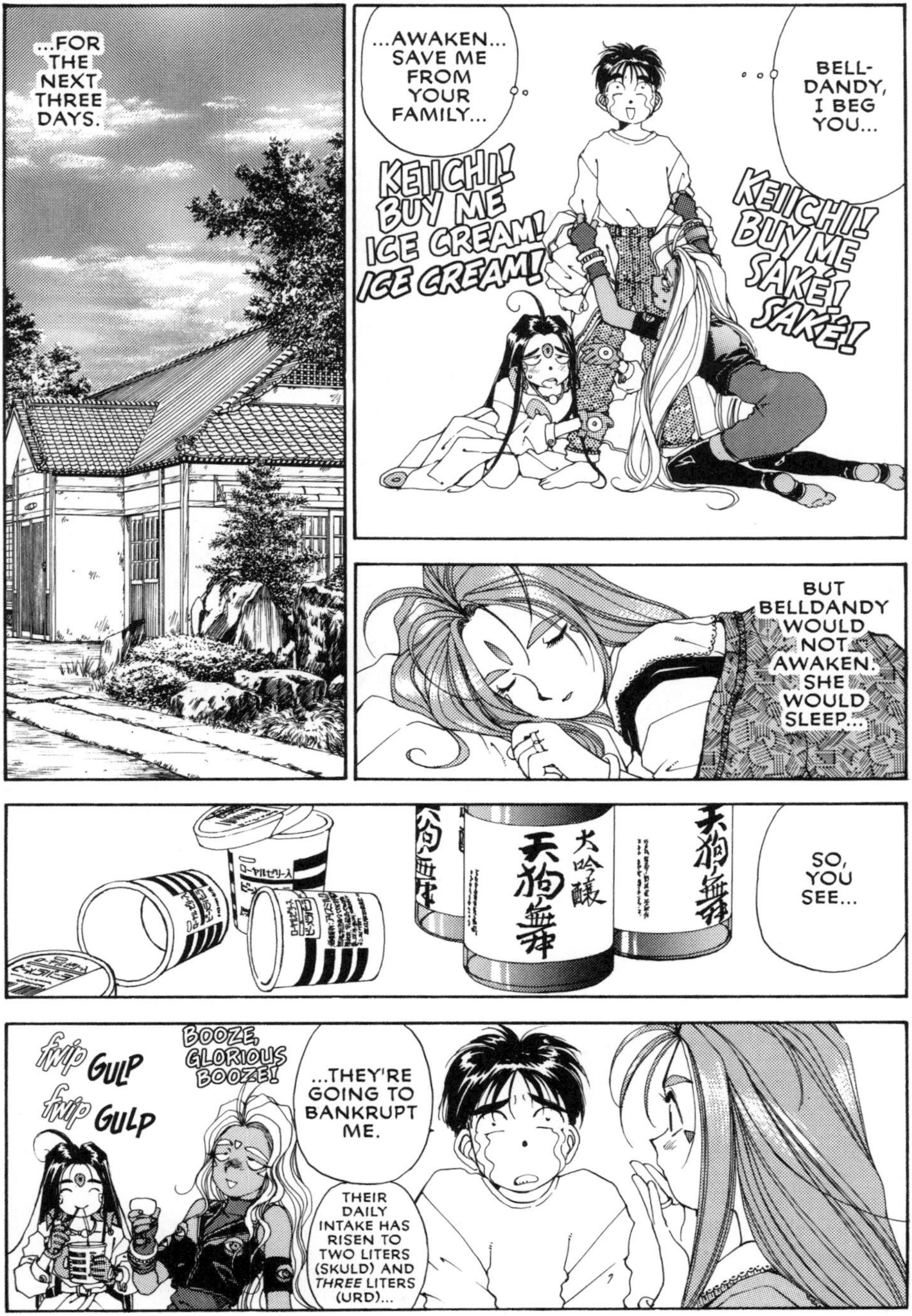

BELL-DANDY, I BEG YOU...
KEIICHI! BUY ME SAKÉ! SAKÉ!
...AWAKEN... SAVE ME FROM YOUR FAMILY...
KEIICHI! BUY ME ICE CREAM! ICE CREAM!
BUT BELLDANDY WOULD NOT AWAKEN. SHE WOULD SLEEP...
...FOR THE NEXT THREE DAYS.
SO, YOU SEE...
天狗舞
大吟醸
天狗舞
...THEY'RE GOING TO BANKRUPT ME.
THEIR DAILY INTAKE HAS RISEN TO TWO LITERS (SKULD) AND *THREE* LITERS (URD)...
BOOZE, GLORIOUS BOOZE!
fwip GULP
fwip GULP

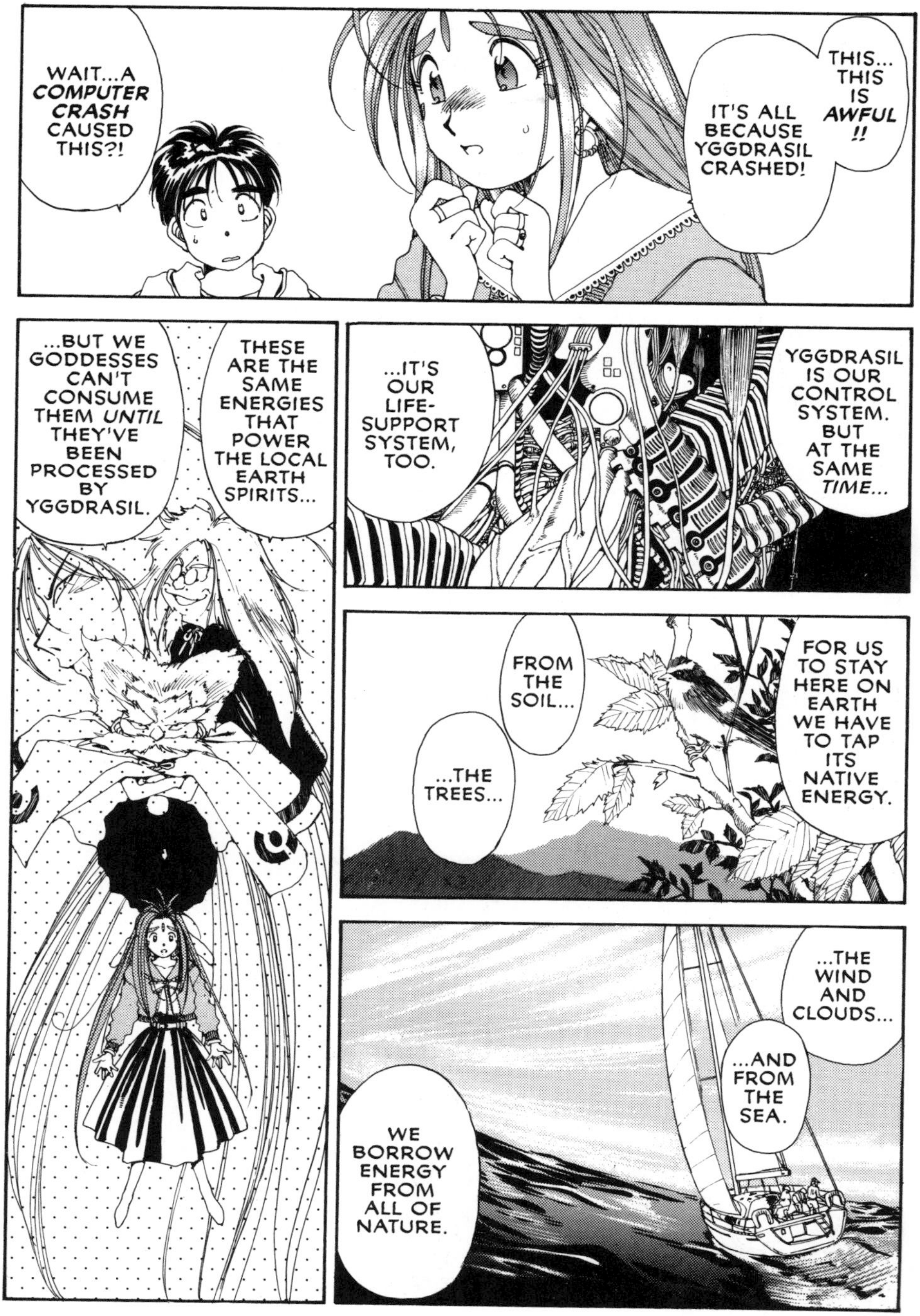
THIS... THIS IS *AWFUL* !!
IT'S ALL BECAUSE YGGDRASIL CRASHED!
WAIT...A *COMPUTER CRASH* CAUSED THIS?!
YGGDRASIL IS OUR CONTROL SYSTEM. BUT AT THE SAME *TIME*...
...IT'S OUR LIFE-SUPPORT SYSTEM, TOO.
FOR US TO STAY HERE ON EARTH WE HAVE TO TAP ITS NATIVE ENERGY.
FROM THE SOIL...
...THE TREES...
...THE WIND AND CLOUDS...
...AND FROM THE SEA.
WE BORROW ENERGY FROM ALL OF NATURE.
THESE ARE THE SAME ENERGIES THAT POWER THE LOCAL EARTH SPIRITS...
...BUT WE GODDESSES CAN'T CONSUME THEM *UNTIL* THEY'VE BEEN PROCESSED BY YGGDRASIL.

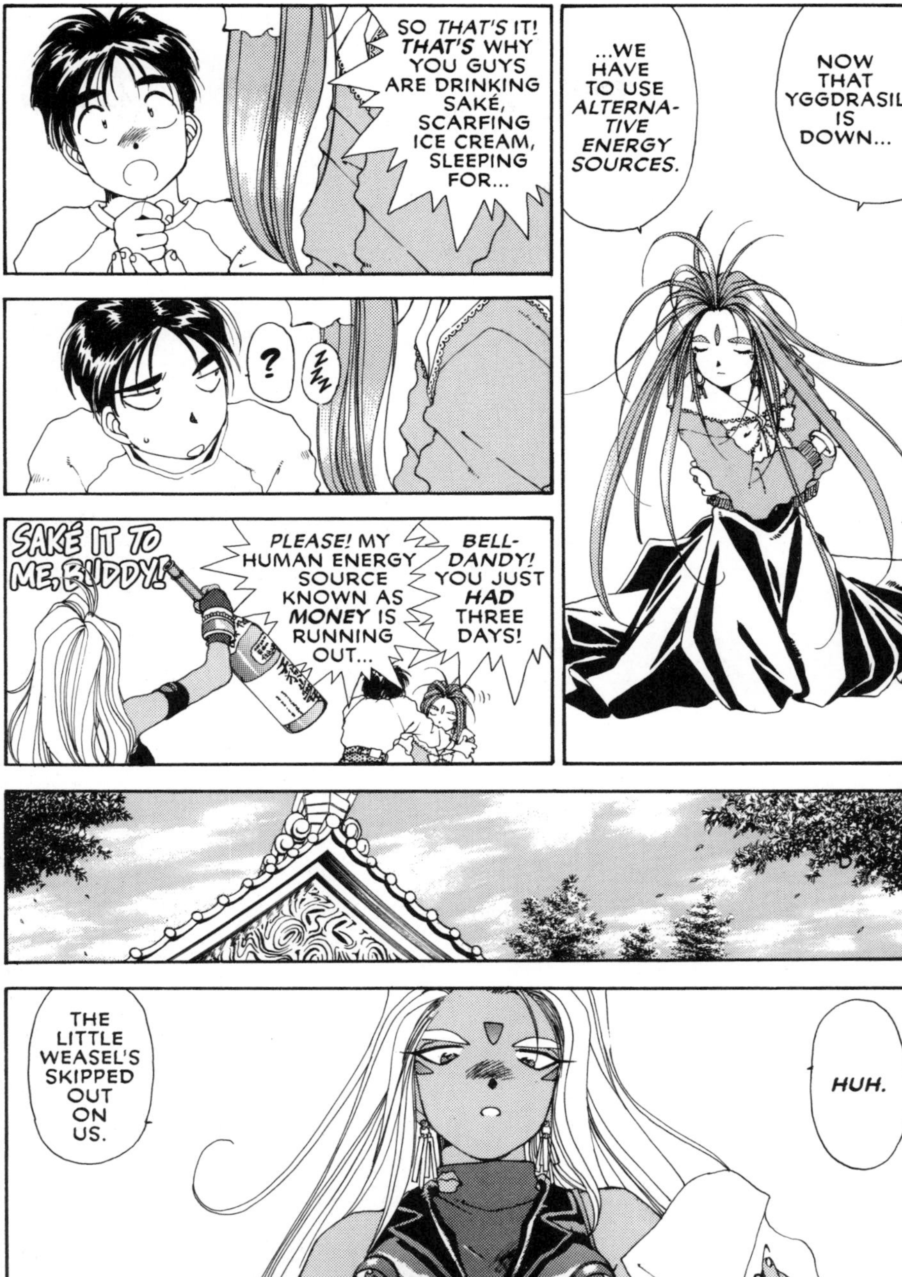
NOW THAT YGGDRASIL IS DOWN...
...WE HAVE TO USE ALTERNATIVE ENERGY SOURCES.
SO THAT'S IT! THAT'S WHY YOU GUYS ARE DRINKING SAKÉ, SCARFING ICE CREAM, SLEEPING FOR...
ZZZ
?
BELL-DANDY! YOU JUST HAD THREE DAYS!
PLEASE! MY HUMAN ENERGY SOURCE KNOWN AS MONEY IS RUNNING OUT...
SAKÉ IT TO ME, BUDDY!
HUH.
THE LITTLE WEASEL'S SKIPPED OUT ON US.

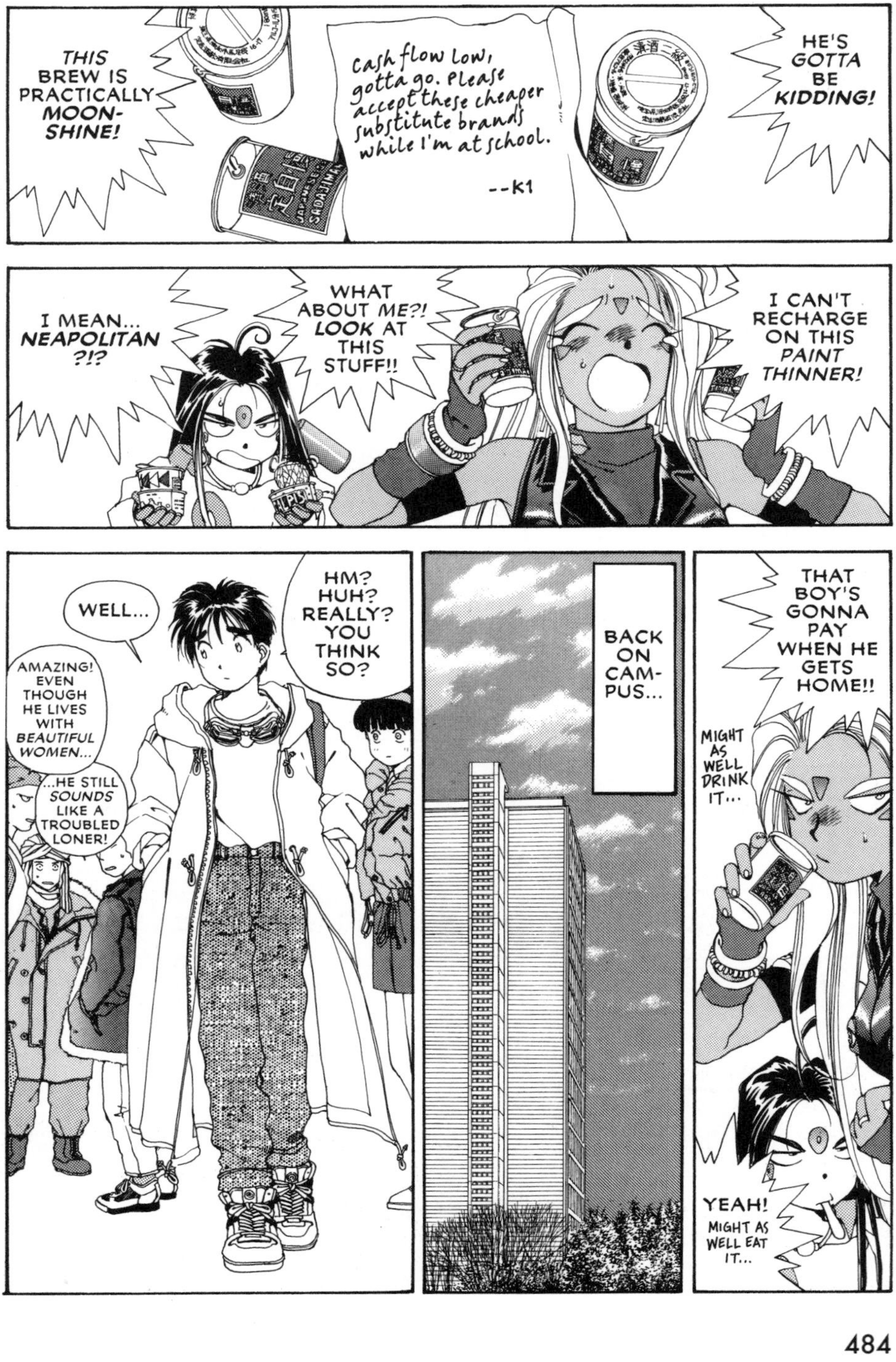
HE'S GOTTA BE KIDDING!
Cash flow low, gotta go. Please accept these cheaper substitute brands while I'm at school.
--K1
THIS BREW IS PRACTICALLY MOON-SHINE!
I CAN'T RECHARGE ON THIS PAINT THINNER!
WHAT ABOUT ME?! LOOK AT THIS STUFF!!
I MEAN... NEAPOLITAN?!?
THAT BOY'S GONNA PAY WHEN HE GETS HOME!!
MIGHT AS WELL DRINK IT...
YEAH! MIGHT AS WELL EAT IT...
BACK ON CAM-PUS...
HM? HUH? REALLY? YOU THINK SO?
WELL...
AMAZING! EVEN THOUGH HE LIVES WITH BEAUTIFUL WOMEN...
...HE STILL SOUNDS LIKE A TROUBLED LONER!

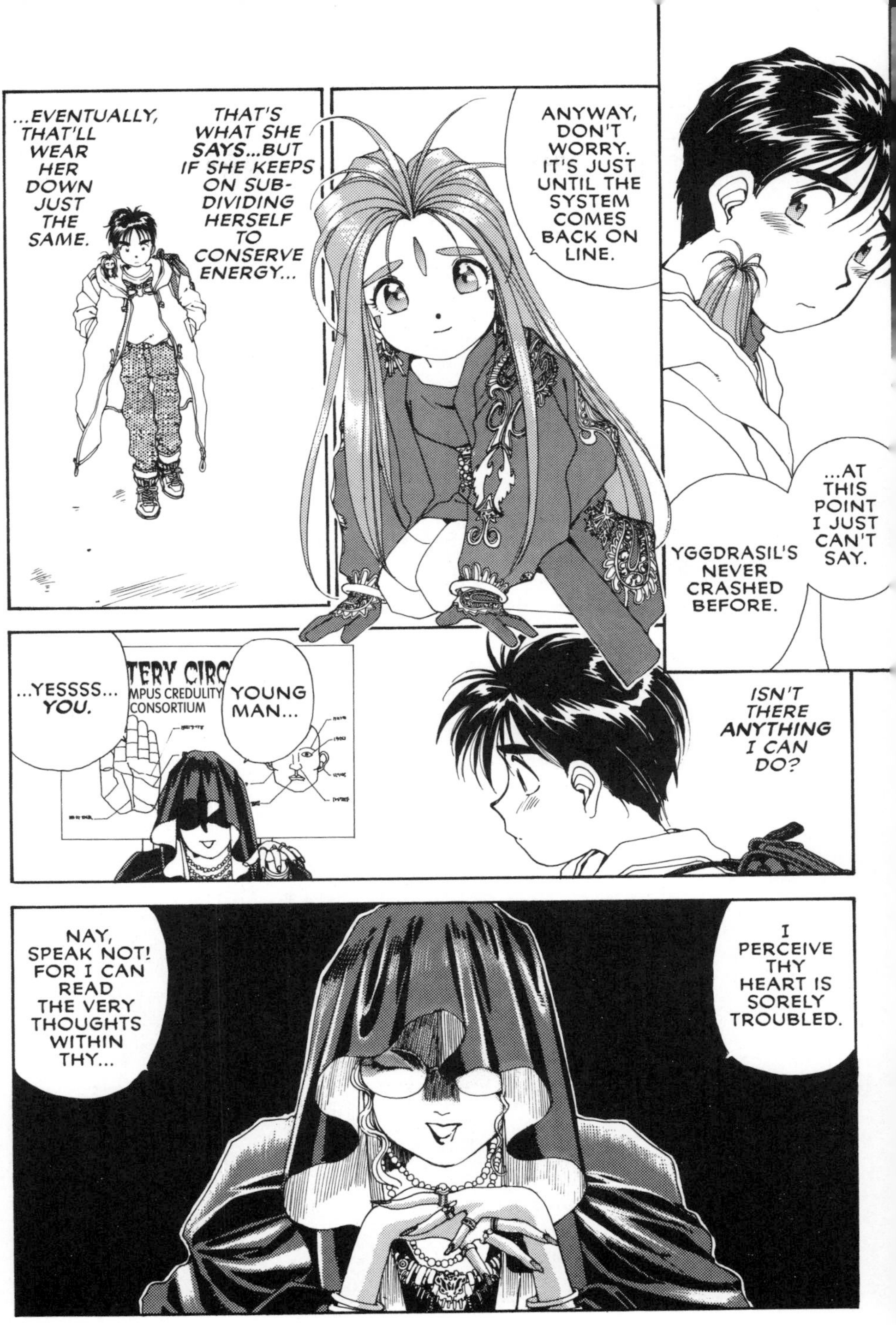
...AT THIS POINT I JUST CAN'T SAY.
YGGDRASIL'S NEVER CRASHED BEFORE.
ANYWAY, DON'T WORRY. IT'S JUST UNTIL THE SYSTEM COMES BACK ON LINE.
THAT'S WHAT SHE **SAYS**...BUT IF SHE KEEPS ON SUB-DIVIDING HERSELF TO CONSERVE ENERGY...
...EVENTUALLY, THAT'LL WEAR HER DOWN JUST THE SAME.
ISN'T THERE **ANYTHING** I CAN DO?
YOUNG MAN...
...YESSSS... **YOU.**
I PERCEIVE THY HEART IS SORELY TROUBLED.
NAY, SPEAK NOT! FOR I CAN READ THE VERY THOUGHTS WITHIN THY...

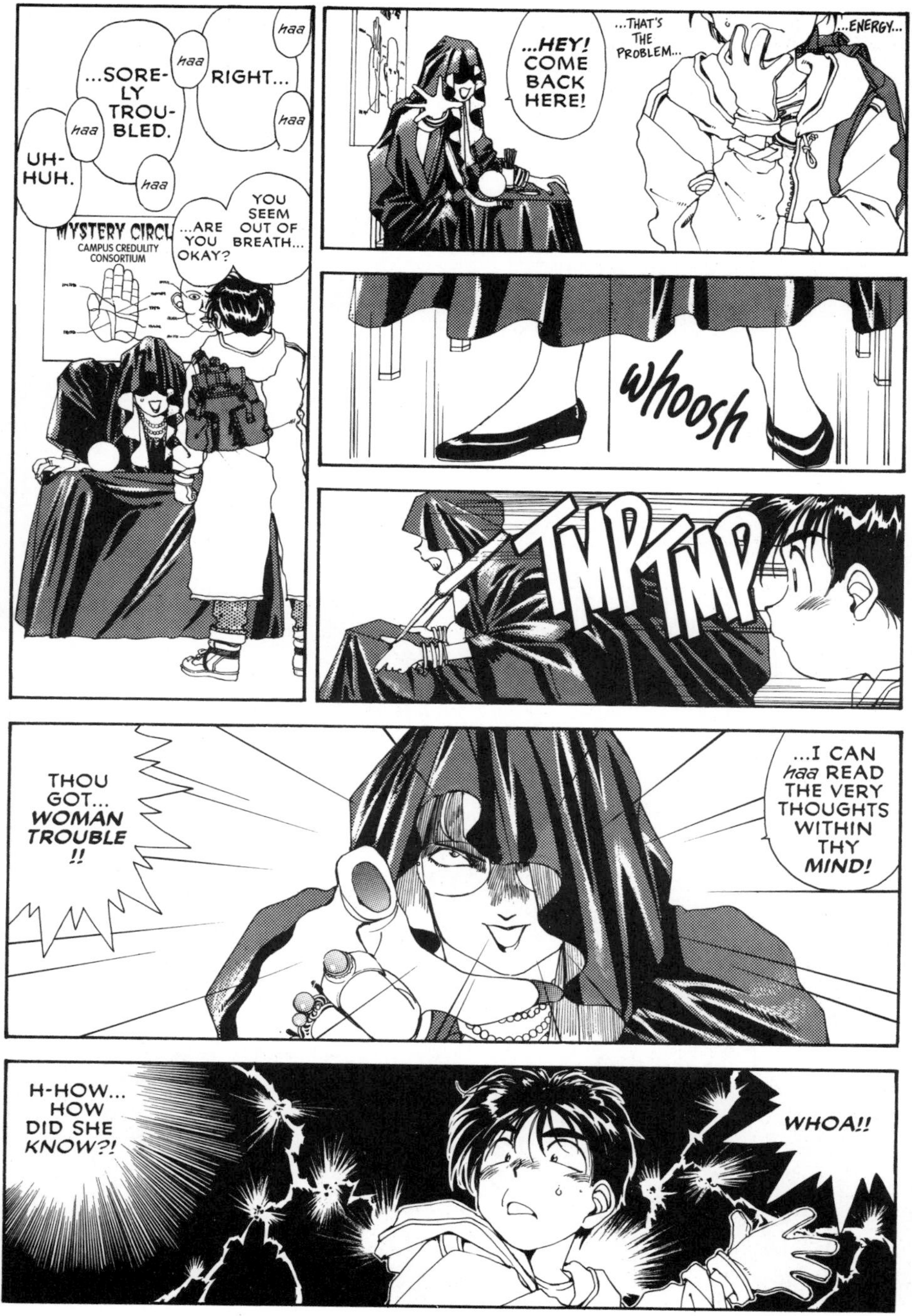
...ENERGY...
...THAT'S THE PROBLEM...
...HEY! COME BACK HERE!
whoosh
TMP TMP
haa
haa
RIGHT...
haa
...SORELY TROUBLED.
haa
UH-HUH.
haa
haa
YOU SEEM OUT OF BREATH...
...ARE YOU OKAY?
MYSTERY CIRCLE
CAMPUS CREDULITY CONSORTIUM
...I CAN haa READ THE VERY THOUGHTS WITHIN THY MIND!
THOU GOT... WOMAN TROUBLE!!
WHOA!!
H-HOW... HOW DID SHE KNOW?!

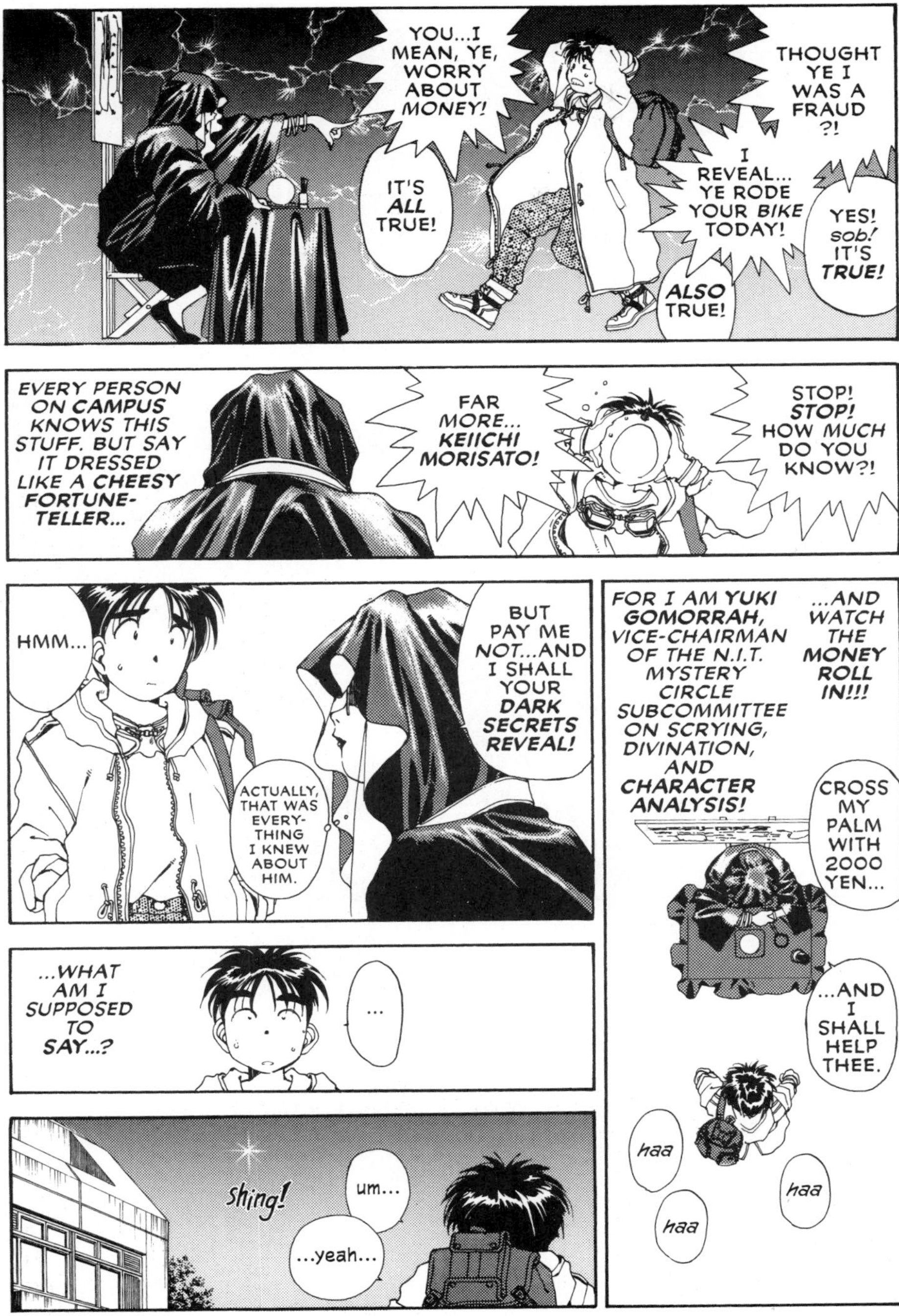
THOUGHT YE I WAS A FRAUD?!
YES! sob! IT'S TRUE!
YOU...I MEAN, YE, WORRY ABOUT MONEY!
I REVEAL... YE RODE YOUR BIKE TODAY!
ALSO TRUE!
IT'S ALL TRUE!
STOP! STOP! HOW MUCH DO YOU KNOW?!
FAR MORE... KEIICHI MORISATO!
EVERY PERSON ON CAMPUS KNOWS THIS STUFF. BUT SAY IT DRESSED LIKE A CHEESY FORTUNE-TELLER...
FOR I AM YUKI GOMORRAH, VICE-CHAIRMAN OF THE N.I.T. MYSTERY CIRCLE SUBCOMMITTEE ON SCRYING, DIVINATION, AND CHARACTER ANALYSIS!
...AND WATCH THE MONEY ROLL IN!!!
CROSS MY PALM WITH 2000 YEN...
...AND I SHALL HELP THEE.
haa
haa
haa
BUT PAY ME NOT...AND I SHALL YOUR DARK SECRETS REVEAL!
HMM...
ACTUALLY, THAT WAS EVERY-THING I KNEW ABOUT HIM.
...
...WHAT AM I SUPPOSED TO SAY...?
um...
Shing!
...yeah...

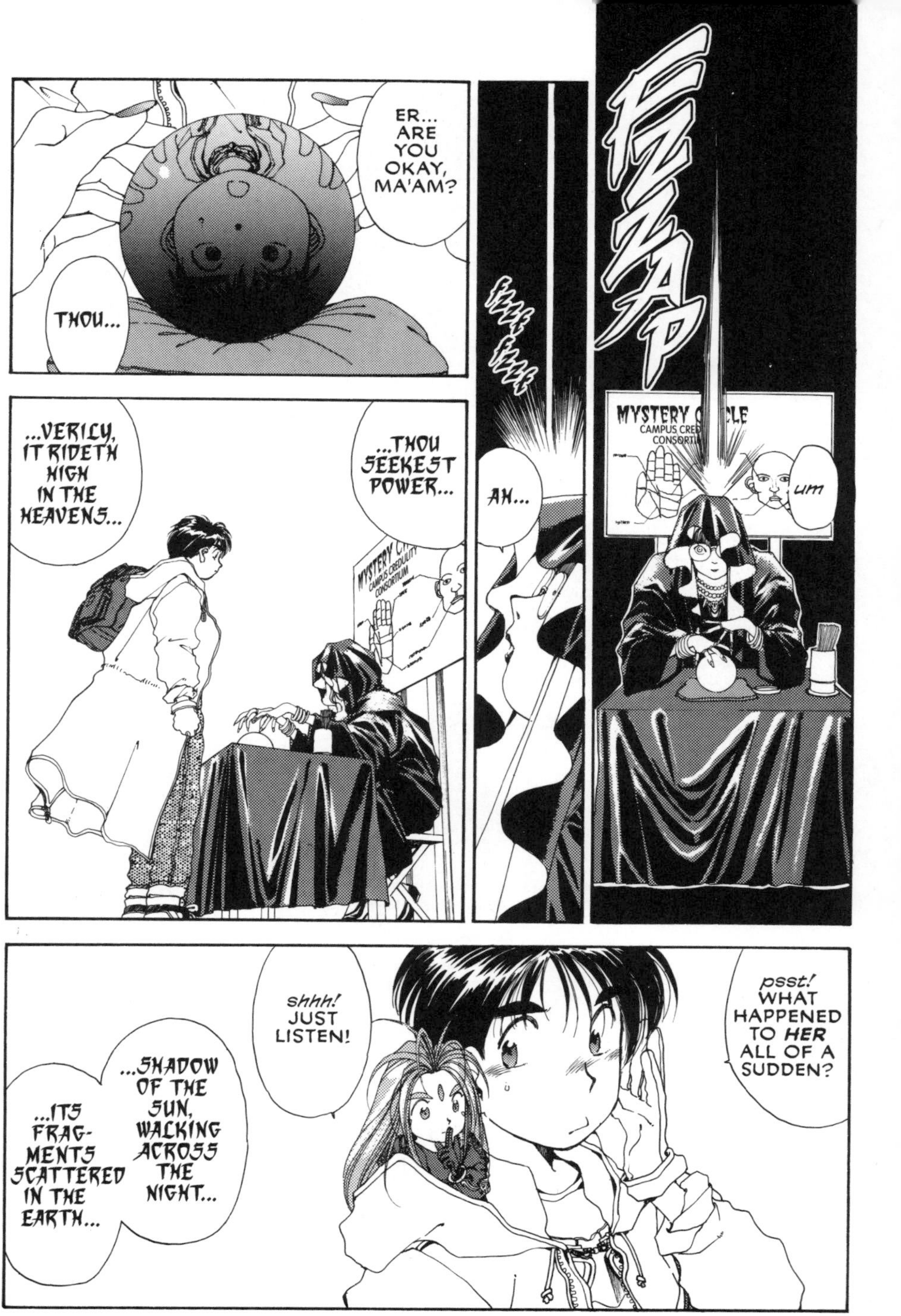
FZZAP
um
AH...
ER... ARE YOU OKAY, MA'AM?
THOU...
...THOU SEEKEST POWER...
...VERILY, IT RIDETH HIGH IN THE HEAVENS...
MYSTERY CIRCLE
CAMPUS CREDULITY CONSORTIUM
*psst!* WHAT HAPPENED TO ***HER*** ALL OF A SUDDEN?
*shhh!* JUST LISTEN!
...SHADOW OF THE SUN, WALKING ACROSS THE NIGHT...
...ITS FRAGMENTS SCATTERED IN THE EARTH...

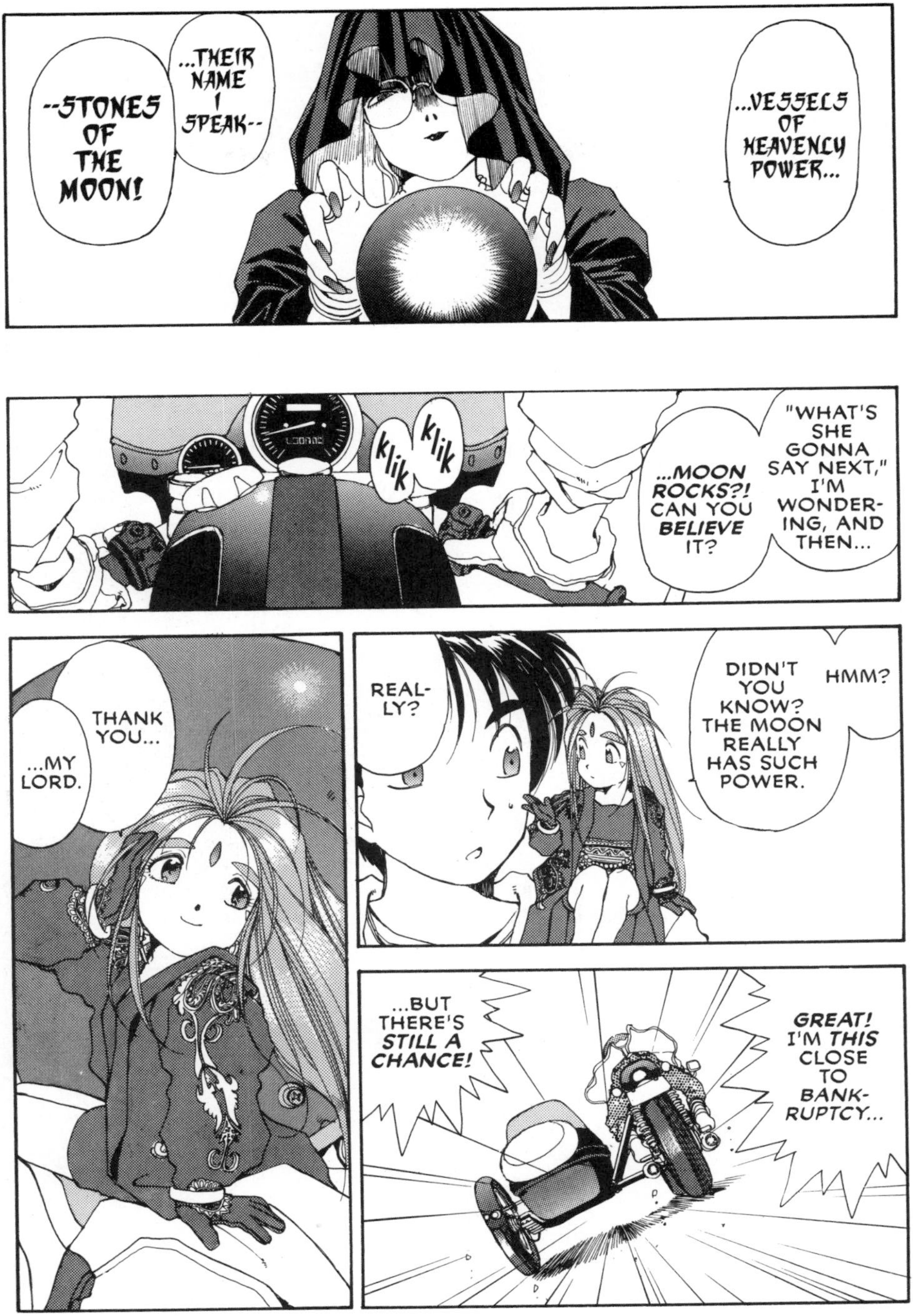
...VESSELS OF HEAVENLY POWER...
...THEIR NAME I SPEAK--
--STONES OF THE MOON!
"WHAT'S SHE GONNA SAY NEXT," I'M WONDERING, AND THEN...
...MOON ROCKS?! CAN YOU *BELIEVE* IT?
klik klik
HMM?
DIDN'T YOU KNOW? THE MOON REALLY HAS SUCH POWER.
REAL-LY?
*GREAT!* I'M *THIS* CLOSE TO BANK-RUPTCY...
...BUT THERE'S *STILL A CHANCE!*
THANK YOU...
...MY LORD.

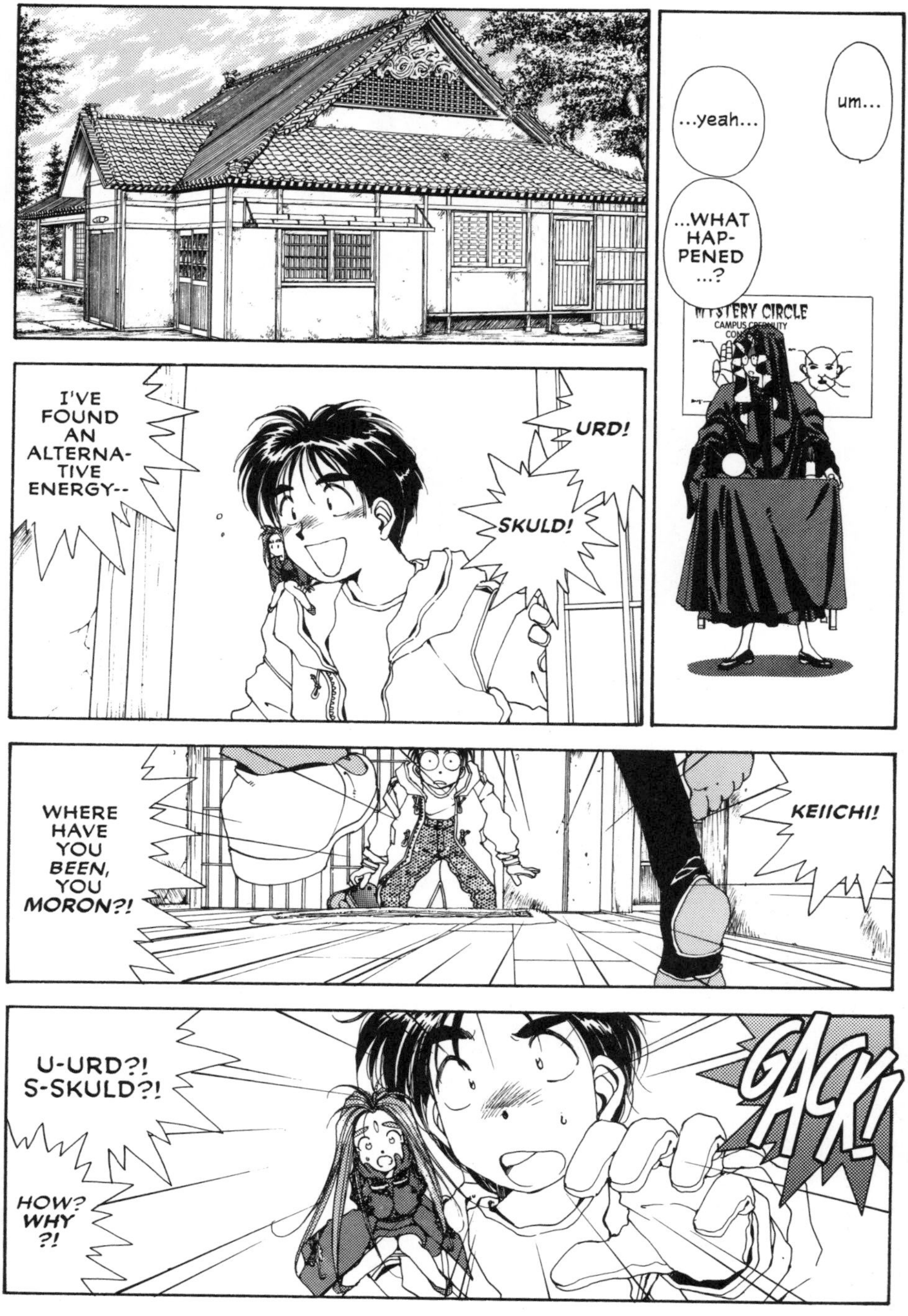
um...
...yeah...
...WHAT HAPPENED ...?
MYSTERY CIRCLE
URD!
SKULD!
I'VE FOUND AN ALTERNATIVE ENERGY--
KEIICHI!
WHERE HAVE YOU *BEEN*, YOU *MORON*?!
GACK!
U-URD?! S-SKULD?!
*HOW? WHY?!*

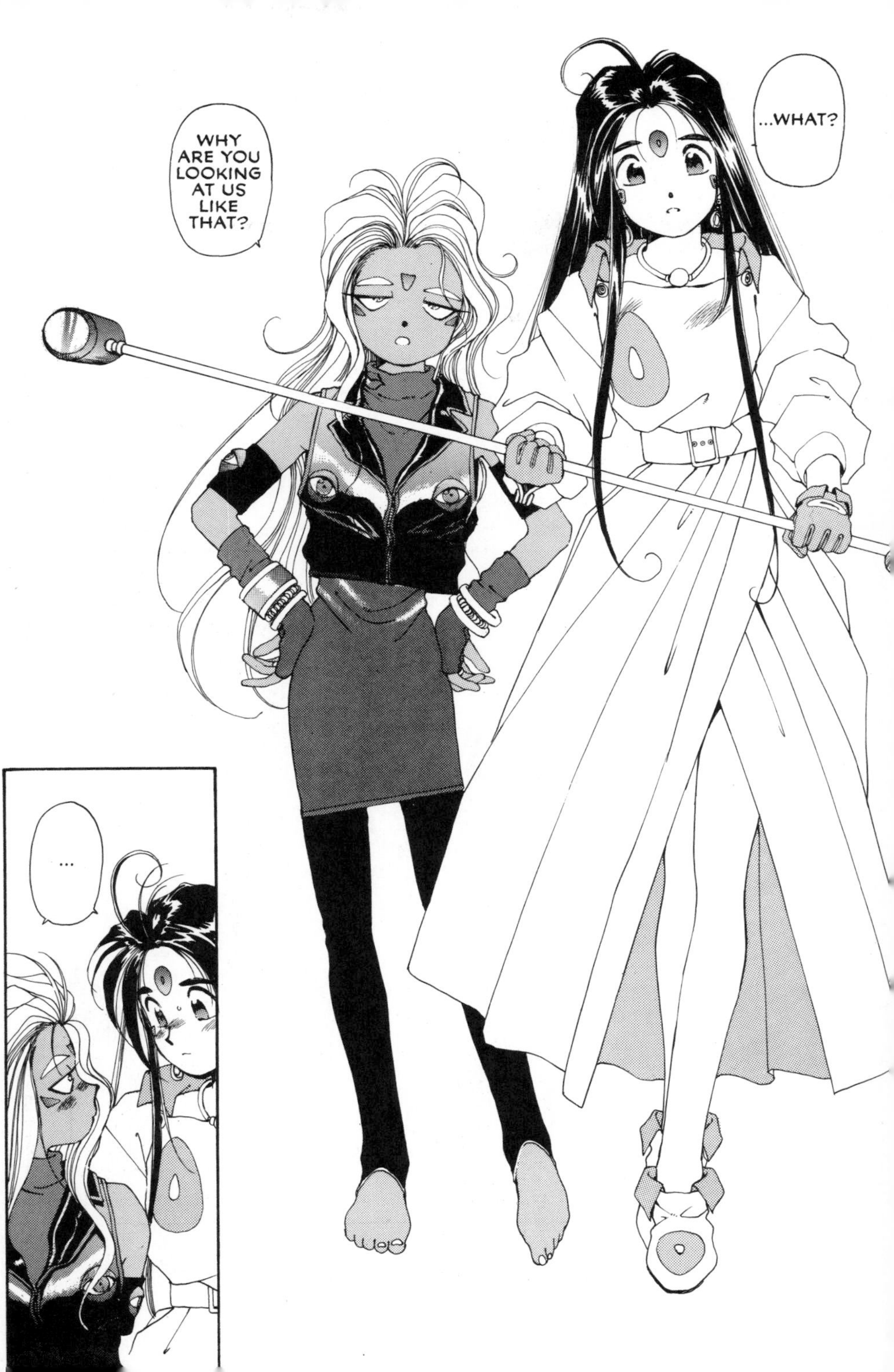
...WHAT?
WHY ARE YOU LOOKING AT US LIKE THAT?
...

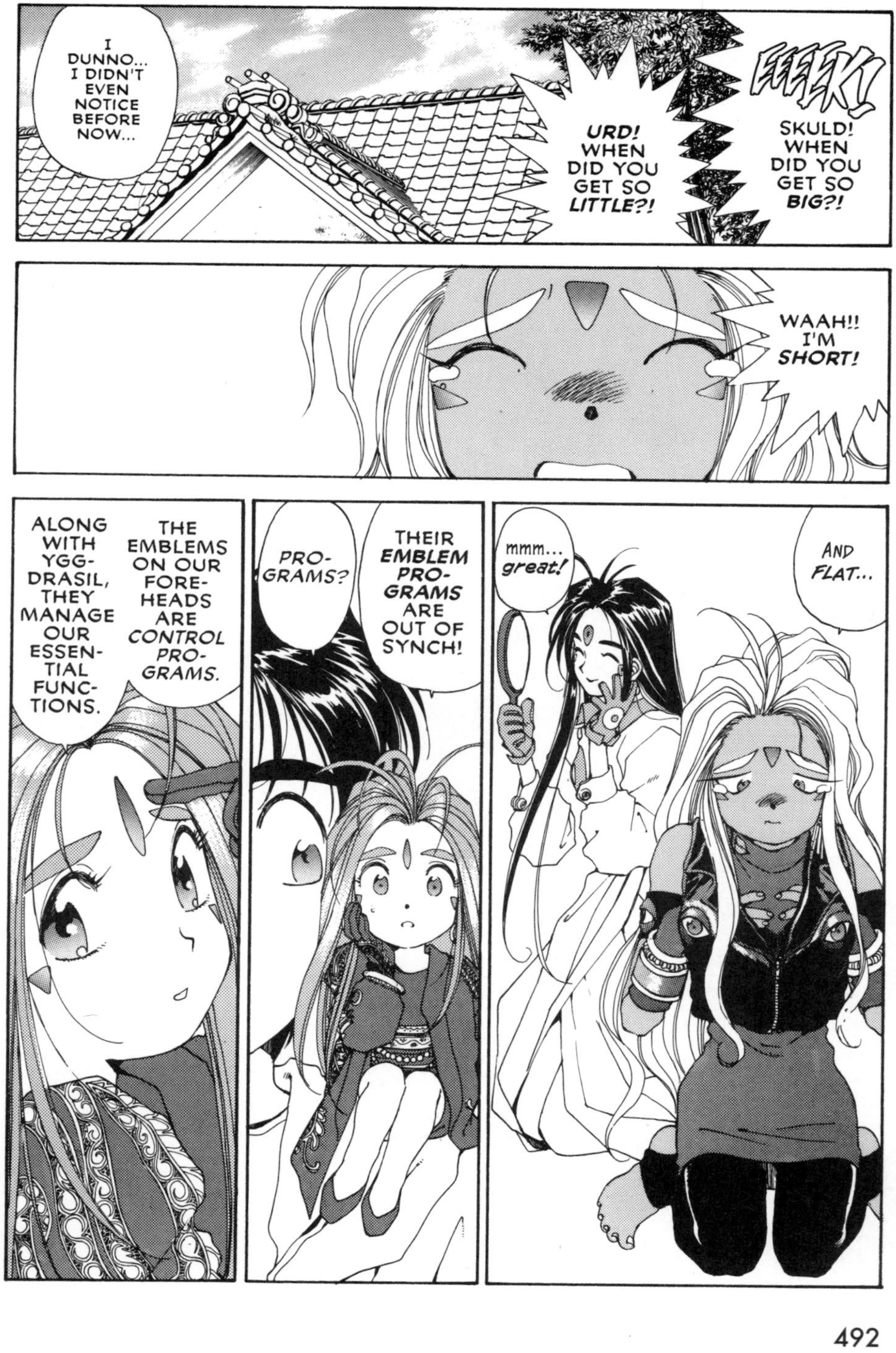
EEEEK!
SKULD! WHEN DID YOU GET SO *BIG?!*
*URD!* WHEN DID YOU GET SO *LITTLE?!*
I DUNNO... I DIDN'T EVEN NOTICE BEFORE NOW...
WAAH!! I'M *SHORT!*
AND *FLAT*...
*mmm... great!*
THEIR *EMBLEM PROGRAMS* ARE OUT OF SYNCH!
*PROGRAMS?*
THE EMBLEMS ON OUR FOREHEADS ARE *CONTROL PROGRAMS.*
ALONG WITH YGGDRASIL, THEY MANAGE OUR ESSENTIAL FUNCTIONS.

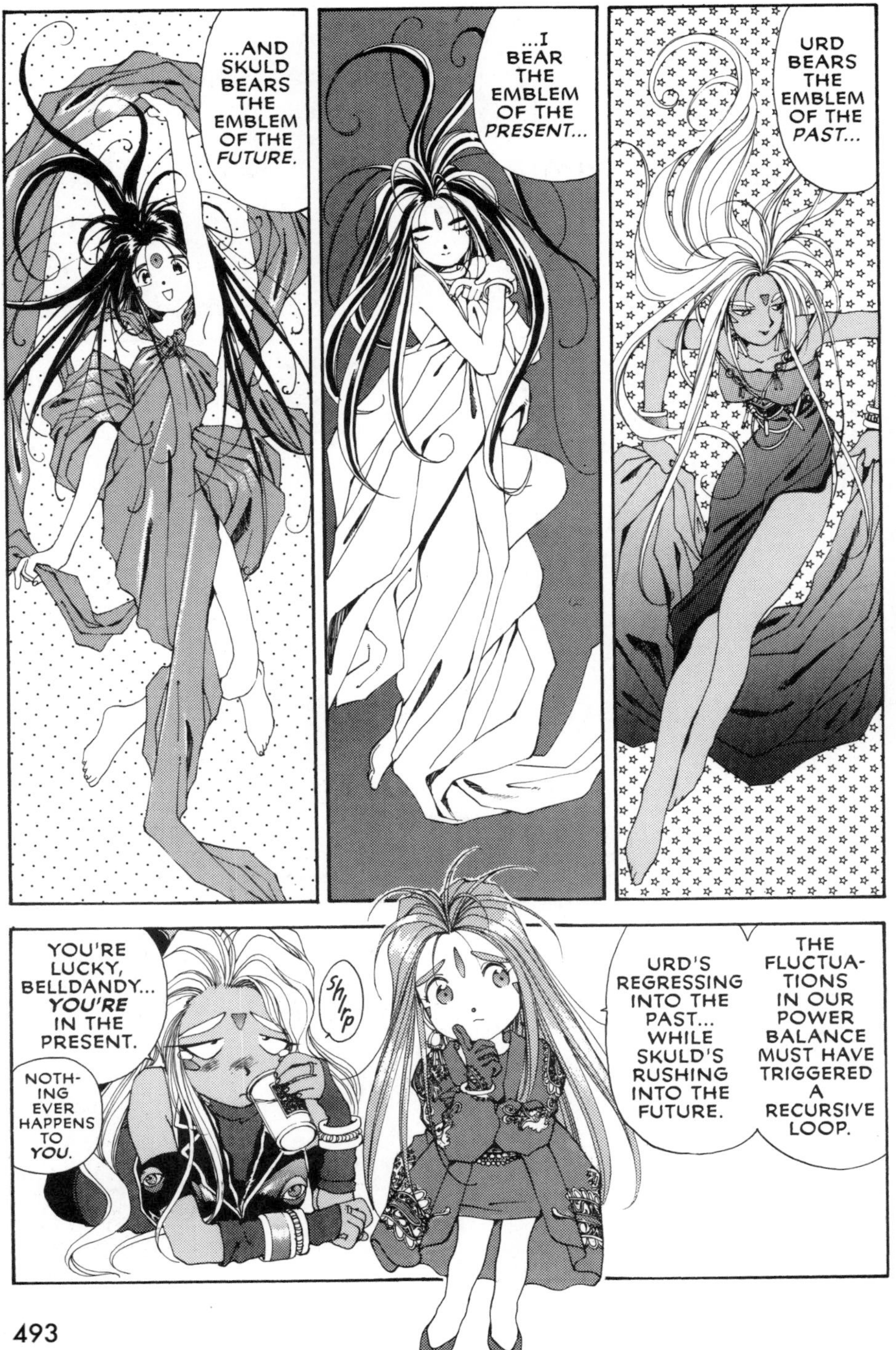
URD BEARS THE EMBLEM OF THE *PAST*...
...I BEAR THE EMBLEM OF THE *PRESENT*...
...AND SKULD BEARS THE EMBLEM OF THE *FUTURE*.
THE FLUCTUATIONS IN OUR POWER BALANCE MUST HAVE TRIGGERED A RECURSIVE LOOP.
URD'S REGRESSING INTO THE PAST... WHILE SKULD'S RUSHING INTO THE FUTURE.
Shlrp
YOU'RE LUCKY, BELLDANDY... ***YOU'RE*** IN THE PRESENT.
NOTHING EVER HAPPENS TO *YOU*.

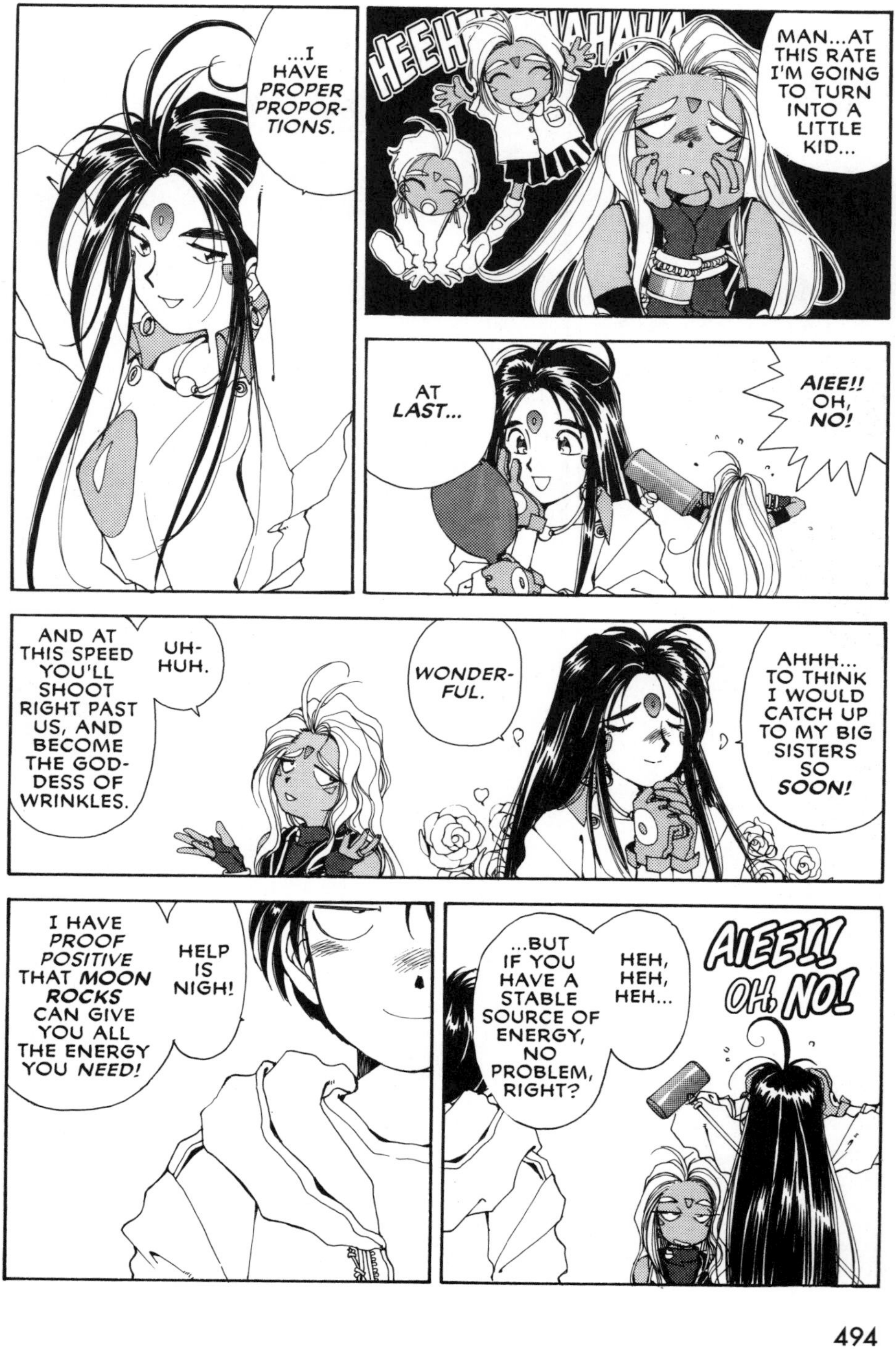
MAN...AT THIS RATE I'M GOING TO TURN INTO A LITTLE KID...
AIEE!! OH, NO!
AT LAST...
...I HAVE PROPER PROPORTIONS.
AHHH... TO THINK I WOULD CATCH UP TO MY BIG SISTERS SO SOON!
WONDERFUL.
UH-HUH.
AND AT THIS SPEED YOU'LL SHOOT RIGHT PAST US, AND BECOME THE GODDESS OF WRINKLES.
AIEE!! OH, NO!
HEH, HEH, HEH...
...BUT IF YOU HAVE A STABLE SOURCE OF ENERGY, NO PROBLEM, RIGHT?
HELP IS NIGH!
I HAVE PROOF POSITIVE THAT MOON ROCKS CAN GIVE YOU ALL THE ENERGY YOU NEED!

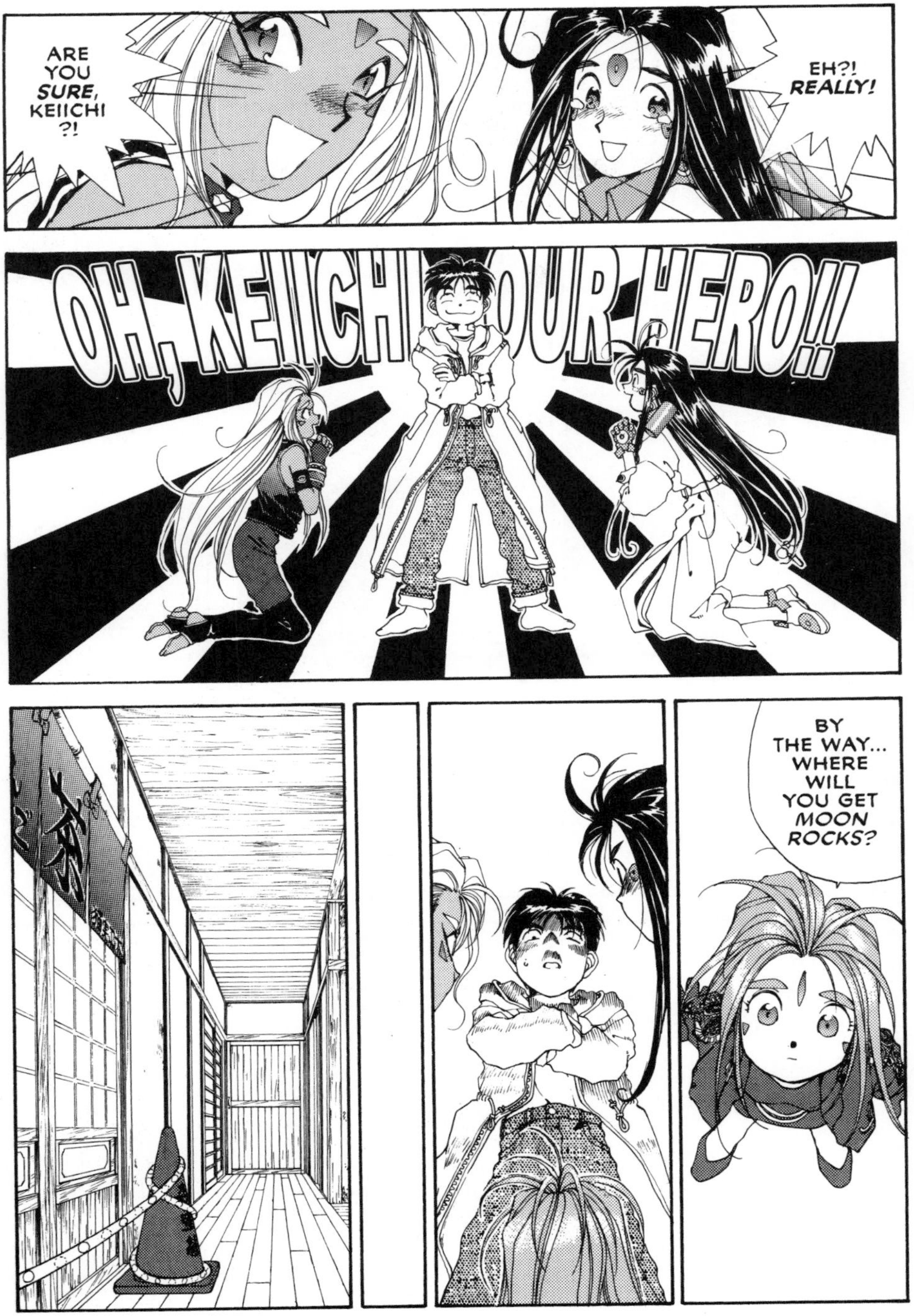
EH?! REALLY!
ARE YOU SURE, KEIICHI?!
OH, KEIICHI, OUR HERO!!
BY THE WAY... WHERE WILL YOU GET MOON ROCKS?

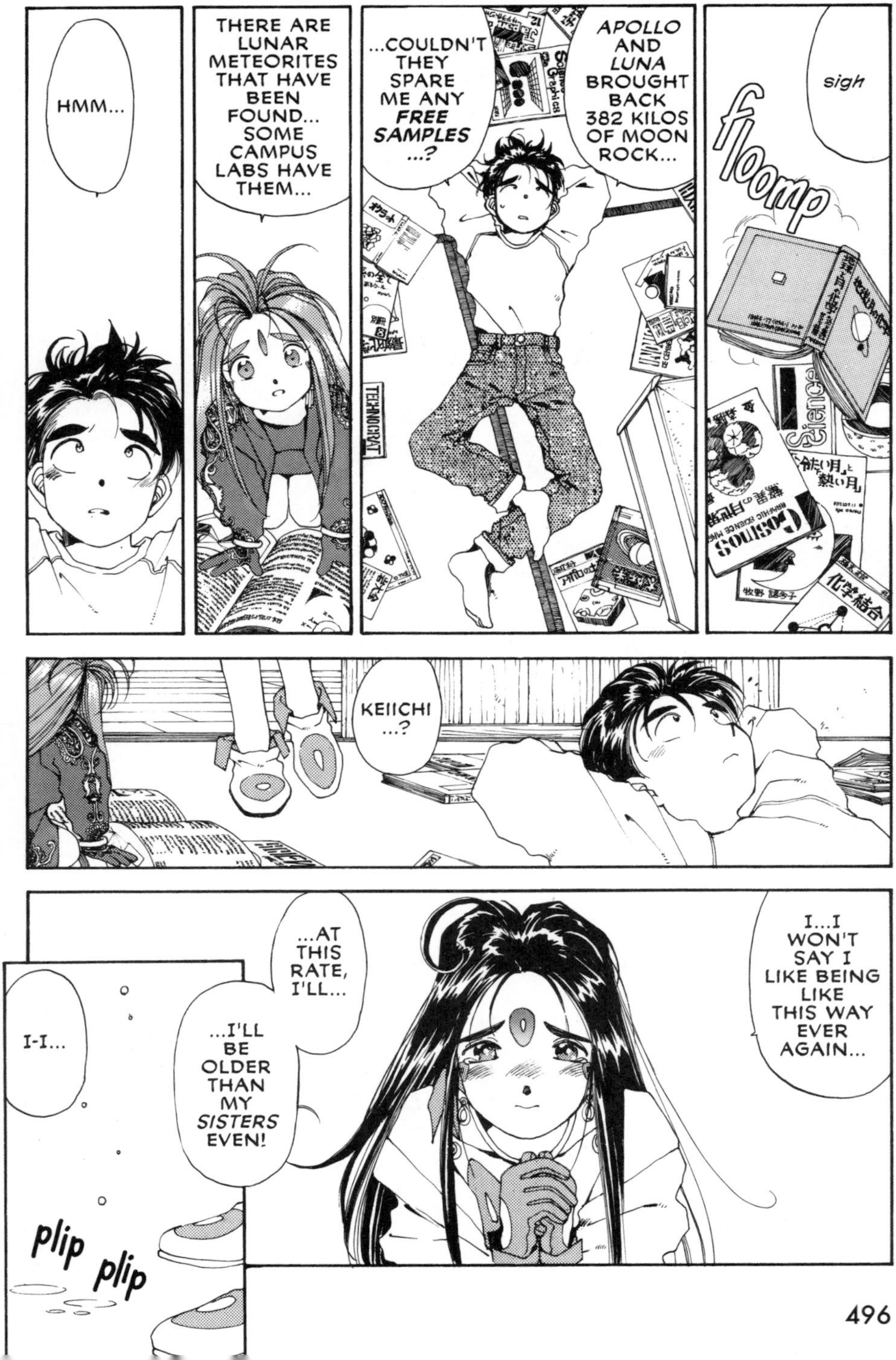
sigh
floomp
APOLLO AND LUNA BROUGHT BACK 382 KILOS OF MOON ROCK...
...COULDN'T THEY SPARE ME ANY FREE SAMPLES ...?
THERE ARE LUNAR METEORITES THAT HAVE BEEN FOUND... SOME CAMPUS LABS HAVE THEM...
HMM...
KEIICHI ...?
I...I WON'T SAY I LIKE BEING LIKE THIS WAY EVER AGAIN...
...AT THIS RATE, I'LL...
...I'LL BE OLDER THAN MY SISTERS EVEN!
I-I...
plip plip

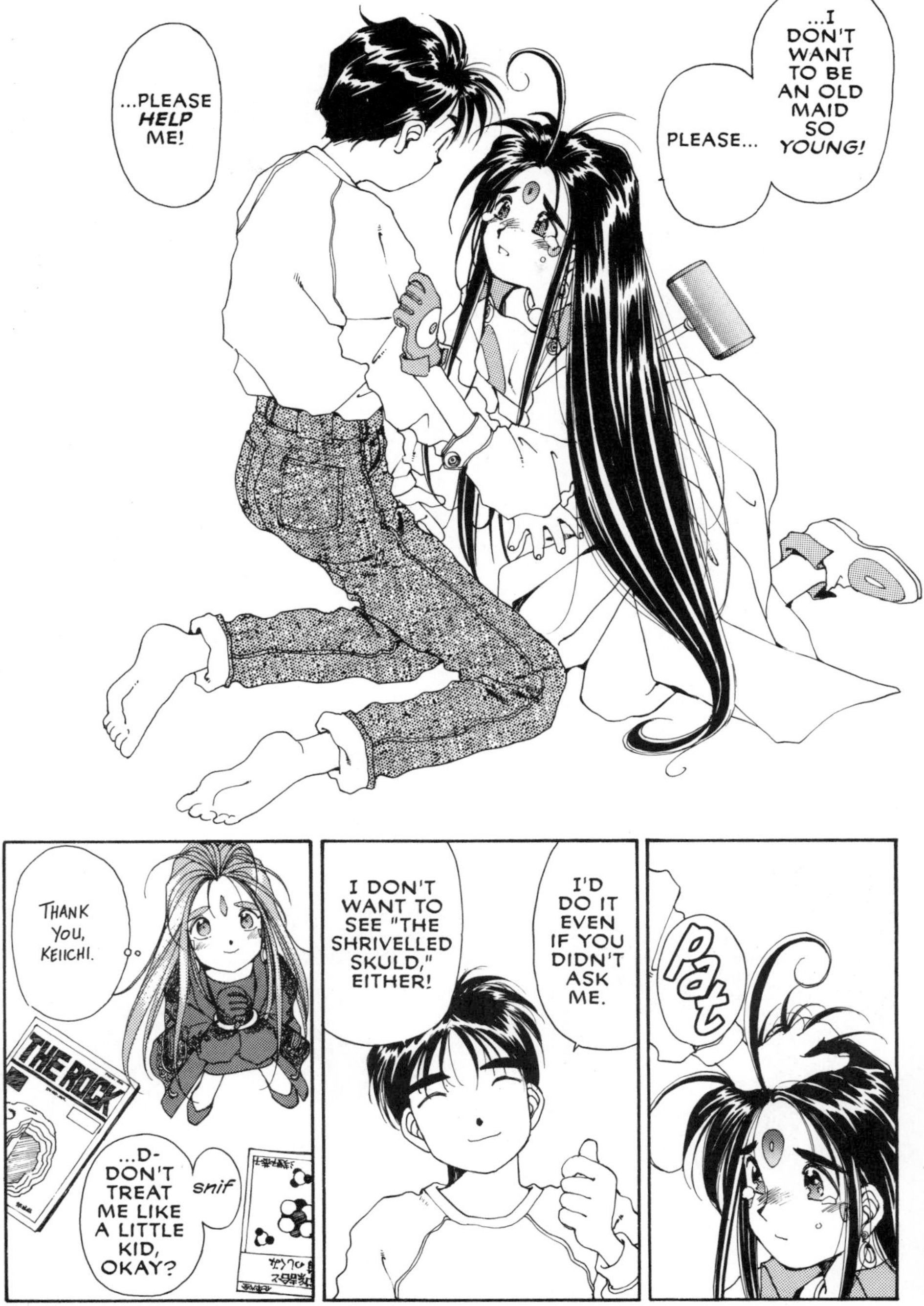
...I DON'T WANT TO BE AN OLD MAID SO *YOUNG!*
PLEASE...
...PLEASE ***HELP*** ME!
*Pat*
I'D DO IT EVEN IF YOU DIDN'T ASK ME.
I DON'T WANT TO SEE "THE SHRIVELLED SKULD," EITHER!
THANK YOU, KEIICHI.
THE ROCK
...D-DON'T TREAT ME LIKE A LITTLE KID, OKAY?
*snif*

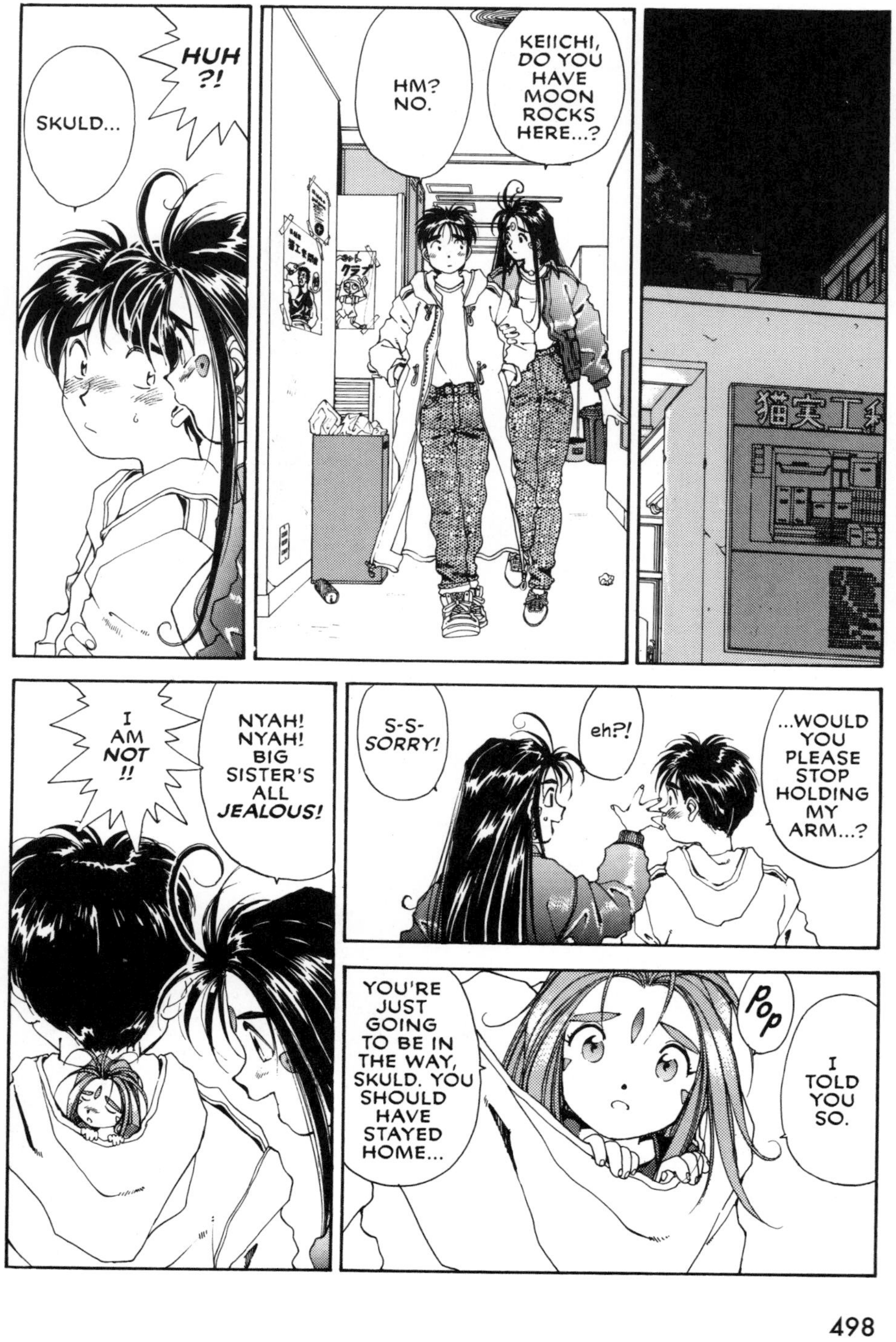
猫実工
KEIICHI, DO YOU HAVE MOON ROCKS HERE...?
HM? NO.
HUH?!
SKULD...
...WOULD YOU PLEASE STOP HOLDING MY ARM...?
eh?!
S-S-SORRY!
I TOLD YOU SO.
Pop
YOU'RE JUST GOING TO BE IN THE WAY, SKULD. YOU SHOULD HAVE STAYED HOME...
NYAH! NYAH! BIG SISTER'S ALL JEALOUS!
I AM NOT!!

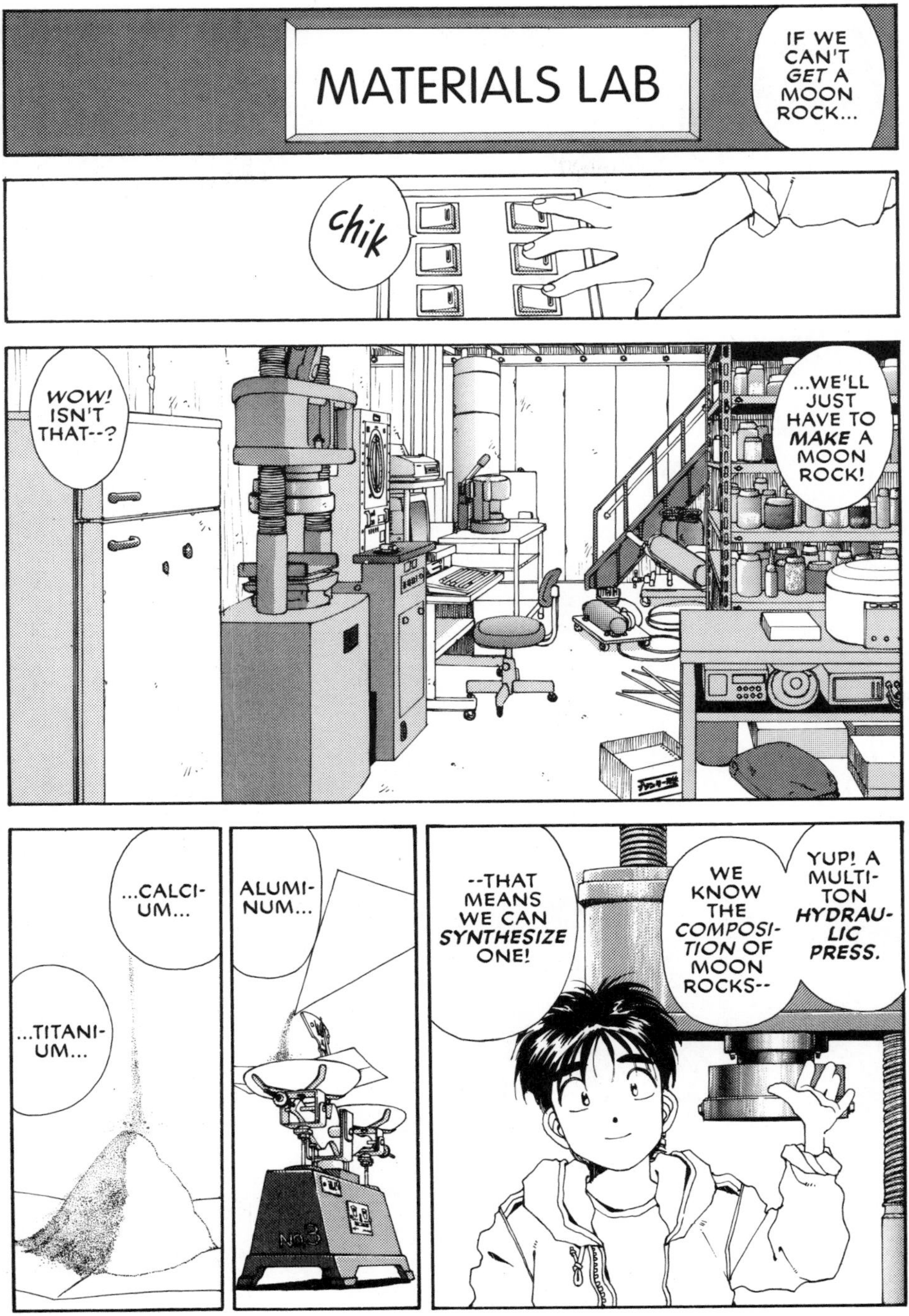
IF WE CAN'T *GET* A MOON ROCK...
MATERIALS LAB
chik
...WE'LL JUST HAVE TO ***MAKE*** A MOON ROCK!
*WOW!* ISN'T THAT--?
YUP! A MULTI-TON ***HYDRAULIC PRESS.***
WE KNOW THE *COMPOSITION* OF MOON ROCKS--
--THAT MEANS WE CAN ***SYNTHESIZE*** ONE!
ALUMINUM...
...CALCIUM...
...TITANIUM...

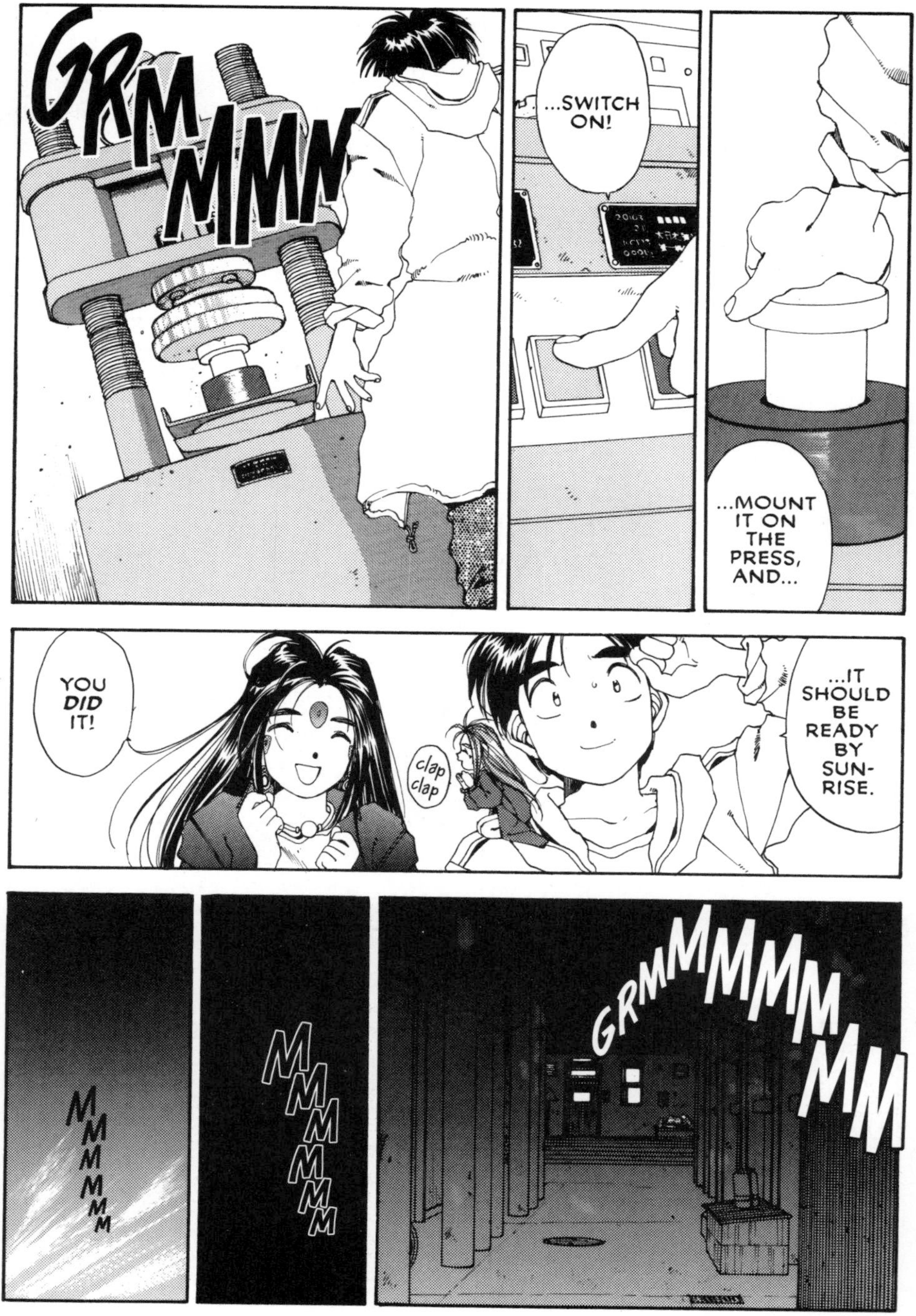
...MOUNT IT ON THE PRESS, AND...
...SWITCH ON!
GRMMMMN
...IT SHOULD BE READY BY SUN-RISE.
clap clap
YOU *DID* IT!
GRMMMMMMMMM
MMMMMMMM
MMMMMM

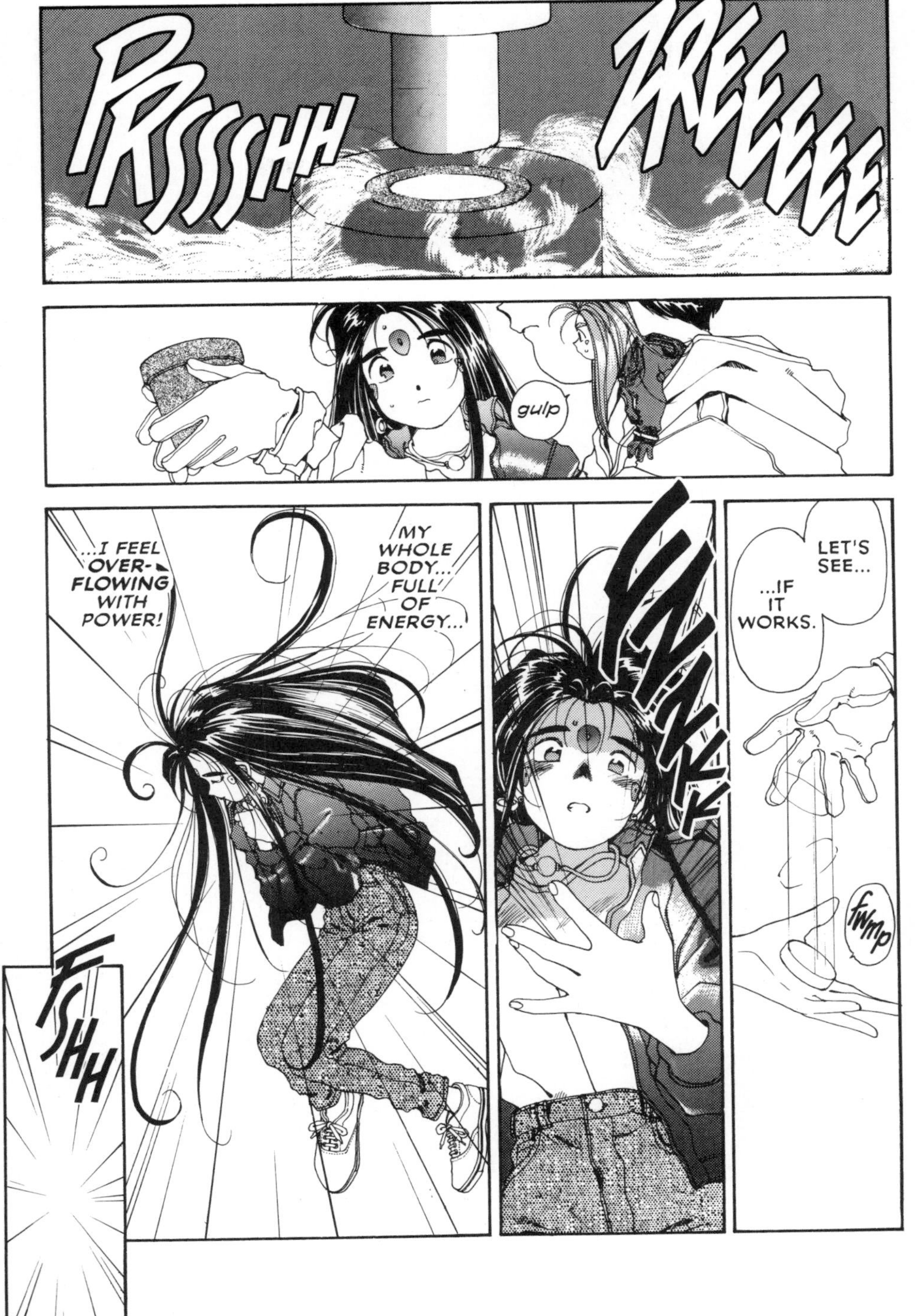
ZREEEEEE
PRSSSHH
gulp
LET'S SEE...
...IF IT WORKS.
fwmp
MY WHOLE BODY... FULL OF ENERGY...
...I FEEL OVER-FLOWING WITH POWER!
FSHH

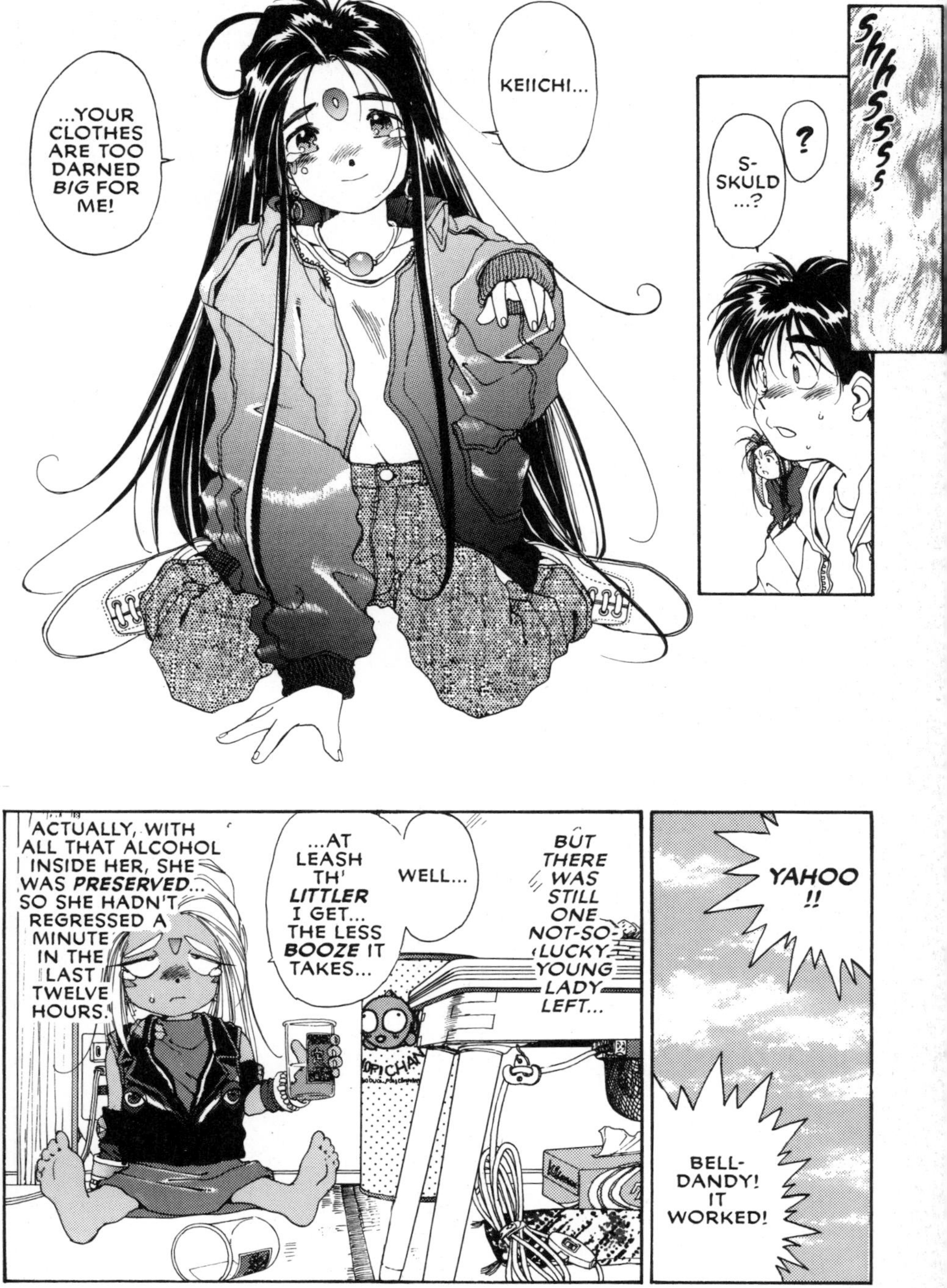
SHHSSSS
?
S-SKULD...?
KEIICHI...
...YOUR CLOTHES ARE TOO DARNED *BIG* FOR ME!
YAHOO!!
BELL-DANDY! IT WORKED!
*BUT THERE WAS STILL ONE NOT-SO-LUCKY YOUNG LADY LEFT...*
WELL...
...AT LEASH TH' *LITTLER* I GET... THE LESS *BOOZE* IT TAKES...
ACTUALLY, WITH ALL THAT ALCOHOL INSIDE HER, SHE WAS *PRESERVED*... SO SHE HADN'T REGRESSED A MINUTE IN THE LAST TWELVE HOURS.

CHAPTER 42

# Urd's Fantastic Adventure

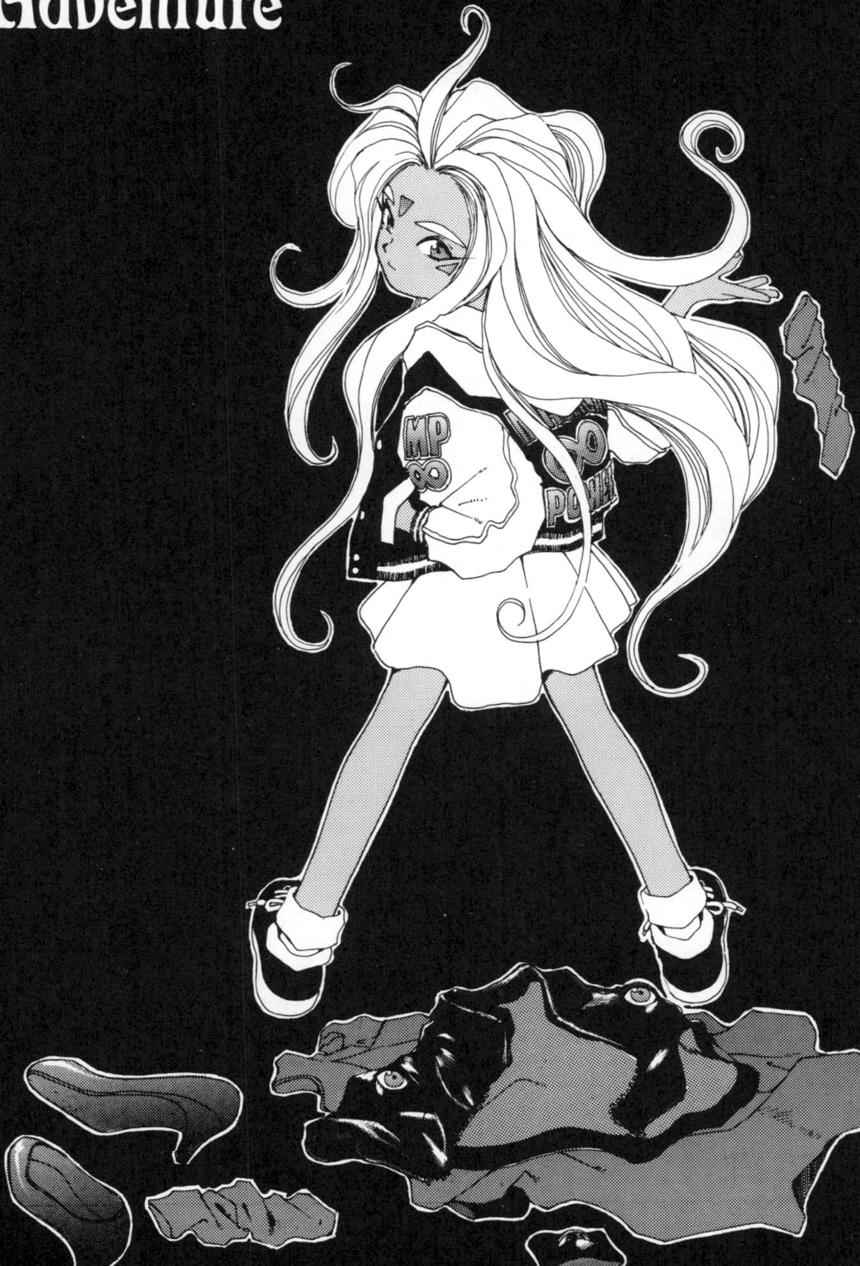

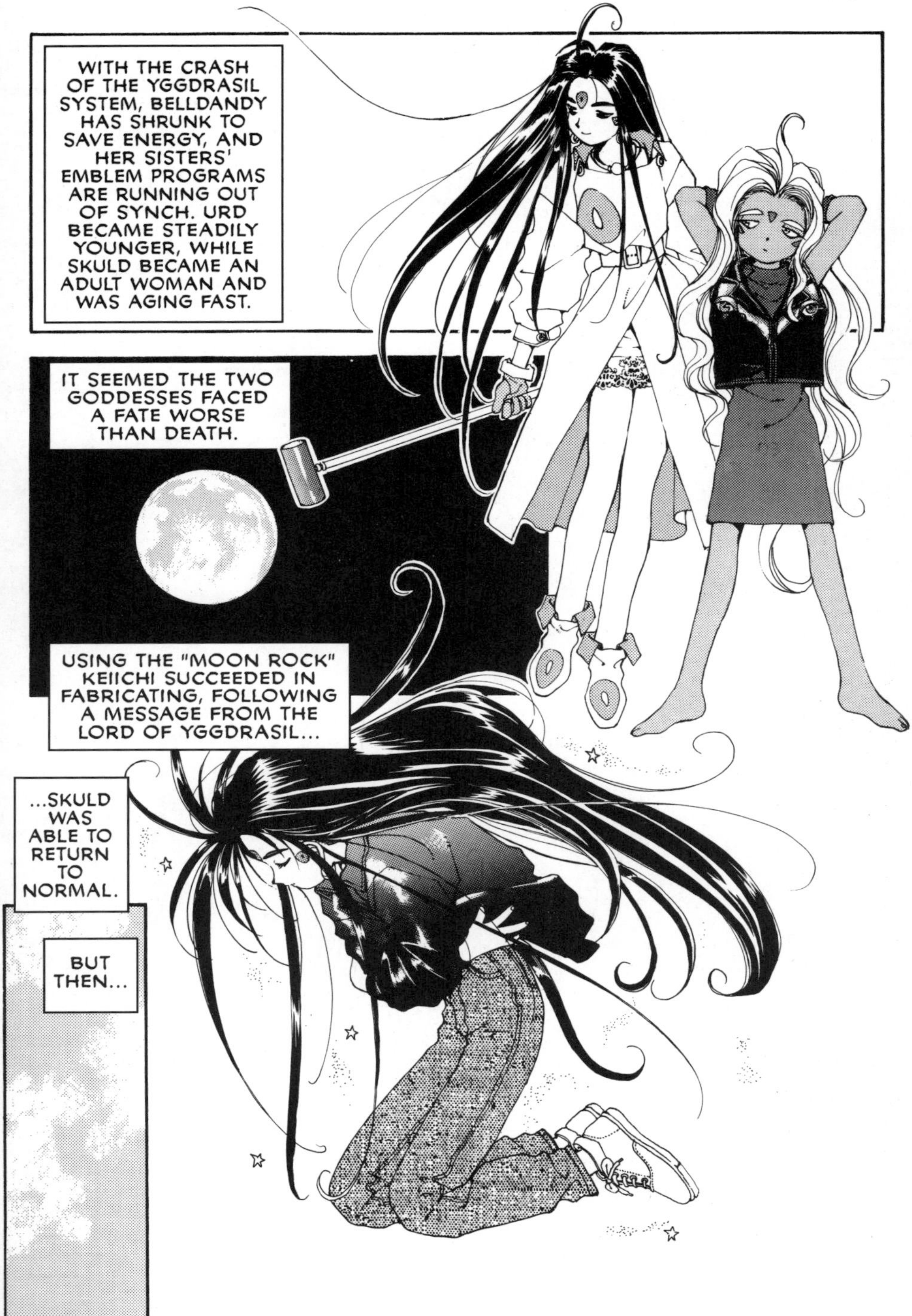
WITH THE CRASH OF THE YGGDRASIL SYSTEM, BELLDANDY HAS SHRUNK TO SAVE ENERGY, AND HER SISTERS' EMBLEM PROGRAMS ARE RUNNING OUT OF SYNCH. URD BECAME STEADILY YOUNGER, WHILE SKULD BECAME AN ADULT WOMAN AND WAS AGING FAST.
IT SEEMED THE TWO GODDESSES FACED A FATE WORSE THAN DEATH.
USING THE "MOON ROCK" KEIICHI SUCCEEDED IN FABRICATING, FOLLOWING A MESSAGE FROM THE LORD OF YGGDRASIL...
...SKULD WAS ABLE TO RETURN TO NORMAL.
BUT THEN...

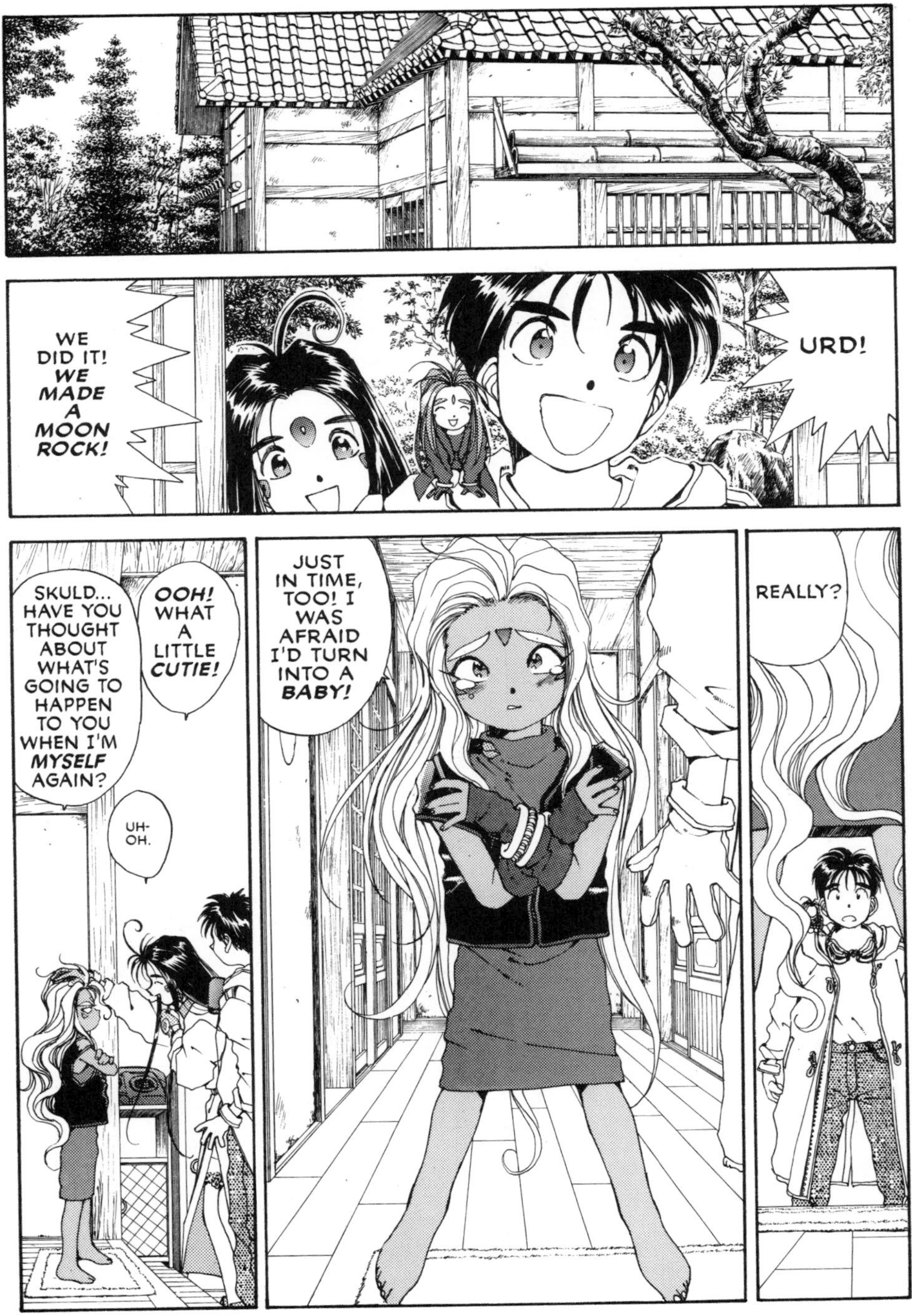
URD!
WE DID IT! WE MADE A MOON ROCK!
REALLY?
JUST IN TIME, TOO! I WAS AFRAID I'D TURN INTO A BABY!
OOH! WHAT A LITTLE CUTIE!
SKULD... HAVE YOU THOUGHT ABOUT WHAT'S GOING TO HAPPEN TO YOU WHEN I'M MYSELF AGAIN?
UH-OH.

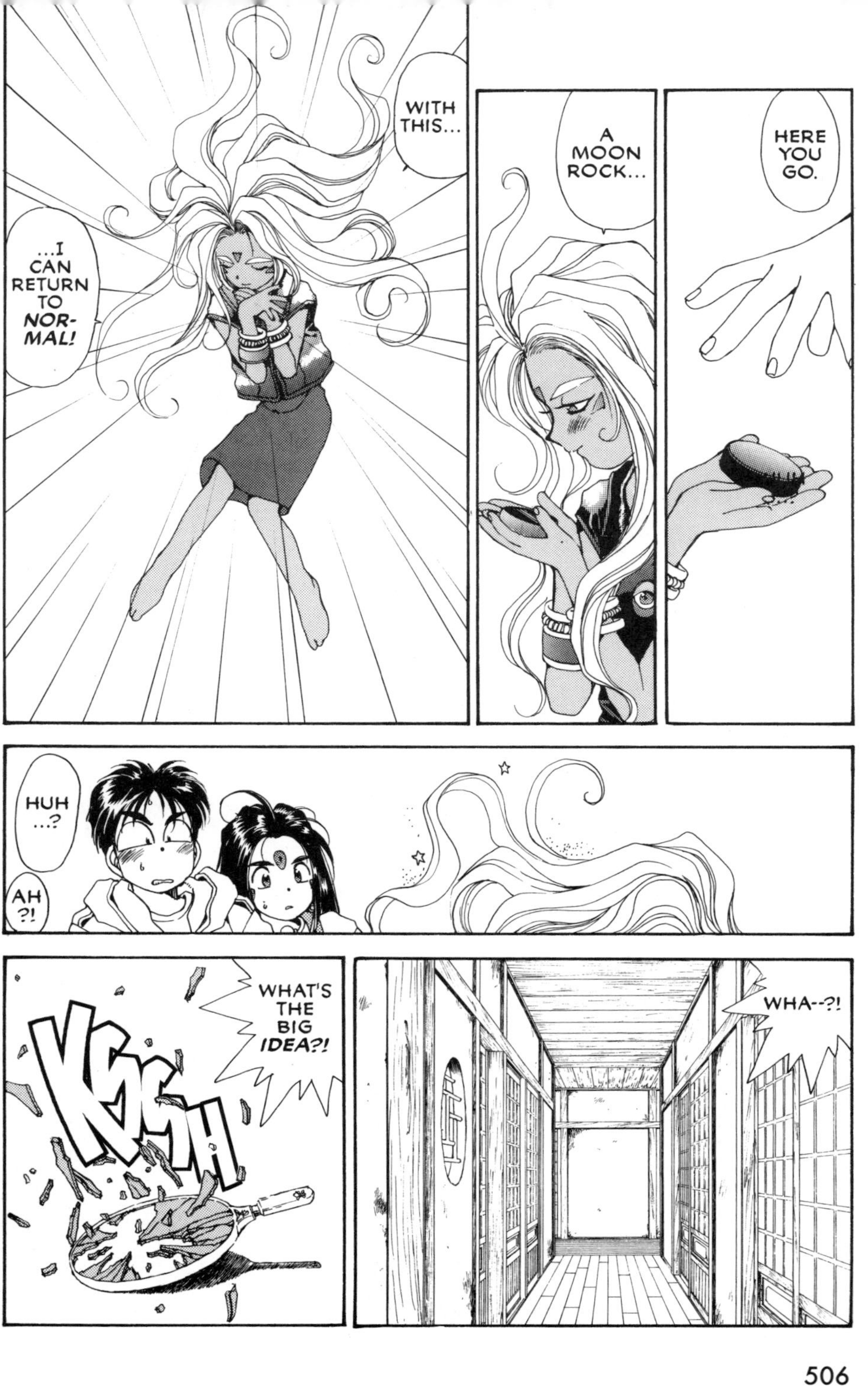
HERE YOU GO.
A MOON ROCK...
WITH THIS...
...I CAN RETURN TO *NORMAL!*
HUH ...?
AH ?!
WHA--?!
WHAT'S THE BIG *IDEA?!*

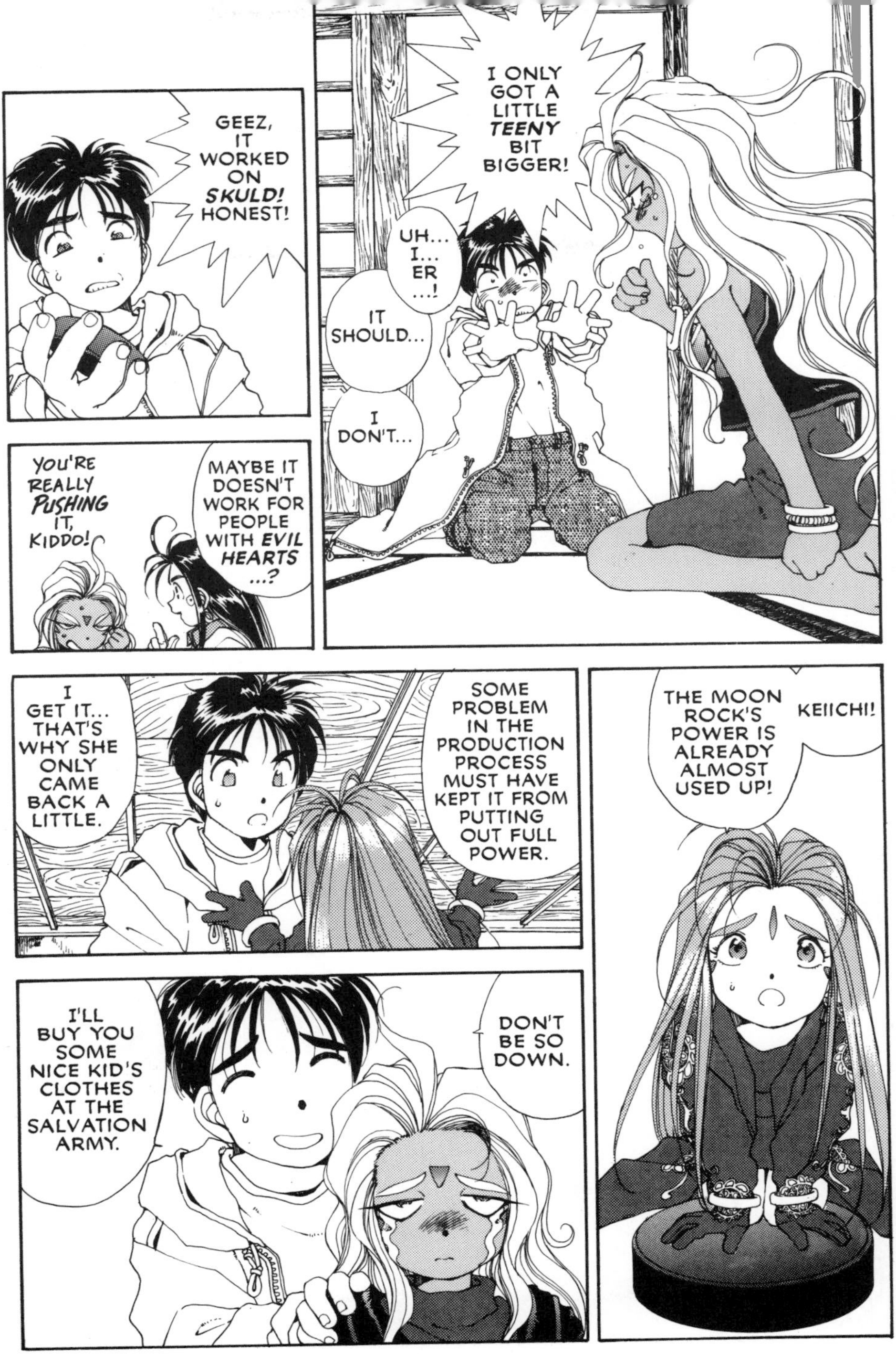
I ONLY GOT A LITTLE TEENY BIT BIGGER!
UH... I... ER ...!
IT SHOULD...
I DON'T...
GEEZ, IT WORKED ON SKULD! HONEST!
MAYBE IT DOESN'T WORK FOR PEOPLE WITH EVIL HEARTS ...?
YOU'RE REALLY PUSHING IT, KIDDO!
KEIICHI!
THE MOON ROCK'S POWER IS ALREADY ALMOST USED UP!
SOME PROBLEM IN THE PRODUCTION PROCESS MUST HAVE KEPT IT FROM PUTTING OUT FULL POWER.
I GET IT... THAT'S WHY SHE ONLY CAME BACK A LITTLE.
DON'T BE SO DOWN.
I'LL BUY YOU SOME NICE KID'S CLOTHES AT THE SALVATION ARMY.

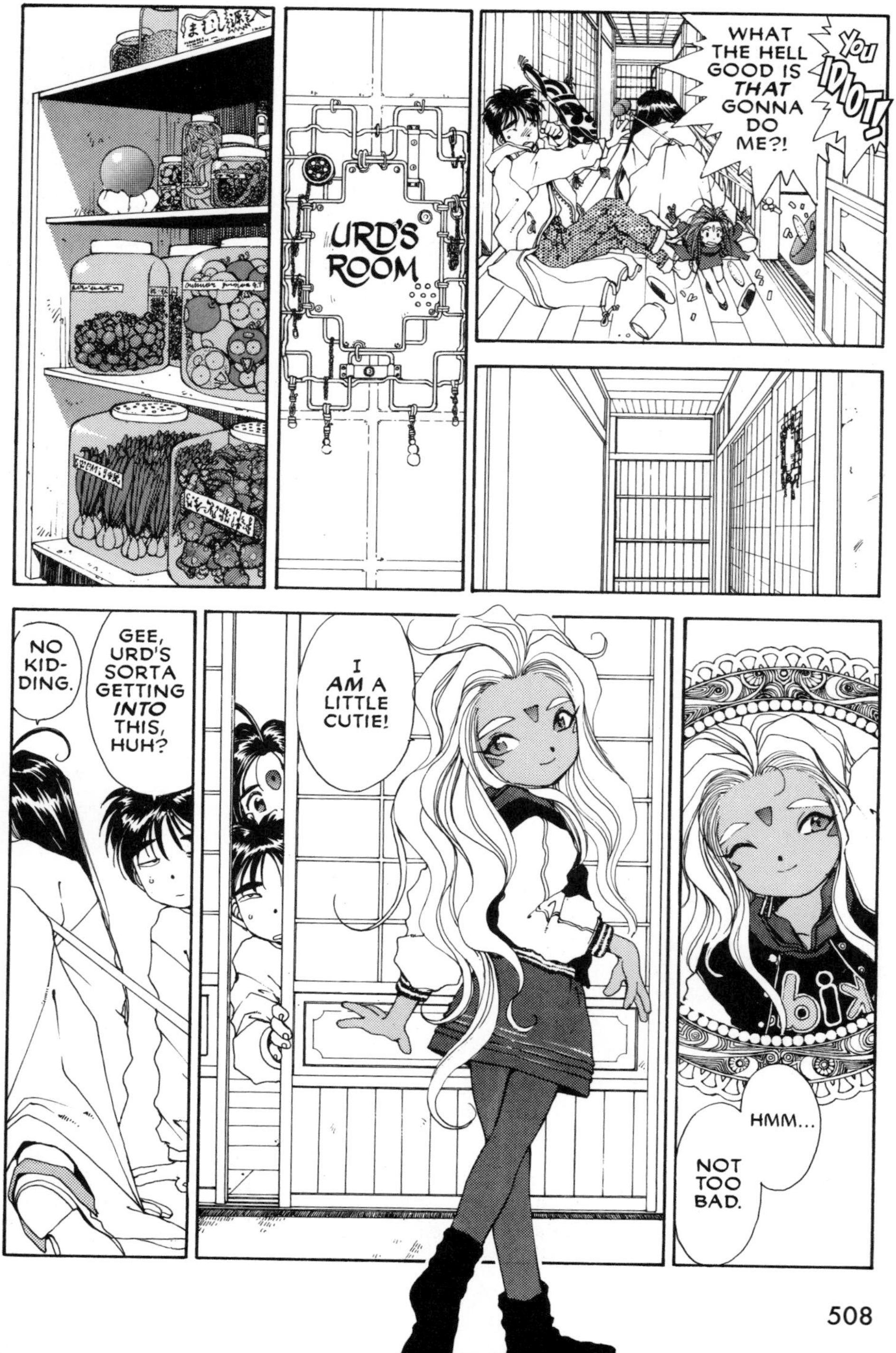
YOU IDIOT!
WHAT THE HELL GOOD IS THAT GONNA DO ME?!
URD'S ROOM
HMM...
NOT TOO BAD.
I AM A LITTLE CUTIE!
GEE, URD'S SORTA GETTING INTO THIS, HUH?
NO KID-DING.

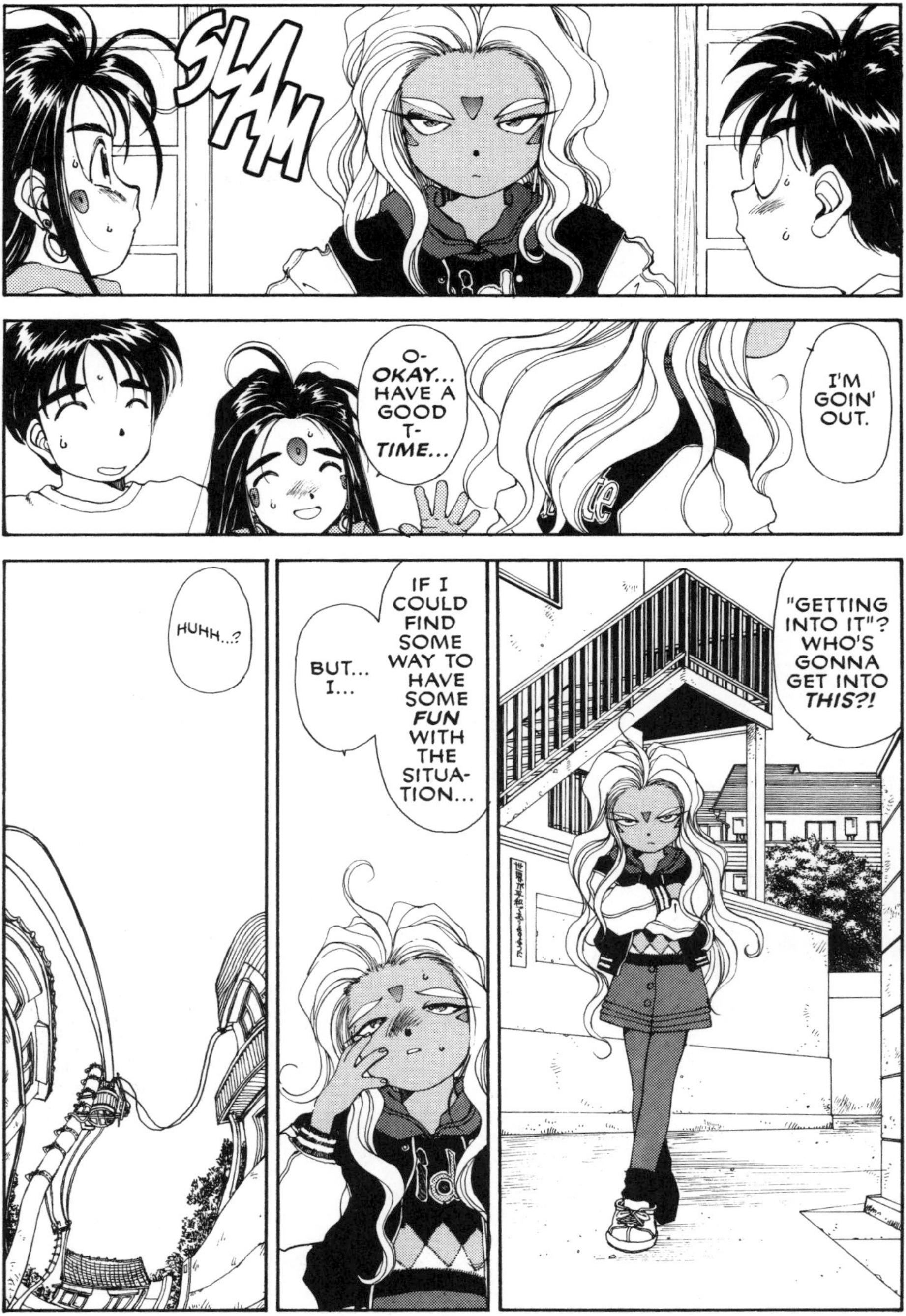
SLAM
I'M GOIN' OUT.
O- OKAY... HAVE A GOOD T- TIME...
"GETTING INTO IT"? WHO'S GONNA GET INTO THIS?!
IF I COULD FIND SOME WAY TO HAVE SOME FUN WITH THE SITUATION...
BUT... I...
HUHH...?

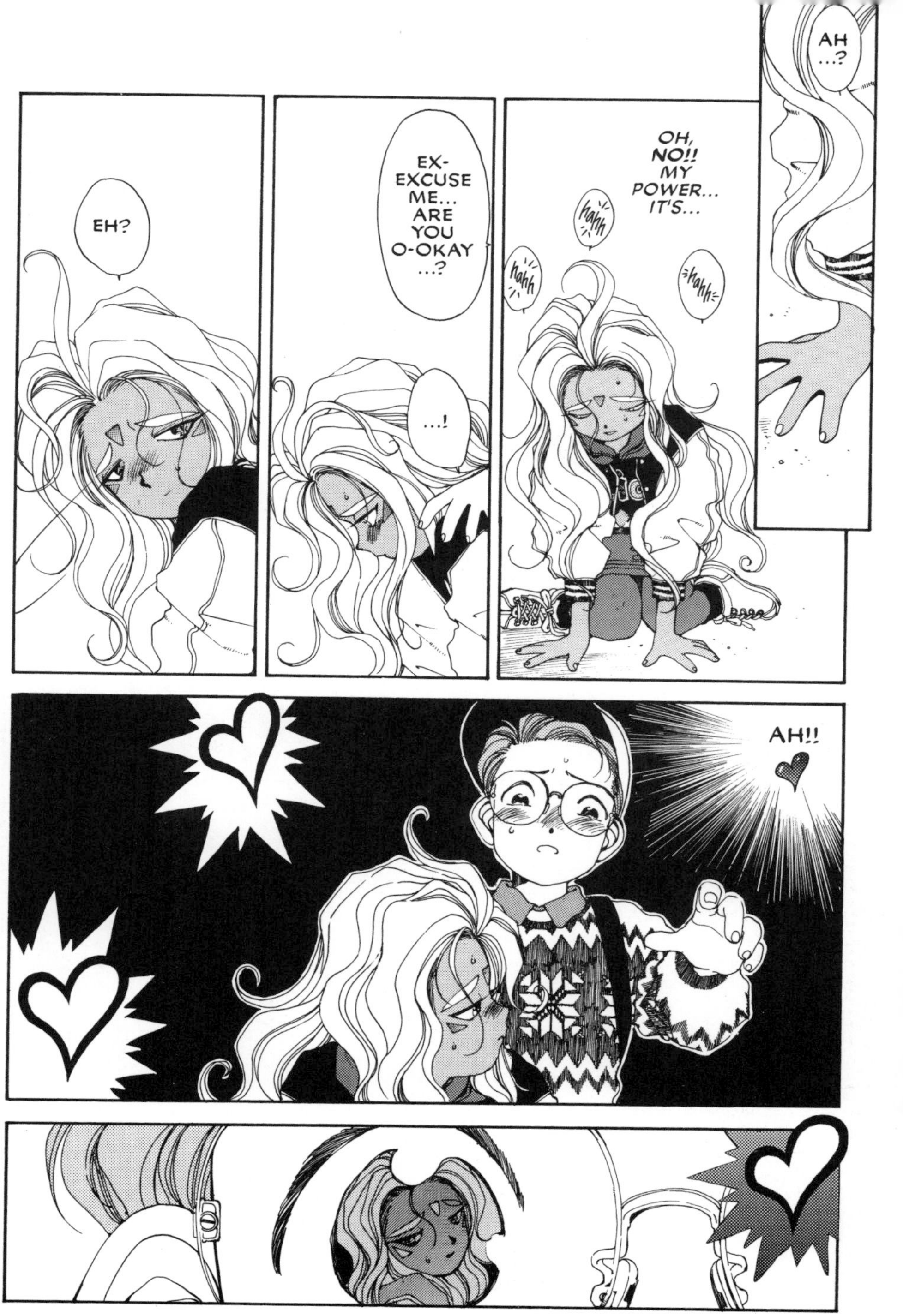
AH ...?
OH, NO!! MY POWER... IT'S...
hahh
hahh
hahh
EX- EXCUSE ME... ARE YOU O-OKAY ...?
...!
EH?
AH!!

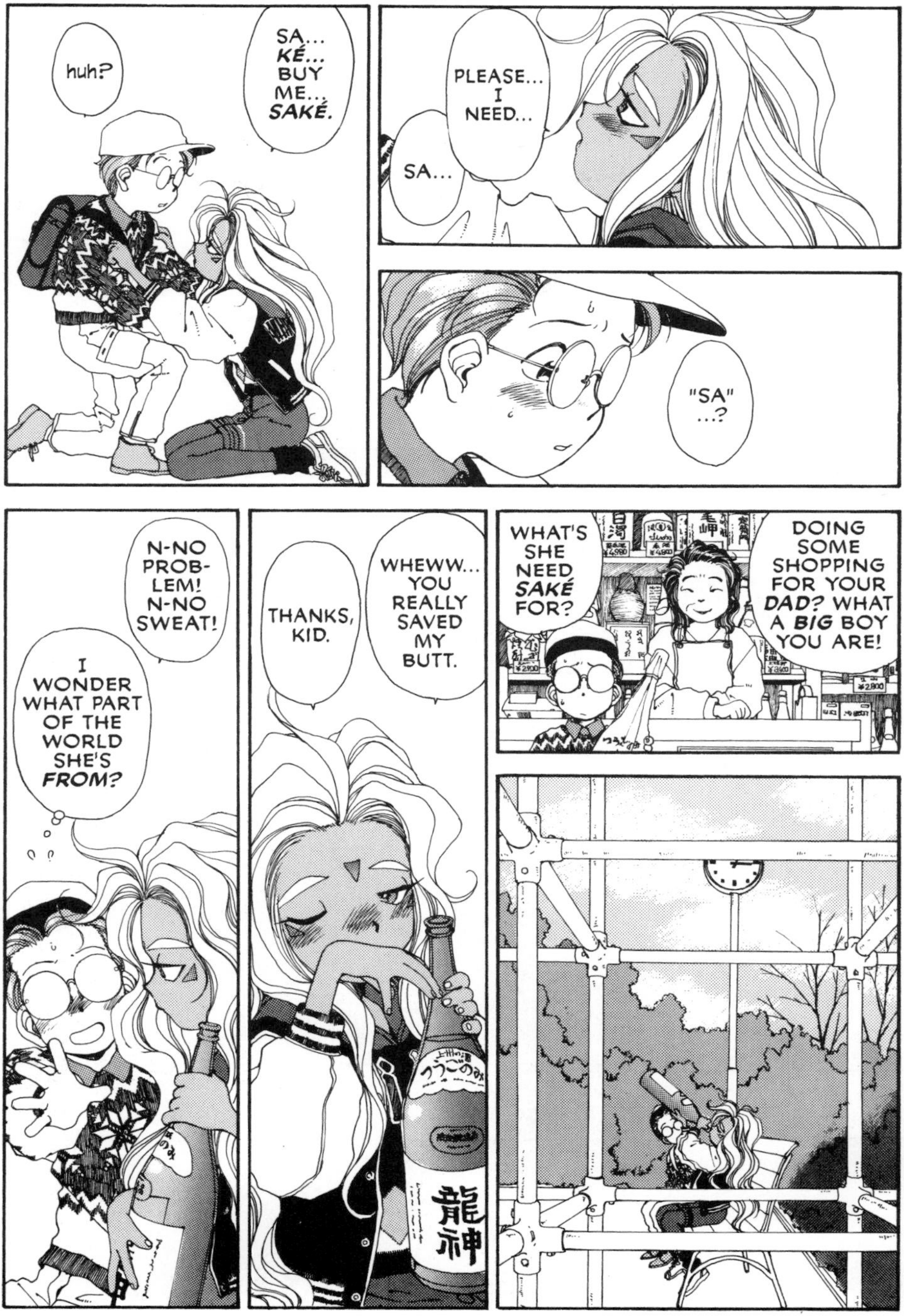
PLEASE... I NEED...
SA...
"SA" ...?
SA... KÉ... BUY ME... SAKÉ.
huh?
DOING SOME SHOPPING FOR YOUR DAD? WHAT A BIG BOY YOU ARE!
WHAT'S SHE NEED SAKÉ FOR?
WHEWW... YOU REALLY SAVED MY BUTT.
THANKS, KID.
龍神
N-NO PROB-LEM! N-NO SWEAT!
I WONDER WHAT PART OF THE WORLD SHE'S FROM?

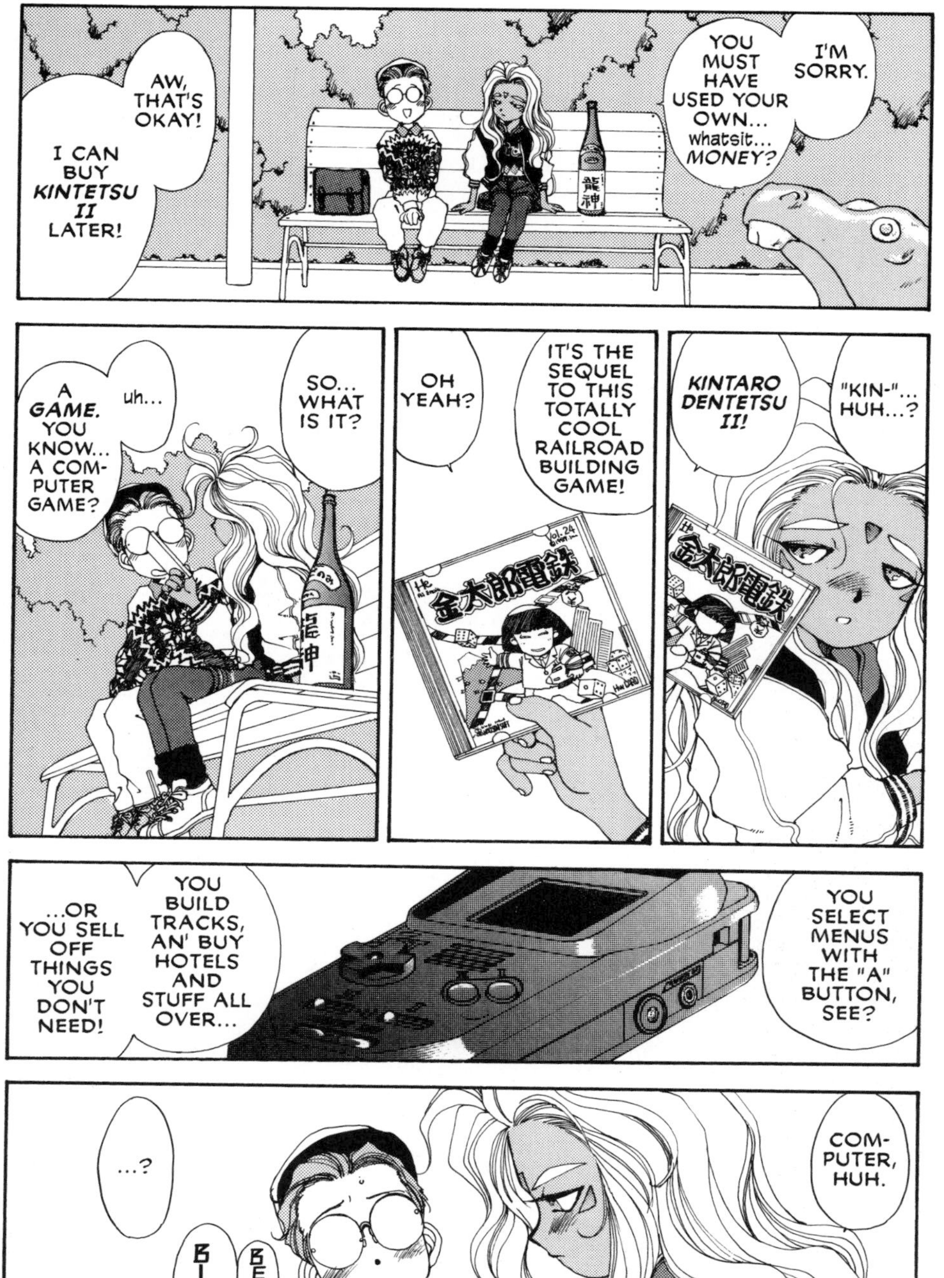

I'M SORRY.
YOU MUST HAVE USED YOUR OWN... whatsit... MONEY?
AW, THAT'S OKAY!
I CAN BUY KINTETSU II LATER!
"KIN-"... HUH...?
KINTARO DENTETSU II!
IT'S THE SEQUEL TO THIS TOTALLY COOL RAILROAD BUILDING GAME!
OH YEAH?
金太郎電鉄
SO... WHAT IS IT?
uh...
A GAME. YOU KNOW... A COMPUTER GAME?
龍神
YOU SELECT MENUS WITH THE "A" BUTTON, SEE?
YOU BUILD TRACKS, AN' BUY HOTELS AND STUFF ALL OVER...
...OR YOU SELL OFF THINGS YOU DON'T NEED!
COMPUTER, HUH.
BEEP
BING!
...?

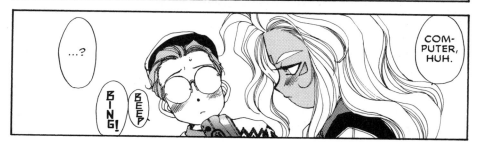

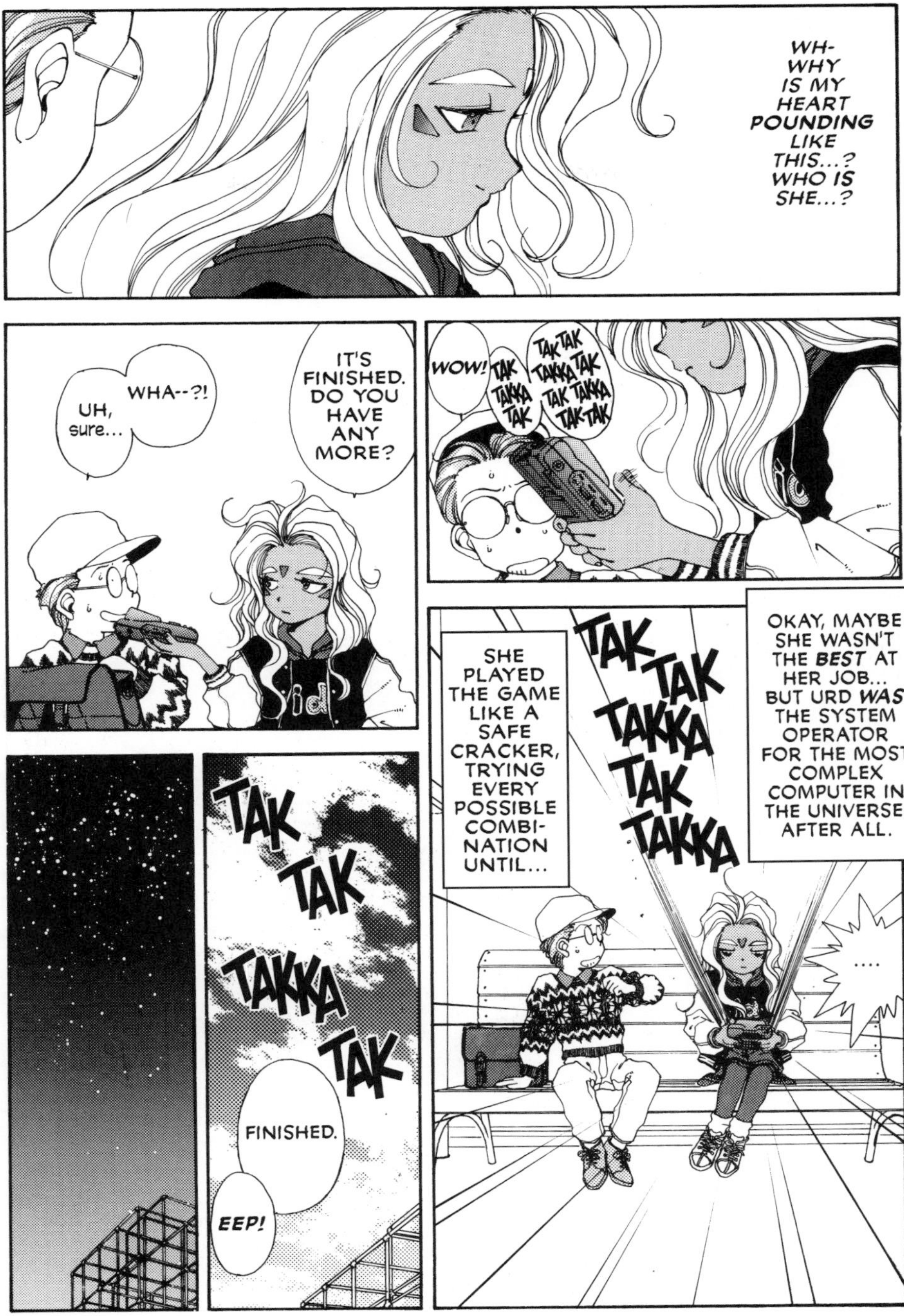
WH- WHY IS MY HEART **POUNDING** LIKE THIS...? WHO **IS** SHE...?
TAK TAK TAKKA TAK TAK TAKKA TAK-TAK
TAK TAKKA TAK
WOW!
IT'S FINISHED. DO YOU HAVE ANY MORE?
WHA--?!
UH, sure...
OKAY, MAYBE SHE WASN'T THE ***BEST*** AT HER JOB... BUT URD ***WAS*** THE SYSTEM OPERATOR FOR THE MOST COMPLEX COMPUTER IN THE UNIVERSE, AFTER ALL.
TAK TAK TAKKA TAK TAKKA
SHE PLAYED THE GAME LIKE A SAFE CRACKER, TRYING EVERY POSSIBLE COMBI- NATION UNTIL...
....
TAK TAK TAKKA TAK
FINISHED.
***EEP!***

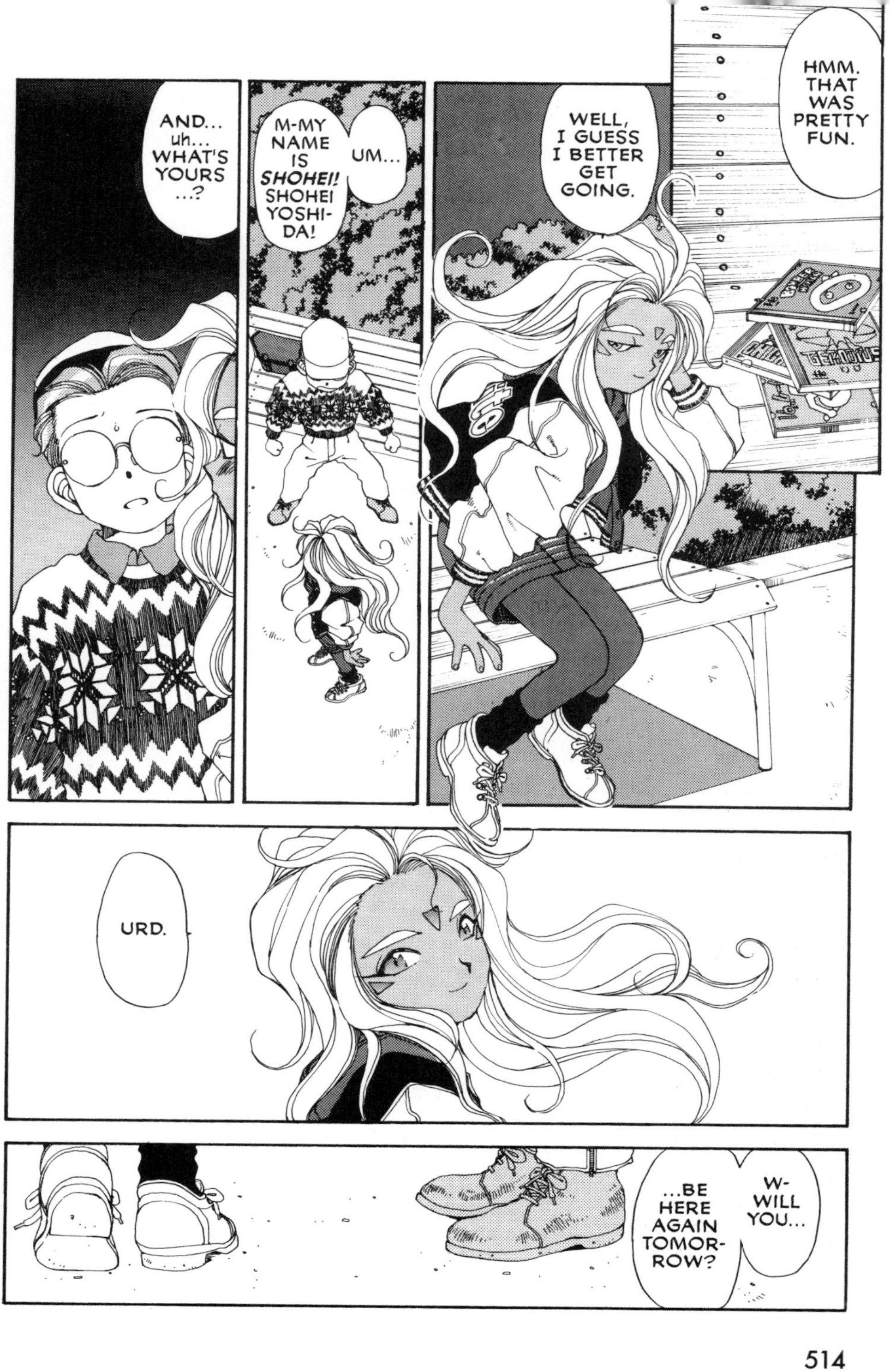
HMM. THAT WAS PRETTY FUN.
WELL, I GUESS I BETTER GET GOING.
UM...
M-MY NAME IS SHOHEI! SHOHEI YOSHIDA!
AND... uh... WHAT'S YOURS ...?
URD.
W-WILL YOU...
...BE HERE AGAIN TOMORROW?

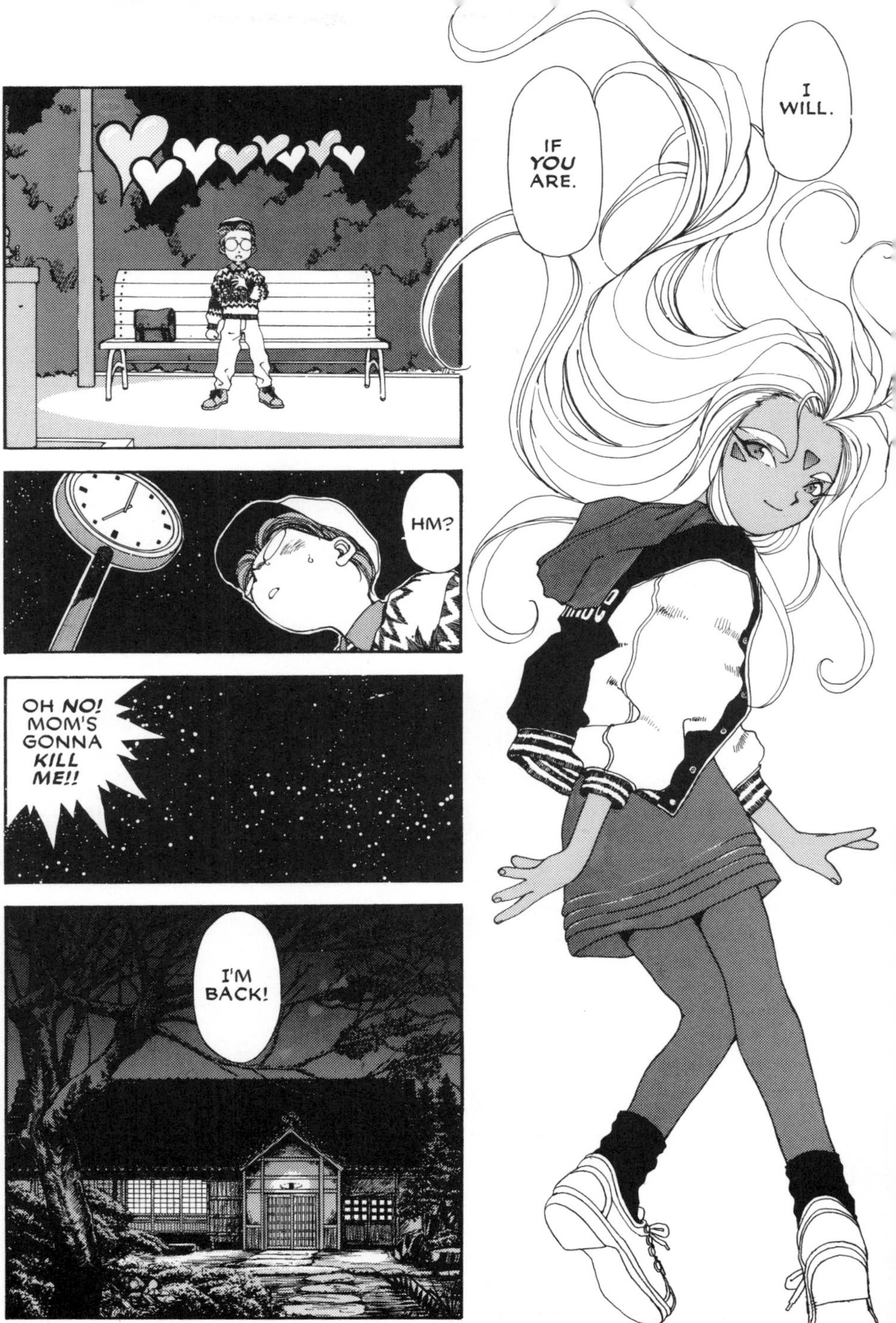
I WILL.
IF *YOU* ARE.
HM?
OH *NO!* MOM'S GONNA *KILL ME!!*
I'M BACK!

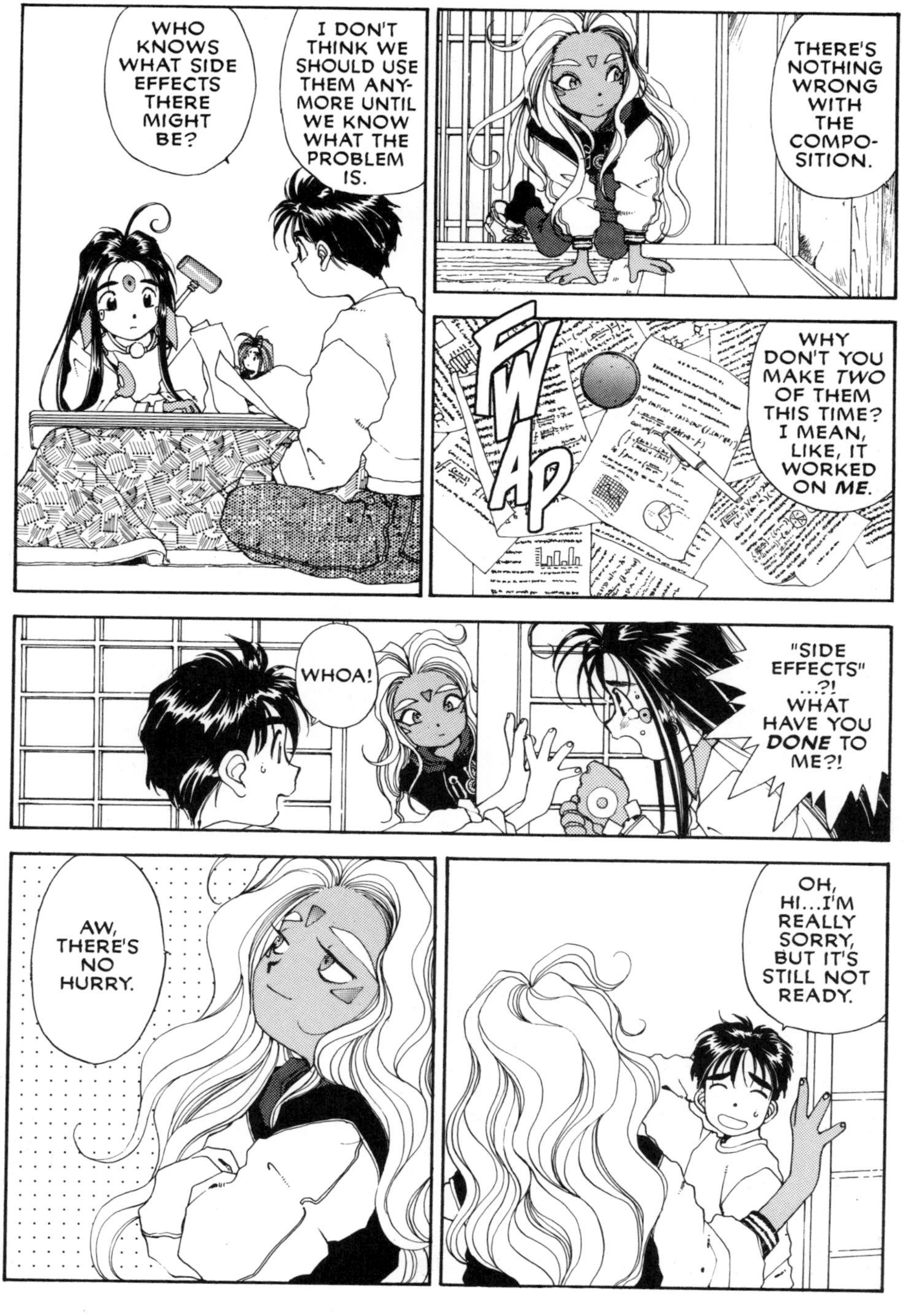
THERE'S NOTHING WRONG WITH THE COMPOSITION.
FWAP
WHY DON'T YOU MAKE *TWO* OF THEM THIS TIME? I MEAN, LIKE, IT WORKED ON ***ME***.
I DON'T THINK WE SHOULD USE THEM ANYMORE UNTIL WE KNOW WHAT THE PROBLEM IS.
WHO KNOWS WHAT SIDE EFFECTS THERE MIGHT BE?
"SIDE EFFECTS" ...?! WHAT HAVE YOU ***DONE*** TO ME?!
WHOA!
OH, HI...I'M REALLY SORRY, BUT IT'S STILL NOT READY.
AW, THERE'S NO HURRY.

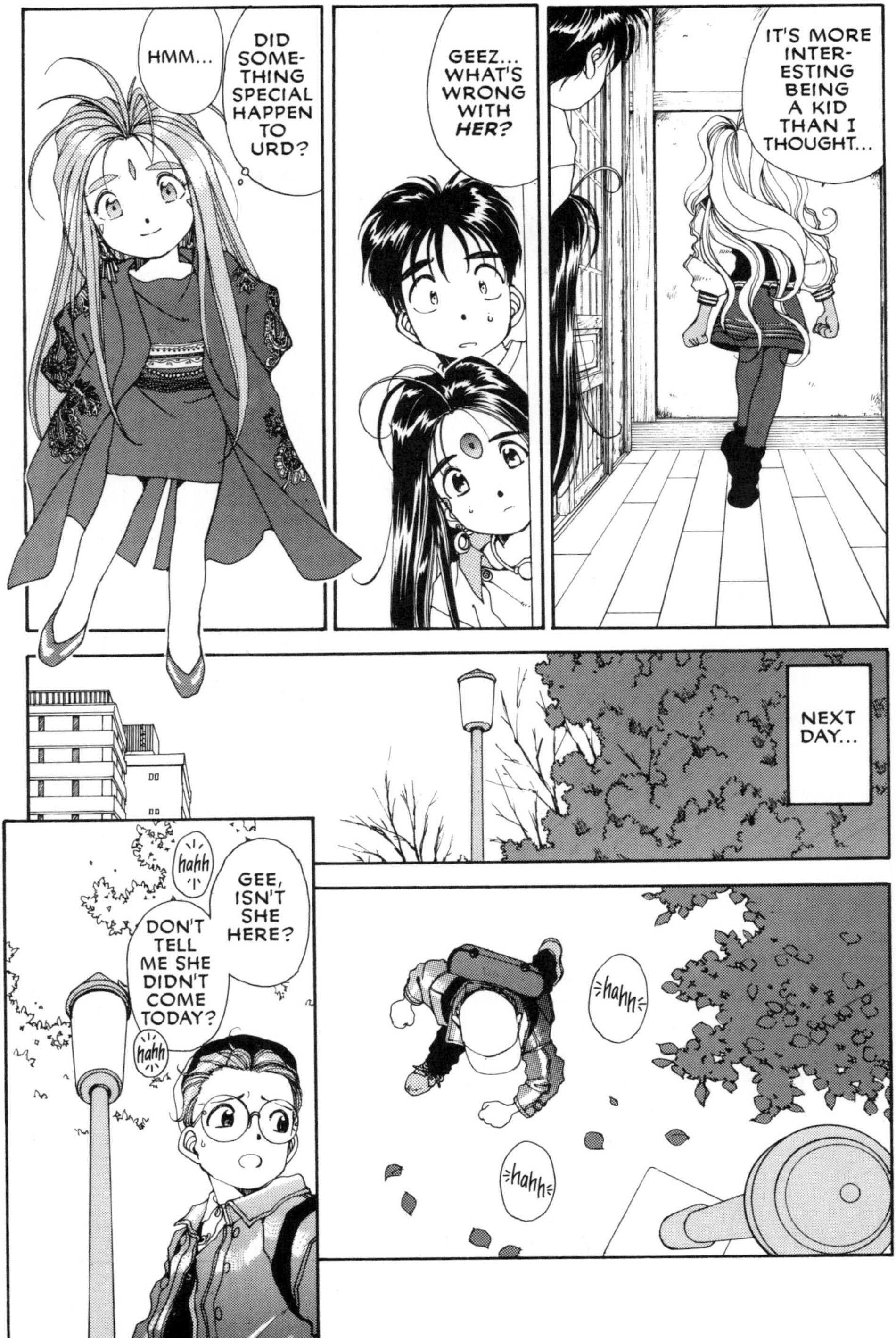
IT'S MORE INTERESTING BEING A KID THAN I THOUGHT...
GEEZ... WHAT'S WRONG WITH *HER*?
DID SOMETHING SPECIAL HAPPEN TO URD?
HMM...
NEXT DAY...
hahh
hahh
hahh
GEE, ISN'T SHE HERE?
DON'T TELL ME SHE DIDN'T COME TODAY?
hahh

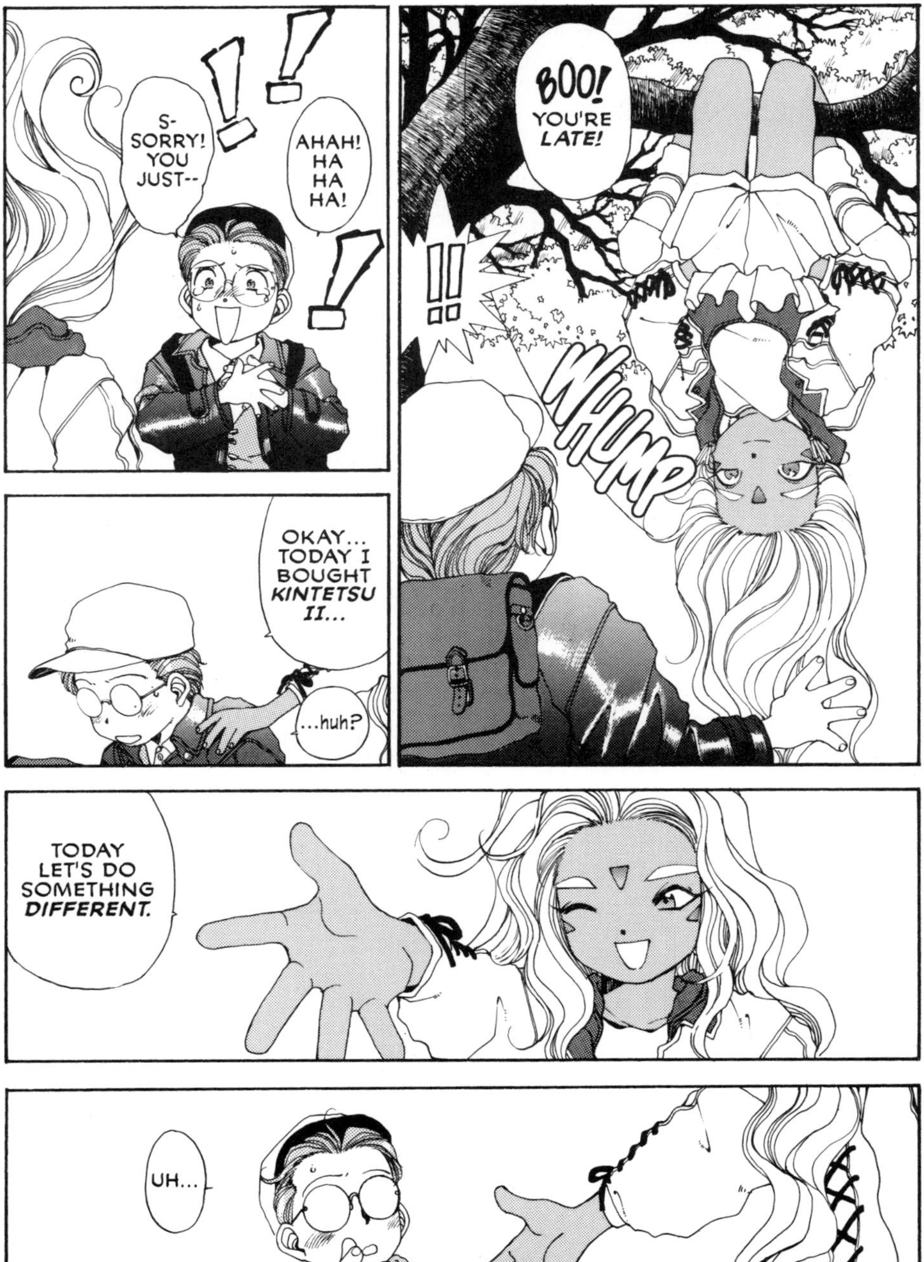
BOO! YOU'RE LATE!
!!
WHUMP
AHAH! HA HA HA!
S-SORRY! YOU JUST--
OKAY... TODAY I BOUGHT KINTETSU II...
...huh?
TODAY LET'S DO SOMETHING DIFFERENT.
UH...

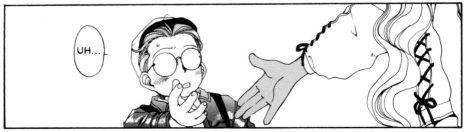

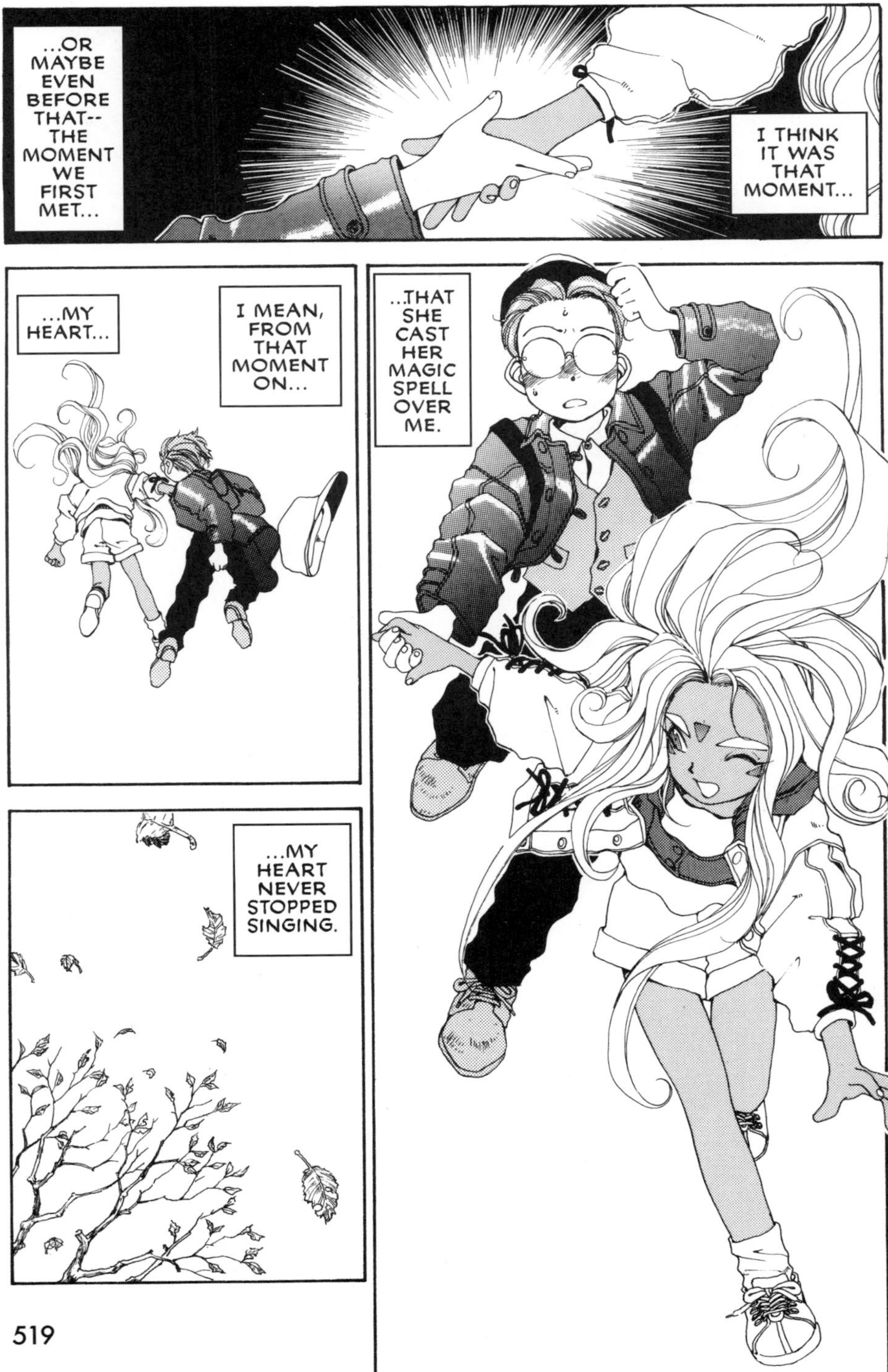
I THINK IT WAS THAT MOMENT...
...OR MAYBE EVEN BEFORE THAT-- THE MOMENT WE FIRST MET...
...THAT SHE CAST HER MAGIC SPELL OVER ME.
I MEAN, FROM THAT MOMENT ON...
...MY HEART...
...MY HEART NEVER STOPPED SINGING.

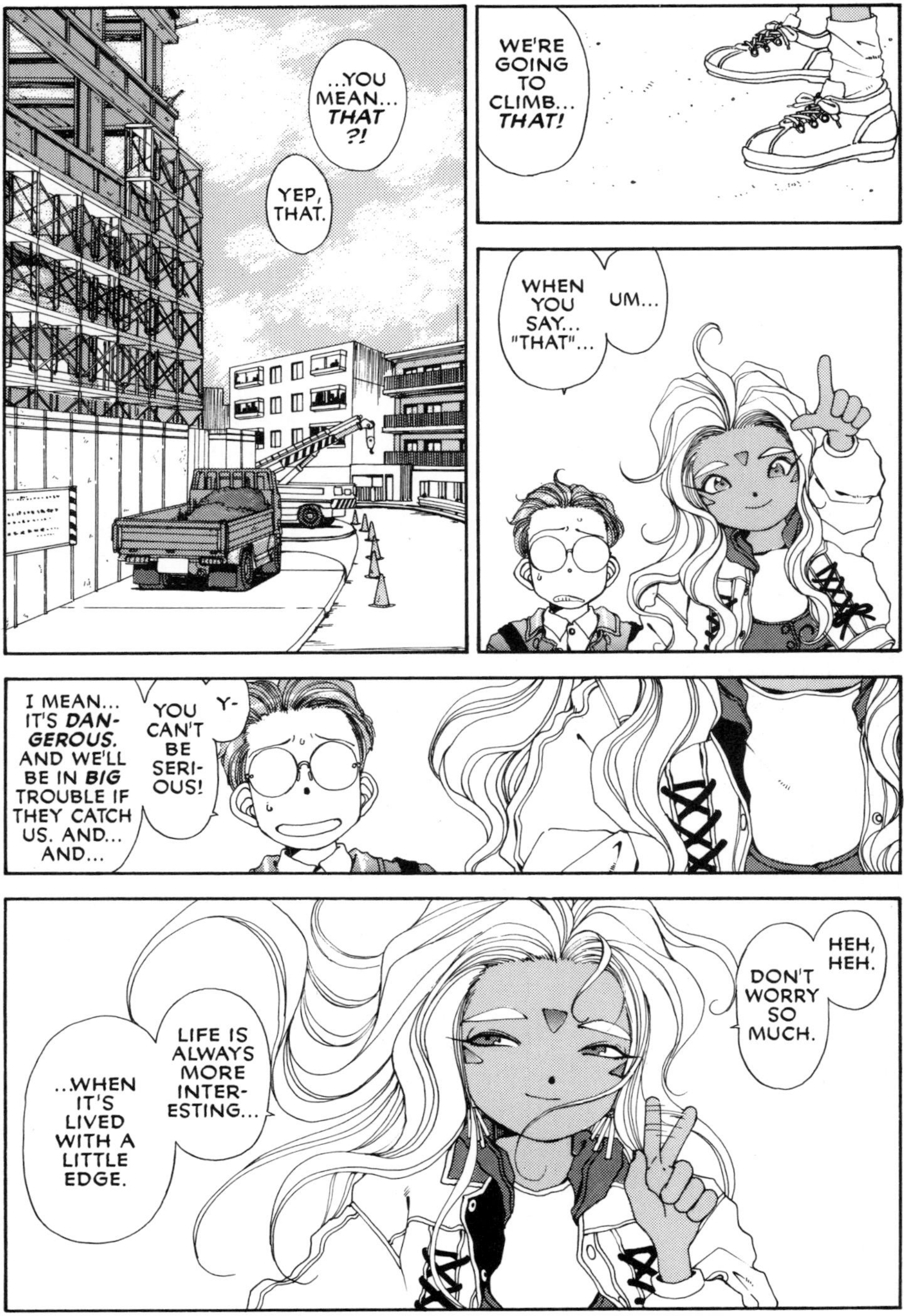

WE'RE GOING TO CLIMB... *THAT!*
UM...
WHEN YOU SAY... "THAT"...
...YOU MEAN... *THAT* ?!
YEP, THAT.
Y-
YOU CAN'T BE SERIOUS!
I MEAN... IT'S *DANGEROUS.* AND WE'LL BE IN *BIG* TROUBLE IF THEY CATCH US. AND... AND...
HEH, HEH.
DON'T WORRY SO MUCH.
LIFE IS ALWAYS MORE INTERESTING...
...WHEN IT'S LIVED WITH A LITTLE EDGE.

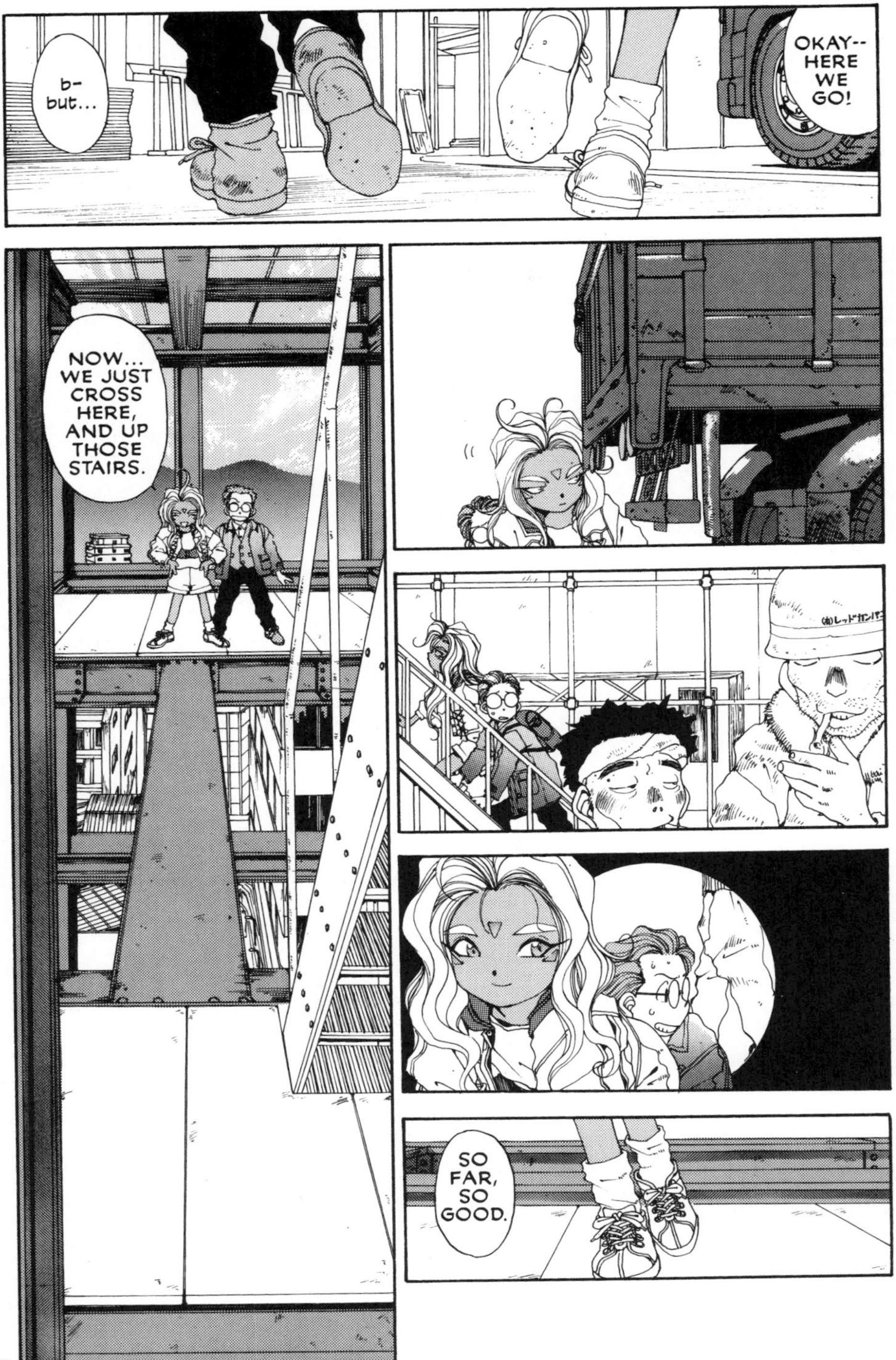
OKAY-- HERE WE GO!
b- but...
SO FAR, SO GOOD.
NOW... WE JUST CROSS HERE, AND UP THOSE STAIRS.

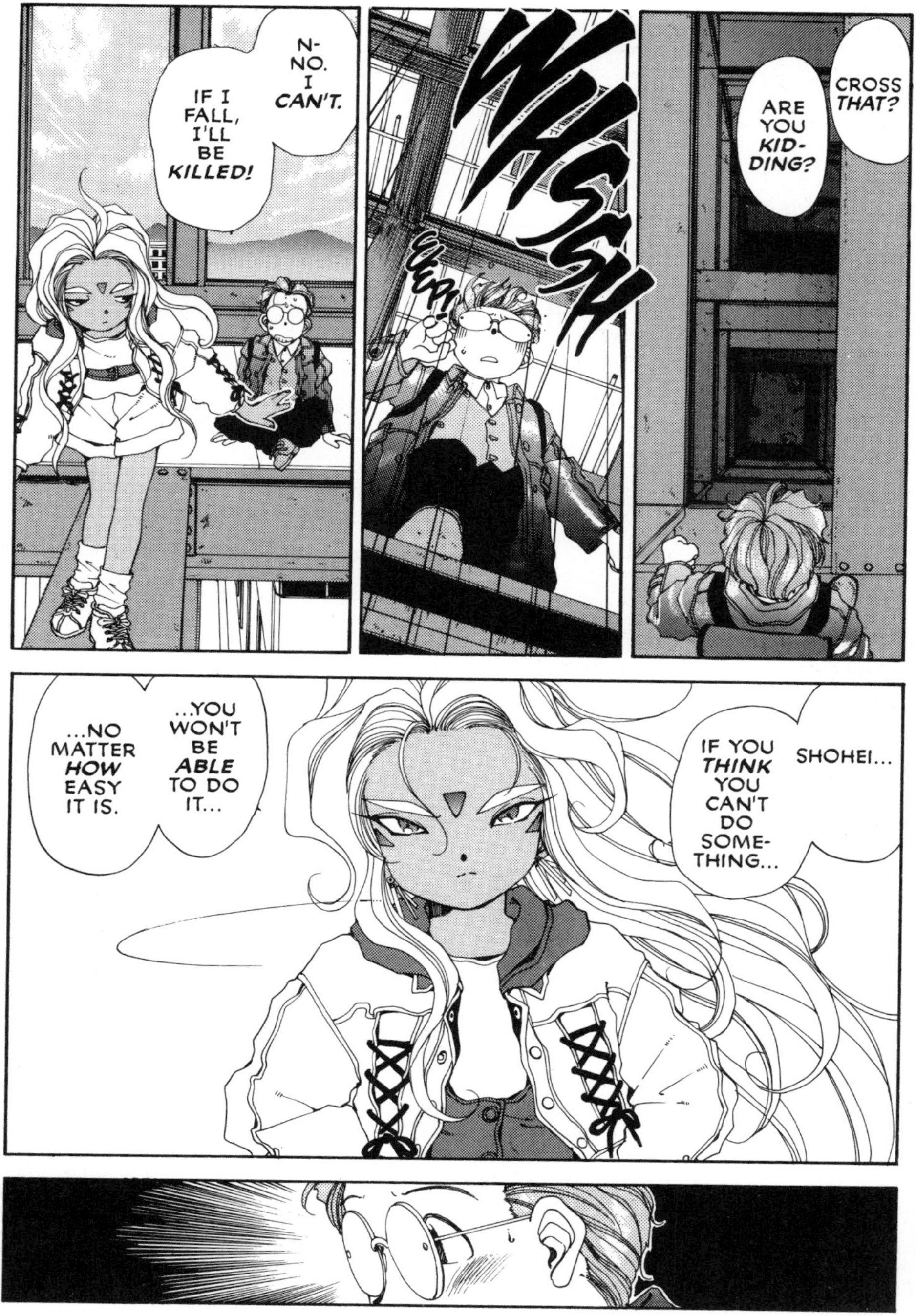
CROSS THAT?
ARE YOU KID-DING?
WHSSH
EEP!
N-NO. I CAN'T.
IF I FALL, I'LL BE KILLED!
SHOHEI...
IF YOU THINK YOU CAN'T DO SOME-THING...
...YOU WON'T BE ABLE TO DO IT...
...NO MATTER HOW EASY IT IS.

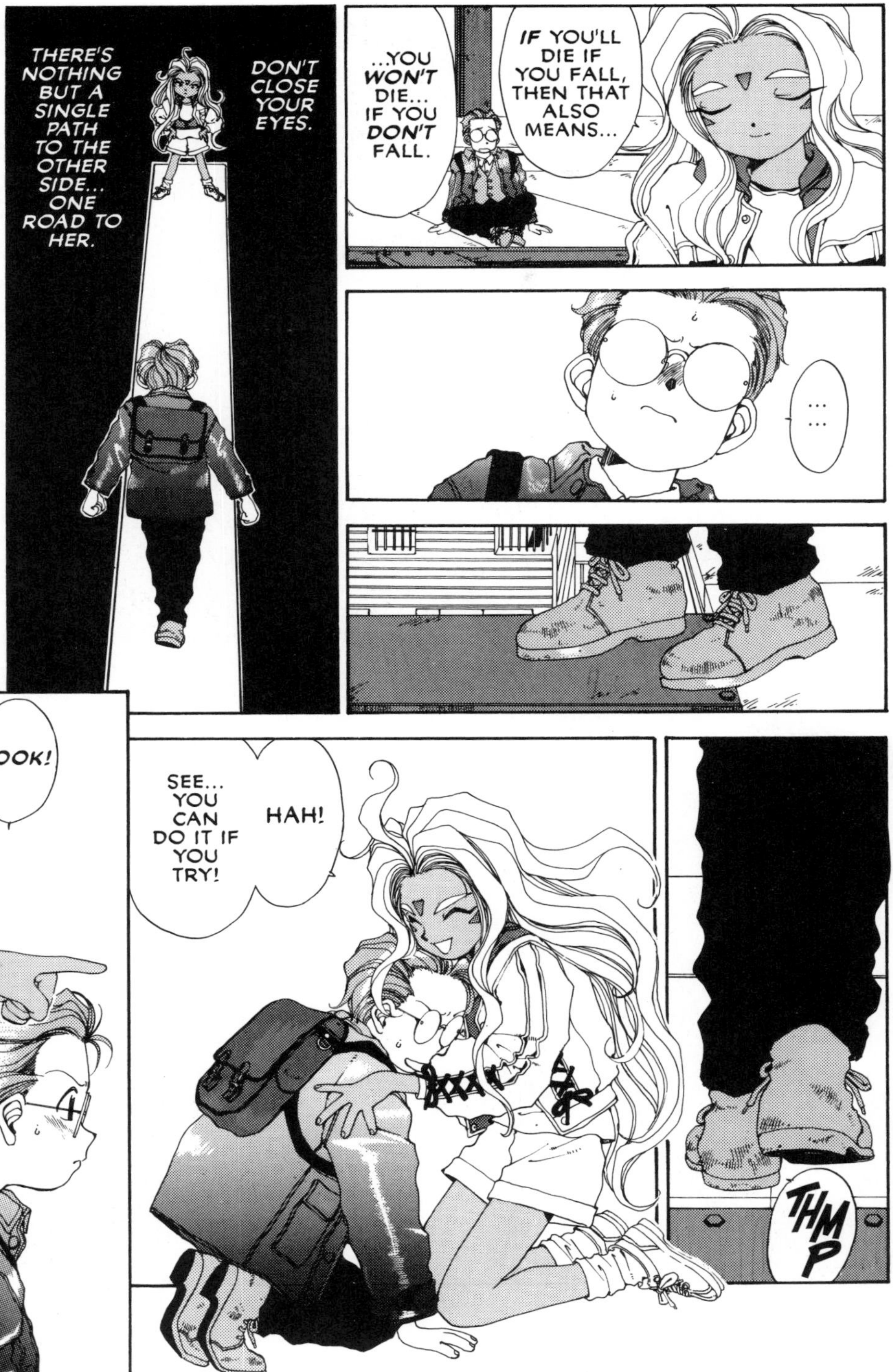
IF YOU'LL DIE IF YOU FALL, THEN THAT ALSO MEANS...
...YOU WON'T DIE... IF YOU DON'T FALL.
......
DON'T CLOSE YOUR EYES.
THERE'S NOTHING BUT A SINGLE PATH TO THE OTHER SIDE... ONE ROAD TO HER.
THMP
HAH!
SEE... YOU CAN DO IT IF YOU TRY!
LOOK!

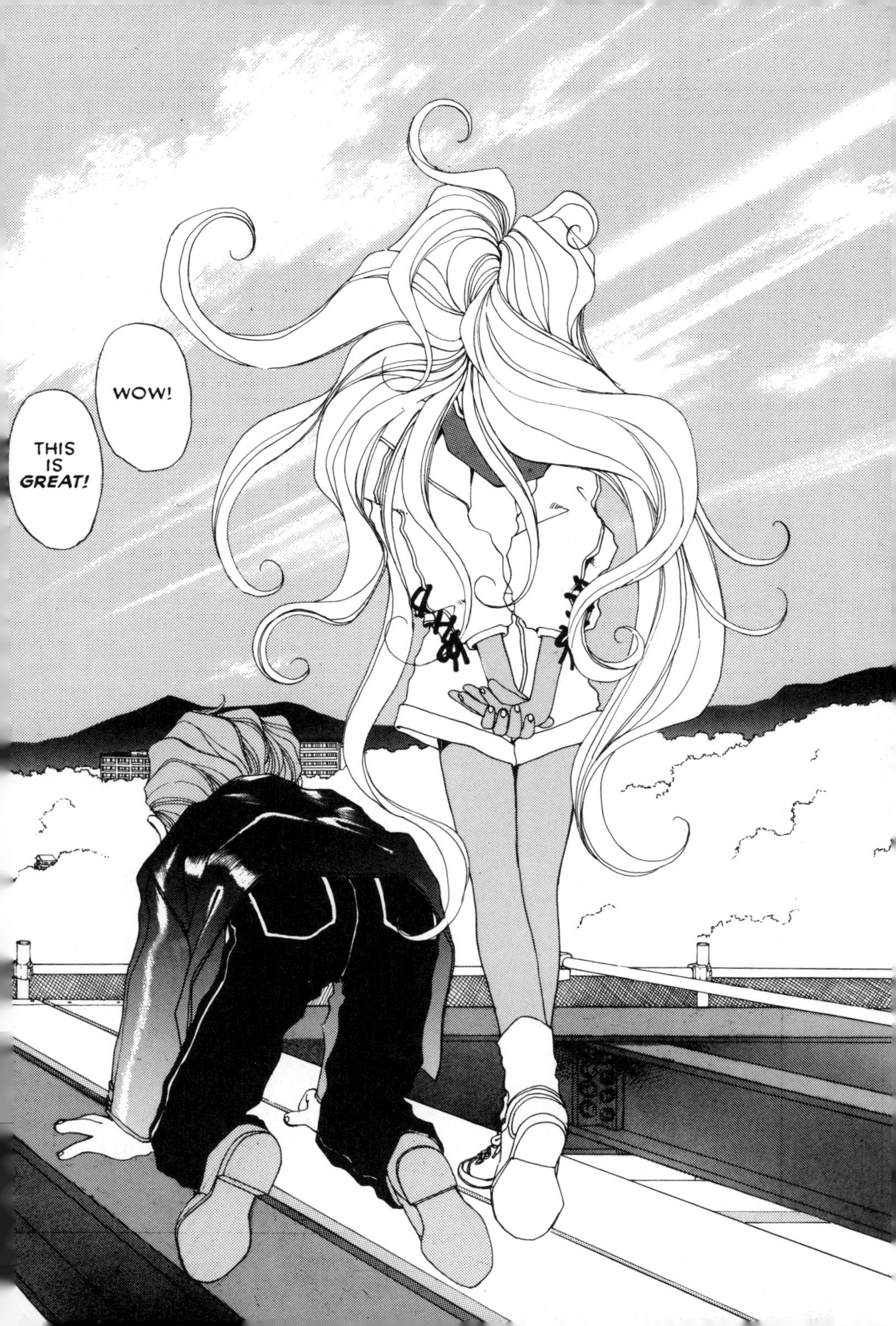
WOW!
THIS IS GREAT!

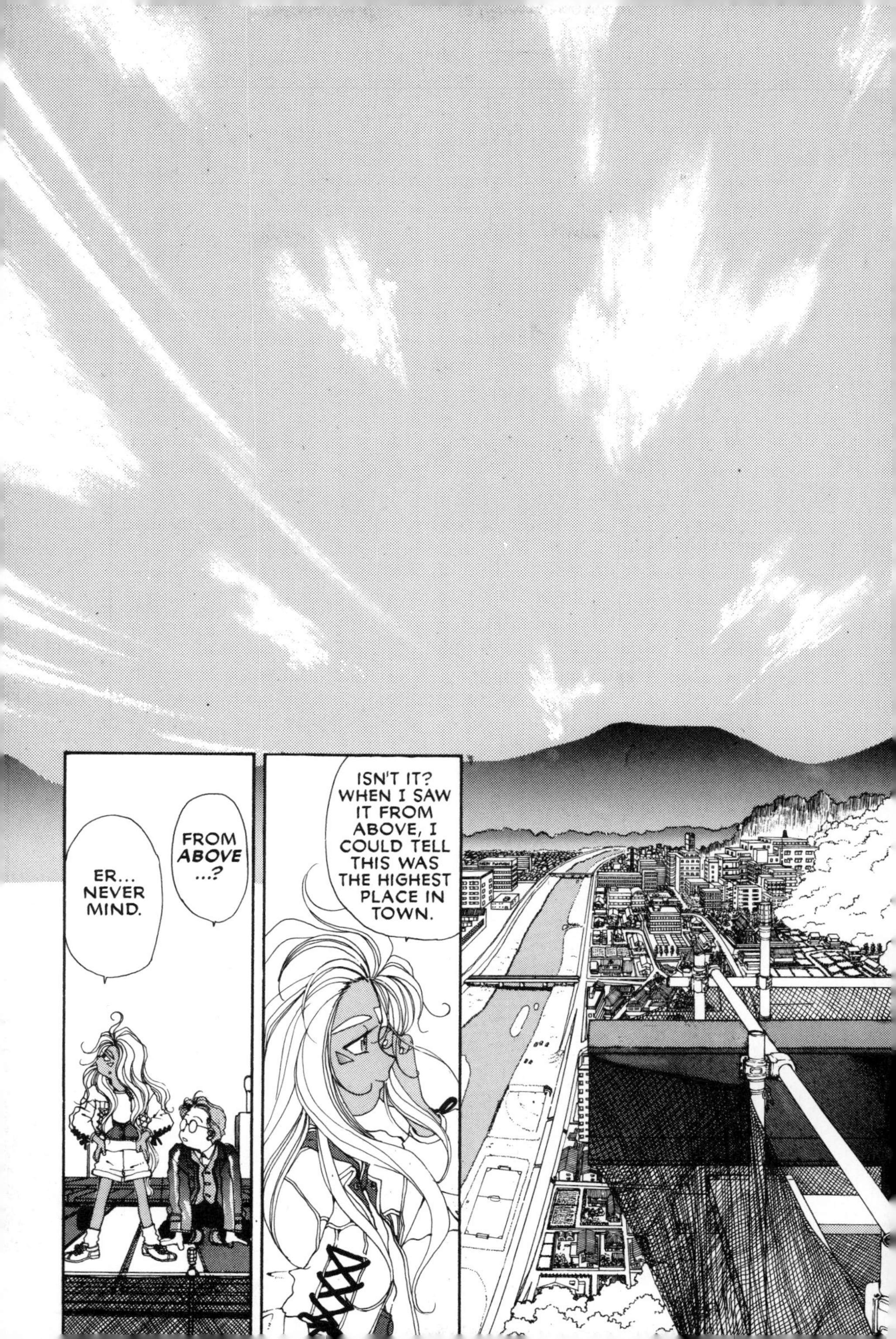
ISN'T IT? WHEN I SAW IT FROM ABOVE, I COULD TELL THIS WAS THE HIGHEST PLACE IN TOWN.
FROM *ABOVE* ...?
ER... NEVER MIND.

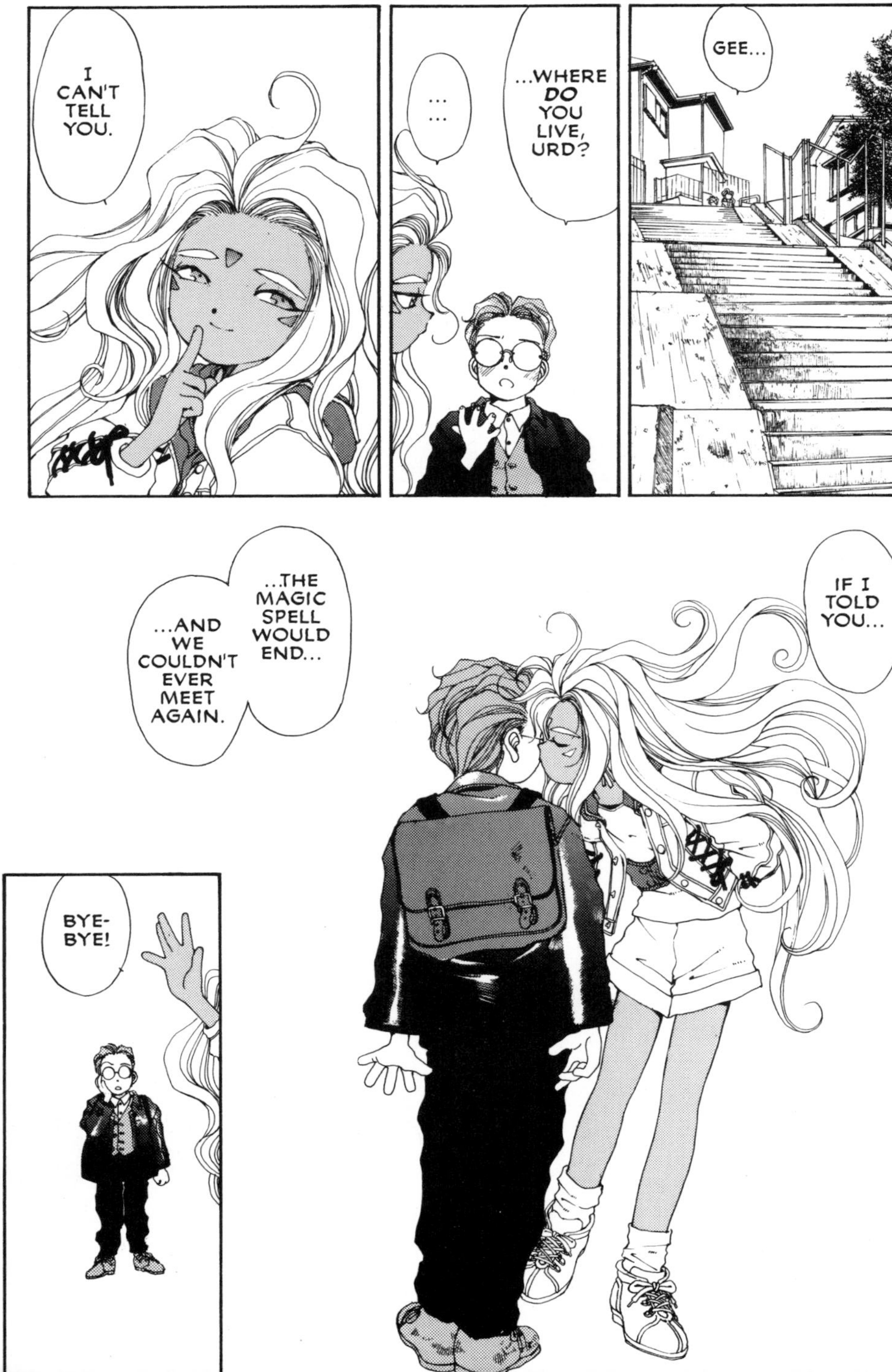
GEE...
...WHERE *DO* YOU LIVE, URD?
... ...
I CAN'T TELL YOU.
IF I TOLD YOU...
...THE MAGIC SPELL WOULD END...
...AND WE COULDN'T EVER MEET AGAIN.
BYE-BYE!

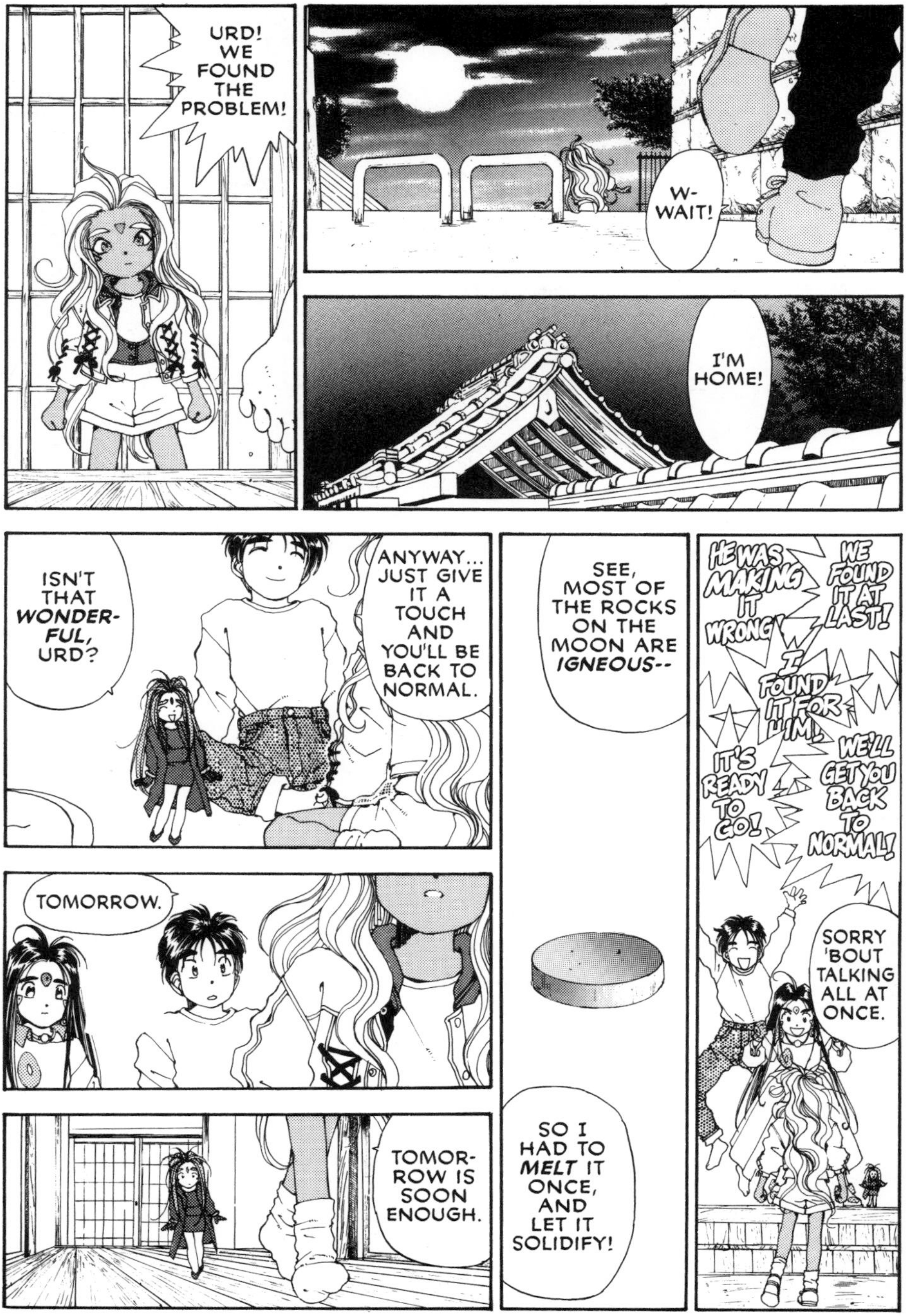
W-WAIT!
I'M HOME!
URD! WE FOUND THE PROBLEM!
WE FOUND IT AT LAST!
HE WAS MAKING IT WRONG!
I FOUND IT FOR HIM!
WE'LL GET YOU BACK TO NORMAL!
IT'S READY TO GO!
SORRY 'BOUT TALKING ALL AT ONCE.
SEE, MOST OF THE ROCKS ON THE MOON ARE *IGNEOUS*--
SO I HAD TO *MELT* IT ONCE, AND LET IT SOLIDIFY!
ISN'T THAT *WONDERFUL*, URD?
ANYWAY... JUST GIVE IT A TOUCH AND YOU'LL BE BACK TO NORMAL.
TOMORROW.
TOMORROW IS SOON ENOUGH.

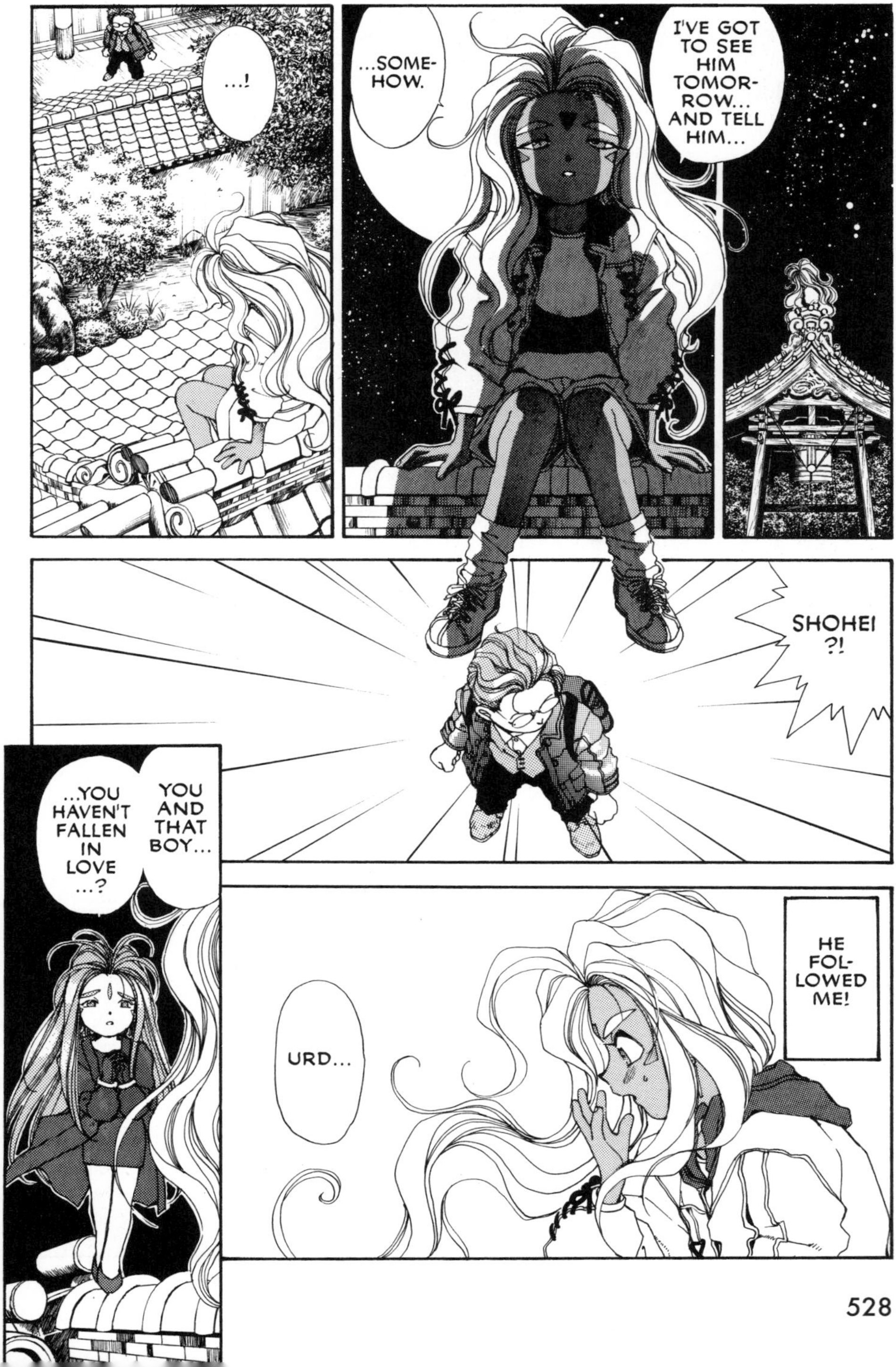
I'VE GOT TO SEE HIM TOMORROW... AND TELL HIM...
...SOMEHOW.
...!
SHOHEI ?!
HE FOLLOWED ME!
URD...
YOU AND THAT BOY...
...YOU HAVEN'T FALLEN IN LOVE ...?

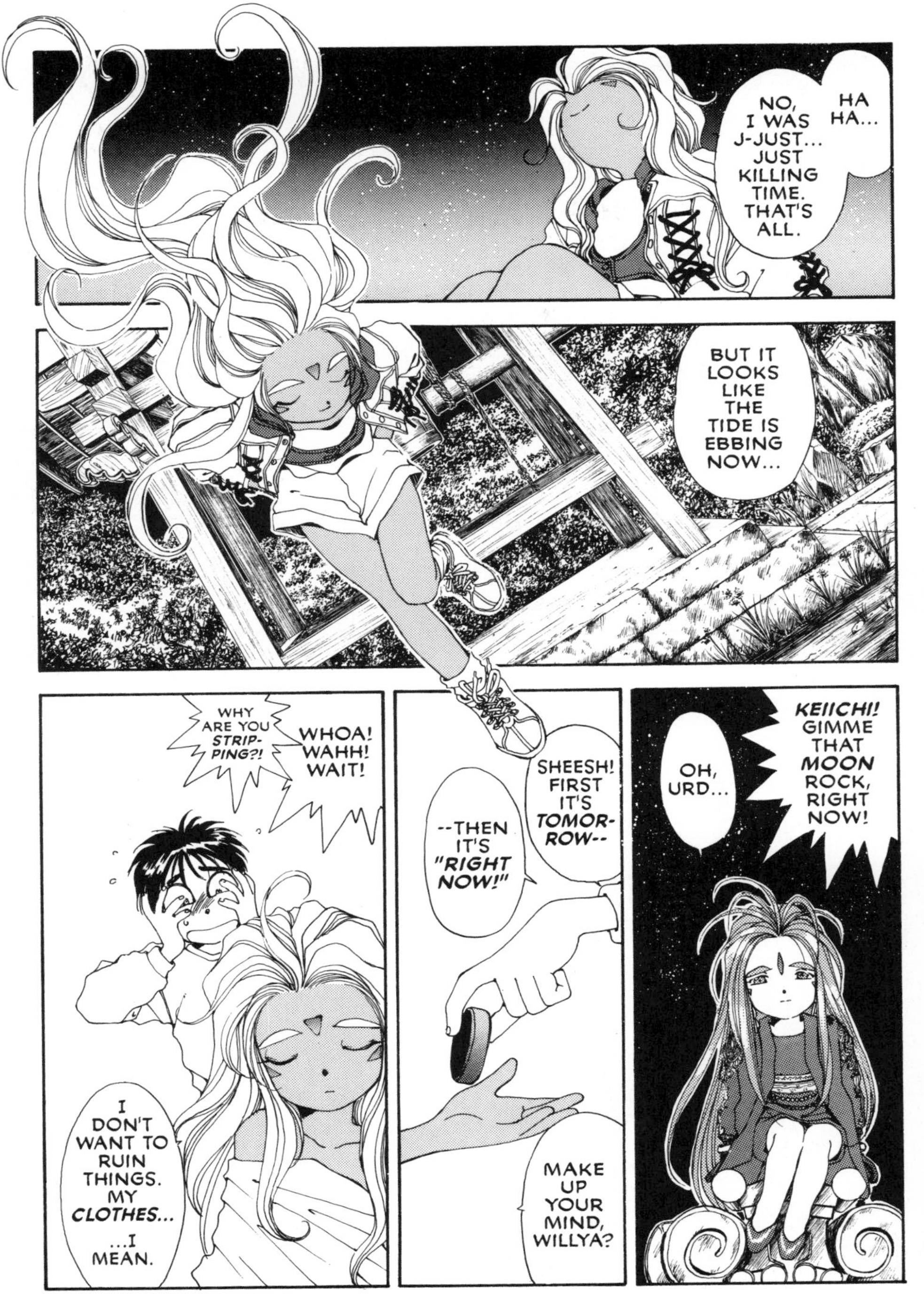
HA HA...
NO, I WAS J-JUST... JUST KILLING TIME. THAT'S ALL.
BUT IT LOOKS LIKE THE TIDE IS EBBING NOW...
KEIICHI! GIMME THAT MOON ROCK, RIGHT NOW!
OH, URD...
SHEESH! FIRST IT'S TOMORROW--
--THEN IT'S "RIGHT NOW!"
MAKE UP YOUR MIND, WILLYA?
WHOA! WAHH! WAIT!
WHY ARE YOU STRIPPING?!
I DON'T WANT TO RUIN THINGS. MY CLOTHES...
...I MEAN.

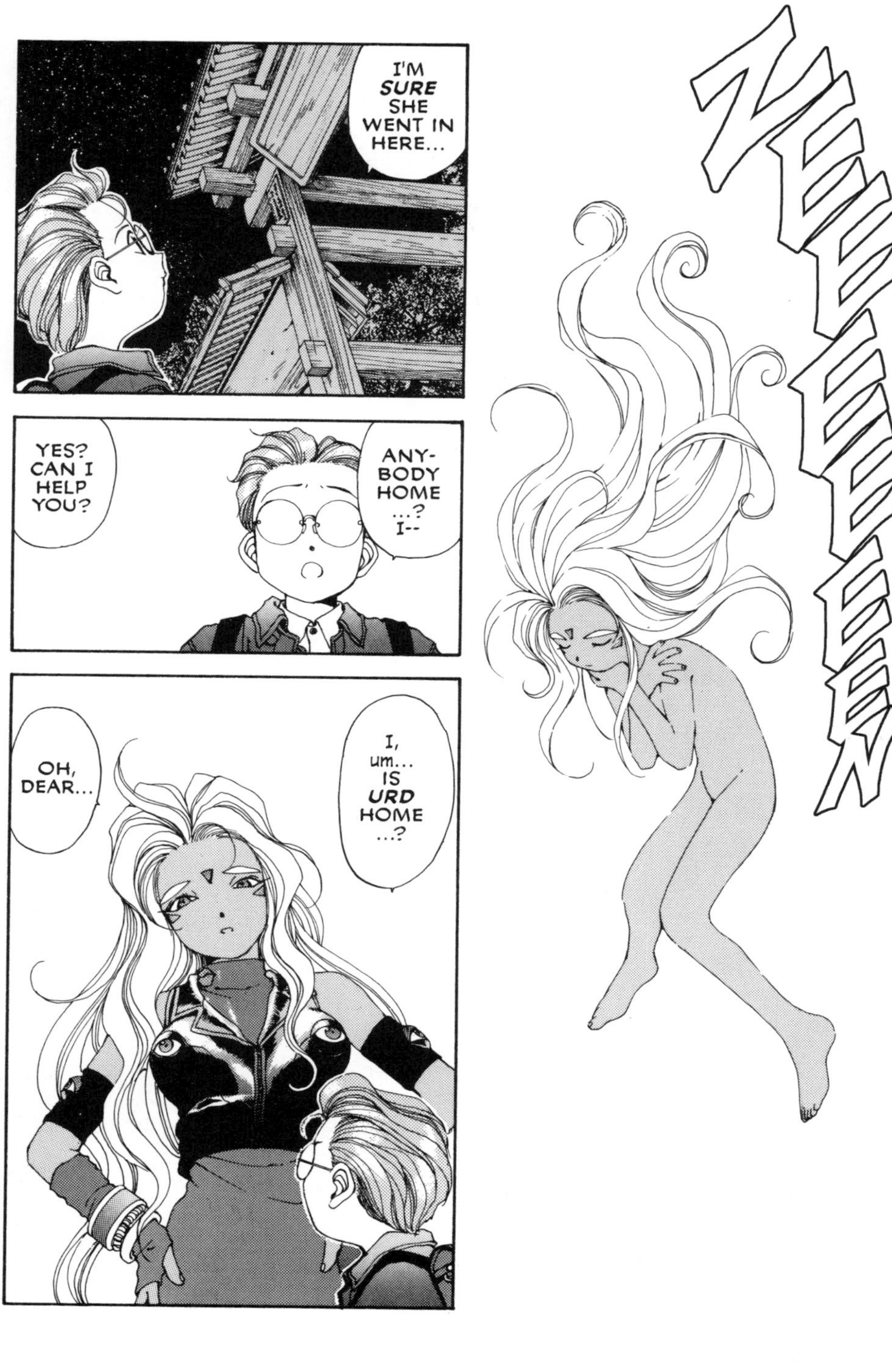
NEEEEEEEEEEEEEEN
I'M **SURE** SHE WENT IN HERE...
ANY-BODY HOME ...? I--
YES? CAN I HELP YOU?
I, um... IS **URD** HOME ...?
OH, DEAR...

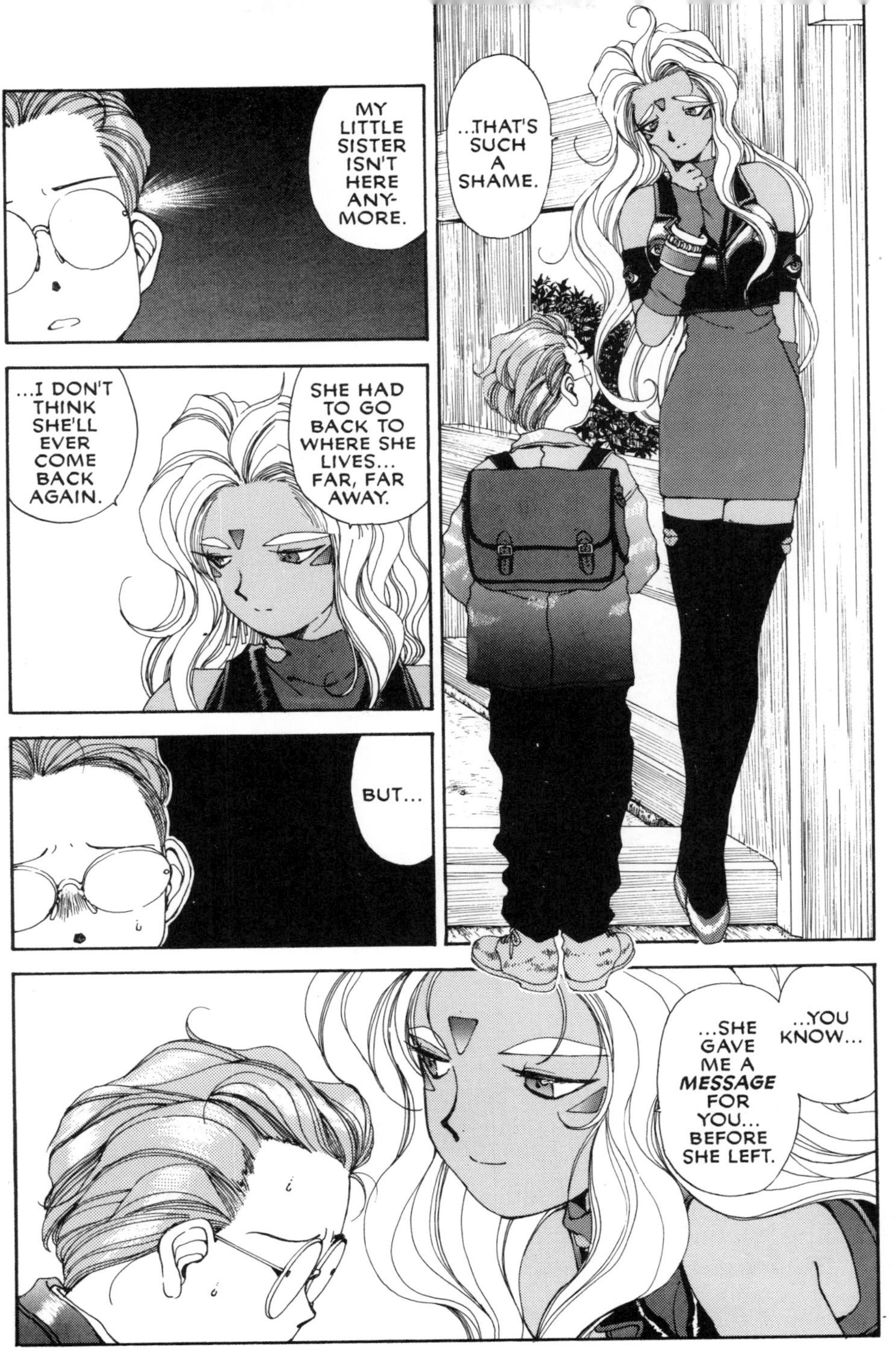
...THAT'S SUCH A SHAME.
MY LITTLE SISTER ISN'T HERE ANY-MORE.
SHE HAD TO GO BACK TO WHERE SHE LIVES... FAR, FAR AWAY.
...I DON'T THINK SHE'LL EVER COME BACK AGAIN.
BUT...
...YOU KNOW...
...SHE GAVE ME A *MESSAGE* FOR YOU... BEFORE SHE LEFT.

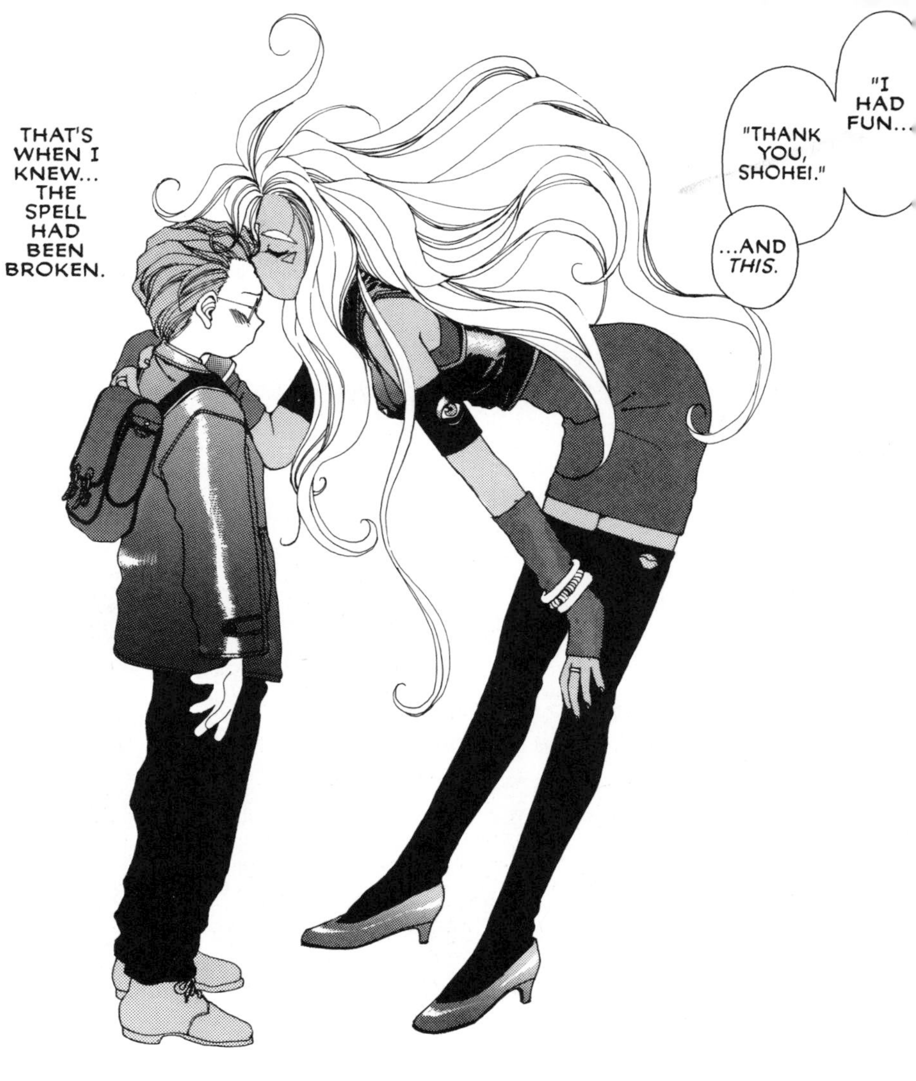
"I HAD FUN...
"THANK YOU, SHOHEI."
...AND *THIS*.
THAT'S WHEN I KNEW... THE SPELL HAD BEEN BROKEN.

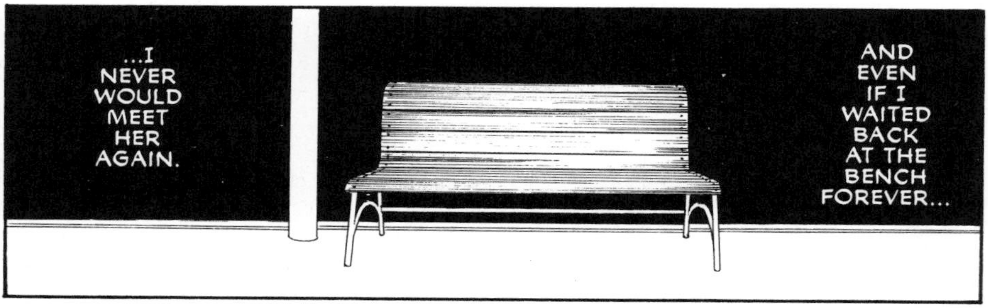
AND EVEN IF I WAITED BACK AT THE BENCH FOREVER...
...I NEVER WOULD MEET HER AGAIN.

# Oh My Goddess!

ああっ女神さまっ

**3**

**OMNIBUS**

藤島康介
**KOSUKE FUJISHIMA**

Strange, cute, and charming new characters are around every corner in *Oh My Goddess! Omnibus* Book 3! First, blond-bombshell demoness Mara descends with a wicked plot to possess the body of Megumi . . . which leads Skuld to *build* a new character, Mini-Banpei RX, to combat their infernal rival! Then, at a mountain resort, the ghost of a long-dead, lovely maid takes form to try to get Keiichi to honor a promise his grandfather made to her . . .

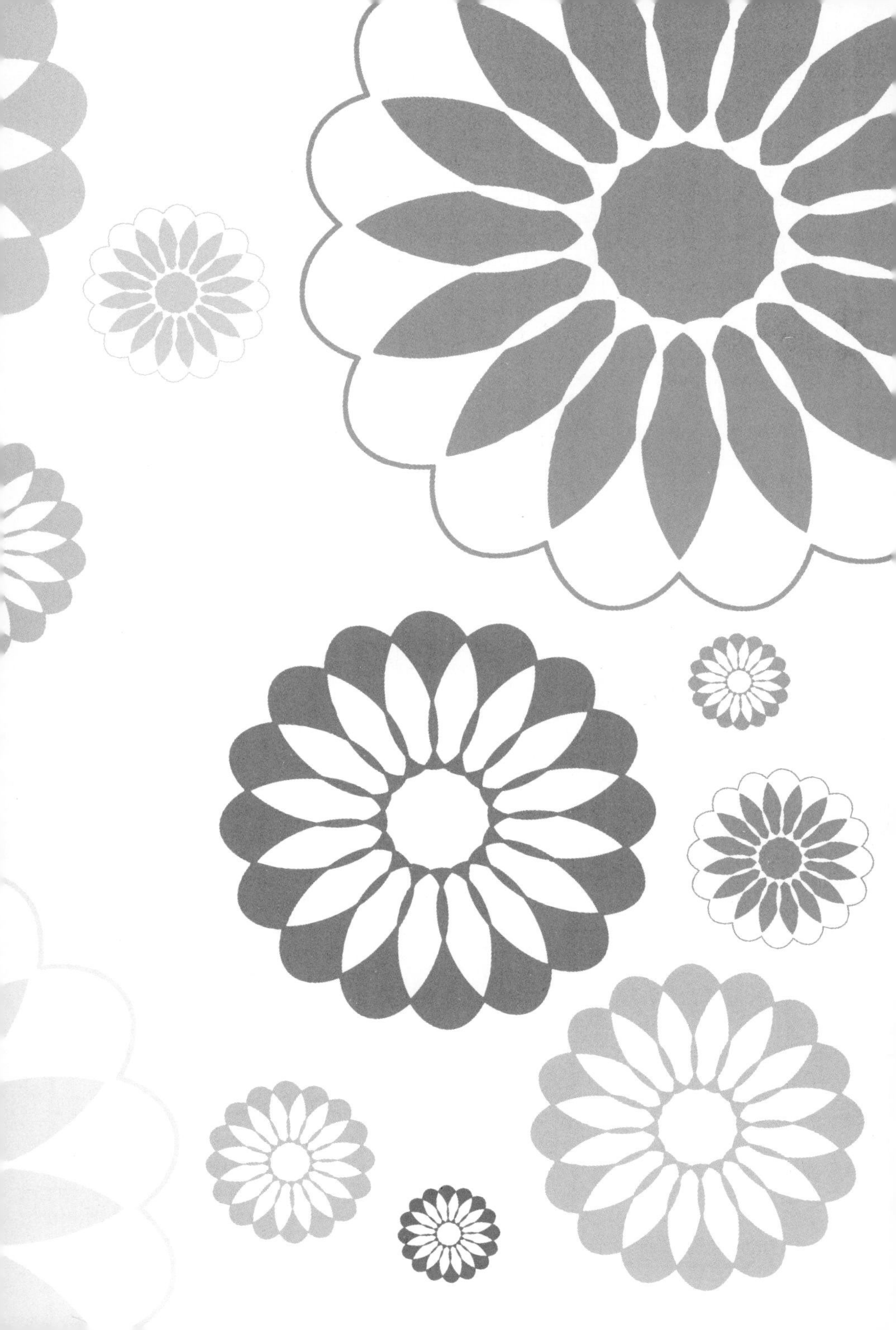

**PUBLISHER**
# Mike Richardson

**EDITOR**
# Carl Gustav Horn

**DESIGNER**
# Kat Larson

**DIGITAL ART TECHNICIAN**
# Christina McKenzie

English-language version
produced by Dark Horse Comics

**OH MY GODDESS! Omnibus Book 2**
© 2015 Kosuke Fujishima. All rights reserved. First published in
Japan by Kodansha, Ltd., Tokyo. Publication rights for this English edition
arranged through Kodansha, Ltd. All rights reserved. No portion of this
publication may be reproduced or transmitted, in any form or by any means,
without the express written permission of the copyright holders. Names,
characters, places, and incidents featured in this publication either are the
product of the author's imagination or are used fictitiously. Any resemblance
to actual persons (living or dead), events, institutions, or locales, without
satiric intent, is coincidental. Dark Horse Manga™ is a trademark
of Dark Horse Comics, Inc. All rights reserved.

Published by Dark Horse Manga
A division of Dark Horse Comics, Inc.
10956 SE Main Street
Milwaukie, OR 97222
DarkHorse.com

To find a comics shop in your area,
call the Comic Shop Locator Service
toll-free at 1-888-266-4226.

First edition: November 2015
ISBN 978-1-61655-784-3

1 3 5 7 9 10 8 6 4 2

Printed in China

# Oh My Goddess!

ああっ女神さまっ

# ANGELIC LAYER

## Story and Art by
## CLAMP

**YOUNG TEEN MISAKI SUZUHARA** has just arrived in Tokyo to attend the prestigious Eriol Academy. But what really excites her is Angelic Layer, the game where you control an Angel—a miniature robot fighter whose moves depend on your mind! Before she knows it, Misaki is an up-and-coming contender in Angelic Layer . . . and in way over her not-very-tall head! How far can enthusiasm take her in an arena full of much more experienced fighters . . . and a game full of secrets?

Don't miss the thrilling prequel to the acclaimed CLAMP manga *Chobits*! These omnibus-sized volumes feature not only the full story of *Angelic Layer* but also gorgeous, exclusive bonus color illustrations!

**VOLUME ONE**
978-1-61655-021-9

**VOLUME TWO**
978-1-61655-128-5

**$19.99 each**

# CLAMP オキモノ キモノ
## Mokona's
# OKIMONO
# KIMONO

CLAMP artist Mokona loves the art of traditional Japanese kimono. In fact, she designs kimono and kimono accessories herself and shares her love in *Okimono Kimono*, a fun and lavishly illustrated book full of drawings and photographs, interviews (including an interview with Onuki Ami of the J-pop duo Puffy AmiYumi), and exclusive short manga stories from the CLAMP artists!

From the creators of such titles as *Clover, Chobits, Cardcaptor Sakura, Magic Knight Rayearth*, and *Tsubasa, Okimono Kimono* is now available in English for the first time ever!

ISBN 978-1-59582-456-1
$12.99

# CLAMP

## IN NEAR-FUTURE JAPAN,

the hottest style for your personal computer, or "persocom," is in the shape of an attractive android! Hideki, a poor student, finds a persocom seemingly discarded in an alley. He takes the cute, amnesiac robot home and names her "Chi."

But who is this strange new persocom in his life? Hideki finds himself having to teach Chi how to get along in the everyday world, even while he and his friends try to solve the mystery of her origins. Is she one of the urban-legendary *Chobits*—persocoms built to have the riskiest functions of all: real emotions and free will?

CLAMP's best-selling manga in America is finally available in omnibus form! Containing dozens of bonus color pages, *Chobits* is an engaging, touching, exciting story.

### BOOK 1
ISBN 978-1-59582-451-6
$24.99

### BOOK 2
ISBN 978-1-59582-514-8
$24.99

MANGA BY
CLAMP

Fourth grader Sakura Kinomoto has found a strange book in her father's library—a book made by the wizard Clow to store dangerous spirits sealed within a set of magical cards. But when Sakura opens it up, there is nothing left inside but Kero-chan, the book's cute little guardian beast…who informs Sakura that since the Clow cards seem to have escaped while he was asleep, it's now her job to capture them!

With remastered image files straight from CLAMP, Dark Horse is proud to present *Cardcaptor Sakura* in omnibus form! Each book collects three volumes of the original twelve-volume series, and features thirty bonus color pages!

**OMNIBUS BOOK 1**
ISBN 978-1-59582-522-3

**OMNIBUS BOOK 2**
ISBN 978-1-59582-591-9

**OMNIBUS BOOK 3**
ISBN 978-1-59582-808-8

**OMNIBUS BOOK 4**
ISBN 978-1-59582-889-7

$19.99 each!

**AVAILABLE AT YOUR LOCAL COMICS SHOP OR BOOKSTORE!**
To find a comics shop in your area, call 1-888-266-4226
For more information or to order direct: • On the web: DarkHorse.com
E-mail: mailorder@darkhorse.com • Phone: 1-800-862-0052 Mon.–Fri. 9 AM to 5 PM Pacific Time

# GATE 7
ゲート セブン

**BRAND NEW FROM CLAMP—COMING TO THE U.S. JUST MONTHS AFTER JAPAN!**

An innocent sightseeing trip to a legendary shrine opens up a magical realm to shy high schooler Chikahito Takamoto! Chikahito finds himself in the mystical world of Hana and an otherworldly band of warriors, and his immunity to their powers leads them to believe he's no ordinary, awkward teenager! Protecting our world from violent elemental beasts, Hana and the team welcome the confused and cautious Chikahito—who isn't quite sure that he wants to be caught in the middle of their war!

| Volume One | Volume Two | Volume Three | Volume Four |
|---|---|---|---|
| ISBN 978-1-59582-806-4 | ISBN 978-1-59582-807-1 | ISBN 978-1-59582-902-3 | ISBN 978-1-59582-961-0 |

### $10.99 each

**DARK HORSE MANGA**

**Available at your local comics shop or bookstore. To find a comics shop in your area, call 1-888-266-4226**
For more information or to order direct: On the web: DarkHorse.com / E-mail: mailorder@darkhorse.com
Phone: 1-800-862-0052 Mon.-Fri. 9 a.m. to 5 p.m. Pacific Time.
Gate 7 © by CLAMP. All rights reserved. English translation rights arranged with PYROTECHNIST CO. LTD., Tokyo. (BL 7072)

# CLOVER

'he long-out-of-print classic from Japan's *shojo*-artist supergroup CLAMP!

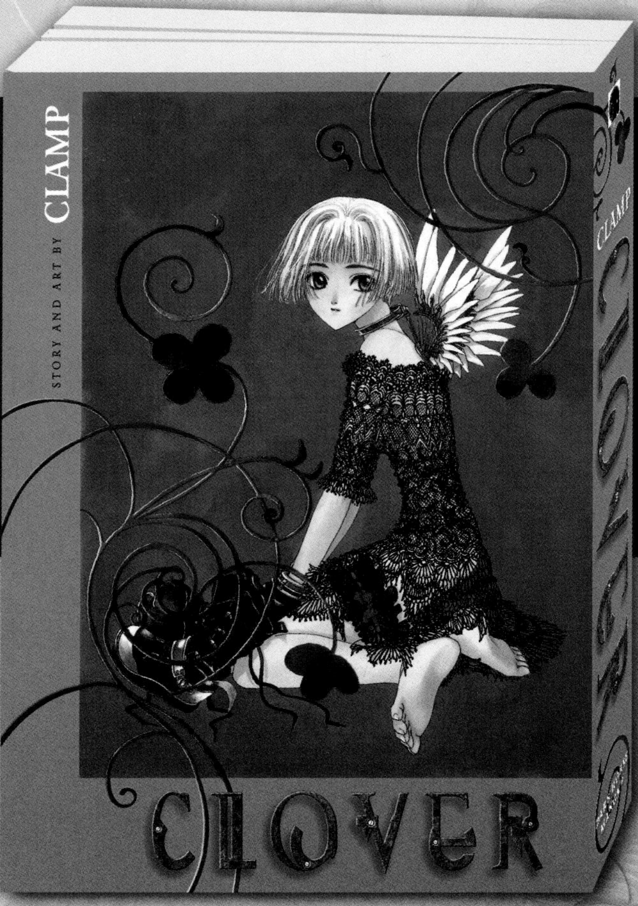
STORY AND ART BY CLAMP
CLAMP
CLOVER

**Clover has never before een available in English 1 its original unflopped, right-to-left reading rmat—until now! Dark Horse collects all four olumes of *Clover* in one argain omnibus format, including 17 pages of bonus art in color!**

**Idgy and genre-bending . . . *Clover* certainly challenges people's erception of what *shojo* manga should be."**

–*Manga: The Complete Guide*

DARK HORSE MANGA

**AVAILABLE AT YOUR LOCAL COMICS SHOP OR BOOKSTORE**

To find a comics shop in your area, call 1-888-266-4226
For more information or to order direct: On the web: **DarkHorse.com** | E-mail: **mailorder@darkhorse.com** | Phone: **1-800-862-0052 Mon.–Fri. 9 AM to 5 PM Pacific Time.**

# NEON GENESIS EVANGELION

**Dark Horse Manga is proud to present these volumes that take a new look at the events and characters from the groundbreaking *Neon Genesis Evangelion* universe!**

### NEON GENESIS EVANGELION: THE SHINJI IKARI RAISING PROJECT
*Story and art by Osamu Takahashi*

Volume 1
ISBN 978-1-59582-321-2
Volume 2
ISBN 978-1-59582-377-9
Volume 3
ISBN 978-1-59582-447-9
Volume 4
ISBN 978-1-59582-454-7
Volume 5
ISBN 978-1-59582-520-9
Volume 6
ISBN 978-1-59582-580-3
Volume 7
ISBN 978-1-59582-595-7
Volume 8

Volume 8
ISBN 978-1-59582-694-7
Volume 9
ISBN 978-1-59582-800-2
Volume 10
ISBN 978-1-59582-879-8
Volume 11
ISBN 978-1-59582-932-0
Volume 12
ISBN 978-1-61655-033-2
Volume 13
ISBN 978-1-61655-315-9
Volume 14
ISBN 978-1-61655-432-3
Volume 15
ISBN 978-1-61655-607-5

**$9.99 each**

### NEON GENESIS EVANGELION: CAMPUS APOCALYPSE
*Story and art by Mingming*

Volume 1
ISBN 978-1-59582-530-8
Volume 2
ISBN 978-1-59582-661-9

Volume 3
ISBN 978-1-59582-680-0
Volume 4
ISBN 978-1-59582-689-3

**$10.99 each**

### NEON GENESIS EVANGELION COMIC TRIBUTE
*Story and art by various creators*
ISBN 978-1-61655-114-8
**$10.99**

### NEON GENESIS EVANGELION: THE SHINJI IKARI DETECTIVE DIARY
*Story and art by Takumi Yoshimura*

Volume 1
ISBN 978-1-61655-225-1

Volume 2
ISBN 978-1-61655-418-7

**$9.99 each**

### TONY TAKEZAKI'S NEON GENESIS EVANGELION
*Story and art by Tony Takezaki*
ISBN 978-1-61655-736-2
**$12.99**

# BRIDE of the WATER GOD

When Soah's impoverished, desperate village decides to sacrifice her to the Water God Habaek to end a long drought, they believe that drowning one beautiful girl will save their entire community and bring much-needed rain. Not only is Soah surprised to be *rescued* by the Water God instead of killed; she never imagined she'd be a welcomed guest in Habaek's magical kingdom, where an exciting new life awaits her! Most surprising, however, is the Water God himself, and how very different he is from the monster Soah imagined . . .

Created by Mi-Kyung Yun, who received the "Best New Artist" award in 2004 from the esteemed *Dokja-manhwa-daesang* organization, *Bride of the Water God* was the top-selling *shoujo* manhwa in Korea in 2006!

**Volume 1**
ISBN 978-1-59307-849-2

**Volume 2**
ISBN 978-1-59307-883-6

**Volume 3**
ISBN 978-1-59582-305-2

**Volume 4**
ISBN 978-1-59582-378-6

**Volume 5**
ISBN 978-1-59582-445-5

**Volume 6**
ISBN 978-1-59582-605-3

**Volume 7**
ISBN 978-1-59582-668-8

**Volume 8**
ISBN 978-1-59582-687-9

**Volume 9**
ISBN 978-1-59582-688-6

**Volume 10**
ISBN 978-1-59582-873-6

**Volume 11**
ISBN 978-1-59582-874-3

**Volume 12**
ISBN 978-1-59582-999-3

**Volume 13**
ISBN 978-1-61655-072-1

**Volume 14**
ISBN 978-1-61655-187-2

**Volume 15**
ISBN 978-1-61655-301-2

**Volume 16**
ISBN 978-1-61655-480-4

**Volume 17**
ISBN 978-1-61655-684-6

**$9.99 each**

Previews for BRIDE OF THE WATER GOD and other DARK HORSE MANHWA titles can be found at darkhorse.com!

## SO BY SATOSHI KON

me director Satoshi Kon (*Paprika, Paranoia Agent, Tokyo Godfathers, Millennium* *rfect Blue*) died tragically young in 2010. But before he directed those unforgettable as a manga artist, and Dark Horse is honored to remember Kon with the release of s most significant books.

SATOSHI KON'S
OPUS

### SATOSHI KON'S OPUS

*OPUS* contains the mastery of both realism and surrealism that would make Kon famous, as a manga artist planning a shocking surprise ending to his story gets literally pulled into his own work—to face for himself what he had planned for his characters!

**ISBN 978-1-61655-606-8**

**$19.99**

seraphim 266613336 wings
mamoru oshii
satoshi kon

### SERAPHIM 266613336 WINGS

***With Mamoru Oshii***

Two of the most acclaimed anime directors of all time, *Ghost in the Shell*'s Mamoru Oshii and Satoshi Kon, collaborated on a work of manga: *Seraphim 266613336 Wings*. *Seraphim* is the story of a future earth devastated by the "Angel Plague," a pandemic that induces apocalyptic visions in the afflicted even as it ossifies their bodies into hauntingly beautiful seraphic forms . . .

**ISBN 978-1-61655-608-2**

**$19.99**

rse.com

**ABLE AT YOUR LOCAL COMICS SHOP OR BOOKSTORE**

**ID A COMICS SHOP IN YOUR AREA, CALL 1-888-266-4226**

**e information or to order direct: ·On the web: DarkHorse.com**

**mailorder@darkhorse.com ·Phone: 1-800-862-0052 Mon.–Fri. 9 AM to 5 PM Pacific Time.**

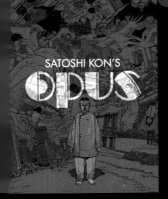

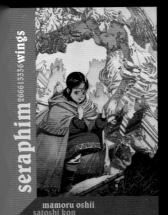

# STOP! This is the back of the book!

This manga collection is translated into English, but arranged in right-to-left reading format to maintain the artwork's visual orientation as originally drawn and published in Japan. If you've never read comics this way before, take a look at the diagram below to give yourself an idea of how to go about it. Basically, you'll be starting in the upper right-hand corner, and will read each word balloon and panel moving right to left. It may take a little getting used to, but you should get the hang of it very quickly. Have fun! If this is the millionth manga you've read this way, never mind. ^_^

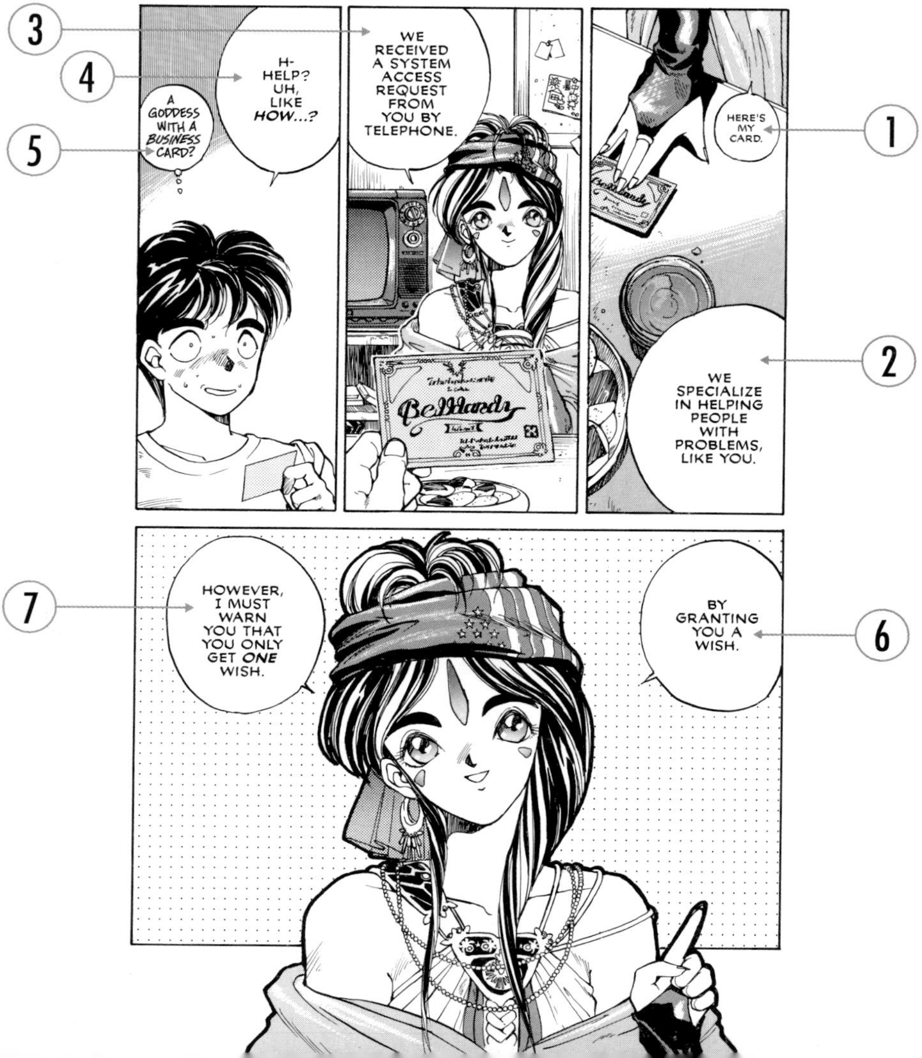

1
HERE'S MY CARD.
2
WE SPECIALIZE IN HELPING PEOPLE WITH PROBLEMS, LIKE YOU.
3
WE RECEIVED A SYSTEM ACCESS REQUEST FROM YOU BY TELEPHONE.
4
H-HELP? UH, LIKE HOW...?
5
A GODDESS WITH A BUSINESS CARD?
6
BY GRANTING YOU A WISH.
7
HOWEVER, I MUST WARN YOU THAT YOU ONLY GET ONE WISH.